About the Companion CD

The *Encyclopedia of Networking*'s accompanying CD contains the entire text of the book, complete with figures, in the Adobe Portable Document Format (PDF), together with the Adobe Acrobat Reader software for the following platforms:

- Windows (including Windows 3.1, Windows 95, and Windows NT)
- DOS
- Sun SPARC
- Solaris
- HP-UX

The Acrobat Reader for the Macintosh is available from http://www.adobe.com, together with installation instructions.

Installing the Acrobat Reader Software

To install the Acrobat Reader software, follow the instructions in the appropriate section below.

Windows

To install the Acrobat Reader for Windows 3.1, Windows 95, and Windows NT:
1. Copy ACROREAD.EXE from the CD to your hard disk.
2. Run ACROREAD.EXE and follow the installation instructions on screen.

DOS

1. Copy ACRODOS.EXE from the CD to your hard disk.
2. Run ACRODOS.EXE and follow the installation instructions on screen.

Sun SPARC

1. Copy the SUNOSREA.GZ file to your hard drive.
2. gunzip and untar the file.
3. Follow the installation instructions in INSTGUID.TXT.

Solaris

1. Copy the SOLARISR.GZ file to your hard drive.
2. gunzip and untar the file.
3. Follow the installation instructions in INSTGUID.TXT.

HP-UX

1. Copy the HPUXREAD.GZ file to your hard drive.
2. gunzip and untar the file.
3. Follow the installation instructions in INSTGUID.TXT.

Running the Encyclopedia

To run the online version of the *Encyclopedia of Networking*, start the Acrobat Reader and open **encyclop.pdf**.

The Encyclopedia
of Networking

INTRODUCING NETWORK PRESS™

You *can* judge a book by its cover.

Welcome to Network Press™, the new and expanded successor to **Sybex's** acclaimed **Novell Press**® book series. If you liked our Novell Press books, you'll be impressed by the improvements we've made in the books that replace them. With **Network Press**, you'll find the same quality from a truly independent and unbiased viewpoint. You'll also find full coverage of not only Novell, but Microsoft and other network environments.

Building on a 20-year history of technical and publishing excellence, **Network Press**™ is dedicated to providing you with the fullest range and depth of networking information available today. You'll find the same commitment to quality, contents, and timeliness that you have come to expect from Novell Press books by Sybex. All previously released Novell Press titles remain available from Sybex.

Network Press books continue to offer you:

- winning certification test preparation strategies
- respected authors you know and trust
- all new titles in a wide variety of topics
- completely updated editions of familiar best-sellers
- distinctive new covers

Our leadership approach guarantees your ongoing success in managing every aspect of your network's software and hardware.

Look for these **Network Press** titles, available now at your local bookstore:

The CNE Study Guide, Second Edition, by David James Clarke IV
(Revised and updated edition of *Novell's CNE Study Guide*)
The Network Press Dictionary of Networking, by Peter Dyson
(Revised and updated edition of *Novell's Dictionary of Networking*)
The Complete Guide to NetWare 4.1, by James E. Gaskin
Managing an Inherited NetWare Network, by Michael J. Miller
The CNE Update to NetWare 4.1, by Michael Moncur

For more information about Network Press, please contact:

Network Press
2021 Challenger Drive
Alameda, CA 94501
Tel: (510) 523-8233/(800) 227-2346
Fax: (510) 523-2373/Email: info@sybex.com

The Encyclopedia of Networking

Second Edition

The First Edition of this
book was published under
the title *Novell's® Complete
Encyclopedia of Networking*

Werner Feibel

San Francisco ▪ Paris ▪ Düsseldorf ▪ Soest

Acquisitions Editor: Kristine Plachy
Developmental Editor: Guy Hart-Davis
Editors: Kristen Vanberg-Wolff and Maureen Adams
Technical Editor: Mary Madden
Book Designer: Seventeenth Street Studios
Technical Illustrators: Cuong Le, Heather Lewis, and Alan Smith
Desktop Publisher: London Road Design
Production Coordinator: Nathan Johanson
Indexer: Matthew Spence
Cover Designer: Archer Design
Cover Photographer: Dewitt Jones

Library of Congress Card Number: 95-72476

ISBN: 0-7821-1829-1

Manufactured in the United States of America

10 9 8 7 6 5 4 3 2 1

[In] a certain Chinese encyclopedia...it is written that animals are divided into:

(a) those belonging to the Emperor
(b) those that are embalmed
(c) tame ones
(d) suckling pigs
(e) sirens
(f) fabulous ones
(g) stray dogs
(h) those included in the present classification
(i) those that tremble as if mad
(j) innumerable ones
(k) those drawn with a very fine camelhair brush
(l) others
(m) those that have just broken the water pitcher
(n) those that look like flies from a long way off

Jorge Luis Borges

Acknowledgments

As with the first edition, this book would never have been completed without the help of many people. These people deserve thanks for all their efforts and energy. Guy Hart-Davis convinced me that it was time for a revision and set me to work. Several people did splendid work during the production process: Kris Vanberg-Wolff, a veteran of the first edition, worked on the revision until her planned departure for the calmer (and tastier) world of cooking school. Maureen Adams, Laura Arendal, and Nathan Johanson took over the production chores after Kris left. They did an excellent job, especially considering the short notice and even shorter revision schedule. My heartfelt thanks to all these folks.

Mary Madden's technical reviews were always full of gentle, constructive corrections and useful suggestions for improvements. Although I may not have been smart enough to act on all of them, the suggestions have improved the book immensely—for which I'm very grateful.

Kris Vanberg-Wolff's eagle eyes and infallible grammatical sense found and fixed my awkward phrasings, stylistic inconsistencies, and grammatical aberrations. I shudder to think what the book would have looked like without the benefit of these efforts.

As always, I'm very grateful to all the people who worked between and behind the scenes to make this book, and also to those who created the compact disc. Thanks also to the many people who sent me information about their products and who took the time to answer my questions.

Finally, I dedicate this book to my wife Luanne and my daughter Molly—for all the joy and fun they provide, during both work and play hours.

Table of Contents

Introduction

What You'll Find in This Book

As in the first edition, I've tried to make this Encyclopedia a comprehensive source of information about matters relating to networking. I've also tried to present the information in a clear and useful manner.

This book contains comprehensive, straightforward summaries of the major concepts, issues, and approaches related to networking. Networking is defined broadly to encompass configurations ranging from a couple of connected computers just a few feet apart to a network of several thousand machines (of all types and sizes) scattered around the world. You'll find discussions of networking as it's done by servers and clients, managers and agents, peers, and even over the telephone.

You probably won't find anything here that you can't find in other places. However, I don't know of any other book or source that collects so much network-related information in one place. To find all the information summarized here, you would need to check hundreds of books, disks, articles, Web pages, or other documents.

Despite its hefty size, this encyclopedia just scratches the surface of what there is to know about networking. After all, how complete can any book be if just the World Wide Web on the Internet has over 10 million hypertext documents. I do think, however, that this book scratches deeper than most other references you'll find.

This revised edition updates entries for concepts and technologies that change rapidly or where there have been major developments. I've also added considerable material about the Internet (and especially about the World Wide Web), since interest in this networking phenomenon is growing at an astounding pace.

Concepts, Not Instructions

As in the first edition, I've tried to cover concepts rather than making this a how-to book. Thus, you won't learn how to install networks or run specific programs. However, you will learn about different types of programs and what they do. For example, you can read about browsers and how they make exploring the World Wide Web possible; you'll also learn about programs such as network operating systems and how they differ from ordinary operating systems.

An Anchor in an Ocean of Words

This book was obsolete from the moment it was written. That's because nothing changes faster than vocabulary in a field where there is money to be made. Since major breakthroughs and advances are still happening in the area of networking, there are new network-related words and concepts to be found in almost every issue of every computer magazine. If you include acronyms and abbreviations, the speed with which the vernacular expands is even faster. For example, the first edition of this book was published under a year ago and it was no trouble finding almost 2,000 new entries for Appendix A.

Given the futility of even trying to stay completely up-to-date, I've chosen to focus on the more enduring concepts and facts—those that provide the foundations and background that underlie the constantly changing terminology. This makes the Encyclopedia more generally useful and enduring.

Helping the Book Grow

While core networking concepts change very little, the core does grow. For example, ten years ago there was much less need to know about wireless communications because there were fewer wireless products, as well as less public interest in the technology. Because of such progress, the body of essential fundamentals grows with each year.

I expect to update and add to the material in the book, and hope to make the Encyclopedia always effective, comprehensive, and useful. Fortunately, an electronic medium makes it easier to grow in this way.

If you need to find out something about networking, look for it in this book. If you find an entry for the topic, we hope you'll be more informed after you've read it. On the other hand, if you can't find the information you need, didn't understand it, or don't think you learned what you should have, please drop us a line and tell us.

Also, if there are concepts or terms you would like to see included, please let us know. If you can provide references, that would be helpful. Even under the best of circumstances, there's little chance that you'll get a reply to individual queries. However, we will read your comments and suggestions and will try to use them to improve future versions of the book.

Symbols &
Numbers

& (Ampersand)

The ampersand is used to indicate special characters in HTML (Hypertext Markup Language) documents—that is, documents for the World Wide Web. For example, *&* specifies the ampersand character (&); *ö* specifies a lowercase o with an umlaut, or dieresis, mark (ö).

< > (Angle Brackets)

Angle brackets are used in pairs to surround *markup tags* in HTML (Hypertext Markup Language) documents for the World Wide Web. For example, *<P>* indicates a paragraph break; *<B>* and *</B>* indicate the start and end of a section that is to be displayed in boldface.

* (Asterisk)

In several operating systems, the asterisk serves as a wildcard character: to represent one or more characters, such as in a file name or extension. For example, *a** matches *act, actor,* and *and,* but not *band.*

In pattern matching involving regular expressions, the asterisk matches the occurrences of the single character immediately preceding it. For example, *ba*th* matches *bth, bath,* and *baaaaath,* but not *bbath.*

In e-mail and in other contexts that use plain text, asterisks are sometimes used around words or phrases to indicate emphasis. For example, "I *really* want to emphasize the second word in this sentence."

@ (At sign)

The *at sign* is used to separate the username from domain specifiers in e-mail addresses. For example, mels@golemxiv.mit.edu would indicate someone with username *mels* on a computer named *golemxiv* at MIT.

\ (Backslash)

In some operating systems, such as DOS, OS/2, and NetWare, the backslash character separates directory names or directory and file names in a path statement. By itself, the backslash represents the root directory in these operating systems.

In various programming and editing contexts, the backslash is used to escape the character that follows. For example, *\n* is an escape code to indicate a newline character in many operating environments.

// (Double Slash)

In URLs (Uniform Resource Locators), double slash characters separate the protocol from the site and document names. For example, if it existed,

>	http://examplehost.ucsc.edu/
>	filename.html

would refer to a file named *filename.html* residing on the *examplehost* machine at the University of California at Santa Cruz. To get to this file, you would use a server that supports the HTTP (Hypertext Transport Protocol).

μ (Mu)

Used as an abbreviation for the prefix micro, as in μsec for microsecond and μm for micrometer. This order of magnitude corresponds to 2^{-20}, which is roughly 10^{-6}, or one-millionth.

SEE ALSO

Order of Magnitude

. and .. (Period and Double Period)

In hierarchically organized directory systems, such as those used by UNIX, DOS, and OS/2, . and .. refer to the current and the parent directories, respectively. In pattern matching involving regular expressions, the . matches any single character, except a newline character.

? (Question Mark)

In many operating systems, a question mark serves as a wildcard character that represents a single character, such as in a file or directory name.

/ (Slash)

The slash (also known as a *forward slash* or a *virgule*) separates directory levels in some operating systems (most notably UNIX), in addresses for gopher, and in *URLs* (Uniform Resource Locators). For example, the following URL specifies the name and location of a hypertext version of the jargon file, which contains definitions for terms and events that have helped define the computer culture:

http://www.phil.uni-sb.de/fun/jargon/index.html

In this URL, the file is named *index.html*, and it is located in the */fun/jargon* directory on a machine in Germany (*de*).

In other operating systems, such as DOS, OS/2, and NetWare, a slash is sometimes used to indicate or separate command line switches or options for a command.

1Base5

The IEEE 802.3 committee's designation for an Ethernet network that operates at 1 megabit per second (Mbps) and that uses unshielded twisted-pair (UTP) cable. This configuration uses a physical bus, with nodes attached to a common cable. AT&T's StarLAN is an example of a 1Base5 network.

SEE ALSO

10BaseX; 10Broad36

4B/5B Encoding

4B/5B encoding is a data-translation scheme that serves as a preliminary to signal encoding in FDDI (Fiber Distributed Data Interface) networks. In 4B/5B, every group of four bits is represented as a five-bit symbol. This symbol is associated with a bit pattern that is then encoded using a standard signal-encoding method, usually NRZI (non-return to zero inverted).

This preprocessing makes the subsequent electrical encoding 80 percent efficient. For example, using 4B/5B encoding, you can achieve a 100 megabit per second (Mbps) transmission rate with a clock speed of only 125 megahertz (MHz).

In contrast, the Manchester signal-encoding method, which is used in Ethernet and other types of networks, is only 50 percent efficient. For example, to achieve a 100 Mbps rate with Manchester encoding, you need a 200 MHz clock speed.

▼ 5B/6B Encoding

A data-translation scheme that serves as a preliminary to signal encoding in 100BaseVG networks. In 5B/6B, every group of five bits is represented as a six-bit symbol. This symbol is associated with a bit pattern that is then encoded using a standard signal-encoding method, such as NRZ (non-return to zero).

▼ 8B/10B Encoding

A data-translation scheme related to 4B/5B encoding that recodes eight-bit patterns into 10-bit symbols. 8B/10B encoding is used, for example, in IBM's SNA (Systems Network Architecture) networks.

▼ 9-Track Tape

A tape storage format that uses nine parallel tracks on 1/2-inch, reel-to-reel magnetic tape. Eight tracks are used for data, and one track is used for parity information. These tapes are often used as backup systems on minicomputer and mainframe systems; digital audio tapes (DATs) are more common on networks.

▼ 10BaseX

The designations 10Base2, 10Base5, 10BaseF, and 10BaseT refer to various types of baseband Ethernet networks.

10Base2

10Base2 uses thin coaxial cable. This version can operate at up to 10 megabits per second (Mbps) and can support cable segments of up to 185 meters (607 feet). It is also known as *thin Ethernet, ThinNet,* or *CheaperNet,* because thin coaxial cable is considerably less expensive than the thick coaxial cable used in 10Base5 networks.

10Base5

10Base5 uses thick coaxial cable. This version is the original Ethernet. It can operate at up to 10 Mbps and support cable segments of up to 500 meters (1,640 feet). It is also known as *thick Ethernet* or *ThickNet.*

10BaseF

10BaseF is a baseband 802.3-based Ethernet network that uses fiber-optic cable. This version can operate at up to 10 Mbps.

Standards for the following special-purpose versions of 10BaseF are being formulated by the IEEE 802.3:

10BaseFP (fiber passive): For desktops

10BaseFL (fiber link): For intermediate *hubs* and workgroups

10BaseFB (fiber backbone): For central facility lines between buildings

10BaseT

10BaseT is a baseband 802.3-based Ethernet network that uses unshielded twisted-pair (UTP) cable and a star topology. This version can operate at up to 10 Mbps. It is also known as *twisted-pair Ethernet* or *UTP Ethernet.*

BROADER CATEGORY
Ethernet

SEE ALSO
1Base5; 10Broad36; 100BaseT

10Broad36

10Broad36 is a broadband, 802.3-based, Ethernet network that uses 75-ohm coaxial (CATV) cable and a bus or tree topology. This version can operate at up to 10 megabits per second (Mbps) and support cable segments of up to 1,800 meters (about 6,000 feet).

A 10Broad36 network uses differential phase shift keying (DPSK) to convert the data to analog form for transmission. Because of the encoding details, a 10Broad36 network actually needs 18 megahertz (MHz) for each channel: 14 MHz to encode the 10 Mbps signal and 4 MHz more for collision detection and reporting capabilities.

In a 10Broad36 network, throughput is 10 Mbps in each direction—that is, a total bandwidth of 36 MHz is needed. This bandwidth can be provided in a single cable or in two separate cables. A split-cable approach uses half the cable for each direction, which means the cable must have a 36 MHz bandwidth. A dual-cable approach uses separate cables for each direction, so that each cable needs only an 18 MHz bandwidth.

BROADER CATEGORIES
Ethernet; Network, Broadband

SEE ALSO
1Base5; 10BaseX

56K Line

A digital telephone circuit with a 64 Kbps bandwidth, but with a bandwidth of only 56 Kbps data, with the other 8 Kbps being used for signaling. Also known as an *ADN* (Advanced Digital Network) or a *DDS* (Dataphone Digital Service) line.

64K Line

A digital telephone circuit with a 64 Kbps bandwidth. Also known as a DS0 (digital signal, level 0) line. When the entire 64 Kbps are allocated for the data, the circuit is known as a *clear channel.* This is in contrast to a circuit in which 8 Kbps are used for signaling, leaving only 56 Kbps for data.

66-Type Punch-Down Block

A device for terminating wires, with the possibility of connecting input and output wires. This type of punch-down block can handle wires with up to 25 twisted pairs. The 66-type have generally been superseded by 110-type punch-down blocks.

SEE ALSO
Punch-Down Block

▼ 100BaseFX

A *100BaseT basal type* variant that runs over multimode fiber-optic cable. Nodes on a 100BaseFX network can be up to 2 kilometers apart. This variant is also written *100Base-FX*.

SEE

100BaseT

COMPARE

100BaseT4; 100BaseTX

▼ 100BaseT

The general name for any of three 100 Mbps Ethernet variants that have just been made a standard by an IEEE 802.3 subcommittee (802.3u). 100BaseT Ethernet is one of the candidates trying to become the standard 100 Mbps Ethernet. This version was developed and proposed originally by Grand Junction, in collaboration with several other corporations.

The term *fast Ethernet* is often used for this version. This is unfortunate, since that term is also used to refer to any Ethernet implementation that supports speeds faster than the official 10 Mbps standard. To add to the confusing terminology, a software product (no longer available) was also named *fastEthernet*.

100BaseT Ethernet retains Ethernet's CSMA/CD (Carrier Sense Multiple Access/ Collision Detect) media access method—in contrast to the 100BaseVG variant (now officially, IEEE 802.12)—which is the other major 100 Mbps Ethernet available.

The main differences between fast (100 Mbps) Ethernet and standard (10 Mbps) Ethernet are:

- A 100BaseT Ethernet allows a much shorter gap between signals.

- A 100BaseT Ethernet requires either higher-grade cable or more wire pairs. It can run at 100 Mbps speeds on Category 3 or 4 cable—provided four pairs are available; Category 5 cable requires only two pairs.

- Currently, a 100BaseT Ethernet can support a network that is only about a tenth of the length allowed for an ordinary Ethernet network. For networks that use copper (as opposed to fiber-optic) cabling: Two nodes of a 100BaseT4 network can be no further apart than 205 meters—regardless of whether the nodes are next to each other.

The following variants of 100BaseT Ethernet have been defined:

100BaseFX: Runs over multimode fiber-optic cable. Nodes on a 100BaseFX network can be up to two kilometers apart.

100BaseTX: Uses two wire pairs, but requires Category 5 unshielded or shielded twisted pair (UTP or STP) wire.

100BaseT4: Can use category 3, 4, or 5 UTP cable. The T4 in the name comes from the fact that four wire pairs are needed: two for sending and two for receiving.

In some configurations, fast and ordinary Ethernet nodes can share the same network. Fast Ethernet devices identify themselves as such by sending a series of FLPs (fast link pulses) at startup.

PRIMARY SOURCES

IEEE 802.3u committee publications

BROADER CATEGORIES

Ethernet

COMPARE

100BaseVG

100BaseT4

A *100BaseT Ethernet* variant that can use category 3, 4, or 5 unshielded twisted pair (UTP) cable. The T4 means that four wire pairs are needed: two for sending and two for receiving. Two nodes of a 100BaseT4 network can be no further apart than 205 meters, regardless of whether the nodes are next to each other. This variant is sometimes written *100Base-T4*.

SEE

100BaseT

COMPARE

100BaseTX; 100BaseFX

100BaseTX

A *100BaseT Ethernet* variant that uses two wire pairs, but requires Category 5 UTP or STP wire. Two nodes of a 100BaseTX network can be no further apart than 205 meters—regardless of whether the nodes are next to each other. This variant is sometimes written *100Base-TX*.

SEE

100BaseT

COMPARE

100BaseT4; 100BaseFX

100BaseVG

100BaseVG is a version of Ethernet developed by Hewlett-Packard (HP) and AT&T Microelectronics, and is currently under consideration by an IEEE 802.12 committee. It is an extension of 10BaseT Ethernet that will support transmissions of up to 100 megabits per second (Mbps) over voice-grade (Category 3) twisted-pair wire. The VG in the name stands for voice-grade.

Differences from 10 Mbps Ethernet

100BaseVG Ethernet differs from ordinary (10 Mbps) Ethernet in the following ways:

- Uses demand priority (rather than CSMA/CD) as the media access method.

- Can use ordinary (Category 3) unshielded twisted-pair (UTP) cable, provided that the cable has at least four wire pairs. Ordinary Ethernet needs only two pairs: one to send and one to receive.

- Uses quartet signaling to provide four transmission channels (wire pairs) instead of just one. All wire pairs are used in the same direction at a given time.

- Uses the more efficient 5B/6B NRZ signal encoding, as opposed to the

Manchester encoding scheme used by ordinary Ethernet.

- For category 3 cable, a VG network can be at most 600 meters from end to end—and only 200 meters if all hubs in the network are connected in the same wiring closet. These values increase by 50%—that is, to 900 and 300 meters, respectively—when category 5 cable is used. For VG using fiber-optic cable, the most widely separated network nodes can be up to 5000 meters, or 5 kilometers, apart.

Upgrading to 100BaseVG

100BaseVG is designed to provide an easy upgrade path from 10 Mbps Ethernet. An upgrade requires two new components:

- A 100BaseVG network interface card (NIC) for each node being upgraded. This NIC replaces the 10 Mbps version in the node.

- A 100BaseVG hub to replace the 10 Mbps hub. This type of hub is plug-compatible with a 10 Mbps hub, so that the upgrade requires simply unplugging a node from one hub and plugging it into the 100BaseVG hub. This can all take place in the wiring closet.

If you are already using twisted-pair Ethernet cabling, you may not need any new wiring, provided that the cable has four wire pairs.

100BaseVG/AnyLAN

100BaseVG/AnyLAN is an extension of 100BaseVG, developed as a joint effort between Hewlett-Packard and IBM. This version also supports the Token Ring architecture, and it can be used with either Ethernet or Token Ring cards (but not both at the same time or in the same network). Because the demand priority access method can be deterministic, the 100BaseVG/AnyLAN architecture could handle isochronous data—that is, data (such as voice or video) that requires a constant transmission rate.

The 100VG-AnyLAN Forum is the advocacy group for this Ethernet variant. This consortium includes over 20 members, including Apple, Compaq, and IBM. 100Base VG/AnyLAN is also known simply as VG or AnyLAN.

BROADER CATEGORY
Ethernet

SEE ALSO
HSLAN (High-Speed Local-Area Network)

COMPARE
100BaseT

100BaseX

100BaseX (sometimes written as 100 Base-X) is a function that translates between the FDDI (Fiber Distributed Data Interface)-based physical layer and the CSMA/CD-based data-link layer in a 100 megabit per second (Mbps) Ethernet proposed by Grand Junction Networks. The term was used more generally to refer to a 100 Mbps Ethernet developed by Grand Junction, among others. This proposed specification has since become known as Fast Ethernet, and has been refined into three variants:

- *100BaseFX*, which runs over fiber-optic cable

- *100BaseT4*, which runs over unshielded twisted pair (UTP) cable rated at Category 3 or higher—provided there are four available wire pairs

- *100BaseTX*, which runs over Category 5 UTP cable

These variants all use the standard CSMA/CD (carrier sense multiple access/collision detection) medium access scheme used by classic Ethernet. (In contrast, the *100BaseVG* variant proposed by Hewlett-Packard and other companies uses a demand priority access scheme.) Specifications and standards for the Fast Ethernet versions have been debated by the IEEE 802.3u subcommittee, and were just approved in June 1995.

BROADER CATEGORY
Ethernet

SEE ALSO
Fast Ethernet

COMPARE
100BaseVG

100 Mbps Ethernet

Any of several proposed 100 Mbps implementations of the Ethernet network architecture. Three different approaches have been proposed: 100BaseVG, 100BaseX, and fastEthernet. These implementations differ most fundamentally in the media-access methods and types of cable they use.

110-Type Punch-Down Block

A device for terminating wires, with the possibility of connecting input and output wires. This type of punch-down block has generally replaced the older 66-type blocks originally used by the telephone company.

SEE ALSO
Punch-Down Block

193rd Bit

In a T1 communications channel, a framing bit that is attached to every group of 192 bits. These 192 bits represent a single byte from each of the 24 channels multiplexed in a T1 line.

SEE ALSO
T1

3174

A cluster control unit for the IBM 3270 family of display terminals.

▼ 3270

The 3270 designation is used for a line of terminals, communications controllers, and printers that are used with IBM mainframes. The 3270 devices use synchronous communications protocols, either SDLC (Synchronous Data Link Control) or BSC (Binary Synchronous Communication), to communicate with the host.

In order for a stand-alone PC to communicate with an IBM mainframe, it must have an add-in board that enables the PC to emulate a 3270 terminal.

▼ 3270 Data Stream

In IBM's SNA (Systems Network Architecture) environment, a stream in which characters are converted and/or formatted, as specified through control characters and attribute settings.

▼ 3274

The designation for a cluster controller that can serve as a front end for an IBM mainframe host. Devices, such as 3270 terminals or printers, communicate with the host through this controller. The 3274 cluster controllers have been replaced by 3174 establishment controllers in newer configurations.

▼ 3278

The designation for a popular IBM terminal used to communicate with IBM mainframes.

▼ 3279

The designation for a color version of the 3278 terminal used to communicate with IBM mainframes.

▼ 3705

The designation for a computer that serves as a data communications controller for IBM's 370-series mainframes. The 3705 also has ports for asynchronous access over dial-up lines.

AA (Auto Answer)

A modem feature in which the modem can automatically respond to a call and establish a connection.

AAL (ATM Adaptation Layer)

The topmost of three layers defined for the ATM network architecture. The AAL mediates between the ATM layer and the various communication services involved in a transmission.

SEE ALSO

ATM (Asynchronous Transfer Mode)

AAR (Automatic Alternate Routing)

In X.25 and other networks, the process by which network traffic is automatically routed to maximize throughput, minimize distance, or balance channel usage.

ABM (Asynchronous Balanced Mode)

In the ISO's HDLC (High-Level Data-Link Control) protocol, an operating mode that gives each node in a point-to-point connection equal status as senders and receivers.

ABP (Alternate Bipolar)

A signal-encoding method.

SEE ALSO

Encoding, Signal

Abstract Syntax

A machine-independent set of language elements and rules used to describe objects, communications protocols, and other items. For example, Abstract Syntax Notation One (ASN.1) was developed as part of the OSI Reference Model; Extended Data Representation (XDR) was developed as part of Sun Microsystems' Network File System (NFS).

AC (Access Control)

A field in a token ring token or data frame.

AC (Alternating Current)

AC (alternating current) is a power supply whose polarity (direction of flow) switches periodically. AC is the type of electrical power supplied for homes and offices.

With AC, the actual amount of power being supplied at any given moment depends on where in the switching process you are. When plotted over time, a "pure" AC power supply produces a sine wave.

Not all countries use the same switching rate. For example, in North America, the current switches polarity 60 times per second; in most European countries, the rate is 50 times per second. These values are indicated as cycles per second, or hertz (Hz). Thus, electrical power in the United States alternates at 60 Hz.

Not all devices can use AC. In some cases the AC power must be converted to direct current (DC), which provides a constant voltage level and polarity. All digital systems (such as computers) must use DC.

COMPARE

DC (Direct Current)

AC (Application Context)

In the OSI Reference Model, AC (application context) is a term for all the application service elements (ASEs) required to use an application in a particular context.

More specifically, in network management, the AC provides the ground rules that serve to define the relationship between two applications during a temporary connection. These ground rules will determine the types of services that can be invoked during the connection and also the manner in which information will be exchanged. Such a context is important for defining the systems management services provided by a CMISE (common management information service element).

SEE ALSO

ASE (Application Service Element); CMISE (Common Management Information Service Element); Acceptable Use Policy (AUP)

Acceptable Use Policy (AUP)

SEE

AUP (Acceptable Use Policy)

Acceptance Angle

In fiber optics, a value that measures the range over which incoming light will be reflected and propagated through the fiber. The size of this angle depends on the relative refractive indexes of the fiber core, the cladding, and the surrounding medium (which is generally air).

Acceptance Cone

In fiber optics, the three-dimensional analog of an acceptance angle. The cone generated by revolving the acceptance angle 360 degrees with the center of the fiber's core as the cone's point.

Access Control

An operating system uses access control to determine the following:

- How users or resources can interact with the operating system

- What a specific user or group of users may do when interacting with the operating system

- Who can access a file or directory and what that user can do after accessing it

- How system or network resources can be used

At the lowest levels, hardware elements and software processes can obtain limited access to the system through mechanisms such as interrupts or polling. For example, low-level access to DOS is through IRQs (interrupt request lines) and through software interrupts, such as INT 21H, which provide programs with access to DOS capabilities and to certain hardware resources.

Access-control measures can be associated with users, files and directories, or resources. When assigned to users or groups of users, these control measures are known as *access rights*, *access privileges*, *trustee rights*, or *permissions*. When associated with files and directories, the access-control

a
b
c
d
e
f
g
h
i
j
k
l
m
n
o
p
q
r
s
t
u
v
w
x
y
z

elements are known as *attributes* or *flags*. Resources and other system objects generally have an associated access control list (ACL), which contains all the users who may use the resource.

Access control is generally specified by a system administrator or by the owner of a particular file or resource. Some access privileges are determined for users during network configuration; others may be assigned when the user logs on to a network or begins a session with an operating system.

Access-control issues can be complex, particularly if multiple operating environments are involved, as on an internetwork. One reason is that operating environments differ in the access-control measures they support. Because there are overlaps, omissions, and definition differences, mapping access controls between environments may be complicated.

SEE ALSO

Access Rights

Access Control Decision Function (ACDF)

SEE

ACDF (Access Control Decision Function)

Access Control Enforcement Function (ACEF)

SEE

ACEF (Accces Control Enforcement Function)

Access Control Information (ACI)

SEE

ACI (Access Control Information)

Access Network

A network attached to the trunk of a backbone network. This type of connection usually requires a gateway or a router, depending on the types of networks that comprise the backbone network.

Access Rights

Access rights are properties associated with files or directories in a networking environment; also known as *access privileges* or *trustee rights*. Access rights determine how users and network services can access and use files and directories. All networking environments and operating systems use some type of access rights settings to control access to the network and its resources.

Access rights are similar to security attributes, which specify additional properties relating to a file or directory. Security attributes can override access rights. In general, rights are assigned to a user for a specific file or directory. Attributes are assigned to a file or directory and control access by any user, regardless of that user's rights. The set of rights a user has been assigned to a file or directory is called his or her *trustee assignment*.

The number of access rights is relatively small. The terminology and particular combination of rights vary from system to system. For example, in Novell's NetWare 3.*x* and 4.*x*, access rights may be associated with directories or files or both, and a right may apply to all the files in a directory or only to individual ones. In NetWare 2.*x*, rights apply only to directories. See the table "Novell NetWare Access Rights" for descriptions of the access rights associated with NetWare.

The meaning or effect of a specific privilege may also be system-dependent. For example, in an AppleShare environment, the following access privileges are defined:

- See Files, which allows a user to see, open, and copy files.

- See Folder, which allows a user to see a folder (but not necessarily the folder's contents). If this privilege is not set, the folder does not even appear on the user's screen.

- Make Changes, which allows a user to change the contents of a file or folder. Even drastic changes such as deletions are allowed.

These AppleShare environment privileges may be granted to any of the following:

- Owner: The user who created (and, hence, owns) the file or folder.

- Group: The collection of users to whom the privilege is granted. This may be a single user.

- Everyone: All users with access to the file server.

NOVELL NETWARE ACCESS RIGHTS

ACCESS RIGHT	USAGE ALLOWED
Access Control (A)	Allows you to modify the trustee assignments and inherited rights mask (IRM) for a file. With Access Control rights, you can grant other users any rights except Supervisory rights.
Create (C)	Allows you to create subdirectories or files within a directory. Also allows you to salvage a file if it is deleted.
Erase (E)	Allows you to delete a file or directory.
File Scan (F)	Allows you to see a file or directory name when listing the parent directory.
Modify (M)	Allows you to change the name and attributes of a file or directory.
Read (R)	Allows you to open and read a file.
Supervisory (S)	Allows you to exercise all rights to a file or directory, including the right to grant Supervisory privileges to the file or directory to other users. (This right does not exist in NetWare 2.*x*.)
Write (W)	Allows you to open, edit, and save a file.

a b c d e f g h i j k l m n o p q r s t u v w x y z

In UNIX, owners, groups, and others may be granted read, write, or execute permissions for a file or a directory, as follows:

- Read access for a file allows a user to read or display the contents of a file. Read permission for a directory means the user can generate a directory listing.

- Write access for a file means the user can edit the file or redirect output to it. Write access for a directory allows the user to create a file or a subdirectory.

- Execute access for a file allows the user to use the file name as a command. Execute permission for a directory means the user can pass through the directory to subdirectories.

When a single machine or network includes more than one environment, there must be a well-defined rule for assigning and determining access rights. For example, in NetWare for Macintosh, the NetWare access rights supersede the AppleShare access privileges.

Similarly, there are mechanisms for ensuring that access rights are applied only as broadly as intended. For example, NetWare uses an Inherited Rights Mask (version 3.*x*) or Inherited Rights Filter (version 4.*x*) to specify which access rights for a directory are also applicable in a subdirectory.

BROADER CATEGORY

Access Control

SEE ALSO

Attribute; IRM/IRF (Inherited Rights Mask/Inherited Rights Filter)

▼
Access Time

In hard-disk performance, the average amount of time it takes to move the read/write heads to a specified location and retrieve data at that location. The lower the value, the better the performance. Currently, hard disks with access times of less than 15 milliseconds are common.

▼
Accounting

A process by which network usage can be determined and charges assessed for use of network resources, such as storage, access, and services. Accounting measures include blocks read, blocks written, connect time, disk storage, and service requests.

Most network operating systems include an accounting utility or support an add-on accounting package. For example, NetWare 3.11 has an accounting option in its SYSCON utility.

▼
Accounting Management

One of five OSI network management domains defined by the ISO and CCITT. This domain is concerned with the administration of network usage, costs, charges, and access to various resources.

SEE ALSO

Network Management

▼
Account Policy

In networking and other multiuser environments, a set of rules that determines whether a particular user is allowed to access the system and what resources the user may use. In

Windows NT Advanced Server, the account policy determines the way in which passwords may be used in a domain (a group of servers with a common security policy and database).

Accumaster Integrator

A network management program from AT&T.

ACD (Automatic Call Distributor)

A device that automatically switches an incoming call to the next available line.

ACDF (Access Control Decision Function)

In open systems, a function that uses various types of information, such as ACI (access control information), and guidelines to decide whether to grant access to resources in a particular situation.

ACE (Adverse Channel Enhancement)

A modem-adjustment method that allows the modem to compensate for noisy lines. For example, the modem might lower the operating speed.

ACEF (Access Control Enforcement Function)

In open systems, a function that enforces the decision made by the ACDF (access control decision function).

ACF (Advanced Communications Function)

ACF (Advanced Communications Function) is the base name for several IBM software packages that operate under IBM's SNA (Systems Network Architecture). In some cases, the programs are revisions or extensions of older programs.

The following programs are included:

- **ACF/NCP (Advanced Communications Function/Network Control Program):** Resides in a communications controller. It provides and controls communications between the host machine and the network devices.

- **ACF/TCAM (Advanced Communications Function/Telecommunications Access Method):** Serves as an ACF/VTAM application and provides message handling and other capabilities.

- **ACF/VTAM (Advanced Communications Function/Virtual Telecommunications Access Method):** Provides and controls communications between a terminal and host programs. ACF/VTAM supersedes and adds capabilities to the older VTAM software.

- **ACF/VTAME (Advanced Communications Function/Virtual Telecommunications Access Method-Entry):** An obsolete program that has been superseded by ACF/VTAM.

BROADER CATEGORY
SNA (Systems Network Architecture)

a b c d e f g h i j k l m n o p q r s t u v w x y z

ACI (Access Control Information)

In the CCITT's X.500 directory services model, any information used in controlling access to a file or directory.

ACID (Atomicity, Consistency, Isolation, and Durability)

In transaction processing (TP), the attributes that are desirable for a transaction.

ACK

In telecommunications, a control character that indicates that a packet has been received without an error. In certain network architectures, ACK is the name for a frame that sends such an acknowledgment. The ASCII ACK character has value 6.

ACL (Access Control List)

In some networking environments, the ACL is a list of services available on a network, along with the users and devices that are allowed to use each service. This list provides one way to control access to network resources.

In NetWare Directory Services (NDS), each object in the directory has a property called the ACL, which lists all the other objects that have trustee assignments (rights) to that object.

ACONSOLE

In Novell's NetWare 3.x, ACONSOLE is a utility that allows a network supervisor to access a server through a modem from a workstation, and to manage the server from this workstation. In NetWare 3.x, the RCONSOLE utility provides the same function across a direct connection.

In NetWare 4.x, RCONSOLE was updated to add ACONSOLE's asynchronous capability, and ACONSOLE was removed.

BROADER CATEGORY
NetWare

ACS (Asynchronous Communications Server)

An ACS is usually a dedicated PC or expansion board that provides other network nodes with access to any of several serial ports or modems. The ports may be connected to mainframes or minicomputers.

To access a modem or a port, the workstation user can run an ordinary communications program in a transparent manner. However, in order for this to work, one of the following must be the case:

- The communications program must include a redirector to route the communication process to the appropriate ACS.

- The workstation must have a special hardware port emulation board installed, which takes up one of the workstation's expansion slots. In this case, the communications package does not need any special rerouting capabilities.

- The user must run a redirection program before starting the communications package. To work with a software-based redirector, the communications package must be able to use DOS interrupt INT 14H. Unfortunately, many communications programs bypass this interrupt to access the UART (universal asynchronous receiver/transmitter) directly for faster operation.

BROADER CATEGORY
Server

ACSE (Association Control Service Element)

In the OSI Reference Model, an application-level service that establishes the appropriate relationship between two applications, so that they can cooperate and communicate on a task, such as exchanging information.

Active

When used to describe hardware or a configuration, *active* generally means that the hardware does some signal processing—cleaning, boosting, or both. For example, an active hub boosts and cleans a signal before passing it on.

Active Hub

In an ARCnet network, a component that makes it possible to connect additional nodes to the network and also to boost signals that go through the hub.

SEE ALSO
Hub

Active Link

In an ARCnet network, a box used to connect two cable segments when both cable segments have high-impedance network interface cards (NICs) connected.

Active Star

A network configuration in which the central node of a star topology cleans and boosts a signal.

SEE ALSO
Topology, Star

ACU (Autocall Unit)

A device that can dial telephone numbers automatically.

AD (Administrative Domain)

In the Internet community, a collection of nodes, routers, and connectors that is managed by a common administrator, such as an organization or a company.

Adapter

A board that plugs into an expansion bus, and that provides special capabilities, such as video, fax, modem, network access, and so on. Besides functionality, adapters are distinguished by the width of the data bus between the adapter and the PC. Adapters may have 8-, 16-, or 32-bit connections.

a
b
c
d
e
f
g
h
i
j
k
l
m
n
o
p
q
r
s
t
u
v
w
x
y
z

ADC (Analog-to-Digital Converter)

A device that converts an analog signal to digital form.

ADDMD (Administrative Directory Management Domain)

In the CCITT's X.500 directory services model, a collection of directory system agents (DSAs) under the control of a single authority.

SEE ALSO

DSA (Directory System Agent)

Address

An address is a value used to specify a location. The location may be an area of local or shared memory, or it may be a node or other device on a network.

Network-Related Addresses

Several types of addresses are distinguished for network locations. The type of address used in a particular context depends partly on which protocol or device is creating the address. Address information may be maintained in any of several ways, such as in look-up tables or directories.

Some common types of network-related addresses are hardware, network, node, Internet, and e-mail (electronic mail). There are other types of addresses, and not all types of addresses are used in the same conceptual model. Devices that connect networks or network segments generally get network and/or node addresses on each network they connect.

Hardware Address

A hardware address, also known as a *physical address* or a *MAC address,* is a unique numerical value assigned to a network interface card (NIC) during the manufacturing process or by setting jumpers or switches during network installation. One part of this address is assigned to the manufacturer by the IEEE (Institute of Electronics Engineers) and is common to all components from that manufacturer; the second part of the hardware address is a unique value assigned by the hardware manufacturer.

Network Address

A network address is an arbitrary value that is assigned identically to each station in a particular network. As long as there is only a single network, this value is automatically unique. If two or more networks are connected, each must have a different network address. If a station (for example, a server) connects to two networks, that station will have two different network addresses.

A network address is also known as a *network number* or an *IPX external network number.*

Node Address

In addition to a common network address, each station in a network has a unique node address. This value identifies a particular node, or more specifically, the NIC assigned to each node, in a particular network. This address is also known as a *node number* or *station address.*

When specified as a source or destination, a network server or workstation may be identified by a network and a node address or by a hardware address.

The node addresses for Ethernet cards are factory-set, and no two cards have the same number. The node addresses for ARCnet and Token Ring cards are set by changing jumpers or switches on the cards. If a node contains two NICs, the node will have two different network addresses.

Internal Address

An internal address is a unique value that specifies a node with respect to a particular server in a network, which is useful in networks that have multiple servers. This is a logical address. Only certain network operating systems, such as NetWare, support internal addresses.

See the figure "Examples of network addresses" for an illustration of the kinds of addresses discussed so far.

Internet Address

An Internet address is a network-layer address that uniquely identifies a node on an internetwork or on the Internet. This type of address uses four bytes of storage, and it is generally represented as four decimal values separated by decimal points, as in 12.34.56.78. Certain bits from an Internet

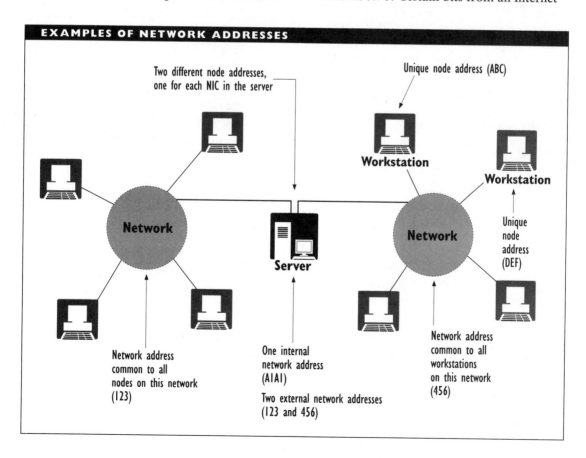

EXAMPLES OF NETWORK ADDRESSES

Two different node addresses, one for each NIC in the server

Unique node address (ABC)

Workstation

Workstation

Network

Network

Server

Unique node address (DEF)

Network address common to all nodes on this network (123)

One internal network address (AIAI)

Two external network addresses (123 and 456)

Network address common to all workstations on this network (456)

a b c d e f g h i j k l m n o p q r s t u v w x y z

address can be masked to identify a subnetwork that contains some of the nodes in the internetwork.

Special protocols, such as the Address Resolution Protocol (ARP), are used to convert from an Internet to a hardware address; other programs, such as the Reverse ARP (RARP), convert from a hardware to an Internet address.

E-Mail Address

An e-mail (electronic mail) address is an application-layer address that identifies a user's mailbox location in a message-handling system. These addresses have little in common with the other types of addresses mentioned; however, the e-mail address must be associated with the station's network and node address or with its hardware address in order for messages to be transferred from a sender to a receiver.

Memory-Related Addresses

Several different formats are used for memory addresses in personal computers: flat address space, segmented address, and paged address.

Flat Address Space

An address in a flat address space is a simple numerical value in the range between 0 and the highest address value. For example, in a machine with 1 megabyte of memory, the addresses range from 0x00000 to 0xfffff.

Segmented Address

An address in a segmented address space consists of a segment and an offset value.

The segment value represents a (usually 16-byte) location that is aligned on a paragraph boundary. The offset value represents the number of bytes to shift from this segment address. DOS uses segmented addresses.

Paged Address

Certain types of address space actually consist of two types of values. For example, in expanded memory, locations in a special set of chips, and hence, in a special set of addresses, are mapped into special memory buffers. These buffers are broken into pages of a specific size.

Virtual memory also uses paged addresses.

Address Bus

An address bus is the electrical signal lines over which memory locations are specified. Each line carries a single bit, so the number of lines on the bus determines the number of possible addresses:

- 20 lines allow access to 1 megabyte (MB) of memory. Examples include Intel's 8086 and 8088 processors.

- 24 lines provide access to 16 MB. Examples include Intel's 80286 and Motorola's 68000 processors.

- 32 lines provide access to 4 gigabytes (AB). Examples include Intel's 80386, 80486, and Pentium; and Motorola's 68020 and later processors.

- 64 lines provide access to 16 exabytes (EB). (An exabyte is a billion billion, or a quintillion, bytes.) Digital Equipment Corporation's Alpha APX chip is an example of a 64-bit address bus.

Address Mask

In the IP (Internet Protocol) addressing scheme, a group of selected bits whose values identify a subnetwork; also known as a *subnet mask*. All the members of that subnetwork share the same mask value. Using an address mask makes it easier for the system to reference a member of a particular subnet.

Address Resolution

The process of mapping one type of address to another; specifically, mapping a network (local) address to a hardware-dependent address. The most widely used method of address resolution is the Address Resolution Protocol (ARP) or a variation of that protocol.

Adjacent Channel

A frequency band immediately before or after the current channel. For example, a channel between 100 MHz and 500 MHz and a channel between 700 MHz and 900 MHz are both adjacent to the channel between 500 MHz and 700 MHz.

ADMD (Administration Management Domain)

In the CCITT's X.400 Message Handling System (MHS) model, an ADMD (Administration Management Domain) is a network or network section operated by the CCITT (Consultative Committee for International Telegraphy and Telephony) or a national PTT (Post, Telegraph, and Telephone). Specific examples of ADMDs include MCImail and AT&Tmail in the United States; British Telecom Gold400mail in Britain.

ADMDs are public carriers, unlike PRMDs (private management domains), which are run by private organizations or companies. In accordance with CCITT guidelines, ADMDs handle any international connections; PRMDs communicate through a local ADMD. ADMDs can connect PRMDs, but a PRMD cannot connect ADMDs. Because all ADMDs run under the auspices of CCITT, the conglomeration of ADMDs in the world forms the backbone for a global X.400 network.

BROADER CATEGORIES

MD (Management Domain); X.400

COMPARE

PRMD (Private Management Domain)

Administration

Administration involves the management and maintenance of a computer system, network, or environment.

Administrative Tasks

An administrator's responsibilities may be grouped into the following general categories:

Configuration management: Handling tasks such as user accounts, hardware settings, access rights, and security.

Data-flow management: Monitoring performance, managing memory

a b c d e f g h i j k l m n o p q r s t u v w x y z

and resources, making sure applications and data files are accessible, and generally ensuring that data is flowing properly.

Hardware maintenance: Installing, maintaining, and diagnosing hardware components.

Software maintenance: Installing applications and other software, software version control, bug reporting and resolution, and so on.

Help: Training users, providing documentation for using the system resources and applications, and offering other support.

Levels of Administration

Various levels of administration are distinguished, including the following:

System: Refers to a particular division in a company or a particular type of hardware, such as mainframes or database servers. System administration responsibilities do not necessarily involve networking issues; that is, a system administrator may or may not need to attend to issues relating to the connections between machines, as well as to the machines themselves.

Network: Usually refers to a LAN (local-area network), but may encompass machines in a larger range, provided these machines are all connected by a common architecture. In addition to the individual machines, a network administrator must keep track of the connections between the machines.

Internetwork: Refers to multiple networks. Some or all of these networks may use different architectures. An internetwork administrator should be able to assume that any subnetworks are under the control of network administrators, so that the internetwork administrator can concentrate on the connections between networks rather than those between machines.

Administration Management Domain (ADMD)

SEE

ADMD (Administration Management Domain)

Administrative Domain (AD)

SEE

AD (Administrative Domain)

Advanced Function Printing (AFP)

SEE

AFP (Advanced Function Printing)

Advanced Intelligent Network (AIN)

SEE

AIN (Advanced Intelligent Network)

Advanced Mobile Phone Service (AMPS)

SEE

AMPS (Advanced Mobile Phone Service)

Advanced Research Projects Agency (ARPA)

SEE

ARPA (Advanced Research Projects Agency)

Advantage Networks

Advantage networks represent a networking strategy from Digital Equipment Corporation (DEC), designed to add support for protocols such as the TCP/IP suite to DEC's OSI-compliant DECnet Phase V architecture.

Adverse Channel Enhancement (ACE)

SEE

ACE (Adverse Channel Enhancement)

Advertising

The process by which a network service makes its presence and availability known on the network. For example, Novell NetWare services use the SAP (Service Advertising Protocol).

AE (Application Entity)

In the OSI Reference Model, an entity (process or function) that runs all or part of an application. An AE may consist of one or more application service elements (ASEs).

AFI (Authority and Format Identifier)

In the OSI Reference Model, part of the address for the network-layer service access point (NSAP). The AFI portion specifies the authority, or administrator, that is allocating the IDI (initial domain identifier) values. The AFI also specifies the format of the IDI and the DSP (domain specific part), which are other parts of the NSAP address.

AFP (Advanced Function Printing)

In IBM's SAA (Systems Applications Architecture) environments, the ability to print text and images; that is, to use all points addressable (APA) printers.

AFT (Application File Transfer)

In the International Standardized Profile (ISP) grouping, a prefix that identifies FTAM (file transfer, access, and management) profiles. For example, AFT11 represents basic file transfer.

Agent

In general, an agent is a program that can perform a particular task automatically, when appropriate or upon request by another program. An agent is commonly used to provide information to an application, such as a network management program. An agent may be machine- or function-specific.

The following are some of the agents that are found in networking-related contexts:

- In a client-server networking model, an element that does work on behalf of a client or a server application. For example, in Novell's SMS (storage management system) backup architecture, a special backup agent, called a *TSA* (*target service agent*), is loaded on every node that you want to back up from a centralized location. The agent allows the central backup program to access and back up the data on that node.

- In an IBM Token Ring architecture, an element on the network interface card that monitors certain aspects of the node and ring performance, and that reports this information to a network management program or to a Ring Error Monitor (REM).

- In network management and monitoring, a terminate-and-stay-resident (TSR) program that runs on a workstation to monitor activity and report this to a network management program.

The data collected by an agent is organized and processed by an agent handler. In network management, an agent handler may organize and analyze data concerning some network function or component.

Aging

A process by which old items or table entries are removed in a systematic manner, such as first in, first out. This process serves both to update such tables and to speed up access.

AI (Authentication Information)

In network security, information used to determine whether a user is legitimate and authorized to access the system.

AIM (Analog Intensity Modulation)

In communications using light (rather than electrical) signals, a modulation method in which the intensity of the light source varies as a function of the signal being transmitted.

AIN (Advanced Intelligent Network)

In telecommunications, the name for a sophisticated digital network of the future.

AIS (Alarm Indication Signal)

A signal used in the OSI network management model and also in broadband ISDN networks to indicate the presence of an alarm or error somewhere on the network.

AL (Application Layer)

The topmost of the seven layers in the OSI Reference Model.

SEE ALSO
OSI Layer

Alarm

In various network environments, particularly network management, an alarm is a signal used to indicate that an abnormality, a fault, or a security violation has been detected. Alarms may be distinguished by type, such as performance, fault, or security, and also by the severity of the event that caused the alarm.

At one extreme are critical events that represent immediate threats to continued network operation; for example, when a crucial LAN (local-area network) node or a

Algorithm   **27**

server goes down. In some network management environments, such critical alarms may trigger automatic response by the network management package.

At the other extreme are events that are not currently serious, but that may eventually become serious enough to threaten network operation; for example, when network traffic is getting close to the network's bandwidth limit. Such events generally do not require immediate correction but should be monitored.

Alarm Indication Signal (AIS)

SEE

AIS (Alarm Indication Signal)

Alarm Reporting Function (ARF)

SEE

ARF (Alarm Reporting Function)

Alert

In network management, an alarm sent by an agent to the administrator. An alert reports that a problem has arisen or that a threshold has been reached.

Algorithm

An algorithm is a predefined set of instructions for accomplishing a task. An algorithm is guaranteed to produce a result in a finite amount of time. Algorithms are used in many ways in networking. For example, there are hashing algorithms for finding file names in a directory and timing algorithms for deciding how long to wait before trying to access a network.

In most cases, the algorithms are of little interest to either the casual or intense network user. However, several algorithms have escaped from behind the scenes and have actually become items in marketing literature and other product discussions. The following are a few of the better-known algorithms:

Auto-partition: An algorithm by which a repeater can automatically disconnect a segment from a network if that segment is not functioning properly. This can happen, for example, when a broken or unterminated cable causes too many collisions. When the collisions have subsided, the network segment can be reconnected.

Bellman-Ford: An algorithm for finding routes through an internetwork. The algorithm uses distance vectors, as opposed to link states. The Bellman-Ford algorithm is also known as the *old ARPAnet* algorithm.

Distance-vector: A class of computation-intensive routing algorithms in which each router computes the distance between itself and each possible destination. This is accomplished by computing the distance between a router and all of its immediate router neighbors, and adding each neighboring router's computations for the distances between that neighbor and all of its immediate neighbors. Several commonly used implementations are available, such as the Bellman-Ford algorithm and the ISO's Interdomain Routing Protocol (IDRP).

Hot potato: In networks, a routing algorithm in which a node routes a packet or message to the output line with the shortest queue.

Link-states: A class of routing algorithms in which each router knows the location of and distance to each of its immediately neighboring routers, and can broadcast this information to all other routers in a link state packet (LSP). If a router updates its LSP, the new version is broadcast and replaces the older versions at each other router. The scheme used to distribute the LSP greatly influences the performance of the routers. These types of algorithm are an alternative to distance-vector algorithms; rather than storing actual paths, link-state algorithms store the information needed to generate such paths. The ISO's open shortest path first (OSPF) algorithm is an example of a link-state algorithm.

Spanning-tree: An algorithm that is used to compute open paths (paths without loops) among networks. The algorithm can generate all such paths and select one. If that path becomes inoperative because a node has gone down, the algorithm can find an alternate path. This type of algorithm is used by bridges to find the best path between two nodes in different networks, and to ensure that no path loops occur in the internetwork. This algorithm is defined in the IEEE 802.1 standard.

▼
Alias

In a computer environment, a name that represents another, usually longer, name. In NetWare Directory Services (NDS), an alias is an object in one part of the Directory tree that points to the real object, which is located in a different part of the tree. Users can access the real object through the alias.

▼
Alignment Error

In an Ethernet or other network, an error in which a packet has extra bits; that is, the packet does not end on byte-boundaries and will have invalid CRC (cyclic redundancy check) values. An alignment error may be caused by a faulty component, such as a damaged network interface card (NIC), transceiver, or cable.

▼
Allocation Unit

In Novell's NetWare, areas that are used to store information from files and tables. Two types of storage are distinguished: blocks, which are used to store data on disk, and buffers, which hold data in RAM temporarily.

SEE ALSO

Block; Buffer, Fiber-Optic Cable; Buffer, Memory.

▼
Alternate Mark Inversion (AMI)

SEE

AMI (Alternate Mark Inversion)

Alternate Route Selection (ARS)

SEE

ARS (Alternate Route Selection)

Alternate Routing

This term describes the use of an alternative communications path, such as a telephone connection, when the primary one is not available.

AM (Accounting Management)

In network management, a function for gathering performance and usage information from a network.

AM (Active Monitor)

In a token ring network, the node that is responsible for creating, passing, and maintaining the token. The performance of the AM is monitored constantly by standby monitors (SMs) to ensure that the token-passing process is not interrupted.

AME (Asynchronous Modem Eliminator)

An AME, also known as a *null modem,* is a serial cable and connector with a modified pin configuration (compared to an ordinary RS-232 cable). This cable enables two computers to communicate directly; that is, without modems as intermediaries.

American National Standards Institute (ANSI)

SEE

ANSI (American National Standards Institute)

America Online (AOL)

SEE

AOL (America Online)

AMF (Account Metering Function)

In the OSI network management model, the function that keeps track of every user's resource usage.

AMH (Application Message Handling)

In the International Standardized Profile (ISP) model, the prefix used to identify MHS (Message Handling System) actions.

AMI (Alternate Mark Inversion)

A signal-encoding scheme in which a 1 is represented alternately as positive and negative voltage, and 0 is represented as zero voltage. It does not use transition coding, but can detect noise-induced errors at the hardware level.

SEE ALSO

Encoding, Signal

AMP (Active Monitor Present)

In token ring networks, a packet issued every 3 seconds by the active monitor (AM) on the ring to indicate that the AM is working and is still in charge.

Amplifier

A device for boosting an analog signal. The same service is provided by a repeater for digital signals.

Amplitude

The magnitude, or level, of a signal. For an electrical signal, it is expressed in volts (voltage) or amperes (current). In computer contexts, current is more likely to be expressed in milliamperes.

AMPS (Advanced Mobile Phone Service)

A cellular telephone service. AMPS is a wireless analog communications service that operates in the 825 to 890 megahertz range.

Analog Communication

A telecommunications system that uses analog (that is, continuous, sinusoidal) signals to represent information. An example of an analog communication system is the classic voice-based telephone system (which is being replaced by the newer, digital systems).

Analog Intensity Modulation (AIM)

SEE

AIM (Analog Intensity Modulation)

Analog-to-Digital Conversion

The process of converting an analog signal (one that can take on any value within a specified range) to digital form. An analog-to-digital converter (ADC) is a device that converts an analog signal to digital form.

ANF (AppleTalk Networking Forum)

A consortium of developers and vendors working to encapsulate AppleTalk in other protocols; for example, within the TCP/IP suite.

ANI (Automatic Number Identification)

In ISDN and some other telecommunications environments, a feature that includes the sender's identification number, such as telephone number, in the transmission, so that the recipient knows who is calling; also known as *caller ID*.

Annex D

In frame-relay technology, a document that specifies a method for indicating permanent virtual circuit (PVC) status. The document is part of the ANSI T1.617 standard.

Anonymous FTP

On the Internet, a protocol that allows a user to retrieve publicly available files from other networks. By using the special user ID, "anonymous" users can transfer files without a password or other login credentials. (FTP is an application-layer protocol in the Internet's TCP/IP protocol suite.)

Anonymous Remailer

An Internet service that can be used to hide the origins of an e-mail message being sent to someone. The anonymous remailer removes any source address information from a message, substitutes any specified pen name, and then sends the message on to the specified destination.

ANSI (American National Standards Institute)

The United States representative in the ISO (International Standardization Organization). ANSI creates and publishes standards for programming languages, communications, and networking. For example, the standard for the FDDI network architecture is ANSI X3T9.5.

Anti-Virus Program

An anti-virus program is used for detecting or removing a computer virus. An anti-virus program looks for suspicious activity, such as unnecessary disk access, attempts to intercept a BIOS or other low-level call, and attempts to format or delete files. In some cases, the anti-virus program detects a pattern characteristic of a particular virus.

Some anti-virus programs are TSR (terminate-and-stay-resident) programs, which monitor computer activity constantly, looking for indications of a virus. In some cases, these types of programs can be extremely annoying and very processor intensive. Users have been known to remove an anti-virus TSR program from memory out of frustration.

Other anti-virus programs are intended to be run periodically. When they are run, the programs look for the tell-tale signs (known as *signatures*) of particular viruses. These programs are minimally disruptive; on the other hand, their effectiveness is directly proportional to the frequency with which they are used.

Because the coding for computer viruses is constantly changing, anti-virus programs must also be updated regularly. It is important to test anti-virus programs thoroughly, which means that every new release must be tested. Make sure an anti-virus program performs to your expectations before installing it on a network. Some programs can eat up a significant amount of working memory.

Recently, a very different (and, consequently, very controversial) type of anti-virus program has become available. InVircible, created by Zvi Netiv, is designed to detect viruses that have already infected a system, and to clean these up. Rather than looking for virus signatures, InVircible uses expert system rules to look for behavior characteristic of viruses: replication, use of memory, attempts to attach to the anti-virus program, etc. InVircible will even put out "virus bait" to get an existing virus to try to infect the bait.

BROADER CATEGORY
Data Protection

RELATED ARTICLE
Virus

▼
AOL (America Online)

America Online is a commercial online service like CompuServe and Prodigy. AOL supports both DOS and Windows users, and provides a range of services (mail, news, reference, financial, entertainment, Internet access, etc.). Users pay a flat monthly fee, which allows a limited number of free hours. Additional hours are billed at a predetermined rate. AOL's graphical interface is highly regarded—in fact, Apple has licensed the interface technology for use in Apple's eWorld interface. AOL provides a very comprehensive set of access opportunities to the Internet.

FOR INFORMATION
Call AOL at 800-827-6364

▼
AOM (Application OSI Management)

In the International Standardized Profile (ISP) model, the prefix for functions and services related to network management.

▼
AOW (Asia and Oceania Workshop)

One of three regional workshops for implementers of the OSI Reference Model. The other two are EWOC (European Workshop for Open Systems) and OIW (OSI Implementers Workshop).

▼
AP (Application Process)

In the OSI Reference Model, a program that can make use of application layer services. Application service elements (ASEs) provide the requested services for the AP.

▼
APD (Avalanche Photodiode)

A detector component in some fiber-optic receivers. The APD converts light into electrical energy. The "avalanche" refers to the fact that the detector emits multiple electrons for each incoming photon (light particle).

▼
APDU (Application Protocol Data Unit)

A data packet at the application layer; also called *application-layer PDU.*

SEE ALSO
OSI Reference Model

▼
API (Application Program Interface)

An abstract interface to the services and protocols offered by an operating system, usually involving a published set of function calls. Programmers and applications can use the functions available in this interface to gain access to the operating system's services.

▼
APIA (Application Program Interface Association)

A group that writes APIs for the CCITT's X.400 Message Handling System (MHS).

▼
APPC (Advanced Program-to-Program Communications)

In IBM's SAA (Systems Application Architecture), APPC is a collection of protocols to enable executing applications to communicate directly with each other as peers (without intervention by a mainframe host).

APPC is defined at a level comparable to the session layer in the OSI Reference Model. It can be supported in various networking environments, including IBM's SNA (System Network Architecture), Ethernet, Token Ring, and X.25.

APPC/PC (Advanced Program-to-Program Communications/Personal Computers) is a PC-based version of APPC.

AppleDouble

In the Macintosh world, a file format that uses separate files for the data and resource forks that make up a Macintosh file. This enables the files—or at least the data portion—to be used on different platforms.

COMPARE

AppleSingle

AppleShare

A network operating system from Apple. AppleShare runs on a Macintosh network server, providing file and printer services. AppleShare uses the AppleTalk protocol suite to carry out its tasks.

SEE ALSO

AppleTalk

AppleSingle

In the Macintosh world, a file format that stores both a file's contents (data fork) and its resources (resource fork) within a single file. Because data and resources are mixed in a proprietary format, such a file cannot be used on other platforms.

COMPARE

AppleDouble

AppleTalk

AppleTalk is Apple's proprietary protocol suite for Macintosh network communications. It provides a multilayer, peer-to-peer architecture that uses services built into the operating system. This gives every Macintosh networking capabilities. AppleTalk can run under any of several network operating systems, including Apple's AppleShare, Novell's NetWare for Macintosh, and Sun Microsystems' TOPS.

AppleTalk was developed in the mid-1980s with the goal of providing a simple, portable, easy-to-use, and open networking environment. To access such a network, a user just needs to "plug in, log in, and join in."

A newer version, Phase 2, was released in 1989. This version provided some new capabilities and extended others.

AppleTalk Layers

AppleTalk is a comprehensive, layered environment. It covers networking services over almost the entire range of layers specified in the OSI Reference Model. The figure "The AppleTalk protocol hierarchy" shows the organization of the AppleTalk layers, as well as the protocols in the AppleTalk Protocol Suite.

a b c d e f g h i j k l m n o p q r s t u v w x y z

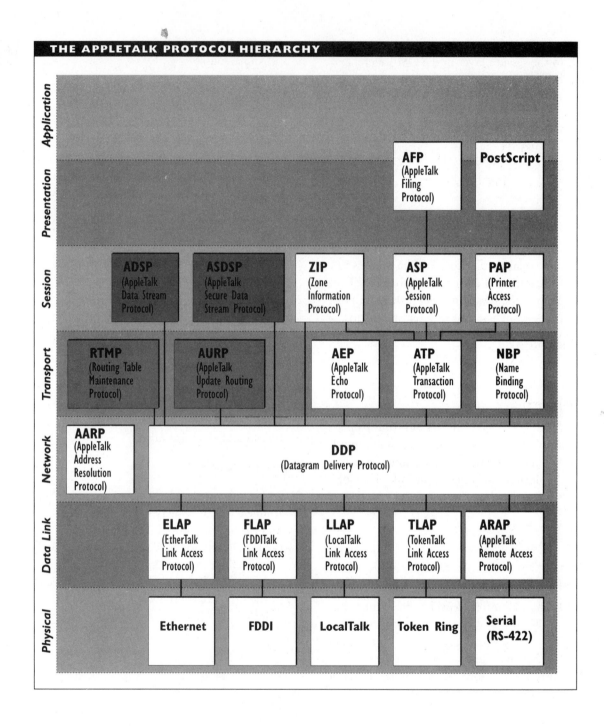

THE APPLETALK PROTOCOL HIERARCHY

Physical and Data-Link Layers

There are AppleTalk implementations for the following network architectures at the physical and data-link layers:

- Apple's 230 kilobit per second (Kbps).

- LocalTalk architecture. LocalTalk provides a media-access method and a cabling scheme for AppleTalk. The architecture uses twisted-pair cables and RS-422 connections, allows nodes to be separated by as much as 305 meters (1,000 feet), and can transmit at up to 230.4 Kbps. The term Local-Talk is sometimes used to refer to an AppleTalk network.

- EtherTalk, Apple's implementation of the 10 megabit per second (Mbps) Ethernet architecture. Two versions of EtherTalk exist. The earlier one, EtherTalk Phase 1, is modeled on the Blue Book Ethernet 2.0 (as opposed to the version specified in the IEEE 802.3 documentation). Its successor, Phase 2, is modeled on the IEEE 802.3 standard. Because these two variants of Ethernet define packets somewhat differently, Phase 1 and Phase 2 nodes cannot communicate directly with each other. EtherTalk has replaced LocalTalk as the default networking capability in newer Macintosh models.

- TokenTalk, Apple's implementation of the token-ring architecture. AppleTalk supports both the 4-Mbps version specified by IEEE 802.5 and the 16-Mbps version from IBM. The token-ring architecture is supported only in AppleTalk Phase 2.

- FDDITalk, Apple's implementation of the 100 Mbps FDDI architecture.

For each of these architectures, a Link Access Protocol (LAP) is defined: LLAP for LocalTalk, ELAP for EtherTalk, TLAP for TokenTalk, and FLAP for FDDITalk.

Network Layer

All AppleTalk networks use the DDP (Datagram Delivery Protocol) at the network layer, regardless of the architecture operating at the data-link layer. This protocol makes a best effort at packet delivery, but delivery is not guaranteed.

Note also the AARP (AppleTalk Address Resolution Protocol) at this layer. The AARP maps AppleTalk (network) addresses to Ethernet or Token Ring (physical) addresses.

Higher Layers

For reliable packet delivery, the ADSP (AppleTalk Data Stream Protocol) and ATP (AppleTalk Transaction Protocol) are available. Each of these protocols is appropriate under different conditions.

The NBP (Name Binding Protocol) and ZIP (Zone Information Protocol) help make addressing easier. NBP associates easy-to-remember names (used by users) with the appropriate address.

ZIP is used mainly on larger networks or internetworks, which are more likely to be divided into zones. A zone is a logical grouping of nodes that together make up a subnetwork. The concept of a zone was introduced to allow for larger networks with more than 255 nodes, and also to make addressing and routing tasks easier.

a b c d e f g h i j k l m n o p q r s t u v w x y z

Applications access an AppleTalk network through the AFP (AppleTalk Filing Protocol); they access printer services by shipping PostScript files through the PAP (Printer Access Protocol).

A few protocols make use of services from more than one lower-level protocol. For example, ZIP relies on ATP and DDP services.

AppleTalk Protocol Suite

The following protocols make up the AppleTalk Protocol Suite (see the figure "The AppleTalk protocol hierarchy," earlier in this article):

AARP (AppleTalk Address Resolution Protocol): A network-layer protocol that maps AppleTalk (network) addresses to physical addresses.

ADSP (AppleTalk Data Stream Protocol): A session-layer protocol that allows two nodes to establish a reliable connection through which data can be transmitted.

AEP (AppleTalk Echo Protocol): A transport-layer protocol used to determine whether two nodes are connected and both available.

AFP (AppleTalk Filing Protocol): A presentation/application-layer protocol used by applications to communicate with the network.

ASDSP (AppleTalk Safe Data Stream Protocol): A session-layer protocol that is similar to ADSP but that provides additional security against unauthorized use.

ASP (AppleTalk Session Protocol): A session-layer protocol used to begin and end sessions, send commands from client to server, and send replies from server to client.

ATP (AppleTalk Transaction Protocol): A transport-layer protocol that can provide reliable packet transport. Packets are transported within the framework of a transaction (an interaction between a requesting and a responding entity {program or node}).

AURP (AppleTalk Update Routing Protocol): A transport-layer routing protocol that is similar to RTMP (Routing Table Maintenance Protocol) but that updates the routing table only when a change has been made to the network.

DDP (Datagram Delivery Protocol): A network-layer protocol that prepares and routes packets for transmission on the network.

LAP (Link Access Protocol): Works at the data-link layer, converting packets from higher layers into the appropriate form for the physical transmission. Each network architecture needs its own LAP.

ELAP (EtherTalk Link Access Protocol): The link-access protocol used for Ethernet networks.

FLAP (FDDITalk Link Access Protocol): The link-access protocol used for FDDI networks.

LLAP (LocalTalk Link Access Protocol): The link-access protocol used for LocalTalk networks.

TLAP (TokenTalk Link Access Protocol): The link-access protocol used for Token Ring networks.

ARAP (AppleTalk Remote Access Protocol): A link-access protocol for accessing the network from a remote location over a serial line.

NBP (Name Binding Protocol): A transport-layer protocol that associates device names with network addresses. If the NBP is successful, this binding process will be completely transparent to the user.

PAP (Printer Access Protocol): A session-layer protocol for creating a path from the user or application to a printer.

RTMP (Routing Table Maintenance Protocol): A transport-layer routing protocol for moving packets between networks.

ZIP (Zone Information Protocol): A session-layer protocol used to help find a node; for example, in a large internetwork.

If installed, an AppleShare server runs on top of these protocols at the uppermost (application) layer. The AppleShare server uses the AFP to provide centralized file sharing for its clients, and can use the PAP to provide printer sharing.

Numbers and Zones

In AppleTalk networks, every node has an official numerical address. In addition, a node may be part of a named group of nodes, which somehow belong together.

Network and Node Numbers

Each AppleTalk network is assigned a unique network number, and each node in that network is assigned this number. Packets addressed to a node on the network must include the network number.

In addition to a network number, each node has a node number that is unique within that network. This is an 8-bit number and can be any value between 1 and 254, inclusive (0 and 255 are reserved as node numbers). However, servers must have node numbers within the range of 128 to 254, and workstations must have numbers in the 1 to 127 range.

Zones

A zone is a logical grouping of nodes. The basis for the grouping can be any criterion that is useful for a particular configuration, as in the following examples:

- Geographical, such as all machines on the second floor

- Departmental, such as all machines in the marketing department

- Functional, such as all machines that can provide access to printers

By restricting routing or searches to machines in a particular zone, network traffic and work can be reduced considerably.

a
b
c
d
e
f
g
h
i
j
k
l
m
n
o
p
q
r
s
t
u
v
w
x
y
z

Accessing resources by zones also makes it easier to determine what is available for specific needs.

A node may belong to more than one zone at the same time, or not be part of any zone. A zone can cross network boundaries; that is, a zone can consist of parts of two or more different networks or include multiple networks.

Phase 2 AppleTalk

Phase 2, an updated version of AppleTalk, was released in 1989. This version provides several improvements over Phase 1, including the following:

- Allows more than 254 nodes per network

- Allows a network to be assigned more than one network number

- Introduced the AppleTalk Internet Router, which allows up to eight AppleTalk networks to be connected

Network Numbering in Phase 2

In AppleTalk Phase 2, a network can be assigned a range of network numbers. A particular node on this network can be associated with any one number in this range. By providing multiple network numbers for a single network, it is possible to have more than the 254 nodes allowed in a Phase 1 network, because each network number can support 253 (yes, 253) individual nodes.

When you are assigning number ranges, a rough guideline is to assign one network number for every 25 to 50 nodes. If you expect a lot of growth, use a smaller number. For example, assigning two network numbers for a 100-node network leaves room for 406 additional nodes.

When a network is part of an internetwork, there are several restrictions on what can be connected and how. These restrictions concern routers and bridges, and the networks they can connect, as follows:

- All routers connected to a particular network must use the same network number range for the interface with that network. For example, if a router thinks the network uses numbers 1,000 to 1,009, another router connected to the same network cannot use 1,002 to 1,008.

- Routers must connect networks with different number ranges that do not overlap. This means that routers cannot connect a network to itself and that networks with overlapping network numbers cannot interact with each other.

- A bridge must connect network segments with the same number range.

The figure "Rules for connecting AppleTalk Phase 2 internetworks" illustrates these rules.

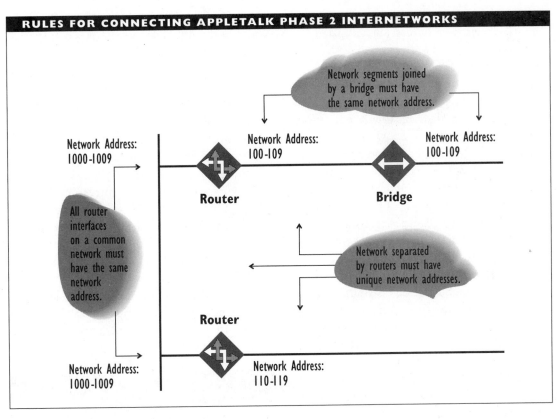

RULES FOR CONNECTING APPLETALK PHASE 2 INTERNETWORKS

Network segments joined by a bridge must have the same network address.

Network Address: 1000-1009

Network Address: 100-109

Network Address: 100-109

Router

Bridge

All router interfaces on a common network must have the same network address.

Network separated by routers must have unique network addresses.

Router

Network Address: 1000-1009

Network Address: 110-119

AppleTalk Networking Forum (ANF)

SEE

ANF (AppleTalk Networking Forum)

Application

An application is a program that calls operating system services and performs work, such as data creation or manipulation, for the user. Applications may be stand-alone, network-based, or part of an integrated package.

Stand-Alone Applications

A stand-alone application can execute only one version of itself at a time and can support only a single user at a time. This type of application executes on a single machine, which may or may not be connected to a network. Single-user versions of spreadsheet, graphics, and database programs are examples of stand-alone applications.

Network-Based Applications

A network-based application executes on a network and is aware of the network, which

a b c d e f g h i j k l m n o p q r s t u v w x y z

means that it can use networking conventions, elements, resources (such as print spoolers and cache buffers), and devices (such as printers, modems, and backup devices).

This type of application can be used by multiple users at the same time. Applications differ in the number of allowable users and in the measures taken to enforce restrictions and to make sure users do not ruin other users' data. Network and data protection measures include the use of flags, access rights, and lock-outs. These serve to help ensure that data is used correctly, only as needed, and with fair access to all users.

Network-based applications may execute on a single machine or be distributed over multiple machines. Client/server computing is an example of a distributed arrangement in which part of an application (the front end) executes on the workstation to provide an interface for the user, and another part (the back end) executes on a server to do the actual work, such as searching a database.

A network-based application may be multiuser or multilaunch. Only one copy of a multiuser application executes, but multiple users can access files in this executing program. A multilaunch application allows multiple users to execute the program separately but at the same time. In effect, each user gets a private version of a multilaunch application.

Integrated Applications

An integrated application is part of a collection, or suite, of programs. Ideally, these programs complement each other in their functionality and allow easy exchange of data. Microsoft Office, Lotus SmartSuite, and Borland Office are examples of such integrated applications.

Accessing Networks from Applications

Users may access networks through or for applications. For example, an application may use a network resource or may need to communicate with an application on another machine. Or a user may log in to a network with the specific intention of using an application available on that network.

Regardless of the details, such network accesses are through the topmost layer in the OSI Reference Model: the application layer. This layer provides users and programs with an interface to the network. At this layer, both the user and the application are isolated from the details of network access and communication.

SHARING DATA AMONG APPLICATIONS

Separate applications can also communicate and exchange data. Using pipes, in which the output from one program is simply "piped" in as input to another program is one of the simplest ways to share data.

OLE (object linking and embedding) is a more sophisticated method, which provides much greater flexibility. OLE makes it possible for updates to be carried over automatically to whatever applications use the updated items.

Application Entity (AE)

SEE

AE (Application Entity)

Application File Transfer (AFT)

SEE

AFT (Application File Transfer)

Application Layer

The topmost layer in the seven-layer OSI Reference Model.

SEE ALSO

OSI Reference Model

Application Process (AP)

SEE

AP (Application Process)

Application Program Interface (API)

SEE

API (Application Program Interface)

Application Program Interface Association (APIA)

SEE

APIA (Application Program Interface Association)

Application Protocol Data Unit (APDU)

SEE

APDU (Application Protocol Data Unit)

APPN (Advanced Peer-to-Peer Networking)

APPN is a network architecture defined within IBM's SAA (Systems Application Architecture) environment. APPN allows peer-to-peer communications between computers without requiring a mainframe in the network.

APPN is also supported within IBM's SNA (Systems Network Architecture) environment. Unlike standard SNA, however, APPN supports dynamic routing of packets.

BROADER CATEGORY

SAA (Systems Application Architecture)

ARA (Attribute Registration Authority)

In the X.400 Message Handling System (MHS), the organization that allocates unique attribute values.

Archie

An Internet service that can find the location of specified files based on the file's name or description. An archie server gets its information by using the FTP program to do a listing of files on accessible servers and also by getting file description information. Currently, archie servers have data about over 2.5 million files on over 1,000 servers.

Archie servers are scattered throughout the Internet, and are accessible using services such as telnet or gopher, through e-mail, or by using archie client programs. Archie servers should be equivalent (except for minor differences arising because not all servers are updated at the same time), so selecting a server is just a matter of convenience. See the table "Example Archie Servers" for a list of some of the available servers.

a
b
c
d
e
f
g
h
i
j
k
l
m
n
o
p
q
r
s
t
u
v
w
x
y
z

EXAMPLE ARCHIE SERVERS	
SERVERS	**LOCATION**
archie.ac.il	Israel
archie.au	Australia
archie.doc.ic.ad.uk	United Kingdom
archie.edvz.uni-linz.ac.at	Austria
archie.funet.fi	Finland
archie.kr	Korea
archie.mcgill.ca	Canada (McGill University)
archie.ncu.edu.tw	Taiwan
archie.rediris.es	Spain
archie.rutgers.edu	USA (Rutgers University)
archie.sura.net	(SURAnet is a service provider)
archie.switch.ch	Switzerland
archie.th-darmstadt.de	Germany
archie.unipi.it	Italy
archie.univ-rennes1.fr	France
archie.unl.edu	USA (University of Nebraska, Lincoln)
archie.wide.ad.jp	Japan

Useful Archie Commands

Once a connection has been established with the archie server, various commands are available. The following list summarizes some useful ones:

help — Displays a list of available commands.

manpage — Displays the reference manual for archie.

list — Displays a list of the anonymous STP servers whose contents are listed in archie's database. If this command is followed by a regular expression, the command displays only the servers that match the expression.

servers — Displays a list of all the available archie servers.

version — Displays the version number of the archie server you're querying. Such information will come in handy if you need to get help with the program.

Various other commands and configuration possibilities are available to make archie more useful and more convenient to use.

Architecture

Architecture is an amorphous term in the area of networking. The term can refer to both the physical layout (topology) of the network and also the protocols (communication rules and data elements) used to communicate.

Architecture can also refer to the basic structure of a networking service, such as a print service architecture. Used this way, it generally indicates the overall scheme of APIs (Application Program Interfaces), agents, and so on, used to fit different pieces of the service together.

You will hear references to network architectures, such as ARCnet, Ethernet, and Token Ring, which are all defined primarily at the two lowest layers of the OSI model: the physical and data-link layers. Each architecture includes an implicit topology.

In the context of hardware, the term refers to the manner in which a computer is constructed. The architecture includes the type of processor (for example, Intel $80x86$ or Pentium, Motorola $680xx$, or RISC chip) and the type of bus that is used to transmit data and other signals to the computer's components and peripherals.

In the IBM PC world, which is currently dominated by Intel processors, the three major buses are ISA (Industry Standard Architecture), EISA (Extended Industry Standard Architecture), and MCA (Micro-channel Architecture). However, two newer bus designs—VL (VESA Local) and PCI (Peripheral Component Interconnect)—are growing in popularity and are likely to become the dominant bus architectures.

SEE ALSO

Network Architecture

Archive

As a noun, a repository for data, applications, and so forth. These materials may be master copies or regular backups of the current hard disk contents. As a verb, the act of backing up data files to provide a safe copy in case of a disaster.

Archive Site

On the Internet, a node that provides access to a collection of files.

ARCnet (Attached Resource Computer Network)

ARCnet is a baseband network architecture originally developed as a proprietary network by Datapoint Corporation in the late 1970s. ARCnet became very popular when Standard Microsystems Corporation (SMC) developed a chip set for PCs. The architecture has been used for years and has become a de facto standard. However, it has not become as popular as other network architectures, such as Ethernet. ARCnet is popular for smaller networks because it is relatively simple to set up and operate, its components are inexpensive (street prices for ARCnet boards are among the lowest), and the architecture is widely supported.

ARCnet has a transmission rate of 2.5 megabytes per second (Mbps). ARCnet Plus is a newer, 20 Mbps version. A third-party, 100 Mbps architecture based on ARCnet is also available from Thomas-Conrad. Although ARCnet Plus was developed by Datapoint Corporation alone, current and future development of ARCnet standards is under the aegis of the ATA (ARCnet Trade Association), a consortium of vendors that market ARCnet products.

ARCnet uses token passing to control access to the network. Each node in an ARCnet network has a unique address (between 1 and 255), and the token is passed sequentially from one address to the next. Nodes with successive addresses are not necessarily next to each other in the physical layout.

Officially, ARCnet uses a bus topology, but in practice ARCnet networks can use a star or a bus wiring scheme. These two types of networks use slightly different components and are sometimes referred to as low-impedance and high-impedance ARCnet, respectively.

a b c d e f g h i j k l m n o p q r s t u v w x y z

The figure "Context and properties of ARCnet" summarizes the characteristics of this architecture.

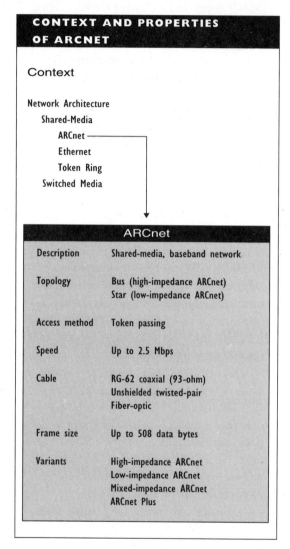

CONTEXT AND PROPERTIES OF ARCNET

Context

Network Architecture
  Shared-Media
    ARCnet
    Ethernet
    Token Ring
  Switched Media

ARCnet	
Description	Shared-media, baseband network
Topology	Bus (high-impedance ARCnet) Star (low-impedance ARCnet)
Access method	Token passing
Speed	Up to 2.5 Mbps
Cable	RG-62 coaxial (93-ohm) Unshielded twisted-pair Fiber-optic
Frame size	Up to 508 data bytes
Variants	High-impedance ARCnet Low-impedance ARCnet Mixed-impedance ARCnet ARCnet Plus

ARCnet Network Components

The hardware components needed in an ARCnet network include an ARCnet network interface card, cable, connectors, hubs, active links, and baluns.

ARCnet Network Interface Card (NIC)

ARCnet NICs include chips to handle the ARCnet protocols and packet formats, as well as a transceiver (usually with a BNC connector) on the card. Most ARCnet NICs have a low-impedance transceiver, which is best suited for a star or tree topology. (A tree topology has features of both star and bus topologies.) Cards with high-impedance transceivers are suitable for a bus topology.

ARCnet cards do not come with hardware addresses in a ROM chip. Instead, they have jumpers that can be set to specify an address for the node in which the card is installed. The network administrator needs to set this address (which must be between 1 and 255) for each card in the network. Each node must have a unique address. The network administrator also needs to set the IRQ (interrupt) and I/O (input/output) addresses on the card. The hardware address is network-dependent; the IRQ and I/O addresses are machine-dependent.

Cable

ARCnet cable can be coaxial, twisted-pair, or even fiber-optic. Coaxial ARCnet networks generally have RG-62 cable, which has a 93-ohm impedance. Other types of coaxial cable, such as RG-59U or RG-11U, are also used.

An ARCnet network might include unshielded twisted-pair (UTP) or IBM's special-design cables (Types 1 and 3), but only if the NIC has the appropriate connectors or if an appropriate adapter is available. If UTP cabling is used, nodes are arranged in a daisy chain and one end of the chain is connected to a hub or to an adapter that connects to coaxial cable. Similar converters can convert from coaxial to fiber-optic cable.

The last node in an ARCnet network must be terminated with a resistor of appropriate strength: 93 ohm for coaxial networks and 105 ohm for networks using twisted-pair wiring.

Connectors, Active Links, and Baluns

For coaxial cable, BNC connectors are used. For twisted-pair cable, the connectors are either the modular RJ-11/RJ-45 telephone type, or the D-shell type used for standard serial and parallel ports.

Active links are boxes used to connect two cable segments when both cable segments have high-impedance NICs connected.

Baluns are used to connect coaxial and twisted-pair cabling.

Hubs

Hubs serve as wiring concentrators. Three types of hubs can be used:

Active hubs: Active hubs have their own power supply. They can clean and boost a signal and then relay it along the network. An active hub serves as both a repeater and a wiring center. Active hubs usually have 8 ports, but they can have as many as 64. The type of hub used must be appropriate for the type of cable being used. Active hubs can extend the maximum distance between nodes.

Passive hubs: Passive hubs simply relay signals without cleaning or boosting them. These types of hubs collect wiring from nodes and must be connected to an active hub. Passive hubs have four ports and are used only in low-impedance networks. Passive hubs cannot be used to extend the distance between nodes.

Intelligent hubs: Intelligent hubs are active hubs that use a low-frequency signal band to monitor the status of a link. These hubs can have up to 16 ports.

ARCnet Operation

ARCnet data transmissions are broadcast to all nodes on the network (a feature characteristic of both bus and star topologies), but the transmitted packets are (presumably) read only by the node(s) to which the destination address applies. Note that even though all nodes can listen at the same time, only one node can transmit.

Structure of an ARCnet Packet

ARCnet has several different types of frames, or packets, which are listed on the table "ARCnet Packets." The figure "ARCnet frame structure" shows the makeup of ARCnet frames.

ARCNET PACKETS	
PACKET TYPE	**FUNCTION**
ITT (Invitation to Transmit)	The token, which determines the node that is allowed to transmit
FBE (Free Buffer Enquiry)	The frame that is used to ask whether the destination node is able to receive packets
ACK (Acknowledge)	The packet used to indicate that a packet was received as transmitted
NAK (Negative Acknowledge)	The packet used to indicate that a packet was not received correctly and should be retransmitted
PAC	The actual ARCnet data frame

The data, control, or check bytes that make up the frame are known as ISUs (information symbol units). ISUs are defined differently in ARCnet and in ARCnet Plus.

All ARCnet frames begin with a 6-bit alert signal, and all bytes begin with the bit sequence 110, so that each byte actually requires 11 bits in an ARCnet transmission.

ARCnet data frames consist of data, header, and trailer. Originally, an ARCnet frame could have up to 252 bytes of data. Almost all ARCnet implementations now support an expanded frame of up to 508 bytes of data (plus a dozen or so header bytes).

An ARCnet header for a PAC frame includes the following:

- A start of header byte

- Source and destination addresses, with values between 1 and 255 (a destination address of 0 indicates that the frame is being broadcast to all nodes)

- One or two bytes indicating the number of data bytes

The trailer is a 16-bit CRC (cyclic redundancy check) value.

Data Frame Transmission

The transmission of data frames in an ARCnet network is controlled by a token, which is a special data frame. This token, in turn, is dispensed by the network's controller, which is the node with the lowest address. The controller is determined when the network is first activated. Each node broadcasts its address and the node with the lowest address becomes the controller. This reconfiguration process, which takes less than a tenth of a second, is repeated each time a new node joins the network.

The controller passes the token sequentially from one address to the next. The node with the token is the only node allowed to transmit, with some exceptions.

ARCNET FRAME STRUCTURE

Frame components are symbols containing the following:

Starting Delimiter (SD)
| 1 | 1 | 1 | 1 | 1 |

ITT Frame
| SD | EQT | NID | NID |

FBE Frame
| SD | ENQ | DID | DID |

ACK Frame
| SD | ACK |

NAK Frame
| SD | NAK |

PAC Frame

| | | | | | 1 or 2 | 1 or 2 | 0-508 | 2 |
| SD | SOH | SID | DID | DID | CP | SC | DATA | FSC |

SD	Starting delimiter, a special bit pattern of six consecutive 1bits, to indicate the start of the frame
EQT	ASCII 0x04, which indicates the frame type
NID	The address of the next node to get the token
ENQ	ASCII 0x85, which identifies the frame type
DID	The address of the destination node for the enquiry
ACK	ASCII 0x86, indicating that the packet was recieved correctly
NAK	ASCII 0x15, indicating that the packet was not recieved correctly
SOH	ASCII 0x01, indicating the start of the header
SID	The address of the source node sending the frame
CP	A continuation pointer value, indicating the number of data bytes
SC	System code
DATA	Up to 508 symbols containing system code and data
FCS	Frame check sequence, verifying the integrity of the frame

a b c d e f g h i j k l m n o p q r s t u v w x y z

Frame transmission is a complicated process in ARCnet. A node (the source) waiting to send a message to another node (the destination) needs to do several things, in the following order:

1. The source waits for the token (ITT).

2. Once it has the token, the source sends an FBE packet to the destination to make sure the destination has room for the frame.

3. The source waits for a positive reply.

4. Once the source gets a positive response (ACK) to the FBE packet, the source broadcasts the frame.

5. The source waits for an acknowledgment from the intended destination. The destination node must acknowledge receipt of the frame. Since acknowledgment is required, ARCnet can guarantee frame delivery.

6. Once the frame has been received at the destination, the controller passes the token to the next address.

Disrupting Data Transmission

Unless something is wrong on the network, every node gets the token at least once every 840 milliseconds. If a node has not seen the token within that time, that node can disrupt the network and force the creation of a new token by sending a reconfiguration burst—a predefined bit pattern sent hundreds of times in succession—to destroy the existing token. After a period, the token is regenerated, the network nodes reannounce

themselves, and the network begins transmitting again.

New nodes on an ARCnet network also send a reconfiguration burst. This pattern announces their presence on the network, and possibly establishes a new node as controller.

Communicating with Higher Layers

ARCnet's small frame size causes compatibility problems with some network-layer protocols, such as Novell's IPX protocol. IPX passes 576-byte packets (known as *datagrams*) to the architecture operating at the data-link layer. This packet size is too large, even for an extended ARCnet frame.

To enable IPX to talk to ARCnet, the fragmentation layer was developed. At this layer, the source node breaks an IPX packet into two smaller frames for ARCnet. At the destination's fragmentation layer, the datagram is reassembled before being passed to IPX.

High-Impedance ARCnet

High-impedance ARCnet networks use a bus topology, as illustrated in the figure "Layout for a high-impedance ARCnet network." The high-impedance NICs make it possible to daisy chain nodes and active hubs. The active hubs serve as collectors for other hubs and nodes.

The following restrictions apply to high-impedance ARCnet networks:

■ No single cable segment connecting nodes can be be more than 305 meters (1,000 feet) long.

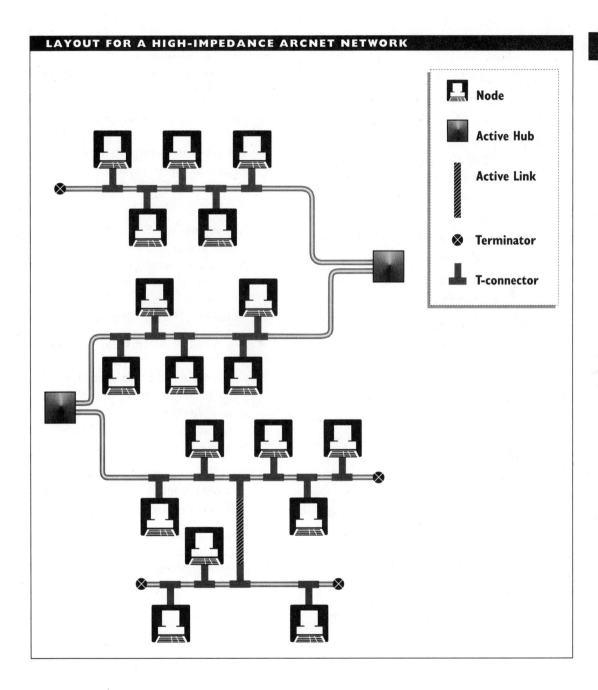

LAYOUT FOR A HIGH-IMPEDANCE ARCNET NETWORK

- Only *active* (or intelligent) hubs may be used.

- Adjacent active hubs (hubs with no intervening nodes) must be within 610 meters (2,000 feet).

- Nodes are connected to the trunk cable using BNC T-connectors. The node's NIC must be connected directly to the T-connector; that is, drop cable is not allowed.

- T-connectors must be at least 1 meter (3.25 feet) apart on the cable.

- At most, eight nodes can be connected in a series (with no intervening hubs).

- Both ends of a cable segment must be terminated with either a BNC terminator or an active hub (or link).

- The cabling cannot loop back on itself. For example, the cable cannot go from an active hub through other hubs and eventually connect back into the original hub.

Low-Impedance ARCnet

Low-impedance ARCnet networks use a star topology, in which passive hubs serve to collect nodes, as illustrated in the figure "Layout for a low-impedance ARCnet network." Each passive hub is connected to an active hub. Active hubs can be linked with each other, and they can also be linked directly with nodes. In the latter case, the active hub also acts as a wiring center.

The following restrictions apply to low-impedance ARCnet networks:

- Active hubs can be connected to nodes, active hubs, or passive hubs. The active hub must be within 610 meters (2,000 feet) of an active hub or a node, or within 30 meters (100 feet) of a passive hub.

- Passive hubs can be used only between a node and an active hub; two passive hubs cannot be next to each other. A passive hub must be within 30 meters (100 feet) of an active hub and within 30 meters (100 feet) of a node.

- Nodes can be attached anywhere on the network, provided the node is within the required distance of an active or passive hub: within 610 meters (2,000 feet) of an active hub or within 30 meters (100 feet) of a passive hub.

- Unused hub ports must be terminated on a passive hub and should be terminated on an active hub.

- The cabling cannot loop back on itself. For example, the cable cannot go from an active hub through other hubs and eventually connect back into the original hub.

LAYOUT FOR A LOW-IMPEDANCE ARCNET NETWORK

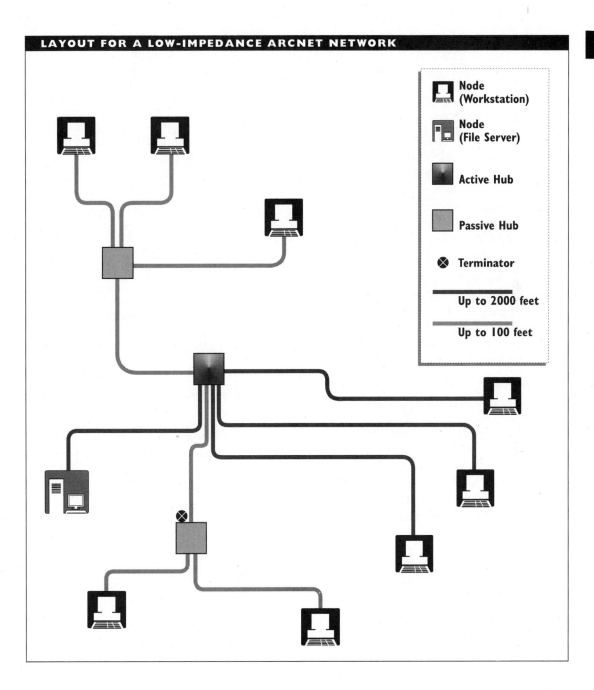

Node (Workstation)

Node (File Server)

Active Hub

Passive Hub

Terminator

Up to 2000 feet

Up to 100 feet

a
b
c
d
e
f
g
h
i
j
k
l
m
n
o
p
q
r
s
t
u
v
w
x
y
z

Mixed-Impedance ARCnet

A mixed ARCnet network is one that includes both high- and low-impedance components in the same network, as illustrated in the figure "Layout of a mixed-impedance ARCnet network, with low-impedance and high-impedance components." In this type of network, all the restrictions for both impedance levels must be observed.

Perhaps the most important constraint for a mixed-impedance ARCnet is that high-impedance NICs can be used in place of low-impedance cards, but the reverse is not possible. Because of this restriction, it is crucial that you keep track of what kind of NIC is in each node.

Restrictions on ARCnet Networks

The following restrictions apply to both high- and low-impedance ARCnet networks:

- The maximum length of a cable segment depends on the type of cable. The general restriction is that the signal attenuation must be less than 11 dB over the entire cable segment at a frequency of 5 MHz. In practice, this leads to the following maximum distances:

Coaxial cable: 450–600 meters (1,500–2,000 feet)

UTP and IBM Type 3 (unshielded) cable: 100 meters (330 feet)

IBM Type 1 (shielded) cable: 200 meters (660 feet)

- The maximum cable length for the entire network is 6,000 meters (20,000 feet)

- The maximum number of cable segments in a series is three. If UTP cable is used, the series of segments can be at most about 130 meters (430 feet); for coaxial cable, the maximum length is about 300 meters (990 feet).

- Each cable segment must be terminated at both ends by being connected to an active hub or terminator.

- An ARCnet network can have a maximum of 255 nodes. Each active hub counts as a node.

- At most, 10 nodes are allowed in a series when UTP cable is used; 8 nodes if coaxial cable is used.

- The maximum distance between any two nodes on the network is determined by the constraint that no ARCnet signal can have a propagation delay of more than 31 microseconds. The total propagation delay is determined by adding the propagation delays in all the devices (nodes, hubs, and cable) connecting the nodes. Network components generally have propagation delays of less than 0.5 microseconds, and much less in some cases.

LAYOUT OF A MIXED-IMPEDANCE ARCNET NETWORK, WITH LOW-IMPEDANCE AND HIGH-IMPEDANCE COMPONENTS

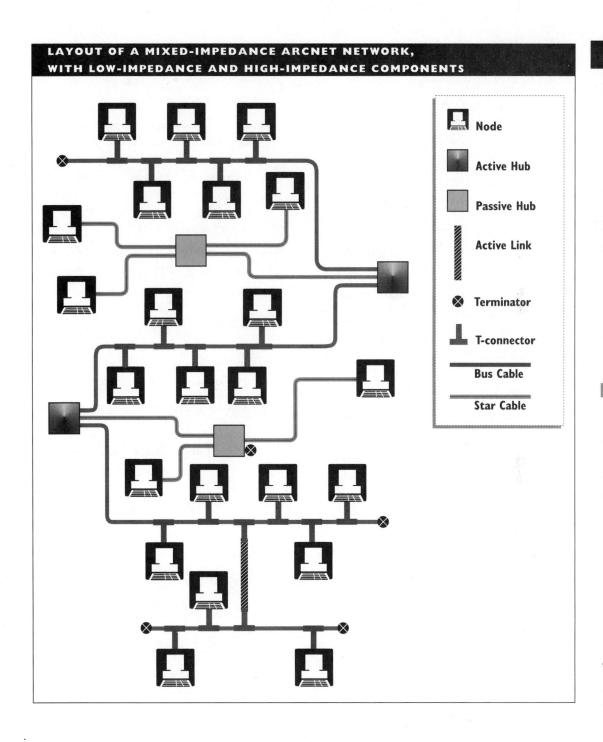

Node

Active Hub

Passive Hub

Active Link

Terminator

T-connector

Bus Cable

Star Cable

a
b
c
d
e
f
g
h
i
j
k
l
m
n
o
p
q
r
s
t
u
v
w
x
y
z

ARCnet Advantages

ARCnet has the following advantages:

- Components are relatively inexpensive. Street prices for basic ARCnet NICs usually are less than those for Ethernet or Token Ring NICs.

- Because the ARCnet architecture and the chip set have been around a long time, the hardware has become stable. The result is that there are few compatibility or reliability problems with ARCnet components.

- Wiring is very flexible, allowing for lots of leeway in placing nodes.

- It is relatively easy to use different types of cabling in an ARCnet network (but adapters must be used to avoid connection incompatibilities).

- A star layout makes diagnostics easy in low-impedance networks.

- Except for the extra cabling a star topology requires, installation is relatively inexpensive.

ARCnet Disadvantages

ARCnet has the following disadvantages:

- Its data transmission is inefficient. ARCnet sends three overhead bits for every byte. Also, administrative exchanges (such as ACK or NAK packets) between source and destination are done on the data bandwidth, which degrades performance further.

- Actual throughput is much less than the maximum 2.5 Mbps. Even for small networks, the throughput is less than 65 percent of maximum, and this value decreases as more nodes are added to the network.

- The network administrator must manually set a unique address by adjusting switches on every NIC in the network. If two nodes have the same address, the administrator will need to track down the conflicting boards by tedious examination of each NIC.

- Because of throughput and addressing restrictions, ARCnet is not particularly well-suited for internetworking.

ARCnet Plus

Datapoint recently released ARCnet Plus, a 20-Mbps version of the ARCnet standard. ARCnet Plus has the following features:

- Backward-compatibility with ARCnet

- Ability to communicate with both ARCnet and ARCnet Plus nodes

- Support for transmission rates of up to 20 Mbps

- Support for data frames up to 4,224 bytes long

- Use of the same RG-62 cable as ordinary ARCnet

- New frames, with enhanced frame formats and command sets

- Support for up to 1 MB of buffer space

ARCnet Plus achieves its greater speed by cutting the time interval for a symbol in half and by using phase and amplitude shifting to encode four bits in every signal; that is, the basic symbol in ARCnet Plus is actually a nibble.

Like its predecessor, ARCnet Plus regulates much network activity by timing. The allowable intervals are much smaller with ARCnet Plus, however. For example, a bit interval is half as long in ARCnet Plus as in regular ARCnet.

Another extension of this type of architecture is TCNS, offered by Thomas-Conrad, which is a 100 Mbps, copper-based network.

BROADER CATEGORY
Network Architecture

SEE ALSO
TCNS (Thomas-Conrad Network System)

TIPS ON ARCNET ADDRESSES

Keep accurate addresses. Make sure you have up-to-date records of the address set for each ARC-net node's NIC. When you need to find duplicate addresses or add nodes, you'll be glad you did.

If you're the administrator, never let anyone else change the node addresses, because you may have to deal with the problems caused by their sloppiness.

Assigning the low address is particularly important. The network controller will be the node with the lowest address, so make sure this machine is fast enough to handle the controlling role. In general, it's best to assign the lowest addresses to servers, bridges, and routers.

▼
ARF (Alarm Reporting Function)

In the OSI network management model, a service that reports failures, faults, or problems that might become faults.

▼
ARM (Asynchronous Response Mode)

In the ISO's HLDC (High-Level Data Link Control) protocol, ARM is a communications mode in which a secondary (slave) node can initiate communications with a primary (master) node without first getting permission from the primary node.

ARM's operation is in contrast to NRM (normal response mode), in which the primary node must initiate any communication, and to ABM (asynchronous balanced mode), in which the two nodes are equal.

BROADER CATEGORY
HDLC (High-Level Data Link Control)

▼
ARPA (Advanced Research Projects Agency)

The agency that was largely responsible for what eventually became the Internet. Now called DARPA (for Defense ARPA).

▼
ARPAnet (Advanced Research Projects Agency Network)

ARPAnet was the first large-scale, packet-switched, wide-area network (WAN). It was originally developed in the early 1970s under the auspices of the U.S. Department of Defense's Defense Advanced Research Projects Agency (DARPA).

a b c d e f g h i j k l m n o p q r s t u v w x y z

Many of the most commonly used networking protocols, including TCP/IP, were developed as part of the ARPAnet project. The ARPAnet was decommissioned in 1991, but parts of the network have become part of the Internet.

ARQ (Automatic Repeat Request)

In communications, a control code that indicates an error in transmission and that requests a retransmission.

ARS (Automatic Route Selection)

In telephony, a process by which a path is selected for a transmission; also called alternate route selection.

AS (Autonomous System)

In the Internet world, AS (autonomous system) is a term for a collection of routers that are part of a larger network but that are under the control of a single organization. The routers, or *gateways* as they are called in the older Internet terminology, communicate with each other using a common protocol, known as an interior gateway protocol (IGP). Currently, the two most widely supported IGPs in the Internet community are the OSPF (Open Shortest Path First) and the Integrated IS-IS protocols.

ASs communicate using an exterior gateway protocol, such as EGP (Exterior Gateway Protocol) and BGP (Border Gateway Protocol).

In the OSI Reference Model, an autonomous system is known as a *routing domain,* IGPs are known as *intradomain routing protocols,* and EGPs are known as *interdomain routing protocols.*

AS/400

A minicomputer line from IBM. The AS/400 was introduced in 1988 to replace the System/36 and System/38 series.

ASCII (American Standard Code for Information Interchange)

ASCII is the character-encoding system used most commonly in local-area networks (LANs). The standard ASCII characters are encoded in seven bits and have values between 0 and 127. The remaining 128 characters form the extended ASCII character set, whose elements may be defined differently depending on the language being used. See the tables "Standard ASCII Character Set" and "Extended ASCII Character Set (IBM PC)."

In common usage, ASCII is used to refer to a text-only file that does not include special formatting codes.

BROADER CATEGORY
Encoding

COMPARE
EBCDIC

STANDARD ASCII CHARACTER SET

DECIMAL	CHARACTER	DECIMAL	CHARACTER	DECIMAL	CHARACTER
0	NUL (null)	21	NAK (negative acknowledge)	43	+
1	SOH (start of heading)	22	SYN (synchronous idle)	44	, (comma)
2	STX (start of text)			45	–
3	ETX (end of text)	23	ETB (end transmission block)	46	.
4	EOT (end of transmission)	24	CAN (cancel)	47	/
5	ENQ (enquire)	25	EM (end of medium)	48	0
6	ACK (acknowledge)	26	SUB (substitute)	49	1
7	BEL (bell)	27	ESC (escape)	50	2
8	BS (backspace)	28	FS (file separator)	51	3
9	HT (horizontal tab)	29	GS (group separator)	52	4
10	LF (line feed)			53	5
11	VT (vertical tab)	30	RS (record separator)	54	6
12	FF (form feed)	31	US (unit separator)	55	7
13	CR (carriage return)	32	space	56	8
14	SO (shift out)	33	!	57	9
15	SI (shift in)	34	"	58	:
16	DLE (data link escape)	35	#	59	;
17	DC1 (device control 1)	36	$	60	<
18	DC2 (device control 2)	37	%	61	=
		38	&	62	>
19	DC3 (device control 3)	39	' (apostrophe)	63	?
20	DC4 (device control 4)	40	(	64	@
		41	)	65	A
		42	*	66	B
				67	C

a
b
c
d
e
f
g
h
i
j
k
l
m
n
o
p
q
r
s
t
u
v
w
x
y
z

DECIMAL	CHARACTER	DECIMAL	CHARACTER	DECIMAL	CHARACTER
68	D	88	X	108	l
69	E	89	Y	109	m
70	F	90	Z	110	n
71	G	91	[	111	o
72	H	92	\	112	p
73	I	93	]	113	q
74	J	94	^	114	r
75	K	95	_	115	s
76	L	96	à	116	t
77	M	97	a	117	u
78	N	98	b	118	v
79	O	99	c	119	w
80	P	100	d	120	x
81	Q	101	e	121	y
82	R	102	f	122	z
83	S	103	g	123	{
84	T	104	h	124	¦
85	U	105	i	125	}
86	V	106	j	126	~
87	W	107	k	127	DEL

EXTENDED ASCII CHARACTER SET

DECIMAL	CHARACTER	DECIMAL	CHARACTER	DECIMAL	CHARACTER
0		25	↓	50	2
1	☺	26	→	51	3
2	☻	27	←	52	4
3	♥	28	∟	53	5
4	♦	29	↔	54	6
5	♠	30	▲	55	7
6	♣	31	▼	56	8
7	◆	32		57	9
8	▣	33	!	58	:
9	○	34	"	59	;
10	◙	35	#	60	<
11	♂	36	$	61	=
12	♀	37	%	62	>
13	♪	38	&	63	?
14	♫	39	'	64	@
15	☼	40	(	65	A
16	►	41	)	66	B
17	◄	42	*	67	C
18	↕	43	+	68	D
19	‼	44	,	69	E
20	¶	45	–	70	F
21	§	46	.	71	G
22	▬	47	/	72	H
23	↨	48	0	73	I
24	↑	49	1	74	J

a b c d e f g h i j k l m n o p q r s t u v w x y z

DECIMAL	CHARACTER	DECIMAL	CHARACTER	DECIMAL	CHARACTER
75	K	100	d	125	}
76	L	101	e	126	~
77	M	102	f	127	Δ
78	N	103	g	128	Ç
79	O	104	h	129	ü
80	P	105	i	130	é
81	Q	106	j	131	â
82	R	107	k	132	ä
83	S	108	l	133	à
84	T	109	m	134	å
85	U	110	n	135	ç
86	V	111	o	136	ê
87	W	112	p	137	ë
88	X	113	q	138	è
89	Y	114	r	139	ï
90	Z	115	s	140	î
91	[	116	t	141	ì
92	\	117	u	142	Ä
93	]	118	v	143	Å
94	^	119	w	144	É
95	_	120	x	145	æ
96	`	121	y	146	Æ
97	a	122	z	147	ô
98	b	123	{	148	ö
99	c	124	|	149	ò

DECIMAL	CHARACTER	DECIMAL	CHARACTER	DECIMAL	CHARACTER
150	û	175	»	200	╚
151	ù	176	▒	201	╔
152	ÿ	177	▓	202	╩
153	Ö	178	▓	203	╦
154	Ü	179	│	204	╠
155	¢	180	┤	205	═
156	£	181	╡	206	╬
157	¥	182	╢	207	╧
158	₨	183	╖	208	╨
159	ƒ	184	╕	209	╤
160	á	185	╣	210	╥
161	í	186	║	211	╙
162	ó	187	╗	212	╘
163	ú	188	╝	213	╒
164	ñ	189	╜	214	╓
165	Ñ	190	╛	215	╫
166	ª	191	┐	216	╪
167	º	192	└	217	┘
168	¿	193	┴	218	┌
169	⌐	194	┬	219	█
170	¬	195	├	220	▄
171	½	196	─	221	▌
172	¼	197	┼	222	▐
173	¡	198	╞	223	▀
174	«	199	╟	224	α

a b c d e f g h i j k l m n o p q r s t u v w x y z

DECIMAL	CHARACTER	DECIMAL	CHARACTER	DECIMAL	CHARACTER
225	β	236	∞	247	≈
226	Γ	237	∅	248	o
227	Π	238	∈	249	·
228	Σ	239	∩	250	·
229	σ	240	≡	251	√
230	μ	241	±	252	n
231	τ	242	≥	253	²
232	Φ	243	≤	254	∎
233	θ	244	⌠	255	
234	Ω	245	⌡		
235	δ	246	÷		

ASCIIbetical Sorting

A sorting strategy that uses the ASCII character set as the basis for the ordering. In ASCII, numbers and special symbols precede letters; uppercase letters precede lowercase ones.

ASE (Application Service Element)

In the OSI Reference Model, an ASE (application service element) is any of several elements that provide the communications and other services at the application layer. An application process (AP) or application entity (AE) requests these services through predefined interfaces, such as those provided by APIs (Application Program Interfaces).

ASEs are grouped into common application service elements (CASEs) and specific application service elements (SASEs). The CASEs provide services for many types of applications; the SASEs represent or provide services for specific applications or genres.

CASE

The following CASEs are commonly used:

ACSE (Association Control Service Element): This element establishes the appropriate relationship between two applications (AEs) to enable the applications to cooperate and communicate on a task. Since all associations or relationships must be established through the ACSE, and since applications must establish a relationship to communicate, the ACSE is needed by all applications.

CCRSE (Commitment, Concurrency, and Recovery Service Element): This element is used to implement distributed transactions which may require multiple applications. The CCRSE helps ensure that distributed data remains consistent by making sure that applications do not interfere with each other when doing their work and that actions are performed completely or not at all.

ROSE (Remote Operations Service Element): This element supports interactive cooperation between two applications, such as between a client and a server. ROSE provides the services needed for the reliable execution of requested operations and transfer of data.

RTSE (Reliable Transfer Service Element): This element helps ensure that PDUs (protocol data units), or packets, are transferred reliably between applications. RTSE services can sometimes survive an equipment failure because they use transport-layer services.

SASE

The following SASEs are commonly used:

DS (Directory Service): This element makes it possible to use a global directory, which is a distributed database with information about all accessible network entities in a communications system.

FTAM: (File Transfer Access and Management): This element enables an application to read, write, or otherwise manage files on a remote machine.

JTM (Job Transfer and Manipulation): This element enables an application to do batch data processing on a remote machine. With JTM, a node could, for example, start a computation on a supercomputer at a remote location and retrieve the results when the computation was complete.

MHS (Message Handling System): This element enables applications to exchange messages; for example, when using electronic mail.

MMS (Manufacturing Message Service): This element enables an application on a control computer to communicate with an application on a slave machine in a production line or other automated operation.

VT (Virtual Terminal): This element makes it possible to emulate the behavior of a particular terminal, which enables an application to communicate with a remote system without considering the type of hardware sending or receiving the communications.

The entire set of ASEs required for a particular application is known as the application context (AC) for that application.

BROADER CATEGORY
AC (Application Context)

ASI (Adapter Support Interface)

ASI (Adapter Support Interface) is a standard interface developed by IBM for enabling Token Ring adapters to talk to any of several higher-level protocols. The most recent version of ASI is marketed as LAN Support Program.

Like other adapter interfaces, such as NDIS (Network Driver Interface Specification) by Microsoft and ODI (Open Data-Link Interface) by Novell, ASI includes at least the following two components:

- A data-link-layer driver to talk to the network interface card (NIC)

- A network-layer driver to talk to the network-level protocols

Asia and Oceania Workshop (AOW)

SEE
AOW (Asia and Oceania Workshop)

ASIC (Application-Specific Integrated Circuit)

Special-purpose chips with logic designed specifically for a particular application or device. ASICs are also known as gate arrays, and they are constructed from standard circuit cells from a library.

ASN.1 (Abstract Syntax Notation One)

In the OSI Reference Model, ASN.1 (Abstract Syntax Notation One) is a notation used to describe data structures, such as managed objects in a network management system.

ASN.1 is machine-independent and is used in many networking contexts. For example, it is used to describe application-layer packets in both the OSI network management framework and in the Simple Network Management Protocol (SNMP) from the Internet TCP/IP protocol suite.

ASN.1 serves as a common syntax for transferring information between two end systems (ESs) that may use different encoding systems at each end.

PRIMARY SOURCES
CCITT recommendations X.208 and X.209; ISO documents 8824 and 8825

BROADER CATEGORY
Abstract Syntax

SEE ALSO
BER (Basic Encoding Rules)

Asserted Circuit

A circuit that is closed; that is, a circuit with a voltage value. Depending on the logic being used, an asserted circuit can represent a 1 (usually) or 0 (rarely).

Assigned Number

In the Internet community, a numerical value that serves to distinguish a particular protocol, application, or organization in some context. For example, assigned numbers distinguish the different flavors of Ethernet protocols used by different implementers. Assigned numbers, which are not addresses, are assigned by the Internet Assigned Numbers Authority (IANA).

ASVD (Analog Simultaneous Voice/Data)

A proposed modem standard that can be used to transmit multimedia materials—voice, video, etc.—over ordinary (analog) telephone lines. The ASVD specifications are being finalized by the ITU (International

Telecommunication Union, formerly known as the CCITT).

ASVD is offered as an inexpensive (and slower) alternative to ISDN (Integrated Services Digital Network). The bandwidth for ASVD is considerably more limited than for ISDN. The version under consideration supports modem speeds of up to 14.4 kbps, but somewhat slower speeds for multimedia data.

Asynchronous

Asynchronous describes a communications strategy that uses start and stop bits to indicate the beginning and end of a character, rather than using constant timing to transmit a series of characters. In a sense, asynchronous transmissions actually synchronize for each character. The figure "A data word sent by asynchronous transmission" shows the bits used in this communications method.

Asynchronous communications methods are generally less efficient but more resistant to disruption than synchronous communications. Asynchronous methods are more efficient for situations in which traffic comes in bursts (rather than moving at a regular pace). Common examples of asynchronous communications devices are modems and terminals.

Asynchronous Modem Eliminator (AME)

SEE
AME (Asynchronous Modem Eliminator)

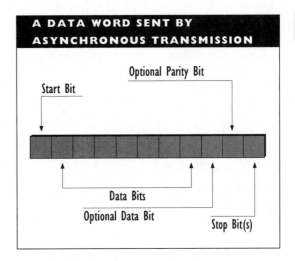

A DATA WORD SENT BY ASYNCHRONOUS TRANSMISSION

Start Bit

Optional Parity Bit

Data Bits

Optional Data Bit

Stop Bit(s)

ATA (ARCnet Trade Association)

A consortium of vendors and other organizations that manages ARCnet specifications.

AT Command Set

The AT command set was developed by Hayes Microcomputer Products to operate its modems. The AT in the title is an abbreviation for attention. This signal precedes most of the commands used to get a modem to do its work. For example, ATDP and ATDT (for attention dial pulse and attention dial tone, respectively) are used to dial a number on either a pulse or Touch Tone phone.

The AT command set quickly became a de facto standard. It is now used by most modem manufacturers and is supported on virtually every modem on the market.

SEE ALSO
Modem

a b c d e f g h i j k l m n o p q r s t u v w x y z

ATCON

A Novell NetWare program that monitors the AppleTalk protocol stack in a multiprotocol network. It reports statistics about the performance of AppleTalk devices and services.

ATDP (Attention Dial Pulse)

In the Hayes modem command set, a command to dial a number using a pulse (rotary) telephone.

SEE ALSO

AT Command Set

ATDT (Attention Dial Tone)

In the Hayes modem command set, a command to dial a number using a Touch Tone phone.

SEE ALSO

AT Command Set

ATM (Asynchronous Transfer Mode)

ATM (Asynchronous Transfer Mode) is a packet-switched, broadband network architecture that is expected to become an established standard by the late 1990s. It forms the core of a broadband ISDN (BISDN) architecture, which extends the digital transmission capabilities defined by ISDN to allow data, voice, and multimedia transmissions on the same lines. It is also known as *cell relay,* to distinguish it from frame relay.

ATM is a real-time architecture that will be able to provide very high bandwidths as needed. The initial implementations will operate at 155.52 megabits per second (Mbps), then at 622.08 Mbps. Speeds up to 2.488 gigabits per second (Gbps) are planned and have been demonstrated in limited tests.

The very high bandwidth and the ability to transmit multiple media make ATM an attractive, high-speed architecture for both local-area networks (LANs) and wide-area networks (WANs). It is useful for enterprise networks, which often connect LANs over wide areas and may need to transport large amounts of data over very long distances.

Long-haul, high-bandwidth capabilities are particularly attractive for WANs, which have until now been shackled by the relatively low bandwidths over long-distance lines. FDDI (Fiber Distributed Data Interface) is a good architecture for LANs, and frame relay has possibilities for WANs, but neither of these architectures is suitable for both LANs and WANs. But note that ATM is still quite expensive.

The figure "Context and properties of ATM" summarizes the characteristics of this architecture.

ATM Features

ATM has the following features:

- Transmission over fiber-optic lines. These can be local or long-distance, public or private lines. Long-distance lines can be leased or dial-up.

- Capability for parallel transmissions, because ATM is a switching architecture. In fact, each node can have a dedicated connection to any other node.

CONTEXT AND PROPERTIES OF ATM

Context

Network Architecture
    Shared-Media
    Switched-Media
        Circuit
        Message
        Packet
            Fixed-Size
                ATM (Cell Relay) ─────────┐
        Variable-Size   │
        Frame Relay   │
                                           ▼

ATM

Properties	Structure		
	Layers	**Planes**	**Cells**
Broadband	Physical	Users	Constant Size (53 Octets)
Core of BISDN	(Two Sublayers)	Management	(48-Octet Payload)
Useful for LANs and WANs	ATM Layer	Control	(5-Octet Header)
Uses short- or long-haul fiber-optic	(Service Independent)		Not Byte-Bound/Oriented
cable	AAL		
Initial speeds up to 166.62 Mbps	(Two Sublayers)		
(eventural speeds up to 2.49	(Four Service Classes)		
Gbps)	A: for Voice, Data		
Can always operate at top speed	B: for Video, etc.		
(provided there is enough traffic)	C: for Connection-		
Can transmit voice, video, data	Oriented Mode		
(simultaneously, if necessary)	D: for Connectionless		
	Mode		

- Operation at maximum speed at all times, provided there is enough network traffic to give the required throughput.

- Use of fixed-length (53-byte) packets, which are known as *cells*.

- Error correction and routing in hardware, partly because of the fixed cell sizes.

- Transmission of voice, video, and data at the same time. The fixed-length cells also make voice transmission more

a b c d e f g h i j k l m n o p q r s t u v w x y z

accurate, because there is less timing variation.

- Easier load balancing, because the switching capabilities make it possible to have multiple virtual circuits between sender and receiver.

ATM Structure

The ATM architecture is organized into layers, as are other network architectures, and also into planes, which specify domains of activity. See the figure "Structure of the ATM architecture" for a graphic representation of the organization of the planes and layers.

Physical Layer

The ATM physical layer corresponds to the OSI Reference Model physical layer. It is concerned with the physical medium and interfaces, and with the framing protocols (if any) for the network.

The physical layer has two sublayers. The lower sublayer, physical medium (PM), includes the definition for the medium (optical fiber) and the bit-timing capabilities. The upper sublayer, transmission convergence (TC), is responsible for making sure valid cells are being created and transmitted. This involves breaking off individual cells from the data stream of the higher layer (the ATM layer), checking the cell's header, and encoding the bit values.

The user network interface (UNI) specified by the ATM forum, an organization dedicated to defining and implementing ATM, allows for various types of physical interfaces for ATM networks, including the following:

- SONET connections at 155.52 Mbps (OC-3, STS-3, or in CCITT terminology, STM-1)

- DS3 connections at 44.736 Mbps

- 100 Mbps connections using 4B/5B encoding

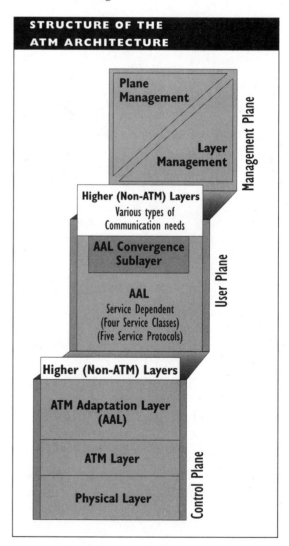

STRUCTURE OF THE ATM ARCHITECTURE

- 155 Mbps connections using 8B/10B encoding

These interfaces all use optical fiber, which is the only medium specified for ATM. A work group is investigating the possibility of defining ATM for Category 3 unshielded twisted-pair (UTP) wire.

ATM Layer

The ATM layer is a service-independent layer at which cell headers and trailers are created, virtual channels and paths are defined and given unique identifiers, and cells are multiplexed or demultiplexed. The ATM layer creates the cells and uses the physical layer to transmit them.

AAL (ATM Adaptation Layer)

The topmost layer, AAL is service-dependent. It provides the necessary protocol translation between ATM and the other communication services (such as voice, video, or data) involved in a transmission. For example, the AAL translates between elements from a pulse-code modulation (PCM) transmission (which encodes voice data in digital form) and ATM cells.

The following four types of services, which each use different AAL protocols, are defined at the AAL:

- Class A is suited for constant bit rate (CBR) data and provides circuit-switching emulation. This is appropriate for voice data. The protocol is AAL 1.

- Class B is for variable bit rate (VBR) data; for example, video transmissions during teleconferences. The protocol is AAL 2.

- Class C is suited for connection-oriented data transmissions. The protocol is AAL 3 or AAL 5.

- Class D is suited for connectionless data transmissions. The protocol is AAL 4 or AAL 5.

AAL 5 supports classes C or D more efficiently than AAL 3 or AAL 4.

AAL Sublayers

The AAL has two sublayers:

- CS (convergence sublayer) is the upper sublayer that provides the interface for the various services. Users connect to the CS through service access points (SAPs). No protocol data units (PDUs) are defined for this level because the data passing through is application- and service-dependent.

- SAR (segmentation and reassembly) is the sublayer that packages variable-size packets into fixed-size cells at the transmitting end, and repackages the cells at the receiving end. The SAR sublayer is also responsible for finding and dealing with cells that are out of order or lost.

A separate PDU is defined for each class of service. Each PDU contains 48 octets, which are allocated for the header, trailer, and data (known as *payload* in ATM terminology). Of these, the AAL 1 PDU can carry the most data at a time: a 47-octet payload. AAL 3 and AAL 4 each have a

a
b
c
d
e
f
g
h
i
j
k
l
m
n
o
p
q
r
s
t
u
v
w
x
y
z

44-octet payload, and AAL 2 has a 45-octet payload. These PDUs become the data (payload) for the ATM cells that are transmitted.

ATM Planes

Three domains of activity, known as planes, are distinguished for ATM:

- The control plane, on which calls and connections are established and maintained.

- The user plane, on which users, or nodes, exchange data. This is the plane at which ordinary user services are provided.

- The management plane, on which network-management and layer-management services are provided. This plane coordinates the three planes and manages resources for the layers.

ATM Operation

The figure "ATM transmission elements" shows the elements used as a transmission gets onto an ATM network. The top part of the illustration represents the higher (non-ATM) service layers; the bottom part represents the ATM and physical layers in the ATM model. The ATM node does the work of the AAL and much of the ATM layer.

Data from the various types of services (voice, video, data, and so forth) is handled at the AAL layer in an ATM node. The data is converted into ATM cells, regardless of the types of packets that came in. The data is handled by the appropriate class of service. For example, the Class A services will handle voice data; Class C or D services will handle data from a network, and so forth.

Data comes into the AAL as packets of varying sizes, but leaves as fixed-size (48-octet) SAR PDUs. The details of these PDUs depend on the type of service (Class A, B, C, or D) being used. The SAR sublayer does the necessary chopping and packing.

The SAR PDUs from the various services are wrapped into ATM cells at the ATM layer and multiplexed for transmission onto the ATM cell stream. These ATM cells contain the virtual channel and path identification required for the cell to reach its destination. The ATM switch uses channel and path information to send the cell out through the appropriate port.

The cell stream contains bits and pieces of various types of packets, all in separate cells. The cells may be routed, or switched, at various points on their path, as appropriate for maintaining connections at the required quality of service.

The cell stream is encoded and transmitted over the physical media connecting the ATM network. At the receiving end, the ATM routes the cells to the appropriate services at the AAL. The cells are repackaged into the appropriate packet form by the AAL service. This service also checks that the entire packet has been received and that everything is correct.

At the receiving end, the transmission sequence is undone, with the services at the topmost (for ATM) sublayer unpacking the ATM cells to reveal the various types of data, which are passed out to the services that handle the data.

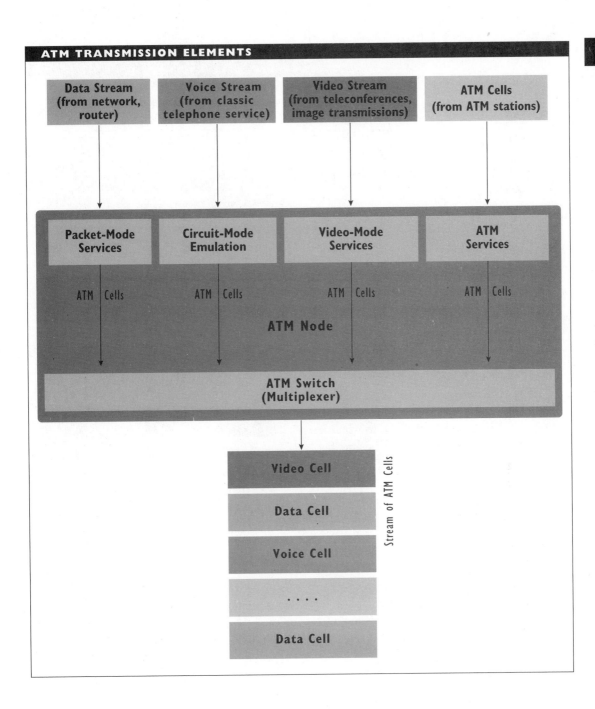

ATM TRANSMISSION ELEMENTS

Data Stream (from network, router)

Voice Stream (from classic telephone service)

Video Stream (from teleconferences, image transmissions)

ATM Cells (from ATM stations)

Packet-Mode Services

Circuit-Mode Emulation

Video-Mode Services

ATM Services

ATM Cells

ATM Cells

ATM Cells

ATM Cells

ATM Node

ATM Switch (Multiplexer)

Video Cell

Data Cell

Voice Cell

. . . .

Data Cell

Stream of ATM Cells

a b c d e f g h i j k l m n o p q r s t u v w x y z

ATM Interfaces

The ATM architecture distinguishes between two interfaces:

- The user-network interface (UNI), which connects an end-user to the network via an ATM switch or other device. This interface supplies network access.

- The network-node interface (NNI), which connects network nodes to each other. This interface makes network routing possible.

Cell Structure

ATM cells are not byte oriented. Even though cells are defined as a specific number of octets, the fields within such a cell often cross byte boundaries.

ATM cells consist of a five-octet header and a 48-octet data, or payload, section. The payload section is an SAR PDU, to which a five-octet ATM header is added. See the figure "Structure of an ATM cell at the UNI."

Most of the bits in the header are used for virtual path and channel identification. The CLP (cell loss priority) bit indicates whether the cell can be discarded if network traffic volume makes this advisable. If the flag is set, the cell is expendable.

Because header fields can extend over multiple octets—for example, the VPI or VCI fields—the ATM specifications include the following guidelines for how bits are to be arranged within a field:

- Within an octet, bit order goes from left to right. For example, in octet 1, the VPI bits are—from highest to lowest—bits 4, 3, 2, and 1, with

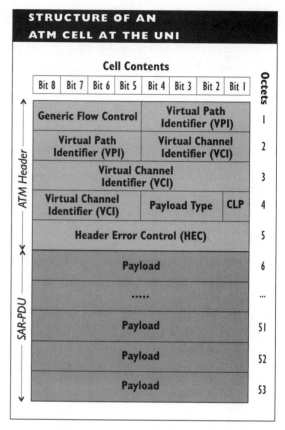

STRUCTURE OF AN ATM CELL AT THE UNI

	Bit 8	Bit 7	Bit 6	Bit 5	Bit 4	Bit 3	Bit 2	Bit 1	Octets
	Generic Flow Control				Virtual Path Identifier (VPI)				1
	Virtual Path Identifier (VPI)				Virtual Channel Identifier (VCI)				2
	Virtual Channel Identifier (VCI)								3
	Virtual Channel Identifier (VCI)				Payload Type			CLP	4
	Header Error Control (HEC)								5
	Payload								6
	.....								...
	Payload								51
	Payload								52
	Payload								53

Cell Contents. ATM Header spans octets 1–5; SAR-PDU spans octets 6–53.

1 being the least significant bit within that octet.

- Across octets, bit order goes downward as octets go upward. Thus, the lowest order bit in the VPI field is bit 5 in octet 2. Similarly, the lowest order bit for the VCI field is bit 5 in octet 4; the highest order bit in this field is bit 4 in octet 2, and the bits in octet 3 are between the high- and low-order quartets.

The cell-structure shown in the figure "Structure of an ATM cell at the UNI" applies to cells that travel onto the network across the UNI. When cells are moving across the NNI—that is, for routing purposes—the VPI field is extended to encompass the entire first octet. That is, cells at the NNI use 12 bits for VPI and 16 for VCI. There is no generic flow control field for these cells.

ATM Variants

Because ATM's progress toward becoming the dominant high-speed architecture has been much slower than anticipated, several variants on the basic technology have been proposed as a means of getting at least some form of ATM into more markets and networks. Two of the more interesting variants are ATM25 and ATM LAN emulation.

ATM25

ATM25 is a 25 Mbps version proposed for use in desktop networks—that is, in LANs. This version was proposed by the Desktop ATM25 Alliance, which includes IBM and Apple among its members. This variant would run on ordinary UTP (unshielded twisted pair) cables, and would allow 25 Mbps transmissions in both directions. The ATM Forum is considering the ATM25 specifications, and Alliance members are currently working on specifications that would enable products from different vendors to work together, and that would enable ATM25 networks to communicate in a transparent manner with other, faster-speed ATM networks.

ATM LAN Emulation

This variant uses software to fool a network operating system into thinking that an ATM interface card is actually an Ethernet or

Token Ring adapter. This software may be included as a driver on the workstation, or client machine. Additional software runs a LAN emulation server—either on an ATM switch or on a separate PC.

With ATM LAN emulation, an ATM device can be made to look like an Ethernet or a Token Ring node to a network server. Below the surface, however, the virtual Ethernet device, for example, is able to operate at blazing ATM speeds by breaking the Ethernet packets into ATM cells before sending them on. The packets might be sent across an ATM network to a receiving device that also supports LAN emulation. The packets could then be reassembled at the receiving end and passed transparently to a receiving Ethernet device. Information in the header area identifies packets as coming from a LAN emulation device. Such an emulation makes ATM devices independent of higher-level protocols (for example, TCP/IP or IPX).

ATM Resources

The ATM Forum is a consortium of several hundred vendors, researchers, and other involved parties. The Forum's charter is to help develop and promote the use of ATM-related products and services. Toward this end, the forum provides information about ATM, helps develop specifications for ATM products and use, and generally keeps ATM on the minds of the appropriate people and groups.

Forum members are companies that are interested in developing or using ATM technology. These companies are readying products for various facets of an ATM network, such as nodes, switches, PBXs, and routers.

a b c d e f g h i j k l m n o p q r s t u v w x y z

Various combinations of forum members/ vendors have formed partnerships to create and market ATM components. Companies such as Sprint and AT&T will offer ATM services to their customers.

While many aspects of the ATM technology and specifications are still in flux, significant portions have been tested and proven viable. Vendors have forged ahead and are selling ATM products. They are still quite expensive, however, partly because the absence of finalized specifications has led to vendor-specific implementations. This, of course, makes interoperability more elusive and customers more reluctant.

ATM variants and emulation schemes have been proposed in an effort to make ATM better known. Major ATM vendors have been cutting their prices, which is also expected to help the established base grow.

BROADER CATEGORIES

Network Architecture; Network, Cell-Switched; Network, Packet-Switched

ATPS (AppleTalk Print Services)

An NLM (NetWare Loadable Module) that provides NetWare nodes with access to printers and Macintosh nodes with access to NetWare print queues. Settings for this module are in the ATPS.CFG file.

ATTACH

In Novell's NetWare 2.x and 3.x, the ATTACH command tells a file server that a workstation exists and wants to join the network. The server will assign the workstation a connection number.

Once attached, the user at the workstation can access any of the server's services (assuming that the user has the necessary access rights to those services). The ATTACH command cannot be used to connect to the network initially. The LOGIN command must be used for the first server. Then the ATTACH command can be used to attach to additional servers. ATTACH does not execute a login script or redefine the workstation's environment. The ATTACH command is not included in NetWare 4.x.

BROADER CATEGORY

NetWare

Attachment

In electronic mail, an attachment is a file that is sent along with a regular e-mail message.

Attack Scanner

An attack scanner is a software package used to probe UNIX networks for security problems or flaws. The package will essentially play the role of an intruder trying to steal or force access to a network. The use of such programs is somewhat controversial.

In April, 1995, a controversial attack scanner product—SATAN (Security Analysis Tool for Auditing Networks) by Wietse Venema and Dan Farmer—was posted to the Internet. Such a product can be used by *crackers* (users trying to break into systems for malicious purposes) as well as by system administrators and security people. As a result, the Internet community is divided as to whether such a product should be made freely available.

Attenuation

Attenuation is the loss of signal strength over distance. It is measured in decibels (dB) per kilometer (expressed as dB/km) or per 100 feet. In the logarithmic decibel scale, a 3 dB loss means a 50 percent loss in power, as computed in the following equation. Specifically, the formula for power loss is:

$$dB = 10 \log_{10} \frac{\text{Power}_{\text{out}}}{\text{Power}_{\text{in}}}$$

In this equation, a 50 percent loss would actually yield a result of −3 dB. Under certain conditions, the coefficient in the equation will be 20, in which case a result of −6 dB would indicate a 50 percent loss. When describing losses, however, the negative sign is dropped, so that a result of −6 dB is expressed as a 6 dB loss.

Attenuation depends on several factors, including the wire composition and size, shielding, and frequency range of the signal. For copper cable, attenuation increases with signal frequency; for optical fiber, attenuation is relatively constant over a large frequency range.

Fiber-optic cable has the least attenuation, usually fractions of a decibel per kilometer. Unshielded untwisted-pair cable (such as the silver, flat-satin cables used in short-distance telephone and modem lines) has the most attentuation of any cable types used in telecommunications. This type of cable is not used directly in networks.

Attenuation Factor

A value that expresses the amount of a signal lost over a given distance, such as decibel loss per kilometer (expressed as dB/km).

Attribute

An attribute is a feature or property associated with an entity. For example, objects in network management and entries in an X.500 Directory Services database have attributes.

An attribute has a type and a value associated with it. The type constrains the form the value can take. For example, an INTEGER type may have only a whole number value, or a BOOLEAN may have only a value that evaluates to TRUE or FALSE.

Much network management or monitoring activity consists of determining or changing attribute values. Attribute values are read or set by functions that provide the relevant network services.

File and Directory Attributes

Among the most important attributes are those associated with files and directories, because these ultimately limit what can be done on a network. The attributes are generally represented as single-bit flag values, with the flag either set or not set.

The specific attributes defined vary from system to system, but attributes are used in every operating system and networking environment. Certain attributes assume or replace others, and certain attributes override access rights. See the table "Novell NetWare File and Directory Attributes" for descriptions of NetWare attributes associated with files and directories.

NOVELL NETWARE FILE AND DIRECTORY ATTRIBUTES

ATTRIBUTE	DESCRIPTION
A (Archive needed)	Set automatically when a file is changed after its most recent backup. (NetWare 2.x, 3.x, 4.x)
C (Copy inhibit)	Set to keep Macintosh files from being copied. Does not apply to DOS files. (NetWare 3.x, 4.x)
Cc (Can't compress)	Set automatically when a file cannot be compressed because it would not save a significant amount of space. (NetWare 4.x)
Co (Compressed)	Set automatically to show that a file has been compressed. (NetWare 4.x)
Di (Delete inhibit)	Set to keep users from deleting a file or directory. (NetWare 3.x, 4.x)
Dc (Don't compress)	Set to prevent a file from being compressed. (NetWare 4.x)
Dm (Don't migrate)	Set to prevent a file from being migrated to a secondary storage medium, such as an optical disk drive. (NetWare 4.x)
X (Execute only)	Set to keep a file from being copied, deleted, changed, or backed up. Since this setting cannot be changed, it's necessary to keep a backup (nonrestricted) copy of the program before freezing it. Assigning this attribute is not recommended; the same effect can be accomplished with the Ro attribute. (NetWare 2.x, 3.x, 4.x)
H (Hidden)	Set to keep a file or directory from being displayed in a directory listing. (NetWare 2.x, 3.x, 4.x)
I (Indexed)	Set to make it faster to access a file with many clusters on a hard disk. (NetWare 2.x, 3.x, 4.x)
Ic (Immediate compress)	Set to make sure that a file is compressed immediately. (NetWare 2.x, 3.x, 4.x)
M (Migrate)	Automatically set to show that a file has been migrated to secondary storage medium. (NetWare 4.x)
P (Purge)	Set to make sure a file or directory is purged (zeroed) immediately after deletion, so that no data from the file is available. (NetWare 3.x, 4.x)
R (Rename inhibit)	Set to make sure a file or directory name is not changed. (NetWare 3.x, 4.x)
Ra (Read audit)	Supported but not used.
Ro/Rw (Read only/ Read write)	Set to specify whether a file can be modified. (NetWare 2.x, 3.x, 4.x)
S (Shareable)	Set to indicate that multiple users or processes can access a file simultaneously. (NetWare 2.x, 3.x, 4.x)

ATTRIBUTE	DESCRIPTION
Sy (System)	Set to indicate that a file or directory is a NetWare or DOS system file or directory. (NetWare 2.*x*, 3.*x*, 4.*x*)
T (Transactional)	Set to allow NetWare's Transactional Tracking System (TTS) to protect a file. (NetWare 2.*x*, 3.*x*, 4.*x*)
Wa (Write audit)	Supported but no AU (Access Unit)

SEE ALSO

Access Rights

AU (Access Unit)

In the 1988 version of the CCITT's X.400 Message Handling System (MHS), an AU is an application process that provides a CCITT-supported service, such as faxing, with access to a Message Transfer System (MTS). The MTS can deliver a message to users or services at any location accessible through the MHS.

AUs supplement user agents (UAs), which give human users access to an MTS.

BROADER CATEGORY

X.400

COMPARE

PDAU; UA (User Agent)

Audio Frequency Range

The range of frequencies that the human ear can hear, which goes from a frequency of 20 hertz to about 20 kilohertz (although few people can hear the extremes well). People can produce sounds within only a small portion of this range, from about 100 to 3,000 hertz, which is the bandwidth of the ordinary, acoustically-based telephone system.

Audit

An examination of network activity to make sure that the network monitoring and data gathering are working correctly. Although this is a management activity, it is done independently of the network management package in some environments (for example, in NetWare). An independent audit can check the reliability of the management software.

AUI (Attachment Unit Interface)

One component of the physical layer, as defined in the IEEE 802.*x* specifications and in the OSI Reference Model. The other two components are the physical layer signaling (PLS) above the AUI and the physical medium attachment (PMA) below it.

SEE ALSO

Connector, AUI (Attachment Unit Interface

AUP (Acceptable Use Policy)

An AUP represents guidelines established for the use of the Internet or of the services from a particular provider. For example, in the early days, commercial traffic was not allowed on the Internet, according to the

NSF's (National Science Foundation) AUP. Internet service providers may also stipulate AUPs. For example, providers may restrict or prohibit distribution of newsletters or other postings to large subscriber lists.

Authentication

In network security and other operations, authentication is the process of determining the identity and legitimacy of a user, node, or process. Various authentication strategies have been developed. Among the simplest are the use of user IDs and passwords.

A relatively new authentication scheme, called *digital signatures,* is very effective and almost impossible to fool (unless one has access to the private encryption key of one party). In digital signatures, a user (user A) uses another user's (user B's) public key to encrypt the transmission, and uses A's private key to "sign" it. At the receiving end, user B uses A's public key to validate the signature, and user B's private key to decrypt the transmission.

The CCITT distinguishes two levels of authentication for directory access in its X.509 recommendations:

- Simple authentication, which uses just a password and works only for limited directory domains.

- Strong authentication, which uses a public key encryption method to ensure the security of a communication.

BROADER CATEGORY
Network Security

Authentication System

An authentication system is a server whose job is to check the validity of all identities on the network and of their requests. Most of the work is done automatically, without requiring any explicit human intervention.

One example of an authentication system is Kerberos, which was created for Project Athena at MIT. Kerberos is a distributed authentication system which verifies that a user is legitimate when the user logs in and every time the user requests a service. Kerberos uses special keys, called *tickets,* to encrypt transmissions between Kerberos and a user.

BROADER CATEGORY
Network Security

Authority and Format Identifier (AFI)

SEE
AFI (Authority and Format Identifier)

Autocall Unit (ACU)

SEE
ACU (Autocall Unit)

AUTOEXEC.BAT

Under DOS, AUTOEXEC.BAT is a special batch file that is executed automatically when the computer boots or reboots. The commands in the file can be used to configure a working environment. For example, commands in an AUTOEXEC.BAT file may load drivers or other files, set a command line prompt, set environment variables, load a network operating system, and so on.

Various solutions have been developed to allow some flexibility in booting to an environment. For example, OS/2 version 2.*x* allows each DOS process to have its own automatically executed file. For DOS, various programs have been developed to allow conditional processing in the AUTOEXEC.BAT file.

BROADER CATEGORY
Boot

SEE ALSO
AUTOEXEC.NCF; CONFIG.SYS

▼ AUTOEXEC.NCF

On a NetWare server, AUTOEXEC.NCF is an executable batch file that is used to configure the NetWare operating system and to load the required modules. The following are some of the tasks of AUTOEXEC.NCF:

- Store the server name and IPX internal network number.

- Load local-area network (LAN) drivers and the settings for the network interface cards (NICs).

- Bind protocols to the installed drivers.

- Load NetWare Loadable Modules (NLMs).

- Set time-zone information on the network.

- Execute certain server commands.

COMPARE
AUTOEXEC.BAT

▼ Automatic Alternate Routing (AAR)

SEE
AAR (Automatic Alternate Routing)

▼ Automatic Call Distributor

A device that automatically switches an incoming call to the next available line.

▼ Automatic Number Identification (ANI)

SEE
ANI (Automatic Number Identification)

▼ Automatic Repeat Request (ARQ)

SEE
ARQ (Automatic Repeat Request)

▼ Automatic Rollback

In NetWare's Transaction Tracking System (TTS), a feature that restores the starting state of a database if a transaction fails before completion.

▼ Automatic Route Selection (ARS)

SEE
ARS (Automatic Route Selection)

▼ Auto-Partition Algorithm

An algorithm by which a repeater can automatically disconnect a segment from a network if that segment is not functioning properly. This can happen, for example, when a broken or unterminated cable causes too many collisions. When the collisions have subsided, the network segment can be reconnected.

A/UX

An implementation of the UNIX operating system on a Macintosh, enhanced with some Macintosh-specific features, such as support for the Macintosh Toolbox. A/UX is based on System V Release 2 (SVR2) of AT&T's UNIX.

AUX

In DOS, AUX is the logical name for an auxiliary device. This is usually the serial communications board, which is more commonly known as *COM1*.

Availability

In network performance management, the proportion of time during which a particular device, program, or circuit is ready for use. Specifically, the availability of a device is the ratio of MTBF to (MTBF + MTTR), where MTBF and MTTR are mean time before failure and mean time to repair, respectively. A device is considered available even if it is in use.

Avalanche Photodiode (APD)

SEE

APD (Avalanche Photodiode)

AWG (American Wire Gauge)

AWG (American Wire Gauge) is a classification system for copper wire. The system is based on the gauge, or diameter, of the conducting wire. The lower the gauge, the thicker the wire and the lower the resistance per unit length. The table "Diameter and Resistance Values for Selected Wire Gauges" shows some gauge values and corresponding diameters.

DIAMETER AND RESISTANCE VALUES FOR SELECTED WIRE GAUGES		
AWG VALUE (GAUGE)	DIAMETER (MM)	RESISTANCE (OHMS/ METER)
30	0.26	0.346
24	0.51	0.080
22	0.64	0.050
20	0.81	0.032
18	1.02	0.020
16	1.29	0.012
14	1.63	0.008
12	2.05	0.005

B8ZS (Bipolar with 8 Zero Substitution)

A signal-encoding scheme in which a 1 is represented alternately as positive and negative voltage, and 0 is represented as zero voltage. B8ZS requires at least one bit of every eight to be a 1.

SEE ALSO
Encoding, Signal

BAC (Basic Access Control)

In the CCITT X.500 directory services model, the more comprehensive of two sets of access-control guidelines. The less comprehensive set is called SAC (Simplified Access Control).

SEE ALSO
X.500

Backbone

In a hierarchically arranged distributed system, the backbone is the top-level, or central, connection path shared by the nodes or networks connected to it.

The backbone manages the bulk of the traffic, and it may connect several different locations, buildings, and even smaller networks. The backbone often uses a higher-speed protocol than the individual local-area network (LAN) segments.

Backbone Network

A backbone network is one with a central cabling scheme (the backbone) to which other networks are attached. Nodes in one network can talk to nodes in other networks by sending packets across the backbone network.

The networks attaching to the backbone are known as *access networks*. Access networks may require a gateway or router to attach to the backbone network.

A backbone network can be useful in decentralized corporations. For example, a backbone network might be used in a company in which each department has set up its own network and several different architectures are used. Since the backbone network leaves the access networks intact, those networks can continue operating as if they were not on the larger network. However, the backbone gives each of the networks access to the resources and data of the other access networks.

One obstacle to a successful backbone network is the high bandwidth that may be required to handle potentially heavy traffic. Because of this consideration, fiber-optic cable is the most sensible cabling for backbone networks.

Back End

In a client/server architecture, the portion of an application that runs on the server and does the actual work for the application. The *front end* runs on the client machine and provides an interface through which the user can send commands to the back end.

Background Process

A process or program that executes incidentally, while another process or program is operating in the foreground. The foreground process gets the main attention of the CPU (central processing unit), and the background process takes CPU cycles when the foreground process is temporarily idle.

Backing Out

In NetWare's TTS (Transaction Tracking System), the process of abandoning an uncompleted database transaction, leaving the database unchanged. TTS takes this action to ensure that the database is not corrupted by information from an incomplete transaction.

SEE ALSO

TTS (Transaction Tracking System)

Backplane

A backplane is a circuit board with slots into which other boards can be plugged, as illustrated in the figure "A backplane." The motherboard in a PC is a backplane.

A *segmented backplane* is a backplane with two or more buses, each with its own slots for additional boards.

Backplate

The metal bracket at one end of a circuit board, usually at the back when the board is plugged into an expansion slot. The backplate, also known as an *end bracket* or *mounting bracket*, typically has cutouts for connectors and switches. PCs usually come with blank backplates over each expansion slot, which are removed when you plug a board into the slot.

Backscattering

In a fiber-optic transmission, light that is reflected back in the direction from which the light came.

Backup

A backup is an archival copy that is stored on an external medium. For example, a backup might contain the contents of a hard disk or a directory.

The creation of regular backups is essential in a networking environment. An effective backup system ensures that data stored on the network can be recreated in the event of a crash or another system failure.

Networking packages differ in the type of backup supported, in the media to which material can be backed up, and in the ease with which parts of the archived material can be restored. Backups are generally made to tape or to erasable optical (EO) media. No serious network should be backed up to floppy disks.

Various types of backups are distinguished, including full, differential, and incremental. In full backups, a copy is made of all the data.

In differential and incremental backups, only the data that has been added or changed since the previous backup is included. Differential and incremental backups assume a full backup has been done and they merely add to this material. Such backups use the Archive flag (attribute), which is supported by DOS and most networking environments. This flag is associated with a file and is set whenever the file is changed after the file is backed up.

a b c d e f g h i j k l m n o p q r s t u v w x y z

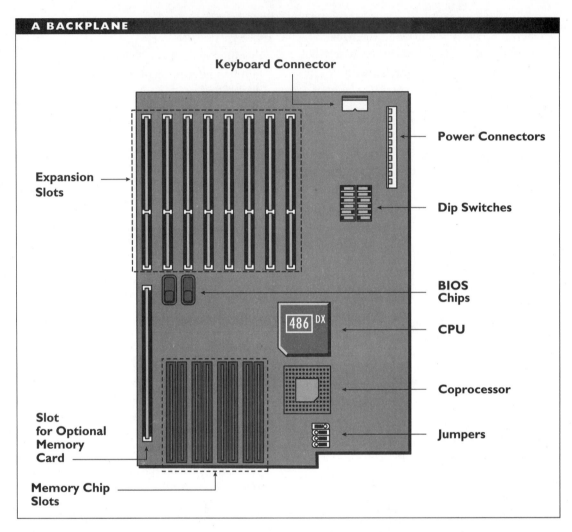

A BACKPLANE

Keyboard Connector

Power Connectors

Expansion Slots

Dip Switches

BIOS Chips

CPU

486 DX

Coprocessor

Slot for Optional Memory Card

Jumpers

Memory Chip Slots

The backed up material should generally be stored in a different physical location from the original material, and should be protected from disasters such as fire, flood, magnets, theft, and so on.

Backup operations should be done at a time when the network is not being used for its ordinary activity, which generally means outside regular working hours. One reason for this is that most backup programs will not back up a file that is open. Truly, the work of a system administrator is never done.

When you restore the data, you restore the last full backup first, then restore each incremental backup made since the last full backup.

SEE ALSO

Archive

RELATED ARTICLES

Data Protection; Disk Duplexing; Disk Mirroring

BACKUP TIPS

- Keep multiple copies of backups; redundancy should be a part of your backup plan.

- Test your backups to make sure that they are what you think they are.

- Store your backups in a secure, off-site location.

- Replace your backup media on a regular basis.

- Consider making incremental backups of critical data at more frequent intervals.

Backward Error Correction (BEC)

SEE

BEC (Backward Error Correction)

Bad-Block Revectoring

In data protection, the process by which material written to a defective area of the hard disk is retrieved and rewritten to a different, nondefective area of storage. The defective area is identified as such in a bad block table, so that future writes will not be made to the area. Bad-block revectoring is known as a *Hot Fix* in Novell's NetWare.

Bad Block Table

In storage management, a table in which all known defective areas of a hard disk are listed to ensure that nothing will be written to these areas. The process of protecting data in this manner is known as *bad-block revectoring*, or *Hot Fix* in Novell's NetWare.

Balun

A balun is a hardware device used to adjust impedances in order to connect different types of cable. The name comes from *bal*anced/*un*balanced, because the device is often used to connect twisted pair (balanced) to coaxial (unbalanced) cable.

Baluns may have different connectors at each end to make them compatible with the cable types being connected. For example, a balun might have a BNC connector at one end and an RJ-45 connector at the other.

A balun makes it possible to use twisted-pair wiring that may already be installed in parts of a building or office in conjunction with coaxial cable that is coming from elsewhere or that has been installed more recently. The balun controls the electrical signal's passage from one cable type to the other, but does not change the signal in any other way. Similarly, a balun enables you to connect a network interface card designed for use with coaxial cables to a hub that uses twisted-pair cabling.

Baluns vary with respect to the cable gauge (thickness) supported and to the maximum cable distance over which the signal is supported. This distance may be as high as 360 to 460 meters (1,200 to 1,500 feet). Coaxial boosters may be used to increase

a
b
c
d
e
f
g
h
i
j
k
l
m
n
o
p
q
r
s
t
u
v
w
x
y
z

signal strength in the coaxial cable, and thus increase the distance over which the signal will be supported by the balun. However, such boosters can cost up to ten times as mach as a balun, and will only double the supported distance.

BROADER CATEGORIES

Connector; Intranetwork Link

▼
Bandwidth

Bandwidth refers to the amount of data a cable can carry; measured in bits per second (bps) for digital signals, or in hertz (Hz) for analog signals such as sound waves. An analog bandwidth is computed by subtracting the lower frequency from the higher one.

For example, the bandwidth of the human voice is roughly 2,700 Hz (3,000 - 300).

A larger bandwidth means greater potential data-transmission capability. For digital signals, a higher bit rate represents a larger bandwidth. However, the higher the frequency, the shorter the wavelength. A higher bandwidth (that is, a higher signal frequency) means faster transmission, which means a shorter signal. With a short signal, there is a smaller margin for error in interpreting the signal. This means that the effects of attenuation and other signal distortion must be kept to a minimum.

A signal traveling along a cable degrades with distance. It is possible to connect the cable to special components that can clean up and rejuvenate a signal. High-frequency electrical signals must be cleaned up

---

WHAT TO LOOK FOR IN A BALUN

Baluns may include a stretch of cable (at extra cost, of course). Here are some things to consider when you're shoppping for a balun:

- Baluns work most reliably when the cable has low capacitance (20 picofarads/foot or less) and when the cable impedance is not too high.

- Baluns are available in different qualities, based on the type and gauge (thickness) of cable at either end. Make sure the balun you select supports the cable properties and distances you need and then some. To be on the safe side, don't use a balun (or any other kind of connector, for that matter) at the maximum rated length.

- Some network interface card manufacturers recommend specific baluns for their boards. Similarly, some manufacturers suggest that you do not use baluns with their hubs or cards. Check with the manufacturer to determine whether either is the case with the network interface card or hub you plan to use.

- When using a balun on a network, you'll almost certainly want a balun designed for data transmission, because this type is made for direct (rather than reversed) pin-to-pin connections.

- Baluns pass signals on, so the balun's reliability depends on the signal's quality. For this reason, it's not a good idea to use a balun with passive hubs, which don't clean and strengthen the signal before passing it on.

frequently, which means single cable segments must be short.

Some commonly used frequency bands for analog transmissions are shown in the table "Bandwidths on the Electromagnetic Spectrum."

Radio Spectrum Bandwidths

Very low frequency (VLF) through super high frequency (SHF) are considered the radio spectrum. The bandwidths are used as follows:

- AM radio broadcasts in the medium frequency (MF) range (535 to 1,605 kHz).

- FM radio and VHF television broadcast in the very high frequency (VHF) range (88 to 108 MHz for FM; the split ranges from 54 to 88 MHz and from 174 to 216 MHz for VHF television).

- Cable stations broadcast over several bands (frequency ranges) in the VHF and ultra high frequency (UHF) ranges (108 to 174 MHz in the VHF range; 216 to 470 MHz in the VHF and UHF ranges).

- UHF television broadcasts in the UHF range (470 to 890 MHz).

- Radar operates at 10 different bands over a huge frequency range (230 MHz to 3 THz).

Digital Transmission Bandwidths

For digital transmissions, bandwidths range considerably. Here are some examples of bandwidth values for digital transmissions:

- Some digital telephone lines: less than 100 kbps

- ARCnet networks: 2.5 Mbps

- ARCnet Plus networks: 20 Mbps

- Ethernet networks: 10 Mbps

- Fast Ethernet networks: 100 Mbps

- Token Ring networks: 1, 4, or 16 Mbps

- Fast Token Ring networks: 100 Mbps

- Fiber-optic (FDDI) networks: About 100 Mbps, but can theoretically be several orders of magnitude higher

- ATM networks: about 655 Mbps, with speeds as high as 2.488 gigabits per second (Gbps) in the future

Bang Path

On the Internet, a bang path is a series of names that specifies a path between two nodes. A bang path is used in uucp (UNIX-to-UNIX copy program) and sometimes for e-mail (electronic mail) or communications on BITNET. The path consists of domain or machine names separated by exclamation points (!), known as *bangs* in some computing circles. For example, in a bang path such as hither!thither!yon, *hither* might be a gateway, *thither* a computer, and *yon* a user.

Bang paths go back to the days before automatic routing, because explicit paths

a
b
c
d
e
f
g
h
i
j
k
l
m
n
o
p
q
r
s
t
u
v
w
x
y
z

BANDWIDTHS ON THE ELECTROMAGNETIC SPECTRUM

NAME	BANDWIDTH (FREQUENCY RANGE)	WAVELENGTH	COMMENTS
Ultra-low frequency (ULF)	.001 Hz (hertz)–1 Hz	300 Gm (gigameter, or billions of meters)— 300 Mm (megameter, or millions of meters)	Subsonic
Extra low frequency (ELF)	30 Hz–300 Hz	10 Mm–1 Mm	Audible spectrum
Voice frequency (VF)	300 Hz–3 kHz (kilohertz)	1 Mm–100 km (kilometer)	
Very low frequency (VLF)	3 kHz–30 kHz 20 kHz–100 kHz	100 km–10 km 150 km–30 km	Ultrasonic
Low frequency (LF)	30 kHz–300 kHz	10 km–1 km	Long wave
Medium frequency (MF)	300 kHz–3 MHz	1 km–100 m	Medium wave
High frequency (HF)	3 MHz–30 MHz	100 m–10 m	
Very high frequency (VHF)	30 MHz–300 MHz	10 m–1 m	
Ultra-high frequency (UHF)	300 MHz–3 GHz	1 m–10 cm	Ultra-shortwave
Super high frequency (SHF)	3 GHz– 30 GHz	10 cm–1 cm	
Extremely high frequency (EHF)	30 GHz–300 GHz 300GHz–300THz	1 cm–1 mm 1 mm–1 micron	Ultramicrowave
Infrared(IR)	300 GHz–430 THz	1 mm–0.7 micron	
Visible	430 THz– 750 THz	0.7 micron–0.4 micron	Visible spectrum
Ultraviolet (UV)	750 THz–30 PHz (petahertz, or quadrillions of hertz; a quadrillion is 10^{15}, or roughly 2^{50})	400 nm - 10 nm	Ultraviolet
X-ray	30 PHz–30 EHz (exahertz, or quintillions of hertz; a quintillion is 10^{18}, or roughly 2^{60})	10 nm–0.01 nm	X-ray

were needed when sending to or communicating with another location.

Banner Page

A banner page is output by a printer in a network environment to separate print jobs. A banner page is also known as a *job separator page*. Printing of this page is controlled by the network operating system.

A banner page might indicate the name of the user who printed the file and other information. You can eliminate banner pages in NetWare and in most other network operating systems.

Base Address

In memory allocation, a base address defines the starting or reference location for a block of contiguous memory. The memory may be general-purpose, or it may serve as cache or port memory. Here are some examples of different types of base addresses:

- A base I/O (input/output) address is the starting location for the memory area allocated for an I/O port. The processor uses this address to find the correct port when the processor needs to communicate with a device.

- A base memory address is the starting location for a block of memory, such as a buffer area.

- A base video address is the starting location for video memory.

Baseband

In networking, a baseband connection is one that uses digital signals, which are sent over wires without modulation; that is, binary values are sent directly as pulses of different voltage levels rather than being superimposed on a carrier signal (as happens with modulated transmissions). Baseband networks can be created using twisted-pair, coaxial, or fiber-optic cable.

Even though only a single digital stream is transmitted over a baseband connection, it is possible to transmit multiple signals. This is done by multiplexing (combining several signals in a transmission by interleaving the signals using, for example, time slices).

This digital signaling is in contrast to broadband, in which analog signals are sent over multiple channels at the same time. Each channel is allocated a different frequency range.

Baseline

In performance analysis, a reference level or the process of determining this level. For example, in a networking context, a baseline measures performance under what is considered a normal load. Commonly used baseline measures include transmission rate, utilization level, and number of lost or erroneous packets.

Basic Access Control (BAC)

SEE

BAC (Basic Access Control)

a b c d e f g h i j k l m n o p q r s t u v w x y z

▼ Basic Information Unit (BIU)

SEE

BIU (Basic Information Unit)

▼ Basic Link Unit (BLU)

SEE

BLU (Basic Link Unit)

▼ Basic Mode

In an FDDI II network, a mode of operation in which data can be transmitted using packet-switching. This is in contrast to hybrid mode, in which both data and voice can be transmitted.

SEE ALSO

FDDI (Fiber Distributed Data Interface)

▼ Basic Rate Access (BRA)

SEE

BRA (Basic Rate Access)

▼ Basic Telecommunications Access Method (BTAM)

SEE

BTAM (Basic Telecommunications Access Method)

▼ Basic Transmission Unit (BTU)

SEE

BTU (Basic Transmission Unit)

▼ Baud Rate

The baud rate is the measure of the number of times an electrical signal can be switched from one state to another within a second. The faster a switch can occur, the higher the baud rate.

The relationship between baud and bit transfer rates depends on the number of bit values that are encoded in a single signal. When each signal represents one bit, the bit and baud rates are equal; when a signal encodes multiple bits, the bit rate is a multiple of the baud rate.

The term *baud* comes from Baudot, the name of a French telegraph operator who developed a five-bit encoding system in the late 19th century. This Baudot code is still used, officially known as International Telegraph Alphabet #1.

Since it is a violation of the bylaws for workers in computers and communications to pass up an opportunity to create an acronym, the term also doubles as the acronym for *bits at unit density*.

COMPARE

Bit Rate

▼ BBS (Bulletin Board System)

A BBS is one or more computers set up with modems so that users can access those computers from remote locations. Users dialing into the BBS can send messages, get technical support from a vendor, upload or download files, and so on.

Many BBSs are set up by vendors to provide users with a forum for communication and with delayed access to technical support. Some BBSs are set up to provide services to a specialized market, generally for a fee. (Fee-based BBSs are often given more aggrandized names, such as Information Services.)

BCC (Block Check Character)

In longitudinal redundancy checks (LRCs), a character inserted at the end of a block to provide error-detection capabilities. Each of the character's bits is a parity bit for a column of bits in the block.

SEE ALSO

CRC (Cyclic Redundancy Check)

BCD (Binary Coded Decimal)

An encoding scheme in which each digit is encoded as a four-bit sequence.

B Channel

In an ISDN system, the bearer channel that carries voice or data at 64 kilobits per second in either direction. This is in contrast to the D channel, which is used for control signals and data about the call. Several B channels can be multiplexed into higher-rate H channels.

SEE ALSO

BRI (Basic Rate Interface); PRI (Primary Rate Interface)

BCN (Beacon)

A frame used in a token ring network to indicate that a hard error (one that is serious enough to threaten the network's continued

operation) has occurred in the node sending the beacon frame or in this node's nearest addressable upstream neighbor (NAUN).

BCP (Byte-Control Protocols)

Protocols that are character- (rather than bit) oriented.

BEC (Backward Error Correction)

Error correction in which the recipient detects an error and requests a retransmission. The amount of material that needs to be retransmitted depends on the type of connection, how quickly the error was detected, and the protocols being used.

COMPARE

FEC (Forward Error Correction)

Bel

A bel is a unit for measuring the relative intensity of two levels for an acoustic, electrical, or optical signal. The bel value is actually proportional to the logarithm (to base 10) of this ratio.

For example, if one voltage is 10 times as strong as another, the higher voltage is one bel higher than the lower one; similarly, if one sound is 100 times as loud as another, the louder sound is two bels louder. The decibel, a tenth of a bel, is used more commonly when computing such values.

Bellman-Ford Algorithm

An algorithm for finding routes through an internetwork. The algorithm uses distance vectors, as opposed to link states. The

a
b
c
d
e
f
g
h
i
j
k
l
m
n
o
p
q
r
s
t
u
v
w
x
y
z

Bellman-Ford algorithm is also known as the *old ARPAnet* algorithm.

SEE ALSO
Algorithm

BER (Basic Encoding Rules)

In the ISO's Abstract Syntax Notation One (ASN.1), the BER are the rules for encoding data elements. Using the BER, it is possible to specify any ASN.1 element as a byte string. This string includes three components, and the encoding may take any of three forms, depending on the information being encoded.

Components of BER

The components of BER are the Type, Length, and Value fields.

The Type, or identifier, field indicates the class of object, as well as the string's form. Examples of ASN.1 types include BOOLEAN, INTEGER, BIT STRING, OCTET STRING, CHOICE, and SEQUENCE OF. Of these, the first two are primitive, the next three may be primitive or constructed types, and the SEQUENCE OF type is always constructed. (A primitive object consists of a single element of a particular type of information, such as a number or logical value; a constructed type is made up of other simpler elements, such as primitive objects or other constructed types.)

The Length field indicates the number of bytes used to encode the value. Values actually may have a definite or an indefinite length. For the latter case, a special value is included in the last byte.

The Value, or contents, field represents the information associated with the ASN.1 object as a byte string. For primitive types, this is a single value; for constructed types, there may be several values, possibly of different types, involved.

BER Encoding

The encoding may be any of the following:

- Primitive/fixed length, which consists only of a primitive object and which is always a fixed length. For example, an integer variable is of this type.

- Constructed/fixed length, which consists of a group of objects and values, with a fixed total length. For example, this might be a record with only predefined components, all of which have a fixed and known length.

- Constructed/variable length, which consists of a group of objects whose total size may vary from case to case, so that a special value is needed to indicate the end of the value.

The BER can provide an encoding for any valid ASN.1 object. One difficulty is that the rules can sometimes provide more than one. In this case, the rules may be too general, because all the "synonymous" rules eat up overhead.

BER Variants

Several variants of the BER have been proposed and are being developed. In general, these are designed to provide faster, simpler, and/or more generic encodings. The following are some of the alternatives that have been proposed:

- CER (canonical encoding rules), which represent a subset of the BER. With the canonical rules, it should be possible to eliminate any redundant paths, which can slow down performance considerably.

- DER (distinguished encoding rules), which are also a subset of BER.

- LWER (lightweight encoding rules), which make faster encoding possible, but may result in larger transmissions.

- PER (packed encoding rules), which are used to compress the information about an object.

PRIMARY SOURCES
CCITT recommendation X.209; ISO document 8825

BROADER CATEGORY
ASN.1

BER (Bit Error Rate)

Number of erroneous bits per million (or billion or trillion) bits in a transmission or a transfer (as from a CD to memory). The BER depends on the type and length of transmission or on the media involved in a transfer.

COMPARE
BLER (Block Error Rate)

Berkeley Internet Name Domain (BIND)

SEE
BIND (Berkeley Internet Name Domain)

BERT (Bit Error Rate Tester)

A hardware device for checking a transmission's bit error rate (BER), or the proportion of erroneous bits. The BERT sends a predefined signal and compares it with the received signal. BERTs are moderately expensive devices that are used most commonly for troubleshooting wiring.

COMPARE
BLERT (Block Error Rate Tester)

BIA (Burned-In Address)

A hardware address for a network interface card. Such an address is assigned by the manufacturer and is unique for each card.

BIB (Bus Interface Board)

An expansion board. In particular, a network interface card (NIC), which serves as an interface between the node (computer) and the network medium.

Big-Endian

In data transmission and storage, the order in which bytes in a word are processed (stored or transmitted). The term comes from Jonathan Swift's *Gulliver's Travels*, in which a war is fought over which end of an egg should be cracked for eating. This

a **b** c d e f g h i j k l m n o p q r s t u v w x y z

ordering property is also known as the processor's *byte-sex*.

In big-endian implementations, the high-order byte is stored at the lower address. Processors in mainframes (such as the IBM 370 family), some minicomputers (such as the PDP-10), many RISC machines, and also the 68000 family of processors use big-endian representations. The IEEE 802.5 (token ring) and the ANSI X3T9.5 FDDI standards use big-endian representations. In contrast, the 802.3 (Ethernet) and 802.4 (token bus) standards use little-endian ordering.

The term is used less commonly to refer to the order in which bits are stored in a byte.

COMPARE

Little-Endian; Middle-Endian

▼
BIND (Berkeley Internet Name Domain)

In the Internet community, a domain name system (DNS) server developed at the University of California, Berkeley, and used on many Internet machines.

▼
Bindery

In Novell's NetWare products, the bindery is a database maintained by the network operating system (NOS) on each server. The bindery is located in the SYS:SYSTEM directory and contains information about all the users, workstations, servers, and other objects recognized by the server.

The bindery information determines the activities possible for the user or node. In the bindery, this information is represented as a flat database.

The bindery has three types of components:

Objects: Users, devices, workgroups, print queues, print servers, and so on. Most physical and logical entities are regarded as objects.

Properties: Attributes, specifically, as assigned to bindery objects, such as full name, login restrictions, or group membership information.

Property data sets: The values that will be stored in an object's property list.

The bindery has been replaced in NetWare 4.*x* by the NetWare Directory Services (NDS), in which information is represented hierarchically in tree format.

However, version 4.*x* includes bindery-emulation capabilities, which makes it possible to integrate bindery-based objects into a network based on NDS. In NetWare 4.1, the *Bindery services* utility creates a bindery context within which the bindery objects appear as a flat database—as required by earlier versions of NetWare. This perspective is valid in only a limited context, which makes it possible to integrate the bindery information into the NDS while still providing a pre-4.*x* server with access to the bindery's contents.

Another 4.1 utility, NetSync, makes it possible to manage up to 12 NetWare 3.*x* servers within a NetWare 4.1 network. This makes all 12 servers look like a single server to users—a user would need only one login to access as many of the NetWare 3.*x* servers as desired. (As always, such access assumes that the user has the necessary privileges.)

With NetSync, it also becomes easier to update resources on different machines.

BROADER CATEGORY

NetWare

Bindery Emulation

In Novell NetWare 4.*x*, bindery emulation is a NetWare Directory Service that makes the Directory database emulate a flat database.

In NetWare 2.*x* and 3.*x*, information about all network objects is stored in a flat database, called the *bindery*. A flat database is one in which all objects in the database exist as entities of equal standing; an object cannot contain another object. In NetWare 4.*x*, network objects and their related information are contained in a hierarchical database called the Directory. A hierarchical database can contain several levels of objects, which means that objects can contain other objects.

Bindery emulation allows programs that were written to run under the NetWare bindery to find the network object information they need in NetWare 4.*x*'s Directory by making the information in the Directory appear as a flat structure.

Such bindery emulation is provided by the Bindery services utility, which makes the bindery's contents look appropriate for whatever server is querying it (i.e, 3.*x* or 4.*x*).

BROADER CATEGORY

NetWare

Binding and Unbinding

In a local-area network (LAN), binding is the process of associating a communication protocol, such as TCP/IP, IPX/SPX, or AppleTalk, and a network interface card (NIC). Unbinding is the process of dissociating the protocol from the NIC.

The LAN driver for a card must have *at least* one communication protocol associated with it. The LAN driver will be able to process only those packets that use the associated protocol.

BIOS (Basic Input/Output System)

The BIOS is a collection of services on a ROM (read-only memory) chip. The BIOS services enable hardware and software, operating systems and applications, and also applications and users to communicate with each other. The BIOS services are loaded automatically into specific addresses and should always be accessible.

BIOS services are updated and expanded to handle newer devices and greater demands. To get a newer BIOS, you simply need to replace the ROM chip in your computer with an appropriate upgrade chip.

BIOS Extensions

A collection of services that supplement those provided by the standard BIOS (Basic Input/Output System). Like the standard BIOS, BIOS extensions are implemented on a ROM (read-only memory) chip, located on the motherboard or on an expansion board.

a b c d e f g h i j k l m n o p q r s t u v w x y z

Bipolar with 8 Zero Substitution (B8ZS)

SEE

B8ZS (Bipolar with 8 Zero Substitution)

BISDN (Broadband ISDN)

BISDN is an extension of the ISDN (Integrated Services Digital Network) to allow multiple types of information to be transmitted. BISDN can handle voice, video, and graphics, as well as data.

Whereas ISDN networks generally use some form of time division multiplexing (TDM) for actual transmissions, BISDN networks generally use ATM (asynchronous transfer mode) as their transmission technology. ATM is often erroneously regarded as being equivalent to BISDN.

BISDN Services

Figure "BISDN Services" summarizes the kinds of capabilities that have been defined for BISDN networks. The services are grouped into two main groups, each with multiple service classes:

- *Interactive services* are those in which the user can initiate the service and influence its direction. Three classes are distinguished, and each class includes several examples. For example, conversational services include video-conferencing and video-telephony (for shopping, learning, etc). Online research is included among interactive services.

- *Distribution services* are those in which information (in the form of video, documents, or data) can be broadcast to whomever has the resources and rights to receive the broadcast. Distribution services are divided into those for which the user has no control over the presentation (other than to turn it on or off) and those where the user can control which elements are received. Examples of the former include TV programming and electronic newspapers; examples of the latter include retrieval of selected news items and certain online courses.

PRIMARY SOURCES

BISDN is discussed in more than a few of the documents in the ITU-T I.xxx document series. For example, I.113 provides a vocabulary for BISDN, and I.121 provides a list of the documents that discuss BISDN or ATM or both. These include I.150 (ATM for BISDN), I.211 (BISDN services), I.311 (General BISDN networking aspects), I.327 (BISDN functional architecture), I.361, I.362, and I.363 (ATM layers), I.413 and I.432 (BISDN User-network interface), and I.610 (Operation and maintenance for BISDN). In some cases, these recommendations must be read in relation to their ISDN counterparts, whose numbers are generally lower than the corresponding BISDN document. For example, I.210 discusses ISDN services.

COMPARE

ISDN (Integrated Services Digital Network)

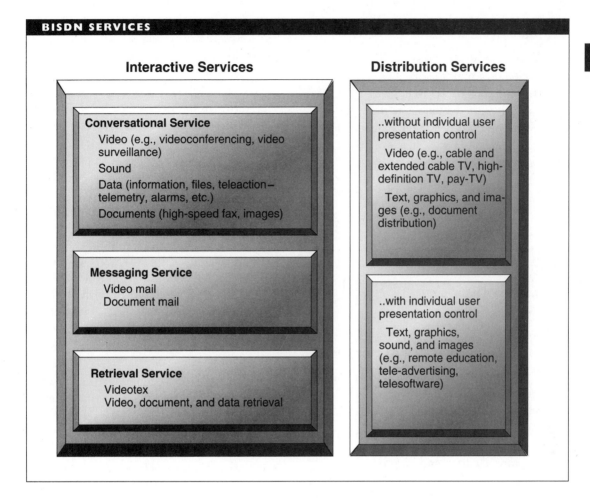

BISDN SERVICES

Interactive Services

Conversational Service
Video (e.g., videoconferencing, video surveillance)
Sound
Data (information, files, teleaction—telemetry, alarms, etc.)
Documents (high-speed fax, images)

Messaging Service
Video mail
Document mail

Retrieval Service
Videotex
Video, document, and data retrieval

Distribution Services

..without individual user presentation control
Video (e.g., cable and extended cable TV, high-definition TV, pay-TV)
Text, graphics, and images (e.g., document distribution)

..with individual user presentation control
Text, graphics, sound, and images (e.g., remote education, tele-advertising, telesoftware)

Bit

A binary digit; the smallest unit of information. A bit can have a value of 0 or 1 in a digital system. All but the low-level protocols move information in larger chunks, such as bytes, which consists of multiple bits.

Bit Error Rate (BER)

SEE

BER (Bit Error Rate)

Bit Error Rate Tester (BERT)

SEE

BERT (Bit Error Rate Tester)

Bit Interval

Bit interval, also known as *bit time*, refers to the amount of time a digital signal is left at a particular voltage level to indicate a value. Usually, the level will indicate the value of a single bit, but it is possible to encode more than a single bit in a voltage level, thereby transmitting more than one bit in a single bit interval.

In general, the longer the bit interval, the slower the transmission rate. For example, when encoding a single bit at a time, a bit interval of .01 second means a transmission rate of only 100 bits per second (bps).

RELATED ARTICLES
Bit Rate; Encoding, Signal

BITNET (Because It's Time Network)

BITNET is a computer network that connects many educational institutions in North America and Europe. BITNET was set up through EDUCOM, a nonprofit educational consortium. It is designed to provide communication facilities and easy access to files—even from remote locations—provided that the user has the appropriate access privileges. Today, BITNET connects more than 1,000 locations.

Partly because the early nodes were predominantly IBM mainframes, BITNET still uses the RSCS (Remote Spooling Communications Subsystem) and NJE (Network Job Entry) protocol suites. Because of this, a gateway is needed to communicate with other networks, such as the Internet.

Once a gateway between the Internet and BITNET is known, it is relatively easy to send a message to a user on BITNET from most Internet installations. An address such as user@computer.bitnet will suffice, because most Internet mail programs recognize *bitnet* as a pseudo domain name.

In Canada, BITNET is known as NetNorth, and in Europe it is known as EARN (for European Academic Research Network).

Bit Rate

Bit rate is a measure of throughput, or rate of data transfer. It represents the number of bits that are transmitted within a second in a digital communication, measured in bits per second (bps). The faster the bit rate, the shorter the bit interval (the interval to signal a bit value). For example, at a bit rate of 5,000 bps, each bit interval can be at most .0002 second when a single bit is transmitted in each bit interval.

Bit rate is often used interchangeably with baud rate, but these two measurements are not exactly the same. *Baud rate* refers to the number of electrical signal transitions made in a second. If a single bit is encoded in each signal, the bit rate and baud rate will be equal. However, if multiple bits are encoded in a single signal, the bit rate will be higher than the baud rate.

Bit Stuffing

In data transmission, a technique for ensuring that specific bit patterns do not appear as part of the data in a transmission. For example, if six consecutive 1 values are encountered in the transmitted data, a 0 bit would be inserted after the fifth consecutive 1 bit. The receiver removes any inserted bits when processing the transmission.

BIU (Basic Information Unit)

In SNA network communications, a packet of information created when the transmission control layer adds a request/response header (RH) to a request/response unit (RU). This unit is passed to the path control layer.

SEE ALSO

SNA (Systems Network Architecture)

BIU (Bus Interface Unit)

An adapter card. In particular, a network interface card (NIC), which acts as an interface between a node (computer) and the network.

BIX (BYTE Information Exchange)

BYTE Magazine's commercial online information service. BIX provides the usual gamut of mail, news, and entertainment services, as well as Internet access—including e-mail (electronic mail), ftp (file transfer protocol), and telnet services. In addition to a base monthly fee (which depends on the amount of access requested), costs for Internet use include access and storage charges.

FOR INFORMATION

Call 800-695-4775; 617-354-4137. You can use telnet to access BIX over the Internet. To do this, telnet to x25.bix.com.

Blackout

A total loss of electrical power. Blackouts can be caused by cut or broken power lines, lightning strikes, and other natural and man-made disasters.

SEE ALSO

Power Disturbances

BLER (Block Error Rate)

In communications, an error rate based on the proportion of blocks with errors. Compare it with BER (bit error rate), which is based on the number of erroneous bits per million (or billion or trillion) bits in a transmission.

BLERT (Block Error Rate Tester)

A hardware device for determining a transmission's block error rate (BER), which is the proportion of blocks with erroneous bits. This device is also known as a BKERT.

Block

A block is an area of memory or storage with a fixed size. A network operating system block can be anywhere from 4 to 64 kilobytes (KB). DOS blocks are typically a multiple of 2 KB. NetWare blocks are typically 4 KB. However, the actual block size depends on the size of the volume on which storage is being allocated.

In some environments, such as in NetWare, a block represents the smallest chunk of storage that can be allocated at a time. (In NetWare, you can accept the suggested block size, which is based on the size of the volume, or you can specify the block size you want to use.)

a b c d e f g h i j k l m n o p q r s t u v w x y z

Two types of blocks are distinguished:

Disk-allocation block: Used to store network data, at least temporarily.

Directory-entry block: Used to store directory information.

NetWare 4.*x* supports block suballocation, in which a block can be broken into 512-byte chunks. These chunks can be used to store the ends of several files. For example, with a 4 kilobyte (KB) block size, three 5 KB files would fit into four blocks. Each of the files would use one block and two 512-byte chunks in the fourth block. In contrast, these files would require six blocks (two per file) in NetWare 3.*x*.

Block Error Rate (BLER)

SEE

BLER (Block Error Rate)

Block Error Rate Tester (BLERT)

SEE

BLERT (Block Error Rate Tester)

BLU (Basic Link Unit)

In IBM's SNA (Systems Network Architecture) networks, a block, or packet, of information at the data-link layer.

SEE ALSO

SNA (Systems Network Architecture)

Blue Book Ethernet

Ethernet version 2.0. This term is sometimes used to distinguish Ethernet 2.0 from the similar, but not identical, Ethernet variant defined in the IEEE 802.3 standard.

SEE ALSO

Ethernet

Bookmark

In gopher environments on the Internet, a bookmark is used to mark a specific menu or directory on a gopher server. Once the bookmark has been created and placed at the desired location, it's possible to get almost immediate access to that location, rather than having to work your way through layers of menus.

SEE ALSO

Gopher

Boot

The process by which a computer is started up and its operating system kernel is loaded into RAM (random-access memory) is called the *boot*, or *bootstrap*, process. Although the details may differ when booting to different disk operating systems or network operating systems, the basic steps are the same:

- Execute a hardware self-test.

- Look in a predefined place for the boot sector and load this code.

- Execute the boot sector program to load other programs.

- Execute these programs to load still other programs or to configure the operating environment.

- Repeat the previous step as often as dictated by the programs being loaded and by their initialization code.

BOOTCONF.SYS

In Novell NetWare, a configuration file that specifies how a diskless workstation can boot the operating system in order to access the network.

Boot ROM

A ROM (read-only memory) chip used in diskless workstations to enable these machines to boot and connect to a network.

Bounce

A term for the action of returning an undeliverable e-mail message. In such a case, the postmaster on the system returns the message, along with a *bounce message*, to the sender.

BRA (Basic Rate Access)

Access to an ISDN Basic Rate Interface (BRI), an interface with two 64 kilobits per second (kbps) B channels (for voice and data) and one 16 kbps D channel (for call and customer information). Compare it with PRA, which is access to a PRI (Primary Rate ISDN).

Braid Shield

In coaxial cable, a braid or mesh conductor, made of copper or aluminum, that surrounds the insulation and foil shield. The braid helps protect the carrier wire from electromagnetic and radio frequency interference.

SEE ALSO
Cable, Coaxial

BRI (Basic Rate Interface)

A BRI is an interface between a user and an ISDN (Integrated Services Digital Network)

THE DOS BOOTSTRAP PROCESS

1. A program (the ROM-BIOS) in ROM (read-only -memory) executes. This program checks the hardware components by doing a POST (power-on self-test).

2. The ROM-BIOS program loads and executes a program from the boot sector on a floppy or hard disk.

3. This boot sector program loads hidden files, which, in turn, load the basic device drivers for DOS (keyboard, disk, and display) and execute the DOS initialization code. Part of this initialization loads the DOS kernel.

4. The DOS kernel builds various tables it will need, initializes device drivers, and executes instructions found in CONFIG.SYS, if this file exists.

5. The DOS kernel loads COMMAND.COM, the DOS command processor.

switch. The BRI specifies two 64 kilobit per second (kbps) B channels (for voice and data) and one 16 kbps D channel (for customer and call information).

This channel combination is sometimes denoted as *2B+D*. It can be compared with PRI (Primary Rate Interface).

Access to a BRI is provided by a BRA (basic rate access).

Bridge

The term *bridge* generally refers to a hardware device that can pass packets from one network to another. Bridges operate at the OSI Reference Model's second lowest layer, the data-link layer. A bridge makes the networks look like a single network to higher level protocols or programs.

A bridge serves both as a medium (the bridge part) and as a filter. It allows packets from a node on one network to be sent to a node on another network. At the same time, the bridge discards any packets intended for the originating network (rather than passing these to the other network).

Bridges versus Routers, Brouters, and Repeaters

The terms *bridge* and *router* are often used interchangeably. In fact, in older documentation, Novell referred to its routers as bridges. A router is a device that can send packets to network segments on the way to their destination. Unlike bridges, routers operate at the network layer of the OSI Reference Model. However, bridges and routers have come to take on some of each others' properties. In fact, a brouter (from *bridging*

router) is a device that has the capabilities of both a bridge and a router.

A bridge's capability to segment, or divide, networks is one difference between a bridge and a repeater. A repeater is a device that moves all packets from one network segment to another by regenerating, retiming, and amplifying the electrical signals. The main purpose of a repeater is to extend the length of the network transmission medium beyond the normal maximum cable lengths.

Protocol Independence of Bridges

A bridge is independent of, and therefore can handle packets from, higher level protocols. This means that different higher level protocols can use the same bridge to send messages to other networks.

To protocols at higher OSI layers (most immediately, the network layer), the presence of a bridge is transparent. This means that two networks connected by a bridge are treated as part of the same logical network by protocols such as Novell's IPX/SPX, IBM's NetBIOS, or the widely used TCP/IP. This transparency makes it possible to access a logical network that is much larger than the largest physical network allowed.

Packet Transmission

Because it operates at the data-link layer, a bridge just checks the address information in a packet to determine whether to pass the packet on. Beyond that checking, a bridge makes no changes to a packet.

A bridge sees each packet that is transmitted on each of the networks the bridge connects. If a packet from network A is addressed to a local node (that is, to one in network A), the bridge discards the packet since the packet will be delivered internally through the network. On the other hand, if a packet from network A is addressed to a remote node (on network B), the bridge passes the packet over to network B. The figure "A simple local bridge" shows how a bridge can connect two networks.

The bridge greatly reduces traffic on both networks by protecting each network from the other's local messages. This makes each of the smaller networks faster, more reliable, and more secure, while retaining transparent communication with the other network (or networks).

When routing packets, a bridge uses only node addresses; it does not take network addresses into account. A node address is a physical address, associated with a network interface card (NIC), rather than with a particular network.

Types of Bridges

Bridges can be categorized by several different features. The table "Bridge groupings" summarizes the various categories.

BRIDGE GROUPINGS	
FEATURE	GROUPING
Level	LLC (logical-link-control) layer versus MAC (media-access-control) layer
Operation	Transparent versus source routing
Location	Internal (card) versus external (stand-alone)
Bridged distance	Local versus remote

LLC Layer versus MAC Layer Bridges

MAC-layer bridges operate at the media-access control (MAC) sublayer, the lower sublayer into which the IEEE divides the data-link layer of the OSI Reference Model. These bridges can connect only networks using the same architecture (Ethernet to Ethernet, Token Ring to Token Ring, and so on), because the bridge expects to handle a particular packet format, such as Ethernet or ARCnet.

LLC-layer bridges operate at the upper sublayer of the data-link layer, the logical link-level control (LLC) sublayer. These types of bridges can connect different architectures (such as Ethernet to Token Ring), because these architectures use the same LLC sublayer format, even if they use different formats at the MAC sublayer.

Most older bridges are of the MAC-layer type and can connect only same-architecture networks; most newer products are of the LLC-layer type and can connect dissimilar architectures.

Transparent Routing versus Source Routing

The manner in which a bridge routes packets depends largely on the architectures involved. Bridges connecting Ethernet networks use transparent routing, a packet-routing method in which the bridge determines a route. Transparent bridges determine "on the fly" where a packet belongs. Such bridges learn and store the location of each node, and then route packets accordingly. A transparent bridge can carry out its routing without explicit instruction or attention from the user. The bridge determines

a
b
c
d
e
f
g
h
i
j
k
l
m
n
o
p
q
r
s
t
u
v
w
x
y
z

A SIMPLE LOCAL BRIDGE

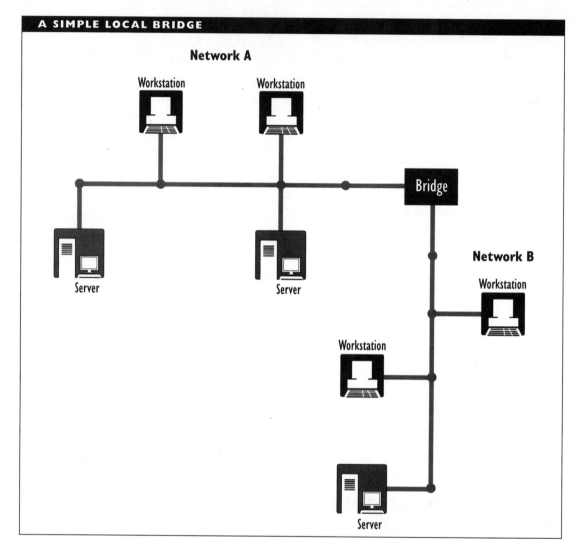

the locations of a node by looking it up in a table the bridge has built.

In contrast, most bridges connecting Token Ring networks use source routing. This is a deterministic routing method in which the source node must provide the route as well as the destination for the packet. The source node learns the available routes through route discovery. The routing

information is inserted by the sender and can be determined by sending a discovery packet. This packet uses the spanning tree algorithm to find the most efficient route to the destination and reports this route to the sender.

Source routing bridges determine an explicit path to the destination node and include this routing information in the packet. Surprisingly, the requirements for source routing capabilities are considerably more complex than for transparent bridges. Accordingly, source routing capabilities are generally available as options for a bridge. Although source routing requires more work to find the path initially, it is more efficient once the path has been established because there is no longer any reason for the bridge to find a path.

According to the IEEE 802.3 specifications, all bridges should be capable of using transparent routing. Some can also do source routing. A bridge can distinguish between the two approaches by checking the packet being sent. Depending on the value of a particular bit in the source address field, a packet may include source-routing information.

Internal versus External Bridges

A bridge may be internal or external. An *internal bridge* is on a card plugged into an expansion slot in a server. The server is part of both networks. An internal bridge gets its power from the PC's bus. Internal bridges generally include multiple types of connectors. A special type of internal bridge is used to connect to wide-area networks (WANs). This type of bridge will have connectors for modem or telephone connections, such as D-shell or RJ-type connectors.

An *external bridge* is a stand-alone component to which each network is connected by cable. The external bridge is part of both networks. An external bridge generally has multiple connectors; for example, BNC for coaxial cable (as in Ethernet or ARCnet networks); modular (RJ-xx) for twisted-pair cable, and possibly DB-9 or DB-25 (for serial connection to a modem). External bridges need their own power supply and they usually include a connector for accessing WANs.

Local versus Remote Bridges

A bridge may be local or remote. A *local bridge* connects two networks in the same geographical location, such as networks on either side of the hall or on either side of an office floor. Usually, these types of bridges are added to break a large, busy network into two smaller networks. This reduces network traffic on each of the newly formed networks.

By using the spanning tree algorithm specified in the IEEE 802.1 standard, local bridges can ensure that only a single path is used to send a packet between a source and a destination. If this path is not usable, the algorithm can find an alternate path.

A *remote bridge* connects two networks separated by considerable geographical distance, large enough to require a telecommunications link. Remote bridges must be used in pairs, with one at each end of the link, as shown in the figure "A simple configuration involving remote bridges."

A remote bridge connects to a local-area network at one end and to a switching network, such as one with an X.25 interface, at the other end. Each remote bridge is connected to a network at one port and to a network cloud at another port. (A *cloud* is a working concept that is used to indicate a connection that is taken for granted, for purposes of the discussion and whose details are not specified.)

a
b
c
d
e
f
g
h
i
j
k
l
m
n
o
p
q
r
s
t
u
v
w
x
y
z

The interfaces are likely to be different at these two ports. For example, a remote bridge may connect to an Ethernet network at one port and to a serial interface (such as RS-232) at the other. The cloud represents the point-to-point link between the two remote bridges.

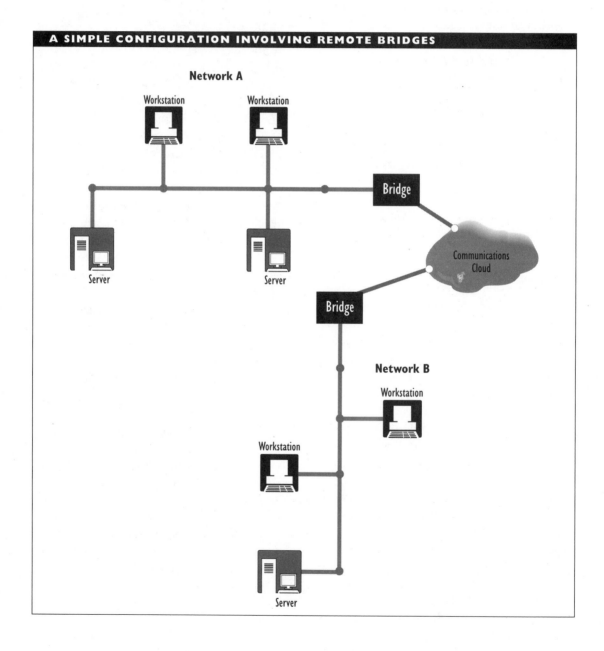

A SIMPLE CONFIGURATION INVOLVING REMOTE BRIDGES

Remote bridges also need a protocol to communicate with each other. For example, if the remote bridges communicate over an ISDN or an X.25 line, the bridge at each end needs to be able to communicate using the switched network (ISDN or X.25) protocol.

The throughput in a remote bridge is likely to be limited by the long-distance connection. At the local end, the bridge will generally have the same nominal speed as the network (10 Mbps for Ethernet, 4 or 16 Mbps for Token Ring, and so on). At the remote end, the throughput will depend on the type of connection. At this end, possible speeds may run from a few kilobits per second to several megabits per second.

Learning Bridges versus Static Bridges

A *learning bridge* is one that automatically builds a table of node addresses, based on the NICs the bridge finds on the network. The bridge builds the table by using the information broadcast when a new node logs on and by checking on the source and destination addresses as packets pass through the bridge.

The performance of a learning bridge improves over time as the bridge completes its table of node locations. Until it knows the location of a node, the bridge assumes the node is on the remote network and so passes on the packets. The bridge is constantly updating its table—adding new addresses and dropping addresses that have not been mentioned within a period of time.

In contrast, a *static bridge* is one that cannot build its own address table. Instead, the addresses must be entered by hand. Fortunately, static bridges have all but disappeared. Just about all modern bridges are

learning bridges, since static bridges do not meet IEEE 802.1 specifications.

Multiple Bridges and the Spanning Tree Algorithm

Multiple bridges may be used to connect several networks. Any one bridge connects only two networks directly, but may connect more than two networks indirectly. The bridge is attached to each network by a port.

If there are multiple bridges, the bridges communicate with each other and establish a layout in order to find a spanning tree for all the networks. A *spanning tree* is one that includes paths to all nodes that can be reached on the network but includes no more paths than are necessary to completely interconnect the nodes and networks involved. Most important, a spanning tree does not include any loops (closed paths) which could trap a packet, thereby effectively shutting down the network.

Because larger network clusters make multiple paths possible, there is the danger that the same message will get broadcast all over the networks through multiple paths. This will produce a great deal of extraneous network traffic and can, in fact, bring down the network. A closed path, or loop, among the networks could be damaging because it could start an unending packet-passing process. The spanning-tree algorithm, specified in IEEE 802.1, is applied to provide a path between every pair of accessible nodes on the network and ensure that there are no loops in the paths to be used by the bridge.

Although the spanning tree algorithm ensures that the same packet won't take multiple paths to the same destination, the algorithm doesn't rule out the possibility of

a
b
c
d
e
f
g
h
i
j
k
l
m
n
o
p
q
r
s
t
u
v
w
x
y
z

WHAT TO LOOK FOR IN A BRIDGE

When you're investigating bridges, you'll want to get details about bridge features and capabilities. Vendors should be able to provide both marketing and technical information about their products. Make sure to get the technical information. The vendors' materials should provide information about at least the following:

- Whether the bridge is local or remote.

- Whether the bridge is internal or external.

- Media and architecture supported for the local network; for example, twisted-pair Ethernet, 16 Mbps Token Ring, or FDDI. It's a good idea to ask explicitly about your particular configuration and to get the answer in writing.

- If applicable, what interface the bridge supports for a remote connection. For example, it may support RS-232, RS-422, V.35, T1, or DSx.

- Number of ports.

- Transmission speeds, both local and long distance, if applicable. The smaller of these values is the critical one. Number of packets passed is generally a more useful figure than the actual bit-transfer rate.

- Whether the bridge supports load balancing.

- Whether the bridge can collect network performance data, such as number of packets received, forwarded, and rejected, number of collisions, and errors during a transmission. Such network management services may require additional software (which may cost several thousand dollars).

- Price, which can range from a few hundred dollars to over $10,000.

When you're selecting a remote bridge, you need to worry about compatibility with the network and also with the long-distance services that will be used. Keep in mind that you may need to budget for two remote bridges if you're responsible for the networks at both ends of the connection.

For more specific and more advanced questions, such as about a bridge's compatibility with a particular network configuration, you may need to talk to the bridge vendor's technical support staff. In many cases, the network vendor (Novell, Banyan, and so on) will have a database of hardware that has been explicitly tested with the vendor's networking products. Be forewarned that these vendors may want to charge you for revealing this information.

multiple paths being used to transmit *different* packets between the same source and destination. Higher-end bridges include the ability to do load balancing by distributing traffic over more than one path between a source and destination.

Recently, wireless bridges have become available for limited-distance remote connections. Remote bridges that use radio waves can be up to 25 or 30 miles apart—provided the terrain and weather allow it, and provided the two bridges have directional antennas available. Remote bridges using lasers can be up to about 3,500 feet apart. Since focused signals must be sent in both cases, such bridges must be within each other's line of sight.

Wireless remote bridges are susceptible to two kinds of interference:

Inward interference, which can occur when another device is operating in the same bandwidth and the two signals interact with each other.

Outward interference, in which the device under consideration is causing interference in a different device.

BROADER CATEGORY
Internetwork Link

SEE ALSO
Brouter; Gateway; Repeater; Router; Switch

▼ ———
Broadband Transmission

A broadband transmission is an analog communication strategy in which multiple communication channels are used simultaneously. The data in a broadband transmission is modulated into frequency bands, or channels, and is transmitted in these channels.

Guard bands, which are small bands of unused frequencies, are allocated between data channels. These provide a buffer against interference due to signals from one data channel drifting or leaking over into a neighboring one. The figure "A broadband transmission" shows how data channels and guard bands are used.

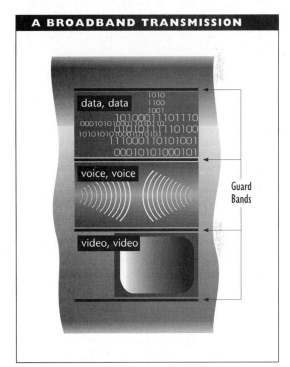

A BROADBAND TRANSMISSION

data, data
1010
1100
1001
10100011101110
000101010011001100
101010101010101011
11000110101001
00010101000101

voice, voice

video, video

Guard
Bands

For example, cable TV (CATV) uses broadband transmission, with each channel getting a 6 megahertz (MHz) bandwidth. Broadband transmissions use coaxial or fiber-optic cable and they can transmit voice, data, or video.

When digital data is being transmitted, a modem or other device demodulates the signals back into digital form at the receiving end. A modem used for broadband transmissions needs two bands of at least 18 MHz bandwidth each: one band for sending and the other for receiving.

Broadcast

In a network transmission, sending a message to all connected nodes. This is in contrast to a transmission that is targeted at a single node. Most packet formats have a special address value to indicate a packet that is being broadcast. Compare broadcast with *multicast*.

Broadcast Storm

In network traffic, a condition in which packets are broadcast, received, and then broadcast again by one or more of the recipients. The effect of a broadcast storm is to congest a network with redundant traffic. Broadcast storms can arise, for example, in bridged networks that contain loops (closed paths).

Broadcast Transmission

In an AppleTalk network that uses the LocalTalk architecture and its LocalTalk Link Access Protocol (LLAP), a transmission sent to each node in the network. Compare broadcast transmission with directed transmission.

Brouter

A brouter (also known as a *bridging router* or, less commonly, as a *routing bridge*) is a device that combines the features of a bridge and a router. A brouter can work at either the data-link layer or the network layer.

Working as a bridge, a brouter is protocol independent and can be used to filter local-area network traffic. Working as a router, a brouter is capable of routing packets across networks.

BROADER CATEGORIES
Bridge; Internetwork Link; Router

Brownout

A short-term decrease in voltage level, specifically when the voltage is more than 20 percent below the nominal RMS voltage. Brownouts can occur when a piece of heavy machinery is turned on and temporarily drains the available power, or when everyone feels the need to run their air conditioners at the same time.

SEE ALSO
Power Disturbance

Browser

A browser is a hypertext file reader. That is, a browser is a program that can display material containing links to other material (perhaps located in other files), and can provide quick and easy access to the contents associated with such links.

Browsers may be text, graphics, or multi-media based:

- A text-based, or line-oriented, browser is unable to display anything but rudimentary graphics, and is generally line-oriented, but can still switch to any material that is formatted in a suitable manner for the browser. WWW and Lynx are examples of such browsers. Both are accessible on the Internet.

- Graphics browsers can handle both text and graphics, require a mouse, and generally have a much nicer display than line-oriented browsers. Cello and Mosaic are examples of graphics-based browsers.

- Multimedia browsers can display sound and video, in addition to the capabilities of graphics browsers. Mosaic is also a multimedia browser. Variants of the mosaic browser are available for several computing environments. For example, XMosaic is a browser for the X Window System. HotJava, a recently announced browser from Sun Microsystems is generally regarded as taking browser technology to a new level. HotJava can handle multimedia material, includes security capabilities, and offers an object-oriented programming language for creating platform-independent applications easily. Because HotJava differs so drastically from existing browsers, it remains to be seen how quickly— or whether—HotJava becomes widely used.

Forms-capable browsers allow users to fill in information on forms or questionnaires. Most graphics-based browsers are forms-capable.

Browsers have long been used in programming environments—for example, in the SmallTalk environment created at Xerox PARC in the 1970s and 1980s. These readers have really come into widespread use with the growth of the World Wide Web (WWW) on the Internet.

SEE ALSO
HotJava; Mosaic; WWW

BSD Socket Layer

In BSD UNIX, the layer that represents the API (Application Program Interface) between user applications and the networking subsystem in the operating system kernel.

BSD UNIX (Berkeley Software Distribution UNIX)

A UNIX version implemented at the University of California, Berkeley. BSD UNIX introduced several enhancements to AT&T's original implementation, including virtual memory, networking, and interprocess communication support.

BTAM (Basic Telecommunications Access Method)

An early access method for communications between IBM mainframes and terminals. BTAM is still used, but is largely obsolete because it does not support IBM's SNA (Systems Network Architecture). ACF/VTAM has replaced BTAM as the method of choice for remote communications with IBM mainframes.

Btrieve

In Novell's NetWare 3.0 and later, Btrieve is a key-indexed record management program that allows you to access, update, create, delete, or save records from a database. Btrieve is a program (actually several programs) that can run in either of two versions: client- or server-based.

In addition to record-management capabilities, Btrieve includes the following:

- Communications facilities, for both local and remote communications between a program and a record base. The Btrieve Message Routers (that is, BROUTER.NLM and BDROUTER.NLM) handle outgoing requests; BSPXCOM handles incoming requests from a remote source (a workstation or another server).

- Requesters (DOS, OS/2, and so on), which provide Btrieve access for applications running on workstations. The requesters are: BREQUEST.EXE (for DOS), BTRCALLS.DLL (for OS/2), and WBTRCALL.DLL (for Windows).

- Utilities for setting up, monitoring, and maintaining the record base, among other things. These utilities are mentioned briefly in the next section.

- Special data-protection measures for dealing with the record base in case of

system failure. In addition to the standard ones such as record locking, data protection measures include *logging*, which records any changes made to designated files so that the changes can be undone later, if necessary. The *roll forward* modules mentioned in the next section provide the mechanism for such corrections. Data protection measures also include *shadow paging*, in which page images are saved before making any changes on the page. Btrieve can back up files even while they're in use by using *continuous operation*.

- Support for NetWare Directory Services (NDS), which are new with NetWare 4.x. This support is available only beginning with version 6.1 of Btrieve.

- Security measures such as the ability to encrypt and decrypt data and also the ability to assign ownership to files.

- Memory management and caching capabilities to help speed up access and other operations.

Btrieve creates and maintains a key-indexed record base (or database). A key-indexed database is one in which keys, or record fields, are used as the basis for creating an index, which is information that guides access to a database.

A Btrieve record base uses a specially defined data format, which is also supported by database programs and other applications from third-party vendors.

Btrieve-Related Modules

The Btrieve programs are provided in Net-Ware Loadable Modules (NLMs). The most fundamental of these are BTRIEVE.NLM and BSPXCOM.NLM.

BTRIEVE contains the Record Manager program that does the work on the server. This program performs disk I/O (input/output) for Btrieve files on the server. This program must be loaded on any server that has Btrieve files.

BSPXCOM handles requests to the server from any workstation or another remote source. BSPXCOM must be loaded on any server that needs to communicate with a Btrieve requester program on a workstation.

Such a Btrieve requester must be loaded on any workstation that needs to communi-cate with a Btrieve record base. This pro-gram relays requests from the user or from an application to the Record Manager on the appropriate server.

Other NLMs handle more specialized duties. For example, BROUTER.NLM and BDROUTER.NLM handle Btrieve-related requests from a server to a remote server. The figure "Relationships of Btrieve ele-ments" shows how the various Btrieve elements fit together.

Several Btrieve utilities provide the more nitty-gritty services needed to handle the record bases:

- BTRMON.NLM monitors Btrieve activity on the server.

- BSETUP.NLM and BREBUILD.NLM are used to change configurations and

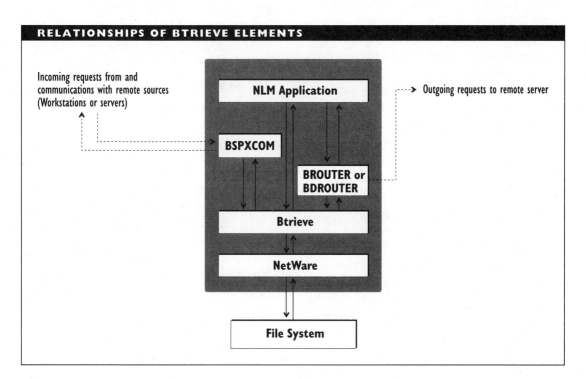

RELATIONSHIPS OF BTRIEVE ELEMENTS

to update Btrieve data files from version 5.x to 6.x, respectively.

- BUTIL.NLM imports and exports Btrieve data, and transfers data between Btrieve files.

- BDIRECT.NLM provides support for the NDS in NetWare 4.x. This NLM is available only in Btrieve versions 6.1 and later.

- BROLLFWD.EXE (for DOS), PBROLL.EXE (for OS/2), and WBROLL.EXE (for Windows) are the roll forward utilities. These are used to restore a Btrieve file in case of some type of system failure.

Server- and Client-Based Btrieve

The server-based version runs the Btrieve Record Manager on the server and a special (operating system dependent) requester program on the workstation. The Record Manager handles the I/O for the database; the requester handles the I/O between workstation and server.

The client-based version does all its processing on the workstation, and makes I/O calls (calls involving the record base) through the workstation's operating system. The client-based version is available only to developers who want to create applications that can use Btrieve data files.

If the calls are for the server's record base, the Btrieve requester redirects the calls to the server. The figure "A client and server using Btrieve" shows this situation. Note that the Btrieve requester is provided as part of a server-based Btrieve implementation.

BROADER CATEGORY
NetWare

BTU (Basic Transmission Unit)

In IBM's SNA communications, an aggregate block of one or more path information units (PIUs) that all have the same destination. Several PIUs can be combined into a single packet, even if they are not all part of the same message. BTUs are created at the path-control layer.

SEE ALSO
SNA (Systems Network Architecture)

Buffer, Fiber-Optic Cable

In fiber-optic cabling, a layer immediately surrounding the cladding (which surrounds the fiber core). The tighter this buffer is wrapped around the cladding, the less opportunity the cladding and core have to move around in the cable.

SEE ALSO
Cable, Fiber-Optic

Buffer, Memory

In memory or storage applications, a buffer is a temporary storage location that is generally used to hold intermediate values, or other types of data, until they can be processed. The storage may be allocated in ordinary RAM (random-access memory), on a hard disk, or in special memory registers (such as on a UART chip, which is used for serial communications).

A print buffer is one common example. A spooler program saves a file to be printed in the print buffer, and deals with the file as

A CLIENT AND SERVER USING BTRIEVE

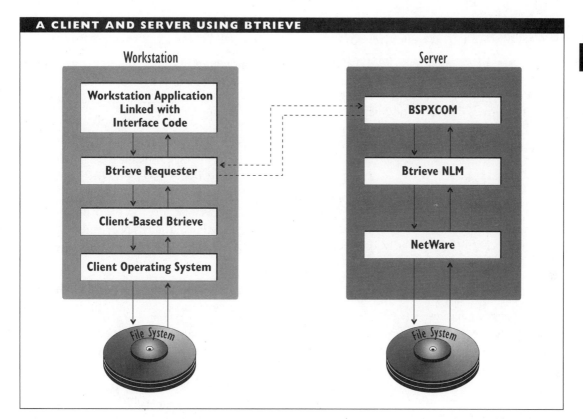

CPU (central processing unit) availability allows. Buffers provide faster access to stored data.

Three types of buffer allocations are distinguished:

File-cache buffer: Used to store disk-allocation blocks temporarily.

Directory-cache buffer: Used to store the DET (directory-entry table) blocks.

Packet-receive buffer: Used to hold incoming packets until they can be processed.

Buffered Repeater

In a network cabling scheme, a device that can clean and boost signals before sending them on. A buffered repeater can hold a message temporarily for example, when there is already a transmission on the network.

SEE ALSO
Repeater

Burned-In Address (BIA)

SEE
BIA (Burned-In Address)

Burstiness

In the CCITT recommendations for B-ISDN, a measure of the distribution of data over time. The definition for the term has not yet been finalized. One definition being considered is the ratio between maximum, or peak, and mean (average) bit rate.

Burst Mode

A high-speed transmission mode in which the transmitter takes control of the communications channel temporarily, until its transmission is complete. This mode is used in internal communications, such as between hard disk and bus, and also in communications between devices. The term is also used to refer to the packet burst protocol in NetWare.

Burst Speed

The maximum speed at which a device can operate without interruption, generally only for short periods. This is in contrast to *throughput,* which indicates the average speed at which a device can operate under ordinary conditions, such as when transmitting or printing an entire file.

Bus

In computer hardware, a *bus* is a path for electrical signals, generally between the CPU (central processing unit) and attached hardware. Buses differ in the number of bit values they can carry at a time, in their speed, and in their control mechanisms:

Bit values: In the PC world, 8-, 16-, and 32-bit data buses are common. On workstations and larger machines, 64- and 80-bit buses are common.

Speed: The speed of a bus depends on the system clock. Bus speed is generally measured in megahertz (MHz). The IBM-PC bus has gone from a 4.77 MHz clock speed in the original PC to 66 MHz in today's high-end machines. Other chips can support clock speeds of over 100 MHz.

Control: Buses may be controlled through interrupts or through polling.

In networking, bus refers to a logical and physical network topology in which messages are broadcast along the main cable, so that all nodes receive each transmission at the same time. Standard Ethernet and certain ARCnet networks use a bus topology.

SEE ALSO
Topology, Bus

Bus Interface Board (BIB)

SEE
BIB (Bus Interface Board)

Bus Interface Unit (BIU)

SEE
BIU (Bus Interface Unit)

Bus Mastering

In general, bus mastering is a bus-access method in which a card or device takes control of the bus in order to send data onto the bus directly, without help from the CPU (central processing unit). In a network, the network interface card takes control of the bus.

Generally, MCA (Microchannel Architecture) and EISA (Extended Industry Standard Architecture) machines support bus mastering, but ISA (Industry Standard Architecture) machines do not. VL (VESA local) and PCI (Peripheral Component Interconnect) buses also support bus mastering.

Bus mastering can improve throughput considerably, but only if the board and the computer support the same bus-mastering method, *and* if the bus mastering doesn't conflict with the hard-disk controller.

Several types of transfer modes are possible with bus mastering, including burst mode, streaming data mode, and data duplexing. A particular bus-mastering scheme may support some or all of these modes.

Bypass

In telephony, a connection with an inter-exchange carrier (IXC) that does not go through a local exchange carrier.

Byte

A collection of—usually eight—bits (but rarely worth a dollar anymore). A byte generally represents a character or digit.

BYTE Information Exchange (BIX)

SEE

BIX (BYTE Information Exchange)

Byte-Sex

For a processor, byte-sex is a feature that describes the order in which bytes are represented in a word. Processors may be little-endian, big-endian, or bytesexual.

In little-endian representations, the low-order byte in a word is stored at the lower address. In big-endian processors or contexts, the high-order byte is stored first. *Bytesexual* is a term used to describe a process that is capable of using either little-endian or big-endian representations for information, depending on the value of a flag bit.

SEE ALSO

Big-Endian; Little-Endian; Middle-Endian

Byzantine Failure/Byzantine Robustness

In networking, a situation in which a node fails by behaving incorrectly or improperly, rather than by breaking down completely and disappearing from the network. A network that can keep working even if one or more nodes is experiencing Byzantine failure has *Byzantine robustness*.

a
b
c
d
e
f
g
h
i
j
k
l
m
n
o
p
q
r
s
t
u
v
w
x
y
z

▼
Cable

It took about 100 years for cable to replace the kite string as a medium for electrical power, but the change was heartily welcomed, particularly by researchers. Cables are currently the most popular medium for transmitting information between nodes in a network, although wireless transmission schemes (radio, infrared, and microwave communications) are becoming more widely used.

Network Cabling Schemes

In a network, the cabling scheme connects nodes (or stations) and also gives the network its characteristic shape (topology) and features. Network cabling schemes distinguish between main and auxiliary cables. The main cable provides the path and defines the shape for the network; the auxiliary cables connect nodes to the main path or to wiring centers that are connected to the main path. Depending on the architecture, the terminology for such cables differs.

Ethernet Trunk and Drop Cables

For Ethernet networks, the main cable is referred to as the *trunk cable*, and the auxiliary cables are called *drop cables*. Trunk cable forms the backbone, or main cabling scheme, of an Ethernet network. Because of its role and location, trunk cable is sometimes called *backbone cable*. Drop cable may be used to attach an individual node to a network trunk cable. Nodes can also be connected to the cable indirectly through a connector or transceiver rather than with drop cable. The different types of connectors are discussed in a separate article.

IBM Token Ring

IBM Token Ring networks distinguish between the main ring path and patch cables. In this context, patch cables attach nodes (called *lobes* in Token Ring networks) to wiring centers. The wiring centers are called multistation attachment units (MAUs) in such networks. The patch cables can also attach to patch panels, which are, in turn, connected to MAUs.

Cable Types

Four main types of cable are used in networks:

- Coaxial cable, also called coax, which can be thin or thick.

- Twisted-pair cable, which can be shielded (STP) or unshielded (UTP).

- IBM cable, which is essentially twisted-pair cable, but designed to somewhat more stringent specifications by IBM. Several types are defined, and they are used primarily in IBM Token Ring networks.

- Fiber-optic cable, which can be single-mode, multimode, or graded-index multimode.

Coaxial, IBM, and twisted-pair cables transmit electricity. Fiber-optic cables transmit light signals. Each of the cable types is subdivided into more specialized categories and has its own design and specifications, standards, advantages, and disadvantages.

Cable types differ in price, transmission speed, and recommended transmission distance. For example, twisted-pair wiring is currently the cheapest (and also the most limited in performance). Fiber-optic cable is more expensive but much faster and more robust. Coaxial cable lies between these two types on most performance and price features.

This article discusses network cabling in general. The specific cable types (coaxial, twisted-pair, IBM, and fiber-optic) are covered in more detail in separate articles. In addition to this cabling, there is a cable infrastructure behind the walls, in shafts, and under the ground. These cables are discussed under the headings Cable, Horizontal and Cable, Backbone.

Cable Components

The different cable types have the following components in common:

- A conductor to provide a medium for the signal. The conductor might be a copper wire or a glass tube.

- Insulation of some sort around the conductor to help keep the signal in and interference out.

- An outer sheath, or jacket, to encase the cable elements. The jacket keeps the cable components together, and may also help protect the cable components from water, pressure, or other types of damage.

In addition to these common features, particular types of cable have other components. Coaxial cable has one or more shields between the insulation and the jacket. Twisted-pair cable has two conductor wires twisted around each other. Fiber-optic cable may include material to help protect the fiber from pressure.

Conductor

For electrical cable, the conductor is known as the *signal*, or *carrier, wire*, and it may consist of either solid or stranded wire. Solid wire is a single thick strand of conductive material, usually copper. Stranded wire consists of many thin strands of conductive material wound tightly together.

Signal wire is described in the following terms:

- The wire's conductive material (for example, copper)

- Whether the wire is stranded or solid

- The carrier wire's diameter, expressed directly (for example, in inches, centimeters, or millimeters), or in terms of the wire's gauge, as specified in the AWG (American Wire Gauge) tables (see the AWG article for a summary of gauges)

The total diameter of the strand determines some of the wire's electrical properties, such as resistance and impedance. These properties, in turn, help determine the wire's performance.

For fiber-optic cable, the conductor is known as the *core*. The core is a glass or plastic tube that runs through the cable. The diameter of this core is expressed in microns (millionths of a meter).

a b **c** d e f g h i j k l m n o p q r s t u v w x y z

Insulation Layer

The insulating layer keeps the transmission medium's signal from escaping and also helps to protect the signal from outside interference. For electrical wires, the insulation is usually made of a dielectric (nonconductor), such as polyethylene. Some types of coaxial cable have multiple protective layers around the signal wire.

For fiber-optic cable, the insulation is known as *cladding* and is made of material with a lower refraction index than the core's material. The refraction index is a measure that indicates the manner in which a material will reflect light rays. The lower refraction index ensures that light bounces back off the cladding and remains in the core.

Plenum Cable Jacket

The outer casing, or jacket, of the cable provides a shell that keeps the cable's elements together. Two main classes of jacket are plenum and nonplenum. For certain environments, plenum cable is required by law. It must be used when the cable is being run "naked" (without being put in a conduit) inside walls, and should probably be used whenever possible.

Plenum jackets are made of nonflammable fluoropolymers (such as Teflon or Kynar). They are fire-resistant and do not give off toxic fumes when burning. They are also considerably more expensive (by a factor of 1.5 to 3) than cables with nonplenum jackets. Studies have shown that cables with plenum jackets have less signal loss than nonplenum cables.

Plenum cable used for networks should meet the NEC's CMP (National Electric Code's communications plenum cable) or CL2P (class 2 plenum cable) specifications. The cable should also be UL-listed for UL-910, which subjects plenum cable to a flammability test. The NEC and UL specifications are discussed in the Cable Standards article.

Nonplenum Cable Jacket

Nonplenum cable uses less-expensive material for jackets, so it is considerably less expensive than cable with plenum jackets, but it can be used only under restricted conditions. Nonplenum cable jackets are made of polyethylene (PE) or polyvinylchloride (PVC), which will burn and give off toxic fumes.

PVC cable used for networks should meet the NEC's CMR (communications riser cable) or CL2R (class 2 riser cable) specifications. The cable should also be UL-listed for UL-1666, which subjects riser cable to a flammability test. See the Cable Standards article for a discussion of cable safety standards and performance levels.

Cable Packaging

Cable can be packaged in different ways, depending on what it is being used for and where it is located. For example, the IBM cable topology specifies a flat cable for use under carpets. Some fiber-optic trunks contain thousands of fibers, each of which can carry multiple messages.

The following types of cable packaging are available:

Simplex cable: One cable within one jacket, which is the default configuration. The term is used mainly for fiber-optic cable to indicate that the jacket contains only a single fiber.

Duplex cable: Two cables, or fibers, within a single jacket. In fiber-optic cable, this is a common arrangement. One fiber is used to transmit in each direction.

Multifiber cable: Multiple cables, or fibers, within a single jacket. For fiber-optic cable, a single jacket may contain thousands of fibers; for electrical cable, the jacket will contain at most a few dozen cables.

Cable Properties

Cable is described in terms of the size and makeup of its components, as well as in terms of its performance. For example, electrical cable specifications include the gauge, or diameter, of the signal wire.

The cable's electrical and physical properties determine the performance you can expect and the range of conditions under which you can use the cable. Cables differ in the electrical properties (signal loss, impedance, and so on) they offer. The table "Cable Properties" lists some of the features that distinguish cables.

CABLE PROPERTIES		
PROPERTY	**MEASUREMENT OR DESCRIPTION**	**COMMENT**
Size		
Conductor wire diameter	Millimeters (mm), inches (in), or gauge (AWG)	For stranded wire, this represents the total diameter of the entire cluster of strands.
Core fiber diameter	Microns	Some core diameters have desirable properties in terms of the paths certain wavelengths of light take in the core. For example, diameters of 62.5 and 100 microns for multimode fiber and of under 10 microns for single-mode fiber are common.
Wire insulation diameter	Millimeters or inches	The diameter of the cable's insulaton layer is needed to calculate certain electrical properties of a cable.
Cladding diameter	Microns	The cladding diameter varies much less than the core diameter, partly because the cladding helps to make the fiber easier to package if the cladding is of an approximately constant size.
Wire shield diameter	Millimeters, inches, or gauge	
Jacket diameter	Millimeters or inches	The diameter of the jacket can be important when installing the cable because it may determine space requirements.

PROPERTY	MEASUREMENT OR DESCRIPTION	COMMENT
Composition		
Conductor wire composition	Materials; solid vs. stranded (# of strands)	Conductor wires may be solid or stranded, or of different types of conductive material (usually copper alone or in some variant). If the wire is stranded, the specifications should note the number of strands.
Wire insulation composition	Materials	
Shield composition	Materials; % area covered by shield mesh	For coaxial cable only, shield composition refers to the makeup of the protective shield around the conductive wire.
Jacket composition	Materials; plenum vs. nonplenum	
Electrical Properties		
DCR (DC Resistance)	Ohms (Ω) per distance (100 or 1000 feet)	Refers to the DC resistance for the conductor wire.
Shield DCR	Ohms (Ω) per distance (100 or 1000 feet)	Refers to the DC resistance for the shield.
Impedance	Ohms	The measure of a wire's resistance to electrical current, which helps determine the wire's attenuation properties. Most networks use cable with a characteristic impedance level. There are devices for connecting cable segments that have diffferent impedances.
Capacitance	Picofarads per foot (pF/ft)	The measure of the cable's ability to store up electrical charge or voltage. This charge storage distorts a signal as it travels along its course; the lower the capacitance the better.
Attenuation	Maximum decibels per distance at a given frequency; common distances include 100 feet, 1000 feet, and 1 kilometer, e.g., dB/1000 ft at 5 MHz	The measure of the signal loss over distance. Data sheets may include several attenuation values for different frequencies. This distinction can be imporant because attenuation of an electrical signal increases with signal frequency.

PROPERTY	MEASUREMENT OR DESCRIPTION	COMMENT
Crosstalk (NEXT)	Minimum decibels per distance (1000 or 100 feet) (dB/distance)	NEXT (near-end crosstalk) is a common measure of interference by a signal from a neighboring cable or circuit. The higher the decibel value, the less crosstalk.
Velocity of Propagation	% (values should be about 60%; preferably above 80%)	Specifies the maximum signal speed along the wire, as a proportion of the theoretical maximum (the speed of light).

Other Properties

PROPERTY	MEASUREMENT OR DESCRIPTION	COMMENT
Weight	Unit weight per distance (oz/ft; gm/meter)	
Maximum recommended cable segment range	Distance (feet, meters, or kilometers)	
Bandwidth	Megahertz (MHz) or megabits per second (Mbps)	
Price	Dollars per distance (100 or 1000 feet)	
Performance/Safety Ratings	NEC CL2, CMP, and CMR; EIA/TIA-568 Categories 1-5; UL Levels 1-5; ETL ratings	See the Cable Standards article for information about these cable safety standards.

You can obtain the specifications for a specific type of cable from the cable manufacturer or vendor. The table "Cable Component Abbreviations" lists some common abbreviations used in cable specifications or data sheets.

Factors Affecting Cable Performance

Cables are good media for signals, but they are not perfect. Ideally, the signal at the end of a stretch of cable should be as loud and clear as at the beginning. Unfortunately, this will not be true.

Any transmission consists of signal and noise components. Even a digital signal degrades when transmitted over a wire or through an open medium. This is because the binary information must be converted to electrical form for transmission, and because the shape of the electrical signal changes over distance.

a
b
c
d
e
f
g
h
i
j
k
l
m
n
o
p
q
r
s
t
u
v
w
x
y
z

CABLE COMPONENT ABBREVIATIONS

ABBREVIATION	FEATURE	COMPONENT(S)
AD	Air dielectric	Insulation
AL	Aluminum braid	Shield
ALS	Aluminum sheath	Shield
AWG	American Wire Gauge (AWG) value for wire	Carrier wire
BC	Bare copper braid	Carrier wire; shield
CCAL	Copper-clad aluminum	Carrier wire
CCS	Copper-covered steel	Carrier wire
FEP	Fluorinated ethylene propylene (Teflon)	Insulation; jacket
FFEP	Foamed fluorinated ethylene propylene (Teflon)	Insulation
FP	Foamed polyethylene	Insulation
K	Kynar/polyvinylidene fluoride (plenum)	Jacket
PE	Polyethylene (solid)	Insulation; jacket
PVC	Polyvinylchloride	Jacket
PVDF	Generic polyvinylidene fluoride (plenum)	Jacket
SC	Silvered copper braid	Carrier wire; shield
TC	Tinned copper braid	Carrier wire; shield
x%	Percentage of surface area covered by braid	Shield
#cond	Number of conductors	Carrier wire

Signal quality degrades for several reasons, including attenuation, crosstalk, and impedance.

Attenuation

Attenuation is the decrease in signal strength, measured in decibels (dB) per 100 feet or per kilometer. Such loss happens as the signal travels over the wire. Attenuation occurs more quickly at higher frequencies and when the cable's resistance is higher.

In networking environments, repeaters are responsible for cleaning and boosting a signal before passing it on. Many devices are repeaters without explicitly saying so. For example, each node in a token ring network acts as a repeater. Since attenuation is sensitive to frequency, some situations require the use of equalizers to boost different frequency signals the appropriate amount.

Crosstalk

Crosstalk is interference in the form of a signal from a neighboring cable or circuit; for example, signals on different pairs of twisted wire in a twisted-pair cable may interfere with each other. A commonly used measure of this interference in twisted-pair cable is near-end crosstalk (NEXT), which is represented in decibels. The higher the decibel value, the less crosstalk and the better the cable.

Additional shielding between the carrier wire and the outside world is the most common way to decrease the effects of crosstalk.

Impedance

Impedance, which is a measure of electrical resistance, is not directly a factor in a cable's performance. However, impedance can become a factor if it has different levels at different locations in a network. In order to minimize the disruptive effects of different impedances in a network, special devices, called baluns, are used to equalize impedance at the connection (at the balun location).

Impedance does reflect performance indirectly, however. In general, the higher the impedance, the higher the resistance, and the higher the resistance, the greater the attenuation at higher frequencies.

Selecting Cable

Cables are used to meet all sorts of power and signaling requirements. The demands made on a cable depend on the location in which the cable is used and the function for which the cable is intended. These demands, in turn, determine the features a cable should have.

Function and Location

Here are a few examples of considerations involving the cable's function and location:

- Cable designed to run over long distances, such as between floors or buildings, should be robust against environmental factors (moisture, temperature changes, and so on). This may require extra jackets or jackets made with a special material. Fiber-optic cable performs well, even over distances much longer than a floor or a building.

- Cable that must run around corners should bend easily, and the cable's properties and performance should not be affected by the bending. For several reasons, twisted-pair cable is probably the best cable for such a situation (assuming it makes sense within the rest of the wiring scheme). Of course, another way to get around a corner is by using a connector; however, connectors may introduce signal-loss problems.

- Cable that must run through areas in which powerful engines or motors are operating (or worse, being turned on and off at random intervals) must be able to withstand magnetic interference. Large equipment gives off strong magnetic fields, which can interfere with and disrupt nearby signals. In commercial and residential settings, this can be a problem with cable that is run, for example, through the elevator shaft. Because it is not affected by such electrical or magnetic fluctuations, fiber-optic cable is the best choice in machinery-intensive environments.

- If you need to run lots of cables through a limited area, cable weight can become a factor, particularly if all that cable will be running in the ceiling above you. In general, fiber-optic and twisted-pair cable tend to be lightest.

- Cables being installed in barely accessible locations must be particularly reliable, and they should probably be laid with backup cable during the initial installation. Some consultants and mavens advise laying a second cable whenever you are installing cable, on the assumption that the installation is much more expensive than the cable and that installation costs for the second cable add only marginally to the total cost. Generally, the suggestion is to make at least the second cable optical fiber.

- Cables that need to interface with other worlds (for example, with a mainframe network or a different electrical or optical system) may need special properties or adapters. For example, UTP cable in a Token Ring network needs a media filter between the cable and the MAU to which the cable is attached. The kinds of cable required will depend on the details of

the environments and the transition between them.

Main Cable Selection Factors

Along with the function and location considerations, cable selections are determined by a combination of factors, including the following:

- The type of network you plan to create (Ethernet, Token Ring, or another type). While it is possible to use just about any type of cable in any type of network, certain cable types have been more closely associated with particular network types. For example, Token Ring networks use twisted-pair cable.

- The amount of money you have available for the network. Keep in mind that cable installation can be an expensive part of the network costs.

- Whatever cabling resources are already available (and usable). You will almost certainly have available wiring that could conceivably be used for a network. It is almost equally certain, however, that at least some of that wire is defective or is not up to the requirements for your network.

- Building or other safety codes and regulations.

Connected versus Bulk Cable

You can get cable with or without connectors at either end. Both connected and bulk cable have advantages and drawbacks. Whether connected or bulk cable is better depends on how you are going to use it.

You have much more flexibility to cut or reroute with bulk cable, because you are not restricted to a precut cable segment. On the other hand, you (or someone you trust) will need to attach the connectors. This requires special tools and involves stripping the end of the cable and crimping the connector to the bare wire.

Cable Prices

Cable prices depend on factors such as the following:

- Type of cable (coaxial, twisted-pair, fiber optic). In general, fiber-optic cable is the most expensive but the price is dropping rapidly. Fiber-optic cable is followed closely by thick coaxial cable. STP and thin coaxial follow in roughly that order, but with considerable overlap in prices. UTP is the least expensive type of cable.

- Whether cable comes in bulk or with connectors at either end. While price is an issue, this question will be answered mainly by your needs for the cable.

- Whether the cable is plenum or nonplenum. Plenum versions can cost from 1.5 to 3 times as much as the nonplenum version.

Cable prices change, so do not be surprised to find considerable variation in prices when you start getting quotes.

UTP cable is grouped into voice- and data-grade. Most telephone wire is just voice-grade. Prices for data-grade UTP cable are a few cents higher per foot.

Cabling Tools

Installation tools for handling cables include wire strippers, dies, and crimping tools for attaching connectors to the end of a stretch of bulk cable. Such tools are often included in adapter kits, which are configured for building particular types of cable (for example, coaxial cable or cable for RS-232 connections). Depending on how comprehensive the toolkit is, expect to pay anywhere from about $30 to $500.

Testing tools for cables include a whole range of line scanners and monitors. The simplest of these can tell you whether there is any electrical activity between one location in a network (or a cable installation) and another. The most sophisticated can do just about everything except tell you where you bought the cable.

The top-of-the-line scanners can test any kind of copper-based cable not only for faults, but also for performance specifications (NEXT, attenuation, and so on). These types of scanners know about the electrical requirements of the most popular network architectures (such as Ethernet/802.3 and Token Ring) and are capable of finding faults or deviations from specifications at just about any location on the network. Of course, you will pay several thousand dollars for this capability.

Cable Vendors and Resources

Many companies sell both electrical and fiber-optic cable, as well as connectors, installation, and testing tools. Some vendors specialize in fiber-optic products, others in copper-based products, and still others offer both.

CABLE TIPS

Here are some tips on purchasing and installing cabling:

- Cables have quite a few properties that should be considered in making decisions. You can find information about these cable properties in cable specifications or data sheets, which are available from cable vendors.

- In general, cable that meets military specifications (MIL-SPECS) is designed to more stringent requirements, and so is a good choice for networks. This is even more true for connectors, because the military specifications insist on durable and reliable connectors. (Connectors are particularly prone to shoddy construction.)

- Fiber-optic connectors are especially tricky to attach because fiber optics has such exact alignment requirements. It's probably worth your while to let a professional attach these connectors.

- When you're ordering cable, make sure it's clear whether you want cable with connectors or "raw" (bulk) cable.

- Make sure the cable is good quality. Otherwise, you'll have trouble after a while, as the insulation within and outside the cable breaks down.

- Test cable both *before* and *after* installing it.

- While present needs are obviously the major determinant of cabling decisions, future plans should also be taken into consideration. In general, at least consider installing cable one level more powerful than you think you'll need.

- When adding cable to an existing cabling system, find out exactly what kind of cable is already in place. The safest thing is to get the actual part and specification information from the cable jacket, then order exactly that from the same distributor (or a certified equivalent from a different manufacturer).

- Before adding to existing cable, test it as thoroughly as possible. If the cable seems likely to have a major breakdown within a few months, it's almost certainly better to replace it now.

- Protect the cable as much as possible. Such measures should include protecting the cable from temperature or moisture changes, which can cause the cable to crack or melt.

- Support the cable as much as possible, so that a hanging cable doesn't stretch because the cable's own weight is pulling it downward.

- Velcro cable ties can help make things neater, by enabling you to collect multiple loose wires into a single cluster. The Rip-Tie Company in San Francisco is one vendor that offers these neatness aids.

When you are ready to start looking for cabling and other components, it will be worthwhile getting the cabling guides and catalogs from several vendors. The guides offer useful general-purpose hints and guidelines for selecting and installing cable.

Here are some cable vendors and their telephone numbers:

AMP Incorporated: (800) 522-6752; (717) 564-0100

Andrew Corporation: (800) 328-2696; Fax (708) 349-5673

Berk-Tek: (800) 237-5835

Black Box Corporation: (800) 552-6816; (412) 746-5500

Comm/Scope: (800) 982-1708; (704) 324-2200; Fax (704) 459-5099

CSP (Computer System Products): (800) 422-2537; (612) 476-6866; Fax (612) 476-6966

FIS (Fiber Instrument Sales): (800) 445-2901; (315) 736-2206; Fax (315) 736-2285

Jensen Tools: (800) 426-1194; (602) 968-6231; Fax (800) 366-9662

Trompeter Electronics: (800) 982-2639; (818) 707-2020; Fax (818) 706-1040

SEE ALSO

Cable, Backbone; Cable, Coaxial; Cable, Fiber-Optic; Cable, Horizontal; Cable, IBM; Connector; Connector, Fiber-Optic

Cable, Adapter

Cable used to connect a Token Ring network interface card (NIC) to a hub or multistation access unit (MAU). IBM Type 1 and Type 6 cable can be used for this purpose. The IBM cables have a DB-9 or DB-25 connector at the NIC end and an IBM data connector at the MAU end.

Cable, Backbone

Backbone cable refers to the cable that forms the main trunk, or backbone, of a network, particularly an Ethernet network. Individual nodes and other devices may be connected to this cable using special adapters (such as transceivers) and a separate stretch of cable (called the *drop cable* in an Ethernet network) to the node.

More generally, backbone cable is defined by the EIA/TIA-568 committee as any "behind the scenes" cable—cable running behind walls, in shafts, or under the ground—that is not classified as horizontal cable. (Horizontal cable is defined by the EIA/TIA-568 committee as any cable that goes from a wiring closet, or distribution frame, to the wall outlet in the work area.) This includes cable used to connect wiring closets and equipment rooms.

The EIA/TIA-568 recognizes four main types of backbone cable, and several optional variants. These types are listed in the table "EIA/TIA-568 Main and Optional Types of Backbone Cable."

a
b
c
d
e
f
g
h
i
j
k
l
m
n
o
p
q
r
s
t
u
v
w
x
y
z

EIA/TIA-568 MAIN AND OPTIONAL TYPES OF BACKBONE CABLE		
CABLE TYPE	**MAIN**	**OPTIONAL**
UTP	100-ohm, multipair UTP cable, to be used for voice-grade communications only	
STP	150-ohm STP cable, such as that defined in the IBM Cable System (ICS)	100-ohm STP cable
Coaxial	50-ohm thick coaxial cable, such as the cable used in thick Ethernet networks	75-ohm (broadband) coaxial cable, such as CATV cable
Optical fiber	62.5/125-micron (step- or graded-index) multimode optical fiber	Single-mode optical fiber

COMPARE

Cable, Horizontal

SEE ALSO

Cable

Cable, Broadcast-Oriented

Cable that is designed to carry video signals sent from one location in the network, known as the *head-end*. This type of cable is generally designed for one-way communication, which makes it of limited value for use as network cable.

Cable, Category *x*

A five-level rating system for telecommunications wiring, specified in the EIA/TIA-568 documents. These describe minimum performance capabilities for unshielded twisted-pair cable.

SEE

Cable Standards

Cable, CATV (Community Antenna Television, or Cable Television)

Wiring used for the transmission of cable television signals. CATV is broadband coaxial cable and is generally wired for one-directional transmission; that is, from the cable station, or a head-end, to the consumer. If the CATV cable is not one-directional, it may be possible to use it for network cabling.

Cable, Coaxial

Coaxial cable, often called coax, is used for data transmissions. This cable's remarkably stable electrical properties at frequencies below 1 GHz (gigahertz) makes the cable popular for cable television (CATV) transmissions and for creating local-area networks (LANs). Telephone company switching offices also use coaxial cable to route long-distance calls. The figure "Context and properties of coaxial cable" summarizes the features of this type of cable.

CONTEXT AND PROPERTIES OF COAXIAL CABLE

Context

Cable
    Electrical
        Twisted-Pair
        Coaxial
    Optical
        Fiber-Optic ⟶

Coaxial Properties

Stable and predictable electrical properties

At least one shield around conductor wire

Subject to electromagnetic interference

Variable impedance levels

Thin and thick varieties

Broadband and baseband varieties

Thin coaxial uses BNC/TNC connectors; thick coaxial uses N-series connectors

Twinaxial runs two cables within a single jacket

Triaxial and quadrax have extra shielding for special uses

Coaxial Uses

Ethernet networks

ARCnet networks

Cable TV lines

Video cable

IBM mainframe and midrange-based networks (twinaxial)

Telephone switching offices

Coaxial Cable Components

A coaxial cable consists of the following layers (moving outward from the center):

Carrier wire: A conductor wire (the carrier, or signal, wire) is in the center. This wire is made of (or contains) copper and may be solid or stranded.

There are restrictions regarding the wire composition for certain network configurations. The diameter of the signal wire is one factor in determining the attenuation (loss) of the signal over distance. The number of strands in a multistrand conductor also affects the attenuation.

a b **c** d e f g h i j k l m n o p q r s t u v w x y z

Insulation: An insulation layer consists of a dielectric (nonconductor) around the carrier wire. This dielectric is usually made of some form of polyethylene or Teflon.

Foil shield: A thin foil shield around the dielectric. This shield usually consists of aluminum bonded to both sides of a tape. Not all coaxial cables have foil shielding; some have two foil shield layers, interspersed with braid shield layers.

Braid shield: A braid, or mesh, conductor, made of copper or aluminum, that surrounds the insulation and foil shield. This conductor can serve as the ground for the carrier wire. Together with the insulation and any foil shield, the braid shield protects the carrier wire from electromagnetic interference (EMI) and radio frequency interference (RFI). The braid and foil shields provide good protection against electrical interference, but only moderate protection against magnetic interference.

Jacket: An outer cover that can be either plenum (made of Teflon or Kynar) or nonplenum (made of polyethylene or polyvinylchloride).

The figure "A coaxial cable has five layers" shows the makeup of a coaxial cable. The layers surrounding the carrier wire also help prevent signal loss due to radiation from the carrier wire. The signal and shield wires are concentric, or co-axial, hence the name.

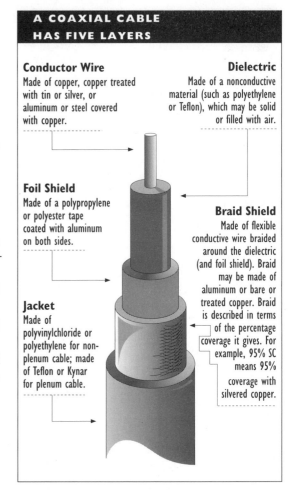

A COAXIAL CABLE HAS FIVE LAYERS

Conductor Wire
Made of copper, copper treated with tin or silver, or aluminum or steel covered with copper.

Dielectric
Made of a nonconductive material (such as polyethylene or Teflon), which may be solid or filled with air.

Foil Shield
Made of a polypropylene or polyester tape coated with aluminum on both sides.

Braid Shield
Made of flexible conductive wire braided around the dielectric (and foil shield). Braid may be made of aluminum or bare or treated copper. Braid is described in terms of the percentage coverage it gives. For example, 95% SC means 95% coverage with silvered copper.

Jacket
Made of polyvinylchloride or polyethylene for nonplenum cable; made of Teflon or Kynar for plenum cable.

Coaxial Cable Performance

The main features that affect the performance of coaxial cable are its composition, width, and impedance.

The carrier wire's composition determines how good a conductor the cable will be. Copper is among the best materials for this purpose. The IEEE specifies stranded copper carrier wire with tin coating for thin coaxial, and solid copper carrier wire for thick coaxial.

Cable width helps determine the electrical demands that can be made on the cable. In general, thick coaxial can support a much higher level of electrical activity than thin coaxial.

Impedance is a measure of opposition to the flow of alternating current. The properties of the dielectric between the carrier wire and the braid help determine the cable's impedance. Each type of network architecture uses cable with a characteristic impedance.

Impedance helps determine the cable's electrical properties and also limits the contexts in which the cable can be used. For example, Ethernet and ARCnet architectures can both use thin coaxial cable, but they have different impedances; therefore, Ethernet and ARCnet cables are not compatible. In networks, the impedances range from 50 ohms (for an Ethernet architecture) to 93 ohms (for an ARCnet architecture).

Coaxial Cable Connectors

A segment of coaxial cable has an end connector at each end. The cable is attached through these end connectors to a T-connector, a barrel connector, another end connector, or to a terminator. Through these connectors, another cable or a hardware device is attached to the coaxial cable.

In addition to their function, connectors differ in their attachment mechanism and components. For example, BNC connectors join two components by plugging them together and then turning the components to click the connection into place. Different size coaxial cable requires a different-sized connector.

For coaxial cable, the following types of connectors are available:

- A BNC (bayonet nut connector) is used for thin coaxial cable.

- The N-series connectors are used for thick coaxial cable.

- A TNC (threaded nut connector) may be used in the same situations as a BNC, provided that the other connector is also using TNC.

Connectors for coaxial cable should be plated with silver, not tin. This improves the contact and the durability of the connector.

Thin versus Thick Coaxial

Descriptively, coaxial cable is grouped mainly into thin and thick varieties. Thin coaxial cable is 3/16-inch in diameter and is used for various network architectures, including thin Ethernet (also known as 10Base2 or CheaperNet) and ARCnet. When using this configuration, drop cables are not allowed. Instead, the T-connector must be connected directly to the network interface card (NIC). This means the NIC must have an on-board transceiver, known as a medium attachment unit (MAU) in the IEEE 802.3 standard.

Thick coaxial cable is 3/8-inch in diameter. It is used for thick Ethernet (also known as 10Base5 or ThickNet) networks, cable TV (CATV), and other connections. Thick coaxial is expensive and is notoriously difficult to install and work with. It is more likely to be inherited than selected for use in a network.

a
b
c
d
e
f
g
h
i
j
k
l
m
n
o
p
q
r
s
t
u
v
w
x
y
z

Cable Content Descriptions

Other descriptions of coaxial cable are based on the contents of the cable, rather than its size, as follows:

Twinaxial: Also known simply as twinax, this coaxial cable has two carrier wires, each with its own dielectric, or insulation, layer. The wires are generally twisted around each other, which helps reduce magnetic interference, and are surrounded by a shield and a jacket whose properties run the same gamut as for ordinary coaxial cable. This type of cable is used in IBM and AppleTalk networks. For example, twinaxial cable is used to connect IBM 5250 terminals to System/36 or AS/400 computers.

Triaxial: Also known simply as triax, this coaxial cable has extra shielding: an inner braid surrounded by an inner (nonplenum) jacket, surrounded by an outer copper braid. This outer braid is, in turn, surrounded by the outer jacket. The extra shielding makes a big difference because of the grounding and improved protection.

Quadrax: This cable is a hybrid of triaxial and twinaxial cable. Quadrax has the extra carrier wire with dielectric, and also has the extra shielding of triaxial.

Quad shield: This cable has four layers of shielding: alternating layers of foil and braid shields. Quad shield cable is used in situations where heavy electrical interference can occur; for example, in industrial settings.

Baseband versus Broadband Cable

Functionally, coaxial cable is grouped into baseband and broadband varieties.

Baseband coaxial cable has one channel over which a single digital message can be sent, at speeds of up to 80 megabits per second (Mbps). Thin coaxial is used for baseband cable.

Broadband coaxial cable can carry several analog signals (at different frequencies) simultaneously. Each of these signals can be a different message or a different type of information. Thick coaxial cable can be used for broadband transmissions in a network.

Broadband coaxial can use a single cable or multiple cables. In single-cable broadband coaxial, frequencies are split; for example, into 6 megahertz (MHz) channels for each station. Some channels are allocated for bidirectional communication. Dual-cable broadband coaxial uses one cable for sending and one for receiving data; each cable has multiple channels.

Note that broadband coaxial requires much more planning than baseband coaxial. For example, a broadband setup will probably need amplifiers for dealing with the different broadband signals.

Coaxial Cable Designations

The following designations are used for coaxial cable used in networks. These are just a few of the available coaxial cable types.

RG-6: Used as a drop cable for CATV transmissions. It has 75 ohms impedance, is a broadband cable, and is often quad-shielded.

RG-8: Used for thick Ethernet. It has 50 ohms impedance. The thick Ethernet configuration requires other cable and a MAU (transceiver). The other cable required is a twisted-pair drop cable to the NIC. The drop cable off RG-8 cable uses a 15-pin DIX (or AUI) connector. RG-8 is also known as N-Series Ethernet cable.

RG-11: Used for the main CATV trunk. It has 75 ohms impedance and is a broadband cable. This cable is often quad shielded (with foil/braid/foil/braid around the signal wire and dielectric) to protect the signal wire under even the worst operating conditions.

RG-58: Used for thin Ethernet. It has 50 ohms impedance and uses a BNC connector.

RG-59: Used for ARCnet. It has 75 ohms impedance and uses BNC connectors. This type of cable is used for broadband connections and also by cable companies to connect the cable network to an individual household.

RG-62: Used for ARCnet. It has 93 ohms impedance and uses BNC connectors. This cable is also used to connect terminals to terminal controllers in IBM's 3270 system configurations.

Advantages of Coaxial Cable

Coaxial cable has the following advantages over other types of cable that might be used for a network. The advantages are general and may not apply in a particular situation. Note also that advantages change or disappear over time, as technology advances and products improve.

- Broadband coaxial can be used to transmit voice, data, and even video.

- The cable is relatively easy to install.

- Coaxial cable is reasonably priced compared with other cable types.

Disadvantages of Coaxial Cable

Coaxial cable has the following disadvantages when used for a network:

- It is easily damaged and sometimes difficult to work with, especially in the case of thick coaxial.

- Coaxial is more difficult to work with than twisted-pair cable.

- This type of cable cannot be used with token ring network architectures.

- Thick coaxial can be expensive to install, especially if it needs to be pulled through existing cable conduits.

- Connectors can be expensive.

- Baseband coaxial cannot carry integrated voice, data, and video signals.

a b **c** d e f g h i j k l m n o p q r s t u v w x y z

USING EXISTING COAXIAL CABLE

It may be tempting to try to use existing coaxial cable—which is likely to be CATV cable—for a network. If you're considering this, here's an important point to keep in mind: Not all CATV cables are the same.

Broadcast-oriented cables are designed to carry video signals sent from one location in the network, known as the head-end. Such cables are designed for one-way communication, which makes them useless for data networks. Even if a bidirectional CATV cable is available, several other considerations must be taken into account before you can use this cable for a local-area network.

If the cable will still be used to transmit TV channels, you need to find two frequency bands that won't be used for TV channels. Each of these bands must have at least 18 MHz band width. The bands are used by a modem, which modulates network data into the appropriate frequency band at one end. A second modem demodulates this signal at the other end. The TV and data networks will be independent of each other.

Because your network may be grafted onto an existing CATV topology, you need to make sure your system can deal with this. Typically, a CATV network uses a tree topology. The head-end is the root, and the signal is transmitted along successive branches. For this setup, you need to make sure that limitations on cable length are not exceeded.

Tools for Working with Coaxial Cable

Almost all cable testers can deal with coaxial cable. (See the Cable article for a discussion of the tools used for cable testing.) For more specialized tasks requiring tools, such as crimpers and dies for attaching connectors to cable, you will need versions specifically designed for coaxial cable.

When in doubt, of course, ask the vendor explicitly whether a particular tool will work with coaxial cable.

SEE ALSO
Cable; Cable, Fiber-Optic; Cable, Twisted-Pair; Connector

Cable, Data-Grade

Twisted-pair cable of sufficiently high quality to use for data transmission. In contrast, voice-grade cable is more susceptible to interference and signal distortion. In the EIA/TIA-568 cable specifications, categories 2 through 5 are data-grade cable.

SEE ALSO
Cable, Twisted-Pair

Cable, Distribution

In broadband networks, a term for cable used over intermediate distances (up to a few hundred yards) and for branches off a network trunk, or backbone. RG-11 cable is commonly used for this purpose.

Cable, Drop

Cable used to connect a network interface card (NIC) to a transceiver on a thick Ethernet network. Drop cable, also known as AUI cable or transceiver cable, has a 15-pin AUI, or DIX, connector at the NIC end and an N-series connector at the transceiver end.

This term may also be applied loosely to other cables that connect a network node to a wiring center of some sort.

SEE ALSO

Cable

Cable, Feeder

A 25-pair cable that can be used for carrying both voice and data signals. This cable can run from equipment to distribution frame.

Cable, Fiber-Optic

Fiber-optic cable, also known as optical fiber, provides a medium for signals using light rather than electricity. Cables of this type differ in their physical dimensions and composition and in the wavelength(s) of light with which the cable transmits. The figure "Context and properties of fiber-optic cable" summarizes the features of this type of cable.

CONTEXT AND PROPERTIES OF FIBER-OPTIC CABLE

Context

Cable
- Electrical
  - Twisted-Pair
  - Coaxial
- Optical
  - Fiber-Optic

Fiber-Optic Properties

- Medium for light signals
- Light at certain wavelengths is best for signaling purposes
- Comes in single-mode (thin fiber core; single light path) and multi-mode (thick fiber core; multiple light paths) versions
- Multimode can be step-index or graded-index
- Cable is very lightweight
- Very high bandwidth
- Immune to electromagnetic inteference, eavesdropping
- Very long cable segments possible

Fiber-Optic Uses

- FDDI networks
- Long-haul lines
- To connect network segments or networks
- To connect mainframes to peripherals
- To connect high-speed, high-performance workstations

a b c d e f g h i j k l m n o p q r s t u v w x y z

Because fiber-optic communication uses light signals, transmissions are not subject to electromagnetic interference. This, and the fact that a light signal encounters little resistance on its path (relative to an electrical signal traveling along a copper wire), means that fiber-optic cable can be used for much longer distances before the signal must be cleaned and boosted.

Some fiber-optic segments can be several kilometers long before a repeater is needed. In fact, scientists have sent signals over fiber-optic lines for thousands of kilometers without any signal boosters. In 1990, researchers sent a 1 gigabit per second (Gbps) signal almost 8,000 kilometers (about 5,000 miles) without a boost!

In principle, data transmission using fiber optics is many times faster than with electrical methods. Speeds of over 10 Gbps are possible with fiber-optic cable. In practice, however, this advantage is still more promise than reality, because the cable is waiting for the transmission and reception technology to catch up.

Nevertheless, fiber-optic connections deliver more reliable transmissions over greater distances, although at a somewhat greater cost. Fiber-optic cables cover a considerable price and performance range.

Uses of Fiber-Optic Cable

Currently, fiber-optic cable is used less often to create a network than to connect two networks or network segments. For example, cable that must run between floors is often fiber-optic cable, most commonly of the 62.5/125 variety with an LED (light-emitting diode) as the light source.

Being impervious to electromagnetic interference, fiber is ideal for such uses because the cable is often run through the elevator shaft, and the elevator motor puts out strong interference when the elevator is running.

One reason fiber-optic networks are slow to catch on is price. Network interface cards (NICs) for fiber-optic nodes can cost several thousand dollars, compared to street prices of about $100 for some Ethernet and ARCnet cards. However, when selecting optical fiber, it is not always necessary to use the most expensive fiber-optic connections. For short distances and slower bandwidths, inexpensive cable is just fine. In general, a fiber-optic cable will always allow a longer transmission than a copper cable segment.

Fiber-Optic Cable Components

The major components of a fiber-optic cable are the core, cladding, buffer, strength members, and jacket. Some types of fiber-optic cable even include a conductive copper wire. This can be used to provide power; for example, to a repeater. The figure "Components of a fiber-optic cable" illustrates the makeup of this type of cable.

Fiber-Optic Core and Cladding

The core of fiber-optic cable consists of one or more glass or plastic fibers through which the light signal moves. Plastic is easier to manufacture and use but works over shorter distances than glass. The core can be anywhere from about 2 to several hundred microns. (A micron, also known as a micrometer, is a millionth of a meter, or about 1/25,000 of an inch.)

COMPONENTS OF A FIBER-OPTIC CABLE

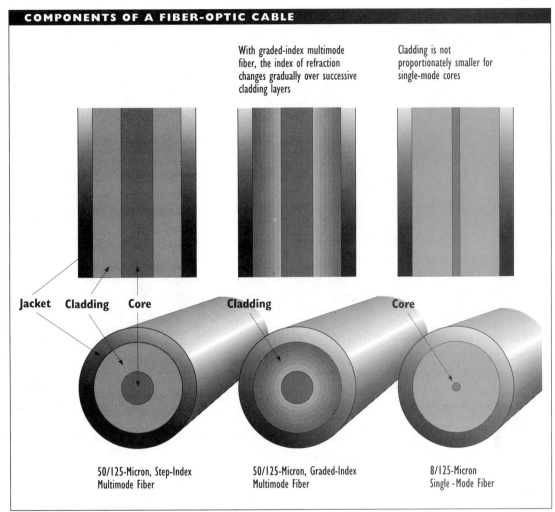

With graded-index multimode fiber, the index of refraction changes gradually over successive cladding layers

Cladding is not proportionately smaller for single-mode cores

Jacket   Cladding   Core   Cladding   Core

50/125-Micron, Step-Index
Multimode Fiber

50/125-Micron, Graded-Index
Multimode Fiber

8/125-Micron
Single-Mode Fiber

In networking contexts, the most popular core sizes are 60, 62.5, and 100 microns. Most of the fiber-optic cable used in networking has two core fibers: one for communicating in each direction.

The core and cladding are actually manufactured as a single unit. The cladding is a protective layer (usually of plastic) with a lower index of refraction than the core. The lower index means that light that hits the core walls will be redirected back to continue on its path. The cladding will be anywhere between a hundred microns and a millimeter (1000 microns) or so.

Fiber-Optic Buffer

The buffer of a fiber-optic cable is one or more layers of plastic surrounding the cladding. The buffer helps strengthen the cable, thereby decreasing the likelihood of micro-cracks, which can eventually grow into larger breaks in the cable. The buffer also protects the core and cladding from potential corrosion by water or other materials in the operating environment. The buffer can double the diameter of some cable.

A buffer can be loose or tight. A loose buffer is a rigid tube of plastic with one or more fibers (consisting of core and cladding) running through it. The tube takes on all the stresses applied to the cable, buffering the fiber from these stresses. A tight buffer fits snugly around the fiber(s). A tight buffer can protect the fibers from stress due to pressure and impact, but not from changes in temperature.

Strength Members

Fiber-optic cable also has strength members, which are strands of very tough material (such as steel, fiberglass, or Kevlar) that provide extra strength for the cable. Each of the substances has advantages and drawbacks. For example, steel attracts lightning, which will not disrupt an optical signal but may seriously disrupt the people or machines sending or receiving such a signal.

Fiber-Optic Jacket

The jacket of a fiber-optic cable is an outer casing that can be plenum or nonplenum, as with electrical cable. In cable used for networking, the jacket usually houses at least two fiber/cladding pairs: one for each direction.

Single-Mode versus Multimode Cable

Fiber-optic cable can be either single-mode or multimode. (Modes are the possible paths for the light through a cable.)

Single-Mode Cable

In single-mode fiber-optic cable, the core is so narrow (generally less than 10 microns) that the light can take only a single path through it. Single-mode fiber has the least signal attenuation, usually less than 2 decibels (dB) per kilometer. This type of cable is the most difficult to install, because it requires the greatest precision, and it is the most expensive of the major fiber-optic types. However, transmission speeds of 50 Gbps and higher are possible. To get a sense of this magnitude, note that a 10 Gbps line can carry 130,000 voice channels.

Even though the core of single-mode cable is shrunk to very small sizes, the cladding is not reduced accordingly, nor should it be. For single-mode fiber, the cladding diameter should be about ten times the core diameter. This ratio makes it possible to make the cladding the same size as for popular multimode fiber-optic cable. This helps create a de facto size standard. Keeping the cladding large also makes the fiber and cable easier to handle and more resistant to damage.

Multimode Cable

Multimode fiber-optic cable has a wider core, so that a beam of light has room to follow multiple paths through the core. Multiple modes (light paths) in a transmission produce signal distortion at the receiving end.

One measure of signal distortion is modal dispersion, which is represented in nanoseconds (billionths of a second) of tail per kilometer (ns/km). This value represents the difference in arrival time between the fastest and slowest of the alternate light paths. The value also imposes an upper limit on the bandwidth, since the duration of a signal must be larger than the nanoseconds of a tail value. With step-index fiber, expect between 15 and 30 ns/km. Note that a modal dispersion of 20 ns/km yields a bandwidth of less than 50 Mbps.

Gradation of Refraction: Step-Index Cable versus Graded-Index Cable

One reason optical fiber makes such a good transmission medium is because the different indexes of refraction for the cladding and core help to contain the light signal within the core. Cable can be constructed by changing abruptly from the core refractive index to that of the cladding, or this change can be made gradually. The two major types of multimode fiber differ in this feature.

Step-Index Cable

Cable with an abrupt change in refraction index is called step-index cable. In step-index cable, the change is made in a single step. Single-step multimode cable uses this method, and it is the simplest, least expensive type of fiber-optic cable. It is also the easiest to install. The core is usually between 50 and 125 microns in diameter; the cladding is at least 140 microns.

The core width gives light quite a bit of room to bounce around in, and the attenuation is high (at least for fiber-optic cable):

between 10 and 50 dB/km. Transmission speeds between 200 Mbps and 3 Gbps are possible, but actual speeds are much lower.

Graded-Index Cable

Cable with a gradual change in refraction index is called graded-index cable, or graded-index multimode. This fiber-optic cable type has a relatively wide core, like single-step multimode cable. The change occurs gradually and involves several layers, each with a slightly lower index of refraction. A gradation of refraction indexes controls the light signal better than the step-index method. As a result, the attenuation is lower, usually less than 15 dB/km. Similarly, the modal dispersion can be 1 ns/km and lower, which allows more than ten times the bandwidth of step-index cable. Graded-index multimode cable is the most commonly used type for network wiring.

Fiber Composition

Fiber core and cladding may be made of plastic or glass. The following list summarizes the composition combinations, going from highest quality to lowest:

Single-mode glass: Has a narrow core, so only one signal can travel through.

Graded-index glass: Not tight enough to be single-mode, but the gradual change in refractive index helps give more control over the light signal.

Step-index glass: The abrupt change from the refractive index of the core to that of the cladding means the signal is less controllable.

Plastic-coated silica (PCS): Has a relatively wide core (200 microns) and a relatively low bandwidth (20 MHz).

Plastic: This should be used only for very short distances.

To summarize, fiber-optic cables may consist of glass core and glass cladding (the best available). Glass yields much higher performance, in the form of higher bandwidth over greater distances. Single-mode glass with a small core is the highest quality. Cables may also consist of glass core and plastic cladding. Finally, the lowest grade fiber composition is plastic core and plastic cladding. Step-index plastic is at the bottom of the heap in performance.

FIBER-OPTIC CABLE QUALITY

Here are a few points about fiber-optic cable (other things being equal):

- The smaller the core, the better the signal.

- Fiber made of glass is better than fiber made of plastic.

- The purer and cleaner the light, the better the signal. (Pure, clean light is a single color, with minimal spread around the color's primary wavelength.)

- Certain wavelengths of light behave better than others.

Fiber-Optic Cable Designations

Fiber-optic cables are specified in terms of their core and cladding diameters. For example, a 62.5/125 cable has a core with a 62.5 micron diameter and cladding with twice that diameter.

The following are some commonly used fiber-optic cable configurations:

8/125: A single-mode cable with an 8 micron core and a 125 micron cladding. This type of cable is expensive and currently used only in contexts where extremely large bandwidths are needed (such as in some real-time applications) or where large distances are involved. An 8/125 cable configuration is likely to broadcast at a light wavelength of 1,300 or 1,550 nm.

62.5/125: The most popular fiber-optic cable configuration, used in most network applications. Both 850 and 1,300 nm wavelengths can be used with this type of cable.

100/140: The configuration that IBM first specified for fiber-optic wiring in a Token Ring network. Because of the tremendous popularity of the 62.5/125 configuration, IBM now supports both configurations.

Make sure you buy fiber-optic cable with the correct core size. If you know what kind of network you plan to build, you may be constrained to a particular core size. IBM usually specifies a core of 100 microns for Token Ring networks; other networks more commonly use cable with a 62.5 micron core.

Components of a Fiber-Optic Connection

In addition to the cable itself, a fiber-optic connection needs a light source to generate the signal, as well as connectors, repeaters, and couplers to route and deliver the signal. The figure "Components of a fiber-optic connection" illustrates how this works.

COMPONENTS OF A FIBER-OPTIC CONNECTION

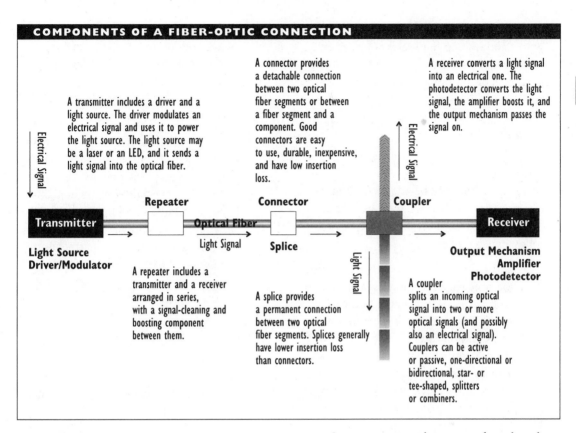

A transmitter includes a driver and a light source. The driver modulates an electrical signal and uses it to power the light source. The light source may be a laser or an LED, and it sends a light signal into the optical fiber.

A connector provides a detachable connection between two optical fiber segments or between a fiber segment and a component. Good connectors are easy to use, durable, inexpensive, and have low insertion loss.

A receiver converts a light signal into an electrical one. The photodetector converts the light signal, the amplifier boosts it, and the output mechanism passes the signal on.

Electrical Signal

Electrical Signal

Repeater

Connector

Coupler

Transmitter

Optical Fiber

Receiver

Light Signal

Splice

Light Signal

**Light Source
Driver/Modulator**

**Output Mechanism
Amplifier
Photodetector**

A repeater includes a transmitter and a receiver arranged in series, with a signal-cleaning and boosting component between them.

A splice provides a permanent connection between two optical fiber segments. Splices generally have lower insertion loss than connectors.

A coupler splits an incoming optical signal into two or more optical signals (and possibly also an electrical signal). Couplers can be active or passive, one-directional or bidirectional, star- or tee-shaped, splitters or combiners.

Transmitter

Fiber-optic transmitters convert an electronic signal into light and send this light signal into the fiber core. The transmitter's light source and output optical power are crucial elements in determining the transmitter's performance.

The transmitter's output power depends on several things, including the fiber and cladding sizes and the fiber's numerical aperture (NA). The NA is a measure of the fiber's ability to gather light and is determined by the angle over which light hitting the fiber will move through it.

Output power values range from less than 50 to over 200 microwatts. Smaller cores generally have lower output power, but also less signal attenuation and higher bandwidth. Output power values should not be too high, since this increases energy requirements and also risks frying the components at the receiving end.

Transmitters use either digital or analog modulation. Analog modulation is used for voice, video, and even radar signals, which require bandwidths ranging from tens of kilohertz to hundreds of megahertz, and even as high as a gigahertz.

a b c d e f g h i j k l m n o p q r s t u v w x y z

Digital modulation is used in computer networks and in long-haul telephone systems, which require transmission speeds ranging from tens of kilobits to more than a gigabit per second. Transmitters differ in speed. Not surprisingly, the faster ones are also more expensive.

Light Source

The light source will be a laser or a light-emitting diode (LED). A good light source in a fiber-optic connection should have the following characteristics:

- Fast rise and fall times. The rise time is the time required for a light source to go from 10 to 90 percent of the desired level. This time limits the maximum transmission rate, so it should be as short as possible. Lasers have a rise time of less than a nanosecond; the rise time for LEDs ranges from a few nanoseconds to a few hundred nanoseconds.

- A narrow spectral width. The spectral width refers to the range of wavelengths emitted by the light source, and it should be as narrow as possible. Spectral widths for lasers are 1 to 3 nm; for LEDs, they are from 30 to 50 nm.

- Light emission at a central wavelength with minimal spectral width. The central wavelength is the primary wavelength of the light being emitted. For various reasons, wavelengths of 820, 850, 1300, and 1550 nm have all been used. LEDs are used for the first three of the wavelengths, but rarely for 1550

nm. Lasers can be used at all of these wavelengths, and single-frequency lasers (possible at the two highest wavelengths) make it possible to emit at a particular wavelength with minimal spectral width.

- A good relationship between the emitting area and acceptance angle. The emitting area is the opening through which the transmitter emits its light. This should be small in relation to the fiber core's acceptance angle, so that all the light emitted by the transmitter will enter the core. Not surprisingly, lasers have a much smaller emitting area than LEDs.

- Steady, strong output power. The higher the output power, the stronger the signal and the further it can travel without becoming too weak. Laser output can be as much as 1000 times that of LEDs.

- A long lifetime. The lifetime of a light source is the amount of time before the source's peak output power is half its original level. This is generally in the millions of hours (longer than ours) and is typically longer for LEDs than for lasers!

Although lasers are clearly the light source of choice, LEDs are generally the light source of record. The most likely reason for this is price; transmitters that use LEDs are usually much less expensive. This is not a problem for networking purposes, however, because LEDs operating at 820 or 850 nm are fine for the short-distance, fiber-optic connections currently most popular.

Despite their performance shortcomings compared with lasers, LEDs are more reliable and less prone to breakdowns.

Receiver

Fiber-optic receivers undo the work of transmitters: they accept a light signal and convert this to an electrical signal representing information in analog or digital form. A receiver's performance depends on how well its three main components work. The following are the main components of a fiber-optic receiver:

- The photodetector, which "sees" the optical signal and converts it into electrical form. This produces a current that is proportional to the level of light detected.

- The amplifier, which boosts the signal and gets it into a form ready for processing.

- The processor, which tries to reproduce the original signal.

The receiver also includes interfaces for the cable carrying the light signal and the device to which the electrical signal is being passed.

The photodetector and amplifier processes are essentially identical for analog and digital signals. The main differences are in the processor.

There are several classes of photodetectors, each suitable for different speed and distance configurations. The receiver sensitivity specifies the weakest signal that the photodetector can detect. This information may be expressed as an absolute value, such

as 10 microwatts, or as a microwatt level needed for a given bit error rate (BER).

Duty Cycle A duty cycle specifies the ratio of high to low signal values in a digital transmission. This is not necessarily equal to the proportion of 0 and 1 bit values in the message, because some signal-encoding methods will encode a 1 as high at one point in a transmission and as low in another point. (See the Encoding, Signal article for examples of such methods.) The ideal duty cycle is 50 percent.

The duty-cycle value is important because receivers use a reference level as the threshold between high and low values. Some receivers adjust this reference during a transmission. If a duty-cycle value deviates from the 50 percent ideal, the altered threshold level could lead to more erroneous values. For example, if a threshold is adjusted downward because of a 20 percent duty cycle, low signals that are marginally but not significantly higher than normal may be misinterpreted as high values. There are two strategies for getting around the potential error problem: signal encoding and reference levels.

Certain signal-encoding methods, such as the Manchester and differential Manchester methods used in Ethernet and Token Ring networks, always have a 50 percent duty cycle. The tradeoff for this nice behavior is that these encoding methods require a clock that runs at twice the data rate (since every interval is associated with two electrical levels).

It is possible to build a receiver that has an absolute reference level; that is, one that will always correspond to the level of a

50 percent duty cycle. This is accomplished by coupling the receiver to a DC power supply. The tradeoff for this is that the receiver has higher power requirements; it requires a signal that is 6 to 8 dB (roughly, four to eight times) stronger than for an ordinary receiver.

Transceiver

A fiber-optic transceiver includes both a transmitter and a receiver in the same component. These are arranged in parallel so that they can operate independently of each other. Both the receiver and the transmitter have their own circuitry, so that the component can handle transmissions in both directions.

Repeater

Like a transceiver, a fiber-optic repeater includes both a transmitter and a receiver in the same component. However, in the repeater, these components are arranged in series, separated by circuitry for cleaning and boosting the signal. The receiver gets the signal and passes it through the booster to the transmitter.

Connectors and Splices

Connectors serve to link two segments of cable or a cable and a device. A connector is used for temporary links. To link two sections of cable permanently, use a splice; to link more than two sections of cable, use a coupler. In general, use a splice when possible; use a connector when necessary.

A good connector or splice should have the following properties:

- Low power loss. There should be minimal loss of signal power going across the connection or splice. For networks and short-distance connections, the loss should be less than 1 dB; for long-haul connections, there should be less than 0.2 dB loss.

- Durability. The connector should be capable of multiple matings (connections) without loosening or becoming unreliable. Durability values typically range between about 250 and 1000 matings.

- Ease of use. The connector or splice should be easy to install.

- Low price. The less expensive, the better, provided all the preceding features are satisfactory.

There are many types of connector designs used for fiber-optic cable. Some of the most commonly used ones in networking are SC, ST, SMA, and the MIC connector specified for the FDDI (Fiber Distributed Data Interface) network architecture. See the Connectors, Fiber-Optic article for more information about fiber-optic connectors.

If a fiber-optic connection is more or less permanent, it may make more sense to splice the cable segments together. Splicing techniques are more reliable and precise than connectors. Because of this, signal loss at splices is much lower (almost always less than 1 dB, and often less than 0.25 dB) than at connectors. Splicing is almost always used for long-haul, fiber-optic cable.

Fusion and mechanical splices are the two most common splicing methods. Of the two, fusion gives the better splices.

A fusion splice welds the two fibers together using a high-precision instrument. This type of splice produces losses smaller than 0.1 dB. The equipment for such splicing is quite expensive, however.

A mechanical splice is accomplished by fitting a special device over the two fibers to connect them and lock them into place. The device remains attached to the splice area to protect the splice from environmental effects, such as moisture or pressure. Mechanical splices have higher signal losses than fusion splices, but these losses may still be less than 0.25 dB.

Couplers

Fiber-optic couplers route an incoming signal to two or more outgoing paths. Couplers are needed in fiber-optic networks. When an electrical signal is split and sent along parallel paths, each derived signal is the same strength. This is not the case with light signals.

After the signal is split, the derived optical signals are each weaker than the original signal. For example, if a fiber-optic coupler splits a signal into two equal signals, each of those derived signals loses 3 dB relative to the original signal, just from the signal halving. Couplers can be designed to split a signal equally or unequally. See the Coupler, Fiber-Optic article for more information.

Optical Switches

Couplers used in networks need some type of bypass mechanism, so that the coupler can be disconnected if the coupler's target nodes are not on the network. This disconnection capability is accomplished with an optical switch, which allows the light to bypass a node and continue around the network.

Fiber-Optic Cable Signal Loss

As mentioned earlier, light signals can be diminished by coupling. In addition, factors that contribute to signal loss across a stretch of cable include the following:

Pulse dispersion: If the cable's core width is large compared with the light's wavelength, light enters the core at different angles and will travel different distances to the destination. As explained earlier, the difference in arrival times between the fastest and slowest signals in a group is measured in nanoseconds of tail over the distance the light must travel. This value limits the maximum transmission rate, because signal pulses must be separated by at least the nanoseconds of tail time. For example, if a signal acquires 10 nanoseconds of tail over the required distance, the maximum transmission rate is 100 Mbps.

Attenuation: Loss of signal strength that occurs because some of the light is absorbed by the cladding, and some light is scattered as a result of imperfections in the fiber.

Fiber bending: Signal loss can occur because the fiber is bent in particular ways. Multiple bands of light (known as modes) enter a core, each at slightly different angles. Bending the fiber can enable certain modes to escape from the core. Since the modes that escape

a
b
c
d
e
f
g
h
i
j
k
l
m
n
o
p
q
r
s
t
u
v
w
x
y
z

will not be random, fiber bending can introduce systematic loss of certain signal components. Simply rolling fiber cable onto a spool for distribution can introduce fiber bending. Cable manufacturers design their cable spools carefully, and some even publish specifications for the spool.

Microbending: Microbends are tiny kinks that can arise in the cable as a result of various stresses (for example, attaching a connector at the end of a cable). Microbends in the fiber can cumulate, and the presence of many kinks can significantly increase the signal loss from bending.

Fiber ovality: If the fiber's core and cladding are not round, the nonuniform shape will distort the signal. This can happen, for example, if the cable was squashed with a heavy weight, so that the core and cladding are partially flattened.

Advantages of Fiber-Optic Cable

Fiber-optic connections offer the following advantages over other types of cabling systems:

- Light signals are impervious to interference from EMI or electrical crosstalk. Light signals do not interfere with other signals. As a result, fiber-optic connections can be used in extremely adverse environments, such as in elevator shafts or assembly plants, where powerful motors and engines produce lots of electrical noise.

- Fiber-optic lines are much harder to tap, so they are more secure for private lines.

- Light has a much higher bandwidth, or maximum data-transfer rate, than electrical connections. (This speed advantage has yet to be realized in practice, however.)

- The signal has a much lower loss rate, so it can be transmitted much further than it could be with coaxial or twisted-pair cable before boosting is necessary.

- Optical fiber is much safer, because there is no electricity and so no danger of electrical shock or other electrical accidents.

- Fiber-optic cable is generally much thinner and lighter than electrical cable, and so it can be installed more unobtrusively. (Fiber-optic cable weighs about an ounce per meter; coaxial cable weighs nearly ten times that much.)

- Cable making and installation are much easier than they were in the early days.

Disadvantages of Fiber-Optic Cable

The disadvantages of fiber-optic connections include the following:

- Fiber-optic cable is currently more expensive than other types of cable.

- Other components, particularly NICs, are very expensive.

- Certain components, particularly couplers, are subject to optical crosstalk.

- Fiber connectors are not designed to be used as often as you would like. Generally, they are designed for fewer than a thousand matings. After that, the connection may become loose, unstable, or misaligned. The resulting signal loss may be unacceptably high.

- Many more parts can break in a fiber-optic connection than in an electrical one.

Fiber-Optic Cable Tools

It is only fitting that the most complex wiring technology should also have the most sophisticated tools. Optical fiber undergoes an extensive set of tests and quality-control inspections before it even leaves the manufacturer.

The manufacturers' tests are designed to get complete details about the cable's physical and optical properties. Optical properties include attenuation, dispersion, and refractive indexes of the core and cladding layers. Physical properties include core and cladding dimensions, numerical aperture and emitting areas, tensile strength, and changes in performance under extreme temperature and/or humidity conditions (or as a result of repeated changes in temperature). The values for these properties are used to evaluate cable performance.

The equipment you might need to test fiber-optic cables in a network setting includes the following:

- An installation kit—a general-purpose tool set for dealing with optical fiber.

Such a toolkit will include cable strippers, scissors, crimping tools, epoxy, pliers, canned air (for cleaning fibers after polishing), inspection microscope, polishing materials, and so on.

- Optical power meter, which is a device that can read levels of optical signals on a fiber-optic line. Using sensors attached to the cable, this device can report absolute or relative signal levels over a range of 110 dB (which means that the weakest and strongest detectable signals differ by a factor of over 10 billion). An optical power meter can also be used to measure light at specific wavelengths.

- An OTDR (optical time domain reflectometer), which is a device that can measure the behavior of the light signals over time and create graphical representations of these measurements. An OTDR can be used to measure signal loss along a stretch of cable and to help locate a fault in a fiber-optic connection.

- Splicer, which is used to create splices, or permanent connections in an optical fiber. Fusion splicers are the most expensive devices of this sort.

- Polishers, which are used to prepare fiber ends for splicing or connection.

- A microscope, so you can inspect the results of a splicing or polishing operation. A microscope may be included in an installation toolkit.

a
b
c
d
e
f
g
h
i
j
k
l
m
n
o
p
q
r
s
t
u
v
w
x
y
z

Fiber-Optic Cable Vendors

Many vendors sell both electrical and fiber-optic cable, as well as connectors, installation, and testing tools. The following vendors offer an extensive selection of fiber-optics products. (See the Cable article for other cable vendors.)

AMP Incorporated: (800) 522-6752; (717) 564-0100

CSP (Computer System Products): (800) 422-2537; (612) 476-6866; Fax (612) 476-6966

FIS (Fiber Instrument Sales): (800) 445-2901; (315) 736-2206; Fax (315) 736-2285

SEE ALSO

Cable; Cable, Coaxial; Cable, Twisted-Pair; Connector, Fiber-Optic; Coupler, Fiber-Optic; FDDI (Fiber Distributed Data Interface)

Cable, Horizontal

Horizontal cable is defined by the EIA/TIA-568 committee as any cable that goes from a wiring closet, or distribution frame, to the wall outlet in the work area. Distribution frames from a floor or building are connected to other frames using backbone cable.

In a sense, horizontal cable is the most crucial in the entire network cabling structure. Since it is installed in the walls, floors, ceiling, or ground, the installation process can be difficult and expensive. Moreover, the cable should be able to handle future standards and technology.

The EIA/TIA-568 recognizes four main types of horizontal cable, and several optional variants. These types are listed in the table "EIA/TIA-568 Main and Optional Types of Horizontal Cable." The EIA/TIA specifications call for at least two cables

EIA/TIA-568 MAIN AND OPTIONAL TYPES OF HORIZONTAL CABLE		
CABLE TYPE	**MAIN**	**OPTIONAL**
UTP	100-ohm, four-pair UTP cable	100-ohm, 25-wire-pair UTP cable
STP	150-ohm STP cable, such as that defined in the IBM Cable System (ICS)	100-ohm STP cable
Coaxial	50-ohm, thin coaxial cable, such as the cable used in thin Ethernet networks	75-ohm (broadband) coaxial cable, such as CATV cable
Optical fiber	62.5/125-micron (step- or graded-index) multimode optical fiber	Multimode fiber with other core/cladding ratios of 50/125-micron, 100/140-micron, etc.
Undercarpet		Flat cable (such as Type 8 in the ICS) that can be run under carpet without posing a hazard

from this list to be run to every wall outlet. At least one of these should be unshielded twisted-pair (UTP).

COMPARE

Cable, Backbone

SEE ALSO

Cable

Cable, IBM

The IBM Cable System (ICS) was designed by IBM for use in its Token Ring networks and also for general-purpose premises wiring. The figure "Context and properties of the IBM Cable System" summarizes the features of this type of cable.

CONTEXT AND PROPERTIES OF THE IBM CABLE SYSTEM

Context

Cable
    Electrical
        Twisted-Pair ─────────────┐
        Coaxial   │
    Optical   │
        Fiber-Optic ──────────────┤
                      ↓

IBM Cable System Properties

Comprises Types 1 through 9 (of which all types but 4 and 7 are defined)

Type 5 is fiber-optic

Type 3 is unshielded twisted-pair (UTP)

Remaining types are shielded twisted-pair (STP)

Type 1 is most common in Token Ring Networks

Type 3 is not recommended for 16 Mbps networks

Type 3 cable generally requires a media filter

Type 6 is used mainly as short-distance patch cable

Type 8 is flat cable for use under a carpet

IBM Cable System Uses

IBM Token Ring networks

10BaseT Ethernet networks

ARCnet networks

ISDN lines

Some IBM 3270 networks

IBM has specified nine types of cable, mainly twisted-pair, but with more stringent specifications than for the generic twisted-pair cabling. The type taxonomy also includes fiber-optic cable, but excludes co-axial cable. The twisted-pair versions differ in the following ways:

- Whether the type is shielded or unshielded

- Whether the carrier wire is solid or stranded

- The gauge (diameter) of the carrier wire

- The number of twisted pairs

Specifications have been created for seven of the nine types. Types 4 and 7 are undefined; presumably, they are reserved for future use.

Type 1 Cable

Type 1 cable is shielded twisted-pair (STP), with two pairs of 22-gauge solid wire. It is used for data-quality transmission in IBM's Token Ring network. It can be used for the main ring or to connect lobes (nodes) to multistation attachment units (MAUs), which are wiring centers.

Although not required by the specifications, a plenum version is also available, at about twice the cost of the nonplenum cable. Compare Type 1 with Type 6.

Type 2 Cable

Type 2 is a hybrid consisting of four pairs of unshielded 22-gauge solid wire (for voice transmission) and two pairs of shielded 22-gauge solid wire (for data). Although not required by the specifications, a plenum version is also available, at about twice the cost.

Type 3 Cable

Type 3 is unshielded twisted-pair (UTP), with two, three, or four pairs of 22- or 24-gauge solid wire. The pairs have at least two twists per foot. This category requires only voice-grade capabilities, and so may be used as telephone wire for voice transmissions. Type 3 is not recommended for 16 Mbps Token Ring networks.

Although not required by the specifications, a plenum version is also available, at about twice the cost.

Type 3 cable is becoming more popular as adapter cable, which is used to connect a node to a MAU. You must use a media filter if you are using Type 3 cable to connect a node to a MAU or if you need to switch between UTP and STP in a Token Ring network. However, you should not mix Type 1 and 3 cable in the same ring. Mixing cable types makes trouble-shooting difficult.

Some manufacturers offer higher-quality Type 3 cable for greater reliability. Such cable has more twists per foot, for greater protection against interference. Many vendors recommend that you use Category 4 cable (with 12 twists per foot). This category of cable costs about 20 percent more than ordinary Type 3 cable, but is rated for higher speeds. The category value represents a classification system for the performance of UTP cable. See the Cable Standards article for more information.

Type 5 Cable

Type 5 is fiber-optic cable, with two glass fiber cores, each with a 100-micron diameter and a 140-micron cladding diameter. (IBM also allows the more widely used 62.5/125-micron fiber.)

This type is used for the main ring path (the main network cabling) in a Token Ring network to connect MAUs over greater distances or to connect network segments between buildings. Plenum versions of Type 5 cable are available at only a slightly higher cost.

Type 6 Cable

Type 6 is STP cable, with two pairs of 26-gauge stranded wire. This type is commonly used as an adapter cable to connect a node to a MAU. In that type of connection, the PC end of the cable has a male DB-9 or DB-25 connector, and the MAU end has a specially designed IBM data connector.

Type 6 cable is also used as a patch cable; for example, to connect MAUs. For this use, the cable has IBM data connectors at each end.

Because Type 6 is used mostly for shorter distances, the price per foot tends to be higher than for other cable types.

Type 8 Cable

Type 8 is STP cable, with two pairs of flat, 26-gauge solid wire. This type is specially designed to be run under a carpet, so the wires are flattened. This makes the cable much more prone to signal loss than Type 1 or Type 2 cable; however, the performance of Type 8 cable is adequate for the short

distances usually involved in under-the-carpet cabling.

Type 9 Cable

Type 9 is STP cable, with two pairs of 26-gauge solid or stranded wire. This type is covered with a plenum jacket and is designed to be run between floors.

SEE ALSO
Cable, Twisted-Pair

Cable, Patch

Cable used to connect two hubs or multi-station attachment units (MAUs). IBM Type 1 or Type 6 patch cables can be used for Token Ring networks.

SEE ALSO
Cable, IBM

Cable, Plenum

Cable that has a fire-resistant jacket, which will not burn, smoke, or give off toxic fumes when exposed to heat. The cable goes through a plenum, a conduit, or shaft, running inside a wall, floor, or ceiling. Fire regulations generally stipulate that cable running through such conduits must be fireproof.

SEE ALSO
Cable

Cable, Quadrax

A type of coaxial cable. Quadrax cable, sometimes known simply as quadrax, is a hybrid of triaxial and twinaxial cable. Like twinaxial cable, quadrax has the extra

a b **c** d e f g h i j k l m n o p q r s t u v w x y z

carrier wire with dielectric; like triaxial cable, quadrax has extra shielding.

SEE ALSO

Cable, Coaxial

Cable, Quad Shield

A type of coaxial cable with four layers of shielding: alternating layers of foil and braid shields. Quad shield cable, sometimes known simply as quad shield, is used in situations where heavy electrical interference can occur, such as in industrial settings.

SEE ALSO

Cable, Coaxial

Cable, Riser

Cable that runs vertically; for example, between floors in a building. Riser cable often runs through available shafts (such as for the elevator). In some cases, such areas can be a source of electrical interference. Consequently, optical fiber (which is impervious to electromagnetic interference) is generally used as rise cable.

Cable Standards

Several cable standards are concerned with the performance and reliability of cables under actual working conditions. In particular, these standards specify the cable's minimal acceptable behavior under adverse working conditions; for example, in manufacturing or industrial environments, where heavy machinery is turned on and off during the course of operations. Such actions can generate strong interference and power-supply variations. Cable environments are often distinguished in terms of the demands made on the cable. The standards also specify the minimum behavior required under extreme conditions, such as fire.

The most commonly used safety standards in the United States are those specified in the National Electric Code and in documents from Underwriters Laboratories. Other standards are specified by the Electronic Industries Association/Telecommunications Industries Association, Electrical Testing Laboratory, and Manufacturing Automation Protocol.

The National Electric Code (NEC)

The NEC is published by the National Fire Protection Agency (NFPA, 617-770-3000), and specifies safety standards for general-purpose cables in commercial and residential environments, and also specifically for cables used for communications. The Class 2 (CL2x) standards apply to general-purpose cables, and the Communications (CMx) standards apply to special-purpose cables capable of carrying data.

Of the CL2 standards, the most stringent ones apply to Class 2 plenum cable (CL2P). Cable that meets or exceeds these standards is said to be CL2P compliant. CMP-compliant cable meets the corresponding standard for plenum communications cable.

The less stringent CL2R standards apply to riser cable (cable that can be used, for example, in a vertical utility shaft between floors in a building). The corresponding standard for communications riser cable is CMR.

Be wary if you intend to use cable that is neither CMx- nor CL2x-compliant. Older cable that is already in the walls may be noncompliant.

Underwriters Laboratories (UL)

UL tests cable and other electrical devices to determine the conditions under which the cable or device will function safely and as specified. UL-listed products have passed safety tests performed by inspectors at the Underwriters Laboratories.

Two tests are most directly relevant to network cable:

UL-910: Tests smoke emissions and the spread of flames for plenum cable. This test corresponds to the CL2P level of safety standards. A cable that passes the UL-910 test is rated as OFNP (optical fiber, nonconductive plenum) by UL.

UL-1666: Tests the performance of riser cable in a fire. This test corresponds roughly to the CL2R level of safety standards. A cable that passes the UL-1666 test is rated as OFNR (optical fiber, nonconductive riser) by UL.

UL also uses a system of markings to categorize cable as falling into one of five levels (I through V). Cables that meet level I and II standards meet minimum UL safety requirements, but the performance of these cables may be inadequate for networking purposes. Cables that meet level III, IV, or V standards meet both safety and various performance requirements. Higher levels allow for less attenuation and interference due to crosstalk than lower levels.

Cable should be UL-listed, and just about every cable is. However, you need to find out which listing applies. For example, OFNR

cable is UL-listed but is not suitable for environments that demand fire protection.

For most networking applications, cable that meets requirements for UL level III or above should be adequate.

UNDERWRITERS LABORATORIES (UL) PHONE NUMBERS

East Coast: (516) 271-6200

Central: (708) 272-8800

West Coast: (408) 985-2400

Electronic Industries Association/Telecommunications Industries Association (EIA/TIA)

A committee for EIA/TIA has created yet another classification system for specifying the performance of unshielded twisted-pair (UTP) cable. The EIA/TIA taxonomy includes the following categories (1 through 5) whose criteria correspond roughly to the performance criteria specified for the UL levels:

Category 1: Voice-grade, UTP telephone cable. This describes the cable that has been used for years in telephone communications. Officially, such cable is not considered suitable for data-grade transmissions (in which every bit must get across correctly). In practice, however, it works fine over short distances and under ordinary working conditions.

Category 2: Data-grade UTP, capable of supporting transmission rates of up to 4 megabits per second (Mbps). IBM Type 3 cable falls into this category.

a b **c** d e f g h i j k l m n o p q r s t u v w x y z

Category 3: Data-grade UTP, capable of supporting transmission rates of up to 10 Mbps. A 10BaseT network requires such cable.

Category 4: Data-grade UTP, capable of supporting transmission rates of up to 16 Mbps. A 16 Mbps IBM Token Ring network requires such cable.

Category 5: Data-grade UTP, capable of supporting transmission rates of up to 155 Mbps (but officially only up to 100 Mbps). The proposed CDDI (Copper Distributed Data Interface) networks and 100Base-X network architecture require such cable.

Performance Levels

Many cable vendors also use a five-level system to categorize their UTP cable. Just as there is overlap in the paths to enlightenment in various religious traditions, there is some overlap between these levels and the other systems discussed here. For example, the references to Level 4, Category 4 cable identify the cable according to the features described here and also according to the features in the EIA/TIA specifications.

Level 1: Voice-grade cable, which is suitable for use in the "plain old telephone system" (or POTS). Such cable can handle data at up to 1 Mbps.

Level 2: Data-grade cable that is capable of transmission speeds as high as 4 Mbps. This level corresponds roughly to the Type 3 cable described in IBM's Cabling System (see the Cable, IBM article). Level 2 cable also meets the requirements for the 1Base5

(StarLAN) Ethernet network developed by AT&T.

Level 3: Data-grade cable that is capable of transmission speeds as high as 16 Mbps. This level corresponds to Category 3 cable in the EIA/TIA-568 specifications. Level 3 cable is used in 4 Mbps or 16 Mbps Token Ring networks, and also in 10BaseT Ethernet/ 802.3 networks.

Level 4: Data-grade cable that is capable of transmission speeds as high as 20 Mbps. This level corresponds to Category 4 cable in the EIA/TIA-568 specifications. Level 4 cable is used for ARCnet Plus, a 20 Mbps version of the ARCnet network architecture.

Level 5: Data-grade cable that is capable of transmission speeds as high as 100 Mbps. This level corresponds to Category 5 cable in the EIA/TIA-568 specifications. Level 5 cable is used for CDDI (or TPDDI), which are copper-based implementations of the 100 Mbps FDDI network architecture. 100Base/X, a proposed 100 Mbps version of Ethernet, is also intended to run on this type of cable.

Electrical Testing Laboratory (ETL)

The ETL is an independent laboratory that tests and rates products for manufacturers. Vendors specify if their cable has been tested and verified by ETL.

Manufacturing Automation Protocol (MAP)

The most commonly observed performance standards, arguably, are those associated with the MAP. Among other things, this standard specifies the expected performance for cables in the highly automated and machinery-heavy industrial working environments of the future.

Cable that meets MAP standards generally has quad shields; that is, four layers of shielding around the central core in a coaxial cable. The four layers of shielding help protect the cable against signal loss from the conductor wire and against electromagnetic interference from the outside world; for example, from heavy machinery being turned on and off. See the MAP article for more information.

Cable Tester

An instrument for testing the integrity and performance of a stretch of cable. Cable testers run various tests to determine the cable's attenuation, resistance, characteristic impedance, and so on. High-end testers can test cable for conformity to various network architecture specifications, and can sometimes even identify a particular type of cable.

Cable, Transceiver

Cable used to connect a network interface card to a transceiver, mainly in Ethernet architectures. A transceiver cable usually has an AUI connector at one end and an N-series or other type of connector at the other end. Coaxial transceiver cable comes in thick and thin versions. You can also get special cable with a built-in right angle.

Cable, Triaxial

A type of coaxial cable. Also called triax, this cable has an inner braid surrounded by an inner (nonplenum) jacket, surrounded by an outer copper braid. The extra shielding makes a big difference because of the grounding and improved protection.

SEE ALSO
Cable, Coaxial

Cable, Twinaxial

A type of coaxial cable. Also called twinax, this cable has two insulated carrier wires, generally twisted around each other, which helps cut down considerably on magnetic interference. Twinaxial cables are used in IBM and AppleTalk networks.

SEE ALSO
Cable, Coaxial

Cable, Twisted-Pair

Twisted-pair cable is very widely used, inexpensive, and easy to install. It can transmit data at an acceptable rate (up to 100 Mbps in some network architectures). The best-known example of twisted-pair wiring is probably telephone cable, which is unshielded and is usually voice-grade, rather than the higher-quality data-grade cable used for networks. The figure "Context and properties of twisted-pair cable" summarizes the features of this type of cable.

In a twisted-pair cable, two conductor wires are wrapped around each other. A signal is transmitted as a differential between the two conductor wires. This type of signal

a b **c** d e f g h i j k l m n o p q r s t u v w x y z

CONTEXT AND PROPERTIES OF TWISTED-PAIR CABLE

Context

Cable
  Electrical
    Twisted-Pair ───────────────────┐
    Coaxial   │
  Optical   │
    Fiber-Optic   │
                                     ▼

Shielded Twisted-Pair (STP) Properties

Includes shield around twisted pairs

150 ohm impedance

Information in differential signal between wires in a pair

Subject to near-end crosstalk (NEXT)

Subject to electromagnetic interference

Generally uses RJ-xx connectors

Shielded Twisted-Pair (STP) Uses

IBM Token Ring networks

ARCnet networks

Rarely in Ethernet networks

Unshielded Twisted-Pair (UTP) Properties

No shield around twisted pairs

100 ohm impedance

Information in differential signal between wires in a pair

Subject to near-end crosstalk (NEXT)

Subject to electromagnetic interference

Generally uses RJ-xx connectors

Performance grades specified in EIA/TIA-568 CATEGORIES 1-5

Unshielded Twisted-Pair (UTP) Uses

10BaseT Ethernet networks

ARCnet networks

Certain sections of IBM Token Ring networks

Telephone lines (voice-grade)

is less prone to interference and attenuation, because using a differential essentially gives a double signal, but cancels out the random interference on each wire.

Twisting within a pair minimizes crosstalk between pairs. The twists also help deal with electromagnetic interference (EMI) and radio frequency interference (RFI), as well as signal loss due to capacitance (the tendency of a nonconductor to store up electrical charge). The performance of a twisted-pair cable can be influenced by changing the number of twists per foot in a wire pair.

IBM has developed its own categorization system for twisted-pair cable, mainly to describe the cable supported for IBM's Token Ring network architecture. The system is discussed in the Cable, IBM article.

Twisted-Pair Cable Components

A twisted-pair cable has the following components:

Conductor wires: The signal wires for this cable come in pairs that are wrapped around each other. The conductor wires are usually made of copper. They may be solid (consisting of a single wire) or stranded (consisting of many thin wires wrapped tightly together). A twisted-pair cable usually contains multiple twisted-pairs; 2, 4, 6, 8, 25, 50, or 100 twisted-pair bundles are common. For network applications, 2- and 4-pair cables are most commonly used.

Shield: Shielded twisted-pair (STP) cable includes a foil shield around each pair of conductors.

Jacket: The wire bundles are encased in a jacket made of polyvinylchloride (PVC) or, in plenum cables, of a fire-resistant material, such as Teflon or Kynar.

The figure "Components of twisted-pair cable" shows the makeup of this type of cable. Note that the shield is not included for unshielded twisted-pair cable.

Twisted-pair cable comes in two main varieties: shielded (STP) and unshielded

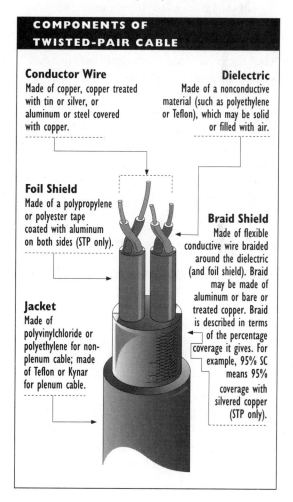

COMPONENTS OF TWISTED-PAIR CABLE

Conductor Wire
Made of copper, copper treated with tin or silver, or aluminum or steel covered with copper.

Dielectric
Made of a nonconductive material (such as polyethylene or Teflon), which may be solid or filled with air.

Foil Shield
Made of a polypropylene or polyester tape coated with aluminum on both sides (STP only).

Braid Shield
Made of flexible conductive wire braided around the dielectric (and foil shield). Braid may be made of aluminum or bare or treated copper. Braid is described in terms of the percentage coverage it gives. For example, 95% SC means 95% coverage with silvered copper (STP only).

Jacket
Made of polyvinylchloride or polyethylene for non-plenum cable; made of Teflon or Kynar for plenum cable.

(UTP). STP contains an extra shield or protective screen around each of the wire pairs to cut down on extraneous signals. This added protection also makes STP more expensive than UTP. (The price of coaxial cable actually lies between UTP and STP prices.)

Shielded Twisted-Pair (STP) Cable

STP cable has pairs of conductors twisted around each other. Each pair is covered with a foil shield to reduce interference and minimize crosstalk between wire pairs.

STP can handle high-speed transmissions, but the cable itself is relatively expensive, can be quite bulky and heavy, and is rather difficult to work with.

STP is used in ARCnet and Token Ring networks, although the special cable versions developed by IBM are more likely to be used in the Token Ring networks. Several of the types specified in the IBM Cable System are STP: Types 1, 2, 6, 8, and 9 (see the Cable, IBM article).

Unshielded Twisted-Pair (UTP) Cable

UTP cable does not include any extra shielding around the wire pairs. This type of cable is used in some Token Ring networks, usually those working at slower speeds. UTP can also be used in Ethernet and ARCnet architectures.

UTP is not the primary choice for any network architecture, but the IEEE has approved a standard for a 10BaseT Ethernet network that uses UTP cabling at 10 Mbps. Networking mavens are divided as to whether 10BaseT and the use of UTP cable in general are welcome additions or dead-ends.

Because it lacks shielding, UTP is not as good at blocking noise and interference as STP or coaxial cable. Consequently, UTP cable segments must be shorter than when using other types of cable. For standard UTP, the length of a segment should never exceed 100 meters (about 330 feet).

On the other hand, UTP is quite inexpensive, and is very easy to install and work with. The price and ease of installation make UTP tempting, but keep in mind that installation is generally the major part of the cabling expense (so saving on the cable won't necessarily help cut expenses very much) and that other types of cable may be just as easy to install.

To distinguish varieties of UTP, the EIA/TIA has formulated five categories. These are summarized in the Cable Standards article.

Performance Features

Twisted-pair cable is described in terms of its electrical and performance properties. The features that characterize UTP and STP cable include the following:

Attenuation: This value indicates how much power the signal has lost and is dependent on the frequency of the transmission. Attenuation is measured in relation to a specified distance; for example, 100 meters, 1000 feet, or 1 kilometer. Attenuation per 1000 feet values range from under 10 dB (for Category 4 cable running at 1 MHz) to more than 60 dB (for Category 5 cable running at 100 MHz). With attenuation, a lower value is better.

USING EXISTING TELEPHONE CABLE WIRES

Most telephone cable is UTP, and many telephone cables have extra wires because the cable comes with four pairs and the telephone company needs only two of the pairs for your telephone connection. (Any additional lines or intercoms require their own wire pairs.)

If there are unused wire pairs, you may be able to use these for your network cabling. While this is a tempting possibility, consider the following points carefully:

- The cable might not run conveniently for your needs, so you may need to add cable segments.

- Make sure you test all the cable you'll be using, and don't be surprised if some of it is defective.

- The telephone cable may be the lower-quality, voice-grade type, and you really should be using data-grade cable, unless you're transmitting over very short distances.

If you're going to use already installed cable for your network, make sure all of it works properly. Use a cable tester, which can provide detailed information about the cable's physical and electrical properties. When you're dealing with a long cable system, the chances are good that at least parts of it will be faulty. Find and replace the bad cable before you set everything up.

Capacitance: This value indicates the extent to which the cable stores up charge (which can distort the signal). Capacitance is measured in picofarads (pF) per foot; lower values indicate better performance. Typical values are between 15 and 25 pF/ft.

Impedance: All UTP cable should have an impedance of 100 +/– 15 ohms.

NEXT: The near-end crosstalk (NEXT) indicates the degree of interference from neighboring wire pairs. This is also measured in decibels per unit distance, but because of notation and expression conventions, a high value is better for this feature. NEXT depends on the signal frequency and cable category. Performance is better at lower frequencies and for cables in the higher categories.

Twisted-Pair Cable Advantages

Twisted-pair cable has the following advantages over other types of cables for networks:

- It is easy to connect devices to twisted-pair cable.

- If an already installed cable system, such as telephone cable, has extra, unused wires, you may be able to use a pair of wires from that system. For example, in order to use the telephone cable system, you need telephone cable that has four pairs of wires, and there can be no intercoms or second lines to use the two pairs not needed for the telephone connection.

- STP does a good job of blocking interference.

- UTP is quite inexpensive.

- UTP is very easy to install.

a
b
c
d
e
f
g
h
i
j
k
l
m
n
o
p
q
r
s
t
u
v
w
x
y
z

- UTP may already be installed (but make sure it all works properly and that it meets the performance specifications your network requires).

Twisted-Pair Cable Disadvantages

Twisted-pair cable has the following disadvantages compared with other types of cable:

- STP is bulky and difficult to work with.

- UTP is more susceptible to noise and interference than coaxial or fiber-optic cable.

- UTP signals cannot go as far as they can with other cable types before they need cleaning and boosting.

- A skin effect can increase attenuation. This occurs when transmitting data at a fast rate over twisted-pair wire. Under these conditions, the current tends to flow mostly on the outside surface of the wire. This greatly decreases the cross-section of the wire being used for moving electrons, and thereby increases resistance. This, in turn, increases signal attenuation, or loss.

Selecting and Installing Twisted-Pair Cable

When you are deciding on a category of cable for your needs, take future developments—in your network and also in technology—into account. It is a good idea to buy the cable at least one category above the one you have selected. (If you selected Category 5 cable to begin with, you should seriously consider fiber-optic cable.)

Check the wiring sequence before you purchase cable. Different wiring sequences can lurk behind the same modular plug in a twisted-pair cable. (A wiring sequence, or wiring scheme, describes how wires are paired up and which locations each wire occupies in the plug.) If you connect a plug that terminates one wiring scheme into a jack that continues with a different sequence, the connection may not provide reliable transmission. See the Wiring Sequence article for more information.

You should find out which wiring scheme is used before buying cable, and buy only cable that uses the same wiring scheme. If you are stuck with existing cable that uses an incompatible wiring scheme, you can use a cross wye as an adapter between the two schemes.

If any of your cable purchases include patch cables (for example, to connect a computer to a wallplate), be aware that these cables come in two versions: straight through or reversed. For networking applications, use straight-through cable, which means that wire 1 coming in connects to wire 1 going out (rather than to wire 8 as in a reversed cable), wire 2 connects to wire 2 (rather than to wire 7), and so on. The tools for installing and testing twisted-pair cable are the same as those used generally for network cables. (See the Cable article for a discussion of cable tools.)

SEE ALSO

Cable; Cable, Coaxial; Cable, Fiber-Optic

Cable, Voice-Grade

Old-time, unshielded twisted-pair, telephone cable; category 1 in the EIA/TIA-568 specifications. This cable is suited to the transmission of voice signals. Officially, such cable is not considered suitable for data-grade transmissions. In practice, it generally works fine at low speeds, over short distances, and under ordinary working conditions.

SEE ALSO

Cable, Twisted-Pair

Cache

As a noun, a cache, also known as a disk cache, is an area of RAM (random-access memory) set aside for holding data that is likely to be used again. By keeping frequently used data in fast RAM, instead of

on a hard or floppy disk with much slower access, a system's performance can be improved greatly.

As a verb, cache refers to the process of putting information into a cache for faster retrieval. Directory information and hard disk contents are examples of data likely to be cached. The figure "Disk cache" shows an example of this process.

Cache Buffer Pool

In Novell's NetWare, the cache buffer pool is the amount of memory available for the network operating system (NOS) after the server module has been loaded into memory.

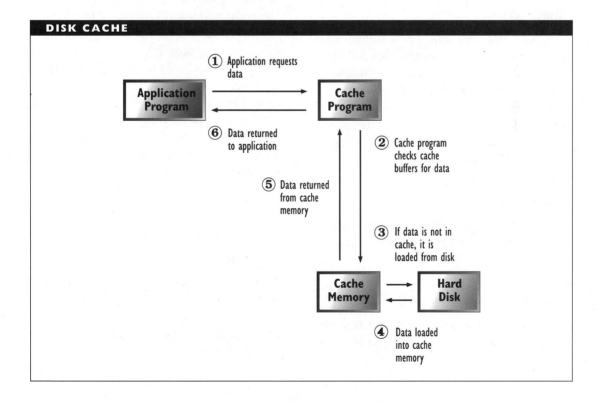

DISK CACHE

① Application requests data

Application Program

⑥ Data returned to application

Cache Program

② Cache program checks cache buffers for data

⑤ Data returned from cache memory

③ If data is not in cache, it is loaded from disk

Cache Memory ⟷ **Hard Disk**

④ Data loaded into cache memory

The memory in this pool can allocated for various purposes:

- To cache the file allocation tables (FATs) for each NetWare volume

- To create a hash table containing directory information

- To provide memory for NetWare Loadable Modules (NLMs) that are needed

Call

A request from one program or node to begin a communication with another node. The term is also used to refer to the resulting communications session.

Caller ID

In ISDN and some other telecommunications environments, a feature that includes the sender's identification number (such as telephone number) in the transmission so that the receiver knows who is calling. Caller ID is also known as ANI (automatic number identification) and CLID (calling line identification).

Call Setup Time

The amount of time needed to establish a connection between two nodes so they can communicate with each other.

Campus Area Network (CAN)

A network that connects nodes (or possibly departmental local-area networks) from multiple locations, which may be separated by a considerable distance. Unlike a wide-area network, however, a campus network does not require remote communications facilities, such as modems and telephones.

Campus-Wide Information System (CWIS)

SEE

CWIS (Campus-Wide Information System)

Capacitance

Capacitance is the ability of a dielectric (nonconductive) material to store electricity and to resist changes in voltage. In the presence of a signal (a voltage change), the dielectric will store some of the charge. Capacitance is usually measured in microfarads or picofarads (millionths or trillionths of a farad, respectively).

Other things being equal, the lower the capacitance, the better the cable. A higher capacitance means that more of the charge can be stored in the dielectric between two conductors, which means greater resistance. At higher frequencies, high capacitance results in greater signal attenuation.

SEE ALSO
Cable

Capacitor

An electrical component in line conditioners, surge protectors, and other equipment. Capacitors help clean incoming power by absorbing surges and noise from electromagnetic and radio frequency interference. Compare it with inductor and MOV (metal oxide varistor).

Carrier Band

A communications system in which the entire bandwidth is used for a single transmission and in which a signal is modulated before being transmitted. This is in contrast to baseband systems, which do not modulate the signal, and to broadband systems, which divide the total bandwidth into multiple channels.

Carrier Frequency

The rate at which the carrier signal repeats, measured in cycles per second, or hertz. In communications, the carrier signal is modulated, or altered, by superimposing a second signal, which represents the information being transmitted. In an acoustic signal, the frequency represents the signal's pitch.

Carrier On

In carrier sense, multiple access (CSMA) media-access methods, a signal that indicates the network is being used for a transmission. When a node detects this signal, the node waits a random amount of time before trying again to access the network.

Carrier Pulse

A signal, consisting of a series of rapid, constant pulses, used as the basis for pulse modulation; for example, when converting an analog signal into digital form.

Carrier Signal

An electrical signal that is used as the basis for a transmission. This signal has well-defined properties, but conveys no information (content). Information is sent by modifying (modulating) some feature of the carrier signal, such as the amplitude, frequency, or timing, to represent the values being transmitted.

Carrier Wire

A conductive wire (capable of carrying an electrical signal); for example, the central wire in a coaxial cable, which serves as the medium for the electrical signal.

SEE ALSO
Cable

CAS (Communicating Application Specification)

An interface standard for fax modems developed by Intel and DCA. This proposed standard competes with the Class x hierarchy developed by EIA.

CAT (Common Authentication Technology)

In the Internet community, CAT is a specification for distributed authentication under development. CAT supports authentication measures based on either public- or private-key encryption strategies.

With CAT, both client and server programs must use the services of a common interface, which will provide the authentication services. This interface will connect to either DASS (Distributed Authentication Security Service), which uses public-key encryption, or Kerberos, which uses private-key encryption.

a b c d e f g h i j k l m n o p q r s t u v w x y z

BROADER CATEGORY

Authentication

SEE ALSO

DASS (Distributed Authentication Security Service); Kerberos

CAU (Controlled Access Unit)

In IBM Token Ring networks, the term for an intelligent hub. CAUs can determine whether nodes are operating, connect and disconnect nodes, monitor node activity, and pass data to the LAN Network Manager program.

CAU/LAM (Controlled Access Unit/ Lobe Attachment Module)

In IBM Token Ring networks, a hub (the CAU) containing one or more boxes (the LAM) with multiple ports to which new nodes can be attached.

CBC (Cipher Block Chaining)

An operating mode for the DES.

SEE

DES (Data Encryption Standard)

CBEMA (Computer Business Manufacturers Association)

An organization that provides technical committees for work being done by other organizations; for example, the committee for the FDDI standard published by ANSI.

CBMS (Computer-Based Messaging System)

An older term for a Message Handling System (MHS), or for electronic mail.

SEE

E-Mail

CBR (Constant Bit Rate)

An ATM connection that uses Class A service, which is designed for voice or other data that are transmitted at a constant rate. Compare it with VBR (variable bit rate).

CC (Clearing Center)

In EDI, a message-switching element through which documents are passed on the way to their destinations.

SEE ALSO

EDI (Electronic Document Interchange)

CCIR (International Consultative Committee for Radiocommunication)

An ITU (International Telecommunication Union) agency that is responsible for defining standards for radio communications. In 1993, the CCIR—together with the IFRB (International Frequency Registration Board)—was replaced by the ITU-R (International Telecommunication Union— Radiocommunication Standardization Sector).

SEE ALSO

ITU

CCIS (Common Channel Interoffice Signaling)

In telephone communications, a transmission method that uses different channels for voice and control signals. The control signals are sent by a fast, packet-switched method, which makes it possible to include extra information (such as caller ID and billing information) in the control channel.

SEE ALSO

CCS 7

CCITT (Consultative Committee for International Telegraphy and Telephony)

The CCITT is a permanent subcommittee of the ITU (International Telecommunications Union), which operates under the auspices of the United Nations. The committee consists of representatives from 160 member nations, mostly from national PTT (Postal, Telephone, and Telegraph) services.

The CCITT is responsible for dozens of standards used in communications, telecommunications, and networking, including the X.25 and X.400 standards, the V.42 and V.42bis standards for modems, and the I.*xxx* series of documents on ISDN (Integrated Services Digital Network).

The CCITT works closely with the ISO (International Standardization Organization), so that many standards and recommendations will appear in documents from both groups. CCITT recommendations appear every four years, with 1992 (the white books) being the most recent.

In March 1993, the CCITT was officially renamed the International Telecommunication Union-Telecommunication Standardization Sector (ITU-T, sometimes written as ITU-TS or ITU-TSS). However, since the CCITT name is so familiar and is likely to remain in widespread use for some time, the older name is used throughout this book.

CCRSE (Commitment, Concurrency, and Recovery Service Element)

In the OSI Reference Model, an application-layer service that is used to implement distributed transactions among multiple applications.

SEE

ASE (Application Service Element)

CCS (Common Channel Signaling)

A signaling method in which control signals are sent across different channels than voice and data signals. This makes it possible to include various types of extra information in the control signal.

SEE ALSO

CCS 7

CCS (Common Communications Support)

One of the pillars of IBM's SAA specifications. CCS includes support for data links, application services, session services, and data streams.

SEE ALSO

SAA (Systems Application Architecture)

a
b
c
d
e
f
g
h
i
j
k
l
m
n
o
p
q
r
s
t
u
v
w
x
y
z

CCS (Continuous Composite Servo)

A compact disc recording technique in which the contents are stored on separate tracks laid out in concentric circles.

COMPARE

SS (Sampled Servo)

CCS (Hundreds of Call Seconds)

In telephone communications, a measure of line activity. One CCS is equivalent to 100 seconds of conversation on a line, so that an hour of line usage is 36 CCS; 36 CCS is equal to one Erlang, and indicates continuous use of the line.

CCS 7 (Common Channel Signaling 7)

A version of the CCITT's Signaling System 7 (SS7); a transmission method in ISDN that makes special services (such as call forwarding or call waiting) available anywhere in a network. CCS 7 is an extension of the CCIS method for transmitting control information.

CD (Carrier Detect)

A signal sent from a modem to a PC, to indicate that the modem is on line and ready for work.

CD (Compact Disc)

Compact discs are the product of a recording and storage technology that makes it possible to fit over half a gigabyte of digital data on a disc about the size of a floppy disk. Unlike floppy or hard disks, which use magnetic technology, compact discs are recorded using optical methods.

To produce a master disc for commercially produced CDs, a laser literally burns the information into the disc by creating tiny pits in the surface. This changes the reflective properties of the disc at these locations relative to the surrounding surface. The information is read by using a laser so that there is never any physical contact during the reading process. The information on a CD is actually contained in the transitions between the pits and the non-pit areas (known as the lands).

CD technology has undergone several revisions and advancements since the first digital audio (DA) discs were developed over 10 years ago.

CD Variants

The following standards and variants have been created and used over the years. Most of these standards are still in use, and many current CD drives can read several of the standards. In addition, newer standards (such as CD-XA) are often back-compatible with earlier standards (such as CD-ROM).

CD standards are distinguished by the color of the laser used in that particular technology—for example, red, yellow, and green. Collectively, these standards documents are known as the Rainbow Books. The following standards are among the most popular:

CD-DA (Digital Audio) (Red Book) This was the first compact disc standard, and was developed for recording musical discs. CD-DA discs can hold about 74 minutes of music recorded at

44,100 samples per second (known as the scanning frequency), using *PCM* (*pulse code modulation*) as the digitization method, and allocating 16 bits for each sample. (With 16 bits, each sample can take on any of 65, 536 (or 2^{16} values). These bits can be allocated in whatever manner one chooses, provided the resulting split is meaningful. For example, by allocating 8 bits to each channel, you can get stereo. CD-DA was not developed for recording data. CD-DA is what everyone correctly thinks of as audio CD.

CD-ROM (Read Only Memory) (Yellow Book) This standard was designed to enable CD technology to be used with computers—and for storing huge amounts of data. Because error rate requirements for data are much more stringent than for music, the bits in a CD-ROM sector are allocated differently than for a musical performance. Whereas a CD-DA sector has 2352 bytes available for storing music in each sector, CD-ROM has only 2048, because 280 extra bits had to be allocated for error-detection and correction. CD-ROM actually does have a less stringent mode, known as mode 2 (in contrast to the mode 1 used for data). This makes 2336 bytes per sector available for use (at the cost of a considerable amount of error correcting).

CD-ROM/XA (Extended Architecture) (Yellow Book and some of the Green Book) This standard was designed to provide a more efficient and flexible storage method, but one that could be made back-compatible with earlier standards. In addition to providing a new, more flexible sector format, CD-ROM/XA uses a different digitization method and compresses the audio data—decompressing the audio on the fly if the audio should ever be needed. At its lowest scanning frequency and highest compression, a CD-ROM/XA disc can hold over nine hours of stereo music—compared to just under 1.25 hours for CD-DA. In addition, CD-ROM/XA uses a new sector format, which allows a file to be nested inside another. Even though it uses special hardware, CD-ROM/XA technology is back compatible with CD-DA and ordinary CD-ROM. (Fortunately, most CD drives available today include this extra hardware, so that these drives can read most kinds of CDs.) CD-ROM discs can hold up to 660 MBytes of data.

Photo-CD This disc format was created by Kodak to provide a way for customers to digitize their photos and to use them at work or home. The Photo-CD technology combines the XA standards with multisession technology. A session is a recording period. Originally, CD's could record only once, which meant that all data or pictures had to be recorded in a single session. With a multisession disc, on the other hand, a customer can have pictures recorded several times up to the disc's capacity.

a
b
c
d
e
f
g
h
i
j
k
l
m
n
o
p
q
r
s
t
u
v
w
x
y
z

CD-WO (Write Once) and CD-MO (Magneto-optical) (Orange Book) These are specifications for recordable CDs. CD-WO—also known as CD-WORM (Write once, read many)—is the older standard. It can create discs with capacities of 128 Mbytes, 650 Mbytes, or 6.5 GBytes, depending on the disc's size. CD-WO discs require a magneto-optical drive and are not compatible with CD-ROM technology. CD-MO discs can hold 128-, 230-, 600-, 650-, or 1300 MBytes, and they must also be read by a special magneto-optical drive. Unlike CD-WO, however, CD-MO discs can be recorded multiple times. Because of this, MO discs are also known as EO (erasable optical) discs.

CD-R (Recordable) (Orange Book) This is a variant of the WO standard. Unlike CD-WO, however, discs recorded using CD-R technology can be read on ordinary CD-ROM drives. Until recently, CD-R machines were much too expensive for personal use; this has begun to change, and such devices are becoming very popular for business use. Discs for use in a CD-R drive are distinguished by their gold surface, as opposed to the silvery surface of a commercially produced disc. One reason for this is that CD-R discs are created using a somewhat different process than commercial CDs. Instead of burning pits into the surface, the recording laser in a CD-R drive simply changes the optical properties of an organic paint in the disc's recording surface. This makes it possible to work with a much weaker laser. CD-R discs can hold up to 660 MBytes of information. These discs are, in essence, just ordinary CD-ROM discs produced by special means.

CD-I (Interactive) (Green Book) This standard allows branching based on interaction between the user and the material. CD-I drives connect to a television set. Any computing capabilities required to run the software are built into the drive. You cannot use or even read CD-I discs in ordinary CD-ROM drives. 3DO is a proprietary variant of the CD-I standard.

High density CD (Blue Book) This technology is still being developed. When perfected, this standard is expected to increase the capacity of a disc tenfold—to about 6.5 GBytes. Look for this technology in the next year or so.

Hybrid standards Several variants have been developed for special purposes or to make use of particular technology. In general, such discs require special hardware. Hybrids include CD+G, CD-MIDI, CD-EB, and CD-V. CD+G (for graphics) is basically an audio CD with additional information such as text or graphics. CD-MIDI (for Musical Instrument Digital Interface) is an audio disc with MIDI information. CD-EB (for Electronic Book) is special size and format that is used mainly to store reference materials. CD-V (for video) is an audio disc with video information recorded in analog form.

The laserdisc is actually a CD-V variant.

The logical structure of the material on a CD is defined in the ISO 9660 documents. These, in turn, are based on the earlier High Sierra specifications.

CDDI (Copper Distributed Data Interface)

A networking configuration that implements the FDDI architecture and protocols on unshielded twisted-pair (UTP) cable—that is, on electrical (rather than optical) cable. A related implementation is SDDI (shielded distributed data interface), which uses shielded twisted-pair (STP) cable. Also known as copper-stranded distributed data interface and as TPDDI (twisted-pair DDI).

SEE ALSO

FDDI (Fiber Distributed Data Interface)

CDFS (CD-ROM File System)

A file structure used for storing information on a compact disc. The file allocation table (FAT) system may not be efficient or even feasible for such a disc because of the large number of files the disc may contain.

CDMA (Code Division Multiple Access)

In cellular communications, CDMA is a proposed transmission method that uses special codes to fit up to ten times as much information into a channel. Each signal that comes in on a given frequency is "spread" using a different code. When the receiver decodes the received signals, only the signal with the appropriate spread will be meaningful; the other signals will be received as noise.

CDMA uses a soft-handoff when switching a transmission from one cell to another to ensure that no bits are lost in the transmission. In this type of handoff, both cells transmit the transitional bits at the same time and on the same frequency. This way, one of the transmissions will be within range of the receiver.

This method is not compatible with the TDMA (time division multiple access) method that was adopted as a standard in 1989.

BROADER CATEGORY

Cellular Communications

COMPARE

TDMA (Time Division Multiple Access)

CDPD (Cellular Digital Packet Data)

A cellular communications technology that sends digital data over unused cellular (voice) channels. CDPD data can be transmitted at 19.2 kbps, but only in service areas that support CDPD. Currently only a few dozen of the major service areas around the country provide direct CDPD support.

CDPD can be used as a mobile computing strategy to stay connected with the company network back at the office. Essentially, a mobile user needs a special CDPD modem and the appropriate software. The user gets an IP (Internet protocol) address, which makes it possible to communicate as well as to make use of Internet services.

Mobile users can remain connected even when they are not using their computers and even when they are outside the range of a cell that supports CDPD. The CDPD specifications support a "sleep" mode for the computer. The network signals periodically to sleeping devices, and a device will "wake" if the signal includes the device's name or address. The monitoring for each device is done by the MDIS (mobile data intermediate system).

Similarly, the MDIS allows a user to remain connected even beyond areas that support CDPD through a technology known as switched CDPD. If the user is outside a service area with CDPD capabilities when called, the MDIS opens a circuit-switched connection over the channel. The connection is circuit-switched as far as the cellular network is concerned, but is essentially packet-switched as far as the device is concerned. This is because the MDIS closes the connection whenever there is silence, and reopens it whenever there is activity.

CDPD supports data compression and encryption. This cuts down on transmission times (and costs) and also helps keep snoopers from getting access to the data. In the CDPD specification, the data are first compressed and then encrypted.

The CDPD specification is being formulated under the auspices of the CDPD Forum, which you can contact at info@forum.cdpd.net or at 800-335-CDPD (2373).

SEE ALSO

Cellular Communications

▼
CD-ROM Drive

CD-ROM stands for compact-disc, read-only memory. A CD-ROM drive is a peripheral device for reading CDs, which have a huge capacity (660 megabytes).

Several features distinguish CD-ROM drives from each other:

- Transfer rate, which represents the amount of data that the drive can read from the disc in a second. Speeds are based on a base rate of 150 kbytes per second, which is known as a single-speed drive. Double speed and quad-speed drives can transfer 300 and 600 kbytes per second, respectively. Quad speed drives are the current norm, but 6x drives (not yet known as "hex speed") are also available.

- Access time, which represents the average time it takes to find a specified item of information on the disc. Currently, access times of less than 200 msec are considered standard.

- Compatibility with various CD standards, which indicates the types of CDs the drive can read. The CD (compact disc) article summarizes these. Briefly, drives should be able to read CD-XA (extended architecture) discs and should support multisession formats.

- Number of discs the drive can handle. Multidisc systems can hold 3, 6, or even 18 discs, and can switch between them within a few seconds. The drive can only read one disc at a time, however.

A CD-ROM drive may be connected to a network, making any available CDs shareable resources. With the appropriate server and drivers, users can share access to the disc currently loaded in the drive. A CD-ROM drive can be accessed just like any other volume, except that you can only read from it. If there are licensing restrictions on the use of a disc, it is essential that the server software be able to restrict simultaneous access to the licensed number of users.

Like any other type of hardware device, CD-ROM drives require hardware drivers to communicate. In addition, a special driver containing extensions is required. These extensions are specific to the operating system, such as DOS, OS/2, or NT, with which the CD-ROM is working. Microsoft has provided such a driver for MS DOS, called MSCDEX, which can be used with most CD-ROM drives. Some hardware manufacturers have also created their own proprietary drivers. If you are connecting a CD-ROM drive to a workstation, you will need to load both the driver's regular hardware driver and either MSCDEX or the manufacturer's own extensions driver.

If you want to make a CD-ROM drive available as a shared volume on a NetWare 3.12 or NetWare 4.*x* network, you do not load the MSCDEX driver. Instead, load the CD-ROM driver's regular hardware drivers and Novell's CDROM.NLM. This NLM manages the interface between the drive and NetWare and enables the CD-ROM device to be viewed and accessed by multiple users, just like any other NetWare volume.

Note that the drivers available for a given CD-ROM drive may or may not work with your system. Verify that the drive is compatible before you install it.

CD-ROM File System (CDFS)

SEE
CDFS (CD-ROM File System)

Cell

In communications or networking, a packet, or frame, of fixed size. In general, fast packet-switching technologies—such as ATM (Asynchronous Transfer Mode) and SDMS (Switched Multimegabit Digital Service)—use cells. Slower packet-switching technologies—such as X.25—are more likely to use variable-sized packets.

In cellular communications, a cell refers to a geographic area. Each cell has its own transmitter and receiver, through which signals can be distributed throughout the cell. Transmissions must be "handed off" from one cell to another when a mobile telephone or networking caller actually moves from one cell to another.

Cell, ATM

In the broadband ATM (Asynchronous Transfer Mode) network architecture, cell refers to a packet. ATM cells are each 53 octets, of which five octets are header and 48 are data.

SEE ALSO
ATM (Asynchronous Transfer Mode)

Cell Loss Priority

In an ATM network, a bit value that specifies whether a cell can be discarded if advisable; for example, if the network

a
b
c
d
e
f
g
h
i
j
k
l
m
n
o
p
q
r
s
t
u
v
w
x
y
z

gets too busy. A value of 1 indicates an expendable cell.

SEE ALSO

ATM (Asynchronous Transfer Mode)

Cellular Communications

Cellular communications is a wireless communications technology. The communications area is divided into smaller areas, called cells, and transmissions are passed from cell to cell until they reach their destinations. Each cell contains an antenna and transmission facilities to pick up signals from another cell or from a caller and to pass them on to an adjacent cell or to a callee within the cell. Cells can be anywhere from a few kilometers to 32 kilometers (20 miles) in diameter.

One cellular communications method, called CDPD (Cellular Digital Packet Data) transmits data over any cellular channels that are not being used. CDPD uses telephone (voice) channels, but can switch to a new frequency, if necessary, when a voice transmission begins in the cell being used. CDPD was developed to provide data communications in the cellular frequency range without interfering with voice calls.

CELP (Code Excited Linear Predictive Coding)

A variant of the LPC voice encoding algorithm. CELP can produce digitized voice output at 4,800 bits per second.

SEE ALSO

LPC (Linear Predictive Coding)

Central Office

The telephone switching station nearest to a customer (residential or business). Customers are connected directly to a CO, which connects them to other points in the telecommunications hierarchy. The CO provides services such as switching, dial tone, private lines, and centrex.

Central Processing

Central processing, also known as centralized processing, is a network configuration in which a single server processes tasks for multiple stations, all of which can communicate with the server. In such a setup, the nodes must share the computing power of the central processor. One consequence is that the more tasks, the slower things get done.

Central processing can be compared with distributed processing, in which tasks are performed by specialized nodes somewhere on a network. A station that needs something done sends a request onto the network. The server responsible for the service takes on the task, does it, and returns the results to the station. The client station need never know who actually did the work.

CERT (Computer Emergency Response Team)

In the Internet community, CERT is a group formed in 1988 (by DARPA) to help respond to, and deal with security problems that may arise on the Internet. The group also provides Internet administrators with information and assistance to help avoid security problems.

Tools and documents related to network security are available through Anonymous FTP from CERT's database in cert.org. See the Protocol, FTP article for more information.

BROADER CATEGORY

Network Security

CFB (Cipher Feedback)

An operating mode for the DES.

SEE

DES (Data Encryption Standard)

CGI (Common Gateway Interface)

An interface specification that defines the rules of communication between information servers, such as HTTP (Hypertext Transport Protocol) servers on the World Wide Web and gateway programs. More specifically, the CGI is used when such a server needs to pass a user request to a gateway program. Being able to pass work off to the gateway program helps take some of the workload off the server.

The gateway program is generally designed to provide a mechanism for getting input from a user—for example, so an authorized user can complete an authentication form in order to get access to restricted areas. Among other things, the CGI specifications define the mechanisms by which information can pass from the server to the gateway program and back.

The CGI specifications, along with many of the other specifications related to HTTP environments, are still undergoing revisions.

PRIMARY SOURCES

You can find the current form of the CGI specifications at

http://hoohoo.ncsa.uiuc.edu.cgi/ overview.html

Channel

A channel is a physical or logical path for a signal transmission. Two particularly important channels in networking are the communications channel and the disk channel.

A communications channel is a path through which data or voice can be transmitted; for example, in a network or a telephone call. In telecommunications, a single cable may be able to provide multiple channels.

A disk channel, in a hard-disk configuration, consists of the components that connect a hard disk drive to an operating environment, such as DOS, OS/2, NetWare, or VINES. These components include cables and a hard disk adapter or controller. A single channel can accommodate multiple hard disks. A computer may have multiple disk channels.

COMPARE

Circuit

Channel Bank

A device that multiplexes low-speed signals into a single high-speed signal.

Character

A byte with an identity. A group of bits, usually, seven or eight bits, that represents a single letter, digit, special symbol, or control code in an encoding scheme, such as ASCII or EBCDIC.

Checksum

Checksum is a simple error-detection strategy that computes a running total based on the byte values transmitted in a packet, and then applies a simple operation to compute the checksum value.

Checksums are very fast and easy to implement, and they can detect about 99.6 percent of errors in a packet. This reliability level is acceptable for most simple communications situations, but is less reliable than the more sophisticated CRC (Cyclical Redundancy Check) calculations, which have an accuracy of more than 99.9 percent.

The receiver compares the checksums computed by the sender and by the receiver. If they match, the receiver assumes the transmission was error-free. If they do not match, there was an error.

BROADER CATEGORY
Error Detection and Correction

COMPARE
CRC (Cyclical Redundancy Check); Parity

Chromatic Dispersion

In a fiber-optic transmission, the dispersion of a light signal because of the different propagation speeds of the light at different wavelengths; also known as material dispersion. The wavelengths around which dispersion is minimal, such as those around 1300 or 830 nanometers, are commonly used for signaling.

CHRP (Common Hardware Reference Platform)

A set of specifications for PowerPC systems. CHRP is being developed by Apple, IBM, and Motorola, and is designed to enable such a machine to run multiple operating systems and cross-platform applications.

While specifications have not been finalized, a minimum machine will have at least 8 MB of RAM and a 1 MB cache; CHRP machines will use the PowerPC 604 or later chip, and will support the PCI (Peripheral Component Interconnect) bus standard. CHRP machines will support at least the following environments:

- AIX (IBM's UNIX port)
- IBM OS/2 for PowerPC
- Mac OS (Apple's new Macintosh operating system)
- Novell NetWare
- Solaris (from SunSoft)
- Microsoft Windows NT

CICS (Customer Information Control System)

A terminal that provides transaction processing capabilities for IBM mainframes. CICS supports the SNA (Systems Network Architecture).

CIDR (Classless Interdomain Routing)

CIDR is a routing strategy that was developed as a partial solution to two difficulties that have developed as the number of networks connected to the Internet has grown very large. One problem was that routers had to deal with too many network addresses and were choking on their routing tables. The second problem was that the supply of Class B network addresses was being used up too quickly. Class B networks can have up to 65,536 hosts, but there can be only 16,384 Class B network addresses. This address class (see **IP Address** for a more detailed discussion) is useful for companies or organizations that have large networks with thousands of hosts for each network. While there are many companies with a few thousand hosts on their networks, there are few that have anywhere near 65,000.

Because of the way address classes are defined, this situation leads to a lot of potential addresses being wasted. The next address class—C—supports networks with 256 or fewer hosts. There can be more than 2 million Class C addresses. So, whereas Class B address spaces are too big, those for Class C are somewhat small for many businesses and organizations. When a mid-size company asks for an Internet address, it must be given either a Class B address from a dwindling supply or several (perhaps several dozen) Class C addresses. For example, a company with just over 8,000 hosts would need 32 Class C addresses. In contrast, by taking a Class B address, it would waste more than 55,000 potential addresses.

CIDR is designed to make a happy medium possible by assigning consecutive Class C addresses to organizations or corporations that have more than 256 machines, but that may not be large enough to merit a Class B address. CIDR takes advantage of the assignment scheme and treats the cluster

of Class C networks as belonging to the same "supernetwork"—as indicated by their common value in the higher order address bits (known as the *prefix* bits in this context). By routing just on the (fewer) higher-order bits, routers can fulfill their functions without having to store all the networks to which they are routing.

For CIDR to be successful, several things are required:

- The internal and external gateway protocols need to be able to represent the "supernetwork cluster" groupings. Earlier gateway protocols (such as BGP-3, IGRP, and RIP-1) cannot do this; newer versions (such as BGP-4, EIGRP, IS-IS, OSPF, and RIP-2) can. The protocol situation is in transition because newer protocols are, in some cases, just becoming available.

- Class C addresses must be assigned consecutively, as assumed in the CIDR strategy. While this can be done easily in some areas, it's much more difficult in others. One important and sticky issue is how to deal with address owners who move, as such a move could entail a switch in providers, which would undoubtedly lead to routing changes. If the address that's moving happens to be in the middle of a "supernetwork," the abbreviated addressing scheme falls apart.

- An effective strategy must be worked out for assigning addresses. Two possible basic approaches are *provider-based* and *geographically based*. In the former, networks that share a provider

a
b
c
d
e
f
g
h
i
j
k
l
m
n
o
p
q
r
s
t
u
v
w
x
y
z

get addresses close to each other, regardless of whether these networks are physically near each other. The geographically based approach would assign addresses within a block to networks in the same geographical area. The current Internet is closer to the provider-based variant.

Cipher Block Chaining (CBC)

An operating mode for the DES.

SEE
DES (Data Encryption Standard)

Cipher Feedback (CFB)

An operating mode for the DES.

SEE
DES (Data Encryption Standard)

Ciphertext

Text that has been encrypted to make it unintelligible to anyone who lacks essential information about the encryption scheme. The required information is generally a specific value, known as the encryption (or decryption) key. Conventional-, public-, or private-key encryption strategies may be used to create ciphertext.

SEE ALSO
Plaintext

CIR (Committed Information Rate)

In frame-relay networks, a bandwidth, or information rate, that represents the average level for a user. If the user's network activity exceeds this rate, the frame-relay controller

will mark the user's extra packets to indicate that they can be discarded if necessary.

Circuit

A closed path through which electricity can flow. The term is also used to refer to components (such as chips) capable of creating such a path.

CIS (CompuServe Information Service)

CIS, better known simply as CompuServe, is the oldest of the major online services, and is still the largest, although America Online, or AOL, is gaining rapidly. CompuServe supports DOS, Windows, and Macintosh users. It offers the usual forums, electronic mail, financial and news services, and software to download or use online. For a flat monthly fee, users have unlimited access to basic services; special services incur additional fees. For a fee, users can also get access to the Internet.

SEE ALSO
AOL (America Online); Prodigy

FOR INFORMATION
Call (800) 848-8199

CISC (Complex Instruction Set Computing)

CISC is a processor design strategy that provides the processor with a relatively large number of basic instructions, many of which are complex but very powerful. These complex instructions may require several clock cycles to complete, which can slow down overall processing.

CISC is in contrast to the RISC (reduced instruction set computing) design strategy. A RISC chip uses a small number of simple operations to do its work. These simple operations are optimized for speed, and most require only a single clock cycle for completion.

CIX (Commercial Internet Exchange)

CIX is an association of domestic Internet access providers that provides connection points between commercial traffic and the Internet. The CIX was formed to route commercial traffic back when such traffic was not allowed according to the AUP (acceptable use policy) for the Internet. CIX members agree to carry each others' traffic when requested. Contact Gopher or Web servers at cix.org for more information about CIX.

Cladding

In fiber-optic cable, the material (usually plastic or glass) surrounding the fiber core. The cladding has a lower index of refraction than the core, which means that light hitting the cladding will be reflected back into the core to continue its path along the cable.

SEE ALSO
Cable, Fiber-Optic

Clamping Time

In power protection, the amount of time needed for a surge protector to deal with a voltage spike or surge; that is, to bring the voltage within acceptable levels.

Class A Certification

An FCC certification for computer or other equipment intended for industrial, commercial, or office use, rather than for personal use at home. The Class A commercial certification is less restrictive than the Class B certification.

Class B Certification

An FCC certification for computer equipment, including PCs, laptops, and portables intended for use in the home rather than in a commercial setting. Class B certification is more restrictive than the commercial Class A certification.

Clearing Center (CC)

SEE
CC (Clearing Center)

CLID (Calling Line Identification)

In ISDN and some other telecommunications environments, a feature that includes the sender's identification number (such as telephone number) in the transmission so that the receiver knows who is calling. It is also known as ANI (automatic number identification) and caller ID.

Client

A client is a machine that makes requests of other machines (servers) in a network or that uses resources available through the servers.

For example, workstations are network clients because they use services from the

a b **c** d e f g h i j k l m n o p q r s t u v w x y z

server. As another example, a client application is an application that makes requests of other applications, on the same or on different machines, for services, information, or access to resources.

COMPARE

Server

SEE ALSO

Workstation

▼

Client-Based Application

An application that executes on the client machine (the workstation) in a network.

▼

Client/Server Computing

Client/server computing is a networking arrangement with the following characteristics:

- Intelligence, defined either as processing capabilities or available information, is distributed across multiple machines.

- Certain machines—the clients—can request services and information from other machines—the servers. For example, a server may have quick access to huge databases that can be searched on behalf of the client.

- The server does at least some of the processing for the client.

Applications capable of running in a client/server environment can be split into a front end that runs on the client and a back end that runs on the server. The front end provides the user with an interface for giving commands and making requests. The application's real work is done by the back end, which processes and carries out the user's commands.

Client/server computing allows for several types of relationships between the server and client, including the following:

- Stand-alone (non-networked) client applications which do not request access to server resources. For example, a local word processor might be a stand-alone client application.

- Applications that run on the client but request data from the server. For example, a spreadsheet program might run on a workstation and use files stored on the server.

- Programs where the physical search of records takes place on the server, while a much smaller program running on the client handles all user-interface functions. For example, a database application might run this way on the server and client.

- Programs that use server capabilities to share information between network users. For example, an electronic-mail system may use the server this way.

The figure "Client/server computing arrangements" illustrates these different arrangements.

SEE ALSO

Back End; Front End

CLIENT/SERVER COMPUTING ARRANGEMENTS

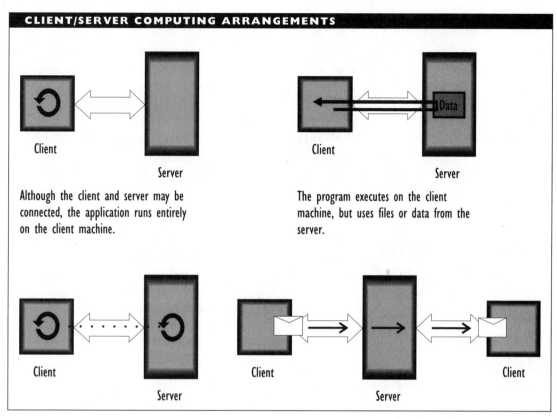

Client

Server

Although the client and server may be connected, the application runs entirely on the client machine.

Client

Server

The program executes on the client machine, but uses files or data from the server.

Client

Server

Client

Server

Client

▼
CLNS (Connectionless Mode Network Service)

In the OSI Reference Model, CLNS is a network-layer service in which data transmission can take place without a fixed connection between source and destination. Individual packets are independent, and they may reach the destination through different paths and in a mixed order. In this type of transmission service, each packet must carry its own destination address and information about the packet's relative position in the message.

CLNS is the most common operating mode for local-area networks (LANs). In contrast, for wide-area networks (WANs), CONS (connection-oriented network service) is more popular.

PRIMARY SOURCE
ISO document 8348

BROADER CATEGORY
Connectionless Service

COMPARE
Connection-Oriented Service

▼
Clock Speed

Activities carried out by and for the processor must all be carefully timed and coordinated. To make this possible, each processor

a b **c** d e f g h i j k l m n o p q r s t u v w x y z

has a clock associated with it. This clock serves as a timing reference by slicing time into very short intervals. The clock speed is defined as the number of such slices in a second.

Clock speed is expressed in millions of cycles per second (megahertz, or MHz). For example, the CPU in the original IBM had a clock speed of 4.77 MHz. This is painfully slow when compared to today's processors, with clock speeds that can be in the 100 MHz range.

CLP (Cell Loss Priority)

In an ATM network, a bit value that specifies whether a cell can be discarded if advisable; for example, if the network gets too busy. A value of 1 indicates an expendable cell.

SEE ALSO

ATM (Asynchronous Transfer Mode)

CLTS (Connectionless Transport Service)

In the OSI Reference Model, a transport-layer service that does not guarantee delivery, but makes a best effort, does error checking, and uses end-to-end addressing.

CLU (Command Line Utility)

In Novell's NetWare and in other operating and networking environments, a program that can be executed at the appropriate command-line prompt. Examples of command line utilities in NetWare include NCOPY and FLAG for manipulating files and file attributes, respectively.

Cluster

In a network, particularly in a mainframe-based network, a group of I/O (input/ouput) devices, such as terminals, computers, or printers, that share a common communication path to a host machine. Communications between the devices in a cluster and the host are generally managed by a cluster controller, such as IBM's 3274 controller.

Cluster Controller

A device that serves as an intermediary between a host machine, such as a mainframe, and a group (cluster) of I/O (input/ouput) devices, such as terminals, computers, or printers. The IBM 3274 is an example of such a device. This controller has been superseded by the 3174 establishment controller.

CMC (Common Mail Calls)

An API (Application Program Interface) developed by the X.400 API Association (XAPIA) to enable message-handling agents—for example, in an email system—to communicate with message stores, or post offices. The calls in the API are designed to be independent of hardware platforms, operating systems, email systems, and messaging protocols. The API is also referred to as common messaging calls.

CMIP (Common Management Information Protocol)

A network management protocol for the OSI Reference Model. CMIP, pronounced "see-mip," defines how management information can be communicated between stations. CMIP is functionally comparable to the older, and arguably more widely used, SNMP (Simple Network Management Protocol).

SEE ALSO

Network Management

CMIPDU (Common Management Information Protocol Data Unit)

In the OSI network management model, a packet that conforms to the CMIP. The packet's contents depend on the requests from a CMISE, which relies on the CMIP to deliver the user's requests and to return with answers from the appropriate application or agent.

SEE ALSO

CMISE (Common Management Information Service Element); Network Management

CMIPM (Common Management Information Protocol Machine)

In the OSI network management model, software that accepts operations from a CMISE user and initiates the actions needed to respond and sends valid CMIPDUs (CMIP packets) to a CMISE user.

SEE ALSO

CMISE; Network Management

CMIS (Common Management Information Service)

In the OSI network management model, a standard for network monitoring and

control services. CMIS, pronounced "see-miss," is documented in CCITT recommendation X.710 and ISO document 9595.

SEE ALSO

CMISE; Network Management

CMISE (Common Management Information Service Element)

In the OSI network management model, a CMISE is an entity that provides network management and control services. Seven types of CMISEs, pronounced "see-mize," are specified:

- Event report
- Get
- Cancel get
- Set
- Action
- Delete
- Create

The services provided by CMISEs are used by the system management functions (SMFs). The SMFs are in turn used to carry out the tasks specified for the five system management functional areas (SMFAs) defined in the OSI network management model. The figure "Major components in the ISO-OSI network management model" shows this relationship.

SEE ALSO

Network Management

a
b
c
d
e
f
g
h
i
j
k
l
m
n
o
p
q
r
s
t
u
v
w
x
y
z

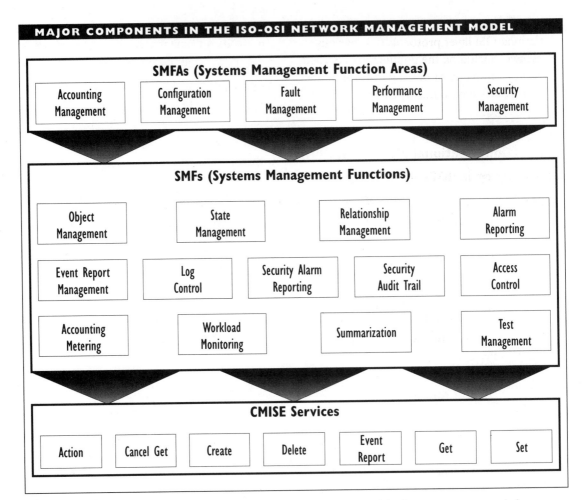

MAJOR COMPONENTS IN THE ISO-OSI NETWORK MANAGEMENT MODEL

SMFAs (Systems Management Function Areas)

| Accounting Management | Configuration Management | Fault Management | Performance Management | Security Management |

SMFs (Systems Management Functions)

Object Management	State Management	Relationship Management	Alarm Reporting
Event Report Management	Log Control	Security Alarm Reporting	Security Audit Trail	Access Control
Accounting Metering	Workload Monitoring	Summarization	Test Management

CMISE Services

| Action | Cancel Get | Create | Delete | Event Report | Get | Set |

CMOS (Complementary Metal-Oxide Semiconductor)

CMOS, pronounced "see-moss," is a logic family for digital circuits. CMOS logic is not exceptionally fast, but it has relatively low power consumption, which makes it ideal for such items as battery-powered PCs.

CMOS is used for RAM chips that need to retain information, such as configuration data or date and time information. The values stored in these RAM chips are maintained by battery power, and they are generally not accessible to the operating system.

COMPARE
TTL (Transistor-Transistor Logic)

CMOT (Common Management Information Services and Protocol Over TCP/IP)

An effort to implement the OSI framework's CMIS and CMIP services on the Internet community's TCP/IP protocol suite, rather than on OSI layer protocols. For various reasons, including the popularity of SNMP and the difficulty of porting the OSI model to a TCP/IP environment, CMOT was never completed.

CMS (Conversational Monitor System)

A subsystem in IBM's SNA.

SEE

SNA (Systems Network Architecture)

CN (Common Name)

In the NetWare Directory Services (NDS) for Novell's NetWare 4.*x*, a name associated with a leaf object in the NDS Directory tree. For a user object, this would be the user's login name.

CNA (Certified NetWare Administrator)

A title given to people who successfully complete Novell-authorized courses on administering a NetWare network and/or pass a comprehensive exam about this topic. The CNA program is designed for people who are responsible for the day-to-day operations and high-level maintenance of their networks. CNAs must know how to add and remove users, grant user rights, load applications, do backups and other maintenance tasks, and maintain network security. Separate tests are required and degrees are offered for NetWare 2.2, 3.11, and 4.*x* environments.

CNAs are discussed in *The CNA Study Guide* (James Chellis, et al. Network Press, 1996).

SEE ALSO

CNE; CNI; ECNE

CNE (Certified NetWare Engineer)

A title given to people who successfully complete a whole series of Novell-authorized courses on becoming technicians or consultants for NetWare networks and/or pass a comprehensive exam about this topic. The CNE program is designed for people who are responsible for designing and installing NetWare networks, and also for the low-level maintenance tasks such as diagnostics, troubleshooting hardware or networking software, and so forth. Separate tracks are available for NetWare 2.2, 3.11, and 4.*x*. In addition to demonstrating mastery of basic and advanced topics related to NetWare, successful CNE candidates must demonstrate mastery of networking technology and operating system concepts.

SEE ALSO

CNA; CNI; ECNE

CNI (Certified NetWare Instructor)

A title given to people who successfully complete a comprehensive and rigorous training program in order to teach Novell courses. Candidates who are accepted for the CNI program must demonstrate a proficiency in their area of specialization by attending each course they want to teach and passing the course test at a more stringent level than is required of ordinary (CNA or CNE) students.

As a final requirement, candidates must pass an IPE (instructor performance evaluation). Among other things, candidates must

a b **c** d e f g h i j k l m n o p q r s t u v w x y z

set up a classroom or lab, and then teach a 45- to 60-minute section of the course for which the candidate wants to become an instructor. Candidates do not know which section they will be asked to teach until the day before their evaluation.

SEE ALSO

CNA; CNE; ECNE

CO (Central Office)

The telephone switching station nearest to a customer (residential or business). Customers are connected directly to a CO, which connects them to other points in the telecommunications hierarchy. The CO provides services such as switching, dial tone, private lines, and centrex.

Coax Booster

A device that strengthens the signal in a coaxial cable, thereby making it possible to run a cable over greater distances.

COCF (Connection-Oriented Convergence Function)

In the DQDB (Distributed Queue Dual-Bus) network architecture, a function that prepares data coming from or going to a connection-oriented service. The service first establishes a fixed, but temporary, connection, then transmits the data, and finally breaks the connection.

Codec

A codec is a device for converting analog signals to digital form. For example, codecs are used in digital telephone systems, such as ISDN (Integrated Services Digital Network), so that voice signals can be transmitted over digital lines. The name is a contraction of coder/decoder.

To make the conversion, a codec must use some type of signal-sampling technique. These samples are converted into discrete signals for transmission across the digital lines.

The most common conversion method is PAM (pulse amplitude modulation), in which samples of the analog signal's amplitude are converted into discrete signals whose amplitude corresponds to the analog signal's amplitude at sampling time. To reproduce the original signal accurately, PAM devices must sample the analog signal at a rate at least twice the frequency's signal. For example, for voice signals, which have a 4 kilohertz bandwidth, the PAM device must sample at least 8,000 times.

The discrete amplitude value is modulated one more time to make it compatible with the digital circuits. PCM (pulse code modulation) converts the PAM signals into a stream of binary values. To make this conversion, the range of amplitudes in a PAM signal is divided into 128 discrete quantizing levels.

To represent 128 possible amplitude values, seven bits are needed for each PAM signal. This means that PCM must work at 56 kilobits per second (kbps) or faster. Digital channels in North America provide a 64 kbps capacity, which means 8 kbps can be used for administrative and system control purposes.

BROADER CATEGORY

Digital Communication

SEE ALSO

Modulation

Code Excited Linear Predictive Coding (CELP)

SEE

CELP (Code Excited Linear Predictive Coding)

Coding

Coding is a general term for a representation, usually by means of a predefined syntax or language. For example, in the OSI Reference Model, an application layer packet, or protocol data unit (APDU), will have a coding that depends on the application involved.

ASCII and EBCDIC are two widely used codings. Abstract Syntax Notation One (ASN.1) coding is used in many contexts that adhere to the OSI Reference Model, such as in network management tasks.

In a communications setting, several types of coding are distinguished, and each type may occur dozens of times:

Source: The coding used by the application that initiates a transmission. That application must be running on an end system—that is, on a network node capable of using all seven layers in the OSI Reference Model.

Target: The coding used by the application that receives a transmission. The receiving application must be running on an end system.

Transfer: A coding used by the applications at both ends of the connection or by the translation program. Transfer coding may be needed if the source and target codings are different.

SEE ALSO

ASCII; ASN.1; EBCDIC

Cold Boot Loader

In Novell's NetWare, a program on the file server's hard disk that will automatically load NetWare after a cold boot.

Collision Detection and Avoidance

In an Ethernet network, a collision is the simultaneous presence of signals from two nodes on the network. A collision can occur when two nodes each think the network is idle and both start transmitting at the same time. Both packets involved in a collision are broken into fragments and must be retransmitted.

Collision Detection

To detect a collision, nodes check the DC voltage level on the line. A voltage level two or more times as high as the expected level indicates a collision, since this means there are multiple signals traveling along the wires at the same time. Collision detection in broadband networks involves a separate bandwidth for collision detection and is somewhat more complex, since there may not be any DC voltage to test.

In the CSMA/CD (carrier sense multiple access/collision detection) media-access method, for example, collision detection involves monitoring the transmission line for

a
b
c
d
e
f
g
h
i
j
k
l
m
n
o
p
q
r
s
t
u
v
w
x
y
z

special signals that indicate that two packets were sent onto the network at the same time and have collided. When this happens, special actions are taken (as described in the CSMA/CD article).

Collision Avoidance

To avoid collisions, nodes can send special signals that indicate a line is being used for a transmission. For example, the CSMA/CD media-access method uses RTS (Ready To Send) and CTS (Clear To Send) signals before sending a frame onto the network. A node transmits only after the node has requested access to the line and been granted access. Other nodes will be aware of the RTS/CTS transmission and will not try to transmit at the same time.

BROADER CATEGORIES
CSMA/CD (Carrier Sense Multiple Access/Collision Detect); Ethernet

COM (Common Object Model)

COM is an object-oriented, open architecture that is intended to allow client/server applications to communicate with each other in a transparent manner, even if these applications are running on different platforms. Objects can also be distributed over different platforms.

The COM model is a joint project of Microsoft and Digital Equipment Corporation (DEC). Their immediate goal is to allow networks or machines that use Microsoft's Object Linking and Embedding (OLE) technology to communicate transparently with networks or machines that use DEC's ObjectBroker technology.

To provide the cross-platform capabilities, COM uses OLE COM, a protocol based on the DCE/RPC (Distributed Computing Environment/Remote Procedure Call) protocol. Once implemented, COM will allow machines running Microsoft Windows, Windows NT, and Macintosh environments to communicate in a transparent manner with machines running DEC's OpenVMS operating system or any of several UNIX implementations.

COMPARE
ObjectBroker; OLE (Object Linking and Embedding)

COM1, COM2, COMx

On a PC, the names associated with successive serial ports. Devices that might be connected to such a port include modems, pointer devices, and some printers.

COMPARE
LPT1

Combiner

A combiner is a fiber-optic coupler (optical signal splitter and redirector) that combines multiple incoming signals into a single outgoing signal.

A particular type of combiner is an essential element for WDM (wavelength division multiplexing), in which signals from multiple channels are sent over the same output channel. The input channels are all transmitting at different wavelengths, and the coupler's job is to combine the signals in the proper manner. A combiner is sometimes known as a combiner coupler.

SEE ALSO

Coupler

Command Line Utility (CLU)

SEE

CLU (Command Line Utility)

Commercial Internet Exchange (CIX)

SEE

CIX (Commercial Internet Exchange)

Committed Information Rate (CIR)

SEE

CIR (Committed Information Rate)

Common Carrier

A private company, such as a telephone company, that supplies any of various communications services (telephone, telegraph, Teletex, and so on) to the public.

Common Mail Calls (CMC)

SEE

CMC (Common Mail Calls)

Common Name (CN)

SEE

CN (Common Name)

Common Programming Interface for Communications (CPIC)

SEE

CPIC (Common Programming Interface for Communications)

Common User Access (CUA)

SEE

CUA (Common User Access)

Communicating Application Specification (CAS)

SEE

CAS (Communicating Application Specification)

Communication, Asynchronous

Asynchronous communications are those in which a transmission may take place at a variable rate, and in which byte boundaries are indicated by a combination of start and stop bits. Transmission elements are distinguished by these special bits. This is in contrast to synchronous communication, in which transmission elements are identified by reference to a clock or other timing mechanism.

Examples of asynchronous processes include voice or data transmissions (commonly using modems), terminal-host communications, and file transfer. Modems, terminals, pointer devices, and printers are all devices that use asynchronous communications.

In asynchronous communication, the occurrence of the special start bit indicates that a byte is about to be transmitted. The duration of the start bit indicates the length of a bit interval (duration of a single signal value), which represents the speed at which that byte is going to be transmitted. In a sense, asynchronous transmissions synchronize for each byte.

a
b
c
d
e
f
g
h
i
j
k
l
m
n
o
p
q
r
s
t
u
v
w
x
y
z

With respect to the communication, both sender and receiver need to agree on the number of start and stop bits, and also on whether a parity bit will be used. This information is necessary to identify the transmission elements. If a parity bit is used, knowing what kind of parity is operating will help interpret the transmission contents. Asynchronous transmissions are less efficient than synchronous (time-based) ones. For example, the start and stop bit around each byte represent 25 percent overhead for an asynchronous byte. Because of this lesser efficiency, asynchronous communications cannot attain the bandwidths possible with synchronous transmissions.

On the other hand, asynchronous transmissions are much more flexible, forgiving, and easier to correct than the faster moving synchronous transmissions.

SEE ALSO

Communication, Synchronous

Communication, Bisynchronous

In bisynchronous, or bisync, communication, a special (SYN) character is used to establish synchronization for an entire data block. Both sender and receiver must be synchronized. The receiver must acknowledge the receipt of each block with alternating ACK characters: ACK0 for one block, ACK1 for the next, ACK0 for the next, and so on. Two successive acknowledgments with the same ACK character indicate a transmission error.

Also known as BSC, bisynchronous communication is used in IBM mainframe environments. It is used primarily when transmitting data in EBCDIC format.

Communication Buffer

RAM set aside on a file server for temporarily holding packets until they can be processed by the server or sent onto the network. The RAM will be allocated as a number of buffers, each with a predetermined size. A communication buffer is also known as a routing buffer or packet receive buffer.

Communication Medium

The physical medium over which a communications signal travels. Currently, the most popular medium is cable. Wireless media, such as infrared wave, microwave, or radio wave, are also becoming more widely used.

Communication, Synchronous

Synchronous communications are those that depend on timing. In particular, synchronous transmissions are those that proceed at a constant rate, although this rate may change during different parts of a communication (or when the line quality changes).

In synchronous communications, transmission elements are identified by reference to either an external clock or self-clocking, signal-encoding scheme. This is in contrast to asynchronous communication, in which transmission elements are identified by special signal values (start and stop bits).

Synchronous communications can achieve very large bandwidths, eventually allowing speeds of over 100 Mbps. Unfortunately, as transmission rate increases, signal quality decreases, because each bit interval becomes extremely short.

External Clocks

When an external clock is used for synchronous communications, the duration of test bits are timed, and the resulting values are used as the bit-interval value. It is necessary to resynchronize the transmission occasionally to make sure that the parties involved do not drift apart in their timing. This is a real danger, because even tiny differences in timing can have a significant effect when millions of bits are transferred every second in a communication.

To avoid such a problem, many synchronous transmission methods insist that a signal must change at least once within a predetermined amount of time or within a given block size. For example, the B8ZS (bipolar with 8 zero substitution) signal-encoding scheme is based on a requirement that a transmission can never contain more than seven 0 bits in succession. Before that eighth consecutive 0, a 1 bit will be inserted.

Self-Clocking Transmissions

Self-clocking, signal-encoding schemes have a transition, such as a change in voltage or current, in the middle of each bit interval. A self-clocking encoding method changes the signal value within every bit interval to keep the two parties in synch during a transmission. This works because each party can recalibrate its timing if it notices a drift.

Self-clocking methods avoid the need to insert extra bits (as in the B8ZS encoding scheme). On the other hand, a self-clocking machine needs a clock at least twice as fast as the transmission speed in order to accomplish the signal changes within each bit interval. Expressed differently, this means you will not be able to transmit any faster than at half the clock speed on a machine. (You can effectively increase the speed by compressing files before transmission, thereby sending more information than the bit rate would indicate.)

COMPARE
Communication, Asynchronous

Compatibility

Compatibility is the ability of one device or program to work with another. Compatibility is sometimes built into the product; in other cases, the compatibility is achieved through the use of drivers or filters.

For example, to ensure that a network interface card will work with a network software package, drivers are used. Rather than creating drivers for every adapter, a more common strategy is to create a more or less generic driver interface, and then try to get developers to adapt the interface for their products to this generic interface. Vendors may also adapt the generic drivers to handle the special features of particular products.

CompuServe

SEE
CIS (CompuServe Information Services)

Computer

Networks consist of computers, along with some means for connecting the computers and enabling them to communicate with each other. The figure "Context of computers in networks" shows the role of computers.

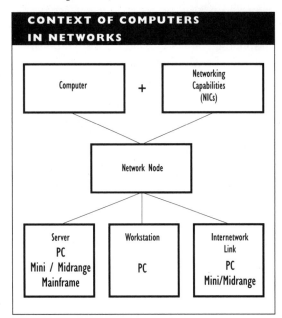

CONTEXT OF COMPUTERS IN NETWORKS

The individual computers that make up a network are known as nodes, or stations. Nodes can be PCs, minicomputers, or even mainframes.

The term PC can refer to any type of personal computer, but there are differences between, for example, a network using IBM PC and compatible machines and one using Macintoshes. Both of these networks will, in turn, differ somewhat from a network that uses Sun workstations.

Almost all PC-class machines are based on one of three processor families: the Intel $80x86$ family (including the analogous processors from third-party manufacturers and Pentium, the newest incarnation from Intel), the Motorola $680x0$ family (used in the

Macintosh and some higher end workstations), and RISC (reduced instruction set computing) chips (used in special-purpose machines, number crunchers, and high-end workstations but starting to migrate down to lower-level machines).

Unless otherwise stated, PC will refer to the IBM PC and compatible computers (as well as to IBM's own Micro Channel Architecture line of computers) based on the Intel architecture. Where the discussion concerns Macintoshes or Sun machines, this will be mentioned.

PCs

PCs can be servers, workstations, or internetwork links in a network. The whole gamut of PCs can be used in a network. You can even attach a palmtop computer to a network. Not all PCs can serve all functions in a network, however.

To work in a network, PCs need a special network interface card (NIC), or adapter. This component provides the appropriate chips and circuitry for translating commands or data into packets and then into electrical signals to be sent over the network. At the receiving end, the NIC captures the received transmission, and again translates, but this time from the electrical format used on the network to a format the networking software understands.

A node may function as a workstation, a server, or an internetwork link (which serves to connect two or more networks). In certain combinations, a computer can serve more than one of these functions at a time.

Server

A server provides access to resources or services, such as files, printers, fax machines, electronic mail, and so on. Servers may be distinguished by the elements to which they control access. For example, you will see references to file servers, print servers, fax servers, and communications servers. A file server generally runs the network, providing access to programs and data, and sometimes also to peripherals.

A network need not have a server. If each node is a workstation, then each node is accessible to other nodes. Networks in which all nodes are workstations are known as distributed, peer-to-peer, or simply peer networks. Artisoft's LANtastic, Novell's NetWare Lite, and Microsoft's Windows for Workgroups are examples of peer-to-peer network packages.

If there is a server, it may be dedicated or nondedicated. A dedicated server cannot be used as a workstation. Networks with a dedicated server are known as centralized networks or server-based networks.

Workstation

A workstation requests access to files, printers, and so on, from a server. Actually, the user simply requests such services as if they were available on the workstation itself. Special shell and redirection software will route the request to the server. Users can also use a workstation for non-network activity.

There is no inherent hardware difference between a server and a workstation. Practical performance considerations, however, dictate that servers should be faster, more powerful machines. In practice, workstations may be any level PC, with 80286 and 80386 being the most common. Servers are almost always 80386 or 80486 machines. In fact, some network operating systems require at least an 80386 processor for the server.

A special class of machines, called diskless workstations, can be used only as workstations on a network. These workstations have their boot instructions in ROM, boot to the network, and can be used only to do work on the network. Since they do not have disk drives, you cannot download any data to the workstations or upload data to the network.

Internetwork Link

An internetwork link serves to connect two networks to each other. A PC may serve as an internetwork link and as a server or workstation at the same time. Examples of internetwork links include bridges, routers, brouters, and gateways.

Non-PC

Networks can include minicomputers, such as the DEC VAX or the IBM AS/400 series, or mainframes, such as the IBM System/370 and System/390 families (although this is more common in older networks and in networks run by or from MIS departments).

Many networks, particularly those in large organizations, include minicomputers and mainframes. For example, it is not uncommon to see a minicomputer serving as a front-end processor (FEP) for a mainframe, to handle incoming transmissions from PCs or terminals.

a
b
c
d
e
f
g
h
i
j
k
l
m
n
o
p
q
r
s
t
u
v
w
x
y
z

Mainframe- and PC-based networks are very different worlds from each other, with different character codes, protocols, frame formats, and operating environments. Despite (or perhaps because of) the obstacles that have always existed to make PC-mainframe communication such a challenge, there are a frightening number of possible configurations in which a PC can talk to a mainframe or minicomputer. IBM alone has dozens of hardware and software products (such as the SNA architecture and the IBM Data Connector) for helping computers of various sizes communicate with each other.

BROADER CATEGORY
Hardware Network

Computer-Based Message System (CBMS)

An older term for a message handling system or for electronic mail.

Computer Business Manufacturers Association (CBEMA)

SEE
CBEMA (Computer Business Manufacturers Association)

Computer-to-PBX Interface (CPI)

SEE
CPI (Computer-to-PBX Interface)

Concentrator

Most generally, in the area of communications, a concentrator is a device that can take multiple input channels and send their contents to fewer output channels. In addition to these multiplexing capabilities, a concentrator can store data until an output channel becomes available.

In networking hardware, a concentrator is essentially an upscale hub. The terms hub and concentrator are often used interchangeably, and the term wiring center is often used to refer to either a hub or a concentrator.

As is the case for a hub, the main function of a concentrator is to serve as a termination point for cable running from individual nodes (stations) in a network. The cable connects to the network or to another wiring center.

A concentrator may have multiple boards or boxes mounted on a rack. Each board is essentially a hub—a wiring center for a single network's nodes. Such boards generally include LEDs (light-emitting diodes) to indicate the status of each port on the board.

The size and complexity of the concentrator depends on the number of boards that have been installed. Partly because of their versatility and power, high-end concentrators can cost as much as $50,000.

Hubs and concentrators can be viewed as the ends of a continuum. Hub manufacturers are likely to include concentrators in their product lines.

Concentrator Operation

Concentrators can be much more versatile than hubs in what they can connect. For example, a concentrator might connect network elements (or networks) with different cabling and perhaps even with different architectures.

Note that the concentrator might not necessarily be connecting these different architectures to each other. Rather, the concentrator may be serving as a wiring conduit for multiple (independent) networks simultaneously; for example, for networks running in different departments in a company. It is possible to include bridging or routing capabilities in the concentrator. With bridging or routing, a concentrator can connect different architectures to each other.

Concentrators are generally located in a wiring closet, which serves as a wire-collection location for a predefined area. In the closet, the concentrator may be connected to another concentrator, to an intermediate distribution frame (IDF), to a main distribution frame (MDF), or perhaps to a telephone line. IDFs collect the wiring from a limited area (such as a floor) and feed this to the MDF for the building. The MDF connects the building to the outside electrical world.

Concentrator Features

All concentrators provide connectivity, serving as wiring centers. Many concentrators also have their own processor and can serve as network activity monitors. Concentrators with processors save performance and other data in a management information base (MIB). This information can be used by network management software to fine-tune the network.

A board in the concentrator may have its own processor for doing its work. In such a case, the board is using the concentrator as a convenient location to use as a base of operations.

BROADER CATEGORY
Intranetwork Link

SEE ALSO
Hub; Wiring Center

Conductor

Any material (for example, copper wire) that can carry electrical current. Compare conductor with semiconductor or insulator.

SEE ALSO
Cable

CONFIG.SYS

In DOS and OS/2 environments, CONFIG.SYS is a file that contains information about various types of configuration and driver settings. For example, CONFIG.SYS may include information about drivers and memory managers that are loaded into memory. The OS/2 configuration file can be quite long and complex.

Configuration Management

Configuration management is one of five OSI network management domains specified by the ISO and CCITT. Configuration management is concerned with the following:

- Determining and identifying the objects on the network and their attributes

- Determining states, settings, and other information about these objects

- Storing this information for later retrieval or modification

a b **c** d e f g h i j k l m n o p q r s t u v w x y z

- Reporting this information if requested by an appropriate and authorized process or user

- Modifying the settings for objects, if necessary

- Topology management, which involves managing the connections and relationships among the objects

- Starting up and shutting down network operations

Identifying Objects and Determining Settings

The first task for configuration management is to identify objects such as stations, bridges, routers, and even circuits. Depending on the sophistication of the management package, this process may be automatic or it may be done manually.

Each object will have configuration states and other information associated with it. For example, a node might have the following settings:

- Interface settings, such as speed, parity, jumper settings, and so on

- Model and vendor information, including serial number, operating system, memory and storage, hardware address, and so on

- Miscellaneous details, such as installed drivers and peripherals, maintenance and testing schedules, and so on

Similarly, leased lines or circuits will have information such as identification number, vendor (or leaser), speeds, and so on.

Operational States for an Object

Within the OSI model, four operational states are defined for an object:

Active: The object is available and in use, but has the capacity to accept services or requests.

Busy: The object is available and in use, but currently is not able to deal with any more requests.

Disabled: The object is not available.

Enabled: The object is operational and available, but not currently in use.

Such values must be determined—manually or automatically—and stored for easy access and updating (for example, in a relational database). If stored in a database, the information will generally be accessed using some type of query language. SQL (Structured Query Language) has become a standard means for accessing object operational state information. The configuration management capabilities include being able to report this information upon request.

Modifying Settings and States

The values and states associated with network objects may be changed. For example, they will be changed when trying to communicate with a network object, correct a fault, or improve performance. Certain values (for example, state information) may be changed automatically when an action is begun on the network. Other values may need to be changed by the system administrator.

BROADER CATEGORY
Network Management

SEE ALSO

Accounting Management; Fault Management; Performance Management; Security Management

Configuration, Network

Network configuration consists of the equipment, connections, and settings in effect for a network at a particular time. Equipment generally refers to hardware (computers, peripherals, boards, cables, and connectors), but may also include software under certain circumstances.

Because compatibility and interoperability can sometimes be elusive in the networking world, a system administrator needs to know considerable detail about the equipment on the network. This information may include specific model numbers, memory specifications, enhancements, and so on. This information must be updated scrupulously or conflicts may occur. Fortunately, most networking systems include a utility for recording configuration information and for updating it as the network changes.

The current settings for each piece of equipment should also be recorded as part of the configuration information. When deciding on specific settings, it is important to avoid conflicts. A conflict can arise, for example, because two boards each wanted to use the same memory location or interrupt line. Again, most network operating systems include a utility to help keep this information organized and to spot potential conflicts before they are made official.

Conformance Requirements

The set of requirements a device or implementation must satisfy in order to be regarded as conforming to a particular specification or recommendation.

Congestion

In data communications, a state in which the data traffic approaches or exceeds the channel's capacity, resulting in a severe performance degradation and, possibly, loss of packets.

Connectionless Service

In network operations, a connectionless service is one in which transmissions take place without a preestablished path between the source and destination. This means that packets may take different routes between the source and destination. Connectionless services are defined at the network and transport layers, with the specifications in CLNS (Connectionless Mode Network Service) and CLTS (Connectionless Transport Service), respectively.

Because packets may arrive by different paths and in random sequences, there is no way to guarantee delivery in connectionless service. Instead, the higher layers, particularly the transport layer, are left with the job of making sure packets reach their destination without error.

CLNP (Connectionless Network Protocol), CLTP (Connectionless Transport Protocol), IP (Internet Protocol), and UDP (User Datagram Protocol) are examples of protocols that support connectionless service.

COMPARE
Connection-Oriented Service

▼————
Connectionless Transport Service (CLTS)

SEE
CLTS (Connectionless Transport Service)

▼————
Connection, Network

A network connection is a linkage between network elements. Network connections exist on two different levels:

Physical connections: Concern the cables and connectors (used to create the physical topology of the network) and the machines connected. When building a network, you must first establish the physical connections.

Logical connections: Concern the way in which nodes on the network communicate with each other. For example, the sequence in which a token is passed in an ARCnet or Token Ring network depends on the network's logical topology, not on the network's physical layout. Thus, node x may communicate with node y in the network, even though the two nodes are not adjacent machines in the physical network.

▼————
Connection Number

A number assigned to any node that attaches to a file server. The network operating system on the file server uses the connection number to control how nodes communicate with each other. A node will not necessarily be assigned the same connection number each time it attaches to the network.

▼————
Connection-Oriented Service

In network operations, a connection-oriented service is one in which a connection (a path) must be established between the source and destination before any data transmission takes place. With this service, packets will reach their destination in the order sent, because all packets travel along the same, "no-passing" path.

With this type of connection, the OSI data-link layer, for example, checks for errors, does flow control, and requires acknowledgment of packet delivery.

X.25 and TCP (Transmission Control Protocol) are two protocols that support connection-oriented services. Connection-oriented services are defined at the network (CONS) and transport (COTS) layers.

COMPARE
Connectionless Service

▼————
Connectivity

The ability to make hardware and/or software work together as needed. The principles and details of how this happens comprise about half of this book and thousands of pages in other books.

Connector

A connector provides the physical link between two components. For example, a connector can link a cable and a network interface card (NIC), a cable and a transceiver, or two cable segments. For electrical cable, a connection is established whenever the conducting wires (or extensions) from the two connectors make and maintain contact. The signal can simply move across the contact.

For fiber-optic cable, good connections take much more work, because the degree of fit between the two fiber cores determines the quality of the connection. This fit cannot be taken for granted, because the diameters involved are smaller than a human hair.

Connectors differ in their shape, size, gender, connection mechanism, and function. These features influence, and sometimes determine, where a connector can be used. Where necessary, special adapters may be used for connections involving different connector combinations. For example, N-series to BNC adapters make it possible to connect thick to thin coaxial cable.

Connectors also differ in how sturdy they are, how easily and how often they can be attached and detached (how many matings they can survive), and in how much signal loss there is at the connection point.

The type of connector needed in a particular situation depends on the components involved and, for networks, on the type of cable and architecture being used. For example, an Ethernet network using coaxial cable will need different connectors between cable and NIC than an IBM Token Ring network using shielded twisted-pair (STP) cable.

The world of connectors includes its own miniworld of acronyms: N, BNC, DB, DIN, RJ, SC, SMA, ST, TNC, V.32, and so on. To make matters even more confusing, some connectors have more than one name.

About half a dozen types of connectors are used with electrical cable in some network-related contexts; about a dozen more types are used with fiber-optic cable. These connector types are discussed in separate articles. This article discusses connectors in general.

Connector Functions

A connector may be passing the signal along or absorbing it (as a terminator does). A connector that passes a signal along may pass it unmodified or may clean and boost it.

Connectors can serve a variety of purposes, including the following:

- Connect equal components, such as two segments of thin coaxial cable

- Connect almost equal components, such as thin to thick coaxial cable

- Connect unequal components, such as coaxial to twisted-pair cable

- Connect complementary components, such as an NIC to a network

- Terminate a segment; that is, connect a segment to nothing

- Ground a segment; that is, connect a segment to a ground

Connector Shapes

In this context, the term shape refers to the component, not to the connection. Specially shaped connectors are used for particular types of connections or for connections in particular locations. For example, a T-connector attaches a device to a cable segment; an elbow connector allows wiring to meet in a corner or at a wall.

The connector shapes used in networking setups are listed in the table "Cable Connector Shapes," and the figure "Some connector shapes" shows examples.

Connector Genders

Connector *gender* basically refers to whether a connector has plugs or sockets. The gender is important because the elements being connected must have complementary genders.

A male connector is known as a *plug;* the female connector is known as a *jack.* With a few notable exceptions, such as the IBM data connectors and certain fiber-optic connectors, all connector types have distinct genders. The figure "Connector genders" shows examples of male and female connectors.

CABLE CONNECTOR SHAPES	
SHAPE	**DESCRIPTION**
Barrel	Used to link two segments of cable in a straight run; i.e., in a location where there are no corners or turns. In networking, BNC and N-series barrel connectors are used to connect sections of thin and thick coaxial cable, respectively.
DB- or D-type	Describes the connector's frame and refers to a whole family of connectors most commonly used for serial, parallel, and video interfaces. DB-9 and DB-25 connectors are used for serial ports on ATs and XTs. 9-pin versions are used for connecting a monitor to the video board. External network cards, which attach to the parallel port, use DB connectors.
Elbow	Connector with a right-angle bend, used to connect two sections of cable in a corner or to accomplish a change of direction.
RJ	Used to connect telephones to the wall or to modems. RJ-11 and RJ-45 are two commonly used types.
T	Used to attach a device to a section of cable. The horizontal bar of the T links two sections of cable, like a barrel connector; the vertical bar attaches the device. In networks, a T-connector is used to link a section of drop cable to the main cable segment in a thick Ethernet network.
Y	Sometimes used in multiplexers; for example, in a component that provides two ports from one. The shape is mainly a matter of convenience.
Miscellaneous	There are no inherent limitations in the shape a connector can have. Special-shaped connectors can be used when necessary.

SOME CONNECTOR SHAPES

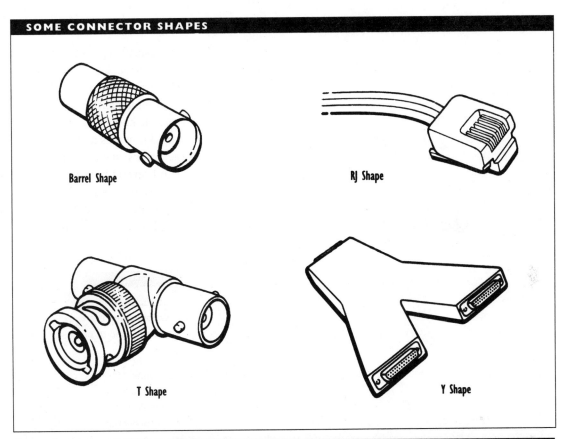

Barrel Shape

RJ Shape

T Shape

Y Shape

CONNECTOR GENDERS

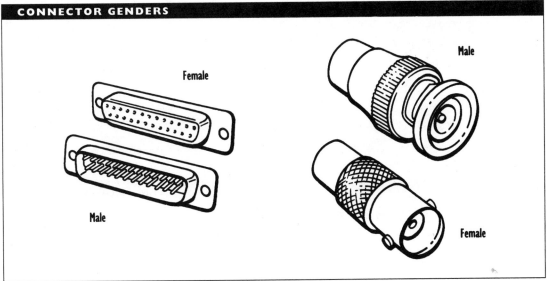

Female

Male

Male

Female

a
b
c
d
e
f
g
h
i
j
k
l
m
n
o
p
q
r
s
t
u
v
w
x
y
z

Connection Mechanisms

The connection mechanism defines how the physical contact is made to allow the signal to pass from one side of the connection to the other.

Connection mechanisms differ considerably in how sturdy they are. For example, the pin-and-socket connection at a serial port can be wobbly without extra support from screws. On the other hand, fiber-optic connectors must be cut to precise proportions, and must not allow any play in the connection, since a cable thinner than a human hair does not need much room to move around.

Connectors are not necessarily named according to the connection mechanism. Rather, the names may have some other basis. The table "Selected Connector Types" illustrates the range of connection mechanisms.

COMPONENTS FOR OTHER TYPES OF LINKS

Connectors connect equal or complementary components. The following components make other types of links possible:

Cable Adapters: Connect almost equal components. Adapters mainly serve to allow size adjustments.

Terminators: Absorb a signal at the end of a network or cable segment to prevent the signal from being reflected back into the cable (thereby causing interference with newer signals traveling out on the cable). Networks have stringent rules about what must be terminated; it's very wise to observe these rules.

Grounded Terminators: Work just like regular terminators, except that grounded terminators have a pigtail or a small metal chain at the end. This needs to be attached to a suitable object to dissipate the charge and to prevent it from being stored up anywhere. (One end of any network or segment must be grounded as well as terminated.)

Baluns: Connect unequal components; that is, components that have different electrical properties (impedances). Baluns are commonly used to connect coaxial to twisted-pair cable.

Transceivers: Connect components and also process signals. Transceivers are receivers and transmitters. Because their main function is passing information (rather than connecting), transceivers may be installed directly on the network interface card. Transceivers establish an electrical, rather than merely a physical, connection.

Repeaters: Clean and boost a signal before passing the signal on to the next cable segment or node. There are often limitations on how repeaters may be distributed on a network. For example, the IEEE 802.3 standards allow at most four repeaters on the signal path between any two stations on an Ethernet/802.3 network. Repeaters are primarily signal boosters, and are connectors only secondarily. Like transcievers, repeaters establish an electrical connection.

SELECTED CONNECTOR TYPES

TYPE	DESCRIPTION
BNC (bayonet nut connector)	Slide together and then lock into place. Ethernet networks with thin coaxial cable use BNC connectors. A variant on the standard BNC connector is used for twinaxial cable. BNC connectors can survive many matings.
TNC (threaded nut connector)	Similar to BNC in construction, except that TNC has threads instead of notches, which create tighter connections.
N-series	Similar to TNC, except that the barrel is somewhat fatter and the plug is somewhat thinner. N-series connectors are used with thick coaxial cable in thick Ethernet networks. N-series connections are quite tight.
Centronics	Use teeth that snap into place. The printer end of a parallel PC-printer connection usually has this type of connector. IEEE-488 interfaces also use Centronics connectors. The term *Telco-type* is also used to describe certain Centronics connectors.
D-type	One of the three classes of connectors that use pins and sockets to establish contact between the elements involved. These are so named because the frame around the pins and sockets that make up the connection resembles a *D*. The connectors for the serial and parallel ports on most PCs use D connectors.
V.35 and M.50	Also use pins and sockets, but they are arranged somewhat differently than for the D-type connectors. V.35 connectors have more rectangular frames.
DIN	Round, but also use pins and sockets. The keyboard connector on most PCs is a DIN connector, as are two of the connectors used for LocalTalk networks.
RJ-*xx*	Connect by catching and locking a plug in place with an overhanging element in the jack connector. RJ-*xx*, or modular, connectors are used in telephone connections and also with twisted-pair cable in networks. Connector versions differ in the number of line pairs they support, e.g., RJ-11 connectors support two pairs; RJ-45 connectors support up to four pairs. A variant on this type is the MMJ (for modified modular jack) connector, which is used in some DEC networks.
IBM Data	A specially designed connector used in IBM Token Ring networks. The connector has a somewhat intricate connection mechanism that can short-circuit when disconnected, so that the network can preserve its structure even when nodes drop out.

a
b
c
d
e
f
g
h
i
j
k
l
m
n
o
p
q
r
s
t
u
v
w
x
y
z

These connection classes are all used for electrical cable. Several of the same connection principles also apply to fiber-optic cable. Numerous types of fiber-optic connectors exist, as discussed in the Connector, Fiber-Optic article.

Connector Mating and Insertion Loss

Attaching two connectors to each other is known as *mating*. Because they involve physical parts and are subject to wear and tear, connectors become less effective as they go through more matings. Because this can lead to increased signal degradation, your choice of connectors may depend on how often you expect to connect and disconnect network segments.

Another factor to consider is *insertion loss*. The signal will undergo a certain amount of loss and distortion at a connection point. This insertion loss will be expressed in decibels (dB). For electrical connections, this value can be 15 dB and more; for fiber-optic cable, this value will generally be less than 1 dB.

SEE ALSO

Connector, AUI; Connector, BNC; Connector, Fiber-Optic

Connector, AUI (Attachment Unit Interface)

An AUI connector is a 15-pin, D-type connector that is used in some Ethernet connections. Typically, it is used to connect a drop cable to a network interface card (NIC). This type of connector is also known as a *DIX* (for Digital, Intel, Xerox) connector.

The figure "An AUI connector" shows an example.

The connection mechanism is the D-type pin and socket, just as for the RS-232 connectors found on most computers. In addition, an AUI connector includes a (sometimes fragile) slide mechanism that can lock the connection into place.

AN AUI CONNECTOR

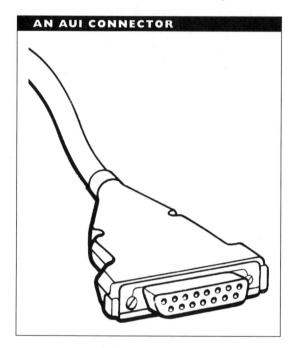

Connector, Barrel

A connector used to link two pieces of identical cable, such as thin or thick coaxial cable. The name comes from the connector's shape. BNC barrel connectors link thin coaxial cable; N-series connectors link thick coaxial.

Connector, BNC

A BNC connector is used with coaxial cable in thin Ethernet networks, in some ARCnet networks, and for some video monitors. Its name may come from Bayonet-Neill-Concelnan, for its developers; from bayonet nut connector, for its attachment mechanism; or from bayonet navy connector, for one of its early uses. The figure "A BNC connector" shows an example of this type of connector.

A BNC CONNECTOR

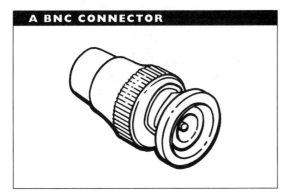

To connect a BNC connector, you insert the plug in the jack, and then lock in the connection by turning the connector. The simple plugging mechanism can survive many matings, and the lock makes the connection more stable.

BNC connectors come in the following shapes and versions:

Barrel connector: Connects two pieces of thin coaxial cable. Each end of the barrel connector is typically female, which means the cable pieces must have a male BNC connector at the end being attached.

Elbow connector: A BNC connector with a right angle in it, for use in corners or in other locations where the cabling needs to change direction.

T-connector: Connects a network node to the cable segment. The T-connector usually has female connections at each end and a male BNC connection forming the descender in the *T*. A network machine is attached to the male connector; the other two ends are connected to the trunk cable segment for the network.

Terminator: Prevents a signal from bouncing back from the end of the network cable and interfering with other signals. The terminator connects to a BNC connector at the end of the trunk cable segment.

Grounded terminator: Grounds and terminates a thin Ethernet trunk segment. A grounded terminator connects to a BNC connector at the end of a trunk cable segment, but includes a ground cable at the end of the terminator. One end of each trunk cable segment must be grounded.

Connector, D-4

A fiber-optic connector that uses a threaded coupling nut for the connection.

SEE

Connector, Fiber-Optic

Connector, D-type

The D-type category of connectors is one of the three classes of connectors that use pins and sockets to establish contact between the elements involved. These are so named because the frame around the pins and sockets that make up the connection resembles a *D*. The connectors for the serial and parallel ports on most PCs use D-type connectors.

D-type connectors are distinguished by the number and arrangement of pins (and/or sockets, depending on the connector's gender) and by the size of the frame. Names such as DB-9, DB-25, or DB-37 refer to connectors with 9, 25, and 37 pins/sockets, respectively.

Common types of D-type connectors include the following:

- DB-9, which is used for some serial (RS-232) interfaces and also for video interfaces. The pin assignments are different for these two uses, so the connectors are not interchangeable.

- DB-15, which is used for video interfaces.

- DB-25, which is used for some serial (RS-232) interfaces and also for a parallel printer interface.

- DB-37, which is used for an RS-422 interface.

The figure "Examples of D-type connectors" illustrates some of these types of connectors. The actual pin assignments depend on the cable's use.

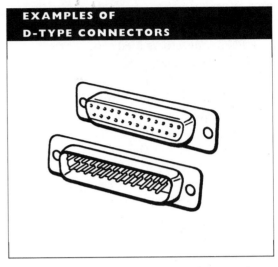

EXAMPLES OF D-TYPE CONNECTORS

In general, connections involving such connectors can be flimsy unless the connectors are locked into place with screws.

Special-purpose variants on the pin-and-socket mechanism (and the D frame) have special names. DIX (for Digital, Intel, and Xerox), or AUI (for attachment unit interface) connectors, are used in Ethernet networks. DIX connectors may also have a slide mechanism to help lock the connection into place.

Connector, Elbow

A connector with a right angle in it, designed for connecting wires in a corner or wherever a change of direction is needed.

Connector, ESCON (Enterprise System Connection Architecture)

A fiber-optic connector for use with multimode fiber in IBM's ESCON channel.

SEE

Connector, Fiber-Optic

Connector, F

A connector used in 10Broad36 (broad-band Ethernet) networks and also in the broadband versions of the (IEEE 802.4) token-bus architecture.

Connector, FC

A connector used for fiber-optic cable, which uses a threaded coupling nut for the attachment and 2.5 millimeter ceramic ferrules to hold the fiber.

SEE

Connector, Fiber-Optic

Connector, Fiber-Optic

A fiber-optic connector must establish a physical link between two segments of optical core, which are just a few nanometers (billionths of a meter, or fractions of a human hair) in diameter. The degree of overlap between the core segments determines the quality of the connection, because this overlap controls how much light is lost or distorted in the crossover from one fiber to the other. The figure "A fiber-optic connector" shows an example of this type of connector.

A fiber-optic connection must not only be precise and smooth, it must also be as immobile as possible. Even the slightest movement can cause unacceptable signal loss. Fiber-optic connections should be put through as few matings as possible, because even a snug connection becomes less snug each time it is made and unmade. (A *mating* is the joining of two connectors.)

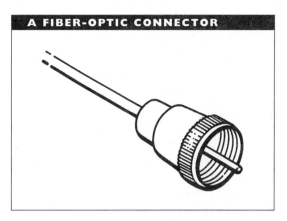

A FIBER-OPTIC CONNECTOR

In fact, to encourage lifelong attachments (instead of random matings), splices are frequently used to make fiber-optic connections. (A *splice* is a permanent connection between two fiber segments.)

To establish a temporary but sound fiber-optic connection, the following tasks are necessary:

- Immobilize each fiber as completely as possible.

- Polish the section that will make contact to as smooth a finish as possible.

- Bring the fiber segments into maximum contact.

- Immobilize the connection.

Features of an Effective Fiber-Optic Connector

An effective connector is one that has very low insertion loss (signal loss that occurs as the signal passes through the connector) and very low return loss (signal that is reflected back through the fiber from which the signal came). Insertion losses of less than 1 decibel (dB), and usually less than 0.5 dB, are the rule with fiber-optic connectors. This means that almost 80 percent of the signal (almost 90 perecent with a 0.5 dB loss) gets past the connector. In contrast, more than 90 percent of an electrical signal may be lost going through a connector.

The reflection loss indicates the amount of the signal that is reflected back; that is, the amount lost to reflection. A large negative decibel value means there was little loss to reflection. For example, a reflection loss of −40 dB means that 0.01 percent of the signal was reflected back. By convention, the negative sign is dropped when speaking of loss; the −40 dB value is simply 40 dB. In this case, and in several others involving signals, a large positive decibel value is better, even though the discussion involves loss.

Several components and steps are important for making a satisfactory fiber-optic connection. Ferrules help guide and immobilize the fiber. To make a good connection, the fiber ends must be properly and evenly polished.

Ferrules

A ferrule grabs the fiber and channels it to a point where it can be put in contact with another fiber. The ferrule (which is derived from a word for bracelet) is a thin tube into which a segment of fiber is inserted. The fiber will be trimmed and polished at the end of the ferrule.

The best (and most expensive) ferrules are made of ceramic. Ceramic is remarkably stable and well-behaved over the temperature range the connector is likely to encounter under ordinary conditions. Plastic is a

poorer (and cheaper) material for ferrules. Stainless steel fits between these two extremes in performance and price.

Even if the ferrule is designed to fit as snugly as possible around the fiber, there may still be movement because of changes in temperature and humidity in the area around the cable. To minimize the movement produced by such climatic conditions, the fiber may be glued to the ferrule using epoxy, or wedged in more snugly by slightly crimping the ends of the ferrule.

Polishing

The fiber will be cut at the end of the ferrule. On the fiber's scale, such a cut will look very jagged and rough—unacceptable for making a connection. To smooth the cut, the end must be carefully and thoroughly polished.

Trying to polish the fiber ends to a completely flat surface is not always the best way to make a clean connection. It is virtually impossible to get both fiber ends smooth enough and angled in the same direction. In practice, there will always be gaps between two smooth and flat surfaces.

A gap between the fiber ends will not only result in a loss of the signal traveling on, it will also cause more of the original signal to be reflected back along the fiber. The return reflection signal will interfere with the newer signals moving along the fiber. Return reflection loss is one of the values that should be as high as possible. As more of a reflected signal is lost, less can actually be reflected back. Losses of 30 to 40 dB are considered good for this variable.

A relatively effective polishing strategy aims for PC (physical contact) connections.

In this strategy, the ends of the fibers are polished to rounded ends. Such fibers *will* be in physical contact, so there will be no air gap to weaken the outgoing signal and reflect it back.

Polishing can be a delicate and tedious process, and is best left to the experts and the machines.

BUILDING YOUR OWN FIBER-OPTIC CABLE CONNECTORS

If you'll be building fiber-optic cable connectors yourself, keep in mind that both the epoxy glue and crimping methods require considerable skill and patience. Newer tools make the job somewhat easier, but you still need to make sure that the fiber is at exactly the right orientation before gluing or crimping.

The fiber protruding through the tube needs to be trimmed and polished so that the surface that connects to the fiber in the other connector will be as smooth as possible. The smoother the surface, the better the connection you can make.

Types of Fiber-Optic Connectors

Like electrical cable connectors, different types of fiber-optic connectors have different kinds of attachment mechanisms. The actual attachments between ferrule shells may be made by threading, snapping, or clicking.

In addition to attachment mechanisms, fiber-optic connectors differ in the following ways:

- The size of the ferrule.

- Whether the connector can be keyed. *Keying* is a technique for making a connector asymmetrical, usually by adding a notch or plug. The asymmetry makes it impossible to plug the connector in incorrectly. It also ensures that the fibers in the connector ends always meet at the same orientation.

- The number of matings the connectors can endure without producing unacceptable signal loss.

- Whether the fiber must be twisted to make the connection. If it needs to be turned, multiple fibers cannot run through the same connector. Nontwisting connectors are becoming much more popular.

Connectors also differ in the way the fiber is attached to the connector itself. You can either use epoxy to glue the fiber into the connector (usually into a tube, or ferrule), or you can crimp the connector and the ferrule together using a special tool. In general, fiber that is attached to the connector using epoxy glue is more robust and less likely to be damaged than fiber attached by crimping.

Fiber-optic connectors can be a source of significant signal loss, so it is important to select connectors carefully. Find out how many matings a fiber connector is specified for. You should also make sure that the cables you are connecting are as similar as possible.

The table "Factors Contributing to Signal Loss at Fiber-Optic Connectors" summarizes problems that can arise with fiber-optic connections. The sum of all these losses is known as insertion loss and can be measured simply by taking readings of signal strength at either end of the connection.

FACTORS CONTRIBUTING TO
SIGNAL LOSS AT FIBER-OPTIC CONNECTORS

FACTOR	DESCRIPTION
Core diameter	Connecting a core with a given diameter to a core with a *smaller* diameter. Depending on the degree of mismatch, you can lose anywhere from 1 dB to more than 10 dB. (Note that there is no loss of this type if the sender's smaller core is connected to a larger core at the receiving end.) This loss source is particularly bothersome for single-mode fiber, since the cores are so small to begin with.
Core concentricity	Connecting two fiber-optic cables whose cores are not both centered in the cladding, so that there is spillage from the transmitter's core into the receiver's cladding.
Core ovality	Connecting cores, one or both of which are elliptical rather than perfectly round. Again, this results in spillage from the sending core.
NA mismatch	Connecting a core with a given NA (numerical aperture) to a core with a smaller NA.
Lateral placement	Connecting two fiber-optic cables that are not properly aligned, which has the same effect as a diameter or concentricity mismatch.
Fiber cuts	Connecting fibers that are not cut cleanly and straight at the ends. The bigger the gap, the greater the signal loss. This potential signal loss is an excellent argument for having the fiber cut professionally, even if you will attach the connectors.
Connection angle	Connecting fibers at an angle. This not only can cause signal loss, it can also cause light to enter the second fiber at an angle different from its original path, which causes signal distortion.
Rough surface	If the surface of either connector end is rough, there will not be a complete union, which will leave space for light to escape.
Gaps	If the two fibers are not actually touching, light can escape into the open area between the fiber. This light is not only lost for the signal, but some of it can also be reflected back into the sender's fiber. Such reflected light can interfere with signals traveling in the proper direction.
Contaminants	Allowing contaminants in the connector can interfere with the connection between the fibers.
Bends	Kinks or bends in the cable, near the connector.
Promiscuity	Using the connector too often; that is, for too many matings, which can loosen the connector and allow play between the two fibers.

Make sure all connectors in your network are compatible. Avoid core or cladding size mismatches if at all possible. Some mismatches won't work together at all; others will introduce unnecessary signal loss.

There are quite a few different types of fiber-optic connectors. One reason for this is that many groups and corporations developed their own during the early days of the technology, and most of those connector types are still around. The most common types are described in the following sections.

ST Connector

An ST (straight tip) connector, developed by AT&T, is the most widely used type of fiber-optic connector. This type of connector is used in premises wiring and in networks, among other places. The connector uses a BNC attachment mechanism, 2.5 mm ferrules (ceramic, steel, or plastic), and either single-mode or multimode fiber. An ST connector will last for about 1,000 matings, *except* when plastic ferrules are used. In that case, the connector is good for only about 250 matings.

Insertion loss is 0.3 dB for ceramic ferrules, but can be more than twice that with plastic ferrules. A return reflection loss of 40 dB is typical with single-mode fiber.

Because this is such a widely used connector type, many other connectors are compatible or can be made compatible with a simple adapter. For example, adapters are available to connect SMA to ST connectors.

FC Connector

Originally developed in Japan for use in telecommunications, an FC connector uses a threaded coupling nut for the attachment, and 2.5 millimeter ceramic ferrules to hold the fiber. An FC connector works with either single-mode or multimode fiber, and will last for about 1,000 matings.

Older style FC connectors used fibers polished to a flat surface. These connectors suffered from signal distortion and loss. Newer FC connectors use a PC polishing approach, which applies polish to a rounded surface to ensure physical contact between the fibers. With PC polished fibers, FC connectors have an insertion loss of about 0.3 dB and a return reflection loss of around 40 dB for single-mode fiber.

FC connectors are becoming obsolete. They are being replaced by SC and MIC connectors.

SC Connector

An SC (subscriber connector) connects two components by plugging one connector into the other. Once the two connectors are latched together, they cannot be pulled apart by sheer pressure. Instead, the connection must be broken (for example, by pressing a button to release a latch).

An SC connector works with either single-mode or multimode fiber, and will last for about 1,000 matings. It has an insertion loss of 0.3 dB, and a return reflection loss of about 40 dB.

SC connectors have replaced the older FC and D-4 connectors used in telecommunications involving fiber-optic cable. SC connectors are also becoming more popular in networking contexts, although they are still not nearly as popular as ST connectors for this application.

MIC Connector

An MIC (medium interface connector), also known as an *FDDI connector,* is a dual-fiber connector designed by an ANSI committee for use with fiber-optic cable in the FDDI (Fiber Distributed Data Interface) network architecture. The connector attaches two fibers that help make up the two rings specified in the FDDI architecture.

MIC connectors use a latching mechanism similar to the one used for SC connectors. An MIC connector works with either single-mode or multimode fiber, and will last for about 500 matings. It has an insertion loss of about 0.3 dB for single-mode fiber, and about 0.5 dB for multimode fiber. Reflection loss is 35 dB or higher, not quite as good as for SC connectors.

The connector is quite flexible and can be attached either to another MIC connector, to two ST connectors, or to a transceiver. Because of this flexibility, MIC connectors are becoming increasingly popular.

SMA Connector

An SMA connector uses a threaded coupling mechanism to make the connection. This type of connector was originally developed in the 1970s by the Amphenol Corporation for use with only multimode fiber; however, SMA connectors can now be used with either multimode or single-mode fiber.

SMA connectors last for only about 200 matings, and they have a relatively high insertion loss of 1.5 dB (which means about 30 percent of the signal is lost).

SMA connectors come in two forms: the SMA-905 uses a straight ferrule, and the SMA-906 uses a ferrule with a step pattern, which is narrowest at the ferrule tip, and widest at the back end of the ferrule.

One reason for their popularity is that SMA connectors have been designed to meet very stringent military specifications.

Adapters are available to connect SMA to ST connectors.

D-4 Connector

A D-4 connector is just like an FC connector, except that the D-4 ferrule (which holds the fiber core in place) is only 2 millimeters. D-4 connectors can be used for single-mode or multimode cable, and will last for about 1000 matings.

ESCON Connector

An ESCON connector is similar to the MIC connector designed for FDDI, except that the ESCON connector uses a retractable cover to make it easier to attach a transceiver. The drawback is that the connection is less robust. An ESCON connector will last for about 500 matings, has a 0.5 dB insertion loss, and a reflection loss of at least 35 dB.

▼
Connector, IBM Data

An IBM data connector is a type designed by IBM for use in its Token Ring networks. These connectors are used to attach a node (or *lobe*) to a multistation access unit (MAU), a wallplate, or a patch panel. MAUs group several lobes into a ring, and may connect to other MAUs. Patch panels serve as wiring way stations.

The attachment mechanism is genderless, and involves a relatively complex mechanism in which two connectors click together to establish the connection.

An IBM data connector is self-shorting, which means that there is a circuit across it even if there is nothing plugged in. This is important for maintaining the ring structure inside a MAU.

Connector, ISO 8877

A variant of the RJ-45 connector that is compatible with international standards.

SEE ALSO

Connector, RJ-*xx*

Connector, MIC (Medium Interface Connector)

A dual-fiber connector designed by an ANSI committee for use with fiber-optic cable in the FDDI network architecture.

SEE ALSO

Connector, Fiber-Optic

Connector, MMJ (Modified Modular Jack)

A special type of modular (RJ-*xx*) connector, developed by Digital Equipment Corporation (DEC) for use with its wiring scheme. An MMJ connector uses the same snap-in attachment mechanism as the RJ-*xx* connector, but the plug and the jack are keyed (made asymmetric).

Connector, N-Series

An N-series, or N-type, connector is used with thick coaxial cable, such as in thick Ethernet networks. N-series connectors come in male and female versions. The connection mechanism uses threads to couple the connectors. The figure "An N-series connector" shows an example of this type of connector.

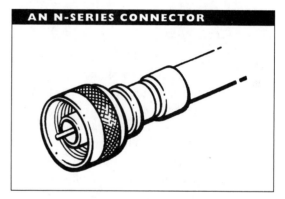

AN N-SERIES CONNECTOR

N-series connectors come in the following shapes and versions:

Barrel connector: Connects two pieces of thick coaxial cable. Each end of the barrel connector is usually female, which means the cable pieces must have a male N-series connector at the end being attached.

Elbow connector: A connector with a right angle in it, for use in corners or in other locations where the cabling needs to change direction.

Terminator: Prevents a signal from bouncing back from the end of the network cable and interfering with other signals. The terminator connects to a

a
b
c
d
e
f
g
h
i
j
k
l
m
n
o
p
q
r
s
t
u
v
w
x
y
z

male N-series connector at the end of the trunk cable segment.

Grounded terminator: Grounds and terminates a thick Ethernet trunk segment. A grounded terminator connects to an N-series connector at the end of a trunk cable segment, but includes a ground cable at the end of the terminator. One end of each trunk cable segment must be grounded.

Connector, RJ-*xx*

An RJ-*xx* connector, also known as a *modular connector,* comes in a plastic plug that snaps into the appropriate socket, or jack. RJ-*xx* connectors are used with twisted-pair cable, such as for telephone cables.

The attachment mechanism involves pushing the plug into the jack until a tooth clicks into place to prevent the plug from coming out.

Several RJ-*xx* versions are available. The most common types are RJ-11, RJ-12, and RJ-45. RJ-11 and RJ-12 connectors are used with two- and three-pair (four- and six-wire) cables. RJ-45 connectors are used with four-pair (eight-wire) cable. Since they have eight wires, RJ-45 connectors are larger than RJ-11 or RJ-12 connectors.

An MMJ (modified modular jack) is a special type of RJ-*xx* connector developed by Digital Equipment Corporation (DEC) for use with its wiring scheme. An MMJ connector uses the same snap-in attachment mechanism as the RJ-*xx* connector, but the plug and the jack are keyed (made asymmetric).

An ISO 8877 connector is a variant of the RJ-45 connector. This type is compatible with international standards.

Connector, SC (Subscriber Connector)

A type of fiber-optic connector that connects two components by plugging one connector into the other.

SEE

Connector, Fiber-Optic

Connector, SMA

A fiber-optic connector type that uses a threaded coupling mechanism to make the connection.

SEE

Connector, Fiber-Optic

Connector, ST (Straight Tip)

A widely used fiber-optic connector developed by AT&T. This type of connector is used in premises wiring and in networks, among other places.

SEE

Connector, Fiber-Optic

Connector, T

A connector that generally links three pieces of cable. Specifically, a T-connector links a device or cable to another cable. In order to add the linked cable, the other cable must be spliced. The connector's name comes from its shape.

Connector, TNC (Threaded Nut Connector)

A connector similar to a BNC connector, except that the TNC connector is threaded and screws into the jack to make the connection. This type of connector is also called a threaded Neill-Concelnan or threaded navy connector.

CONS (Connection-Mode Network Service)

In the OSI Reference Model, a network-layer service that requires an established connection between source and destination before data transmission begins. The logical-link control and media-access control sublayers can do error detection, flow control, and packet acknowledgment. CONS is common in wide-area networks, and is in contrast to the CLNS (connectionless-mode network service) more popular with local-area networks.

Console

In a Novell NetWare environment, the monitor and keyboard from which the network administrator can control server activity is called the *console*. The administrator (or any other user, if there is a security breach) can give commands to control printer and disk services, send messages, and so on.

To prevent unauthorized use of the console, several steps are possible:

- Lock the console to prevent physical access to it.

- Use the lockup feature in the Monitor NLM (NetWare Loadable Module) to disable keyboard entry until the user enters the correct supervisor password.

- Use the Secure Console command to secure the console and also to prevent access to the debugger (which can be used to bypass security measures).

- Be on the lookout for unauthorized activity in the SYS:SYSTEM directory.

- Before loading an NLM, check to make sure it is approved, which means the module has been tested by Novell and was found to work.

BROADER CATEGORY
NetWare

Container

A *container* is an element in the directory tree for Novell's NetWare 4.*x*'s NetWare Directory Services (NDS). The Directory tree contains information about all the objects connected to all the servers in a NetWare network or internetwork. Containers help to group these objects into a hierarchical structure.

A container is an object that may contain other containers or leaf objects or both. Within the Directory tree, a container is allowed only below the root or below another container, as illustrated in the figure "An example of an NDS Directory tree."

a
b
c
d
e
f
g
h
i
j
k
l
m
n
o
p
q
r
s
t
u
v
w
x
y
z

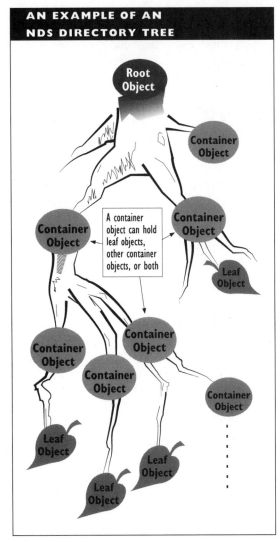

AN EXAMPLE OF AN NDS DIRECTORY TREE

Root Object

Container Object

Container Object

Container Object

A container object can hold leaf objects, other container objects, or both

Leaf Object

Container Object

Container Object

Container Object

Container Object

Leaf Object

Leaf Object

Leaf Object

In an actual network, a container generally corresponds to some meaningful level of organization or administration within the world connected by the network, such as a division or department of a company. A leaf object corresponds to information about a specific network element (node, peripheral, user, and so on).

Two types of container objects are commonly used:

O (**Organizations**): Help to organize and group objects in the tree. There must be at least one organization in a directory tree. All organizations in a tree must be at the same level: immediately below the root.

OU (**Organizational Units**): Help to organize subsets of leaf objects in the tree. OU levels are not required in a Directory tree.

BROADER CATEGORY

NetWare

SEE ALSO

NDS (NetWare Directory Services)

Contention

The basis for a first-come-first-serve media access method. In a contention-based access method, the first node to seek access when the network is idle will get to transmit. Contention is at the heart of the CSMA/CD access method used in Ethernet networks. Compare it with the polling and token-passing methods.

Context

In the CCITT's X.500 Directory Services (DS) model, a portion of the Directory Information Tree (DIT), which contains information about all directory objects. In Novell's NetWare 4.*x* NDS, the current location in the Directory tree.

SEE ALSO

NDS (NetWare Directory Services)

Control Character

A control character is any of several character values that have been reserved for transmission and other control functions, such as cursor movement. For example, in the ASCII character set, the characters with codes below 32 are control characters. Character 9 (Ctrl-I) is a Tab code, character 7 (Ctrl-G) is the code for a beep, and so on.

Control characters are also known as *control codes, communication control codes,* or *communication control characters.*

Controlled Access Unit (CAU)

SEE

CAU (Controlled Access Unit)

Controller

In a mainframe environment, a controller is a device that communicates with a host computer and mediates between this host and the terminals accessing the host.

In a PC environment, a controller is a device, usually a board, that is responsible for accessing another device, and for writing and possibly retrieving material on this device. For example, a hard disk controller accesses the hard disk. Controllers, also called *controller boards,* mediate between the computer and a CD-ROM or tape drive. The controller board generally manages the connected device, including input and output.

The operating system uses a *controller address* to locate a disk controller. This value is usually set directly on the controller board, by setting jumpers or DIP switches.

Control Unit Terminal (CUT)

SEE

CUT (Control Unit Teminal)

Convergence

A process by which network activity is resynchronized after a change in routing; for example, because a node was added or dropped.

Cooperative Processing

A program execution technology that allows different tasks in a program to be carried out on different machines. Cooperative processing is important for client/server computing, in which an application front end executes on a client (workstation), and a back end executes on the server.

Coprocessor

A microprocessor chip that carries out a certain class of tasks on behalf of another processor (the central processing unit, or CPU), in order to leave the CPU available for other work. The most commonly used coprocessors do floating-point arithmetic. Other types are for graphics, disk management, and input/output.

CORBA (Common Object Request Broker Architecture)

A specification created by the Object Management Group (OMG) to provide a way for applications operating in object-oriented environments to communicate and exchange information, even if these applications are

a b **c** d e f g h i j k l m n o p q r s t u v w x y z

running on different platforms. By going through an ORB (object request broker) applications can make requests of objects or other applications without knowing anything about the structure of the called entity.

The ORB enables applications to communicate through an object-oriented front end, which makes it unnecessary to use application- or platform-specific RPCs (remote procedure calls) to make requests or to route and deliver responses.

In addition to ORB clients and servers, the CORBA specification includes an IDL (interface definition language) and APIs (application program interfaces). The IDL provides the ORB client with a way to specify each desired operation and any required parameters. CORBA makes provisions for two classes of APIs:

- A static invocation API, which can be used to specify requests and parameters in advance, so that these can be compiled directly into the application.

- A dynamic invocation API, which must be used to specify requests and parameters that will not be known until runtime.

While CORBA version 2.0 is new, CORBA-compliant products have been appearing almost since the original specification in 1992. For example, Digital's Object-Broker software implements CORBA on a variety of platforms including various flavors of UNIX, Windows and Windows NT, DEC OSF/1, and Macintoshes. (Object-Broker is implemented only partially on some of these platforms.) Microsoft is expected to develop a competing technology

based on its OLE (Object Linking and Embedding) standard.

PRIMARY SOURCE

OMG's *Common Object Request Broker Architecture* specification

Core

In fiber optics, the transparent central fiber (usually glass, but sometimes plastic) through which a light signal travels. The core is surrounded by cladding, which has a lower index of refraction than the core, so that light is reflected back into the core when it hits the cladding.

SEE ALSO

Cable, Fiber-Optic

Core Gateway

On the Internet, any one of several key routers (*gateways,* in older Internet terminology). All networks on the Internet must provide a path from a core gateway to the network.

Corporation for Open Systems (COS)

A group concerned with the testing and promotion of products that support the OSI Reference Model.

Corporation for Research and Educational Networking (CREN)

SEE

CREN (Corporation for Research and Educational Networking)

▼ Count to Infinity

In a distance-vector routing strategy, *count to infinity* is an artifact in which certain networks may come to be classified as unreachable because routers are relying on each others' incorrect information.

The *infinity* in this case refers to the distance to the network. In practice, this value will be one more than the maximum hop count allowed for a route. In a Novell NetWare network, 16 hops (steps to the destination) would be infinite, since at most 15 hops are allowed.

BROADER CATEGORY
Routing, Distance-Vector

▼ Coupler, Fiber-Optic

Most generally, a coupler is a device for transferring energy between two or more channels. In fiber-optic networks, a coupler is a device that routes an incoming signal to two or more outgoing paths, or a device that routes multiple incoming signals into a single outgoing path.

Couplers are important in fiber-optic networks. When an electrical signal is split and sent along parallel paths, each derived signal is the same strength. This is not the case with light signals. After the signal is split, the derived optical signals are each weaker than the original signal.

For example, if a fiber-optic coupler splits a signal into two equal signals, each of those derived signals is half as strong; it loses 3 decibels (dB) relative to the original signal. Couplers can be designed to split a signal equally or unequally.

Couplers are often described in terms of the number of input and output signals. For example, a 3 × 5 coupler has three input and five output channels. If the coupler is bidirectional, you can also describe it as 5 × 3.

Under certain conditions, particularly when using wavelength as a basis for splitting or multiplexing a signal, couplers are subject to optical crosstalk. This can happen, for example, if the wavelengths being used are too similar, so that they are transformed in similar ways by the coupler. Generally, the wavelengths used will be made different deliberately to minimize the possibility of crosstalk.

Fiber-optic couplers can be grouped in any of several ways, based on their form and function:

- Whether the coupler is created by using mirrors (CSR) or by fusing fibers (fused).

- Whether the coupler splits a signal (splitter) or combines multiple signals into a single one (combiner).

- Whether the coupler has its own power supply to boost signals (active) or simply splits signals (passive).

- Whether the coupler sends signals in one direction (directional) or both directions (bidirectional).

- Whether the coupler splits the signal into two (tee) or more (star) parts.

CSR versus Fused Couplers

CSR (centro-symmetrical reflective) couplers use a concave mirror that reflects the light from incoming fiber(s) to outgoing ones. By adjusting the mirror, the light distribution can be controlled.

In a fused coupler, incoming and outgoing fibers are gathered at a central point and wrapped around each other. By applying heat to the wrapping point, the fibers can be fused at this location, so that light from any of the incoming fibers will be reflected to all the outgoing ones.

Splitter versus Combiner Couplers

A splitter coupler breaks a signal into multiple derived signals. An important type of splitter is a wavelength-selective coupler, which splits an incoming signal into outgoing signals based on wavelength.

In contrast, a combiner coupler, also known simply as a *combiner*, combines multiple incoming signals into a single outgoing one. A particular type of combiner is an essential element for WDM (wavelength division multiplexing), in which signals from multiple channels are sent over the same output channel. The input channels are all transmitting at different wavelengths, and the coupler's job is to combine the signals in the proper manner.

Active versus Passive Couplers

An active coupler has its own electrical power supply, which enables the coupler to boost each of the derived signals before transmitting it. Active couplers include electrical components: a receiver that converts the input signal into electrical form, boosting capabilities, and transmitters to convert the electrical signal into an optical one before sending it. An active coupler may also send the signal, usually in electrical form, to a node on a network.

A passive coupler simply splits the signal as requested and passes the weakened signals on to all fibers. There is always signal loss with a passive coupler.

Directional versus Bidirectional Couplers

A directional coupler can send a split signal in only one direction. A bidirectional coupler can send a split signal in both directions.

Tee versus Star Couplers

A tee coupler splits an incoming signal into two outgoing signals. This type of coupler has three ports, and is used in bus topologies.

A star coupler splits the signal into more than two derived signals. Star couplers are used in star topologies.

Passive Star Couplers

A passive star coupler is an optical signal redirector created by fusing multiple fibers together at their meeting point. This type of coupler serves as the center of a star configuration. Because the fibers are fused, a signal transmitted from one node will be transmitted to all the other nodes attached when the signal reaches the coupler.

Passive star couplers are used for optical (IEEE 802.4) token-bus networks that have a passive star topology.

COW (Character-Oriented Windows) Interface

In OS/2, an SAA (Systems Application Architecture) compatible interface.

CPE (Customer Premises Equipment)

Equipment used at the customer's location, regardless of whether this equipment is leased or owned.

CPI (Computer-to-PBX Interface)

In digital telecommunications, an interface through which a computer can communicate with a PBX (private branch exchange).

CPIC (Common Programming Interface for Communications)

APIs (Application Program Interfaces) for program-to-program communications in IBM's SAA (Systems Application Architecture) environment. The CPIC APIs are designed for LU 6.2 protocols; that is, for interactions in which the programs are equals.

CPU (Central Processing Unit)

The main processor in a computer. The CPU may be aided in its work by special-purpose chips, such as graphics accelerators and the UART (universal asynchronous receiver/transmitter).

Cracker

Someone who tries to access computers or networks without authorization—generally with malicious intentions. In contrast, the term *hacker* is used to refer to someone who tries to access systems out of curiosity. The latter term, however, is also used as a general term for anyone trying to access a computer without authorization.

CRC (Cyclic Redundancy Check)

An error-detection method based on a transformation of the bit values in a data packet or frame.

SEE

Error Detection and Correction

CREN (Corporation for Research and Educational Networking

Part of the Internet, along with ARPAnet, MILnet, and several other research and government networks.

CRF (Cable Retransmission Facility)

In a broadband network, the starting point for trammsissions to end-users. For example, the CRF might be the cable network's broadcast station. End-user stations can generally transmit control and error information, but not data to the CRF.

Crimper

A tool for crimping the end of a piece of cable in order to attach a connector to the cable. This tool is essential if you plan to cut and fine-tune cable.

Cross-Connect Device

A cross-connect device is a punch-down block. A *cross-connect* is a connection between two punch-down blocks. This device is used to establish a physical connection between the horizontal cable running from a machine to the cable running to the wiring center, or hub.

The device is used to terminate incoming wire pairs in an orderly manner, and to distribute these wires to end users or to wiring centers. By connecting a device, such as a node in a network, to the more accessible punch-down block instead of directly to a wiring center or to a hub, you can switch connections more easily; for example, to test different wiring configurations.

Crosstalk

Crosstalk is interference generated when magnetic fields or current from nearby wires interrupt electrical currents in a wire. As electrical current travels through a wire, the current generates a magnetic field. Magnetic fields from wires that are close together can interfere with the current in the wires. Crosstalk leads to *jitter,* or signal distortion.

Shielding the wire and twisting wire pairs around each other help decrease crosstalk. If twists are spaced properly, the magnetic fields in the wires cancel each other out. However, crosstalk can also be induced if the twists in a wire are badly spaced.

Crosstalk comes in near and far-end varieties, known as NEXT and FEXT, respectively. FEXT (far-end crosstalk) is the interference in a wire at the receiving end of a signal sent on a different wire. NEXT (near-end crosstalk) is the interference in a wire at the transmitting end of a signal sent on a different wire. NEXT is the value generally measured when evaluating or testing cable.

Cross Wye

A cable used to switch the wiring arrangement from one sequence to another; for example, from USOC wiring to EIA-568B. This type of switch effectively changes the pin assignments of the incoming cable.

SEE ALSO
Wiring Sequence

CSFS (Cable Signal Fault Signature)

In electrical line testing, a unique signal reflected back when using time domain reflectometry (TDR) to test the electrical activity of a line. Based on the CSFS, a trained technician may be able to identify the source and location of a problem.

CSMA/CA (Carrier Sense Multiple Access/Collision Avoidance)

CSMA/CA is a media-access method used in Apple's LocalTalk networks. CSMA/CA operates at the media-access-control (MAC) sublayer, as defined by the IEEE, of the data-link layer in the OSI Reference Model.

The CSMA/CA Process

When a node wants to transmit on the network, the node listens for activity (CS, or carrier sense). Activity is indicated by a carrier on signal. If there is activity, the node waits a period of time and then tries again to access the network. The figure "Summary of the CSMA/CA process" illustrates how the method works.

The wait, known as the *deferral time,* depends on the following:

- The activity level of the network. The deferral time is longer if there is a lot of network activity; it is shorter when there is little activity.

- A random value added to the base deferral time. This ensures that two nodes who defer at the same time do not try to retransmit at the same time.

SUMMARY OF THE CSMA/CA PROCESS

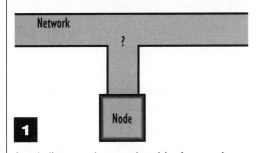

1

A node listens to the network activity for a carrier signal (CS) that indicates the network is in use. At any given time, multiple nodes may be listening. If a node hears a signal, the node defers (backs off) for an amount of time determined by network activity level and a random number generator.

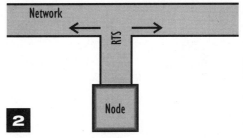

2

Hearing no CS, a node with something to say sends a request to send (RTS) signal onto the network. The signal is broadcast in both directions.

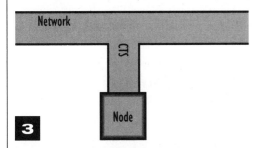

3

If it is sending to a particular node (directed transmission), the would-be sender waits for a clear to send (CTS) reply. If no reply is received within a predefined time, the node assumes there is a collision, and backs off for a random amount of time.

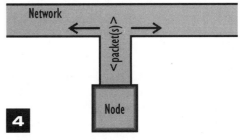

4

If a CTS is received, or if the message is intended as a broadcast transmission, the node begins sending its packet(s). In the case of a broadcast transmission, the node doesn't wait for a CTS.

If the network is currently idle, the node sends a Request To Send (RTS) signal. This signal is sent regardless of whether the node wants to send a directed transmission (one with a particular destination) or a broadcast transmission (one sent to each node on the network).

Directed versus Broadcast Transmissions

In a directed transmission, the RTS is addressed to a particular node, and the sending node waits for a Clear To Send (CTS) signal in reply from this node. The RTS and the CTS must be sent within a predefined amount of time; otherwise, the sending node assumes there is a collision and defers.

In Apple's LocalTalk network architecture, the minimum interframe gap (IFG)—the time between successive frames (such as RTS and CTS or between CTS and data transmission)—is 200 microseconds.

In a broadcast transmission, the RTS is addressed to a predefined address (255) that indicates broadcasts. The sending node does not wait for a CTS; instead, the node begins the transmission. In a broadcast transmission, the RTS serves more as a statement of intent than as a request.

Type of Access Method

CSMA/CA is a probabilistic and contentious access method. This is in contrast to the deterministic token-passing and polling methods. It is contentious in that the first node to claim access to an idle network gets it. CSMA/CA is probabilistic in that a node may or may not get access when the node tries. A disadvantage stemming from this

probabilistic access is that even critical requests may not get onto the network in a timely manner.

Collision avoidance requires less sophisticated circuitry than collision detection, so the chip set is less expensive to manufacture. Collisions cannot always be avoided, however. When they occur, LocalTalk lets a higher level protocol handle the problem.

BROADER CATEGORY
Media-Access Method

SEE ALSO
CSMA/CD; Polling; Token Passing

▼

CSMA/CD (Carrier Sense Multiple Access/Collision Detect)

CSMA/CD is a media-access method used in Ethernet networks and in networks that conform to the IEEE 802.3 standards. CSMA/CD operates at the media-access-control (MAC) sublayer, as defined by the IEEE, of the data-link layer in the OSI Reference Model.

The following network architectures use this access method:

- Ethernet (and 802.3 compliant variants)

- EtherTalk, Apple's implementation of the Ethernet standard

- G-Net, from Gateway Communications

- IBM's PC Network, which is a broadband network

- AT&T's StarLAN

The CSMA/CD Process

In CSMA/CD, a node that wants to transmit on a network first listens for traffic (electrical activity) on the network. Activity is indicated by the presence of a carrier on signal on the line. The figure "Summary of the CSMA/CD process" illustrates how the method works.

If the line is busy, the node waits a bit, then checks the line again. If there is no activity, the node starts transmitting its

---

SUMMARY OF THE CSMA/CD PROCESS

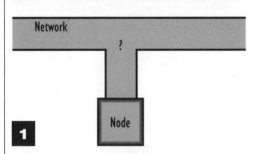

1 A node listens to the network activity for a carrier signal (CS) that indicates the network is in use. At any given time, multiple nodes may be listening. If a node hears a signal, the node defers (backs off) for an amount of time determined by network activity level and a random number generator.

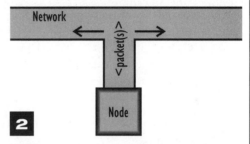

2 Hearing no carrier signal, a node with something to say sends its packet(s) onto the network. Note that the transmission moves in both directions along the bus. This is necessary to ensure that all nodes get the message at the same time, so that each node hears the same network.

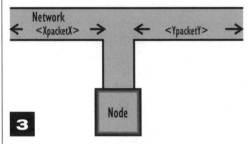

3 Because of the multiple access (MA) property, another node may have done the same thing, so that two messages are moving along the bus at the same time.

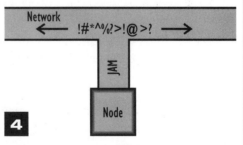

4 In such a case, a collision occurs. The packets are garbled, and electrical activity on the line is higher than usual. When a node hears a collision, the node starts sending a jam signal to indicate the collision. A node involved in a collision backs off for a randomly determined amount of time before trying again to access the network.

---

a b c d e f g h i j k l m n o p q r s t u v w x y z

packet, which travels in both directions on the network cable.

The node continues monitoring the network. However, it is possible for two nodes to both detect no activity on the line and start transmitting at the same time. In that case, a collision occurs, and the network has packet fragments floating around.

When a collision is detected, a node follows this procedure:

1. Cancels its transmission by sending a jam signal (to indicate there is a collision and thereby prevent other nodes from joining the fun)

2. Waits a random amount of time (the *deferral time*), determined by a backoff algorithm

3. Tries to access the network again

Internally, nodes keep track of the number of unsuccessful transmission attempts for each packet. If this number exceeds some predefined value, the node decides the network is too busy and stops trying.

Each node in a network that uses CSMA/CD listens to every packet transmitted. The listener first checks whether the packet is a fragment from a collision. If so, the node ignores it and listens for the next packet.

If a packet is not a fragment, the node checks the destination address. The node will further process the packet if any of the following is the case:

- The destination address is the node's address.

- The packet is part of a broadcast (which is sent to every node).

- The packet is part of a multicast and the node is one of the recipients.

As part of this further processing, the destination node checks whether the packet is valid. (For a summary of invalid Ethernet packets, see the section on the Ethernet frame in the Ethernet article.)

Type of Access Method

CSMA/CD is a probabilistic, contentious access method, in contrast to the deterministic token-passing and polling methods. It is contentious in that the first node to claim access to an idle network gets it. CSMA/CD is probabilistic in that a node may or may not get access when the node tries. A disadvantage stemming from this probabilistic access is that even critical requests may not get onto the network in a timely manner.

CSMA/CD works best when most network activity is light. The access method works most poorly when the network traffic consists of many small messages, because nodes spend much of their time colliding, then waiting to retransmit.

To use this access method, a node must be able to detect network activity (carrier sense, or CS) and to detect collisions (collision detect, or CD). Both of these capabilities are implemented in hardware, on board the network interface card.

Because CSMA/CD is a contentious access method, any node can access the network, provided that node puts in the first request when the network line is idle. This makes the method multiple access (MA). Unlike CSMA/CA, a CSMA/CD node must be able to detect a collision on the line.

BROADER CATEGORY
Media-Access Method

SEE ALSO
CSMA/CA; Polling; Token Passing

CS-MUX (Carrier-Switched Multiplexer)

In the FDDI (Fiber Distributed Data Interface) II architecture, CS-MUX is a component that passes time-dependent data, such as voice or video, to the architecture's media-access-control (MAC) layer. At that layer, the data is handled by a special isochronous media-access-control (IMAC) component.

The CS-MUX is not part of the FDDI II definition. Rather, the CS-MUX provides certain types of data for FDDI. Functionally, a CS-MUX operates at a level comparable to the logical-link-control (LLC) sublayer of the ISO model's data-link layer.

BROADER CATEGORY
FDDI (Fiber Distributed Data Interface)

CSU (Channel Service Unit)

A CSU is part of the integrated services unit (ISU) component that replaces a modem on a digital line. The CSU is mainly responsible for making the signals well-behaved and protecting the public carrier's lines from a malfunctioning data service unit (DSU).

In particular, a CSU prevents faulty customer-premises equipment (CPE), such as DSUs, from affecting a public carrier's transmission systems and ensures that all signals placed on the line are appropriately timed and formed. All CSU designs must be approved and certified by the FCC (Federal Communications Commission).

BROADER CATEGORY
Digital Communications

SEE ALSO
DSU/CSU (Data Service Unit/Channel Service Unit)

CTI (Computer-Telephone Integration)

A strategy for connecting standalone or networked computers to telephone switches in such a manner that the computer can receive, initiate, and route calls over the switch.

There are various strategies for accomplishing this. For example, a special connection—a *CTI link*—can be used to provide a single link between a network and a switch. All traffic passes through the CTI link, which may have a table or other means of determining which client is the recipient or initiator of a call.

Standards for CTI must be developed at two levels: the physical and the API, or programming, level.

- At the physical level, the rules for basic connections between computers and switches must be specified. For example, a standard must specify the electrical characteristics of such a connection. The CSTA (computer-supported telecommunication applications) standard was developed by the ECMA (European Computer Manufacturers' Association). It has been around for a few years, and it is being implemented

a b c d e f g h i j k l m n o p q r s t u v w x y z

by several vendors. A competing standard—SCAI (switch computer applications interface)—is still under development by ANSI.

- The API level provides functions that enable programmers to gain access to and use the capabilities of the lower level protocols. Little has been standardized at this level. Two widely used APIs are Microsoft's *TAPI* (Telephony Application Programming Interface) and Novell's *TSAPI* (Telephony Services API).

In addition to a CTI link, various other elements can be introduced into a configuration that integrates computers and telephony devices and services. For example, a CTI server can connect to the CTI link at one end and to APIs running on network nodes at the other end. This makes it easier to coordinate and control traffic between network and telephony services.

Data distributors, voice response units (VRUs), and automatic call distributors can also help make the services relying on CTI more efficient. For example, an ACD can help route incoming calls to the next available person in a technical support pool. As standards for Computer Telephony become more completely defined and accepted, we can expect considerable activity in this area.

SEE ALSO

TAPI; TSAPI

CTS (Clear To Send)

CTS is a hardware signal sent from a receiver to a transmitter to indicate that the transmitter can begin sending. CTS is generally sent in response to a Request To Send (RTS) signal from the transmitter. The CTS signal is sent by changing the voltage on a particular pin.

CTS is used most commonly in serial communications, and is sent over pin 5 in an RS-232 connection. The RTS/CTS combination is used in the CSMA/CA (carrier sense multiple access/collision avoidance) media-access method used in Apple's LocalTalk network architecture.

BROADER CATEGORY

Flow Control

SEE ALSO

RTS (Request To Send)

CTS (Conformance Testing Service)

A series of programs developed to create test methods for determining how well (or whether) a product implements a particular protocol correctly. CTS projects have developed or are developing test suites for LAN protocols (*CTS-LAN*), for wide area networks (*CTS-WAN*), and for such ISO or ITU standards as *FTAM* (File Transfer, Access, and Management), X.400 (message handling), and X.500 (directory services). In general, the tests conform to guidelines for abstract test suites established by the ITU.

CUA (Common User Access)

In IBM's SAA environment, specifications for user interfaces that are intended to provide a consistent look across applications and platforms.

SEE ALSO

SAA (Systems Applications Architecture)

CUT (Control Unit Terminal)

A terminal operating mode that allows only one session, such as running an application, per terminal. (If a CUT terminal is attached to an IBM 3174 establishment controller with multiple logical terminal support, it can support multiple sessions.)

COMPARE

DFT (distributed function terminal)

Cut-Off Wavelength

In single-mode fiber optics, the shortest wavelength at which a signal will take a single path through the core.

Cut-Through Switching

A switching method for Ethernet networks. The switch reads a destination address and immediately starts forwarding packets, without first checking the integrity of each packet. This reduces latency.

There are two switching strategies for implementing cut-through switches:

- Cross-bar switching, in which each input port (segment) establishes a direct connection with its target output port. If the target port is currently in use, the switch waits, which could back packets up at the input port.

- Cell-backplane switching, in which all ports share a common backplane (bus) along which all packets are sent. Incoming packets are broken up and repackaged with target addresses. These fragments are then sent onto the common backplane, from which the

fragments will get themselves to the specified output port. The backplane should have a bandwidth at least as high as the cumulative bandwidths of all the ports.

COMPARE

Store-and-Forward Switching

CWIS (Campus-Wide Information System)

An online repository of information about a particular school or campus. The CWIS contains information such as campus-event calendars, course listings, and job openings. Although they are created for use by students on the individual campuses, CWISs are accessible over the Internet.

Cycle, Periodic Analog Signal

One complete repetition of a periodic analog signal. A cycle goes from a high point (peak) in the signal's level to a low point (trough) and back to the peak. The cycles per second value defines the frequency of a periodic signal. Frequency is measured in hertz (Hz). For example, a 50 Hz signal travels at 50 cycles per second.

Cycle, FDDI II

In an FDDI (Fiber Distributed Data Interface) II network operating in hybrid mode, a cycle is a 12,500-bit protocol data unit (PDU), or packet, that provides the basic framing for the FDDI transmission. The cycle is repeated 8,000 times per second, which yields 100 megabits per second (Mbps) of bandwidth for the network.

a b c d e f g h i j k l m n o p q r s t u v w x y z

The cycle contains the following components:

Cycle header: Specifies how the cycle is to be used. One part of the information specified in the 12 bytes in the header is whether each of the wideband channels is being used for packet-switched or isochronous data.

DPG (dedicated packet group): Used for packet-transfer control. The DPG consists of 12 bytes.

WBC (wideband channel): Used for actual data transmission. There are 16 WBCs in each cycle. Each WBC consists of 96 bytes, or octets, and may be subdivided into subchannels. Depending on the number of bits allocated each cycle, subchannels may have bandwidths ranging from 8 kilobits per second (kbps) to 6.144 Mbps. For example, an 8-bit-per-cycle subchannel yields a 64 kbps data rate, corresponding to a B channel in the ISDN telecommunications model; using 193 bits per cycle yields a 1.544 Mbps T1 line. The default FDDI II WBC uses all 768 bits for a single channel.

BROADER CATEGORY
FDDI (Fiber Distributed Data Interface)

Cylinder

On a hard disk, the term for the collection of concentric tracks at the same position on each of the hard disk platters.

D4 Framing

In digital signaling, D4 framing is a method for identifying the individual channels in a DS1 channel.

D4 framing groups twelve 193-bit frames into one D4 superframe so that each DS1 channel consists of two D4 superframes.

Within each D4 superframe, the values in every one hundred ninety-third bit—in bits 193, 386, and so on—are used to identify the individual (DS0) channels. Also in each D4 superframe, the eighth bit in every channel of frames 6 and 12 is used for signaling between central offices. The figure

"Elements in D4 framing" illustrates this method.

COMPARE
ESF Framing

DA (Destination Address)

In many types of packets, a header field that specifies the node to which the packet is being sent. Depending on the type of address involved, this field may be four, six, or more bytes.

SEE ALSO
SA (Source Address)

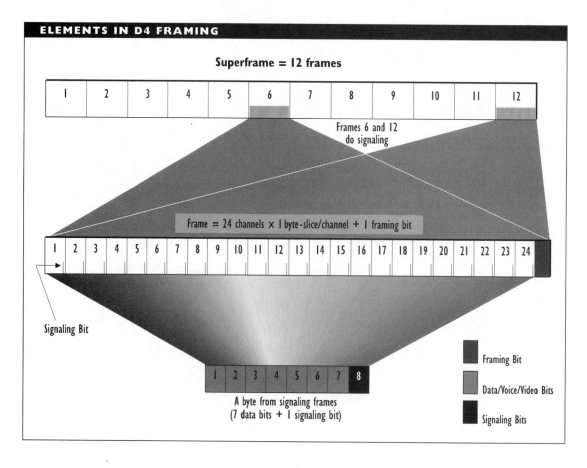

ELEMENTS IN D4 FRAMING

Superframe = 12 frames

| 1 | 2 | 3 | 4 | 5 | 6 | 7 | 8 | 9 | 10 | 11 | 12 |

Frames 6 and 12 do signaling

Frame = 24 channels × 1 byte-slice/channel + 1 framing bit

| 1 | 2 | 3 | 4 | 5 | 6 | 7 | 8 | 9 | 10 | 11 | 12 | 13 | 14 | 15 | 16 | 17 | 18 | 19 | 20 | 21 | 22 | 23 | 24 |

Signaling Bit

| 1 | 2 | 3 | 4 | 5 | 6 | 7 | 8 |

A byte from signaling frames
(7 data bits + 1 signaling bit)

Framing Bit

Data/Voice/Video Bits

Signaling Bits

DAA (Data Access Arrangement)

In telephony, a device required as protection for the public telephone network if the user's equipment does not meet FCC standards.

DAC (Digital-to-Analog Converter)

A device for converting a digital signal to an analog one. An ADC (analog-to-digital converter) changes an analog signal to a digital signal.

DAC (Dual-Attachment Concentrator)

In an FDDI (Fiber Distributed Data Interface) network architecture, a concentrator used to attach single-attachment stations or station clusters to both FDDI rings.

DACS (Digital Access and Cross-Connect System)

In digital telecommunications, a mechanism for switching a 64 kilobit per second (kbps) DS0 channel from one T1 line to another. The DACS method was originally developed for use in telephone company switching, but it has proven useful in networking contexts.

Daemon

In many operating environments, a background program that begins executing automatically when a predefined event occurs. Daemons (pronounced "demons") are common in the OS/2 and UNIX environments and are used in artificial intelligence work. Certain terminate-and-stay resident (TSR)

programs in a DOS environment behave like daemon programs.

Daisy Chain

A serial linkage of components, also known as *cascading*. In a daisy chain, device A is connected to device B, which is connected to C, and so on. A daisy chain arrangement may be used in networks based on a bus topology. Hard drives or other devices may be daisy chained if they are all connected to a SCSI adapter.

DAL (Data Access Language)

In Macintosh-based client/server environments, an extension to the SQL database language. DAL is intended to provide a uniform access to any database that supports SQL.

DAM (Data Access Manager)

In the System 7 operating system software for Macintoshes, DAM is a built-in capability for accessing databases on a network. The DAM mediates between an application and the database being accessed.

The DAM uses *database extensions* to communicate with the database. These are database-specific system files that contain the commands necessary to interact with a particular database.

BROADER CATEGORIES
Macintosh

DAMA (Demand-Assigned Multiple Access)

In telecommunications, a method for allocating access to communications channels. Idle channels are kept in a pool. When a channel capacity is requested, an idle channel is selected, allocated the requested bandwidth, and assigned to the requesting party.

DAN (Departmental-Area Network)

In government offices, a network that services a single government department.

Dark Fiber

A term for optical fiber that has been installed but is not being used. According to some estimates, over 99% of the installed fiber-optic cable is still dark fiber.

DARPA (Defense Advanced Research Projects Agency)

The government agency largely responsible for the development of the ARPAnet government/university network, which eventually became part of the Internet. DARPA, originally known just as ARPA, is part of the U.S. Department of Defense (DoD).

DAS (Disk Array Subsystem)

The carriage, cabling, and circuitry for using multiple hard disks.

DAS (Dual-Attachment Station)

In an FDDI (Fiber Distributed Data Interface) network architecture, a station, or node, that is connected physically to both the primary and secondary rings. A station can be connected directly to the ring through a port on the DAS. In contrast, a SAS (single-attachment station) must be attached to a concentrator.

DAS (Dynamically Assigned Socket)

In an AppleTalk internetwork, a DAS is a unique socket value, assigned, upon petition, to a particular client.

A *socket* is an entity through which a program or process, known as a *socket client,* communicates with a network or with another process. Each AppleTalk socket is associated with an 8-bit value.

Values between 128 and 254, inclusive, are allocated for DASs. A process running on a node can request a DAS value. An available value in this range is assigned to the process. While this process is executing, the assigned value cannot be used for another socket.

DASs are in contrast to statically assigned sockets (SASs). SASs are allocated for use by various low-level protocols, such as NBP and RTMP in the AppleTalk protocol suite. Values between 1 and 127, inclusive, are used for SASs. Values between 1 and 63 are used exclusively by Apple, and values between 64 and 127 can be used by whatever processes request the values.

BROADER CATEGORY
Socket

DASS (Distributed Authentication Security Service)

DASS is a system for authenticating users logging into a network from unattended workstations. These workstations must be considered suspect, or untrusted, because their physical security cannot be guaranteed.

DASS uses public-key encryption methods, which support the more stringent authentication methods defined in the CCITT's X.509 specifications. In contrast to DASS, Kerberos is a distributed authentication system that uses a private-key encryption method.

BROADER CATEGORIES

Authentication; Encryption

COMPARE

Kerberos

DAT (Digital Audio Tape)

A DAT is a popular medium for network and other backups. Information is recorded in digital form on a small audio tape cassette, originally developed by Sony and Hewlett-Packard (HP). The most common format was a 4-millimeter tape in a helical-scan drive, which can hold more than a gigabyte of information.

DATs use a logical recording format called *Data/DAT*. This format supports random data reads and writes. It also allows data to be updated in place, rather than requiring the modified data, and perhaps some of the unchanged data as well, to be rewritten to a new location.

Data Access Language (DAL)

In Macintosh-based client/server environments, an extension to the SQL database language. DAL is intended to provide a uniform access to any database that supports SQL.

Database

A database is an indexed collection of information. The index imposes an order on the information and also provides access to the information in the database.

The information in a database can be accessed, modified, or retrieved using a query language. The most widely used query language is SQL (Structured Query Language), which forms the basis for most other query languages currently in use. See the SQL article for more information about this language.

The overwhelming majority of databases are still text-based, rather than graphics- or multimedia-based, but this is changing. This development has implications, particularly for distributed databases. Until high-speed, long-distance telecommunications facilities are affordable for ordinary consumers, transmitting video over long-distance lines will seldom be worth the price.

Database types include flat file, relational, object-oriented, inverted-list, hierarchical, network, and distributed.

Flat File Database

In a flat file database, all the information is contained in a single file. A flat file database consists of individual records that are, in turn, made up of fields. Each field may

a
b
c
d
e
f
g
h
i
j
k
l
m
n
o
p
q
r
s
t
u
v
w
x
y
z

contain a particular item of information. There is not necessarily any relationship between records. The records are not organized in any particular way. Instead, lookup tables are created, and these are used to find and manipulate records.

A flat file database makes considerable demands of a user, who may need to "program" the required information into appropriate lookup tables.

NetWare versions prior to 4.x use a flat database, called the bindery, to store information about nodes and devices on the network.

Relational Database

In a relational database, the contents are organized as a set of tables in which rows represent records and columns represent fields. Certain fields may be found in multiple tables, and the values of these fields are used to guide searches. Database access and manipulation are a matter of combining information from various tables into new combinations. For example, a request might look for all records for people who work in a particular department and whose last raise was more than one year ago.

The overwhelming majority of databases currently available on PCs are relational databases. Fortunately, the theory of relational databases is well-developed, so that robust DBMS (database management system) packages and powerful query and manipulation tools are available.

Object-Oriented Database

In an object-oriented database, the information is organized into objects, which consist of properties and allowable operations involving the objects.

Objects can be defined in terms of other objects (for example, as special cases or variants of a specific object), and can inherit properties from such "ancestor" objects. The Directory tree based on the information in the NetWare Directory Services (NDS) is an example of an object-oriented database.

Inverted-List Database

In an inverted-list database, the contents are also organized in tables, but these tables are more content-bound (less abstract), and therefore less easy to manipulate and modify.

In addition to tables, an inverted-list database also has records whose contents help simplify certain searches. For example, a database might have a record for each department in a corporation, and the contents of that record might be a listing of all the employees in that department. Indexes are used to keep track of records and to speed access.

Hierarchical Database

In a hierarchical database, the contents are organized hierarchically, as one or more trees. Each record in a tree has exactly one parent and may have children. Any two records in a hierarchical database are related in exactly one way.

The DOS directory and file system is an example of a hierarchical database. The relationships involved include "is a subdirectory of" and "in the same directory as."

Network Database

A network database is similar to a hierarchical database in that there are links between records. The main difference is that records in a network database may have no parents or one or more parents. This is because a network database consists essentially of records and links. These links do not necessarily form a hierarchically organized tree.

Note that the *network* in this label is not a computer network. It is a network in the mathematical sense: elements (records) connected by links (relationships).

Distributed Database

Any of the database types can be developed as a distributed database, because this is a matter of database storage rather than structuring. A distributed database is simply one whose contents are stored on multiple machines.

The fact that two employee records are on different machines does not change the relationship between the employees (for example, if both work in the same department). DBMS software will hide the distributed nature of the database from the user, so that users need not make any adjustments to their queries or methods for retrieving and changing data.

Data Bits

In asynchronous transmissions, the bits that actually comprise the data. Usually, 7 or 8 data bits are grouped together. Each group of data bits in a transmission is preceded by a start bit, then followed by an optional parity bit, as well as one or more stop bits.

Data Bus

The internal bus over which devices and system components communicate with the central processing unit (CPU) is called a *data bus*. Buses differ in their width, which is the number of data bits that can be transported at a time, and in their clock speed.

In general, maximum supported clock speeds keep getting higher, with 100 megahertz (MHz) speeds already available on some processors. While processor manufacturers continuously leap-frog each other's highest speeds, official bus standards change more slowly.

In the following summaries, the quoted clock speeds are those specified in the bus specifications or in de facto standards. You will be able to find faster processors than the ones discussed.

PC Data Bus Architecture

The following bus architectures are (or have been) popular for PCs:

ISA (Industry Standard Architecture): The bus for the earliest PCs. Early PC versions were 8-bit and ran at 4.77 MHz; later AT versions were 16-bit and ran at 8 MHz.

EISA (Extended Industry Standard Architecture): A 32-bit extension of the ISA bus. This architecture also runs at 8 MHz.

MicroChannel: A 32-bit proprietary architecture from IBM, for use in most of its PS/*x* and Model *xx* series of computers. The MicroChannel bus operates at 10 MHz.

a
b
c
d
e
f
g
h
i
j
k
l
m
n
o
p
q
r
s
t
u
v
w
x
y
z

VESA (Video Electronics Standards Association): An enhanced version of the EISA architecture, also known as *local bus*. The original version was 32-bit at 40 MHz; the newer version is 64-bit at 50 MHz.

PCI (Peripheral Component Interconnect): A newer architecture from Intel, PCI is 64-bit and operates at 33 MHz.

These bus architectures are discussed in more detail in separate articles.

Macintosh Data Bus Architecture

In contrast, Apple's Macintosh line of computers has, for the most part, used the NuBus architecture developed by Texas Instruments. This architecture is processor-specific, which means that it is not applicable to an entire processor family.

SEE ALSO

EISA (Extended Industry Standard Architecture); ISA (Industry Standard Architecture); MicroChannel; PCI (Peripheral Component Interconnect); VESA (Video Electronics Standards Association)

▼

Data Communications

Data communications is the transmission of data, commonly by electronic means, over a physical medium. Any potentially relevant Zen koans aside, it is generally agreed that, to be useful, data communications require both a sender and a receiver.

Components of Data Communications

The sender and receiver are also known as the *data source* and *data sink,*

respectively. These are connected by a *data link*. The data link includes a transmission medium (for example, wire) and the appropriate transmission and receiving devices at the data source and sink. The figure "Elements in data communications" shows these components.

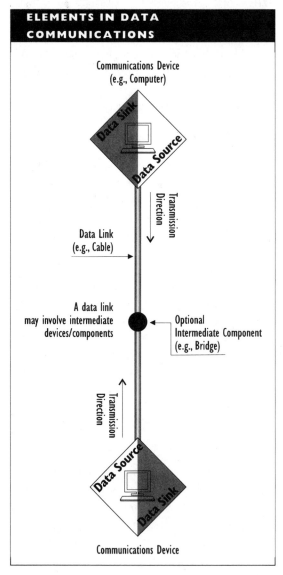

ELEMENTS IN DATA COMMUNICATIONS

Communications Device (e.g., Computer)

Data Sink

Data Source

Transmission Direction

Data Link (e.g., Cable)

A data link may involve intermediate devices/components

Optional Intermediate Component (e.g., Bridge)

Transmission Direction

Data Source

Data Sink

Communications Device

The sender must encode and transmit the data, and the receiver must receive and decode the data. Data encoding may include special treatment, such as compression to eliminate redundancy or encryption to prevent, or at least discourage, eavesdropping.

Types of Data Transmission

The data transmission may be any of the following types:

Point-to-point, or direct: Over a direct (unmediated) link between sender and receiver. Point-to-point connections are commonly used in small networks and dedicated communications lines.

Mediated: Handled, and possibly modified, by intermediate stations or parties en route to the receiver. A transmission may be mediated simply because there are stations between the sender and the receiver. In such a case, all transmissions take the same path.

Switched: Mediated and possibly routed along different paths. A switched transmission may be diverted to any of multiple possible paths. Different transmission elements—fixed-size blocks, variable-sized packets, or entire messages—can be used as the basis for the switching.

Broadcast: Transmitted to any station or party capable of receiving, rather than to a specific receiver. A radio transmission is broadcast.

Multicast: Transmitted to any station on a stored or specified list of addresses. For example, electronic newsletters or mail from special interest groups are multicast when they are sent only to subscribers.

Stored and forwarded: Sent to a holding location until requested or sent on automatically after a predefined amount of time.

Time division multiplexed (TDM): Combined with other transmissions. In this multiplexing method, transmissions share the entire capacity of a single channel. For example, the transmission might be divided into brief transmission slices that are interspersed in the channel.

Frequency division multiplexed (FDM): Combined with other transmissions, as in TDM, but the multiplexed transmissions split a single channel, with each transmission taking some portion. For example, a transmissions may use a small frequency range within the channel's entire range.

The figure "Common data transmission schemes" shows the most common types of transmission.

a b c d e f g h i j k l m n o p q r s t u v w x y z

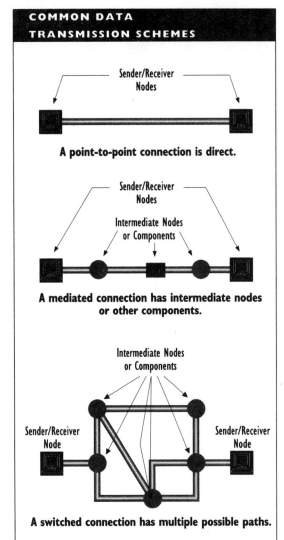

COMMON DATA TRANSMISSION SCHEMES

Sender/Receiver Nodes

A point-to-point connection is direct.

Sender/Receiver Nodes

Intermediate Nodes or Components

A mediated connection has intermediate nodes or other components.

Intermediate Nodes or Components

Sender/Receiver Node

Sender/Receiver Node

A switched connection has multiple possible paths.

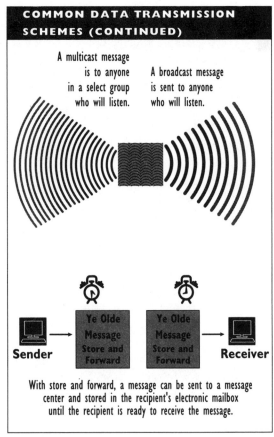

COMMON DATA TRANSMISSION SCHEMES (CONTINUED)

A multicast message is to anyone in a select group who will listen.

A broadcast message is sent to anyone who will listen.

Sender

Ye Olde Message Store and Forward

Ye Olde Message Store and Forward

Receiver

With store and forward, a message can be sent to a message center and stored in the recipient's electronic mailbox until the recipient is ready to receive the message.

Data Compression

Data compression is a method of reducing the amount of data used to represent the original information. This can be accomplished by eliminating redundancy.

Compression Bases

The basis for the compression can be any of the following:

- Patterns in bit sequences, as in run-length limited (RLL) encoding

- Patterns of occurrences of particular byte values, as in Huffman or LZW encoding

- Commonly occurring words or phrases, as in the use of abbreviations or acronyms

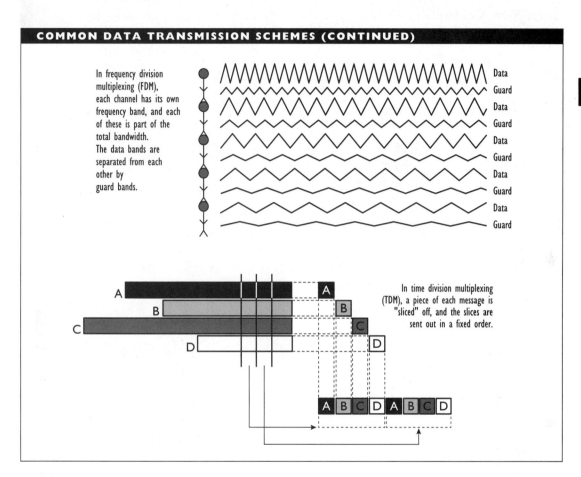

COMMON DATA TRANSMISSION SCHEMES (CONTINUED)

In frequency division multiplexing (FDM), each channel has its own frequency band, and each of these is part of the total bandwidth. The data bands are separated from each other by guard bands.

Data
Guard
Data
Guard
Data
Guard
Data
Guard
Data
Guard

In time division multiplexing (TDM), a piece of each message is "sliced" off, and the slices are sent out in a fixed order.

Compression Methods

The two types of compression methods are lossless and lossy. In lossless compression, all the original information can be recovered. Lossless methods generally compress data to about 50 or 33 percent of the original size. These values represent compression ratios of 2:1 and 3:1, respectively. Lossless compression methods rarely reach ratios higher than 5:1 or so.

In lossy compression, some of the original information will be lost. Lossy methods can

attain compression ratios of 100:1 and even higher.

Data Encryption Algorithm (DEA)

SEE

DEA (Data Encryption Algorithm)

Data Encryption Key (DEK)

SEE

DEK (Data Encryption Key)

Data-Flow Control

The fifth layer in IBM's SNA.

SEE

SNA (Systems Network Architecture)

Data Fork

The data fork is the data portion of a Macintosh file. It is the part of a Macintosh file that is transferred to non-Macintosh environments, such as DOS or UNIX.

SEE ALSO

Macintosh

Datagram

A datagram is a packet that includes both source and destination addresses provided by the user, rather than by the network. A datagram can also contain data. A message might be sent as multiple datagrams, which may be delivered to the destination in nonconsecutive order. Receipt of a datagram is not acknowledged.

Datagram routing takes place at the network layer of the OSI Reference Model. Datagram transmission takes place at the data-link layer.

Datagram services are provided in connectionless (as opposed to connection-oriented) transmissions. Because connectionless transmissions do not necessarily deliver datagrams in order, datagram services cannot guarantee successful message delivery. Receipt verification is the responsibility of a higher-level protocol, which must be able to assemble the message from the datagrams. Protocols that provide this type of service include UDP (User Datagram Protocol) in the Internet's TCP/IP protocol suite, CLNP (Connectionless Network Protocol) in the OSI Reference Model, and DDP (Datagram Delivery Protocol) in the AppleTalk protocol suite.

SEE ALSO

Connectionless Service; Connection-Oriented Service

Datakit VCS

A data-switch product from AT&T. Datakit VCS offers communications channels ranging from 9.6 kilobits per second to 8 megabits per second, and can be linked to X.25 networks.

Data Link

In communications, the components and medium necessary for communication between two stations or parties. The medium is generally (but not necessarily) a wire or fiber-optic cable, and the components are the transmitting and receiving facilities at either end of the link.

Data-Link Connection Identifier (DLCI)

SEE

DLCI (Data-Link Connection Identifier)

Data-Link Control (DLC)

SEE

DLC (Data-Link Control)

Data Network Identification Code (DNIC)

SEE

DNIC (Data Network Identification Code)

Data Over Voice (DOV)

In communications, a strategy for transmitting data over the voice channel at the same time as a voice transmission. A human listener would not hear the data being transmitted. DOV requires special equipment.

SEE ALSO

DUV (Data Under Voice)

Data Packet

In general, a data packet is a well-defined block that contains user or application data. When transmitted, a data packet will also include a considerable amount of administrative information (not data) in the packet header and footer.

A data packet is defined for a particular protocol. The term is also used to refer to such packets within a particular protocol or architecture. For example, an X.25 data packet can contain up to 1024 bytes of user data.

Data-PCS (Data Personal Communications Services)

Data-PCS is a type of wireless communications service defined by Apple in a proposal to the FCC (Federal Communications Commission). The proposal was a petition to have the FCC set aside a 40 megahertz

(MHz) bandwidth in the 140 MHz range between 1.85 and 1.99 gigahertz (AHz).

The bandwidth is to be used for wireless communications using radio waves. Transmissions within the allocated bandwidth could have a maximum power of 1 watt. This maximum is strong enough for a 50 meter (165 feet) transmission range, but weak enough to allow multiple wireless networks to operate in different parts of the spectrum without interference.

BROADER CATEGORY

Transmission, Wireless

Data Protection

Data protection involves the safeguarding of data being transmitted across the network or stored somewhere on the network. Various steps can be taken to protect network data. Most of the measures cost money, but the more steps you take, the better protected your data is likely to be. This article summarizes techniques for protecting your data from equipment failures. See the Security article for information about how to protect data from unauthorized or malicious users.

Protecting Data Against Power Disturbance

The first line of defense—at the power lines—includes measures such as the following:

- Make sure the outlets you are using for the network machines are properly grounded. Without grounding, power protection measures may be pointless.

- Use a UPS (uninterruptible power supply) to ensure that a sudden power sag or failure does not cause the server or other crucial computers to crash. When a brownout or blackout occurs, the UPS provides emergency power from batteries. In case of a total power loss, the UPS should be able to power the server long enough to permit an orderly shutdown. A UPS can also clean a power signal (to make it closer to a pure waveform) before it reaches the networking hardware.

- Use surge protectors to protect against spikes (or surges) and sags. The former are very short bursts of very high voltage; the latter are temporary drops in voltage. When selecting surge protectors, be aware that the less expensive surge protectors are designed to protect against a single spike (or at most against a few spikes). These protectors are not designed to withstand repeated spikes. More expensive protectors will provide such long-term protection. Make sure surge protectors and all other electrical devices are UL listed.

- Use isolation transformers to protect against noise and static (smaller variations in voltage). These transformers clamp (suppress) any voltages that lie outside a predefined range.

Backups, Diagnostic, and Anti-Virus Measures

Other data protection measures include the following:

- Doing regular backups, so that a minimum amount of data (such as no more than a day's worth) will ever be lost because of system failure. See the Backup article for more information.

UPS TIPS

If a UPS on every machine is too expensive, put one on just the most crucial network components. Make sure to protect at least the file servers. Put surge protectors on as many other nodes as possible.

When calculating costs, keep in mind that research has found that networks with UPSs have lower maintenance costs than networks with just surge protectors and isolation transformers.

Don't put a UPS on a printer. Not only is this unnecessary, it's also futile, since the printer's power demands will drain the UPS battery.

- Running regular and rigorous diagnostics on your hard disks. Diagnostic programs will detect bad sectors or sectors that are about to go bad, will move any data from these sectors to safe areas of the disk, and will lock out the defective sectors. Some network packages can do this type of redirection on the fly. See the Diagnostic Program article for more information.

- Monitoring for viruses, and having well-defined recovery procedures in case of a virus attack. To reduce the possibility of virus infections, limit users' ability to upload software from personal floppy disks. See the Anti-Virus Program article for more information.

Data Protection through Software and Hardware

NetWare provides a variety of data-protection features that can be grouped into a category called *fault tolerance*. Other networking software may have similar features. NetWare's fault-tolerance features include the following:

Disk duplexing: Uses two hard disks attached to the server, and automatically copies all data to both hard disks. The disks are each accessed through separate channels (which means that each disk has its own controller board). If one disk or channel fails, the network operating system will notify the system administrator, and will continue writing to the working disk. Not all network software packages support disk duplexing.

Disk mirroring: Also uses two hard disks and copies all data to both hard disks, but both disks share the same channel (which means that they are connected to the same controller board). Failure of the controller board makes both disks inaccessible.

Hot Fix: Uses a special area of the hard disk (called the *redirection area*) to hold data from defective areas. When a write operation indicates there is a problem at the location being written, the Hot Fix capability rewrites the data in question to the redirection area, and stores the address of the defective location in a table set aside for that purpose.

Read-after-write verification: Checks newly written data before discarding the source data from memory. After writing data to the hard disk, the networking software reads the newly written data and compares it with the original data (which is still stored in RAM). If the new data and the original data match, the original data is discarded from RAM, and the next disk operation can take place. If there is a discrepancy, some corrective action (for example, a Hot Fix) is taken.

FAT duplication: Maintains duplicate file allocation tables (FATs) and directory entry tables (DETs). This method helps prevent files from becoming corrupted because of addressing errors (rather than because of media defects). FAT duplication is done automatically by most networking software.

SEE ALSO
Anti-Virus Program; Backup; Diagnostic Program; Security

Dataset

In some network management programs, a term for a collection of data gathered by an agent (a program that performs a particular task automatically or on command). The data will generally pertain to a particular network function or device.

Data Set

In telecommunications, the telephone company's name for a modem.

▼
Data Set Ready (DSR)

A signal from a modem, sent to indicate the modem is ready to operate. In an RS-232C interface, this signal is sent on pin 6.

COMPARE
DTR (Data Terminal Ready)

▼
Data Sink

In data communications, the receiver of a data transmission. This is in contrast to the *data source,* which is the sender.

▼
Data Source

In data communications, the sender of a data transmission. This is in contrast to the *data sink,* which is the receiver.

▼
Data Stream Compatibility (DSC)

In IBM's SNA (Systems Network Architecture), a basic, bare-bones printing mode.

COMPARE
SCS (SNA Character String)

▼
Data Switch

A location or device in which data can be routed, or switched, to its destination. Data-switch devices are used in switching networks, in which data is grouped and routed on the basis of predetermined criteria or current network traffic.

▼
Data Terminal Ready (DTR)

A signal from a modem, sent to indicate that a device (for example, a computer) is ready

to send and receive data. In an RS-232C interface, this signal is sent on pin 20.

COMPARE
DSR (Data Set Ready)

▼
Data Transparency

Data transparency is a data-transmission strategy designed to ensure that data will not be interpreted as control signals. Bit or byte sequences that might be interpreted as flags or commands are modified before transmission and restored upon receipt.

For example, LLAP (LocalTalk Link Access Protocol), which is used in some AppleTalk networks, uses a data transparency method called *bit stuffing* to ensure that the data bit sequence 01111110 is never transmitted, since this specific value represents a flag. In bit stuffing, a 0 bit is inserted after the fifth 1 value in the 01111110 sequence.

▼
Data Warehousing

An information management strategy in which a company's information is all accessible through a single database. The corporate information may come from many sources and departments, may come in a variety of forms, and may be stored at different levels of detail. Corporate information includes such things as product, customer, and other "departmental" databases; sales, inventory, and other transaction data; archival, or legacy, data, and so forth.

The data warehouse will also contain *meta-data,* which is information about the general organization of the warehouse, the format and location of the various materials in the warehouse, the operations or uses allowed for various items, and possibly connections between data items. The meta-data needs to be updated whenever the actual data is changed.

The warehouse contents may be distributed over various machines and locations, but should be accessible in a transparent manner through a server. It is this transparent access of the entire corporate database with simple commands that makes data warehousing so attractive. By making the entire database accessible, it becomes easier to spot trends, coordinate updates, and generally keep the data organized and consistent.

Access to the data warehouse always assumes user authorization. That is, the integration of various databases should not make it possible for users to get access to data that were off limits before warehousing. Warehouse data should be accessible to authorized users in raw form or for analyses—and the necessary retrieval and analysis tools should be part of the data warehouse system.

Warehouse data will vary in level of detail, or *granularity*. Current data, which is more likely to be active and in flux, will be more detailed (finer-grained) than older materials, which may be just summary data. Other types of data may lie between these two extremes.

The material in a data warehouse need not all be online all the time. Dormant (or, at least napping) materials may be stored on secondary media (such as tapes or compact discs), which may need to be mounted before users can access them. For these materials to belong to the data warehouse,

it's only necessary for the meta-data to include information about these materials and their location.

A Data Warehousing System

A complete data warehousing system should have resources for:

- Defining and organizing the warehouse contents, and storing this as meta-data

- Acquiring, displaying, and distributing data

- Managing and overseeing both the data and the warehouse operations

- Displaying information about the warehouse contents and organization

- Analyzing and manipulating the data

The advantages of data warehousing are many, as are the obstacles. One of the major issues that must be considered is how to organize and connect very heterogeneous information. The degree to which updates and reorganizations can be automated will depend strongly on the quality of the basic organization.

dB (Decibel)

A decibel (abbreviated dB—from a unit named in honor of Alexander Graham Bell) is a tenth of a bel. It is a logarithmic unit used to measure relative signal intensity. For example, decibels are used to measure the relative intensity of acoustic, electrical, or optical signals.

A decibel value is computed by taking the logarithm (to base 10) of a ratio, and then multiplying this value by 10 (or 20, for some

a b c **d** e f g h i j k l m n o p q r s t u v w x y z

measures). For example, doubling the level of a magnitude (such as a voltage) represents a 3 decibel increase; conversely, halving a level represents a 3 decibel decrease.

The decibel value may be computed in terms of a reference level, such as a watt (W) or a milliwatt (mW). For such measures, the reference level is one of the values in the ratio. These referenced measures are denoted by dbW for decibel with reference to one watt, and dbm for decibel with reference to one milliwatt.

DBMS (Database Management System)

A DBMS is application software that controls the data in a database, including overall organization, storage, retrieval, security, and data integrity. In addition, a DBMS usually has the following features:

- Support for formatting reports for printed output

- Support for importing and exporting data from other applications using standard file formats

- A data-manipulation language to support database queries

SEE ALSO
Database

DBS (Direct Broadcast Satellite)

A satellite that broadcasts signals directly to subscribers; that is, without going through a central station.

DC (Direct Current)

Electrical power that travels in only one direction, as opposed to alternating current (AC), which changes directions many times a second. Batteries and most electronic components (such as computers) use DC power; power supplied for homes and offices is AC.

DCA (Document Content Architecture)

DCA is a data stream defined by IBM for using text documents in various computer environments. Three standard formats are specified for text transfer:

RFT (Revisable Form Text): The primary format, in which text can still be edited

FFT (Final Form Text): The format in which text has been formatted for a particular output device and cannot be edited

MFT (Mixed Form Text): The format that contains more than just text, such as a document that also includes graphics

COMPARE
DIA (Document Interchange Architecture)

DCB (Disk Coprocessor Board)

A DCB is an expansion board that serves as an interface between the central processing unit (CPU) and the hard disk controller. Because the DCB is intelligent, the CPU need not worry about reading and writing data.

A DCB is also called an *HBA (host bus adapter)*.

A disk channel consists of a DCB and other components needed to connect to one or more hard disks. Novell's NetWare supports up to four channels. For SCSI (Small Computer System Interface) drives, up to eight controllers can be associated with each DCB, and each controller can support two hard disks.

DCD (Data Carrier Detect)

In telecommunications, a signal in an RS-232 connection that is asserted (True) when the modem detects a signal with a frequency appropriate for the communications standard the modem is using.

DCE (Data Communications Equipment)

DCE, which stands for data communications equipment or data circuit-terminating equipment, refers to a modem that is used in conjunction with a computer as the DTE (data terminal equipment).

More generally, a DCE is any device capable of communicating with the appropriate DTE, and of providing access to the appropriate type of line. For example, a modem can speak to a computer and can provide access to analog telephone lines. In digital telecommunications, a DSU (data service unit) and a CSU (communications service unit) together make up a DCE, and provide access to the digital lines.

DCE (Distributed Computing Environment)

DCE is an open networking architecture promoted by the Open Software Foundation (OSF), which is a consortium of vendors that includes Digital Equipment Corporation (DEC), Hewlett Packard (HP), and IBM. The DCE architecture provides the elements needed to distribute applications and their operation across networks in a transparent fashion.

If DCE is implemented, the entire network should appear to a user as one giant, very fast and powerful computer. Regardless of whether the network consists of two identical PCs or a few dozen different machines, DCE protects the user from any implementation details.

DCE sits on top of whatever network operating system is running, so that a user interacts with the DCE environment. This environment provides the following tools and services for a user or an application:

- RPC (Remote Procedure Call), which makes it possible to call an application or function on any machine, just as if the resource were local or even part of the application.

- Threads (independently executable program segments), which can be distributed across different machines and executed simultaneously. Threads can speed work up considerably. The RSA encryption algorithm—which was expected to require over 15 years to crack—was cracked within months using threads.

a
b
c
d
e
f
g
h
i
j
k
l
m
n
o
p
q
r
s
t
u
v
w
x
y
z

- Security measures, which automatically apply to the entire network. This means that a user on a machine is protected automatically from a virus or unauthorized user on another machine, just as if the intruder on the other machine were an intruder on that machine.

In a DCE, all nodes can be synchronized to the DCE's clock, which effectively provides precise timing capabilities. DCE offers both global X.500 and also local CDS (cell directory services).

By making the entire network's resources available in a completely transparent manner, DCE helps make the fullest use of available resources, and also makes it more likely that a resource will be available when needed.

D Channel

In an ISDN (Integrated Services Digital Network) system, the D channel is the "data," or signaling, channel. The D channel is used for control signals and for data about the call. This is in contrast to the B channel, which serves as a bearer for data and voice.

For BRI (Basic Rate Interface), the D channel has a data rate of 16 kilobits per second (kbps); for PRI (Primary Rate Interface), the D channel has a data rate of 64 kbps. These two forms of the D channel are denoted as *D16* and *D64,* respectively.

BROADER CATEGORY
ISDN (Integrated Services Digital Network)

SEE ALSO
BRI (Basic Rate Interface), PRI (Primary Rate Interface)

COMPARE
B Channel, H Channel

DCS (Defined Context Set)

In the CCITT's X.216 recommendations, an agreed-upon context for the delivery and use of presentation-level services.

DCS (Digital Cross-Connect System)

In digital telephony, a special-purpose switch for cross-connecting digital channels (for switching a digital channel from one piece of equipment to another). With a DCS, this cross-connect can take place at the rate supported by the slower of the two lines.

DDB (Distributed Database)

A database whose contents are stored on different hard disks or in different locations. Each disk or location may be managed by different machines. The Internet's domain name system (DNS) is an example of a distributed database.

SEE ALSO
Database

DDBMS (Distributed Database Management System)

Database management software that can handle a distributed database (DDB).

DDD (Direct Distance Dialing)

In telephony, the ability to dial a long-distance number without going through an operator.

DDE (Dynamic Data Exchange)

DDE is a technique for application-to-application communications. It is available in several operating systems, including Microsoft Windows, Macintosh System 7, and OS/2.

When two or more programs that support DDE are running at the same time, they can exchange data and commands, by means of *conversations*. A DDE conversation is a two-way connection between two different applications.

DDE is used for low-level communications that do not need user intervention. For example, a communications program might feed stock market information into a spreadsheet program, where that data can be displayed in a meaningful way and recalculated automatically as it changes.

DDE has largely been superseded by a more complex but more capable mechanism known as Object Linking and Embedding (OLE).

DDL (Data Definition Language)

Any of several languages for describing data and its relationships, as in a database.

DDM (Distributed Data Management)

In IBM's SNA (Systems Network Architecture), services that allow file sharing and remote file access in a network.

DDN NIC (Defense Data Network Network Information Center)

The DDN is a global network used by the U.S. Department of Defense (DoD) to connect military installations. Parts of the DDN are accessible from the Internet, and parts are classified.

The DDN NIC is a control center that provides information and services through the Internet. The DDN NIC does the following:

- Serves as a repository for the Requests for Comments (RFCs), which are used to define standards, report results, and suggest planning directions for the Internet community.

- Assigns IP (Internet Protocol) network addresses.

- Assigns numbers to domains (or *autonomous systems*, as they are called in the Internet jargon).

SEE ALSO

IR (Internet Registry)

DDP (Distributed Data Processing)

Data processing in which some or all of the processing and/or I/O (input/output) work is distributed over multiple machines.

DDS (Dataphone Digital Service)

DDS is an AT&T communications service that uses digital signal transmission over leased lines. Because data is transmitted digitally, no modem is required; however, a DSU/CSU (digital service unit/channel service unit) is needed at the interface between the digital lines and the customer's equipment. The customer equipment will generally be a remote bridge or router, because DDS is commonly used for providing point-to-point links in a wide-area network (WAN).

DDS uses four wires, supports speeds between 2.4 and 56 kilobits per second (kbps), and is available through most LECs (local exchange carriers) and IXCs (interexchange carriers); that is, it is available through local or long-distance telephone companies.

DDS (Digital Data Service)

Leased lines that support transmission rates between 2.4 and 56 kilobits per second.

DE (Discard Eligibility)

In a frame-relay packet header, a bit that can be set to indicate that the packet can be discarded if network traffic warrants it. If network traffic gets too heavy, the network can discard packets that have this bit set.

DEA (Data Encryption Algorithm)

In general, an algorithm, or rule, for encrypting data. In the DES, the DEA is an algorithm for encrypting data in blocks of 64-bits each.

SEE ALSO

DES (Data Encryption Standard)

DECmcc (DEC Management Control Center)

Network management software for Digital's DECnet networks. Products based on this core, such as DECmcc Director, are available for specific environments.

DECnet

DECnet is a proprietary network architecture from Digital Equipment Corporation (DEC). DECnet has gone through several major revisions during its lifetime. The two most recent versions, Phases IV and V, were released in 1982 and 1987, respectively. Both versions are still used.

Historically, DECnet networks consisted mainly of PDP-11s and VAXen, but the architecture can support a broad range of hardware, including PCs and Macintoshes. Gateways also exist for remote access and for access to SNA (System Network Architecture) networks.

DECnet Phase IV

The eight layers in the DECnet Phase IV model correspond roughly—sometimes very roughly—to the seven layers in the OSI Reference Model. The Phase IV layers are as follows:

Physical: Corresponds to the OSI physical layer. This layer establishes a physical connection and manages the actual data transmission. This layer supports Blue Book (as opposed to IEEE 802.3) Ethernet protocols.

Data link: Corresponds to the OSI data-link layer. This layer supports Blue Book Ethernet, X.25, and DDCMP (Digital Data Communications Messaging Protocol) protocols.

Routing: Corresponds to the OSI network layer. This layer routes packets to their destination and helps manage intra- and internetwork traffic. It permits adaptive routing, gathers network management data, and supports various routing protocols.

End-to-end communications: Corresponds roughly to the OSI transport layer. This layer helps maintain network links, and segments and reassembles information (at sending and receiving ends, respectively). It supports the VAX OSI Transport Service (VOTS) protocol and DEC's own Network Services Protocol (NSP).

Session control: Corresponds roughly to the OSI session layer. This layer stores network name and address information, for use when establishing a connection. It is also responsible for breaking the network link when the transmission is finished. The session control layer supports both proprietary and OSI session protocols.

Network application: Corresponds roughly to the OSI presentation layer. This layer enables local and remote file and terminal access. It supports OSI presentation layer protocols and also DEC's Data Access Protocol (DAP).

Network management: Corresponds very roughly to part of the OSI application layer. This layer handles peer-to-peer network management. It supports DEC's Network Information and Control Exchange (NICE) protocol.

User: Corresponds very roughly to part of the OSI application layer—the part concerned with user applications.

DECnet Phase V

DECnet Phase V was designed to comply fully with the OSI Reference Model. This version has only seven layers, which correspond to the OSI layers. In general, DECnet Phase V supports OSI-compliant protocols at each level. It also supports DEC's own protocols (such as DDCMP and DAP) for backward-compatibility with Phase IV networks.

Designed to handle large networks, DECnet Phase V can use up to 20 bytes for address information. A network can be divided into domains for routing or administrative purposes. The address field includes an Initial Domain Part (IDP) value, which is unique for every network.

Dedicated Circuit

A path that goes directly from a user location to a telephone company point of presence (POP); that is, it goes to the location at which a subscriber's leased or long-distance lines connect to the telephone company's lines.

SEE ALSO
IXC (Interexchange Carrier), POP (Point of Presence)

Dedicated Line

A dedicated line is a permanent connection—a connection that is always available—between two locations. This connection is provided on private, or leased, lines, rather than the public, dial-up lines, and so a dedicated line is also known as a *leased,* or *private, line.*

Available dedicated-line services include the following:

DDS (Dataphone Digital Services): Provide synchronous transmission of digital signals at up to 56 kilobits per second (kbps). Subrate (lower-speed) services are also available, at 2,400 to 19,200 bps.

56/64 kbps lines: In Europe, these lines provide a full 64 kbps; in the United States and in Japan, 8 kbps are used for administrative and control overhead, leaving only 56 kbps for the subscriber. Such lines are also available through dial-up (nondedicated lines).

Fractional T1 lines: Lines built up in increments of 64 kbps, to a maximum rate of 768 kbps.

T1/E1 lines: Provide 1.544 megabits per second (Mbps) for T1 (available in the United States and Japan) and 2.048 Mbps for E1 (available in Mexico and Europe) service.

The availability and pricing of these dedicated-line services vary greatly in different geographical areas.

COMPARE
Dial-Up Line

De Facto Standard

A standard that results from widespread usage by the user community, rather than from the work of an official standards committee. This is in contrast to a *de jure standard,* which gets its legitimacy from a standards committee. De facto standards may be just as explicitly specified as de jure standards. De facto standards simply have not been given a "Good Standardizing" seal of approval. ARCnet is one of the best-known de facto standards.

Default Path

In packet routing, a path used by a router to forward a packet when the packet itself contains no explicit routing instructions, and the router has no predefined path to the packet's ultimate destination. The default path is generally one to a router that is likely to have more detailed routing information.

Default Server

For a node, the default server is usually the server the node logs in to. If a user is logged in to more than one server, the default is the server that the user is currently accessing.

Default Value

A value used for a parameter or setting when no other value is specified by the user through a program or in a data file.

Default Zone

In an AppleTalk Phase 2 network, the zone to which a device or node belongs until it is assigned to a specific zone.

SEE

AppleTalk

Deferral Time

In a CSMA (collision sense, multiple access) media access method, the amount of time a node waits before trying again to access the network after an unsuccessful attempt. The time depends on a random value and on the network's activity level.

SEE

CSMA (Collision Sense, Multiple Access)

Deferred Procedure Call (DPC)

SEE

DPC (Deferred Procedure Call)

De Jure Standard

A standard that has been officially approved by a recognized standards committee, such as ANSI, CCITT, or IEEE. De jure standards may be national or international. Popular de jure standards include IEEE 802.3 (Ethernet) and IEEE 802.5 (Token Ring) for networks,

and CCITT V.42bis (data compression) for modems.

COMPARE

De Facto Standard

DEK (Data Encryption Key)

A value used to encrypt a message. The DEK is used by an encryption algorithm to encode the message, and may be used by a decryption algorithm to decode the message. More sophisticated encryption strategies use different keys for encrypting and for decrypting.

SEE ALSO

DES (Data Encryption Standard)

Delay

In an electrical circuit, a *delay* is a property that slows down high-frequency signals, causing signal distortion. An equalizer can be used to help deal with this problem.

In a network or communications connection, a delay is a latency, or lag, before a signal is passed on or returned. This type of delay may be due to switching or to distances involved (for example, in satellite or cellular communications).

Some devices and connections will not tolerate delays longer than a predefined amount of time, and they may time-out if this time limit is exceeded. For example, a printer may time out if there is too long a wait before the next instruction arrives. For some time-sensitive devices, you can change the default waiting time.

a
b
c
d
e
f
g
h
i
j
k
l
m
n
o
p
q
r
s
t
u
v
w
x
y
z

Delphi Internet

Delphi Internet is a commercial online service—like America Online, CompuServe, or Prodigy. While Internet access has been the focus of its advertisements, Delphi Internet also offers other facilities commonly associated with online service providers. These include forums, mail, online shopping, news and financial information, and games and other software to use online or to download. Delphi Internet's Custom Forums allow users to host and manage their own forums. Delphi's Internet services include e-mail, Telnet, FTP, gopher, Usenet, and IRC (Internet Relay Chat).

FOR INFORMATION
Delphi Internet at (800) 695-4005

Demand-Assigned Multiple Access (DAMA)

SEE
DAMA (Demand-Assigned Multiple Access)

Demand Priority

Demand priority is a media-access method used in 100BaseVG, a 100 megabit per second (Mbps) Ethernet implementation proposed by Hewlett-Packard (HP) and AT&T Microelectronics. Demand priority shifts network access control from the workstation to a hub. This access method works with a star topology.

In this method, a node that wishes to transmit indicates this wish to the hub and also requests high- or regular-priority service for its transmission. After it obtains permission, the node begins transmitting to the hub.

The hub is responsible for passing the transmission on to the destination node; that is, the hub is responsible for providing access to the network. A hub will pass high-priority transmissions through immediately, and will pass regular-priority transmissions through as the opportunity arises.

By letting the hub manage access, the architecture is able to guarantee required bandwidths and requested service priority to particular applications or nodes. It also can guarantee that the network can be scaled up (enlarged) without loss of bandwidth.

Demand priority helps increase bandwidth in the following ways:

- A node does not need to keep checking whether the network is idle before transmitting. In current Ethernet implementations, a wire pair is dedicated to this task. By making network checking unnecessary, demand priority frees a wire pair. This is fortunate, because the 100BaseVG specifications use quartet signaling, which needs four available wire pairs.

- Heavy traffic can effectively bring standard Ethernet networks to a standstill, because nodes spend most of their time trying to access the network. With demand priority, the hub needs to pass a transmission on only to its destination, so that overall network traffic is decreased. This means there is more bandwidth available for heavy network traffic.

By giving the hub control over a transmission, so that the message is passed to only its destination node or nodes, demand priority also makes it easier to prevent eavesdropping.

BROADER CATEGORIES
100BaseVG; Media-Access Method

Demarcation Point

In telephone communications, the point at which the customer's equipment and wiring ends and the telephone company's begins.

Demodulation

In communications, the process of removing and isolating the modulating signal that was added to a carrier signal for purposes of communication. For example, in serial communications involving computers and modems, the demodulation process converts the acoustic signal that has traveled over the telephone line into an electrical form from which the transmitted data can be determined.

Demultiplexer

A device that takes multiplexed material from a single input, and sends the individual input elements to several outputs.

De-osification

A term for the conversion from definitions that conform to the OSI network management model to definitions that conform to the IP network management model. The term is used in TCP/IP environments that

use SNMP (Simple Network Management Protocol).

Departmental-Area Network (DAN)

SEE
DAN (Departmental-Area Network)

Departmental LAN

A small- to medium-sized network (up to about 30 users) whose nodes share local resources.

DES (Data Encryption Standard)

DES is the official United States data encryption standard for nonclassified documents. DES uses a single, 64-bit value as a key and a private-key encryption strategy to convert ordinary text (*plaintext*) into encrypted form (*ciphertext*). (See the Encryption article for details on plaintext and ciphertext, as well as *private*- versus public-key encryption.)

In a *private*-key strategy, only the sender and the receiver are supposed to know the key (bit sequence) used to encrypt the data. The encryption *algorithm,* on the other hand, is publicly known.

Although it is relatively difficult to crack, DES cannot protect against fraud by the sender or the receiver. For example, there is no way to identify a sender who has learned the key and is pretending to be the legitimate sender.

An ardent early advocate for DES, the National Security Agency (NSA) has campaigned to remove DES as the official encryption standard. The NSA is advocating a classified algorithm (one under the NSA's

a
b
c
d
e
f
g
h
i
j
k
l
m
n
o
p
q
r
s
t
u
v
w
x
y
z

control) as the basis for the encryption standard. To date, this suggestion has met with considerable resistance from the business and computing communities.

DEA (Data Encryption Algorithm)

When the DES is used for encryption, a message is divided into 64-bit blocks, and each block is encrypted separately, one character at a time. During the encryption of a block, the computer plays an electronic shell game: the characters in the block are scrambled 16 times during encryption, and the encryption method changes after each scrambling. The key determines the details of the scrambling and the character encryption. In short, each 64-bit block goes through over a dozen transformations during encryption.

Of the 64 bits used for the encryption key, 56 are used for encryption, and 8 are used for error detection. The 56 bits yield about 70 quadrillion possible keys—almost 15 million possible keys for each person alive today. (Imagine the key chain you would need.)

The encryption algorithm involves several steps:

- Permuting (switching the order of) the bits in the block.

- Repeating a computation that uses the data encryption key (DEK) and that involves substitution and transposition operations.

- Permuting the bits in the block to restore the original order.

DES Modes

DES can operate in any of four modes:

ECB (Electronic Cookbook): The simplest encryption method. The encryption process is the same for each block, and it is based on the encryption algorithm and the key. Repeated character patterns, such as names, are always encoded in the same way.

CBC (Cipher Block Chaining): A more involved encryption method in which the encryption for each block depends on the encryption for the preceding block, as well as on the algorithm and key. The same pattern is encoded differently in each block.

CFB (Cipher Feedback): A still more involved method in which ciphertext is used to generate pseudo-random values. These values are combined with plaintext and the results are then encrypted. CFB may encrypt an individual character differently each time it is encountered.

OFB (Output Feedback): Similar to CFB, except that actual DES output is used to generate the pseudo-random values that are combined with plaintext. This mode is used to encrypt communications via satellite.

PRIMARY SOURCE
FIPS publication #46

BROADER CATEGORY
Encryption

Desktop

In the Macintosh environment, a file server that provides access to applications and documents through the use of icons. On a workstation, the desktop provides a graphical representation of the files and programs located on that workstation. The term also refers to workstations that reside on users' desks (as opposed to laptops and palmtops, for example).

Destination Address

In many types of packets, the address of the station to which the packet is being sent. The address of the station that is sending the message is called the *source address*.

DET (Directory Entry Table)

In Novell's NetWare, the DET is one of two tables used to keep track of directory information. The other table is the file allocation table (FAT). The DET is stored on a hard disk.

The DET contains information about a volume's file and directory names and properties. For example, an entry might contain the following:

- File name

- File owner

- Date and time of last update

- Trustee assignments (or user rights)

- Location of the file's first block on the network hard disk

The DET also accesses the FAT, which is an index to the locations of the blocks that make up each file.

The contents of the DET are stored in special storage allocation units, called directory entry blocks (DEBs). Each DEB is 4 kilobytes, and NetWare can support up to 65,536 of these blocks.

To improve performance, NetWare can use directory caching or hashing. *Directory caching* keeps currently used directory blocks and the FAT in a reserved area of RAM. Frequently used directory entries will be loaded into a cache memory. *Directory hashing* is the indexing of the directory entries, which speeds access to directory information.

Device Driver

A driver program designed to enable a PC to use or communicate with a particular device, such as a printer or monitor. A device driver generally has a more specific name, such as printer driver or screen driver, depending on the type of device involved.

Device Numbering

Device numbering is a method for identifying a device, such as a hard disk, scanner, or floppy drive. Three numbers serve to define each device:

Hardware address: The address associated with the board or controller for the device. This value is set either through software or by setting jumpers in the required configuration. Drivers that need to deal with the device can

a b c **d** e f g h i j k l m n o p q r s t u v w x y z

read the hardware address from the jumper settings.

Device code: A value determined by the location of the device's board, the device itself, and possibly by auxiliary components (such as controllers) associated with the board. For example, a device code for a hard disk includes values for disk type, controller, board, and disk numbers.

Logical number: A value based on the boards to which the devices are attached, on the controller, and on the order in which devices are loaded.

Device Sharing

Use of a centrally located device by multiple users or programs. For example, a printer or hard disk may be shared among several workstation users. Since most devices are idle a high proportion of the time, sharing them is a cost-effective way to make a resource more widely available and more likely to be used.

DFS (Distributed File System)

A file system with files located on multiple machines, but accessible to an end-user or a process as if the files were all in a single location.

DFT (Distributed Function Terminal)

In IBM's SNA (System Network Architecture), a terminal mode in which a terminal may support up to five different sessions, so that a user can access up to five applications through the same terminal.

COMPARE
CUT (Control Unit Terminal)

DIA (Document Interchange Architecture)

DIA is software and services defined by IBM, to make it easier to use documents in a variety of IBM environments. DIA includes the following services:

- APS (Application Processing Services)
- DDS (Document Distribution Services)
- DLS (Document Library Services)
- FTS (File Transfer Service)

COMPARE
DCA (Document Content Architecture)

Diagnostic Program

A diagnostic program tests computer hardware and peripheral devices for correct operation. Some problems, known as *hard faults,* are relatively easy to find, and the diagnostic program will diagnose them correctly every time.

Other problems, called *soft faults,* can be difficult to find, because they occur sporadically or only under specific circumstances, rather than every time the memory location is tested.

Most computers run a simple set of system checks when the computer is first turned on. The PC tests are stored in read-only memory (ROM), and are known as power-on self tests (POSTs). If a POST detects an error condition, the computer will stop and display an error message on the screen.

Some computers will emit a beep signal to indicate the type of error.

Dial-Back

In network operations, dial-back (also known as *call-back*) is a security measure to prevent unauthorized dial-up access to a network. The networking software maintains a list of users and the numbers from which they might dial in.

When a user wants to dial into the network, the server takes the call, gets the user's login information, then breaks the connection. The software then looks up the user in the dial-up table and calls back the number listed for the user.

As an access control and security measure, dial-back works reasonably well. However, it can fail when the user needs to dial in from a different location, or when an unauthorized person has gained access to the location from which the user generally dials in (the network calls a number, not a person).

Dial-up Line

A dial-up line is a nondedicated communications line in which a connection can be established by dialing the number, or code, associated with the destination. A common example of a dial-up line, also called a *switched line* or *public line,* is the public telephone line. Dial-up lines generally support speeds of 2,400 to 9,600 bps.

The connection is created at dial-up time, and it is destroyed when the call is finished. This is in contrast to a *leased line* (also called a *private* or *dedicated line*), in which

a connection between two specific points is always available.

With a dial-up line, the same calling node can be connected with an arbitrary number of destinations. Costs accrue only for the duration of a particular connection.

COMPARE
Dedicated Line

DIB (Directory Information Base)

In the CCITT X.500 Directory Services model, the body of directory-related information. Directory system agents (DSAs) access the DIB on behalf of directory user agents (DUAs).

SEE ALSO
DIT (Directory Information Tree); X.500

DIBI (Device Independent Backup Interface)

An interface proposed by Novell to make it easier to move material between different environments on the network.

Dibit

A pair of bits treated as a single unit. For example, a dibit is used in certain modulation methods that can encode two bits in a single modulated value. The four possible dibits are 00, 01, 10, and 11.

DID (Destination ID)

In an ARCnet packet, the address of the destination node.

a
b
c
d
e
f
g
h
i
j
k
l
m
n
o
p
q
r
s
t
u
v
w
x
y
z

DID (Direct Inward Dialing)

In telephone communications, a system in which an outside caller can reach a number in a private branch exchange (PBX) directly, without going through a switchboard.

Dielectric

A nonconducting material, such as rubber or certain types of plastic, used as an insulating layer around the conductive wire in coaxial and twisted-pair cable.

Digital Access and Cross-Connect System (DACS)

SEE

DACS (Digital Access and Cross-Connect System)

Digital Circuit

In communications, lines that transmit data as unmodulated square waves, which represent 0 or 1 values. Digital circuit lines are provided by common carriers, such as telephone companies.

Digital Communication

Digital communication is a telecommunications method that uses digital (discrete) signals, usually binary values, to represent information. The original information may be in analog or digital form.

A digital transmission uses digital, rather than analog, signals. Digital signals are encoded as discrete values, representing 0 or 1. These binary values may be encoded as different voltage or current levels, or as changes in voltage levels.

In an analog signal, information is represented as variations in a continuous waveform's amplitude or frequency. To transmit analog information, the analog signal passes through a codec (coder/decoder), which functions as an analog-to-digital converter (ADC). The codec samples the analog signal thousands of times a second, representing each sample value as a unique 8-bit digital value.

The codec's output is a sequence of discrete voltage levels, which represent the sample values. This sequence is transmitted over the appropriate lines, which may support speeds ranging from 2,400 bits per second to more than 200 megabits per second.

The received digital signal is cleaned to recover the signal information. A codec then converts the digital signal back to analog form. At this end, the codec serves as a digital-to-analog converter (DAC). The sampled values are used as reference points for synthesizing a continuous waveform that tries to reproduce the original analog signal.

The quality of the synthesized signal depends on the sampling frequency (usually 8000 times per second) and on the number of bits used to represent the possible signal levels (usually 8 bits).

The elements involved in the process are illustrated in the figure "Digital communication of an analog signal."

Compared with analog transmissions, digital transmissions are generally less susceptible to noise, are easier to work with for error detection and correction, and require somewhat less complex circuitry.

DIGITAL COMMUNICATION OF AN ANALOG SIGNAL

Analog Signal: Information is represented as variations in a continuous waveform's amplitude or frequency.

Codec: The analog signal is converted to digital form.

Digital Signal: The codec's output is a sequence of discrete voltage levels, which represent the sampled values.

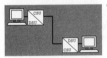

Transmission: The digital signal is transmitted over the appropriate lines.

Digital Signal: The received digital signal is cleaned, to recover the signal information.

Codec: The digital signal is converted back to analog form.

Analog Signal: The quality of the synthesized signal depends on the sampling frequency and on the number of bits used to represent the possible signal levels.

Digital Cross-Connect System (DCS)

SEE

DCS (Digital Cross-Connect System)

Digital ID

An element attached to an electronic message to authenticate the message and sender. The digital ID is assigned by a certification, or authentication, authority, and is valid for only a limited period. A digital ID contains the following elements:

- The sender's name, address, and organization
- The sender's public key
- A digital signature from the certification authority
- A serial number for the digital ID
- Validity period for the digital ID

Digital Multiplexed Interface (DMI)

SEE

DMI (Digital Multiplexed Interface)

Digital Network Architecture (DNA)

SEE

DNA (Digital Network Architecture)

Digital Signal Processor (DSP)

SEE

DSP (Digital Signal Processor)

a b c d e f g h i j k l m n o p q r s t u v w x y z

Digital Signature

In network security, a digital signature is a unique value associated with a transaction. The signature is used to verify the identity of the sender and also the origin of the message. Digital signatures cannot be forged.

To illustrate how digital signatures can be used, suppose user A and user B are communicating using an encryption strategy, such as the RSA public-key encryption strategy. With the RSA strategy, user A has a public and a private key, and user B has a private and a public key, which differs from user A's keys.

The figure "Communications using digital signatures and a public-key encryption method" shows what must happen for user A and user B to communicate using a digital signature.

BROADER CATEGORIES

Encryption; Security Management

Digital Speech Interpolation (DSI)

SEE

DSI (Digital Speech Interpolation)

Digital Termination Service (DTS)

SEE

DTS (Digital Termination Service)

DIP (Dual In-line Package) Switch

A DIP switch is a block with two or more switches, each of which can be in either of two settings. DIP switches are used as alternatives to jumper settings when configuring a component. The figure "A DIP switch" illustrates an example of a rocker-type DIP switch.

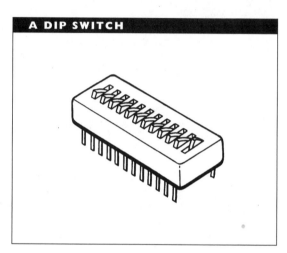

A DIP SWITCH

DIP switches are used in printed circuit boards, dot-matrix printers, modems, and many other peripheral devices.

Direct Connection

In networking, a direct connection is an unmediated connection to the network. For example, a direct connection might be through a network cable attached to the network interface card (NIC).

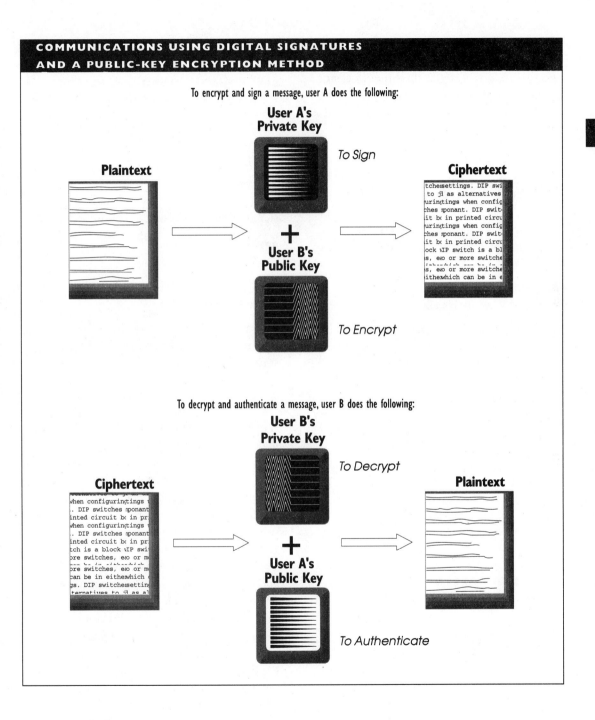

COMMUNICATIONS USING DIGITAL SIGNATURES
AND A PUBLIC-KEY ENCRYPTION METHOD

To encrypt and sign a message, user A does the following:

User A's Private Key

To Sign

Plaintext

Ciphertext

User B's Public Key

To Encrypt

To decrypt and authenticate a message, user B does the following:

User B's Private Key

To Decrypt

Ciphertext

Plaintext

User A's Public Key

To Authenticate

In telecommunications and wide-area networks (WANs), direct connection is a connection to long-distance lines that does not go through a local carrier. This type of connection is in contrast to the switched-digital access method, in which the connection does go through the local carrier.

Direct-Control Switching

In switching technology, a system in which the path is established directly, by signals in the network, rather than through a central controller.

Directed Transmission

In an AppleTalk network using the Local-Talk network architecture and its LocalTalk Link Access Protocol (LLAP), a directed transmission is one intended for a specific node. It is in contrast to a *broadcast transmission,* which is intended for all nodes.

In infrared communications, directed transmission is a method in which a signal is aimed at a central reflective target, and read by receiving nodes as the signal bounces off the target. This is in contrast to a *diffuse transmission,* which travels in multiple directions, but is much weaker in each direction.

BROADER CATEGORIES
AppleTalk; Infrared Transmission; LLAP

COMPARE
Broadcast Transmission

Direct Inward Dialing (DID)

SEE
DID (Direct Inward Dialing)

Directional Coupler

A coupler that can send a split signal in only one direction. This is in contrast to a bidirectional coupler, which can split a signal in more than one direction.

SEE ALSO
Coupler

Direct Link

A connection, or circuit, that connects two stations directly, without any intervening stations.

Directory

A directory is an organizational concept that makes it possible to group files, so that files can be accessed more easily. For example, all files related to a particular project or application may be grouped in a single directory. To further group files, they can be placed in subdirectories within directories.

Grouping files in a directory makes it possible to organize these files on a logical basis and at a logical level. Creating subdirectories makes it possible to impose a hierarchical structure on files. A subdirectory is said to be contained in a *parent directory.*

Grouping certain files distinguishes them implicitly from other files that are *not* in the directory. Because files in a directory are effectively partitioned from files outside, it's possible to use the same file names in different directories.

The Directory Hierarchy

Directories can contain other directories, which can contain still other directories, so that multiple levels of containment are possible. A directory structure looks like a tree. This tree has an infelicitously named *root directory* at the top of the tree, (sub)directories as branches, and files as individual leaves at the ends of the branches.

A file can be referred to or located by specifying a path to it. This path consists of a sequence of directory (or subdirectory) names that are passed in traversing the tree to the file. Such a path usually begins with the root and ends with the file name.

File Path

In a file path, directory names are separated by a special character, which differs from environment to environment. For example, in DOS, the separator character, or delimiter, is the backslash (\); in UNIX it is the forward slash (/). Some operating environments will accept either delimiter.

In crowded or complex environments, such as in a directory structure with many subdirectory levels, file paths can get quite long. Unfortunately, most operating systems limit the number of characters allowed in a path formulation. For example, DOS path names can be at most 127 characters; NetWare's can be up to 255 characters. Length limitations can be a problem when trying to pass material from one program to another.

To avoid problems with such limits, most operating environments provide mechanisms for specifying relative partial paths. For example, a *relative path* is one that "begins" at the current directory location (as opposed to beginning at the root).

Fake Root Directory

Versions 3.*x* and later of Novell's NetWare allow you to define a subdirectory as a *fake root* directory. To an application, this directory looks just like the root, and administrators can assign user rights from the fake root directory.

One advantage of a fake root is that the real root directory need not be cluttered because of an inflexible application. Also, the true root directory is not compromised because user rights must be assigned at that level.

Directory Structure

As stated, a directory structure is inherently hierarchical, and can be represented as a tree with the root at the top. This hierarchical property can be used to keep a hard disk organized and easy to use. It can also help contribute to network security by making certain types of accidents much less likely.

Directory structure refers to the way in which directories and subdirectories are organized in relation to each other; that is, it refers to how they are laid out conceptually on a hard disk or partition.

Flat versus Deep Directory Structure

A directory structure can be *flat* or *deep*—depending on the number of subdirectories at the root and on the number of subdirectory levels.

a
b
c
d
e
f
g
h
i
j
k
l
m
n
o
p
q
r
s
t
u
v
w
x
y
z

A flat directory structure has lots of subdirectories under the root, but few, if any, sub-subdirectories. Such a structure is likely to arise if there are no commonalities in the kinds of directories being created (and, therefore, little or no need to create higher-level groupings). The figure "A flat directory structure" shows an example of this structure.

A deep directory structure, on the other hand, may have many levels of subdirectories. For example, this type of structure might be used if there are a few categories of programs, with various possible activities for these programs. The figure "A deep directory structure" illustrates this type of setup.

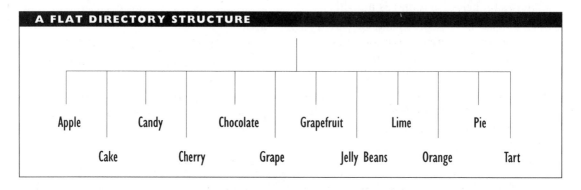

A FLAT DIRECTORY STRUCTURE

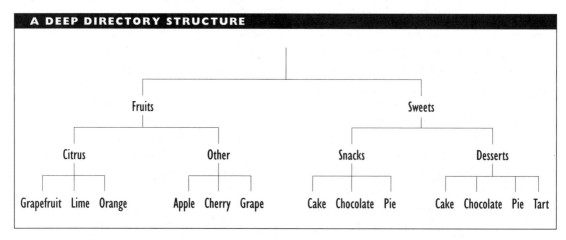

A DEEP DIRECTORY STRUCTURE

a
b
c
d
e
f
g
h
i
j
k
l
m
n
o
p
q
r
s
t
u
v
w
x
y
z

DIRECTORY STRUCTURE SUGGESTIONS

Various computer mavens and kibitzers have offered suggestions about what types of directory structures are best:

- In terms of accessibility, for example, structures with no more than four or five levels are recommended. With too many levels, paths can get unacceptably long.

- Groupings and structures should be "logical" or "reasonable"—terms whose definitions are generally left to the reader or the administrator.

- A directory should not contain "too many" files. In some environments, the operating system will provide at least an upper bound on what constitutes "too many." In other cases, the software will dictate how many files are to be included in the directory.

- In a network, it's often useful to structure directories so that one set of access rights at the top-level directory applies to all that directory's subdirectories and files. For example, you might put all applications in a PRO-GRAM directory and all working files in a WORK directory, and assign the appropriate access rights to those two main directories.

Network Directory Structures

In a networking context, much of the directory structure will be determined by how the networking software sets itself up and on the needs of users on the network. Networking packages try to isolate system-critical files and programs from general access. This means that the structure will have at least two directories: one for the system and one for users. In practice, directory structures for networks will be more complex than those for stand-alone machines.

For example, Novell's NetWare creates four predefined directories on its SYS volume: SYSTEM, PUBLIC, LOGIN, and MAIL. Administrators and users can build around this "proto-structure," by adding more directories on this volume, or by creating additional volumes with different directories. UNIX-based networking software will be installed within the existing UNIX directory structure.

Administrators will build the files and directories needed to run the network around and under the predefined directories. For example, each user may get his or her own "home" directory, which will generally be a subdirectory in some "user" area. Applications should be placed in separate directories.

When creating a directory structure and naming directories, it is important to determine any restrictions that apply. In particular, you need to find out which application requires the shortest file/directory names and the shortest paths. The resulting directory structure must be accessible even with the most severe restrictions.

Higher-Level Grouping Concepts

Directories are created, in part, to deal with the proliferation of files. Similarly, partitions on a hard disk can be created to deal with the proliferation of directories and with the storage requirements imposed by thousands of files and directories.

A network file server may have to manage gigabytes of material—possibly more material than can fit on a single hard disk. To make it possible to deal with elements at this next level of storage requirements, higher-level grouping concepts are introduced. In fact, from an information management perspective, a file server is nothing more than a way of grouping a few megabytes of material.

Within this framework, the concept of a directory is just a middle-level management element. For example, in the NetWare environment, a file is associated with:

- A file server

- A volume (which may encompass one or more hard disks)

- Directories and subdirectories

To specify a file path, all the elements are included, as in this example of a full NetWare path:

MYSERVER/SYS:PUBLIC/INFO/TECH/
CABLE.TEX

Do not confuse the NetWare Directory Services (NDS) Directory (which is written with an uppercase *D* in Novell's documentation) with the file system directory (lowercase *d*) structure maintained by the NetWare operating system. The Directory contains information about objects (resources, users, and so on); the directory contains information about files and subdirectories.

COMPARE

NDS (NetWare Directory Services)

Directory Caching

Directory caching is a method that uses a fast storage area to help speed up the process of determining a file's location on disk. File allocation table (FAT) and directory entry table (DET) information about the most commonly used directory entries can be written to the directory cache memory, from which the information can be retrieved quickly. Directory caching is a feature of Novell NetWare.

The advantages of directory caching can be augmented if the file server uses a cache and if the requested file's contents happen to be in the server's cache. As the directory cache fills up, the least-used directory entries are eliminated from the cache.

Directory Hashing

A method for organizing directory entries to minimize the search time for an entry. The hashing provides guided access to the desired entry, so that fewer entries need to be checked along the way.

Directory ID

In an AppleTalk network, a unique value associated with a directory when the directory is created.

Directory Information Base (DIB)

SEE

DIB (Directory Information Base)

Directory Management Domain (DMD)

SEE

DMD (Directory Management Domain)

Directory Rights

In various networking environments, restrictions and privileges that define which activities the *trustee* (the user or process) logged in to the network is allowed to perform.

SEE ALSO

Access Rights

Directory Service (DS)

SEE

DS (Directory Service)

Directory Service Area (DSA)

SEE

DSA (Directory Service Area)

Directory Synchronization

In directory management, the task of maintaining multiple directories, and of avoiding or resolving inconsistencies by making sure all directories are updated properly.

Directory System Agent (DSA)

SEE

DSA (Directory System Agent)

Directory User Agent (DUA)

SEE

DUA (Directory User Agent)

Direct Outward Dialing (DOD)

SEE

DOD (Direct Outward Dialing)

Direct Wave

In wireless communications, an electromagnetic signal that is transmitted through the air, but low enough to reach the destination without being reflected off the earth or off the ionosphere. A direct wave requires a line of sight between sender and receiver.

DIS (Draft International Standard)

For international standards committees, an early version of a proposed standard. The DIS is circulated to all committee members for consideration and comment.

DISA (Data Interchange Standards Association)

The DISA was created in 1987 to serve as the secretariat for ASC X12 (Accredited Standards Committee for X12), which is the committee charged by ANSI (American National Standards Institute) with formulating EDI (electronic data interchange) standards. Since then, the Association has taken on other responsibilities, including publication of the X12 documentation, and providing support to other standards bodies about EDI.

a b c **d** e f g h i j k l m n o p q r s t u v w x y z

Disk Driver

Software that serves as the interface between the operating system and the hard disk; also known as a *disk interface driver.* The network vendor usually includes drivers for the most common types of hard disks (ESDI, SCSI, and IDE), and the hard disk manufacturer may include drivers for specific network operating systems.

Disk Duplexing

Disk duplexing is a data-protection mechanism that uses two or more hard disks, with a separate channel from the PC to each disk. (A *channel* is the hard disk and the components that connect the drive to an operating environment.) A disk-duplexing system automatically writes everything to both disks, using the separate channels. The figure "Disk duplexing" illustrates this process.

If one disk or channel fails, the networking software notifies the system administrator. The administrator should fix or replace the defective disk or channel, to get it back on line as quickly as possible. Until the disk is replaced, the disk duplexing software will continue writing to the working disk.

Some implementations of disk duplexing support *split seeks,* in which data are read from whichever disk finds the data first.

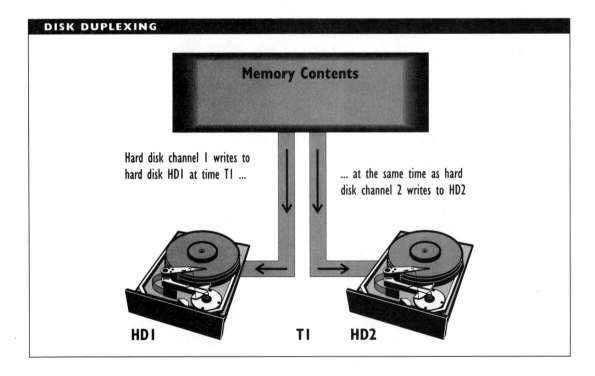

DISK DUPLEXING

Memory Contents

Hard disk channel I writes to hard disk HDI at time TI ...

... at the same time as hard disk channel 2 writes to HD2

HDI   TI   HD2

BROADER CATEGORY

Data Protection

COMPARE

Disk Mirroring

▼

Disk Mirroring

Disk mirroring is a data-protection strategy that uses two hard disks, which are accessed through a single disk channel. (A *channel* is the hard disk and the components that connect the drive to an operating environment.) All the data is written to both hard disks, but using the same channel. The figure "Disk mirroring" illustrates this process. This is in contrast to disk duplexing, in which separate channels are used.

Note that all the data is written twice in succession with disk mirroring. Note also that failure of the disk channel makes both disks inaccessible.

BROADER CATEGORY

Data Protection

COMPARE

Disk Duplexing

IDE DRIVES AND DISK MIRRORING

IDE drives are not suitable for disk mirroring, because one of the IDE drives is automatically designated master and the other slave. The master does diagnostics for both drives and controls the slave drive. This relationship has the following consequences, which limit the desirability of IDE drives for disk mirroring:

- If the master crashes, the slave is useless, since the master runs the show for both drives.

- If the slave crashes, the master won't find it. Rather, the master will keep searching when there is no response from the slave drive, and will eventually time out.

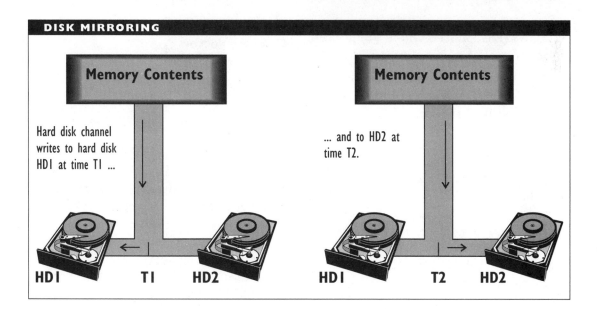

DISK MIRRORING

Memory Contents

Memory Contents

Hard disk channel writes to hard disk HD1 at time T1 ...

... and to HD2 at time T2.

HD1   T1   HD2

HD1   T2   HD2

Disk Striping

Disk striping is a data-storage strategy that combines comparable partitions on separate hard disks into a single volume. Data can be read from or written to multiple partitions at the same time, because each partition is on a separate disk, and each disk has its own read/write heads.

Disk striping with parity distributes parity information across the partitions. If one partition fails, the information on the other partitions can be used to reconstruct the missing data.

Disk Subsystem

The components that make up a hard disk drive: drive unit, hard disk, controller, interface card, and cable. When discussed as a separate entity, a disk subsystem is generally housed as an external drive.

DISOSS (Distributed Office Supported System)

An IBM mainframe-based package that provides document preparation and electronic mail (e-mail) capabilities.

Dispersion

In a fiber-optic signal, dispersion refers to the broadening of the light signal as it travels through the fiber. Dispersion is directly proportional to distance traveled. Dispersion also imposes a limit on bandwidth, because two light signals cannot become so dispersed that they overlap.

In a wireless (infrared, radio, or microwave) transmission, dispersion refers to the scattering of the signal, which is generally caused by the atmospheric conditions and by any particles or objects in the transmission path.

In an electrical transmission, dispersion is the distortion of the signal as it travels along the wire.

Disruptive Test

In network management, a diagnostic or performance test that requires a break in ordinary network activity in order to run. Some network management packages require verification before running the test, or make it possible to run such a test automatically at certain times, such as when there is little other network activity.

COMPARE
Nondisruptive Test

Distance Vector

Distance vector refers to a class of routing algorithms. Distance vector algorithms compute distances from a node by finding paths to all adjacent nodes and by using the information these nodes have about continuing on the paths adjacent to them.

Distance vector algorithms can be computationally intensive, a problem that is alleviated somewhat by defining different routing levels.

Examples of distance vector algorithms are the ISO's Interdomain Routing Protocol (IDRP) and the routing information protocols (RIPs) supported in the TCP/IP suite and in Novell's IPX/SPX suite.

Distortion

Any change in a signal, particularly, in the signal's shape. The factors that can cause or contribute to distortion include attenuation, crosstalk, interference, and delay. *Nonlinear distortion* occurs because the signal's harmonics (multiples of the signal's fundamental frequency) are attenuated (weakened) by different amounts.

Distributed Application

A *distributed application* is one that executes on multiple machines in a network, generally, with specialized portions of the application executing on each machine.

For example, in a client/server network, an application front end may execute on the user's workstation to provide an interface for the user, and a back end for the application may execute on a server to do the work requested through the front end. The back end will pass the results to the front end, and then to the user.

This is in contrast to a *centralized application,* which executes entirely on a single machine.

Distributed Architecture

A configuration in which processors are located in multiple devices, possibly in multiple locations. Each processor is capable of functioning independently or in cooperation with other elements in the architecture.

Distributed Database (DDB)

SEE

DDB (Distributed Database)

Distributed Data Management (DDM)

SEE

DDM (Distributed Data Management)

Distributed Data Processing (DDP)

SEE

DDP (Distributed Data Processing)

Distributed File System (DFS)

SEE

DFS (Distributed File System)

Distributed Function Terminal (DFT)

SEE

DFT (Distributed Function Terminal)

Distributed Network Architecture (DNA)

SEE

DNA (Distributed Network Architecture)

Distributed Office Supported System (DISOSS)

SEE

DISOSS (Distributed Office Supported System)

Distributed Processing

In networking, distributed processing describes a setup in which responsibilities and services are spread across different nodes or processes, so that particular tasks are performed by specialized nodes somewhere on a network. This is in contrast to

a b c **d** e f g h i j k l m n o p q r s t u v w x y z

central processing, in which multiple nodes share the computing power of a single server.

In distributed processing, a station that needs something done sends a request onto the network. The server responsible for the service takes on the task, does it, and returns the results to the station. The station need never know who actually did the work.

Distributed processing is much less susceptible to high activity levels, because the extra work can be spread out among many servers. On the other hand, distributed processing requires much more extensive bookkeeping and administration, and much more passing on of information.

COMPARE

Central Processing

▼
Distributed Relational Data Architecture (DRDA)

SEE

DRDA (Distributed Relational Data Architecture)

▼
Distributed System

A distributed system consists of multiple autonomous computers that are linked and that can—through software—give the appearance of being a single, integrated computer system. The individual computers may be parts of a local, wide, or global area network. Figure "A sample distributed system" shows an example of such a system.

Examples of distributed systems abound, including the Internet, various University computing centers, and ATM (automatic teller machine) networks.

Features of Distributed Systems

Several features and capabilities are considered desirable for distributed systems. These include:

- *Resource sharing.* This refers to the ability for users to share hardware (e.g., CPU time, peripherals), application software (e.g., groupware), or data (e.g., reference materials). A resource manager can coordinate resource allocation and sharing. Two approaches to resource sharing are common: client-server and object-based. These are described more fully below.

- *Concurrency.* This refers to the fact that multiple users may be requesting or accessing system resources at the same time. Ideally, processors should be able to deal with multiple users simultaneously. A distributed system automatically demonstrates concurrency each time two or more users do things at the same time on their own machines.

- *Openness.* An open system is one for which specifications and interfaces have been made public, so that developers can create products for the system. An open system can more easily handle new hardware or software configurations because there are officially accepted specifications. Open systems also adhere to open principles for internal operations. For example, IPC (interprocess communication) calls provide a standard mechanism for processes or components to communicate with each other.

A SAMPLE DISTRIBUTED SYSTEM

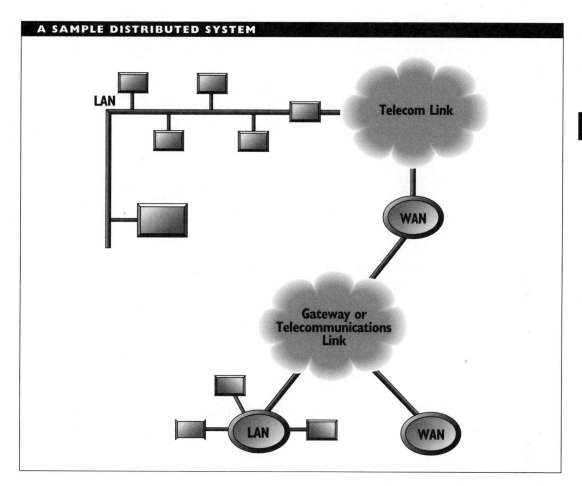

- *Transparency.* This refers to the fact that a user doesn't need to know that different resources being used may be scattered all around the world. For the user, there should be no significant difference between requesting a local resource and one at some remote location.

- *Scalability.* This refers to the ability of the system to grow—for example, through the addition of new computers or by the creation of internetworks. When a distributed system grows, certain information may need to be duplicated at multiple locations in order to maintain the efficiency of the original, smaller system. Such *replicas* must be updated and corrected in a synchronized manner.

- *Fault tolerance.* This refers to the system's ability to continue functioning after one or more components become unavailable because of either hardware or software failure. One way to handle hardware failure is to include redundant components in the system. This is

a
b
c
d
e
f
g
h
i
j
k
l
m
n
o
p
q
r
s
t
u
v
w
x
y
z

an effective but expensive solution. In a fault tolerant system, a software failure will affect only the process or processes that failed. Among other things, this means that a process should not be able to freeze another process or overwrite the memory or data for another process.

In a client-server approach to resource sharing, each server process is a centralized resource manager—that is, transactions generally go through a server. Servers may provide only certain services, and may complement each other with respect to the services they provide. A client-server approach works well for general-purpose sharing of information and resources.

In an object-based approach, each resource is regarded as an object that can be moved anywhere in a distributed system while still remaining accessible. In an object-based approach, all shared resources can be viewed in the same way. An object manager can control access to objects or classes of objects.

An important task in a distributed system is the handling of the file and directory system. Various approaches have been developed for this task. These include the Network file system (NFS) from Sun and the Andrew File System (AFS) from Carnegie-Mellon University. Currently, distributed systems are most likely to use UNIX machines, partly because useful file systems have been developed for UNIX environments.

Distributed systems are in contrast to centralized systems in which multiple users may be connected via terminals or PCs to a single host machine, which may itself be a PC. Mainframe-based centralized systems are sometimes known as *monolithic systems*.

Distribution Frame

A location at which wiring is concentrated. In a sub- or intermediate distribution frame (SDF or IDF), wiring from components (such as nodes in a network) is concentrated at a single location. A backbone cable runs from such SDFs to the main distribution frame (MDF), which serves as a wiring center for all the voice and data cable in a building, and which connects the building to the larger power structures in the outside world.

Distribution List (DL)

SEE

DL (Distribution List)

DIT (Directory Information Tree)

In the CCITT's X.500 Directory Services (DS) model, a directory information tree (DIT) contains the information for a directory information base (DIB).

The information in a DIT will generally be distributed. This provides faster access to the information at the distributed locations. Since a DIT can get quite large, distributing it also helps keep down the size of the DIT materials at any single location.

Objects in a DIT

The objects in a DIT may represent intermediate categories, such as country, organization, or organizational unit, or they may represent specific objects, such as a device, a person, or an alias for either of these. The root of the DIT is an imaginary entry with a null name. This serves as a base for naming elements in the tree.

An object gets its name from the path between the tree's root and the object. A particular object may be found in multiple locations in the tree; that is, the object may have multiple names. For example, a particular end-user might be found in the DIT as a CPA by day (on a path through the user's employer) or as a rock guitarist by night (on a path through a musician's union).

A DIT does not contain the actual objects, just information about them. Each location in the tree has predefined attributes associated with it. The attributes will depend on the object class to which the entry belongs. An *object class,* such as country or organization, determines which attributes are mandatory and which are optional for objects belonging to that class.

Objects in the tree will have specific values associated with these attributes. Although an object may appear at multiple locations in the DIT, each object will have only one body of information associated with it.

Operations on the DIT

Two general classes of operations are possible in a DIT: retrieval (reading) and modification (creating and writing). A given DIT operation may apply to a single entry or to a group of entries. The X.500 model supports three of the four possible operation classes:

- Retrieve a single entry

- Retrieve a group of entries

- Modify a single entry

The fourth operation class, Modify a group of entries, is not supported in X.500.

Using the DIT

End-users or processes can access the information in the DIT as follows:

- A directory user agent (DUA) provides the user with access to the DIT through an *access point.* A particular access point may support one or more of the operation classes.

- A directory system agent (DSA) provides the requested services for the DUA, and can also provide services for other DSAs. Since the DIT can be large and may be distributed, more than one DSA may be involved. A particular DSA is generally responsible for a portion of the DIT. This portion is known as a *context.*

BROADER CATEGORY
X.500

▼
Diversity

In microwave communications, diversity refers to either of two strategies for providing safeguards against equipment failure:

Frequency diversity: A separate frequency band is allocated for use in case the main band cannot be used (for example, because of noise or other interference).

a
b
c
d
e
f
g
h
i
j
k
l
m
n
o
p
q
r
s
t
u
v
w
x
y
z

Space diversity: Two receiving antennas are set up close—but not too close—to each other. If the primary target antenna malfunctions, the auxiliary antenna will be used to pull in the signals.

DIX (Digital Intel Xerox)

The three companies whose early work on networking eventually led to the development of the Blue Book Ethernet standard.

DL (Distribution List)

In the 1988 version of CCITT's X.400 Message Handling System (MHS), a tool for reaching multiple recipients with a single transmission. The DL includes all addresses to which a message is to be sent.

DLC (Data Link Control)

As a general term, DLC refers to the functions provided at the data-link layer of the OSI Reference Model. These functions are generally provided by a logical-link-control (LLC) sublayer.

SEE ALSO

Protocol, DLC

DLCI (Data Link Connection Identifier)

In frame-relay communications, a field in the frame-relay header. The DLCI represents the virtual circuit number associated with a particular destination.

DLL (Dynamic Link Library)

A DLL is a precompiled collection of executable functions that can be called in programs. Instead of linking the code for called DLL functions into a program, the program merely gets a pointer to the DLL at runtime. The required DLL file must be accessible at runtime, however. Multiple programs can use the same DLL.

DLLs are used extensively in Microsoft Windows, OS/2, and in Windows NT. DLLs may have file-name extensions of .DLL, .DRV, or .FON.

DLS (Data-Link Services)

The services provided at the data-link layer in the OSI Reference Model.

DMA (Direct Memory Access)

Direct memory access is a method for transferring data from a drive or other peripheral device directly to the computer's memory, without involving the CPU (central processing unit).

The DMA process is managed by a specialized DMA controller chip, which is generally faster than the processor. When the data transfer is finished, the controller chip informs the processor, which can then proceed as if the processor had managed the transfer. Each DMA controller can handle up to four devices.

DMD (Directory Management Domain)

In the CCITT's X.500 Directory Management Services, a collection of one or more directory system agents (DSAs), and possibly of some directory user agents (DUAs), all managed by a single organization.

SEE ALSO
X.500

DMI (Desktop Management Interface)

DMI provides a standard method for identifying PC hardware and software components automatically, without intervention from the user. At a minimum, DMI identifies the following information about any component installed in a PC:

- Manufacturer

- Component name

- Version

- Serial number (if appropriate)

- Installation time and date

DMI is supported by Digital Equipment Corporation (DEC), IBM, Intel, Microsoft, Novell, Sun, and more than 300 other vendors.

DMI (Digital Multiplexed Interface)

In digital telecommunications, a T1 interface between a private branch exchange (PBX) and a computer.

DNA (Digital Network Architecture)

A layered architecture from Digital Equipment Corporation (DEC). DNA is implemented in the various incarnations of DECnet.

SEE ALSO
DECnet

DNA (Distributed Network Architecture)

A term for a network in which processing capabilities and services are distributed across the network, as opposed to being centralized in a single host or server.

DNIC (Data Network Identification Code)

A unique, four-digit value assigned to public networks and to services on those networks.

DNIS (Dialed Number Identification Service)

A telephony service that retrieves information about the number being called. This information can include the name of the number's owner and the number's location. DNIS is very commonly used with 800 and 900 lines. For example, when multiple lines—each with different numbers—all come into the same call distributor, DNIS can tell which number a caller used.

COMPARE
ANI (Automatic Number Identification)

a b c **d** e f g h i j k l m n o p q r s t u v w x y z

DNS (Domain Naming System)

DNS is the distributed naming service used on the Internet. The DNS can provide a machine's IP address, given domain names for the machine. Various products have been developed to provide DNS, such as the Berkeley Internet Name Domain (BIND). DNS is described in RFCs 1101, 1183, and 1637.

Internet Domains

The basis for the domains in the DNS may be geographical, such as an entire country, or organizational, such as a common group or activity. The top-level domains represent the most general groupings, and these domain names are standardized. There are currently 7 top-level organizational domains and 59 top-level geographical domains. See the tables "Internet Top-Level Organization Domains" and "Internet Top-Level Geographic Domains" for lists of these domains.

INTERNET TOP-LEVEL ORGANIZATIONAL DOMAINS	
DOMAIN NAME	**INTERPRETATION**
com	Commercial organization
edu	Educational institution
gov	Government agency or organization
int	International organization
mil	U.S. military
net	Networking organization
org	Nonprofit organization

Domain Names in Internet Addresses

An Internet name consists of a *userid* followed by an *at* sign (@), which is followed by one or more names separated by dots. The most general of these names refers to domains. Domain names are found at the *end* of an Internet name.

A particular name may include references to one or more domains. The rightmost of these is a top-level domain. The ordering from specific to general in an Internet name is in contrast to the elements in an IP (Internet Protocol) address, in which the first (leftmost) number represents the most general division.

DOAM (Distributed Office Applications Model)

DOAM is an overarching OSI (Open Systems Interconnection) model for several application-layer processes. The DOAM deals with document and data organization and transmission. Its functions include the following:

- Document Filing and Retrieval (DFR)
- Document Printing Application (DPA)
- Message-Oriented Text Interchange System (MOTIS)
- Referenced Data Transfer (RDT)

Document Management

Document management refers to the range of tasks and considerations that may arise in relation to the online creation, modification, and storage of simple, compound, or hypertext documents.

INTERNET TOP-LEVEL GEOGRAPHICAL DOMAINS

DOMAIN NAME	INTERPRETATION	DOMAIN NAME	INTERPRETATION	DOMAIN NAME	INTERPRETATION
aq	Antarctica	FR	France	nl	Netherlands
ar	Argentina	GB	Great Britain	no	Norway
at	Austria	GR	Greece	nz	New Zealand
au	Australia	HK	Hong Kong	pl	Poland
be	Belgium	HR	Croatia	pr	Puerto Rico
bg	Bulgaria	HU	Hungary	pt	Portugal
br	Brazil	IE	Ireland	re	Reunion
ca	Canada	IL	Israel	se	Sweden
ch	Switzerland	IN	India	sg	Singapore
cl	Chile	IS	Iceland	si	Slovenia
cn	China	IT	Italy	su	Soviet Union
cr	Costa Rica	JP	Japan	th	Thailand
cs	Czech and Slovak Republics	KR	South Korea	tn	Tunisia
		KW	Kuwait	tw	Taiwan
de	Germany	LI	Liechtenstein	uk	United Kingdom
dk	Denmark	LT	Lithuania	us	United States
ec	Ecuador	LU	Luxembourg	ve	Venezuela
ee	Estonia	LV	Latvia	yu	Yugoslavia
eg	Egypt	MX	Mexico	za	South Africa
es	Spain	MY	Malaysia		
fi	Finland				

- A *simple document* contains text and possibly formatting commands, but no graphics, voice, etc.

- A *compound document*—also known as a *multimedia document*—can include graphics, sound or video, in addition to text.

- A *hypertext document* is one that contains links to other documents or other locations in the same document. With

a b c d e f g h i j k l m n o p q r s t u v w x y z

the appropriate software, a user can access the material associated with such links from within the document. Hypertext documents may be simple or compound. The materials accessible through a hypertext document may be located in different places. For example, the material accessible from a home page on the World Wide Web (WWW) might be located on machines scattered all around the world.

Tasks such as the following are considered part of document management. Note that in some cases the required tools are generic, and are not tied to document management systems. For example, encryption or compression programs are used for purposes other than document management.

- *Creation.* Documents may be created in many different ways: by scanning existing documents for text (and possibly also for graphics), with an ordinary text editor, word processor, desktop publishing program, or hypertext (e.g., HTML) editor. Depending on the method used to create the document, the result may be a simple or a compound one.

- *Storage.* A document can be stored as one or more elements. The media on which a document is to be stored may be considered primary, secondary, or tertiary. Primary media are those that are almost always available and very frequently used. Hard disks are the best example of a primary medium. Secondary media are also almost always available, but have much

slower access times than primary media. CD-ROM drives are a good example of secondary media. Tertiary media are available only upon request, and they usually have slower access times than primary media. Tapes or discs that must first be mounted are examples of tertiary media.

- *Retrieval.* Users must be able to call up and view documents. Ideally, the online view of a retrieved document should be comparable to a printed version. That is, formatting and layout information should be preserved. This requires the use of special viewers or browsers that can interpret the formatting and layout commands and can translate them into the appropriate display instructions. Popular viewers include Acrobat from Adobe, World-View from Interleaf, and DynaText from Electronic Book Technologies.

- *Transmission.* To be truly useful, a document management system must be accessible to multiple users. These may be in different geographical locations. Consequently, it may be necessary to send a document from one location to another. The transmission should be as efficient and inexpensive as possible, but should be error-free, and should leave the document unchanged.

- *Reception.* Just as it must be possible to send a document to specified locations, it must also be possible to receive the document at that location. Resources must be available to reconstruct the document (for example, if it was sent in packets) and to check its integrity.

- *Revision.* Very few documents are perfect right from the start. As a result, users must be able to revise documents. For simple documents, this can be done using a text editor; for compound documents, more sophisticated editing capabilities are needed. Editors that can use markup languages such as HTML (HyperText Markup Language) or its more general and powerful predecessor SGML (Standard Generalized Markup Language) are becoming increasingly popular.

- *Compression.* Compression reduces a document's size by taking advantage of redundancy in the document. This saves storage and also saves money when the document is transmitted. Compression of compound documents can get complicated since different types of compression algorithms are most appropriate for text and images.

- *Encryption.* Encryption makes a document more difficult to use if stolen—since the document will be gibberish to anyone who doesn't know the encryption method or key. Document encryption is particularly important with personal and financial data. Encryption and compression are often used together. In such cases, it's extremely important to do things in the correct order. For example, compressing and then encrypting is most effective for text documents. If such

a document is transmitted, the algorithms must be applied in reverse order at the receiving end—that is, decryption then decompression.

Document management software can be grouped into three categories:

- *File managers,* which generally work with only a single or a limited number of file formats. During storage, documents may be converted to the supported format, which may be proprietary.

- *Library managers,* which handle documents in their native formats and which include security capabilities. Library managers can also track document versions.

- *Compound Document Managers,* which treat documents as virtual entities that are always subject to change. Instead of handling a document as a static object, a compound document manager sees a document more as a set of pointers to various elements, any of which may be revised between one viewing and the next.

▼ DOD (Direct Outward Dialing)

In a Centrex or a private branch exchange (PBX), a service that makes it possible to get an outside line directly, without going through the system's switchboard.

▼ Domain

In both the Internet and OSI (Open System Interconnection) communities, the term *domain* refers to an administrative unit. The details of such a unit, however, differ in the Internet and OSI environments.

In the Internet community, a domain is an element in the DNS (Domain Naming System), which is a naming hierarchy. See the DNS article for more information about Internet domains.

In the OSI community, a domain is also a division created for administrative purposes. In this context, the details are based on functional differences. The five management domains defined in the OSI model are accounting, configuration, fault, performance, and security. See the Network Management article for more information about these domains.

The term has several other meanings in different networking contexts:

- In IBM's SNA (Systems Network Architecture), a domain represents all the terminals and other resources controlled by a single processor or processor group.

- In Novell's NNS (NetWare Name Service), the collection of servers that share bindery information constitutes a domain.

- In NetWare 4.*x*, a domain is a special area in which an NLM (NetWare Loadable Module) can run.

NetWare 4.*x* actually has two domains for NLMs: OS_PROTECTED and OS. In the OS_PROTECTED domain, you can run untested NLMs to ensure that they do not corrupt the operating system memory. The OS domain is where NLMs that are proven reliable can run more efficiently.

SEE ALSO

DNS (Domain Naming System); Network Management

▼
Domain Specific Part (DSP)

SEE

DSP (Domain Specific Part)

▼
DOS Client

A workstation that boots DOS and gains access to the network using workstation software.

▼
DOS Extender

Software that enables DOS programs to execute in protected mode, and to make use of extended memory. Two widely used DOS extender specifications are VCPI (Virtual Control Program Interface) and DPMI (DOS Protected Mode Interface).

SEE ALSO

DPMI, Protected Mode, VCPI

▼
DOS Requester

In Novell's NetWare 3.12 and 4.*x*, the DOS Requester is client software that runs on a workstation and mediates between applications, DOS, and NetWare. The DOS Requester replaces the NETX.COM network shell program used in earlier versions of NetWare.

The software actually consists of a terminate-and-stay resident (TSR) manager (VLM.EXE) and several Virtual Loadable Modules (VLMs), which can be loaded at startup or as needed. The software also includes modules for dealing with security, DOS redirection, transport-layer protocols, and NDS (NetWare Directory Services) or bindery commands. The figure "Structure of NetWare's DOS Requester" illustrates the components.

VLM.EXE is the VLM manager, and is responsible for loading the appropriate module at the appropriate time. VLM also controls memory usage and communication between relevant modules.

CONN.VLM is the *Connection Table Manager,* which allows clients to connect to a network (assuming, at least for now, that the user is authorized to do so).

The DOS Requester's components fit into a three-layer structure:

- The DOS Redirector, the REDIR.VLM module, resides at the *DOS Redirection Layer.* This module provides DOS file services and callouts. This is the topmost of the three layers.

- The *Service Protocol Layer* has modules for providing NetWare-specific services, and also file, print, and security services. The components that make up this layer are described below.

- The *Transport Protocol Layer* is the lowest of the three layers, and is responsible for making sure packets are transmitted and that the connection is maintained. The TRAN.NLM module is the Transport protocol multiplexor, and is responsible for enabling communications between the available protocols (IPX or TCP) and the resources at the service protocol layer. The IPX and TCP protocols

are handled by IPXNCP.NLM or TCPNCP.NLM, respectively. If necessary, the AUTO.VLM module can be used to reconnect a workstation to a server automatically—for example, to reestablish a broken connection. AUTO.VLM will automatically reconfigure the system to its original state.

The following services are provided at the Service Protocol Layer:

- NetWare services are provided to handle the different flavors of NetWare: NetWare 2.*x* and 3.*x* (which use binderies), NetWare 4.*x* (which uses NetWare Directory Services, or NDS), and Personal NetWare. These flavors are handled, respectively, by BIND.VLM (for 2.*x* and 3.*x*), NDS.VLM (for 4.*x*), and PNW.VLM (for Personal NetWare). The module for the appropriate protocols is determined and called by NWP.VLM—the NetWare Protocol multiplexor.

- File services are handled by the FIO.VLM (file input/output) module. This module uses a basic file transfer protocol by default. If desirable or necessary, however, FIO can use special methods when reading or writing. These measures include using a cache (CACHE) or a packet-burst protocol (PBODI), or transmitting large internet packets (LIP).

a
b
c
d
e
f
g
h
i
j
k
l
m
n
o
p
q
r
s
t
u
v
w
x
y
z

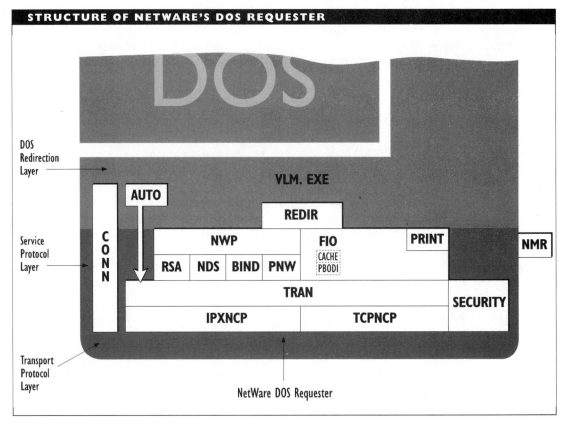

STRUCTURE OF NETWARE'S DOS REQUESTER

DOS Redirection Layer

Service Protocol Layer

Transport Protocol Layer

VLM. EXE
AUTO
REDIR
CONN
NWP
RSA NDS BIND PNW
FIO
CACHE
PBODI
PRINT
NMR
TRAN
SECURITY
IPXNCP
TCPNCP
NetWare DOS Requester

- Print services are provided by the PRINT.VLM module. Since PRINT.VLM uses the FIO capabilities, it can use any of the special measures listed for FIO.VLM. The print module's behavior depends on the settings it finds in the NET.CFG configuration file.

- Security services (both encryption and authentication) are provided through RSA.NLM, a module that implements the Rivest, Shamir, and Adleman public-key encryption algorithm.

Unlike the NetWare shell, the DOS Requester may be called by DOS to do a task that is network-based and that DOS is, therefore, unable to perform. For example, DOS may use the DOS Requester to access file services on a remote machine.

The DOS Requester still processes NetWare requests to get them into the appropriate format and then sends the requests on to the server.

BROADER CATEGORY
Network Shell

COMPARE
NETX

Dotted Decimal

Dotted decimal, also known as *dotted digit,* is the notation system used to represent the four-byte IP (Internet Protocol) addresses. An address in this format is called a *dot address.*

SEE

IP Address

Double Buffering

The use of two buffers for input and output in order to improve performance and increase throughput. In a double-buffered environment, one buffer is processed while the other is filling.

DOV (Data Over Voice)

In communications, a strategy for transmitting data over the voice channel at the same time as a voice transmission. A human listener would not hear the data being transmitted. DOV requires special equipment.

COMPARE

DUV (Data Under Voice)

Downgrading

In the CCITT X.400 Message Handling System (MHS), the process of converting a message from the 1988 MHS version format to a format suitable for an MHS based on the 1984 version of X.400.

Downlink

In telecommunications, a communications link between a satellite and one or more earth stations.

Download

To transfer data, such as a file, from a host computer to a remote machine. For example, the host may be a mainframe or a BBS (bulletin board system) computer. Downloading requires a communications protocol that both the host and recipient can understand and use.

COMPARE

Upload

Downsizing

Downsizing refers to the redesign of mainframe-based business applications to create applications capable of running on smaller, less expensive systems, often local-area networks (LANs) of PCs. A client/server architecture is the model most often implemented during downsizing.

In moving applications from large computer systems to PCs, it is possible that security, integrity, and overall control will be compromised. Development and training costs for the new system can be high. However, a collection of appropriately configured PCs, networked together, can provide more than ten times the power for the same cost as a mainframe computer supporting remote terminals.

A more accurate term might be *rightsizing,* to match the application requirements of the corporation to the capabilities of the hardware and software systems available.

Downtime

A machine or other device that is not functioning is said to be down. Downtime is a period during which a computer or other device is not functioning. This is in contrast to *uptime,* during which the machine is functioning.

Note that uptime and downtime are not synonymous with availability and unavailability. A device may be unavailable during uptime (for example, because of heavy activity).

DP (Draft Proposal)

For some standards committees, a preliminary version of specifications or standards. The DP is circulated for a limited time, during which comments and critiques are collected by the standards committee.

DPA (Demand Protocol Architecture)

In Microsoft's LAN Manager network operating system, DPA is a feature that makes it possible to load and unload protocol stacks dynamically. This capability makes it possible to support other network environments, such as VINES or NetWare, in the same machine.

DPA was originally added by 3Com to its implementation of LAN Manager, but it has since been added to versions supported by other vendors.

BROADER CATEGORY
LAN Manager

DPC (Deferred Procedure Call)

In Windows NT and NT Advanced Server, a called function whose task is less important than the currently executing function. As a result, execution of the called function is deferred until higher priority tasks are completed.

DPMI (DOS Protected Mode Interface)

DPMI is an interface specification from Microsoft. The interface is designed to provide DOS extension. By providing this capability, DPMI enables DOS programs to run in protected mode, so that they can make use of extended memory, take advantage of system safeguards afforded in protected mode, and so on.

The data and execution safeguards provided in protected mode allow most programs to run as DOS tasks on their own or under Windows 3.*x*. DPMI provides enhanced capabilities for 80286 and higher processors.

DPMI was developed partly in response to the older VCPI (Virtual Control Program Interface). DPMI and VCPI are incompatible, so these two interfaces should not be mixed on a network.

COMPARE
VCPI (Virtual Control Program-Interface)

SEE ALSO
DOS Extender; Protected Mode

DQDB (Distributed Queue Dual Bus)

DQDB is a network architecture that has been recommended by the IEEE 802.6 committee for use in metropolitan-area networks (MANs). DQDB has the following characteristics:

- Operates at the bottom two layers of the OSI Reference Model: the physical and data-link layers. Actually, DQDB operates at the physical layer and at the media-access-control (MAC) sublayer, as defined by the IEEE 802.2 committee.

- Uses two buses for the network. Each bus operates in a single direction, and the buses operate in opposite directions. A node on the network may transmit and receive on one or both buses, depending on where the node is located in relation to the bus ends.

- Generally uses fiber-optic cable as the physical medium. Copper cable is generally not used, because it has difficulty supporting both the distances and the bandwidth that may be required for a MAN. This may change, however, as higher-grade copper cable becomes available. (Note that copper cable *is* used in many MANs, but as access cable to connect individual nodes or subnetworks to the MAN bus.)

- Can support circuit-switched voice, data, and video, and can handle synchronous or asynchronous transmissions.

- Provides connection-oriented, connectionless, and isochronous communications services.

- Allocates bandwidth dynamically, using time slots.

- Supports transmission speeds of at least 50 megabits per second (Mbps), and will eventually support speeds of about 600 Mbps.

- Uses 53-octet slots for transmissions.

The performance of a DQDB configuration is independent of the number of nodes and of the distances involved, which makes DQDB ideal for high-speed transmissions.

DQDB Topology

DQDB uses a dual-bus topology, with the buses transmitting in opposite directions. The first node in each direction is the head of the bus. This node has special responsibilities for the bus, including the task of generating the slots in which data are transmitted.

Since the head node is at the starting end of the bus, all other nodes on the bus are *down the line,* or to move the metaphor (and the bus) to the water, *downstream* from the head node. Conversely, the head node is *up the line* or *upstream* from all the other nodes on the bus. Node positioning is important when controlling access to the network.

The DQDB architecture may use either the "traditional" open bus topology shown in the figure "DQDB with open bus topology," or the looped bus shown in the figure "DQDB with looped bus topology." Because the looped bus topology is easier to reconfigure if a node goes down, it is used more

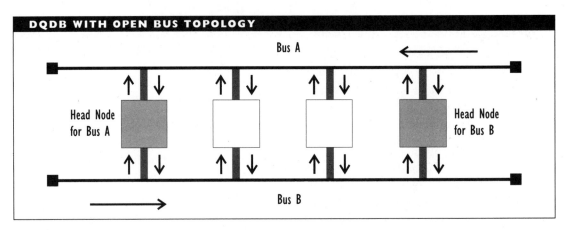

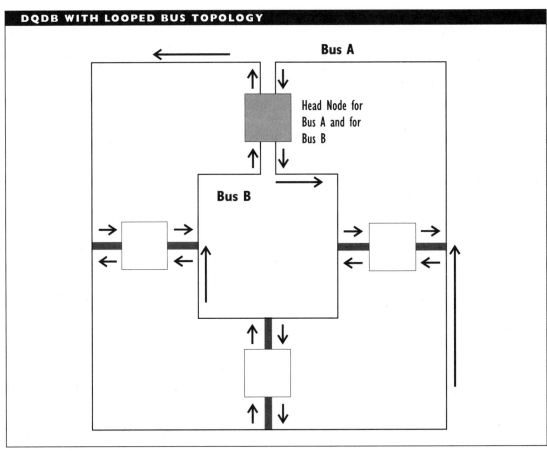

commonly. In fact, when a looped bus is reconfigured to compensate for a lost node, the result is an open bus.

In a looped bus topology, the head node is also the endpoint, or tail, for the bus. While this looks just like a ring topology, the looped bus differs because the head node does not pass on a transmission it receives as the tail. Note also that the same node serves as the head for both buses on a looped bus.

DQDB Structure

The DQDB architecture is described in terms of three layers in the 802.6 specifications, as illustrated in the figure "Layers in the DQDB architecture."

The DQDB layers are as follows:

Physical layer: The lowest layer, which supports several transmission schemes. At its lower end, this layer interfaces to the physical medium; at the upper end, the layer uses a convergence function to get data from the upper layer and to prepare the data for transmission across the medium.

DQDB layer: The workhorse layer of the DQDB architecture. It corresponds to the lower half of the OSI Reference Model's data-link layer, or the MAC sublayer as specified by the IEEE 802.2 committee. The DQDB layer can provide services for any of several types of connections. This layer is divided into three sublayers (described later in this article).

Outside layer: The third "layer" is not really part of the DQDB architecture,

nor is the layer's name official. This level is included in the specifications in order to specify the services that the DQDB layer must be able to provide. The description of required services is quite heterogeneous, largely because the DQDB architecture supports such a variety of connections and transmissions.

DQDB Layer Services

To accommodate the requirements of the layers above it, three types of services have been defined for the DQDB layer in the 802.6 specifications: connectionless, connection-oriented, and isochronous.

The connectionless services do not establish a fixed connection before transmitting data. Instead, individual packets are sent independently of each other, possibly by different paths. This type of service might be requested by the LLC sublayer, which makes up the upper half of the data-link layer. The MAC convergence function (MCF) does the translation and preparation needed to have the data passed down into the proper form for transmission.

The connection-oriented services establish a connection first, then send the data and, finally, break the connection. Because a fixed (if temporary) connection is established, all the data takes the same path. This makes both the sender's and the receiver's jobs a bit easier.

The isochronous services assume a constant transmission pace. Such transmissions are often synchronous, but this is not required.

a
b
c
d
e
f
g
h
i
j
k
l
m
n
o
p
q
r
s
t
u
v
w
x
y
z

LAYERS IN THE DQDB ARCHITECTURE

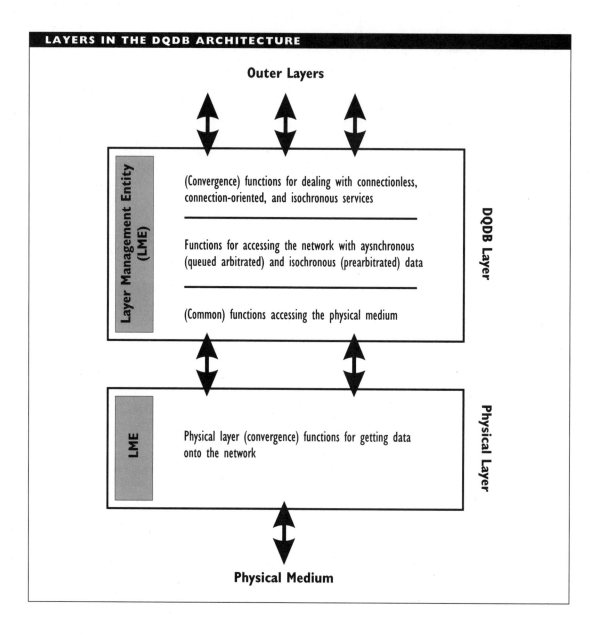

DQDB Sublayers

The DQDB layer is divided into three sublayers:

- The topmost layer interacts with the "outside" layer; that is, it interacts with the applications that want (or need) to use the DQDB. At this layer, functions are specified and/or defined for the three main types of services (connectionless, connection-oriented, and isochronous) provided by the DQDB layer.

- The middle layer provides functions for arbitrating access to the network. Two types of slots are used: queued arbitrated (QA) and prearbitrated (PA). The QA slots carry asynchronous data from either connectionless or connection-oriented services. The PA slots carry isochronous data.

- The bottom sublayer provides access to the physical medium for both asynchronous and isochronous data. This sublayer also includes functions for controlling the configuration and for serving as the head of the bus.

An MCF is defined for the top DQDB sublayer. This function does the preparations for data using connectionless services. A connection-oriented convergence function (COCF) has been proposed in the 802.6 documents, but has not yet been defined. Similarly, the function needed for handling isochronous data has been proposed but not defined.

DQDB Operation

Information moves around a DQDB network in 53-octet slots, and slots from different nodes are intermingled in the network traffic. This means that nodes need to be able to break higher-layer packets into 52-byte chunks before sending the information. Nodes also must be able to reconstruct a packet from the slots received in a transmission. The 52 bytes will contain pieces of a higher-level packet. The fifty-third byte in a slot is for access control information.

The head node is responsible for creating empty slots and sending these down the line, where the slots will be used by nodes to send their messages. By generating as many slots as needed, the head node can make sure that each node on the bus gets access.

To do this, the head node must know how many slots are needed by the nodes. Suppose a node (N) wants to transmit on one of the buses (let's say bus A). In order to get a slot on bus A, N must indicate—*on bus B*—that N needs a slot. This request will eventually reach the head node for bus A, which will increment a counter that indicates the number of slots A needs to create.

Bus A creates empty slots and sends these down the line. As the slots move down the line, they are taken by the nodes that have requested them. These nodes fill the slots and send them toward their destination. A node will take only the slot it has requested, even if that node needs additional slots since its last request.

There are restrictions built into the slot request and generation process to help ensure that the slots are being allocated fairly and that the architecture's bandwidth is being allocated in a balanced fashion.

Draft Proposal (DP)

For some standards committees, a preliminary version of specifications or standards. The DP is circulated for a limited time, during which comments and critiques are collected by the standards committee.

DRAM (Dynamic Random-Access Memory)

DRAM is a type of chip memory in which information is stored in capacitors, whose charge must be refreshed periodically. This is in contrast to SRAM (static random-access memory) in which information is stored differently.

Dynamic RAM is slower but much cheaper than SRAM and is, therefore, much more widely used. Most of the chip memory in a PC (stand-alone machine or network-based workstation) is DRAM. If SRAM chips are used at all, they may be used for cache storage.

BROADER CATEGORY
Memory

COMPARE
SRAM (Static Random-Access Memory)

DRDA (Distributed Relational Data Architecture)

A distributed database architecture from IBM. DRDA forms the core of the database management capabilities in IBM's SystemView network management package.

Drive

A drive is a data storage location. Drives may be the following:

- Physical, such as floppy disk drives, hard disk drives, or tape drives.

- Logical, such as hard disk partitions or NetWare drives. Logical drives represent organizational entities.

- Virtual, such as RAM disks or virtual disks. These use physical resources to mimic physical drives, but their contents disappear when the computer is turned off.

In the DOS environment, drives are referenced by letters. For example, A: and B: represent floppy disk drives on a PC. In a NetWare network, drives A: through E: represent local drives on a workstation; drives F:, G:, and so on, are logical *network drives*.

SEE ALSO
Directory; Drive Mapping

Drive Mapping

The process of assigning a hard disk volume or directories on this volume to a particular logical disk drive is called *drive mapping,* or simply *mapping.* For example, a workstation user might use drive mapping to designate the server's hard disk as logical drive H: (from the workstation's perspective).

Each user can have his or her own set of drive mappings, which can be loaded into the user's working environment when logging on to the network or specified during regular operation.

In NetWare and other operating systems, it is possible to map a drive letter to a particular directory on the server. In effect, this mapping makes the directory the root of the specified drive. Drive mapping gives a user immediate access to the directory, and is one way of dealing with path name restrictions (as discussed in the Directory article).

NetWare supports four types of drive mappings:

- Local mappings, which are to local hard disks and floppy drives. By default, drives A: through E: may be used for local mappings.

- Network mappings, which are to volumes and directories on the network. By default, drives F: through Z: may be used for network mappings.

- Network search mappings, which are to directories that contain programs or data files. Users can specify conditions and rules under which search directories will be checked. See the Search Drives article for more information.

- Directory map objects mappings, which allow a Directory map object to reference the location of commonly used files or applications.

Drive mappings can be temporary or permanent in NetWare. Temporary mappings disappear when a session is ended.

SEE ALSO
Search Drives

Driver

A program that serves as an interface between two programs or between a program and a hardware component. For example, to ensure that a network interface card (NIC) will work with a network software package, drivers are used.

In Windows NT and NT Advanced Server (NTAS), the term *driver* is used more broadly, and also encompasses file systems, such as the file allocation table (FAT) used by DOS and the high performance file system (HPFS) used by OS/2.

Types of Drivers

Drivers can be written for virtually any kind of device or interface, including the following:

- Printers, scanners, disks, monitors, and other devices

- SCSI, RS-232, RS-422, IDE, and other interfaces

- NICs, such as for Ethernet and Token Ring

Drivers are often specialized; a particular driver may support a single device model for a particular program. However, rather than creating drivers for every model, manufacturers may create a more or less generic driver interface, and then encourage developers to adapt the interface for their products to this generic interface. Vendors may also adapt generic drivers to handle the special features of particular products.

UPDATING DRIVERS

Because the driver program is generally a small piece of software, it's relatively easy to change. For this reason, drivers tend to be updated fairly frequently. Vendors can generally tell you whether their drivers have been updated, and several magazines list driver updates as a regular feature.

Keep your drivers up to date, but make sure you can return to an older driver—in case incompatibilities develop with the newer version.

NIC Driver Interfaces

In local-area networking, two generic driver interfaces are widely supported:

- NDIS (Network Driver Interface Specification), developed jointly by Microsoft and 3Com for LAN Manager, but now used for other network packages as well.

- ODI (Open Data-link Interface), an alternative to NDIS developed by Novell for its NetWare products. It is currently less widely used than NDIS, but is nonetheless widely supported.

Both of these represent efforts to provide a general interface between NICs and the higher-level protocols supported in a particular network.

NDIS and ODI provide generic interfaces, but specific drivers for particular adapters are also still used, partly because specific drivers can optimize the performance of the product. Most adapters ship with dozens of drivers.

SEE ALSO

NDIS (Network Driver Interface Specification); ODI (Open Data-link Interface)

Drop

An attachment to a horizontal cabling system (for example, through a wallplate). This is generally the point through which a computer or other device is connected to the transmission medium on a network. A drop is also known as a *drop line*.

Drop Box

In an AppleShare server, a term for a folder for which write (Make Changes) but not read privileges are granted. Users can add items to the folder but cannot open the folder or see its contents.

Dropout

Temporary loss of the signal in a transmission, such as through malfunction, power loss, or interference.

Drop Set

All the components needed to connect a machine or other component to the horizontal cabling. At a minimum, this includes cable and an adapter or connector.

Drop Side

All the components needed to connect a machine or other component to the patch panel or punch-down block that connects to the distribution frame.

DS (Digital Service)

DS is a communications service that uses digital signaling methods. More specifically, DS represents a telecommunications service in North America, which defines a four-level transmission hierarchy, with increasing bandwidths.

DS uses pulse code modulation (PCM) to encode an analog signal in digital form. The signal is sampled 8000 times per second, and each sample value is encoded in an 8-bit value. The signal transmission uses time division multiplexing (TDM).

DS1–DS4 Levels

DSx, (Digital Signal, where x is 0, 1, 1C, 2, 3, or 4) represents a hierarchy of channel capacities for digital signals. The hierarchy defines protocols, framing format, and even the signal frequency used at the specified level.

The *DS* in DS0, DS1, and so on, is sometimes expanded to *digital service*. The terms are sometimes written as DS-0, DS-1, and so on.

The data signals are transmitted over T-carrier lines, such as T1 or T3. The higher-capacity channels are based on the 64 kilobit per second (kbps) DS0 channel. The DS0 channel is based on the 4 kilohertz (kHz) analog channel used for ordinary voice communications.

The 1.544 megabit per second (Mbps) DS1 channel is constructed of the smaller DS0 channels. Twenty-four DS0 channels are multiplexed into a single DS1 channel, yielding a 1.536 Mbps bandwidth for data. An extra *framing bit* is added to each 192-bit (eight bits per channel × 24 channels)

frame. This is known as the 193rd bit, and it represents the extra 8 kbps in the DS1 channel capacity.

Either of two techniques is commonly used to handle framing in DS1 channels: D4 or ESF. The signals in a DS1 channel can be transmitted over T1 lines.

Lower-capacity digital channels are also possible. These channels are also built up by combining DS0 channels, which can be transmitted over fractional T1 (FT1) lines. An FT1 line consists of one or more DS0 channels.

Higher-capacity channels are built by multiplexing lower-bandwidth channels, together with framing and administrative overhead. The overhead bits are transmitted in separate channels, which may have 8, 16, or even 64 kbps bandwidths.

The figure "Digital signal hierarchy for North America" summarizes the digital signal hierarchy as it is defined in North America. The channel configurations are somewhat different in Europe and Asia.

To give you a sense of the relative sizes involved in the DS hierarchy, if a DS0 channel were represented as being an inch thick, a DS4 channel would be wider than a football field.

SEE ALSO

D4 Framing; DACS (Digital Access and Cross-Connect System)

DS (Directory Service)

Directory-related services, as defined in the CCITT X.500 model, or naming services as provided in Novell's NDS and Banyan's StreetTalk. Directory services are provided at the application layer.

DIGITAL SIGNAL HIERARCHY FOR NORTH AMERICA

Two 1.544 Mbps DS1 channels are multiplexed into a single 3.152 Mbps DS1C channel

Two DS1C channels are multiplexed into a single 6.312 Mbps DS2 channel

Seven DS2 channels are multiplexed into a single 44.736 Mbps DS3 channel

Six DS3 channels are multiplexed into a single 274.176 Mbps DS4 channel

SEE ALSO

NDS (NetWare Directory Services); StreetTalk; X.500

DSA (Directory Service Area)

In telephony, a term used to describe the calling area covered by a directory service.

DSA (Directory System Agent)

In the CCITT X.500 Directory Services model, software that provides services for accessing, using and, possibly, for updating a directory information base (DIB) or tree (DIT), generally for a single organization.

SEE ALSO

X.500

DSA (Distributed Systems Architecture)

An OSI-compliant architecture from Honeywell.

DSC (Data Stream Compatibility)

In IBM's SNA (Systems Network Architecture), a basic, bare-bones printing mode.

COMPARE

SCS (SNA Character String)

DSE (Data Switching Equipment)

Equipment used in a switching network, such as X.25.

DSI (Digital Speech Interpolation)

In digital telecommunications, a strategy for improving the efficiency of a communications channel. DSI works by transmitting during the "quiet" periods that occur in normal conversation. DSI can nearly double the number of voice signals that can be carried on the line.

DSOM (Distributed System Object Model)

IBM's implementation of the CORBA (Common Object Request Broker Architecture) object request broker from the OMG (Object Management Group).

SEE ALSO

CORBA

DSP (Digital Signal Processor)

A device that can extract and process elements from a stream of digital signals.

DSP (Domain Specific Part)

In the OSI Reference Model, part of the address for the network-layer service access point (NSAP). The DSP is the address within the *domain,* which is the part of the network under the control of a particular authority or organization.

SEE ALSO

SAP (Service Access Point)

DSPU (Downstream Physical Unit)

In a ring topology, a device that lies in the direction of travel of packets.

DSR (Data Set Ready)

A signal from a modem, sent when the modem is ready to operate. In the RS-232C interface, this signal is transmitted on pin 6.

DSU/CSU (Data Service Unit/Channel Service Unit)

In digital telecommunications, the DSU and CSU are two components of a DCE (Data-Communications Equipment) device. These components provide access to digital services over DDS, T1, and other types of lines. The DSU performs the following tasks:

- Connects to the DTE (usually a router or remote bridge) through a synchronous serial interface, which is a V.35

or an RS-422 connection; RS-232 connections are also possible for subrate (low-speed) services

- Formats data for transmission over the digital lines

- Controls data flow between the network and a CSU

The CSU, which must be certified by the FCC (Federal Communications Commission), does the following:

- Terminates the long-distance connection at the user's end

- Processes digital signals for the digital lines

- May test remote loopback on the lines

- Serves as a buffer to keep faulty subscriber equipment from bringing down the digital service

Functionally, the DSU/CSU component is comparable to a modem; each mediates between a digital computing element and a transmission medium. The medium is analog in the case of the modem and digital for the DSU/CSU.

The figure "DSU/CSU devices provide access to digital lines" shows how this component fits into a networking scheme.

DSX1/3 (Digital Signal Cross-Connect between Levels 1 and 3)

In digital communications, DSX1/3 specifies the interfaces for connecting DS1 and DS3 signals (which entails connecting T-1 and T-3 lines).

DTAM (Document Transfer and Manipulation)

DTAM provides the communication functions for the ITU's (International Telecommunication Union) application-layer Telematic services. Telematic services are communications services other than telephony and telegraphy. These include teletex (basically, souped-up telex), fax transmission, and telewriting (transmission of hand drawing or writing, so that the resulting image is duplicated at the receiving end).

The DTAM specifications cover three *service classes,* which specify—at a very general level—the actions allowed on documents. The service classes are *bulk transfer* (BT), *document manipulation* (DM), and *bulk transfer and manipulation* (BTM). Each service class is defined by more primitive functional units and by communication support functions.

To transfer documents, DTAM uses either application level support functions or session layer services. In the latter case—known as *transparent mode bulk transfer*—DTAM bypasses the presentation layer and sends the material directly to the session layer. This is allowed only in cases where the received document just needs to be sent on to another location. Since the recipient acts as an intermediary, no presentation of the document is necessary. Transparent mode is allowed only for Group 4 faxes, which are not yet widely used.

In *normal mode,* DTAM uses the services of the ACSE (Association Control Service Element), the RTSE (Reliable Transfer Service Element), or the ROSE (Remote

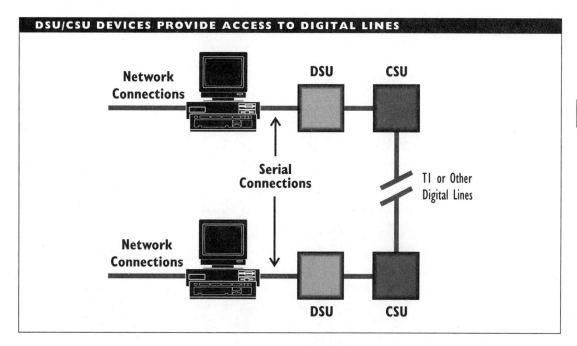

DSU/CSU DEVICES PROVIDE ACCESS TO DIGITAL LINES

Network Connections

DSU

CSU

Serial Connections

TI or Other Digital Lines

Network Connections

DSU

CSU

Operation Service Element)—depending on the required task.

Documents that the DTAM can handle must conform to the *ODA* (Open Document Architecture) standard. This standard is used for the interchange of compound documents—that is, of documents that may contain graphics, video, or sound in addition to text.

The DTAM protocols provide the means by which two DTAM service elements (DTAM-SEs)—or rather two applications using DTAM—communicate. The communication support functions help pass packets (known as PDUs, or protocol data units) up or down in the OSI hierarchical model. The Figure "DTAM model" illustrates the hierarchical as well as the lateral relationships.

So far, the DTAM protocol supports over a dozen different types of PDUs. For example, the DINQ (D-initiate request) PDU is

used for the Association Use Control functional unit. This unit is the one that controls whether there is any association between DTAM entities at either end of the connection.

Since several of the functional units have yet to be finalized, there's a good chance that more PDU types will be defined.

PRIMARY SOURCES

ITU recommendations T.431, T.432, and T.433. T.62bis provides guidelines for transmissions that bypass the presentation layer and communicate directly with the session layer.

SEE ALSO

ACSE, ODA, ROSE, RTSE

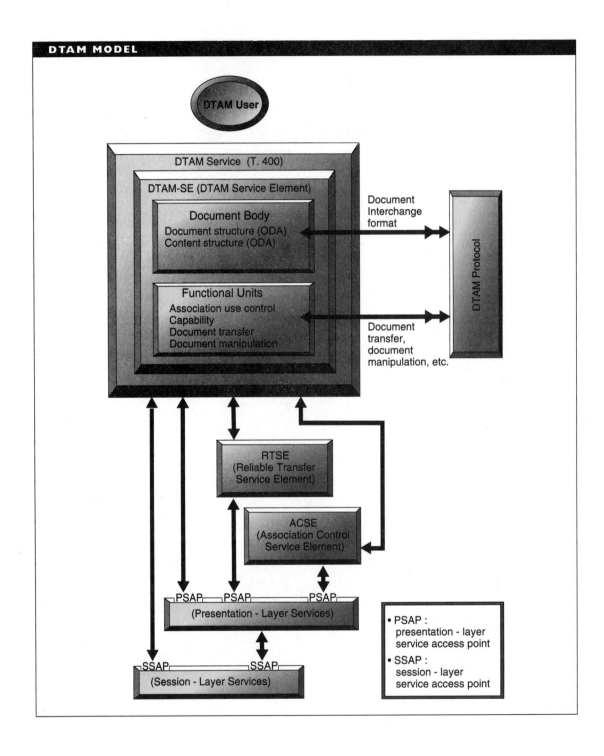

DTAM MODEL

DTAM User

DTAM Service (T. 400)

DTAM-SE (DTAM Service Element)

Document Body
Document structure (ODA)
Content structure (ODA)

Functional Units
Association use control
Capability
Document transfer
Document manipulation

Document Interchange format

Document transfer, document manipulation, etc.

DTAM Protocol

RTSE (Reliable Transfer Service Element)

ACSE (Association Control Service Element)

PSAP   PSAP   PSAP
(Presentation - Layer Services)

SSAP   SSAP
(Session - Layer Services)

• PSAP : presentation - layer service access point
• SSAP : session - layer service access point

DTE (Data Terminal Equipment)

In telecommunications, a terminal, a PC, or another device that can communicate with a DCE (data communications equipment) device. For example, in analog telecommunications, a modem serves as a DCE, and provides access to the telephone lines; in digital communications, a DSU/CSU provides access to the lines for a DTE.

DTMF (Dual Tone Multifrequency)

DTMF is a telephone technology that makes it possible to create 16 different tones using eight frequencies. These 16 tones suffice to provide a unique tone for each of the 12 base buttons on a Touch Tone telephone, as well as for up to four additional keys.

The figure "Frequencies for buttons on a Touch Tone telephone" shows how the frequencies are assigned to the buttons.

DTR (Data Terminal Ready)

In the RS-232 interface, a control signal used to indicate that a device (for example, a computer) is ready to send and receive data. This signal is sent on pin 20.

DTR (Dedicated Token Ring)

DTR is a variant of the standard token ring technology. In DTR, a direct connection is possible between a node and the token ring switch. Such a node could then make use of the entire network bandwidth, since there are no other nodes that can share it.

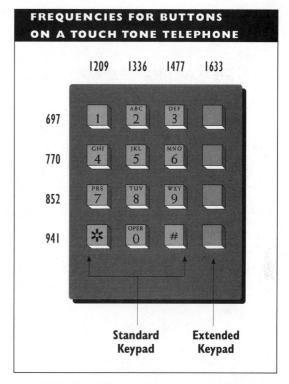

FREQUENCIES FOR BUTTONS ON A TOUCH TONE TELEPHONE

Standard Keypad

Extended Keypad

ASTRAL (Alliance for Strategic Token Ring Advancement and Leadership) is supporting both DTR and token ring switches. The IEEE 802.5 committee—which is the working group for token ring topology—will wait and see whether it proves viable and becomes widely used before committing to the new technology.

BROADER CATEGORY
Token Ring

DTS (Digital Termination Service)

In telecommunications, a service by which private networks can get access to carrier networks using digital microwave equipment within a frequency band allocated by the FCC (Federal Communications Commission) for this purpose.

DUA (Directory User Agent)

In the CCITT X.500 Directory Services model, a program that provides access to the directory services. The DUA mediates between an end-user or a client program and a directory system agent (DSA), which provides the requested services.

SEE ALSO
X.500

Dual-Attachment Concentrator (DAC)

SEE
DAC (Dual-Attachment Concentrator)

Dual-Attachment Station (DAS)

SEE
DAS (Dual-Attachment Station)

Dual Cable System

A broadband wiring arrangement in which separate cables are used for transmission and receiving. Such a wiring system may be used, for example, in a 10Broad36 broadband Ethernet or a broadband (IEEE 802.4) token-bus architecture.

COMPARE
Split Cable System

Dual Homing

In networking, a configuration in which a node can be connected to the network through more than one physical link. If one link fails, the station can still communicate via the other link.

Duty Cycle

In an electrical signal, the proportion of a time period during which the signal is on, which is when it represents a bit value of 1.

DUV (Data Under Voice)

In telecommunications, a strategy for transmitting voice and data over the same line.

COMPARE
DOV (Data Over Voice)

Dynamic Addressing

In an AppleTalk network, dynamic addressing refers to a strategy by which nodes automatically pick unique addresses. A new node keeps trying addresses until it finds one that is not already claimed by another node. Dynamic addressing is also referred to as *dynamic node addressing*.

Dynamic addressing works as follows:

- The node selects a valid address at random and sends an *enquiry control packet* to that address.

- If the address belongs to a node, the node responds with an *acknowledge control packet*. The new node then selects another address at random and repeats the process.

- If the address does not belong to a node, the enquiring node takes it as the node's new address.

BROADER CATEGORY
AppleTalk

▼
Dynamic Configuration

In networking, a system capability in which the file server can allocate memory as needed, subject to availability, while the network is running. Dynamic reconfiguration enables the server to allocate more resources (such as buffers, tables, and so on) as necessary in order to avoid congestion or overload on the network.

▼
Dynamic Routing

In various networking environments, automatic rerouting of data transmissions in order to maximize throughput or to balance traffic on transmission channels. Routing decisions are based on available and acquired data about network traffic patterns. Dynamic routing is also known as *dynamic adaptive routing*.

a
b
c
d
e
f
g
h
i
j
k
l
m
n
o
p
q
r
s
t
u
v
w
x
y
z

▼
E1 Carrier

In digital telecommunications, E1 is a carrier channel configuration defined by the CCITT and used in Europe, Mexico, and South America. Like the T carrier channels (T1, T2, and so on) defined in North America, the E1 carrier channel is built up of 64 kilobit per second (kbps) voice channels. See the DS (Digital Service) article for a discussion of how the T-carrier channels are defined.

The E1 carrier is defined as thirty 64 kbps voice channels and two 64 kbps signaling channels. In ISDN B and D channel terminology, this type of carrier is known as 30B+2D. The E1 carrier has a bandwidth of 2.048 megabits per second (Mbps).

E1 links can be multiplexed into higher-capacity carriers. The figure "Hierarchy of E1-based digital carriers" shows the E1 carrier hierarchy, which is analogous to the T1 hierarchy defined for digital communications in North America, Australia, and Japan. Because the hierarchy also allocates channels for link management and signaling, the data rates are higher than the number of 64 kbps channels indicates.

BROADER CATEGORY
Digital Communication

COMPARE
T1 Carrier

▼
EARN (European Academic and Research Network)

A European network that provides file transfer and e-mail (electronic mail) services for universities and research institutions.

▼
Earth Station

The ground-based portion of a satellite communications system is called an *earth station* or a *ground station*. The station consists of an antenna and receiver (or transceiver) that are in communication with a satellite in geosynchronous orbit.

Signals can be beamed from an earth station to the satellite and from there to the destination node (another earth station). These communications services can be leased from various companies. For long distances, the prices are competitive with earth-based connections (such as leased or public lines).

The size of the antenna required to receive signals at an earth station depends on the transmission frequency. For 19.2 kilobit per second (kbps) lines, an antenna of about 1.2 to 3 meters (4 to 10 feet) in diameter is sufficient. For faster speeds (such as the 1.544 megabit per second speed of T1 lines), larger antennas are required. These are harder to install and maintain, and may require special permits.

▼
EBCDIC (Extended Binary Coded Decimal Interchange Code)

EBCDIC (pronounced "eb-se-dic") is an 8-bit character encoding scheme used on IBM mainframes and minicomputers. Compare it with ASCII, which is used on PCs.

▼
ECB (Electronic Cookbook)

An operating mode for the Data Encryption Standard.

HIERARCHY OF E1-BASED DIGITAL CARRIERS

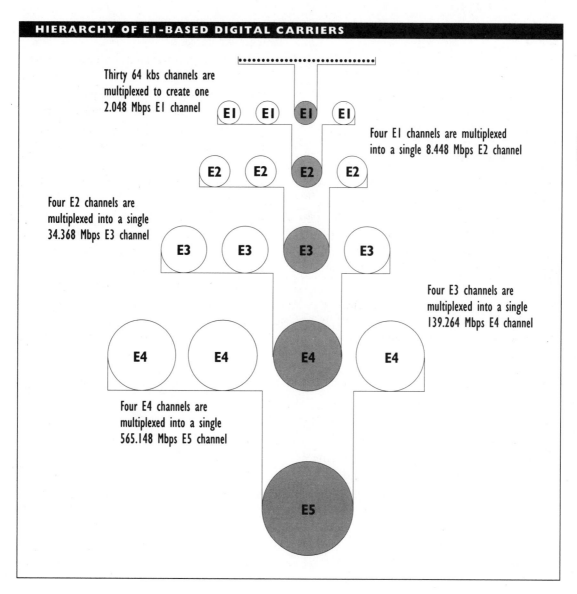

Thirty 64 kbs channels are multiplexed to create one 2.048 Mbps E1 channel

Four E1 channels are multiplexed into a single 8.448 Mbps E2 channel

Four E2 channels are multiplexed into a single 34.368 Mbps E3 channel

Four E3 channels are multiplexed into a single 139.264 Mbps E4 channel

Four E4 channels are multiplexed into a single 565.148 Mbps E5 channel

SEE

DES (Data Encryption Standard)

▼
ECC (Error Correction Code)

In digital communications, a term applied (sometimes incorrectly) to any of several types of codes used to detect or correct errors that may arise during transmission.

SEE

Error Detection and Correction

a b c d **e** f g h i j k l m n o p q r s t u v w x y z

Echo

As a verb, echo refers to the display of typed text on the screen. Other definitions discuss the term in particular contexts, such as electrical signaling.

Echo, Electrical

In electrical transmissions, an *echo* is a signal that "bounces off" the destination station (or an intermediate station) and is reflected back toward its source. The echo is a weaker version of the original signal, and it will interfere with any incoming signal, which can lead to noise and transmission errors.

An echo can occur if the transmission lines are not properly terminated or if there is an electrical mismatch (for example, in impedance levels) between the sending and receiving stations.

To eliminate the disruptive effect of an echo, a device called an echo canceler can be used. This device makes a copy of the echo and superimposes a displaced copy on the echo in order to cancel the echo signal and remove it from the transmission lines.

An echo suppressor can also be used to eliminate echo signals. An echo suppressor does the same thing as an echo canceler, but works differently.

Echo/Echo Reply

In networking environments, echo signals can be used to determine whether target nodes are able to receive and acknowledge transmissions. The echo signal is sent out, and the sender waits for an acknowledgment.

The method provides a simple mechanism for checking network connections. With this scheme, a node sends an Echo packet to a destination to determine whether the destination is connected. If the destination is connected and able to communicate, it responds with an Echo Reply packet.

This echoing strategy is quick and dirty, but only minimally informative. Furthermore, packet delivery may be unreliable because most Echo/Echo Reply schemes are transmitted at the network layer, which may not guarantee packet delivery. One way to increase reliability is to repeat the echo signal a number of times to test the connection. The proportion of trials that are successful will shed light on the reliability of the connection.

The error-signal strategy for simple network monitoring is used in several network protocols, including ICMP (Internet Control Message Protocol), AppleTalk, XNS (Xerox Network Services), and Novell's IPX (Internet Packet Exchange).

Most network management packages use more powerful protocols, such as SNMP or CMIS/CMIP for monitoring network activity. See the SNMP (Simple Network Management Protocol) and CMIS (Common Management Information Services) articles for more information about these protocols.

ECL (Emitter-Coupled Logic)

A logic scheme for very high-speed digital circuitry. Compare ECL with CMOS (complementary metal-oxide semiconductor) and TTL (transistor-transistor logic).

ECMA (European Computer Manufacturers Association)

An association that provides technical committees for other standards organizations, such as the ISO and CCITT.

ECN (Explicit Congestion Notification)

In frame-relay transmissions, ECN is a mechanism for indicating that there is traffic congestion on the network. Such congestion can be indicated in either or both of two bit values in a packet header:

- The BECN (Backward Explicit Congestion Notification) bit is set in frame-relay headers moving in the direction opposite the congestion and serves to warn source nodes that congestion is occurring "down the line."

- The FECN (Forward Explicit Congestion Notification) bit is set in frame-relay headers to warn a destination node that there is congestion.

The figure "Use of ECN bits to signal congestion" shows how these bits are used for signaling if there is congestion around node B.

BROADER CATEGORY
Frame Relay

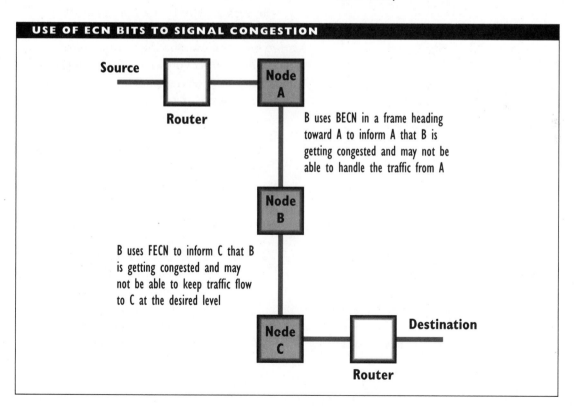

USE OF ECN BITS TO SIGNAL CONGESTION

Source — Router — Node A

B uses BECN in a frame heading toward A to inform A that B is getting congested and may not be able to handle the traffic from A

Node B

B uses FECN to inform C that B is getting congested and may not be able to keep traffic flow to C at the desired level

Node C — Router — Destination

ECNE (Enterprise Certified NetWare Engineer)

A title given to people who have successfully met the requirements for CNE (Certified NetWare Engineer) and who pass several additional courses and tests in order to be able to troubleshoot and operate enterprise-wide networks.

In addition to being a CNE, ECNE candidates must demonstrate mastery of advanced concepts related to the NetWare operating system (either version 3.11 or 4.x—depending on the candidate's specialization) and of topics selected from various electives. Elective areas include such topics as Internetworking products, UnixWare, and NetWare programming.

SEE ALSO

CNA; CNE; CNI

ED (End Delimiter)

A field in a token ring token or data frame. ED indicates the end of a token or data frame.

SEE

Token Ring

EDI (Electronic Data Interchange)

EDI provides specifications for business transactions that are done electronically—for example, on a network. EDI standards specify the type of information that needs to be available or exchanged for various types of transactions. The standards also specify the format this information must have.

EDI Services

EDI services can translate data into the appropriate formats and can send and receive such formats. EDI services and standards support multiple protocols and multiple platforms. For example, EDI services may run on mainframes, minicomputers, or PCSs; the services may run under VMS, MVS, UNIX, Windows, and so on. Data can be transmitted using various protocols, including the ITU's (International Telecommunication Union, formerly the CCITT) X.400 message handling systems.

EDI activities are broken down into transaction sets and functional groups. A *transaction set* consists of data that is exchanged between parties to produce an interchange (of forms, funds, etc.). For example, the transmission of a purchase order, an insurance form, or an invoice can all be transaction sets. A *functional group* consists of several similar transaction sets (such as five invoices).

The transaction set is made up of segments. Each segment is either an administrative chunk (such as a header or trailer) or part of the data being exchanged (for example, an invoice, purchase order, or other type of form). With certain exceptions, segments are transmitted in a predefined sequence, and some segments may be repeated. Each segment in a transaction set is either mandatory, optional, or floating. Allowable data segments are defined and described in the *Data Segment Dictionary*.

Data segments are, in turn, made up of data elements. A *data element* is the smallest unit of information in EDI. The allowable data elements are described in the *Data Element Dictionary*. In their respective dictionaries, each data segment and data element are assigned unique identification numbers, and each will have one or more attributes and values associated with it. When reading articles about EDI, it's not uncommon to find references to particular forms or items by number.

The corpus of documents, forms, and other items in the world of EDI is enormous. This is so, in part, because standards have been developed for entire industries (transportation, health care, finance, etc.). Some of these industries are known for their bureaucratic excesses, and one of the goals of EDI is to help save time, work, paper, and money by automating much of the work and by maintaining records in electronic (as opposed to paper) form as much as possible.

Various surveys and studies have found that companies can save anywhere from a few percent to almost 90 percent on relevant transactions by switching to EDI. It's not uncommon for a company to report savings of $10 or more on each purchase order, for example.

Note that for such savings to be realized, both parties involved in a transaction must use EDI. In fact, one reason EDI continues to grow is that companies who are using EDI may require prospective suppliers or partners to use EDI in their dealings with the company. Once these suppliers have switched, they may, in turn, require that *their* clients use EDI.

EDI Standards and Variants

In the United States, most of the work on EDI specifications and standards has been done by ANSI X12 committees—actually, by subcommittees that address more specific topics. Over two dozen task and work groups from the various subcommittee areas have met or are meeting. For example, an Interactive EDI work group and a Data Security task group have been formed by the X12C subcommittee, which is concerned with communication and controls. That is, the X12C subcommittee is concerned with making sure information can move smoothly, quickly, and securely over electronic lines. Other subcommittees include: X12E (product data), X12F (Finance), X12G (Government with, surprisingly, just two task groups), X12I (Transportation), and X12N (Insurance with, not surprisingly, a dozen Work Groups and ten task groups).

Other standards for EDI also exist. For example, continental Europe uses ODETTE (Organization for Data Exchange by Tele-Transmission in Europe) and the United Kingdom uses TRADACOMS (Trading Data Communications Standards).

Internationally, the ISO's (International Standardization Organization) EDIFACT (EDI for Administration, Commerce, and Transport) standard is considered the official specification. This is sometimes also known as the UN/EDIFACT standard, where UN represents the United Nations.

The various national standards organizations all have the option of being represented in the EDIFACT committees—either directly or through another organization. For example, the United States and several South American countries comprise the PAEB (Pan American EDIFACT Board). Members of the PAEB represent US interests in EDIFACT—at least in part.

a b c d **e** f g h i j k l m n o p q r s t u v w x y z

The X12 and the EDIFACT specifications are not identical, and there is some controversy as to whether the United States will accept the ISO version as official. Currently, the agreement is that by 1997, there will be only a single EDI standard.

Eventually, EDI is expected to make up a large part of the traffic in X.400 systems—possibly as e-mail traffic—and also in CTI (computer-telephone integration) systems.

PRIMARY SOURCES

ISO recommendation 9735; various ANSI documents including X12.3 (Data Element Dictionary) and X12.22 (Data Segment Dictionary); CCITT recommendation x.435

EDO (Extended Data Out)

A variant of dynamic random access memory (DRAM) that helps improve memory speed and performance. By altering the timing and sequence of signals that activate the circuitry for accessing memory locations, EDO keeps data in currently accessed locations available even while beginning the next memory access. Not all processor chip sets support EDO RAM.

EEMA (European Electronic Mail Association)

A European association of developers and vendors of electronic mail products. The EMA (Electronic Mail Association) is the counterpart in the United States.

EFF (Electronic Frontier Foundation)

The EFF is an organization founded in 1990 to help ensure that the "electronic frontier" remains accessible and open to everyone. The EFF tries to accomplish its goals by providing a forum for the discussion of issues related to the use of electronic networks, and a voice for end-users in public policy and other debates.

On occasion, EFF also provides a legal-defense fund for Sysops and other computer-using individuals being prosecuted by the government.

GETTING IN TOUCH WITH EFF

To contact the EFF, write, phone, fax, or modem:

Electronic Frontier Foundation
1001 G Street NW, Suite 950
East Washington, DC 20001
Telephone: (202) 347-5400 (voice)
E-mail: eff@eff.org

Effective Bandwidth

The central part of the total bandwidth in a communications channel. This is the section in which the signal is strongest and clearest. The effective bandwidth is generally the area within which the total attenuation is less than 3 decibels (dB). (A 3 dB attenuation corresponds roughly to a 50 percent reduction in signal strength.)

Effective Isotropic Radiated Power (EIRP)

SEE

EIRP (Effective Isotropic Radiated Power)

Effective Rights

In Novell's NetWare environment, effective rights refer to the rights a user can exercise in a particular directory or file (versions 2.*x* and later) or in the Directory tree created by the NetWare Directory Services (NDS, in version 4.*x*).

Effective rights are defined with respect to the following:

Directory rights in the file system: Directory effective rights are determined by any trustee assignments. If no such assignments exist, the effective rights of a directory are determined by the user's effective rights in the parent directory and the directory's Inherited Rights Mask (in NetWare 3.*x*) or Maximum Rights Mask (NetWare 2.*x*).

File rights in the file system: File effective rights are determined by any trustee assignments for the file. Otherwise, the user's effective rights in the directory apply.

Object rights in the NDS: Object effective rights (in NetWare 4.*x* only) define what a user is allowed to do with an object entry in the NDS Directory tree. These rights apply to the object as a single structure in the tree, not to the properties associated with the object or to the object itself. For example, if a user has a Browse right for an object, the user does not automatically have access to property information.

Property rights in the NDS: Property effective rights (in NetWare 4.*x* only) define what kind of access a user has to the information associated with an object.

Effective rights for NDS objects and properties are determined by:

- Inherited rights associated with the object or property, taking into account any Inherited Rights Filters (IRFs) that apply.

- Trustee assignments associated with a user or group

- Applicable security restrictions

BROADER CATEGORY

NetWare

Effective Throughput

The number of data bits transmitted within a given time (such as a second). This is in contrast to ordinary, or simple, throughput, which represents the total number of bits (both data and administrative) transmitted.

EFS (End Frame Sequence)

The last field in a token ring data packet.

SEE

Token Ring

EFS (Error Free Second)

One second of transmission without errors. The total or average number of EFS can be used as an index of transmission quality.

a b c d **e** f g h i j k l m n o p q r s t u v w x y z

EIA (Electronic Industries Association)

An association that represents American manufacturers in standards organizations. The EIA has published several widely used standards, such as RS-232C, EIA-232D, RS-422, and RS-449. These standards govern the electrical characteristics of connections between computers and other electronic devices (such as modems or printers). The CCITT has created international versions of several EIA standards.

Reports that are concerned more directly with communications are produced jointly with the TIA (Telecommunications Industry Association). For example, EIA/TIA-568 defines five categories for unshielded twisted-pair (UTP) cable and specifies the minimal performance requirements for each category.

EIB (Enterprise Information Base)

In enterprise networks, the information base containing management- and performance-related information about the network. The information in this type of database is used by network management or monitoring software.

EIRP (Effective Isotropic Radiated Power)

The strength of a signal received at an earth station in a satellite communications system; that is, the strength of the satellite's signal by the time it reaches the ground. This value is generally measured in decibels (dB).

EISA (Extended Industry Standard Architecture)

EISA is an architecture for the PC expansion bus that provides 32-bit bus access but remains compatible with the 8- and 16-bit ISA (Industry Standard Architecture) that characterizes the IBM-PC and its descendants.

This architecture was developed by a consortium of hardware manufacturers in response to the 32-bit proprietary Micro-Channel architecture developed by IBM.

BROADER CATEGORY
Data Bus

COMPARE
ISA; MicroChannel; PCI; VESA

EKTS (Electronic Key Telephone System)

In telephony, a key telephone system (KTS) that uses electrical switches. By shrinking the entire KTS down to electronic circuitry, it becomes easier to add features and to install the KTS in a telephone.

SEE ALSO
KTS

Electrical Signal

Electrical energy (voltage or current) transmitted as a waveform. Signals are distinguished by their amplitude (strength), frequency or period (repetition rate), and phase (timing).

Communication occurs when a *modulating signal* (which represents information) is superimposed on a fixed *carrier signal* (which serves as a baseline) and is then transmitted. The information is represented by changing one or more of the modulating signal's distinguishing features.

Electromagnetic Interference (EMI)

SEE

EMI (Electromagnetic Interference)

Electronic Cookbook (ECB)

SEE

ECB (Electronic Cookbook)

Electronic Key Telephone System (EKTS)

SEE

EKTS (Electronic Key Telephone System); KTS

Electronic Mail Association (EMA)

SEE

EMA (Electronic Mail Association)

Electronic Mailbox

In an e-mail (electronic mail) system, a directory provided to store messages for a single user. Each e-mail user has a unique ID and a unique mailbox.

SEE ALSO

E-Mail

Electronic Switching

In circuit switching, hardware in which the connections are made electronically (rather than electromechanically).

Elevator Seeking

Elevator seeking is a technique for optimizing the movement of the read/write heads in a file server's hard disk.

Requests for disk access from different nodes are queued on the basis of the heads' position; that is, requests for data from the same area of the disk are fulfilled together. The heads move in a sweeping motion from the outside of the disk to the inside. This strategy reduces read/write head activity and greatly increases the throughput.

The name *elevator seeking* comes from the fact that people going to a particular floor get off together, regardless of when each person got on the elevator. Similarly, the elevator stops at floors as they are reached, not in the order in which the floors were requested.

ELS (Entry Level System) NetWare

ELS NetWare refers to low-end NetWare products that support a limited number of stations and a limited range of hardware. ELS NetWare comes in two configurations:

- ELS Level I supports up to four nodes, a few different network interface cards, and a limited set of operating environments.

a b c d **e** f g h i j k l m n o p q r s t u v w x y z

- ELS Level II supports up to eight nodes and a much broader range of hardware and operating environments.

ELS products are no longer sold.

EMA (Electronic Mail Association)

An association of developers and vendors of electronic mail products.

EMA (Enterprise Management Architecture)

EMA is a network management model from Digital Equipment Corporation (DEC). With this model, DEC hopes to provide the tools needed to manage enterprise networks, regardless of the configurations that make up the network. The architecture is designed to conform to the ISO's CMIP (Common Management Information Protocol).

The DEC Management Control Center (DECmcc) Director implements the current version of the EMA model. This product is extended by several add-on products that are designed for specialized management tasks.

In order to achieve vendor and protocol independence, the EMA isolates the Director as much as possible from implementation details. The Director is in charge of managing network elements, and it uses several kinds of modules for its tasks:

- Access modules, to provide a path to the network elements being managed. Each access module supports a single type of network element, such as a bridge or a device belonging to a particular type of network. Access modules use widely supported protocols, such as the CMIP and the Internet community's SNMP, to communicate.

- Functional modules, to provide the capabilities for carrying out the performance, configuration, security, and other types of management tasks.

- Presentation modules, which provide an integrated, standardized interface for the Director.

The other major component of the EMA model is the Executive. This element contains the information about the network elements in a Management Information Repository.

BROADER CATEGORY
Network Management

E-Mail (Electronic Mail)

E-mail (also written as *email*) is an application that provides a message transfer and storage service for the nodes on a network or internetwork or for a stand-alone machine through a dial-up service. Each user has an electronic mailbox (a unique directory for storing electronic mail), and other users can send e-mail messages to the user at this mailbox.

The e-mail messages are sent to an *e-mail address*. For the end-user, an e-mail address is generally written as a sequence of names, separated by periods or other special characters, as in *fiddle@faddle.edu*.

Once the message is stored in the recipient's mailbox, the owner of the mailbox can retrieve whatever messages look important and/or interesting. E-mail packages differ in the ease with which such selections can be made and also in the services the packages provide.

All e-mail packages will send and deliver mail, and all can let users know when they have mail. Most packages allow you to create the message by using the e-mail software or by using your own resources. Many packages also allow recipients to reply to a message by simply annotating the original message. Some packages allow voice mail, which requires additional hardware.

Setting up a proprietary e-mail service on a single network is generally straightforward, but may be of little value in the long run. In order to exchange e-mail with users on other networks or in remote locations, more powerful software is needed.

E-mail services are also available through dial-up services such as CompuServe and MCI Mail.

If an e-mail message cannot be delivered, it may be stored temporarily in a *post office*. This is just a service with available storage and with the ability to check periodically whether the recipient is ready to take delivery. E-mail handling is an example of the more general store-and-forward strategy.

History and Overview of Electronic Mail

The first e-mail systems were developed in the late 1960s and early 1970s. These were mainly small-scale, departmental systems—although the ARPANET was a major factor in the development of electronic messaging. These systems were also mainly proprietary, with little effort being made to enable e-mail systems to communicate with each other—even within the same company. The first

e-mail systems consisted of little more than file transfer capabilities.

In the late 1970s and early 1980s, public e-mail services became available through service providers such as AT&T Mail, MCI Mail, and CompuServe. For the most part, mail services on these providers were used by businesses and by individuals. Research and academic e-mail services developed on what was becoming the Internet.

At the same time, PCs appeared and quickly became extremely popular. By the mid- to late 1980s, e-mail packages for LANs were appearing and proliferating. As was the case with public and corporate e-mail services, each package had its own formats and protocols.

As mail and messaging services became more popular and more widely used, the need for interoperability grew. As a result, standards were developed:

- The X.400 series of recommendations from the CCITT (Consultative Committee for International Telegraphy and Telephony, now going under the name International Telecommunications Union, or ITU) provided standards for electronic messaging and mail. The first version of the X.400 standards appeared in 1984, and these are known as MHS 84 (for message handling system, 1984). X.400 systems commonly serve as a backbone for delivering mail between (possibly incompatible) e-mail systems.

- The SMTP (Simple Mail Transfer Protocol) in the IP (Internet protocol) suite provided e-mail standards and protocols for the Internet.

In the late 1980s and early 1990s, e-mail continued to grow rapidly in popularity. During this period, formats became more standardized, and even the LAN-based packages began to support either X.400 or SMTP or both.

Two other events have helped make electronic mail a truly international service:

- The appearance of the CCITT X.500 standards for directory naming and services helped make it possible to keep track of addresses and locations more easily and in a more consistent manner. During this same period, a new version of the X.400 MHS standards appeared—known as MHS 88.

- The appearance of gateways, which could serve as a transfer place between incompatible mail systems—sort of like the locks in the Panama canal provide a transfer between incompatible oceans.

The mid- to late 1990s promise to be an even more exciting period for electronic mail. Several kinds of developments are likely to take place during this period:

- Increasing bandwidth, so that even huge files can be sent quickly and easily via e-mail. The planning and work are already underway for gigabit-level bandwidths for such services, and even terabit-speed networks are beginning to be discussed.

- Support for video, audio, and graphics in a mail or message service. The Multi-purpose Internet Mail Extensions (MIME) provide guidelines for how such materials should be handled. While these represent a start, it's likely that major developments will occur in this area.

- The appearance of intelligent agents to help in mail handling and delivery, and also to help users screen their mail.

- The development of wireless mail services will continue, helping to spur advances in wireless networking.

- The generalization of electronic mail and messaging to encompass electronic commerce—for example, through EDI (electronic data interchange).

- The use of e-mail as a medium for workflow messages and traffic. Workflow software is used to specify or manage the sequence of tasks needed to carry out and complete a project—particularly when the project requires the participation of multiple workers.

- The use of encryption, digital signatures, and other security techniques to keep the content of e-mail messages hidden from unauthorized eyes. This is an essential development if e-mail is to become a vehicle for electronic commerce. *PEM* (privacy enhanced mail) is an example of such a security measure. The more general *PGP* (pretty good privacy) algorithm may also be used for encryption).

E-Mail System Components

The architecture of an e-mail system can vary, but all e-mail systems need to provide the following types of services:

- Terminal and/or node handling, so that the mail service can understand user requests and respond to those requests.

- File handling, so that electronic messages can be stored as files in the appropriate mailbox. These are general file handling abilities, with a few exceptions.

- Communications handling, so that a mail server (for example) can talk to and exchange messages with another server at a remote site. For the most part, these are general communications capabilities.

- Local mail services, so that a mail server can receive and deliver mail from local users.

- Mail transfer, so that a mail server can deliver electronic messages to another server and can receive electronic messages from the other server.

Encryption and multicast capabilities are also common e-mail system features.

MHS (Message Handling Service) is Novell's e-mail system for NetWare. MHS is a store-and-forward system that also provides gateways into other messaging systems, most notably, into X.400 systems.

E-Mail Protocols

Until recently, the e-mail universe was filled with proprietary protocols, few of which could talk to each other. Fortunately, this has changed. Most e-mail products now support either or both of two widely used standards: the SMTP (Simple Mail Transfer Protocol) from the TCP/IP protocol suite or protocols specified in the CCITT's X.400 series of standards.

SEE ALSO

MHS (Message Handling System); MIME (Multipurpose Internet Mail Extensions); PEM (Privacy Enhanced Mail); PGP (Pretty Good Privacy)

Embedded SCSI

A hard disk with a SCSI interface and a controller built into the hard disk.

EMI (Electromagnetic Interference)

Random or periodic energy from external sources that can interfere with transmissions over copper cable. EMI sources can be artifacts (such as motors or lighting—particularly fluorescent lighting) or natural phenomena (such as atmospheric or solar activity). Compare this with RFI (radio frequency interference).

EMM (Expanded Memory Manager)

An EMM is a program that provides access to expanded memory.

SEE ALSO

Memory Management

Emoticon

In electronic communication, *emoticons* are special symbols that are used to convey emotions (elation, disappointment, and so on) or commentary (sarcasm, irony, and the like) related to the text. Emoticons are also known as *smileys*.

Emoticons are built using characters available on any keyboard. For example, the emoticon ;-) represents a wink, which can convey irony, sarcasm, or a conspiratorial "nudge-nudge, know what I mean." The following are examples of emoticons:

:-)	Smile; happiness; agreement; laughter
:-(	Frown; unhappiness; disagreement; anger
;-)	Half-smile; irony; sarcasm; joking
(@w@)	Amazement; incredulity
;-o	Shout
;-r	Disgust; displeasure (tongue sticking out)

PRIMARY SOURCE

Smileys by David W. Sanderson (O'Reilly & Associates) includes more than 650 symbols.

EMS (Expanded Memory Specification)

In the DOS environment, the specification for expanded memory (a type of memory that is allocated on separate boards and whose contents are paged into "ordinary" memory piecemeal). Although the EMS calls for expanded memory to have its own hardware, various memory managers and drivers can emulate expanded memory in extended memory.

SEE ALSO

Memory

Emulation

A complete functional duplication of one machine or device by another. For example, a PC may emulate a 3270 terminal in order to communicate with an IBM mainframe. A hardware device or a software package that provides emulation is called an *emulator*.

SEE ALSO

Terminal Emulation

Encapsulation

In a layered networking model, encapsulation refers to a process by which each layer subsumes the PDU (protocol data unit) from the layer above into a larger PDU by adding a header to the higher-layer PDU. (A PDU is a packet built at a particular layer, which is used for communicating with a program at the same layer on a different machine). For example, a transport-layer protocol encapsulates a PDU from the session layer.

The layer is often indicated by adding an initial letter to *PDU*. For example, a presentation layer PDU would be written as PPDU or P-PDU.

Encapsulation is used by internetwork links, such as certain routers or gateways. *Encapsulating routers* operate at the network layer, and *transport-layer gateways* operate at the higher, transport layer.

The inverse process—removing the lower-layer headers at the receiving end—is known as *decapsulation*.

▼ Encoding

Encoding is a process by which information in one form or at one level of detail is represented in a different form or at a different level.

Encoding Contexts

The term is widely used, and encoding is practiced in many contexts. For example, encoding may be used in the following ways:

- In text processing, characters, digits, and other symbols are represented as decimal values between 0 and 128 or between 0 and 255. ASCII and EBCDIC are examples of character-encoding schemes.

- In telegraphy, characters and digits are represented as sequences of dots and dashes. Morse code is an example of this encoding scheme.

- In the transmission of digital signals over networks, binary values (0 and 1) are represented as changes in voltage or current levels. Signal-encoding schemes include AMI (Alternate Mark Inversion), Manchester, Differential Manchester, and MLT-3.

Special Forms of Encoding

Special forms of encoding include translation and compression. In translation, one encoding scheme is converted to another, such as from EBCDIC to ASCII. In compression encoding, redundant information is represented in a more efficient manner.

In the X.400 Message Handling System (MHS), a distinction is made between two types of encoding for a packet: definite or indefinite. A definite encoding scheme includes explicit length information in a packet. This information is generally stored in a *length field*.

An indefinite encoding scheme uses a special character (EOC, for end of content) to indicate when the end of a packet is reached.

Note that encoding here refers to the form a packet takes, rather than the form an electrical signal takes.

▼ Encoding, Signal

Signal encoding is a set of rules for representing the possible values for an input signal in some other form. For example, in digital communications, the signal-encoding rule will determine what form an electrical signal will take to represent a 1 or a 0.

Dozens of rule sets have been proposed just for digital signals. Each has its advantages and disadvantages. In the simplest encoding scheme, a particular voltage level represents one value and a different (or zero) voltage represents a different value. For binary inputs, just two different voltage levels are needed.

Note that the actual voltage levels and charges used to represent the bit values depend on the logic being used for the circuitry. TTL logic is used in situations where circuit speed is important; because of its lower voltage requirements, CMOS logic is used where low power consumption is more important (for example, in battery-powered computers).

It is possible to encode more than one bit in a digital signal. For example, by allowing four different voltages, you can represent two bits in each signal; with eight voltages,

a b c d **e** f g h i j k l m n o p q r s t u v w x y z

you can represent three bits at a time, and so on. The trade-off is that the components must be able to make finer discriminations, which makes them more expensive to manufacture or more error prone, or both.

Signal Timing

Each signal has a predefined duration, so that the voltage for a single signal will be held for a specified amount of time. The shorter this time needs to be, the faster the potential transmission speed. The trade-off is that the faster signal allows less room for distortion by noise, so that the error rate may increase.

In order to distinguish the individual bits in a series of the same bit values, such as a series of 1 values in succession, sender and receiver may use clocking (a timing mechanism used to determine the start of a bit signal) to establish the duration of a signal for a single bit, which is called the *bit interval*. Each party in the communication uses its own clock to time the signal.

Since transmission speeds can be more than 100 megabits per second (Mbps), the clocks must be very closely synchronized. In practice, the clocks may need to be resynchronized millions of times per second.

To avoid the overhead of inserted clocking bits, most encoding schemes use actual bit values (generally a 1) as the clocking bit. This works fine unless there are long stretches without any 1 values. (At high speeds, a "long" stretch can be as short as a single byte.) For these cases, special, adaptive encoding schemes, such as B8ZS (bipolar with 8 zero substitution), have been developed to make sure such a sequence never occurs.

Self-Clocking Encoding Schemes

Some encoding schemes are self-clocking, in that the clocking is built into the signal itself. This clocking usually takes the form of a voltage change at the middle of the bit interval.

Although self-clocking schemes make external clocks and adaptive encoding unnecessary, they cannot operate at more than half the speed of the system clock. This is because two clock cycles must be used to split a bit interval in half.

Transition Coding

Some encoding schemes use transition coding in which a value is encoded by a transition (from one voltage level to another) *during* the bit interval. For example, the representation of a 1 in a scheme with transition coding may consist of a positive voltage for half the bit interval and zero voltage for the other half. This type of encoding scheme is also self-clocking. Transition coding tends to be less susceptible to noise.

A Sampling of Encoding Schemes

The following general encoding schemes summarize a few of the strategies used to represent binary values.

Unfortunately, there is little consistency in signal-encoding terminology, so that the same term may refer to two different encoding schemes. If the encoding method is important for your purposes, ask the vendor for sample timing diagrams, so that you can see the actual encoding.

Unipolar: Uses a positive or a negative voltage (but not both in the same scheme) to represent one value (for example, 1) and a zero voltage to represent the other. Unipolar encoding does not use transition coding, and it requires an external clock.

Polar: A positive voltage represents one value and a negative voltage represents the other. Polar encoding does not use transition coding, and it requires an external clock.

Bipolar: Uses positive, negative, *and* zero voltages, usually with zero voltage representing one value and a nonzero voltage representing the other. Bipolar encoding may use transition coding, and it may be self-clocking.

Biphase: Includes at least one transition per bit interval. In addition to making this scheme self-clocking, the transition coding also makes it easier to detect errors. Biphase schemes are often used for networks.

Of these schemes, variants on bipolar and biphase are the most widely used. The following sections describe some specific versions of bipolar and biphase strategies. In a specific communications context, a binary value may undergo several encoding schemes before actually being transmitted.

AMI (Alternate Mark Inversion)

AMI, also known as *ABP (alternate bipolar) encoding,* is a bipolar scheme. This signal-encoding method uses three possible values: +V, 0V, and −V (positive, zero, and negative voltage). All 0 bits are encoded as 0V (zero voltage); 1 bits are encoded as +V and −V (positive and negative voltage) in

alternation. The figure "AMI encoding for a bit sequence" shows an example of AMI encoding.

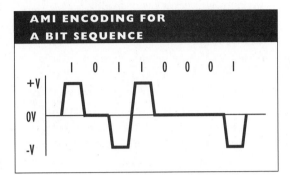

AMI ENCODING FOR A BIT SEQUENCE

AMI encoding is used in DS*x*-level transmissions, as in ISDN (Integrated Services Distributed Network), FDDI (Fiber Distributed Data Interface), and other high-speed network architectures.

AMI encoding is not self-clocking. This means that synchronous transmissions, such as those using digital signal methods, must use an external clock for timing. The positive and negative voltages associated with 1 bits are used for this timing.

In order to ensure that the transmission never gets out of synch, some environments require a minimum density of 1 values in any transmission. The minimum pulse density is generally set to at least one in every eight bits. To ensure that this pulse-density requirement is met, a variant encoding method, called B8ZS, is used.

B8ZS (Bipolar with 8 Zero Substitution)

Like AMI, B8ZS uses three possible values: +V, 0V, and −V (positive, zero, and negative voltage). All 0 bits are encoded as 0V (zero voltage); 1 bits are encoded as +V and −V (positive and negative voltage) in alternation. Unlike AMI, however, B8ZS requires that at least one bit out of every eight must be a 1; that is, eight consecutive 0 values will never occur in B8ZS.

If eight consecutive 0 bits are encountered, the encoding will insert a 1 before the eighth 0. This value will be removed at a later point. A minimal density of 1 values is needed because these values are used for timing. If the transmission contains too long a string of 0 values, the sender and receiver can get out of synch without knowing it. By ensuring there will be at least one opportunity to synchronize every eight bits, the transmission can never get too far out of synch.

Differential Manchester

Differential Manchester is a biphase signal-encoding scheme used in Token Ring local-area networks (LANs). The presence or absence of a transition at the beginning of a bit interval indicates the value; the transition in mid-interval just provides the clocking.

For electrical signals, bit values will generally be represented by one of three possible voltage levels: positive (+V), zero (0V), or negative (–V). Any two of these levels are needed—for example, +V and –V.

There is a transition in the middle of each bit interval. This makes the encoding method self-clocking and helps avoid signal distortion due to DC signal components.

For one of the possible bit values but not the other, there will be a transition at the start of any given bit interval. For example, in a particular implementation, there may be a signal transition for a 1 bit. The figure "Differential Manchester encoding for a bit sequence" shows an example of a signal

using +V and –V, with signal transition on 1 bits.

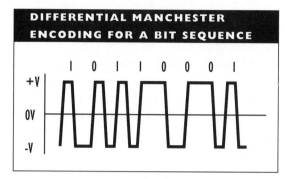

DIFFERENTIAL MANCHESTER ENCODING FOR A BIT SEQUENCE

In differential Manchester encoding, the presence or absence of a transition at the beginning of the bit interval determines the bit value. In effect, 1 bits produce vertical signal patterns; 0 bits produce horizontal patterns, as shown in the figure. The transition in the middle of the interval is just for timing.

Manchester

Manchester is a biphase signal-encoding scheme used in Ethernet LANs. The direction of the transition in mid-interval (negative to positive or positive to negative) indicates the value (1 or 0, respectively) and provides the clocking.

The Manchester scheme follows these rules:

- +V and –V voltage levels are used.

- There is a transition from one to the other voltage level halfway through each bit interval.

- There may or may not be a transition at the start of each bit interval, depending on whether the bit value is a 0 or 1.

- For a 1 bit, the transition is always from –V to +V; for a 0 bit, the transition is always from +V to –V.

In Manchester encoding, the beginning of a bit interval is used merely to set the stage. The activity in the middle of each bit interval determines the bit value: upward transition for a 1 bit, downward for a 0 bit. The figure "Manchester encoding for a bit sequence" shows the encoding for a sample bit sequence.

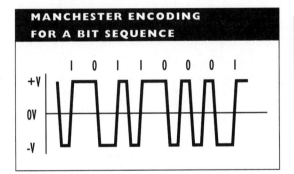

MANCHESTER ENCODING FOR A BIT SEQUENCE

MLT-3 Encoding

MLT-3 is a three-level encoding scheme that can also scramble data. This scheme is one proposed for use in FDDI networks. An alternative is the two-level NRZI.

The MLT-3 signal-encoding scheme uses three voltage levels (including a zero level) and changes levels only when a 1 occurs. It follows these rules:

- +V, 0V, and –V voltage levels are used.

- The voltage remains the same during an entire bit interval; that is, there are no transitions in the middle of a bit interval.

- The voltage level changes in succession: from +V to 0V to –V to 0V to +V, and so on.

- The voltage level changes only for a 1 bit.

MLT-3 is not self-clocking, so that a synchronization sequence is needed to make sure the sender and receiver are using the same timing. The figure "MLT-3 encoding for a bit sequence" shows an example of this encoding.

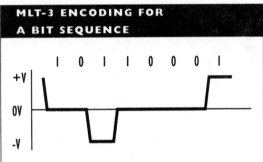

MLT-3 ENCODING FOR A BIT SEQUENCE

NRZ (Non-Return to Zero)

NRZ, also known as *differential encoding,* is a bipolar encoding scheme that changes voltages between bit intervals for 1 values but not for 0 values. This means that the encoding changes during a transmission. For example, 0 may be a positive voltage during one part and a negative voltage during another part depending on the last occurrence of a 1. The presence or absence of a transition indicates a bit value, not the voltage level.

a
b
c
d
e
f
g
h
i
j
k
l
m
n
o
p
q
r
s
t
u
v
w
x
y
z

NRZ is inexpensive to implement, but it is not self-clocking. It also does not use transition coding.

The figure "NRZ encoding for a bit sequence" shows the encoding for a sample bit sequence.

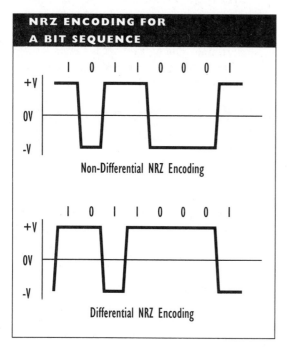

NRZ ENCODING FOR A BIT SEQUENCE

Non-Differential NRZ Encoding

Differential NRZ Encoding

RZ (Return to Zero)

RZ is a bipolar signal-encoding scheme that uses transition coding to return the signal to a zero voltage during part of each bit interval. It is self-clocking.

The figure "Differential and nondifferential RZ encoding of a bit sequence" shows both differential and nondifferential versions of the RZ encoding scheme. In the differential version, the defining voltage (the voltage associated with the first half of the

bit interval) changes for each 1 bit and remains unchanged for each 0 bit.

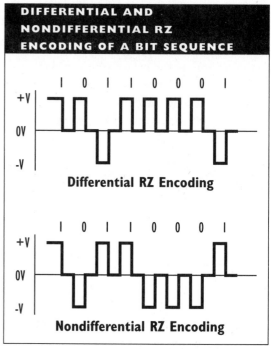

DIFFERENTIAL AND NONDIFFERENTIAL RZ ENCODING OF A BIT SEQUENCE

Differential RZ Encoding

Nondifferential RZ Encoding

In the nondifferential version, the defining voltage changes only when the bit value changes, so that the same defining voltages are always associated with 0 and 1. For example, +5 volts may define a 1, and –5 volts may define a 0.

FM 0 Encoding

FM 0 (frequency modulation 0) is a signal-encoding method used for LocalTalk networks in Macintosh environments. FM 0 uses +V and –V voltage levels to represent bit values. The encoding rules are as follows:

- 1 bits are encoded alternately as +V and –V, depending on the previous voltage level. The voltage level remains constant for an entire bit interval for a 1 bit.

- 0 bits are encoded as +V or −V, depending on the immediately preceding voltage level. The voltage changes to the other value halfway through the bit interval.

The figure "FM 0 encoding for a bit sequence" shows the encoding for a sample bit sequence.

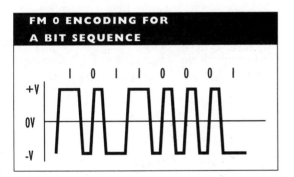

FM 0 ENCODING FOR A BIT SEQUENCE

FM 0 is self-clocking because the encoding for a 0 bit can be used to determine the length of a bit interval and to synchronize the sender and receiver.

Encryption

Most simply, encryption is a process in which ordinary text or numerical information (*plaintext*) is converted into an unintelligible form (called *ciphertext,* among other terms) using a well-defined (and reversible) conversion algorithm and a predefined bit value (known as a *key*). The key provides a starting value for the encryption algorithm.

For various reasons, some information must be kept encrypted. Because of the fervor with which this statement is believed, encryption has become an active area of research and study. Much computing and brain power has been expended in developing encryption algorithms that are impossible to crack and then cracking them.

Three broad strategies can be used for encryption: the traditional strategy, the private-key strategy, and the public-key strategy.

Traditional Encryption

The traditional encryption strategy is simply to devise and apply a conversion algorithm. The receiver must know the algorithm and the key in order to reverse the conversion and decrypt the information. This approach has two weaknesses:

- The algorithms and keys used tend, as a class, to be easier to crack than those used in the other strategies.

- The algorithm or key may be stolen or intercepted while being communicated to the receiver.

Secret-Key Encryption

Secret-key encryption strategies use a single key—known only to the sender and the receiver—and a public encryption algorithm. Private-key encryption is also known as *one-key key, single key,* or *symmetric key encryption.*

The Data Encryption Standard (DES), which was adapted in 1977 as the official United States encryption standard for nonclassified data, uses a secret-key strategy. The encryption algorithm is quite complex and involves numerous permutations and transpositions of message elements. See the DES article for more information. Different levels of encryption can be used to make the ciphertext even more unintelligible.

As long as the secret keys are kept secret, this encryption strategy is very effective. For example, even though it uses only 56 bits for the encryption key, the DES has an extremely small likelihood of being cracked.

Secret-key strategies have one major disadvantage: it is not possible to protect a message against fraud by either the sender or the receiver.

Public-Key Encryption

Public-key encryption strategies use the two halves of a very long bit sequence as the basis for the encryption algorithm. Public-key encryption is also known as *double-key encryption* or *asymmetric key encryption*

One key (one half of the bit sequence) is placed in a public-key library to which everyone has access. The other key is known only to a single party, and is this party's private key. Either half of the bit sequence can be used to encrypt the information; the *other half* is needed to decrypt it. Someone wishing to send a message can use the receiver's public key to encrypt the message; the receiver can use the private key to decrypt it. To reverse the process, the erstwhile receiver uses the private key to encrypt the message. The destination party can use the public key to decrypt the message.

This encryption strategy is simple to implement. It is also relatively easy to crack unless the initial bit sequence is quite long. The RSA algorithm is an exception to this weakness and has the advantage of being able to protect against fraud by the sender

or receiver. See the RSA Algorithm article for more information.

End Bracket

A circuit board with slots into which other boards can be plugged. The motherboard in a PC is a backplane. A *segmented backplane* is a backplane with two or more buses, each with its own slots for additional boards.

End Node

In a network, a station that serves as a source or a destination for a packet. An end node should be able to communicate through all the layers in the OSI Reference Model or an equivalent layered model.

SEE ALSO
Node

End of Content (EOC)

In telecommunications, a special character used to indicate the end of a message or page.

End Office (EO)

SEE
EO (End Office)

End System (ES)

In the OSI Reference Model, an end system (ES) is a network entity, such as a node, that uses or provides network services or resources. An end system is known as a *host* in Internet terminology.

Architecturally, an end system uses all seven layers of the OSI Reference Model. This is in contrast to an intermediate system (IS), or router, which uses only the bottom three layers (the subnet layers) of the model. The figure "Communications involving intermediate and end systems" shows the relationship between intermediate and end systems.

BROADER CATEGORY
OSI Reference Model

COMPARE
Intermediate System (IS)

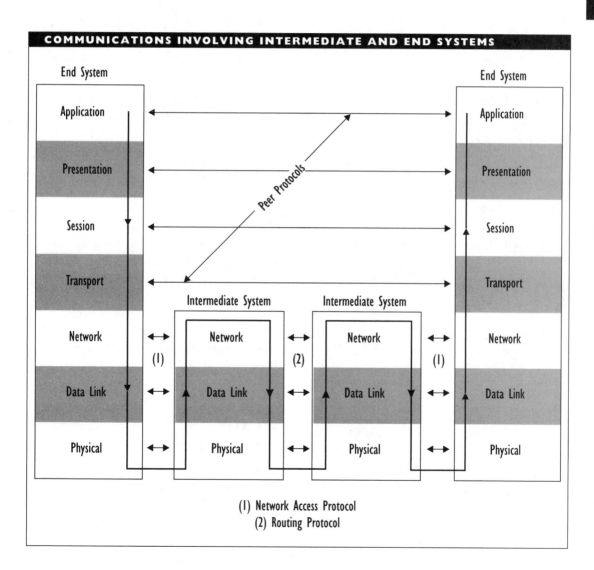

COMMUNICATIONS INVOLVING INTERMEDIATE AND END SYSTEMS

(1) Network Access Protocol
(2) Routing Protocol

End-to-End Routing

A routing strategy in which the entire route is determined before the message is sent. This is in contrast to node-to-node routing, in which the route is built step-by-step.

End-User

In a network, the ultimate consumer of a networking service.

Enhanced Parallel Port (EPP)

SEE

EPP (Enhanced Parallel Port)

ENS (Enterprise Network Services)

ENS is an extension to Banyan's VINES network operating system (NOS). ENS enables StreetTalk to keep track of servers using NOSs other than VINES, such as any version of Novell's NetWare 2.*x* and later or of Apple's AppleTalk.

StreetTalk is the global naming service for VINES. A naming service keeps track of which nodes and devices are attached to the network and assigns a global name to each node. The name is independent of the particular network in which the node is located and makes it possible for a user connected to one server to use resources attached to a different server, without knowing which specific server has the resources.

ENS for NetWare is a special version for use in NetWare versions 2.2 or later. Naming services are not needed in version 4.0, because this version provides global naming

through the NetWare Directory Services (NDS).

ENS for NetWare includes four components:

- Server software, which runs the dedicated server that is needed to run ENS for NetWare

- A StreetTalk agent, which runs as a VAP (Value-Added Process, for NetWare 2.*x*) or as an NLM (NetWare Loadable Module, for NetWare 3.*x*)

- Client software, which must run on each workstation that wants to use ENS

- ENS utilities, which are used instead of NetWare utilities

Enterprise Computing

A term for networks that encompasses most or all of a company's computing resources. In most cases, an enterprise computing network will include a whole range of computers, which may be running different operating systems and belong to different types of networks. Consequently, one of the biggest challenges for enterprise computing is to achieve interoperability for all its components.

SEE ALSO

Network, Enterprise

Enterprise Information Base (EIB)

SEE

EIB (Enterprise Information Base)

Entity

In networking models, entity refers to an abstract device, such as a program, function, or protocol, that implements the services for a particular layer on a single machine. An entity provides services for entities at the layer above it and requests services of the entities at the layers below it.

The term entity is also used to refer to a device on a network, at least when that device is running a program or providing a service.

Entrance Facilities

In a premises distribution system (PDS), the location at which the building's wiring and the external wiring meet.

Entry Point

For networking hardware, the point at which a node is connected to the network; for software, the point at which a program, module, or function begins executing. In IBM's NMA, *entry point* refers to the software through which an SNA-compliant device can communicate with the network management program.

SEE ALSO

NMA (Network Management Architecture)

Entry State

In a routing table for an AppleTalk network, a value that indicates the status of a path. Such an entry may have the value good,

suspect, or bad, depending on how recently the path was verified as being valid.

Envelope

In communications or electronic mail (e-mail) systems, *envelope* refers to information that is added to a data packet in order to make sure the packet reaches its destination and is received correctly. This information is generally appended as a header (and possibly also a trailer) for the data packet.

In relation to an electrical signal, envelope is used as a term for the signal's shape, such as sine, square, or trapezoidal.

The term *enveloping* refers to a process by which multiple faxes are included in a single transmission.

Envelope Delay Distortion

In an electrical signal, the amount of delay between different frequencies. The greater this delay, the greater the distortion.

EO (End Office)

In telephony, a central office, which is where a subscriber's lines are terminated and connected to other exchanges.

SEE

CO (Central Office)

EOC (End of Content)

In telecommunications, a special character used to indicate the end of a message or page.

a b c d **e** f g h i j k l m n o p q r s t u v w x y z

EPP (Enhanced Parallel Port)

A parallel port with a maximum signal rate of 16 megabits per second (Mbps). The EPP specifications were developed jointly by Xircom and Zenith, and the developers plan to produce a 64 Mbps version. The faster port makes external LAN cards (such as those produced by Xircom) more viable.

Equalization

The process by which a device's frequency-response is made uniform over a specified frequency range. This is done to eliminate, or at least decrease, distortion in a signal due to high-frequency signals being slowed to a greater degree than lower-frequency waves. A device that performs equalization is called an *equalizer.*

Erlang

In communications, a measure of the degree to which a communications channel is being used to capacity. One Erlang is defined as 36 CCS (hundreds of call seconds), which amounts to an entire hour of channel usage at capacity.

Error Detection and Correction

In communications, an *error* is a situation in which the received material does not match what was sent. Errors can arise for any of many reasons, including the following:

- Problems with the signal, such as noise, interference, or distortion

- Protocol problems, so that sender and receiver cannot understand each other

- Buffer overflow, such as when the capacity of a channel or a device is exceeded

Error correction is a term for any of several strategies for ensuring that the receiver ends up with the same message as the one originally sent. To accomplish this, two steps are necessary: detecting an error and correcting it. In digital communications, errors are at the level of individual bits, so the task becomes one of ensuring that the bit sequence received matches the one sent.

Various precautions and measures can be taken to identify and possibly even correct errors. These measures vary in how effective they are, and all impose a transmission penalty in the form of extra bits that must be sent.

Error-Detection Methods

Detecting errors involves the identification of an incorrect or invalid transmission element, such as an impossible character or a garbled (but not encrypted) message.

In general, error-detection strategies rely on a numerical value (based on the bytes transmitted in a packet) that is computed and included in the packet. The receiver computes the same type of value and compares the computed result with the transmitted value. Error-detection strategies differ in the complexity of the computed value and in their success rate.

Error-detection methods include cyclic or longitudinal redundancy checks and the use of parity bits. Parity bits, CRC (cyclic redundancy check), and LRC (longitudinal redundancy check) values are sometimes referred to as ECCs (error correction codes), even though, strictly speaking, they can only help *detect* errors. *Hamming codes,* on the other hand, are true ECCs, because they provide enough information to determine the nature of the error and to replace it with a correct value.

CRC (Cyclic Redundancy Check)

CRC is an error-detection method based on a transformation of the bit values in a data packet or frame. The transformation involves multiplying the bit pattern by a polynomial equation, whose order depends on the number of bits allocated for the computed value. The more bits, the better the error-detection capabilities.

The sender computes a CRC value and adds this to the data packet. The receiver computes a CRC value based on the data portion of the received packet and compares the result with the transmitted CRC value. If the two match, the receiver assumes the packet has been received without error. Note that a matching CRC value is no guarantee of an error-free transmission, although it does make it almost certain that any errors overlooked involved more than two bits in the packet.

The following are some of the CRC tests that have been developed and that are used in communications and networking contexts:

CRC-12: A 12-bit CRC check, used with older protocols, most notably, IBM's BSC (Binary Synchronous Communication) protocol.

CRC-16: A 16-bit CRC check, used in many file transfer protocols. CRC-16 can detect all single- and double-bit errors, all errors in which an odd number of bits are erroneous, and most error bursts (signals in which multiple bits in succession are erroneous, for example, because of some temporary glitch or interference in the power supply).

CRC-CCITT: A 16-bit CRC check, intended as an international standard.

CRC-32: A 32-bit CRC check, used in local-area network (LAN) protocols because it can detect virtually all errors.

Parity, or Vertical Redundancy Checking (VRC)

Parity, also known as *vertical redundancy checking* (VRC), is a crude error-detection method, which is used in serial transmissions. With this method, an extra bit is added at regular locations, such as after seven or eight data bits. The value of the parity bit depends on the pattern of 0 and 1 values in the data byte and on the type of parity being used.

Bits 3, 4, and 5 in the UART (universal asynchronous receiver/transmitter) line control register (LCR) determine the parity setting in a serial communication. The following values are used (with bit values displayed in the order 345):

None (000): The value of the parity bit is ignored.

Odd (100): The parity bit is set to whatever value is required to ensure that the bit pattern (including parity bit) has an odd number of 1 values. For example, with 1010 1101, the parity bit would be set to 0.

Even (110): The parity bit is set to whatever value is required to ensure that the bit pattern (including parity bit) has an even number of 1 values. For example, with 1010 1101, the parity bit would be set to 1.

Mark (101): The parity bit is always set to the mark value (1).

Space (111): The parity bit is always set to the space value (0).

Block Parity, or Longitudinal Redundancy Checking (LRC)

Another type of parity, called *block parity* or *longitudinal redundancy checking (LRC)*, is computed for each bit place value in a block of bytes. For example, after every eight bytes, an additional byte is set. One of these extra bits corresponds to each place value for the preceding set of bytes. Block parity is always set to even (according to ISO standard 1155), so that each block parity bit is set to whatever value is required to give the column of bits an even number of 1 values.

The figure "LRC and VRC parity" shows these two types of parity in a single transmission.

LRC AND VRC PARITY

```
1001  011-1
0011  111-0
1100  110-1
1001  000-1
1101  101-0          Byte Parity Bits
1010  101-1
0001  100-1
---------------
1001  110-1
```

Block Parity Bits

Error-Correction Methods

Once an error is detected, the most common correction scheme is to request a retransmission. The retransmission may consist of either just the erroneous material or the corrected material *and* all the material that was sent after the error but before the receiver alerted the sender. Needless to say, correcting errors can become expensive if there are a lot of them.

It is possible to develop automatic error-correction tools. For example, *forward error correction (FEC)* methods enable the receiver to correct an error without requiring a retransmission. Popular FEC methods include Hamming and HBC (Hagelberger, Bose-Chaudhuri) coding.

To do error-correction on the fly, many extra bits must be added to the message in order to locate and correct errors. (Once located, correcting a bit-level error is really not difficult: if 0 is wrong, then 1 must be the value). Such methods may be used in communications in which retransmissions are more disruptive and/or costly than the overhead of sending correctable information.

Error Correction Code (ECC)

In digital communications, a term applied (sometimes incorrectly) to any of several types of codes used to detect or correct errors that may arise during transmission.

SEE ALSO

Error Detection and Correction

Error Rate

A measure of erroneous transmission elements in relation to the total transmission. This information can be conveyed in several ways. A widely used index is the BER, which specifies the number of erroneous bits per million (or billion or trillion) bits.

SEE ALSO

BER (Bit Error Rate)

ESCON (Enterprise System Connection Architecture)

ESCON is a fiber-optic communications channel. IBM developed this architecture for use as a back-end network for connecting its ES/9000 series (or compatible) mainframes and peripheral devices, such as controllers, channel extenders, and storage devices.

ESCON uses either 50/125 or 62.5/125 (core/cladding diameter) multimode fiber. The light source for ESCON is an LED (light-emitting diode), which sends signals at a wavelength of approximately 1,325 nanometers (nm). This wavelength is popular because of its optical properties.

ESCON uses a 4B/8B signal-encoding scheme, in which groups of four or eight bits are encoded as 5- or 10-bit symbols, respectively. 4B/8B is more efficient than the Manchester or differential Manchester signal-encoding schemes used in most local-area networks (LANs). ESCON supports transmission speeds of up to 200 megabits per second (Mbps).

The optical fiber runs from the mainframe's channel controllers to a copper-based (not optical), switched-star concentrator, which IBM calls a *director*. Control units for the mainframes are connected to the director. Concentrator and mainframe can be 2 or 3 kilometers (1 to 2 miles) apart, depending on whether the 50 or 62.5 nanometer fiber core is used.

The director keeps channel activity down by sending signals only to lines for which the signals are intended, as opposed to passing the signals on to all lines (as a passive concentrator would do).

BROADER CATEGORIES

Cable, Fiber-Optic; Network Architecture

ESDI (Enhanced Small Device Interface)

An interface and storage format for hard disks. ESDI can support relatively high-capacity (up to a gigabyte or so) drives and supports access times as low as about 20 milliseconds.

COMPARE

IDE; SCSI

ESF (Extended Superframe Format) Framing

In digital signaling, ESF is a method for framing a DS1 channel. (*Framing* is identifying the individual channels in the DS1 channel). ESF framing groups 24 (193-bit) frames into an ESF superframe, so that each DS1 channel consists of one ESF superframe.

In each ESF superframe, the values in every 193rd bit (in bits 193, 386, and so on) are used for any of three purposes:

- Framing, as originally intended (frames 4, 8, 12, …, 24).

- A 4 kbps link between endpoints (frames 1, 3, 5, …, 23).

- A 6-bit cyclic redundancy check (CRC) value (frames 2, 6, 10, …, 22)

The eighth bit in every channel of frames 6, 12, 18, and 24 is used for signaling between central offices. The signaling capabilities for ESF framing are more sophisticated than for D4 framing, because four frames provide signaling for ESF, compared with only two frames for D4. The figure "Elements in ESF framing" illustrates this method.

COMPARE

D4 Framing

ESN (Electronic Switched Network)

An ESN is a telecommunications service for private networks. A *private network* is one consisting of multiple PBXs (private branch exchanges) at various locations. ESN provides automatic switching between PBXs, so that a PBX can be called from any other PBX in the network without the need for a dedicated connection between the two PBXs.

Because a private network is also known as a *tandem network,* an ESN is said to provide "electronic tandem switching."

Establishment Controller

In an IBM environment, an *establishment controller* can support multiple devices, such as IBM or ASCII terminals or token ring nodes, for communication with a mainframe host. The controller communicates with the host's front-end processor (FEP). The IBM 3174 establishment controller is an example of this type of controller.

If local, the link between controller and device can be over a parallel line, an ESCON link, or through a token ring network. Remote connections can use V.24, V.35, or X.21 interfaces, and SNA/SDLC, X.25, or BSC protocols.

In IBM's SNA (Systems Network Architecture) environment, an establishment controller is a type 2.0 PU (physical unit).

BROADER CATEGORY

SNA (Systems Network Architecture)

SEE ALSO

Cluster Controller

ELEMENTS IN ESF FRAMING

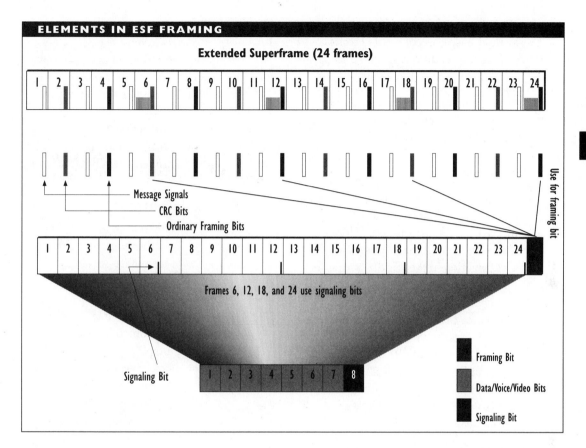

Extended Superframe (24 frames)

Message Signals
CRC Bits
Ordinary Framing Bits

Use for framing bit

Frames 6, 12, 18, and 24 use signaling bits

Signaling Bit

Framing Bit

Data/Voice/Video Bits

Signaling Bit

Ethernet

Ethernet is a shared-media network architecture. Its elements are the result of work by Xerox, Intel, and Digital Equipment Corporation. Ethernet, along with variants defined in the IEEE 802.3 standard, is currently the most widely used architecture for local-area networks (LANs). According to some estimates, there are more than 10 million Ethernet nodes around the world. Estimates of Ethernet's share of the LAN configurations range between 60 and 90 percent.

An Ethernet network has the following characteristics:

- Operates at the two lowest layers in the OSI Reference Model: the physical and data-link layer.

- Uses a bus topology. Nodes are attached to the trunk segment, which is the main piece of cable in an Ethernet network. (10BaseT, a variant architecture based on the IEEE 802.3 standard, can use a star topology.)

- Can operate at a speed of up to 10 megabits per second (Mbps). Several variants operate at slower speeds, and newer variants promise faster speeds.

- Uses CSMA/CD, a media-access method based on collision detection. This access method is specified as part of the IEEE 802.3 document.

- Broadcasts transmissions, so that each node gets the transmission at the same time. A broadcast strategy is necessary for a collision detection type of media-access method.

- Uses Manchester encoding to represent the 0 and 1 values that make up the physical signal. This is a self-clocking encoding method that includes a voltage transition in the middle of each bit interval. To break a bit interval into two halves, the clock rate must be at least twice the maximum transmission speed, so that a 20 megahertz (MHz) clock is required for 10 Mbps Ethernet. (Implementations don't actually achieve the maximum transmission rate, so that you can get by with slower clocks.)

- Uses 50-ohm coaxial cable. Variants can use 50- or 75-ohm coaxial, twisted-pair, and fiber-optic cable. Each type of cable has its characteristic add-ons (connectors and terminators).

- Is a baseband network, although variants also support broadband networks.

The figure "Context and properties of Ethernet" summarizes this architecture.

Ethernet Versions

Ethernet's roots go back to Project ALOHA at the University of Hawaii in the 1960s.

The CSMA/CD access method was developed for the ALOHA WAN.

Ethernet version 1.0 was superseded in 1982 by Ethernet 2.0, which is currently the official Ethernet standard. This is also known as DIX (for Digital, Intel, Xerox) Ethernet or Blue Book Ethernet.

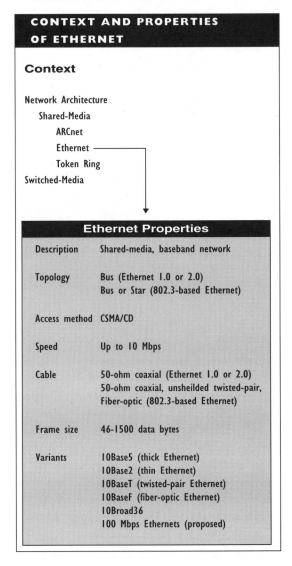

CONTEXT AND PROPERTIES OF ETHERNET

Context

Network Architecture
  Shared-Media
    ARCnet
    Ethernet
    Token Ring
Switched-Media

Ethernet Properties

Description	Shared-media, baseband network
Topology	Bus (Ethernet 1.0 or 2.0) Bus or Star (802.3-based Ethernet)
Access method	CSMA/CD
Speed	Up to 10 Mbps
Cable	50-ohm coaxial (Ethernet 1.0 or 2.0) 50-ohm coaxial, unsheilded twisted-pair, Fiber-optic (802.3-based Ethernet)
Frame size	46-1500 data bytes
Variants	10Base5 (thick Ethernet) 10Base2 (thin Ethernet) 10BaseT (twisted-pair Ethernet) 10BaseF (fiber-optic Ethernet) 10Broad36 100 Mbps Ethernets (proposed)

A variant on this standard was formulated by the IEEE 802.3 work group. This variant is sometimes called Ethernet as well. However, although Ethernet and 802.3 are similar, there are differences in the way the data-link layer is handled and in the format of a packet. These differences are explained later in this article.

Because of these differences, difficulties will arise if you try to mix different types of Ethernet on the same network. 802.3 and Ethernet 2 nodes cannot coexist on the same network. Fortunately, most implementations allow you to select which flavor of Ethernet you want to use on the network.

Some networking environments let you have different types of packets on the network under certain conditions. For example, NetWare allows both 802.2 and 802.3 packets to coexist on a network. (Packet types are discussed later in this article.)

Ethernet Groupings

Ethernet networks are grouped by their broadcast method, type of cable, and physical properties.

Baseband versus Broadband

In a baseband network, one node can broadcast at a time. In a broadband network, multiple nodes can broadcast at the same time.

Blue Book Ethernet operates only in baseband mode. Ethernet 802.3-based implementations can operate in either baseband or broadband mode.

Thick, Thin, and Twisted-Pair

Ethernet networks are also categorized according to the type of cable used. Thin and thick Ethernet use thin and thick coaxial cable, respectively. Twisted-pair Ethernet is actually an 802.3 architecture that uses unshielded twisted-pair (UTP) cable. The following are some of the synonyms for these Ethernet varieties:

Thick Ethernet: ThickNet, Standard Ethernet, 10Base5

Thin Ethernet: ThinNet, CheaperNet, 10Base2

Twisted-pair Ethernet: UTP Ethernet, 10BaseT

Physical Layer Properties

The IEEE 802.3 working group developed a simple notation system to characterize various physical-layer properties of an Ethernet network. Ethernet networks are described using three elements related to the wiring and the physical signal. Each description has three elements:

Speed/Band/Length or Cable-type

as in

10Base5

The first element, *Speed,* specifies the approximate maximum transmission speed, or bandwidth, in megabits per second (Mbps) for the network. This will be a 1, 5, 10, or 100 (for newer, experimental networks).

The second element, *Band,* is either Base or Broad, depending on whether the network is baseband or broadband. For example, 10Base5 specifies a baseband network; 10Broad36 specifies a broadband network.

The third element, *Length* or *Cable-type,* usually specifies the approximate maximum length of a network segment in hundreds of meters. For example, 10Base5 can have network segments of up to 500 meters (1,650 feet). In some cases, the length value is specified in 50-meter increments. For example, the 1Base5 network supports network segments up to 250 meters, not 500 meters.

In other cases, the third element is used to specify cable type. For example, 10BaseT and 10BaseF specify networks with twisted-pair and fiber-optic cable, respectively.

The table "Types of Ethernet Networks" summarizes the types of Ethernet networks that have been defined in IEEE 802.3 or by other groups. See the 10Base*x*, 10Broad36, and 100BaseT articles for more details.

Ethernet Hardware

Although the details differ, Ethernet networks all use a limited number of components, which include Ethernet network interface cards (NICs), cables, connectors, transceivers and receivers, hubs, punchdown blocks, and baluns.

Ethernet NICs

Each node must have an Ethernet NIC, which provides the computer with access to the network. An NIC converts, packetizes, and transmits data from the computer and receives, unpacketizes, and converts data received over the network. NICs are architecture-specific. This means that you cannot use an Ethernet NIC for a Token Ring network. It also means that you may not be able to use an 802.3 card for an Ethernet network or vice versa.

An Ethernet and an 802.3 card *can transmit* packets to each other, because the Ethernet and 802.3 packets have the same general structure. However, the variant cards *cannot read* each other's packets, because certain fields in the packets have different types of information. Some NICs support both Ethernet and 802.3 formats, and are therefore able to read and create both types of packets. Even if the cards cannot communicate directly, the networking software will generally be able to translate.

Ethernet NICs can have any or all of the following connectors: BNC, DIX, RJ-*xx*. On NICs with multiple connectors, you will generally need to set DIP switches or jumper settings on the board to indicate the type of connector you will be using.

Ethernet cards include a hardware address on a ROM chip. This address is assigned by the IEEE and the vendor and is unique to that particular NIC. Part of the address contains vendor information, and part identifies the board itself. This address can be used by bridges and routers to identify a particular node on a network.

TYPES OF ETHERNET NETWORKS	
TYPE	**DESCRIPTION**
10Base2	Thin Ethernet using thin (3/16-inch), 50-ohm coaxial cable. This is arguably the most popular Ethernet configuration.
10Base5	Thick Ethernet using thick (3/8-inch), 50-ohm coaxial cable. Although it's the cabling for Blue Book Ethernet, this is not a very popular configuration because thick coaxial cable is difficult to handle and install.
10BaseT	Twisted-pair Ethernet using UTP cable. This configuration was adopted as the 802.3i standard in 1990, and it is becoming popular because UTP is inexpensive and easy to install and work with.
1Base5	The StarLAN network developed by AT&T. StarLAN uses UTP cable and a star topology, and was defined long before the 10BaseT standard was proposed.
10Broad36	The only broadband network defined in the 802.3 standard. This network uses 75-ohm coaxial cable (CATV cable).
10BaseF	The only network in the 802.3 standard that explicitly calls for fiber-optic cable. This type is actually divided into three variations: 10BaseFB, 10BaseFP, and 10BaseFL.
10BaseFB	This network uses optical fiber for the backbone, or trunk, cable. Trunk segments can be up to 2 kilometers (1.25 miles) in length.
10BaseFP	This specifies a network that uses optical fiber and a star topology. The coupler used to distribute the signal is passive (does not regenerate the signal before distributing). As a result, such a network needs no electronics except for those in the computer. Maximum length for a piece of such cable is 500 meters (1,650 feet).
10BaseFL	This specifies a network that uses optical fiber to connect a node to a hub, or concentrator. Cable segments can be up to 2 kilometers in length.
100BaseVG	A 100 Mbps Ethernet network developed by Hewlett-Packard and AT&T Microelectronics.
100BaseT	A 100 Mbps Ethernet network developed by Grand Junction Networks. This is a proposed standard of the IEEE 802.3 study group. Variants include 100BaseT4, 100BaseTX, and 100BaseFX

Ethernet Cable

Blue Book Ethernet networks use coaxial cable. Networks based on the 802.3 architecture can use coaxial, fiber-optic, or twisted-pair cable. The cable in an Ethernet network may have any of several functional uses:

- Trunk cable is used for the main network segment, which is known as the *trunk segment*. Nodes are attached, directly or indirectly, to the trunk segment.

- Drop cable is used to attach nodes indirectly to a trunk segment in a thick Ethernet network. This type of cable is also known as transceiver cable (because it connects the node to a transceiver) and as AUI cable (because of the type of connectors at either end of such a cable).

- Patch cable is used in 802.3 networks to connect any of the following: two hubs, a node from the wallplate to a punch-down block, or a wiring hub to a punch-down block.

See the Cable article for more information about network cabling.

Ethernet Connectors

Connectors are used to connect cable segments. An Ethernet (bus) network also needs terminators and grounded terminators, because network segments must be properly grounded and terminated to prevent signals from being reflected back over the network.

The following types of connectors are used:

- Thick Ethernet networks use N-series connectors and terminators on the trunk and AUI, or DIX, connectors on the NIC.

- Thin Ethernet networks use BNC connectors and terminators on the trunk and on the NIC.

- Twisted-pair Ethernet networks use RJ-45 connectors or variants on these. These networks do not require separate terminators.

See the Connector; Connector, AUI; Connector, BNC; and Connector, RJ-*xx* articles for more information.

Repeaters and Transceivers

Repeaters clean and regenerate a signal. Repeaters are used in the middle of a stretch of cable that is so long that the signal quality would deteriorate to an unacceptable level without regeneration. Hubs often act as repeaters.

Transceivers can transmit and receive signals. Transceivers provide the actual point at which the node makes contact with the network. Ethernet/802.3 transceivers may be internal (on the NIC) or external, depending on the type of Ethernet. External transceivers, which are used for thick Ethernet, are attached to the trunk cable with an N-series connector or with a vampire tap.

Transceivers are called *MAUs* (*medium attachment units*) in the IEEE 802.3 document.

Hubs

Hubs are wire collectors. They are used in 802.3 networks that use twisted-pair cable. Wires from nodes in a twisted-pair Ethernet network may be terminated at the hub. Hubs may be internal (boards installed in a machine) or external (stand-alone components). These components are also known as concentrators.

Hardware manufacturers have created special-purpose hubs that enhance the operation of an Ethernet network or that extend the capabilities of certain components.

Examples of these are enhanced hubs and switched hubs.

Enhanced hubs for 10BaseT networks have been enhanced with various capabilities and features by different manufacturers. These enhancements include the following:

- Network monitoring and management capabilities.

- Nonvolatile memory to save settings and performance information even during a power outage.

- Security features, such as the ability to send a packet only to its destination while sending a busy signal to all other nodes. This helps increase the security on the system by preventing a meaningful message from being intercepted by an unauthorized node.

Switched-hub technology can increase the effective bandwidth of an Ethernet network by allowing multiple transmissions on the network at the same time. For this technology to work, the network must have multiple servers, and the hub must be able to switch to any of multiple network segments.

Ethernet Switches

An Ethernet switch connects a limited number of network segments. This is in contrast to a simple bridge, which connects two segments. Each network segment communicates over the switch through its own port on the switch. Ethernet switches operate at the data link level (level two of the OSI hierarchy) and work in many ways like a multiport bridge.

Like a multiport bridge, an Ethernet switch can segment a larger network—for example, to help relieve traffic congestion by not allowing transmissions within a segment to leave that segment.

However, Ethernet switches have some additional features that help make them very popular. By placing switches intelligently in a large network, it's possible to produce more efficient network arrangements, thereby resulting in faster throughput. Some switches can even provide dedicated connections between two network segments.

Kalpana developed the first Ethernet switch just a few years ago. Since then, switches have become extremely popular as one solution to the increased traffic on Ethernet networks—with faster Ethernets being the other. Because of their popularity, numerous vendors now supply Ethernet switches.

Two basic classes of Ethernet switches are available:

- *Workgroup* switches communicate with only a single node on each port. Such a switch can provide dedicated services between segments. Because only a single machine can communicate at each port, a workgroup switch doesn't need to check for collisions at the port, and it only needs minimal resources for storing addresses. Such switches require simpler circuitry and so are relatively inexpensive—often less than $300 per port.

- *Network,* or *segment,* switches are more sophisticated and more expensive. Such switches support multiple nodes at each port—and must, therefore, be able to store all the addresses and forwarding information. Network switches use the spanning tree algorithm to prevent redundant paths between segments.

Punch-Down Block

A punch-down block may be used in a twisted-pair network to provide a more convenient location to terminate wires from nodes in such a network. A punch-down block is a device for making physical contact with the wire inside a cable jacket, thereby establishing the necessary connection for electrical activity. Using such an intermediate connection makes it easier to change the wiring scheme.

Baluns

Baluns are used to connect coaxial cable segments (for example, an AUI cable attached to a node) and twisted-pair cable segments (for example, a cable attached to a hub).

Ethernet Layout

Ethernet uses a bus configuration. Ethernet 802.3 networks can also use a star topology.

In a bus, nodes are attached to the network's backbone, or trunk segment. Nodes are attached directly in thin Ethernet and with a drop cable in thick Ethernet. The figure "A thick Ethernet (bus) layout" shows an example of a layout of a bus network.

The number of nodes that can be attached to a trunk segment depends on the type of cabling: a 10Base5 (thick coaxial) segment can support up to 100 nodes; a 10Base2 (thin coaxial) segment can support no more than 30 nodes.

A link segment connects two repeaters. A link segment is not treated as trunk segment. You cannot attach a node to link segment cable; you must attach the node to the trunk segment.

Both ends of *each* Ethernet trunk cable segment need to be terminated, and one of these ends need to be grounded. Depending on the type of cable, N-series or BNC terminators are used. If there are repeaters connecting trunk segments, each of the segments must be terminated separately at the repeater.

A fiber-optic inter-repeater link (FOIRL) uses special transceivers and fiber-optic cable for a link segment. With an FOIRL link, the segment between the transceivers can be up to 2 kilometers (1.25 miles).

In a star topology, such as in twisted-pair Ethernet, the nodes are attached to a central hub rather than to a backbone cable. The hub serves to broadcast transmissions to the nodes and to any other hubs attached. The figure "Layout of a twisted-pair (star) Ethernet network" shows the layout for a simple star network.

Ethernet Operation

An Ethernet network works as follows:

- Access: A node that wants to send a message listens for a signal on the network. If another node is transmitting, the node waits a randomly determined amount of time before trying again to access the network.

A THICK ETHERNET (BUS) LAYOUT

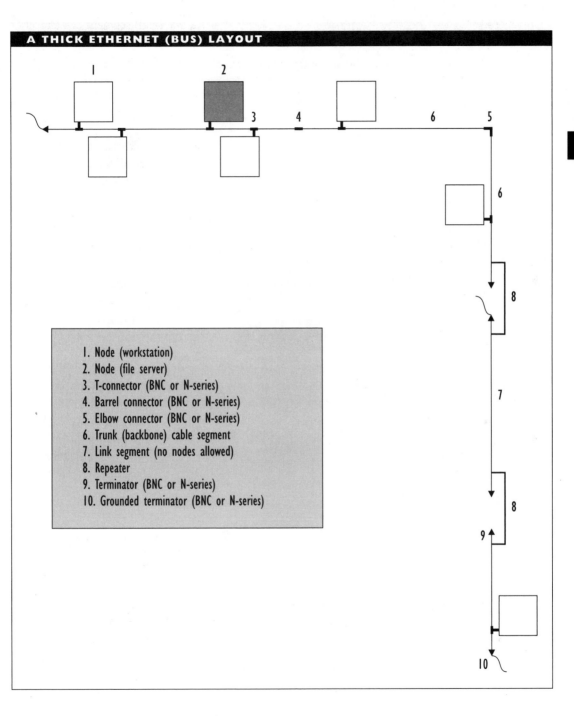

1. Node (workstation)
2. Node (file server)
3. T-connector (BNC or N-series)
4. Barrel connector (BNC or N-series)
5. Elbow connector (BNC or N-series)
6. Trunk (backbone) cable segment
7. Link segment (no nodes allowed)
8. Repeater
9. Terminator (BNC or N-series)
10. Grounded terminator (BNC or N-series)

a b c d **e** f g h i j k l m n o p q r s t u v w x y z

LAYOUT OF A TWISTED-PAIR (STAR) ETHERNET NETWORK

The gray area around the hub indicates that the connections to the hub may not be direct. A node or MAU may be connected directly to a wallplate, from there to a punch-down panel, and from there to the hub.

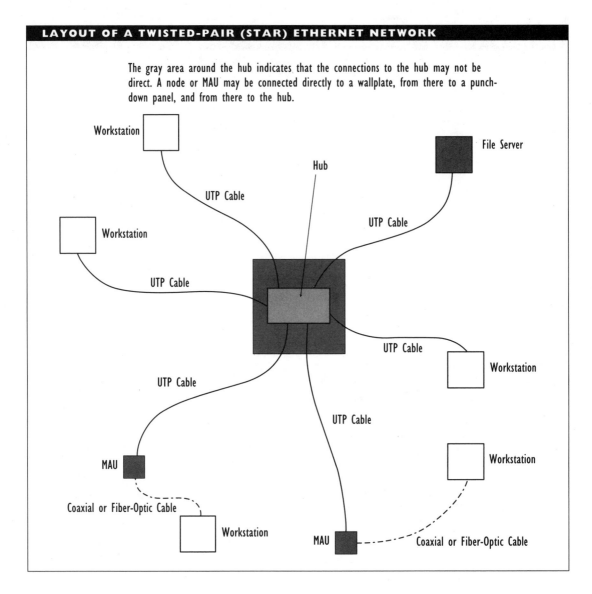

- Transmission: If there is no activity on the network, the node starts transmitting and then listens for a collision. A collision occurs if another node also found the network idle and started transmitting at the same time. The two

packets collide, and garbled fragments are transmitted across the network.

- Collision handling: If there is a collision, the first node to notice sends special jam packets to inform other nodes of the collision. The colliding nodes both retreat and wait a random amount of time before trying again to access the network.

- Reception: If there is no collision, the frame is broadcast onto the network. All nodes listen to each packet transmitted. Each node checks the packet's destination address to determine whether the packet was intended for that node. If so, the node processes the packet and takes whatever action is appropriate. If the node is not the recipient for the packet, the node ignores the packet. (This eavesdropping feature of Ethernet networks—actually, of bus topologies in general—makes it difficult to implement message-level security on an Ethernet network.)

SQE SUPPORT

All Ethernet variants except version 1.0 expect a SQE (signal quality error) signal from transceivers. This signal, which is also known as a heartbeat, "proves" that the component is working and is, therefore, capable of detecting collisions.

Mixing components that do and don't support SQE on the same network is asking for trouble. If a component sends an SQE signal to a component (such as NIC) that doesn't support SQE, the receiver may assume the signal indicates a collision and will send a jam signal (the signal used to stop transmission when a collision occurs).

Ethernet Frames

Ethernet frames, or packets, come in several flavors. However, all Ethernet frames consist of preamble, header, data, and trailer components.

Ethernet Frame Elements

Each of the Ethernet frame elements has a predefined structure:

Preamble (8 bytes): Consists of eight bytes, which are divided into seven preamble bytes and one start frame delimiter (SFD) byte for certain packet flavors. These bytes are used to mark the start of a packet and to enable the sender and receiver to synchronize.

Header (14 bytes): Consists of three fields: a 6-byte destination address, a 6-byte source address, and a 2-byte field whose value is interpreted as a length for some packet flavors and as information about the network-level protocol for other flavors. Interpreting this third field as length or type distinguishes the two main types of Ethernet packets (Ethernet 2 and 802.3-based packets).

Data (46–1,500 bytes): Contains whatever packet was passed by the higher-level protocol. Ethernet 2 packets contain network-layer packets in the data component; 802.3-based packets get the data component from a sublayer that may add to the network-layer packet. The data component must be at least 46 bytes, so it may include padding bytes.

Trailer (4 bytes): Consists of a frame check sequence (FCS). These bytes represent a CRC (cyclic redundancy

a b c d **e** f g h i j k l m n o p q r s t u v w x y z

check) value, which provides information for detecting errors in a transmission. This component is the same in all packet flavors.

Not counting the preamble, the three remaining components yield Ethernet packets that are between 64 and 1,518 bytes.

Ethernet Packet Flavors

The major distinction in packets is between Ethernet 2 and 802.3-based flavors. This distinction depends on how the values in the third header field are interpreted. The Ethernet packet flavors include Ethernet 2, 802.3, 802.2, and Ethernet SNAP.

File servers for Ethernet networks will generally be able to handle multiple frame flavors, although you may need to run a utility to take advantage of this capability. With a multi-flavor server, nodes that use different Ethernet versions may be able to communicate with each other, but only through the server. For example, nodes using 802.3 and Ethernet 2 NICs may be able to pass packets, but they will not be able to communicate directly with each other.

Ethernet 2: This is the simplest of the packet flavors. The third header field is Type, and its value specifies the source of the network layer protocol being used. The table "Selected Ethernet Type Field Values" lists some of the possible values for this field. The data component is whatever was received by the data-link layer from the network layer above it. (The other packet formats receive the data component from a data-link sublayer.)

802.3: This flavor has Length as the third header field. The field's value specifies the number of bytes in the data component. The 802.3 flavor is sometimes known as *802.3 raw,* because it does not include LLC (logical-link control) sublayer information in the data component (as does, for example, an 802.2 frame).

802.2: This packet is similar to the 802.3 format in that it has a Length (rather than a Type) header field, but differs in that part of the data component is actually header information from the LLC sublayer defined above the MAC sublayer in the IEEE 802.2 standard. The first three or four bytes of an 802.2 packet's data component contain information of relevance to the LLC sublayer. The first two bytes contain values for the DSAP (Destination Service Access Point) and SSAP (Source Service Access Point). These values identify the protocols being used at the network level.

The third byte is the Control field, which contains information regarding the type of transmission (such as connectionless or connection-oriented) being used. The packet passed by the network layer follows after these three values.

Ethernet_SNAP (Sub-Network Access Protocol): This variant of an 802.2 packet contains LLC sublayer information as well as five additional bytes of information as part of the data component. Two of the five bytes specify the type of protocol being used at the network layer. This is the same

SELECTED ETHERNET TYPE FIELD VALUES

VALUE (HEXADECIMAL)	SOURCE	VALUE (HEXADECIMAL)	SOURCE
0x0600	Xerox XNS IDP	0x80c0	Digital Communications Associates (DCA)
0x0800	IP (Internet Protocol)		
0x0801	X.75 Internet	0x80d5	IBM SNA Services over Ethernet
0x0805	X.25 Level 3	0x80e0	Allen-Bradley
0x0806	ARP (Address Resolution Protocol)	0x80f3	AARP (AppleTalk ARP)
0x0807	XNS Compatibility	0x80f7	Apollo Computer
0x0a00	Xerox 802.3 PUP	0x8137	Novell NetWare IPX/SPX
0x0bad	Banyan Systems	0x9000	Loopback (Configuration test protocol)
0x6003	DEC DECnet Phase IV	0x9001	Bridge Communications XNS Systems Management
0x6004	DEC LAT		
0x6005	DEC DECnet diagnostics	0x9002	Bridge Communications TCP/IP Systems Management
0x6010	3Com Corporation		
0x7030	Proteon		
0x8008	AT&T		
0x8035	Reverse ARP		
0x8038	DEC LANBridge		
0x803d	DEC Ethernet CSMA/CD Encryption Protocol		
0x803f	DEC LAN Traffic monitor		
0x8046	AT&T		
0x8065	University of Massachusetts, Amherst		
0x809b	EtherTalk (AppleTalk running on Ethernet)		
0x809f	Spider Systems Ltd.		

a
b
c
d
e
f
g
h
i
j
k
l
m
n
o
p
q
r
s
t
u
v
w
x
y
z

information as in the Type field for an Ethernet 2 packet, except that the field is in a different location in the packet. This Ethernet Type field is preceded by a three-byte Organization Code field, which specifies the organization that assigned the Ethernet Type field value.

The table "Selected Ethernet Type Field Values" shows a list of selected Ethernet Type field values.

The figure "Structure of an Ethernet frame" shows the components of the different flavors of Ethernet frames.

Invalid Frames

A destination node checks for several types of errors that can creep into Ethernet packets (or frames). In particular, the node checks for each of the following types of invalid packets:

- Long (oversized) packets are longer than the allowed size (1,518 bytes for Ethernet) but have a valid CRC value. These may be caused by a faulty LAN driver.

- Runt (undersized) packets are shorter than the minimum size (64 bytes), but have a valid CRC value. These may be caused by a faulty LAN driver.

- Jabber packets are longer than 1,518 bytes and have an *invalid* CRC value. These may be caused by a faulty transceiver.

- Alignment errors are packets that have extra *bits,* which means that they do not end on byte-boundaries. Such packets will also have invalid CRC

values. These may be caused by a faulty component (NIC, transceiver, or cable).

- CRC errors are packets that have a valid number of bytes and end on a byte-boundary but have an invalid CRC value. These may be caused by noise on the cable or because a cable segment was too long.

- Valid packets are packets that have none of the preceding problems. Only valid packets are passed on the higher-level protocols in a transmission. Valid packets are created by properly functioning networking software and hardware.

802.3 Differences

The IEEE 802.3 working group, whose task was to formulate a standard for CSMA/CD-based networks, came up with something that looks like Blue Book Ethernet, but that differs in several important ways. The Ethernet 802.3 standard was adopted in 1985, and the addition (802.3i) was adopted in 1990. The table "Differences between Ethernet 802.3 and Blue Book Ethernet" summarizes the distinctions between these variants.

Because 802.3 distinguishes between the LLC and MAC sublayers, the process of creating a packet for transmission goes through an extra level of handling. In 802.3 networking, a network-layer packet becomes the data for a PDU (protocol data unit) at the LLC sublayer. A PDU, in turn, becomes the data when an MAC sublayer packet is constructed for transmission over the physical connection. In Blue Book Ethernet networking, the network-layer

STRUCTURE OF AN ETHERNET FRAME

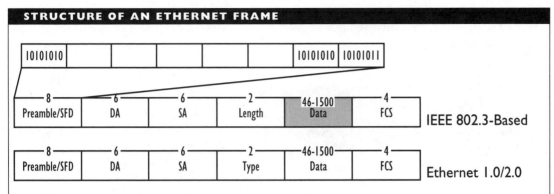

8	6	6	2	46-1500	4	
Preamble/SFD	DA	SA	Length	Data	FCS	IEEE 802.3-Based

8	6	6	2	46-1500	4	
Preamble/SFD	DA	SA	Type	Data	FCS	Ethernet 1.0/2.0

Preamble: 7 identical bytes; used for synchronization

SFD (Start Frame Delimiter): Indicates the frame is about to begin

DA (Destination Address): Contains the address of the frame's destination

SA (Source Address): Contains the address of the frame's sender

Length: Indicates the number of data bytes (IEEE 802.3-based variants)

Type: Indicates the upper-level protocol that is using the packet (Ethernet 1.0/2.0 variants)

Data: Contains the information being transmitted, which may consist of a higher-layer packet (may be padded)

FCS: A frame check sequence

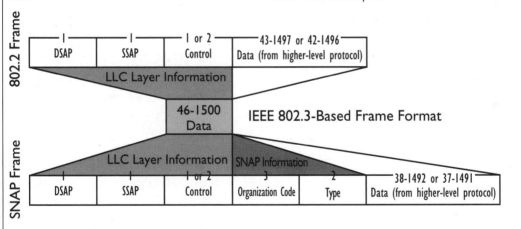

IEEE 802.3-Based Frame Format

DSAP (Destination Service Access Point): Specifies the process receiving the packet at the destination's network layer

SSAP (Source Service Access Point): Specifies the process sending the packet from the source's network layer

Control: Specifies the type of LLC service requested

Organization Code: Specifies the organization that assigned the following Type field

Type: Indicates the upper-level protocol that is using the packet

packet becomes the data portion of a packet. The figure "Layers involved in handling Blue Book and 802.3 Ethernet packets" illustrates the process.

DIFFERENCES BETWEEN ETHERNET 802.3 AND BLUE BOOK ETHERNET	
802.3	**ETHERNET**
Supports bus or star topologies.	Supports only a bus topology.
Supports baseband or broadband networks.	Supports only baseband networks.
Defines only the MAC sublayer of the data-link layer. Uses the LLC sublayer defined in the IEEE 802.2 standard for the rest of the data-link layer.	Does not divide the data-link layer into sublayers.
Uses 7 bytes for a preamble and 1 byte as a start of frame delimiter (SFD) for a packet.	Uses 8 bytes for a preamble; does not distinguish a separate SFD byte.
Uses the third header field to indicate the length of the frame's data component.	Uses the third header field to specify the type of higher-layer protocol using the data-link services.
Can use the SQE signal as a network management device.	Can use the SQE signal as a network management device only in version 2.0.

Twisted-Pair Ethernet

A 10BaseT, or twisted-pair Ethernet, network uses unshielded twisted-pair (UTP) cable and a star topology, as opposed to the coaxial cable and bus topology of Blue Book Ethernet. In this architecture, each node is connected to a central wiring hub, which serves as the relay station for the network. This 802.3-based variant was officially adopted as IEEE standard 802.3i in 1990.

A twisted-pair Ethernet network needs the following components:

- NIC with on-board MAU (or transceiver), to mediate between the node and the network (one per node)

- External MAU, for mediating between the network and nodes that use coaxial or fiber-optic cable (optional)

- UTP cable, to connect nodes to a wiring hub

- Wiring hubs (stand-alone or peer)

- Punch-down block, to make wire termination more flexible and easier to change (optional)

- RJ-45 connectors, for connecting to wall plates and to NICs

In order to be sufficiently free of interference, UTP cable for a network should have enough twists in the wire. Some telephone cable may not be suitable, because it is too flat and has too few twists. The cable also must have enough conductors for the eight-wire RJ-45 connectors.

Each node in a 10-BaseT network is connected directly or indirectly to a wiring hub. Indirect connections can be through wall plates or by connecting the PC to an external MAU, which is connected to a wall plate or to a hub.

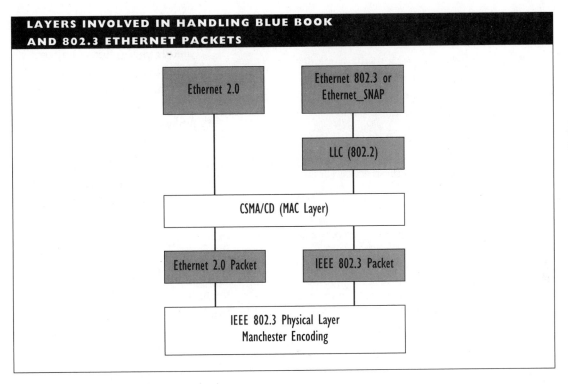

LAYERS INVOLVED IN HANDLING BLUE BOOK AND 802.3 ETHERNET PACKETS

10BaseT networks can use either of two kinds of hubs:

- A stand-alone hub is an external component with RJ-45 connections to link the nodes. This type of hub has its own power supply.

- A peer hub is a card that can be installed in one of the machines on the network. This internal hub must be connected physically to the NIC in the machine, and it depends on the PC for its power.

Nodes are connected to one of these hubs—from a distance no greater than 100 meters (330 feet)—using UTP cable with RJ-45 connections at each end. A 10BaseT network can have up to four linked hubs.

Thick Ethernet

A 10 Base5, or thick Ethernet, network uses thick ($3/8$-inch) coaxial cable (with 50-ohm impedance) for the network backbone. The 50-ohm cable is specially designed for this version of Ethernet, but standard thick coaxial cable can also be used.

Thick Ethernet Components

A thick Ethernet network uses the following components:

- Ethernet NICs to mediate between node and network (one per node)

- Thick coaxial cable for trunk cable segments (with nodes attached) or for

a b c d **e** f g h i j k l m n o p q r s t u v w x y z

link segments (between repeaters, and with no nodes attached)

- Transceivers to attach to the trunk segment and to do the required conversions when the node transmits or receives (one per node)

- Transceiver, or drop, cable with DIX connectors on each end, to connect the NIC in the node to the transceiver attached to the trunk segment (one per node)

- N-series barrel connectors, to connect pieces of cable in the trunk segments (the fewer the better)

- N-series terminators, to terminate one end of a trunk segment (one per trunk segment)

- N-series grounded terminators, to terminate *and ground* one end of a trunk segment (one per trunk segment)

- Repeaters (optional), to extend the network by regenerating the signal before passing it on

The thick cable is relatively difficult to manage and install. Most networks that use thick cable use it as the network backbone, which is not expected to change. The nodes in the network are attached using additional cable, called drop cable or transceiver cable.

Thick Ethernet Configuration

The following configuration rules and restrictions apply for thick Ethernet.

- The maximum length of a trunk segment is 500 meters (1,640 feet).

- The network trunk can have at most five segments, for a total trunk of 2,500 meters (8,200 feet). Of these five cable segments, up to two can be link segments (without nodes attached) and up to three can be trunk segments (with nodes attached).

- Within a thick coaxial trunk segment, you can use N-series barrel connectors to link shorter pieces of cable. You can use repeaters to connect two segments into a longer network trunk. A repeater counts as a node on each of the segments the repeater connects.

- You can have at most 100 nodes (including repeaters) attached to each trunk cable segment.

- A thick Ethernet network can have at most 300 nodes, of which 8 will actually be repeaters.

- Each trunk segment must be terminated at one end; the segment must also be terminated and grounded at the other end. When using thick coaxial cable, this is accomplished using N-series terminators, which are connected to the male N-series connectors at each end of the trunk segment.

- Nodes are connected to the trunk cable using a transceiver cable from an AUI, or DIX, connector on the NIC to an AUI connector on a transceiver. The male connector attaches to the NIC and the female connector to the transceiver.

- The transceiver is connected to the trunk cable with a vampire tap or with an N-series T-connector.

- Transceivers must be at least 2.5 meters (8 feet) apart on the trunk, although the machines themselves can be closer together.

- The transceiver cable can be at most 50 meters (165 feet) long, which is the maximum distance a node can be from the network cable trunk.

The figure "Major components of a thick Ethernet network" shows an example of a thick Ethernet network.

Thin Ethernet

A 10Base2, or thin Ethernet, network uses thin ($3/16$-inch) coaxial cable (with 50-ohm) impedance for the network backbone. Thin coaxial cable is much easier to prepare and install than thick Ethernet cable.

Thin Ethernet Components

A thin Ethernet network uses the following components:

- Ethernet NICs, containing a transceiver, to mediate between node and network (one per node)

- Thin coaxial cable for trunk cable segments

- BNC barrel connectors, to connect pieces of cable in the trunk segments (the fewer the better)

- BNC T-connectors, to attach a node to the network (one per node)

- BNC terminators, to terminate one end of a trunk segment (one per trunk segment)

- BNC grounded terminators, to terminate *and ground* one end of a trunk segment (one per trunk segment)

- Repeaters (optional), to extend the network by regenerating the signal before passing it on

Thin Ethernet Configuration

The following configuration rules and restrictions apply for thin Ethernet:

- Each trunk segment can be at most 185 meters (607 feet). Each trunk segment can consist of multiple pieces of cable, linked using BNC barrel connectors.

- The network trunk can have at most five segments, for a total trunk of 925 meters (3,035 feet). Of these five cable segments, up to two can be link segments (those with no nodes attached) and up to three can be trunk segments (without nodes attached).

- You can use repeaters to connect two segments into a longer network trunk. A repeater counts as a node on each of the segments the repeater connects.

- You can have at most 30 nodes (including repeaters) attached to each trunk cable segment.

- A thin Ethernet network can have at most 90 nodes, of which 8 will actually be repeaters.

a b c d **e** f g h i j k l m n o p q r s t u v w x y z

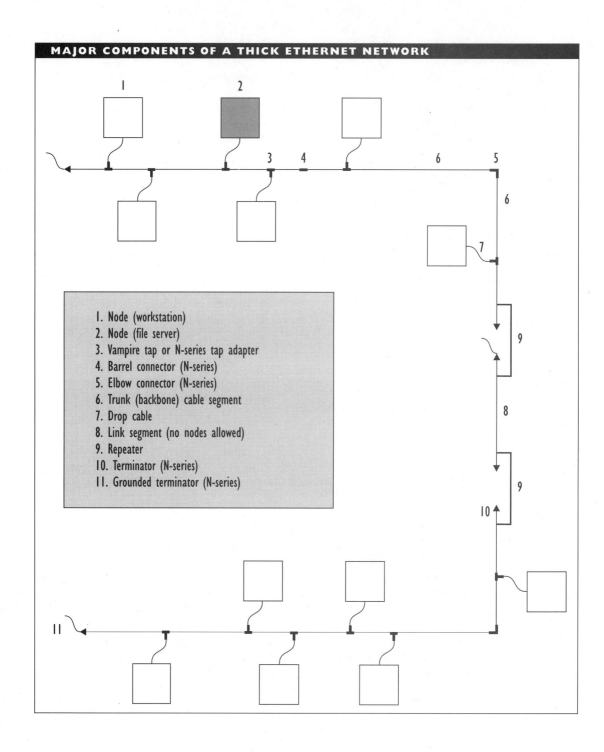

MAJOR COMPONENTS OF A THICK ETHERNET NETWORK

1. Node (workstation)
2. Node (file server)
3. Vampire tap or N-series tap adapter
4. Barrel connector (N-series)
5. Elbow connector (N-series)
6. Trunk (backbone) cable segment
7. Drop cable
8. Link segment (no nodes allowed)
9. Repeater
10. Terminator (N-series)
11. Grounded terminator (N-series)

- Each trunk segment must be terminated at one end; the segment must also be terminated and grounded at the other end using BNC terminators, which are connected to the male BNC connectors at each end of the trunk segment.

- Nodes are connected to the trunk cable using a BNC T-connector that is attached to the NIC.

- T-connectors must be at least 0.5 meter (1.6 feet) apart on the trunk, although the machines themselves can be closer together.

The figure "Major components of a thin Ethernet network" shows an example of a thin Ethernet network.

Hybrid Ethernet

You can combine thin and thick coaxial cable in the same Ethernet network, provided that the network elements meet the appropriate cable specifications. This approach can be less expensive than a pure thick Ethernet configuration and more robust than a pure thin Ethernet configuration.

One approach is to combine thick and thin coaxial cable within a trunk segment. In this case, the connection is made using hybrid (BNC/N-series) adapters. One end of the adapter is a BNC connection and the other end is an N-series connection. Two versions of this adapter are available: one has female connections at either end, and the other has male connections.

When thin and thick coaxial cables are combined within the same segment, you need a formula to determine the amount of each type of cable you can use. The following formula assumes that no trunk segment is longer than 500 meters (1,640 feet):

$$(1,640 - Len)/3.28 = MaxThinCoax$$

where *Len* is the length of the trunk segment and *MaxThinCoax* represents the maximum length of thin coaxial cable you can use in the segment.

You can also build a network trunk using thin and thick trunk segments. In this case, the transition is made at the repeaters. Each segment must meet the specifications for that type of cable, just as if the entire trunk were made of the same type of cable.

As with thin or thick Ethernet segments, each end of a hybrid segment must be terminated. The terminator must match the type of cable at the end. Thus, if one end of the segment ends in thin coaxial and the other ends in thick coaxial, you need a BNC terminator at the first end and an N-series terminator at the second end. You can ground either of the ends.

Note that all the cable used in both thick and thin Ethernet networks has the same impedance: 50 ohms. This is one reason why it is relatively easy to combine thin and thick Ethernet segments.

Trends: Fast Ethernet

Several companies have developed *fast Ethernets,* which are implementations capable of 100 Mbps transmission speeds over

a
b
c
d
e
f
g
h
i
j
k
l
m
n
o
p
q
r
s
t
u
v
w
x
y
z

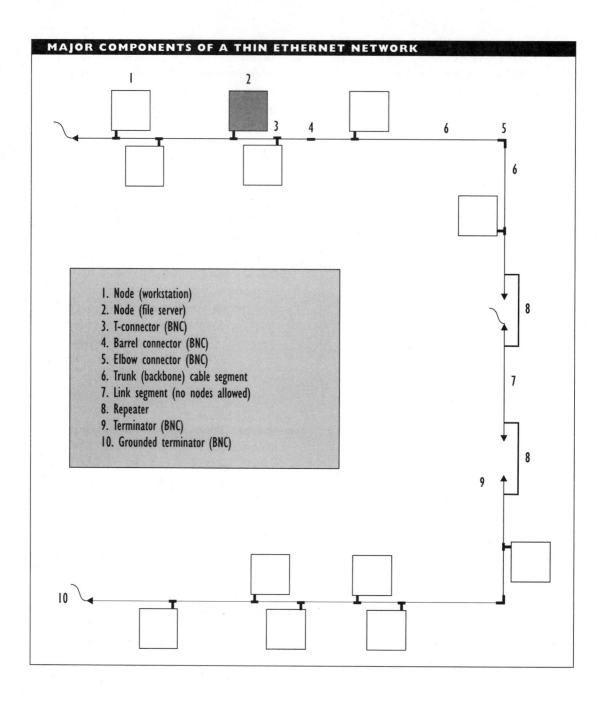

MAJOR COMPONENTS OF A THIN ETHERNET NETWORK

1. Node (workstation)
2. Node (file server)
3. T-connector (BNC)
4. Barrel connector (BNC)
5. Elbow connector (BNC)
6. Trunk (backbone) cable segment
7. Link segment (no nodes allowed)
8. Repeater
9. Terminator (BNC)
10. Grounded terminator (BNC)

UTP cable. These implementations are also known as 100 Mbps Ethernets.

Two fast Ethernet variants were accepted as official standards in June 1995. 100BaseVG, developed by Hewlett-Packard and several other vendors, was recently accepted as a standard by the IEEE 802.12 study group. On the same day, several variants of Grand Junction's 100BaseT were accepted as extensions of the 802.3 10BaseT standard. The variants are: 100BaseFX (for fiber optic cable), 100BaseT4 (for connections with four available wire pairs), and 100BaseTX (for high-quality Category 5 cable).

In order to achieve such high speeds, developers have found it necessary to take liberties with certain Ethernet features, as follows:

Access method: A major controversy concerns the access method to be used. Hardware vendors have formed camps behind the HP and Grand Junction versions, depending partly on whether they want to retain the familiar CSMA/CD. HP's 100BaseVG uses demand priority as its media-access method. This strategy involves packet switching and takes place in the hubs that serve to concentrate nodes on a twisted-pair network. Grand Junction's 100BaseT uses CSMA/CD.

Cable Type: Current versions of twisted-pair Ethernet run on cable that meets the TIA-568 standards for Category 3 cable or higher. Category 3 cable is rated for transmission speeds of up to 10 Mbps, and standard Ethernet requires two pairs of cable—one pair for each direction. 100BaseT Ethernet requires either four pairs of Category 3 cable or else two pairs of Category 5 cable (which *is* rated for 100 Mbps speeds). 100BaseVG uses special signaling methods, and so it can use ordinary Category 3 cable.

NICs: Cards that support a 100 Mbps Ethernet must be capable of switching to the slower 10 Mbps speed, and must be able to detect when it is necessary to do so.

Fast Ethernet cards send a fast link pulse (FLP) signal to indicate that they are capable of 100 Mbps transmission. If this signal is not detected, it is assumed that the node is an ordinary (10 Mbps) one.

Other proposed features, such as the frame format and configuration restrictions, are the same as for the current 802.3 Ethernet.

Isochronous Ethernet

An isochronous transmission is one that occurs at a constant rate. This is required, for example, when sending voice or video, since the information could become unintelligible if sent at varying speeds or with pauses in mid-transmission. Such time-dependent transmissions are not possible with ordinary Ethernet—largely because the media access method (MAC) is probabilistic and is not designed for constant activity.

To make it possible to transmit voice and video over Ethernet networks, National Semiconductor has submitted specifications for *isoENET*—an isochronous version of Ethernet—to the IEEE 802.9 committee.

a b c d **e** f g h i j k l m n o p q r s t u v w x y z

802.9 is the committee that deals with the integration of voice and data (IVD).

The isoENET specs support transmissions using ISDN (Integrated Services Digital Network) signaling methods—but running over Category 3 UTP (unshielded twisted pair) cable. IsoENET's 16 Mbps bandwidth is broken into two major components. In addition to the 10 Mbps bandwidth for ordinary Ethernet transmissions, isoENET supports up to 96 B channels, each with a 64 kbps capacity—for a total throughput of about 6 Mbps—for the isochronous part of the transmission.

Advantages of Ethernet

Ethernet networks offer the following advantages:

- Good for networks in which traffic is heavy only occasionally or in which traffic consists of a few long transmissions.

- Easy to install.

- Technology is well-known and thoroughly tested.

- Moderate costs.

- Flexible cabling, especially when using twisted-pair cable.

Disadvantages of Ethernet

Ethernet networks have the following disadvantages:

- Heavy traffic can slow down a network that uses a contention access system such as CSMA/CD. Such congestion is less likely to be a problem

with the 100 Mbps Ethernets—at least until the traffic catches up with the greater bandwidth.

- Since all nodes are connected to the main cable in most Ethernet networks, a break in this cable can bring down the entire network.

- Troubleshooting is more difficult with a bus topology.

- Room for incompatibilities because of frame structure (such as 802.3 versus Blue Book Ethernet).

SEE ALSO
100BaseT; 100BaseVG; isoENET

BROADER CATEGORY
Network Architecture

COMPARE
ARCnet; ATM; FDDI; Token Ring

Ethernet Meltdown

A situation in which traffic on an Ethernet network approaches or reaches saturation (maximum capacity). This can happen, for example, if a packet is echoed repeatedly.

EtherTalk

EtherTalk is the driver used to communicate between the Macintosh and an Ethernet network interface card. It is Apple's Ethernet implementation for the AppleTalk environment.

Two versions of EtherTalk have been developed:

- EtherTalk Phase 1 is based on the Ethernet 2 version, also known as Blue Book Ethernet.

- EtherTalk Phase 2 is based on the IEEE 802.3 Ethernet variant.

BROADER CATEGORIES
AppleTalk; Ethernet

COMPARE
ARCTalk; LocalTalk; TokenTalk

ETR (Early Token Release)

ETR is a frame, or packet, control process used in 16 megabit per second (Mbps) token ring networks. ETR makes it possible for multiple packets to be moving in the ring at once, even with just a single token for packet control.

Ordinarily in a token ring network, only the node with the token can send a packet, so that only one packet is moving around the network at any one time. This packet travels around the ring. Each node passes the packet on, and the destination node reads the packet. When the packet returns to the sender (with acknowledgment and verification of its receipt), that node strips the packet and passes the token to the next active node on the ring.

With ETR, the sender releases the token immediately after releasing its packet. The next node on the ring sends the packet on. Since this node now has the token, the node can send its own packet. Immediately after sending the packet, the node releases the token. Successive nodes pass on whatever packets they receive, and they send their own packets (if they have any to send) when the token reaches them.

Note that ETR allows multiple packets on the network, but that there is only one token on the network at any time.

BROADER CATEGORIES
Token Passing; Token Ring

ETSI (European Telecommunications Standards Institute)

A European standards committee that has defined a subset of ISDN's proposed functionality for use in Europe. This variant is known as EuroISDN and is analogous to the National ISDN versions (NI-1, NI-2, and a planned NI-3) developed in the United States. The ETSI is also looking into specifying guidelines for providing interoperability between EuroISDN and National ISDN.

European Academic and Research Network (EARN)

A European network that provides file transfer and e-mail (electronic mail) services for universities and research institutions.

European Electronic Mail Association (EEMA)

A European association of developers and vendors of electronic mail products. The EMA (Electronic Mail Association) is the counterpart in the United States.

Event Reporting

In network management, a data-gathering method in which agents report on the status of the objects under the agents' purview. The agent generates a report containing the relevant information and sends this report to the management package. This is in contrast to polling, in which the management program periodically requests such reports from agents.

eWorld

An online service newly developed by Apple for Macintosh users. eWorld is based on AOL (America Online) software. It uses a city as the metaphor for its graphics-based interface. In this interface, city locations (such as buildings or kiosks) provide access to the available services. Currently, eWorld supports Internet access only for e-mail, but other services are planned.

SEE ALSO

AOL; CompuServe; Prodigy

FOR INFORMATION

Call 800-775-4556

EWOS (European Workshop for Open Systems)

One of three regional workshops for implementers of the OSI Reference Model. The other two are AOW (Asia and Oceania Workshop) and OIW (OSI Implementers Workshop).

Exchange

In telephone communications, an exchange is an area serviced by a central office, or CO. An exchange consists of a sequential block of phone numbers, each associated with the same three-digit value (known as the *exchange ID*, or *XID*).

Each exchange in North America is characterized by an office class and a name. The table "North America Exchange Classes and Names" summarizes how the classes are defined.

Exchange Carrier

A *local exchange carrier* (LEC), which is a company that provides telecommunications services within an exchange, or LATA (local access and transport area).

Expansion Bus

A set of slots, such as those on a motherboard, into which expansion cards can be plugged in order to provide the computer with additional capabilities and access to external devices.

Expansion Chassis

A structure that includes a backplane (circuit board with slots for other boards) and a power supply. The chassis may be closed and self-standing, or it may be rack mountable for installation into a larger component.

Explorer Frame

In networks that use source routing, such as IBM Token Ring networks, an explorer frame is used to determine a route from the source node to a destination. An explorer frame is also known as a *discovery packet*, particularly in the Internet community.

There are two types of explorer frames:

- An all-routes explorer frame explores all possible routes between source and destination

- A spanning-tree explorer frame follows only routes on the spanning tree for the network. (A spanning tree is an optimal set of paths for all possible connections in a network.)

Extended Addressing

In AppleTalk Phase 2, extended addressing is a scheme that assigns an 8-bit node number and a 16-bit network number to each station. Extended addressing allows for up to 16 million (2^{24}) nodes on a single network.

This is in contrast to the *nonextended addressing* used in AppleTalk Phase 1 networks and also in networks that use a Local-Talk architecture. Nonextended addressing uses just the 8-bit node number, which limits networks to 254 nodes (not 256, because two of the node numbers are reserved).

Packets for extended networks use the *long DDP* packet format; packets for non-extended networks use the *short DDP* packet format, which omits network address bytes (since these are either undefined or 0).

Extensible MIB

In an SNMP environment, a MIB for which a vendor can define new variables when implementing the MIB.

SEE ALSO

MIB (Management Information Base); SNMP (Simple Network Management Protocol)

NORTH AMERICA EXCHANGE CLASSES AND NAMES	
EXCHANGE CLASS	NAME
1	Regional centers (RCs) or points (RPs). These have the largest domains: a dozen or so cover all of North America. The class 1 offices are all connected directly to each other.
2	Sectional centers (SCs) or points (SPs).
3	Primary centers (PCs) or points (PPs).
4	Toll centers (TCs).
4P	Toll points (TPs).
4X	Intermediate points (IPs). These are used only with digital exchanges, and are designed to connect to remote switching units (RSUs).
5	End offices. These are owned by local telephone companies. Ownership of the broader centers varies. Individual subscribers are connected to class 5 offices, of which there are many thousand in North America.
5R	End offices with remote switching capabilities.

a b c d e f g h i j k l m n o p q r s t u v w x y z

Facility

In telephone communications, a transmission link between two locations, or stations. In an X.25 packet, a facility is a field through which users can request special services from the network.

Facility Bypass

In telecommunications, a communication strategy that bypasses the telephone company's central office. For example, wireless transmissions might use facility bypass.

Facility Data Link (FDL)

SEE

FDL (Facility Data Link)

Fading

In electrical or wireless signaling, *fading* is the decrease in the signal's strength because of any of the following:

- Obstruction of the transmitter's or the receiver's antenna

- Interference (from other signals or from atmospheric conditions)

- Increased distance from the transmission source

Fading is sometimes referred to as just *fade,* as in *fade margin.* The fade margin refers to the amount of signal (in decibels) that can be lost before the signal becomes unintelligible.

FADU (File Access Data Unit)

In the OSI's FTAM (File Transfer, Access, and Management) service, a packet that contains information about accessing a directory tree in the file system.

Fail-Safe System

A computer system that is designed to keep operating, without losing data, when part of the system seriously malfunctions or fails completely.

Fail-Soft System

A computer system that is designed to fail gracefully, with the minimum amount of data or program destruction, when part of the system malfunctions. Fail-soft systems close down nonessential functions and operate at a reduced capacity until the problem has been resolved.

Fake Root

In Novell's NetWare versions 3.*x* and 4.*x*, a fake root is a drive mapping to a subdirectory that makes the subdirectory appear to be the root directory.

A fake root allows you to install programs into subdirectories, even though they insist on executing in the root directory. With the programs in a subdirectory, administrators can be more specific about where they allow users to have rights, and avoid granting rights at the true root of the volume.

Fake roots are not allowed in all environments. For example, fake roots cannot be used with OS/2 clients. When a fake root is used, there are also restrictions on how certain commands work and on how certain actions—for example, returning to the original (non-fake) root—must be performed.

BROADER CATEGORY
NetWare

FAL (File Access Listener)

In Digital Equipment Company's DECnet environment, a program that implements the DAP (Data Access Protocol) and that can accept remote requests from processes that use DAP.

Fall Time

The amount of time it takes an electrical signal to go from 90 percent of its level down to 10 percent. This value is important, because it helps set an upper limit on the maximum transmission speed that can be supported. Compare it with rise time.

Fanout

In communications and signaling, a configuration in which there are more output lines than input lines.

FAQ (Frequently Asked Questions)

In the Internet community, FAQ is a compilation of the most commonly asked questions, *with answers,* about any of dozens of topics. Many of these questions might be asked by newcomers, who may know little or nothing about a topic.

FAQs are posted in order to minimize the number of users who actually do ask the questions. Users can download and read the answers at their leisure, rather than tying up the lines by mailing these questions across the Internet and waiting for the answers to come pouring in.

FAQs can be found in archives on the Internet, and will have names such as disney-faq/disneyland, audio-faq/part1, or usenet-faq/part1. In FAQ archives, you can find a variety of information, such as where to look for old, out-of-print Disney videos, what to listen for when evaluating speakers (the electronic kind), and so on.

Far End Block Error (FEBE)

In broadband ISDN (BISDN) networks, an error reported to the sender by the receiver when the receiver's computed checksum result does not match the sender's checksum.

Far End Receive Failure (FERF)

In broadband ISDN (BISDN) networks, a signal sent upstream to indicate that an error has been detected downstream. An FERF might be sent, for example, because a destination has reported an error.

Fast Ethernet

Any of several Ethernet variants based on an approach developed by Grand Junction and others. The official name for this brand of Ethernet is 100BaseT (for twisted pair, which refers to the type of cable), and there are actually three variants, as described in the article "100BaseT."

a b c d e **f** g h i j k l m n o p q r s t u v w x y z

The term is also used to refer to any 100 Mbps Ethernet implementation—for example, 100BaseT or 100BaseVG. Finally, fastEthernet was the name for a now-defunct product.

Fastconnect Circuit Switching

The use of fast, electronic switching to establish a path (circuit) between two stations.

FastPath

A high-speed gateway between AppleTalk and Ethernet networks.

FAT (File Allocation Table)

The FAT (file allocation table) is where DOS keeps its information about all the files on a partition and about the disk location of all the blocks that make up each file. Because losing a FAT can be fatal in the PC world, DOS maintains a second copy of the FAT.

Some network operating systems, such as NetWare, also use FATs as part of their file handling. For example, NetWare uses a directory entry table (DET) and a FAT. Access to the FAT is through the DET.

The total storage a FAT can map depends on the size of each block (or allocation unit). Hard disk blocks can be 4, 8, 16, 32, or 64 kilobytes (KB) each.

The *number* of blocks that can be covered by the FAT is constant, at least for all but the earliest versions of the FAT. Large blocks are good for large files; smaller blocks are best for lots of small files.

Various tricks can be used to speed up access to the FAT, including caching and indexing the FAT. *Caching* the FAT involves storing it in chip memory (RAM) for faster access. Indexing information in a FAT can be accomplished by using a hashing function.

Fault

A break or other abnormal condition in a communications link. A fault generally requires immediate attention. The fault may be physical or logical.

Fault Management

One of five basic OSI network management tasks specified by the ISO and CCITT, fault management is used to detect, diagnose, and correct faults on a network.

Fault Detection and Assessment

A network management package can detect faults by having nodes report when a fault occurs, as well as by polling all nodes periodically. Both capabilities are necessary for thorough fault management. It may not be possible to get reliable reports about certain types of faults, such as one that causes an entire network to go down. For such cases, polling will provide at least the negative information of no response to a poll.

On the other hand, polling uses bandwidth that could be used for transmitting information. As in the real world, the more time spent on administrative work (polling), the less opportunity for doing real work (transmitting information). The value of the information obtained through polling must be weighed against the loss of bandwidth.

The bandwidth consumed by polling depends also on the complexity of the polling method. For example, a simple method sends a signal and waits for an echo to acknowledge that the channel is open. All network management environments include facilities for echo polling. More complex polling may check for more details, such as whether the node has something to send and whether a higher-priority level is requested.

When a fault is detected, the network management package must assess the fault to determine whether it is necessary to track it down and correct it immediately. Certain types of faults affect or shut down vital network services, and these faults must be dealt with as soon as possible. Other faults may involve only a path between locations, and they may not be crucial because alternate paths exist.

To determine the type of fault and its locations, the network management package may need to do some testing. For example, if a poll does not get the expected echo, the management package needs to determine whether the fault is in the poller, the pollee, or the link between them. This may require signal monitoring or loopback testing.

Fault Correction

Once the fault has been detected, identified, and located, measures must be taken to correct it. In some cases, such as when there is redundancy in the system, the management package may be able to correct the fault automatically. More likely, the network administrator or engineer will need to intervene in order to correct the fault. The ease with which this happens depends on the reliability of the detection and diagnosis, and on the type of information provided about the fault.

The fault-management system must be able to trace faults through the network and carry out diagnostic tests. Fault correction requires help from the configuration management domain.

Fault Reporting

To collect the information necessary to detect and report faults, fault-management systems use either of two families of protocols: the older SNMP (Simple Network Management Protocol) or the OSI standard CMIP (Common Management Information Protocol).

Faults can be reported in various ways. The simplest (and least informative) is an auditory alarm signal, which merely alerts the system administrator.

Actual information about the fault can be reported as text, or through a graphical interface that shows the network layout schematically, with the fault located in this diagram.

BROADER CATEGORY
Network Management

SEE ALSO
Accounting Management; Configuration Management; Performance Management; Security Management

Fault Point

In networking, a location at which something can go wrong. Fault points often tend to be at connection locations.

Fault Tolerance

Fault tolerance is a strategy for ensuring continued operation of a network even when certain kinds of faults arise. Fault-tolerant networks require some sort of redundant storage medium, power supply, or system.

For example, a fault-tolerant cabling system will include extra cables, in case one cable is cut or otherwise damaged. A fault-tolerant disk subsystem will include multiple copies of data on separate disks and use separate channels to write each version.

In some configurations, it is possible to remove and replace the malfunctioning component (for example, a hard disk) without shutting down the system. See the SFT (System Fault Tolerance) article for information about Novell NetWare's fault-tolerant features.

BROADER CATEGORIES
Data Protection; Security

Fax

A fax is a long-distance photocopy; it is a reproduction of a text or graphics document at a remote location. The document is scanned (or already available in digitized form), encoded into a standard format for faxes, transmitted over telephone or private lines, and printed (or stored) at the receiving end. *Telecopy* and *telefax* are other terms for fax. The figure "The fax transmission process" illustates how a fax is sent.

Fax images have resolutions that range from about 100×200 (vertical $\times$ horizontal) dots per inch (dpi) to about 400×400 dpi.

The CCITT has formulated fax format and transmission standards, referred to as Groups 1–4, which represent a range of signaling methods and formats, as follows:

- Group 1 uses frequency modulation of analog signals and supports only slow transmission speeds (6 minutes per page). Group 1 offers low (100 dpi) resolution.

- Group 2 uses both frequency and amplitude modulation to achieve higher speeds (between 2 and 3 minutes per page). Group 2 also offers low (100 dpi) resolution.

- Group 3 uses quadrature amplitude modulation (QAM) and data compression to increase transmission speeds to about one page per minute. Group 3 supports various automatic features and offers 200 dpi resolution. Commercially available fax machines support at least the Group 3 format.

- Group 4 supports higher-speed digital transmissions, so that a page can be transmitted in about 20 seconds. Group 4 offers 200 or 400 dpi resolution. Three classes are distinguished under the Group 4 format (which is not yet in wide use).

SEE ALSO
Modulation

THE FAX TRANSMISSION PROCESS

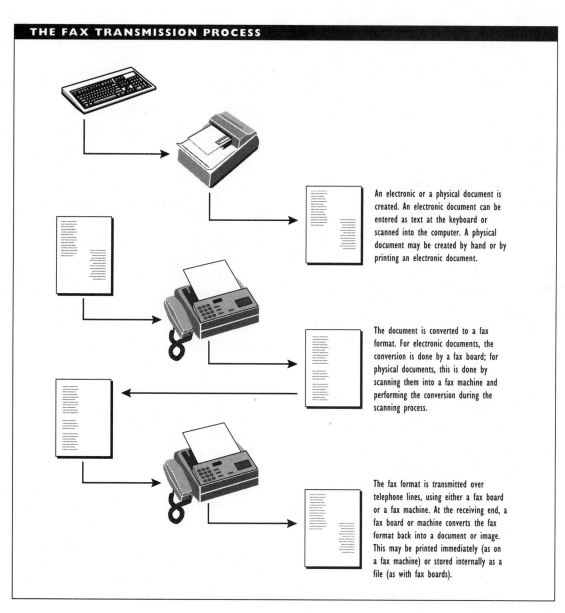

An electronic or a physical document is created. An electronic document can be entered as text at the keyboard or scanned into the computer. A physical document may be created by hand or by printing an electronic document.

The document is converted to a fax format. For electronic documents, the conversion is done by a fax board; for physical documents, this is done by scanning them into a fax machine and performing the conversion during the scanning process.

The fax format is transmitted over telephone lines, using either a fax board or a fax machine. At the receiving end, a fax board or machine converts the fax format back into a document or image. This may be printed immediately (as on a fax machine) or stored internally as a file (as with fax boards).

Fax Device

A fax device can be used to send and receive faxes on a network, under the control of a fax server. This may be a machine or a board. Machines may use thermal or plain paper.

In general, thermal paper comes in rolls, fades and cracks quickly, and must be cut as the fax leaves the machine. The main (and

a b c d e **f** g h i j k l m n o p q r s t u v w x y z

only) advantage of thermal paper fax machines is price.

Fax *boards* can generally accept text or graphics files (in the appropriate format), can convert these into fax format, and can transmit the resulting information. Fax boards can also receive faxes and convert them to the appropriate form for use. Because fax boards have no paper supply of their own, most boards can send their files to a printer for hard copy.

Although the speed and resolution capabilities for most fax machines are similar—thanks, in part, to the CCITT fax standards—there are certain considerations when selecting a fax device for use on a network.

For example, if your network receives many faxes daily, you will not want to use a thermal paper fax machine that insists on printing every fax received. On a busy day, there might be a 100-foot roll of faxes to wade through (literally) in order to find your fax. For a network, you will probably want the fax device to suppress printing (if requested) and pass an electronic version of the received fax to the appropriate program.

BROADER CATEGORY
Peripheral

SEE ALSO
Modem; Server; Fax

FBE (Free Buffer Enquiry)

A field in an ARCnet frame.

SEE
ARCnet

FC (Frame Control)

A field in a token ring data packet, or frame. The FC value tells whether the frame is a MAC-layer management packet or whether it is carrying LLC (logical-link control) data.

FCC (Federal Communications Commission)

A federal regulatory agency that develops and publishes guidelines to govern the operation of communications and other electrical equipment in the United States.

Perhaps the best-known FCC regulations are those that define and govern class A and class B devices, and those that allocate the electromagnetic spectrum. The device certifications are based on the amount of radio frequency interference (RFI) the device may cause for other devices in the vicinity.

Class A certification is less stringent, and it is assigned to equipment for use in business contexts. The more stringent class B certification applies to devices that are used in the home.

The FCC also allocates portions of the electromagnetic spectrum for particular uses, such as the following:

- The frequency band between 88 and 108 megahertz (MHz) is allocated for FM radio broadcasting.

- The bands between 54 and 88 MHz and between 174 and 216 MHz are allocated for VHF television.

- The band between 470 and 638 MHz is allocated for UHF television.

- Bands in the 4, 6, and 11 gigahertz (AHz) ranges have been allocated for long-haul telecommunications using a common carrier.

- Bands in the 18 and 23 GHz ranges have been allocated for short-haul transmissions, such as those in private networks.

FCS (Fiber Channel Standard)

The specifications for optical fiber in the FDDI (Fiber Distributed Data Interface) network architecture.

FCS (Frame Check Sequence)

In network or other transmissions, a value that is used to check for errors in a transmitted message. The FCS value is determined before sending the message, and it is stored in the packet's FCS field. If the new FCS value computed from the received packet does not match the original, a transmission error has occurred.

SEE ALSO
Error Detection and Correction

FDDI (Fiber Distributed Data Interface)

FDDI is a proposed ANSI standard specification (X3T9.5) for a network architecture that is designed to use fiber-optic lines at very high speeds.

An FDDI network has the following characteristics:

- Uses multimode or single-mode fiber-optic cable.

- Supports transmission speeds of up to 100 megabits per second (Mbps).

- Uses a ring topology. Actually, FDDI uses dual rings on which information can travel in opposite directions.

- Uses token-passing as the media-access method. However, in order to support a high transmission rate, FDDI can have multiple frames circulating the ring at a time, just as with ETR (early token release) in an ordinary Token Ring network.

- Uses light, rather than electricity, to encode signals.

- Uses a 4B/5B signal-encoding scheme. This scheme transmits 5 bits for every 4 bits of information. (This means that an FDDI network needs a clock speed of 125 Mbps to support a 100 Mbps transmission rate.) The actual bits are encoded using an NRZ-I strategy.

- Uses an LED (light-emitting diode) or a laser operating at a wavelength of roughly 1,300 nanometers (nm). This wavelength was chosen because it provides suitable performance even with LEDs.

- Supports up to 1,000 nodes on the network.

- Supports a network span of up to 100 kilometers (62 miles).

- Supports nodes up to 2 kilometers (1.25 miles) apart when using multimode cable and up to 40 kilometers (25 miles) when using single-mode cable.

- Supports a power budget (allowable power loss) of 11 decibels (dB) between nodes. This value means that about 92 percent of the signal's power can be lost between two nodes. (The signal is at least partially regenerated by the transceiver at each node.)

- Can handle packets from either the LLC (logical-link control) sublayer of the data-link layer or from the network layer.

- Supports hybrid networks, which can be created by attaching a subnetwork (for example, a collection of stations arranged in a star or a tree) to the ring through a concentrator.

The figure "Context and properties of FDDI" summarizes this architecture.

FDDI Applications

The FDDI architecture can be used for three types of networks:

- In a backbone network, in which the FDDI architecture connects multiple networks. Optical fiber's very high bandwidth makes FDDI ideal for such applications.

- As a back-end network to connect mainframes, minicomputers, and peripherals. Again, the high bandwidth makes FDDI attractive.

- As a front-end network to connect special-purpose workstations (such as graphics or engineering machines) for very high-speed data transfer.

FDDI Documents

The FDDI standard consists of four documents: PMD, PHY, MAC, and SMT. Each of which describes a different facet of the architecture.

PMD (Physical Medium Dependent)

PMD represents the lowest sublayer supported by FDDI. This document specifies the requirements for the optical power sources, photodetectors, transceivers, MIC (medium interface connector), and cabling. This is the only optic (as opposed to electrical) level and corresponds roughly to the lower parts of the physical layer in the OSI Reference Model.

The power source must be able to send a signal of at least 25 microwatts (25 millionths of a watt) into the fiber. The photodetector, or light receptor, must be able to pick up a signal as weak as 2 microwatts.

The MIC for FDDI connections serves as the interface between the electrical and optical components of the architecture. This connector was specially designed by ANSI for FDDI and is also known as the FDDI connector.

The cabling specified at this sublayer calls for two rings running in opposite directions. The primary ring is the main transmission medium. A secondary ring provides redundancy by making it possible to transmit the data in the opposite direction if necessary. When the primary ring is working properly, the secondary ring is generally idle.

CONTEXT AND PROPERTIES OF FDDI

Context

Network Architectures
    Electrical
        Ethernet, ARCnet, etc.
        Coaxial
    Optical
        FDDI ────────────────────────┐

FDDI Properties

Medium	Multi-mode or single-mode optical fiber
Light source	LED or laser operating at approximately 1300 nm wavelength
Encoding scheme	4B/5B + NRZI
Topology	Dual rings, traveling in opposite directions
Access method	Token passing, but with multiple frames allowed
Data frame size	Maximum of 4500 data bytes plus 8+ bytes for a preamble
Layers	PMD optical, PHY, MAC, SMT
Performance	Supports transmission speeds of up to 100 Mbps
	Can provide and maintain a guaranteed bandwidth
	Supports up to 1000 nodes on the network
	Supports a network span of up to 100 km
	Supports nodes up to 2 km apart with multimode cable; up to 40 km with single-mode cable
Variants	FDDI-I and FDDI-II

PHY (Physical)

The PHY layer mediates between the MAC layer above and the PMD layer below it. Unlike the PMD layer, this is an electronic layer. Signal-encoding and signal-decoding schemes are defined at the PHY layer. Functionally, this corresponds to the upper parts of the OSI Reference Model physical layer.

MAC (Media Access Control)

The MAC layer defines the frame formats and also the media-access method used by the network. This corresponds to the lower part of the OSI Reference Model data-link layer. The MAC and PHY layers are implemented directly in the FDDI chip set.

The MAC layer gets its data from the LLC sublayer above it.

SMT (Station Management)

The SMT component monitors and manages the node's activity. The SMT facility also allocates the architecture's bandwidth as required.

There are three elements to the SMT component:

- Frame services generate frames for diagnostics.

- Connection management (CMT) controls access to the network.

- Ring management (RMT) troubleshoots the network.

If there is a fault in the primary ring, the SMT facility redirects transmissions to use the secondary ring around the faulty section. This component can also use the secondary ring to transmit data under certain conditions, achieving a potential transmission rate of 200 Mbps. This component has no counterpart in the OSI Reference Model. SMT capabilities may be implemented in hardware or software.

FDDI Versions

The original FDDI specification (retroactively named FDDI-I) called only for asynchronous communications using packet-switching. (Actually, there was a synchronous traffic class in FDDI-I, but this did not guarantee a uniform data stream as would be required, for example, for voice or certain video data.)

To handle voice, video, and multimedia applications in real-time, a uniform data-transmission capability was added in a revision that is generally known as FDDI-II, but that is officially named hybrid ring control (HRC) FDDI. This new capability uses circuit-switching, so that FDDI-II supports both packet- and circuit-switched services. The figure "FDDI-I and FDDI-II organization" shows the major differences between the two versions.

The major structural additions to FDDI-II are a medium access control element capable of dealing with circuit-switched data and a multiplexer capable of passing either packet- or circuit-switched (that is, data, voice, video, and so on) material to the physical layer. This hybrid multiplexer (HMUX) gets frames from both the MAC connected to the LLC sublayer and from the isochronous MAC, or IMAC, added in FDDI-II.

The IMAC interacts with one or more circuit-switched multiplexers (CS-MUXs), which are capable of delivering voice, video, or any other kind of data that requires a continual connection and a constant rate. The IMAC and the HMUX together make up the HRC element that distinguishes FDDI-II.

An FDDI-II network can operate either in basic or hybrid mode, depending on whether circuit-switched services are needed. By default, FDDI networks operate in basic mode, which can handle only packet-switched data.

FDDI-I AND FDDI-II ORGANIZATION

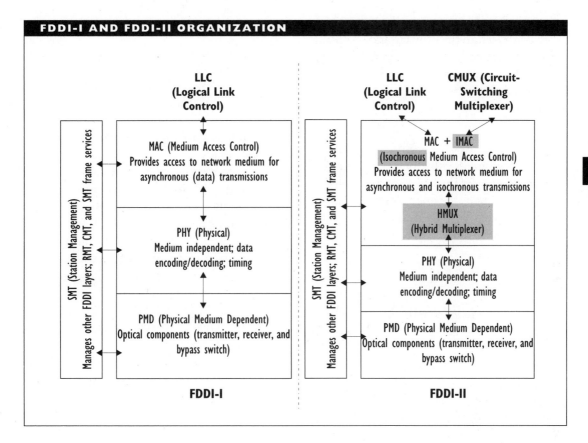

The standard has been broadened in several other ways to support a greater variety of components. For example, the original standard called for 62.5/125 micron multimode cable and for LEDs as the power source. Extensions have made other diameters of multimode cable and also single-mode cable acceptable, and have made lasers a possible power source.

FDDI Hardware

An FDDI network contains the following hardware elements: stations, NIC, cable, connectors, concentrators, and couplers.

FDDI Stations

A station, or node, on an FDDI network may be a single-attachment station (SAS) or a dual-attachment station (DAS).

An SAS node has only one transceiver, which is connected to the primary ring. This node cannot be connected directly to the network backbone. Instead, it must be attached through a concentrator, which is connected to both rings. The advantage of this method is apparent when SAS transceivers fail, because the failure will be contained by the concentrator and will not bring down the entire network. SAS nodes are also known as class B stations.

A DAS node has two transceivers, which are connected to the primary and secondary rings, respectively. This node can be connected directly to the network backbone. DAS nodes are also known as class A stations.

NIC

The NIC contains either one or two transceivers that meet the PMD specifications. Not surprisingly, the one-transceiver NICs are less expensive. An FDDI NIC has both a power source and a photodetector on the NIC.

Cable

Either single-mode cable or 62.5/125 micron multimode cable can be used. (The two values represent the diameter of the optical fiber's core and cladding components, respectively.) Often, cable with two core segments is used. One core is used for the primary ring, and the other is used for the secondary ring.

Even though only one multimode cable configuration is officially supported, in practice, FDDI networks may also support 50/125, 85/125, and 100/140 micron cables. The restriction depends on the power budget (allowable power loss) for the cable.

See the Cable, Fiber-Optic article for more information.

Dual Bypass Switch

A dual bypass switch is an optional component. It is often attached to nodes to make it easier to bypass the node in case of failure.

Connectors

The FDDI standard calls for specially designed connectors: MIC connectors. The MIC was designed to protect the ferrules that hold the fiber for the actual connection. The MIC is also expected to provide a snug, robust fit and to minimize signal loss at the connection.

The connection ends are polarized (asymmetrically cut), so that it is not possible to inadvertently link primary or secondary cables to each other. The connectors are also keyed to make it impossible to connect the wrong components to each other. There are different keys for connecting cable segments and for connecting nodes to a concentrator or a concentrator to a backbone. The FDDI MIC is a duplex connector, so that cables for both rings can be connected simultaneously. Special adapters are available to enable an MIC to connect to two ST connectors or to a transceiver.

FDDI variants have been developed that support SC, ST, and other types of fiber-optic connectors, partly because these are less expensive than FDDI connectors. Within a stretch of cable (at locations other than interfaces) the FDDI standard actually allows any kind of connector, provided the total power loss for the entire stretch of cable does not exceed the 11 dB power budget.

If you plan to use non-MIC connections in your FDDI setup, be sure to do your research carefully. Make sure that all the components you will be using will support the nonstandard connectors.

See the Connector, Fiber-Optic article for more information.

Concentrators

Concentrators serve as wiring centers for FDDI nodes. For example, concentrators may be used in a front-end network. Concentrators are connected to both the primary and secondary rings. Because of this, concentrators provide a link between the SAS and the secondary ring. As such, the concentrator assumes the function of secondary transceiver for each of the SASs attached to the concentrator.

Concentrators also come in single-attachment or dual-attachment forms (SAC and DAC, respectively). DACs can be connected to any of the four node types (SAS, DAS, SAC, and DAC) and can be used to attach stations or clusters of stations to the logical ring, even though these nodes are physically elsewhere.

SACs, in contrast, are used primarily for attaching SASs and other SACs. A SAC must connect to to a DAC, which is part of the ring.

Couplers

A coupler serves to split a light signal into two or more signals. For example, a coupler may be used to transmit the signal to multiple nodes.

The efficiency of a coupler can be an important factor in a fiber-optic setup. Whereas an electrical signal retains its strength when split, the same is not true of light. Splitting a light beam into two equal beams is equivalent to a 3 dB loss for each beam.

See the Coupler, Fiber-Optic article for more information.

GETTING FDDI COMPONENTS

There are still enough complexities and variations in the world of fiber optics that you should seriously consider going with a single vendor for your fiber-optic needs. Get that vendor to guarantee that the components will work together so that you won't have to worry about all those details. Make sure to give that vendor a list of performance specifications that the network must meet.

FDDI Ports

Stations on an FDDI network communicate through ports. Four types of ports are defined for FDDI stations:

- Port A is defined only for dual-attachment devices (DACs and DASs) and is connected to the incoming primary ring and the outgoing secondary ring.

- Port B is defined only for dual-attachment devices (DACs and DASs) and is connected to the incoming *secondary* ring and the outgoing primary ring.

- Port M (Master) is defined only for concentrators (DAC or SAC) and connects two concentrators. This port can also be used to communicate with both DASs and SASs.

- S (Slave) is defined only for single-attachment devices and is used to connect two stations or a station to a concentrator.

a b c d e **f** g h i j k l m n o p q r s t u v w x y z

FDDI Operation

In creating an FDDI network, the first task is to configure the ring. After each station on the network is identified, it is assigned a unique address, usage priorities, and so on.

Initially, the network operates in basic mode and continues to do so until a station requests a switch to hybrid mode. If this is feasible, the stations go through a process to determine the cycle master, which essentially runs the hybrid mode by controlling the creation and transmission of the cycles (bit-filled time slots) that provide the structure for a network in hybrid mode.

In basic mode, a token circulates from node to node, as follows:

1. When an unused (available) token reaches a node (node A), the node grabs the token and transmits a frame. Then node A releases the token. First the frame and then the token reach the node's nearest downstream neighbor (node B).

2. If the frame is addressed to node B, the recipient copies the pertinent information (source address and data), sets the Frame Status field to an appropriate value, and sends the frame on to make its way back to the sender (node A). If node B is not the destination for the frame, the node simply passes the frame on unchanged.

3. Next, node B gets the token that node A released immediately after the frame. If node B has something to say, node B grabs the token, sends its frame, and follows this immediately with the token.

Note that there are now two frames circulating, but only one token. Allowing multiple frames to circulate simultaneously is one way to achieve a high-transmission speed in an FDDI network.

When things are working smoothly, the FDDI configuration is as illustrated in the figure "An FDDI network with the primary ring working properly," with the secondary ring idle. When a connection between two stations is broken, the station with a frame but no destination information sends the frame onto the secondary ring, as shown in the figure "An FDDI network with a break, forcing a switch over to the secondary ring." On that path, the frame reaches the station that was the next destination before the break.

An FDDI network can have both synchronous and asynchronous transmissions occurring at the same time. These transmissions are controlled by the SMT facility. The SMT component can allocate a fixed portion of the bandwidth for synchronous transmissions, leaving the rest of the bandwidth available for asynchronous transmissions. Different priority schemes are used to control access to the synchronous and asynchronous portions of the bandwidth.

As is the case with any token-passing network, it is necessary to monitor the network to make sure the token does not get corrupted, lost, or trapped by a node that goes off line. The SMT is responsible for such monitoring.

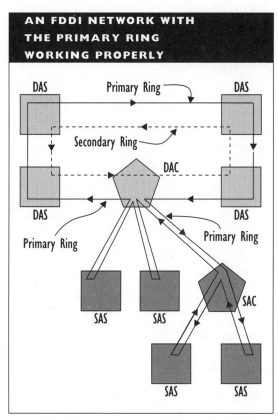

AN FDDI NETWORK WITH THE PRIMARY RING WORKING PROPERLY

AN FDDI NETWORK WITH A BREAK, FORCING A SWITCH OVER TO THE SECONDARY RING

All nodes monitor the ring to check for problems. If a node detects a token problem—a problem that might require the network to be reinitialized—the node initiates a claim token process. This is a contest in which one node finally wins the right to reinitialize the ring and issue a new token.

If a node detects a serious error (such as a break in the ring), that node sends a beacon frame. As other nodes detect the error or receive a beacon frame, they also start sending beacon frames. A node stops sending beacon frames as soon as the node receives such a frame from its nearest upstream neighbor (NAUN).

The frame immediately downstream from the problem will be the last node transmitting beacon frames, and this node will stop as soon as it receives its own beacon frame back, because this will indicate that the problem has been resolved (usually by switching to the secondary ring to bypass the fault).

Once the problem has been resolved, the last beaconing node starts the claim token process.

a b c d e **f** g h i j k l m n o p q r s t u v w x y z

Extended Dialogs

FDDI allows a node to seize control of the token temporarily and to restrict its use in order to carry out an extended interaction with a specific other node. Only the nodes involved in the interaction can use this token. These two nodes will communicate with each other until the interaction is finished, at which point one of them will release an unrestricted token.

Note that a restricted token will not trigger a claim token process because each node gets to see the token. Nonprivileged nodes (those not involved in the extended interaction) simply are not allowed to use the token.

Station Management for FDDI

As stated, the SMT component has three major responsibilities: connection management, ring management, and frame services.

CMT (Connection Management)

CMT is concerned with the station's coordination with the network, the physical connection (PCM), and the station's configuration. The coordination task is known as entity-coordination management (ECM), and it makes sure that all the required ports are working properly, with the network and with each other.

The PCM is responsible for the negotiations that determine the type of port associated with the station, availability of a MAC component for testing the link, and also for connecting the station. If these negotiations are successful, the CMT switches to the settings required to connect the station to the

network and to enable it to communicate once connected.

RMT (Ring Management)

RMT is used to keep the ring in working order. Toward this end, RMT checks for duplicate addresses and for stuck beacons (a frame sent to indicate a major error on the ring, such as a break).

A stuck beacon arises when a station keeps sending beacon frames. This happens when the station never gets a beacon from another node (which would indicate that other nodes are also aware of the failure). In case of a stuck beacon, the RMT uses a trace function to help isolate the error and to recover from the stuck beacon.

Frame Services

Like all good management services, the SMT has its own communications facilities, which provide the required information independently of the data being transmitted across the network. The station management functions are implemented through several special-purpose frames, which are used to allocate and check resources, exchange information with stations, and so on. The SMT frames are described in the next section.

FDDI Frames

FDDI has three types of frames: tokens, command, and data frames. These are used in basic FDDI operation. When the system is operating in hybrid mode, transmissions are defined by cycles (125 microsecond intervals), with bit sequences defined within this framework. Cycles are discussed later in this article.

Frames consist of the preamble, header, contents, and trailer. The preamble is generally not included when determining the frame's length.

Discussions of FDDI frames can be confusing, because FDDI signal encoding uses a five-bits-for-four encoding scheme. When describing the size of frame elements, the number of bits involved before encoding will be based on octets, or more directly, on 4-bit nibbles; after encoding, 25 percent more bits will be floating around, because each nibble is encoded into a 5-bit symbol.

For consistency with the discussion of frames for other architectures, the following descriptions use the byte-based bit counts that hold prior to encoding. For example, the preamble for an FDDI frame consists of at least 8 bytes; that is, the preamble has 16 nibbles or 64 bits. In post-encoding terms, this amounts to 16 symbols, or 80 bits.

Token Frames

A token frame consists of three bytes plus the preamble, as follows:

Preamble (8+ bytes): Consists of 64 or more bits, each with a predefined value. The preamble serves as a pattern with which the receiver can set the signal clock.

Starting Delimiter (1 byte): Indicates the actual start of the frame.

Frame Control: Only the two most significant bits are used for the token frame. A byte value of 1000 0000 indicates an unrestricted token, which can

be used without restrictions for both synchronous and asynchronous communication. A value of 1100 0000 indicates a restricted token, whose use in asynchronous transmissions has constraints.

Ending Delimiter (1 byte): Indicates the end of the frame.

The figure "An FDDI token frame" shows the components of a token frame in FDDI.

AN FDDI TOKEN FRAME

64 bits Preamble	8 bits SD	8 bits FC	8 bits ED

SD = Starting Delimiter
FC = Frame Control
ED = Ending Delimiter

Data Frame

A data frame contains packets that were received from higher-level protocols and that are being sent to another node. A data frame consists of at most 4,500 bytes (9,000 symbols), not counting the preamble.

Preamble (8+ bytes): Same as for a token frame.

Starting Delimiter (1 byte): Same as for a token frame.

Frame Control (1 byte): Provides the following information through four bit groupings: Whether the frame is part of a synchronous or an asynchronous transmission (1 bit), whether the frame is using 2- or 6-byte addresses (1 bit), whether the frame is a data (LLC-layer) or command (MAC-layer) frame (2 bits), and the type of command if the frame is a command (4 bits).

Destination Address (2 or 6 bytes): Contains the address of the frame's recipient. The receiving node saves the source address and the frame's data before passing the frame to the next node in the ring.

Source Address (2 or 6 bytes): Contains the address of the frame's sender.

Information (at most 5601 nibbles): Contains the packet received from the higher protocol layer.

Frame Check Sequence (4 bytes): Contains the results of a CRC (cyclic redundancy check) to determine whether an error has crept into the frame.

Ending Delimiter (4 bits): Same value as in a token frame, but stored only once.

Frame Status (12+ bits): Used to indicate the result of the frame's trip around the ring. The recipient uses this field to indicate whether the frame was received correctly. An unchanged Frame Status field indicates that the destination node was not found on the ring.

The figure "An FDDI data frame" shows the components of this frame.

Command Frames

Command frames have the same structure as data frames, except that the information field is always 0 bytes long. A command frame contains instructions for doing maintenance on the network ring. These instructions are contained in the Frame Control field.

Command frames cannot have the same structure as token frames because the Frame Status field provides information about the results from carrying out the command.

AN FDDI DATA FRAME

64 bits Preamble	8 bits SD	8 bits FC	16 or 48 bits DA	16 or 48 bits SA	0+ bits Info	32 bits FCS	4 bits ED	12 bits FS

SD = Starting Delimiter   FCS = Frame Check Sequence
FC = Frame Control   ED = Ending Delimiter
DA = Destination Address   FS = Frame Status
SA = Source Address

SMT Frames

The SMT component uses various special-purpose frames to keep things running smoothly:

ECF (Echo Frame): Used for tests within the SMT operation.

ESF (Extended Services Frame): Provides a mechanism for user-defined frames.

NIF (Neighbor Information Frame): Used to contact the frame's downstream neighbor.

PMF (Parameter Management Frame): Makes remote management possible.

RAF (Resource Allocation Frame): Used to allocate the bandwidth as needed.

RDF (Request Denied Frame): Indicates that the SMT component has encountered an invalid frame or ID.

SIF (Station Information Frame): Used to pass information about a station's configuration and operation.

SRF (Status Report Frame): Used to keep other stations updated about a station's status.

Transmissions in Hybrid Mode

When an FDDI-II station operates in hybrid mode, the transmission is structured around a cycle, which is a packet that is repeated continuously during a session. Cycles are generated by a special node that functions as the cycle master.

Each cycle is 125 microseconds long and contains 12,500 bits. Each cycle has room for the following:

Preamble (5 nibbles): As usual, the preamble is used for synchronization.

Cycle Header (12 bytes): Provides information about the contents of the rest of the cycle.

DPG (Dedicated Packet Group, 12 bytes): Can be used for handling transmissions that involve packet transfers.

WBC (Wideband Channel, 96 bytes per channel per cycle): Provides multiple transmission channels, each with up to 6.144 Mbps bandwidth.

This cycle arrangement helps ensure that every channel can get maximum use. Toward this end, each WBC can be divided into lower bandwidth channels, which enables traffic from a greater number of stations to travel simultaneously along the network. This would not increase the bandwidth, because each of the channels would have a smaller capacity. Since not all stations will have over 6 million bits of information to send every second, turning a WBC into a few dozen 64 kbps channels can actually help increase traffic on the network.

The cycle header is a crucial element in the hybrid mode of operation, because the contents of this header help ensure that each station is properly synchronized and also provide the information that enables stations to interpret the contents of the rest of the cycle. For example, the header might indicate whether the data is to be treated as packet-switched or isochronous (circuit-switched) data.

a b c d e **f** g h i j k l m n o p q r s t u v w x y z

Variants

Some vendors are supporting an architecture similar to FDDI on electrical cable. This variant is known as CDDI (Copper Distributed Data Interface) or TPDDI (Twisted Pair Distributed Data Interface), and it is an effort to extend the FDDI specifications to copper shielded or unshielded twisted-pair wiring. There are as yet no official standards for CDDI, so there is little guarantee of interoperability with products from different vendors.

See the ESCON, Fiber Channel, and SONET articles for discussions of other variants.

BROADER CATEGORY
Network Architecture

SEE ALSO
Cable, Fiber-Optic; Connector, Fiber-Optic; Coupler, Fiber-Optic

FDDITalk

Apple's implementation of FDDI (Fiber Distributed Data Interface) protocols and drivers for use in an AppleTalk network.

SEE ALSO
EtherTalk; LocalTalk; TokenTalk

FDL (Facility Data Link)

In an ESF digital transmission format, a 4 kilobit per second (kbps) communications link between the sender's station and the telephone company's monitors. This 4 kbps band is created by taking half of the 24 framing bits in an ESF and using them for the link.

SEE ALSO
ESF (Extended Superframe)

FDM (Frequency Division Multiplexing)

A multiplexing scheme in which the bandwidth of a medium is divided into distinct and mutually exclusive frequency ranges. FDM is generally used for analog transmissions and is in contrast to TDM (time division multiplexing).

SEE ALSO
Multiplexing

FDMA (Frequency Division, Multiple Access)

In communications, a strategy for assigning multiple channels within a large bandwidth. Once channels are assigned, signals can be sent along these channels using a multiplexing strategy such as FDM (frequency division multiplexing). Compare it with CDMA (cell division multiple access) and TDMA (time division multiple access).

SEE ALSO
Multiplexing

FDX (Full Duplex)

A communication setup in which transmissions can go in both directions at the same time. This is in contrast to simplex and half-duplex connections.

FEBE (Far End Block Error)

In broadband ISDN (BISDN) networks, an error reported to the sender by the receiver when the receiver's computed checksum result does not match the sender's checksum.

FEC (Forward Error Correction)

A type of error correction in which a transmission includes enough additional information for the receiver to locate and correct any bit-level errors that arise during transmission.

SEE ALSO

Error Detection and Correction

FECN (Forward Explicit Congestion Notification)

A frame-relay term.

SEE ALSO

ECN (Explicit Congestion Notification)

Federal Information Exchange (FIX)

SEE

FIX (Federal Information Exchange)

Federal Networking Council (FNC)

SEE

FNC (Federal Networking Council)

Feed

In telecommunications, a circuit through which data is sent to a central station or for transmission along a network backbone.

FEP (Front-End Processor)

In an IBM SNA (Systems Network Architecture) network, an FEP is a component that controls access to the host computer (the mainframe). The FEP, also known as a *communication controller,* is generally attached to the host by a fast, direct connection (often a fiber-optic link) and is controlled by the host through a network control program (NCP) loaded and executed on the FEP.

Through the NCP, the FEP relieves the host of tasks such as establishing connections and monitoring links. The FEP is also responsible for doing any data compression or translation as the data moves between host and remote device.

In IBM hardware terms, the FEP is a controller in the 37*xx* series; in SNA terms, the FEP is a Type 4 PU (physical unit). 37*xx* controllers vary in the number of lines they can handle and in the speed these lines can support.

BROADER CATEGORY

SNA (Systems Network Architecture)

FERF (Far End Receive Failure)

In broadband ISDN (BISDN) networks, a signal sent upstream to indicate that an error has been detected downstream. An FERF might be sent, for example, because a destination has reported an error.

Ferrule

In a fiber-optic connection, a component that serves to keep the optical core and cladding aligned and immobile. The fiber cladding may be glued to the ferrule with epoxy. Ferrules may be made of ceramic (the most reliable), plastic, or stainless steel.

a b c d e **f** g h i j k l m n o p q r s t u v w x y z

SEE ALSO
Connector, Fiber-Optic

▼
FEXT (Far End Crosstalk)

In an electrical signal, interference, or leakage, of a transmitted signal from one wire into another wire. FEXT is measured at the *receiving* end, in contrast to NEXT (near end crosstalk).

▼
Fiber Bandwidth

A measure of a fiber-optic cable's ability to carry information, usually expressed in terms of megahertz (MHz) or megabits per second (Mbps) per kilometer or some other distance.

▼
Fiber Bundle

In fiber optics, a collection of fibers that are routed together. Two types of bundles are distinguished:

- *Flexible bundle.* A collection of fibers that are grouped, or bundled, at either end of the cable, but that are free to move between these endpoints.

- *Rigid bundle.* A collection of fibers that are melted together to form a single rod that is bent into the desired shape during manufacture. Rigid, or *fused,* bundles are less expensive to manufacture than flexible ones.

BROADER CATEGORY
Cable

▼
Fiber Channel

Fiber Channel is a technology for very high-speed, switching-based serial transmissions. The Fiber Channel Standard (FCS) is being developed by ANSI X3T9.3 committees. The standard includes specifications for physical media and connections, packet encoding and framing strategies, and interfaces to higher-level protocols. More specifically:

- FCS supports both single- and multi-mode fiber optic cable. Coaxial and shielded twisted-pair (STP) cable are also supported as physical media.

- FCS transmissions use an 8B/10B encoding strategy in which every 8-bit input element is recoded as 10 outgoing bits.

- FCS packets can be up to 2,148 bytes long. This is divided into five fields: 4 bytes for Start of Frame (SOF), 24 bytes for the Frame Header, anywhere between 0 and 2,112 bytes for the data field, 4 bytes for a CRC (cyclical redundancy check), and a 4-byte End of Frame (EOF) field. The data field can include up to two Optional Header fields of 32 bytes each.

- FCS services are defined in a way that allows a common transmission to be split across multiple ports of a single node.

- FCS includes mappings between the lower-levels covered by FCS and higher level protocols such as Intelligent Peripheral Interface (IPI), High-Performance Parallel Interface (HIPPI), Small Computer System Interface (SCSI), or Internet Protocol (IP). Note that these higher-level interfaces may be either for bus- or telecommunications-based connections.

An FCS connection can support any of a range of bandwidths, including 100-, 200-, 400-, and 800 Mbps. In fact, FCS supports mulitple speeds in a single session. The FCS specifies three classes of service:

- Class 1 is connection-oriented and can guarantee a specified bandwidth for a specified connection period.

- Class 2 is a connectionless, multiplexed service with acknowledgement for delivery.

- Class 3 is a connectionless, multiplexed service without delivery acknowledgement.

FCS is comparable to other high-speed switching technologies such as ATM (Asynchronous Transfer Mode).

BROADER CATEGORY
Cable, Fiber-Optic

Fiber Optics

Fiber optics refers to a communications technology that uses light signals transmitted along special fibers, instead of electrical signals transmitted along copper wire.

Networks based on fiber optics offer numerous advantages over those based on copper wiring and electrical signals, including the following:

- Immunity to electromagnetic interference, eavesdropping, and jamming

- Higher bandwidth

- Greater distances allowed

Currently, fiber-optic networks also offer a major disadvantage: price.

SEE ALSO
Cable, Fiber-Optic; FDDI (Fiber Distributed Data Interface)

Field

Most generally, a field is an element in a compound data structure, such as a packet database record, or form. In connection with networking packets, a field refers to a packet element that begins at a specific position in the bit block that makes up the packet. For example, in an Ethernet 2 packet, the source address field begins at the seventh byte in the packet.

FIFO (First In, First Out)

The processing strategy for the queue abstract data type. In this strategy, the element added least recently is the element removed first. For example, the single line bank queues for the next available teller are FIFO queues. Compare FIFO with LIFO (last in first out).

a
b
c
d
e
f
g
h
i
j
k
l
m
n
o
p
q
r
s
t
u
v
w
x
y
z

File Attribute

A value, or status, associated with a file. The value specifies, for example, the kinds of actions allowed with the file. Examples of file attributes include read-only, read/write, and archive. Files on a network will generally also have attributes that pertain to the access and usage rights and restrictions associated with the file.

SEE ALSO

Attribute

File Caching

File caching is a scheme in which an area of RAM is reserved for use as fast-access *cache memory*. Frequently used files (or file chunks) are kept in this cache area for faster access.

When there is a request for a file, the operating system first checks whether the file is in the cache. If so, the file is retrieved from the cache rather than from its permanent storage, and the cache version will be modified if the file is changed. If the file is not in the cache, it is retrieved from disk (and may be written to the cache area).

There are various trade-offs and several strategies for deciding when to write the contents of a file in the cache to disk. These decisions are made when configuring (or possibly when creating) the cache program; they are not made by the end-user.

The use of file caching can speed up performance, sometimes by a considerable amount. Other steps to improve performance include elevator seeking, which speeds up the storage and retrieval of data

from the hard disk, and directory caching and hashing, which speed up the retrieval of information from the directory entry tables.

File Extension

In many operating systems, a file extension is a suffix added to a file name. In many cases, the extension identifies the type of file (text, program, graphics, and so on).

In DOS, a file extension can be at most three characters and must be separated from the file name (maximum eight characters) by a period. In the name PROGRAM.EXE, for example, *PROGRAM* is the name and *EXE* is the extension. It is not uncommon to include the leading period when specifying the extension, as in .EXE, for a program file.

The number of possible extensions is quite large, even if just letters are used.

The following are some examples of common file extensions and the types of files they represent:

- EXE, COM, and BAT indicate DOS files that can be executed. Files ending in BAT are batch files.

- NLM indicates a NetWare Loadable Module.

- DXF, GIF, PCX, and TIF indicate types of graphics files.

- C, CPP, ASM, and PAS indicate source files in particular programming languages: for C, C++, Assembler, and Pascal programs, respectively.

- ASC and TXT generally indicate files containing ordinary text.

- PS and EPS files are usually PostScript files, which may contain instructions for drawing a graphics image. PS files are text files; an EPS file can include a binary image.

Along with these, there are a score or so of other conventional extensions—just enough variety and overlap to ensure that there is always doubt as to a file's format.

File Indexing

In Novell's NetWare, file indexing is a strategy by which FAT (file allocation table) entries are indexed for faster access. This makes it possible to move directly to a particular block in a file without needing to move through all the blocks that precede it. NetWare versions 3.11 and later automatically index a FAT entry with more than 64 blocks, which is a file whose contents are scattered over more than 64 blocks on the disk.

A more powerful indexing strategy is used for files with more than 1,023 blocks. Note that 4 kilobytes is the smallest block size supported by NetWare, which makes a file with 1,024 blocks equal to 4 megabytes, or almost twice the size of the original text files for this book.

File Name

A file name is the name of a file on a disk, used so that both you and the operating system can find the file again. Every file in a directory must have a unique name, but files in different directories can share the same name.

In DOS, file and directory names have two parts. They can have up to eight characters in the name and up to three characters in the optional file-name extension, separated from the name by a period. Many applications take over the extension part of the file name, using specific groups of characters to designate a particular file type.

In the Macintosh operating system, file names can be up to 31 characters and can contain any character except a colon (:), which is used to separate elements of a path name.

In the OS/2 HPFS, files can have names of 254 characters, including many characters that are illegal in DOS file names, such as spaces. The Windows NT File System allows 255-character file names and also provides some degree of security by including permissions when sharing files.

SEE ALSO

File Extension

File Sharing

An arrangement by which multiple users can access the same file(s) simultaneously. File access has restrictions, and it is generally controlled by both application and networking software. For example, certain parts of the file may be locked (made inaccessible) if a user is already accessing that file.

SEE ALSO

Access Rights; Attribute; Security

File System

In an operating system, the file system is the structure used for file entries. The file system organizes information about files, such as their names, attributes, and locations.

Examples of file systems include the following:

CDFS (CD-ROM File System): Used to store information about files on a compact disk.

FAT (File Allocation Table): Used by various versions of DOS.

HPFS (High Performance File System): Used in OS/2.

NTFS (NT File System): Used by Windows NT and NT Advanced File Server.

HFS (Hierarchical File System): Used on the Macintosh by the System 7 operating system.

NFS (Network File System): A distributed file system originally developed by Sun Microsystems to make it easier to handle files on remote systems, but now used widely on UNIX and other distributed systems—for example, on the Internet.

AFS (Andrew File System): Another distributed file system, originally developed at Carnegie-Mellon University, and a major contender to become the file system of the future on large networks such as the Internet.

In Novell's NetWare 4.*x*, the term *file system* is used in preference to *directory structure* (the term in pre-4.0 NetWare versions) to describe the structure of the system and the user's files and directories. This revised usage is to avoid confusion between the file

system information and the contents of Novell's Directory (the information tree created by the global naming service that replaced the NetWare bindery from earlier versions).

Novell's file system has three major levels:

- Volume, which is the highest level, and which refers to a partition created by the NetWare installation program. A volume may encompass any amount from as little as part of a hard disk to as much as multiple disks.

- Directory, which is an intermediate level that contains other directories or files.

- File, which is the most specific level. This is the level at which a user or a process generally works.

▼
File Transfer

File transfer is the process of copying a file from one machine or location to another. File transfer is a common networking task.

When a file is transferred over a network, the file must first be divided into smaller packets for transmission. The details of this "packetization" depend on the transfer protocol (communications and packaging rules) being used. This protocol also determines how the transfer instructions are given.

In networking contexts, FTP (File Transfer Protocol) and FTAM (File Transfer, Access, and Management) are two popular protocols. For transfer over modems, Kermit, XMODEM, YMODEM, and ZMODEM are some of the available protocols.

If the file is being transferred between different operating environments, the file may also be reformatted during the transfer. For example, in transferring text files between UNIX and DOS environments, the ends of lines must be changed; in transferring from a Macintosh to a DOS environment, the Macintosh file's resource fork will be discarded, and the data fork may also need to be reformatted.

Filter

In electrical signaling, a device used to allow certain frequency bands to pass, while blocking other bands.

Filtering

In hardware, filtering is a process of frequency selection and exclusion. Signals within one or more frequency bands are allowed to pass unmodified, but all other signals are blocked.

In network operations, filtering is a process for selecting and discarding packets in order to control access to a network or to resources, such as files and devices. The basis for the filtering can be addresses or protocols.

For example, bridges filter network traffic so that local packets stay on their networks, rather than being passed to another network. Various security measures can be used to filter user access to files.

Packets that are not filtered are generally forwarded to an intermediate or final destination.

The rate at which packets are checked and filtered is called the *filtering rate*. For a bridge, this is generally a better index of the bridge's performance than simple throughput.

Finder

In Apple's Macintosh environment, an application that provides access to applications and documents.

Finger

An Internet utility that can be used to determine whether a particular user is logged onto a particular machine, and also to find out something about the user. To use this command, type `finger` followed by the name of the user about whom you want information. If the user is on a machine different from yours, you also need to include the user's address.

If the specified user has an account on the specified machine, the finger command will display information such as the person's login and real-life names, office and phone number, and the person's last login. Finally, finger will display (or act upon the commands from) any plan or proj files found in the fingered person's files. The details that are shown depend in part on the fingered person's configuration. Finger is generally considered a point of vulnerability in network security, since the program can tell a would-be intruder quite a bit about the users—or, rather, the accounts—on a network. For example, knowing when users last logged on can help identify rarely-used accounts.

a b c d e f g h i j k l m n o p q r s t u v w x y z

▼
Firewall

A firewall is a network component that provides a security barrier between networks or network segments. Firewalls are generally set up to protect a particular network or network component from attack, or unauthorized penetration, by outside invaders. However, a firewall also may be set up to protect vital corporate or institutional data or resources from internal attacks or incompetence. Internal firewalls are generally placed between administrative, or security, domains in a corporate or institutional network. For example, a firewall might be set up between the network domain that houses the payroll and personnel information and other parts of the corporate network.

All traffic to or from the protected network must go through the firewall; the firewall is designed to allow only authorized traffic. If the firewall does its filtering job successfully, attacks will never even reach the protected network.

To be effective, the firewall must also be able to protect itself from penetration. To help ensure this, firewalls are generally designed to be special-purpose machines. That is, the firewall will not provide services beyond those necessary to authenticate the user and to decide whether to allow the traffic through. If a received packet is legitimate, the firewall will pass on the traffic to the appropriate machine.

Firewalls are not gateways, but they do often work in association with gateways. One reason for this is that both firewalls and gateways tend to sit between networks. The gateway's job is to translate packets as they move between different network environments; the firewall's job is to filter them.

In some cases, however, the gateway and firewall functions will be provided by the same network components. This can happen, for example, if a network is communicating with an alien network, so that the communication requires a gateway. In such a case, however, the filtering and gateway (i.e., translating) elements will still be distinct and will communicate with each other through an internal filter.

Three broad categories of firewall are distinguished, although a particular firewall installation may include more than one of these.

- *Packet-filtering.* Such low-level filters pass or drop packets based on their source or destination addresses or ports. This level of filtering is already provided by routers. Such a firewall is easy and inexpensive to set up, but its capabilities are quite limited. A packet-filtering firewall can fail if its table of valid and invalid addresses is incorrect. Such a firewall is also susceptible to address-spoofing (making a filter believe that a packet is coming from a different address).

- *Application-filtering.* These higher-level filters screen traffic involving specific applications or services (for example, ftp or e-mail). The advantage of such a filter is that it allows for more sophisticated evaluation and authentication measures. For example, such a firewall could be designed to protect against a gopher server moving a renegade file onto a machine or to check for an attack entering with an application. A major disadvantage of a filter operating at the application level is that such programs can be very complex and have many possible action sequences. The large number of possibilities—for example, an application calling another application—makes it very difficult to build in safeguards against every possible attack.

- *Circuit-level.* Such a filter looks not only at source and destination addresses but also at the circuits (temporary paths) that have been established for a connection. Such circuits are established—for example, when using TCP (transport control protocol)—during an initial handshaking session. Such a filter can detect address-spoofing, for example, because such a misleading packet would have no way of getting the circuit information that is set up during the handshaking. While very effective for certain protocols, circuit filters are of limited use with connectionless protocols (such as UDP), which may send packets over various paths.

Like all security measures, firewalls can be useful, but they are not foolproof. They have the advantage of concentrating security measures and issues, making it easier to set up and maintain them. Of course, such centralization also provides an Achilles heel—that is, a point of vulnerability. If an intruder can get around (or, more often, under) the firewall, then an attack is possible.

A firewall's effectiveness depends on all traffic going through the firewall. This is not a sufficient condition for security, however. In *tunneling*, one packet is encapsulated inside another. With this strategy, a packet from an untrusted machine or user could be placed into a packet from a trusted machine, and the latter packet could then be sent through a firewall. Unless the firewall actually takes each packet apart and examines its contents, there is no guaranteed effective protection against tunneling.

FIRL (Fiber-Optic Inter-Repeater Link)

An FIRL (sometimes written as *FOIRL*) is a link segment that uses fiber-optic cable to connect two repeaters in a standard Ethernet or an 802.3-based Ethernet network. An FOIRL cannot have any nodes. The standard connector for such a link is the SMA connector (IEC 874-2).

Firmware

Instructions encoded permanently in ROM (read-only memory) on a chip. Certain operating system components or boot instructions are encoded as firmware.

First-Level Interrupt Handler (FLIH)

SEE

FLIH (First-Level Interrupt Handler)

FIX (Federal Information Exchange)

A connection point between the Internet and any of the federal government's internets.

a
b
c
d
e
f
g
h
i
j
k
l
m
n
o
p
q
r
s
t
u
v
w
x
y
z

Fixed Priority-Oriented Demand Assignment

In networking, an access protocol in which stations must reserve slots on the network. These slots are allocated according to the stations' priority levels.

Fixed Routing

A routing strategy in which packets or messages are transmitted between the source and destination over a well-defined and constant path.

Flag

A flag is a value that represents a setting or condition. Since a flag represents a yes or no, on or off, or similar choice, only a single bit is needed to represent a flag value. Because of this, multiple flags are generally combined into a byte or word. For example, in bit-oriented protocols, a flag byte is a bit sequence used to mark the start and/or the end of a frame.

To determine a flag setting, you can mask (screen out) all the bits except the flag bit of interest. The mask byte (word) would contain 0 bits everywhere except in the position corresponding to the flag bit. A mask has 0 bits at every location except at the desired flag bits, where it has a 1 bit. By taking the logical AND (which is 1 only if both the mask and flag bits are 1) of the bit sequence, it is possible to determine a flag setting.

In NetWare security, the attributes that determine the access and use rules for a file or directory are also known as *flags*.

Flag Byte

In bit-oriented protocols, a bit sequence used to mark the start and/or the end of a frame.

Flag Character

In X.25 packet-switching technology, a special character (0111 1110) that is included at the beginning and end of every LAPB frame to indicate a frame boundary. The protocol uses *bit stuffing* to ensure that this bit sequence never occurs elsewhere in the packet (for example, as part of the packet's data).

Flame

On the Internet, a flame is a nasty message usually aimed at the author(s) of particular postings or the perpetrator(s) of actions to which the flamer (the flame's author) has taken exception. Breaches of *netiquette* (unofficial rules of behavior on the Internet) often incur flames. The flame is sometimes used to express the flamer's anger and sometimes to insult the target (i.e., the flamee). The word can also be used as a verb.

Flamers generally warn of a flame by specifying "FLAME ON!" in the posting's subject header. Users have been known to deliberately provoke flames by posting *flame bait,* and simple flames have been fanned into long-running *flame wars.*

Flash Memory

Nonvolatile RAM, which retains its contents even when power is shut off. Flash memory can, however, be erased or reprogrammed. Flash memory is useful for storing configuration information, which must be retained between sessions but may change during any session.

Flat Name Structure

A naming strategy in which each name is unique and in which there is no logical, physical, or other relationship between names. For example, this strategy may be used for files or network nodes. Such names are accessible only through table lookup. Compare this with a hierarchical name structure.

FLIH (First-Level Interrupt Handler)

In a network, an interrupt handler whose job is to determine which device or channel generated the interrupt and then to invoke a second-level interrupt handler to actually process the request behind the interrupt.

Floating Point Unit (FPU)

SEE

FPU (Floating Point Unit)

Flooding

In a network, the uncontrolled propagation of discovery or other packets.

Flow Control

In communications, flow control refers to an action used to regulate the transfer of information between two locations. Flow control is helpful if the device at one location is

much faster than at the other. For example, flow-control may be necessary when a computer is communicating with a printer or modem.

Hardware flow-control methods use signals on the pins used for RTS (request to send) and CTS (clear to send); software methods send specific byte values (XON and XOFF) to control the transmission of data. In internetworks, flow control is handled by a router, which is a device that sends transmissions in the appropriate direction and also reroutes transmissions around troubled or congested locations.

FLP (Fast Link Pulse)

One of a series of identical signals sent at startup by a fast Ethernet device—that is, by a device (Ethernet adapter, bridge, or switch) capable of supporting a transmission rate of up to 100 Mbps.

SEE ALSO

Fast Ethernet

Flux Budget

In FDDI networks, the amount of light that can be lost between adjacent nodes without having the transmission become unintelligible.

FNC (Federal Networking Council)

A committee consisting of representatives from government agencies that are involved with networks that connect to the Internet.

a
b
c
d
e
f
g
h
i
j
k
l
m
n
o
p
q
r
s
t
u
v
w
x
y
z

Focal Point

In IBM's NMA (Network Management Architecture), *focal point* is a term for the node on which the network management software is running. This is generally a mainframe host in NMA.

Other nodes and devices communicate with the focal point either through entry points (in the case of SNA-compliant devices) or service points (in the case of non-IBM devices or networks).

BROADER CATEGORY
NMA (Network Management Architecture)

SEE ALSO
Entry Point; Service Point

Foil Shield

In some coaxial cable, a thin shield, usually made of aluminum bonded to both sides of a tape, that surrounds the dielectric and is, in turn, covered by a braid shield. Together, the foil and braid shields provide good protection against electrical interference.

SEE ALSO
Cable, Coaxial

FOIRL (Fiber-Optic Inter-Repeater Link)

An FOIRL (sometimes written as *FIRL*) is a link segment that uses fiber-optic cable to connect two repeaters in a standard Ethernet or an 802.3-based Ethernet network. An FOIRL cannot have any nodes. The standard connector for such a link is the SMA connector (IEC 874-2).

Footprint

In satellite communications, a footprint refers to the earth area covered by a radio signal from the satellite. In networking, the term is used to refer to the amount of RAM (random-access memory) an application uses during execution.

Foreground Process

A process or program that gets the highest priority for execution. Other processes or programs get attention when the foreground process does not need the processor at a particular instant. These lower-priority processes are said to run in the *background*.

Foreign Exchange (FX)

SEE
FX (Foreign Exchange)

Fork

In the Macintosh file system, a *fork* is either of two components for a file: the data fork, which contains the actual information in the file, or the resource fork, which contains application-specific data.

SEE ALSO
Macintosh

Forward Explicit Congestion Notification (FECN)

SEE

FECN (Forward Explicit Congestion Notification)

Forwarding

In a network bridge, router, or gateway, or in a packet-switching node, *forwarding* is the process of passing a packet or message on to an intermediate or final destination. This is in contrast to *filtering,* in which a packet is discarded. The basis for the filtering or forwarding can be addresses or protocols.

Ordinarily, a bridge or another forwarding device does the following:

- Reads and buffers the entire packet.

- Checks the address or protocol.

- Filters or forwards the packet, depending on the value found and on the filtering criteria.

In *on-the-fly forwarding,* a device begins forwarding the packet as soon as the device determines that this is the appropriate action. This means that the packet can be on its way to a new destination while still being read by the bridge.

For Your Information (FYI)

SEE

FYI (For Your Information)

Four-Wire Circuit

In telephone communications, a circuit made up of two pairs of conducting wires. One pair is used for transmitting and the other pair for receiving. This provides full-duplex (FDX) operation. A four-wire terminating circuit is a hybrid circuit in which four-wire circuits are connected to two-wire (one-pair) circuits.

FPODA (Fixed Priority-Oriented Demand Assignment)

In networking, an access protocol in which stations must reserve slots on the network. These slots are allocated according to the stations' priority levels.

FPS (Fast Packet Switching)

In certain packet-switching architectures, FPS is a switching strategy that achieves higher throughput by simplifying the switching process. Steps to accomplish this include the following:

- Leaving error-checking and acknowledgments to higher-level protocols

- Using fixed-size packets

- Using simplified addresses, where possible

- Switching packets as they come in, rather than buffering the entire packet before sending it on

Not all architectures use each of these techniques. FPS is used, for example, in frame- and cell-relay implementations. This strategy is feasible only when the

a b c d e f g h i j k l m n o p q r s t u v w x y z

communications lines are clean, so that all but a tiny fraction of transmissions are error-free.

FPU (Floating Point Unit)

A math coprocessor chip that specializes in doing floating-point arithmetic. Examples include the 80x87 family of processors from Intel, as well as third-party FPUs, such as those from Cyrix and AMD.

FQDN (Fully Qualified Domain Name)

In the naming system for the Internet, the complete name for a machine on the network. The FQDN includes both the machine's name (the hostname) and domain name(s). For example, if *sand* is a hostname and it is located at the University of Antarctica, the machine's FQDN might be sand.antarcticau.edu.

SEE ALSO
DNS (Domain Naming Service)

Fractional T1 (FT1)

SEE
FT1 (Fractional T1)

Fragment

A fragment is part of a packet, which may be created deliberately or by accident.

In the context of an Ethernet network, packet fragments may be created unintentionally by a collision between two packets transmitted at the same time. These fragments may circulate for a brief period, but will soon disappear. Until that happens, jam

packets are sent along the network to ensure that one of the nodes does not try to do something with the fragments.

In the context of the IP (Internet Protocol), a packet is deliberately broken into fragments if the packet is too large for service from the lower layer.

This process is known as *fragmentation* in the Internet environment. The same process is known as *segmentation,* and the packet parts are known as *segments,* in environments that conform to the OSI Reference Model.

When a packet is fragmented, the data portion is broken in parts. Each part is combined with the header and is passed down to the layer below for further processing, such as for encapsulation into the lower-layer packets.

The reverse process—removing redundant headers and recombining several fragments into the original packet—is known as *reassembly.*

Frame

In some network architectures, such as Token Ring, X.25, and SNA (Systems Network Architecture), frame is a term for a data packet, particularly for a packet at the data-link layer of the OSI Reference Model.

In connection with non-multiplexed communications, the terms *frame* and *packet* have come to be used interchangeably. *Packet* was originally the broader term, with *frame* being restricted to packets only at the data-link level of particular protocols.

In the frame-relay network architecture, a frame is a fixed-size packet. See the Frame

Relay article for more information about these frames.

The term "frame" is also used to refer to one or more bits that occur in a predefined location in a time interval and that are used for control and synchronization purposes.

In transmissions that use TDM (time division multiplexing), a frame is a sequence of time slots, each of which contains a chunk from one of the channels being multiplexed. For example, in a DS1 signal, a frame contains 24 such chunks: one from each of the 64 kbps channels being multiplexed. Several such frames may, in turn, be grouped into larger frames, called *superframes,* as in the ESF (extended superframe) grouping strategy.

SEE ALSO

Packet

▼

Frame Check Sequence (FCS)

SEE

FCS (Frame Check Sequence)

▼

Frame Reject Response (FRMR)

SEE

FRMR (Frame Reject Response)

▼

Frame Relay

Frame relay is one of several contenders for a wide-area networking standard. Other contenders include ATM, BISDN, and cell relay. Frame relay was originally intended as a bearer service for ISDN (Integrated Services Digital Network). It is suitable for transmitting data only, not for transmitting voice or video, because these require constant transmission capabilities.

An Overview of Frame Relay

Frame relay provides fast packet-switching by leaving various checking and monitoring to higher-level protocols. Frame relay has a high throughput and low delays. It also is efficient, making maximum use of available bandwidth. Frame relay can have a bandwidth as high as 2 megabits per second (Mbps). In contrast, X.25, which also uses packet-switching, is much slower, because the X.25 protocol will ask for data to be retransmitted if packets are lost or garbled.

The standard is packet-oriented and well-suited to "bursty" data, which is data with very high traffic volume at some times, almost no traffic at others. In contrast, circuit-switched networks are inefficient with bursty data, because assigned circuits cannot be used for other transmissions when both parties on the circuit are idle.

Frame relay discards any packets that cannot be delivered either because their destination cannot be found or because there are too many packets coming in at once. Discarding packets is frame relay's way of telling its users that they are overdoing it. Discarding is a viable error-handling strategy, because transport-layer protocols (such as SPX, NetBIOS, and TCP) have their own error-detection mechanisms. Frame relay relies on higher-level protocols to do error correction and to request retransmissions if packets are lost or discarded. This means that frame relay should be used over "clean" lines, so that there are not too many errors for the higher-level protocols to discover.

a
b
c
d
e
f
g
h
i
j
k
l
m
n
o
p
q
r
s
t
u
v
w
x
y
z

The standard can notify sources and/or destinations if there is heavy traffic (congestion) on the network. Notified nodes are expected (but not required) to adjust their transmissions in order to reduce the congestion.

Because it operates at the physical layer and the lower part of the data-link layer of the OSI Reference Model, frame relay is protocol-independent, and it can transmit packets from TCP/IP, IPX/SPX, SNA, or other protocol families.

The figure "Context and properties of frame-relay networks" summarizes the characteristics of this standard.

Frame Relay Operation

Frame relay uses statistical multiplexing to move frames across the network. Actually, for the user, frame relay provides access to the network by getting whatever packets it can onto the network.

Frame-Relay Packets

As illustrated in the figure "A frame-relay packet," packets are variable-length, and the header can be as small as 2 bytes. Bit values in the header and flag fields are used for control and signaling.

CONTEXT AND PROPERTIES OF FRAME-RELAY NETWORKS

Context

WAN/Telecommunications Standards
   Circuit Switching
    Packet Switching
      Fixed-size Packets
        ATM
      Variable-size Packets
       Frame Relay ⎯⎯
Message Switching

Frame Relay Properties

Uses digital telephone lines for wide-area transmissions

Fast, with high throughput and low delays

Efficient (makes use of any available bandwidth)

Transmission rates up to 2 Mbps

Packet-oriented and well-suited to "bursty" data

Suitable only for data, not for voice or video

Suitable for use over clean lines

Discards any packets it cannot route or deliver

Operates at physical and lower data-link layers

Protocol-independent (can transmit any higher-layer protocol)

Leaves error correction and retransmissions to higher-layer protocols

Routing is over virtual circuits

Can report network congestion to source and/or destination nodes

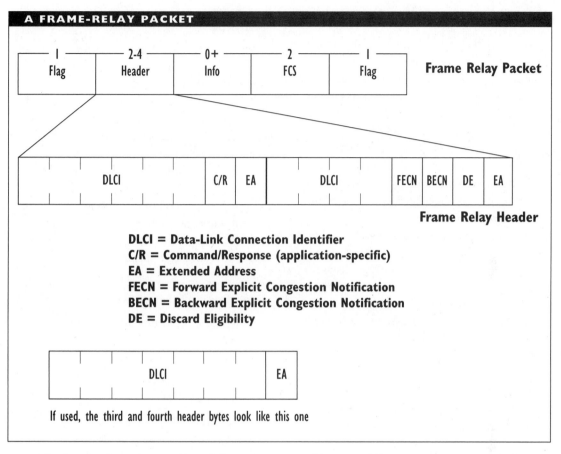

A FRAME-RELAY PACKET

1	2–4	0+	2	1
Flag	Header	Info	FCS	Flag

Frame Relay Packet

DLCI	C/R	EA	DLCI	FECN	BECN	DE	EA

Frame Relay Header

DLCI = Data-Link Connection Identifier
C/R = Command/Response (application-specific)
EA = Extended Address
FECN = Forward Explicit Congestion Notification
BECN = Backward Explicit Congestion Notification
DE = Discard Eligibility

DLCI	EA

If used, the third and fourth header bytes look like this one

The header for a frame-relay packet includes a 10-bit DLCI (data link connection identifier) value, which is split over 2 bytes. This value represents the port to which the destination network is connected. When a packet reaches a node, the node sends it on to the appropriate port or else discards the packet. The routing algorithm used to determine paths can be a major factor in the network's performance.

The header also includes 2 bits for explicit congestion notification (ECN), which is to inform nodes in either direction of heavy traffic. (See the ECN article for information about how these bits are used.)

One bit is used to indicate whether the packet can be discarded, if necessary. The EA (extended address) bits are available if more header bytes might be needed, which may be the case if a network is so large that 1,024 DLCI values will not suffice. (Actually, fewer than 1,024 DLCI values are available; DLCI 1,023 is reserved for passing information about the virtual circuits that have been established, and other DLCI values are reserved for internal use.)

a
b
c
d
e
f
g
h
i
j
k
l
m
n
o
p
q
r
s
t
u
v
w
x
y
z

Deciding If Packets Can Be Discarded

One way the network decides whether a packet can be discarded is by considering the network activity of the packet's source. Each node on a frame-relay network has a committed information rate (CIR) associated with it. This rate represents the user's estimate of the node's average bandwidth requirements.

When network traffic starts approaching the congested stage, each user's traffic is compared against the CIR for that user. If the node is below the node's CIR, packets from that node get through. When a node is slightly above its CIR, the network will try to deliver the node's packets if possible, but will discard them if necessary. If the node's activity is above its CIR by some predefined amount, the node's packets are automatically discarded.

Sender and receiver can exchange limited status information, provided that the two nodes both adhere to LMI (Local Management Interface) specifications. (Actually, the communication will be between the router and the network, standing in for the source and destination, respectively.)

PRIMARY SOURCES

CCITT publications I.233, I.370, Q.922 and Q.92; ANSI documents T1.606, T1.617, and T1.618. The ANSI and CCITT documents are very similar, showing good agreement on the part of the standards committees.

BROADER CATEGORY

Packet-Switching

Framing

In asynchronous communications, framing is the process of inserting start and stop signals before and after data being transmitted. These framing elements delimit the data by serving as borders for the data. They allow the receiver to determine the sender's timing, because the duration of the start bit indicates the bit interval size being used by the sender.

A *framing error* occurs in asynchronous communication when the receiver incorrectly identifies the start and stop signals, or the framing, in a transmission.

Free Space Attenuation

In wireless communications, the amount of signal loss between the transmitting and the receiving stations.

Frequency

For periodic phenomena, such as sound or light waves, a measure of the number of times a cycle repeats within a given interval (such as a second). The cycle frequency is expressed in hertz (Hz). One hertz equals one cycle per second.

Frequency-Agile Modem

In a broadband system, a frequency-agile modem can switch frequencies in order to allow communications over different channels (different frequency bands) at different times.

Frequency Band

A range of frequencies within which a transmission occurs. For example, the frequency band for ordinary telephone signals is between about 300 and 4,000 hertz.

Frequency Converter

A device that can be used to convert between the sender's and the receiver's frequency ranges in a broadband system. For example, in a broadband network (or in a cable TV system), the headend (main transmitter) may need to convert the incoming signals before sending them on to network nodes (or cable subscribers).

Frequency Delay

In signaling, a delay that may be caused by the fact that signals of different frequencies travel at slightly different speeds through a given medium and, therefore, reach the destination at slightly different times. This delay can result in signal distortion. Various devices, such as an equalizer, can correct the problem.

Frequency Translator

In a broadband cable system, an analog device that converts from one block of frequencies to another.

Frequency Division Multiplexing (FDM)

SEE

FDM (Frequency Division Multiplexing)

FRMR (Frame Reject Response)

In a connection using the SDLC (Synchronous Data Link Control) protocol, a signal from the receiving station indicating that an invalid frame or packet has been received.

Frogging

In broadband communications, inversion of the signal frequencies in order to equalize the distortion and loss across the transmission's bandwidth. The incoming channel with the highest frequency will go out as the lowest frequency band, the second highest in will be the second lowest out, and so on.

FS (Frame Status)

A field in a token ring data packet.

SEE ALSO

Token Ring

FSF (Free Software Foundation)

FSF is an organization, based in Cambridge, Massachuesetts, dedicated to creating high-quality software and making both the executable and source code freely available. The foundation is headed by Richard Stallman, who is a well-known consultant and guru in the UNIX community.

Perhaps the best-known product from the foundation is the GNU (for GNU's Not UNIX) operating environment. GNU includes dozens of work-alike versions of popular applications. For example, Oleo is the GNU spreadsheet program.

a b c d e f g h i j k l m n o p q r s t u v w x y z

FSP (File Service Process)

On a file server, a process that executes and responds to file-handling requests.

FT1 (Fractional T1)

In digital communications, a portion of a 1.544 megabit per second T1 carrier, or line. Fractional T1 lines are available from IXCs (interexchange carriers) and can have bandwidths of 384, 512, or 768 kilobits per second, corresponding roughly to a quarter, a third, and half of a full T1 carrier.

FTS (File Transfer Service)

FTS refers to any of a broad class of application-layer services for handling files and moving them from one location to another. The following are just some of the services that have been developed within the OSI framework:

CGM (Computer Graphics Metafile): A format for storing and exchanging graphics information. It is documented in ISO document 8632.

DFR (Document Filing and Retrieval): A proposed ISO standard for allowing multiple users to work with documents on a remote server. DFR is part of the DOAM (Distributed Office Applications Model).

DPA (Document Printing Application): Also part of the DOAM.

EDI (Electronic Data Interchange): Any of several proposals for exchanging data electronically, using predefined formats. Several special-purpose "EDI-fices" have been developed, including EDIME (EDI messaging environment), EDI-MS (EDI message store), and EDIFACT (EDI for administration, commerce, and transport). They are documented in ANSI document X.12.

ILL (Interlibrary Loan): A proposed standard to allow the loan of books and other documents among libraries all over the world. It is documented in ISO documents 10160 and 10161.

JTM (Job Transfer and Manipulation): A standard that specifies how jobs can be distributed for remote processing, and how reports and output can be sent wherever specified. It is documented in ISO documents 8831 and 8832.

MHS (Message Handling System): As defined in the CCITT's X.500 series of specifications.

ODA/ODIF (Open Document Architecture/Open Document Interchange Format): Standards for the structure of a document and for the document's format during transmission. These standards are documented in CCITT documents T.411 through T.418 and ISO 8613.

RDA (Remote Database Access): A standard for accessing data in remote databases.

RDT (Referenced Data Transfer): Part of DOAM.

TP (Transaction Processing): A standard that specifies how data from online transactions is to be distributed. It is documented in ISO document 10026.

VT (Virtual Terminal): Specifications for a "generic terminal," which can be emulated in software and used to access any host.

Full Duplex (FDX)

SEE

FDX (Full Duplex)

Function Management Layer

The topmost layer in IBM's SNA. An end-user deals directly with this layer which, in turn, deals with the data-flow control layer.

SEE

SNA (Systems Network Architecture)

FX (Foreign Exchange)

In telephone communications, a line or service that connects a user's (subscriber's) telephone to a central office (CO) other than the one that provides basic service for the subscriber's exchange.

FYI (For Your Information)

The name for a series of Internet documents intended to provide basic information about the Internet, its services, and about certain topics related to the Internet. While they are published as *RFC* (*Request For Comments*) documents, FYI papers differ from most RFCs in that the FYI papers are generally (but not always) less technical, and FYIs do not specify standards. Example FYI titles include:

- FYI 24 : "How to use Anonymous FTP" (1994, RFC 1635)

- FYI 23 : "Guide to Network Resource Tools" (1994, RFC 1580)

- FYI 18 : "Internet Users' Glossary" (1993, RFC 1392)

- FYI 10 : "There's Gold in them thar Networks! or Searching for Treasure in all the Wrong Places" (1993, RFC 1402; 1991, RFC 1290)

- FYI 1 : "F.Y.I. on F.Y.I. : Introduction to the F.Y.I. Notes" (1990, RFC 1150)

FYI 10 illustrates a common occurrence in the FYI and RFC literature. The more recent version makes the older one obsolete. Thus, RFC 1402 is the newer (and, hence, more correct) version of FYI 10.

a
b
c
d
e
f
g
h
i
j
k
l
m
n
o
p
q
r
s
t
u
v
w
x
y
z

G

An abbreviation for the prefix *giga,* as in GHz (gigahertz) or Gbps (gigabits per second). This order of magnitude corresponds to 2^{30}, which is roughly 10^9, or billions (in the United States counting system).

SEE ALSO

Orders of Magnitude

Gain

In electrical signaling, an increase in a signal's voltage, power, or current. This type of increase can occur only through amplification. Noise caused by a momentary increase in signal amplitude is called a *gain hit*.

Gatedaemon

In the Internet environment, a program that can be used for routing packets. Gatedaemon, or *gated* (pronounced "gate dee"), as it is called, supports multiple routing protocols, such as exterior gateway protocols, and protocol families.

SEE ALSO

Protocol; Routing

Gateway

In the context of local-area networks (LANs) and mainframe connections, a gateway is a hardware and/or software package that connects two different network environments. For example, a gateway can be used to connect a PC-based network and an IBM mainframe, or a Token Ring network and an AppleTalk network. The figure "Context and properties of gateways" summarizes the characteristics of this type of internetwork link.

CONTEXT AND PROPERTIES OF GATEWAYS

Context

Internetwork Links
- Bridge
- Gateway
- Router

Gateway Properties

Connects dissimilar networks, such as different architectures, LAN to mainframe or WAN, . . .

Some provide access to special services, such as e-mail or fax

Operates at upper layers of the OSI Reference Model

Takes transmission capabilities for granted in order to focus on content and format

Often does data translation or conversion

Needs a network interface card for each architecture supported

More generally, the term can refer to any device or software package that connects two different environments, regardless of whether networks are involved. As such, a gateway can also be considered a communications server or, in some cases, an access server.

In the Internet community, the term *gateway* has been used to refer to anything that connects networks. The connecting device is generally a router, and this term has replaced gateway in Internet contexts.

Gateways in Networks

A gateway provides a LAN with access to a different type of network, an internetwork, a mainframe computer, or a particular type of operating environment. A gateway serves to connect networks with very different architectures, for example, an Ethernet LAN and an SNA network, or a LAN and an X.25 packet-switching service. Gateways are also used to provide access to special services, such as e-mail (electronic mail), fax, and Telex.

Gateways can operate at several of the higher OSI Reference Model levels, most notably at the session, presentation, and application layers. Gateways usually operate above the communications subnet (which comprises the bottom three layers in the OSI Reference Model). This means that gateways take transmission capabilities for granted and concentrate on the content of the transmission.

In the course of doing their work, gateways may very likely change the representation of data before passing it on. For example, a gateway may convert from ASCII to EBCDIC on the way to an IBM mainframe, encrypting or decrypting data between the source and destination environments. Gateways also must do protocol conversion, since the different environments connected by a gateway will generally use different protocol families.

The multilayer operation of gateways is in contrast to repeaters, bridges, and routers, which each operate at a single level (the physical, data-link, and network layers, respectively), and which do not change the data in any way.

Essentially, a gateway, which is generally a dedicated computer, must be able to support both of the environments it connects. To each of the connected network environments, the gateway looks like a node in that environment. To provide this support, the gateway needs an interface card and at least some shell software for both of the environments being connected. In addition, the gateway runs special software to provide the necessary conversion and translation services and to communicate with the two environments. Practically speaking, a gateway needs a considerable amount of storage and RAM (random-access memory). The operation of a network gateway is illustrated in the figure "A gateway looks like a different environment to each of the networks it connects."

a
b
c
d
e
f
g
h
i
j
k
l
m
n
o
p
q
r
s
t
u
v
w
x
y
z

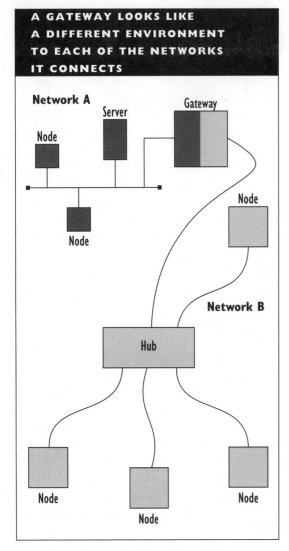

A GATEWAY LOOKS LIKE A DIFFERENT ENVIRONMENT TO EACH OF THE NETWORKS IT CONNECTS

Some gateways are unidirectional, which means that they handle traffic in one direction only. In such cases, you may need to install two separate gateways for bidirectional communication.

Gateway Operation

The behavior of a gateway depends on the type of connection being established. For example, when connecting a PC to an IBM mainframe, the gateway may also provide terminal-emulation capabilities, in addition to translating between EBCDIC and ASCII character codes. Terminal-emulation capabilities make it unnecessary to install a terminal-emulation card in each node that wants to access the mainframe. In this type of connection, the mainframe will think it is talking to a controller that is channeling sessions from multiple terminals, and the workstation will behave and look like a terminal.

A gateway for message-handling services needs to be able to package and represent messages in whatever form is necessary for the destination. In particular, the gateway needs to be able to access remote networks through public or private data-transmission services (for example, X.25).

In general, a gateway may provide a variety of services, including the following:

- Packet format and/or size conversion
- Protocol conversion
- Data translation
- Multiplexing

Gateways as Bottlenecks

Gateways are often bottlenecks in network communications. For example, a gateway that connects remote locations may need to use a synchronous protocol (such as SDLC), which operates at a relatively slow 19,200 bits per second (bps). Even if gateways use faster transmission protocols, they may slow down a network because of all the data translation and other tasks (such as terminal emulation) they must perform.

Depending on the environments being connected, it may be possible to get around certain speed limitations, almost always at the expense of a few (or a few dozen) "kilobucks."

Gateway Categories

Gateways can be grouped in various ways. A common general grouping scheme uses the attributes on which the gateway services operate:

- An *address gateway* connects networks that have different directory spaces but that use the same protocols. This type of gateway is common, for example, when dealing with a Message Handling Service (MHS).

- A *protocol gateway* connects networks that use different protocols. The gateway does the protocol translations.

- A *format gateway* connects networks that use different representation schemes (for example, ASCII versus EBCDIC). The gateway maps between the two formats.

Special-purpose gateways that provide access to specific services are becoming more widely used. As with servers, the terminology regarding gateways is quite variable and is extensible. Gateways are sometimes named after the devices to which they connect. You may also see some kinds of gateways, particularly those involving mainframes, marketed as access servers.

The following list contains just a sample of the types of gateways that have been developed. These types are not mutually exclusive.

X.25: Provides access to X.25 packet-switching services for remote communications. This type of gateway may be used by a wide-area network (WAN) or an enterprise network.

Fax: Provides access to fax machines at remote locations. The gateway will convert messages to fax format.

E-mail: Provides services (such as e-mail connections) between LANs. E-mail gateways often connect network-operating-system-specific MHSs to an X.400 mail service.

Internet: Provides access to the Internet backbone network. An Internet gateway is used by an intermediate-level network or by an outernet (a network that is not part of the Internet).

SAA: Provides access to machines using IBM's SAA (Systems Applications Architecture) environment.

SNA: Provides access to machines using IBM's SNA (Systems Network Architecture) environment, which is the architecture for the entire IBM mainframe line.

Mainframe: Connects a LAN to a network of one or more mainframes. These gateways require a PC, a (3270) emulation board, and the appropriate gateway software. By dedicating a single machine as a gateway, you can

WHAT TO LOOK FOR IN A GATEWAY

Because of the overwhelming number of combinations that might be connected by gateways, it's important to make sure you get a gateway that's suitable for your environment and needs. The following list contains just some of the things you need to determine when selecting a gateway.

- What specific networking environment(s) does the gateway support? What restrictions, if any, are there on this support?

- What protocols does the gateway support? This will be determined, in part, by the networking environments supported.

- If it's a special-purpose gateway, what particular implementations of the service does the gateway support? For example, which e-mail packages does an e-mail gateway support? Be aware that a gateway may support some packages for certain networking environments and other packages for other environments.

- If the gateway will provide access or communications capabilities, what interfaces are supported?

- What are the hardware requirements for the gateway? For example, does the gateway require a card for each end? Does the gateway require a stand-alone machine? If so, what capabilities does the machine need?

- Is the gateway bidirectional?

- Do nodes attached to the gateway need to run special software (for example, emulation packages) or does the gateway take care of that?

- How many nodes (or terminals or sessions) can the gateway support at a time?

- What's the gateway's throughput?

- What management capabilities does the gateway provide/support?

save the cost of outfitting all nodes with terminal-emulation cards and capabilities. An SNA gateway is a mainframe gateway.

BROADER CATEGORY
Internetwork Link

SEE ALSO
Bridge; Brouter; Router; Switch

▼
Gauge

A measure of electrical wire diameter. Under the American Wire Gauge (AWA) standards, higher gauge numbers indicate a thinner cable. See the AWG article for a table of some sample gauge values.

Gaussian Noise

In electrical signaling, noise resulting from the vibration of atoms or molecules. This noise occurs over all frequencies, and it increases with temperature.

GDMO (Guidelines for the Definition of Managed Objects)

An ISO specification that provides notation for describing managed objects and actions involving such objects.

GDS (Generalized Data Stream)

The format for mapped data in the APPC (Advanced Program-to-Program Communications) extension of IBM's SNA (Systems Network Architecture). Data from high-level applications is converted to GDS format before transmission. This helps protect from format differences, such as when one application uses the ASCII character format and the other uses EBCDIC.

Geosynchronous Orbit

An orbit around the earth, such as the orbit of a communications satellite. A satellite in geosynchronous orbit is known as a geosynchronous or *geostationary satellite*. The orbit is "synchronous" because the satellite makes a revolution in about 24 hours. The satellites are about 36,000 kilometers (22,350 miles) above the earth, and they appear to be stationary over a location.

GFC (Generic Flow Control)

In the ATM networking model, a protocol that is used to make sure all nodes get access to the transmission medium. This service is provided at the ATM layer in the model.

GFI (General Format Identifier)

In an X.25 packet, a field that indicates packet formats and several other features.

Glare

In certain bidirectional telephone circuits, such as private branch exchange (PBX) lines, a condition in which an incoming and outgoing call "meet," possibly causing crossed connections. One way to avoid this problem is to use a *ground start* signaling technique.

Global Group

In Windows NT Advanced Server, a global group is one whose users have access to servers and workstations in the users' own domains and also in other domains (provided that the other domains allow access from the user's group or domain).

Global Name

In a network or an internetwork, a name known to all nodes and servers. This is in contrast to a local name (a name associated with a particular server). A global name is fully qualified; that is, it includes all the intermediate levels of membership associated with the name.

a b c d e f **g** h i j k l m n o p q r s t u v w x y z

SEE ALSO

Global Naming Service

Global Naming Service

A global naming service provides mechanisms for naming resources that may be attached to any of several file servers in a network. First developed in the StreetTalk service in Banyan's VINES software, these capabilities have been added to other network operating systems, such as version 4.0 of Novell's NetWare.

Names in a global naming service have a predefined format, which reflects the different levels of operations in the network. For example, StreetTalk names have the format:

Item@Group@Organization

Global naming services are in contrast to local naming services, such as those provided by the bindery in NetWare versions 3.*x* and earlier.

Global Tree

Global tree is an unofficial term for a tree that uses Abstract Syntax Notation One (ASN.1) to represent objects related to networking, particularly to network management. The root of this tree is unnamed, and the tree's main subtrees are administered, respectively, by the CCITT, the ISO, and by a joint ISO-CCITT committee.

Most management and much Internet-related information is found in the iso(1) (sub)tree. Subtrees under iso(1) are administered by various groups and organizations. These organizations may, in turn, grant a subtree under theirs to other groups. For example, under its subtree, the ISO set up a

branch for different organizations. For reasons that will be explained, this subtree is named *org(3)*. The figure "Partial view of the global ASN.1 tree" shows some branches on this tree.

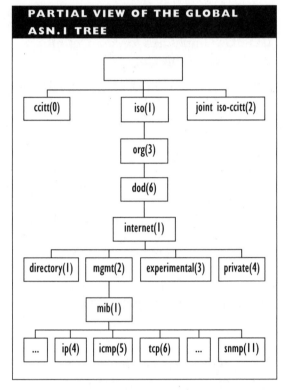

PARTIAL VIEW OF THE GLOBAL ASN.1 TREE

The global tree has appeared under various names, including the following:

- *MIB tree,* because the tree includes entries for a management information base (MIB)

- *ASN.1 tree,* because the tree's information is represented using the Abstract ASN.1 notation

- *SMI tree,* for structure of management information tree

Notation

Each node in the tree has a name and a number associated with it. Each of these values identifies an object (very loosely and broadly defined) for the tree. The numbers correspond, with some exceptions and restrictions, to the sequence in which subtrees were assigned.

Two ways of referencing elements in the tree are commonly used: global notation and local notation.

Global notation uses just the numbers associated with each node, with the values for the individual nodes on the path separated by decimal points. In this notation, the full name for the internet(1) node would be 1.3.6.1; the last 1 is the one for internet.

Local notation lists just the new node's parent and the new node's number. (The parent of node A is the node immediately above node A.) In this notation, internet(1) is named {dod 1}, because, as illustrated in the figure "Partial view of the global ASN.1 tree," dod is just above internet. The *dod* part represents internet subtree's parent, and the 1 indicates that *internet* is the subtree with index 1 under *dod*. This notation assumes that the application reading it will be able to determine the full name for *dod*.

Levels of Detail

At the higher levels of the tree, the nodes are quite "large" (international and national organizations or agencies). Further down in the tree, the topics are more specific. The global tree covers a huge range of detail, from international standards organizations at the highest level to the value for the setting on a particular model of network interface card.

Networking-related protocols and objects will have their own nodes somewhere in the tree. Each of these objects will have a unique path to it. For example, information relating to the TCP protocol begins at *tcp(6)*, which is found at location 1.3.6.1.2.1.2.1.6 in the tree; information about the IP protocol begins at 1.3.6.1.2.1.2.1.4 in the tree.

As part of the descriptions for these protocols, the subtrees will include nodes for particular functions and entities for the protocol. These can, in turn, be refined. By the time you get to the bottom of a subtree, the trail will have accumulated all there is to tell (as far as the network is concerned) about the object at that node.

In order to avoid conflicts, specific locations in the tree are reserved and allocated for particular purposes. The *internet(1)* subtree includes *experimental(3)* and *private(4)* subtrees. Within *private(4)*, for example, specific companies can be provided with "space" to define their extensions or variations for elements described elsewhere in the tree.

As standards are revised or updated, portions of the tree will change. For example, the *mib-2(1)* subtree under *mgmt(2)* replaced the *mib(1)* subtree when the revised management information base, MIB-II, was defined.

BROADER CATEGORIES
MIB (Management Information Base); Network Management

SEE ALSO
Internet

GMT (Greenwich Mean Time)

The time at the Greenwich observatory. This is generally used as the reference time when a standardized value is needed. This official name has been changed to UTC (a permuted acronym for Universal Coordinated Time).

Gopher

On the Internet, a gopher is a popular distributed service that can organize, retrieve, and provide access to hierarchically related information. The information can be in various forms: library catalogs, databases, newsgroups, and so on. Gopher servers are available at various locations throughout the Internet and are accessible through TELNET or through a gopher client.

A gopher client can make use of any accessible gopher servers. The details of a gopher session depend on which gopher server you use to access the Internet and on the information that you request.

In a gopher session, you can access the requested information through a single, dynamic menu system, regardless of where on the Internet the information is actually located. This is because a gopher, in essence, organizes and presents all the information within a single "gopherspace."

For retrieval, a gopher (which comes from the expression "go fer") server must know a file's type in order to determine how to handle the file when passing it on to the client. For example, plain text or HTML (Hypertext markup language) files are passed as stored, unless the file has been compressed. In that case, the server will decompress the file before passing it to the client.

To make gopher easier and more efficient to use, two tools are often used:

- *Veronica* makes it easier to search for an item. Veronica will search all accessible gopher servers, check all their menus, and return information about those items that satisfy the specified search criteria. Veronica servers can search on substrings and can even handle Boolean (AND, OR, NOT) operators in the search strings. (The name comes from the *Archie* comic strip, which features a character named Veronica. The name is in recognition of the fact that Veronica does for gopher servers what the archie service does for FTP sites—namely, collect and search a summary of their contents.)

- *Jughead* makes it possible to limit searches to a specified set of gopher servers. (This time the name is in honor of Archie's other friend in the comic strip.)

In addition, gopher clients allow you to create *bookmarks* to mark a menu or directory. Once a bookmark has been created, you can jump immediately to the menu or directory at the bookmark. This saves the time of moving manually through a hierarchy of gopher menus. Using a variant of the bookmark, you can record a gopher search so you can repeat the search regularly, if desired.

SEE ALSO
Internet; WAIS

GoS (Grade of Service)

In telephony, a general measure of performance with respect to a particular variable. Most commonly, GoS refers to the probability that a call will get a busy signal or a long delay before connection. For example, if 1 call in 500 gets a busy signal, the GoS probability would be 0.002.

GOSIP (Government OSI Profile)

The OSI Reference Model as defined by the United States government. Compliance with this standard is required for many types of purchases for government installations, particularly for those purchases having to do with networking.

GPIB (General-Purpose Interface Bus)

A parallel interface that is very popular for connecting scientific apparatus to computers. This interface was developed at Hewlett-Packard (HP) for in-house use and is sometimes still known as the *HPIB*. GPIB has been standardized by the IEEE as IEEE-488.

Grace Login

A login in which the user logs in with an expired password. In many networks, passwords are valid only for a limited time. After that time has elapsed, a user must change his or her password. Most networks allow a limited number of grace logins before the user must change the password.

Graded-Index Fiber

In fiber optics, cable in which the cladding, or cover, around the fiber core consists of multiple layers, each with a slightly different index of refraction. This provides a cleaner signal than single-step fiber.

SEE ALSO
Cable, Fiber-Optic

Graphical User Interface (GUI)

SEE
GUI (Graphical User Interface)

Ground

An electrical reference voltage for other voltages in a system. Any network must be grounded, as must network segments. In a circuit, a ground is a common return path for electric current. A ground and polarity checker is a tool for testing the grounding and polarity (direction of flow) of a circuit.

Ground Start

In telephone communications, a signaling technique in which a party gets a dial tone by grounding the circuit in a private branch exchange (PBX). This grounding helps to prevent a collision between incoming and outgoing calls, which is a condition known as *glare*. Pay telephones and phones in a PBX often use ground start.

Ground Wave

In wireless communications, a low-frequency radio signal that travels over the earth's surface.

Group, Network

In networking, a group is an organizational concept that can help make network administration easier. A group contains multiple members, all of whom share resources, files, or data. The network administrator can assign rights to an entire group, making these rights available to every member of that group.

Most network operating systems support the creation and use of groups, but these systems differ in the number of groups allowed and in the ease with which a group can be created, modified, or retrieved.

In Novell's NetWare versions 2.*x* and 3.*x,* the special group EVERYONE contains all users.

Group, Telecommunications

In telecommunications, a communications channel formed by combining twelve 4-kilohertz (kHz) voice channels, each using a different carrier frequency. This 48-kHz "superchannel" is transmitted in broadband fashion, with all channels transmitted simultaneously, using frequency division multiplexing (FDM). A group in the telecommunications context is also known as a *group channel.* The frequency spectrum used by a group is known as a *group signal.*

Group Object

In Novell's NetWare 4.0 Directory tree, a type of *leaf object* that has several user objects associated with it. Group objects allow administrators to grant several users rights at the same time, in the same way rights can be granted to network groups.

Groupware

Groupware is a client-server based software genre that shares features with several other types of applications but generally puts its own unique slant on these features.

Like a database, groupware allows multiple individuals to share a common pool of information. Unlike a database, however, each group member can view and handle the information in a manner tailored to that group member's needs.

In fact, groupware can be designed to enforce domain-specific views of the information. That is, particular group members may have limited views of the material. For example, personnel or customer information in a corporate database may be available to people in several departments, but each department may get a different view of the data. Thus, a technical support person may need to know a customer's configuration and software purchases, but that person doesn't need access to information about the customer's credit, occupation, or demographics.

Groupware also shares features with integrated software (for example, Lotus Smart-Suite, Microsoft Office, or Novell's Office Professional) in that various types of tools are available within an integrated environment. Unlike such suites, however, groupware is designed for use by multiple individuals who need to exchange information and to update it in a synchronized manner. In contrast, a software suite is designed to provide a single individual with a variety of tools in an integrated, easy-to-switch environment. It's irrelevant whether the individual uses the different tools on a single body of material or on independent content. For example, the user of a software suite may decide to use a spreadsheet for sales data, presentation software for dealing with product information, and a document processor to create ad copy.

Like workflow software, groupware allows users to develop material and then pass it off to other project members. Unlike workflow software, however, groupware need not be restricted to time- or sequence-dependent exchanges.

Like document management software, groupware uses a document (rather than a database record) as its standard element. Document management packages are designed to provide archiving capabilities and to allow multiple users access to the documents. Such packages are generally designed to allow document users to communicate indirectly—through the document, so to speak. In contrast, groupware is designed to allow users to communicate directly with each other—either about or with documents. To make this possible, a groupware product will include some type of electronic mail service.

In addition to its application-based features, groupware also includes development tools. These are essential because the software's capabilities must be tailored to a group's particular needs. To make this possible, it is often necessary to create services that can handle the group's documents in the appropriate manner.

Lotus Notes is arguably the best-known example of groupware.

SEE ALSO

Integrated Software Suite; Lotus Notes; Workflow Software

GSTN (General Switch Telephone Network)

A public telephone network.

Guaranteed Bandwidth

In networking or telecommunications, the capability for transmitting continuously and reliably at a specified transmission speed. The guarantee makes it possible to send time-dependent data (such as voice, video, or multimedia) over the line.

Guard Band

In telecommunications and electrical transmissions, a guard band (sometimes written *guardband*) is a thin frequency band used to separate bands (channels) above and below the guard band. By providing a gap between the two channels, the guard band helps prevent interference and signal leakage.

In cellular communications, a guard band is a 3 megahertz (MHz) band that separates two voice channels in order to keep the channels from interfering with each other.

a
b
c
d
e
f
g
h
i
j
k
l
m
n
o
p
q
r
s
t
u
v
w
x
y
z

In the never-ending quest to transmit more and more quickly, some vendors have developed products that transmit data along these guard bands.

Guard Time

In time division multiplexed (TDM) signaling, a brief interval of "silence" between transmissions. This period can be used for synchronization and compensating for signal distortion. This is the temporal analog to a *guard band*.

Guest

In many networks, Guest is a special account or user name. This account is for the use of anyone who needs to log in to the network for public information. The access must be temporary, and the account is afforded only restricted access rights.

GUI (Graphical User Interface)

A graphically based interface, such as Microsoft Windows, Motif, or Macintosh. In GUIs (pronounced "gooeys"), information and commands are presented through icons, and the user gives commands by pointing to or manipulating the icons. GUIs are in contrast to character-based interfaces, such as the default interfaces for DOS or UNIX.

Guided Media

Transmission media that constrain the electromagnetic, acoustic, or optical signal because of physical properties of the medium. For example, in fiber-optic transmissions, the cladding reflects the signal back into the core. Similarly, coaxial or twisted-pair cable constrains the electrical signal, and telephone lines constrain an acoustic signal.

Guidelines for the Definition of Managed Objects (GDMO)

SEE

GDMO (Guidelines for the Definition of Managed Objects)

Hacker

An avid computer user who enjoys exploring and testing the limits of computers, and who enjoys "hacking together" solutions to programming or other computing problems. Hackers often extend their zealous explorative tendencies to others' computers—breaking into networks, corporate or university computers, etc. Generally, however, these explorations don't have any malicious or destructive goals.

In contrast, the term *cracker* is used to describe users who do have destructive plans when they break into other computer systems. Unfortunately, in general parlance, hacker has come to be used for both of these sometimes intrusive types.

HAL (Hardware Abstraction Layer)

In Windows NT and NT Advanced Server, the HAL mediates between the operating system kernel and specific hardware. By implementing functions for interfaces, caches, interrupts, and so on, the HAL can make every piece of hardware look the same to the higher layers. This helps make NT more transportable to other machines.

Half Bridge

In wide-area networks, either of a pair of bridges that are separated by a telecommunications link. Instead of connecting directly to another network, the half bridge is connected to another half bridge by telephone or other long-distance cable.

Half Duplex (HDX)

SEE

HDX (Half Duplex)

Half-Open Connection

A "wannabe" (an incomplete) connection, half of which is already established. The other half is still open (not connected). For example, a half-open connection exists after you finish dialing a telephone number but before the call starts ringing.

Half Router

Either of a pair of routers that are separated by a telecommunications link. The link is transparent to non-router stations, so that the two halves of the router together look like a single, full-function router.

Hamming Code

A true error-correcting code, which works by inserting extra bits at predefined locations in a transmission. Mathematically, the spacing and values of these bits makes it possible to determine if an error has occurred, where the error is, and how to correct it.

SEE ALSO

Error Detection and Correction

Handle

In an operating system, a pointer to a resource or a feature, such as a file or device. The supply of handles may be limited by the operating system or environment. For example, DOS allows up to 20 file handles by default.

In a networking context, handle refers to a user's name or nickname online. This may be a *username* or a name used to identify the user in online discussion or chat groups. The term *nick* is also used to refer to a discussion group member's name.

Hand-off

In cellular communications, hand-off refers to the transfer of a connection from one cell to another. Hand-off time is generally between 200 and 1,200 milliseconds (ms), which accounts for the delay you will sometimes hear when talking to someone on a cellular telephone.

Such a delay can cause problems for devices that require frequent reassurance that a connection still exists. For example, some modems will disconnect if a long delay occurs in a connection.

You will see this term written as both *hand-off* and *handoff*. Hats off to the language coiners, because so far they have kept their hands off making it two separate words.

Handshaking

Handshaking is an exchange of signaling information between two communications systems. Handshaking establishes how the two systems will transmit data.

Two broad classes of handshaking are distinguished:

- *Hardware handshaking* uses the request to send (RTS) and clear to send (CTS) pins to control transmissions.

- *Software handshaking* uses the XON and XOFF characters to signal when to stop and start the transmission.

Hard Disk

A hard disk is a magnetic storage device consisting of multiple spinning platters (disks), each with its own read/write heads. Hard disk drives have a much higher storage capacity (up to a gigabyte or more) than floppy disks. They also have a much faster access time and higher transfer rate than floppy disk drives. The access times of hard disks are as low as 5 to 20 milliseconds (ms); floppy disk access times are 200 msec or more.

Hard disks differ from each other (and from floppy disk drives) in the interfaces and formats (encoding techniques and rules) used.

Hard Disk Interfaces

Interfaces differ in the capacities and transfer speeds they support. The following are some widely used hard disk interfaces:

- ESDI (Enhanced Small Device Interface), which supports medium- to high-capacity drives with capacities of up to 2 gigabytes (GB). Transfer speeds of 1 to 3 megabytes per second (MBps) are typical.

- IDE (Integrated Drive Electronics), which combines controller and hard disk into a single integrated, and more intelligent unit. The disadvantage is that you cannot format such a drive yourself. This interface is often used on laptops, partly because it is an

a b c d e f g **h** i j k l m n o p q r s t u v w x y z

integrated drive. It can support capacities of up to .5 GB, but it is typically used for drives with capacities of a few hundred megabytes. Transfer rates can be as high as 2 MBps.

- EIDE (Enhanced Integrated Drive Electronics), which is a superset of the IDE interface. EIDE can handle 1 GB and larger hard disks. Support for this enhanced interface is provided by a controller chip on the motherboard. While the EIDE (and the IDE) specifications were developed originally for the ISA (Industry Standard Architecture) bus architecture, the interface is also used with other bus standards, such as PCI (Peripheral Component Interconnect). The EIDE interface's popularity was somewhat tarnished recently when a silent, data-corrupting bug was found if certain EIDE controllers were used in a particular way. This flaw affects certain PCI motherboards that contain a particular EIDE controller chip. It was reported in August 1995 in the comp.os.os2.bugs newsgroup.

- IPI (Intelligent Peripheral Interface), which supports transfer rates of up to 25 MBps and storage capacities of several gigabytes.

- SCSI (Small Computer System Interface), which provides a generic interface for other devices (scanners, CD-ROM drives, other hard disks, and so on) and can support very high-capacity drives. SCSI can support up to eight devices in a single expansion slot. Two major versions of this interface have appeared: SCSI-1 and SCSI-2. SCSI-1, the slower, less capable of the pair, supports drives of up to 2 GB and transfer rates as high as 5 MBps. An ordinary SCSI-2 interface supports transfer rates of up to 10 MBps. *Wide* SCSI, a 32-bit interface, can transfer up to 40 MBps. SCSI-2 can support drives with capacities of 3 GB or more.

- SMD (Storage Module Device), which is a medium speed (up to 4 MBps) interface. SMD is commonly used with minicomputers and mainframes. SMD supports drives of up to 2 GB.

Hard Disk Formats

Two encoding strategies provide the basic formats used on most hard drives: MFM and RLL. MFM (modified frequency modulation) encoding is used for low-capacity disks of 50 MB or less and for floppy disks.

RLL (run length limited) encoding can store twice as much in the same area as MFM, and can support very high-capacity drives. Because of this, RLL encoding is used with all the major hard disk interfaces.

Various flavors of RLL encoding can be defined. These differ in the fewest and most consecutive 0 values they can handle. For example, RLL 2,7 means a signal must receive at least two 0 values in succession but no more than seven. (MFM is actually a low-level version of RLL: RLL 1,3.)

▼
Hard Error

In a Token Ring network, a serious error that threatens the continued operation of the network. This is in contrast to a soft error, which will not bring down the network.

Hardware Abstraction Layer (HAL)

SEE

HAL (Hardware Abstraction Layer)

Hardware, Network

The hardware for a network includes the following types of components: nodes, topology, connection elements, and auxiliary components. This article presents an overview of the hardware items. See the article about the specific component for more details on that component.

Nodes

The computers in a network may be used for workstations, servers, or both. A network can include PCs, Macintoshes, minicomputers, and even mainframes. PCs need a network interface card (NIC) installed for networking capabilities. Macintoshes and Sun workstations come with networking capabilities built in, so that a special card is not required to use the native network architecture for these machines.

The NICs mediate between the computer and the network by doing the necessary processing and translation to enable users to send or receive commands and data on the network. NICs are designed to support particular network architectures, such as Ethernet, ARCnet, or Token Ring.

Connection Elements

Network connection elements include the following:

- Cable: Coaxial, twisted-pair, IBM type, or fiber-optic

- Wiring centers: Hubs, concentrators, or MAUs (multistation access units)

- Intranetwork links: Connectors, repeaters, transceivers, and so on

- Internetwork links: Bridges, routers, gateways, and so on

- Wireless components: Transceivers, antennas, cells, and so on

Cable provides a transmission medium as well as a physical link between the nodes on the network. Connectors and repeaters attach cable sections to each other; connectors and transceivers attach NICs to a cable and thereby to the network. Transceivers and baluns enable different types of cable to be connected to each other under certain conditions. Terminators absorb a transmission at the end of a network, thereby preventing the signal from traveling back in the other direction on the network. The types of intranetwork links allowed in a particular network will depend on the cable used and on the network topology.

Wiring centers serve as focal points for network elements, and may also influence the logical arrangement of nodes on the network.

Internetwork links may be bridges, routers, gateways, and so on. Such components serve to connect networks to other networks. The type of internetwork connector used depends on whether the two networks are of the same type; that is, it depends on the type and amount of translation that is needed.

The details of wireless components and the conditions under which they can be used depend on the type of wireless connection (infrared, microwave, or radio wave transmission).

Auxiliary Components

Auxiliary components can include peripheral devices, safety devices, and tools.

Peripherals include printers, fax machines, modems, tape drives, CD-ROM drives, and so on. Such devices will generally be attached to a server machine, which will control access to the devices by the nodes on the network.

Safety devices include UPSs and SPSs (uninterruptible and standby power supplies), surge protectors, and line conditioners.

Tools include line analyzers, crimping tools, and so on. These tools are not part of the network itself, but should be available if needed.

Topology

The arrangement of cable and nodes in the network, known as the network *topology*, is also considered part of the hardware.

The physical topology represents the physical layout of the network, and is distinguished from the logical topology, which determines how communication takes place on the network. The logical topology may be bus or ring; the physical topology

might be bus, ring, star, mesh, tree, and so on.

Harmonica

In cabling, a device than can convert a 25-pair cable into multiple 2-, 3-, or 4-pair cables.

Harmonica Block

In cabling, a wiring block that can be used to connect a limited number (up to a dozen) of RJ-11 plugs, each coming from different nodes, into a common wiring center.

Hashing

A process by which access to files or other information can be accelerated. This is accomplished through the use of an indexing function that decreases the number of elements that need to be searched. Hashing is commonly used for improving access to lists, such as dictionaries and directory lists.

HBA (Host Bus Adapter)

A special-purpose board designed to take over data storage and retrieval tasks, thereby saving the CPU (central processing unit) some work. A disk channel consists of an HBA and the hard disk(s) associated with it. Novell's Disk Coprocessor board is a SCSI HBA adapter.

H Channel

In an ISDN (Integrated Services Digital Network) system, an H channel is any of several "higher-rate" channels that can be used for

HARDWARE COMPATIBILITY

Check hardware compatibility very early in the network design and implementation process. The following are some tips on planning the hardware for your network:

- Several network vendors have certification programs through which particular hardware combinations are tested and certified as compatible with each other and with the vendor's networking software. If you have the opportunity to do so, ask the vendors specific questions regarding compatibility.

- If you have access to it, check the Support on Site for Networks CD-ROM (from Ziff-Davis) for information about the components and configuration you're planning or that you have.

- If a consultant or vendor is configuring your network for you, get a written guarantee that you will be provided with a working network. Note that this is not the same as a guarantee that you're getting a network that does what you need it to do.

When you're configuring a network, there are trade-offs with respect to the number of different vendors you deal with. Try to avoid buying all your equipment from a single source, because that makes you much too dependent on that source. If that source goes out of business, your own business could be threatened as the network components start breaking.

On the other hand, buying from too many different vendors is asking for compatibility and support problems. The greater the number of different components you have, the greater the likelihood that one or more of those components will have quirks that will cause difficulties when you least expect them. Keep in mind that support people tend to assume that the fault lies with a component other than theirs. Each vendor will try to get you to talk to the other vendors.

transmitting user data. An H channel can be leased as a single unit, and can then be subdivided into lower-bandwidth channels. These higher-speed channels are defined for situations where high bandwidth is required, such as when transmitting video or other graphics information.

The following H channels are defined:

H0: A 384 kilobit per second (kbps) channel, which is equivalent to six B, or bearer, channels, each of which has a 64 kbps capacity.

H10: A 1.472 megabit per second (Mbps) channel, which represents just the 23 B channels for a PRI (Primary Rate Interface) line. This H channel is used only in the United States.

H11: A 1.536 Mbps channel, which is equivalent to the PRI in the United States, Canada, and Japan. This 1.536 channel actually consists of 23 64 kbps B channels and one 64 kbps D channel. The D channel is generally being used for signaling.

H12: A 1.92 Mbps channel, which is equivalent to the 30 B channels in the European PRI.

SEE ALSO
B Channel; D Channel

HCSS (High-Capacity Storage System)

In Novell's NetWare 4.*x*, a storage system that includes optical disks as part of the file system. These provide slower, but much higher-capacity, storage for files. The HCSS oversees the use of these media, so that access to files on optical disks is transparent to the user.

The HCSS can move user data to and from the writable optical storage, as required. These processes are known as *data migration* (moving to) and *demigration* (moving from). Such migrations will be transparent to the user—even in directory listings.

Because the data migration and demigration processes are transparent, they must be able to start up automatically when required. Two criteria are used to determine when to migrate or demigrate data:

- *Capacity threshold,* which specifies the percentage of a hard disk that can be filled before the HCSS automatically moves some of the material to secondary storage

- *LRU,* or *least recently used* selection criterion, which specifies that the file(s) with the oldest "last used" date will be the first to be moved to secondary storage; the second oldest will be stored second, and so forth

HDX (Half Duplex)

A communication setup in which transmissions can go in either direction, but in only one direction at a time. With half-duplex operation, the entire bandwidth can be used for the transmission. In contrast, full-duplex operation must split the bandwidth between the two directions.

Head End

In a broadband network, the starting point for transmissions to end users. For example, cable network's broadcast station is a head end. End-user stations can generally transmit control and error information, but no data, to the head end. The term is also used to refer to the base, or root, node in a tree topology, or a node on either of the buses in a DQDB (Distributed Queue, Dual Bus) architecture.

Header

In a transmission packet, the header contains control and other information that precedes the data in the packet. Header fields include source and destination addresses, packet type information, various types of identifier information, and so on.

In addition to header and data portions, a packet may also have a trailer section *after* the data. The trailer generally includes error-detection fields, such as cyclic redundancy checks (CRCs).

In an e-mail (electronic mail) message, the header is the information that precedes the actual message. The message header includes information such as the sender's address, message subject, date, and time.

HEC (Header Error Control)

An 8-bit field in an ATM-cell header. Its value is calculated using the remaining 32 bits of the header in order to detect errors in the header. Because the HEC field is relatively large (compared with the cell size), this value can even be used to *correct* single-bit errors.

SEE ALSO

ATM (Asynchronous Transfer Mode)

Hertz (Hz)

A unit of frequency. Hertz is used, for example, to describe the periodic properties of acoustic, electrical, and optical signals. One hertz is equal to one cycle per second.

Heterogeneous Network

A network that is using multiple protocols at the network layer. In contrast, a homogeneous network uses a single protocol at the network layer.

Hexadecimal

Hexadecimal is a number system that uses 16, instead of the more common 10, as the base for place value holders. Each place value is 16 times the preceding place value. For example, 1, 16, and 256 represent the hexadecimal place values corresponding to the 1, 10, and 100 values in the decimal (base 10) system.

To supplement the ten digits (0 through 9), hexadecimal notation uses the letters *a* through *f* (in uppercase or lowercase) in order to represent the values 10 through 15,

respectively. Thus, the hexadecimal value B9 represents 185: $11 \times 16 + 9$.

Hexadecimal values are written with a leading *0x* (zero and *x*) or with a trailing *H*. For example, 0xb9 and B9H represent the same decimal value.

Each hexadecimal value takes four bits, so that a byte consists of two hexadecimal digits. The table "Binary, Decimal, and Hexadecimal Values" shows the decimal and hexadecimal values corresponding to the 16 possible 4-bit sequences, and to a few select byte values.

HFS (Hierarchical File System)

The file system for the Macintosh operating system.

HGopher

A Windows-based gopher client program. You can use *anonymous FTP* to download HGopher from the lister.cc.ic.ac.uk FTP site.

Hiccup

A transmission error in which data is dropped and must be retransmitted. Hiccups may be caused by momentary line or port interference, buffer overflow, power losses or surges, or by simple computer or program perversity.

BINARY, DECIMAL, AND HEXADECIMAL VALUES		
BIT SEQUENCE	HEXA-DECIMAL	DECIMAL
0000	0H	0
0001	1H	1
0010	2H	2
0011	3H	3
0100	4H	4
0101	5H	5
0110	6H	6
0111	7H	7
1000	8H	8
1001	9H	9
1010	aH	10
1011	bH	11
1100	cH	12
1101	dH	13
1110	eH	14
1111	fH	15
1111 0000	f0H	240
1111 0111	f7H	247
1111 1111	ffH	255

Hierarchical Name Structure

A naming strategy that relies on the hierarchical relationship between two entities. This strategy is used, for example, for files or network entities. In a network context, a node's name is based on the name of the parent node, which sits immediately above the node in a hierarchy. Compare this with a flat name structure.

Hierarchical Routing

In an internetwork, hierarchical routing is routing in which multiple levels of networks (or of routers) are distinguished.

For example, in the Internet, three routing levels may be used: backbone, midlevel, and stub. At the backbone level, routing among midlevel networks is supported; at the mid-level networks, routing between sites (stub networks) is supported. At a particular site, internal routing among the network's nodes is supported.

High-Capacity Storage System (HCSS)

SEE

HCSS (High-Capacity Storage System)

High Level Language Application Program Interface (HLLAPI)

SEE

HLLAPI (High Level Language Application Program Interface)

High-Speed Circuit

In telecommunications, circuits capable of faster transmission rates than are needed for voice communication. High-speed circuits generally support speeds of 20 kilobits per second or more.

High-Speed Serial Interface (HSSI)

SEE

HSSI (High-Speed Serial Interface)

High-Usage Trunk Group

In telecommunications, a cable group that is intended as the primary path between two switching stations. As the primary path, this trunk will get the majority of the traffic between the two stations.

Hit

A momentary change in the phase (timing) or amplitude (strength) of a signal. This produces signal distortion and can increase the error rate.

HLLAPI (High Level Language Application Program Interface)

In the IBM environment, a PC-based package used for creating interfaces between mainframes and PC applications. HLLAPI is designed for use with high-level programming languages, such as C, Pascal, and BASIC.

HMA (High Memory Area)

In extended memory (memory with addresses above 1 megabyte), the first 64 kilobyte block of allocatable memory. More specifically, the HMA is the memory between addresses 100000H and 10ffffH.

SEE ALSO

Memory

HMUX (Hybrid Multiplexer)

In the FDDI-II network architecture, a component at the media-access-control (MAC) layer. The HMUX multiplexes network data from the MAC layer and also isochronous (time-dependent) data, such as voice or video, from the isochronous MAC (IMAC) layer. The HMUX passes the multiplexed stream to the PHY (medium-independent physical) layer. See the figure "FDDI-I and FDDI-II Organization" in the FDDI entry.

Hogging

In network communications, hogging occurs when a transmitting node takes more than its share of the network's bandwidth for transmission. For example, in a slotted-ring network, hogging occurs when a node takes all available empty slots, leaving none for "upring" nodes.

Holding Time

In telecommunications, the amount of time for which a call keeps control of a communications channel.

Home Directory

In various multiuser environments, such as UNIX or Novell NetWare systems, a directory created specifically for a user, and intended as the user's root directory on the network. The user's login script generally includes an instruction that maps a drive designation to the home directory after the user logs on to the network.

a
b
c
d
e
f
g
h
i
j
k
l
m
n
o
p
q
r
s
t
u
v
w
x
y
z

Home Page

A home page is the starting point for a hypertext document on the World Wide Web (WWW). The links from a home page may lead to other documents at the same site or to documents that belong to other people or corporations, and that may be scattered around the world. These linked *Web pages* may themselves be home pages.

Each home page is associated with a *URL (Uniform Resource Locator),* which specifies the page's location. For example, the following URL gets you to the home page for information about the best Web services—as determined by user votes—in various categories.

http://wings.buffalo.edu
/contest/awards/index.html

A URL provides three essential items of information:

- The protocol required to request the page. In most cases, this will be HTTP (Hypertext Transfer Protocol), but other protocols (such as FTP) are possible.

- The machine on which the document is found. In most cases, this information will be specified with domain names. In rare instances, this information will consist of the Internet addresses (that is, of four decimal values in succession).

- The path information for the file under discussion. This includes the file's name at the end.

Home pages have many uses. Corporations or organizations may use a home page to provide information to customers or others interested in the company's products. Individuals may use home pages to provide easy access to their favorite documents.

Some example home pages are shown in the following list. Keep in mind, however, that home pages may disappear or move, and frequently do so. After a home page moves, a message may be displayed for a limited period of time. Some browsers can move immediately to the new location.

http://lycos.cs.cmu.edu This document is the starting point for Lycos, a search engine for finding documents on the World Wide Web. This page is updated regularly.

http://www.cis.upenn.edu/~lwl/mudinfo.html This document contains links to various types of information about MUDs (multi-user dimensions) and related game environments. This page is updated regularly.

http://www.cs.colorado.edu/home/mcbryan/WWWW.html This document provides the starting point for the WWWW, the World Wide Web Worm search engine. This page is updated regularly.

http://www.ucc.ie/info/net/acronyms/acro.html This home page gives you access to a regularly updated list of over 13,000 acronyms and abbreviations related to computing. The list is updated approximately weekly, and there is a provision for submitting new acronyms.

A home page makes up part of an HTML (Hypertext markup language) document, and can be stored as an ordinary ASCII file—albeit one containing HTML markup tags.

Home Run

In a wiring plan, a cable that runs from the wallplate to a distribution frame. This is generally two-, three-, or four-pair cable.

Homogeneous Network

A network that is using a single protocol at the network layer. In contrast, a hetero-geneous network uses multiple protocols at the network layer.

Hop Count

In message or packet routing, a *hop* is a transmission between two machines, which may be nodes or routers, depending on the size of the network or internetwork across which transmissions must go.

In network routing, the number of nodes or routers through which a packet must (or may) pass in going from the source to the destination is called the *hop count*. Some protocols or services will keep track of the number of hops for a packet and will discard the packet and display an error mes-sage if the hop count exceeds a predefined value. For example, a hop count of 20 for an IP (Internet Protocol) packet means that a packet must reach its destination before it is passed through 20 routers.

In calculating the cost of a route, the number of nodes or routers the packet *must* pass through is used. In determining a

packet-lifetime value, the number the packet *may* pass through is used.

Host

In the mainframe and minicomputer envi-ronments, a host or host computer is a machine that provides processing capabili-ties for attached terminals or nodes. Often, a front-end processor (FEP) or a controller (or host controller) mediates between the host and the terminals. PCs accessing such a host generally must run a terminal-emulation program in order to pretend they are terminals.

In the PC environment, the host is the computer to which a device is connected. For example, a PC can be the host for a network interface card (NIC), or a printer, or both.

On the Internet, a host is a machine through which users can communicate with other machines. For example, a minicom-puter at a university may serve as a host for access to the Internet.

Host Bus Adapter (HBA)

SEE

HBA (Host Bus Adapter)

Hostname

In the Internet environment, the name for a machine, such as *thelma* or *henry*. The host-name is part of the more complete fully qualified domain name (FQDN).

a b c d e f g **h** i j k l m n o p q r s t u v w x y z

Host-to-Terminal

In communications and networking, a connection in which a central machine (the master) handles multiple terminals (the slaves).

Hot Fix

Hot Fix is a NetWare data-protection strategy in which data are redirected "on the fly" from defective to safe locations on a hard disk.

NetWare's Hot Fix capability verifies data by reading the newly written data and comparing it with the original data, which is stored in RAM until it is verified. If there is a discrepancy that can be attributed to defects in the media, the software writes the data in question to a specially allocated holding area and stores the address of the defective sector(s) in a table set aside for that purpose.

HotJava

HotJava is an extremely powerful browser (hypertext reader) program introduced recently by Sun Microsystems. In addition to being able to display graphics, sound, and text, HotJava can display animation and can even distribute and execute applets (simple programs).

HotJava is written in Java, which is a high-level, object-oriented language designed to be architecture-independent and usable in distributed environments. Applets written in Java can be run on any machines for which a Java interpreter and run-time system are available.

Current browsers—even those capable of handling multimedia materials—are written to understand a limited number of file formats and protocols. If new protocols or formats are introduced, the browser must be rewritten. In contrast, HotJava can dynamically link in the ability to handle new formats or protocols, provided Java applets for handling the new material are available on the server.

These applets will reside with the material so that the browser itself need not be changed. If a HotJava user requests a format or a protocol that HotJava doesn't understand, the browser simply asks the server for the support code, downloads it, and then downloads the requested material. This is all done in a manner that is completely transparent to the user.

Even more impressively, HotJava can literally download and "display" programs with which the user can interact and work. For example, with a HotJava browser, a science class could download an interactive program illustrating concepts being studied; a math or accounting class could download calculators or special computation programs—for example, to generate sample data on the fly.

Because of the way Java is designed, such applets are secure, so that users don't need to worry that a virus or other type of bug is being downloaded with it.

Because of its ability to dynamically link in content and protocols, HotJava seems an ideal way to deal with the ever changing set of tools and materials on the Internet. Commercial users are evaluating the few available HotJava implementations with interest, and Netscape has licensed Java in order to incorporate its capabilities into future versions of the Netscape browser software.

PRIMARY SOURCES
http://java.sun.com

BROADER CONCEPT
Browser

Hot Key

In general, a hot key is a keystroke or keystroke combination that causes a particular action or function to be executed, usually regardless of the current state of a program or process.

In PCs communicating with a mainframe, a hot key is a special keystroke or keystroke combination used to switch between using a PC as a terminal (connected to a mainframe) or a PC (as a stand-alone machine). Most terminal-emulation and communications packages provide this capability. The specific key sequence differs for different packages.

Hot Line Service

A private, point-to-point telephone connection. With such a connection, there is no need to dial; one telephone rings as soon as the other is picked up.

Hot Potato Algorithm

In networks, a routing algorithm in which a node routes a packet or message to the output line with the shortest queue.

Hot Standby

In microwave communications, a strategy in which two transmitters and two receivers are connected to an antenna. At a given time, only one of these is doing any work. If that transceiver unit malfunctions, the hot standby immediately replaces it and takes over the transmission and receiving duties.

HPFS (High Performance File System)

A file system developed for OS/2, versions 1.2 and later—including the newer OS/2 Warp. The HPFS was designed to overcome limitations of the DOS file system, including file name restrictions, inability to associate attributes with a file, and so on.

HPFS supports the following:

- File names of up to 255 characters

- Up to 64 kilobytes of extended attributes for each file

- Advanced caching methods for faster disk access

- Very high-capacity hard disks (up to 64 gigabytes)

- On-the-fly write-error recovery

DOS does not support the HPFS, but Windows NT does. HPFS cannot be used on a floppy disk.

HPPI (High-Performance Parallel Interface)

A very high-speed ANSI interface standard used to connect supercomputers to "mere mortal" devices such as routers or other computers. HPPI supports speeds of up to 1.6 Gbps over short distances.

a b c d e f g **h** i j k l m n o p q r s t u v w x y z

HSLAN (High-Speed Local-Area Network)

HSLAN is a term used to describe the generation of local-area network (LAN) architectures currently being developed with transmission speeds of 100 megabits per second (Mbps) or more. Most of the architectures proposed for HSLANs are designed for larger networks, such as metropolitan-area networks (MANs) or wide-area networks (WANs).

Architectures that show promise for HSLANs include the following:

- ATM (Asynchronous Transfer Mode), which is a broadband extension of the ISDN (Integrated Services Digital Network) architecture that has been poised for great things for many years now. ATM is most suitable for WANs.

- FDDI (Fiber Distributed Data Interface), which uses optical signals and media to achieve its high speeds. FDDI is already widely used for special-purpose networks, such as those connecting mainframes to controllers or connecting high-end workstations to each other.

- 100 Mbps Ethernets, which include proposed implementations from Hewlett-Packard (100BaseVA) and Grand Junction (100BaseX).

HSM (Hierarchical Storage Management)

A data storage strategy in which data are distributed across three levels of storage media:

- Primary, or online, storage refers to disks that are immediately accessible. Active material will be stored in online storage.

- Secondary, or near-line, storage refers to devices that can be made accessible automatically—that is, without operator intervention. Secondary storage is used for material that is currently dormant (but that may need to be consulted or reactivated). CD-ROM or optical drive jukeboxes are commonly used for secondary storage.

- Tertiary, or off-line, storage refers to media and other hardware that must be requested and mounted or installed each time the material is needed. Material that is unlikely to be needed again is stored in such files.

HSSI (High-Speed Serial Interface)

A term applied to serial connections that transmit at more than 20 kilobits per second.

HTML (Hypertext Markup Language)

HTML is the language used to create hypertext documents for the World Wide Web (WWW). HTML is a markup language, which means that formatting commands, or *tags,* are written directly into the source file. Tags are interspersed with ordinary text, and are not interpreted until the file is displayed or printed by a *browser* program.

HTML files have two main components: a head and a body.

- The *head* contains administrative information—for example, the document title or reference locations for relative addressing. (In relative addressing, links, or references, are assumed to be in the same directory as the source file. The location of this directory must be specified.) In general, the head contains information about the document.

- The *body* contains the materials (files, images, etc.) that make up your document—that is, the content along with markup tags.

Three types of HTML elements are defined:

- *Character entities* are special characters or symbols that aren't part of a minimal alphanumeric character set and that may not be available on a particular keyboard. Examples of character entities include angle brackets (< and >), ampersands (&), characters with cedillas (such as Ç), etc. HTML character entities begin with & and end with a semicolon. For example, *<, >, &,* and *Ç* are the codes for <, >, &, and Ç, respectively.

- *Empty markup* tags are instructions that take no special arguments. For example, <P> and <HR> represent, respectively, a new paragraph indicator and a command to draw a horizontal line.

- *Nonempty markup tags* are instructions that include parameters, and that

apply to a limited section of text or other material. Such tags generally come in pairs, with one member of the pair indicating the beginning and the other member the end of the material being affected. For example,

> <B>In an HTML document, this text will be in boldface</B>

produces something like: **In an HTML document, this text will be in boldface.** One of the most important elements in an HTML document—the anchor—is also indicated using nonempty markup tags. This element is discussed later in the entry.

When displayed, the actual appearance of an HTML document depends on the browser controlling the display. Browsers differ in the way in which they interpret specific tags—to the extent allowed by the HTML specifications. In a way, tags represent suggestions, so that different browsers might produce different displays. For example, the **<EM>** and **</EM>** tags indicate the start and end of material that is to be emphasized. The way to do this (for example, using boldface or italic) is left up to the browser. Browsers can also differ in the basal typefaces and sizes they use, which can give a document very different appearances.

Anchors

The *anchor* is one of the most important and most versatile elements in an HTML document. This element can indicate a cross-reference that can be reached at

a b c d e f g **h** i j k l m n o p q r s t u v w x y z

the click of a button. The anchor can also represent the name of a location to which readers might jump. Consider the following:

<A HREF= http://www.ncsa. uiuc.edu/demoweb/htmlprimer.html> Introduction to HTML </A>

This anchor associates a link with the "Introduction to HTML" text. When displayed by a browser, this line will appear underlined (or will be made to look different by other means)—to indicate that there is more information available about this topic. (Note that only "Introduction to HTML" will be displayed. The other material in the anchor is administrative.) Clicking on the "Introduction to HTML" text (or selecting it by other means) will cause the browser to retrieve and display the contents of the file html-primer.html. The long piece of text following the HREF field is an example of a URL (universal resource locator)—essentially an address in Webspeak. The browser will retrieve information from this location.

The *http* indicates that the material is to be retrieved using the Hypertext Transfer Protocol. The *www.ncsa.uiuc.edu* portion specifies the machine on which this file is located. In this case, the URL indicates that the file is found on a specific computer (www.ncsa) at the University of Illinois at Urbana-Champaign (uiuc.edu). Note that the Web server names in the URL must be available (i.e., up and running) for this retrieval process to work. Finally, the */demoweb/html-primer.html* portion specifies the path leading to the file on the WWW machine. (Note that the file name does not conform to DOS restrictions on file names. For historical reasons, most of the files on

the Internet are, in fact, UNIX files. Such files can have multiple letter-extensions and long names—at least when presented by a UNIX file system.)

PRIMARY SOURCES

Many introductions to HTML exist on the Web. These include:

http://info.cern.ch/hypertext/ WWW/MarkUp/MarkUp.html

http://www.ncsa.uiuc.edu/General/ Internet/WWW/HTMLPrimer.html

http://www.utirc.utoronto .ca/HTMLdocs/NewHTML/ intro.html

In addition, books about HTML are appearing almost as quickly as Web pages.

SEE ALSO

WWW (World Wide Web)

HTTPD (Hypertext Transfer Protocol Daemon)

An HTTPD is a program that can recognize and respond to requests using HTTP (the Hypertext Transfer Protocol). HTTP is the primary protocol for requesting and providing documents on the Internet's World Wide Web (WWW). In essence, an HTTPD is the simplest form of Web server.

The first HTTPDs were written for UNIX systems (hence the "daemon" in the name). However, as other platforms (for example, Windows) have joined the WWW, Web servers have been created for these newer environments. As demands and capabilities have grown, the simple daemon program has given way to more sophisticated Web servers that are capable of more than just retrieving and sending hypertext documents: on-the-fly text searches, handling URL redirection (document address changes), etc.

Hub

A hub is a component that serves as a common termination point for multiple nodes and that can relay signals along the appropriate paths. Generally, a hub is a box with a number of connectors to which nodes are attached, as shown in the figure "A stand-alone hub." Hubs usually accommodate four or eight nodes, and many hubs include connectors for linking to other hubs.

A hub usually connects nodes that have a common architecture, such as Ethernet, ARCnet, FDDI, or Token Ring. This is in contrast to a concentrator, which can generally support multiple architectures. Although the boundary between concentrators and hubs is not always clear, hubs are generally simpler and cheaper than concentrators. Token Ring hubs are known as multistation access units (MAUs or MSAUs).

Hub-node connections for a particular network all use the same type of cable, which may be coaxial, twisted-pair, or fiber-optic. Regardless of the type of cabling used for hub-*node* connections, it is often advisable to use fiber-optic cable for hub-*hub* connections.

Hubs may be located in a wiring closet, and they may be connected to a higher-level wiring center, known as an intermediate distribution frame (IDF) or main distribution frame (MDF).

In light of its central role, you should seriously consider connecting a hub to a UPS (uninterruptible power supply).

Hub Operation

All hubs provide connectivity; they pass on signals that come through. The simplest hub broadcasts incoming signals to all connected

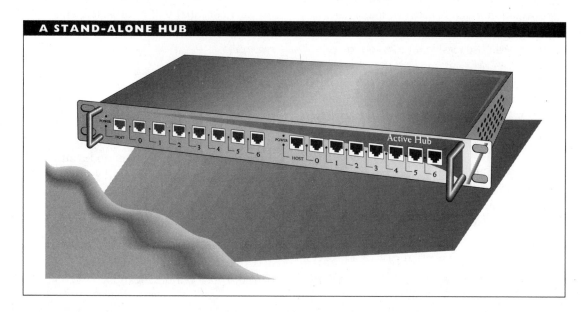

A STAND-ALONE HUB

nodes; more intelligent hubs will selectively transmit signals. Any other services a hub provides will depend on the capabilities that have been built into the hub. For example, MAUs (Token Ring hubs) and active hubs (used in the ARCnet architecture) also boost a signal before passing it on. MAUs also do some internal routing of the node connections in order to create a ring arrangement for the nodes.

There are constraints on the distances that can separate a hub from a node or from another hub. These constraints depend on the type of hub (active or passive) and on the network architecture. In general, allowable node-hub distances are shorter than hub-hub distances.

Hub Features

In addition to connectivity, some hubs also provide management capabilities. Some hubs include an on-board processor which can monitor network activity and can store monitoring data in a MIB (management information base). A network management program—running on the hub or on a server—can use these data to fine-tune the network in order to improve the network's performance.

Just about all hubs have LEDs (light-emitting diodes) to indicate the status of each port (node). Many hubs can also do partitioning, which is a way to isolate a nonfunctioning node.

Other capabilities can be built into hubs or can be provided through software. For example, hubs can be provided with non-volatile memory, which can retain states and configuration values in case of a power outage.

Hubs can also be built or imbued with security capabilities. For example, with the help of software, certain high-end hubs can be made to send data packets to a destination node and garbage packets to all other nodes. This makes it much more difficult for a node to read packets not intended for that node.

Various types of special-purpose or enhanced hubs have been developed to incorporate some subset of these features. The hub variants are discussed in the following sections. In some cases, devices may be considered hubs or concentrators.

Peer versus Stand-Alone Hubs

A *peer hub* is implemented on a card that plugs into an expansion slot in a PC. Such a hub can use the computer's power supply. (The computer's power supply should be adequate, but is not guaranteed to be so.)

A *stand-alone hub* is an external hub that requires its own power supply. This type of hub is generally a box with connectors for the nodes that will be attached, and possibly with special connectors for linking two hubs.

Intelligent Hubs

An *intelligent hub* is a hub with special capabilities for configuration and/or management. For example, an intelligent hub may be able to partition nodes automatically in order to isolate a defective node. Similarly, an intelligent hub (such as in a 10BaseT network) can monitor network activity and report the data to a management program somewhere on the network. Some intelligent hubs can be controlled from a remote location.

The dividing line between intelligent hubs and concentrators is not always clear. In this gray area, vendors may use either *hub* or *concentrator* to refer to their product, presumably using whichever term is expected to generate more interest and sales.

Multi-Architecture Hubs

A device that that is capable of supporting multiple network architectures (for example, Ethernet and FDDI, or Ethernet and Token Ring) is sometimes called a *multi-architecture hub,* but is more likely to be called a concentrator. This flexibility is accomplished by having separate network interface cards for each architecture supported.

Active versus Passive Hubs

In ARCnet networks, an *active hub,* in addition to serving as a wiring and signal relay center, cleans (adjusts the timing of) and boosts a signal. To perform these tasks, an active hub needs its own power supply.

In contrast, a passive hub, used in low-impedance ARCnet networks, merely serves as a wiring and relay center. The signal is properly directed as it passes through, but it is not cleaned in any way. Because passive hubs do not change the signal in any way, they do not require a power supply.

Active hubs can be connected to nodes (servers or workstations), other active hubs, or passive hubs. Active hubs can be separated from each other by up to 610 meters (2,000 feet) when using coaxial cable, and by up to 1.6 kilometers (1 mile) with fiber-optic cable.

A passive hub may be connected to a node or to an active hub, but not to a passive hub. Passive hubs generally support distances of only about 30 meters (100 feet).

BROADER CATEGORY
Intranetwork Link

SEE ALSO
Concentrator; Wiring Center

Hub and Spoke

A term for an arrangement with a central component and multiple peripheral, or outlying components. For example, a central office with connections to smaller branch offices would have a hub-and-spoke arrangement.

Hub Card

In 10BaseT networks, a multiport card that can be used in place of a hub.

Hundred (Centum) Call Seconds (CCS)

In telephone communications, a measure of line activity. One CCS is equivalent to 100 seconds of conversation on a line, so that an hour of line usage is 36 CCS; 36 CCS is equal to one Erlang, and indicates continuous use of the line.

Hunt Group

In telephony, a group of lines which are tried (hunted) in succession, until an available one is found to make a call. If a selected line is busy, the next line is tried.

Hybrid Circuit

In telephone wiring, a circuit in a four-wire (two-pair) cable that can be used to divide these into two-wire (one-pair) paths.

Hybrid Mode

In an FDDI-II network, a mode of operation that makes both packet- and circuit-switched services available, so that both data and voice can be transmitted on the network. This is in contrast to basic mode, which supports only packet-switching and can transmit only data (no voice).

SEE ALSO
FDDI (Fiber Distributed Data Interface)

Hybrid Multiplexer (HMUX)

In the FDDI-II network architecture, a component at the media-access-control (MAC) layer. The HMUX multiplexes network data from the MAC layer and also isochronous (time-dependent) data, such as voice or video, from the isochronous MAC (IMAC) layer. The HMUX passes the multiplexed stream to the PHY (medium-independent physical) layer. See the figure "FDDI-I and FDDI-II Organization" in the "FDDI" entry.

Hyperlink

A link or cross-reference in a hypertext or hypermedia document.

SEE ALSO
Hypermedia; Hypertext

Hypermedia

Material that is arranged with *hyperlinks*—that is, directly accessible connections. With hyperlinks, the contents of the file or document can be examined in a non-linear sequence. A hypermedia document differs from a hypertext file in that the document can include sounds and pictures in addition to text. Thus, when "reading" a hypermedia document about Mozart, a user might be able to click on hyperlinks to get descriptions of Mozart's contemporaries, a picture of Mozart, or perhaps even an excerpt from one of his musical compositions.

COMPARE
Hypertext

Hypertext

Text that is arranged with *hyperlinks*—directly accessible connections—so that the contents of the document can be "read" in a non-linear fashion. By clicking on a hyperlink, the reader can jump around within the document, and even to other documents.

COMPARE
Hypermedia

HYTELNET

HYTELNET (also written Hytelnet or hytelnet) provides a menu-driven, hypertext front end for the Telnet remote terminal emulation program. Written by Peter Scott at the University of Saskatchewan, HYTELNET provides an index of all known Telnet servers, so you can use it to search for catalogs, databases, bulletin boards, etc. Once you've used HYTELNET to access the desired Telnet server, however, you may still have to deal with that server's interface and constraints.

If HYTELNET is available on your system, you can start it by typing **hytelnet**. If not, you can access it through a HYTELNET gateway, such as the one provided by EINet (now known as TradeWave). To do this, use a browser (hypertext file reader), and set it to the following URL (uniform resource locator—essentially a Web address):

http://galaxy.einet.net/hytelnet/
HYTELNET.html

You can also try HYTELNET through the University of Saskatchewan. To do this, you need to telnet to herald.usask.ca, and use **hytelnet** as the login ID.

Hz (Hertz)

A unit of frequency. Hertz is used, for example, to describe the periodic properties of acoustic, electrical, and optical signals. One hertz is equal to one cycle per second.

a b c d e f g **h** i j k l m n o p q r s t u v w x y z

IA5 (International Alphabet 5)

IA5 is a seven-bit code that defines the character set used for message transfers, according to the CCITT X.400 Message Handling System (MHS) specifications.

In its default coding, IA5 is almost identical to the ASCII system. However, because certain character encodings can be changed, IA5 can take on a non-ASCII form. In particular, the following encodings may be redefined:

- Two possible representations can be used for each of the characters corresponding to codes 35 and 36 (decimal). The ASCII encoding uses # and $, respectively.

- Ten characters may be redefined according to national needs. For example, characters may be redefined to represent characters with diacritical marks (umlauts, accents, or tildes, depending on the country). These have codes 64, 91 through 94, 96, and 123 through 126.

You can create and register a particular variant of IA5 encoding, provided that your variant is defined according to these constraints. Various national alphabets have been registered with the ECMA (European Computer Manufacturers Association).

A different character set, defined for Teletex (an international electronic-mail service), uses eight bits, and so provides twice as many possible characters.

PRIMARY SOURCES

CCITT recommendation T.50;
ISO document 646

IAB (Internet Architecture Board)

An organization (originally Internet Activities Board) that oversees standards and development for the Internet. This board also administrates, with the help of the IANA (Internet Assigned Numbers Authority), the internet(1) subtree in the global tree in which all networking knowledge is stored. The IAB has two task forces: IETF (Internet Engineering Task Force) and IRTF (Internet Research Task Force).

IAC (Inter-Application Communication)

In the System 7 operating system for the Macintosh, a process by which applications can communicate with each other and exchange data, IAC can take any of several forms, depending on what is being communicated and who is involved in the communication.

- Copy and paste provides the most perfunctory form of IAC. This type of communication uses a commonly accessible storage area, the Clipboard, as the communication point. Copy and paste is best suited for communicating or exchanging information that is not going to change or be updated, such as a list of the fields in a packet for a particular networking protocol.

- Publish-and-subscribe is used for information that may be revised and updated, such as spreadsheets or text files. A most recent version of the information is always stored in a file known as the edition. Applications that need this information subscribe to the edition, so that the application is always notified when the edition is updated. This makes it possible to create a document from materials drawn together from various sources, even as these sources are being created.

- Events are used to drive program execution and also to control the flow of data in a communications or other type of program. Apple events are lower level, and they adhere to a predefined protocol (the Apple Event Interprocess Messaging Protocol). Macintosh processes and servers use Apple events to get other processes to do their work. Higher-level events are requests from an application to the operating system or to another application. Either Apple or higher-level events can be used to enable one program to control or give orders to another.

- The Program to Program Communications (PPC) Toolbox provides low-level, but flexible and powerful, routines to enable applications to communicate with each other.

IANA (Internet Assigned Numbers Authority)

A group in the Internet community that is responsible for assigning values for networks, attributes, and so on. This service, which is operated by the University of Southern California Information Sciences Institute (USC-ISI), makes sure that the same identifier values are not assigned to two different entities.

IAP (Internet Access Provider)

An IAP is a service provider that provides some way to connect to the Internet. Several access methods are possible, and a particular IAP may allow any or all of these methods. IAPs—or ISPs (Internet Service Providers)—fall along a spectrum with respect to service. At one end, IAPs provide only Internet access; at the other end, online service providers have Internet access as only a small part of their business.

Most IAPs charge a flat monthly rate, which allows the subscriber a limited number of hours online; additional hours cost extra. Some IAPs will provide unlimited access for a (higher) flat fee. A particular IAP generally services only a limited calling area, and provides access numbers only for certain area codes—although a significant percentage of IAPs provide 800 numbers. Depending on how telephone access is provided, there may be a connect-time charge for the call.

The following types of accounts are common:

UNIX shell account: With this type of account, the user is just dialing into a UNIX server that allows public access. To the server, the user's computer looks like a dumb terminal. With such an account, the subscriber can use the server's Internet utilities. Since UNIX interfaces can be Spartan (even to a Spartan), many subscribers with such an account use *The Internet Adapter*

a b c d e f g h **i** j k l m n o p q r s t u v w x y z

(TIA) to give them a friendlier interface.

SLIP or PPP account: With this type of account, the user's computer becomes an Internet host—that is, a machine on the Internet. The subscriber's computer gets its own Internet address (although this may be different each time the user logs on), and Internet utilities (FTP, Telnet, etc.) must be available on the subscriber's machine. The subscriber accesses the Internet by using SLIP (Serial line Internet Protocol), CSLIP (Compressed SLIP), or PPP (Point-to-Point Protocol) over a modem.

BBS account: With this type of account, the user is just calling up the BBS, and then using BBS software to access the Internet. Any file transfers, etc., must go through the BBS machine, and will incur any storage or transport fees for such storage.

IAPs usually provide at least the SLIP or PPP software, and may include some utilities for navigating on the Internet. The IAP will also provide a script or other file to make it easier to log in. Most commonly, new subscribers will begin with a free set of Internet Tools—such as the Chameleon Sampler from NetManage—and will add to these by downloading client, viewer, and other programs from the Internet itself.

Eventually, a subscriber's expertise and needs may grow, and the added features of commercial products will become more attractive. In fact, many of the companies who sell Internet access products are counting on this happening. NetScape's fantastically successful debut with its initial stock offering is an indication that investors feel the same way.

IBMNM (IBM Network Management)

A protocol used for network management in an IBM Token Ring network.

IDA (Integrated Digital Access)

A facility that provides access to multiple digital channels, such as voice, video, and data channels.

IDAPI (Integrated Database Application Programming Interface)

A proposed standard for interfaces between applications that serve as user front-end programs and back-end programs that actually access databases. IDAPI was developed by Borland, IBM, Novell, and WordPerfect as an alternative to Microsoft's ODBC (Open Database Connectivity).

IDC (Insulation Displacement Contact)

In cabling, a type of wire termination in which the connector cuts the cable's insulating jacket when the connector is attached. Most unshielded twisted-pair cable is terminated at an IDC.

IDE (Integrated Drive Electronics)

IDE is a hard disk interface and technology in which the controller is on the hard disk. Because the controller circuitry is small enough to fit on the drive, IDE hard disks have long been popular for laptop and note-book computers. Transfer rates for IDE drives can be as high as 2 megabytes per second (MBps).

A recently released enhanced IDE (EIDE) standard supports drives with a capacity of 1 GB or more. These high-capacity IDE drives are becoming increasingly popular, and this enhanced technology may give SCSI (Small Computer Serial Interface) technology competition in the high-capacity storage market.

BROADER CATEGORY
Hard Disk

Identifier Variable

In NetWare login scripts, a variable used as a placeholder for special values, such as a user's login name. This makes it possible to create scripts that can be used by multiple users or in various contexts simply by changing the values associated with the script's identifier variables.

IDF (Intermediate Distribution Frame)

An intermediate location for routing wiring in a building. An IDF is connected to an MDF (main distribution frame) at one end and to end users at the other end. In a multi-floor building, each floor is likely to have an IDF, partly because of the difficulty in running multiple wires vertically in buildings. An IDF is generally located in a wiring closet.

IDG (Inter-Dialog Gap)

In the LocalTalk variant for AppleTalk, the minimum gap between dialogs. For LLAP (LocalTalk Link Access Protocol), this gap is about 400 microseconds.

IDI (Initial Domain Identifier)

In the OSI Reference Model, the part of a network address that represents the domain (an administrative unit).

Idle Cell

In ATM, a cell that is transmitted when there is not enough network traffic to keep the rate at a specified level. An idle cell can be discarded at any point in the transmission, such as when the network traffic reaches a level at which the idle cell is no longer needed.

SEE ALSO
ATM (Asynchronous Transfer Mode)

IDN (Integrated Digital Network)

A network that uses digital signaling and circuitry.

IDT (Interrupt Dispatch Table)

In Windows NT and NT Advanced Server (NTAS), a table used by the operating system kernel to determine and locate the routine for handling a particular interrupt. The kernel maintains a separate table for each processor, since the processors may use different interrupt handlers.

▼
IDU (Interface Data Unit)

In the OSI Reference Model, a data structure that is passed between layers, as when an entity at one level provides a service for an entity at a higher level.

▼
IEC (International Electrotechnical Commission)

An international organization, with members from more than three dozen countries, that sets electrical standards. The acronym is sometimes used for *interexchange carrier*, which is more commonly denoted by IXC.

▼
IEEE 802.*x*

The IEEE (Institute of Electrical and Electronics Engineers) is an American professional organization that defines standards related to networking and other areas. The IEEE 802.*x* standards are perhaps the best-known IEEE standards in the area of networking. These are a series of standards, recommendations, and informational documents related to networks and communications.

The IEEE publications are the products of various technical, study, and working groups, some of which have been meeting for over a decade, others of which are just a few months old.

The recommendations are mainly concerned with the lower two layers in the OSI Reference Model: the data-link and physical layers. The IEEE recommendations distinguish two sublayers in the OSI model's data-link layer: a lower, MAC (media-access-control) sublayer and an upper, LLC (logical-link-control) sublayer.

Note that several of the standards (802.1 through 802.11) have been adopted and superseded by newer versions (8802-1 through 8802-11, respectively) from the ISO, whose standards are internationally accepted. The literature has not yet caught up with these revisions, so you will still see references to IEEE 802.3, for example, rather than to ISO/IEC 8802-3.

The following are the IEEE 802.*x* standards:

- 802.1 specifies standards for network management at the hardware level, including the spanning tree algorithm. This algorithm is used to ensure that only a single path is selected when using bridges or routers to pass messages between networks and to find a replacement path if the selected path breaks down. This document also addresses systems management and internetworking.

- 802.2 defines the operation of the LLC sublayer of the OSI model's data-link layer. LLC provides an interface between media-access methods and the network layer. The functions provided by the LLC, which are to be transparent to upper layers, include framing, addressing, and error control. This sublayer is used by the 802.3 Ethernet specifications, but not by the Ethernet 2 specifications.

- 802.3 describes the physical layer and the MAC sublayer for baseband networks that use a bus topology and

CSMA/CD as their scheme for accessing the network. This standard was developed in conjunction with Digital, Intel, and Xerox, so that it matches the Ethernet standard very closely. Ethernet 2 and IEEE 802.3 are *not* identical, however, and special measures are required to allow both types of nodes to coexist on the same network. The 802.3u working group recently (in June 1995) adopted a standard for several variants of 100BaseT Ethernet— that is, a version of Ethernet operating at up to 100 Mbps over twisted pair wiring. (100 BaseVG, the main competitor for 100BaseT was adopted as a standard the same day by the 802.12 working group.)

- 802.4 describes the physical layer and the MAC sublayer for baseband or broadband networks that use a bus topology, token passing to access the network, and either CATV or fiber-optic cable. The specifications in this document are closely related to the MAP (Manufacturing Automation Protocol), which was developed by General Motors and which is widely accepted in industrial settings.

- 802.5 describes the physical layer and the MAC sublayer for networks that use a ring topology and token passing to access the network. IBM's 4Mbps Token Ring product line conforms to this standard, as does IBM's faster (16 Mbps) Token Ring network.

- 802.6 defines standards for MANs (metropolitan-area networks), whose nodes are scattered over distances of more than 5 kilometers (3 miles). Part of the 802.6 committee's goal was to find an acceptably fast and inexpensive technology for transmitting among nodes in a MAN. The document recommends the use of DQDB (Distributed Queue Dual Bus) technology for such networks, rather than more expensive leased lines or less expensive but slower public packet-switched networks.

- 802.7 is the report of a TAG (Technical Advisory Group) on broadband networks. The document specifies the minimal physical, electrical, and mechanical features of broadband cable, and also discusses issues related to installation and maintenance of such cable.

- 802.8 is the report of a TAG on fiber-optic networks. The document discusses the use of optical fiber in networks defined in 802.3 through 802.6, and also provides recommendations concerning the installation of fiber-optic cable.

- 802.9 is the report of a working group addressing the integration of voice and data (IVD). This document specifies architectures and interfaces for devices that can transmit both voice and data over the same lines. The 802.9 standard, which was accepted in 1993, is compatible with ISDN, uses the LLC sublayer specified in 802.2, and supports UTP (unshielded twisted-pair) cable.

- 802.10 is the report of a working group addressing LAN (local-area network) security issues, including data exchange and encryption, network management, and security in architectures that are compatible with the OSI Reference Model. An 802.9 working group has been studying the *isoENET* proposal, which attempts to provide bandwidth and protocol support for voice or other time-sensitive transmissions over Ethernet networks.

- 802.11 is the name for a working group addressing wireless networking standards.

- 802.12 is a relatively new working group. It was convened to study the 100BaseVG Ethernet proposal from Hewlett-Packard and other companies.

This architecture supports speeds of up to 100 Mbps, but uses a different media access scheme than the Ethernet versions defined by 802.3 committees. In June of 1995, the 802.12 committee adopted 100BaseVG as a standard. This is one of the two 100 Mbps standards adopted at that time. The other was the 100BaseT, adopted by 802.3u.

The figure "The IEEE 802 committees and working groups" shows the various committees. Note that the work of the 802.2 committee serves as a basis for several other standards (802.3 through 802.6, and 802.12). Several of the committees (802.7 through 802.11) serve primarily informational functions, in principle, for any of the architecture committees.

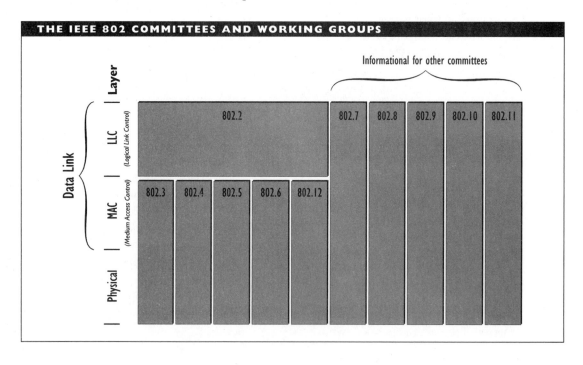

THE IEEE 802 COMMITTEES AND WORKING GROUPS

Note that different 802.*x* committees have specified different bit orders for transmissions. For example, 802.3 (CSMA/CD) and 802.4 (token bus) have specified LSB (least significant bit) first; 802.5 (token ring) has specified MSB (most significant bit) first, as has ANSI X3T9.5, the committee responsible for the FDDI architecture specifications. These two approaches are known as little-endian and big-endian, respectively.

This difference in bit ordering has consequences for bridges and routers, which must do bit switching when routing between networks, so that addresses and frames are interpreted correctly.

IESG (Internet Engineering Steering Group)

In the Internet community, the executive committee for the Internet Engineering Task Force (IETF).

IETF (Internet Engineering Task Force)

A committee that operates under the auspices of the Internet Activities Board (IAB) to help establish standards relating to the Internet. The IETF is largely responsible for formulating the Remote Network Monitoring Management Information Base (RMON MIB), which is expected to become the standard for monitoring and reporting network activity in the Internet environment.

IFG (Interframe Gap)

The maximum amount of time between successive frames, or packets, in a network transmission. For example, in the LocalTalk variant of the AppleTalk software, an IFG of 200 microseconds is considered normal.

IFRB (International Frequency Registration Board)

An ITU (International Telecommunications Union) agency that is responsible for allocating frequency bands in the electromagnetic spectrum. Together with the *CCIR* (International Consultative Committee for Radiocommunication), the IFRB was replaced in 1993 by the ITU-R (International Telecommunication Union—Radiocommunication Standardization Sector).

SEE ALSO
ITU

IFS (Installable File System)

An IFS is a file system that can be loaded dynamically into an operating system. Being able to treat an existing file system, such as the FAT (file allocation table) system used in DOS, as an IFS can help make newer operating systems or releases backward-compatible with earlier environments.

For example, Windows NT has an IFT, which can do the following:

- Read directories using FAT, CDFS (CD-ROM file system), or HPFS (high-performance file system, used in OS/2 formats).

- Read and write files using the formats appropriate for the file system.

Similarly, IFS is a feature of Windows 95 that enables it, among other things, to provide 32-bit file access (32BFA), long file names, and built-in support for networks.

The Windows 95 IFS services are provided by the IFSMgr VxD (IFS Manager virtual device driver).

IHL (Internet Header Length)

A field in an IP (Internet Protocol) datagram, or packet. The field's 4-bit value specifies the length of the datagram's header in 32-bit words.

IMAC (Isochronous Media Access Control)

In the FDDI II architecture, an element in the architecture's media-access-control (MAC) layer that can handle time-dependent data, such as voice or video, received through a circuit-switched multiplexer (CS-MUX). This element is in contrast to the ordinary MAC component, which gets network data (packets) and processes them for transmission over the architecture's physical layer.

Impairment

Any of various types of degradation in electrical signals because of interference, loss, or distortion. Signal-to-noise ratio (SNR), echo, and response at different frequencies are examples of impairment measures.

Impedance

Impedance is the opposition alternating electrical current encounters as it moves along a circuit. Impedance is analogous to friction and is one cause of signal attenuation. Impedance represents the ratio of voltage to current along the transmission line, and it is measured in ohms.

Factors that determine the impedance of a cable segment include distance between conductors (such as between the signal wire and the conductive shield in coaxial cable), and the type of insulation surrounding the wire.

Most network architectures use cable with characteristic impedance. For example, Ethernet cabling is usually 50-ohm, and ARCnet uses 93-ohm cable.

Implicit Congestion Notification

A means of determining that there is congestion on a network. Certain transport protocols, such as TCP from the Internet TCP/IP protocol suite, can infer when network congestion is occurring. This notification is in contrast to explicit notification methods, such as the ECN (explicit congestion notification) method, used in frame-relay networks.

IMR (Internet Monthly Report)

Notices of news and developments that are posted monthly on the Internet. You can get the report by joining the mailing list for the report or by downloading a copy whenever you feel curious.

IMS (Information Management Systems)

A mainframe-based database management and communications package from IBM for use in its SNA (Systems Network Architecture). IMS uses a hierarchical database model.

IMTS (Improved Mobile Telephone Service)

In mobile telephony, a type of service that allows direct dialing between a mobile telephone and an ordinary (wired) phone. (In this context, the ordinary telephone is known as a *wireline*.)

Inband Signaling

Signaling and control information that is transmitted at frequencies that lie within the regular, data channel bandwidth, rather than using frequencies that lie outside this bandwidth (as in *out-of-band signaling*). The term may also be written as *in-band signaling*.

Independent Telephone Company (ITC)

SEE

ITC (Independent Telephone Company)

Index of Refraction

A measure of the degree to which light will travel at a different speed in a given medium, such as in water or in a fiber-optic core made of a particular type of material.

Inductor

An electrical component in line conditioners and surge protectors. Inductors help remove noise caused by electromagnetic and radio frequency interference. Compare this with a capacitor or MOV (metal oxide varistor).

Industry Standard Architecture (ISA)

SEE

ISA (Industry Standard Architecture)

Information Agent

A program that can search databases for information specified by the user. The information agent will search a predefined set of databases, or may allow the user to specify the database(s) to use.

Information Management Systems (IMS)

SEE

IMS (Information Management Systems)

Information Systems Network (ISN)

SEE

ISN (Information Systems Network)

Infrared Transmission

Infrared transmission is wireless communications over a relatively small area, using infrared components to transmit and receive signals. Infrared transmissions use a frequency range just below the visible light spectrum. These waves are used in wireless networks, but require a line of sight connection between sender and receiver or between each of these and a common cell or target.

An infrared signal can be focused or diffuse. A focused signal is aimed directly at the target (receiver or cell); or the signal may be beamed at a surface and reflected off this to a receiver. A focused signal can travel over a greater range but only to a specific target. In contrast, a diffuse signal travels in multiple directions, but is much weaker in each direction. As a result, the range of a diffuse signal is much smaller than for a focused signal.

Transmissions that use reflection fall into two categories:

- *Directed transmissions* use a common central target, and all transceivers bounce and read signals off this target. A directed transmission is useful if the network configuration stays constant (if nodes do not move around). There are generally restrictions on the number of transceivers that can see the target and the range over which these transceivers are distributed.

- *Diffuse transmissions* use everyday objects, so that the target can change if necessary. This newer technology is useful if nodes are moved around a great deal.

In contrast to reflected transmissions, a point-to-point transmission aims the signal directly at the target.

Advantages of infrared transmissions include the following:

- Components are relatively inexpensive.

- Very high bandwidths, from about 400 gigahertz (GHz) to about 1 terahertz (THz) are possible.

- Signals can be reflected off surfaces (such as walls), so that direct line of sight is not necessary.

- Transmissions can be multidirectional.

Disadvantages of infrared transmissions include the following:

- Transmission distance is limited.

- Transmission cannot penetrate walls.

- Possible health risks from infrared radiation.

- Atmospheric conditions (such as rain or fog) can attenuate the signal.

Infrared transmissions are used in contrast to cable-based transmissions or to other types of wireless transmissions (such as those using microwaves).

No license is required for infrared networks.

BROADER CATEGORY
Network, Wireless

COMPARE
Microwave Transmission; Radio Wave Transmission

Initial Domain Identifier (IDI)

SEE
IDI (Initial Domain Identifier)

In-Place Upgrade

An in-place upgrade is one that is installed over an earlier version. Because the previous version of files will be destroyed when you are using this type of upgrade, it is crucial to first back up the entire hard disk or partition and make sure you have a floppy boot disk.

If you have many files in the old format—*and* you can spare the space during installation—consider renaming the directory containing the old version, and then installing the new version in the directory structure that had been used.

Insertion Loss

The amount of signal loss at a connection in the cable or between the cable and a device, such as a transceiver or a node. This loss is measured in decibels (dB). With electrical cable, losses in the 10 dB range are not uncommon; with fiber-optic cable, losses are generally 2 dB or less.

Inside Wire

On a customer's premises, the wiring between an individual workstation and the demarcation point for the public wiring.

INSTALL

A Novell NetWare server utility used for managing, maintaining, and updating NetWare servers. INSTALL can be used for the following tasks:

- Creating, deleting, and managing hard-disk partitions and NetWare volumes on the server

- Installing NetWare and other additional products, and updating the license or registration disk

- Loading and unloading disk and LAN drivers

- Adding, removing, repairing, checking, and unmirroring hard disks

- Changing server startup and configuration files

Installable File System (IFS)

SEE

IFS (Installable File System)

INT 14H

The PC interrupt used to reroute messages from the serial port to the network interface card. This interrupt is used by some terminal-emulation programs. The bit-oriented INT 14H is generally regarded as being badly documented, but it is widely used nonetheless. An alternative is to use INT 6BH. This is the approach taken, for example, in Novell's NASI (NetWare Asynchronous Services Interface). NASI is generally considered faster than the INT 14H approach, but it is not as widely supported.

Integral Controller

A controller built into a mainframe, as opposed to an external controller, which is a separate device.

Integrated Digital Access (IDA)

SEE

IDA (Integrated Digital Access)

Integrated Digital Network (IDN)

SEE

IDN (Integrated Digital Network)

a
b
c
d
e
f
g
h
i
j
k
l
m
n
o
p
q
r
s
t
u
v
w
x
y
z

Integrated Software

Software in which several applications are mutually accessible and able to exchange and update data in a consistent and transparent manner. While it is not required, the component applications are generally on a single machine—either a stand-alone computer or on a server. Arguably, office suites (such as Microsoft Office, Novell Perfect-Office, and Lotus SmartSuite) are among the best known and most widely used examples of integrated software.

Various techniques are available to enable programs to exchange data. These vary in their level of sophistication, power, and complexity. At the most basic level, IPC (interprocess communication) capabilities can be used to accomplish such exchanges—provided one is willing and able to write the necessary programs. Prefab capabilities include the Windows Clipboard, DDE (Dynamic Data Exchange), and OLE (Object Linking and Embedding). Of these, OLE is the most powerful. The office packages use Microsoft's OLE technology to make possible automatic updates in applications whenever data or documents are revised. Database and network access may be provided through other package components—generally add-on modules.

Generally, such integrated packages are controlled by a task management component, through which the user can get access to any of the applications in the suite. For example, Microsoft Office is controlled by the Microsoft Office Manager (MOM) and Office 95 by the Microsoft Shortcut Bar; Novell's Perfect Office is managed by the Desktop Application Director (DAD). Lotus SmartCenter controls the components in SmartSuite. Usually, these components can also be configured to launch other Windows applications.

Integrated Terminal

A terminal capable of handling multiple streams, such as voice, video, and data.

Intelligent Printer Data Stream (IPDS)

SEE

IPDS (Intelligent Printer Data Stream)

Interactive Voice Response (IVR)

SEE

IVR (Interactive Voice Response)

Interconnect Company

A company that supplies telecommunications equipment to connect to telephone lines. Such equipment must be registered with the telephone company before it can be connected to the telephone company's lines.

Inter-Dialog Gap (IDG)

SEE

IDG (Inter-Dialog Gap)

Interdomain Routing Protocol

The ISO equivalent of an exterior gateway protocol (EGP) in the Internet vocabulary. This type of protocol routes packets between different domains (subnetworks under the control of a single organization) in an internetwork. IDRP is also the name of a specific interdomain routing protocol.

SEE ALSO

Protocol, IDRP

Interface, Hardware

A hardware interface is a hardware connection between two devices. A hardware interface requires physical, electrical, and functional specifications that define how the two devices connect and communicate.

The physical interface specifies features such as the number of pins, wires, and so on, and the manner in which these are arranged and attached.

The electrical interface specifies the magnitude, duration, and sign of electrical signals. For example, it specifies the voltage level and duration for 0 and 1 values. Three types of electrical interface are commonly used: voltage, current loop, and contact closure.

The functional interface specifies the interpretation of the signals on each wire. For example, for the EIA-232D serial interface, pins 2 and 3 are for transmitting and receiving data, respectively; pins 4 and 5 are request to send (RTS) and clear to send (CTS), respectively.

Some common hardware interfaces include the following:

- EIA-232D, which specifies 25-pins, asynchronous or synchronous serial transmissions at up to 19,200 bits per second (bps) for up to 15 meters (50 feet). This revision has replaced the old, familiar RS-232C interface.

- EIA-530, which specifies 25-pins, asynchronous or synchronous serial transmissions at up to 2 megabits per second (Mbps) for up to 610 meters (2000 feet). This interface is getting considerable support from the United States government, and may eventually supplant EIA-232D.

- V.24/V.28, which is a CCITT standard that is functionally equivalent to EIA-232D.

Interface, Software

A software interface is a software connection between two programs or two program elements, such as procedures or functions. Software interfaces are characterized by several features, including the following:

- Parameters, which are slots used to pass information between processes. Parameters may be typed (passed as characters, digits, or other pre-interpreted values, as in Pascal or C functions) or untyped (passed as bytes or blocks, as when streams are used).

- Parameter format, which determines how the bits in a byte are ordered, such as whether the least or most significant bit is passed first.

- Evaluation order, which determines whether parameters are evaluated from left to right or from right to left.

- Clean-up responsibilities, which determine whether the calling or the responding process is responsible for getting rid of parameters from the stack after the interaction is complete

a b c d e f g h **i** j k l m n o p q r s t u v w x y z

and the parameters are no longer needed.

Application program interfaces (APIs) provide a commonly used means of passing information between programs, in particular, between an application program and an operating system. APIs provide predefined calls for accomplishing this.

Interface Data Unit (IDU)

SEE

IDU (Interface Data Unit)

Interference

Unanticipated input that affects the definition or quality of data being transmitted. The sources of interference depend on the type of signals involved and on the context. For example, electrical signals are susceptible to other electrical signals, magnetic fields, jamming, and atmospheric conditions. In contrast, optical signals are relatively impervious to these types of interference.

Interframe Gap (IFG)

SEE

IFG (Interframe Gap)

InterLATA

In telephony, circuits or services that cross between two exchanges, which are known as local access and transport areas, or LATAs. InterLATA services are provided by interexchange carriers (IXCs).

INTERLNK

In MS DOS 6.*x*, INTERLNK is a program that makes it possible to connect two computers through serial or parallel ports, and to share drives and printer ports on the computers.

One of the computers (the client) can access the drives and printers on the other (the server). For the connection to work, the following conditions must be met:

- For serial connections: three-wire serial cable or seven-wire null-modem cable and a free serial port on each computer

- For parallel connections: a bidirectional parallel cable and free parallel ports on each computer

- DOS 6.*x* on one computer and DOS 3.3 or later on the other

- The INTERLNK.EXE program on client computers, and an entry in the client's CONFIG.SYS file to load this driver

- 16 kilobytes (KB) and 130 KB of available memory on the client and server, respectively

To start the server, the INTERSVR command is used.

Intermediate Cross-Connect

In a premises distribution system (PDS), a cross-connect (connection between blocks) between wiring closets.

Intermediate Distribution Frame (IDF)

SEE

IDF (Intermediate Distribution Frame)

Intermediate System (IS)

SEE

IS (Intermediate System)

Internal PAD

In an X.25 or other packet-switching networks, a packet assembler and disassembler (PAD) that is located within a packet-switching node.

Internal Routing

In networks using Novell's NetWare, internal routing provides access to multiple networks within a single file server. Each network is represented by a separate network interface card (NIC) in the server. The routing between cards (that is, between networks) is accomplished by using the file server's NetWare operating system to move material.

The use of internal routing increases flexibility because each NIC can be connected to its own physical network. In fact, these networks can use different protocols. For example, one NIC can be connected to an Ethernet network, and another to an ARCnet or Token Ring network, as shown in the figure "Internal routing."

International Numbering Plan

In telecommunications, a strategy developed by the CCITT for allocating telephone numbers around the world. There are several subplans, each for different regions of the world, including ones for North America and Europe.

International Reference Version (IRV)

SEE

IRV (International Reference Version)

International Standardization Organization (ISO)

SEE

ISO (International Standardization Organization)

Internet

As a general term, an internet is an internetwork, which is a network consisting of two or more smaller networks that can communicate with each other. See the Internetwork article for a discussion of this type of networking.

As a specific reference, *the* Internet (note the uppercase *I*) is the giant internetwork created originally by linking various research and defense networks (such as NSFnet, MILnet, and CREN). Since then, various other networks—large and small, public and private—have become attached to the Internet. With about a million registered nodes, many of which are servers for smaller networks, the Internet is by far the largest network in the world. Just a list of all the nodes would be a book much larger than this one.

The Internet, its ancestors, and its subnetworks have been the developing grounds for many of the most commonly used protocols and networking principles. For example, the TCP/IP protocol suite was developed as part of the ARPAnet project, which was a predecessor to many of the subnetworks, and also to the Internet itself.

Internet Structure

The Internet has a three-tiered structure:

- The *backbone* is the highest level in the Internet hierarchy; it is the level that holds the entire Internet together. It consists of networks such as NSFNET and EBONE. The backbone will carry traffic and do routing for the intermediate (transit) level networks. Because this high-level traffic volume can get heavy, the backbone networks have a very high bandwidth. For example, the NSFNET runs over T3 lines, which have a bandwidth of about 45 Mbps.

- The *mid-level networks*—also known as *regional*, or *transit, networks*—lie below the backbone. These carry data and do routing for the lower-level (stub) networks and for their own

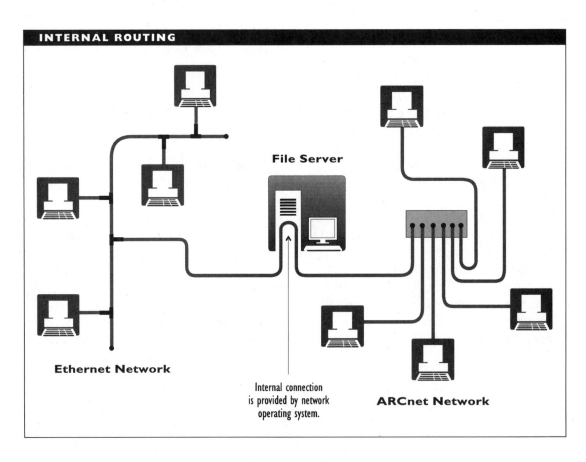

INTERNAL ROUTING

File Server

Ethernet Network

Internal connection is provided by network operating system.

ARCnet Network

hosts. A mid-level network must have paths to at least two other networks. Examples of transit networks include NEARNET, PSINet and SURANET. A mid-level computer is sometimes known as a rib site because it's an appendage off the backbone. (How's that for rib-tickling humor on the Internet?)

- The *stub networks* are basically local or metropolitan area networks. These carry packets only between hosts, but not between networks. This is the level with which most users communicate. A stub network may be connected to other networks, but will not carry traffic for them. Examples of stub networks include MHVNet and the Santa Cruz Community Internet.

This structure is sketched in the figure "Three levels of Internet networks."

The Internet grows very rapidly: at the rate of 10 to 20 percent per *month*. The number of networks branching off the Internet backbone more than doubled within a 16-month period. There are now over a million nodes, and planning is already underway for managing a *billion*-node internetwork.

Internet Organizations

The IAB (Internet Architecture Board, formerly Internet Activities Board), which oversees standards and development for the Internet. This board also administrates, with the help of the IANA (Internet Assigned Numbers Authority), the internet(1) subtree

in the global tree in which all networking knowledge is stored.

The IANA is responsible for assigning values for networks, attributes, and so on. This service, which is operated by the University of Southern California Information Sciences Institute (USC-ISI) makes sure that the same identifier values are not assigned to two different entities.

The IAB has two task forces: IETF (Internet Engineering Task Force) and IRTF (Internet Research Task Force). The IETF is the committee largely responsible for formulating the Remote Network Monitoring Management Information Base (RMON MIB), which is expected to become the standard for monitoring and reporting network activity in the Internet environment.

The IRTF works on long-term research projects. These projects may have to do with any aspect of Internet operations, and some results have led or may lead to major changes in certain aspects of Internet activity. Topics on which the IRTF has worked include how to increase the privacy of electronic mail, and how to make services available to mutually suspicious participants.

The IESG (Internet Engineering Steering Group) is the executive committee for the IETF. The IRSG (Internet Research Steering Group) is the group that oversees the IRTF.

The ISOC (Internet Society) is an international organization that promotes the use of the Internet for communication and collaboration. It provides a forum for the discussion of issues related to the administration and evolution of the Internet. The ISN (Internet Society News) is the official newsletter of ISOC. The figure "Internet administrative

a b c d e f g h **i** j k l m n o p q r s t u v w x y z

layout" shows how these various committees and groups are related.

There are hundreds (possibly thousands)
of services and resources available on the
Internet. These include the following:

- Electronic mail (e-mail)

- Remote login services (Telnet)

- Special interest and other discussion
  groups and forums (Usenet)

THREE LEVELS OF INTERNET NETWORKS

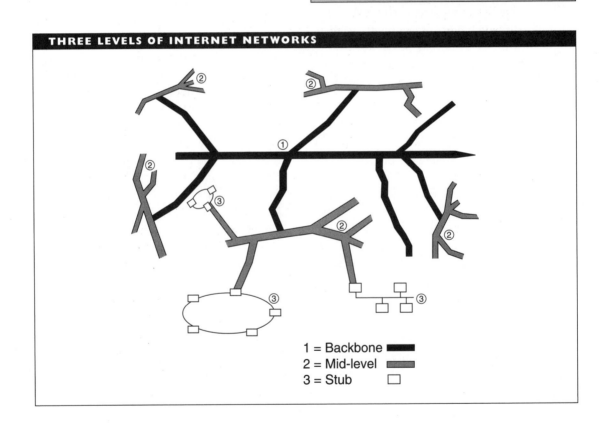

1 = Backbone
2 = Mid-level
3 = Stub

- File retrieval and transfer services (FTP)

- Various services to find files, interest groups, and even individual users (including Archie, Veronica, Jughead, Gopher, Finger, and World Wide Web, or WWW)

- Magazines, news services, directories, and other information (including White Pages Directories and mailing lists)

- Real-time, node-to-node or conference communications (Talk and Internet Relay Chat, or IRC)

- Games, jokes, and other diversions for passing, enjoying, or wasting your time

The following is a very brief summary of some of the more commonly used services and resources on the Internet. Just a list of the Usenet discussion groups runs longer than 50 pages in small print.

Archie: A service for gathering, indexing, and displaying information (such as a list of the files available through anonymous ftp). See the Archie entry for information about specific Archie clients and servers.

Browsers: Programs that can read hypertext files, such as those found on the World Wide Web (WWW). Various browsers are available, ranging from the line- and text-oriented Lynx to the graphics- and multimedia-browsers such as Mosaic and NetScape. See the

entry on browsers and entries for specific browsers for more information.

Finger: A service that can provide information about the person associated with a particular userid.

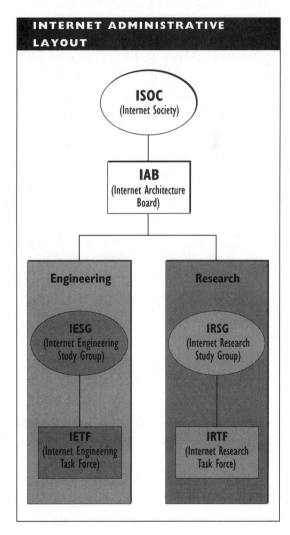

INTERNET ADMINISTRATIVE LAYOUT

ISOC
(Internet Society)

IAB
(Internet Architecture Board)

Engineering

IESG
(Internet Engineering Study Group)

IETF
(Internet Engineering Task Force)

Research

IRSG
(Internet Research Study Group)

IRTF
(Internet Research Task Force)

a b c d e f g h **i** j k l m n o p q r s t u v w x y z

FTP: A program that allows you to transfer files between computers. Many Internet nodes contain files that are available to the general public through anonymous FTP. An FTP program is generally provided by Internet Access Providers as part of their basic software package.

Gopher: A distributed service that can organize and provide access to hierarchically related information. The information can be in various forms: library catalogs, databases, newsgroups, and so on.

Internet Hunt: A monthly information scavenger hunt in which participants try to find the answers to 10 questions using only resources available on the Internet. The Internet hunt is an excellent, fun, and nonthreatening way to learn about the Internet and its available services and resources.

IRC (Internet Relay Chat): A service that extends Talk capabilities to allow multiparty conversations.

Jughead: A service that helps make certain Gopher searches easier and more manageable.

Lycos: A tool for searching for documents on the World Wide Web (WWW). Lycos is a search engine with information on over 6 million Web documents.

Mail: A very basic mail service developed for UNIX systems, but also available on the Internet. Other mail programs are easier and/or more powerful. These include Elm and Pine (for UNIX) and Eudora and Pegasus (for Windows).

MUDs: These multiuser dimensions (or dungeons) are sophisticated descendants of earlier dungeons and dragons games. MUDs and related resources (MUSHes MOOs, MUSEs, etc.) provide interactive games or virtual environments in which players can assume roles or characters, can manipulate simulated environments (labs, societies, etc.), or just socialize. Each MUD environment has its own client and server programs.

News: Various newsreaders (programs for searching and reading news items) are available on the Internet. UNIX newsreaders include rn (read news), nn (no news, a more selective newsreader), and tin (threaded Internet newsreader). Windows newsreaders include News Xpress, WinTrumpet, and WinVN.

Ping: A simple program that can be used to determine whether a connection is available between your machine and a specified other machine. You can also use Ping to test whether you're connected properly to your Internet Access Provider.

Players: Programs for playing various kinds of audio or sound files. Players differ in the file formats they can handle, in the speakers and sound boards they support, and in the platforms on which they run. Example players for Windows include Wham and WPlany.

Readers: Programs for interpreting and displaying the contents of formatted documents (such as PostScript files). Such programs must be able to understand formatting and layout commands and must also be able to translate these into instructions for displaying the material on the screen. Arguably, the best known reader is the one for Adobe Acrobat. Readers are essentially viewers (see below) for documents.

Talk: A service that allows two users logged onto the Internet to communicate with each other in real time (subject to any transmission and routing delays).

Telnet: A program that provides terminal-emulation capabilities for logging in to a network from a remote location.

Usenet: A loose network of thousands of discussion groups about various topics ranging from the mainstream and mundane to the esoteric and "out of this world," with some topics being even further out than that.

Veronica: A service that helps make Gopher searches easier and more manageable.

Viewers: Programs for displaying various types of graphics or video files. Viewers differ in the kinds of files they can handle, in whether they can handle compressed files (either on-the-fly or through preprocessing), and in whether they can handle animation or video formats. Viewers generally fall into one of three categories: those that can handle images (possibly compressed), those for displaying animation, and those for displaying video.

Wais: A service that can be used to gather information about a topic from various locations and provide easier access to the information.

White Pages Directories: Resources that provide electronic address listings for users on the Internet.

WWW (World Wide Web): A giant information network containing millions of hypertext documents that are accessible through Web server programs. To access and read or print such documents, users need a browser program that can request the documents from the server and display them for the user. The WWW is currently the fastest growing segment of the Internet as individuals and corporations are discovering the advantages of putting their own Web pages (hypertext documents) on the Web.

WWWW (World Wide Web Worm): A search engine for finding hypertext documents on the Web. WWWW can search for keywords or keyword combinations in titles, authors, or contents of the documents, and will display the addresses of documents that match your search criteria. WWWW has information about more than 3 million documents.

a b c d e f g h **i** j k l m n o p q r s t u v w x y z

internet(1)

In the global tree of network information, a subtree administered by the Internet Activities Board (IAB). The full name for this subtree is 1.3.6.1; the local name is {dod1}. Notable subtrees under this one include *mgmt*(2), which contains the definitions for network management objects and packages.

SEE ALSO

Global Tree

Internet Architecture Board (IAB)

SEE

IAB (Internet Architecture Board)

Internet Assigned Numbers Authority (IANA)

SEE

IANA (Internet Assigned Numbers Authority)

Internet Engineering Steering Group (IESG)

SEE

IESG (Internet Engineering Steering Group)

Internet Engineering Task Force (IETF)

SEE

IETF (Internet Engineering Task Force)

Internet Hunt

A monthly quiz that poses 10 questions. All the answers must be found using only the Internet and its resources. The hunt is both entertaining and enlightening. It provides an excellent, nonthreatening way to learn about the Internet. To get the list of questions, point a gopher client to the gopher.cic.net host.

Internet Registry (IR)

SEE

IR (Internet Registry)

Internet Relay Chat (IRC)

SEE

IRC (Internet Relay Chat)

Internet Research Steering Group (IRSG)

SEE

IRSG (Internet Research Steering Group)

Internet Research Task Force (IRTF)

SEE

IRTF (Internet Research Task Force)

Internet Router (IR)

SEE

IR (Internet Router)

Internet Services List

A list of services available on the Internet. The list is maintained by Scott Yanoff and is updated regularly. You can use anonymous ftp to get the list from the /pub directory of the csd4.csd.uwm.edu ftp site.

Internet Standard (IS)

SEE

IS (Internet Standard)

Internetwork

A network that consists of two or more smaller networks that can communicate with each other, usually over a bridge, router, or gateway.

Internetworking is one of the major buzzwords in the world of networking. Implementing the concepts behind the term is one of the major problems and sources of confusion in the world of networking.

Internetworking is the process of establishing and maintaining communications, and of sending data among multiple networks. The goal in an internetworking task is to get data from one user (the source) to another (the destination). This is known as end-to-end service.

Stating the goal is easy; accomplishing it is something else entirely. The details of how to provide the end-to-end service depend to a large extent on the ends, but also on the intermediaries: the nodes and other devices encountered along the way. The following types of connections are common:

LAN to LAN: The local-area networks (LANs) are assumed to be close

enough so that such a connection does not need telecommunications capabilities. Difficulties can arise if the LANs use different network architectures.

LAN to mainframe: A connection between a LAN and a mainframe may or may not require telephone communications. The task will almost certainly involve data translations (for example, on their way through a gateway), and will probably require terminal emulation on the part of the LAN's representative in the connection.

LAN to WAN: A connection between a LAN and a wide-area network (WAN) requires telecommunications capabilities. The distance-related phase can be either slow or expensive. With ordinary telephone lines, the slow speeds (up to about 19,200 bits per second) create a bottleneck, since LAN speeds are several hundred times as fast. Fast lines, on the other hand, are still expensive. Once the telecommunications problems are resolved, network protocol compatibility remains a potential problem.

The details of how to accomplish internetwork connections have filled many thousands of pages, because internetworking can take many forms and may take place at any of several layers. For example, for relay systems such as X.25, the internetworking takes place through the three lowest layers of the OSI Reference Model. In particular, X.25 protocols operate at the network layer.

In contrast, for Message Handling Systems such as the CCITT X.400 recommendations, communications between networks may take place at the application layer. In all cases, however, the lower layers eventually need to get involved in order to do the actual relaying of packets.

Connectionless and Connection-Oriented Services

One fundamental distinction has guided much of the work on internetworking: the distinction between connectionless and connection-oriented services.

Connection-Oriented Services

When the network services are connection-oriented, a temporary (for the duration of the communication) path is established, and data is relayed along this connection.

Because the path is preestablished, certain routing information can be assumed, which simplifies the packets that need to be constructed and sent. In all acceptable internetworking implementations, these details should be completely transparent to the users. As far as users are concerned, the connection between the endpoints is direct. Because connection-oriented services are so tidy, it is easier to do error-checking and flow control.

Various protocols have been developed to provide connection-oriented services. For example, the CCITT's X.25 is a connection-oriented network layer protocol, as is CONP (Connection-Oriented Network Protocol). The X.25 protocol has been adapted for connection-oriented services by both the OSI and the Internet communities. COTP (Connection-Oriented Transport Protocol) is a protocol for the transport layer. The NetWare SPX (Sequenced Packet Exchange) protocol is connection-oriented.

Connectionless Services

In connectionless service, data transmission does not need to wait for a path to be established. Packets are routed independently to their destinations, so that two packets from the same message or transmission might take two different paths.

Because packets travel independently, they probably will not arrive in order. Consequently, the original sequence needs to be reconstructed at the destination end. This is generally done at the transport layer in the OSI Reference Model.

CLNP (Connectionless-mode Network Protocol), CLTP (Connectionless-mode Transport Protocol), and UDP (User Datagram Protocol) are connectionless service protocols. The first two are used in OSI environments; the UDP is used in TCP/IP-based environments. The IPX (Internetwork Packet Exchange) and the MHS (Message Handling Service) protocols are two examples of connectionless NetWare protocols.

Internetworking Features

Internetworking may involve only local networks, or there may be long-distance connections between networks, so that WAN connections come into play. Paths between endpoints can get quite long, particularly if there are many networks between the two end users.

Regardless of the layer under consideration or of the types of networks involved, the internetworking process always has the same type of structure:

- Any required internetworking services are supplied for a layer by the layer below it. For example, transport-layer protocols get routing (pathfinding) and relaying (data-movement) services from the network layer.

- The services are requested and provided through well-defined service access points (SAPs). These SAPs not only provide interfaces, but they also provide unambiguous addresses by which to refer to the user of the network services.

- The actual data-transmission path may include one or more intermediate

systems, which are usually routers. The routers will make use of the lower three OSI layers, known as the *subnet layers,* to move the data along to the next router or to the destination node.

The figure "Layer-oriented view of an internetworking path" shows the elements involved in an internetworking process. Note that the service users need to know nothing about the details of the transmission path.

In addition, several features are *desirable* in any internetworking service:

- The use of the services should be completely transparent to the end users. Any required routing and relaying should be done by the service providers, and should be of no concern to the end users.

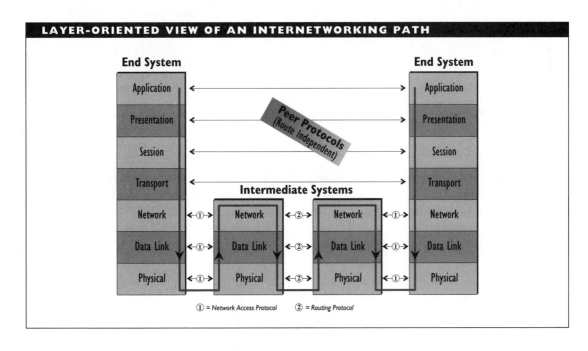

LAYER-ORIENTED VIEW OF AN INTERNETWORKING PATH

① = Network Access Protocol ② = Routing Protocol

a b c d e f g h **i** j k l m n o p q r s t u v w x y z

- The use of the services should not affect the transmitted data in any way. This means that the data that reaches the destination should be identical to the data that left the user, regardless of where the data has been during its journey. The exception is when a gateway is used to send data to a different type of network, so that the data may need to look different when it reaches its destination.

- The end users should be able to expect a given quality of service when using the network services.

PRIMARY SOURCES

ISO documents 8208 and 8878 (X.25); ISO document 8208 (CONP); ISO document 8073 and CCITT recommendation X.224 (COTP); ISO document 8348 (connectionless services); ISO documents 8473 and 8880-3 (CLNP); ISO 8602 (CLTP); RFC 768 (UDP).

SEE ALSO

Internetwork Link

COMPARE

Interoperability

Internetwork Link

An internetwork link serves to connect two or more networks. The networks may be identical, similar, or dissimilar. They may be located near each other or far apart. The figure "Context of internetwork links" summarizes these types of connections.

Identical networks use the same PC and network architectures and the same or comparable cabling. For example, a bridge may link two Token Ring networks or a thin (10Base2) Ethernet network to a twisted-pair (10BaseT) network. These types of networks are often created for convenience. For example, an internetwork may be created to turn a large network into two smaller ones, in order to reduce network traffic.

Similar networks use the same PC architecture (for example, Intel-based) but may use different network architectures, such as Ethernet and Token Ring. Dissimilar networks use different hardware and software, such as Ethernet and an IBM mainframe.

Internetwork links differ in the level at which they operate. This difference also affects the kinds of networks they can link. The following links may be used:

- A *bridge* provides connections at the data-link layer, and it is often used to connect networks that use the same architecture. A bridge serves both as a link and as a filter: passing messages from one network to the other, but discarding messages that are intended only for the local network. This filtering helps reduce traffic in each network.

- A *router* determines a path to a destination for a packet, and then starts the packet on its way. The destination may be in a network removed from the router by one or more intermediate networks. To determine a path, a router communicates with other routers in the larger (inter)network. Routers operate at the network layer, and most are protocol-dependent; that is, each router generally can handle only a single network-layer protocol.

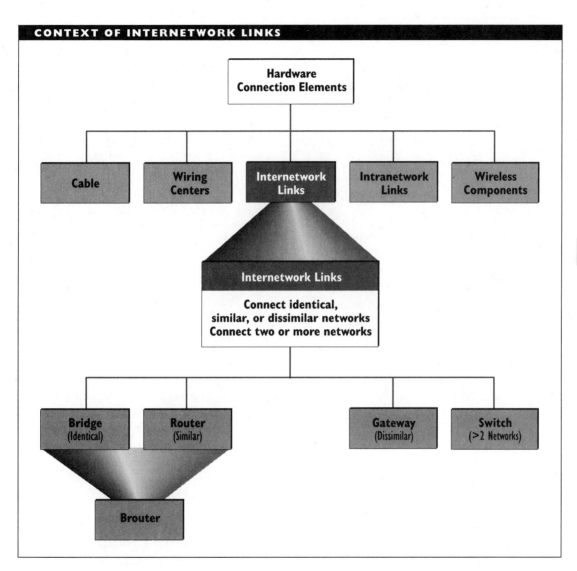

CONTEXT OF INTERNETWORK LINKS

Special multiprotocol routers, such as Novell's Multiprotocol Router, are available. Because they need to do much more work to get a packet to its destination, routers tend to be slower than bridges.

- A *brouter* combines the features of a bridge and a router. It has the forwarding capabilities of a router, and the protocol independence of a bridge. Brouters can process packets at either the data-link or network level.

- A *gateway* moves packets between two different computer environments, such as between a local-area network and a mainframe environment or between Macintosh and PC networks. Gateways operate at the session layer and above. Because they connect dissimilar networks, gateways may need to do data translation (for example, between ASCII and EBCDIC), compression or expansion, encryption or decryption, and so on.

- A *switch* (in this context) is a multiport bridge or gateway. Whereas a gateway connects two environments (for example, two electronic-mail systems), a mail switch can connect several such systems. Similarly, an Ethernet switch can direct packets to any of several Ethernet subnetworks to which the switch is attached.

SEE ALSO

Bridge; Brouter; Gateway; Intranetwork Link; Router; Switch

▼
Interoffice Channel (IOC)

SEE

IOC (Interoffice Channel)

▼
Interoperability

The other great buzzword, along with *internetworking,* in the network world is *interoperability.* This term refers to the ability of two different networks to work together. For example, interoperability describes how networks can communicate or share data

with each other, regardless of whether these networks use the same network architecture.

Interoperability is taken for granted when the networks are homogeneous; that is, when they use the same architecture. Even when the networks are heterogeneous, some degree of interoperability is almost always possible, although the costs in performance degradation or in required equipment may be unacceptably high.

One way to think of these terms is to regard interoperability as the capability for working together and internetworking as the actual cooperation.

The term interoperability is also used to refer to the ability of different software products to work together in the same environment.

SEE ALSO

Internetwork

▼
Interpersonal Messaging Service (IPMS)

SEE

IPMS (Interpersonal Messaging Service)

▼
Inter-Repeater Link

In an Ethernet network, a cable segment between two repeaters. An IRL cannot have any nodes attached. If the cable is optical fiber, it is known as a FOIRL (fiber-optic inter-repeater link).

▼
Interrupt

An interrupt is a mechanism by which one computing element, such as a drive or a program, can get the attention of another element, such as the CPU (central processing unit) or another program. Operating systems that use interrupts have a mechanism for weighting and dealing with the interrupts. Interrupts may be generated by hardware or software.

For hardware interrupts in a PC environment, there are 8 or 16 interrupt request lines (IRQs). Machines with an 80286 or higher processor have 16 lines. Each device attached to a computer can be assigned an IRQ. When it wants a service from the CPU, the device signals on this line and waits. In principle, each line may be assigned to a device; in practice, certain IRQ lines are reserved by the system for its own needs.

IRQs have different priority levels, and the higher priority lines are assigned to the most important functions on the PC. By doing this, an operating system or interrupt handler can be sure that no vital activities are interrupted.

IRQ values for a device may be set through software or by setting jumpers or DIP switches on the expansion board for the device. When configuring devices on your machine, it is important that you do not have two devices that use the same IRQ (at least if there is any chance that the two devices will be used at the same time).

Hardware Interrupts

Hardware interrupt signals are conveyed over specific interrupt request lines (IRQs).

The number of IRQs in a particular machine, 8 or 16, depends on the number of *interrupt controller chips* on the processor. In machines that conform to the ISA (Industry Standard Architecture), the Intel 8259A Programmable Interrupt Controller chip is used. Each 8259A has 8 IRQs. Machines with an 80286 or higher processor have two chips, and therefore have 16 IRQs. The second 8259A is controlled by the first, and must announce interrupts on its lines (IRQs 8 through 15) by signaling on the first chip's IRQ 2. The figure "IRQ lines" shows these interrupt lines.

The figure also shows the standard IRQ assignments for ISA machines. Note that there are some differences in the assignments for single- and double-chip processors. Note also that extensibility is built into both controller chips. The IRQ 2 on the primary interrupt controller chip makes it possible to cascade the IRQs from the second chip. In a similar manner, IRQ 9 on the second chip allows for additional signals. Network-related interrupts can be indicated through this IRQ.

Software Interrupts

Executing programs also use interrupts to get resources needed to perform some action. For example, there are software interrupts to access a monitor screen or disk drive, to handle a keystroke or a mouse click, and so on.

There are software interrupts for handling specific requests and for performing specific actions (for example, determining memory size). There are also interrupts that provide access to more functions (for example, DOS interrupt 21H, which provides a function dispatcher that can access any of several dozen different functions).

a b c d e f g h **i** j k l m n o p q r s t u v w x y z

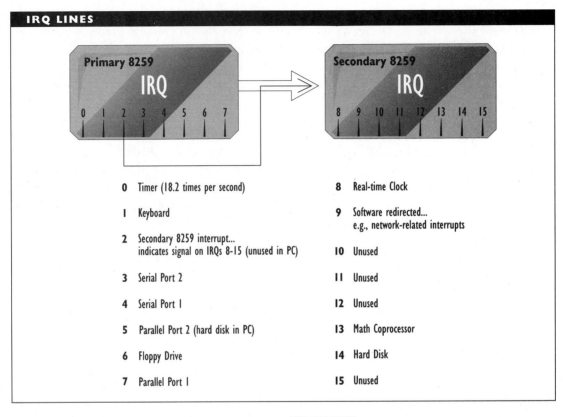

IRQ LINES

Primary 8259 IRQ
0 1 2 3 4 5 6 7

Secondary 8259 IRQ
8 9 10 11 12 13 14 15

0	Timer (18.2 times per second)	**8** Real-time Clock
1	Keyboard	**9** Software redirected... e.g., network-related interrupts
2	Secondary 8259 interrupt... indicates signal on IRQs 8-15 (unused in PC)	**10** Unused
3	Serial Port 2	**11** Unused
4	Serial Port 1	**12** Unused
5	Parallel Port 2 (hard disk in PC)	**13** Math Coprocessor
6	Floppy Drive	**14** Hard Disk
7	Parallel Port 1	**15** Unused

Handling Interrupts

Each type of interrupt invokes its own *interrupt handler,* which is a program designed to deal with the interrupt. The location of a specific interrupt handler is found in an *interrupt vector table.* DOS provides a 256-entry table for storing such addresses. It is possible to preempt the default interrupt handlers by substituting the address of an alternate handler in the appropriate vector table cell.

Interrupt Dispatch Table (IDT)

SEE

IDT (Interrupt Dispatch Table)

Interrupt Request Level (IRQL)

SEE

IRQL (Interrupt Request Level)

Intraexchange Carrier

A local telephone company; that is, a carrier that handles calls within an exchange. These are known as *intraLATA* calls, because exchanges are known as local access and transport areas, or LATAs. An intraexchange carrier is also known as an *LEC* (local exchange carrier).

Intraframe Encoding

In video signal transmission, a compression strategy in which only those parts of a video frame that have changed are encoded for transmission.

IntraLATA

In telephony, circuits that lie within a single exchange (known as a local access and transport area, or LATA). IntraLATA service is provided by a local exchange carrier (LEC); that is, by a local telephone office.

Intranetwork Link

An intranetwork link is a component that serves to connect two elements in the same network. This link may be physical or electrical. The figure "Context of intranetwork links" summarizes this type of connection.

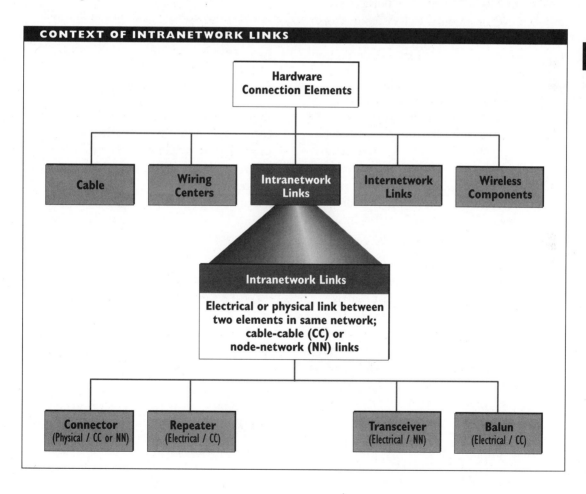

CONTEXT OF INTRANETWORK LINKS

Hardware Connection Elements

- Cable
- Wiring Centers
- Intranetwork Links
- Internetwork Links
- Wireless Components

Intranetwork Links

Electrical or physical link between two elements in same network; cable-cable (CC) or node-network (NN) links

- Connector (Physical / CC or NN)
- Repeater (Electrical / CC)
- Transceiver (Electrical / NN)
- Balun (Electrical / CC)

a b c d e f g h i j k l m n o p q r s t u v w x y z

Node-network and cable-cable links can be distinguished. The following components create these links:

- *Connectors* establish a physical link between two components. There are more than a dozen connector types, some of which come in several shapes and sizes. For a given network configuration, only a small number of connectors will be appropriate. For example, an ARCnet network will use either BNC or modular (RJ-*xx*) connectors. A connector is a passive component, and some signal loss (the insertion loss) is involved.

- *Transceivers* establish an electrical connection between a workstation and the network. The transceiver may be located on the network interface card or it may be attached to the workstation by a drop cable. In the latter case, the transceiver will include connectors to attach to both the drop and the network (trunk) cable.

- *Repeaters* establish an electrical connection between two cable segments. Repeaters clean and boost signals before passing them on to the next segment. Because signals are boosted, repeaters can be used to extend the maximum distance over which a signal can travel. In order to accomplish this task, repeaters need their own power supplies.

- *Baluns* establish an electrical link between different types of cables, such as twisted-pair and coaxial. In particular, a balun connects cables that have

different impedances, and it makes the necessary impedance conversions as signals pass through the balun.

SEE ALSO

Balun; Connector; Connector, Fiber-Optic; Internetwork Link; Repeater; Transceiver

INWATS (Inward Wide Area Telephone Service)

In telephone communications, an 800 service; that is, a service in which the called party pays for the call.

IOC (Interoffice Channel)

In digital telecommunications, a communications link between two carrier offices (for example, two local telephone offices) or between points-of-presence (POPs) for two interexchange carriers (IXCs). For high-speed lines (such as T1), the cost for such a channel is on a per-mile basis. This term is also written as *inter-office channel*.

IONL (Internal Organization of the Network Layer)

In the OSI Reference Model, IONL is a detailed specification for the network layer. This specification was made in order to distinguish more clearly the levels of service provided by the network layer.

In IONL, the network layer is divided into three sublayers:

Subnetwork access: At the bottom of the network layer, the subnetwork access sublayer provides an interface over which to send data across a network or subnetwork. Services at this level are provided by a subnetwork access protocol (SNAcP). The X.25 packet-level protocol is an example of a sub-network access protocol.

Subnetwork-dependent: Protocols operating at this sublayer assume a particular type of subnetwork, such as an Ethernet local-area network. This type of subnetwork-dependent convergence protocol (SNDCP) has been defined by the ISO.

Subnetwork-independent: This sublayer provides *inter*networking capabilities for the layers above it. Protocols at this sublayer can work with multiple sub-networks. The services provided by a subnetwork-independent control protocol (SNICP) are independent of particular subnetworks. CLNP (Connectionless-mode Network Protocol) is an SNICP.

PRIMARY SOURCE

ISO document 8648

IP (Internet Protocol) Address

An IP address is an address for a station or other device on the Internet. This type of address consists of 4 bytes, which are represented as decimal values separated by periods, as in 123.45.67.89. In order to ensure uniqueness, IP addresses are assigned in part by the Internet Assigned Numbers Authority (IANA).

To deal with the rapid growth of the Internet, IP addresses have become hierarchical, and the address bits can be given any of several interpretations.

The bits in an IP address are allocated for Net and Host (*Node* in Internet terminology) fields, which specify a network and host number, respectively. Originally, 8 bits were allocated for networks and the remaining 24 bits for the host information. Since there are well over 255 networks now attached to the Internet, such an addressing scheme is no longer adequate.

To help handle the growth of the Internet, several classes of addresses have been defined. These differ in how they allocate bits for the Net and Host fields.

IP Address Classes

The following classes are defined for IP addresses:

- Class A is used for very large networks (networks with a large number of nodes). This class uses 7 bits for Net and 24 bits for Host. The high-order bit is 0 in such an address. There are 128 class A networks possible. The now-defunct ARPANET, which had a network address of 10, is an example of a network in this class.

- Class B is used for medium-size networks, such as networks that span a large college campus. This class uses 14 bits for Net and 16 bits for Host. The two high-order bits are set to 10. This address class is also popular for local-area networks (LANs), particularly if they use subnetting.

- Class C is used for small networks (those with no more than 255 nodes). This class allocates 21 bits for Net and only 8 bits for Host. The three high-order bits are 110.

a b c d e f g h **i** j k l m n o p q r s t u v w x y z

- Class D allocates 28 bits for a special multicast address, which is an address in which a group of targets are specified. The first 4 bits of such an address are always 1110.

- Class E is a reserved address class. Addresses in this class are for experimental use, and cannot be guaranteed to be unique. The first 4 bits of this type of address are always 1111.

In summary, address classes are distinguished by the high-order bits: 0 for class A, 10 for class B, 110 for class C, 1110 for class D, and 1111 for class E. Two particular Net addresses—0 and those with all 1s—are reserved. Net address 0 is reserved for the originating entity (network or host), and address 255 is used for broadcasts. Figure "IP address breakdown" shows how the bits are allocated for the different address classes.

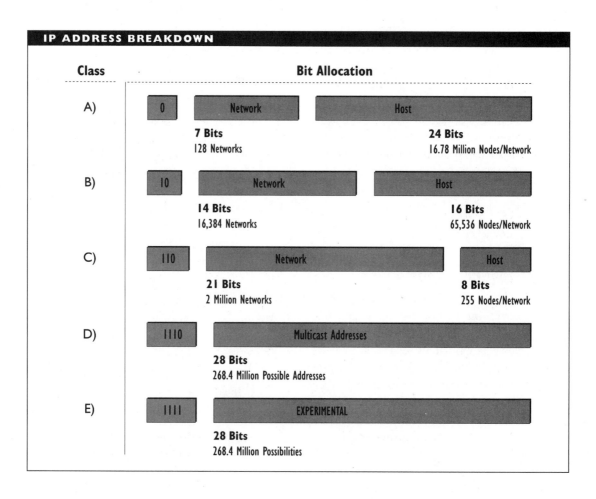

IP ADDRESS BREAKDOWN

Class	Bit Allocation

A) 0 | Network — **7 Bits** 128 Networks | Host — **24 Bits** 16.78 Million Nodes/Network

B) 10 | Network — **14 Bits** 16,384 Networks | Host — **16 Bits** 65,536 Nodes/Network

C) 110 | Network — **21 Bits** 2 Million Networks | Host — **8 Bits** 255 Nodes/Network

D) 1110 | Multicast Addresses — **28 Bits** 268.4 Million Possible Addresses

E) 1111 | EXPERIMENTAL — **28 Bits** 268.4 Million Possibilities

IP Subnet Addresses

The use of subnetting provides additional flexibility in addressing. A subnet is a portion of a network or an internetwork that can be viewed from the outside as a single element.

An IP address that uses subnetting has three types of information: network, subnet, and host. Subnets are identified by combining an address with a mask, which is a bit pattern that cancels out unwanted bits, so that only the bits of interest remain.

PRIMARY SOURCE
RFC 1349

IPC (Interprocess Communication)

IPC is a set of services for exchanging control information and data between separate processes or programs on the same or different hosts. OS/2 implements IPC as part of its multitasking capabilities.

IPC between processes on the same machine can use any of several mechanisms, including the following:

- Shared memory, in which the two processes both access a common area of memory.

- Named pipes, in which a two-way virtual circuit is established. For sharing on a network, named pipes (which allow two-way communications) must be used.

- Semaphores, in which the processes signal when there is something to communicate.

IPC capabilities are particularly important for applications that run in client/server computing environments.

IP (Internet Protocol) Datagram

The basic packet sent across the Internet. An IP datagram contains source and destination addresses, fields for various bookkeeping and tracking information, and data.

IPDS (Intelligent Printer Data Stream)

In an SNA (Systems Network Architecture) environment, a printing mode that provides access to advanced function printer (AFP) capabilities, such as the ability to output text, graphics, and color (if supported) simultaneously on a printer.

IPI (Intelligent Peripheral Interface)

A hard disk interface that supports transfer rates of up to 25 megabytes per second and storage capacities of several gigabytes.

SEE ALSO
Hard Disk

IPM (Interpersonal Messaging)

In the ITU X.400 series of recommendations for message handling systems (MHS), one of the two major categories of message handling, with the other being a message transfer system (MTS). IPM represents a type of message handling for use in ordinary business or private correspondence. The handled elements—interpersonal messages—consist of *heading* and *body* components. Headings are made up of fields (such as name, address,

a b c d e f g h **i** j k l m n o p q r s t u v w x y z

subject) and values for these fields. The actual content of a message makes up the body. The entire content can be broken into smaller chunks (*body parts*), each of which may be manipulated separately.

The interpersonal messaging process is assumed to take place in an IPME (Interpersonal Messaging Environment) under the control of an IPMS (Interpersonal Messaging System). In IPM, users exchange messages and replies over the IPMS, as depicted in the figure "IPM and its components").

As shown in the figure, users in IPMEs have three main kinds of capabilities:

Originate, in which the user initiates a message transmission or exchange. Various types of originate actions are possible—including a probe to determine whether anyone is listening, and transmitting the start of a message.

Receive, in which the user receives a message or a probe through the IPMS.

Manage, in which the user can change material associated with the user's headings (name, address, etc.).

PRIMARY SOURCES
ITU recommendations X.400, X.402, X.420

BROADER CATEGORY
MHS (Message Handling System)

COMPARE
MTS (Message Transfer System)

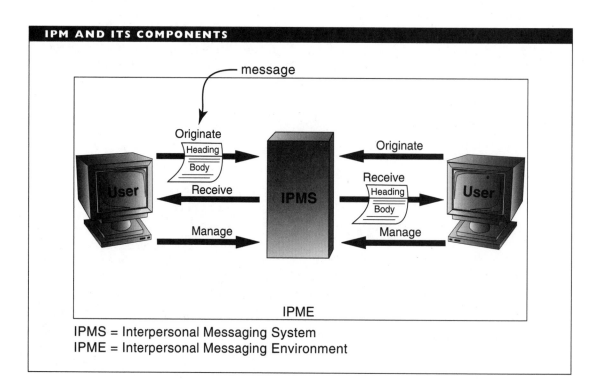

IPM AND ITS COMPONENTS

message

Originate
Heading
Body
Receive
Manage

IPMS

Originate
Receive
Heading
Body
Manage

User

User

IPME

IPMS = Interpersonal Messaging System
IPME = Interpersonal Messaging Environment

IPMS (Interpersonal Messaging Service, or System)

In the 1984 version of the X.400 Message Handling Services recommendations, a user-to-user service that provides electronic-mail capabilities. The other major class of services provided in the 1984 version was Message Transfer Service (MTS).

IPX Network Numbers and Internetwork Addresses

In Novell NetWare networks, IPX external and internal network numbers are assigned. The IPX external network number is a unique hexadecimal value associated with a network or network cable segment. The value may be from one to eight hexadecimal digits (up to 4 bytes), and is assigned arbitrarily.

The IPX internal network number is a hexadecimal number that uniquely identifies an individual file server. This value can also be from one to eight hexadecimal digits, and it is assigned arbitrarily to the server during the installation of the networking software.

An IPX internetwork address in NetWare is a three-part, 12-byte address. The first part (4 bytes) is the IPX external network number. The middle part (6 bytes) is the node number. The third part (2 bytes) is the socket number, which is the number associated with a particular device or process. IPX internetwork addresses are generally represented as hexadecimal values, so they can have as many as 24 digits associated with them. (And you thought that 10 telephone digits were too much trouble!)

SEE ALSO
Address

IPXODI (Internet Packet Exchange Open Data-Link Interface)

In Novell NetWare 3.*x* and later, IPXODI is a protocol driver that can prepare workstation requests intended for the network. The preparation may involve attaching the appropriate header to the packet, packaging the packet in the appropriate manner, and passing the packet on to the link-support layer (LSL). (The LSL mediates between the LAN driver for the network interface card and the protocol stack running on the network.)

Data sent using IPXODI is handled as datagrams, which means the packager makes a best effort but cannot guarantee delivery. The next higher layer, SPX (Sequenced Packet Exchange), makes sure the data is received correctly.

BROADER CATEGORY
NetWare

IR (Internet Registry)

A central database that contains the network addresses of machines and ID numbers of autonomous systems (domains) on the Internet. The task of maintaining the IR is delegated by the Internet Assigned Numbers Authority (IANA) and is being carried out by the Defense Data Network Network Information Center (DDN NIC).

This process has become considerably more difficult as the corporate world joins the Internet, wanting to use its trademarked

a
b
c
d
e
f
g
h
i
j
k
l
m
n
o
p
q
r
s
t
u
v
w
x
y
z

names, and willing to put its lawyers to work to get its way.

IR (Internet Router)

In an AppleTalk internetwork, a device that uses network numbering to filter and route packets.

IRC (Internet Relay Chat)

A protocol that provides access to a global talk network in which participants can communicate in real time to converse about topics of mutual interest. Different conversations take place over different channels. IRC is an extension and enhancement of the UNIX *talk* program to, among other things, allow more than two users to talk at a time. IRC can serve as an inexpensive conference call method.

Iridium Project

A project, initiated by Motorola, for making worldwide mobile communications possible. The project calls for 77 satellites to blanket the earth. These would allow point-to-point communications between any two locations. Compare this project with Project 21.

IRL (Inter-Repeater Link)

In an Ethernet network, a cable segment between two repeaters. An IRL cannot have any nodes attached. If the cable is optical fiber, it is known as an FOIRL (fiber-optic inter-repeater link).

IRM/IRF (Inherited Rights Mask/ Inherited Rights Filter)

In environments for Novell NetWare 3.*x*, the IRM is a security measure that determines which trustee rights a user can carry over (inherit) from a directory into a subdirectory in the NetWare file system.

The IRM does not grant any new rights (trustee rights the user does not already have). Rather, the IRM controls which of the trustee rights *already granted in a parent directory* can also be used in the current directory.

The IRM does not take away trustee rights granted in a particular subdirectory. For example, if the IRM for directory X filters out all but the File Scan right, then a user with a Modify right in directory X will not be able to carry that right over to subdirectories of X. If, however, the user is granted a Modify right for subdirectory Y, then the IRM for X has no effect on that right.

NetWare 4.*x*: Inherited Rights Filter

In NetWare 4.*x*, the inheritance mechanism is known as the Inherited Rights Filter (IRF). For files and directories, the IRF works the same way as the IRM.

In addition, the IRF controls access to objects and properties in containers on the NetWare Directory Services (NDS) tree. Because the IRF can block Supervisor rights under certain conditions, it is wise to grant a trustee all rights that are appropriate, rather than granting just the Supervisor right.

BROADER CATEGORY
Access Rights

IRP (I/O Request Packet)

Used in Windows NT and NT Advanced Server for communication between drivers.

IRQ (Interrupt Request Line)

An IRQ is a mechanism for signaling an interrupt in PC hardware. Each device attached to a computer is assigned an IRQ. When it wants a service from the CPU (central processing unit), the device signals on this line and waits.

IRQs have different priority levels. The higher priority lines are assigned to the most important functions on the PC. By doing this, an operating system or interrupt handler can be sure that no vital activities are interrupted.

When configuring devices on your machine, it is very important that you do not have two devices that use the same IRQ—at least if there is any chance that the two devices will be used at the same time.

IRQL (Interrupt Request Level)

In Windows NT and NT Advanced Server (NTAS), a measure of relative priority for interrupt request lines. During program or thread execution, a processor uses a cutoff interrupt request level. Interrupts below that level are blocked (masked), while interrupts at or above that level are handled. A thread can change the IRQL.

IRSG (Internet Research Steering Group)

In the Internet community, the group that oversees the Internet Research Task Force (IRTF).

SEE ALSO
Internet

IRTF (Internet Research Task Force)

A group within the Internet community that works on long-term research projects. These projects may concern any aspect of Internet operations, and some results have led or may lead to major changes in certain aspects of Internet activity.

IRV (International Reference Version)

A particular variant of the IA5 (International Alphabet 5) character-encoding scheme. IRV is identical to the ASCII encoding scheme.

IS (Intermediate System)

In the OSI Reference Model, an Intermediate System is a network entity that serves as a relay element between two or more subnetworks. For example, repeaters, bridges, routers, and X.25 circuits are all intermediate systems at the physical, data-link, network, and network layers, respectively.

Architecturally, an intermediate system uses at most the bottom three layers of the OSI Reference Model: network, data-link, and physical. These are the so-called subnet layers. This is in contrast to an end system

a
b
c
d
e
f
g
h
i
j
k
l
m
n
o
p
q
r
s
t
u
v
w
x
y
z

(ES), which uses all seven layers of the model. A node is an end system.

An intermediate system is also known as a *relay open system* in the OSI Reference Model. You will also see *internetworking unit*, or *IWU*, used to refer to an intermediate system.

BROADER CATEGORY
OSI Reference Model

COMPARE
End System (ES)

IS (Internet Standard)

An Internet Standard is a specification that has undergone a formal evaluation and testing process, has proven stable and viable, and has been widely implemented. For example, an Internet Standard might be a specification for a protocol.

Internet Standard is the final level in a three-stage process:

Proposed Standard (PS): A specification that appears robust is submitted for testing. This specification is sufficiently detailed and stable to warrant implementation.

Draft Standard (DS): A specification that has been a Proposed Standard for at least six months and which has been tested in at least two implementations that have interacted with each other.

Internet Standard (IS): A specification that has been a Draft Standard for at least four months and has general acceptance as worthy of implementation and use.

ISA (Industry Standard Architecture)

The architecture for the PC expansion bus used in the original IBM PC and in its descendants (including the XT, AT, and models based on the 386, 486 and higher chips). This architecture provides for 8- and 16-bit access to the PC and allows limited control of the bus. Compare it with EISA, MCA, PCI, and VESA.

ISDN (Integrated Services Digital Network)

ISDN is a potential telecommunications standard that is capable of sending digitally encoded voice, data, video, and other signals on the same lines. ISDN can also provide access to a variety of communications, information processing, and supplementary services. The figure "Context and properties of ISDN" summarizes the characteristics of ISDN.

ISDN is a completely digital service. An ISDN implementation must provide any adapters needed to translate analog or non-ISDN compatible signals. ISDN has the following features:

- Supports bandwidths of about 2 megabits per second (Mbps)—enough to fill a European E1 transmission channel

- Uses a single digital link to get the gamut of a user's communications devices (telephone, fax, computer, or video) onto the ISDN lines

---

**CONTEXT AND
PROPERTIES OF ISDN**

Telecommunications

Analog
    Telephone Service
Digital
    ISDN
    BISDN

ISDN

Provides bearer services
(for digital communications),
teleservices
(for information processing),
and supplementary services
(for convenience and flexibility).

BRI (Basic Rate Interface) provides a throughput of
144 kbps.

PRI (Primary Rate Interface)
provides a throughput of up to 2 Mbps.

Supported bearers include: X.25, frame relay,
circuit-switching.

Supported teleservices include:
fax, teletex, videotex, electronic mail.

Supplementary services include:
call waiting, conferencing, fast dialing.

Supports switching within a PBX or across a
network of unlimited size.

- Provides bearer services for communications, teleservices for information processing, and supplementary services

- Allows for internal and external switching, so that calls can stay within a PBX (private branch exchange) or travel across a vast network to a destination that might be halfway around the world

ISDN Services

ISDN provides access to a wide variety of services, as illustrated in the figure "ISDN services."

Bearer Services

Bearer services are concerned with moving information from one location to another. Several bearers are supported:

- Frame relay, which uses fast packet-switching and stripped down processing to provide 2 megabits per second (Mbps) throughput

- X.25, which provides packet-switched services at modest speeds, but with good error handling and flexible routing services

- Circuit-switched connections capable of carrying voice or data at up to 64 kilobits per second (kbps), and even at multiples of this rate

ISDN SERVICES

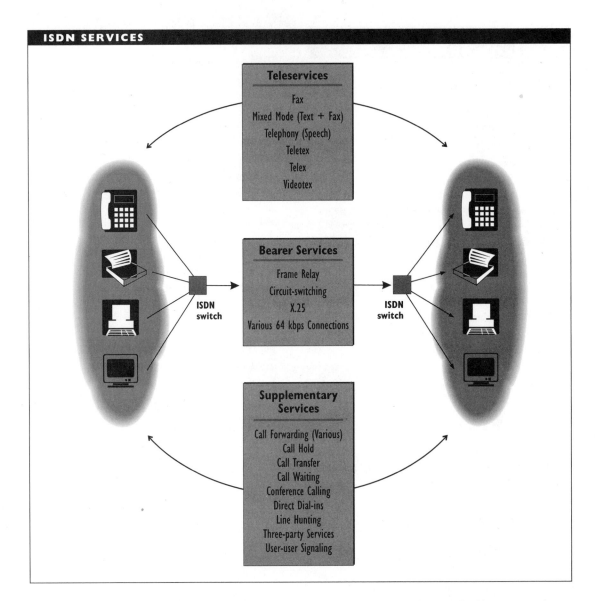

Teleservices

Teleservices are concerned with processing information in various ways. Teleservices include the following:

- Mixed mode, which allows a combination of text and image (facsimile) information to be sent together

- Telefax, which provides fax transmission, store, and forward capabilities

- Teletex, which provides text communication capabilities using a standardized alphabet

- Telex, which provides interactive communication capabilities

- Videotex, which includes capabilities for sending, storing, and retrieving text and graphics information

Supplementary Services

The supplementary services are designed to make it easier to use the bearer and teleservices. Supplementary services include telephony's greatest hits, including caller ID, call forwarding and waiting, and conference calling.

ISDN Equipment

The CCITT has provided detailed recommendations concerning the types of

equipment that can be used with ISDN and also how to accomplish this. Several categories of equipment are distinguished. The categories and their functions are summarized in the table "ISDN Equipment Categories." The figure "ISDN hardware and interfaces" shows how these elements fit together.

ISDN Transmission Rates

ISDN supports either medium- or high-speed transmission rates. Rates are based on the number of B and D channels allocated.

D channels are used for signaling; B (for bearer) channels carry data. D channels may be 16 or 64 kbps; B channels are 64 kbps.

The BRI (Basic Rate Interface) rate consists of two B and one 16 kbps D channel (2B+D), which equal a bandwidth of 144 kbps.

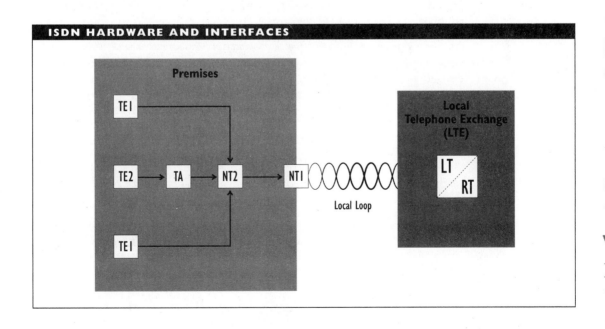

ISDN HARDWARE AND INTERFACES

a b c d e f g h i j k l m n o p q r s t u v w x y z

The configuration for the PRI (Primary Rate Interface) rate depends on where the lines are. In the United States, Canada, and Japan, a PRI line consists of 23B+D. This D channel is 64 kbps, so the PRI rate is 1.536 Mbps. In Europe, the PRI rate is 30B+D, for a bandwidth of 1.920 Mbps.

ISDN transmission channels can also be grouped in other ways. The following H channels have been defined:

- H_0, which consists of six B channels, for a bandwidth of 384 kbps.

- H_10, which consists of the 23 B channels from the PRI, and has a transmission rate of 1.472 Mbps. This channel is used only in the United States.

- H_11, which is just another name for the PRI and has a transmission rate of 1.472 Mbps. It is used only in the United States.

- H_12, which again is just another name for the PRI and has a transmission rate of 1.920 Mbps. It is used in Europe.

ISDN EQUIPMENT CATEGORIES

CATEGORY	DESCRIPTION
TE2	Hardware that is not compatible with ISDN, such as telephones, computers, video devices, and fax machines. TE2 equipment is connected over an R Interface to a terminal adapter, which makes the incoming signals ISDN-compatible.
TEI	Hardware that is compatible with ISDN.
TA (Terminal Adapter)	Mediates between a TE2 device and the ISDN network. The TA is connected to the NT2 (the user's switching exchange) over an S interface. The TA's output will conform to the appropriate one of four CCITT standards: V.110, V.120, X.30, or X.31.
NT2	Provides a switching exchange on the user's premises. Such an exchange can take supported input from the appropriate device, either directly or through a TA. The NT2 can then move the signal to an internal network (such as a PBX) or send it on to the service provider's lines. The NT2 is connected to the TE2 or TA components over an S interface; the NT2 is connected to the NT1 over a T interface.
NT1	The point at which the service provider's lines and switches terminate and the user's equipment (CPE) begins. There is a T interface between an NT1 and an NT2 at the customer's end. The NT1 is connected to a local carrier's central office over a U interface, which gets the 4-wire configuration on the user's premises down to the 2-wire configuration on the phone lines.
LT (Line Termination)	The point in the central office at which the lines from the user's NT1 terminate. This location communicates over a V interface with the analogous termination for exchanges (ET).
ET (Exchange Termination)	Also located at the central office.

ISDN has long been popular in Europe, but was always an up-and-coming technology here—until recently. It has taken several years, but ISDN is finally getting established in North America. This growth is being spurred, in part, by the rapid drop in rates for individual subscribers and also by installation fee waivers being offered as incentives by providers. Its growing popularity is spurring developers and other workers in the field to revise or upgrade existing methods or protocols. For example, in the Internet community, a multilink version of the PPP (Point-to-Point Protocol) has been developed.

Despite the healthy growth rate due to its new-found popularity, it's still not clear whether it will be ISDN or its broadband big brother—broadband ISDN (BISDN)—that will become *the* digital technology.

PRIMARY SOURCES

The CCITT's I-series of recommendations are all concerned with ISDN in one form or another. Recommendations I.112, I.120, and I.200 provide general definitions and orientations.

ISM (Industrial, Scientific, and Medical)

A term used to refer to three frequency ranges made available in 1985 by the FCC for unlicensed spread spectrum communication. Prior to this action, these ranges—902–928 MHz, 2.4–2.5 GHz, and 5.8–5.9 GHz—had been allocated for industrial, scientific, and medical use, respectively.

ISN (Information Systems Network)

A high-speed switching network from AT&T. ISN can handle both voice and data transmission, and can connect to many popular networks, including Ethernet and SNA-based mainframes.

ISN (Internet Society News)

The official newsletter of the Internet Society (ISOC).

ISO (International Standardization Organization)

A worldwide body made up of representative groups from member nations. The ISO develops communications and other types of standards, including the seven-layer OSI Reference Model for connecting different types of computer systems. It is also sometimes called the International Standards Organization.

iso(1)

In the global tree of networking information, a top-level subtree administered by the ISO. Objects found under this subtree include the Internet, and network management topics.

SEE ALSO

Global Tree

Isochronous

Isochronous means time-sensitive. In particular, an isochronous transmission or communication session is one whose operation is dependent on constant time intervals.

An isochronous connection ensures that there will always be an integral number of time intervals between any two transmissions, whether synchronous or asynchronous. This type of transmission capability is needed, for example, for digitized voice or video signals.

Isochronous Media Access Control (IMAC)

SEE

IMAC (Isochronous Media Access Control)

ISOCON

A Novell NetWare tool for managing and monitoring the OSI-compliant protocol stack in a multiprotocol network. ISOCON provides data- and error-rate information for devices that use protocols based on the OSI Reference Model. Compare it with ATCON and TCPCON.

ISODE (International Standards Organization Development Environment)

An implementation of the higher layers of the OSI Reference Model, to enable them to operate in a TCP/IP network. It is pronounced "I sew dee ee."

isoENET

A variant of Ethernet designed for isochronous (constant rate) transmissions, which are required, for example, when sending video or voice. The isoENET specifications were developed largely by National Semiconductor, and have been submitted as a proposed standard to the IEEE 802.9 committee. These specifications support transmissions using ISDN (Integrated Services Digital Network) signaling methods—but running over Category 3 UTP (unshielded twisted pair) cable.

IsoENET has a 16 Mbps bandwidth, which is broken into two major components. In addition to the 10 Mbps bandwidth for ordinary Ethernet transmissions, isoENET supports up to 96 B channels, each with a 64 Kbps capacity—for a total throughput of about 6 Mbps—for the isochronous part of the transmission.

The Ethernet channel travels just as on an ordinary Ethernet network. The isochronous data is removed at a Hub/Switch, and is sent to a PBX (private branch exchange) or to a TDM (time division multiplexer). The isochronous channel's signaling is compatible with both ISDN and ATM networks.

BROADER CATEGORIES

Ethernet; Isochronous

SEE ALSO

PACE (Priority Access Control Enabled)

ISP (International Standardized Profile)

A standardized subset of a not-yet-finalized specification—that is, one still under development. A *profile* (also known as a *functional standard*) is a clearly defined subset of an emerging standard—presumably a subset that provides enough of the specification to permit a working implementation of at least the subset.

In an effort to avoid, or at least minimize, the chaos that can result when vendors, countries, or areas implement different parts of a not-yet-standardized specification, the ISO (International Standardization Organization) published a set of guidelines for creating standardized subsets. These guidelines are published in ISO Technical Report 10000, and they provide a mechanism whereby the individual profiles created by regional working groups or standards committees can be coordinated by a Regional Workshop Coordinating Committee (RWCC).

ISU (Integrated Service Unit)

In digital telephone services, a device that consists of CSU (Channel Service Unit) and DSU (Digital Service Unit), and that replaces a modem on a DDS (Digital Data Service) line.

ITC (Independent Telephone Company)

A local exchange carrier (LEC) that is not a Bell operating company (BOC). There are currently more than 1500 such companies in the United States.

ITR (Internet Talk Radio)

Audio programs distributed over the MBONE (multicast backbone) attached to the regular Internet. For information about ITR, send an e-mail message to the info-server at info@radio.com.

SEE ALSO
MBONE

ITT (Invitation To Transmit)

In an ARCnet network architecture, the token frame.

ITU (International Telecommunications Union)

ITU is a United Nations agency formed to help develop and standardize telecommunications around the world. The ITU had three subagencies:

- The ubiquitous CCITT (Consultative Committee for International Telephony and Telegraphy), which is responsible for dozens of communications, interface, and other types of standards. On March 1, 1993, the CCITT was officially replaced by the ITU-T (International Telecommunication Union—Telecommunication

Standardization Sector). CCITT publications are now known as ITU-T publications.

- The IFRB (International Frequency Registration Board), which is responsible for allocating frequency bands in the electromagnetic spectrum for telecommunications. Together with the CCIR (next item), the IFRB has been replaced by the ITU-R (International Telecommunication Union—Radiocommunication Standardization Sector).

- The CCIR (Consultative Committee on International Radio), which is responsible for recommendations relating to radio communications. Together with the IFRB, the CCIR has been replaced by the ITU-R (International Telecommunication Union—Radiocommunication Standardization Sector).

ITU-T (International Telecommunication Union—Telecommunication Standardization Sector)

The official designation for the committee that replaced the CCITT (Consultative Committee for International Telegraphy and Telephony) on March 1, 1993. Sometimes also written as *ITU-TS* or *ITU-TSS*.

IVD (Integrated Voice and Data)

The physical integration of voice and data in a single network is the primary focus of the working group for IEEE 802.9. In practice, this amounts to the integration of ISDN (Integrated Services Digital Network) and LAN (local-area network) architectures and protocols. This has resulted in the Integrated Services for Local Area Networks (ISLAN) standard, which was approved in 1993 as IEEE standard 802.9.

IEEE 802.9 specifies the interface between equipment that produces packetized or time-sensitive (isochronous) data and an access unit, which uses TDM (time division multiplexing) to combine the data for further transmission.

IVR (Interactive Voice Response)

A term for various computer telephony configurations that include voice processing technology. Generally, a user uses a touch tone phone to communicate with such a system, and the system uses digitized voice or voice synthesis to respond.

Examples of IVR systems include automated order entry lines, crossword puzzle answer services, and college registration lines (electronic rather than human ones). In an automated order entry system, the caller enters product codes by pressing buttons on the phone, the system confirms the item name, availability, and price by voice response, and the order is entered into the system.

IWU (Internetworking Unit)

An intermediate system.

SEE ALSO

IS (Intermediate System)

IXC (Interexchange Carrier)

A level of telephone company service that
provides long-distance connections between
local exchange carriers (LECs), or local telephone companies, also called an interexchange channel. Some of the better-known
IXCs include AT&T InterSpan, MCI Communications, Sprint, and WilTel.

a
b
c
d
e
f
g
h
i
j
k
l
m
n
o
p
q
r
s
t
u
v
w
x
y
z

Jabber Detector

In a network that uses the CSMA/CD media access method, a device that helps prevent a node from transmitting constantly (for example, if the node is malfunctioning).

Jabber Packet

In an Ethernet network, a meaningless transmission generated by a network node because of a network malfunction (such as a faulty transceiver) or other error. A jabber packet is larger than the maximum size (1,518 bytes for Ethernet) and contains a bad CRC value. In contrast, long frames exceed the maximum frame length, but have a valid CRC value.

Jack

A female connector; specifically, a connector with sockets, or slots. This is in contrast to a male connector, known as a plug.

SEE ALSO
Connector

Jacket

The outer cover, or sheath, on a cable. The material of which the jacket is made will determine, in large part, the cable's safety properties. For example, a plenum cable jacket must be constructed from fire-resistant material such as Teflon.

SEE ALSO
Cable

Jamming

Jamming refers to the radiation of a specific range of frequencies in order to make it more difficult or impossible to use signals in that frequency range for communication. Jamming may be deliberate or accidental.

Active jamming—by far the most common type—is deliberate jamming.

In *passive jamming*, the interference arises as an incidental side effect of another action. For example, passive jamming may occur because someone in the vicinity happens to be using the same frequency range.

Jam Signal

In an Ethernet network, a signal sent to tell other nodes on the network that a packet collision has taken place.

SEE ALSO
CSMA/CD; Ethernet

JANET (Joint Academic Network)

An electronic-mail (e-mail) network run by universities and other academic institutions in Great Britain. JANET is an X.25 network, and provides e-mail access to just about anywhere in the world through connections to other networks, such as BITNET and JUNET.

Jargon File

A file containing various informative, amusing, and enlightening terms related to computers and the computing culture. The file is available on the World Wide Web (WWW) at the following URL (uniform resource locator, essentially a document address):

http://www.ccil.org/jargon/jargon.html

It is also available as a highly recommended book: *The New Hacker's Dictionary, 2nd edition,* edited by Eric Raymond (MIT Press).

JCL (Job Control Language)

A command language that provides the instructions for an operating system to run an application program.

JDA (Joint Development Agreement)

An agreement between IBM and Microsoft to develop various operating system technology, such as OS/2. The agreement has since been terminated. Each vendor went in its own development direction: OS/2 for IBM and Windows NT for Microsoft.

JEDI (Joint Electronic Data Interchange)

A United Nations task force that represents the United Nations in meetings and events related to EDI (Electronic Data Interchange).

Jitter

In signaling, a variation in the timing between the source's and receiver's clocks or in the constancy of the source clock rate. *Phase jitter* can cause the signal to be slightly out of phase. In *amplitude jitter,* the amplitude of a signal varies over time.

Job Control Language (JCL)

SEE

JCL (Job Control Language)

Job Transfer and Manipulation (JTM)

SEE

JTM (Job Transfer and Manipulation)

Journaling

In transaction processing, a strategy in which every transaction is recorded, so that a database or file can be re-created in case of failure or malfunction.

JPEG (Joint Photographic Experts Group)

An image compression standard that uses a discrete cosine transformation to achieve compression ratios as high as 100:1. JPEG, pronounced "jay peg," is an example of a lossy algorithm, which means that some image details will be lost at high compression ratios.

Originally implemented only in hardware, JPEG compression schemes are now available in many image viewing or handling packages. JPEG compression occurs in three steps:

1. Discrete cosine transformation (DCT), which converts image data into a breakdown based on frequencies.

2. Quantization, which adjusts the granularity (number of bits) used to represent various frequencies, so that little storage is wasted to represent rarely

occurring frequencies. The coarser granularity for these infrequent frequencies introduces the loss during the compression. The degree of compression (and concomitant loss of information) depends on how the granularity is adjusted.

3. Lossless compression of the quantization data. Once the data have been reduced by dropping out details of rarely occurring information, the remaining information is reduced again by applying a common compression algorithm (such as Huffman or run length encoding).

JSA (Japanese Standards Association)

The Japanese counterpart to ANSI (American National Standards Institute) in the United States or to the CSA (Canadian Standards Association) in Canada.

JTC (Joint Technical Committee)

Any of several such committees formed by the ISO (International Standards Commitee) and IEC (International Electrotechnical Commission). Perhaps the best known is JTC1, which is the committee that was largely responsible for the OSI Reference Model.

JTM (Job Transfer and Manipulation)

In the OSI Reference Model, one of several file transfer services (FTSs) defined at the application layer. JTM enables an application to do data processing on a remote machine.

SEE ASO

ASE (Application Service Element)

Jughead (Jonzy's Universal Gopher Hierarchy Excavation and Display)

In the world of gophers (file finders and fetchers) on the Internet, Jughead is a program that makes it possible to limit a search to a specified set of gopher servers. Jughead accomplishes this by searching only the higher-level menus of "gopherspace"—which are more likely to be associated with particular servers.

To use Jughead, you must point a gopher client to a Jughead server—for example, the one at gopher.utah.edu. On many servers, you can also get Jughead by selecting a menu item that reads something like "Search Gopherspace by Top-level Menus." Such a menu may not mention Jughead at all.

BROADER CATEGORY

Gopher

COMPARE

Archie; Veronica

Jukebox

An optical storage system that can hold multiple disks at the same time, allowing one of these to be selected at any given time.

Jumbo Group

In telecommunications, a jumbo group is a multichannel group consisting of six master groups. A *master group* is itself a conglomerate of a large number of channels. The jumbo group consists of 3,600 voice channels, all transmitted simultaneously over a

JUMBO GROUP CONSTITUENTS		
NAME	BANDWIDTH	NUMBER OF VOICE CHANNELS
Channel	4 kHz	1
Group	48 kHz	12
Super Group	240 kHz	60 (5 groups)
Master Group	2,400 kHz	600 (10 super groups)
Jumbo Group	14.4 MHz	3,600 (6 master groups)

broadband connection. The table "Jumbo Group Constituents" shows the way a jumbo group is built up.

Jumper

A wire or metal bridge whose placement can be used to close a circuit. A jumper can establish electrical connections that indicate configuration settings. Jumpers are alternatives to DIP switches for storing configuration values. A group of jumpers is called a *jumper block*.

JUNET (Japanese UNIX Network)

A research network for noncommercial institutions and organizations.

a
b
c
d
e
f
g
h
i
j
k
l
m
n
o
p
q
r
s
t
u
v
w
x
y
z

K

Used, generally in lowercase, as an abbreviation for the prefix *kilo*, as in kbps (kilobits per second). This order of magnitude corresponds to 2^{10} which is 1,024, or roughly 10^3. A kilobyte (KB) is 1,024 bytes. A kilohertz (kHz) is 1,024 cycles per second.

SEE ALSO
Orders of Magnitude

KA9Q

An implementation of the TCP/IP protocol suite for packet radio systems. KA9Q is discussed in RFC 1208.

KDC (Key Distribution Center)

In data-encryption terminology, a KDC is a center for storing, managing, and distributing encryption keys.

KDD (Kokusai Denshin Denwa)

A Japanese long-distance telephone service provider.

Kerberos

Kerberos is a network security system originally developed for Project Athena at MIT (Massachusetts Institute of Technology). Kerberos is a *distributed authentication system*. It verifies that a user is legitimate when the user logs in, as well as every time the user requests a service. The system is designed to provide authentication for users who may be logging in to the network from an unattended workstation. Such stations must be regarded as suspect, or untrusted, because their physical security cannot be guaranteed.

Kerberos protects transmissions by using special keys, called *tickets*, to encrypt transmissions between Kerberos and a user. Kerberos uses private-key encryption methods. This is in contrast to a service such as Digital Equipment Corporation's (DEC's) DASS (Distributed Authentication Security Service), which uses public-key encryption.

BROADER CATEGORIES
Authentication; Security

SEE ALSO
DASS (Distributed Authentication Security Service)

Kermit

A popular file transfer protocol. Kermit has been implemented on most types of hardware, and it is widely used, particularly when logging on to bulletin board systems (BBSs).

Kernel

The kernel is the core of an operating system. The kernel contains the most essential operating system services, such as task schedulers and interrupt handlers, and is always loaded whenever the operating system is active. It can call other operating system services (such as file or other I/O services) when requested by a user, a function, or an application.

Keyboard Send and Receive (KSR)

SEE

KSR (Keyboard Send and Receive)

Key Distribution Center (KDC)

SEE

KDC (Key Distribution Center)

Keying

The process of making components non-symmetrical in order to make sure they are connected properly. Keying is important in situations in which incorrect connections can cause damage to circuitry and components. For example, modular telephone (RJ-*xx*) plugs and jacks may be keyed; MMJ connectors are a keyed variant of RJ-*xx* connectors. Cables connecting disk drives to power supplies may also be keyed.

Key Management Protocol (KMP)

SEE

KMP (Key Management Protocol)

Killer Channel

In digital telecommunications, a transmission channel whose timing is off, so that the channel overlaps and interferes with other channels.

Kill file

On the Internet, a data file that contains instructions to filter out ("kill") news postings and e-mail from certain persons or about certain topics. Also called a *bozo filter.*

KIS (Knowbot Information Service)

On the Internet, an experimental service that can query directory services in order to retrieve requested information. KIS uses knowbot programs to search the directory services for the information.

KMP (Key Management Protocol)

In a secure network, KMP is a protocol used for checking security keys.

Knowbot

A program that can track down information, even if it is in a remote location. Knowbots (from *knowledge robots*) are still mainly an experimental technology, although there is one well-known and widely used example: In the Internet environment, knowbots are used in the KIS (knowbot information service) to get directory service ("white pages") information.

Kokusai Denshin Denwa (KDD)

SEE

KDD (Kokusai Denshin Denwa)

KSR (Keyboard Send and Receive)

A KSR device is a telephoneless telephone—a communications device that consists of a keyboard and printer. Because the device has no storage, messages are printed as they are received and transmitted as they are typed at the keyboard.

a
b
c
d
e
f
g
h
i
j
k
l
m
n
o
p
q
r
s
t
u
v
w
x
y
z

KTS (Key Telephone System)

In telephony, a KTS is an arrangement of multiline phones in which users can press keys to access lines to a central office or to a PBX (private branch exchange), or to access KTS features. KTS features include the following:

- Putting a caller on hold
- Calling or answering on a selected line
- Contacting a party over an intercom
- Transferring a call to another line

The KTS signals are sent to and processed by a *key service unit,* or KSU.

An EKTS is a KTS that uses electrical switches. By reducing the entire KTS down to electronic circuitry, it becomes easier to add features and to install the KTS in a telephone.

LAA (Locally Administered Address)

In a Token Ring network connected to a mainframe, the LAA is a parameter used by a 3174 controller to determine whether the node can access the mainframe.

LAM (Lobe Attachment Module)

In a Token Ring network, a LAM is a box with multiple interfaces to which new nodes (known as *lobes*) for the network can be attached. A LAM may have interfaces for up to 20 lobes. Functionally, a LAM is like a multi-station access unit (MAU), but with a larger capacity: 20 nodes, as opposed to 8 for the MAU. The LAM interfaces may use either IBM connectors or RJ-45 plugs.

LAMs can be daisy-chained and connected to a hub, known as a *controlled access unit (CAU)* in token-ring terminology. Each CAU can handle up to four LAMs, for a total of 80 lobes.

LAMA (Local Automatic Message Accounting)

The process by which the local telephone company handles automatic billing for local and toll calls. This accounting method requires automatic number identification (ANI), a capability that has been adapted to provide caller ID services. An alternative accounting strategy, CAMA (centralized automatic message accounting), accomplishes the same thing but at a central office.

LAN (Local-Area Network)

A LAN is a collection of two or more computers that are located within a limited distance of each other and that are connected to each other, directly or indirectly. LANs differ in the way the computers are connected, in how information moves around the network, and in what machine (if any) is in charge of the network. The figure "Context and properties of a LAN" summarizes some of the features of LANs.

The computers in a LAN may be PCs, Macintoshes, minicomputers, mainframes, or machines with other architectures. However, there are restrictions on the combinations that are feasible and sensible. This article focuses on PC-based LANs, although other configurations are also mentioned.

LAN Terminology

The PCs in a LAN are called *nodes,* and nodes may be either *servers* or *workstations.* Workstations are sometimes known just as *stations.*

Minicomputers or mainframe computers in a LAN generally serve as *hosts* for PCs or terminals that are connected to the computer. Most computer-terminal connections are over telephone or dedicated lines, so that these configurations are generally considered *wide-area networks,* or *WANs.*

Nodes are connected to a network by means of a *network interface card (NIC),* which is also called a *network adapter card, network board,* and a dozen other names. The NIC is installed in an expansion slot in the node. This NIC is connected directly or indirectly to the network cable. Each

CONTEXT AND PROPERTIES OF A LAN

Context
Network Types
    CAN
    DAN
    Enterprise Network
    GAN
    MAN
    WAN
    LAN ─────────────────────────────┐

LAN Properties

LANs can be PC-based (servers and workstations) or host-based (hosts and terminals).

Server-based LANs have a dedicated server. The NOS usually replaces the native OS, and security can be well-controlled. Such LANs are suited for a large range of network sizes.

On peer-to-peer LANs most machines can be server or workstation. The NOS often runs under the machine's native OS, and security is not well-controlled. Peer LANs are not suitable for large networks.

LAN architectures include ARCnet, Ethernet, FDDI, and Token Ring.

Architecture determines network size, distance limitations, and lower-level protocols.

NOS determines higher-level protocols and available services.

node must have its own NIC. A server can have multiple NICs, which allow that server to be connected to multiple networks simultaneously.

Types of LANs

LANs differ in their configuration at two levels:

- In the administrative relationship between nodes. In this sense, LANs are divided into *server-based* and *peer-to-peer* (or just peer) varieties.

- In the physical and logical relationships among nodes. This has to do with the manner in which information moves around the network. LANs differ in the *architecture* (Ethernet, Token Ring, FDDI, and so on) and *topology* (bus, ring, or star) they use.

Server-Based LANs versus Peer-to-Peer LANs

In a *server-based network,* a server controls access to some resource (such as a hard disk or printer) and serves as a host for the workstations connected to the server. A workstation requests services, such as access to files or programs on the hard disk or use of a printer, from a server.

a
b
c
d
e
f
g
h
i
j
k
l
m
n
o
p
q
r
s
t
u
v
w
x
y
z

SERVER-BASED AND PEER-TO-PEER NETWORK OPERATING SYSTEMS

Examples of peer-to-peer NOSs include:

- 10net 5.1 from Tiara Systems

- Complete Network from Buffalo Products

- LANsmart from D-Link Systems

- LANstep from Hayes Microcomputer Products

- LANtastic from Artisoft

- Personal NetWare from Novell

- PowerLAN from Performance Technology

- Web from Webcorp

- Windows for Workgroups from Microsoft

All of these NOSs support peer-to-peer networking, but some also provide more of the capabilities (for example, security) expected of server-based NOSs. Examples of such NOSs are Hayes LANstep version 2.0 from Hayes Microcomputer Products and Personal Netware from Novell.

NOSs for server-based networks include:

- LAN Manager from Microsoft

- LAN Server from IBM

- NetWare from Novell

- PacerShare from Pacer Software

- PathWorks from Digital Equipment Corporation (DEC)

- StarGroup System from NCR

- TotalMac from Syntax

- VINES from Banyan Systems

- Windows NT Advanced Server (NTAS) from Microsoft

Servers run the network operating system (NOS) software; workstations run client software that manages the communication between the workstation and the network.

Servers may be dedicated or not. A *dedicated server* can be used only as a server; it cannot be used as a workstation as well. A *nondedicated server* can be used as a workstation, as needed, even when it continues to perform server duties.

A server-based LAN, in which each node may be either a server or workstation as the need arises, is in contrast to a *peer-to-peer network*. In general, large networks—those with more than a few dozen nodes—are more likely to be server-based. This is because the reliability and security of server-based networks are easier to test than those of peer-to-peer networks.

Peer-to-peer LANs, also known simply as *peer LANs,* are more egalitarian in that each node can initiate actions, access other nodes, and provide services for other nodes without requiring a server's permission, although access or password restrictions may be in effect.

For example, in a peer-to-peer LAN, a given node (node A) may provide services for another node (node B) at one point; at another time, node B may provide similar or different services for node A.

Network software for peer LANs is more likely to work *with* the native operating system (for example, DOS). In contrast, the network software for server-based LANs generally replaces the native operating system. One reason for this is the server in a large network is kept very busy, and it becomes too inefficient to go through two layers of operating systems. In the case of DOS, there is another, more fundamental reason: DOS cannot do multitasking.

LAN Topologies

A topology describes the physical or logical layout of a LAN. The *physical topology* is concerned with how the cabling connects nodes. There are several physical topologies, including bus, ring, star, tree, and star-wired ring. Some of these are variants of others; some are hybrids.

A *logical topology* describes how information is passed among nodes. There are only two fundamental logical topologies:

- *Bus,* in which all information is broadcast, so that every node gets the information at (just about exactly) the same time. Since information is generally intended only for a single node, the other nodes discard the message as soon as they determine they are not the destination.

- *Ring,* in which information is passed around from node to node until it reaches its destination.

LAN Architectures

A LAN architecture includes cabling, topology, media (network) access method, and packet format. The architectures that are commonly used for LANs are based in electrical wiring, although some of these architectures also support optical fiber as an alternative transmission medium.

LAN architectures are in a transition period. The traditional architectures, including ARCnet, Ethernet, and Token Ring, are being replaced by high-speed versions, which are an order of magnitude faster than their predecessors. It is not yet clear just how rapid the transition to the high-speed versions will be.

The current, but obsolescing, generation of LAN architectures support transmission speeds ranging from about 2.5 megabits per second (Mbps) for ARCnet networks to 16 Mbps for some Token Ring

a
b
c
d
e
f
g
h
i
j
k
l
m
n
o
p
q
r
s
t
u
v
w
x
y
z

implementations. Ethernet supports speeds up to 10 Mbps.

The up-and-coming architectures are either high-speed variants of existing ones or new, fiber-based architectures, such as FDDI (Fiber Distributed Data Interface) or ATM (Asynchronous Transfer Mode). The fiber-based architectures are also used for WANs. Examples of high-speed variants include several fast Ethernet versions, which support speeds of up to 100 Mbps, and ARCnet Plus, which supports a 20 Mbps rate.

LAN Hardware

The hardware for PC-based LANs includes computers, NICs, cables, connectors, wiring centers, safety devices, and tools.

Computer

For most PC-based networking packages, server machines must be at least AT-class, and in many cases, 80386 models or better. Workstations can be lower-level machines. See the Computer article for more information about computers used in networks.

NIC (Network Interface Card)

A NIC makes a PC network-capable. Each PC needs at least one NIC. NICs are designed for particular network architectures (Ethernet, Token Ring, and so on). Note that some computers (for example, Macintoshes) come with networking capabilities built-in and do not need a special NIC as long as you use the native networking resources.

In general, ARCnet and Ethernet cards are cheaper than Token Ring cards, and fiber-optic cards are currently more expensive than some PCs.

Cable

The cable can be coaxial, twisted-pair (possibly telephone cable), or fiber-optic, depending on the resources and on the network architecture. For certain network types, you need cable for both the main network trunk and also for attaching individual nodes to this trunk or to wiring centers (such as hubs or concentrators). This "attachment" cable is known in various contexts as *drop, patch, adapter,* or *transceiver cable.*

In some cases, the cost of the actual cable will be low compared with the cost of testing and installing the cable. In fact, the cable installation costs can sometimes be so high that it may be wise, economically, to install fiber-optic cable for the future while installing copper (twisted-pair or coaxial) cable for the present. See the Cable article for general information about network cabling and the Cable, Coaxial; Cable, Fiber-Optic; and Cable, Twisted-Pair articles for information about the specific cable types.

Connectors

The connectors must be suitable for the cable being used. Connectors are used to link cable segments, to attach nodes to a network trunk, and to connect a cable to a wiring center. Certain connectors are used to terminate a cable segment to prevent spurious signals on the network. Some of the terminators must have special grounding caps.

See the Connector and Connector, Fiber-Optic articles for more information about connectors.

Wiring Center

Wiring centers are components to which multiple nodes are connected in some network architectures. Wiring centers may simply collect connections and relay signals (as passive hubs do), or the centers may clean and regenerate the signal before directing and relaying it (as active or intelligent hubs do).

Depending on how big and how capable you need them, wiring centers may cost you anywhere from a few hundred to many thousands of dollars.

Safety Devices

Safety devices protect the network from crashes or damage due to electrical irregularities or power loss. You should protect at least your servers with an uninterruptible power supply (UPS), and you should protect each workstation with at least a surge protector.

These components are mainly insurance purchases. Unlike many types of insurance, however, network insurance is always a good investment. Results of various studies show that network hardware malfunctions are disconcertingly common, and that the costs of malfunctions—in both repair expenses and in lost data and revenues—can be astronomical. On the other hand, limited protection may cost as little as $50 per workstation for surge protectors to a few

hundred dollars for a UPS for a server with a large hard disk.

Tools

The tools are partly insurance and partly convenience devices. Since networks are often most expensive when they are down or functioning incorrectly, it is important to be able to test components when things go wrong. You should also test components before installing them, to ensure that you do not install a faulty component, and then test them periodically to make sure they are functioning properly. Special tools are available for testing network components.

Network testers can be quite expensive (thousands of dollars). Convenience tools, such as wire crimpers and voltmeters, are quite inexpensive (from a few dollars to a few hundred). The amount you will need to spend on tools depends on the size of the network, the importance of the network's contents, and who will be doing network maintenance. Of course, if you do not spend the money for these tools (and for training yourself or the other person who will use them), you may end up paying even more money to have an expert come in and repair your network.

Miscellaneous Hardware

Your network might include other special hardware. For example, special disk controller boards can speed up disk access and overall performance. Remote access boards can enable users to call into a network from a remote location.

Like automobile options, network add-ons can be expensive items.

LAN Software

The software for LANs includes drivers, NOSs, network shells or requestors, network applications, management programs, diagnostic programs, and backup software. Some or all of these software components may be included in the NOS package, or they may be available as add-on products.

NIC Drivers

Drivers mediate between the NIC and the networking software running on either a workstation or the server. Drivers are hardware-specific. However, two "generic" driver interfaces have been developed: ODI (Open Data-link Interface) and NDIS (Network Driver Interface Specification).

Drivers are usually included with the NIC or with the NOS. If neither is the case, you can almost certainly download whatever driver you need from a vendor's bulletin board. (Unfortunately, the drivers are just about the only free software when it comes to networking.)

NOS

The NOS runs on the server and is responsible for processing requests from workstations, for maintaining the network, and for controlling the services and devices available to users. An NOS may replace the native operating system or run as a program on top of the native operating system. In addition, NOSs may use the native file system or introduce their own file system. For example, Novell's NetWare and Banyan VINES replace the existing operating system and use their own file systems. Novell's NetWare

for OS/2 runs simultaneously with OS/2 in a different disk partition. NetWare for UNIX runs as a process within UNIX. Artisoft's LANtastic supplements DOS and uses the DOS file system for its own directories.

The NOS can be a considerable expense. NOS software is generally priced as a function of the number of nodes you plan to attach to the network. Most vendors give you packages for predefined network sizes, such as for 5-, 10-, 25-, and 100-node networks. This vendor-biased pricing scheme may mean extra up-front expense, since you may need to pay for nodes you do not need at the moment. However, your network will probably grow to use the extra nodes, so the investment will not be wasted.

Workstation Software

Each workstation on a network needs software to handle the communication between the workstation and the network. This software is known by various names, such as *shell, redirector, requestor,* or *client.* Generally, this software works with the workstation's native operating system. Some tasks are performed by the operating system, and some are redirected to the network. How the task allocation decision is made depends on the type of network software being used.

Network-Aware Applications

Network-aware versions of applications are designed specifically to run on a network. Network-aware versions keep track of whether a file or application is already being accessed, and they may prevent additional users from accessing the same file or running the same program. Sophisticated programs designed for a client/server computing environment can run in multiple pieces on separate machines. For example, a database program may run a front end (an interface for the user) on the workstation, and a back end (to process and carry out user commands) on the server.

Network versions of software packages may not always be different from the stand-alone versions, but they will, however, almost always cost more. You may need to pay five or ten times as much for a network version as for a single copy. However, the network copy will include a license for use by multiple users, so that the cost of the network version will generally be comparable to the cost of buying multiple stand-alone versions of the software.

Network Management Software

Network management programs can monitor activity on the network and gather data on network performance. The information can be used to fine-tune and improve the performance of the network. Management software is optional and tends to be expensive, but it may help save lots of money at some later time.

Diagnostic and Backup Software

Diagnostic and backup programs can be used to help anticipate problems or to catch them early, and also to help deal with the problems once they have arisen. As with management software, network versions of some packages may be expensive, but they can save your system (and *you*) under some circumstances. For example, virus detection

can save you hours of grief and job hunting. Similarly, software for testing the hard disk can identify bad disk sectors (or sectors about to go bad) before data is written there and lost, and can move any data from bad sectors to safe locations.

Some networking software includes both diagnostic and backup capabilities. If this suits your needs, and if it works with the hardware you have, you can save yourself some money. Otherwise, you *need* to get backup software, and you should also get diagnostic software.

LAN Costs

Just as with any large-scale project, the start-up costs for LANs tend to be the major share of the expenses.

Many of the costs are one-time expenses. These will become less painful with the passage of time. If a network runs successfully for even a year without a major malfunction, the cost of a UPS will seem like small potatoes.

Depending on the network architecture you selected, the power you want, and the quality of components you intend to use, costs per node may range from a few hundred dollars (above the cost for the node itself) to many thousands of dollars (for example, for fiber-optic networks).

While you may be able to keep the price of your workstations down, you will probably need to count on a few thousand dollars (perhaps as high as $10,000 or $15,000) for each server, particularly for servers with hard disks. If you want built-in safety features (such as duplicate storage of information), this will cost even more. Again, such an additional expense may be advisable for servers but is usually unnecessary for workstations.

LAN Development

The process of developing a LAN from a gleam in someone's eye (or a sentence in a memo) to a working network has four main phases:

Planning: There may be several rounds of planning. The early rounds should be mainly research and just a little planning; with time, the relative prominence of research and planning should invert. Later planning phases involve investigating what is feasible, given your resources and needs.

Design: During the LAN design phase, you need to select a network architecture and begin specifying the details for the network. Your choices depend on what you have discovered during the planning phases.

Implementation: During this phase, the network is actually put together, debugged, and set into action. Depending on what needs to be done, this phase will include tasks ranging from buying and installing cable to connecting the hardware, installing the software, and basically getting the network up and running. Make sure you have a plan for LAN implementation.

Operation: This phase overlaps with the implementation phase. These phases may last for weeks or even months. Major revisions to the network are not uncommon in the first few months of operation. After everything is installed and has been found to work, you are ready for the day-to-day network activity. Unfortunately for a LAN administrator, even ordinary operations may not provide any respite. This is the phase during which the tasks described in the LAN Administration section become relevant.

LAN Planning

In the early planning phases, you need to investigate whether there is a need for a LAN and also an interest in having one. The goal of the first planning phase—*assessing need and desirability*—is to decide whether there is any point in trying to design a network. If you decide a network is appropriate, you next need to investigate what approaches are feasible for developing a network in your specific situation.

Need and Desirability Planning

One of the most important steps in planning a network is to investigate as thoroughly as possible the pre-network context. Study current operations to determine working patterns, bottlenecks, and needs. This will also help determine likely future needs.

Talk to the people who will be affected to determine their needs and wants, and also their expectations and fears. You will need the cooperation of the users. Be aware of and take into account company, office, and interoffice politics.

Determine the needs or problems that make a LAN desirable or necessary. If the orders for a LAN came from higher up, there may be difficulty convincing the staff; if the impetus comes from the trenches, you will need to convince the money holders. These two different audiences may require very different strategies.

Although it may be necessary or desirable to create a LAN, there are often alternatives—for example, additional stand-alone machines or the use of switchboxes—and you need to consider these as well. One way to be sure of doing this is to evaluate different ways of fulfilling employees' or management's needs.

You will need to decide whether a network will fulfill the needs identified or if an alternative will fulfill the needs as effectively at a lower cost. Be sure to keep future plans in mind. For example, a network might be more expensive up front but may be easier and cheaper to expand later on.

Determine particular resources and constraints that may influence the eventual LAN. For example, hardware and software, employee skills, and power and wiring constraints can affect your decision. Evaluate these with respect to the audience you will need to convince. For example, the front office may assume that you will be using existing cable. This may have implications for your strategy.

Once you have gathered all your data, summarize and write up this information. Be sure to reference the source of each item, and also indicate what information is verified, verifiable, unverified, and questionable (or whatever categories make the most sense for your purposes). It is always easier to go back and verify something if you know where the information came from.

Feasibility Planning

After you have finished the background research and have established a need for a network (or at least for some type of change from the present situation), you need to start thinking about what is available and what can be done.

For example, you should determine which resources (machines, cabling, software, and so on) are available and which of these resources will be usable *and useful* for a network.

Next, determine the costs for a network. Make sure to remember both the obvious and less obvious sources of expenses. Obvious ones include the following:

- Cabling for both materials and installation (keep in mind that installation costs can be high)

- Hardware (computers, NICs, and so on)

- Safety devices (UPSs, surge protectors, and so on)

- Networking and application software

- Fees: for consultants, designers, architects, and anyone else who can think of an excuse to bill you

- Ongoing costs, such as those for line leasing, the system administrator's salary, maintenance contracts, technical support, upgrades, and so on

- Training costs, for network users and administrators

a b c d e f g h i j k **l** m n o p q r s t u v w x y z

Less obvious costs include those for company downtime: the downtime during the switch over to networked operation, and then when you need to do the switch again because something went wrong with the first installation. Then there will be downtime after you have installed and implemented the system and the network goes down. It is a good idea to include emergency resources in your initial planning, so that at least some work can be done.

And also consider the costs due to temporary productivity decreases while employees get used to working on a network.

LAN Design

By the end of the network design phase, you should have detailed descriptions of what the network will look like and how it will operate. You should also have a detailed list of the components, a timetable, and an implementation procedure.

The network design process is a mystic mixture of art, science, CPA and *spendthrift* mentalities (at the same time), luck (good or bad), and accident. The design process is a detailed planning phase, operating within the constraints imposed through the feasibility study.

As with any mysterious process, there are many ways to go about it. The following sections outline a few design strategies.

Counting Nodes and Assigning Tasks

Many planning issues and tasks are simplified if you can determine the exact number of nodes on the network. Once you have some numbers, and perhaps location

information, you can begin assigning tasks and responsibilities to different nodes.

For example, if a network expects to have 500 nodes, you may want to assign tasks and capabilities in a way that minimizes the distance traveled to use those resources. One way to do this is with duplicate (or triplicate) function assignments. For example, you might define three separate print servers (each with its own printer) for three crowded areas.

Defining Network Operations

It is a good idea to begin formulating a network usage and resource statement. By sketching out how the network will function—including how information will flow, who will control its flow, and so on—you will get some insight into the most appropriate type of relationship between stations. This, in turn, will help you decide what kind of topology to use.

In some cases, the network operations may have implications for the kind of cable you will need to use. For example, if you decide to situate nodes from the same LAN on multiple floors, you may want to insist that the *riser cable* (which runs between floors) should be optical fiber.

Defining Network Administration and Security

The amount and type of security a network needs will depend on the kinds of data on the network and also on the kinds of users who are logging in to the network. For example, if it is better to destroy data than to let a competitor see it, there will be heavy emphasis on encryption and less concern with safeguarding.

In part, the security needs will help shape the type of administration the network will have. The type of network (for example, server-based or peer-to-peer) will also influence the way it will be administered.

Defining Administrative Policy

Part of the network design task includes defining a policy for how the network will be administered. It is important to have an explicit, written policy for LAN use that is ready when the LAN goes into operation.

An administrative policy will include guidelines for every important aspect of the network's operation, including the following:

- Backup and maintenance (when and how to do backups, maintenance schedules, and so on)

- Software monitoring or regulation, to ensure that licensing limits are not being violated

- Software upgrade procedures, to ensure that everyone is working with the same version of a software package

- Operating procedure for emergencies, such as virus attacks, power outages, or component malfunctions

- Security setup and enforcement, for example, to specify regulations concerning password format, required password changes, and so on

For example, you will need to decide how the use of applications will be managed. It is essential for each network user to be using the same version of application programs. Explicit procedures for ensuring this should be part of the LAN policy document.

Also, if a user's workstation becomes infected with a virus, the entire network is at risk. Therefore, if data integrity is crucial or if network downtime is unacceptably expensive, it may be necessary to set policies regarding the kinds of software users are allowed to install on a workstation. Such a policy will not be completely enforceable, but making the restrictions explicit will help emphasize the importance of the issue. Users may comply with the policy because they see the reasons for doing so.

It is also important to include in the administrative policy explicit plans for dealing with specific tasks or problems before you actually need to deal with them. While it is useful advice in general, it is crucial in relation to networks: When confronted with a problem or task, stop!

The policy should include measures for dealing carefully with the situation, to ensure that no irreversible actions are taken before the network is backed up in its current state (if possible).

The administrative policy should be updated regularly and modified as necessary.

Checklists and Worksheets

Lists represent one of the most useful general-purpose tools for just about any type of task. Because the individual items are distinct, lists are easy to expand, rearrange, and edit. They can even be organized into a more useful format, such as in a tree structure.

a b c d e f g h i j k **l** m n o p q r s t u v w x y z

A LAN DESIGN CHECKLIST

The following annotated list illustrates the kinds of questions you may find in LAN design checklists.

What services will be provided on the network? What machines will provide the services?

The answers to these questions will depend on your reasons for setting up a network in the first place, and also on the hardware you have or will make available for the network.

- Who will control access to these machines, and how will access be controlled?

    The LAN administrator will "control" access by assigning user privileges and access rights. The actual security measures instituted will depend on how costly a security breach would be. The simplest measures used to introduce such controls include logins, passwords, user IDs, and so on.

- How will access to files and services be controlled?

    As with access to machines, the LAN administrator can assign file or command privilege levels to network users.

- How will users be added and removed?

    In most cases, the processes for managing users will be fairly mechanical and will be carried out by the LAN administrator. However, it's important to establish clearly from the outset how user accounts will be managed.

- How will new users be trained? How will current users be kept up to date? Who will be responsible for providing the required training?

    Initial user training is crucial to the network's success, since inexperienced and ignorant (regarding the network) users will be unproductive, frustrated, and, eventually, stand-alone users. Depending on the situation, you may want users trained by in-house or outside staff.

- How will user operation be monitored?

    The information from monitoring users can be useful, at least during early phases. However, monitoring can be tricky, because it's imperative that users feel they have privacy on the network and do not need to worry about being watched.

- How will new software be evaluated, tested, and installed? Once tested, who will be responsible for installing it on the network and making sure it works?

    Testing software for a network can be a nightmare. Software testing may be done by an independent testing company. The advantage is that a good testing company will have a more comprehensive and systematic test suite than the more haphazard methods of most end-users. The disadvantage is that the testing will be aimed at the general network user and may not include tests that are appropriate for specific users.

- How will application programs be managed? Who will be responsible for upgrades and for making sure all users are working with the same versions of applications and files? What kinds of restrictions, if any, will there be on applications that users can run on their workstations?

  You need to ensure that network users are all using the same version of applications. Also, to avoid viruses, which can cause data loss and company downtime, you may need to set policies regarding the software that users can install on their workstations.

- How will file management and backup be managed?

  Although this is generally the LAN administrator's responsibility, the question needs to be asked because backups are so vital for a network.

- How will connections to other networks be managed, if applicable?

  The answer to this will depend, in part, on the type of networks that are to be connected. For example, connecting two Ethernet networks is less of a task than connecting an Ethernet and an SNA network.

- How will the network be maintained? For example, who will be responsible for periodic hardware checks: testing the cable integrity, hard disk, and so on?

  While it is important to be conscientious about doing maintenance on stand-alone hardware, it is essential to be compulsively so when it comes to networks. A hardware malfunction on a network can be much more costly than on a stand-alone machine. Regular and careful maintenance can help minimize the likelihood of such a malfunction.

- What provisions will be built in for network expansion?

  Network expansion is more than just adding some extra machines. It may require additional network cabling or electrical wiring. There may also be tradeoffs (such as size versus performance) to be considered. Networking software and network-based applications may need to be upgraded to allow for more users. These and other possibilities make it important to build expansion into a network design.

Several of the books in the Novell Press series have useful checklists. Two recent ones include Logan Harbaugh's *Problem Solving Guide for NetWare Systems* and David Clarke's *CNA Study Guide*.

Two types of lists are common for network design planning:

- Checklists, usually consisting of tasks and/or questions. Task lists are useful for accomplishing something; question lists are useful for verifying or checking something. Because they can be open and freeform, task lists are useful for ill-structured tasks—those that do not have simple instructions but involve multiple steps.

- Worksheets, either property summaries or action charts, such as flow charts or Booch diagrams. Property summaries are handy for making comparisons. Action charts are useful for well-defined tasks of medium complexity.

Maintenance Sheets

Make sure you set up an explicit, completely defined, and thorough hardware maintenance procedure. The maintenance should include not only event-driven troubleshooting and repair, but also preventative maintenance, such as diagnostics and cleaning to keep the hardware from failing in the first place.

Develop a checklist and a worksheet for this maintenance. These records will help ensure that maintenance tasks are done the same way every time.

LAN Implementation

The actual construction of the LAN and installation of the networking software takes place during an implementation phase. This process requires carrying out the installation plan slowly and systematically, testing each component before it is added to the network, and then again after it has been added to the network. The original installation *plan* may be revised several times during this phase, as a result of information derived from the actual installation *process*.

An implementation plan should outline on paper each phase of the installation process and should describe what happens during each phase. The plan should also note what the prerequisites and results are for each phase. Finally, the plan should specify what tests are to be run to make sure that each phase has been carried out successfully.

The implementation phase should include frequent meetings to review the progress, deal with any unanticipated problems or findings, and make any modifications suggested or required by the progress to date. The first of these meetings should take place before you begin the installation and should evaluate the "raw" implementation plan—the plan before any steps are actually carried out. After all the steps are completed, a final review meeting should be held to evaluate and sign off on the implementation.

Network Installation

The following are some general considerations and suggestions to keep in mind during LAN installation:

- If possible, keep users informed of what is happening at all times.

- If possible, get a diagram of all existing cabling, whether you plan to use the cabling or not. If you are using it, you need to test it, and you may need to repair, update, or extend it. If you do not plan to use the cabling, you may be able to use any conduits already built for installing the cable that you *will* be using.

- Test components as early in the installation as possible. For example, test cable *before* it is installed. Then test it again after it is installed.

- Cable should be installed by people who know what they are doing.

- Do not proceed to the next step in the installation until you have confirmed that the previous step was successful.

- Actual hardware installation should always include an overseer or an oversight process, just to make sure there are no obvious mistakes or oversights.

- Detailed records of the exact type of cable and connectors, including source and part numbers, are important. The same is true for components such as hubs, bridges, routers, NICs, and so on. Record this information as the components are added to the network.

- Also record *where* in the network each component is installed.

- All hardware to be used in the network should be run for an extended time before installation to give the machine's components an adequate burn-in time. Hardware should be checked very carefully after installation. Each piece should be tested as it is installed.

- Once all nodes are attached, test the entire system.

- If possible, test application software first on a non-network machine, to make sure it actually works and is free of viruses and of obvious bugs or defects.

- Install applications onto the network, and test each one carefully. Do not test software on actual data. Test only with data you can afford to lose. Back up your system before testing.

- Back up all machines before adding them to the network.

Network User and Administrator Manuals

Develop detailed manuals for all persons involved with the network, from supervisors and administrators to users. The manuals should be tailored for the audience, using a "need-to-know" criterion for deciding what to include.

User manuals need contain only information about such things as logging in to the network, accessing network services, and running applications.

Administrator manuals should include detailed information about the hardware configuration of each node, and also the basic software configuration (operating system version, RAM and storage capabilities, and so on) for all the application and network software. The administrator's manual should also include a cable map showing all cables, connectors, and NICs on the network.

Try to make the administrator manuals sufficiently detailed and complete so a trained outsider can maintain the system if necessary.

Training

The implementation plan should include training of users and of the administrator. Think very carefully about whether user training should be done by in-house or outside staff. There are advantages and disadvantages to each approach.

In-house people are more likely to know your personnel, as well as the exact needs and layout of the organization. If the LAN administrator is someone already experienced with networks *and* good at conveying

a b c d e f g h i j k **l** m n o p q r s t u v w x y z

this experience and knowledge, user instruction may be added to the list of administrative tasks.

If the administrator does not meet these standards, it is probably wiser to bring in an outside person to provide the necessary training. Keep in mind that someone who is doing a training course as a one-shot deal—whether it is the administrator or another person on your company's staff—will probably have much less experience in training than someone who is a professional trainer. The trainer must not only know the material but must also be able to present it. Not all companies have such a person.

If you pick the proper outside trainers, you can be reasonably assured that they know their stuff and can present it. (Get recommendations and references for potential trainers.) Someone who does lots of training is more likely to know the kinds of problems and difficulties users typically encounter. The trainer may arrange for a portion of the training to be dedicated just to problems.

On the other hand, outsiders are generally (but not always) more expensive than in-house trainers, especially in a rapidly growing and changing field in which information is a premium commodity. Also, outsiders do not know your company or your staff as well (but this can also be an advantage in some cases). A presentation by someone who gives presentations all the time is more likely to be formulaic, rather than being tailored to your company's particular needs.

Whether you use in-house or outside trainers, the training costs may seem high. But keep in mind that the money you invest in training can save many times that amount through improved ability and accelerated learning (and, presumably, productivity) curves. In some touchy political situations, it may even be worthwhile paying for some training before installing a network. This can be helpful, for example, if the staff is resisting the network. Getting some exposure to a network may help the staff develop a more favorable attitude.

Implementing a LAN in a Working Environment

The discussion of the implementation process has assumed that the network was being created from fresh machines. In practice, this is rarely the case. Instead, you may need to implement a network with machines that already have their applications and operating environments. Even worse, you may need to do this while these machines are expected to conduct business as usual, so that there is pressure to get the network up as quickly and smoothly as possible.

The transition between old and new systems must be planned very carefully. The network developer should remain involved during such a transition. You should have a contingency plan if the transition fails.

Various changeover strategies are possible, including the following:

Cold conversion: This is a complete and immediate changeover; it is the simplest and least expensive. However, cold conversion is not suited for operations with critical applications. Make sure you have a way of retrieving the last state of the old system and starting up from that state, in case the new system does not work.

Conversion with overlap: In this strategy, the old system keeps operating as the new one is started, so that both systems operate simultaneously for a short period. If the resources are available, this method is clearly the most desirable. The longer you can afford to run both systems, the more opportunity you have to fine-tune the network.

Piecemeal conversion: In this approach, the new system is implemented in phases. These phases must be planned, and a phase must begin only after the previous phase has been successfully completed. This strategy requires fewer resources (but more time) than conversion with overlap. Because of the time scales involved, piecemeal conversion makes it more difficult to retreat to the older method if something goes wrong.

Once the transition is complete and the network becomes the normal mode of operation, the system administrator and any developers or planners still involved must observe everything carefully and must talk to users to get as much information about network usage and user reaction as possible.

This information will enable you to identify the following types of problems:

- Bugs in the system, which may produce incorrect results or which may crash the system.

- Bottlenecks in the network, which lead to inefficiency and slow down network performance. These can be fixed or at least minimized by fine-tuning the network.

- User problems, which may indicate software problems or inadequate training.

LAN Access

LAN access refers to the process of getting commands or information onto a network. The access can be at either of two levels:

- Access to the network medium at the physical layer. Physical access to the network medium is discussed in the Media-Access Method article.

- User access to the network by logging in. Logical access is discussed in the Login article.

LAN Administration

A LAN administrator, or supervisor, runs the network. The administrator is responsible for "doing whatever is necessary to make sure the network keeps working." More specifically, an administrator's duties include tasks such as assigning access and security levels to users, making sure the equipment is functioning, verifying that resources are not being used inappropriately, and checking that users are keeping their storage use in check.

The following sections describe some task areas that may be involved in LAN administration. Note that these are by no means the only types of tasks a LAN administrator must handle. In fact, all but the simplest, most vanilla-flavored networks will introduce oddities and requirements of their own.

a b c d e f g h i j k **l** m n o p q r s t u v w x y z

Security

Security and access control involve making sure the contents and components of the network are safe from corruption by user error or by attack from inside or outside. This will generally require taking measures to control user access to the network and its resources.

As a security guardian, the LAN administrator must allocate user access rights to the information and resources available on the network. By allowing users only into certain directories, the core of the operating environment is kept secure and safe from accidental damage.

Specifically, LAN security deals with the following types of concerns:

- Only authorized users can access the LAN and its components.

- Unauthorized users cannot accidentally or deliberately destroy files.

- Unauthorized users cannot copy or otherwise steal files or data.

- Files and data are not corrupted or destroyed by viruses, worms, or Trojan horses (all types of invasive programs that can cause direct or indirect damage to your files and/or your running programs).

- Files, data, and hardware components are not destroyed by power irregularities (surges, sags, and so on) or other electrical phenomena.

Security Measures Administrators can take various types of measures to help increase network security, including the following:

- Exercise access control and user authentication through login procedures and password requirements. User IDs and passwords are important for maintaining system security. Users should *not* use as passwords such items as nicknames, names of family members, telephone numbers, or other data associated directly with the user. Users should also change passwords regularly. Some administrators require periodic changes.

- Assign access privileges (or trustee rights) to users to control who has access to what and to help keep vital files secure, at least from accidental and casual attack.

- Be vigilant about policing user IDs and accounts. Accounts should be closed and IDs invalidated immediately whenever users are removed from the network.

- Be aware of any back doors into the networking software. A *back door* is a special command or action that allows unrestricted access to the software and, usually, to the hardware on which the software is running. System developers often build such back doors into their creations to allow emergency access (and possibly for other reasons).

- Limit physical access to nodes, especially to a file server node, to help reduce security breaches. For example, only the LAN administrator should have access to the file server running the network. Ideally, this machine should be locked or have its keyboard removed when it is unattended.

- Protect the system from viruses and other invaders. Always install from write-protected disks, and keep master disks and boot disks write-protected. Never install a program whose provenance you do not know, and do not let users do so either. Virus-detection software should be installed on any bridges or other devices that communicate with other networks. This is because a different network is comparable to a disk of unknown provenance.

- Provide power protection, at least for network servers. For other nodes, surge suppressors might suffice.

- Use call-back modems to help protect against unauthorized access. When a user calls in to access the network, the modem takes the call and gets some required information from the caller. The caller hangs up, and the modem checks on the user and the information provided. If everything looks legitimate, the modem calls the user back, and the user is on the network.

- If LAN tapping is a concern, consider using fiber-optic cable because it is the most difficult to tap.

- If sensitive data is involved, consider using encryption strategies. There are various methods for data encryption. See the DES (Data Encryption Standard) and Encryption articles for more information.

You can use special-purpose machines and boards to do complete audits of network access and use, and even to record all activity on the network. This information can help you identify security weaknesses and breaches (but can also give users the impression that they are being watched).

Programs exist to help with network security. Such programs can be instructed to watch for viruses, watch for changes or attempted changes to network or applications software, or allow only "approved" programs to execute on the network.

Configuration

The system administrator needs to be able to determine the configuration of a network at all times. To do this, the administrator should have the following information:

- An up-to-date list of every component on the network, with exact model number, location, and with information about factory and current settings

- A complete cabling diagram

- A complete list of all application software on the network, with version and default settings information

This information should be updated scrupulously and checked obsessively for correctness. Having incorrect information that is believed correct is much, much worse than having no information at all.

In addition, the administrator should be able to get, if necessary, information about network activity (over time or at a given time), storage and memory usage, and ongoing user sessions.

It is important to keep configuration information on a non-networked PC or else make sure to print a copy of the most recent configuration information anytime you update the file. This way, you will have the necessary information if the network goes down.

User Support

User support entails answering user questions about applications on the network and about the network in general, resolving user problems with applications or with the network, training new users, and keeping users informed as the network changes.

Documentation

The LAN administrator should see that adequate documentation is available about using the hardware and software on the network. In some cases, the administrator may need to create local release notes, which are special additions to official documentation. These release notes will describe any unique features of the local installation or implementation.

Operations

To keep a network operating normally, it is useful to monitor the network during day-to-day operation. This involves making sure all components are working and resolving any user problems that arise.

Maintenance and Upgrades

In addition to making sure a network is operating smoothly, an administrator should try to ensure that the network will continue

to do so. Regular maintenance checks on the equipment help keep things running or at least help to ensure that problems will be caught before they become major. Regular backups help ensure that data loss is kept to a minimum in the event of network malfunction.

Make sure to keep at least one backup copy of all software and data. If possible, have one such copy off-site. Backups should be scrupulously done and carefully labeled, so that it is always possible to restore a relatively up-to-date version of the network in case of disaster.

As a network ages and evolves, equipment and software will need to be replaced. These processes open up several barrels of worms:

- As new software versions are released, they need to be installed. Older versions should be removed and should be replaced completely, if at all possible. Doing this is not always easy and may not even be possible. For example, if some project is dependent on a particular version of a package, you will not be able to remove it.

- New software may not be an improvement over older versions, and it may need to be uninstalled and replaced with the older software. To avoid this nightmare, it is advisable to test new versions thoroughly before installing them. (A "baby" network, with just a few nodes, might be a good place to do this.) Before installing new software, make sure there is a way to uninstall it if necessary.

- New hardware may be incompatible with existing equipment, and may force a decision as to whether to replace more than anticipated or to forego whatever technological advances the new hardware promises.

- New hardware may be incompatible with existing software. This can happen, for example, if there is a lag before drivers appear for the new hardware.

In short, while advances in hardware and software may sound wonderful to end-users and "techweenies," these improvements are just more things to help make an administrator's life miserable.

To keep software maintenance and upgrades manageable, make sure to keep detailed information such as the following about all software on the network:

- Name, version, and serial number of each package

- Detailed installation and usage instructions

- A log of user reports of difficulties or problems with the software

Performance Monitoring

Performance monitoring and analysis involve tracking the network's behavior (counting packet collisions, measuring traffic and response times, and so on) with an eye toward identifying inefficiencies and bottlenecks so they can be eliminated. Various software and hardware products are available to help with this task.

While monitoring system performance, keep careful track of the following:

- Operating costs

- Threats to security

- User satisfaction

- User productivity

Track these indexes especially thoroughly during the first few weeks after network installation. Do not be surprised if some of the measures change quite drastically during this period. For example, costs may drop drastically after the startup period. In contrast, user satisfaction and productivity may rise after the initial problems and frustrations are resolved.

Network Accounting

Accounting involves overseeing costs incurred by users, charges to be paid by users, and so on. An administrator needs to make sure that the users do not exceed their usage allowances and that accounts are paid up.

Problems

Problem and fault handling involve identifying problems, failures, or bottlenecks in the hardware or software, determining their cause, deciding how to correct them, and taking whatever steps are necessary (including calling a service technician, if that is what the LAN administration plan calls for) to correct the problem.

a
b
c
d
e
f
g
h
i
j
k
l
m
n
o
p
q
r
s
t
u
v
w
x
y
z

Design

If he or she is lucky, an administrator's duties will include helping to design and implement the network. While both of these are major tasks, input during these initial phases can help make the later administrative tasks much easier. (Of course, this opportunity has been known to backfire on occasion, and an administrator may be "stuck" with the network he or she helped design.)

See the LAN Design section in this article for more information.

Other Task Groupings

Other task breakdowns have been proposed. For example, the OSI has specified five categories of network management tasks:

- Accounting management
- Configuration management
- Fault management
- Performance management
- Security management

These are discussed in separate articles, as well as in the Network Management article.

LANalyzer

A network monitoring and management product from Novell. LANalyzer (and other products of its type) can inventory network components and configurations, perform various types of network mapping, and monitor packet traffic. It also can do trend analyses on this traffic (in order to anticipate congestion and warn the network administrator).

LAN ADMINISTRATION VERSUS LAN MANAGEMENT

The terms *LAN administration* and *LAN management* are often used interchangeably. However, there are some differences between the two tasks.

The functions defined for LAN management can at least be summarized officially by reference to the five management domains specified by the OSI network management model. In contrast, the duties of a LAN administrator are often vaguely defined and may even be defined dynamically; as a new type of issue, problem, or crisis arises, the LAN administrator's duties are (re)defined to include its resolution.

LANAO (LAN Automation Option)

In IBM's NMA (Network Management Architecture), an optional add-on to the NetView package that implements the NMA. LANAO simplifies and, for certain data, automates the monitoring and management of one or more Token Ring networks.

SEE ALSO
NetView

LAN Driver

A LAN driver is a hardware-specific driver program that mediates between a station's operating system and the network interface card (NIC). A LAN driver is also known as a *network driver*.

The LAN driver must be loaded in order to access the NIC, and the network protocols must be able to communicate with the NIC through this driver, as illustrated in the figure "LAN drivers sit between the hardware and the network shell."

To make NICs accessible to any of multiple protocols that might be running on a network, generic interfaces for LAN drivers have been created. The best known of these interfaces are ODI (Open Data-link Interface) from Novell and Apple and NDIS

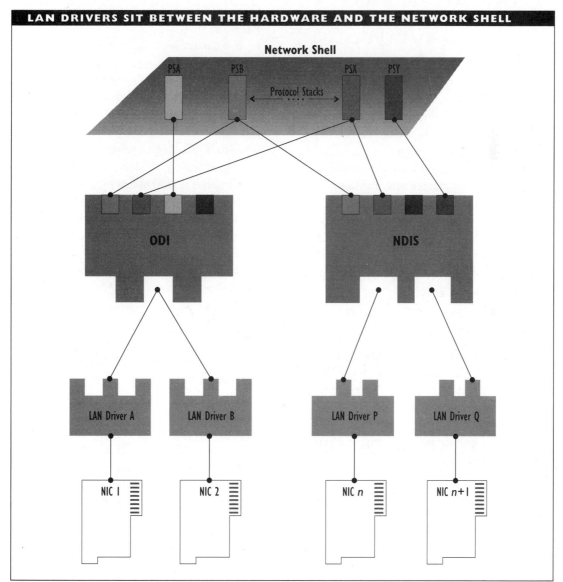

LAN DRIVERS SIT BETWEEN THE HARDWARE AND THE NETWORK SHELL

(Network Driver Interface Specification) from Microsoft and 3Com.

BROADER CATEGORY

Driver

SEE ALSO

NDIS (Network Driver Interface Specification); ODI (Open Data-link Interface)

LAN Inventory Package

A LAN inventory package is any of several products that can automatically create an inventory of the components and configuration on a local-area network (LAN). This type of software is used to keep track of changes to the network configuration.

LAN inventory packages may also be able to do at least some monitoring of network activity or performance. You can find listings of LAN Inventory and other networking-related products in the Annual Buyers Guide issue of *LAN* magazine, which comes out in the fall.

LAN Manager

LAN Manager is a much-licensed, server-based network operating system (NOS) from Microsoft. The LAN Manager server capabilities have also been implemented as Windows NT Advanced Server (NTAS). LAN Manager supports various low-level network architectures, including ARCnet, Ethernet, and Token Ring cabling and protocols. With the introduction of Windows NT and Windows NT Advanced Server, LAN Manager is no longer updated.

LAN Manager Servers and Clients

LAN Manager supports servers running under OS/2, UNIX, and certain Windows NT configurations. It supports clients running under various operating systems or environments, including DOS, Windows, OS/2, and System 7 (the Macintosh operating system).

The capabilities and hardware requirements for workstations depend on the operating environment. For example, DOS workstations can be anything from 8088-based PCs to the high-end machines, and can run any version of DOS from 3.3 onward. OS/2 workstations, in contrast, require at least an 80286 machine.

Windows and Windows for Workgroups machines can also be used as LAN Manager workstations. Machines in a Novell NetWare network can be workstations on both the LAN Manager and the NetWare networks. Macintosh machines must be able to use AppleShare to be LAN Manager workstations.

LAN Manager Protocol Support

LAN Manager uses NetBEUI (NetBIOS Extended User Interface) as its main transport- and session-layer protocol but includes support for the TCP/IP protocol stack used for the Internet and most UNIX systems. NetBEUI is an efficient protocol *within* a network but is not well-suited for use across subnetworks. The figure "LAN Manager architecture" shows LAN Manager's components.

LAN MANAGER ARCHITECTURE

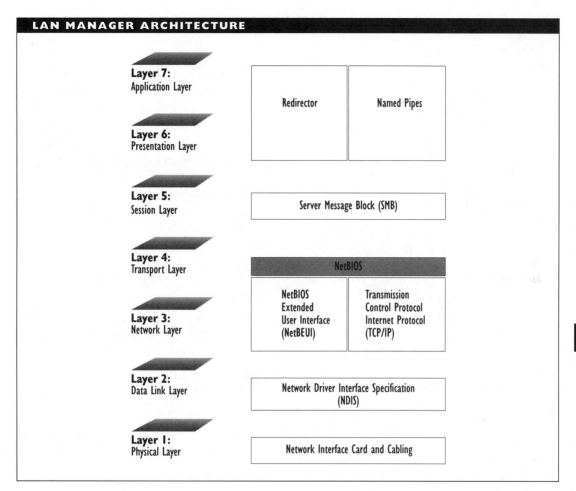

Layer 7:
Application Layer

Layer 6:
Presentation Layer

| Redirector | Named Pipes |

Layer 5:
Session Layer

| Server Message Block (SMB) |

Layer 4:
Transport Layer

NetBIOS

| NetBIOS Extended User Interface (NetBEUI) | Transmission Control Protocol Internet Protocol (TCP/IP) |

Layer 3:
Network Layer

Layer 2:
Data Link Layer

| Network Driver Interface Specification (NDIS) |

Layer 1:
Physical Layer

| Network Interface Card and Cabling |

The NOS supports other protocol stacks, including several proprietary ones developed by LAN Manager licensees, through add-on products. For example, it can support Microsoft's own MS-DLC protocol, which helps provide workstations with access to mainframes in an SNA (Systems Network Architecture) environment. This protocol is used by terminal-emulation products, such as IRMA Workstation for Windows and Rumba from Wall Data, for access to the data-link layer. It may access this layer through an NDIS (Network Driver Interface Specification) interface.

LAN Manager also supports various network management capabilities and protocols, including SNMP (Simple Network Management Protocol) developed for TCP/IP networks, and NetView, IBM's network management package for SNA networks.

a
b
c
d
e
f
g
h
i
j
k
l
m
n
o
p
q
r
s
t
u
v
w
x
y
z

Other LAN Manager Features

LAN Manager includes support for the following additional features:

- Server-based capabilities such as file and printer services.

- Distributed computing and communications capabilities, such as named pipes (two-way communications channels between processes or machines) and mailslots (one-way channels).

- Peer-to-peer networking in Windows for Workgroups environments.

- Remote booting, access, and monitoring, as well as shared modems for dial-out capabilities.

- LAN security at both the user and share levels. User-level security is more stringent: a user must be able to log in to the network and have access privileges to the desired resource. With share-level security, the user requests access to a device rather than actually logging in to the network.

- The definition of *domains,* which are larger subnetworks that are managed by a single organization.

In addition, LAN Manager 2.2 includes several windows-based utilities.

Both versions 1.0 and 2.0 have been licensed by Microsoft to other vendors, who have marketed the same basic product under different names. For example, IBM's LAN Server 1.*x* is based on LAN Manager 1.0, as is 3Com's 3+Open software. DEC Path-Works is based on LAN Manager 2.0.

LAN Network Manager (LNM)

LNM is an SAA-compliant network management product from IBM. The product is used to help manage Token Ring networks. Because it can work with NetView (a mainframe-based network management program), LNM is particularly useful for managing networks that are part of larger, SNA (Systems Network Architecture) networks. The product can use both CMIP and SNMP network management protocols.

LAN Network Manager runs under OS/2 Presentation Manager. When running as a stand-alone product, it can function as a focal point (data gatherer) for a network. Running in conjunction with NetView, it can function as an entry point (an SNA-compliant reporter, or agent) for NetView.

LAN/RM (Local-Area Networks Reference Model)

A term for the IEEE 802.*x* series of specifications, most of which are related to local-area networks (LANs).

SEE ALSO

IEEE 802.*x*

LAN Server

A server-based network operating system (NOS) from IBM. The package is based on Microsoft's LAN Manager, and it supports servers running in the OS/2 environment.

SEE ALSO

LAN Manager

▼
LANstep

LANstep is a networking environment from Hayes Microcomputer Products. It supports up to 255 users on a peer-to-peer network that includes features usually associated with larger and server-based networks.

LANstep Services

Network services may be distributed over one or more nondedicated servers, and an authorized user anywhere on the network can access a service by name, without needing to specify the location of the server that provides the service. This transparent access is provided by LANstep's Smart Directory Services, which maintain a global resource directory and which can direct a user's request for a named service to the appropriate server. Access rights are also distributed, along with the resources to which the rights relate.

Just as the network can provide services, users can provide resources in the form of data or other files. The user owns the resource, and he or she can set the access rights for the resource. Only users with access rights will get information about the resource.

LANstep supports the "classic" network architectures: ARCnet, Ethernet, and Token Ring, and it supports the appropriate network adapters, provided these are compliant with the NDIS (Network Driver Interface Specification). LANstep uses NDIS to support multiple protocol stacks. This makes it possible to communicate with different networking and operating environments (such as Novell's NetWare or UNIX).

LANstep Environment

LANstep provides its own operating system and interface. It also allows DOS and Microsoft Windows applications to execute and includes support for application software that uses NetBIOS protocols. LANstep can also provide access to network resources through Microsoft Windows.

LANstep allows users to map drive letters to specific drives or directories. In addition, the environment includes predefined mappings for certain drive letters to important or frequently used locations. For example, drive F: is mapped to the directory of the currently executing application. These predefined mappings can be changed.

LANstep Management

Although LANstep services and access rights can be distributed, LANstep management is centralized. Smart Directory Services provide a centralized database of available services.

Network security is centralized by having users log into the network, rather than into each server on the network or into each service. Once authenticated, the user can use any of the resources to which the user has access.

The menu-based interface displays references only to resources, files, and directories accessible to the user. If a user does not have access rights to the color printer, then this resource does not appear in the user's menus. This helps provide increased security by making it more difficult for users to get unauthorized access to any resource. The user's menus are updated dynamically if the system or user configuration changes.

a
b
c
d
e
f
g
h
i
j
k
l
m
n
o
p
q
r
s
t
u
v
w
x
y
z

Network management utilities are available to perform both service- and server-based tasks, such as version control or server activity monitoring, respectively.

Other Features

LANstep provides a proprietary electronic mail (e-mail) service but can also use an optional mail gateway to allow access to other mail services. These services must support the ISO's MHS (Message Handling System) standard, however.

▼ LANtastic

LANtastic is a term used loosely to refer to an extended family of products that provide various types of networking capabilities on proprietary and standard local-area networks (LANs). The core product associated with the term is a network operating system (NOS) that provides flexible and efficient peer-to-peer networking capabilities. The LANtastic series of products is by Artisoft.

LANtastic Features

The LANtastic NOS has the following capabilities and features:

- Runs as a DOS process and uses the DOS file system. However, LANtastic can provide limited multitasking in some configurations.

- Can run on proprietary network interface cards (NICs) or on Ethernet cards.

- Supports networks ranging in size from two to a few hundred nodes.

LANtastic is aimed at the small- to medium-sized network market, and it is on the low end of the price range.

- Supports peer-to-peer LANs (allows any node to serve as either a server or a workstation) or server-based LANS (with a dedicated server).

- Can provide various types of servers, including file, print, CD-ROM, and access. Some of these capabilities require add-on hardware or software products. LANtastic is particularly efficient in providing CD-ROM services: only the machine that has the CD drive needs to load the Microsoft CD-ROM extensions driver. This saves memory on the other machines.

- Supports e-mail (electronic mail) and real-time chatting services.

- Supports a variant that runs over a NetBIOS protocol. This version is independent of particular NICs in that it will run (in principle) in any environment that supports NetBIOS, including Token Ring or ARCnet networks.

- Allows servers to control access to files, directories, and services, by requiring passwords for access and controlling access privileges.

- Allows network activity to be logged through an auditing feature. This log will include a record of any unsuccessful attempts to log in or to access forbidden services.

LANtastic Variants and Add-Ons

The following variants on the core LANtastic program are available:

- LANtastic Starter Kit: Provides the items necessary for a two-node network, including the software, cable, and NICs. The kit comes with either proprietary or Ethernet cards.

- LANtastic Z: Provides for a two-node LANtastic network whose nodes communicate through parallel or serial ports. (The Z in the name stands for *zero slot*.)

- LANtastic/AI: A version that is independent of any particular NIC.

- LANtastic for NetWare: Enables a single machine to use both NetWare and LANtastic servers (with some restrictions). On this machine, drive F: might map to a NetWare server, while drive G: maps to a LANtastic server. LANtastic for NetWare actually runs on a special NetBIOS emulation provided by Novell.

- LANtastic for Windows: Allows Windows applications to pass information through Dynamic Data Exchange (DDE) across the entire network. With DDE, a file created using a Windows application can be sent to other nodes on the network. When a recipient clicks on the file, it will start up the application that created it.

With hardware and software add-ons, LANtastic also supports modem sharing and remote network access. ArtiCom provides any node on a network with access to a modem. The Network Eye (TNE) provides remote access to any machine on the network. For example, with TNE, you can see the screen of any other node on the network or you can display your screen on any other node or nodes. You can even run programs on any number of other nodes.

Voice mail support is provided with the hardware and software add-ons Sounding Board and ArtiSound Recorder.

LAN, Transparent

A networking service that makes it possible for two LANs to communicate over telecommunications links without having to deal explicitly with the long distance connection. That is, a node on one LAN talking to a node on another one will not need to be concerned with the fact that the communication is going over telephone lines.

LAN, Virtual

A network configuration that can be created as needed by software and that can span physical LANs and topologies. Virtual LANs can be helpful when using workflow or other software that allows interaction on a larger project by multiple users.

LAN, Wireless

In a wireless LAN, communication is accomplished using infrared signals, radio waves, or microwaves. Although the actual transmission is through open air, the configuration is not completely wireless. The PC is usually connected via cable to the wireless transmitter.

The states of the art and the world for wireless LANs are still rudimentary and in flux. Currently, the market is small, the technology is relatively simple, and the wave spectrum has yet to be completely allocated and standardized.

Many wireless LANs have very limited range, often on the order of a few dozen or a few hundred meters. There are still decisions to be made about what frequency bands should or must be used for wireless transmissions, and also about whether these bands will be licensed. Similarly, there is little standardization of the technology. Rather, each vendor does things slightly differently.

For example, the following wireless LAN products are available:

- NCR's WaveLAN, which uses an unregulated 902 to 928 megahertz (MHz) bandwidth, can transmit over about 30 to 60 meters (100 to 200 feet) indoors and about 250 meters (800 feet) outdoors between nodes. AIRLAN CAN (Campus Area Network) products from Solectek use the 902–928 MHz frequency band for communicating within in-building LANs and a higher, 2.4 GHz frequency for transmitting between bridges in different buildings. In both cases, the products use spread spectrum technology. These products can transmit up to 800 feet.

- BICC Communications' InfraLAN, which uses infrared signals, has a range of only 25 meters (80 feet) or so.

- Motorola's Altair, which uses radio waves in the 18 to 19 gigahertz (GHz) range, works for only about 20 meters (70 feet) indoors and about twice that distance outdoors.

- Data Race has several wireless LAN products, which operate in the 2 to 4 GHz range.

Costs for installations with just a few nodes are still quite high compared with those for cabled networks. Prices are becoming competitive for networks with many nodes.

BROADER CATEGORY
Transmission, Wireless

Large Internet Packet (LIP)

SEE
LIP (Large Internet Packet)

Laser Transmission

A laser is a source of exceptionally coherent, or focused, light. The name comes from *light amplification by stimulated emission of radiation.*

The light is of a single wavelength or of a small spectrum around a single wavelength. The light source is used to read signals off a CD-ROM and may also be used as a signal source in a fiber-optic network. LEDs (light-emitting diodes) are an alternative signal source in fiber-optic communications.

Laser line width, more commonly known as *spectral width,* refers to the range of light wavelengths (or frequencies) emitted by a laser.

Laser transmission refers to wireless communications using lasers. A laser sends the pulses (which can represent 0 and 1 values) over a narrow path to a receiver. Photodiodes at the receiving end convert the light pulses back into bits.

Advantages of laser transmissions include the following:

- Very high bandwidths, generally above 1 terahertz (THz) and even in the hundreds of THz range, are possible, even when infrared light is used.

- Light is impervious to interference and jamming.

Disadvantages of laser transmissions include the following:

- A line of sight is usually required between sender and receiver, which also limits the maximum distance between parties.

- Because the transmission uses a very narrow beam of extremely focused light, sender and receiver must be precisely aligned.

- Atmospheric conditions (such as rain or fog) can attenuate or distort the signal.

Laser transmissions are used in contrast to cable-based transmissions or to other types of wireless transmissions, such as those using microwaves.

RELATED ARTICLES
Cable, Fiber-Optic; Fiber Optics

Last Mile

In telephony, a somewhat poignant term used to refer to the link between the customer's premises and the local telephone company's central office. For various reasons, this is the most expensive and least efficient stretch in the entire telephone network's cabling system.

LAT (Local-Area Transport)

A Digital Equipment Corporation (DEC) protocol for high-speed asynchronous communication between hosts and terminal servers over Ethernet.

LATA (Local Access and Transport Area)

A telephone exchange; that is, a geographical and administrative area that is the responsibility of a local telephone company. Calls that cross LATA boundaries are handled by interexchange carriers (IXCs), or long-distance carriers.

Latency

For a network or communications channel, latency represents the amount of time before a requested channel is available for a transmission. In data transmissions, latency is the amount of time required for a transmission to reach its destination.

a b c d e f g h i j k **l** m n o p q r s t u v w x y z

Layer

In an operating, communications, or networking environment, layers are distinct levels of capabilities or services that build upon each other. A layer uses the services of the layer below it and provides services to the layer above it.

Layers communicate with layers above and below them through well-defined interfaces. As long as interfaces do not change, internal changes in a layer's implementation have no effect on the layers above or below. Such vertical communication generally takes place within a single machine. The process is illustrated in the figure "Communications between and over layers."

A given layer on a machine uses a predefined protocol to communicate with the layer's counterpart on another machine. This horizontal communication generally takes place between different machines. However, the communication is direct only at the lowest, physical layer. Horizontal communication between higher layers is indirect; it requires vertical communication in both machines.

A transmission from a particular layer on a particular machine needs to move down through the other layers to the first layer on that machine. At this level, the machine communicates directly with the first layer on the other machine. On the other machine, the transmission is then passed upward through its layers.

Layer Models

In the worlds of communications and networking, layers are used to distinguish the types of network- and application-based activities that are carried out.

For example, perhaps the best-known layer model is the seven-layer OSI Reference Model for describing network activities. Its layers range from the physical layer, at which details of cable connections and electrical signaling are specified, to the application layer, at which details of the immediate interface between an application and network services are defined. Other layer models include IBM's SNA (Systems Network Architecture), Digital's DECnet, and the TCP/IP model used on the Internet.

Layered Architecture

A *layered architecture* is a hardware or software design in which operations or functions at one level (layer) build upon other operations or functions at a lower level. One of the best-known examples of such a design is the UNIX operating system.

In a layered architecture, each layer uses the layer immediately below it and provides services to the layer above it. For example, in the OSI Reference Model, the data-link layer uses the physical layer below it to transmit bits across a cable link. The data-link layer, in turn, provides the network layer above it with logical (and, indirectly, physical) access to the network. In such a model, a network layer packet becomes the data component of a data-link level packet, through a process known as *encapsulation*.

COMMUNICATIONS BETWEEN AND OVER LAYERS

Network access for applications — **Application** ↔ **Application**

Data massaging (conversion, formatting, translation) for applications — **Presentation** ↔ **Presentation**

Connection and dialog management, security — **Session** ↔ **Session**

Error checking and delivery verification — **Transport** ↔ **Transport**

Packet routing; internetwork communication — **Network** ↔ **Network**

Interface for higher layers; access to physical medium — **Data Link** ↔ **Data Link**

Bit values, not packets, are transferred — **Physical** **Physical**

Cable, optical fiber, or wireless medium

Layered architectures for networking environments generally distinguish at least two classes of layers:

- Transport-based layers, which are concerned with the problem of getting data from one location to the other

- Application- or user-based layers, which are concerned with making sure the transmitted data is in a form suitable for the application that will use it

These layer classes can be refined into smaller groups.

SEE ALSO
OSI Reference Model

Layer Management Entity (LME)

SEE
LME (Layer Management Entity)

LBRV (Low Bit Rate Voice)

Digitized voice signals that are being transmitted at speeds lower than the 64 kilobits per second channel capacity, generally either at 2,400 or 4,800 bits per second. Voice data will either be compressed or will use sophisticated encoding methods.

LBS (LAN Bridge Server)

In an IBM Token Ring network, a server whose job is to keep track of and provide access to any bridges connected to the network.

LBT/LWT (Listen Before Talk/ Listen While Talk)

LBT represents the fundamental rule for a CSMA/CD (carrier sense multiple access/ collision detect) media-access method. A node wishing to send a packet onto the

a b c d e f g h i j k **l** m n o p q r s t u v w x y z

network first listens for a special signal that indicates that the network is in use. If no such signal is heard, the node begins transmitting.

A related concept is called *LWT (listen while talk)*. LWT says that a node should keep listening for an "in use" signal even while transmitting. (By extension, the LBT and LWT rules could be applied to other aspects of life, no doubt with wonderful effects.)

LC (Local Channel)

In digital telecommunications, a link between a customer's premises and the central office.

LCC/LCD (Lost Calls Cleared/ Lost Calls Delayed)

In switching systems, LCC is a call-handling strategy in which blocked calls are lost, or discarded. This is in contrast to a LCD strategy, in which blocked calls are queued for later, or delayed, processing.

LCD (Liquid Crystal Display)

A veteran display technology that has been around since the early days of calculators and digital watches. An LCD screen element is lit by passing voltage through the special liquid crystal at the element's location and then bending the light that the crystal emits.

The use of bent light makes the display dependent on the viewing angle and also on the amount of ambient light, with the latter being important for contrast. A constant internal light source can be used to produce fixed contrast and thereby reduce the importance of ambient light. Such a light source is generally placed at the back of the screen and is known as backlighting. If placed at the edge, the light source is known as edgelighting or sidelighting.

LCI (Logical Channel Identification)

In an X.25 (or other switching) packet, a field that indicates the virtual circuit (logical channel) being used for the packet.

LCR (Least Cost Routing)

In a PBX (private branch exchange) telephone system, a feature that selects the most economical path to a destination.

LCR (Line Control Register)

In a UART (universal asynchronous receiver/transmitter), a register that is used to specify a parity type.

LDDS (Limited-Distance Data Service)

In telecommunications, a class of service offered by some carriers. LDDS provides digital transmission capabilities over short distances using line drivers instead of modems.

LDM (Limited-Distance Modem)

A short-haul modem, which is designed for very high-speed transmissions (more than 1 megabit per second) over short distances (less than 20 miles or so).

Leaf Object

In Novell's NetWare NDS, an object that represents an actual network entity, such as users or devices. Five types of leaf objects are defined: user-related, server-related, printer-related, informational, and miscellaneous. Each of these types includes several more specific object types.

SEE ALSO

Container Object; NDS (NetWare Directory Services)

Leaf Site

On the Internet, a computer that receives newsfeeds from other Usenet sites but does not pass these feeds on to other computers.

Leased Line

In telecommunications, a private line, which is a communications loop reserved for a single customer. The bandwidth on a leased line depends on the type of service. For example, a T1 line has a 1.544 megabits per second bandwidth; fractional T1 lines come in 64 kilobits per second chunks. A leased line is in contrast to a *dial-up line,* which is accessible to any user.

Least Cost Routing (LCR)

SEE

LCR (Least Cost Routing)

Least Significant Bit (LSB)

SEE

LSB (Least Significant Bit)

LEC (Local Exchange Carrier)

A local telephone company; a company that provides telephone service within an exchange, or calling area. LECs are connected by IXCs (interexchange carriers). LECs are also known as *local carriers.*

LED (Light-Emitting Diode)

A semiconductor device that can convert electrical energy into light. LEDs are used in calculator displays and for the lights on computers and modems. LEDs are also used as light sources in communications using fiber-optics. The more expensive alternative to this use is the laser.

Legacy Wiring

Wiring that is already installed in a business or residence. Legacy wiring may or may not be suitable for networking purposes.

LEN (Low-Entry Networking)

An IBM term for peer-to-peer configurations in IBM's SNA (Systems Network Architecture).

LEOS (Low Earth Orbit Satellite)

A satellite whose orbit is at a low altitude above the earth. This is in contrast to a *geosynchronous satellite,* which remains stationary relative to the earth at 23,000 miles or so in space.

a
b
c
d
e
f
g
h
i
j
k
l
m
n
o
p
q
r
s
t
u
v
w
x
y
z

LFN (Long Fat Network)

An LFN is a very high bandwidth, long-distance network. LFNs have bandwidths of several hundred megabits per second with proposed gigabit per second speeds. Because of the high bandwidths, LFNs can cause performance and packet-loss problems for TCP/IP protocols.

For example, some LFNs will have such high bandwidths that all the segment numbers possible under TCP/IP will be used in less than 30 seconds. Since TCP/IP segments may be allowed up to 120 seconds to reach their destination, packets with duplicate numbers may coexist.

Various fixes are currently being explored for these problems, but so far none has received general acceptance.

LID (Local Injection/Detection)

In fiber-optics, a device used to align fibers when splicing them together.

Lifetime

In general, a value that represents the length of time a particular value, feature, or link should be considered valid. In Internet router advertisement messages, lifetime indicates the amount of time a router's information should be considered valid.

LIFO (Last In, First Out)

The queuing strategy for a stack. In this strategy, the element added most recently is the element removed first. For example, in employment situations where seniority is observed, the most recently hired employee is the first one to be laid off if business gets slow. The FIFO (first in, first out) strategy takes the opposite approach.

Light-Emitting Diode (LED)

SEE

LED (Light-Emitting Diode)

Limited-Distance Data Service (LDDS)

SEE

LDDS (Limited-Distance Data Service)

Limited-Distance Modem (LDM)

SEE

LDM (Limited-Distance Modem)

LIMS (Lotus Intel Microsoft Specifications)

The acronym LIM refers to the members of the consortium that originally created the expanded memory standard.

LIMS refers to specifications developed for implementing expanded memory. This is memory allocated on special chips, and then mapped into 16 kilobyte (KB) pages allocated in the area of memory between 640 KB and 1 megabyte (MB).

The memory specification was developed in order to make more memory available to 8086 processors, which cannot operate in protected mode, as is needed to access memory addresses above 1 MB.

Line

A circuit or link used in data or voice communication.

Linear Predictive Coding (LPC)

SEE

LPC (Linear Predictive Coding)

Line Card

In communications, a line card serves as the interface between a line and a device.

Line Circuit

In telephony, the circuit that detects whether a line is on- or off-hook and that handles call origination and termination.

Line Conditioner

A line conditioner is a device for keeping the voltage supply to a device within a "normal" range.

Line conditioners are most useful in places where there are likely to be brownouts or power sags (lower than normal voltages). Over time, sags can damage systems just as badly as voltage spikes (excess voltage) can. Studies indicate that sags alone account for almost 90 percent of all electrical disturbances.

In addition to massaging the voltage supply, most line conditioners can also detect some common line anomalies: reversed polarity, missing ground, or an overloaded neutral wire. In some cases, these problems can also damage data or equipment.

Although a line conditioner is limited in the load it can handle, a typical conditioner can serve for multiple outlets. The power requirements of the devices connected to these outlets cannot exceed the line conditioner's capacity, however.

Line conditioners are known by several other names, including *voltage regulator, power conditioner, line stabilizer/line conditioner,* or *LS/LC.*

Line Conditioning

In analog data communications, line conditioning refers to any of several classes of services available through the telephone company for improving the quality of a transmission. Line conditioning tries to attenuate or eliminate the effects of certain types of distortions on the signal.

Line conditioning becomes more necessary as transmission speeds increase. For example, on ordinary telephone lines, transmissions at more than 9,600 bits per second often require line conditioning.

Two types of line conditioning are available:

- C conditioning tries to minimize the effects of distortion related to signal amplitude and distortion due to *envelope delay.* Five levels of type C conditioning (C1, C2, through C5) are distinguished, with level C5 the most stringent.

- D conditioning tries to minimize the effects of *harmonic distortion* in addition to the amplitude and envelope delay distortions handled by type C conditioning.

a b c d e f g h i j k **l** m n o p q r s t u v w x y z

Line Driver

A component that includes a transmitter and a receiver, and is used to extend the transmission range between devices that are connected directly to each other. On some lines, line drivers can be used instead of modems but only for short distances of up to 15 kilometers (10 miles) or so. Line drivers are used in limited-distance data services (LDDS) offered by some telephone companies.

Line Group

In telephony, a line group represents multiple lines that can be activated or deactivated as a group.

Line Hit

In electrical transmissions, a brief burst of interference on a line.

Line Insulation Test (LIT)

SEE

LIT (Line Insulation Test)

Line Level

In an electrical transmission, the line level represents the power of a signal at a particular point in the transmission path. This value is measured in decibels (dB).

Line Load

In telephony, the line load represents the amount of usage a line is getting at a particular time, expressed as a percentage of capacity.

Line Monitor

In telecommunications, a line monitor is a device for spying on a line. The device can be attached to the line and can record or display all transmissions on the line.

Line-of-Sight Communications

In line-of-sight communications, a signal from one location is transmitted to another through the open air, without reflection off a satellite or off the earth.

Line Printer Daemon (LPD)

SEE

LPD (Line Printer Daemon)

Line-Sharing Device

A multiplexing device that allows two or more devices to share the same line.

Line Speed

In telephony, line speed refers to the transmission speed a line will support for a given grade of service (GoS).

Line Status

In telephony, line status refers to a setting that indicates whether a telephone is idle (on-hook) or in use (off-hook).

Line Termination Equipment

In telecommunications, any equipment that can be used to send signals. This type of equipment includes line cards, modems, multiplexers, hubs, and concentrators.

Line Trace

In networking, a service that logs all network activity for later examination and analysis.

Link

A physical or logical connection between two points.

Link State Algorithm

A class of routing algorithms in which each router broadcasts connection information to all other routers on an internetwork. This saves the routers from checking for available routes but adds the memory requirement of storing all the routing information.

SEE ALSO

Algorithm

Link State Packet (LSP)

SEE

LSP (Link State Packet)

Link Station Address

In network communications, the sending and receiving addresses for a station, or node. The sending address must be unique, but there may be multiple receiving addresses associated with each node. Each receiving address beyond the first for a node represents a group address. This can be used to identify the recipients of a multicast, for example.

Linux

Linux is a UNIX clone for Intel 386, 486, and Pentium systems. The first versions of the kernel were developed by Linus Torvalds at the University of Helsinki. After he had a somewhat stable version, Torvalds released the source code across the Internet, and soon programmers and wizards around the world were busy fixing, improving, and adding to the kernel, file systems, drivers, and so forth.

Linux is a complete multiuser, multitasking environment, and is compatible—at the source level—with the IEEE POSIX.1 standard for portable UNIX systems, as well with most features of other popular UNIX versions (System V, BSD, etc.).

Linux implementations generally come with a full complement of utilities: word processors, compilers, applications, etc. Many of these were developed as part of the Free Software Foundation's GNU (which stands for GNU's Not UNIX) project. However, many applications written for "official UNIX" compile and run with no modification under Linux.

Linux supports the full complement of protocols in the TCP/IP stack, as well as the client and server programs associated with the Internet environment (Telnet, FTP, NNTP, etc.). It also supports other telecommunications and BBS protocols and environments.

Linux can run the various UNIX shells—Bourne (sh), C (csh), Korn (ksh), and Bourne again (bash)—as well as the X Window graphical user interface. Unlike other versions of UNIX, Linux can coexist with MS-DOS—even in the same partition, if necessary.

a b c d e f g h i j k **l** m n o p q r s t u v w x y z

Linux is freely available even though it's neither shareware nor public domain software. It is covered by the GNU GPL (General Public License). Under the GPL, people can modify the source code and sell their own versions; however, the new versions must also be sold under the GPL. That is, the resulting software cannot be restricted; it must be available for modification and reselling.

As a result, numerous Linux implementations and developer's or administrator's packages are available. Linux makes an ideal and inexpensive operating system for setting up an Internet server.

PRIMARY SOURCES

The best and most complete all around source of information about Linux is *The Linux Bible: The GNU Testament,* 3rd edition (Yggdrasil Computing). For information about this, send email to info@yggdrasil.com. *The Linux Journal* is another good source of information.

LIP (Large Internet Packet)

In Novell's NetWare, LIP represents a packet format that allows for packets larger than the normal NetWare limit of 576 bytes. This feature is useful for transmissions over an inter-network, because the larger packets can help increase throughput over bridges and routers.

LIT (Line Insulation Test)

In telephony, a test that automatically checks lines for shorts, grounds, and interference.

Little-Endian

In data transmission and storage, little-endian is a term that describes the order in which bytes in a word are processed (stored or transmitted). The term comes from Jonathan Swift's *Gulliver's Travels,* in which a war is fought over which end of an egg should be cracked for eating.

In little-endian storage, the low-order byte is stored at the lower address. This arrangement is used in Intel processors (such as the 80x86 family), in VAX and PDP-11 computer series, and also in various communications and networking contexts. Most notably, it is used in the IEEE 802.3 (Ethernet) and 802.4 (Token Bus) specifications. In contrast, the IEEE 802.5 (Token Ring) specification uses big-endian ordering.

The term is less commonly used to describe the order in which bits are stored in a byte.

COMPARE

Big-Endian; Middle-Endian

LLC (Logical-Link Control)

In the IEEE's LAN/RM (local-area network reference model) the LLC is a sublayer above the MAC (media-access control) sublayer. Together, MAC and LLC are equivalent to the data-link layer in the OSI Reference Model.

The LLC provides an interface and services for the network-layer protocols, and mediates between these higher-level protocols and any of the various media-access methods defined at the lower, MAC sublayer. The figure "The layer and sublayer arrangement for a LAN" illustrates the arrangement.

The details of the LLC are provided in the IEEE 802.2 document. Details of the MAC sublayer protocols are specified in the IEEE 802.3, 802.4, and 802.5 documents. The IEEE 802.1 recommendations provide a broader context for the sublayers and protocols. LLC is modeled after the SDLC link-layer protocol.

SAPs

Requests to the LLC are communicated through SAPs (service access points). SAPs are locations where each party, for example, a network-layer protocol and an LLC layer service, can leave messages for the other. Each SAP has a 1-byte "address" associated with it.

The same LLC sublayer may need to provide services for more than one network-layer protocol. For example, it may work with IP and IPX. The use of SAPs makes this possible, since each of these protocols will have a different SAP address value. A SAP uniquely identifies a protocol.

Delivery Services

The LLC can provide three types of delivery services. Type 1 is a connectionless service without acknowledgment. This is the fastest but least reliable type of service offered at the LLC sublayer. In a connectionless service, there is neither a predefined path nor a permanent circuit between sender and receiver. Without acknowledgment, there is no way of knowing whether a packet reached its destination.

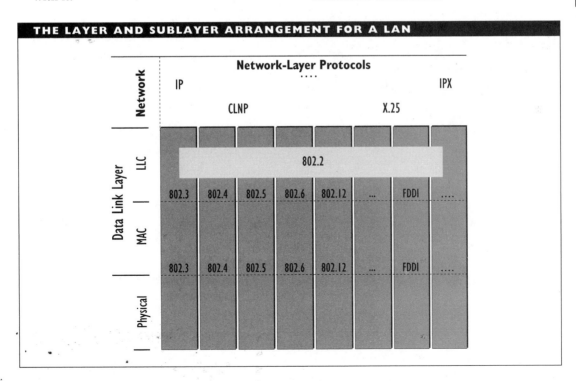

THE LAYER AND SUBLAYER ARRANGEMENT FOR A LAN

Despite its relative unreliability, Type 1 is the most popular service at this level, because most higher-level protocols *do* include delivery and error checking, so there is no need to duplicate this checking at the LLC layer. The network layer IP protocol (of TCP/IP fame) is connectionless, as is NetWare's IPX protocol.

Type 2 is a connection-oriented service. In a connection-oriented service, a circuit is established before data transmission begins. The transport-layer TCP protocol, used on the Internet and on many other systems, is connection-oriented, as are the X.25 network-layer protocol and NetWare's SPX protocol. With a connection—even if it is only virtual—the service can provide sequence control (so that message elements are assembled in the correct order by the receiver), flow and error control, and so on. Two flow control methods are commonly used at the LLC sublayer:

- Stop and wait, in which each LLC frame must be acknowledged before the next one is sent.

- Sliding window, in which x LLC frames can be sent before an acknowledgment is required. The value of x represents the window size.

Type 3 is a connectionless service, but with acknowledgment.

The LLC Frame

An LLC frame is known as a PDU (protocol data unit). Its structure is defined in the IEEE 802.2 document. There are four major components to a PDU:

DSAP (destination service access point): An 8-bit value that identifies the higher-level protocol using the LLC services.

SSAP (source service access point): An 8-bit value that indicates the local user of the LLC service. In many cases, this value will be the same as for the DSAP.

Control: A 1- or 2-byte field that indicates the type of PDU. The contents of this field depend on whether the PDU is an information (I), supervisory (S), or unnumbered (U) frame. I frames, used for transmitting data, and S frames, used to oversee the transfer of I frames, are found only in type 2 (connection-oriented) services. U frames are used to set up and break the logical link between network nodes in either type 1 or type 2 services. They are also used to transmit data in connectionless (type 1 or type 3) services. NetWare's IPX packets are unnumbered.

Data, or information: a variable-length field that contains the packet received from the network-level protocol. The allowable length for this field depends on the type of access method being used (CSMA/CD or token passing). S frames do not have a data field.

The figure "Examples of LLC frames" illustrates the frame components.

EXAMPLES OF LLC FRAMES

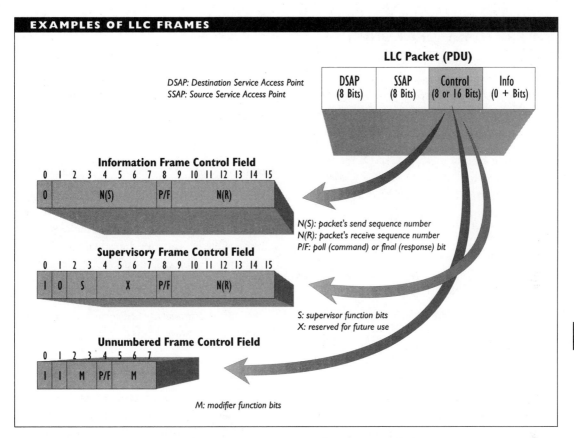

LLC Packet (PDU)

DSAP: Destination Service Access Point
SSAP: Source Service Access Point

| DSAP (8 Bits) | SSAP (8 Bits) | Control (8 or 16 Bits) | Info (0 + Bits) |

Information Frame Control Field

| 0 | 1 | 2 | 3 | 4 | 5 | 6 | 7 | 8 | 9 | 10 | 11 | 12 | 13 | 14 | 15 |

0 | N(S) | P/F | N(R)

N(S): packet's send sequence number
N(R): packet's receive sequence number
P/F: poll (command) or final (response) bit

Supervisory Frame Control Field

| 0 | 1 | 2 | 3 | 4 | 5 | 6 | 7 | 8 | 9 | 10 | 11 | 12 | 13 | 14 | 15 |

1 | 0 | S | X | P/F | N(R)

S: supervisor function bits
X: reserved for future use

Unnumbered Frame Control Field

| 0 | 1 | 2 | 3 | 4 | 5 | 6 | 7 |

1 | 1 | M | P/F | M

M: modifier function bits

▼ LLC2 (Logical Link Control Type 2)

A protocol and packet format for use in SNA-based networks. This format is newer, more versatile, and more widely supported than the SDLC protocol also common in SNA environments.

▼ LME (Layer Management Entity)

In the OSI network management framework, a mechanism by which layers can communicate with each other to exchange information and also to access management elements at different layers. LMEs are also known as *hooks*.

SEE ALSO
Network Management

▼ LMI (Local Management Interface)

A specification regarding the exchange of management-related information between a network and any of various hardware devices (such as printers, storage devices, and so on).

LMU (LAN Manager for UNIX)

An implementation of LAN Manager, Microsoft's server-based network operating system, for UNIX servers.

LMX (L Multiplex)

In analog communications, LMX represents a hierarchy of channel groupings (group, super group, master group, and jumbo group).

LOAD and UNLOAD

In Novell's NetWare, the LOAD command is used to link modules or drivers to the network operating system (NOS). The UNLOAD command is used to unlink modules when they are no longer needed.

When a module is loaded, the NOS allocates a limited amount of memory for the module. The module may request more memory, temporarily, when actually doing work. When a module is unloaded, any memory that had been allocated to the module will be returned to the available memory pool.

NetWare Loadable Modules (NLMs) can be loaded and unloaded as needed. However, you need to be careful when unloading certain "low-level" modules (such as disk or LAN drivers) that may be needed by other modules.

BROADER CATEGORY
NetWare Loadable Module (NLM)

Load Balancing

In switching systems, a strategy in which callers are distributed across all available channels. Load balancing makes the traffic on the channels as evenly distributed as possible.

Loading Coil

A device attached to copper cabling to help reduce distortion of analog signals traveling across the cable. Loading coils make it impossible to transmit digital signals over the copper cables. This has consequences for premises that lie within a few miles of the telephone company office, because these very short connections generally use copper cable with loading coils.

Load Sharing

In internetwork communications, load sharing refers to the ability of two or more bridges to divide network traffic between them. For example, the bridges might provide parallel paths to other networks.

Lobe

In a Token Ring network architecture, lobe is a term for a node, or workstation.

Local-Area Networks Reference Model (LAN/RM)

SEE
LAN/RM (Local-Area Networks Reference Model)

Local-Area Transport (LAT)

SEE

LAT (Local-Area Transport)

Local Automatic Message Accounting (LAMA)

SEE

LAMA (Local Automatic Message Accounting)

Local Carrier

A local telephone company; a company that provides telephone service within an exchange, or calling area. Local carriers are connected by IXCs (interexchange carriers). Local carriers are also known as *local exchange carriers (LECs)*.

Local Channel (LC)

SEE

LC (Local Channel)

Local Loop

In telecommunications, a local loop is a connection between a home or business and the local telephone exchange, or central office.

Local Management Interface (LMI)

SEE

LMI (Local Management Interface)

Local Name

In a network or an internetwork, a local name is known only to a single server or domain in a network.

COMPARE

Global Name

LocalTalk

LocalTalk is Apple's proprietary network architecture, for use in networks that run the AppleTalk networking software, such as Macintosh networks. LocalTalk operates at the data-link and physical layers, which are the two lowest layers in the OSI Reference Model.

LocalTalk has the following characteristics:

- Uses twisted-pair cable.

- Uses an RS-422 interface.

- Uses either a DB-9 or a DIN-8 connector and two DIN-3 connectors. The DIN-3 connectors are designed so that a node can easily drop out of a network without disrupting the electrical activity of the now smaller network.

- Supports transmission speeds of up to 230.4 kilobits per second.

- Uses operating system services, so that all Macintoshes come with built-in networking capabilities.

- Supports up to 255 nodes in a network.

- Allows nodes to be separated by up to 1,000 feet.

- Uses the LocalTalk Link Access Procedure (LLAP) at the data-link layer to access the network.

- Uses the CSMA/CA (carrier sense multiple access/collision avoidance) method to access the network.

- Allows only one network number per network.

SEE ALSO
AppleTalk

Locking

Locking is a mechanism for ensuring that two network users or programs do not try to access the same data simultaneously. A lock may be advisory or physical. An *advisory* lock serves mainly as a warning, and it can be overridden; a *physical* lock serves as a control mechanism, and it cannot.

The following types of locks are distinguished:

File locking: A scheme in which a file server prevents a user from accessing any part of a file while another user is already accessing that file. This is the crudest and least efficient of the locking methods.

Record locking: A scheme in which a file server prevents a user from accessing a record in a file while another user is already accessing that same record. This is more efficient and less restrictive than file locking.

Logical locking: A scheme in which logical units (for example, records or strings) in a file are made inaccessible as required.

Physical: A scheme in which actual sectors or sector groups on a hard disk are made inaccessible as required. This is the standard locking scheme used by MS-DOS and is in contrast to logical locking.

Files can also be locked to prevent or restrict general user access to files.

BROADER CATEGORY
Data Protection

Lockout

In networking, a lockout is an action or state in which a potential network user or application is denied access to particular services on the network or to the network itself.

Logical Address

In a network, a software-based value that is assigned during network installation or configuration, or when a workstation is added to a network. Network and node addresses are logical and are in contrast to hardware addresses, which are fixed during the manufacturing process.

SEE ALSO
Address

Logical Channel Identification (LCI)

SEE
LCI (Logical Channel Identification)

Logical Number

A value assigned in a device-numbering scheme for a hardware device. The logical number is based on several factors and conditions, such as what other devices are attached, and the order in which these were attached and installed.

Logical versus Physical

Logical versus physical represents both a descriptive and functional distinction for several important concepts related to networks. In general, a logical configuration is based on function or on software; a physical configuration is based on hardware, possibly aided or enhanced by software.

For example, logical versus physical distinctions include the following:

- A PC may be physically attached to a network, but may be logically detached if the machine is operating in a stand-alone fashion (rather than as a workstation on the network).

- A network may be using a logical bus topology, which is implemented as a star in the physical wiring.

- A file server's hard disk may be logical drive H: in a workstation's configuration, and the physical drive may be in another room or building.

Login

A login is a process by which a workstation or terminal makes itself known to a server or host, and the workstation's user makes himself or herself known to the network, for authentication and security clearance.

The terms *login* and *logon* (or *log in* and *log on*) are used synonymously. In general, *logon* (or *log on*) is more likely to be used when discussing mainframe environments.

The Login Process

The login process generally involves booting or starting network software on the workstation to announce the machine's presence, and then providing a session through which a user can provide a valid ID and a password to prove that the user is allowed to be operating a workstation, or perhaps just *that* workstation, on the network.

The files and programs used to carry out the login process and validate a particular user logging in are stored in a *login directory*. This directory is created during the network operating system (NOS) installation process. The name and exact contents of a login directory may differ, depending on the NOS. The login directory in Novell's NetWare is named SYS:LOGIN.

Once the network security is convinced of the user's authenticity, the user is given security clearance for access to the network and to some or all of the network's services. In NetWare, the network software runs a *login script* associated with the user. This script may contain commands to assign usage and access rights to the user, initialize the user's local environment on the network (load drivers, change directories, and so forth), map network drives for the user's environment, and execute programs or other commands.

a b c d e f g h i j k **l** m n o p q r s t u v w x y z

Login Restrictions

The login restrictions that can be set to limit a user's ability to log in to a network fall into any of several management areas:

Security: Requiring a user ID and a password helps control network access. The details surrounding password requirements may vary. For example, users may be allowed (or required) to change their passwords every so often. Users may be limited in the number of incorrect passwords they can type before being shut out of the network.

Configuration: If memory usage or other system requirements are of concern, users may have limited access. For example, a login restriction may limit the amount of disk space a user is allowed to use.

Accounting: Various accounting restrictions can be imposed. For example, restrictions may apply to the account's total access time, amount of time open, range of hours during which it is accessible, or number and range of machines from which it is accessible.

▼
Login Script

In Novell's NetWare, a login script is a sequence of commands executed when a user wants to log in to a network. These commands will initialize a node's and a user's operating environments, map directories, allocate resources, and perform other startup tasks for the user.

Three classes of login scripts are distinguished:

- Container, or System: The system script is created by the network administrator. It is used to set general parameters and mappings and to execute commands that are appropriate for all users. In NetWare 3.*x*, the system script is server-specific, which means that all users who log in to the server will have the server's system script executed. In NetWare 4.*x*, the system script is a property of a container object, so that all users in the container get the system script. The container, or system, login script is executed first.

- User: The user script belongs to an individual user, and it does whatever remains to be done to initialize the environment for a particular user.

- Profile: In the NetWare Name Service (NNS) and in NetWare 4.*x*, the profile script initializes the environment for all the users in a group. If defined, such a script executes between the system and user script.

If a configuration includes a system login script, this script is executed before either profile or user scripts.

Logins from Remote Locations

Remote access refers to logins from remote locations. These login procedures are accomplished by dialing into an *access server* (a special modem or computer) and logging in through this server.

The *network modems* that can be used as remote access servers must have an NIC compatible with the network to which the modem is providing access.

Login Service

A login service is a tool for simplifying the login and authentication processes for users. The service consists of four main components, which reside on different machines.

- Client software, which runs on the client's workstation, and which the client can use to access the network and begin the login process.

- Server software, which runs on the target machine, and which will evaluate the user's authenticity and privileges before providing access to the requested services.

- Authentication service, which verifies that the user logging in is legitimate and is allowed on the network. If so, the authentication service gives the user a special ticket that serves as an ID. The authentication service should be running on a secure server.

- Privilege service, which ensures that the user is given access only to the applications and services for which the user has the required privileges. The privilege service should also be running on a secure server.

To use a login service, the user:

1. Checks in with the authentication service to get the validation ticket.

2. Checks in with the privilege service to get the user's PAC (Privilege Attribute Certificate).

Once the user has the PAC, he or she can use the network's facilities—to the extent allowed in the PAC.

To increase security, any or all of the information can be encrypted at any or all of the login phases. The encryption methods can be different for each of the phases, if desired.

With the authentication and security possible when using a login service, SSO (single sign on) becomes a real possibility. In SSO, a user needs to have only a single user ID and password to access any part of a network allowed to the user.

Logout

A logout is a process by which a user's session on a network or a host is closed down and terminated in an orderly fashion. The user's workstation or terminal may be removed as an active node on a network. The workstation may remain physically attached, even though the logical connection between the node and the network is severed.

The terms *logout* and *logoff* (or *log out* and *log off*) are used synonymously; however there are some differences in usage. In general, *logoff* (or *log off*) is more likely to be used when discussing mainframe environments.

Long-Haul Carrier

A long-haul carrier is the carrier system for long-distance signals, which can range from

a b c d e f g h i j k l m n o p q r s t u v w x y z

hundreds of miles to transcontinental or international distances. The term encompasses cabling and signaling (including modulation) specifications. The currently used system was developed as the L carrier system just before World War II, but its capacity and reliability have been increased over the years.

For example, the first long-haul carrier L1 included 480 channels. This has since been increased to 13,200 channels in the L5E system. The end of the L carrier system may finally be in sight, however, as the switchover to digital communications progresses.

Long-haul carriers use mainly coaxial cable and analog signaling. Long-haul carriers are expensive, but this cost is offset by their tremendous capacity. This is in contrast to short-haul carriers.

A *short-haul carrier,* which is used for distances of a hundred miles or so, uses a less expensive technology because the shorter distances involved produce less signal loss. Short-haul carriers use less expensive (and less robust) modulation techniques and have much smaller capacities (usually no more than 24 channels or so) than long-haul carriers. This is because there are no provisions in the short-haul specifications for higher-order modulation. Short-haul carriers also have noisier channels than long-haul carriers.

Long-Haul Microwave Communications

Microwave (that is, gigahertz-level) transmissions over distances of 40 or 45 kilometers (about 25 or 30 miles).

Look-Ahead/Look-Back Queuing

In telephony, look-ahead queuing represents an automatic call distribution feature in which the secondary queue is checked for congestion before traffic is switched to it. This is in contrast to look-back queuing, in which the secondary queue can check whether congestion on the primary queue has cleared up and, if so, return calls to that queue.

Loop

A circuit between a customer's premises and the central office (CO). This can take several forms, with the most common being a line (a pair of wires, in the simplest case).

Loopback

Loopback involves shorting together two wires in a connector, so that a signal returns to its source after traveling around the loop. The term also refers to a test that relies on a loopback process. A *loopback plug* is a device for doing loopback testing.

Loopback Mode

An operating mode for certain devices, such as modems. Loopback mode is used for line testing: signals are sent back to their origin (hence, the *loopback*), rather than being sent on.

Loop Start

In analog telephone communications, a method by which a telephone can seize a line, or circuit. When a would-be caller picks up the telephone receiver, a circuit is closed and current flows, indicating that the telephone is off-hook and that the person wants to make a call.

Loop Timing

In digital communications, a synchronization method in which a clock signal (timing information) is extracted from incoming pulses.

Loose Source and Record Route (LSRR)

SEE

LSRR (Loose Source and Record Route)

Loss

In electrical signals, a loss represents a decrease in signal level, or strength. In call or packet transmissions, loss is the disappearance of a packet or a call, which can occur if a packet is discarded because of heavy traffic or because of an addressing error.

Loss Budget

In electrical or optical signaling, the loss budget represents the combination of all the factors that cause signal loss between the source and destination.

Lost Calls Cleared/Lost Calls Delayed (LCC/LCD)

SEE

LCC/LCD (Lost Calls Cleared/Lost Calls Delayed)

Lotus Notes

Lotus Notes—or, simply, Notes—is arguably the best-known example of *groupware* in the PC-based networking world. Notes is, among other things, a distributed client-server database application for the Windows environment. A Notes server (which is not the same as a network file server) is responsible for running the Notes configuration at a particular installation. The Notes server is also responsible for enforcing access privileges when dealing with client requests.

Most fundamentally, Notes works with databases—albeit databases of a very flexible and free-form nature. The Notes database is built around documents, document groupings, and representations of document content. Documents can be form-oriented or unstructured.

Unlike standard database programs, Notes allows users to view the information in individualized ways, and to expand the database in just about any direction or manner desired. Thus, document contents can be organized and made available in different ways to different users or groups.

A view is a listing of documents available for a particular context or user. From a view, a user can select the specific document or documents of interest, and can access or use the documents as allowed by the user's access level.

Documents can contain links to other documents so that a user can switch quickly to the other end of the link—regardless of whether the document at the end of the link is in the same database or even on the same machine. For example, a document might include links to elaborations, addenda, or tips. A customer's record in a vendor's database might include a link to technical support or complaint calls from the user.

Documents can also include buttons, which will cause predefined actions to be carried out when the button is pressed. For example, a document can include a button to forward material to other users or groups. Links or buttons built into forms become part of all documents based on that form; links and buttons built into a document appear only in that document (and any copies that might be made of it).

The presentation possibilities for a document's contents depend on whether the document is unstructured or whether it is based on a form. The views and capabilities for a particular Notes installation are created by the administrator. That is, the Notes administrator must set up all the views that will be available for users. Similarly, the administrator, or someone else, must create new forms if needed or desired.

In addition to its main functions, Notes provides useful auxiliary features—for example, electronic mail capabilities enable communication among members of the group. Development tools are available to create customized applications that can become accessible through Notes.

Notes users can communicate via electronic mail or through document attachments and links. The Notes e-mail component is compatible with the VIM (Vendor-Independent Messaging) standard, so that Notes users can communicate with any electronic mail systems that also adhere to this standard. Notes also includes dial-in capabilities, so that users can log into Notes from a remote location.

Electronic mail facilities form the basis for one of the *workflow automation* schemes supported by Notes: *routing applications*. In this approach, a project is passed along by mail from person to person as it is developed. Each person makes whatever additions or revisions are required from that user.

Shared applications are the other variant of workflow automation supported by Notes. In a shared application, a project is available at all phases to all relevant and authorized users. Each user contributes as required at the appropriate point, and each user can check on the project's status at any point.

Notes includes encryption capabilities, and a Notes server can require user authentication. Domestic and international versions of Notes use different encryption algorithms—in part because of export restrictions on encryption technology.

Third-party databases and forms are available commercially and from online services. For example, Lotus provides a calendar database, which can be downloaded from online services. With this database, users can do group scheduling.

In early 1995, Lotus released Office Suite, which integrates Notes and the applications in Lotus SmartSuite into an integrated package. It remains to be seen what, if any, other changes will occur in the capabilities, packaging, and marketing of Notes now that Lotus has been bought by IBM.

Lotus SmartSuite

Lotus SmartSuite—or just SmartSuite—is a Windows product that integrates several applications into a single package. The components are:

- Lotus 1-2-3, which is the spreadsheet program that has produced fortunes and lawsuits galore. 1-2-3 is used for doing various types of charts and numerical worksheets. The Version Manager in 1-2-3 allows users to do "what if" analyses—in which certain data values are changed or extrapolated in order to see how these changes would affect the rest of the financial or numerical picture.

- Ami Pro, which was Lotus' word processing package in SmartSuite versions 3.x and earlier. Beginning with version 4.0, the word processor's name has been changed to WordPro. The functionality of this application has also been increased to make it easier for users to collaborate on shared documents. Also, a new implementation of the LotusScript scripting language is included with WordPro.

- Approach, which is a relational database program. Approach includes predefined templates for databases, and various other tools to make it easier to automate database creation and report generation.

- Freelance Graphics, which enables users to create slides, notes, and transparencies for presentations and other

purposes. In addition to various chart and table templates, Freelance Graphics includes capabilities for adding sound, animation, and special transitions to presentations.

- ScreenCam is an application that lets users record activities on the screen and then play these back inside a Freelance Graphics presentation. With the appropriate hardware, you can also record audio.

- Organizer, which is a personal information manager (PIM)—that is, a program for setting appointments, reminders, and alarms, for storing address and phone book information, for keeping to-do lists, and for doing the kinds of things that can (but don't always) help make one more productive.

The various SmartSuite applications can be accessed from the SmartCenter. This is essentially a task manager designed to make it as easy as possible to use the included applications together. It's possible to add new applications to SmartCenter and to make these just as accessible as the included components.

SmartSuite applications can use any of three ways to communicate and exchange data with each other. Of these three methods, only OLE—the most sophisticated—makes it possible to update all versions of a document or project automatically:

- Cutting and copying material to the Windows clipboard, and then retrieving the material in order to paste it in the new location.

a b c d e f g h i j k **l** m n o p q r s t u v w x y z

- Using dynamic data exchange (DDE).

- Using object linking and embedding (OLE).

While not designed specifically for group or network use, SmartSuite can be licensed and used in such a context. In such a setting, working groups can take advantage of information exchange and application access capabilities.

In addition to the basic components, SmartSuite supports macros, and third party macro packages are available as freeware, shareware, and commercial ware. In fact, SmartSuite includes a Working Together Bonus Pack that contains macros to further integrate components and even third party Windows applications.

Lotus SmartSuite for Windows 95 is expected to be available by Q4 of 1995 and to have even more features. Several of the major enhancements are designed to make it easier for work teams to collaborate and cooperate on their projects.

Low-Speed Modem

A low-speed modem is one operating at speeds of 600 bits per second or less.

LPC (Linear Predictive Coding)

A voice-encoding algorithm for use in narrowband transmissions, which can produce a digitized voice signal at 2,400 bits per second (bps). LPC is used in secure telephone units (STU-III), which were developed by the National Security Agency.

A variant, CELP (code excited linear predictive) coding can produce digitized voice output at 4,800 bps.

LPD (Line Printer Daemon)

In UNIX implementations, a daemon program that controls printing from a UNIX machine or network. The LPD program knows which printer or print queue it is printing to and so can make adjustments if necessary.

LPT1

The logical name for the primary parallel port. Additional parallel ports are LPT2 and LPT3. As a device, this port is also known as PRN.

COMPARE
COM1

LSAP (Link Service Access Point)

Any of several SAPs at the logical-link control (LLC) sublayer of the OSI Reference Model's data-link layer. SAPs are addresses through which services are requested or provided.

SEE ALSO
SAP (Service Access Point)

LSB (Least Significant Bit)

The bit corresponding to the lowest power of two (2^0) in a bit sequence. The actual location of this bit in a representation depends on the context (storing or transmitting) and on the ordering within a word.

COMPARE
MSB

SEE ALSO
Big-Endian; Little-Endian

LSL (Link-Support Layer)

In Novell's ODI (Open Data-link Interface), the LSL is an intermediate layer between the network interface card's LAN driver and the protocol stacks for various network and higher-level services, such as IPX and TCP/IP. This layer makes it possible for the same board to work with several types of protocols.

The LSL directs packets from the LAN driver to the appropriate protocol stack or from any of the available stacks to the LAN driver. To do its work, the LSL uses interrupt vectors INT 0x08 and INT 0x2F.

The LSL for DOS can support up to eight boards.

BROADER CATEGORY
ODI (Open Data-link Interface)

LSP (Link State Packet)

In a protocol that uses link state routing, an LSP contains information about all the connections for a router, including information about all the neighbors for that packet and the cost (in money, time, error rate, or other currency) of the link to each neighbor. This packet is broadcast to all other routers in the internetwork.

LSRR (Loose Source and Record Route)

In Internet transmissions, an IP (Internet Protocol) option that enables the source for a datagram to specify routing information and to record the route taken by the datagram. This option helps ensure that datagrams take only routes that have a level of security commensurate with the datagram's security classification.

LTA (Line Turnaround)

In half-duplex communications, the amount of time it takes to set the line to reverse the transmission direction.

LTM (LAN Traffic Monitor)

A device for monitoring the activity, or traffic, level in a network.

L-to-T Connector

In telecommunications, a component that connects two (analog) frequency division multiplexing (FDM) groups into a single (digital) time division multiplexing (TDM) group. This allows the analog channels to be sent over a digital signal 1 (DS1) line.

LU (Logical Unit)

In IBM's SNA (Systems Network Architecture), an LU is an entry point into a network. LUs are one of three types of addressable units in an SNA network. The other two units are PUs (physical units) and SSCPs (system services protocol units).

a b c d e f g h i j k **l** m n o p q r s t u v w x y z

LUs differ in the types of communications possible with them and in the types of protocols used. The table "Logical Unit Types" lists the types of LUs defined.

Lurking

On a network or an internetwork, lurking is listening without participating in an interactive user forum, special interest group, or newsgroup.

Lycos

Lycos is a World Wide Web (WWW) *search engine*. This means you can use Lycos to find hypertext documents that satisfy the search criteria you specify. Lycos has information about the more than six million articles on the Web, and this information is updated frequently to help keep up with the rapid pace of growth on the Web.

Lycos allows you to specify a search string or to fill out a form to set search criteria. You can search either a small or a large catalog of documents. To access Lycos, set

LOGICAL UNIT TYPES	
TYPE	**DESCRIPTION**
LU 0	Communication from program to device.
LU 1	Communication from program to device, with a master/slave relationship between the elements. Used for mainframe batch systems and printers that use the SNA character string (SCS) data format.
LU 2	Communication from program to device, with a master/slave relationship between the elements. Used for 3270 terminals.
LU 3	Communication from program to device, with a master/slave relationship between the elements. Used for 3270 Data Stream terminals.
LU 4	Communication from program to program or from program to device, with a master/slave or a peer-to-peer relationship between the elements. Used for printers using the SCS data format.
LU 6.0	Communication from program to program, with a peer-to-peer relationship between programs. Used for host-to-host communications using either CICS or IMS subsystems.
LU 6.1	Same as LU 6.0.
LU 6.2	Communications from program to program, with a peer-to-peer relationship between programs. Used for dialog-oriented connections that use the General Data Stream (GDS) format. Also known as APPC.
LU 7	Data Stream terminals used on AS/400, System 36, System 38, and so on.

a Web browser to the following URL (Uniform Resource Locator—essentially, a Web document address).

http://lycos.cs.cmu.edu

Figure "Lycos home page" shows what this URL looks like at the time of this writing. For information about Lycos, consult the FAQ (Frequently Asked Questions) file at

http://lycos.cs.cmu.edu/lycos-faq.html

BROADER CATEGORY

Search engine

COMPARE

WWWW (World Wide Web Worm)

▼
Lynx

Lynx is a character-based browser (hypertext file reader) for UNIX and other platforms. While Lynx cannot display graphics, it does give you the option of saving images on disk for later examination with an appropriate viewer program.

To use Lynx, just type the program name at a UNIX prompt. On the same line, specify the Web server you want to use. Once started, Lynx will display the requested

LYCOS HOME PAGE

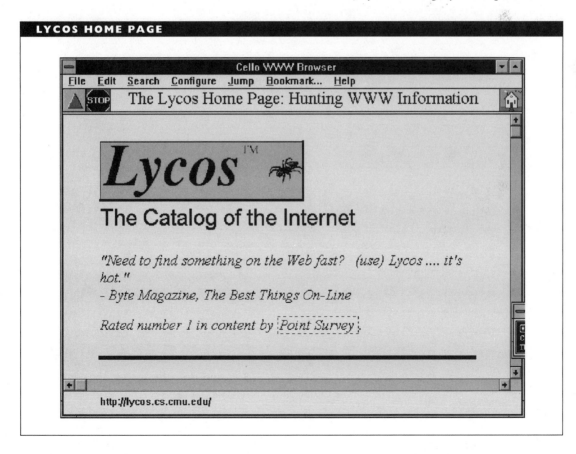

a b c d e f g h i j k **l** m n o p q r s t u v w x y z

home page but without graphics. Where a graphics-based browser would display an image, Lynx will simply have "[image]" or some other text designed into the page.

Figure "Lynx home page" shows the starting page (at the time of this writing) for Lynx, which is found is at the following location:

http://www.cc.ukans.edu

BROADER CATEGORY

Browser

COMPARE

Mosaic; Netscape Navigator

LYNX HOME PAGE

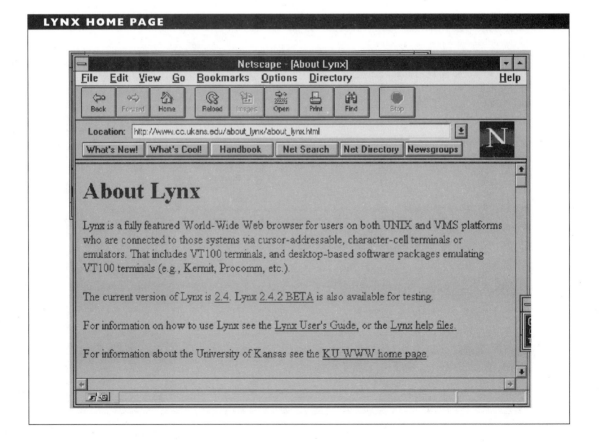

M

In uppercase, an abbreviation for the prefix *mega,* as in MHz (megahertz) or Mbps (megabits per second). This order of magnitude corresponds to 2^{20}, which is roughly 10^6, or millions. In lowercase, *m* is used as an abbreviation for the prefix *milli,* as in msec (millisecond) or mA (milliampere). This order of magnitude corresponds to 2^{-10}, which is roughly 10^{-3}, or one thousandth.

SEE ALSO
Order of Magnitude

MI3

In telecommunications, the method used to multiplex 28 T1 (1.544 Mbps) channels into a T3 (44.736 Mbps) channel.

SEE ALSO
T1 Carrier

MAC (Media Access Control)

In the IEEE 802.*x* networking model, the lower sublayer of the OSI data-link layer. The MAC and the LLC (logical link control) sublayer above it provide higher-level protocols (such as TCP/IP or IPX/SPX) with access to the physical network medium.

SEE ALSO
OSI Reference Model

MAC Convergence Function (MCF)

SEE
MCF (MAC Convergence Function)

Mach

Mach is an operating system created at Carnegie-Mellon University. A UNIX variant, Mach is based on the BSD 4.3 version developed at UC Berkeley. Although it has UNIX roots, Mach was written from scratch, and it was designed to support advanced features such as multiprocessing (support for multiple processors, or CPUs) and multitasking (the ability to work on more than one task at a time).

Mach is also significant for introducing the microkernel as an alternative to the traditional operating system kernel, which is much larger and feature-filled. The NeXT-STEP operating system is a version of Mach implemented originally on NeXT computers and now ported to Intel processors.

Macintosh

Macintosh is the shared name for a family of graphics-based computers from Apple. Until very recently, these computers were built around the Motorola 680*x*0 family of processors (for example, the 68030 or 68040).

The rather large Macintosh family consists of several classes of computers, with high- and low-end models in most classes.

Models in the classic series look similar to the original Macintosh, released in 1984. Examples include the Classic and Classic II, as well as the LC (for low-cost color) and LC II. For both monochrome and color versions, the II versions are higher-end models than the others, but neither is very high-end when compared with other classes in the family.

Models in the desktop Mac II line look more streamlined than models from the classic line. These models also include one or more NuBus expansion slots. Compact versions have the screen and computer in a single unit. At the low end are the Mac II, MacIIx, and MacIIcx, which use 68030 or earlier versions of the processor. High-end desktop machines can be found in the Quadra series, whose members have a 68040 processor.

Models in the portable PowerBook lines are self-contained, lightweight machines. Low-end models include the PowerBook 100 and the PowerBook 140. Higher-end models include the PowerBook 180.

Models in the newly released PowerPC series use a RISC (reduced instruction set computing) processor built through a joint effort of Apple, IBM, and Motorola. Models include the Power Macintosh 6100/60, 7100/66, and 8100/80. These machines include emulation software that enables DOS and Microsoft Windows programs to run on the machine.

Macintosh Networking Capabilities

All but the earliest Macintoshes come with built-in networking capabilities, so these machines require no special network inter-face cards (NICs) or adapters. By default, Macintoshes use AppleTalk as their net-working system, with support for several different network architectures at the data-link level. You will need an NIC if you intend to use something other than Apple-Talk as the networking software and LocalTalk as the data-link architecture.

Macintosh File Format

A Macintosh file has two distinct types of information associated with it: data and resources. The contents are stored in *fork*s.

The *data fork* contains the actual file information, such as the text that makes up a letter or the code that makes up a pro-gram. When a PC reads a Macintosh file, only the data fork is read.

In addition to a data fork, a Macintosh file has a *resource fork,* which contains the resources (applications, windows, drivers, and so on) that are used with the file. Non-Macintosh environments ordinarily are not designed to deal with the resource fork. However, under certain circumstances, non-Macintosh environments may store the resource forks. For example, a NetWare server can store both data and resource forks for Macintosh files if the Macintosh name space is loaded on the server. DOS workstations can access the Macintosh files through the appropriate applications, but they will not handle the files in the same way as a Macintosh.

Despite the difference in format, most network operating systems have provisions for storing, or at least accessing, Macintosh files.

RELATED ARTICLES
AppleTalk; LocalTalk

a
b
c
d
e
f
g
h
i
j
k
l
m
n
o
p
q
r
s
t
u
v
w
x
y
z

> ### WARNING: MANIPULATING ALIEN FILES
>
> Be sure to use the *network* operating system commands (rather than DOS commands) when moving, copying, or otherwise manipulating files with an alien format on a network.
>
> For example, don't use the DOS COPY command to copy a Macintosh file. If you do, only the data fork will be copied. Use Novell NetWare's NCOPY command instead.

Macintosh Client

A Macintosh computer connected to a network. For example, a Macintosh client may be connected to a Novell NetWare network. If a NetWare server is running NetWare for Macintosh modules, the Macintosh can retrieve files from that server. A Macintosh client can also run executable Macintosh files on the network.

Macintosh File System (MFS)

SEE

MFS (Macintosh File System)

Mailbomb

A very large file or a very large number of messages sent to an e-mail address as a prank or in an effort to crash the recipient's mail program.

Mailbot

An automated mail server—also known as an *infoserver*. A mailbot is a program that can automatically carry out actions specified in an e-mail message or reply to e-mail requesting specific information. The mailbot is activated by an incoming message addressed to the program. A common name for such a infoserver is *info* (surprise, surprise).

Mailbox

A file or directory used to store electronic mail messages.

Mail Bridge

A device that connects two networks and filters mail transmissions between them. Only mail that meets specified criteria will be passed from one network to the other. The two networks need not be using the same mail protocol. If they use different protocols, however, the mail bridge needs to be able to handle both protocols.

Mail Delivery System

A mail delivery system consists of the elements needed to get electronic mail (e-mail) from one location to another. The following elements may be used in a mail delivery system:

Mail server: A program that manages delivery of mail or other information upon request. Mail servers are generally implemented at the topmost layer (the applications layer) in the OSI Reference Model.

Mail directory: The directory for a network in which each user on a network has a unique electronic mailbox. This mailbox, which is usually a subdirectory, is used to store e-mail messages until the mailbox owner is ready to read them.

Mailbox: A directory provided to store messages for a single user. Each e-mail user has a unique ID and a unique mailbox. A mailbox is more commonly referred to as an *electronic mailbox.*

Mail exploder: A program used to deliver a message to all the addresses on a mailing list, which is a list containing addresses for all the destinations for a message. With a mail exploder available, a user just needs to send a message to a single address. The mail exploder will make sure that all names on the relevant mailing list get the message.

E-mail is not always intended for a local user, or even for someone using the same kind of mail server. Because of such complexities, there may be routing or translation difficulties. To help avoid or overcome these types of obstacles, a *mail gateway* can be used to connect two or more e-mail services. Mail gateways generally use a store-and-forward scheme to transfer mail between services.

The mail services connected by a gateway may be similar or dissimilar. Gateways that connect similar mail services are known as *mail bridges.* One reason for using a store-and-forward strategy is to give the gateway time to translate messages before passing them to a different mail service.

Another device that can be used to connect multiple e-mail environments to each other is a *mail switch.* A mail switch can route an input e-mail message to the appropriate output system. In addition to making the connection and passing the materials, a mail switch may also need to translate the messages from one e-mail format to another. In many cases, mail switches write the input to a standardized intermediate format, such as MHS or the X.400 format. The intermediate version is then translated into the output format.

In many ways, mail switches are coming to replace gateways. Most mail switches run on a minicomputer or a RISC (reduced instruction set computing) machine for better performance.

Mailing List

In a message-handling or an electronic mail (e-mail) service, a mailing list is a list of e-mail addresses. For example, a mailing list might contain the addresses of users interested in a specific topic. Messages about the topic can be sent automatically to all the addresses.

The delivery of messages to the addresses on a mailing list is handled by a *mail exploder.* On some networks, particularly those with heavy network traffic, a human may be asked first to determine whether the message should be transmitted to the entire mailing list. Manual filtering of messages can greatly reduce network traffic.

a
b
c
d
e
f
g
h
i
j
k
l
m
n
o
p
q
r
s
t
u
v
w
x
y
z

You can subscribe to, or join, special-interest mailing lists so that you will receive information about specific topics. When you do, it's important to observe the guidelines and etiquette associated with the list.

For example, you should adhere to these basic guidelines:

- Follow the local rules for joining or quitting a mailing list.

- Quit the list when you're no longer interested in the topic that binds the list members. This cuts down on the electronic junk mail traffic and also saves you the chore of wading through the messages.

- Refrain from repeating messages that have already been distributed to the addresses on the mailing list.

Major Resource

In a NetWare 4.*x* environment, a category of data used to guide backups. For example, a server or a volume might be categorized as a major resource. The data in a major resource can be backed up as a single group. Subdivisions within a major resource, such as directories or subdirectories, are known as *minor resources*.

Malachi

A product that can be used to download software through your TV. Malachi consists of an adapter for the PC, a cable to connect your PC to the TV, and software to handle the work. Malachi—from En Technology (Keene, NH)—accomplishes its task by using the VBI (vertical blank interval). This is a non-visible component of the TV signal. (Currently, the VBI is used for closed-captioning.)

The long-range significance of such a product is that it makes possible home delivery of software over cable TV lines.

MAN (Metropolitan-Area Network)

A MAN is a network with a maximum range of about 75 kilometers (45 miles) or so, and with high-speed transmission capabilities. Most MANs include some type of telecommunications components and activity to handle long-distance transmissions. Because the distances are generally short enough to incur minimal telecommunications costs, the connections usually use very high-speed lines, such as T3, at almost 45 megabits per second (Mbps).

MANs versus LANs and WANs

MANs have much in common with two other network categories: local-area networks (LANs) and wide-area networks (WANs). The following are the major differences:

- MANs generally involve higher speeds and greater distances than LANs.

- Unlike LANs, MANs generally include provisions for both voice and data transmissions.

- MANs generally involve higher speeds than WANs.

MANs often include several LANs connected to each other via telephone lines. The figure "A MAN made up of several LANs connected by high-speed lines" shows such an arrangement.

MAN Architecture

Most MAN networks use either of two network architectures:

- FDDI (Fiber Distributed Data Interface), which supports transmission speeds of 100-plus Mbps, uses a dual-ring topology and has optical fiber as the medium.

- DQDB (Distributed Queue Dual Bus), which is specified in IEEE 802.6. DQDB supports transmission speeds ranging from 50 to 600 Mbps over distances as large as 50 kilometers (30 miles). As the name implies, DQDB uses a two-bus topology.

RELATED ARTICLES

DQDB (Distributed Queue Dual Bus); FDDI (Fiber Distributed Data Interface)

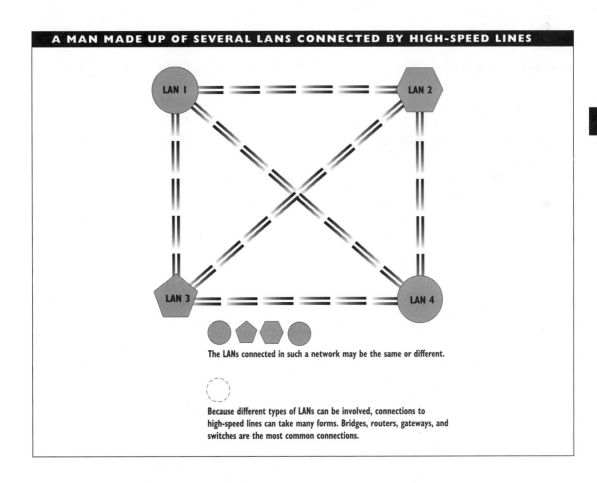

A MAN MADE UP OF SEVERAL LANS CONNECTED BY HIGH-SPEED LINES

LAN 1 LAN 2 LAN 3 LAN 4

The LANs connected in such a network may be the same or different.

Because different types of LANs can be involved, connections to high-speed lines can take many forms. Bridges, routers, gateways, and switches are the most common connections.

a b c d e f g h i j k l **m** n o p q r s t u v w x y z

SEE ALSO

LAN (Local-Area Network); WAN (Wide-Area Network)

Managed Object

In a network management model, any element in the network that can be managed (used or monitored). In addition to objects such as nodes, hubs, and so on, less tangible elements—services and protocols, files and programs, and even algorithms and connections—are also considered managed objects.

SEE ALSO

Network Management

Managing Process

In network management, the managing process is the software that is in charge of management chores. The managing process initiates the requests for data and performs any supported and requested analyses on the data.

The managing process requests data and reports from *managing agents*. These agents are programs that monitor the activity of network stations with respect to whatever attributes are of interest and report the data from this monitoring to the managing process.

The programs for each managing agent (also known as a *management* agent) generally run on the node the agent is monitoring.

A managing process executes on the *managing station,* which is the machine collecting the performance data.

SEE ALSO

Network Management

Manufacturing Message Service (MMS)

SEE

MMS (Manufacturing Message Service)

MAP (Manufacturing Automation Protocol)

MAP is a specification for how to automate tasks in computer integrated manufacturing (CIM) and other factory contexts. An early version of MAP was formulated by General Motors to guide its own procurement strategies. The most recent version, 3.0, differs considerably from the original specifications. By agreement, the MAP 3.0 specifications were left unchanged for a six-year period, which ended in 1994. These specifications are expected to undergo numerous revisions.

MAP Network Types

Three types of networks are distinguished in the MAP model:

Type 1: These networks connect mainframes, minicomputers, and PCs operating at the highest levels in the automation hierarchy. The main tasks are information management, task scheduling, and resource allocation. Electronic mail (e-mail) and files are exchanged, and database operations may be carried out. This type of network does not involve time-critical activity.

Type 2: These networks connect work cells and workstations. The devices serve as process or machine controllers. They exchange programs, alarms, and synchronization signals. Certain exchanges are time-critical.

Type 3: These networks connect machines and their components, including individual sensors or actuators and the machine's controllers for these components. The components must operate in real-time and must be able to operate in full-duplex mode; that is, being able to transmit in both directions at the same time. Commands and data are exchanged constantly but almost always in small chunks because of the real-time restrictions.

The MAP network types differ in the following ways:

- The manufacturing hierarchy level at which the network is defined. The upper levels correspond to offices and shops. Intermediate levels correspond to work cells and stations (machines). The lowest levels correspond to individual pieces of equipment (components).

- The type of equipment involved. At the higher levels, mainframes and other large computers plod along at their own paces to process data destined to determine corporate destinies. At the lower levels, simple processors work in real-time to give specific commands and to pass simple data values.

- The kind of traffic on the network. This may be file transfers, database operations, e-mail, programs, data, commands, and so on. At the upper levels, information and general plans are exchanged; at the lower levels, data and specific commands are exchanged.

MAP Network Components

The MAP 3.0 specifications define three types of end systems in MAP networks: FullMAP, MiniMAP, and EPA.

FullMAP System

FullMAP stations are used in Type 1 networks, where time is not a factor. These stations use a full protocol suite for their activities, as shown in the figure "Protocol suite for FullMAP stations."

MiniMAP System

MiniMAP stations are used in Type 2 and 3 networks, which may handle time-critical traffic. In order to speed things up sufficiently, these nodes communicate with a barebones protocol suite, as shown in the figure "Protocol suite for MiniMAP stations."

a b c d e f g h i j k l **m** n o p q r s t u v w x y z

PROTOCOL SUITE FOR FULLMAP STATIONS

Protocol	Layer
ACSE (Association Control Service Element)	Application
DS (Directory Service)	
FTAM (File Transfer and Management)	
MAP Network Management	
MMS (Manufacturing Message Specification)	
COPP (Connection-Oriented Presentation-Layer Protocol)	Presentation
COSP (Connection-Oriented Session-Layer Protocol)	Session
COTP (Connection-Oriented Transport-Layer Protocol)	Transport
CLNP (Connectionless Network-Layer Protocol)	Network
CONP (Connection-Oriented Network-Layer Protocol)	
SNA Protocol (Subnet Access Protocol)	
SNDC Protocol (Subnet Convergence-Dependent Protocol)	
SNIC Protocol (Subnet Convergence-Independent Protocol)	
LLC Class 1 **LLC Class 3**	Data Link
Token-Bus MAC	
Token-Bus Broadband **Token-Bus Carrier Band**	Physical

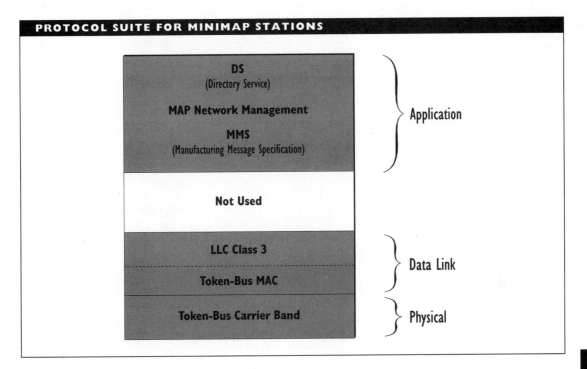

PROTOCOL SUITE FOR MINIMAP STATIONS

DS
(Directory Service)

MAP Network Management

MMS
(Manufacturing Message Specification)

} Application

Not Used

LLC Class 3

} Data Link

Token-Bus MAC

Token-Bus Carrier Band

} Physical

The MiniMAP protocol suite includes only the top layer and the bottom two layers from the OSI hierarchy. The four middle layers are not used. This has important consequences in addition to speeding up communications:

- Only certain application level protocols are allowed.

- No routing is possible, so packets must stay within a network segment.

- Full-duplex communication is necessary because there is no session control.

- No packet fragmentation is possible, since there is no transport layer to do the fragmenting and reconstructing.

EPA System

In the EPA (Enhanced Performance Architecture) system, elements are defined in order to provide a mediator between the incompatible FullMAP and MiniMAP devices. EPA objects use a protocol suite that supports both the FullMAP and MiniMAP suites.

▼ ───────
MAPI (Messaging Application Program Interface)

An interface for messaging and mail services. Microsoft's MAPI provides functions for using Microsoft Mail within a Microsoft Windows application. Simple MAPI consists of 12 functions, such as *MapiDeleteMail()*, *MapiReadMail()*, and *MapiSendMail()*. By calling these functions in the appropriate manner and combination, a Windows application can address, send, and receive mail messages while running.

Mapping

The process of assigning a drive letter to a particular logical disk drive.

SEE

Drive Mapping and Search Drives

Margin

In a signal transmission, the allowance for a certain amount of signal loss, either through attenuation or over time.

Markup Tag

A markup tag is a formatting or inclusion command that is embedded as an annotation in a file being edited. The tag is an instruction for some type of processing or reading program—for example, a typesetting package or a Web browser (hypertext file reader).

Although the tags are visible in the original file, the effects of the tags are not. They are not visible to the user, or to anyone else, until the file is passed through the appropriate program. Such markup systems are in contrast to WYSIWYG (what you see is what you get) environments in which formatting commands are implemented immediately so that the user can see the effects right away.

Editing environments that use markup tags include such languages as TeX, SGML (Standard Generalized Markup Language), and HTML (Hypertext Markup Language).

Of these, HTML is currently the language getting the most attention, because it is used to create hypertext pages for the World Wide Web (WWW).

In HTML, tags represent instructions about the document's layout and about links to other documents or to other places in the file. Tags are denoted by placing them within angle brackets, or <> . HTML tags may be empty or nonempty.

- An *empty tag*—for example, <HR> or <P>—takes no arguments. Thus, the first tag (HR) is an instruction to draw a horizontal line at the location where the instruction was found. Similarly, <P> indicates a paragraph break.

- A *nonempty tag*—for example, <B>—applies only to certain elements or portions of text. This "scope" of influence is indicated by having a second version of a tag to indicate the end of the tag's influence. Ending tags are identical to their starting counterparts, except that they have a forward slash after the opening left angle bracket. For example, the tag </B> ends the section of text that began with <B>. All text between these two tags is written in boldface.

Masquerade

A security threat in which a user, process, or device pretends to be a different one. For example, a process may pretend to be the password-checking program in order to intercept user passwords; a user may pretend to be a different user (generally someone who rarely logs in or who has a very easy-to-guess password).

Mating

The physical linking of two connectors to establish a connection. Since mechanical parts are involved in this linkage, there will be wear and tear on the connectors, and the quality of the connection may eventually deteriorate.

SEE ALSO

Connector; Connector, Fiber-Optic

MAU (Medium Attachment Unit)

In the IEEE 802.3 specifications, a MAU refers to a transceiver.

MAU (Multistation Access Unit)

MAU (sometimes abbreviated MSAU) is IBM's term for a wiring hub in its Token Ring architecture. This hub serves as the termination point for multiple nodes and can be connected to the network or to another hub, as illustrated in the figure "MAUs in a Token Ring network."

Each MAU can have up to eight nodes (*lobes* in IBM's terminology) connected, and each MAU can be connected to other MAUs. The MAU has connectors for the lobes and two special connectors—ring in (RI) and ring out (RO)—for connecting MAUs to each other. A MAU organizes the nodes connected to it into an internal ring and uses the RI and RO connectors to extend the ring across MAUs.

When MAUs are connected, it is possible to create a main and a secondary ring path.

This redundancy can be helpful if the main ring path breaks. In that case, packets can be routed via the secondary ring path.

In the process of passing packets around the ring, a MAU can clean and boost a signal; that is, it can serve as a repeater. MAUs differ in the additional capabilities they provide.

The most widely supported MAU standard is that for IBM's MAU model 8228. You will often see references to "8228-compliant MAUs." This standard serves as a common denominator; it is a minimal set of capabilities that just about all MAUs support. Most MAUs have capabilities beyond those of the 8228. These capabilities can make a network more efficient but can also increase the likelihood of compatibility problems.

Most MAUs have LEDs (light-emitting diodes) to indicate the status of each port (lobe) on the MAU. MAUs can automatically disconnect faulty lobes without affecting the other lobes or disrupting the network.

Lobes are connected to MAUs using Type 1, 2, or 3 IBM cable. Because Type 3 cable is unshielded, you also need a media filter between the cable and the MAU, to clean certain noise from the signals before they reach the MAU. Type 6 cable is sometimes used to connect MAUs to each other, provided the distance between MAUs is just a few meters.

When using IBM Type 1 or 2 cable, more than 30 MAUs may be connected, supporting up to 260 nodes altogether. When using IBM Type 3 cable, up to 9 MAUs can be connected, supporting up to 72 nodes altogether.

a
b
c
d
e
f
g
h
i
j
k
l
m
n
o
p
q
r
s
t
u
v
w
x
y
z

MAUS IN A TOKEN RING NETWORK

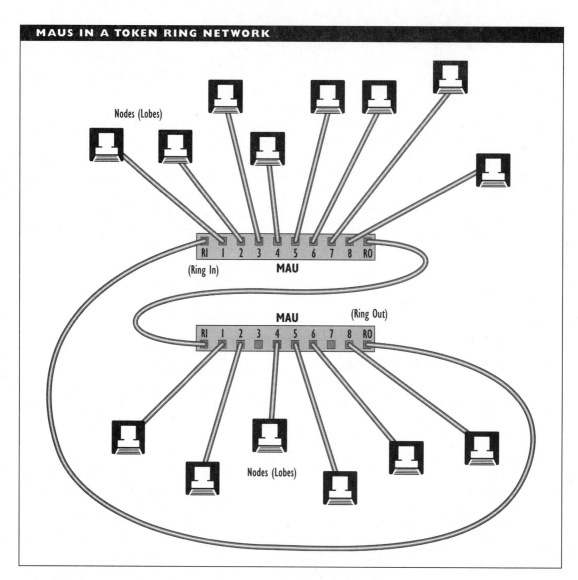

Maximum Transmission Unit (MTU)

SEE

MTU (Maximum Transmission Unit)

MBONE (Multicast Backbone)

The MBONE is a multicast network that adds live audio and video capabilities to the Internet; however, this technology and architecture are still in an experimental phase. A multicast network is one in which a packet is sent to all addresses on a subscriber or other type of list. This is in contrast to a unicast network (in which only a single user gets the packet at a time) and to a broadcast network (in which a packet is sent to all users, regardless of whether they are on lists or not).

The MBONE is a virtual network that sits on top of the Internet and provides multicast and real-time capabilities that are not yet widely available on the Internet proper. The MBONE is organized as clusters ("islands") of networks that can support multicast IP (Internet Protocol) transmissions.

These islands are connected via *tunnels*, which are paths between endpoints that support multicast transmissions. Although the tunnel generally goes through ordinary (i.e., non-multicast) networks, it does provide a virtual point-to-point connection between the endpoints. These are usually ordinary workstations that can run *mrouted* (multicast routing daemon) programs.

Because of its multicast capabilities, the MBONE can be used to reach large audiences and can be used for two-way communications in real time. Real-time capabilities mean that voice or video data can be exchanged. In fact, the IETF (Internet Engineering Task Force) currently broadcasts its conferences over the MBONE. The MBONE requires special hardware, and it uses special protocols to handle the multicast packets quickly and efficiently.

The MBONE can cause potential security problems. One reason is that multicast packets are often encapsulated (stuffed) into ordinary Internet Protocol (IP) packets—so they can be transmitted through ordinary

(ie, non-MBONE) routers. The multicast packet will then be removed at an MBONE host for further processing.

This strategy causes a problem for security devices (such as firewalls) that check addresses but not the contents of packages that travel through them. With such a setup, it would be possible to send a rogue packet past a firewall by putting it into an MBONE transmission.

Although the MBONE is still in an experimental stage, it is already international and considerably larger than most networks. As of May 1994, the MBONE spanned 20 countries and had over 900 routers. (You can get a PostScript graphic showing the high-level MBONE topology by using anonymous FTP to get the file /mbone /mbone-top.ps from the ftp.isi.edu FTP site.)

Primary Sources The most recent FAQ (frequently asked question) file is available by getting /mbone/faq.txt from the ftp.isi .edu FTP site. Hypertext documents are available from http://www.research.att.com/ mbone-faq.html and from http://www.cl .cam.ac.uk/mbone/ in theUnited Kingdom. Other information sources are listed in the FAQ file.

MCF (MAC Convergence Function)

In the DQDB network architecture, a function that is responsible for preparing data from a connectionless service (a service in which each packet is sent independently of other packets, and different packets may take different routes to the same destination).

a b c d e f g h i j k l **m** n o p q r s t u v w x y z

SEE ALSO
DQDB (Distributed Queue Dual Bus)

MD (Management Domain)

In the CCITT's X.400 Message Handling System (MHS), a limited, but not necessarily contiguous, area whose message-handling capabilities operate under the control of a single management authority. This authority can be the CCITT, a university, an organization, or other group. Two types of management domains are defined: ADMD (Administrative Management Domain) and PRMD (Private Management Domain).

MD5 (Message Digest 5) Algorithm

The MD5 algorithm is a proposed encryption strategy for the Internet's SNMP (Simple Network Management Protocol). The algorithm uses a message, an authentication key, and time information to compute a checksum value (the *digest*).

MDF (Main Distribution Frame)

The central distribution point for the wiring to a building. The wiring from an MDF may be routed to IDPs (intermediate distribution points) or directly to end-users. An MDF is generally located in a wiring closet.

Mean Time Between Failures (MTBF)

SEE
MTBF (Mean Time Between Failures)

Mean Time To Repair (MTTR)

SEE
MTTR (Mean Time To Repair)

Media Access Control (MAC)

SEE
MAC (Media Access Control)

Media-Access Method

The media-access method is the strategy used by a node, or station, on a network to access a network's transmission medium. Access methods are defined at the data-link layer in the OSI Reference Model. More specifically, they are defined at the MAC sublayer (as defined by the IEEE). The figure "Media-access methods" shows how these methods fit into the network architecture.

Probabilistic versus Deterministic Access Methods

The two main classes of access methods are probabilistic and deterministic.

With a probabilistic media-access method, a node checks the line when the node wants to transmit. If the line is busy, or if the node's transmission collides with another transmission, the transmission is canceled. The node then waits a random amount of time before trying again.

Probabilistic access methods can be used only in networks in which transmissions are broadcast so that each node gets a transmission at just about the same time. The best-known probabilistic access method is

CSMA/CD (carrier sense multiple access/ collision detect), which is used in Ethernet networks.

With a deterministic media-access method, nodes get access to the network in a predetermined sequence. Either a server or the arrangement of the nodes themselves determines the sequence. The two most widely used deterministic access methods are token-passing (used in ARCnet and in Token Ring networks) and polling (used in mainframe environments). Slots and registers are older access methods that have been superseded by token passing in most applications.

In general, probabilistic methods are most suitable for smaller networks with relatively light traffic. Deterministic networks are better suited to large networks and those with heavy traffic. Some network architectures, such as IBM's SNA (Systems Network Architecture), and some applications (real-time applications, such as process control) must use deterministic methods.

Media access may be determined at a station on a network or at a wiring center. The traditional media-access methods, such as CSMA/CD and token-passing, are determined at each node. As network traffic

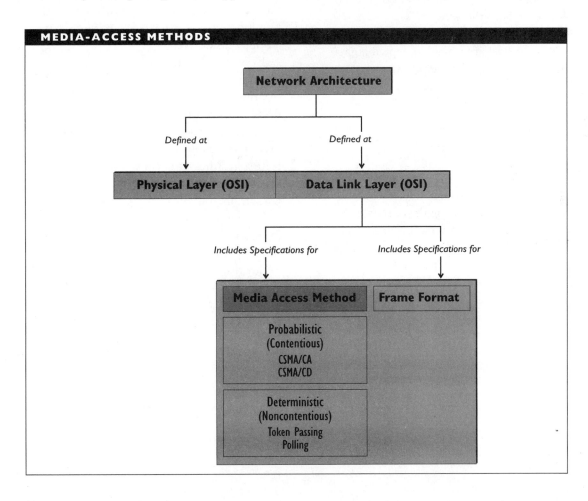

MEDIA-ACCESS METHODS

Network Architecture

Defined at → Physical Layer (OSI)

Defined at → Data Link Layer (OSI)

Includes Specifications for → Media Access Method

- Probabilistic (Contentious)
  - CSMA/CA
  - CSMA/CD
- Deterministic (Noncontentious)
  - Token Passing
  - Polling

Includes Specifications for → Frame Format

increases, stations (nodes) will spend more time waiting to access the network.

Other Access Methods

Higher bandwidth networks and networks with very heavy traffic require more efficient media-access methods. One way to accomplish this is to move access control to a wiring center (such as a hub). Then the nodes in the network do not need to worry about accessing the network. A node just transmits to the hub whenever the node has something to say. The hub then becomes responsible for getting each node's bits of wisdom onto the network.

Demand priority, which is used in Hewlett-Packard's highly-adapted high-speed 100BaseVG Ethernet standard, is an example of a media-access method that uses hub control.

BROADER CATEGORY
Network Architecture

Media Filter

A device for converting the output signal of a Token Ring network interface card to work with a particular type of wiring, such as unshielded twisted-pair (UTP) cable. Specifically, a device that can convert between UTP and shielded twisted-pair (STP) cables. A media filter is a passive device, designed mainly to eliminate undesirable high-frequency emissions.

Media Manager

In Novell's NetWare 4.*x*, a collection of resources for keeping track of and providing access to various types of storage devices (disk, compact disc, tape, jukebox, and so on) without requiring special device drivers.

Memory

Memory is randomly addressable storage in a computer that is used to run programs, temporarily store data, and for other purposes. Memory is implemented in very fast access chips, which can be accessed several hundred times as quickly as a hard disk or a floppy disk drive.

Every location in a memory space has an address that identifies that particular location in the space. The form this address takes depends on the type of memory involved and also on the type of addressing used. For example, in IBM PC-based architectures, addresses in conventional memory are represented in terms of segment (16-byte paragraph) and offset components.

The chips used for the memory and the location of these chips depend on the type of memory. Four types of memory are commonly distinguished: conventional, upper, extended (including HMA), and expanded. The figure "Memory layout" shows how these memory areas are related.

Conventional Memory

In IBM PCs, *conventional memory* is the first 640 kilobytes (KB) of memory. The

MEMORY LAYOUT

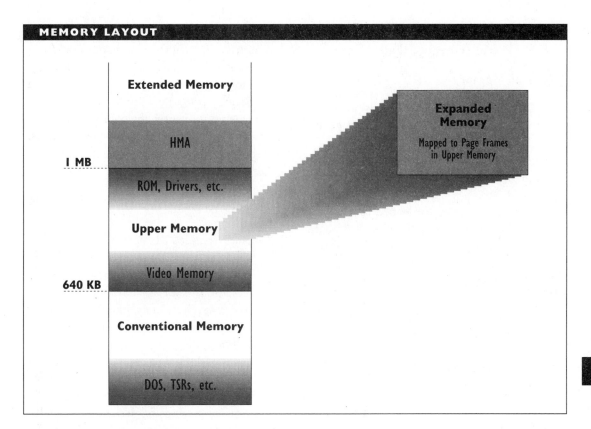

architecture of the early Intel processors restricted the original IBM PC to accessing 1 MB of memory, 640 KB of which was available for applications; the remaining 384 KB was reserved for system use, the BIOS, and the video system. At that time, 640 KB was more than ten times the amount of memory available in other personal computers. However, as both applications and DOS grew, they began to run out of room.

Conventional memory is generally represented in chips installed on the motherboard. The DOS kernel is loaded into conventional memory when you boot your computer. Most application programs execute in conventional memory.

Upper Memory

In IBM PCs, *upper memory* refers to the area of memory between 640 KB and 1,024 KB, or 1 megabyte (MB). Traditionally, this area, also known as *system memory*, was accessible only to the system, not to user programs. Programs such as memory managers provide access to upper memory, and can store drivers, terminate-and-stay-resident (TSR) programs, and other necessary material in available locations in upper memory.

Upper memory is allocated in presized chunks called *upper memory blocks*

(UMBs). Upper memory is allocated in the same chips as conventional memory.

Extended Memory

In IBM PCs, *extended memory* is memory above 1 MB. This type of memory is available only in machines with 80286 and higher processors because the machine must be in protected mode to access memory above 1 MB.

Extended memory is defined by the Extended Memory Specification (XMS), and it is generally accessed through XMS drivers, such as HIMEM.SYS.

Extended memory is allocated in presized *extended memory blocks* (EMBs). Allocation for the EMBs begins at the location 64 KB above the 1 MB extended memory border; that is, above the high memory area (HMA). Extended memory is allocated on chips installed on the motherboard or in added memory banks.

HMA (High Memory Area)

The first 64 KB of extended memory is called the *HMA*. In DOS versions 5.0 and later, the operating system kernel can be loaded into this area, freeing a considerable amount of conventional memory. In order to access the HMA, address line A20 must be enabled.

Expanded Memory

Expanded memory is a DOS mechanism by which applications can access more than the 640 KB of memory normally available to them.

Expanded memory is provided in storage on a separate expansion board (or it is emulated in extended memory), and a special driver is used to map memory on these chips to 16 KB pages allocated in upper memory.

Because programs cannot access this memory directly, the contents of expanded memory are moved piecemeal into pages that are allocated in the memory area between 640 KB and 1 MB. The more pages that are allocated, the larger the chunk of expanded memory that can be accessed at a given time.

The Expanded Memory Specification (EMS) LIM 4.0 (LIM is for Lotus Intel Microsoft, the companies that developed the specification) is the standard method of accessing expanded memory. This specification lets programs running on any of the Intel 8086 family of processors access as much as 32 MB of expanded memory. Although the EMS calls for expanded memory to have its own hardware, various memory managers and drivers can emulate expanded memory in extended memory.

Memory Uses

Memory chips can also be categorized in terms of the manner in which the memory is used. In this regard, the two main categories are ROM (read-only memory) and RAM (random access memory). Each of these general classes comes in several variants, which are discussed in their own entries.

SEE ALSO

RAM (Random Access Memory); ROM (Read-Only Memory)

Memory Managers

A *memory manager* is a program that controls access to available memory and can manipulate available memory in order to make its use more efficient.

In particular, memory managers can do the following types of tasks:

- Provide access to expanded and/or extended memory.

- Emulate expanded memory (which assumes its own memory board) in extended memory.

- Move drivers and programs into upper and high memory in order to make more conventional memory available.

For example, a memory manager can load drivers or certain programs into non-conventional memory areas. Because more conventional memory is available, users have greater flexibility in the kinds of programs they can run. Memory managers can also improve program performance because programs have more memory to work with.

Most programs support extended memory, but some older programs require expanded memory. Memory manager programs, such as 386MAX from Qualitas and QEMM-386 from Quarterdeck Systems, can simulate expanded memory in extended memory. This leads to the somewhat perverse situation in which information stored in one area of extended memory (the LIM simulation) is paged to another area of extended memory (the expanded memory pages allocated in upper memory) for use by a program most likely running in conventional memory.

Memory Dump

A displayed, saved, or printed copy of a specified area of internal memory, which should show the current values of the variables stored in the selected memory area. A memory dump provides "state-of-the-machine" (at that address) information.

Memory Pool

In Novell's NetWare, a memory pool of a finite supply of memory, not necessarily contiguous. NetWare 4.*x* uses only a single memory pool, whose resources are allocated for whatever functions request them. NetWare version 3.*x* defines several memory pools, including a short-term and a file cache pool.

Memory Protection

In a Novell NetWare 4.*x* environment, memory protection is a memory management strategy that protects the server's memory from being corrupted by NetWare Loadable Modules (NLMs).

To accomplish its goals, NetWare 4.*x*'s memory protection uses two different domains: OS and OS_PROTECTED. These domains are associated with two of the four privilege levels, or rings, managed by the Intel architecture. These privilege levels are protected from each other so that programs or processes running in different levels cannot interfere with each other.

Novell recommends running third-party or untested NLMs in the OS_PROTECTED domain, at least until you are confident that the NLM is well-behaved. To do this,

a
b
c
d
e
f
g
h
i
j
k
l
m
n
o
p
q
r
s
t
u
v
w
x
y
z

type the following commands at the server console before loading the NLM:

LOAD DOMAIN

DOMAIN=OS_PROTECTED

If you want to load the NLM from within the AUTOEXEC.NCF file, add these same two lines to that file. To load an NLM in the OS domain, use the same commands but change the second one to DOMAIN=OS.

Message-Oriented Text Interchange System (MOTIS)

SEE

MOTIS (Message-Oriented Text Interchange System)

Message Switching

In message switching, a message makes its way from sender to receiver by being passed through intermediate nodes. Each node may store the entire message, and it will forward it to the next node when the opportunity arises.

Under certain types of connections, different parts of the message may take different routes to the destination during transmission. By using message switching and a store-and-forward method, a network operating system can make the most effective use of the available bandwidth.

Metering

The tracking of software availability and use on a network. One major goal of metering is to ensure that software licenses are not being violated. Some software products can meter themselves by using built-in metering concepts. More sophisticated products can do trend analyses of the metering data to help predict when new copies of a software product will need to be purchased or licensed.

MFM (Modified Frequency Modulation)

An encoding method for floppy disks and low-capacity (50 megabytes or less) hard disks. MFM hard disks can transfer more than 600 kilo*bytes* per second.

MFS (Macintosh File System)

An older file system used in earlier Macintosh models. The MFS used a flat file structure rather than the hierarchical file system used in more recent versions. Newer Macintoshes can read disks that use the MFS.

MHS (Message Handling System), CCITT X.400

An MHS is an application-level service element that enables applications to exchange messages. An electronic mail (e-mail) facility with store-and-forward capabilities is an example of an MHS.

In the CCITT's X.400 recommendations, an MHS can transfer messages between end-users or between end-users and a variety of CCITT-defined services, such as fax, videotext, and so on.

MHS Components

The CCITT's X.400 MHS includes the following components:

- User agents (UAs) to provide interfaces for the end-users at one end and the

Message Transfer System (MTS) at the other end.

- Access units (AUs) to provide interfaces for the CCITT services at one end and the MTS at the other end.

- A message store (MS) to provide temporary storage for messages before they are forwarded to their destination. The MS is a general archive in which mail can be held until the appropriate user retrieves it through a UA or until the allowable storage time for the message is exceeded. The MS is distinct from the mailboxes associated with individual users. UAs and other services use the MSAP (Message Store Access Protocol) to access the message store.

- An MTS, complete with message transfer agents (MTAs), to perform the actual transfer of the message from one end to the other. The MTAs are responsible for storing and/or forwarding messages to another MTA, to a user agent (UA), or to another authorized recipient. (An MTA is comparable to a mail agent in the TCP/IP environment.)

The MTS is a connectionless but reliable transfer capability. *Connectionless* means that parts of the message are transported independently of each other and may take different paths. *Reliable* means that a message part will be delivered correctly or the sender will be informed that this was not possible.

Message Handling Layers

In the 1984 version of the X.400 MHS recommendations, the message transfer layer (MTL) is the lower sublayer of the OSI application layer. This sublayer provides access to the transfer services. Message transfer agent entities (MTAEs) carry out the functions at this sublayer. The 1984 version defines a protocol known as P1 for communications between MTAEs.

The user agent layer (UAL) is the sublayer above the MTL. The services for this sublayer may be implemented on a different machine than the one containing the MTL. For example, in a local-area network (LAN) workstations may run the UAL to communicate with a server that provides the actual message transfer server. For configurations in which the MTL and UAL are on different machines, the recommendations provide a submission and delivery entity (SDE) to carry out the functions of the MTL.

MHS Management Domains

In the CCITT's X.400 MHS, a management domain (MD) is a limited, but not necessarily contiguous, area whose message-handling capabilities operate under the control of a single management authority. This authority can be the CCITT, a university, an organization, or other group.

Two types of management domains are defined:

ADMD (Administrative Management Domain): A domain which is always run by the CCITT, such as national PTT (Postal, Telegraph, and Telephone) systems

PRMD (Private Management Domain):
A domain created by a local organization, such as a store, together with all its branches in the state, or a university campus

BROADER CATEGORY
X.400

RELATED ARTICLES
E-Mail; IPMS (Interpersonal Messaging Service)

MHS (Message Handling System), NetWare

In the Novell NetWare environment, MHS refers both to a protocol for mail handling and routing and to mail delivery service products for NetWare 2.*x* and later.

NetWare Global MHS

NetWare Global MHS is a collection of NetWare Loadable Modules (NLMs) that provide mail delivery service for networks using NetWare 3.*x* or later. MHS provides store-and-forward capabilities for various types of messaging services, including electronic mail, fax services, calendar and scheduling services, and also workflow automation.

Optional modules provide capabilities for accessing different messaging environments, including the following:

- UNIX and other TCP/IP-based networks, by using a module that supports the SMTP (Simple Mail Transfer Protocol).

- OSI environments, by using a module that provides support for X.400 protocols and services.

- IBM mainframes and AS/400 systems, by using the SNADS (SNA Distribution Services) module.

- Macintosh, OS/2, and other environments over gateways.

The related products NetWare MHS 1.5N and NetWare MHS 1.5P provide services for other environments. NetWare MHS 1.5N provides support for NetWare 2.*x* networks. MHS 1.5P supports laptops and remote PCs.

MIB (Management Information Base)

An MIB contains data available to a network management program. MIBs are created by management agents so that each machine with an agent will have an associated MIB. The network manager will query these MIBs and may use an MIB of its own. The management MIB has more general information; the individual MIBs have machine-specific information.

The details of the MIB's format and the communication between manager and agents depend on the networking and network management model being used. For example, the Internet, OSI-compliant networks, and IBM SNA-based networks are based on different models, and so they have different MIBs. Translation capabilities are available for many environment combinations.

In the IP (Internet Protocol) network management model, the SNMP (Simple Network Management Protocol) contains *MIB views* (also known as *SNMP MIB views*), which are selective subsets of the information available in an agent's MIB. An MIB view can be created for a single station or for all the stations in an SNMP community.

Microbend/Microcrack

In fiber optics, microbends are tiny bends in fiber, and microcracks are microscopic cracks in fiber. Both of these flaws can affect a transmission.

SEE ALSO

Cable, Fiber-Optic

MicroChannel

MicroChannel is a proprietary bus architecture developed by IBM for its PS/2 series of computers. Expansion boards for Micro-Channel machines may have up to 32-bit data channels, but they are incompatible with machines that conform to ISA (Industry Standard Architecture) or EISA (Extended Industry Standard Architecture).

A MicroChannel environment allows you to use software to set addresses and interrupts for hardware devices. This means you do not need to adjust jumpers or dip switches on the boards. This also helps reduce the number of address and interrupt conflicts. MicroChannel was formerly known as *MCA,* but this name was dropped after a lawsuit filed by the Music Corporation of America.

BROADER CATEGORY

Data Bus

COMPARE

EISA (Extended Industry Standard Architecture); ISA (Industry Standard Architecture); PCI (Peripheral Component Interconnect); VL Bus

Microkernel

A streamlined and stripped-down operating system kernel. A microkernel handles only the scheduling, loading, and running of tasks. All other operating system functions (such as input/output and virtual memory management) are handled by modules that run on top of this microkernel. The concept of a microkernel was developed at Carnegie-Mellon University and was implemented in the Mach operating system developed there.

Micron

A unit of measurement corresponding to one millionth of a meter (roughly $1/25,000$ inch), also called a *micrometer.* Units of this magnitude are used in networking to specify the diameter of optical fibers, as in 62.5 or 100 micron fibers.

Microsoft Mail

Microsoft's electronic mail package. Client software for Mail is available as a part of Microsoft Office and Office Professional, Windows for Workgroups, and Windows 95. Windows 95 also includes a post office (temporary message storage area). Mail *servers* are part of the Microsoft BackOffice suite and the Windows NT server.

Mail is compatible with Microsoft's Messaging Application Program Interface

a
b
c
d
e
f
g
h
i
j
k
l
m
n
o
p
q
r
s
t
u
v
w
x
y
z

(MAPI) and is one of the messaging services supported by Microsoft Exchange in Windows 95.

SEE ALSO

Microsoft Exchange; Microsoft Office; Windows 95

Microsoft Network (MSN)

SEE

MSN (Microsoft Network)

Microsoft Office

Microsoft Office—or just Office for simplicity—is an integrated suite of applications, with implementations for Windows, Windows NT, and Windows 95. Office comes in two versions: Office and Office Professional. The major difference between these packages is the inclusion of Microsoft Access in Office Professional.

Office includes the Windows applications in the following list. You can add other Windows applications to the Office environment.

- *Excel,* which is Microsoft's entry in the electronic spreadsheet world. Excel provides all the standard features of a spreadsheet program. You can enter numerical or text data, create and apply formulas where appropriate, call functions to modify the data, and format and modify the spreadsheet's content as you need. Excel allows you to create and print charts and graphs based on the numbers in your spreadsheets.

- *Mail,* which provides electronic mail services. You can use Mail to correspond electronically with others on a local area network or even across long-distance telephone lines. Each user has his or her own mailbox, which may be a directory on a network server. Mail is delivered to the network post office, which is set up and run by a network administrator. Users can retrieve their mail from the post office. Within the Mail application, you can compose, read, print, and forward messages. You can attach images or other files to mail messages.

- *Powerpoint,* which is a presentation program. You can use Powerpoint to create slides, transparencies, handouts, speaker notes, etc. Powerpoint supports text and graphics in the presentation elements, and it allows you to use any of various transitions between slides. Powerpoint allows you to leave a predefined sequence and branch to specific slides in mid-presentation; you can also jump from a slide to any material (Excel spreadsheets, Word documents, etc.) that may be linked to the slide. The application includes several wizards, which are programs that help accomplish certain tasks (such as specifying the format of slides or other elements).

- *Word,* which is a widely used word processing program. In addition to the usual word processing capabilities, Word includes over a dozen predefined templates to help you create certain types of documents, and each template comes in as many as four different "flavors" for creating different kinds of looks. Example templates include: brochure, fax cover sheet, letter, memo, press release, and purchase order. Word also has wizards, which help you create specific documents by asking you questions about what you want to do and then creating a document style based on your answers. Example wizards include: Calendar, Directory, Invoice, and Letter. Add-on products (ranging from freeware to buyware) expand Word's capabilities. Generally these add-ons take advantage of the fact that you can define macros to perform new actions. For example, one type of add-on enables Word to create HTML (hypertext markup language) documents, which are documents found on the World Wide Web (WWW). You can also get free macros to convert an existing Word file to HTML format, which can save you the work of creating new files. Word also includes spelling, style, and grammar checkers.

- *Access,* which is a relational database management program and is included only in Office Professional. (You can, however, buy it separately and then add it to the regular Office environment.) You can use Access to create, query, and generate reports from databases containing just about whatever information you want. Access comes with 30 predefined database templates, including book inventories, personal or business contact lists, expense trackers, mailing lists, recipe collections, and wine inventories. Access

also has wizards—special programs to help you do such things as setting up queries, creating tables, reports, mailing labels, and even controls and buttons. Access supports both macros and a programming language (Access Basic), which makes it possible to create modules that can perform tasks that are too difficult to accomplish with just macros.

You can start the component applications from either the Windows Program Manager or the Microsoft Office Manager (or Microsoft Shortcut Bar, as it's called in Office 95). The Office Manager serves as a task manager for the integrated suite. You can start any or all of the component applications from the Office Manager, and you can switch easily between applications. The applications in Office and Office Professional can exchange data using either the Windows Clipboard or OLE (Object Linking and Embedding).

Office Professional also comes in a CD-ROM version that includes Microsoft Bookshelf and Microsoft Office Assistant. Bookshelf includes several reference works (a dictionary, thesaurus, encyclopedia, atlas, almanac, chronology, and dictionary of quotations). The Office Assistant includes 54 business tools, including financial statements, templates for business plans, and five-year projections. These auxiliary programs are also accessible from the Office Manager.

Microwave Transmission

Microwave transmission is unbounded or wireless network communication that makes use of microwaves to transmit the signals. Microwaves are in the 1 gigahertz (GHz) and higher region of the electromagnetic spectrum. Various sources put the upper frequency limit for microwaves at 30 GHz, 300 GHz, and 1 terahertz (THz). Whichever limit is used, microwaves still offer a potentially very high bandwidth; in practice, most microwave connections are in the low gigahertz range.

Microwave transmissions are used in wireless networks but require a line of sight between sender and receiver.

This type of transmission is in contrast to cable-based transmission and to transmission using radio or infrared waves or laser signals. Like radio waves, the microwave spectrum requires licensing from the FCC (Federal Communications Commission). Microwave transmissions are very susceptible to eavesdropping, jamming, and interference (from natural or electrical sources).

Microwave transmissions can be broadband or baseband, and they can use earth-based or satellite receivers.

Earth-Based versus Satellite Receivers

With earth-based receivers, the microwave signal is beamed over a line-of-sight path to a parabolic antenna. The signal may be passed from antenna to antenna (with each of these functioning as a repeater). These antennas cannot be more than about 30 or 40 kilometers (20 or 25 miles) apart (because of the earth's curvature). In practice, earth-based microwave connections are rarely this large. Rather, the transmissions are usually just between buildings (less than 100 meters, or a few hundred feet).

With satellite-based receivers, the signal is beamed between an earth-based parabolic antenna and a satellite in geosynchronous orbit over the earth. The signal is then beamed from the satellite to other locations, possibly over thousands of miles. The signal from the satellite can be broadcast or focused, and the receiving antennas can be fixed or mobile.

Advantages of Microwave Transmission

Advantages of microwave transmission include the following:

- They have a very high bandwidth.

- Repeater antennas may be much less expensive to build over terrain where cable is inadvisable.

- The transmissions can reach remote locations, even if these are in hostile terrain.

- With satellite-based communications, long distances can be covered without intervening repeaters.

- Both transmitter and receiver can be mobile if necessary.

- The signals can be sent to a narrow or wide area.

Disadvantages of Microwave Transmission

Disadvantages of microwave transmissions include the following:

- Line of sight is required between stations or intermediate antennas.

- FCC licensing and approval for equipment are required.

- Microwave transmissions are very susceptible to eavesdropping, interference, and jamming.

- Microwave signals are also susceptible to atmospheric conditions. For example, rain and fog will attenuate the signals. More important, higher frequencies will be attenuated more, which distorts a transmission.

- Equipment is still expensive.

BROADER CATEGORY
Network, Wireless

COMPARE
Infrared Transmission; Radio Wave Transmission

MID (Message ID)

In electronic mail (e-mail) or message handling, the MID represents a unique value associated with a particular message.

Middle-Endian

On 32-bit systems, a middle-endian byte representation strategy is one that is neither little-endian (low-order byte at lower address) or big-endian (high-order byte first).

The bytes in a 16-bit word are stored 1-2 or 2-1 (for little- and big-endian representations, respectively). In proper 32-bit systems, these representations extend to 1-2-3-4 or 4-3-2-1. In contrast, middle-endian systems use representations such as 2-1-4-3 (big-endian bytes in little-endian words) or 3-4-1-2 (little-endian bytes in big-endian words).

Such ambiguous representations give rise to what is known as the *NUXI problem:* how to represent the letters of the word "UNIX" in a 32-bit word. The two "proper-endian" solutions are "UNIX" and "XINU." The middle-endian representations are "NUXI" and "IXUN."

COMPARE
Big-Endian; Byte-Sex; Little-Endian

Middleware

Middleware refers to a level of hardware or, more commonly, software that sits between an application program and its operating environment—that is, its operating system (OS) or network operating system (NOS). A network shell is an example of middleware, as is an object broker program (see **CORBA**).

The term is used particularly in reference to distributed application software. Communication between application software and middleware is generally through APIs (Application Program Interfaces). Middleware can help make it possible to achieve communication between incompatible environments or protocols.

The term is also used to refer to a class of development tools. Middleware of this type allows users to build simple products for performing specific tasks by linking together available services using a scripting language.

a
b
c
d
e
f
g
h
i
j
k
l
m
n
o
p
q
r
s
t
u
v
w
x
y
z

▼
Migration

In networking and other computing contexts, migration is the process of moving operations from one technology to another. For example, a company might migrate from electrical to optical media. Migration is an important way of keeping up with emerging technologies.

A *migration path* specifies the details of the migration. The more clearly the path is defined, the smoother the migration should be.

In NetWare environments, migration refers to the conversion of a server and its contents from an earlier version of NetWare or from a different network operating system (NOS) to NetWare version 4.*x*.

The term is also used to refer to the progress of data from the primary storage area, such as the server's hard disk, to a secondary storage area, such as a tape or an erasable optical disk.

▼
MILnet

One of the networks that make up the Internet. This network was originally used for unclassified military information.

▼
MIME (Multipurpose Internet Mail Extensions)

MIME is a mail handling standard developed by the IETF (Internet Engineering Task Force) to provide support for multimedia and multipart messages. MIME makes it possible to encode and transmit sound, video, and formatted data in a single message, and also to receive and handle (read, see, or hear) the message.

MIME User Agents

MIME capabilities are provided by MIME user agents (UAs), which can create, transmit, receive, and parse multimedia or multipart messages. The figures "MIME agents in composition" and "MIME agents in display" show the UA's role in these processes.

To create a multimedia message, the MIME UA uses separate composition agents for each message type supported. These agents are used to create the message in an appropriate format. A UA might have agents for specific text or word processors (to handle formatting and other commands correctly), for audio, and for video. To help create audio or video messages, the respective agents might provide support for a microphone or camera, respectively. Because the MIME standard and UAs are extensible, new composition agents can be added.

A MIME UA also uses a MIME Message Designer and a MIME Message Builder. The Message Designer calls the appropriate composition agents to create the desired message. This component is also extensible and can be modified to use newly added composition agents. The Message Builder does the conversions needed to send the message using a mail delivery service. The Message Builder mediates between the Message Designer and the mail service, and it provides the interface between the MIME UA and the mail service.

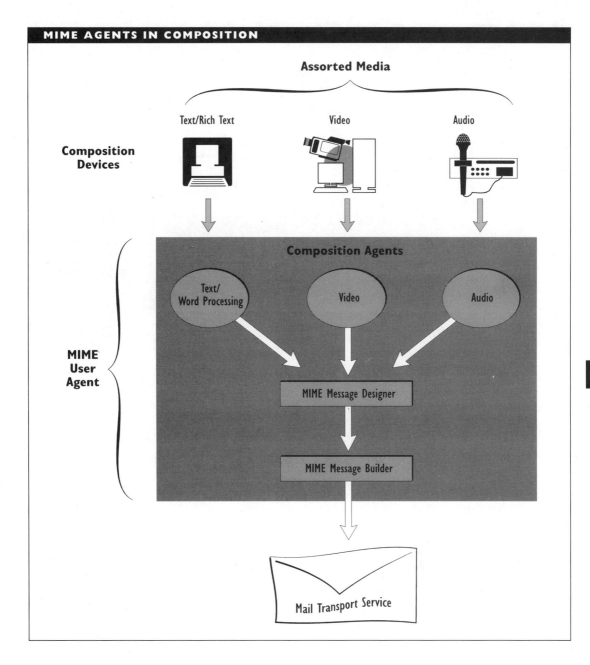

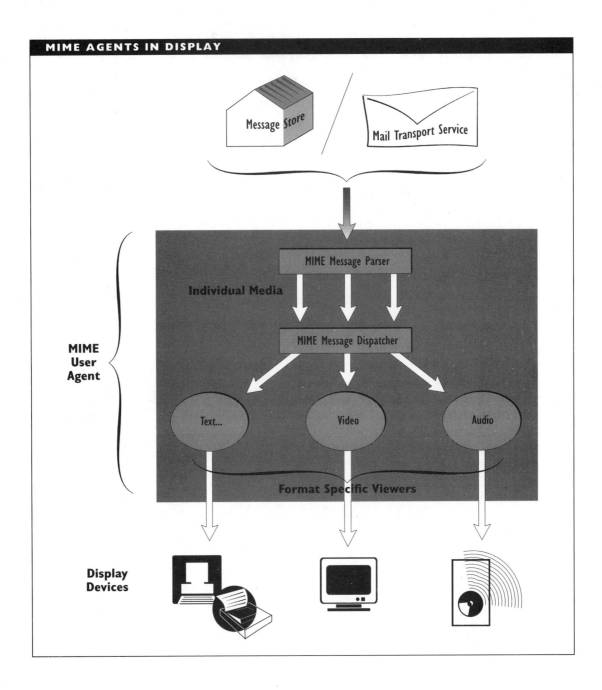

MIME AGENTS IN DISPLAY

At the receiving end, the MIME UA uses a MIME Format Message Parser to identify the different parts in a message. The Parser then passes the message parts to a Dispatcher, which calls Viewers designed specifically for a particular type of message.

MIME Capabilities

Originally developed for the Internet, MIME was designed as an open and extensible standard. It is independent of specific platforms and can (in principle) be used to send multimedia messages across different platforms and operating environments. Support for MIME has been built into several e-mail packages.

Because of its flexibility and extensibility, MIME opens many possibilities for making messaging services much more powerful. For example, a message might contain a program that can execute as part of the message, to do a demonstration or a calculation.

However, these possibilities also raise unresolved issues relating to security and compatibility. For example, it is important to be able to keep a message from doing damage to the recipient's files or system. It is also useful to be able to select which parts of a message to read so that a laptop with minimal graphics capabilities does not need to receive the multimegabyte animation component in a message.

PRIMARY SOURCES

RFCs 1521, 1522, 1343, and 1344; approved as draft standards in RFCs 1590 and 1522

Minicomputer

A computer that is smaller than a mainframe, bigger than a breadbox, and (traditionally) more powerful than a PC. Minicomputers, particularly VAX machines from Digital Equipment Corporation (DEC), are popular as components in distributed networks, such as the ARPAnet.

Mirror

Also known as a *mirror site* or an *FTP mirror site*. An Internet site that contains a copy of the contents of an archive site. A mirror site is created in order to take some of the workload off a heavily-accessed archive. Mirror sites are updated on a regular basis from the archive. Two well-known archives that have mirrors are the SimTel archive of DOS programs and the CICA archive of Windows programs.

MLI (Multiple Link Interface)

Part of the ODI generic network driver interface. Specifically, the MLI sits under the link-support layer (LSL). The latter deals with the protocol stacks, and the MLID (MLI driver) deals with the various network interface cards, or adapters, that support ODI.

SEE ALSO

ODI (Open Data-link Interface)

MLT (Multiple Logical Terminals)

In an SNA environment, a feature of an IBM 3174 establishment controller. With MLT, even CUT (control user terminal)

a b c d e f g h i j k l **m** n o p q r s t u v w x y z

components can support multiple sessions simultaneously.

SEE ALSO

SNA (Systems Network Architecture)

MMF (Multimode Fiber)

In fiber-optical signaling, multimode fibers can support multiple light paths at once. Multimode fibers are less expensive to make than single-mode fibers, but they are also noisier.

SEE ALSO

Cable, Fiber-Optic

MMJ (Modified Modular Jack)

A variant on the RJ-*xx* jacks. The MMJ was developed by Digital Equipment Corporation (DEC) for use in its premises cabling. The wiring (and sequencing) is compatible with the RJ-*xx* wiring, but the MMJ is keyed to make it impossible to use with an ordinary RJ-*xx* connector.

MMS (Manufacturing Message Service)

In the OSI Reference Model, the MMS enables an application on a control computer to communicate with an application on a slave machine. For example, MMS can be used in a production line or other automated operation context.

MMT (Multimedia Multiparty Teleconferencing)

MMT allows the transmission of data, voice, and/or video in a teleconferencing context.

MNP (Microcom Networking Protocol)

MNP refers to a family of protocols, developed by Microcom but licensed for use by third parties, for facilitating telecommunications. Some of the protocols are concerned with error correction; others are concerned with data compression.

Mobitex

A collection of wireless networks, operated by RAM Mobile Data. Mobitex connects more than 6,000 cities in the United States, and is also found in Canada, the United Kingdom, and Scandinavia.

Modal Dispersion

In fiber optics, modal dispersion refers to the gradual spreading of an optical signal with increasing distance. A *mode* is a path for light to take through a fiber.

SEE

Cable, Fiber-Optic

Modem

A modem (from *mo*dulation-*dem*odulation) is a communications device that converts binary electrical signals into acoustic signals for transmission over telephone lines and converts these acoustic signals back into binary form at the receiving end. Conversion to acoustic form is known as *modulation*; conversion back to binary form is known as *demodulation*. The process is illustrated in the figure "Modem operation."

MODEM OPERATION

...11010011...

At the transmitting end, a serial stream of bits arrives at the modem from the computer's serial port.

These bit values are modulated (converted into analog acoustic form) using a predefined modulation technique.

This analog signal is transmitted along telephone lines.

At the receiving end, the analog signal is demodulated (converted back to digital form).

...11010011...

The resulting serial stream is sent on to the computer at the receiving end.

In the terminology used in the RS-232C communications standard, modems are DCEs (data circuit-terminating equipment), which means they are connected at one end to a DTE (data terminal equipment) device. The DTE (a PC) sends instructions and data to the DCE for processing and further transmission.

Modems differ in the modulation methods they use and in the communications and transmission standards with which they comply. Modems are grouped in the following ways:

- Class: Narrowband, voice-grade, wideband, or short-haul

a b c d e f g h i j k l **m** n o p q r s t u v w x y z

- Modulation method: Frequency, amplitude, phase, quadrature amplitude, or trellis coded modulation

- Signaling method: Any of several methods defined in Bell and CCITT standards

- Error-correction method: None, trellis coded modulation, Microcom Networking Protocol, Link Access Protocol D (LAPD), or V.42

- Location: Internal or external

Modem Class

The following classes of modems are currently used:

- Narrowband, which are low bandwidth, 300 bit per second (bps) modems used with teletypes.

- Voice-grade, which has three levels: low speed (up to 1,200 bps), medium speed (up to 4,800 bps), and high speed (above 4,800 bps).

- Wideband, which are high bandwidth, up to 64 kilobits per second (kbps), modems used for computer-to-computer transmissions over a dedicated channel.

- Short-haul, which are very high bandwidth, up to 1.5 megabits per second (Mbps), modems used for short distances (up to 20 miles). These are also known as *limited-distance modems* (*LDMs*).

Modulation Method

Modems can encode the 0 and 1 values that come from the computer (the DTE) in any of several ways. This encoding process is known as *modulation*, and it entails making some change to the electrical wave that is being used to transmit the message. Modulation techniques involve signal frequency (pitch), amplitude (strength), phase (timing), or some combination of these.

Modulation methods include the following:

- Frequency modulation (FM) or frequency shift keying (FSK), which uses different frequencies for 0 and 1 values. The exact frequencies used depend on the modem's compatibility. FSK can encode 1 bit per baud (signal transition) so that the maximum transmission speed with FSK is 2,400 bps.

- Amplitude modulation (AM) or amplitude shift keying (ASK), which uses different amplitudes for 0 and 1 values. AM can encode 1 bit per baud.

- Phase modulation (PM) or phase shift keying (PSK) in which each value is encoded as a signal wave beginning at different points in the wave's cycle. PSK can encode up to 3 bits per baud (which requires eight unique offsets). For example, the bit pattern 000 might be encoded as a signal 45 degrees out of phase, 001 might be 90 degrees, and so on.

- Quadrature amplitude modulation (QAM), which combines AM and

PSK and can encode between 4 and 7 bits per baud.

- Trellis coded modulation (TCM), which uses an encoding scheme similar to the one used for QAM but adds extra bits for its error-correction work.

The various shift keying methods may involve absolute values or they may involve differential values. For example, an FSK method may use specific frequencies to encode the binary 1s and 0s, or it may use a change in frequency to encode one value and a constant frequency to encode the other. This is a DFSK (with D for differential) method, which is less expensive and less error-prone, because it is easier to recognize a change in value than to recognize a specific value. See the Modulation article for more information about these methods.

Signaling Methods

Modems have been designed to two families of signaling specifications. One feature of the specifications concerns the allowed signal or transmission speeds. The other feature determines the kind of interaction possible between the two machines involved in a communication. The following types of connections are possible:

- Simplex, which is one-directional. For example, a connection to a ticker-tape machine or from a cable head end to a subscriber's box is a simplex connection.

- Half-duplex, which is two-directional, but not simultaneously.

- Full-duplex, which is two-directional at any time.

Specifications from Bell provide the signaling guidelines for lower-speed modems. The table "Bell Modem Specifications" lists these standards.

The CCITT family provides the specifications for higher-speed modems and for modems that do error correction. The table "ITU Modem Specifications" lists these standards.

BELL MODEM SPECIFICATIONS

BELL SPECIFICATION	USE
103/113	300 bps half-duplex (used rarely, if at all)
201C	2,400 bps half-duplex
202S	1,200 bps half-duplex
202T	Up to 1,800 bps half-duplex on dial-up lines and full-duplex on leased lines
208A	4,800 bps half- or full-duplex over leased lines
208B	4,800 bps half-duplex over dial-up lines
212A	300 or 1,200 bps half- or full-duplex

ITU MODEM SPECIFICATIONS	
ITU SPECIFICATION	**USE**
V.17	14,400 bps for faxes of 2-wire lines
V.21	300 bps half-duplex over 2-wire lines (like its Bell counterpart, nearly obsolete)
V.22	1,200 bps full-duplex over 2-wire lines
V.22bis	2,400 or 1,200 bps full-duplex over 2-wire lines
V.23	600 or 1,200 bps full-duplex over 2-wire lines
V.26	2,400 bps full-duplex over 4-wire leased lines
V.26bis	2,400 bps half-duplex over 4-wire dial-up lines
V.26ter	2,400 bps full-duplex over 2-wire dial-up or leased lines
V.27	4,800 bps full-duplex over 4-wire leased lines
V.27bis	2,400 or 4,800 bps full-duplex over leased lines
V.27ter	2,400 or 4,800 bps half-duplex over dial-up lines
V.29	9,600 bps on 4-wire leased lines
V.32	9,600 bps full-duplex over 2-wire lines; uses an error correction scheme specified by V.42
V.32bis	V.32 at up to 14,400 bps
V.32ter	V.32 at up to 19,200 bps
V.33	14,400 bps on 4-wire leased lines
V.FAST	19,200 bps over dial-up lines
V.34	28,800 bps over dial-up lines (up to 115,200 bps possible when using V.42 bis compression

Any standard that supports dial-up lines also supports leased lines; the converse is not true.

Hayes Command Set

Virtually all modems support the Hayes AT command set, which is a modem command format developed by Hayes Microcomputing for use in its modems.

The command format uses special signals and timing to distinguish commands from data in a modem session. Since its inception, the AT command set has been extended and updated to work with the more powerful modems as they have appeared.

Error Correction

Error-correction capabilities save on re-transmissions, which can help increase throughput. Protocols with error-correction capabilities include the following:

- Link Access Protocol D (LAPD), which is based on the High-level Data Link Control (HDLC) synchronous protocol.

- Microcom Networking Protocol (MNP), which is actually a family of several protocols. MNP 5 and MNP 6 are used with high-speed, voice-grade modems. MNP 10 is still proprietary to Microcom and is used in applications where error correction is crucial (for example, in wireless modems).

- Trellis Coded Modulation (TCM), which is used primarily with modems on leased lines.

- V.42, which provides error detection and correction; V.42bis also provides data compression.

Internal versus External Modems

A modem may be internal so that it is implemented on a card that plugs into your computer, or external so that it is contained in a separate box connected to your computer by a cable.

Internal modems are less expensive, take up less space on your desk, and can use the computer's power supply. However, they do not provide a convenient way of signaling modem activity (such as the use of lights on the modem's panel). An internal modem also requires an interrupt request line (IRQ) and a serial port address.

External modems take up more space on your desk but less inside your computer. Because they use a serial port (which is included on most computers), they do not take up one of your expansion slots. External modems will generally have lights to indicate various types of information during operation. External modems need their own power supply.

Modem Variants

A modem is nothing but a conversion machine. This basic capability has been packaged in a variety of ways: as cellular, fax, PCMCIA, portable, and wireless modems, to name just a few.

Cellular Modem

A cellular modem is one designed for use with cellular telephones. In order to deal with the uncertain world of wireless transmissions, cellular modems differ from their generic counterparts in several ways:

- They do not expect to hear a dial tone from a modem at the other end.

- They generally come with very advanced error-correction capabilities, such as the MNP 10 protocol from Microcom.

- They are more tolerant of timing fluctuations, which can arise, for example, when a transmission is handed off from one cell to another.

- They are more expensive, with prices that can go well over $1,000.

It is possible to use a regular modem with a cellular telephone. This requires special adapters, however. The adapter must be able to fool the modem with a dial tone.

Fax Modem

A fax modem is a device that combines the capabilities of a fax machine and a modem. Fax modems can be distinguished by the fax format(s) they support and also by the type of interface they use.

Virtually all fax modems support the CCITT group 3 fax format. This standard calls for fax transmission at 9,600 or 14,400 bps and for a fax resolution of 200×100 dots per inch (dpi) (horizontal × vertical) or 200×200 dpi in fine mode. (Groups 1 and 2, which preceded the group 3 standard by over a decade, are obsolete.)

The EIA is developing a class hierarchy to define the interface between a fax modem and the computer, and also to divide the work between these two devices. This hierarchy includes three classes:

Class 1: Defines six commands which a fax modem must be able to understand. This class leaves most of the work (creating the fax and so on) up to the computer. Currently, only class 1 is widely supported and (more or less) finalized.

Class 2: In this class, the modem does more of the work. Modems that support this interface understand about 40 commands. This is not yet an official standard and is likely to be revised. Some fax modems support this class *as currently defined.*

Class 3: This class will turn over the entire task of creating and transmitting the fax to the modem. This standard is far from completion.

In addition to this hierarchy, Intel and DCA have proposed a standard, called the Communicating Application Specification (CAS). The CAS is supported on all Intel fax modems and on models from several other vendors.

In addition to differing in the interfaces supported, fax modems differ in their capabilities. Some can send and receive faxes (called S/R fax modems); others can only send.

PCMCIA Modem

A PCMCIA modem is one that can be implemented on a Type II PCMCIA card. This card can be plugged into any notebook or palmtop computer that is compatible with this generation of PCMCIA card.

Portable Modem

A portable modem is compact and external. This type of modem can be transported easily and can be plugged into the appropriate port on any computer.

As technology progresses, components get smaller, faster, and more powerful. Portable modems are about the size of a deck of cards. To say such modems can be transported easily in a pocket would be stretching both the truth and the pocket. Although portable modems are bulkier than the PCMCIA modems, they have the advantage of being external and, therefore, more maneuverable.

Wireless Modem

A wireless modem is wireless when it is communicating with another modem, not with the computer. A wireless modem plugs into the computer's RS-232 port but broadcasts over a wireless data network, such as the Mobitex networks run by Mobile Data.

Modem Pooling

Many networks, especially larger ones and those with a lot of dial-in activity, have multiple modems through which users can connect to the network. These will generally be handled as a pool of available resources, with each incoming call being passed to the next available modem.

Such modem pooling is commonly used, for example, by Internet access providers (IAPs). Users dial into a general access number at which calls are handled in the order received. Each call is assigned to the next available modem. A user will then be assigned to a port for the session. This means that a user may not know what port or address will be assigned until the call and the connection are actually made. It also means that the details of a user's connection may be different each time the user calls in.

Multiport serial boards, which have two or more serial ports, can be used to handle multiple modems through a single board or card.

BROADER CATEGORY
Peripheral

Modulation

Modulation refers to the process of converting an informational signal (the modulating signal) into a form suitable for transmission using another (carrier) signal. This is accomplished by superimposing the information onto the (constant) carrier signal. The superimposed signal represents the information to be transmitted.

For example, a modem converts a binary value (communicated as an electrical signal) into acoustic form for transmission over a telephone line.

Modulation can involve either analog signals, digital signals, or both.

Analog Modulation

Analog modulation converts an analog signal (the information) into another analog signal (the carrier). The type of modulation depends on the feature of the carrier signal that is used to represent the information. Analog modulation can be of the following types:

Amplitude modulation (AM): Varies the amplitude (strength) of the carrier signal. AM is used in radio and television broadcasting.

Frequency modulation (FM): Varies the frequency (pitch) of the carrier signal. FM is used in radio and television broadcasting and in satellite communications.

Phase modulation (PM): Varies the phase (time displacement) of the

a b c d e f g h i j k l **m** n o p q r s t u v w x y z

signal. PM is used in radio and television broadcasting and in satellite communications.

RF Modulation

RF modulation converts a digital signal to analog form (as is done in a modem, for example). The type of modulation and the amount of information that can be represented at a time depend on the features of the carrier signal that are modified. RF modulation can be of the following types:

Amplitude shift keying (ASK): Varies the amplitude (strength) of the carrier signal. This method is used in low-speed (300 bps) modems. This type of modulation is also known as *on-off keying* (*OOK*).

Frequency shift keying (FSK): Varies the frequency (pitch) of the carrier signal. This method is used in medium-speed (1,200 and 2,400 bps) modems.

Phase shift keying (PSK): Varies the phase (time displacement) of the carrier signal. Depending on how many different displacements are used, more than 1 bit can be represented in a single modulated signal. For example, by using four shift amounts (such as 0, 90, 180, and 270 degrees), 2 bits can be represented at a time. This method is used in medium- and high-speed (2,400 and 4,800 bps) modems and is also known as *binary phase shift keying* (*BPSK*).

Quadrature amplitude modulation (QAM): Varies both the phase and the amplitude of the carrier signal. This makes it possible to encode as many as four bits in a single signal. QAM is used in high-speed (4,800 bps and faster) modems.

Quadrature phase shift keying (QPSK): This method uses part of each cycle to indicate 0 or 1. It is similar to QAM.

Trellis coded modulation (TCM): This is equivalent to QAM or QPSK, but includes extra bits for error correction.

The figure "Quadrature amplitude modulation encoding" shows a QAM modulation scheme that encodes four bits in each signal by using eight phase values with two amplitudes at each value.

The shift keying modulation methods come in plain and differential forms. The differential versions encode different values simply as *changes* in the relevant signal feature, for example, as a change in frequency rather than as a change to a specific frequency. The following are the differential versions:

Differential amplitude shift keying (DASK): Different digital values are encoded as changes in signal *amplitude*. This is in contrast to ASK.

Differential frequency shift keying (DFSK): Different digital values are encoded as changes in signal *frequency*. This is in contrast to FSK.

Differential phase shift keying (DPSK): Different digital values are encoded as changes in signal *phase* (timing offset). This is in contrast to PSK.

QUADRATURE AMPLITUDE MODULATION ENCODING

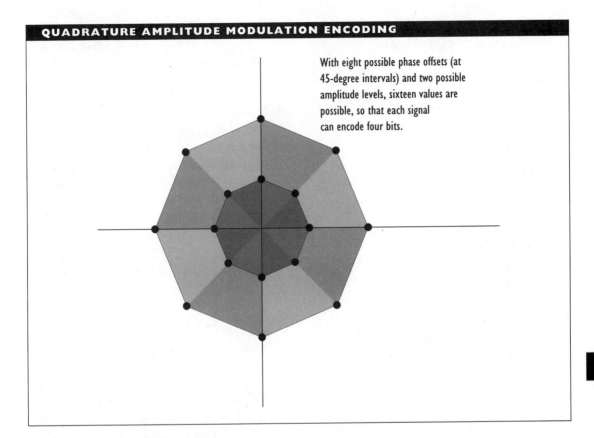

With eight possible phase offsets (at 45-degree intervals) and two possible amplitude levels, sixteen values are possible, so that each signal can encode four bits.

Duobinary AM/PSK: A digital signal is represented in analog form by varying both the amplitude and the phase (timing offset) of an analog carrier signal. The PSK element is used to reduce the bandwidth required for the transmission, not to encode a signal value. This modulation method is used in broadband versions of the IEEE 802.4 Token Bus architecture.

Differential modulation methods are easier to implement and are more robust than ordinary shift keying methods because the differential forms just look for differences, rather than for specific values.

Digital Modulation

Digital modulation converts an analog signal into a digital carrier (as in compact discs and digital telephone lines, for example). The basic strategy is to convert an analog wave into discrete pulses by taking multiple samples of the analog signal and converting each sample into a corresponding discrete signal.

It has been demonstrated mathematically that the conversion can be made without any loss of information if enough samples are taken. The type of modulation used depends on what aspect of the pulse is modified to convey a value.

a b c d e f g h i j k l **m** n o p q r s t u v w x y z

For example, pulse time modulation refers to a class of digital modulation methods in which a time-dependent feature of a pulse (for example, width, duration, or position) is varied to encode an analog signal that is being converted to digital form.

Digital modulation can be any of the following types:

Delta modulation (DM): Represents the analog signal as a series of bits, whose values depend on the level of the analog signal relative to the previous level. If the signal is going up (increasing), the method sets a 1; otherwise, it sets a 0. This modulation method discards information on the rate at which the analog signal is changing.

Adaptive delta modulation (ADM): Represents the analog signal as a weighted train of digital pulses. ADM differs from delta modulation in weighting the signal, which means that it takes into account the rate of change in the analog signal.

Adaptive differential pulse code modulation (ADPCM): Amplitudes are represented using 4-bit values (rather than the 8 bits used in PCM), and a 32 kilobit per second (kbps) data-transfer rate is used (rather than 64 kbps, as for PCM).

Pulse amplitude modulation (PAM): Represents the amplitude of the analog signal at sampling time with a carrier pulse of comparable amplitude. In short, PAM simply chops a continuous analog signal into a series of discrete signals.

Pulse code modulation (PCM): Converts a signal into a serial stream of bit values. The signal is based on an analog signal that has already been modulated (generally by using PAM, but possibly using PDM, PPM, or PWM). The pulses are grouped into any of a predefined number of different levels using a quantizer, and each of the possible levels is represented by a unique bit stream. The number of possible values in this stream determines the granularity of the modulation. In most applications, 127 different levels are used, so that 7 bits are needed for each pulse. More sophisticated multimedia applications may use as many as 24 bits to represent pulses.

Pulse duration modulation (PDM): Represents an analog signal by varying the duration, or width, of a discrete pulse. The dots and dashes used for Morse code represent such a modulation. This type of modulation is also known as pulse width modulation (PWM).

Pulse position modulation (PPM): A pulse time method that represents an analog signal by varying the positioning (the time displacement) of a discrete pulse within a bit interval. The position is varied in accordance with the sampled value of an analog signal.

Pulse width modulation (PWM): Represents an analog signal by varying the width (the duration) of a discrete pulse. This method is also known as *pulse duration modulation (PDM).*

Digital modulation methods differ in their goals. Waveform coding methods try to provide as complete a representation of the analog signal as possible; that is, they try to represent the original waveform in the output signal. The methods summarized above use waveform coding.

Source coding methods try to minimize the number of bits needed to provide an acceptable (but not necessarily identical) representation of the analog signal. Source coding methods are quite complex.

SEE ALSO
Pulse Modulation

MONITOR.NLM

A Novell NetWare Loadable Module (NLM) for monitoring the status and performance of the NetWare server and network activity. The monitor also observes memory and processor use, and can do garbage collecting to clear memory when necessary.

Monitor, Standby

A standby monitor is a reserve device that can be put into operation as soon as the main monitor malfunctions.

Mosaic

Mosaic is the original name for a Web browser (hypertext file reader) developed at the NCSA (National Center for Supercomputing Applications) at the University of Illinois at Urbana-Champaign. The NCSA version of Mosaic was developed largely with federal funds and is freely available for downloading and use. Like most freeware,

however, NCSA Mosaic has not undergone the testing expected of a commercial product. Similarly, its features are more a reflection of its developers' needs and preferences than of the needs of a general audience.

While releasing *its* version as freeware, the NCSA also licensed the Mosaic software to third parties. These companies were free to enhance and develop Mosaic as they chose. Several of them have released commercial versions of Mosaic.

The following versions of Mosaic are among the better known and more widely available:

- NCSA Mosaic: This is the free version. While it has not been tested and debugged as exhaustively as a commercial product, NCSA Mosaic is quite robust and reasonably fast. It has a considerable set of features, including the ability to keep a history of accessed Web pages, and also a hotlist of popular pages—that is, pages you are likely to visit frequently. To use NCSA Mosaic with Windows 3.1, you also need to install the Win32s 32-bit package. Self-extracting versions of both Win32s and NCSA Mosaic are available through FTP from the ftp.ncsa.uiuc.edu site. The browser and 32-bit package are both in the /Web/Mosaic/Windows directory. The browser will have a name such as mos20fb.exe. (The last part of the name will change as new versions are released.) The 32-bit Windows package is named w32sole.exe. This package is freely available but is quite large and will take up several megabytes of storage. Windows NT and Windows 95 users don't need to install the 32-bit package because these are already 32-bit environments.

- Air Mosaic: This version, from Spry, is included in the company's Mosaic in a Box and Internet in a Box products. These products are designed and configured for easy installation so that even a new user can be up and exploring the Internet very quickly. These packages also include auxiliary software needed to log in and use the Internet. Air Mosaic supports multiple hotlists (lists of popular Web sites) and makes it easy to find and retrieve such pages.

- Quarterdeck Mosaic: This version also supports multiple hotlists. In addition, Quarterdeck's Mosaic lets you keep a complete history of all pages viewed—from the first day you installed the browser to the present. Quarterdeck's package includes a set of Internet tools to make access and search easier. Mosaic is optimized so that the first page is shown very quickly while other material is still being downloaded. In this way, users can start reading right away—without having to wait for the entire screen to fill.

- Enhanced NCSA Mosaic: This version is from Spyglass and is, in some ways, a tested and debugged version of the freeware NCSA Mosaic. In addition to being sold to end users, Spyglass is marketed as an OEM item (and is

bundled with various hardware and software products).

The Mosaic variants have much in common but also differ in important ways. All support FTP and gopher; only Quarterdeck Mosaic supports Telnet. All four let you read news and look for text in a document. Similarly, all support a history list and forms.

Beyond that, the versions differ in various features. For example, only the Quarterdeck and Spyglass versions support document encryption. All versions except Enhanced Mosaic allow you to send e-mail and to post (send a message) to a newsgroup. Only Quarterdeck's Mosaic lets you *receive* e-mail.

Be aware, however, that because of the tremendous competition in this market, such feature lists are almost certain to change (probably toward more features) as new releases appear.

BROADER CATEGORIES

Browser, WWW (World Wide Web)

COMPARE

Lynx; NetScape Navigator

Motherboard

The main circuit board in a computer. This board will hold the CPU (central processing unit) and may include a math coprocessor, various other controller chips, and RAM chips. In its role as a backplane, the motherboard provides slots for expansion.

SEE ALSO

Backplane

MOTIS (Message-Oriented Text Interchange System)

A message-handling system developed by the ISO. The basic elements of this system are compatible with the model in the CCITT's X.400 specifications.

SEE ALSO
MHS (Message Handling System)

MOV (Metal Oxide Varistor)

An electrical component in a line conditioner or surge protector. MOVs help clip high-energy spikes from an incoming supply. Compare MOV with capacitor and inductor.

MPI (Multiple Protocol Interface)

The top part of the link-support layer (LSL) in the generic ODI (Open Data-link Interface) for LAN drivers.

MPR (Multi-Port Repeater)

A repeater in an Ethernet, usually thin Ethernet, network.

MRM (Maximum Rights Mask)

In Novell's NetWare 2.2, the MRM is a list of the trustee rights that users are allowed to exercise in a directory. An MRM is assigned to every directory. The MRM can block both inherited rights and specific trustee assignments. This means that, even if a user has been given all trustee rights to a directory, the directory's MRM can prevent the user from exercising some or all of those rights.

NetWare 2.2 uses the following rights to control file access and use:

- R (Read), which allows the user to open and read a file

- W (Write), which allows the user to open and write to an existing file

- C (Create), which allows a user to create a new file or directory

- E (Erase), which allows a user to delete a file or a directory, including its files and subdirectories

- M (Modify), which allows a user to change a file's or a directory's names and attributes, but not content

- F (File Scan), which allows a user to see files in directory listings

- A (Access Control), which allows a user to change trustee assignments and also the MRM

The MRM was replaced by the Inherited Rights Mask (IRM) in NetWare 3.*x* and by the Inherited Rights Filter (IRF) in NetWare 4.*x*.

COMPARE
IRM (Inherited Rights Mask)/IRF (Inherited Rights Filter)

MRU (Maximum Receive Unit)

In network communications, the MRU represents the size of the largest packet that can be received over a physical link between two nodes. The MRU will generally depend on

a
b
c
d
e
f
g
h
i
j
k
l
m
n
o
p
q
r
s
t
u
v
w
x
y
z

several factors, including the channel bandwidth and any timing constraints or considerations associated with the network architecture.

Under certain circumstances—in particular, when there are multiple links between two devices—it's possible to get throughput that exceeds the MRU. This is accomplished by combining several channels into a larger logical channel that can accommodate faster (combined) traffic than any of the individual physical channels. To actually accomplish this increased throughput, however, special protocols must be used, otherwise packets may not be reassembled correctly at the receiving end.

MS (Message Store)

In the 1988 version of CCITT's X.400 Message Handling Service (MHS), an MS is a general archive in which mail can be held until the appropriate user retrieves it through a user agent (UA) or until the allowable storage time for the message is exceeded. The MS is distinct from the mailboxes associated with individual users.

UAs and other services use the MSAP (message store access protocol) to access the message store.

MSB (Most Significant Bit)

In a bit sequence, the MSB is the bit corresponding to the highest power of 2 for the sequence. In a byte, this would be the 128s digit (corresponding to 2^7); in a 16-bit word, the bit would correspond to the 2^{15} place value.

The actual location of this bit in a representation depends on the context (storing or transmitting) and on the ordering within a word. See the Big-Endian and Little-Endian articles for a discussion of these issues.

COMPARE
LSB (Least Significant Bit)

MST (Minimum Spanning Tree)

In bridged networks or in an internetwork, the MST is the "shortest" set of connections that includes all the possible connections and that does not contain any loops (closed paths, in which a packet could get trapped).

SEE ALSO
Bridge

MTA (Message Transfer Agent)

In an X.400 model, a component of a Message Handling System (MHS) that is responsible for storing and/or forwarding messages to another MTA, to a user agent (UA), or to another authorized recipient. The MTA is comparable to a mail agent in the TCP/IP environment.

MTBF (Mean Time Between Failures)

A measure of the durability of an electronic component. This value, also known as mean time before failure, represents the average amount of time that elapses between breakdowns.

SEE ALSO
MTTR (Mean Time To Repair)

MTL (Message Transfer Layer)

In the 1984 version of the X.400 MHS (Message Handling System) recommendations, the MTL is the lower sublayer of the OSI Reference Model's application layer. This sublayer provides access to the transfer services. Message transfer agent entities (MTAEs) carry out the functions at this sublayer. The 1984 version defines a protocol known as P1 for communications between MTAEs.

The user agent layer (UAL) is the sublayer above the MTL. The services for this sublayer may be implemented on a different machine than the one containing the MTL. For example, in a LAN, workstations may run the user agent sublayer to communicate with a server that provides the actual message transfer server. For configurations in which the MTL and UAL are on different machines, the recommendations provide a submission and delivery entity (SDE) to carry out the functions of the MTL.

BROADER CATEGORY:
   X.400

MTS (Message Transfer Service)

In the 1984 version of the CCITT's X.400 Message Handling System (MHS), the MTS is a connectionless but reliable transfer capability. (*Connectionless* means that parts of the message are transported independently of each other, and may take different paths; *reliable* means that a message part will be delivered correctly or the sender will be informed that this was not possible.)

The 1988 and 1992 versions of the MHS elaborated on the MTS. In the revised standards, the MTS is a worldwide, application-independent store-and-forward service for message transfers. This means that the MTS will deliver messages from one user to another, regardless of the relative locations of sender and recipient. Such actions assume, of course, that it is possible to deliver messages to the recipient.

The general-purpose MTS is distinguished from the more specialized IPMS (Interpersonal Messaging System)—the other major component of the MHS. The IPMS is used for personal or simple business correspondence. The MTS, on the other hand, is intended more for EDI (Electronic Data Interchange) documents. Such documents represent a cost-effective and environmentally sound (i.e., paperless) way of exchanging business forms, invoices, etc.

The MTS deals with requests from:

- User agents (UAs), which generally just front for ordinary users. UAs are abstract service elements, and each active UA will be associated with a real user at some level.

- Message stores (MSs), which hold messages until they are picked up by the user (agent).

- Access units (AUs), which serve as gateways between user requirements and low-level demands.

- Message transfer agents (MTAs), which work within the MTS and which—effectively—bind the MTS together. MTAs may connect to each other or to an end user. MTAs also deal with the message store and with access units.

PRIMARY SOURCES

The MHS model is covered in the X.400 series of ITU (formerly CCITT) recommendations. The MTS specifically is the subject of recommendation X.411.

MTSO (Mobile Telephone Switching Office)

In cellular communications, an MTSO is a central computer that monitors all transmissions. If a connection is too noisy, the MTSO searches for a less noisy channel and does a hand-off by transferring the connection to another channel in the next cell.

The hand-off takes between 200 and 1,200 milliseconds, which is quite a long time for some devices to wait. For example, some modems will disconnect if there is such a long break in the connection.

MTTR (Mean Time To Repair)

The average amount of time required to repair an electrical or other component. For many types of equipment, this value is in the 15- to 45-minute range.

MTU (Maximum Transmission Unit)

The largest packet that can be sent over a given medium. If a packet is larger than an MTU, the packet must be fragmented (or segmented), sent as two (or more) properly sized packets, and then repackaged at the receiving end.

The MTU between any two nodes in a single network is the same. However, for a connection that goes through several networks, the MTU for the entire connection—known as the *path MTU*—is determined by the shortest MTU anywhere in the path. (The Path MTU is abbreviated PMTU.)

MUD (Multi-User Dimension)

Also known as a multi-user dungeon, a MUD is an online environment for doing role playing and other types of interactions in adventure games or simulations. MUD activities are interactive, and in most of them players can take on roles or personalities of their own choosing. The laws that govern a particular MUD have either been defined in advance by the MUD's creator, or they can be created as the game develops.

Players cooperate with or compete against each other. Some games provide tests of mental skill; others involve warfare. Still others may call for interpersonal (or societal or even global) planning and action. Many of the games are text-based, but some of the more sophisticated ones involve virtual reality. Players may prosper, wither, or even die—figuratively, of course.

Variants include MOOs (MUDs, Object-Oriented), MUSEs (Multi-User Simulated Environments), and MUSHes (Multi-User Shared Hallucinations). Of these, MUSEs are most likely to be educational—for example, in the form of science labs or other types of experimental or empirical endeavors.

PRIMARY SOURCES

The web page at http:/www.cis .upenn.edu/~lwl/mudinfo.html provides a rich set of resources about MUDs. Figure "MUD information web page" shows one browser's (Cello's) view of the home page for this file. While this page is updated at irregular intervals, the pages to which this document has links may be updated more frequently.

Multibyte Character

In encoding, a character represented by 2 or more bytes. These characters arise in languages whose alphabet contains more than 256 characters, as is the case with ideographic languages such as Chinese and Japanese.

Multicast

A transmission method in which one source node communicates with one or more destination nodes with a single transmission. However, in contrast to a *broadcast,* which is sent to all connected nodes, a multicast message is transmitted only to some of the possible recipients.

Multi-CPU Architecture

A computer architecture that uses multiple processors, either to work together on the same tasks or separately on different tasks.

MUD INFORMATION WEB PAGE

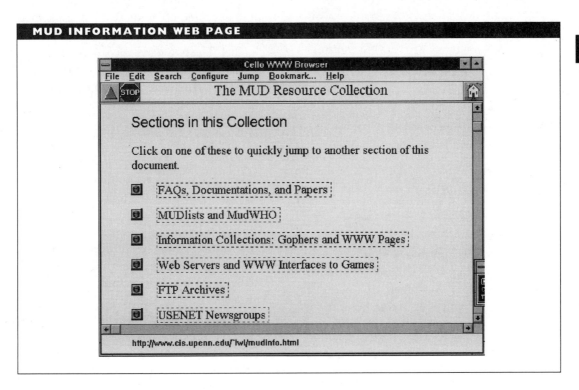

a b c d e f g h i j k l **m** n o p q r s t u v w x y z

This type of architecture can be used in local-area networking contexts, such as in super-servers. However, in many cases, the extra processor is included for redundancy, rather than for efficiency.

Multidrop Connection

In networking, a connection in which multiple nodes are connected by a single line. For example, an Ethernet bus topology provides a multidrop connection.

Multi-homed Host

In the Internet environment, a single machine connected to multiple data links, which may be on different networks.

Multimode

In fiber optics, a class of fibers with a core thick enough for light to take several paths (known as *modes*) through the core. This is in contrast to a single mode fiber, whose core is thin enough that light can take only a single path through the core.

SEE ALSO
Cable, Fiber-Optic

Multipath

In radio communications, a multipath refers to signals that are reflected back and that are out of phase with each other. Multipaths can arise in areas with a lot of communications traffic, for example.

Multiple Access

Simultaneous access to the same file for multiple users. Multiple access is generally allowed only for reading files. If users are allowed to make changes to a file, some sort of locking mechanism is required to prevent users from interfering with each other's work.

Multiple Logical Terminals (MLT)

SEE
MLT (Multiple Logical Terminals)

Multiplexing

In communications or signaling, multiplexing is a technique for allowing multiple messages or signals to share a transmission channel. The two main ways of sharing a channel are time division multiplexing (TDM) and frequency division multiplexing (FDM).

Time Division Multiplexing (TDM)

In TDM, small slices from each input channel are sent in sequence so that each input channel has some of the time on the output channel. If each of n input channels is given an equal time slice, then each channel gets only $1/n$ of the time on the output channel. This multiplexing process is illustrated in the figure "Time division multiplexing strategy."

TDM is sometimes used to create a secondary channel that operates at the limits of the main channel's bandwidth—which is generally not used for transmission.

TIME DIVISION MULTIPLEXING STRATEGY

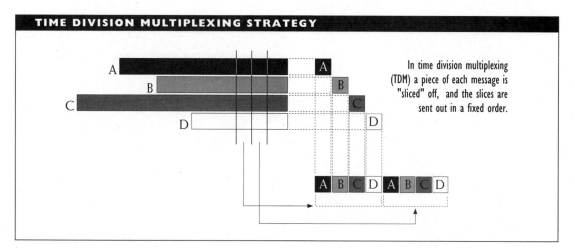

In time division multiplexing (TDM) a piece of each message is "sliced" off, and the slices are sent out in a fixed order.

The following variants on TDM are distinguished:

- ATDM (asynchronous time division multiplexing): Multiplexing in which the data is transmitted asynchronously.

- STDM (statistical time division multiplexing): A multiplexing method that polls nodes and immediately skips any nodes that have nothing to send.

- STM (synchronous transfer mode): Designed for use in BISDN (broadband ISDN) and also supported in the SONET (Synchronous Optical Network) architecture.

Frequency Division Multiplexing (FDM)

In FDM, the output channel is divided into multiple, smaller bandwidth channels. Each of these output "channelettes" is defined in a different frequency range, and each is allocated for transmitting one of the input channels. The output channels all have a capacity that is inversely proportional to the number of input channels. The figure "Frequency division multiplexing strategy" shows this process.

Wavelength Division Multiplexing (WDM)

Since frequency and wavelength are inversely related for electromagnetic and optical signals, WDM is analogous to FDM, except that different signals are transmitted at different wavelengths along the same wire or fiber.

Multiplexers

A *multiplexer* (or *multiplexor*) is a device for selecting a single output from among several inputs or for channeling several data streams into a single communications channel. The input channels are generally low-speed, while the single output channel is high-speed with enough bandwidth to accommodate the multiple slower channels. This term is often abbreviated as *MUX*.

a
b
c
d
e
f
g
h
i
j
k
l
m
n
o
p
q
r
s
t
u
v
w
x
y
z

FREQUENCY DIVISION MULTIPLEXING STRATEGY

In frequency division multiplexing (FDM) each channel gets its own frequency band. Each of these is part of the total bandwidth. The data bands are separated from each other by guard bands.

Data
Guard
Data
Guard
Data
Guard
Data
Guard
Data
Guard

The multiplexer uses a predetermined strategy for combining multiple streams. For example, in TDM, the multiplexer gives each stream a time slice in the transmission. At the other end of such a transmission, another multiplexer (known as a *demultiplexer*) reverses the process to extract the individual channels from the multiplexed stream.

Multipoint Connection

In networking, a connection in which multiple nodes are connected by a single line. For example, an Ethernet bus topology provides a multipoint connection.

Multiport Repeater

In an Ethernet network, a repeater that connects multiple network segments in parallel.

Multiprocessing

A computing strategy in which multiple processors work on the same task. This is in contrast to *multitasking,* in which the same processor works on multiple tasks, apparently at the same time.

Multiserver Network

A multiserver network has two or more file servers on a single network. As with a single-server network, the nodes can access each server in accordance with their access rights. However, some nodes may not be able to communicate with every server, because the node and server may have different architectures (or be of different types), such as a Macintosh on a NetWare network.

The servers in a multiserver network have the same physical network number but are distinguished by different node numbers within that physical network. For example, on physical network AAA3, the servers might be nodes 1 and 2.

Each server also has a unique internal network number, such as FFFA and FFFD for the two servers.

Multiserver networks involve only a single physical network address. This means that all network traffic flows across the entire network. The manner in which it flows—broadcast or sequentially—depends on the network architecture. Each server may generate its own network traffic, which will traverse the entire network. On the other hand, no special routing or filtering processes are necessary on a multiserver network.

In contrast, an internetwork includes at least two different physical network addresses. There must be a device that links the two networks. This will generally be either a bridge or a router, but may also be a gateway. If more than two networks are being linked, the connection is likely to be a switch. Because they can filter, network links can help reduce the traffic on the component networks. These links must do work—to check an address, find a route, or translate and route a packet.

Multitasking

In multitasking, a single processor seems to be running two or more programs at the same time (concurrently). Actually, only one of these tasks gets the processor's attention at any given moment, so that the concurrency is only apparent. The currently running task is said to be in the *foreground;* the other tasks are running in the *background.*

Multitasking is different from *multiprocessing,* in which multiple processors work on the same task.

Preemptive versus Non-Preemptive Multitasking

Multitasking may be preemptive or non-preemptive. In *preemptive multitasking,*

the operating system (or whatever program is controlling the multitasking) controls switching between tasks, and every task gets its turn in a predictable fashion. Windows NT and UNIX support preemptive multitasking.

In *non-preemptive multitasking,* an application or process gets to execute until it stops itself. The application cannot be interrupted, and it must be trusted to give up control. Novell's NetWare does non-preemptive multitasking.

Although non-preemptive environments run the risk of greedy or runaway applications that will not give up the chip, non-preemptive multitasking has certain advantages for server-based arrangements such as a NetWare network. An important one is that there is less need for synchronization of shared data and memory, because no other application or process is competing with the application that is executing.

Non-preemptive environments also have resources available to prevent an application from hogging the CPU (central processing unit), including direct intervention by the operating system itself.

Types of Multitasking

The following types of multitasking are distinguished:

Context-switching: This is the simplest form of multitasking. Two or more processes, or tasks, are loaded, each with its own data and execution environment, or context. Only one task at a time gets the processor's attention. The operating system switches between tasks, usually when it wants to run another program. Task managers, which can be part of an operating system or of a shell, provide context-switching capabilities. Among other things, a task manager must provide and manage storage for each of the loaded tasks.

Cooperative: In cooperative multitasking, a background process is allowed to get the processor's attention during moments when a foreground process is temporarily idle. For example, a data analysis program may be running in the background while you are doing text editing. While you are thinking, the operating system will let the data analysis program do a bit of work. System 7, the Macintosh operating system, supports cooperative multitasking, which is non-preemptive.

Time-slice: In time-slice multitasking, each process gets a slice of the processor's time. All tasks may get equal time slices, or each will get a time slice whose size is proportionate to the task's priority. The operating system runs each of the tasks in succession for the duration of the task's time slice. OS/2 and various mainframe operating systems support time-slice multitasking, which is preemptive.

▼
Multithreading

A thread is an executable object, which belongs to a single process or program. Each thread comes with its own stacks, registers, and instruction counter.

Multithreading is a special form of multitasking in which all the tasks come from the same program. In multithreading, multiple processes from a single program execute, seemingly at the same time. This concurrency is only apparent because, as with multitasking, the processor is actually switching its attention very rapidly among all the threads.

▼
Multiuser

Refers to an environment or operating system that supports more than one user at a time. UNIX is an example of a multiuser operating system; DOS and OS/2 are single-user systems.

▼
MUP

In Windows NT, MUP (Multiple UNC provider, where UNC stands for *uniform naming convention*) refers to a driver that can determine which network to access when an application wants to open a remote file.

▼
MVS (Multiple Virtual Storage)

MVS is an operating system used by IBM in many of its mainframes. MVS is basically a batch-oriented system that can manage large amounts of memory or storage.

Originally introduced in 1974, MVS has been modified and extended as the need has arisen. For example, MVS/XA (Extended Architecture) and MVS/ESA (Enterprise Systems Architecture) were introduced in the 1980s to handle IBM's newer mainframes, such as the ESA/370 product line and the ES/9000 models in the System/390 line.

MX (Mail Exchange) Record

In the Internet's DNS, a record is a data structure that indicates which machine(s) can handle electronic mail (e-mail) for a domain (particular portion or region of the Internet).

SEE ALSO

DNS (Domain Naming System)

a
b
c
d
e
f
g
h
i
j
k
l
m
n
o
p
q
r
s
t
u
v
w
x
y
z

N

Used, usually in lowercase, as an abbreviation for the prefix nano, as in nsec (nanoseconds) or nm (nanometers). This order of magnitude corresponds to 2^{-30} which is roughly 10^{-9}, or one billionth (in the United States counting system).

SEE ALSO

Order of Magnitude

NA (Numerical Aperture)

In fiber optics, the NA indicates the range of angles over which a fiber core can receive incoming light. In the ASCII encoding system, character 21 is used for NAK.

NAC (Network Access Controller)

An NAC is a device that provides access to a network, for remote callers or for another network.

NAK (Negative Acknowledgment)

A signal used to indicate that an error has been detected in a transmission.

Named Pipe

In many operating environments, a stream that can be used for the exchange of information between two processes. The pipe can be referred to by name, and the storage allocated for the pipe can be accessed and used for reading and writing, much like a file, except that the storage and the pipe disappear when the programs involved finish executing.

Name Resolution

In a network or internetwork, name resolution refers to the process of mapping a name of a device or node to an address.

Name Space

A name space is a NetWare Loadable Module (NLM) that makes it possible to store non-DOS files on a Novell NetWare file server. You can store Macintosh, UNIX, OS/2, or other types of files on a NetWare 3.*x* or later server by linking the appropriate name space NLM to the operating system. You also must use the ADD NAME SPACE utility to add configuration information for the name space.

The volume to which the alien file is being added will create two directory entries for the file: a DOS entry and an entry with the information for the file's native format.

Adding a name space to a volume has its costs:

- More cache memory is needed to store the additional directory entries.

- Removing the name space is a major chore.

BROADER CATEGORY

NetWare

Naming Service

A naming service is a mechanism that makes it possible to name resources on the network and to access them through those names. This service associates a more easily remembered name with a network entity, and that name can then be used instead of the resource's network address. Naming services are available in most network operating systems.

A naming service can be either of two types:

- A *local naming service,* which is associated with a single server

- A *global naming service,* which is associated with a network or an internetwork

For example, Novell's NetWare versions prior to 4.0 use a local naming service; information about the resources associated with a server is stored in a resource database known as the *bindery.* The NetWare Directory Services (NDS) used in NetWare 4.*x* is an example of a global naming service. Another example is StreetTalk, the global naming service for Banyan's VINES. With a global naming service, each object on the internetwork has a unique name, so you do not need to know the name of a server to find an object associated with that server.

SEE ALSO

Bindery; NDS (NetWare Directory Services); StreetTalk

Narrowband ISDN (NISDN)

SEE

NISDN (Narrowband ISDN)

NAS (Network Application Support)

NAS is Digital Equipment Corporation's (DEC's) attempt to provide a uniform environment for software running on different platforms (such as VAXen and PCs), so that applications can be integrated with each other, regardless of the platforms involved.

NAS is designed to use international standards to support the multiple platforms. This is in contrast to the strategy used with SAA (Systems Application Architecture), which is IBM's counterpart to NAS. SAA relies on proprietary protocols to provide support for multiple platforms.

When completed, NAS will be incorporated into DEC's EMA (Enterprise Management Architecture).

NASI (NetWare Asynchronous Services Interface)

NASI provides specifications for accessing communications servers across a Novell NetWare network. The NASI SDK (software developer's kit) can be used to create applications that use the interface.

NAU (Network Addressable Unit)

In IBM's SNA networks, an NAU is any location with one or more ports for communicating over the network. The three types of NAUs are PUs (physical units), LUs (logical units), and SSCPs (system service control points).

SEE ALSO

SNA (Systems Network Architecture)

NAUN (Nearest Addressable Upstream Neighbor)

In a Token Ring network, the NAUN for a particular node (A) is the node (B) from which A receives packets and the token. Each node in a Token Ring network receives transmissions only from its NAUN.

SEE ALSO
Token Ring

NCC (National Computer Center)

The NCC in Britain is one of the centers that has developed automated software for testing compliance with X.400 and X.500 standards. These centers develop test engines based on the abstract test suites specified by the ITU (International Telecommunication Union). Other centers include the NVLAP (National Voluntary Laboratory Accreditation Program) in the U.S., Alcatel in France, and Danet GmbH in Germany.

NCC (Network Control Center)

In a network, the NCC is a designated node that runs the managing process for a network management package. This process is in charge of the network management task, and receives reports from the agent processes running on workstations.

SEE ALSO
Network Management

NCCF (Network Communications Control Facility)

NCCF is a component of IBM's NetView network management software. It can be used to monitor and control the operation of a network.

SEE ALSO
NetView

NCP Packet Signature

In Novell's NetWare 4.*x*, the NCP packet signature is a security feature that helps prevent a workstation from forging an NCP (NetWare Core Protocol) request packet and using it to get SUPERVISOR rights on the network. (NCP is the protocol used in NetWare to encode requests to the server and responses to the workstation.)

Each NCP packet must be signed by the server or workstation sending the packet. The signature is different for each packet. If an invalid NCP packet is received, an alert is entered into the error log and sent to both server and workstation. This alert specifies the workstation and its address.

Four packet signature levels are possible for the server and also for the workstation, or client. The table "Server and Workstation Packet and Signature Levels" shows the levels and their meanings for server and client.

Server levels are set using the SET parameter; client levels are set in the NET.CFG file.

The four possible levels for each party yield 16 possible effective packet signature combinations, only some of which actually result in signatures. Some of these levels can slow down performance considerably, and others make it impossible to log in to the network. For example, if either the server or workstation is set to 3 and the other party's level is set to 0, log in will not be possible. There is a packet signature only if both server and client are set to 2 or higher or if either is set to 1 and the other to 2.

SERVER AND WORKSTATION PACKET AND SIGNATURE LEVELS		
LEVEL	SERVER	CLIENT
0	Server does not sign packets.	Client does not sign packets.
1	Server signs packets only if client requests it (if client level is 2 or 3).	Client signs packets only if server requests it (if server level is at 2 or 3). This is the default.
2	Server signs packets if client can sign (if client level is 1 or higher). This is the default.	Client signs packets if server can sign (if server level is 1 or higher).
3	Server signs packets and requires clients to sign (or else login will fail).	Client signs packets and requires server to sign (or else login will fail).

BROADER CATEGORY
Security

RELATED ARTICLE
Digital Signature

NCS (Network Control System)

A software tool used to monitor and modify network activity. NCS is generally used to refer to older systems, which were run in a low-speed, secondary data channel created using time-division multiplexing. These components have been replaced by the more sophisticated network management systems (NMSs).

NCSA (National Center for Supercomputer Applications)

A computing center at the University of Illinois at Urbana-Champaign (*uiuc*). The NCSA is active in providing information and developing resources for the World Wide Web (WWW). In fact, the widely-used Mosaic browser (hypertext file reader) was originally developed at NCSA. The NCSA version of Mosaic is freeware and is available for downloading from many FTP or Web sites. Commercial versions—developed by companies who licensed the original Mosaic technology from NCSA—are also available.

The NCSA's web server provides links to lots of interesting places. The "Starting Points for Internet Exploration" home page is at the following URL (Uniform Resource Locator, which is essentially a Web page address):

http://www.ncsa.uiuc.edu/SDG/
Software/Mosaic/StartingPoints/
NetworkStartingPoints.html

Note that this entire beast is a single "gigaword" and should all be on a single line, with no spaces. The URL is also case sensitive.

NDIS (Network Driver Interface Specification)

NDIS provides a standard interface for network interface card (NIC) drivers. The NDIS standard was developed by Microsoft and 3Com, and it is supported by many NIC manufacturers. Because it allows multiple transport protocols to use the same NIC, this interface helps ensure the NIC's compatibility with multiple network operating systems.

NDIS matches a packet from the NIC's driver with the proper protocol stack by polling each stack until one claims the packet. This is in contrast to the competing ODI (Open Data-link Interface) standard from Novell and Apple. In ODI, the LSL (link-support layer) matches the packet with the appropriate protocol.

If the NIC can buffer a received packet, only the packet's header is checked to determine the protocol. If the NIC cannot buffer the packet, the entire packet is checked. Buffering saves work and can actually improve performance.

BROADER CATEGORIES

Driver; LAN Driver

COMPARE

ODI (Open Data-link Interface); ODINSUP (ODI/NDIS Support)

▼

NDS (NetWare Directory Services)

NDS is a global naming service used in NetWare 4.*x*. This service provides a global directory containing information about all the objects in a network, regardless of their location.

The NetWare Directory Database

The global directory for the NDS is the NetWare Directory Database (NDD), often called simply the Directory (with a capital *D*).

The Directory is organized as a tree, and it contains information about the following types of objects:

- Physical objects, such as users, nodes, and devices

- Logical objects, such as groups, queues, and partitions

- Objects that help to organize other objects in the Directory, such as Organization and Organizational Unit objects

Portions of this Directory tree will be copied to other locations where the information can be used and administered by a server. Note that while the Directory contains information about network objects, it does not contain information about the network's file system. The files and directories on a file server are not represented in the Directory at all. However, certain utilities, such as NetWare Administrator, display both NDS objects and files in what looks like a uniform manner, which makes it easier for a network administrator to manipulate both objects and files.

Objects in NDS

An object consists of *properties* and the values, or data, for those properties. For example, a User object includes address and telephone number properties; individual users will be distinguished in part by the information stored in these slots.

In the Directory structure, two categories of objects are distinguished: container and leaf objects. A third object, called the root object, is also recognized. This object is created during installation as the parent directory for any other objects. Once created, the root object cannot be deleted or changed.

Container Objects

Container objects are intermediate elements in the Directory tree. These help provide a logical organization for other objects in the Directory tree. A container can include other containers, leaf objects, or both.

Two main kinds of container objects are defined: Organization and Organizational Unit.

An Organization (O) object represents the first level of grouping for most networks. Depending on the scope of a corporate network, this level could represent a company, division, or department. At least one Organization object is required in each NDS Directory tree. An Organization object can contain Organizational Unit or leaf objects.

An Organizational Unit (OU) object can be used as a secondary grouping level. For example, Organizational Unit objects may be created for networks in which the contents of each Organization container are still too large. In a large network, Organizational Unit objects might be departments or project groups. These objects are optional, but they must be below an Organization or another Organizational Unit object if they are included. An Organizational Unit object can contain Organizational Unit or leaf objects.

The other two kinds of container objects are Country (C) and Locality (L). These objects are defined for compatibility with X.500 Directory Services, but are rarely used and are not required for compliance with the X.500 specifications.

Leaf Objects

Leaf objects represent information about actual network entities, such as users, devices, and lists. The table "NDS Leaf Objects" lists the types of leaf objects defined.

NDS LEAF OBJECTS	
LEAF OBJECT	**DESCRIPTION**
AFP Server	A NetWare node that supports the AppleTalk Filing Protocol and that is probably functioning as a server in an AppleTalk network.
Alias	Refers, or points, to a different location. An alias can be used to help simplify access to a particular object (for example, by using a local object to point to the object entry in a different part of the Directory).
Bindery	Included for backward-compatibility with earlier NetWare versions. Bindery objects are placed in the Directory by the migration (network upgrade) utilities, so the binderies from version 3.*x* servers have something to access in the Directory.
Bindery Queue	Included for backward-compatibility with earlier NetWare versions.
Computer	Represents a particular node on the network.

a b c d e f g h i j k l m **n** o p q r s t u v w x y z

LEAF OBJECT	DESCRIPTION
Directiry Map	Contains information about the network's file system, which is *not* encompassed by the NDS Directory. The information in a Directory Map provides path information, rather than actually showing the structure of the file system's directory. This information is useful for login scripts.
Group	Represents a list of User objects. The network supervisor can assign rights to all the users on this list simply by assigning the rights to the group.
NetWare Server	Represents any server running any version of NetWare.
Organizational Role	Represents a function or position within an organization, such as Leader, Consultant, or Moderator.
Printer	Represents a network printer.
Print Queue	Represents a network print queue.
Print Server	Represents a network print server.
Profile	Represents a shared login script. The script might be shared, for example, by users who need to do similar things during the login process but who are located in different containers.
User	Represents an individual who can log in to the network and use resources. Properties associated with User objects include those concerned with the actual person as an individual (name, telephone number, address, and so on) and as a network entity (password and account information, access rights, and so on).
Unknown	Used for an object that cannot be identified as belonging to any other object type, possibly because the object has become corrupted in some way.
Volume	Represents a physical volume on the network.

Object Rights

Object rights apply to the objects contained in the NDS global database. Trustee rights may be assigned for an object or they may be inherited from the object above it. The database objects provide information about the actual objects on the network. The following object rights are defined:

Supervisor: Grants all access privileges to the object and to its properties.

Browse: Grants the right to see an object in the Directory tree that contains the global database.

Create: Grants the right to create an object *below* the current one in the Directory tree.

Delete: Grants the right to delete an object from the Directory tree.

Rename: Grants the right to change an object's name.

Property Rights

Property rights apply to the properties of an NDS object. Note that object rights do not affect property rights. The following property rights are defined:

Supervisor: Grants all rights to the property, but can be nullified by a specific object's Inherited Rights Filter (IRF).

Compare: Grants the right to compare the property value to any other value. This right shows only how the two values compare; it *does not* allow seeing the property values.

Read: Grants the right to see a property's value.

Write: Grants the right to add, change, or even remove the values of a property.

Add or Delete Self: Grants a trustee the right to remove only the trustee as one of the property's values.

Partitions and Replicas

To help keep things manageable, NetWare divides the Directory into partitions. A *partition* is a grouping of related or nearby container objects and their contents. In particular, a partition consists of a container object, the objects contained in it, and data about those objects. It does not contain information about the network's file system.

A partition might consist of a server and the stations and resources associated with it. A particular object belongs to only one partition, although the object can be accessed from anywhere on the network.

This grouping is then used as the basis for creating replicas for each partition. A *replica* is simply a copy of a partition, and it is created in order to make the information in the partition more easily available by copying the information to a local source. Replicas also ensure that there is no single point of failure for the Directory. This means that if a server that contains a partition goes down, but another server contains a replica of that partition, users can still access the Directory. The replicas are stored on servers throughout the network. This replication across the network has two purposes:

- It speeds up access to Directory information, since an object can be found by checking a smaller partition tree on a local server instead of searching the entire Directory tree at a central location (which every other query would also be pestering).

- It provides redundancy which, in turn, provides fault tolerance and a measure of network protection.

Replicas distribute Directory information across the network. In some cases, a replica may be updated, and this change will eventually be incorporated into the partition from which the replica was created. This makes it possible to change the Directory from anywhere on the network (provided the appropriate resources are available).

a b c d e f g h i j k l m **n** o p q r s t u v w x y z

In order to help make such changes more manageable and better controlled, a replica may be designated as read only. A read-only replica cannot be changed and need not be checked when updating the partition. In contrast, changes made to replicas with read and write properties are incorporated into the partition when updating. The synchronization of this updating process involves the use of time servers, as explained in the following section.

Using Time Servers to Coordinate Changes

Information about objects changes as a print queue grows or shrinks, a user changes a password, or an application is executed. Since these changes may be recorded in replicas, it is essential to keep track of the timing and sequence of events when updating the Directory. That way, if two people change the same object from different replicas, the Directory can ensure that the changes occur in the correct order.

NetWare 4.x uses time synchronization for this purpose. In time synchronization, the NDS marks each event that occurs, along with the exact time of its occurrence, with a unique value, known as a *time stamp*.

To make time stamps useful, the network must ensure that all servers are keeping the same time. To accomplish this, special time servers are designated. These time servers provide the correct time to other time servers or to workstations. Three types of time-providing servers are distinguished in NetWare 4.x: Single Reference, Reference, and Primary. All other servers that accept time information from any of these servers are called *secondary* time servers.

In any network with more than one time server, the time servers work together to achieve a network time. The time servers influence each other until a kind of "average" time is achieved, and the servers deliver that time to the secondary servers. See the article on Time Synchronization for more information about time servers.

STRUCTURING YOUR DIRECTORY TREE

All Directory trees have the root object and at least one organization object. If there are multiple organization objects, all of them are at the same level. Beyond this, the details of a Directory tree are completely open-ended.

The final configuration of your Directory tree can have profound effects on the ease with which users can access information in the tree, on the amount of traffic on the network, and on network administration. Your tree needs to be good as a data structure (to make searches efficient); it also needs to work as a representation of the available information.

Despite the importance of the Directory structure, finding the best one is more art than science. And modifying the Directory structure after it's set up is currently not simple, although tools to simplify Directory tree management should be released soon.

Novell's Application Notes, including those collected in the book, *Novell's Application Notes for NetWare 4.01* (Novell Press, 1993), provide helpful guidelines and information for designing a Directory tree.

Backward-Compatibility with Earlier NetWare Versions

NetWare 4.*x* is the first major version of this network operating system to use a global and hierarchical naming service. Previous versions include a *bindery,* which uses a flat database associated with a single, local server. The NDS replaces the bindery.

To make it possible for bindery-based NetWare servers to access information in the Directory, the NDS includes a *bindery-emulation* feature which can present the Directory information in flat database form for the server's bindery.

BROADER CATEGORIES
Global Naming Service; NetWare

RELATED ARTICLE
StreetTalk

Nearest Addressable Upstream Neighbor (NAUN)

SEE
NAUN (Nearest Addressable Upstream Neighbor)

NEP (Noise-Equivalent Power)

In a fiber-optic receiver, NEP represents the amount of optical power needed to produce an electric current as strong as the receiver's base noise level.

NetBEUI (NetBIOS Extended User Interface)

An implementation and extension of IBM's NetBIOS transport protocol.

NetBEUI (pronounced "net-boo-ee") is used in Microsoft's LAN Manager and LAN Server. NetBEUI communicates with a network through Microsoft's NDIS interface for the network interface card.

SEE ALSO
Protocol, NetBIOS

NETBIOS.EXE

A NetBIOS emulator program used in Novell's NetWare network operating system. This emulator makes it possible to run applications that use NetBIOS-based peer-to-peer or distributed communications (as opposed to using a server-based communications model, as in NetWare).

SEE ALSO
Protocol, NetBIOS

NetPartner

A network management system from AT&T. NetPartner can monitor voice and data links for wide-area networks.

Netscape Navigator

Navigator, from Netscape Communications, is arguably the most widely-used graphics-based browser (hypertext reader). The program was designed and co-written by Marc Andreessen—the leader of the team that created the the NCSA Mosaic browser. While it can claim Mosaic as an inspiration, Navigator was designed from scratch to improve on, and add features not available in, the NCSA version of that browser.

a b c d e f g h i j k l m **n** o p q r s t u v w x y z

Navigator is available in both free and commercial versions. Figure "Navigator home page" shows the opening screen for a version commonly used in Windows 3.1 environments. Versions are also available for Windows NT and Windows 95, UNIX (various flavors), and Macintosh environments.

Among other things, Navigator knows how to:

- Access and view Web pages from just about anywhere in the world

- Search the Web using hypertext-oriented WebCrawlers (Worms, spiders, etc.) or the more linearly-oriented tools such as Gopher, Archie, Veronica, and WAIS (Wide Area Information Service)

- View images in any of several common formats (AIF, JPEG, and XBM, in Navigator's case)

- Install viewers that support other file formats

- Install players that support audio and video files

- Download hypermedia (text, image, video, or sound) files using Navigator, or text and binary files using FTP

- Send e-mail

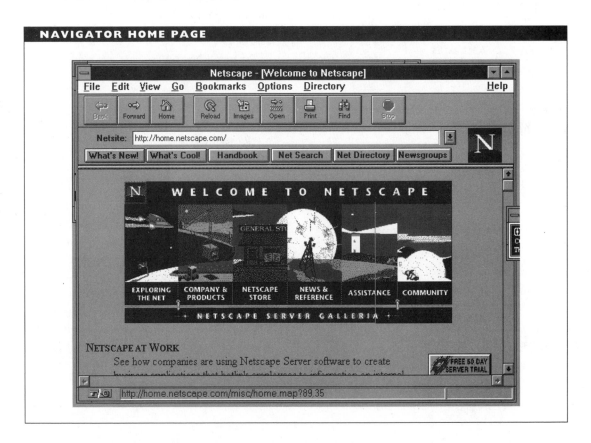

NAVIGATOR HOME PAGE

- Install a mail program to receive e-mail

- Read and post messages to Usenet newsgroups

- Encrypt communications if necessary or desirable, and if the contacted server supports it

E-mail and security capabilities are among the most notable improvements Netscape has made over NCSA Mosaic. Users can send the contents of Web pages using e-mail, and can do online transactions and other interactions in reasonable safety. Under normal operation, the screen shown in the figure "Navigator home page (secure)" differs from the "Navigator home page" figure only in having a key on the status bar.

In the program's operation, however, there are important differences. In secure mode, the browser uses the SSL (Secure Socket Layer) protocol and RSA public key encryption to ensure that web pages and other transmissions are (almost) completely protected from snoopers.

Navigator comes in 16- and 32-bit versions. The latter are for Windows NT and Windows 95 environments; the 16-bit version is for Windows 3.1. A freely usable version of Navigator works well with the Chameleon Netmanage sampler, which has

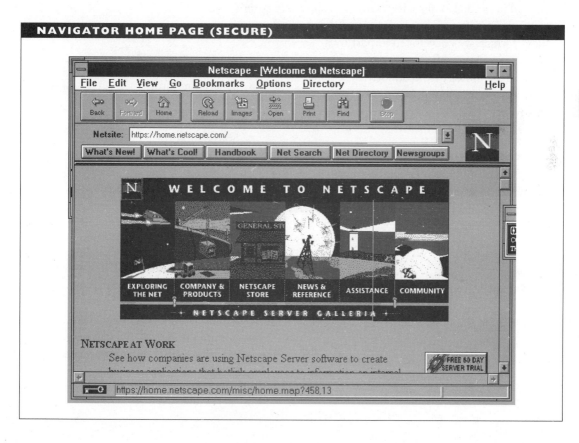

NAVIGATOR HOME PAGE (SECURE)

a
b
c
d
e
f
g
h
i
j
k
l
m
n
o
p
q
r
s
t
u
v
w
x
y
z

provided thousands of first-time Internet users with their basic tools.

Netscape Communications is dedicated to supporting open standards and to making its own protocols (such as SSL) available for use by other parties. In keeping with this strategy, Navigator (and other Netscape products) supports over a dozen protocols and formats, including TCP/IP, HTML, HTTP, NNTP, URLs, CGI, SOCKS, MIME, Gopher, FTP, SMTP, and the RFC822 format for e-mail over the Internet.

Netscape's development and marketing strategies are willing to adopt various technologies—as can be seen, for example, in their licensing of RSA public key encryption algorithms and also in their intention to support S-HTTP (Secure hypertext transfer protocol), which was developed in part by a rival player. Similarly, Netscape has licensed the Java technology from Sun Microsystems. This Web programming language promises to advance the capabilities of browsers and of Web communications by a giant step.

PRIMARY SOURCES

Information about Navigator, as well as about Netscape Communications and its other products is available through the company's home page:

http://home.netscape.com

From there, you can move all around Netscape's world; you can also explore a generous and wide-ranging slice of the Web's offerings. This is the Web page to which Navigator will move by default. There's a very good chance that a high proportion of the more than two million copies of Navigator in use have this as their default home page.

NetView

NetView is a mainframe network management product from IBM. It is used for monitoring SNA (Systems Network Architecture)-compliant networks. NetView runs as a VTAM (Virtual Telecommunications Access Method) application on the mainframe that is serving as network manager.

NetView Components

NetView includes the following components:

- Access services
- Performance monitor
- Session monitor
- Hardware monitor
- Status monitor
- Distribution manager
- Host command facility
- Help desk facility
- Customization facilities

NetView uses the NMVT (Network Management Vector Transport) protocol to communicate with management agents operating at entry points (which connect SNA-compliant devices to NetView) and service points (which connect non-IBM devices or networks).

Many of NetView's features have been incorporated into IBM's LAN Network Manager, which is used to manage Token Ring networks. LAN Network Manager can work together with NetView, such as when the LAN is part of a larger, SNA network. Novell's NetWare Management Agent for NetView also provides NetView support for NetWare servers running a Token Ring network. This product consists of several NetWare Loadable Modules (NLMs) that can forward NetView alerts to a NetView host machine and can also respond to requests from a NetView host for maintenance statistics.

NetView/PC

A related product, NetView/PC, provides an API (Application Program Interface) that enables developers to interface NetView with new hardware or software.

NetView/PC can be used as a manager for its own network. As such, the program can gather performance, usage, and billing information. NetView/PC also makes it possible for non-IBM devices, LANs, or even certain types of PBXs (private branch exchanges) to connect to an IBM NMA (Network Management Architecture) network.

BROADER CATEGORIES

Network Management; NMA (Network Management Architecture)

▼ NetWare

NetWare is a network operating system (NOS) from Novell. Several different versions of NetWare are currently (or have been) available. These versions differ in the hardware they support, in the networking services they provide, and in special features (such as fault tolerance).

Early NetWare Versions

The earliest versions of NetWare—Advanced NetWare 286, SFT (System Fault Tolerant) NetWare 286, and ELS (Entry Level System) NetWare—are no longer available.

Newer NetWare Versions

Valuable features from earlier versions (for example, fault tolerant capabilities such as disk mirroring) were incorporated into NetWare 2.2, which was released in 1991. The table "NetWare Versions and Features" lists the newer NetWare versions and summarizes some of their features.

Note that later versions of NetWare generally inherit the features of earlier versions (a NetWare 3.*x* server can do anything a NetWare 2.*x* server can, a NetWare 4.*x* server can do whatever a NetWare 3.*x* server can and so on). Also note that the NetWare versions have many more specific features along with the ones included in the table's summary.

a
b
c
d
e
f
g
h
i
j
k
l
m
n
o
p
q
r
s
t
u
v
w
x
y
z

NETWARE VERSIONS AND FEATURES	
VERSION	**FEATURES**
NetWare Lite	Maximum of 25 nodes per server
	Peer-to-peer network only (no dedicated server)
	Limited file, printer sharing
	Limited security features
	Runs as a DOS process
	No SFT features
	Can coexist with other NetWare versions
	Replaced by Personal NetWare
NetWare 2.2	Maximum of 100 nodes per server
	Use of dedicated or nondedicated server
	Full file, printer sharing
	SFT capabilities: disk mirroring, disk duplexing, and transaction tracking system (TTS)
	Security features
	Supports Macintosh file system
	Optional support for Macintosh clients
	Extensible through VAPs (Value Added Processes)
NetWare 3.x	Maximum of 250 nodes per server
	Supports only dedicated servers
	Supports multiple protocol stacks
	Supports multiple file systems (DOS, Macintosh, OS/2, UNIX)
	Optional support for multiple clients (DOS, Macintosh, OS/2, UNIX)
	Extensible through NLMs (NetWare Loadable Modules)

VERSION	FEATURES
NetWare 4.x	Maximum of 1000 nodes per server
	Supports global resource, global naming (NDS)
	Supports up to 12 NetWare 3.x servers as part of NDS (NetWare 4.1)
	Supports on-disk file compression
	More stringent security, including auditing of network activity
	Extensive network management capabilities
	Improved storage management (SMS) and message handling (MHS) capabilities
	E-mail capabilities
	Supports High Capacity Storage Systems (HCSS), such as optical drives
	Supports multiple drives in a jukebox for optical discs
	Special protocols and packet formats to speed up WAN connections
	Better routing protocols (NLSP)
	Supports data migration from earlier NetWare versions
Personal Netware	Up to 50 nodes per server
	Up to 50 interconnected servers
	Distributed, replicated, object database allows a single login to entire network
	Fully compatible with other NetWare versions
	Supports NMS and SNMP management standards
	Built-in security, including access restrictions, password encryption, and audit trails
	Automatic reconnection if a server goes down
	Supports Client VLMs (Virtual Loadable Modules) for configuration flexibility

a
b
c
d
e
f
g
h
i
j
k
l
m
n
o
p
q
r
s
t
u
v
w
x
y
z

NetWare Components

Server-based versions of NetWare (NetWare 2.*x*, 3.*x*, and 4.*x*) consist of two components:

- The operating system software for the server. This component manages the network's files and resources, communicates with workstations, and deals with workstation requests.

- Workstation software, which is a network shell or redirector program. This component provides the workstation with access to the network and, therefore, to the resources and files on the server or on another workstation.

Server Software

The NetWare program running on the server is an NOS. NetWare has its own partition on the hard disk, and it may replace the native operating system (for example, DOS) as the program with which applications and other processes deal. In other cases, NetWare may run as a process under the operating system, as does NetWare for UNIX. Even when it becomes the primary operating system, NetWare may still rely on the native operating system. For example, NetWare for DOS uses some DOS services as well as the DOS file system.

The capabilities of the NOS running on a server depend on several things, including the following:

- The version of NetWare running

- For version 2.*x*, the combination of Value-Added Processes (VAPs) loaded with the NOS

- For versions 3.*x* and 4.*x*, the combination of NetWare Loadable Modules (NLMs) loaded with the NOS kernel

- Any auxiliary programs or modules being used to supplement the networking services

- The network size and resources

- The traffic load and patterns for the network

- The configuration of the hardware on which the NOS is running

Several core capabilities are available with any NetWare version:

- Controlled file and directory access. NetWare provides access controls and file and record locking.

- Shared access to printing resources. The NOS (or a process controlled by the NOS) makes sure that print jobs are added to the appropriate queue and are printed.

- Electronic mail (e-mail) capabilities. In NetWare, this is provided through Novell's MHS (Message Handling Service) protocol, which third-party e-mail packages can use.

- Security controls. For example, NetWare can require user log in and authentication procedures and limit user access rights.

- Interprocess Communication (IPC), which enables processes on the network to communicate with each other.

Workstation Software

The software on the workstation in a Net-Ware network must be able to communicate with the network and also with the workstation's operating system.

The workstation software determines whether a request from a program or user is intended for the workstation (that is, for DOS) or for the network. If the request is for the workstation, the software passes it on to DOS. If it is a network request, the software does the following:

- Converts the request into the appropriate format.

- Packs the request into a packet, together with routing and other administrative information. NetWare uses the NCP (NetWare Core Protocol) to formulate (and respond to) the requests and the IPX (Internetwork Packet Exchange) protocol to create the packet to be transmitted.

- Passes this packet on to a network interface card (NIC) for packaging in a format suitable for the actual network architecture.

- Verifies that the packet was received correctly, and requests a retransmission if an error occurred.

Once the packet is passed to the NIC, the workstation component of the NOS is finished with its task. The software running the NIC does further processing and makes sure the packet gets onto the network.

For DOS workstations, the program that does these things is called the *NetWare shell* in versions preceding 4.*x*. In NetWare 4.*x*, this software is known as the *NetWare DOS Requester.* The DOS Requester software runs as a DOS process, but takes considerable control by intercepting certain key DOS interrupts. This is done so that network-related requests go on to the network.

The workstation software consists of several utilities, each responsible for one of the shell's tasks. These utilities include NET*x*.COM, SPX.COM, and IPX.COM. NET*x* does the intercepting, redirecting, and the first round of processing (into NCP form); SPX and IPX create packets designed for their counterpart programs at the destination.

The DOS Requester (NetWare 4.*x*) consists of a collection of Virtual Loadable Modules (VLMs), which are modules running on a workstation. The VLMs accomplish generally the same kinds of tasks as the shell utilities, but do so in different ways.

NetWare Protocols

The NetWare NOS software corresponds roughly to the layers defined in the OSI Reference Model. The protocols supported within this framework are listed in the table "NetWare Protocol Suite."

By default, NetWare uses the protocol stack shown in the figure "Default NetWare protocol stack." In addition to these protocols, NetWare supports frame formats for different network architectures (Ethernet, Token Ring, ARCnet, and so on). Add-on modules also provide support for other protocol suites, such as the TCP/IP (used in UNIX systems) and AppleTalk protocol families.

a
b
c
d
e
f
g
h
i
j
k
l
m
n
o
p
q
r
s
t
u
v
w
x
y
z

NETWARE PROTOCOL SUITE	
PROTOCOL	**DESCRIPTION**
Burst Mode	Used instead of NCP for situations in which large amounts of data need to be transmitted.
IPX (Internetwork Packet Exchamge)	NetWare's standard network-layer protocol. IPX is used to route data packets from the transport layer across a network.
NCP (NetWare Core Protocol)	The protocol NetWare uses to formulate and respond to workstation requests. It includes procedures for dealing with any service a workstation might request (such as file or directory handling, printing, and so on). Burst mode can be used to make NCP more efficient when transmitting large blocks of data (such as entire files) over slower WAN links.
NLSP (NetWare Link State Protocol)	A routing protocol that improves upon and has largely replaced RIP and SAP. NLSP is more efficient and reliable than these older protocols. It also supports multiple paths between NLSP nodes, which affords a measure of fault tolerance in addition to improving performance.
RIP (Routing Information Protocol)	Used by routers and servers to exchange routing information on an internetwork. RIP packets use NetWare's IPX protocol to move between stations. RIP is generally known as IPX RIP to distinguish Novell's version from the RIP protocol in the TCP/IP protocol suite. RIP has largely been replaced by NLSP.
SAP (Service Advertising Protocol)	Used by NetWare services to broadcast their availability across the network. The protocol supports broadcast, query, and response packets. SAP has largely been replaced by NLSP.
SPX (Sequenced Packet Exchange)	NetWare's standard transport-layer protocol. It is used to ensure that data packets have been delivered successfully by the IPX services. SPX requests and receives acknowledgments from its counterpart on the receiving node, and also keeps track of fragmented messages consisting of multiple packets.
Watchdog	Used for maintenance purposes. It can determine whether the NetWare shell is still running on workstations that have been idle for a long time.

DEFAULT NETWARE PROTOCOL STACK

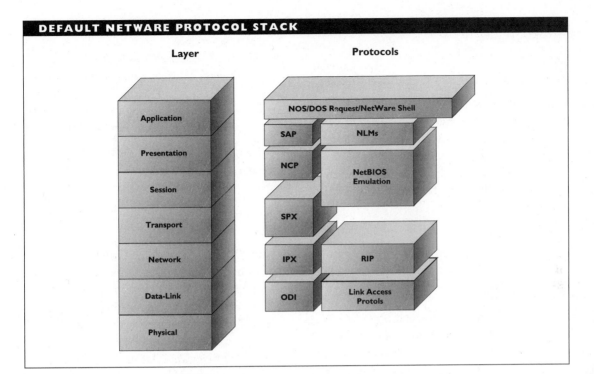

Layer / Protocols

The NetWare protocol collection also includes a NetBIOS emulation that provides access from peer-to-peer networks and from networks that support IBM's APPC (Advanced Program-to-Program Communication) protocols.

The SPX and IPX protocols are the ones most characteristically identified with NetWare. Access to the NIC and to the actual physical network depends on the network architecture and also on the LAN drivers being used.

SEE ALSO

NDS (NetWare Directory Services);
Personal NetWare

NetWare Access Server

NetWare Access Server is a software product that enables up to 16 users to dial into a network from remote locations at the same time. The product works with Novell's NetWare version 2.1 and later.

The NetWare Access Server software is installed on a dedicated 386 (or higher) computer with a communications board installed. Users at remote workstations can use asynchronous modems, public or private X.25 packet-switching services, or ISDN services to connect to the access server. Once connected, remote users can access network resources or run DOS and Microsoft Windows programs.

a b c d e f g h i j k l m **n** o p q r s t u v w x y z

BROADER CATEGORY
NetWare

NetWare Directory Database (NDD)

In the NDS for Novell NetWare 4.*x*, the NetWare Directory Database contains the object information. This information is represented in a hierarchically organized tree structure. This database is commonly known simply as the Directory (with capital *D*).

SEE ALSO
NDS (NetWare Directory Services)

NetWare Express

A private electronic information service from Novell. Subscribers can access the Novell Support Encyclopedia and the NetWare Buyer's Guide, and they can get product information and technical support. To access this service, delivered over the GE Information Services Network, users need the appropriate software and an asynchronous modem. There is a fee for this service.

NetWare for Macintosh

A collection of NetWare Loadable Modules (NLMs) that provide various NetWare services, including file handling, printing, network administration, and AppleTalk routing, for Macintosh clients on a Novell NetWare network. With NetWare for Macintosh, Macintosh users can access network resources, files, and applications, send print jobs to network printers, and take advantage of NetWare features, such as network security.

Users also get access to the NetWare Directory Services (with version 4.*x* of the product), as well as access to AppleTalk print services. Thus, by running NetWare for Macintosh, users can get the benefits and resources accessible through a NetWare network, while keeping their familiar Macintosh interface.

BROADER CATEGORY
NetWare

NetWare for SAA

Novell's gateway package for connecting NetWare networks to various machines that support IBM's SNA (Systems Network Architecture), including AS/400s, 3090s, and 370s. NetWare for SAA is installed as a series of NetWare Loadable Modules (NLMs) in NetWare 3.*x* or 4.*x*, and it supports up to several hundred sessions for each gateway.

Once NetWare for SAA is loaded, a client on a NetWare network can get access to the applications and data on the IBM mainframe or midrange system—assuming that the user has the required access privileges. The client can be running any of the operating systems supported by NetWare: DOS, Macintosh, OS/2, UNIX, or Windows.

NetWare for SAA emulates PU2.0 and PU2.1 devices, which are both peripheral devices with access only through a communications controller or a front end processor. NetWare for SAA also supports 3270 and TN3270 (a Telnet variant) terminal emulation.

BROADER CATEGORY
NetWare

NetWare for UNIX

A program that provides NetWare support on machines running general-purpose operating systems, such as UNIX. NetWare for UNIX (formerly Portable NetWare) runs as a set of applications on the host. The software enables the host to provide file handling, printing, and backup services to clients, regardless of whether clients are running DOS, Microsoft Windows, or the Macintosh operating system. NetWare for UNIX is sold by the host system vendors.

NetWare/IP

NetWare Loadable Modules (NLMs) that provide support for the IP (Internet Protocol) as a routing protocol for NetWare 3.*x* and 4.*x* servers. With NetWare/IP, a NetWare server can function as a gateway between NetWare and TCP/IP networks.

NetWare Management Agents

NetWare Management Agents are NetWare Loadable Modules (NLMs) that enable communication between a NetWare 3.*x* or 4.*x* server and external management software. If the external software is Novell's NetWare Management System, then the agent will carry out commands for the management software.

NetWare Management Agents can provide statistical information about the server and its performance: configuration, disk, memory and CPU usage, file activity, protocols and frames passed across the network, etc. The agents can also send alarms in case a server goes down or has exceeded

threshold on a parameter. The agents support standard management and networking protocols—SNMP (Simple Network Management Protocol), IP (Internet Protocol), and IPX (Internetwork Packet Exchange).

Once a NetWare Management Agent has been installed, it can be used by multiple administrators at multiple locations. That is, more than one administrator can request statistics and information from the agent—provided, as always, that the administrator has the appropriate privileges.

BROADER CATEGORIES

NetWare; Network Management

NetWare Management System (NMS)

The NMS is a Novell software product that provides centralized network monitoring and management capabilities. NMS monitors resource usage, configuration and traffic changes, etc., and can reconfigure the network, if necessary.

NMS provides monitoring and management capabilities in the following domains:

Asset management—NMS can determine and map all devices on the network, can provide configuration information, and can help configure the network.

Fault management—NMS monitors devices, checking for changes that might indicate trouble; it constantly checks the network's connectivity, and issues a real-time alarm if necessary.

Address management—NMS stores all IPX and SPX addresses in a database, and then searches for duplicates. NMS

a b c d e f g h i j k l **m** n o p q r s t u v w x y z

continues to monitor for duplicate addresses, to make sure none are assigned later.

Hub management—NMS works with a NetWare Hub Services Agent to provide monitoring and management of hub adapters and ports.

Router management—NMS can monitor routers, can supply them with IP and IPX addresses, and can monitor and display port usage.

NetWare server management—NMS works with a NetWare Management Agent to monitor and manage multiple NetWare servers.

Critical device monitoring—NMS will monitor any devices the system administrator specifies as critical, will track their performance, and will raise an alarm if a device is going to have or cause problems.

Record keeping—NMS will store data in a central Btrieve database, so that the data can be used for analyses or just summaries.

BROADER CATEGORIES

NetWare; Network Management

NetWare Multiprotocol Router (MPR)

The MPR is a collection of software routing products. These products can route protocols from the IPX/SPX, TCP/IP, SNA, and AppleTalk stacks concurrently. MPR can use a variety of network architectures and topologies, and supports long distance communications at speeds ranging from 1,200 bps to 2.048 Mbps.

MPR also supports *dial on demand routing,* in which a server—for example, at a branch office—may ask for a line only when there's something to be sent or communicated. This is more cost effective than keeping a permanent connection with outlying offices or areas.

MPR consists of four main products:

- A two-port *branch-link router*

- A multiple-port (up to 16) *enterprise router*

- An SNA*Extensions package, which provides access to IBM SNA communications

- A WAN*Extensions package, which provides access to X.25 and frame relay networks

MPR (version 3.0) supports the following protocols:

IPX RIP: NetWare's routing information protocol

(IPX) NLSP: NetWare Link Services Protocol, which has largely replaced IPX RIP and SAP protocols, because it's more efficient

TCP/IP RIP: The Internet's slightly different routing information protocol

TCP/IP OSPF: The Internet's Open Shortest Path First protocol for trading packets among routes within an autonomous system

SNA: IBM's System Network Architecture

AppleTalk AURP: The AppleTalk Update Routing Protocol

AppleTalk RTMP: The Routing Table Maintenance Protocol

In addition, MPR supports many WAN configurations, including ISDN, SMDS, PPP, and—with the WAN*Extension—frame relay and X.25. MPR also supports data compression and packet filtering to help keep WAN traffic to a minimum.

MPR supports the Internet's Simple Network Management Protocol (SNMP) for monitoring and managing routers.

BROADER CATEGORIES

NetWare; Protocol, Routing; Router

NetWare NFS

A collection of NetWare Loadable Modules (NLMs) that provide file handling and printing services for UNIX clients in a NetWare network. NetWare NFS uses the Network File System (NFS) application-layer protocol from Sun Microsystems.

NetWare NFS Gateway

The software that is installed on a Novell NetWare server and allows NetWare clients (using DOS or Microsoft Windows) to access files on an NFS (Network File System) server. To the client, the files on the NFS server appear to be on the NetWare server.

NetWare Peripheral Architecture (NPA)

SEE

NPA (NetWare Peripheral Architecture)

NetWare Requester for OS/2

Software that runs on an OS/2 workstation and enables the workstation to connect to a Novell NetWare network. In addition to providing the necessary redirection services, this Requester allows application servers to communicate with the workstations without involving NetWare.

NetWare Runtime

NetWare Runtime is a version of the Novell NetWare operating system designed for use by one or two users. This version can be used as an application server, with applications based on NetWare Loadable Modules (NLMs) installed on it. This frees the regular NetWare server for other network tasks, such as file and print services.

NetWare Runtime can provide basic services, such as e-mail and communications, and database services. The database capabilities are particularly important for applications that may have front- and back-end components (programs that run in part on a client and in part on a server).

Applications running with the NetWare Runtime system can use the NetWare protocol stack (SPX and IP) or other protocols (such as TCP/IP or AppleTalk).

BROADER CATEGORY

NetWare

NetWare Shell

In NetWare versions prior to 4.0, a terminate-and-stay-resident (TSR) program loaded on a workstation. The shell

a b c d e f g h i j k l m n o p q r s t u v w x y z

sits between the application environment and DOS.

SEE ALSO

NetWare

NetWare TCP/IP

A collection of NetWare Loadable Modules (NLMs) that implement the TCP/IP protocol suite in order to provide routing services for stations using the TCP/IP format.

NetWare Telephony Services

NetWare Telephony Services is a software/ hardware product from Novell that makes it possible to integrate a Novell NetWare network with a telephone PBX (private branch exchange). The product includes a hardware link between the NetWare server and the PBX. This link is administered through the server, and it is used for all the communications between network and PBX. Workstations that want access to the PBX must be running the appropriate part of the software and must communicate with the PBX through the network server.

The hardware link between the network and PBX consists of a PBX-specific board (installed in the server) and cabling. Details of the link (whether serial, ISDN, TCP/IP, or another type) and of the board will depend on the board's manufacturer, which is likely to be the PBX vendor. Fortunately, just about every board manufacturer supports the telephony services standard used in the Novell product. An appropriate PBX driver will make the board and the PBX accessible to the network.

In addition to board and driver, NetWare Telephony Services includes a NetWare Loadable Module (NLM) that enables and controls the communications between the network and the PBX. Actual telephony services, such as call forwarding or unified messaging of fax, voice, electronic mail, and other transmissions, are provided through applications. A Telephony Service Application Program Interface (TSAPI) is available for developers who want to provide such services in their products.

NetWare Telephony Services is eventually expected to encompass voice processing and speech synthesis, in addition to the call-control capabilities currently provided. For example, instead of clicking on an icon to dial a number or transfer a call, a user may be able to give the required commands verbally.

NetWare Tools

A collection of basic end-user utilities for NetWare version 4.*x*. The NetWare Tools utilities are installed separately from the NetWare server installation program. They can be used to accomplish various tasks on the network, such as mapping drives, sending messages, and setting up printing. NetWare tools are designed for end-user tasks. In contrast, administrative tasks are performed using utilities such as the NetWare Administrator.

NetWare Utilities

NetWare utilities are programs that can be used to accomplish specific tasks.

Utilities can be grouped in various ways, including graphics- versus text-based and server- versus workstation-based. Server-based utilities execute on the server, and they are generally used to manipulate the server. Some server-based utilities are NetWare Loadable Modules (NLMs). These are loaded using the LOAD command.

The NLMs actually hook into the operating system and execute until they are unloaded. Other server-based utilities are simply commands that the user types at the server console.

Workstation-based utilities execute on the workstation, even though they are installed on the server. These utilities are generally used to manipulate the networking environment: files, users, print queues, and so on. Some workstation-based utilities can be used by any legitimate user; others can be used only by administrators.

Graphics-based, or GUI, utilities use icons, dialog boxes, and so on, just as in Microsoft Windows or OS/2.

Text-based utilities run under DOS, and they can be command lines (for example, at the DOS prompt) or menus.

Utilities are added, dropped, consolidated, and divided as NetWare evolves. For example, NetWare 3.x has more than 120 utilities, whereas one counting method yields fewer than 75 utilities in NetWare 4.x. One reason for this is that some NetWare 4.x utilities consolidate several 3.x utilities.

GETTING INFORMATION ABOUT NETWARE UTILITIES

It is not possible to summarize all the NetWare utilities without adding a medium-length book to this Encyclopedia. For more information about these utilities, you can read the following:

- The Utilities manuals and the *Quick Access Guides* for NetWare versions 3.x and 4.x provide detailed and terse summaries, respectively, of the utilities for these versions.

- The *Complete Guide to NetWare® 4*, by James Gaskin, is a comprehensive source.

NetWire

An online information service run by Novell. NetWire provides product and technical information, and an opportunity to submit technical questions to Novell Technicians. NetWire is available through CompuServe.

Network

A network consists of computers, called nodes or stations. The computers are connected to, or can communicate with, each other in some way. Nodes run special software for initiating and managing network interactions. With the help of networking software, nodes can share files and resources.

Network Components

The following are the main hardware components of a network:

Nodes: Computers and network interface cards (NICs)

Topology: Logical and physical

Connection elements: Cabling, wiring centers, links, and so on

Auxiliary components: Peripheral devices, safety devices, and tools

See the Hardware, Network article for more information about the hardware components.

The software components include the following:

Networking systems: Network operating system (NOS) and workstation software

Resources: Server software and drivers

Tools: Utilities, LAN analyzers, network monitoring software, and configuration managers

Applications: Network-aware software

The component groupings, particularly for the software, are not mutually exclusive. The same software may be viewed as belonging in multiple categories. For example, a NOS can include various network resources and tools.

Because of the connection and the software, nodes on the network can communicate and interact with each other. The interaction may be directly between two nodes, via one or more intermediate nodes, or through a server node. The interaction can be over a physical medium (such as electrical or fiber-optic cable) or by wireless means (using radio waves, microwaves, or infrared waves).

Users working on a network node can make use of available files and resources on other nodes as well. Each user generally has a limited range of access and usage privileges, which are monitored and controlled by the NOS. A (human) network administrator, or manager, oversees the NOS's configuration and operations. The administrator sets the user privileges.

Network Categories

Networks come in all shapes and sizes, and can be categorized using a variety of features and functions. These categorizations are neither exclusive nor exhaustive, but they do yield a rich crop of terminology, as summarized in the table "Network Groupings."

The various groupings are described in the following sections. Keep in mind that networking categories and terminology may overlap, complement, or be independent. For example, one person's local-area network (LAN) may be another's campus-area network (CAN).

Networks Classified by Message Capacity

A network may be able to transmit one or more messages at a time. A *baseband* network can transmit exactly one message at a time. Most LANs are baseband networks. A *carrierband* network is a special case of a baseband network. In this type of network, the channel's entire bandwidth is used for a single transmission, and the signal is modulated before being transmitted.

A *broadband* network can transmit more than one message at a time by using a different frequency range for each message and then multiplexing these multiple channels (sending all the messages out on a single channel).

NETWORK GROUPINGS

CATEGORY	DESCRIPTION
Message Capacity	Whether the network can transmit one or more messages at a time. Networks are either baseband, carrierband, or broadband.
Range	The geographical or bureaucratic range over which the nodes are distributed. Networks can be categorized as LANs, WANs, MANs, CANs, DANs, and GANs, which are local-, wide-, metropolitan-, campus-, departmental-, and global-area networks, respectively.
Node types	Nodes in a network may be PCs, minicomputers, mainframes, or even other networks. Networks used for general-purpose computing and operations are most likely to be PC-based. MIS departments and universities are most likely to have networks that include minicomputers or mainframes. Backbone networks are networks whose "nodes" are actually smaller networks, known as access networks.
Node Relationships	The relationship among the nodes that make up the network. Networks categorized along these lines are known as distributed, peer-to-peer, server-based, and client/server.
Topology	Topology refers to both the network's logical topology (logical layout of nodes in the network) and physical topology (physical layout, including the wiring scheme by which nodes are connected). The main logical topologies are bus and ring. Physical topologies include bus, star, ring, and star-wired ring.
Architecture	The network architecture, which is defined by the cabling used, by the method used to access the network, and by the format of a data packet on the network. Common LAN architectures include Ethernet (and the very closely related 802.3), Token Ring, ARCnet, and FDDI.
Access Possibilities	At one extreme are shared-media networks, in which exactly one node can have access to the network medium at a given time. In contrast to this, switching networks allow multiple nodes to use the network at the same time. Switching networks accomplish this by multiplexing.

Networks Classified by Transmission Rate

In general, broadband networks support higher transmission rates. However, there is considerable variation in transmission rates for baseband networks, and there is considerable overlap in transmission rates. That is, there are lots of baseband networks that are faster than some broadband networks, even though broadband networks tend to support higher rates.

Very roughly, we can distinguish four generations of networks:

- The earliest networks operated at kilobit per second (kbps) speeds, anywhere from fewer than ten to a few hundred kilobits per second.

a b c d e f g h i j k l m **n** o p q r s t u v w x y z

- The next generation encompasses the transmission speeds for the "traditional" LAN architectures: Ethernet, Token Ring, and ARCnet. These have speeds in the 1 to 20 megabit per second (Mbps) range. The traditional speeds are 10 Mbps or slower; the 16 Mbps Token Ring and 20 Mbps ARCnet Plus are improvements on the original designs.

- The up-and-coming generation supports transmissions in the 100+ Mbps range. This includes FDDI (100 Mbps), ATM (up to 600+ Mbps), and fast Ethernet (100 Mbps).

- The next generation of networks will support transmissions at 1+ gigabits per second (Gbps) rates. At these speeds, the entire *Oxford English Dictionary* could be transmitted several times in a single second. These rates can be obtained only through multiplexing, since hardware devices (such as disk or tape drives) cannot supply data fast enough.

Networks Classified by Range

Networks are distinguished by the range over which the nodes are distributed. Interestingly, the *number* of nodes is not used as a major distinction (except by network software vendors when they sell packages to end-users). The table "Network Range Categories" summarizes the types of networks in this classification. See the article about the specific network type for a more detailed discussion.

The most common categories are LANs, WANs (wide-area networks), and MANs (metropolitan-area networks), but GANs (global-area networks) will become increasingly popular as multinational corporations connect all their operations.

LANs generally include only PCs. WANs generally include some type of remote connection. Enterprise networks typically require gateways to access the mainframe-based networks.

Networks Classified by Types of Nodes

PC-based networks are the fastest growing segment of the networking world. Such networks offer the greatest flexibility in where to put servers and how to divide the services among nodes on the network. References to "LANs" generally assume a PC-based network.

Most PC-based networks use either Macintoshes or IBM PC and compatible machines. Macintoshes come with networking capabilities built in; PCs require extra hardware (an NIC) to join a network.

The whole gamut of PCs may be used in networks. For example, an IBM-based network may have machines ranging from an XT to a machine with an 80486 or a Pentium processor. Of course, key functions may be restricted to certain classes of machines. For example, some networking software allows only 80386 or 80486 machines as file servers; older machines can be used only as workstations or "smaller" servers (such as print or tape servers).

Use of *superservers,* which are souped-up PCs specially designed to be used as file servers, is becoming more popular. This is

NETWORK RANGE CATEGORIES

RANGE CATAGORY	DESCRIPTION
LAN (Local-area network)	Consists of machines that are connected within a relatively small geographical radius (for example, within an office, floor, or a building) and by a particular type of medium. Functionally, a LAN consists of a group of computers interconnected so that users can share files, printers, and other resources. A LAWN (local-area wireless network) is a special type of LAN that uses microwave, infrared, or radio transmissions instead of cabling.
CAN (Campus-area network)	Connects nodes (or possibly departmental LANs) from multiple locations, which may be separated by a considerable distance. Unlike a WAN, however, a campus network does not require remote communications facilities, such as modems and telephones.
Dan (Departmental-area network)	A small network, which may connect up to 20 or 30 nodes so that they can share common resources. DANs are typically used in government agencies.
WAN (Wide-area network)	Consists of machines that may be spread out over larger areas, such as across a college campus, an industrial park, a city, or a state. WANs usually include some type of remote bridges or routers, which are used to connect groups of nodes by telephone or other dedicated lines. Because of this, the bandwidth for WANs tends to be considerably smaller than for LANs. A SWAN is a satellite-based WAN.
MAN (metropolitan-area network)	Generally defined as a network that covers a radius of up to 50 or 75 miles. These types of networks use fast data transmission rates (over 100 Mbps) and are capable of handling voice transmission.
GAN (global-area network)	Usually an internetwork that extends across national boundaries and that may connect nodes on opposite sides of the world. As with very widely distributed WANs, most GANs are likely to be internetworks in disguise.
Enterprise	Connects machines for an entire corporate operation. The network may connect very diverse machines from different parts of the company. These machines may be in different rooms, buildings, cities, or even countries. Enterprise networks are increasingly likely to cross national boundaries in this age of multinational corporations.

a
b
c
d
e
f
g
h
i
j
k
l
m
n
o
p
q
r
s
t
u
v
w
x
y
z

because hardware capabilities have reached a level at which it is feasible for a single machine to serve dozens of nodes, and possibly to serve nodes with different network architectures at the same time. To manage multiple architectures, a superserver needs the appropriate hardware for each architecture. (See the articles about servers, NICs, and the individual network architectures for more information.)

Networks that include minicomputers or mainframes are usually located in either business or university environments. In the business world, such networks are generally run by an MIS department. Historically, these network environments have been dominated for several decades by IBM mainframes. Minicomputers, produced by companies such as Digital Equipment Corporation (DEC) or Wang (and even IBM), made inroads only slowly in the business world. In the early days, minicomputers were used as front-end processors (FEPs) for mainframes.

Mainframe-based networks generally consist mainly of terminals, which communicate directly with the mainframe or through FEPs. PCs can be used in the place of terminals, but the PCs must run terminal-emulation software and may need to "play dumb" (pretend to be nothing more than a terminal) to communicate with the mainframe.

Mainframe-based networks generally use software that complies with IBM's SNA (Systems Network Architecture) and, if PCs are to be included as more than dumb terminals, SAA (Systems Applications Architecture). SNA and SAA provide comprehensive models (comparable to the seven-layer OSI Reference Model) for controlling the details of network operation and communication at several levels.

DEC's alternative to SNA is DNA (Digital Network Architecture), which provides a framework for networks built around minicomputers (such as DEC's VAX machines). DECnet is one example of networking software based on the DNA framework.

In university settings, distributed networks are quite common. In such networks, there is no centralized controller. Instead, nodes are more or less comparable, except that certain nodes provide the services available on the network. UNIX environments are particularly likely to use a distributed network architecture.

Minicomputer- and mainframe-based networks often provide services to LANs. Nodes on the LAN get access to the mainframe-based network through gateways. The real advantages of layered architectures become particularly clear in such interactions between the very different worlds of the LAN and an SNA-based network.

Backbone networks are designed with smaller, access networks as nodes. Such networks are able to provide the advantages of very large, heterogeneous networks while also allowing the simplicity of a LAN. The access networks can operate as independent networks for the most part, but can get access to resources in any of the other networks linked to the backbone, provided, of course, that the access network has the appropriate usage privileges.

Networks Classified by Relationships among Nodes

Nodes on a network can be servers or workstations. A workstation makes requests, and a server fulfills them. The "server" actually controls the network by providing the user at the workstation with only the resources the server sees fit.

With the introduction of products such as NetWare Lite, Personal NetWare, LANTastic, and Microsoft Windows for Workgroups, peer-to-peer networks have been gaining in popularity.

The following terms are used to describe the relationship between nodes in a network:

Peer-to-peer: Every node can be both client and server; that is, all nodes are equal. Peer-to-peer (or just peer) networks are useful if you need to connect only a few machines (generally, fewer than 10) and if no one will be running programs that push available resources to the limit.

Distributed: A network with no leader; that is, one in which any node can talk to any other. An example of a distributed network is Usenet, which is popular in the UNIX community. In a distributed network, servers are just that—machines, devices, or programs that provide services, as opposed to controlling network activity.

Server-based: A network with a dedicated file server. The server runs the network, granting other nodes access to resources. Most middle- to large-sized networks are server-based, and the most popular PC-based network operating systems (Novell's NetWare, Microsoft's LAN Manager, IBM's LAN Server, and Banyan's VINES) assume a server-based network.

Client/server: A sophisticated version of a server-based network. While workstations in server-based networks can get access to all sorts of resources through the server, the workstation must do most of the work. The server doles out the resources (downloads files and, possibly, applications to the workstation), and then lets the workstation run the programs.

In the most general form of client/server computing, the workstation makes a query or request, and the server processes the query or request and returns the results to the workstation. In a commonly used form, a front-end process running on the client sends a query or request to the back end running on the server. The back end does the requested work and returns the results to the client.

Networks Classified by Topology

There are thousands of ways you can connect computers into a network. Fortunately, these possibilities all reduce to a few fundamental types (just as all the possible wallpaper patterns reduce to about two dozen basic patterns).

When discussing network layouts, or topologies, it is useful to distinguish between the physical and logical layouts. The logical topology specifies the flow of information and communication in the network. The physical topology specifies the wiring that links the nodes in the network.

a
b
c
d
e
f
g
h
i
j
k
l
m
n
o
p
q
r
s
t
u
v
w
x
y
z

Logical Topologies   The two main logical topologies are bus and ring. In a bus topology, information is broadcast along a single cable, called the *trunk* cable. All nodes attached to the network can hear the information, and at roughly the same time. Only nodes for whom the information is intended actually read and process the transmitted packets. The information broadcast and simultaneous access characterize a bus topology.

Because all nodes hear a transmission at the same time, contentious network-access methods, such as CSMA/CD, can be used. In contentious media-access methods, nodes get transmission rights by being the first to request them when there is no network activity.

The figure "A linear bus topology" illustrates this logical topology.

In a ring topology, information is passed from node to node in a ring. Each node gets information from exactly one node and transmits it to exactly one node. Nodes gain access to the message sequentially (in a predetermined sequence), generally based on network addresses. As with all networks, a node is expected to process only those packets with the node as a destination.

Because all nodes do not hear a transmission at the same time, network-access methods cannot be based on contention for transmission rights. Instead, deterministic-access methods, such as token passing, are used. The figure "A ring topology" illustrates this logical topology.

Physical Topologies   Whereas the logical topology controls how information moves across a network, the physical topology, or

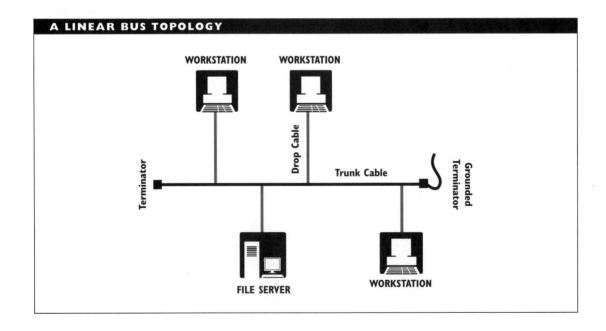

A LINEAR BUS TOPOLOGY

WORKSTATION   WORKSTATION

Terminator

Drop Cable

Trunk Cable

Grounded Terminator

FILE SERVER

WORKSTATION

A RING TOPOLOGY

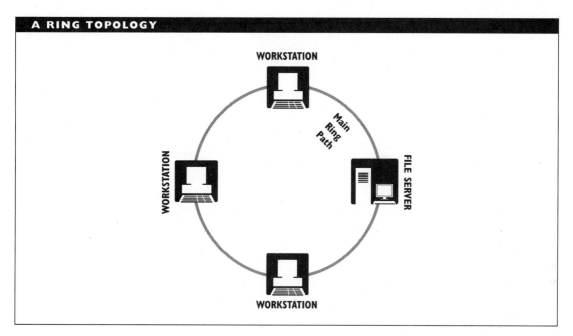

WORKSTATION

Main Ring Path

FILE SERVER

WORKSTATION

WORKSTATION

wiring scheme, controls how electrical signals move across the network. This has consequences for the status of a network if a node breaks down.

For example, a bus wiring scheme requires minimal cable, but can make troubleshooting more difficult than with, for example, a star wiring scheme. If a node attached to the bus over a drop cable goes down, there may be no way for the server to know this until the server tries to send the node a message and gets no response. In contrast, a star wiring scheme uses lots of cable, since each node may be a considerable distance from the central node or hub, but it is easy to determine when a node goes down because the central node can communicate directly with each node.

Although there are dozens of ways to label network wiring schemes, most of these fall into the following major groups:

Bus: A central cable forms the backbone of the network, and individual nodes are attached to this bus, either directly or by means of a shorter piece of cable. Signals travel along the bus, and each node eavesdrops on all messages, reading only those addressed to the node. Ethernet and certain versions of ARCnet use a bus topology. Variants on a bus topology include tree and branching tree. The figure "Bus networks" shows a bus network and two common variants.

a b c d e f g h i j k l m **n** o p q r s t u v w x y z

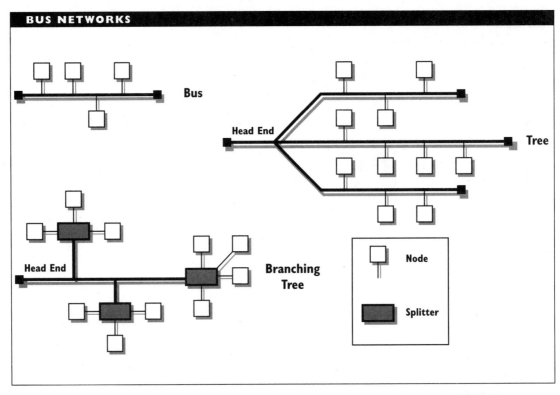

BUS NETWORKS

Bus

Head End

Tree

Head End

Branching
Tree

Node

Splitter

Ring: The nodes are arranged in a (more or less imaginary) circle. Each node is connected to the node immediately before and immediately after it. Messages are passed around the ring (more or less) in sequence. Again, a node takes the message if the node is the recipient, and passes the message on otherwise. FDDI and IBM Token Ring networks use a ring topology. Variants on the basic ring wiring scheme include slotted-ring, backbone, and multiple-ring topologies.

Star: All nodes are connected to a central machine or to a wiring center (such as a hub). Messages can be sent directly

to their destinations from the center. Some versions of ARCnet use a star topology. A distributed star network is a variant in which several hubs, each of which forms a star, are connected to each other.

Star-wired ring: All nodes are attached to a wiring center in a star topology, but the nodes are accessed as if they were in a ring. Some IBM Token Ring networks actually use a star-wired ring topology.

The figures "A star topology" and "A star-wired ring topology" illustrate these two types of physical topologies.

A STAR TOPOLOGY

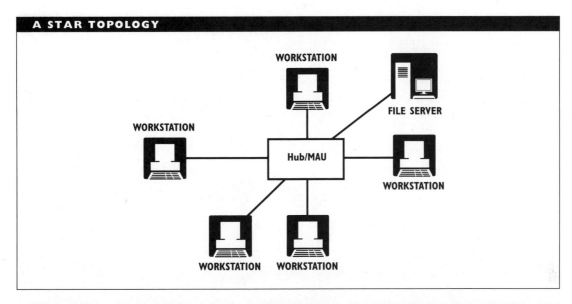

A STAR-WIRED RING TOPOLOGY

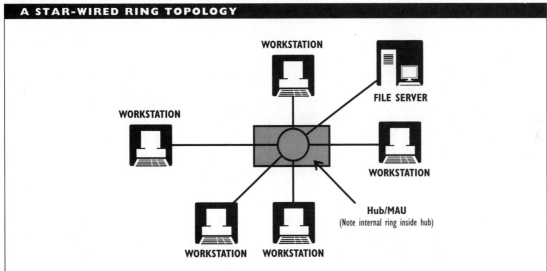

These four schemes capture most of the network wiring configurations, but there are other ways of categorizing the network layout. For example, in a *mesh topology,* a node may be connected to one or more other nodes. In the extreme case, every node is connected directly to every other node. The advantage of direct access to each node is more than offset by the wires that will be running everywhere and by the fact that each node will need a port for connecting to every other node.

a b c d e f g h i j k l m n o p q r s t u v w x y z

Networks Classified by Architecture

Network architectures differ in the cabling used (coaxial, twisted-pair, fiber-optic), the methods used to access the network (CSMA/CD, token passing, polling), the format of data packets sent across the network, and the network topology.

In general, different network architectures need translators in order to talk to each other. Routers and multiarchitecture hubs help to make such cross-architecture communications transparent to users.

The most commonly used network architectures are Ethernet/IEEE 802.3, ARCnet, Token Ring, and FDDI. See the Network Architecture article for more information.

Networks Classified by Access Possibilities

Networks can be shared-media or switched. In standard, shared-media network architectures (such as Ethernet or Token Ring), only one node can transmit at a time. That is, access to the network medium is exclusive. How a node gets access to the medium depends on the access method used (for example, CSMA/CD versus token passing versus polling).

Switched networks, in contrast, establish temporary connections as needed between parties. Such networks use multiplexing to enable multiple nodes to transmit at the same time. The basis used for the switching distinguishes such networks. Networks can be packet-switched, circuit-switched, or message-switched.

ALTERNATIVES TO NETWORKS

The following alternatives to networks have been used and should be considered before you go to the trouble and expense of creating your own network, especially if your main needs are for file sharing:

- SneakerNet: This involves the use of removable media—usually floppy disks—whose contents are transferred by carrying them from machine to machine, as needed. As befits this age of commercialization, SneakerNet has also been referred to as Adidasnet, Nikenet, and Reeboknet.

- Portable Drives: Portable hard disks and erasable optical drives are available, and at affordable prices. Portable drive interfaces allow such drives to be plugged into a parallel port for easy access. Erasable optical drives have capacities of over 200 megabytes per disk.

- File Transfer Programs: These set up fast, short-distance links for rapid file or other data transfer between two machines. Such programs usually use the parallel port, and many use special cables for fast transmissions. In this context fast means only about 100 kbps or so.

- Switch Boxes: These allow two or more users to switch a resource (for example, a printer) from one machine to another. This technique isn't convenient, but it's inexpensive.

- Multiuser Systems: In these, a single processor does work for multiple users who are logged in through separate terminals. UNIX is a popular operating system for multiuser systems; DOS is not.

Planning a Network

If you are planning to set up a network, you should seriously consider hiring a professional consultant to help you. Be sure to make the prospective consultant prove to you that he or she is competent.

Before investing in a network, planning is essential. Always make sure you have all available information to guide your planning. The following are some guidelines to follow when you begin planning for a network:

- Formulate your needs as completely and clearly as possible. This will help you decide what components and services the network (or other solution) will need to include.

- Determine what resources (financial, equipment, and expertise) are available for planning, implementing, and running a network. This information will determine whether you are in a position to create and operate a network.

- Determine who will need access to the network and where these people are located. This information will help determine whether a network is a necessary or feasible solution for your needs. It will also give you information regarding possible cabling requirements. The cabling details will depend on the type of network (if any) you end up creating.

- Get to know your current usage and needs *in detail*. This will mean convincing the people using the (currently, stand-alone) PCs to start paying attention to what they do, how often, and for how long. This information will also help you decide whether a network is the best solution for your needs.

- Get detailed drawings of existing wiring. Once you have designed the network, you will be able to determine whether it is feasible to use some or all of the existing wiring, assuming that the wiring meets your performance requirements and that enough of the wiring is available to meet your cabling needs.

CALCULATING AVAILABLE RESOURCES

To play it safe, after you've determined the available resources, use only a portion of these for your working calculations. This downgrading will protect you against the inevitable resource losses and sags due to people leaving, becoming involved in other projects, and so forth.

The amount by which you need to decrease your estimates depends on the possible costs if your network is a failure and also on how stable the resources are. As a general rule of thumb, assume your available resources will be anywhere from 10 to 50 percent less than you estimated.

The converse of this coin concerns *cost* calculations. When you decide how much time and money things will cost, it's a good idea to *add* an amount or a percentage—as a hedge against Murphy's laws.

Chances are only moderate (at best) that you will be able to use the wiring—except, possibly, for short-hauls and special-purpose connections. On the other hand, if you can do it, this can save a considerable amount of money, since cable installation is a major chunk of network cabling expenses.

Once you've decided that a network is the appropriate solution for your needs, a second phase of planning begins. In this phase, the components and details of the network are designed. Later phases include implementing and actually running the network. See the LAN article for a more detailed discussion of LAN planning.

SEE ALSO

Network, Circuit-Switched; Network, Message-Switched; Network, Packet-Switched

Network Access Controller (NAC)

SEE

NAC (Network Access Controller)

Network Addressable Unit (NAU)

SEE

NAU (Network Addressable Unit)

Network Administration

Network administration refers to the task of managing and maintaining a network, to make sure all programs are up to date, all hardware is functioning properly, and all authorized users are able to access and work on the network.

A network administrator, or manager, must do tasks such as the following:

- Setting up new accounts

- Assigning user privileges, permissions, and so on

- Doing billing and other accounting chores

- Testing and installing new software or hardware

- Troubleshooting existing hardware and software

- Backup and file management

SEE ALSO

LAN (Local-Area Network)

Network Analyzer

A network analyzer is a product that can be used to monitor the activity of a network and the stations on it, and to provide daily summaries or long-term trends of network usage and performance. A network analyzer can do tasks such as the following:

- Count or filter network traffic. For example, a network analyzer may count the total number of packets processed or count just the packets between specific nodes.

- Analyze network activity involving specified protocols or frame structures.

- Generate, display, and print statistics about network activity, either as they are being generated or in summary form (at the end of a shift or a day, for example).

■ Send alarms to a network supervisor or network management program if any of the statistics being monitored exceeds predetermined thresholds. For example, if the program detects too many discarded or lost packets, it may send an alarm.

■ Do trend or pattern analyses of network activity. For example, a network analyzer may identify network bottlenecks or find statistics whose average behavior is approaching a threshold. If the network analyzer program cannot do the trend analyses, it will at least allow you to export the data in a format that another program can use to do the desired analyses.

Network analyzers may be software only or may consist of both software and hardware. The latter may include an interface card for testing the network directly. This card may even include an on-board processor. Because of their greater capabilities, hardware/software analyzers are considerably more expensive than software-only products. Prices for the hardware/software packages can be several times as high as for software-only products.

Network Architecture

Depending on the scope of the discussion, a network architecture may refer to a model that encompasses an entire computing environment or to one that specifies just low-level features (cabling, packet structure, and media access) of a network.

Examples of global (encompassing) architectures include IBM's SNA (Systems Network Architecture), DEC's DNA (Network Architecture), and the ISO's OSI Reference Model. Such architectures are used for wide-area networks (WANs) as well as local-area networks (LANs). See the articles about the specific architectures for more information about global architectures.

This article focuses on the more circumscribed PC-based architectures that specify a smaller range of features. PC-based architectures are most often used for LANs.

Architecture Functions

A PC-based network architecture encompasses the physical and data-link layers (the bottom two) of the OSI Reference Model. As such, the architecture specifies cabling, signal encoding, performance (such as transmission speed), packet structure, and the strategy used to access the network (media-access method). The figure "Context and properties of network architectures" illustrates the role of an architecture.

In turn, a network architecture determines the selection of various networking components, including network interface cards (NICs), wiring centers, cables, and connectors.

Network architectures are also built around particular topologies, although variant topologies exist for the electrically based architectures. For example, an Ethernet architecture uses a bus topology, but variants that use a star topology have been developed.

Generations of Architectures

Architectures for LANs can be split into at least two generations. The first generation

a b c d e f g h i j k l m **n** o p q r s t u v w x y z

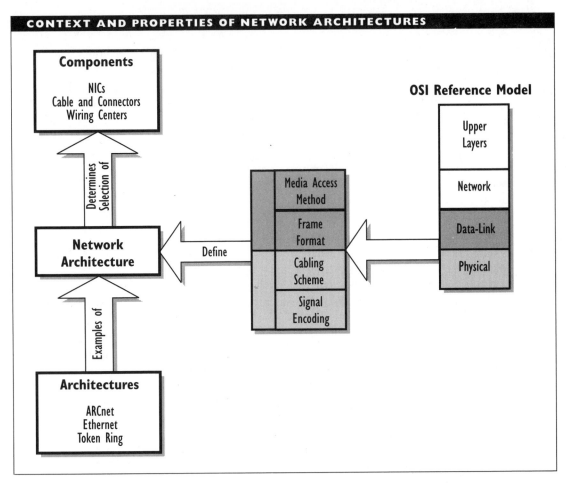

CONTEXT AND PROPERTIES OF NETWORK ARCHITECTURES

saw the development of low- to medium-bandwidth architectures: LocalTalk (230 kbps), Ethernet (10 Mbps), Token Ring (16 Mbps), and ARCnet (2.5 Mbps). These architectures are exclusively copper-based, at least in their original formulations.

The second generation consists of high-bandwidth architectures: FDDI (100 Mbps), ATM (155 Mbps and higher), and high-speed versions of first-generation architectures, such as 100 Mbps Ethernet and 20 Mbps ARCnet Plus. The fast variants are copper-based, and are an effort to speed up

networks using existing cable resources. The new architectures are fiber-based, and are designed to carry multiple types of data (voice, video, and digital).

The table "Common Network Architectures" summarizes the main types of architectures. See the article about the specific architecture for a detailed discussion.

SEE ALSO

ARCnet; ATM; Ethernet; FDDI; Token Ring

COMMON NETWORK ARCHITECTURES

ARCHITECTURE	VARIANTS	DESCRIPTION
ARCnet	ARCnet Plus; TCNS	A widely used, easy-to-implement architecture for small- to medium-size networks (maximum, 255 nodes). Uses coaxial, twisted-pair, or fiber-optic cable and can transmit at a maximum of 2.5 Mbps. Its media-access method is token-passing.
Ethernet	Blue Book Ethernet (Ethernet 2.0); 802.3 Ethernet; 1Base5; 0Base2; 10Base5; 10BaseF; 10BaseT; 10Broad36;100Base VGAnyLAN; 100Base-T	Blue Book Ethernet uses coaxial cable; 802.3-based variants can use coaxial, unshielded twisted-pair, or fiber-optic cable. Both types specify transmission speeds of up to 10 Mbps, and both use CSMA/CD as their media-access method.
LocalTalk		A proprietary architecture developed by Apple, and used in networks that run the AppleTalk networking software. LocalTalk supports data-transfer rates of 230.4 kbps for up to 32 nodes in a network. This architecture usually uses coaxial cable, but also supports twisted-pair cable.
Token Ring	1, 4, 16 Mbps	Usually associated with IBM. Token Ring is becoming increasingly popular as a network choice, despite its higher cost compared with Ethernet or ARCnet. Token Ring nodes are connected into a logical ring, regardless of the physical arrangement of the nodes in the network. Token Ring networks generally use special IBM cable, but fiber-optic cable can also be used. Token Ring architectures transmit at 4 or 16 Mbps. Token Ring networks use a token-passing media-access method.
ATM (Asynchronous Transfer Mode)		A packet-switched network architecture that can be used for both LANs and WANs. ATM uses either Category 5 unshielded twisted-pair (UTP) or fiber-optic cable. ATM networks have a very high potential bandwidth: initially 155 Mbps, but eventually reaching gigabit per second speeds. ATM uses a switching technology, so that multiple transmissions are possible at the same time.
FDDI (Fiber Distributed Data Interface)	FDDI-I, FDDI-II (HRC), CDDI, TPDDI	Uses light rather than electrical signals, and requires special optical fiber. FDDI networks can transmit at up to 100 Mbps. The architecture actually uses two rings, which carry the signal in opposite directions. FDDI networks also use a token-passing scheme to control media access. Several companies have implemented electrically-based versions of FDDI. These "copper" variants are sometimes known as CDDI or TPDDI (for twisted-pair distributed data interface).

a
b
c
d
e
f
g
h
i
j
k
l
m
n
o
p
q
r
s
t
u
v
w
x
y
z

Network Backbone

The main cabling for a network. This is the common cable to which servers and workstations are attached. For example, in a bus topology, each node on the network is attached either directly or over a shorter cable to the main network cable (the backbone).

Network, Back-End

A network that connects mainframes, mini-computers, and peripherals. A back-end network needs a very high bandwidth, so optical fiber is generally used as the transmission medium. FDDI is a popular architecture for this type of network.

Network, Baseband

A baseband network is one in which only a single channel is used for the entire network traffic. Unless specified otherwise, networks use baseband architectures.

A baseband network may actually use two channels, one in each direction, with each sharing part of the bandwidth. Even with just a single channel, it is possible for more than one packet to be on the network path at a given time. The two packets must be separated from each other by a time amount whose magnitude depends on the size of the network.

COMPARE
Network, Broadband

Network Board

An expansion board that makes a computer network-capable, also called *network adapter, LAN card, network interface card, NIC,* along with other names.

SEE
NIC (Network Interface Card)

Network, Broadband

A broadband network is one that either uses multiple channels simultaneously or that shares a total bandwidth with transmissions that are not part of the network activity. In either case, a single channel in a broadband network represents only part of the total bandwidth supported by the cable and the transmission scheme.

Broadband networks use special cable that is capable of supporting multiple channels. For example, CATV cable (the sort used for cable television connections) may be used for a network.

Filters

Because signals in a broadband network must be confined to a portion of the total bandwidth, filtering and other signal-cleaning measures are necessary. This confinement makes the signal more delicate and subject to distortion (for example, because some of the signal's harmonics, and therefore, some of its power, are lost).

Several types of filtering may be used to help clean a broadband transmission. The filters are distinguished by the filtering technique they use, as well as by where in the transmission process they are applied.

For example, filters applied early in the transmission, prior to modulation, are known as *baseband*, or *premodulation*, filters. Those applied after the modulation are known as *passband*, or *postmodulation*, filters. More complex filters, such as the raised-cosine type, operate in a more sophisticated manner.

Packet Padding

To compensate for the transmission errors that can arise because of distortion through filtering, broadband network architectures generally add additional header and trailer elements around the standard network packet.

For example, in a broadband Ethernet network, the Ethernet packet is framed with preambles and postambles. (The preamble actually uses some of the bits from the standard Ethernet packet, but encodes them differently to make the information more useful for a broadband transmission.)

Another way to reduce signal distortion is to use a more robust encoding method. For example, baseband Ethernet networks, along with most electrically based networks, use Manchester encoding to represent a bit value electrically. For various reasons, broadband Ethernet networks generally use NRZ (non-return to zero) encoding over parts of the transmission path.

Amplifiers

Amplifiers for broadband networks must perform to more stringent specifications and must produce much less distortion than amplifiers for baseband networks. Specifically, an amplifier for a broadband network must not have different amounts of distortion at different frequencies, because different channels would be affected differently in that case.

The amplifiers must also deal with much smaller voltages than in baseband networks. For example, whereas a signal in a baseband network may use two or more volts to represent a 1, the same value in a baseband network might be encoded with less than 100 millivolts (mV), and sometimes as low as 5 or 10 mV.

Collision Detection

Broadband networks cannot rely on the same methods as baseband networks to detect collisions. For example, a broadband Ethernet network must use a separate 4 megahertz (MHz) channel for collision detection. In contrast, a baseband Ethernet network simply needs to check the DC voltage on the wire.

COMPARE
Network, Baseband

Network, Campus

A network that connects nodes, or possibly departmental local-area networks, from multiple locations, which may be separated by a considerable distance. Unlike a wide-area network, a campus network does not require remote communications facilities, such as modems and telephones. This type of network is also known as a *campus-area network (CAN)*.

a
b
c
d
e
f
g
h
i
j
k
l
m
n
o
p
q
r
s
t
u
v
w
x
y
z

Network, Cell-Switched

A network that combines the guaranteed bandwidth of a circuit-switched network with the efficiency of a packet-switched network. ATM is an example of a cell-switched network. Compare this with circuit-switched, message-switched, and packet-switched networks.

Network, Cellular

A cellular network is an example of a wireless network. A cellular network uses frequencies in the 825 to 890 megahertz (MHz) range, and special stations (cells) for passing a signal from sender to receiver. The information is transmitted through the open air between the sender's antenna and transceivers in cells surrounding the sender.

To transmit data, the networks compete with cellular voice channels in the bandwidth. Various strategies have been developed for maximizing the amount of data that can be sent over cellular channels, even while those channels are used for voice transmissions.

Cellular networks can be an attractive alternative for corporations in which a few nodes may be scattered over several nearby buildings. The cost of cabling between those nodes may be prohibitive.

Because of the transmission medium, transceivers must be in the line of sight. This means that transmissions will often be noisy, and the range of the cellular network may be limited in cities where tall buildings can interfere.

One way to improve the performance of cellular systems is to digitize the voice signal, then compress the data before transmission. Another method is to use multiplexing methods for digital transmissions, such as TDMA (time division muliplexing access).

Radio frequency (RF), infrared, and microwave networks offer alternatives to the cellular approach.

Cellular Network Advantages

Cellular networks have the following advantages:

- Nodes can be mobile.

- Frequency ranges being used have a large potential bandwidth.

- There are cells in just about all the major metropolitan areas in the United States.

Cellular Network Disadvantages

Cellular networks have the following disadvantages:

- Line of sight is required between transceivers and nodes.

- Because transmissions are through open air, they are susceptible to eavesdropping and interference.

- Components and services are still relatively expensive.

- Because signals may need to be passed from cell to cell, there may be delays in the transmission. Some software and devices (for example, modems) get upset by such timeouts, and may stop working properly.

COMPARE

Network, Radio Wave; Network, Infrared; Network, Microwave

Network, Centralized

A network in which control of the network is concentrated in a single machine, known as the *host* (mainframe) or the *server* (PC). This is in contrast to a *distributed network,* in which control is shared by several or all of the nodes on a network. Mainframe-based networks are generally centralized; PC-based networks may be centralized (server-based) or distributed (peer-to-peer).

Network, Circuit-Switched

A circuit-switched network is one in which a dedicated circuit, or connection, is established temporarily between two parties on the network. This circuit remains in effect until the communication between the parties is completed. Each connection that is established gets a limited but guaranteed bandwidth for the duration of the connection.

The best example of circuit switching is the telephone system, which uses this method to route calls to the appropriate telephone exchange. Since a telephone conversation takes place in real time, it is important that the connection remain established until the parties are ready to hang up.

A circuit-switched network has a low latency (time before the network is ready for the transmission). Circuit-switched networks are most useful for constant bit rate data (such as voice), and are wasteful for data that comes in bursts.

COMPARE

Network, Cell-Switched; Network, Message-Switched; Network, Packet-Switched

Network Control Center (NCC)

SEE

NCC (Network Control Center)

Network Control System (NCS)

SEE

NCS (Network Control System)

Network, Departmental

A small- to medium-sized network (generally up to about 30 users) whose nodes share local resources, also known as a *departmental LAN* or a *departmental-area LAN (DAN).*

Network, Distributed

A network in which control of the network is shared among some or all of the nodes on a network. The best examples of distributed networks are peer-to-peer local-area networks (LANs) and UNIX-based networks. Distributed networks are in contrast to centralized networks, which may be host- or server-based, depending on whether the control is in a mainframe or a PC.

Network, Enterprise

An enterprise network is one that connects an entire organization. For example, an enterprise network may connect all branches of a bank or a corporation with a chain of

a
b
c
d
e
f
g
h
i
j
k
l
m
n
o
p
q
r
s
t
u
v
w
x
y
z

factories and stores. This type of network will often cover a wide area, and may even transcend national boundaries.

Components of Enterprise Networks

An enterprise network is likely to consist of multiple local-area networks (LANs), and may involve diverse hardware, network architectures, and operating environments. For example, an enterprise network may include everything from mainframes to palmtop (or at least subnotebook) computers. As a consequence, enterprise networks usually require routers or gateways.

Enterprise networks are both an attraction and a challenge. The challenge is to make very different and incompatible environments compatible with each other, or at least able to communicate. Existing environments were created without any thought to networking or integrating beyond the local group or department. The attraction is to succeed in unifying all the various means of communicating and computing.

Achieving Interoperability in Enterprise Networks

Interoperability refers to the ability of two different networks to communicate and work together, regardless of whether these networks use the same network architecture. This is vital to the success of enterprise networks.

In most cases, the difficulties arise when trying to connect the PC-based departmental and local-area networks (LANs) with the centralized and mainframe-based MIS (management information system), or "corporate," networks. This is because these two computing environments were created for different purposes and, as a result, the architectures and communications protocols are very different in these two worlds.

LANs and PC-based networks have been developed largely to assist personal and group productivity—by sharing files, data, and resources. Until recently, DOS-based PCs have been limited to 16-bit operation, with true 32-bit programming and operating environments appearing only recently in the DOS world. This processing bottleneck has imposed limitations on the kinds of tasks that are feasible in PC networking environments. Mainframe-based environments have been used for heavy-duty processing, such as processing of large databases, and for providing centralized access to computing resources.

Allowing LANs and Mainframes to Communicate

Network operating systems (NOSs) have various strategies available to enable LANs and mainframe networks to work together. The approach taken depends partly on whether the NOS is primarily a LAN- or a mainframe-based system.

LAN-based operating systems (for example, Novell's NetWare or Banyan's VINES) generally use their native protocol stack to communicate with the LAN end of the enterprise network. For example, a NetWare server might use NCP (NetWare Core Protocol) and the IPX/SPX protocols to communicate with stations on an Ethernet network and to provide file and print services to these workstations. Lower-level communications can be accomplished through ODI (Open Data-link Interface) drivers. This allows the server to support other protocol stacks (for example, the AppleTalk or TCP/IP stacks) when communicating with Macintosh or UNIX-based clients.

To communicate with the mainframe end of the enterprise network, NOSs may use a gateway that supports a protocol stack and networking architecture compatible with the mainframe environment. Because the mainframe will often be an IBM, the gateway will generally use the SNA (Systems Network Architecture) protocols.

With this approach, the server (with its gateway) sits between the LAN and the mainframe. The server provides the usual file and printing services to the LAN; the mainframe may provide processing for larger tasks. Workstations generally run their own applications.

Mainframe-based operating systems (such as MVS, VSE, or VMS) generally use a module that makes it possible to treat the LAN as just another session for the mainframe. For example in IBM environments, the SNA's APPC (Advanced Program to Program Communication) component allows a LAN (for example, a Token Ring network) to communicate with the mainframe as if the LAN were just another device on the mainframe's network. In this approach, the LAN is just another node on the mainframe's network. The mainframe provides print, file, and application services for its nodes.

Integrating a 32-Bit Operating System with a NOS

The distributed computing capabilities of a 32-bit operating system such as UNIX provide another way to create and control enterprise networks. By integrating a 32-bit operating system (for example, UnixWare)

with a NOS (for example, NetWare), it is possible to provide greater processing power on the server so that some of the critical applications can be done on servers instead of mainframes. UnixWare can provide application server capabilities, and NetWare can provide file and printer services.

Another benefit of this type of integration is that storage and data can be distributed. For example, files or data may be managed by UnixWare or by the NetWare server, depending on available storage and on user needs. Also, applications and processing power can be distributed. Workstations can run their personal applications just as on a LAN, but can get access to the capabilities of the UnixWare system if necessary.

BROADER CATEGORY
Network

▼ Network, Front-End

A network of high-performance, special-purpose workstations (such as graphics or engineering machines). For maximum bandwidth, such machines will be connected using optical fiber.

▼ Network, Global-Area (GAN)

SEE
GAN (Network, Global-Area)

▼ Network, Heterogeneous

A network that is using multiple protocols at the network layer. In contrast, a homogeneous network uses a single protocol at the network layer.

Network, Homogeneous

A network that is using a single protocol at the network layer. In contrast, a heterogeneous network uses multiple protocols at the network layer.

Network, Host-Based

A network in which control of the network is concentrated or centralized in a mainframe. If the controller node is a PC, the network is said to be *server-based*. Host-based networks are examples of centralized networks, and are in contrast to distributed networks in which no single node has control of the network.

Network, Hybrid

A network that includes a mixture of topologies, such as both bus and star.

Network, Infrared

An infrared network is a type of wireless network. An infrared network uses signals in the infrared range of the electromagnetic spectrum, in which the frequencies are in the hundreds of terahertz (THz).

Infrared networks work only over relatively short distances. They require either a line of sight between sender and receiver or a surface off which the signal can be reflected to the receiver.

No license is required for infrared networks. InfraLAN from BICC Communications is an infrared network that operates like a Token Ring network.

SEE ALSO
Infrared Transmission

Network Management

The purpose of network management is to automate the processes of monitoring and adjusting the performance of a network, as well as providing reports about network activity. Network management models are built around managed objects, which are any network elements that can be used or monitored. These models generally specify the kinds of attributes managed objects must have and the kinds of functions associated with them.

A network management configuration generally involves a *managing process*, which runs on a *managing station*. The managing process collects performance and other data about the network or about particular nodes on the network. This information is actually gathered by *managing agents*, which are programs that monitor workstations and that can report this information to a managing process. The details of this monitoring and reporting process help distinguish different network management models.

Network management is generally implemented as a high-level application, so that the management software uses well-established protocol suites, such as the TCP/IP protocols, to do its work and to move its information around.

Various models have been proposed for network management. The two most comprehensive proposals are the models developed for the Internet Protocol (IP, or TCP/IP) and for the ISO's seven-layer

OSI (Open Systems Interconnection) model. In addition, major network management packages still rely on mainframe-based management models, such as those developed by IBM, DEC, and AT&T.

The IP Management Model

The IP management model was developed for the Internet community in a series of RFC (Request For Comment) documents. The model's simplicity and portability have made it popular even outside the Internet community; it is arguably the most widely implemented network management model available. Most network management packages support it.

The components of the IP model have been updated and improved (as MIB-II and SNMP version 2). The effort and improvements indicate clearly that this "interim" network management solution is not going away.

The major components within this model are SMI (structure of management information), MIB (management information base), and SNMP (Simple Network Management Protocol).

SMI

The SMI component specifies how information about managed objects is to be represented. This representation uses a restricted version of the ISO's Abstract Syntax Notation One (ASN.1) system.

SMI relies heavily on ASN.1 notation, and represents a flexible way to organize and represent information—a method that is, for all practical purposes, infinitely extendible.

Information about management and other network elements is represented as properties associated with the element (object), along with values for some or all of these properties. To help organize or group this object information, additional elements are introduced.

The body of such information can be represented as a tree. Each managed object (network, station, application, function, setting, and so on) has a unique location in the tree. A tree can have branches, called *subtrees,* and these subtrees can have branches of their own. Each subtree is anchored by a root element. The intermediate root elements are generally organizational elements (as opposed to managed objects).

Leaf elements are those at the ends of branches; that is, they are the elements with no branches extending from them. These elements contain information about objects, often about specific objects.

Each managed network can provide content for a local information tree. In order to help provide order and common references, a global information tree is being constructed. This tree contains information about the objects defined in specifications for networking and other computer- and communications-related projects.

One of the branches on this global tree is administered by the ISO. This branch, which is named iso(1), contains the information used by network management packages. The administrator for a branch can grant branches on the subtree to particular organizations or vendors who can, in turn, grant branches on their branches to other organizations, etc. For example, the ISO administers a branch, org(3), under which nonprofit organizations can grow subtrees. The figure "Management information in the global information tree" illustrates this relationship.

Of most relevance for network management is the fact that special-purpose objects or MIBs can be defined and added to the global tree. Specific products can thus draw on a large standardized body of management information, which makes it much easier to create standardized and portable network management products.

The syntax for defining objects in this way is discussed in several RFCs, which are available through the Internet.

MIB

In the IP management model, the MIB contains the definitions and values for the managed objects relevant to a particular network. The information for the MIB component is acquired and updated by a *management agent,* which is a program whose task is to determine and report the information desired by a network management program. Each agent has an information base for the agent's network element; the management station can get information from this MIB through the agent.

The original version of this database was released in May 1990. The intent was to release successive versions of MIB, with each being a back-compatible extension. In this spirit, MIB-II (or MIB-2) was released in March of 1991.

For various reasons, the continued expansion of a generic MIB has been abandoned in favor of a scheme that allows extensions (such as those for a specific network or

networking product) to be defined as separate nodes.

SNMP

SNMP is the protocol used to represent management information for transmission. Originally conceived as an interim protocol, to be replaced by the ISO's CMIS/CMIP model, SNMP has proven remarkably durable. In fact, a new and improved version, SNMP version 2, was proposed in 1992.

SNMP provides communications at the applications layer in the OSI Reference Model. This protocol is simple but powerful enough to accomplish its task. SNMP uses a management station and management agents who communicate with this station. The station is located at the node that is running the network management program.

SNMP agents monitor the desired objects in their environment, package this information in the appropriate manner, and ship it to the management station, either immediately or upon request.

In the global tree, there is a branch for SNMP under the MIB-2 node. (This branch was not defined in MIB-I.) There are also entries for SNMPv2 (an extended implementation that includes security features) in other parts of the global tree.

In addition to packets for processing requests and moving packets in and out of a node, the SNMP includes traps. A *trap* is a special packet that is sent from an agent to a station to indicate that something unusual has occurred. Novell's management products, including NetWare Management System (NMS) Runtime, NetWare Management Agent, NetWare Hub Services, and LANalyzer for Windows, support SNMP.

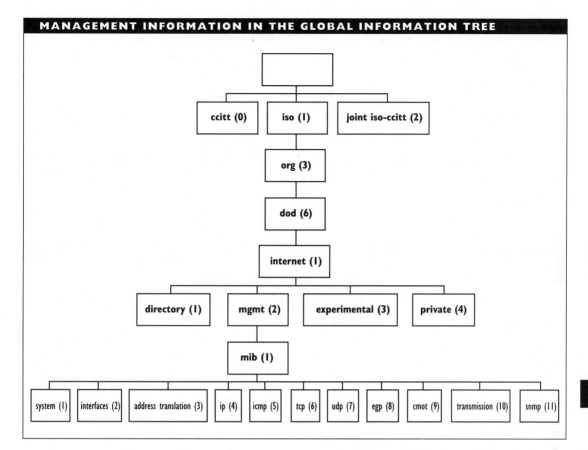

MANAGEMENT INFORMATION IN THE GLOBAL INFORMATION TREE

The OSI Management Model

The open systems-based management model from the OSI is arguably the most widely discussed network management model (the IP model is almost certainly more widely *implemented*).

With its emphasis on open systems, the OSI model is designed to operate in any conceivable environment. By building on the seven-layer OSI model, the OSI system is guaranteed to have at least functional portability at each of the layers.

The OSI model has several important components:

- SMAP (systems management application process), which carries out the network management functions on a single machine. The SMAP may serve as a network manager or as an agent.

- SMAE (systems management application entity), which communicates with other nodes, including the network manager, which is the machine that is in charge of the network management tasks. SMAEs use CMIP (Common Management Information Protocol) packets to communicate.

- LME (layer management entity), which provides network management functions that are specific to a particular layer. Each layer has its own LME.

- MIB (management information base), which contains the network management information received from each node.

The relationship of these elements is summarized in the figure "Major components in the OSI network management model."

SMAE

An SMAE must do a lot of work to process management information and to communicate with other nodes. Functionally, an SMAE is organized as shown in the figure "The internal structure of an SMAE."

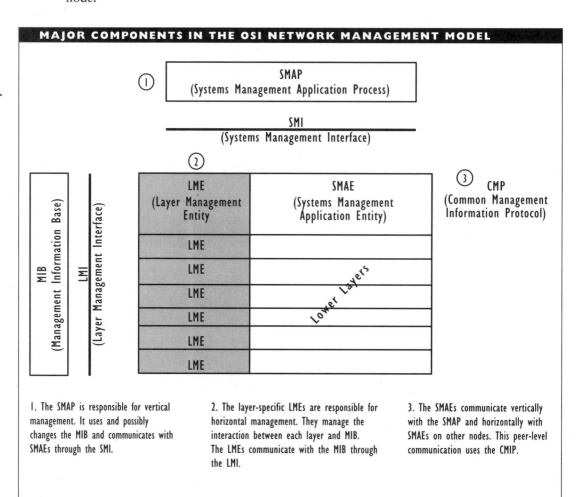

MAJOR COMPONENTS IN THE OSI NETWORK MANAGEMENT MODEL

1. The SMAP is responsible for vertical management. It uses and possibly changes the MIB and communicates with SMAEs through the SMI.

2. The layer-specific LMEs are responsible for horizontal management. They manage the interaction between each layer and MIB. The LMEs communicate with the MIB through the LMI.

3. The SMAEs communicate vertically with the SMAP and horizontally with SMAEs on other nodes. This peer-level communication uses the CMIP.

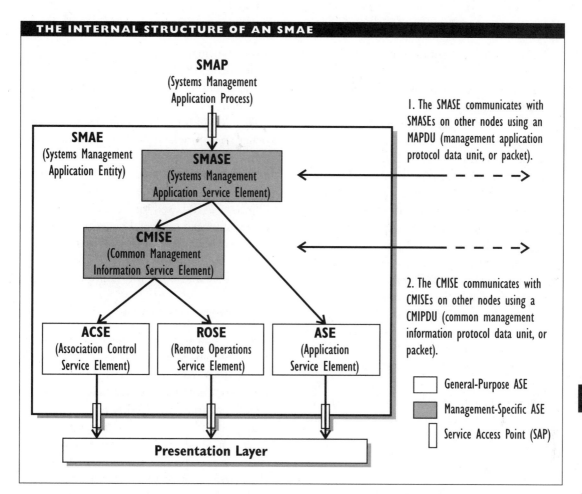

THE INTERNAL STRUCTURE OF AN SMAE

SMAP
(Systems Management
Application Process)

SMAE
(Systems Management
Application Entity)

SMASE
(Systems Management
Application Service Element)

CMISE
(Common Management
Information Service Element)

ACSE
(Association Control
Service Element)

ROSE
(Remote Operations
Service Element)

ASE
(Application
Service Element)

Presentation Layer

1. The SMASE communicates with SMASEs on other nodes using an MAPDU (management application protocol data unit, or packet).

2. The CMISE communicates with CMISEs on other nodes using a CMIPDU (common management information protocol data unit, or packet).

☐ General-Purpose ASE
▨ Management-Specific ASE
☐ Service Access Point (SAP)

The SMASE (systems management application service element) represents the working element in the SMAE. This element relies on both a management service element, called CMISE (common management information service element), and a non-management service element, called ASE (application service element).

Both SMASE and CMISE have well-defined packet formats, and may exchange information with their counterparts in other nodes. Such communications use management application protocol data units (MAP-DUs) or common management protocol data units (CMIPDUs).

a b c d e f g h i j k l **m** n o p q r s t u v w x y z

Management Levels

The components operate at either of two levels of network management specified in the ISO model: systems management or layer management.

Systems management encompasses five major areas and more than a dozen function classes. This is what is generally meant when network management is discussed. The SMAP and SMAE together make up the systems management capabilities.

Layer management encompasses the objects and functions that provide network management services at specific layers in the OSI Reference Model. These capabilities are needed to ensure that the network management package can communicate at whatever level is necessary.

In addition to these levels of management, the OSI model describes services and protocols that can be used to carry out network management tasks, as well as the format in which management information can be stored and retrieved.

CMIS and CMIP

Network management tasks are accomplished using CMIS (common management information services), which rely on CMIP to transfer information. Together, the services and protocol can provide all the capabilities needed to accomplish the network management tasks.

MIB

Storage format is specified through a MIB, which determines the representation, storage, and retrieval of management information.

The MIB for the OSI model is much richer and more flexible than the information base for the IP model. For example, whereas functions using SNMP can manipulate only attribute values for existing objects, CMIP-based functions can create or delete managed objects if necessary. Both models rely on the global information tree created by the ISO and CCITT to represent networking and other information.

Systems Management Domains

The OSI management model describes five major systems management domains, as well as the functions used by these domains. The domains, known as systems management functional areas (SMFAs), are accounting management, configuration management, fault management, performance management, and security management. Each of these areas is discussed in its own article.

The SMFAs use the lower-level systems management functions (SMFs) listed in the table "Systems Management Functions" to accomplish their work.

Each node being monitored will have an agent (an SMAE) whose job is to monitor the node's performance in the functional areas of interest. The information collected by the agent is passed to a managing process and stored in a MIB.

SYSTEMS MANAGEMENT FUNCTIONS	
SMF	**DESCRIPTION**
Object management	Create, delete, examine, and update objects; report that such manipulations have taken place
State management	Monitor objects' management states; report when these states are changed
Relationship management	Establish, monitor, and view the relationships among objects
Alarm reporting	Provide notice of and information about faults, errors, or other abnormalities in network operation
Event reporting	Select events to be reported; specify the destinations for such reports
Log control	Specify how to handle event logs, such as what to add, when to add events, and how often to create new logs
Security alarm reporting	Provide notice of and information about faults, errors, or other abnormalities related to network security
Security audit trail	Specify the events and event formats to be used for a security log
Access control	Control access to management information and operations
Account metering	Specify a model for the objects and measures needed to keep track of resource usage, generate accounting and billing for such use, and enforce any accounting limits associated with a particular user
Workload monitoring	Specify a model for the objects and attributes needed to monitor; report on the performance of network components
Summarization	Specify a model for objects used to analyze and summarize network management information
Test management	Specify a model for objects that are used to test network components and services

CMISE

SMFs rely on CMISEs to do the necessary work. The figure "Components and their relationships in systems management in the OSI model" shows the chain of commands used to perform systems management.

A CMISE consists of two components: CMIS and CMIP. The CMIS provides an interface through which a user can access the available services. The CMIP provides a way to package the data and service requests.

A CMISE provides three types of service:

- Management association services, which are necessary to enable applications to establish connections with

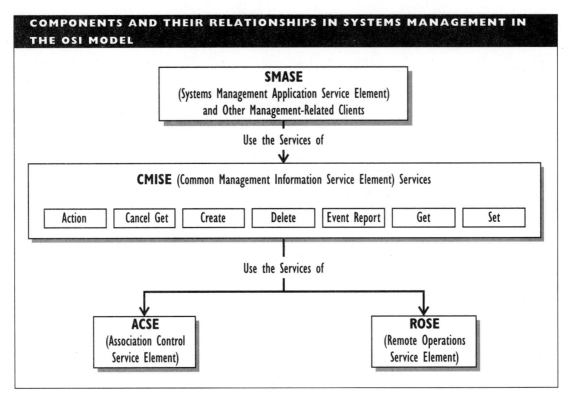

COMPONENTS AND THEIR RELATIONSHIPS IN SYSTEMS MANAGEMENT IN THE OSI MODEL

SMASE
(Systems Management Application Service Element)
and Other Management-Related Clients

Use the Services of

CMISE (Common Management Information Service Element) Services

| Action | Cancel Get | Create | Delete | Event Report | Get | Set |

Use the Services of

ACSE
(Association Control
Service Element)

ROSE
(Remote Operations
Service Element)

each other. Using these services (which are actually provided for the CMISE by the ACSE), two applications can establish the ground rules for their connection, the types of information they can exchange, and the types of application service elements and common management information services allowed in the communication. These ground rules form an application context.

- Management notification services, which report events involving managed objects to an authorized user (that is, client). Actually, this category consists of only a single action. The management notification service is analogous, in some ways, to the SNMP trap messages, which also serve to report about a particular state in an object.

- Management operation services, which carry out the tasks necessary to manage the network. These tasks include creating or deleting objects, reading or changing attribute values, and so on.

Certain services (for example, those that create or delete an object) require confirmation from the process involved that the service was carried out. Other services, such as changing attribute values, do not require such confirmation. (To determine whether an unconfirmed action was carried out, a process needs to check the new value.)

Actions can be performed on multiple objects, which can be specified using special parameters. In addition, CMIS provides sophisticated filtering capabilities that can be used to select just the attributes (or attribute values) to be selected or changed.

These powerful selection capabilities, along with the ability to create or delete managed objects, make the OSI management model more complex than the IP model, and also make the two models relatively incompatible. Converting from OSI to IP format, known in the IP community as *de-osifying,* is not a simple task.

Note that the CMISE relies on lower-level and more specialized service elements, the application control service element (ACSE) and the remote operations service element (ROSE), to accomplish some of its tasks. CMIP also uses ROSE to transfer CMPIDUs.

ROSE operations may be synchronous or asynchronous; they may be confirmed, unconfirmed, or partially confirmed (report success or failure, but not both). Applications that use ROSE to work together may do so under any of three relationships (association classes):

- Association class 1: Only the application that initiates the association can invoke operations.

- Association class 2: Only the application that responds to the association can invoke operations.

- Association class 3: Either the initiating or responding application can invoke operations.

CMISE always uses association class 3, so that either application can invoke any required operations.

Mainframe-Based Management Models

Network management models based on mainframe networks operate from a central host. The most widely used mainframe model is IBM's NMA (Network Management Architecture), which is an extension of SNA (Systems Network Architecture).

NMA is concerned with four types of management: configuration management, problem management, performance and accounting management, and change management.

NMA is implemented through NetView, which has long been IBM's premier management package for SNA-based networks. The management software will run on the host, which is the focal point for the network management. This host will request various types of data from SNA-compliant devices at entry points and from non-IBM devices at service points. NetView uses the NMVT (Network Management Vector Transport) protocol to transmit management information. See the NMA article for more information.

Other Models

Although they are not as comprehensive as the ISO management model, other network management models have been proposed. Two of the more comprehensive are AT&T's UNMA (Unified Network Management

Architecture) and Digital Equipment Corporation's EMA (Enterprise Management Architecture). Both models are discussed in their own articles.

These models can be distinguished on the basis of a few fundamental features:

- Whether the model is centralized, distributed, or both.

- Whether the model is concerned primarily with applications or with hardware.

- Whether the model is limited to LANs or WANs or whether it is independent of network size.

Location of Management Components

In a centralized model, all the management work is carried out by a single process or node. Such models tend to be CPU-based, and are similar to the host-centric models that have prevailed for so long in the mainframe world.

In a distributed model, each node has certain network management capabilities. The monitoring and data gathering are done independently by each node, and the results are reported to the central processing node, which will do the data analyses.

Some models may include both centralized and distributed features. For example, nodes on a network may be able to gather data, but may need to do so at the command of a central machine.

Focus of Model

Some network management models are concerned primarily with monitoring applications and transmissions; others are concerned with monitoring the state of the hardware during network activity.

A software-based model will provide usage, availability, and performance data about the applications on the network. In contrast, a hardware-based model will provide information about how hardware resources are used.

Scope of Model

While LAN and WAN management share many features, there are some important differences, including the following:

- Much LAN traffic is broadcast, which means a management package can collect at least some data passively. In contrast, the telecommunications link used in a WAN forces the management package to take an active part in the transmission.

- LAN networks are generally homogeneous; WAN networks may be heterogeneous.

- Because WAN transmissions may need to go through multiple switching networks, response times become much less reliable as indicators of network activity than in LANs.

Network Management Tools

The network management capabilities are usually implemented in software. The management tools may be specialized (for example, collecting just performance data) or comprehensive.

Tools must have monitoring, reporting, and analysis capabilities. Those tools that will serve as managing processes—as the control programs for the network management—also need control capabilities.

In general, the management models do not specify the details of how these capabilities are to be implemented. For example, programs may report data in text or graphics form. Programs will also differ in their monitoring capabilities.

The tools may be designed for LAN or WAN management or both. Although many of the tasks are the same for managing both LANs and WANs, there are some important differences, mainly with respect to reporting and timing.

Management tools that are designed to manage both LANs and WANs are sometimes known as SuperManagers, and they are part of even more comprehensive architectures. Examples of SuperManagers include the following:

- IBM's NetView, which operates within IBM's SNA

- AT&T's Accumaster Integrator, which operates within AT&T's UNMA (Universal Network Management Architecture)

- DEC's DECmcc Director, which operates within Digital's EMA (Enterprise Management Architecture)

Management tools may use text, graphics, sound, or some combination of these, to report data and analyses.

A comprehensive catalog of network management tools is published occasionally as an RFC. The most recent of these is RFC 1470, published in June 1993.

PRIMARY SOURCES

IP management model: RFC 1155 (SMI), RFCs 1156 and 1213 (MIB-I and II), RFC 1157 (SNMP); RFCs 1441 through 1452 (SNMPv2)

OSI network management model: ISO documents 10733 and 10737 (layer management), CCITT X.73x and X.74x series and the ISO 10164-x series (systems management), CCITT X.71x series and ISO 9595-x and 9596-x series (CMIS and CMIP), CCITT X.72x series and ISO 10165-x series (MIB)

SEE ALSO

Accounting Management; Configuration Management; EMA (Enterprise Management Architecture); Fault Management; Global Tree; MIB (Management Information Base); NetView; NMA (Network Management Architecture); Performance Management; Protocol, SNMP; Security Management; SMI (Structure of Management Information); UNMA (Unified Network Management Architecture)

▼
Network Management Entity (NME)

SEE

NME (Network Management Entity)

▼
Network Management Vector Transport (NMVT)

SEE

NMVT (Network Management Vector Transport)

Network, Message-Switched

A message-switched network is one in which messages from multiple users can travel along the network at the same time. The messages may be stored temporarily, and then forwarded to the destination by routing, or switching, the message through intermediate nodes until the message reaches its destination. Because of this message handling technique, message-switched networks are also known as store-and-forward networks. Electronic mail (e-mail) handling services are examples of message switching.

This method collects an entire message and then passes the message to its destination. This is in contrast to packet switching, in which the individual packets that make up a message are passed from source to destination (possibly in a haphazard order), and are then reassembled at the destination.

COMPARE

Network, Circuit-Switched; Network, Packet-Switched

Network, Microwave

A microwave network is an example of a wireless network. A microwave network uses signals in the gigahertz (GHz) range of the electromagnetic spectrum. Such networks beam signals at antennas, from which the signal is broadcast to other nodes.

Networks use either an earth-based antenna or a satellite in geosynchronous orbit as the retransmission point. With a satellite, the signal can be transmitted thousands of miles; with earth-based antennas, the signal is limited to a few kilometers.

Microwave technology uses transmissions in the gigabit per second range, so that this technology begins at the upper limit of radio waves.

Like radio waves, the microwave spectrum requires licensing from the FCC (Federal Communications Commission). Microwave transmissions are very susceptible to eavesdropping, jamming, and interference (from natural or electrical sources).

SEE ALSO

Microwave Transmission

Network Modem

A modem that is also a separate station on a network. This modem has its own network interface card, and it is connected directly to the network as a node. A remote caller accesses the network through this node. A network modem can work as an access server.

Network Number

In a Novell NetWare environment, a hexadecimal value that uniquely identifies a network or a network cable segment. It is also known as the *IPX external network number.*

SEE ALSO

IPX Network Numbers and Internetwork Addresses

Network, Packet-Switched

A packet-switched network is one in which packets from multiple transmissions can travel along the network at the same time. The packets are simply routed, or switched, from source to destination using whatever temporary path is appropriate. A packet contains source and destination addresses (and also sequence information), so that packets can be passed from node to node until they reach their destination, and reassembled there.

For packet switching to work, the receiver must be able to reconstitute the transmission from the individual packets. This chore generally is the responsibility of a component or program that operates at the transport layer of the OSI Reference Model.

Networks that involve large-scale data transmissions for many users at the same time (for example, private or public data lines) use packet switching. Many of these services comply with the X.25 standard, which provides an interface between a user and the packet-switched network. This interface includes PADs (packet assemblers/disassemblers) to make sure that a transmission is in packets before being sent onto the network and that the transmitted packets are reassembled before being passed to the receiver.

The performance of a packet-switched network depends in part on the protocol preparing the packets for the network. In some cases, packets are quite small (for example, 128 bytes in the XMODEM communications protocol), which can slow down the transmission. On the other hand, if packets are too large, the likelihood of an erroneous bit in the packet increases, as does the cost of retransmission if that happens.

Packet-switched networks are most useful for data that come in bursts. Such networks are unsuited for voice transmission (which requires a constant data rate) because delays can occur in transmission, packets can reach their destination "out of order," and the network may not be available immediately for transmission.

COMPARE
Network, Circuit-Switched; Network, Message-Switched

▼ Network, Peer-to-Peer

A network in which each node is assumed to have processing capabilities, and in which nodes can be servers or workstations as required, so that nodes are functionally equal. In a peer-to-peer network, nodes can use each other's resources and can provide available resources to other nodes. This is in contrast to a server-based network, in which one or more machines have special status as dedicated servers. Novell's Personal NetWare, Microsoft's Windows for Workgroups, and Artisoft's LANTastic are examples of peer-to-peer networks.

SEE ALSO
LAN (Local-Area Network)

▼ Network, Premises

A premises network is confined to a single building, but covers that building completely.

▼ Network, Radio

A radio network is an example of a wireless network. In such a network, communication is accomplished using radio wave transmissions. In such a transmission strategy, radio waves are broadcast in all directions,

a b c d e f g h i j k l m **n** o p q r s t u v w x y z

and can be picked up by any station with a suitable receiver. This makes radio waves suitable for broadcast situations in which security is not an issue.

Radio waves can penetrate walls, and do not require a line-of-sight connection between sender and receiver, which makes radio networks more flexible than wireless networks based on infrared or microwave transmissions.

Radio waves may be used for single-frequency or spread-spectrum transmissions. In single-frequency transmissions, the signal is encoded within a narrow frequency range. With such a signal, all the energy is concentrated at a particular frequency range. This signal is susceptible to jamming and eavesdropping. Depending on the frequency range being used, you may need a license to operate a single-frequency network.

Motorola's Altair system is an example of a single-frequency network. These networks operate within a frequency range that requires licensing, but the vendor takes care of that. Motorola must also assign you a frequency within which to operate, to ensure that your network does not interfere with another such network in the area. The Altair system operates as an Ethernet network.

In spread-spectrum transmissions, the signal is distributed over a broad frequency range, or spectrum. Spread-spectrum signals are extremely unlikely to interfere with other transmissions, since the other transmission would need to be using the same spreading algorithm. Spread-spectrum networks do not require licensing, at least not within the frequency range covered by such products (see ISM).

WaveLAN from NCR is an example of a spread-spectrum network. The hardware comes on an adapter card, and includes a transmitter and an antenna. The transmitter is capable of sending a 250 milliwatt signal for up to 245 meters (800 feet) under ideal outdoor conditions, or about a third of that distance under ordinary indoor conditions.

SEE ALSO
Radio Wave Transmission

Network, Server-Based

A network in which one or more nodes have special status as dedicated servers. Other nodes must go through a server for resources on other machines. This is in contrast to a peer-to-peer network, in which each node may be either server or workstation as the need arises. Larger networks are more likely to be server-based, as are networks with sensitive or critical information. NetWare from Novell, VINES from Banyan Systems, and AppleTalk from Apple can each be used to create server-based networks.

SEE ALSO
LAN (Local-Area Network).

Network Service Access Point (NSAP)

SEE
NSAP (Network Service Access Point)

Network, Shared-Media

A shared-media network is one in which all nodes share the same line, so that only a single transmission is possible at one time. This is in contrast to a switched network, in which multiple lines can be active at a time. Adding nodes to a shared-media network merely increases the traffic; it does not increase the capacity.

The standard network architectures—Ethernet, ARCnet, and Token Ring—create shared-media networks, at least in the architectures' basic forms.

In contrast, up-and-coming architectures, such as ATM (Asynchronous Transfer Mode), are switched networks. These architectures can support multiple channels at a time. In the case of ATM architectures, these channels can have very high bandwidths.

Enhancements for standard architectures can also provide limited switching capabilities. For example, switched-hub technology can enable multiple transmissions at the same time over an Ethernet network. Similarly, ETR (early token release) makes it possible to have multiple packets moving around a Token Ring network at the same time.

COMPARE
Network, Switched

Network Station

A machine that is linked to a network. The network station can be either a workstation or a server.

Network, Switched

A switched network is one in which temporary connections between two nodes are established when needed. Routing a transmission through such temporary connections is known as *switching*. Switching is used for networks on which many nodes, or parties, may be accessing the network at the same time.

Three types of switched networks are in common use:

- Circuit-switched. The telephone system is the best example of a circuit-switched network.

- Message-switched. Electronic mail (e-mail) handling services that store messages and then forward them to their destination are examples of message-switched networks.

- Packet-switched: Networks designed for large-scale data transmission. For example, public or private phone services using the X.25 standard or the proposed Data Highway, generally use packet switching.

Each of these types of networks is discussed in a separate article.

Because connections are established as needed, switched networks can handle transmissions from multiple nodes at the same time. This is in contrast to a shared-media network (such as an Ethernet network), in which only a single transmission can be traveling at a time.

COMPARE
Network, Shared-Media

Network, Wireless

A wireless network is one that does not rely on cable as the communications medium. Such networks are also known as LAWNs (local-area wireless networks). The IEEE 802.11 workgroup is responsible for developing a standard for wireless networking.

a b c d e f g h i j k l m **n** o p q r s t u v w x y z

Wireless networks are used for purposes such as the following:

- Connecting machines within a building

- Connecting portable or mobile machines to a network

- Keeping a mobile machine in contact with a database

- Ad hoc networks (for example, in committee or business meetings)

Wireless networks use signals that cover a broad frequency range, from a few megahertz to a few terahertz. Depending on the frequencies involved, the network is known as a radio wave, microwave, or infrared network.

Wireless Network Groupings

Radio wave networks operate at frequencies anywhere from a few megahertz (MHz) to about 3 gigahertz (GHz), and they use either a single-frequency or spread-spectrum transmission strategy. Radio frequencies must be licensed from the FCC (Federal Communications Commission).

A single-frequency strategy transmits within a single, generally small, frequency band. This is susceptible to eavesdropping, interference, and jamming. In contrast, a spread-spectrum strategy distributes the transmission across a broader frequency range. The "spreading" sequence may be determined at random, and must be known to the receiver. This strategy is difficult to intercept without knowing the spreading sequence, and is unlikely to interfere with other transmissions.

Microwave networks use frequencies in the gigahertz range. At the low end, microwave overlaps with radio wave, since these terms are not associated with explicit boundaries. In fact, only some sources distinguish a separate microwave category. Others use radio wave to refer to the spectrum up to about 6 GHz.

Microwave networks use either an earth-based antenna or a satellite in geosynchronous orbit as the retransmission point. With a satellite, the signal can be transmitted thousands of miles; with earth-based antennas, the signal is limited to a few kilometers.

The microwave spectrum requires licensing from the FCC. Microwave transmissions are very susceptible to eavesdropping, jamming, and interference (from natural or electrical sources).

Infrared networks use frequencies ranging from a few hundred GHz to about 1 terahertz (THz), just below the visible light spectrum. These waves require a line-of-sight connection between sender and receiver or between each of these and a common cell. An infrared signal can be focused or diffuse.

A focused signal is aimed directly at the target (receiver or cell), or the signal may be beamed at a surface and reflected off this to a receiver. This type of signal can travel over a greater range but only to a specific target. In contrast, a diffuse signal travels in multiple directions, but is much weaker in each direction. As a result, the range of a diffuse signal is much smaller than that of a focused signal.

No license is required for infrared networks.

Wireless Network Standards

The IEEE 802.11 working group on wireless networking has published comprehensive specifications for wireless network architectures. Separate protocols are needed for the data-link and the physical layers.

The DFWMAC (Distributed Foundation Wireless Media Access Control) protocol was adopted in 1993 as the standard MAC protocol. DFWMAC supports transmissions of at least 1 megabit per second (Mbps), and uses the CSMA/CA (carrier sense multiple access/collision avoidance) medium-access method, but requires acknowledgment that a transmitted packet was received.

The DFWMAC protocol can work with any of multiple physical layer protocols. These protocols are distinguished in part by the frequency band in which they are being used. The table "Frequency Band Allocations" shows the frequency bands that have been allocated (or freed) by the FCC for the specified uses.

With the help of a PCF (point coordination function), DFWMAC can even handle time-sensitive transmissions such as video. This is possible because the PCF helps grab the transmission for enough time to transmit a superframe, which contains the time-sensitive information.

NETX.COM

NETX.COM is a network shell program for workstations in pre-4.*x* versions of Novell's NetWare. NETX is used to establish a connection with the NetWare operating system running on the server. Earlier versions of this program are DOS version-specific, and are named NET3, 4, 5, or 6, depending on the major DOS version. For example, NET5.COM was for DOS version 5.*x*. NETX.COM was developed to be DOS

FREQUENCY BAND ALLOCATIONS	
BANDWIDTH	**USE**
824-849 MHz, 869-894 MHz	Cellular communications
896-901 MHz, 930-931 MHz	Private, land-based mobile communications (for example, radio and mobile data services)
902-928 MHz	Unlicensed commercial use (for example, cordless phones and wireless LANs). Formerly allocated for industrial, scientific, and medical (ISM) usage
931-932 MHz	Common-carrier paging services
932-935 MHz, 941-944 MHz	Point-to-point or point-to-multipoint communications
1.85-1.97 GHz, 2.13-2.15 GHz, 2.18-2.2 GHz	Commercial and noncommercial PCS (personal communications services)
2.4-2.5 GHz, 5.8-5.9 GHz	Unlicensed commercial use

a b c d e f g h i j k l m **n** o p q r s t u v w x y z

version-independent, effectively replacing these earlier versions.

NETX runs on top of DOS, and takes over certain critical DOS interrupts:

- 21H (the standard function dispatcher)

- 17H (used to send data to printer ports)

- 24H (the critical error handler vector)

With control of these interrupts, NETX intercepts user or application requests. If these are intended for the network, NETX encodes the requests or commands using the NCP (NetWare Control Protocol), and passes the constructed packet down through the IPX and data-link layers for transmission on the network. NETX communicates with the network driver either through Novell's ODI (Open Data-link Interface) or through a hardware-specific driver.

In NetWare version 4.*x*, NETX.COM has been replaced by the NetWare DOS Requester.

BROADER CATEGORY
NetWare

COMPARE
DOS Requester

RELATED ARTICLES
IPX.COM, SPX.COM

▼
NETx.VLM

In Novell's NetWare 4.*x*, NETx.VLM is a Virtual Loadable Module (VLM) that runs as part of the NetWare DOS Requester and that serves to provide backward-compatibility with earlier NetWare versions, which use

a network shell (NETx.COM) to direct user and application requests to DOS or to the network.

News

On the Internet, News is an information-sharing service that enables users to exchange messages about topics of mutual interest or just to look in and see what messages others are contributing to the exchange. In short, network news provides an interactive forum in which users can discuss ideas about particular or general topics. News is also known as *Net News, Network News* and *Usenet News.*

This open forum, in which messages are available for public viewing and reaction, is in contrast to the more personal mail service. One of the reasons a news service was developed on UNIX systems was to provide a more convenient way to exchange ideas and to hold conferences.

News messages are *posted* to a *newsgroup,* which is a collection of messages about a topic. Newsgroups are organized hierarchically, using subgroupings under seven general newsgroup categories. The newsgroups in these categories—or the network locations that distribute these newsgroups—make up the Usenet. As of mid-1995, there were almost 15,000 newsgroups.

Usenet sites mirror (maintain copies of) or distribute the messages for the following top-level categories, and possibly more.

comp: computer science and related topics

news: announcements and information about Usenet and news-related software

rec: hobbies, arts, crafts, music, and other recreational activities

sci: scientific research, advances, and applications for scientific fields other than computer science

soc: topics of social relevance—with "social" defined just about any way you want it to be

talk: debate and heated (or long-winded) discussion about controversial topics

misc: categories that don't fit into any of the others in the list

The first of the following categories is not officially one of the high-level categories handled by Usenet machines. It is, however, distributed by most of them. The other categories may not be as easily accessible.

alt: groups that haven't been officially accepted as official by the Usenet community or groups that don't (want to) fit into any of the categories (including **misc**)

bix: business-related topics and announcements—including advertisements

gnu: the GNU (GNU's Not UNIX) development project and the works of the Free Software Foundation (FSF)

k12: teaching-related topics for grades kindergarten through high school

de and fj: discussions in German and Japanese, respectively

Within the high-level categories, there are subcategories, which have their own subcategories. This process can go through several levels. For example, *rec.sport.football.australian*, *rec.sport.football.canadian*, *rec.sport.football.college*, *rec.sport.football.fantasy*, and *rec.sport.football.pro* can all be found under the rec category. Similarly, you can find newsgroups such as *alt.gopher* (Gopher internet utility), *comp.lang.perl.misc* (Perl programming language), *at.astronomie* (astronomy in Austria), and *scruz.poetry* (poetry readings in Santa Cruz, CA). Note that the highest level in the hierarchy is the leftmost part of the name, with deeper levels being further to the right.

Newsreader programs generally keep a list of available newsgroups, and update this list each time you connect to the news server. Many newsreaders keep this list in text format. It's sometimes more convenient to just read this file to determine what newsgroups are available. It's possible to configure most newsreaders so that they report any newsgroups formed since the user last logged on.

Certain newsgroups—those in the *alt.binaries.** hierarchy—deal almost entirely in image files. While many of these are sexually-oriented, others contain computer art, graphs of fractal equations, etc. Files containing binary images must be processed in a special manner.

a b c d e f g h i j k l m **n** o p q r s t u v w x y z

Getting the News

The news materials—that is, the messages posted to the various newsgroups—are delivered to news servers. Such deliveries are known as *feeds;* servers agree to deliver, exchange, or distribute feeds for each other.

The servers use Network News Transfer Protocol (NNTP) as their protocol when doing newsfeeds. One reason is that NNTP is interactive, so servers can select which newsgroups and articles they want. This can save many megabytes of transmissions and many hundreds of file deletions.

Users can read the news articles by getting them from a news server or by downloading them and reading them off-line. A newsreader program is used to connect to a news server and then to retrieve and read the news articles. Newsreaders are generally text-based programs that can display a list of articles in a particular newsgroup, and that can display at least the text portion of the articles.

Newsreaders can download, and usually upload, article files, and keep track of which articles the user has read or downloaded, which articles are new, etc. Newsreaders may include or support viewers for various graphics or other formats. They may also include or support special utilities for encoding or decoding a file, or for converting a file from one format to another.

In this context, file encoding and decoding refer to the conversion of 8-bit data chunks, which might produce bizarre or destructive effects during transmission, into safe ASCII characters. This is done by recoding three bytes from the source as four bytes in the converted version. Utilities such as BinHex and the UNIX environment's uuencode make such conversions.

The rapidly growing ability to include various types of information in a mail or news message has led to the development of the MIME (Multipurpose Internet Mail Extension) specifications. These provide a notation and syntax for including various types of material in a file, and even include provisions for attaching required viewers or other simple programs to a message. MIME messages use Base64 encoding, which is another four-bytes-for-three encoding scheme.

Reading the News

A newsreader must be configured before use. The first time the newseader is used, it will retrieve a list of all the newsgroups available on the connected news server and will give the user an opportunity to subscribe to any or all of them. There are currently almost 15,000 newsgroups, and news servers will typically accept feeds from at least several thousand of them. Not surprisingly, downloading the list for the first time will take a while.

You can subscribe to any or all of the newsgroups. If you subscribe, your newsreader will automatically retrieve information about the newsgroups whenever you connect to the news server. Depending on your configuration settings, the newsreader may deliver information only about new postings.

Finding the News

Pick just about any topic, and there's a good chance that you'll find a newsgroup that discusses it. To find out what newsgroups are available, subscribe to the *news.lists* newsgroup. You'll generally find an article containing a list of active newsgroups (see the figure "Newsgroups list"). Other useful newsgroups for new news users include: *news.newusers.questions* and *news.announce.newusers*.

by topic, then subtopic, and so forth. Seven of the top-level groupings are carried over the Usenet; other newsgroups fall into the *alt* category or into any of the several dozen special interest categories. See the "News" article for more details and specific examples. News servers may carry and distribute some or all of the available newsgroups.

Newsgroup

On the Internet, a newsgroup is any of the 14,500 (and counting) article (posting, or message) collections that have been created. These collections are named and organized

Newsreader

A newsreader is a program that can retrieve, organize, display, and send *postings* (messages, or articles) from newsgroups (named message collections, which may contain news, opinions, or just drivel). A series of

NEWSGROUPS LIST

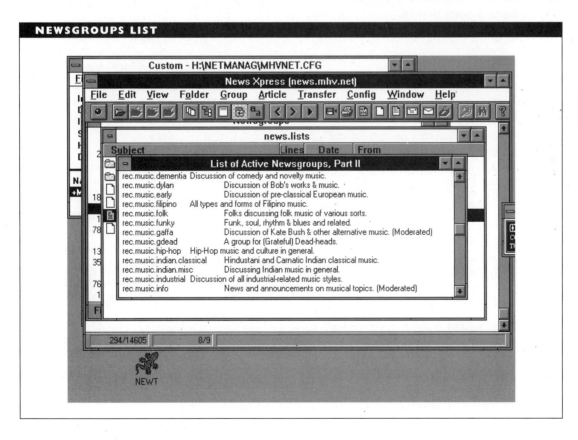

articles that are part of a single discussion is known as a *thread*.

With a newsreader, you can perform actions such as the following:

- Select newsgroups to which you want to subscribe. This is a task for which there is considerable variation with respect to how they let you accomplish this. Some newsreaders start off by assuming you want to subscribe to all available newsgroups—all 14,500+ of them (if your news server carries them all); others let you specify to which newsgroups you want to subscribe.

- Select the newsgroup articles that you actually want to read.

- Read the articles. Most newsreaders will keep track of the articles you've read from that newsgroup. Read articles won't reappear on your list of available articles for the newsgroup.

- Follow threads of a discussion over multiple articles. Some newsreaders are threaded (see below), which means that they will determine links between articles so that you can read them in the proper sequence if you like. If your newsreader isn't a threaded one, you can still do this, except that you'll have to find the thread yourself.

- Save articles to disk.

- Use e-mail to reply directly to the writer of an article.

- Post a response to an article, in which case your response will become part of the thread for the original article.

- Post an article of your own, in which case your article will become the start of a new thread.

- Create a file in which you can specify posters (that is, article writers) or topics you want to exclude (or, more rarely, include) automatically when the newsreaders retrieves news for you. The file containing the selection criteria is called a *killfile,* or a "bozo filter" because it's generally used to screen out rather than to include.

Newsreaders may be grouped in several ways:

- Newsreaders may be *character-based* or *windowed,* with the latter being more sophisticated.

- *Threaded* newsreaders arrange articles so that you can read the entire "conversation" (article series) without having to determine the sequence yourself. This is in contrast to *unthreaded* newsreaders, which make you determine the proper sequence yourself.

- *Online* newsreaders let you look at articles while you're connected to the Internet, whereas *offline* versions download the articles so you can read them at your leisure. The latter can save telephone and connect time, but they can also download a lot of useless postings.

Many browsers include newsreaders, or at least some limited capabilities for reading news articles. You won't necessarily be able to post things yourself, however.

Unix newsreaders include *rn* (read news), *trn* (threaded rn), *tin* (threaded internet newsreader), and *nn* (no news). Windows-based newsreaders include News Xpress, WinVN, and Free Agent. Newswatcher is a widely-used Macintosh-based newsreader.

Handling Newsgroup Subscriptions

In some environments, the most convenient way to handle newsgroup subscriptions is to edit the newsgroup list that the newsreader maintains. This file will be named something like *newsrc* (or *.newsrc* in UNIX environments), and will generally be an ASCII file.

Each available newsgroup will be listed in this file. Newsgroups to which you subscribe will contain a special character to distinguish them from the newsgroups to which you don't subscribe. For example, in UNIX environments (and in certain Windows newsreaders, such as News Xpress), newsgroup names will end in either a colon (:) or an exclamation point (!)—also known as a bang sign in UNIXese. The colon indicates a newsgroup to which you subscribe; the bang sign a newsgroup to which you don't.

Your most effective editing strategy will depend on how your newsreader starts you out—that is, with all bang signs (unsubscribed) or all colons (over-subscribed). In the former case, it's probably easiest to change only the newsgroups to which you want to subscribe. For newsreaders that start out by having you subscribe to all the newsgroups, it will probably be easier to change all the colons to bang signs, and then proceed as in the previous case. This assumes, of course, that you don't actually want to subscribe to all 14,500+ newsgroups.

NEXT (Near End Crosstalk)

In a cable containing multiple wires, such as twisted-pair cable, NEXT (for near end crosstalk or near end differential crosstalk) refers to the leakage of a signal from one wire pair to an adjacent one. This interference is measured at the transmitting end, in contrast to FEXT (far end crosstalk). In analog systems, this can take the form of an echo, or a second signal. For example, when you can hear other voices on a telephone line, this may be caused by NEXT.

In digital systems, the crosstalk is much more likely to take the form of random noise. As such, it can be filtered out easily, so that the disruptive effects of NEXT are generally minimal in digital systems.

NEXT is generally measured in decibels per 100 or 1000 feet, and is usually denoted by a *positive* numerical value. For reasons having to do with the notation conventions, a high positive value is better; that is, the higher the value, the lower the effect of crosstalk. You will often see this figure reported as a minimum value.

BROADER CATEGORY
Crosstalk

COMPARE
FEXT (Far End Crosstalk)

Next Station Addressing (NSA)

SEE
NSA (Next Station Addressing)

a
b
c
d
e
f
g
h
i
j
k
l
m
n
o
p
q
r
s
t
u
v
w
x
y
z

NeXTSTEP

NeXTSTEP is an object-oriented variant of the UNIX operating system. It is based most immediately on the Mach variant developed at Carnegie-Mellon University. Like Mach and Windows NT, NeXTSTEP uses a microkernel architecture in which only a barebones operating system core (the microkernel) stays loaded; other services are provided in modules that can be loaded as needed.

NeXTSTEP machines come with built-in support for thin and twisted-pair Ethernet. As a UNIX variant, NeXTSTEP supports the TCP/IP protocol suite, and NeXTSTEP machines can be either servers or clients on a TCP/IP network. They can also be NetWare or Macintosh clients; NeXTSTEP includes software that allows a NeXT machine to access file and print services on NetWare or AppleTalk networks.

Optional add-ons provide support for ISDN (Integrated Services Digital Network) and terminal-emulation capabilities for communications with IBM mainframes.

NeXTSTEP can support file servers and services, using the NFS (Network File System) popular in certain UNIX networks. The operating system also supports NetInfo databases and provides servers for these databases. In addition, NeXTSTEP can provide mail, printing, and fax modem services.

NeXTSTEP was designed originally as the native operating system for NeXT's hardware line. However, following the disappointing sales of NeXT machines, NeXT dropped out of the hardware business and has ported NeXTSTEP to Intel processors.

NIC (Network Interface Card)

The NIC is the network component with a thousand names, including LAN adapter, LAN card, NIU (network interface unit), network adapter, and network board.

An NIC enables a PC to connect to and access a network. The NIC communicates through drivers with the node's networking software (shell or operating system) at one end, and with the network (the cabling to the other nodes) at the other end.

NICs usually fit into expansion slots in a PC.

NICs and Network Architectures

NICs differ in the network architectures they support. This support is implemented in chips on the board. A network adapter might have Ethernet or Token Ring or FDDI chips, for example. (Chips and Technologies has developed ChipsLAN, a chip set that supports both Ethernet and Token Ring architectures, although not at the same time.)

There are dozens of NIC manufacturers and vendors, with hundreds of models. In practice, network operating systems officially support anywhere from a small number (usually fewer than a dozen) to several dozen specific cards. Other cards actually get their compatibility by emulating one or more of the officially supported cards.

Fortunately, these emulations are good enough, because NICs from different vendors are generally compatible, provided they support the same architecture. Thus, an Ethernet card from one vendor can communicate perfectly well with an Ethernet card from another vendor. However, an Ethernet NIC cannot communicate with a Token Ring NIC, even if both cards are from the same vendor, unless there is a translation component (such as a router) between the networks that are home to the two NICs.

The network architecture supported determines various performance features and restrictions for the NIC and, therefore, for the network. The architecture may constrain the cabling possibilities. For example, an Ethernet NIC may have only a BNC connector or only a DIX connector. However, if necessary, you can use a transceiver (for Ethernet) or a media filter (for Token Ring) to mediate between the NIC and the network cabling.

NIC Operation

The NIC mediates between the computer (and its user) and the network. For the sender, the NIC is responsible for getting the user's commands onto the network; for the receiver, the NIC is responsible for getting a transmission off the network and to the networking software running on the receiving machine.

Outgoing Network Activity

At the transmitting end, the NIC in a workstation translates user requests into a form suitable for transmission across the network. The NIC in a server translates system responses into the appropriate form to send them over the network. This translation process involves the following:

- Converting a parallel data chunk into a serial stream of bits.

- Dividing the bit stream into packets, whose form is determined by the network architecture the NIC supports. Some higher-end cards have multi-architecture chip sets, so that a single NIC can support two different network architectures.

- Converting the bit values into electrical signals, using the encoding scheme appropriate for the architecture.

After the transmission is converted, the NIC accesses the network—using whatever media-access method the supported architecture specifies—and transmits the user's message in the appropriate packets.

Incoming Network Activity

At the receiving end, the NIC monitors the network, checking the current transmission to determine if the NIC's node fits the destination address. Any of the following are considered a "fit":

- The packet's destination address matches the address of the NIC's node.

- The packet's destination address indicates the packet is being broadcast to all nodes on the network.

- The packet's destination address indicates the packet is being multicast to a group of nodes, including the NIC's node.

After capturing a packet addressed to the node, the NIC translates the packet into a form suitable for the networking software. Part of this translation process strips off any overhead bits from the serial bit stream, and

a b c d e f g h i j k l m **n** o p q r s t u v w x y z

converts the remaining bits into a parallel data chunk. When the transmission is in an appropriate form, the NIC passes it to the application running on the node.

In addition to checking the network on their own, NICs also do various administrative tasks independently of the networking software running on the node. For example, the token-passing process, which controls media access for certain types of networks, is done entirely by the NICs. Similarly, some NICs include components for monitoring the network and the NIC, and for reporting any errors.

NICs and LAN Drivers

NICs communicate with the networking software through LAN drivers. The driver provides a crucial link between network and software.

In the ordinary world, a separate driver is needed for each operating system, card, and networking protocol combination. In order to save programming time and effort, and to avoid a driver population explosion, several efforts have been made to create generic interfaces, so that a single driver can handle multiple protocols for a given adapter and operating system combination.

Microsoft and 3Com developed the NDIS (Network Driver Interface Specification) standard, and Novell and Apple developed the ODI (Open Data-link Interface) standard. These generic interfaces differ in how they route a packet to the appropriate protocol stack, but both help reduce the number of drivers needed. With an NDIS- or ODI-compliant card, a single driver will handle packets for the DoD's TCI/IP, Novell's

IPX/SPX, Apple's AARP, and even IBM's NetBIOS protocols.

Keep in mind that an NIC driver is involved in much activity and can be a performance bottleneck if not properly written.

Card Sizes and Features

NICs differ in the following features:

- The size of the card's data bus. NICs come in 8-, 16-, and 32-bit versions. In general, 8-bit cards are adequate for workstations, but servers should get more powerful 16- or 32-bit cards.

- *Bus mastering* support. The NIC may support bus mastering, a bus access method in which the card takes control of the bus directly, so that the card can bypass the CPU and send data onto the bus. In general, MCA and EISA machines support bus mastering, but ISA machines do not. Several types of transfer modes are possible with bus mastering, including burst mode, streaming data mode, and data duplexing. A particular bus-mastering scheme may support some or all of them.

- The board speed. Regardless of whether a NIC uses bus mastering, it needs to interact with the bus. Like other operations on the computer, interactions rely heavily on the timing (and speed) afforded by the computer's clock. In general, the bus speed will be one-third of the clock's speed, and the processor will operate at half the clock speed.

- The network architecture supported. The most widely used architectures include ARCnet, Ethernet, FDDI, and Token Ring. Newly available chip sets support both Ethernet and Token Ring architectures.

- Whether the NIC includes a processor. Some NICs include a processor (generally in the 80186 or 80286 class) to make the board more "intelligent." This intelligence will enable the board to do more of the work, freeing the node's processor for other duties. This is particularly important for the file server, since that processor gets requests from multiple sources.

- Whether the NIC has on-board RAM. Optional on-board RAM can serve as a buffer when necessary. That is, any available RAM on the NIC can be used to store parts of a transmission, such as while the NIC waits to pass the received material to the node's networking software or to send the packets onto the network. For certain types of checking, the NIC may store a packet in RAM, passing only required fields to the networking software. If no RAM is available, the NIC must pass the entire packet to the software, which will slow down performance.

- Whether the NIC supports boot ROM. Most NICs include a socket for an optional diskless boot ROM. When this chip is installed, boot information is read from the ROM instead of from a boot disk (which becomes unnecessary). Such a chip is necessary for diskless workstations. These enable users to access network files and resources, but do not allow the user to take files off the network or to copy files to the network, since the workstation has neither a floppy nor a hard disk.

- Whether the NIC has LEDs (light-emitting diodes). Some of the fancier NICs may include LEDs at the interface. These LEDs will indicate board state or network activity.

Other things being equal, and assuming any network or other restrictions are met, the following points apply to all NICs:

- 32-bit NICs are faster than 16-bit NICs, which in turn are faster than 8-bit NICs.

- NICs with on-board RAM will generally work faster. The RAM is used as a buffer, so that the NIC is never the bottleneck in communication between the PC and the network.

- NICs with an on-board processor will be able to do more of the work. These NICs will also, of course, cost more.

Installing NICs

Standard NICs are snapped into an available expansion slot of your computer, just like a board for any other add-on. When installed in a PC expansion slot, each NIC must get an I/O address and an IRQ, and the card may also be assigned a DMA channel. For some boards you also need to specify a memory address, which specifies a location

a
b
c
d
e
f
g
h
i
j
k
l
m
n
o
p
q
r
s
t
u
v
w
x
y
z

WHAT TO LOOK FOR IN AN NIC

When you're shopping for NICs, find out about the product's reliability and the vendor's faith in that reliability. First, ask about the manufacturer's warranty. Five-year warranties are not uncommon for NICs and some vendors even offer lifetime warranties.

One index of a product's reliability is the mean time before failure (MTBF). This value represents the amount of time before about half the units have broken down. For NICs, manufacturers quote times of 10 or 20 years. Such reliability is essential, since the costs of downtime will be several times the cost of an NIC.

The drivers included with a NIC are very important. An adapter should support either the NDIS or the ODI interface standard for NIC drivers (preferably both), because these two driver interfaces provide generic driver services. Having both these driver interfaces available makes the adapter considerably more portable and flexible. Above all, however, make certain the board includes a driver that will support your particular configuration.

Make sure any NIC you plan to buy is compatible with the PC architecture of your machines. In particular, make sure you don't buy an MCA-compatible card for an ISA or EISA machine.

If you're purchasing a NIC that supports bus mastering, you also need to know if its bus-mastering method is compatible with the method your computer uses. Bus mastering can improve throughput considerably, but only if the board and the computer support the same bus mastering method, *and* if the bus mastering doesn't conflict with the hard disk controller. Since incompatibilities in this area can lead to lots of complaints and support calls, vendors do extensive product compatibility testing. Your particular configuration may be in their database, so check with the vendors involved before you buy and assemble the hardware.

You can sometimes save considerable money if you're in a position to buy multiple adapters at a time from a vendor. Many vendors feature 5- or 10-packs of a particular adapter at a reduced price.

Although speed enhances performance, an investment in superfast boards doesn't guarantee you the speed you desire. Vendors and users are constantly trying to get components to go faster—for example, to speed up interactions with the bus—and sometimes they succeed. The developed products may include superfast boards, which can operate at half or even full clock speed. These boards may work with a particular configuration created by the vendor, but are very likely to be incompatible with other products, at least in fast mode. To have the superfast board work with a generic computer, it may be necessary to operate the board at a slower speed, so the higher price for the extra speed might be wasted.

used as a buffer for board-related operations. These settings become part of the system configuration for your computer. Usually, the vendor's default settings will work, unless you already have multiple add-on cards in your computer. If there is a conflict, you may need to assign different values.

NIC Addresses

NICs and nodes have several types of addresses associated with them. NICs have hardware addresses, whose values are "wired" into or set on the board.

For Ethernet and Token Ring cards, the hardware address is assigned by the manufacturer and is built into the card. The hardware address is completely independent of the network in which the board is ultimately used. Rather, the hardware address identifies the card's manufacturer and includes a unique "serial" number for that manufacturer's products. Part of this address is assigned according to guidelines specified by the IEEE.

For ARCnet cards, the network address is a value between 1 and 255, recorded in jumper or DIP switch settings. The system administrator must set this address manually. It is the administrator's responsibility to make sure that each card has a unique address. Failure to keep good records in this regard could lead to lots of frustrating trial and error until the machines with the duplicate addresses are identified.

As representative of a node in a particular network, an NIC also has network and node (or station) addresses.

As the network address, each physical network is assigned an eight hexadecimal-digit (four-byte) value between 0x1 and 0xFFFFFFFF. This network address value must be unique if the network is connected to other networks (via a router, bridge, or gateway). In an internetwork, each network can have only one network address.

Individual nodes in a network also get node, or station, addresses. A node address uniquely identifies the node *within* the network. A file server that is attached to two different networks will have two network and two node addresses. Routers, bridges, and gateways have addresses in both of the networks they connect.

In Novell's NetWare 3.*x* and later, each *server* also has a unique IPX internal network number. This logical address is an eight-digit value between 1 and FFFFFFFF, and must differ from any other internal or network address associated with any network associated with the server.

Alternatives to Plug-In NICs

A node on a network needs some component that will mediate between the network and the computer's software. Usually, this capability is provided by an NIC that plugs into an expansion slot in the computer.

There are other ways of providing a mediating component. The variants are useful for attaching non-desktop machines, such as laptops, notebooks, and palmtops, to a network. Alternatives include docking stations, external adapters, and PCMCIA cards.

External LAN drivers are generally available from the adapter's vendor. Before buying an external NIC, make sure this is the case and also make sure the driver supports your networking software. (Since a docking

TIPS ON CONFIGURING NICS

The following are some tips and considerations for configuring NICs:

- Before changing any NIC settings, record the factory settings (or find these settings in the documentation), so you can restore them if necessary.

- If the default settings won't work, try the alternatives recommended by the vendor. Vendors will usually have two or three alternative settings.

- To change settings, you may need to move jumpers or change DIP switch settings. (On MCA and EISA machines you can make such changes through software.)

- If you change the board settings, make sure to change the values in any software configuration files.

- Most cards will want the DMA setting turned off, since this access method has outlived its usefulness and is often slower than ordinary CPU-controlled data transfer methods. (If DMA lines are used, line 3 is generally used for ATs and line 2 for XTs.)

- If you change the IRQ, try to avoid certain values that are likely to cause conflict. These include IRQ 5 (particularly in XTs) and IRQ 2.

- If you need to specify memory addresses and you use memory management software, you may need to exclude the memory range the NIC uses from the memory manager's purview. To do this, most memory managers have an exclude command.

Even if the settings for an NIC seem to work, check them explicitly anyway. Conflicts may arise only under relatively unlikely conditions. To check for such rare interactions, find out all the IRQ and I/O address assignments for the boards in your machine, and see whether any of these match the NIC's settings. If so, you may encounter conflicts at some point when both functions are used at the same time.

For example, if your NIC settings match those for the floppy disk controller, you'll run into problems if you try to access the floppy drive while accessing the network.

It's a good idea in general to have a record of the internal settings for your computer. Having this information easily accessible makes technical support and troubleshooting much easier. It will also save you time on technical support calls.

station will be using an ordinary NIC, special drivers are not necessary.)

Docking Station

A docking station is essentially an expansion box that turns a laptop, notebook, or palmtop computer into a desktop machine. The docking station has expansion slots, into which you can put whatever types of cards you want. To use the attached laptop (for example) on a LAN, you need to plug an NIC into one of the expansion slots.

Docking stations are hardware-dependent, and generally work with only a single model computer from a single manufacturer. Docking stations can cost several hundred dollars. Note that you still need an NIC with a docking station.

External Adapter

An external adapter, or NIC, attaches to the laptop's parallel port. This adapter is just an NIC in a different case. External adapters can be pocket-size (*aka* portable) or desk-size. The desk-size version may support multiple types of cable in the same unit; the pocket-size adapter will have room for only a single type of connector.

External NICs generally include a pass-through parallel port, which provides an additional parallel port to replace the one bound to the external adapter. Note, however, that this additional port will be accessible only if it can be assigned a valid and accessible address.

The pocket-size adapter does not include a parallel port, but the adapter can be used with a parallel port multiplexor. Prices depend in part on the architecture being supported; ARCnet is cheapest; Token Ring, most expensive.

Unlike docking stations, external adapters are hardware-independent (as is the case for ordinary NICs). This makes it possible to use these adapters with just about any laptop. Newer laptops have the EPP (enhanced parallel port), which supports burst speeds of up to 16 Mbps. Support for this port is built into Intel's 386/25 SL chip set, which is currently very popular for laptops.

External adapters are portable, hardware-independent, and easy to install. Because they communicate through the parallel port, such adapters do not need an address and IRQ line, which make setup much easier. External adapters use the IEEE hardware addressing algorithm (just like other types of NICs).

External adapters are slower because the parallel port is slower. Fortunately, these adapters will not slow down other network activity, because tasks such as token passing are handled right on board, without going to the port.

PCMCIA Cards

PCMCIA cards are very small (about the size of a credit card) and are designed to plug into small computers, such as notebooks and palmtops, and some peripherals. The PCMCIA interface standard is still relatively new (with PCMCIA 2 being the current major version), so such products are just beginning to appear.

ARCnet NIC

An ARCnet NIC has chips to handle the ARCnet network architecture. ARCnet NICs come with either a low- or high-impedance transceiver. A low-impedance card is generally used in ARCnet networks that use a star-topology; high-impedance cards are used in networks that use a bus topology. ARCnet cards generally have a BNC connector (since ARCnet typically uses coaxial cable).

ARCnet cards do not come with hardware addresses in a ROM chip. Instead, these cards have jumpers that can be set to specify an address for the node in which the card is installed. The network administrator needs to set this address (which must be between 1 and 255) for each card in the network. Each node must have a unique address. The administrator also needs to set the IRQ and I/O address on the card.

ARCnet cards are arguably the least expensive of the major architectures (such as Ethernet and Token Ring), with Ethernet adapters right down there as well.

Ethernet NI

An Ethernet NIC supports the Ethernet network architecture. NICs that support the slightly different IEEE 802.3 standard are sometimes loosely called Ethernet NICs as well. Many boards support both Ethernet and 802.3.

Ethernet NICs can have BNC, DIX, and/or RJ-*xx* connectors. On boards with multiple connectors, you will generally need to set DIP switches or jumper settings on the board to indicate the type of connector you will be using. Some of the higher-end boards can sense automatically which interface you are using, or they will let you specify this in software.

Ethernet cards include a hardware address on a ROM chip. This address is assigned by the IEEE and the vendor and is unique to that particular board. Part of the address contains vendor information, and part identifies the board itself. This address can be used by bridges and routers to identify a particular node on a network.

Token Ring NIC

A Token Ring NIC supports IBM's Token Ring network architecture. Token Ring NICs can have DB-9 and/or RJ-*xx* connectors.

Either shielded twisted-pair (STP) or unshielded twisted-pair (UTP) cable can be attached to the board using the proper types of connectors. On most Token Ring cards, you will need to set jumpers or DIP switches in the hardware to specify the type of connector being used. Other values that may need to be set using jumpers or DIP switches include the IRQ, I/O address, and operating mode, or speed, to either 4- or 16-Mbps. Not all cards will support both speeds.

Token Ring NICs are considerably more expensive than ARCnet or Ethernet cards.

One reason Token Ring cards cost more is that they include more complex circuitry. For example, each Token Ring NIC includes an agent that can report node activity and NIC states to network management nodes.

The proliferation of Token Ring chip sets in the past few years will help bring prices down. Chip manufacturers include Texas Instruments, IBM, Western Digital, Chips & Technologies, and National Semiconductor.

Token Ring NIC Enhancements

Because Token Ring NICs have the most complex requirements and capabilities, they also offer the most opportunity for ingenuity and enhancements. Various enhancements have been added to Token Ring cards to make them more attractive, including the following:

- ETR (early token release) capabilities. ETR is a token-passing strategy that makes it possible to have more than one data packet circulating at a time around the ring.

- Interface sensing. Some NICs can automatically determine which of the available interfaces is being used for the network.

- Dual protocol chips. Several chip manufacturers, including Texas Instruments and Chips & Technologies, have developed chip sets that support both Token Ring and Ethernet architectures on the same board. This makes the board considerably more flexible and portable.

- Tools. Since Token Ring controllers are essentially processors, it is possible to program them to do new things. Adapter manufacturers are using a set of tools, developed by Proteon, for adding capabilities to the controller chip.

- On-chip protocols. Madge Networks has built adapters with the ability to run network protocols (such as Novell's IPX protocol) right on the adapter, which can help speed up performance.

NID (Next ID)

In an ARCnet frame, the NID is the address of the next node to receive the token.

NII (National Information Infrastructure)

A government term for the Internet and other public networks, which will form a seamless communications web that will make huge amounts of information easily accessible to users.

The term is intended to encompass more than just the equipment and the connections between networks. It also includes the protocols—transmission, and network standards—the access and applications software, the information, and even the service providers.

PRIMARY SOURCES

Documents related to the government's plans and pontifications about this infrastructure are generally available in the */pub* directory at the *ftp.ntia.doc.gov* FTP site. The file should be called something like *niiagenda.asc*.

NIM (Network Interface Module)

A network interface card, or network adapter.

SEE ALSO

NIC (Network Interface Card)

NISDN (Narrowband ISDN)

A term sometimes used for the ordinary ISDN (Integrated Services Digital Network) architecture, to distinguish it from BISDN (Broadband ISDN).

SEE ALSO

ISDN (Integrated Services Digital Network)

Nitwork

Nitwork refers to the kind of work that means the difference between a network and a notwork. Nitwork is a term for the dozens, possibly hundreds, of details that need to be considered and dealt with in order to keep a network running properly. Overlooking or failing to resolve such details can cause frustrating problems that may be expensive and time-consuming to correct.

NIU (Network Interface Unit)

A network interface card, or network adapter.

SEE ALSO

NIC (Network Interface Card)

NLM (NetWare Loadable Module)

In Novell's NetWare 3.x and later, an NLM is a program that can be loaded and linked to function as part of the network operating system (NOS). These modules can be loaded and unloaded as needed.

NLMs can be used to link different types of resources or services into the NOS, to make these available temporarily or for the entire time the network is running. When an NLM is loaded, NetWare allocates memory for the NLM to use. This memory and any resources used are returned for reuse when the NLM is unloaded.

NLMs help make network operation more efficient because services can be loaded more selectively. With the availability of NLMs, servers only need to load the core of the NOS. The core capabilities

can be extended by adding only the modules that are likely to be needed.

NLM Classes in NetWare 4.x

NetWare 3.x and 4.x distinguish four classes of NLMs:

- Disk drivers, which enable communication between the NOS and the hard disks on the server. Such drivers have a DSK extension.

- LAN drivers, which control communication between the NOS and the network interface cards (NICs) in the server. Such drivers have a LAN extension.

- Management utilities and server applications modules, which make it possible to monitor and change the network configuration and activity. Such modules have an NLM extension.

- Name space modules, which allow non-DOS files and naming conventions to be used in the directory and file systems. Such modules have an NAM extension.

Some NLMs, such as LAN and disk drivers, will be loaded every time the network server is booted. These can be specified in the STARTUP.NCF and AUTOEXEC.NCF files, along with any options or commands for the NLMs.

With an open interface, the NOS's capabilities can also be extended or modified by creating new or different NLMs. Since these NLMs may not be tested as thoroughly as those included with NetWare (or they may be tested during network operation), it is important to protect the core NOS and NLMs from corruption by errant NLMs.

In order to increase network security, and also to protect the NOS from uncertified NLMs, which may be unreliable, NetWare takes advantage of privilege levels supported by the Intel processor architecture. This feature establishes a hierarchy of four rings (numbered 0, 1, 2, and 3). Of these, ring 0 is the most privileged. Any application or module can execute in a specified ring, and the application's operations are confined to the application's ring or to rings further out (with lower privilege levels).

Novell uses rings 0 and 3. By default, NetWare and any NLMs execute in ring 0, in the OS domain. However, in NetWare 4.*x* you can specify that an NLM should run in an OS_PROTECTED domain. In that case, the NLM will execute in ring 3, and will not be able to tamper with or corrupt the contents of ring 0.

BROADER CATEGORY
NetWare

COMPARE
VAP (Value-Added Process)

NMA (Network Management Architecture)

NMA is IBM's network management model. This model is mainframe-oriented and centralized. It is used in IBM's NetView network management package and, more recently, in the more flexible SystemView.

In the NMA model, network management tasks fall into four categories:

- Configuration management, which is concerned with identifying the network elements and the relationships among them.

- Problem management, which is concerned with identifying, diagnosing, tracking, and resolving problems that arise.

- Performance and accounting management, which is concerned with monitoring the availability and use of the network's elements, and also with managing the billing for use of these resources.

- Change management, which is concerned with changes in hardware, software, or microcode.

These tasks are carried out by (or under the control of) the central host, which serves as the network manager. Under the NMA model, the network manager is the focal point for the network. Devices from IBM (that is, SNA-based) and non-IBM networks may be connected to the focal point in two different ways.

- Devices that support IBM's SNA (Systems Network Architecture) can connect through entry points. Such entry points serve as agents in reporting to the network manager at the focal point.

- Non-IBM devices must be connected through service points, which are nodes running special software (for example, NetView/PC) that can communicate with the NMA package. Such devices can also be connected if they can function as LU 6.2 (logical unit 6.2) devices.

The NetView/PC software can be used to connect a wide range of devices and networks to an NMA network. For example, NetView/PC can connect one or more Ethernet or Token Ring LANs, a PBX, or a single machine to a network using NetView. NetView itself runs as a VTAM application on the host machine.

Novell's NetWare Management Agent for NetView allows a NetWare server to function as a Token Ring network agent for a NetView host. The NetWare server can report alarms from the Token Ring network to the host, and it can also respond to requests from the host for maintenance statistics.

The NMVT (Network Management Vector Transport) protocol is used to exchange management data. This protocol uses management service request units to request and return information about the status or performance of elements on the network.

BROADER CATEGORY
Network Management

NME (Network Management Entity)

In the OSI network management model, the NME is the software and/or hardware that gives a network node the ability to collect, store, and report data about the node's activities.

SEE ALSO
Network Management

NMS (NetWare Management System)

Novell's NMS is a software product that provides centralized management of a local-area or enterprise network. NMS runs on a dedicated, Microsoft Windows-based machine. It provides a Windows-based interface and uses NetWare Management Agents, NetWare LANalyzer Agent, and NetWare Hub Services for data gathering and reporting.

NMS Features

NMS includes the following management capabilities and features:

- Asset management: NMS can identify, monitor, and protect network components. For example, NMS can automatically discover and map the configuration of a network. NMS can also use password protection to prevent unauthorized changes to the configuration.

- Fault management: NMS can monitor activity and changes in the network, issue real-time alarms, and execute programs in response to alarms. NMS can keep a log of faults and alarms, and it can be used to test the connectivity of IPX and IP devices.

- Address management: NMS can automatically determine and store all IP and IPX addresses on the network.

- Router management: NMS can monitor and report on routers that support the MIB II (Management Information Base II) standard.

- Monitoring and analysis: NMS can monitor critical devices selected by the network administrator. NMS can also monitor and analyze traffic on a distributed network, even from a remote location.

- Data storage and reporting: NMS can summarize and report on the information provided up to the time of the summary and report.

NMS supports SNMP (Simple Network Management Protocol) as its management protocol, and provides an SNMP Browser to monitor and control SNMP devices.

NMS Agents

NMS uses several types of agents to get information or suggestions about network operation. Each is appropriate for a different type of task.

A NetWare Management Agent (NMA) is installed on a server and provides statistics about the server's configuration, memory allocation and central processing unit (CPU) usage. NMAs can also send alarms. An NMA makes it possible for the same network to be managed from multiple locations, provided each of the managing administrators has the appropriate access rights.

A NetWare LANalyzer Agent provides information about the interactions among devices and workstations, and it can also do analyses of the collected data.

The NetWare Hub Services Agent can be used to provide information about the network activity of its hub, which must conform to the Hub Management Interface (HMI).

NMVT (Network Management Vector Transport)

In IBM's NMA, NMVT is the protocol used to exchange management data.

SEE ALSO

NMA (Network Management Architecture)

Node

On a network, a node is simply an element with a network interface card (NIC) installed. A node is generally a computer (a workstation or a server), but may be another type of device, such as a printer or modem. Nodes that are not computers may have an NIC preinstalled.

Node Address

A node address is a unique numerical value associated with a specific node in a particular network. In general, this value is assigned to the network interface card (NIC) installed in the node.

This value may be assigned through software or in the hardware. For example, an NIC for an Ethernet network has a unique address assigned by the manufacturer. In contrast, boards for an ARCnet network or a Token Ring network are assigned addresses through jumper or switch settings.

A complete address for a node will include a network address that is common to all nodes in the same physical network, as well as the node address that is unique to the node within its physical network.

a
b
c
d
e
f
g
h
i
j
k
l
m
n
o
p
q
r
s
t
u
v
w
x
y
z

A node address is also known as a *node number,* a *physical node address,* or as a *station address.*

Node-to-Node Routing

A routing method used to get a packet from its source node to its destination, as opposed to simply routing a packet to the router nearest to the destination node.

Noise, Electrical

Noise is the term for random electrical signals that become part of a transmission, and that serve to make the signal (information) component of the transmission more difficult to identify. Noise can take various forms, including the following:

  Impulse noise: Voltage increases that last for just a short period, on the order of a few milliseconds. Examples include power surges or spikes, lightning, and switching on the line.

  Gaussian, or white, noise: Random background noise.

  Crosstalk: Interference on one wire from another.

There are limits set on the allowable levels for each of these types of noise.

To remove random noise from a signal, a *noise filter* can be used.

Nominal Velocity of Propagation (NVP)

SEE
NVP (Nominal Velocity of Propagation)

Nondisruptive Test

In network management, a nondisruptive test is a diagnostic or performance test that can be run in the background, and that has little or no effect on ordinary network activity. Compare this with a disruptive test.

Non-Repudiation

A network security measure that makes it impossible for a sender to deny having sent a message (*origin non-repudiation*) and for a recipient to deny having received the message (*destination non-repudiation*).

Non-Return to Zero (NRZ)

NRZ is a signaling method in which the voltage does not necessarily return to a zero, or neutral, state after each bit is transmitted. Therefore, the signal remains at the same level for the entire bit interval and may remain at this level for several bit intervals if the same value is transmitted multiple times in succession. Such a signal method is not self-clocking.

SEE ALSO
Encoding, Signal

Nonshareable

A nonshareable file, device, or process is available to only one user at a time.

NOS (Network Operating System)

A NOS is a software package that makes it possible to implement and control a network and that enables users to make use of resources and services on that network. Examples of NOSs include Novell's NetWare, Banyan's VINES, Artisoft's LANtastic, and Microsoft's LAN Manager.

A NOS's responsibilities include the following:

- Providing access to files and resources (for example, printers) on the network

- Providing messaging and/or electronic mail (e-mail) services

- Enabling nodes on the network to communicate with each other

- Interprocess Communications (IPC); that is, enabling processes on the network to communicate with each other

- Responding to requests from applications or users on the network

- Mapping requests and paths to the appropriate places on the network

Server-Based versus Peer-Based NOSs

A NOS may be server- or peer-based. Server-based NOSs are considerably more complex (and usually more powerful) than NOSs for peer-to-peer networks. In the former case, the NOS and the server run the show. The NOS becomes the server's native operating system.

For example, Novell's NetWare requires its own hard disk partition, and the computer boots to this, rather than to DOS. NetWare does use some DOS services and also retains the DOS file structure. Most NOSs at least support the file structure from the native operating system; many use this file system as if it were the NOS's own native file system.

In peer-to-peer networks, any station can function as file server or as a client (consumer) for network services. Peer-to-peer NOSs are generally simpler than NOSs for server-based networks. Such NOSs often run simply as an ordinary process. In such a case, the NOS generally will run on top of the computer's native operating system (DOS, OS/2 or UNIX, for example). Even for a peer-to-peer network, however, the NOS takes over at least those operating system functions that relate to the network.

In server-based networks, workstations will generally run a network shell, or redirection, program, rather than the entire NOS. The station's native operating system (for example, DOS, OS/2, or UNIX) will still be running and will share the workload with the networking software.

The networking shell may intercept user requests to determine whether the request is for the station's operating system or for the network. In the latter case, the shell redirects the request to the network interface card (NIC), through which the request will be passed to the NOS on the server. This is how the shell program for Novell's NetWare versions 3.x and earlier works.

In other arrangements, the native operating system does the screening, and the networking module is called only when necessary. This is how the DOS Requester used in NetWare 4.x workstations works.

Built-In NOSs

Some operating systems have networking capabilities built-in, including the following:

- The operating system used on Macintoshes

- The NeXTSTEP operating system from NeXT Computers, now available for Intel platforms

- UNIX

- Windows NT

- Novell DOS 7

In most such cases, the operating system's networking capabilities can be greatly enhanced through the use of utilities or other third-party programs.

RELATED ARTICLES
LAN Manager; LANtastic; NetWare; VINES

Notarization

In network security, notarization is the use of a trusted third party, called a *notary,* to verify that a communication between two entities is legitimate. The "notary" has information that is used to verify the identity of the sender and receiver and also of the time and origin of a message.

Notwork

Notwork is a term used to describe a network that is operating unreliably or not at all.

Novell AppWare

Novell AppWare is a software layer that helps simplify the development of network-based software by shielding developers from

the details of network access and operation. Because AppWare sits above the operating system layer, a uniform set of APIs (Application Program Interfaces) can provide access to different operating systems, interfaces, or network services. AppWare makes network services more easily available to all developers, regardless of the operating system or user interface for which the developer is writing.

Three components make up the AppWare environment: the AppWare Foundation, AppWare Loadable Modules (ALMs), and the AppWare Bus. The figure "AppWare components and context" shows how these elements fit together, as well as how AppWare fits into the networking framework.

AppWare Foundation

The AppWare Foundation provides a set of APIs that can be used to access various environments or services. Applications written to these APIs can be compiled to run in any environment with which the Foundation can communicate. Thus, an application written to run in a Microsoft Windows environment just needs to be recompiled to run in a UNIX or OS/2 environment, for example.

The AppWare Foundation is the component that makes cross-platform development easier by protecting developers from the differences associated with each platform. The Foundation is, itself, built upon CORBA (Common Request Broker Architecture), which was developed to provide a platform- and language-independent way for objects to communicate within and across applications. By making such communication both language- and platform-independent,

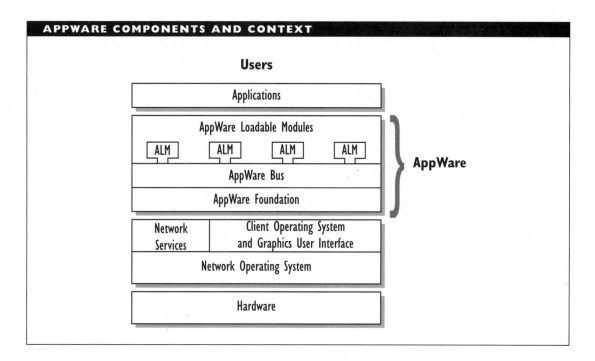

APPWARE COMPONENTS AND CONTEXT

CORBA helps make components more easily interchangeable, which helps bring true plug-and-play capabilities closer to reality.

AppWare Loadable Modules (ALMs)

ALMs are large-grained code packages that provide specific services or capabilities. For example, ALMs may be written to provide messaging or other communications capabilities; to provide access to files, databases, printers, and so on; or to help provide network security.

Unless one explicitly uses or builds on another, ALMs are independent of each other but can be used together. The ability to create and combine ALMs makes development much easier by making it possible to reuse existing code at a very high level. It

is possible to create an AppWare-based application by simply combining ALMs in the proper way. Thus, ALMs can be used as very high-level building blocks for customized and generic applications. Novell provides Novell Visual AppBuilder as a high-level tool for combining ALMs to create applications.

ALMs can be created using third-generation languages and compilers (such as C or C++). ALM code makes calls to the APIs provided in the AppWare Foundation. The services available through ALMs are limited only by the imagination of developers. In addition to traditional network services such as file handling and messaging services, ALMs have been created for accessing Oracle and Sybase databases, for imaging and

a b c d e f g h i j k l m **n** o p q r s t u v w x y z

document management, and to provide telephony services.

AppWare Bus

The AppWare Bus is used to coordinate ALMs so that each can do its work and so that the ALMs can work together, if necessary. Novell describes the relationship between the AppWare Bus and ALMs as comparable to the relationship between a motherboard and expansion cards. The AppWare capabilities and integration are achieved in software, however.

The Novell ALM Construction Kit provides interfaces for plugging an ALM into the AppWare Bus.

Novell DOS 7

Novell DOS 7 is a version of DOS developed by Digital Research, released after Digital Research was acquired by Novell. As did earlier versions, which were known as DR DOS, Novell DOS 7 extends the capabilities of DOS significantly, providing significant advances in the areas of memory management, multitasking, and networking. This operating system also supports Microsoft Windows.

Novell DOS 7 includes utilities for improving system performance through disk compression, or caching. It also includes built-in virus scanning and CD-ROM extensions.

Memory Management

Novell DOS 7 uses an API (Application Program Interface) called DOS Protected Mode Services (DPMS) that allows device drivers

and terminate-and-stay-resident (TSR) programs to use protected mode on 80286 and higher processors.

The open DPMS specification, developed by Novell, makes it possible to load such drivers and programs into extended memory, thereby freeing more of the upper memory area between 640 kilobytes (KB) and 1 megabyte (MB). For example, the CD-ROM extension, which is equivalent to Microsoft's MSCDEX, can be loaded into extended memory using the DPMS API.

To load programs into extended memory, the DPMS Server must be loaded into conventional or upper memory. This server will then manage the DPMS clients which are loaded into extended memory. The figure "Memory use with and without DPMS" compares memory with and without DPMS capabilities.

Several of the drivers and utilities included with Novell DOS 7 support DPMS, so they can be loaded as DPMS clients. The DPMS specification is general-purpose, and its use is not limited to Novell products. Novell has made the specifications public, and grants developers royalty-free distribution rights.

Multitasking

Novell DOS 7 supports an operating system kernel for preemptive multitasking, which is multitasking in which a higher-priority program can interrupt the foreground execution of a lower-priority program while the higher-priority program executes.

Interrupted programs may continue to execute in the background, even if they are doing graphics. The ability to interrupt can help make a computer more efficient; the

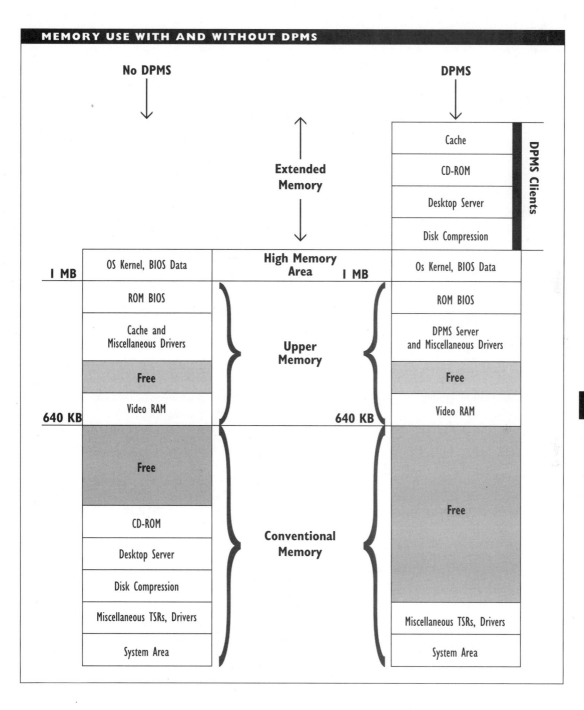

MEMORY USE WITH AND WITHOUT DPMS

No DPMS

DPMS

DPMS Clients

Cache

CD-ROM

Desktop Server

Disk Compression

Extended
Memory

1 MB

High Memory
Area

1 MB

OS Kernel, BIOS Data

Os Kernel, BIOS Data

ROM BIOS

ROM BIOS

Cache and
Miscellaneous Drivers

Upper
Memory

DPMS Server
and Miscellaneous Drivers

Free

Free

Video RAM

640 KB

640 KB

Video RAM

Free

Free

CD-ROM

Desktop Server

Conventional
Memory

Disk Compression

Miscellaneous TSRs, Drivers

Miscellaneous TSRs, Drivers

System Area

System Area

a b c d e f g h i j k l m **n** o p q r s t u v w x y z

ability to execute in the background helps make possible a more complete use of available resources.

Networking

Novell DOS 7 includes Personal NetWare, which provides built-in capabilities for peer-to-peer networking. This allows users on a network to share data and other files. The Novell Desktop Server software provides these capabilities.

A workstation running Novell DOS 7 can use the NetWare Universal Client component to communicate with a server on a NetWare network. Such a workstation can provide performance and diagnostic information using a built-in SNMP (Simple Network Management Protocol) agent.

Novell DOS 7 supports various types of security measures, including the following:

- The ability to restrict the resources (drives, ports, servers, and so on) a user can access, and also restrict the hours during which a user can access the network

- Support for file and directory passwords

- Secure disk partitions

Novell Groupwise

Novell's Groupwise 4.1 is an integrated messaging-system package that combines the functionality of e-mail, personal appointment management, group scheduling, workflow routing, and message and task management. The task management capabilities can help with workflow routing because

it's possible to move tasks around a network (that is, assign tasks to specific users) on a timed basis. For example, depending on the command, a task from a project can be moved (assigned) to a different user manually or automatically, according to a schedule.

Groupwise consists of client and server components, and can include an administrator component (Admin) and gateways. The client provides an interface to give users access to the messaging system. Client programs are available for DOS, Windows, Macintosh, and UNIX. The Admin element is used to configure and maintain the messaging capabilities for a network.

The gateways allow Groupwise networks to exchange messages with other, alien messaging systems. Over a dozen different gateway modules are available, including APIs for DOS and OS/2 programs, DOS or OS/2 modules for Lotus Notes, cc:Mail, VMS Mail, X.25 and X.400.

A single-user demo of Groupwise is included with Novell's PerfectOffice integrated software package.

NPA (NetWare Peripheral Architecture)

A Novell driver architecture in which NetWare drivers are built out of two components:

- HAM (Host Adaptor Module), which controls a server's adapter card for a particular peripheral.

- CDM (Custom Device Module), which controls the specific device attached to the adapter.

In addition to these modules, the NPA also has APIs that provide the hooks necessary for these components to communicate with the Media Manager (NetWare's database about available peripherals). The HAI (Host Adapter Interface) and the CDI (Custom Device Interface) allow the HAM and CDM, respectively, to deal with the Media Manager.

This architecture makes it easier to provide support for new hardware as it appears, because only part of the driver software— the CDW—needs to be rewritten when the hardware attached to a server is upgraded.

NPAP (Network Printing Alliance Protocol)

A proposed standard for a bidirectional protocol to be used for communication among printers on a network. The protocol allows exchange of configuration and other data independent of the printer-control or page-description language being used.

NPSI (Network Packet Switch Interface)

An interface used in IBM's SNA.

SEE ALSO
SNA (Systems Network Architecture)

NRZ (Non-Return to Zero)

NRZ is a signaling method in which the voltage does not necessarily return to a zero, or neutral, state after each bit is transmitted. Therefore, the signal remains at the same level for the entire bit interval, and may

remain at this level for several bit intervals if the same value is transmitted multiple times in succession. Such a signal method is not self-clocking.

SEE ALSO
Encoding, Signal

NSA (Next Station Addressing)

In FDDI, NSA is an addressing mode by which a station can send a packet, or frame, to the next station in the ring, without knowing that station's address.

SEE ALSO
FDDI (Fiber Distributed Data Interface)

NSAP (Network Service Access Point)

In the OSI Reference Model, the NSAP represents the location through which a transport layer entity can get access to network layer services. Each NSAP has a unique OSI network address.

SEE ALSO
SAP (Service Access Point)

NTFS (NT File System)

NTFS is the native file system for Windows NT. NTFS features include the following:

- File names of up to 255 characters. Because NTFS supports the 16-bit Unicode character representation scheme, it is possible to include foreign characters in file names.

- Automatic creation of a DOS-compatible file name. NTFS automatically creates a version of the file name that is compatible with the 8.3 (name.extension) rule for DOS file names.

- Support for both the FAT (file allocation table) from DOS and HPFS (High-Performance File System) from OS/2.

- Special storage methods to help increase file access speed. For example, NTFS can actually store the contents of small files in its master file table (the table that contains file name, attribute, and location information). This provides almost immediate access.

- The ability to assign permissions for using and sharing files and directories.

- The use of a log to keep track of file transactions, to aid in recovery in case of malfunction.

- The ability to recover from disk crashes or errors. In some cases, the recovery can be done on the fly.

NuBus

NuBus is a bus specification that provides expansion capabilities for later Macintosh models. Based on a Texas Instruments design, the NuBus is a general-purpose bus that supports 32-bit data and address transfer. This bus connects to the Macintosh using a 96-pin DIN connector.

NuBus slots can be used to provide video capabilities (for example, color), extra memory, and networking capabilities. NuBus cards are self-configuring, and all NuBus expansion slots map to different internal addresses. To communicate with an expansion board, an application or process writes to a memory location associated with the board.

Null Modem

A serial cable and connector with a modified pin configuration, compared to an ordinary RS-232 cable. The null modem enables two computers to communicate directly (without modems as intermediaries). A null modem cable is also known as an *asynchronous modem eliminator* (AME). The figure "Null modem pin assignments" shows the pin assignments for the various 9- and 25-pin combinations used on PCs.

NVE (Network Visible Entity)

In an AppleTalk network, NVE refers to a resource that can be addressed through the network. An NVE is identified by name, type, and zone. The *entity type* specifies the generic class (such as LaserWriter or AFPServer) to which the resource belongs. Apple maintains a registry of entity types.

NVLAP (National Voluntary Laboratory Accreditation Program)

The NVLAP in the United States is one of the centers that has developed automated software for testing compliance with X.400 and X.500 standards. These centers develop test engines based on the abstract test suites specified by the ITU (International Telecommunication Union). Other centers include the NCC (National Computer Center) in the UK, Alcatel in France, and Danet GmbH in Germany.

NULL MODEM PIN ASSIGNMENTS

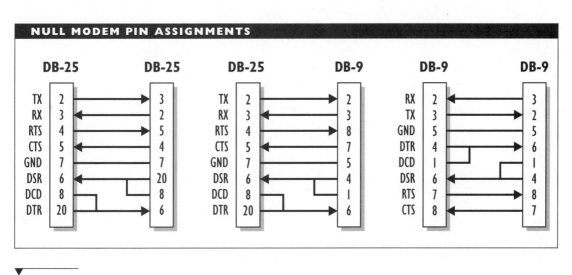

NVP (Nominal Velocity of Propagation)

In a network, NVP is a value indicating the signal speed as a proportion of the maximum speed theoretically possible. This value varies with cable and with architecture. Values for electrically based local-area networks range from about 60 to 85 percent of maximum. This value is also known as *VOP* (*velocity of propagation*).

a
b
c
d
e
f
g
h
i
j
k
l
m
n
o
p
q
r
s
t
u
v
w
x
y
z

OAI (Open Application Interface)

In telecommunications, OAI refers to an interface that can be used to program and change the operation of a PBX (private branch exchange).

OAM (Operations, Administration, and Maintenance) Functions

The OAM functions are a set of functions defined by the CCITT for managing the lower layers in an ATM (Asynchronous Transfer Mode) network, or more generally, a broadband ISDN (BISDN) network. The functions are implemented in a bidirectional flow of information between corresponding sublayers.

The functions fall into the following categories:

- Performance monitoring: These functions check that the network is functioning at the required level. They also generate information that can be used for maintenance.

- Defect detection: These functions identify defects or malfunctions in the network.

- System protection: These functions are responsible for isolating a malfunctioning element and switching over to other elements in order to keep the system running properly.

- Failure reporting: These functions inform other management entities (such as network management software or the other party) of a malfunction.

- Fault localization: These functions determine *where* a detected malfunction occurred, in order to enable the system to take the appropriate protection and failure-reporting measures.

Object

In its role as a current computing buzzword, the term *object* may refer to any type of entity that can have properties and actions (or methods) associated with it. Each property represents a slot into which specific information (a value for the property) can be filled. A particular combination of properties defines an object or object type, and a particular combination of values for the properties defines a specific instance of that object type.

In networking, the term object refers to an entity in some type of grouping, listing, or definition. For example, users, machines, devices, and servers are considered network-related objects. Abstract entities, such as groups, queues, and functions, can also be treated as objects.

Objects are mainly of interest in relation to specific networking contexts or models. For example, *managed objects* are elements that can be used to accomplish a task or monitored to get a performance overview and summary. These objects are important because they provide the data for the network management programs that network supervisors may be running.

In a Novell NetWare network, an object is any entity that is defined in a file server's bindery in NetWare versions 2.*x* and 3.*x*, or in the NetWare Directory Services (NDS) in version 4.*x*. *NDS objects* are the objects contained in the database for the NDS. These are discussed in the NDS article.

The global information tree contains definitions of many of the objects used in network management and other network-related activities.

In *object-oriented programming (OOP),* an object is a self-contained component that consists of both data (properties) and code (actions). Programming objects may be defined in terms of other objects, in which case the derived object may inherit properties and methods from the parent object. An actual instance of an object type will contain specific data values and methods that can distinguish it from other instances of that object type.

Inheritance and polymorphism, which enable a single object type to look and behave differently (but appropriately) in different instances, are two features that help give OOP the power and flexibility for which it is noted.

RELATED ARTICLES

Global Information Tree; NDS (NetWare Directory Services)

ObjectBroker

ObjectBroker, from Digital Equipment Corporation (DEC), is a package that allows applications running in object-oriented environments, but on different hardware, to communicate with each other in a transparent manner. It also enables developers to create object-oriented applications and services that are distributed across a network.

ObjectBroker runs on a variety of platforms, including DEC's own OpenVMS, ULTRIX, and OSF/1 environments, several other UNIX variants, Macintosh System 7, Microsoft Windows, and Windows NT.

COMPARE

OLE (Object Linking and Embedding)

Octet

A group of eight bits. The term is generally used when describing frame, or packet, formats.

ODA (Open Document Architecture)

The ODA is an ISO standard for the interchange of *compound documents,* which are documents that may contain fonts and graphics in addition to text.

The ISO 8613 standard specifies three levels of document representation:

- Level 1: Text-only data

- Level 2: Text and graphical data from a word processing environment

- Level 3: Text and graphical data from a desktop publishing environment

The standard is mainly concerned with preserving the layout and graphics information in the document. That is, a physical connection is taken for granted; it is the logical connection that is being standardized.

PRIMARY SOURCE

ISO document 8613

ODBC (Open Database Connectivity)

An API (Application Program Interface) developed by Microsoft for accessing databases under Windows. An alternative to

ODBC is IDAPI (Integrated Database Application Programming Interface), which is a standard proposed by Borland, IBM, Novell, and WordPerfect.

▼
ODI (Open Data-link Interface)

ODI is an architecture developed jointly by Novell and Apple that provides a standard interface for network interface cards (NICs) or device drivers. This makes it possible to use multiple protocols and multiple LAN drivers with a single NIC. For example, ODI can give a single workstation access to a Novell NetWare network through one protocol stack and to a UNIX-based or an AppleTalk network through another. In effect, ODI can make communications (partially) independent of both protocols and media.

ODI sits between LAN drivers (which talk to the NIC) and the protocol stacks. By providing separate interfaces to the protocols and the NICs, ODI allows these two levels to be mixed and matched in a transparent manner. The figure "ODI sits between protocol stacks and network interface cards" shows this arrangement.

The interface for ODI actually consists of two main components: LSL and MLI. The LSL (link-support layer) mediates between the protocols and the drivers. The LSL checks an incoming packet and sends it to the appropriate protocol stack. Outgoing packets are directed in an analogous manner to the appropriate MLID (multiple link interface driver).

The MLI (multiple link interface) communicates with the NICs through an MLID.

The MLI itself has three main components, each with a special focus:

- MSM (media-support module) provides the interface to the LSL. This ODI component is relatively stable.

- TSM (topology-specific module) provides the functions needed to deal with a particular network topology, such as Ethernet, Token Ring, or ARCnet. This component comes in several flavors, each of which is relatively stable. The module for a particular topology (such as Ethernet) handles all the variants for that topology (for example, Blue Book 802.3).

- HSM (hardware-specific module) provides the interface to a particular NIC. This is the element that is most subject to change.

Novell also provides ODINSUP, a driver that serves as an interface between ODI and NDIS (Network Driver Interface Specification), which is Microsoft's counterpart to ODI. When ODINSUP is available, the LSL will pass any unrecognized packets to ODINSUP. This driver will, in turn, pass the packet to NDIS, on the assumption that the NDIS driver will be able to deal with it.

BROADER CATEGORIES
Driver; LAN Driver

COMPARE
NDIS (Network Driver Interface Specification)

ODI SITS BETWEEN PROTOCOL STACKS AND NETWORK INTERFACE CARDS

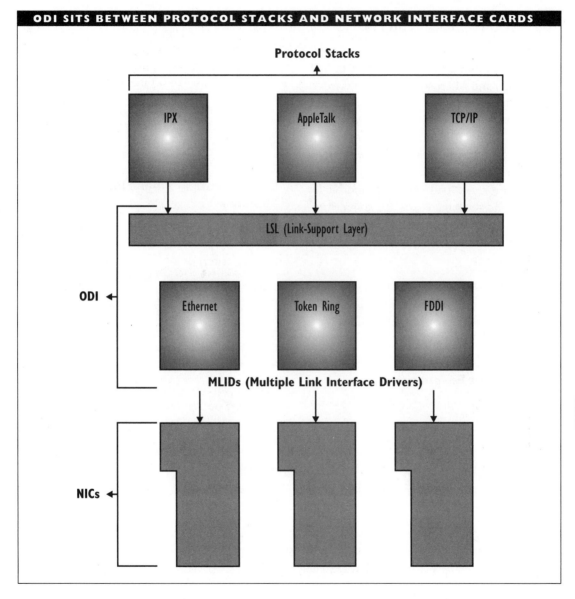

Protocol Stacks

IPX   AppleTalk   TCP/IP

LSL (Link-Support Layer)

ODI

Ethernet   Token Ring   FDDI

MLIDs (Multiple Link Interface Drivers)

NICs

a b c d e f g h i j k l m n o p q r s t u v w x y z

ODINSUP (ODI/NDIS Support)

ODINSUP is a Novell driver that can mediate between Novell's ODI (Open Data-link Interface) and Microsoft's NDIS (Network Driver Interface Specifications) interfaces for connecting protocol stacks and LAN drivers.

With ODINSUP, it is possible for protocol stacks supported by NDIS to communicate through the ODI's interfaces, so that a workstation can load both ODI and NDIS drivers and stack managers at the same time. The workstation can then log into different networks with a single network interface card (NIC).

BROADER CATEGORY

LAN Driver; NDIS (Network Driver Interface Specification); ODI (Open Data-link Interface)

OFB (Output Feedback)

An operating mode for the Data Encryption Standard (DES).

Office Drop

The network cable that goes to a node.

Offline Newsreader

An offline newsreader is one that can download files from a newsgroup so that a user can look at the postings at a later time. (A newsreader is a program for accessing, retrieving, and reading newsgroup postings.) Such a program can save in connect time charges, but may end up using a lot of storage and, in the end, taking just as much time as doing things online. Creating a useful *killfile* (news posting filter and selector) can help make an offline newsreader more effective.

BROADER CATEGORY

Newsreader

OFNP (Optical Fiber, Nonconductive Plenum)

A UL (Underwriters Laboratory) designation for optical fiber that meets certain fire-safety criteria.

SEE ALSO

Cable, Fiber-Optic; Cable Standards

OFNR (Optical Fiber, Nonconductive Riser)

A UL (Underwriters Laboratory) designation for optical fiber that meets certain fire-safety criteria.

SEE ALSO

Cable, Fiber-Optic; Cable Standards

OH (Off Hook)

In telephony, OH is used to indicate that a telephone line is in use.

Ohm

An ohm is the unit of resistance; the electrical counterpart to friction. This unit is symbolized by the uppercase Greek omega (Ω).

OIW (OSI Implementers Workshop)

OIW is one of three regional workshops for implementers of the OSI Reference Model. This workshop is for the North American region. The other workshops are EWOS (European Workshop for Open Systems) and AOW (Asia and Oceania Workshop).

OLE (Object Linking and Embedding)

OLE (pronounced "olay") is a mechanism by which Microsoft Windows applications can include each other's creations in files. For example, a graphics image or a spreadsheet can be incorporated into a document under the appropriate conditions. Once incorporated, this object can be modified or edited using the program that created it; the user can invoke this program by double-clicking on the object incorporated in the document file.

Currently, OLE is application-based, which means that OLE support must be written into the applications (as opposed to being available automatically as part of the Microsoft Windows environment). Any applications involved in an OLE transaction must explicitly support OLE. Two major versions of the OLE specifications, 1.0 and 2.0, have been released, and these have different capabilities. The possibilities in a given exchange are determined by the lowest version of OLE involved.

The *linking* and *embedding* in the name are actually alternatives. That is, you can do either of the following:

- *Link* a reference to the actual object to the document file. Before you can print the document or access the object through the document, the object needs to be loaded from disk. By retrieving the object only when needed, you ensure that the latest version of the object will be retrieved.

- *Embed* an object into a document file by making a copy of the object at the desired location. You can invoke the creating program from the embedded object; however, the embedded object is no longer affected by changes to the original object. That is, after embedding an image into a document, you can invoke the image creation program from the embedded copy, but editing the original image does not change the embedded copy.

COMPARE

DDE (Dynamic Data Exchange)

ONC (Open Network Computing)

A model for distributed computing, originally developed by Sun Microsystems but now supported in most UNIX implementations, including Novell's UnixWare. The ONC model uses Sun's NFS (Network File System) for handling files distributed over remote locations. Communication with remote servers and devices is through RPCs (remote procedure calls). The ONC model supports the TCP/IP protocol stack.

Open

In a cable, an *open* refers to a gap or separation in the conductive material somewhere along the cable's path, such as in one wire in a pair. Depending on the gap, this may impede or preclude the transmission of data along the cable.

In networking and other computer-related contexts, *open* is used as an adjective to refer to elements or interfaces whose specifications have been made public so they can be used by third parties to create compatible (or competing) products. This is in contrast to *closed,* or *proprietary,* environments.

Open Pipe

A term used to describe the path between sender and receiver in circuit-switched and leased-line communications. The intent is to indicate that the data flows directly between the two locations (through the open pipe), rather than needing to be broken into packets and routed by various paths.

Open System

Generally, a system whose specifications are published and made available for use, in order to make it easier to establish a connection or to communicate with the system. This is in contrast to a closed, or proprietary, system. Within the context of the OSI Reference Model, an open system is one that supports this model for connecting systems and networks.

SEE ALSO
OSI Reference Model

Open Systems Interconnection (OSI)

SEE
OSI (Open Systems Interconnection)

Operating System (OS)

SEE
OS (Operating System)

Optical Drive

An optical drive provides mass storage using optical or magneto-optical encoding. Optical drives are becoming more popular for networks because of their large storage capacity, which ranges from hundreds of megabytes to several gigabytes.

Optical drives are not yet supported directly in most network operating systems. One problem is the relatively slow access times for CD-ROM drives (200 to 350 milliseconds, or up to 30 times as long as hard disk access). This can cause network processes to time out (assume the device is not available and to return with an error condition). In some cases, however, the drive manufacturers can provide drivers and possibly other software to enable you to use the drive on a network.

Currently the following types of optical drives are available:

CD-ROM (compact disc–read-only memory): A read-only drive for a medium with a huge storage capacity of 660 megabytes (MB). CD-ROM drives cannot be used for recording data, only for reading. Compact discs can be useful as data, documentation, or software sources. Jukebox versions of CD-ROM drives can hold from 5 to 100 discs, and can provide access to any one of these discs within a few seconds.

WORM (write once, read many):
A WORM drive can record on its medium, but can write only once to each location on the disk. Once written, the information can be read as often as desired. Like compact discs, WORM disks have a very high storage capacity.

EO (erasable optical): An EO drive uses a medium similar to a compact disc, but encased in its own cartridge. This is a read/write medium on which information is stored in optical form. Novell's NetWare version 4.*x* supports a high capacity storage system (HCSS), which allows infrequently used network files to be stored on EO disks instead of on the hard disk.

OROM (optical read-only memory):
This storage method uses a storage format similar to that of CD-ROM, but an OROM disk can be read by a magneto-optical drive.

MO (magneto-optical): This is a general term for drives that use optical means to store data.

BROADER CATEGORY
Peripheral

Optical Switch

An optical switch uses light to carry out a switching function, such as to connect an input stream to an output channel. Optical switches are much faster than electromechanical or electrical switches, and they are needed for the very high-speed communications technologies beginning to arrive.

Optical Time Domain Reflectometer (OTDR)

SEE
OTDR (Optical Time Domain Reflectometer)

ORB (Object Request Broker)

An object request broker is a service that can enable existing applications to communicate with object-oriented applications or frontends. This makes it possible for an application to request a service without knowing the directory structure of the environment from which the service is being requested. Once a request has been made, the ORB will find the requested object, if possible, and will apply the appropriate method—all in a manner that should be transparent to the requester.

The ORB is a central part of the CORBA (Common Object Request Broker Architecture) that has been developed by the OMG (Object Management Group).

SEE ALSO
CORBA

Order of Magnitude

An order of magnitude refers to a change in a numerical value that is a multiple of the original, or reference, value. In decimal systems, changes that are powers of 10 are commonly used as orders of magnitude. Thus, A and B differ by one order of magnitude if one is 10 times the other; they differ by two orders of magnitude if one is 100 times the other. Note that A and B are still

a b c d e f g h i j k l m n o p q r s t u v w x y z

said to differ by an order of magnitude even if one is 90 times the other. For some computations, powers of 1,000 (10^3) are used as (decimal) orders of magnitude.

The order of magnitude is determined by the base being used. Thus, in a binary system, powers of 2 determine orders of magnitude. The table "Prefixes for Selected Orders of Magnitude" lists some of the prefixes used.

Note that the orders of magnitude are referenced to powers of two. That is, a "mega"

is defined as 2^{20} (1,048,576), rather than as 10^6 (1,000,000 exactly). Both binary and decimal references can be used. The context will determine which is more appropriate. For example, binary values are more meaningful when speaking of storage or memory quantities; decimal values are more meaningful when speaking of time or frequency values.

ADVANTAGES OF EO DRIVES

For all practical purposes, EO drives are mass storage devices, and they may soon be the storage device of choice. The medium has several significant advantages:

- Capacity: A disk the size of a 3.5 inch floppy disk can hold over 200 MB; a disk not much larger than a 5.25 inch floppy disk can hold a gigabyte of information.

- Security: The storage capacities are high enough to make it feasible to store entire working environments on a single disk, so that everyone can have his or her own working environments.

- Access Time: Access times of under 20 milliseconds are already possible, making EO drives competitive with hard disk drives.

- Data Integrity: Data is stored optically rather than magnetically. This makes the data impervious to corruption or accidental erasure by electrical or magnetic disturbances.

- Life Expectancy: Since the read/write components never actually touch the medium, there is minimal wear and tear. EO discs have an expected lifetime of 30 to 40 years.

- Price: Street prices for such disks are already competitive with floppy disk prices and considerably better than hard disk prices. With economies of scale that can be expected as the market grows, these prices will fall even more.

- Portability: Portable EO drives, for example, the Tahoe and Tahoe-230 from Pinnacle Micro, make it easy and convenient to take your working environment when moving from place to place.

Fujitsu Computer Products (800-626-4686) offers 128 MB and 230 MB EO drives: the DynaMO and the DynaMO-230.

Pinnacle Micro (800-533-7070) has a whole line of EO drives, with capacities ranging from 128 MB to over 10 GB. The latter is actually a jukebox device, capable of holding several disks and of switching between them.

PREFIXES FOR SELECTED ORDERS OF MAGNITUDE

PREFIX	NAME	2^x	10^y	TERM
B	Bronto	$x = 70$	$y = 21$	Sextillions
E	Exa	$x = 60$	$y = 18$	Quintillions
P	Peta	$x = 50$	$y = 15$	Quadrillions
T	Tera	$x = 40$	$y = 12$	Trillions
G	Giga	$x = 30$	$y = 9$	Billions
M	Mega	$x = 20$	$y = 6$	Millions
k	kilo	$x = 10$	$y = 3$	Thousands
m	Milli	$x = -10$	$y = -3$	Thousandths
&m	Micro	$x = -20$	$y = -6$	Millionths
n	Nano	$x = -30$	$y = -9$	Billionths
p	Pico	$x = -40$	$y = -12$	Trillionths
f	Femto	$x = -50$	$y = -15$	Quadrillionths
a	Atta	$x = -60$	$y = -18$	Quintillionths

Originate Mode

In communications, the originate mode is the mode of the device that initiates the call and waits for the remote device to respond.

COMPARE
Response Mode

OS (Operating System)

The operating system is the software that runs a computer. DOS, OS/2, UNIX, and System 7 are examples of widely used operating systems.

An operating system does the following:

- Deals with the computer's hardware

- Provides an environment and an interface for users

- Carries out (executes) user commands or program instructions

- Provides input and output, memory and storage, file and directory management capabilities

An operating system generally provides a generic interface and command set for users. This interface can be replaced with a different operating system shell. Such shells may also include additional commands you can use while running a particular shell. Microsoft Windows provides a graphics-oriented shell for DOS-based environments;

the Thompson shell (from Thompson Automation) or the mks Toolkit (from Mortice Kern Systems) provide UNIX-like shells for DOS.

A computer's "native" (built-in or default) operating system may be supplemented or replaced by a different operating system, such as a network operating system (NOS).

In addition to the responsibilities of an ordinary operating system, a NOS must be able to do the following:

- Provide access to files and resources (for example, printers) on the network

- Provide messaging and/or electronic-mail (e-mail) services

- Enable nodes on the network to communicate with each other

- Support interprocess communications (IPC), which enable processes on the network to communicate with each other

- Respond to requests from applications or users on the network

- Map requests and paths to the appropriate places on the network

The NOS may actually perform the regular operating system's duties, or it may rely on the native operating system to carry these out.

OS/2

OS/2—or OS/2 Warp, as the latest version is called—is a 32-bit operating system for Intel-based machines. The system was originally developed jointly by IBM and Microsoft, but is now being developed completely by IBM. In this entry, "OS/2" refers to any version of the operating system. The "Warp" was added to the product name with version 3, and this word will be included only where that specific version of the operating system is under discussion.

OS/2 supports true preemptive multitasking, multiple threads, flat (i.e., non-segmented) memory addressing, an object-oriented graphical user interface (GUI), various types of networking, and installable file systems. A major benefit of true multitasking is that crashing an application will crash only that one application, and will not freeze the entire machine. Other tasks will continue executing.

File System Support

Support for the file allocation table (FAT) based system used in DOS, and OS/2's own HPFS (High-Performance File System) is built into OS/2. The system can also support add-on file systems, such as a CDFS (CD-ROM file system).

The HPFS has two particularly useful features: long names and extended attributes. HPFS names can be up to 254 characters and can include spaces. The extended attributes feature can be used to associate whatever information or properties are appropriate for a file. For example, icons, version or other special information, and resources used for the file can be stored in the extended attributes. An extended attribute can even be another file. These attractive features can cause compatibility problems, however. DOS and Microsoft Windows programs won't be able to use HPFS files.

OS/2's Workplace Shell provides a powerful object-oriented GUI that integrates the capabilities of both the Microsoft Windows Program and File Manager. Being object-based, the Workplace Shell knows how to manipulate various types of elements (such as text or data files, icons, applications, and devices), and can be taught to handle others. REXX is a command and macro programming language, which can be used to write scripts and enhance the Workplace Shell.

OS/2 Interfaces and Resources

REXX is a command and macro language that is included with OS/2. In fact, REXX is a full-fledged programming language, so you can use it to write scripts that are much more complex and sophisticated than the batch files that DOS supports. Such scripts can help enhance the Workplace Shell or make the user's work easier in other ways.

Version 3—that is, OS/2 Warp—also includes a Bonus Pak of resources that help make the OS/2 environment more intelligent and more capable. Properly used, such features can also make the user more useful and more capable. For example, the Bonus Pak includes a Personal Information Manager (PIM), which provides many of the elements you need to organize your life—at least on disk. The PIM includes a phone book, a calendar, and an appointment scheduler; it has a daily planner, note pad, and a to-do list. There is even a program, called Event Monitor, that will sound alarms and even carry out automated tasks for you.

IBM Works is an integrated software suite that provides several of the most commonly used applications—word processing, spreadsheet, database, and charting programs, and a report generator—in a single package. Collectively, the applications may not be as powerful as those included in the integrated office packages by Lotus (SmartSuite), Microsoft (Office and Office Professional), and Novell (PerfectOffice). Nevertheless, each application is a full-featured and fully-functional example of its genre.

The Bonus Pak also includes a multimedia viewer, which can handle image, video, and sound files. The viewer will call the appropriate component to display or play non-text material that appears in a program or file.

Several of the added resources have to do with networking or other forms of telecommunication. These resources include:

- HyperACCESS Lite, which is a general communications program that can serve as a front end for connections to online services or bulletin board systems (BBSs).

- FaxWorks for OS/2, which provides the ability to send, receive, view, manipulate, and print... (surprise, surprise) faxes.

- CIM (CompuServe Information Manager) for OS/2, which can provide access to CompuServe's online services.

- Internet Connection Services, which provide the software needed to connect to the Internet over a modem (using a SLIP connection), and which also includes programs for using the Internet. This package provides Gopher, FTP, and Telnet programs,

a
b
c
d
e
f
g
h
i
j
k
l
m
n
o
p
q
r
s
t
u
v
w
x
y
z

as well as a newsreader, e-mail client, and a browser (hypertext file reader) for viewing World Wide Web (WWW) files. You can use this package to connect to an Internet Access Provider. The program is preconfigured to connect you to the IBM Global Network, but you can sign up with a different provider if you wish.

OS/2 Versions

Version 1 of OS/2 was actually a 16-bit operating system. Current versions of OS/2 can, however, run these 16-bit programs by using a readdressing scheme. OS/2 2.0, which was released in 1992, was a major revision, but it could still run OS/2 1.*x* and DOS programs. Microsoft Windows support was limited to Windows 3.0, and programs running in enhanced mode were not supported.

Version 2.1, released in 1993, added support for Microsoft Windows 3.1 enhanced-mode programs. This version also added support for PCMCIA cards and improved support for other devices, such as CD-ROMs and monitors. OS/2 for Windows made OS/2 available to users who have Microsoft Windows 3.1 installed.

OS/2 Warp

With version 3.0, IBM added the word Warp to the name. It also simplified many of the system's networking capabilities and added a few. Version 3 packages come in either of two configurations:

- Those that include WIN-OS/2, which is IBM's emulation of Microsoft Windows 3.1. This form is more expensive but does not require you to have Microsoft Windows installed on your system. Once WIN-OS/2 is installed, it can run most Windows programs. It's possible to install this version even if Microsoft Windows is installed, although it's not clear why you would want to pay the extra money and use up extra storage, unless you need to run a 16-bit Windows application that can't run under WIN-OS/2, but can run under Windows.

- Those that don't include a Windows emulator. In this configuration, OS/2 can use Microsoft Windows to run Windows programs, provided Microsoft Windows is installed on your system.

OS/2 Warp Connect

OS/2 Warp Connect adds support for local area networks to the telecommunications and internetworking capabilities of plain OS/2 Warp. Warp Connect provides the software needed to support your machine as a network node—either at home or from a remote location. The additional networking support comes from:

- IBM Peer for OS/2, which enables users to share information and resources—that is, to function as peers in a network. These machines can also connect to PCs running Windows for Workgroups or other networking software.

- LAN Client solution, which makes the node a client machine for either a LAN Server or a NetWare network.

- TCP/IP for OS/2, which provides a TCP/IP protocol stack and access to the Internet (after subscribing to an Internet Access Provider).

- LAN Distance Remote, which lets you connect a remote PC to the PC, and to get onto the network from the remote location.

Warp Connect also includes Lotus Notes Express, which enables users on the network to collaborate on projects. Finally, Warp Connect comes with or without a WIN-OS/2 component. These versions come in blue and red boxes, respectively.

OS/2 for SMP

In the past few years, machines with multiple processors have become increasingly popular. In Symmetric Multiprocessing (SMP), all the processors are equals, and a task can always be passed on to the next available processor.

OS/2 for SMP can support machines with between 2 and 16 processors, and provides the same multitasking and multiple thread support to a multiple processor system as regular OS/2 provides for a single processor. OS/2 for SMP conforms to version 1.1 of the Multiprocessor System Specification.

OS/2 for SMP must be pre-installed, and both pricing and configuration depend on the number of processors in the machine.

OS/2 LAN Server

This is actually a version of IBM's LAN Server network operating system built on OS/2. It provides support for a network server running DOS, Windows, and OS/2

clients or applications. An entry-level version supports up to 100 nodes, and an Advanced version supports up to 1,000.

LAN Server 4.0 includes all of OS/2's features and capabilities, and adds its own enhancements and improvements—for example, fault tolerance and disk mirroring for extra data protection. Extensions to OS/2's HPFS make file access much faster.

LAN Server provides peer-to-peer capabilities so that machines—even DOS clients—can communicate with each other. Interestingly, IBM has made TCP/IP the default protocol stack in LAN Server 4.0. LAN Server can communicate with servers from other environments—including NetWare, Solaris, LAN Manager, Windows NT, MVS, and VM.

OS/2 and Networking

OS/2 is network-friendly, and IBM is marketing OS/2 in part as an operating environment that can integrate various environments. In fact, both Microsoft's LAN Manager and IBM's LAN Server network operating systems are built on OS/2. LAN Manager runs on top of OS/2 1.3, but OS/2 2.0 and 2.1 machines can be clients on a LAN Manager network. LAN Manager is unlikely to be ported to newer versions, however, since Microsoft has built its capabilities into Windows NT.

LAN Server also runs on top of OS/2, and it does support the newer versions as well. LAN Server 3.0 includes all of OS/2's features and capabilities and adds its own enhancements and improvements, such as fault tolerance and disk mirroring, which help provide data protection. Extensions to

OS/2's HPFS provide more features and also make file access much faster.

OS/2 machines can be either servers or clients in a Novell NetWare network. With OS/2 machines, NetWare runs alongside OS/2. OS/2 systems can be clients in UNIX and VINES networks.

OS/2 and Windows

OS/2's influence is probably greater than its market share might suggest. While OS/2 has only a small share of the market when compared to DOS and Windows, this operating system is found in some mission-critical and widely-used applications. For example, ATM machines are almost all controlled by OS/2.

OSI (Open Systems Interconnection)

In networking and telecommunications, OSI is used to express the main concept of the ISO's seven-layered model. In this context, an open system is a computer (with software and peripherals) that supports this model for connecting systems on a network and for transmitting information among these systems.

SEE ALSO

OSI Reference Model

OSI Implementers Workshop (OIW)

SEE

OIW (OSI Implementers Workshop)

OSI Network Management Model

A network management model that provides a set of concepts and guidelines for various aspects of network management. The model does not provide standards or specifications; rather, it is intended as the conceptual basis for such specifications. Also known as the ISO network management model, for the International Standardization Organization, which developed the model.

SEE

Network Management

OSI Network Address

In the OSI Reference Model, an address associated with an entity at the transport layer. This address may be up to 20 bytes long. OSI network addresses have two components: a standardized initial domain part, and a domain-specific part, which is under the control of the network administrator.

OSI Presentation Address

In the OSI Reference Model, an address associated with an entity at the application layer. This address consists of an OSI network address and of selectors that identify service access points (SAPs) for the presentation, session, and transport layers. The selector values provide layer-specific addresses.

OSI Reference Model

The OSI (Open Systems Interconnection) Reference Model is a seven-layer model developed by the ISO (International Standardization Organization) to describe how to connect any combination of devices for purposes of communications.

This model describes the task in terms of seven functional layers, and specifies the functions that must be available at each layer. The seven layers form a hierarchy from the applications at the top to the physical communications medium at the bottom. The functions and capabilities expected at each layer are specified in the reference model; however, the model does not prescribe how this functionality must be implemented.

The focus in this model is on the "interconnection" and on the information that can be passed over this connection. The OSI model does not concern itself with the internal operations of the systems involved.

Communications Models

The OSI Reference Model incorporates two communications models:

- A horizontal, protocol-based model by which programs or processes on different machines communicate

- A vertical, service-based model by which layers on a single machine communicate

These are illustrated in the figure "Communications in the OSI Reference Model."

A program or protocol (P) on a particular machine (A) communicates with a counterpart program or protocol (Q) operating at the same layer on another machine (B). In order to do this, the program on each machine must rely on the services of the layer below the program's.

The sending program on machine A must rely on its service layer to encapsulate P's information properly, so that P's packets reach their destination. The receiving program (Q) on machine B must rely on its service layer to deliver a packet from P correctly. Q's service layer may, in turn, rely on its service layer to verify that the delivered material is error-free.

Communications Elements

In order to communicate, the following elements are needed:

- At least two parties wishing to communicate. These can be the same or different programs on each machine, or they can be two layers on the same machine.

- A common language, or protocol, with which these parties can communicate. Horizontally (that is, between machines) the two programs need a common protocol or an interpreter to translate for each program. Vertically, layers communicate through APIs (Application Program Interfaces). The APIs define the available functions for a layer and provide the mechanisms for invoking these functions.

OSI Layers

The OSI Reference Model uses seven functional layers to define the communication capabilities needed to enable any two machines to communicate with each other.

The seven layers range from the application layer at the top to the physical layer at the bottom. The top layer is where users and application programs communicate with a

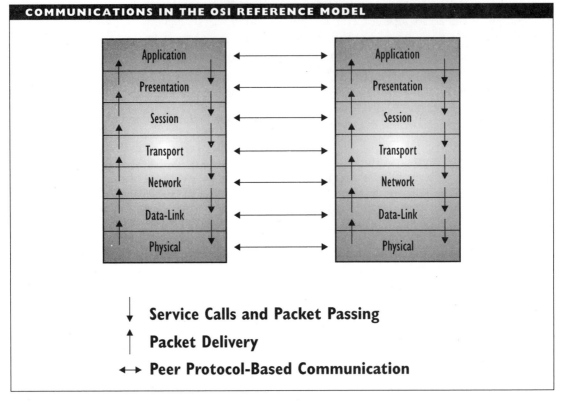

COMMUNICATIONS IN THE OSI REFERENCE MODEL

↓ **Service Calls and Packet Passing**

↑ **Packet Delivery**

↔ **Peer Protocol-Based Communication**

network. The bottom layer is where the actual transmissions take place. Services at one layer communicate with and make use of services at adjacent layers.

The middle layer (transport) is pivotal. It separates the application- and service-oriented upper layers from the network- and communication-oriented lower layers, which are known as the *subnet layers*. The figure "OSI layer groupings" shows this division.

The individual layers are discussed in the sections that follow, from highest to lowest layer. The discussion includes examples of programs and protocols, but be aware that many programs have capabilities that span or straddle two or more OSI layers. This is particularly true of programs developed in

other (non-OSI) communications frameworks (IBM mainframe, UNIX/Internet, and so on). It is also more likely to be true with upper-layer programs.

For example, it is not unusual for a "hyperthyroid" application to include data translation capabilities (conversions, encryption, or compression), which are assigned to the presentation layer in the OSI model. Such a program can fit as an example in either layer.

Application Layer

The application layer is the topmost layer in the OSI Reference Model. This layer is responsible for giving applications access to

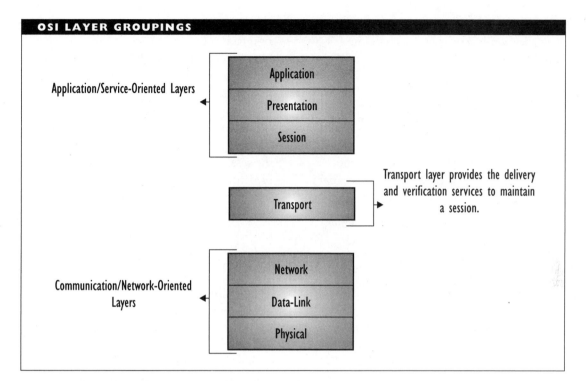

OSI LAYER GROUPINGS

Application/Service-Oriented Layers

- Application
- Presentation
- Session

Transport

Transport layer provides the delivery and verification services to maintain a session.

Communication/Network-Oriented Layers

- Network
- Data-Link
- Physical

the network. Examples of application-layer tasks include file transfer, electronic mail (e-mail) services, and network management.

Application-layer services are much more varied than the services in lower layers, because the entire gamut of application and task possibilities is available here. The specific details depend on the framework or model being used. For example, there are several network management applications. Each of these provides services and functions specified in a different framework for network management.

Programs can get access to the application-layer services through application service elements (ASEs). There are a variety of such ASEs, each designed for a class of tasks. See the ASE article for details.

To accomplish its tasks, the application layer passes program requests and data to the presentation layer, which is responsible for encoding the application layer's data in the appropriate form.

Application Layer Protocols Not surprisingly, application programs are found at this layer. Also found here are network shells, which are the programs that run on workstations and that enable the workstation to join the network. Actually, programs such as network shells often provide functions that span or are found at multiple layers. For example, NETX, the Novell NetWare shell program, spans the top three layers.

a
b
c
d
e
f
g
h
i
j
k
l
m
o
p
q
r
s
t
u
v
w
x
y
z

Programs and protocols that provide application-layer services include the following:

- NICE (Network Information and Control Exchange), which provides network monitoring and management capabilities

- FTAM (File Transfer, Access, and Management), which provides capabilities for remote file handling

- FTP (File Transfer Protocol), which provides file transfer capabilities

- X.400, which specifies protocols and functions for message handling and e-mail services

- CMIP, which provides network management capabilities based on a framework formulated by the ISO

- SNMP, which provides network management within a non-OSI framework. This protocol does not conform to the OSI model, but does provide functionality that is specified within the OSI model

- Telnet, which provides terminal emulation and remote login capabilities. Telnet's capabilities go beyond the application layer

- rlogin, which provides remote login capabilities for UNIX environments

Presentation Layer

The presentation layer is responsible for presenting information in a manner suitable for the applications or users dealing with the information. Functions such as data conversion from EBCDIC to ASCII (or vice versa), use of special graphics or character sets, data compression or expansion, and data encryption or decryption are carried out at this layer.

The presentation layer provides services for the application layer above it, and uses the session layer below it. In practice, the presentation layer rarely appears in pure form. Rather, application- or session-layer programs will encompass some or all of the presentation-layer functions.

Session Layer

The session layer is responsible for synchronizing and sequencing the dialog and packets in a network connection. This layer is also responsible for making sure that the connection is maintained until the transmission is complete, and ensuring that appropriate security measures are taken during a session (that is, a connection). Functions defined at the session layer include those for network gateway communications.

The session layer is used by the presentation layer above it, and uses the transport layer below it.

Session Layer Protocols Session-layer capabilities are often part of other configurations (for example, those that include the presentation layer). The following protocols encompass many of the session-layer functions.

- ADSP (AppleTalk Data Stream Protocol), which enables two nodes to establish a reliable connection for data transfer

- NetBEUI, which is an implementation and extension of NetBIOS

- NetBIOS, which actually spans layers 5, 6, and 7, but which includes capabilities for monitoring sessions to make sure they are running smoothly

- PAP (Printer Access Protocol), which provides access to a PostScript printer in an AppleTalk network

Transport Layer

In the OSI Reference Model, the transport layer is responsible for providing data transfer at an agreed-upon level of quality, such as at specified transmission speeds and error rates.

To ensure delivery, outgoing packets are assigned numbers in sequence. The numbers are included in the packets that are transmitted by lower layers. The transport layer at the receiving end checks the packet numbers to make sure all have been delivered and to put the packet contents into the proper sequence for the recipient.

The transport layer provides services for the session layer above it, and uses the network layer below it to find a route between source and destination. The transport layer is crucial in many ways, because it sits between the upper layers (which are strongly application-dependent) and the lower ones (which are network-based).

Subnet Layers and Transmission Quality In the OSI model, the three layers below the transport layer are known as the *subnet* layers. These layers are responsible for getting packets from the source to the destination. In fact, relay devices (such as bridges,

routers, or X.25 circuits) use only these three layers, since their job is actually just to pass on a signal or a packet. Such devices are known as intermediate systems (ISs). In contrast, components that *do* use the upper layers as well are known as *end systems* (ESs). See the End System and Intermediate System articles for more information.

The transmission services provided by the subnet layers may or may not be reliable. In this context, a *reliable service* is one that will either deliver a packet without error or inform the sender if such error-free transmission was not possible.

Similarly, the subnet layer transmission services may or may not be connection-oriented. In connection-oriented communications, a connection between sender and receiver is established first. If the connection is successful, all the data is transmitted in sequence along this connection. When the transmission is finished, the connection is broken. Packets in such a transmission do not need to be assigned sequence numbers because each packet is transmitted immediately after its predecessor and along the same path.

In contrast, in connectionless communications, packets are sent independently of each other, and may take different paths to the destination. With such a communications mode, packets may get there in random order, and packets may get lost, discarded, or duplicated. Before transmission, each packet must be numbered to indicate the packet's position in the transmission, so that the message can be reassembled at the destination.

Since the transport layer must be able to get packets between applications, the services needed at this layer depend on what the subnet layers do. The more work the subnet layers do, the less the transport layer must do.

Subnet Service Classes Three types of subnet service are distinguished in the OSI model:

- Type A: Very reliable, connection-oriented service

- Type B: Unreliable, connection-oriented service

- Type C: Unreliable, possibly connectionless service

Transport Layer Protocols To provide the capabilities required for whichever service type applies, several classes of transport layer protocols have been defined in the OSI model:

- TP0 (Transfer Protocol Class 0), which is the simplest protocol. It assumes type A service—that is, a subnet that does most of the work for the transport layer. Because the subnet is reliable, TP0 requires neither error detection nor error correction; because the connection is connection-oriented, packets do not need to be numbered before transmission. X.25 is an example of a relay service that is connection-oriented and sufficiently reliable for TP0.

- TP1 (Transfer Protocol Class 1), which assumes a type B subnet; that is, one that may be unreliable. To deal with this, TP1 provides its own error detection, along with facilities for getting

the sender to retransmit any erroneous packets.

- TP2 (Transfer Protocol Class 2), which also assumes a type A subnet. However, TP2 can multiplex transmissions, so that multiple transport connections can be sustained over the single network connection.

- TP3 (Transfer Protocol Class 3), which also assumes a type B subnet. TP3 can also multiplex transmissions, so that this protocol has the capabilities of TP1 and TP2.

- TP4 (Transfer Protocol Class 4), which is the most powerful protocol, in that it makes minimal assumptions about the capabilities or reliability of the subnet. TP4 is the only one of the OSI transport-layer protocols that supports connectionless service.

Other transport layer protocols include:

- TCP and UDP, which provide connection-oriented and connection-less transport services, respectively. These protocols are used in most UNIX-based networks.

- SPX, which is used in Novell's NetWare environments.

- PEP, which is part of the XNS protocol suite from Xerox.

- VOTS, which is used in Digital Equipment Corporation networks.

- AEP, ATP, NBP, and RTMP, which are part of the AppleTalk protocol suite.

Network Layer

The network layer (also known as the *packet layer*) is the third lowest layer, or the uppermost subnet layer. It is responsible for the following tasks:

- Determining addresses or translating from hardware to network addresses. These addresses may be on a local network or they may refer to networks located elsewhere on an internetwork. One of the functions of the network layer is, in fact, to provide capabilities needed to communicate on an internetwork.

- Finding a route between a source and a destination node or between two intermediate devices.

- Establishing and maintaining a logical connection between these two nodes, to establish either a connectionless or a connection-oriented communication.

The data is processed and transmitted using the data-link layer below the network layer. Responsibility for guaranteeing proper delivery of the packets lies with the transport layer, which uses network-layer services.

Network Layer Protocols Two important classes of network layer protocols are address resolution protocols and routing protocols. Address resolution protocols are concerned with determining a unique network address for a source or destination node.

Routing protocols are concerned with getting packets from a local network to another network. After finding the destination network, it is necessary to determine a path to the destination network. This path will usually involve just routers, except for the first and last parts of the path.

Protocols at the network layer include the following:

- ARP (Address Resolution Protocol), which converts from hardware to network addresses.

- CLNP (Connectionless Network Protocol), which is an ISO-designed protocol.

- DDP (Datagram Delivery Protocol), which provides connectionless service in AppleTalk networks.

- ICMP (Internet Control Message Protocol), which is an error-handling protocol.

- IGP (Interior Gateway Protocol), which is used to connect routers within an administrative domain. This is also the name for a class of protocols.

- Integrated IS-IS, which is a specific IGP.

- IPX (Internetwork Packet Exchange), which is part of Novell's protocol suite.

- IP (Internet Protocol), which is one of the UNIX environment protocols.

- X.25 PLP (Packet Layer Protocol), which is used in an X.25 switching network.

a
b
c
d
e
f
g
h
i
j
k
l
m
n
o
p
q
r
s
t
u
v
w
x
y
z

Data-Link Layer

The data-link layer is responsible for creating, transmitting, and receiving data packets. The data-link layer provides services for the various protocols at the network layer, and uses the physical layer to transmit or receive material.

The data-link layer creates packets appropriate for the network architecture being used. Requests and data from the network layer are part of the data in these packets (or *frames,* as they are often called at this layer). These packets are passed down to the physical layer; from there, the data is transmitted to the physical layer on the destination machine.

Network architectures (such as Ethernet, ARCnet, Token Ring, and FDDI) encompass the data-link and physical layers, which is why these architectures support services at the data-link level. These architectures also represent the most common protocols used at the data-link level.

The IEEE's (802.*x*) networking working groups have refined the data-link layer into two sublayers: the logical-link control (LLC) sublayer at the top and the media-access control (MAC) sublayer at the bottom. The LLC sublayer must provide an interface for the network layer protocols. The MAC sublayer must provide access to a particular physical encoding and transport scheme.

Data-Link Layer Protocols Link access or data-link control protocols are used to label, package, and send network-layer (properly addressed) packets. The following protocols are used at the data-link layer:

- ELAP (EtherTalk Link Access Protocol), which provides a Macintosh with access to an Ethernet network.

- HDLC (High-level Data Link Control), which is based on IBM's SDLC and which has been standardized by the ISO. HDLC is a very flexible protocol for accessing data-link services.

- LAPB (Link Access Protocol, Balanced), which is used in X.25 networks.

- LAPD (Link Access Protocol, D channel), which is used in ISDN (Integrated Services Digital Network).

- LLAP (LocalTalk Link Access Protocol), which provides a Macintosh with access to a LocalTalk network.

- PPP (Point-to-Point Protocol), which provides direct medium-speed communication between two machines. PPP operates over serial lines.

- SLIP (Serial Line Interface Protocol), which provides access to an Internet protocol network over serial lines. This protocol can be used to access the Internet.

- TLAP (TokenTalk Link Access Protocol), which provides a Macintosh with access to a Token Ring network.

Physical Layer

The physical is the lowest layer in the OSI Reference Model. This layer gets data packets from the data-link layer above it, and converts the contents of these packets into a series of electrical signals that represent 0 and 1 values in a digital transmission.

These signals are sent across a transmission medium to the physical layer at the receiving end. At the destination, the physical layer converts the electrical signals into a series of bit values. These values are grouped into packets and passed up to the data-link layer.

Transmission Properties Defined The mechanical and electrical properties of the transmission medium are defined at this level. These include the following:

- The type of cable and connectors used. Cable may be coaxial, twisted-pair, or fiber-optic. The types of connectors depend on the type of cable.

- The pin assignments for the cable and connectors. Pin assignments depend on the type of cable and also on the network architecture being used.

- Format for the electrical signals. The encoding scheme used to signal 0 and 1 values in a digital transmission or particular values in an analog transmission depend on the network architecture being used. Most networks use digital signaling, and most use some form of Manchester encoding for the signal.

Physical Layer Specifications Examples of specifications for this layer include the following:

- EIA-232D, which specifies both the interface and electrical signal

characteristics for a serial connection between a DTE (data terminal equipment) and DCE (data communications equipment). This standard is a revision and extension of the more familiar RS-232C standard that has connected so many computers to modems and printers over the years. Equivalent to CCITT V.24 (interface) and V.28 (electrical characteristics) standards.

- RS-422A and RS-423A, which specify the electrical characteristics of balanced and unbalanced voltage circuits for a digital interface. Equivalent to CCITT standards V.10 and V.11, respectively.

- RS-449, which specifies general-purpose serial interfaces for 37- and 9-pin connectors.

- RS-530, which specifies the interface for a high-speed 25-pin serial connection between a DTE and a DCE.

- ISO 2110, which defines the connector pin assignments for 25-pin serial connectors. These assignments correspond to those defined in CCITT V.24 and RS-232D.

- IEEE 802.3, which defines various flavors of Ethernet, including the physical connections and signaling methods.

- IEEE 802.5, which defines the physical connections and signaling rules for Token Ring networks.

a b c d e f g h i j k l m n o p q r s t u v w x y z

Model Operation

The ultimate goal of the activity in the OSI Reference Model is peer communication: that is, to allow comparable layers on two different machines to communicate. Thus, an application on machine A wants to communicate with the same or a different application on machine B. Similarly, the transport layer on machine A is communicating with its counterpart on machine B.

Since there is no direct connection between peer layers, the communication must take an indirect course: down the layer hierarchy on one machine and up the hierarchy on the other machine. Thus, in order to communicate, the application layer on A must first communicate with A's presentation layer. This layer must, in turn, communicate with the session layer below it.

SAPs (Service Access Points)

The actual interfaces between layers are through service access points (SAPs). These are unique addresses that the layers involved can use to exchange requests, replies, and data. Because multiple programs may be running at a given layer, each needs its own SAPs for communicating with the layers above and below it.

SAPs represent the generic communications slots between layers. To identify the layer under discussion, it is common practice to include a letter identifying the lower layer in the pair. For example, a SAP linking a presentation layer process to the session layer below it would be known as an SSAP.

PDUs (Protocol Data Units) and SDUs (Service Data Units)

Information is passed between layers in the form of packets, known as PDUs (protocol data units). The packet size and definition depends on the protocol suite involved in the horizontal communications. The basic strategy for passing PDUs is as follows:

- Packets are padded as they make their way down the layers on the sending machine, and are stripped as they make their way up the layers on the receiving machine.

- Once passed to the lower layer (layer Y), a data packet from the layer above (layer X), known as an XPDU or X-PDU (after the layer), is padded by adding Y-specific header and trailer material. Once padded, the XPDU is passed as layer Y's data—as a YPDU—down to layer Z, where the padding process is repeated with different information. For example, in going from the presentation to the network layer, a packet is padded at the session and transport layers before being passed to the network layer.

- The header materials in a PDU provide handling and delivery information for the process that receives the packet. Trailer materials typically provide error-checking information.

PDUs are sometimes known as SDUs (service data units) when being passed vertically, which is when the services of an adjacent layer are used to process or deliver the packet. Thus, a TPDU (a transport layer packet) may be considered an SDU when the packet is passed down to the network layer for routing. The literature is inconsistent as to whether this would be a TSDU or an NSDU—whether an SDU is named after the source or target layer.

As packets are padded, they may get too big to pass downward as single packets. When this happens, the packets must be segmented (divided into smaller packets), numbered, and sent on as properly sized PDUs. Segmented packets will need to be reconstructed on the receiving end.

PCI (Protocol Control Information)

Each sending layer gets material received from the layer above it, adds new material (which contains the layer's communication with its peer on the other machine), and passes this to the layer below for further processing.

At the sending station, this information is passed down until it reaches the physical layer. At this layer, the material is transmitted over an electrical or optical connection as a bit sequence. At the receiving station, the bit sequence is converted to bytes and is passed up the layers.

As it reaches each layer on the receiving machine, the layer removes the material included for the layer, takes whatever actions are appropriate for the message and the request, and then passes the stripped packet on to the next higher layer.

The header information that is added and stripped is known as the PCI (protocol control information) component. Depending on the protocols involved, this may contain information such as source and destination addresses and control settings.

Each layer adds its own PCI as the packet is passed down to the layer. By the time a packet from an application reaches the data-link layer, it will have five PCIs attached: from the application, presentation, session, transport, and network layers.

In summary, the following is added and created at each layer:

APCI + data = APDU

PPCI + APDU = PPDU

SPCI + PPDU = SPDU

TPCI + SPDU = TPDU

NPCI + TPDU = NPDU

DPCI + NPDU = DPDU

SEE ALSO
End System (ES); Intermediate System (IS); Network Management

OS Kernel

The core portion of an operating system. The kernel provides the most essential and basic system services (such as process and memory management).

OSME (Open Systems Message Exchange)

OSME refers to an IBM application for exchanging X.400 messages.

OSTC (Open System Testing Consortium)

A European consortium that developed a suite for testing conformance to the 1984 ITU X.400 series of recommendations about MHS (Message Handling System). This suite is used, for example, in the United States to assess conformance to the MHS requirements for GOSIP (Government Open Systems Interconnection Profile) certification. The Corporation for Open Systems (COS) in the US has developed a similar test suite.

OTDR (Optical Time Domain Reflectometer)

In fiber optics, an OTDR is a tool for testing the light signal. An OTDR can analyze a cable by sending out a light signal and then checking the amount and type of light reflected back.

Out-of-Band Communication

A type of communication that uses frequencies outside the range being used for data or message communication. Out-of-band communication is generally done for diagnostic or management purposes.

Output Feedback (OFB)

SEE

OFB (Output Feedback)

PABX (Private Automatic Branch Exchange)

A telephone exchange that provides automatic switching and other communication capabilities. Since almost all exchanges are automatic these days, the term has come to be used almost synonymously with PBX (private branch exchange).

PAC (Privilege Attribute Certificate)

In a *login service,* a note given to a user by the privilege service. This certificate, which cannot be forged, specifies the privileges accorded to the certificate's holder. When a user wants to access an application or a service, the PAC is checked to determine whether the user should be given the requested access.

PACE (Priority Access Control Enabled)

A proprietary variant of the Ethernet architecture developed by 3Com and collaborators for transmitting time-sensitive data, such as digitized video or audio, over Ethernet networks.

The strategy behind PACE is to prioritize the materials being transmitted, giving highest priority to data that must be sent at a constant rate to be comprehensible.

COMPARE
isoENET

Pacing

In communications, the temporary use of a lower transmission speed. For example,

pacing may be used to give the receiver time to catch up and process the data that has already been sent.

Packet

A packet is a well-defined block of bytes, which consists of header, data, and trailer. In a layered network architecture, packets created at one level may be inserted into another header/trailer envelope at a lower level.

Packets can be transmitted across networks or over telephone lines. In fact, network protocols and several communications protocols use packet switching to establish a connection and route information.

The format of a packet depends on the protocol that creates the packet. Various communications standards and protocols use special-purpose or specially defined packets to control or monitor a communications session. For example, the X.25 standard uses diagnostic, call clear, and reset packets (among others), as well as data packets.

Packets are sometimes also known as *frames,* although that term originally referred specifically to a packet at the data-link layer in the OSI Reference Model.

Packet, Dribble

A packet that ends on an odd byte.

Packet, Jabber

A meaningless transmission generated by a network node because of a network malfunction, such as a faulty transceiver or other error. A jabber packet is larger than the maximum size (1,518 bytes for Ethernet) and contains a bad CRC (cyclic redundancy check) value. In contrast, long frames exceed the maximum frame length but have a valid CRC value.

Packet, Ping

In an Ethernet network, a diagnostic packet sent by the NODEVIEW (or SERVERVU) applications in Novell's LANalyzer. The packet is used to test whether workstations or servers on the network are working correctly (are capable of receiving packets).

Packet Radio Network

A network that uses radio waves to transmit packets. Timing considerations aside, this approach may be the most plausible for long-distance wireless communications.

Packet Receive Buffer

RAM (random-access memory) set aside on a file server for holding packets temporarily until they can be processed by the server or sent onto the network. The RAM is allocated as a number of buffers, each of a predetermined size. This is also known as a *routing buffer* or a *communication buffer*.

Packet, Runt

A packet with too few bits. Compare this with a dribble packet, which is a packet that ends on an odd byte.

Packet Switching

Packet switching is a transmission method in which packets are sent across a shared medium from source to destination. The transmission may use any available path, or circuit, and the circuit is available as soon as the packet has been sent. The next packet in the transmission may take a different path.

With packet switching, multiple packets from the same transmission can be on their way to the destination at the same time. Because of the switching, the packets may not all take the same paths, and they may not arrive in the order in which they were sent.

The X.25 telecommunications standard uses packet switching, as do many local- and wide-area networks.

COMPARE
Circuit Switching; Message Switching

Packet-Switching Service

Any of several commercial enterprises that offer packet-switching capabilities to subscribers. CompuServe, SprintNet, and Tymnet are a few of the available services.

Packet Switch Node (PSN)

SEE
PSN (Packet Switch Node)

a b c d e f g h i j k l m n o **p** q r s t u v w x y z

PAD (Packet Assembler/Disassembler)

A hardware or software component that mediates between a packet-switching network and a PC or other asynchronous device (such as a bridge or router). For example, PADs are essential components of an X.25 connection.

The PAD's function is to assemble the PC's data into packets suitable for transmission on the network and to disassemble packets received from the network into a form suitable for the application running on the PC. The PAD can also create certain predefined administrative packets, such as call request and call clear in an X.25 network.

Paging

Paging is a memory-allocation strategy that effectively increases memory or allows more flexible use of available memory. A page is a contiguous chunk of memory of predefined size. Pages may be allocated as needed, usually in some area of RAM (random-access memory), such as the upper memory area between 640 kilobytes (KB) and 1 megabyte (MB). The original location of a page's contents may vary, depending on implementation.

The details of paging strategies can differ quite drastically. For example, a common use of paging is to create virtual memory on disk. When portions of working memory need to be removed temporarily, those portions can be stored on disk to make room. In contrast, Novell's NetWare assigns 4 KB memory pages to processes for use as needed. Page tables map between the physical memory associated with the page and the logical address space (for the process) provided by the pages.

Parameter

A variable that can be assigned a value in order to change a configuration or to provide input for an instruction. In most instances, a parameter will have or get a default value if neither the user nor the application specifies such a value.

Parameter RAM (PRAM)

SEE
PRAM (Parameter RAM)

Parity

An error-detection method in which an extra bit is added at regular locations in a serial transmission (for example, after seven or eight data bits). The value of the parity bit depends on the pattern of 0 and 1 values in the byte and on the type of parity being used. Parity is also known as *vertical redundancy checking (VRC)*.

SEE ALSO
Error Detection and Correction

Parity, Block

A type of parity that is computed for each bit place value in a block of bytes. For example, after every 8 bytes, an additional byte is set. One of these extra bits corresponds to each place value for the preceding set of bytes. Block parity is also called *longitudinal redundancy checking (LRC)*.

SEE ALSO
Error Detection and Correction

Partition, Disk

In hard disk storage, a partition is a logical division of a physical hard disk. Partitions may be created to divide a large storage region into smaller, more manageable regions, or to store different operating systems.

Disk partitions were essential in earlier versions of DOS, which could not support more than 32 megabytes (MB) of storage on a single "disk." Partitions are still common on high-capacity hard disks, because the FAT (file allocation table) DOS uses to store file and directory information can hold only a limited number of entries.

Each FAT entry represents a single, contiguous region of storage, called a *cluster*, or allocation unit. For a given configuration, all clusters are the same size, which may be 2, 4, or 8 kilobytes (KB), or even larger. Under DOS, the smallest unit of storage that can be allocated is a single cluster. This means that a file containing a single character will still need an entire cluster. Large clusters are wasteful if you have many small files. Since each partition gets its own FAT, breaking a large-capacity hard disk into multiple partitions can make storage more efficient, because smaller clusters can be used.

In Novell's NetWare, a partition is a logical subdivision of a server hard disk, or volume. For example, a NetWare server may have a DOS and a NetWare partition on the same hard disk.

Passive Coupler

In fiber-optic communication, a coupler that simply splits a signal as requested and passes the weakened signals on to all fibers. There is always signal loss with a passive coupler.

SEE ALSO
Coupler, Fiber-Optic

Passive Hub

A component in low-impedance ARCnet networks. A passive hub merely serves as a wiring and relay center. It merely passes the signal on, without changing it in any way. Passive hubs do not require a power supply.

SEE ALSO
ARCnet; Hub

Passive Star

A network configuration in which the central node of a star topology passes a signal on, but does not process the signal in any way. This is in contrast to an active star configuration, in which signals are processed before being passed on.

SEE ALSO
Topology, Star

Passive Star Coupler

A fiber-optic coupler (optical signal redirector) created by fusing multiple optical fibers together at their meeting point. This coupler serves as the center of a star configuration. This type of coupler is used for an optical (IEEE 802.4) Token Bus network that uses a passive star topology.

a b c d e f g h i j k l m n o **p** q r s t u v w x y z

Password

Many networks require users to enter a password as part of the login process, to verify that they are authorized to access the network. The characters in a password do not appear on the monitor as the user types them in, to keep the password from being observed by others.

Assigning Passwords

A password will generally be some letter or alphanumeric sequence. The network administrator usually assigns a password to a user when first creating that user's account. In most cases, the user should change the assigned password to one that he or she can remember easily. Only the user should know the password and be able to provide it during logging in.

Users can change their passwords when they wish and should do so frequently. Some networks *require* users to change their passwords periodically. Passwords should not be based on letters or numbers significant in the user's life (address, birthday, nickname, first and/or last name, and so on).

Dynamic Passwords

Dynamic passwords provide a special type of password scheme in which a user's password is changed every time the user logs in to a network. In this type of system, the user uses a special device, called a remote password generator (RPA), to generate a new password. When the user wants to log in to the network, the network responds with a special number that the user must type into the RPG together with the user's own personal identification number (PIN). The RPG then generates the password to use for the session.

Networks that use dynamic passwords need special software to generate the numbers used for generating the passwords. Each user must be provided with an RPG.

BROADER CATEGORY
Security

RELATED ARTICLE
Authentication

Patch Cable

Cable used to connect two hubs (or MAUs). IBM Type 1 or Type 6 patch cables can be used for Token Ring networks. These cables will have special IBM data connectors at each end.

SEE ALSO
Cable

Patch Panel

A centralized wiring location in which twisted-pair or coaxial cables can be interconnected without connecting the cable to punch-down blocks. Using a patch cord, the cable is plugged into a modular outlet, which is linked to the desired location. This makes it easier to switch connections in order to test or work around certain circuits.

Path Information Unit (PIU)

SEE
PIU (Path Information Unit)

PathWorks

A network operating system (NOS) from Digital Equipment Corporation (DEC). DEC's PathWorks is based on Microsoft's LAN Manager.

Payload

In ATM network terminology, the payload is the data portion of an ATM cell, or packet. This cell consists of a five-octet header and a 48-octet payload. More generally, payload refers to the data portion of a packet (for example, of an IP packet, or datagram).

PBX (Private Branch Exchange)

A telephone switching system configured for communications in a private network but with possible access to a public telephone system. A PBX may use analog or digital signaling, and the switching may be done automatically or manually (for example, through an operator).

PC (Physical Contact)

A term applied to indicate that the cable or fiber elements involved in a connection are actually touching. The term is used mainly in connection with optical fiber.

PCI (Peripheral Component Interconnect)

PCI is a local-bus design from Intel. A *local bus* is one that is connected directly to the central processing unit (CPU).

The PCI design supports 64-bit data paths, arbitrated bus mastering (interrupt

handling based on priority levels), and secondary caches to help speed up operations. The PCI bus is designed to accommodate increases in processor speeds.

This bus design is one of two main candidates to replace ISA and EISA as the next PC bus standard. The other contender is the VL (VESA local) bus design.

PCI (Protocol Control Information)

In the OSI Reference Model, protocol-dependent information added to a data packet before the packet is passed to a lower layer for further processing.

SEE ALSO

OSI Reference Model

PCMCIA (Personal Computer Memory Card International Association)

PCMCIA is an I/O standard that supports services or devices provided on boards the size of a credit card. PCMCIA specifies a 68-pin connection, which is used for all three of the cards described below. Originally developed for use in palmtop computers, the PCMCIA is being included in printers, laptops, and even larger computers.

The PCMCIA version 1.0 specifications were released in 1990. These support Type I cards, which are 3.3 millimeters (mm) thick and can provide volatile or nonvolatile storage (RAM, ROM, or flash memory).

The PCMCIA version 2.01 specifications were released in 1991. These support Type II cards, which are 5 mm thick and can be network interface cards (NICs), fax/modem cards, and so on. These also support a 10.5 mm thick Type III card. This card can

a b c d e f g h i j k l m n o **p** q r s t u v w x y z

actually provide a miniature hard drive. Type III cards are also used for wireless networks.

Socket Services software provides a standard interface to PCMCIA hardware, and Card Services software coordinates access to the actual cards. In theory, up to 4,080 cards can be supported on a single computer.

PCMCIA Modem

A modem on a Type II PCMCIA card.

PCS (Personal Communications Services)

In telecommunications, a term used to describe the intended use for three sections of the electromagnetic spectrum that the FCC (Federal Communications Commission) is setting aside for unrestricted use by individuals and organizations.

PCS (Plastic-Clad Silica)

A type of optical fiber, with a glass core and plastic cladding. The performance of such fiber is inferior to all-glass fiber.

SEE ALSO

Cable, Fiber-Optic

PDAU (Physical Delivery Access Unit)

In the 1988 version of the CCITT's X.400 Message Handling System (MHS), an application process that provides a letter mail service with access to a Message Transfer System (MTS). The MTS can deliver an image of the letter to any location accessible through the MHS.

SEE ALSO

X.400

PDN (Public Data Network)

In communications, a PDN is a circuit- or packet-switched network that is available to the public and that can transmit data in digital form.

A *PDN provider* is a company that provides access to a PDN and that provides any of X.25, frame relay, or cell relay (ATM) services.

Access to a PDN generally includes a guaranteed bandwidth, known as the committed information rate (CIR). Costs for the access depend on the guaranteed rate. PDN providers differ in how they charge for temporary increases in required bandwidth (known as *surges*). Some use the amount of overrun; others use the surge duration.

PDS (Premises Distribution System)

A cabling system that covers an entire building or campus. Also, the name of a premises wiring system from AT&T.

PDS (Processor-Direct Slots)

In the Macintosh environment, a general-purpose expansion slot. A PDS card is hardware-specific because the card is connected directly to the computer's processor rather than being connected indirectly via a bus. The other expansion architecture used in Macintoshes is the NuBus.

PDU (Protocol Data Unit)

In the OSI Reference Model, a packet. Specifically, a PDU is a packet created at a particular layer in an open system. The PDU is used to communicate with the same layer on another machine.

SEE

OSI Reference Model

PDU Lifetime

A value that indicates the number of routers a PDU (protocol data unit) can use before it must reach its destination or be discarded. Such a pruning measure is necessary to keep packets (PDUs) from traveling around and around on the network.

Peak Load

For a network, the maximum load that can be (or is) placed on a network. This value may be expressed in any of several performance measures, including transactions, packets, or bits per second.

Peer

In communications, a device that is considered equal to another device with respect to communication capabilities.

Peer Hub

A hub that is implemented on a card that plugs into an expansion slot in a PC. A peer hub can use the computer's power supply. (The computer's power supply should be adequate but is not guaranteed to be so.)

SEE ALSO

Hub

Peer Layers

In a layered network architecture, corresponding layers on two stations. Communication between nodes at a particular layer uses a protocol supported at that layer. For example, nodes on a Novell NetWare network could communicate with each other at the transport layer by using the SPX protocol.

PEM (Privacy Enhanced Mail)

PEM is one of the two major enhancements to the Internet mail message format defined in RFC 822. PEM provides mechanisms for encrypting, signing, and authenticating messages so that users can send e-mail that is reasonably secure against prying eyes, modems, or daemons.

PEM provides any or all of four types of "privacy enhancement services":

Message confidentiality: by encrypting the message. PEM supports either public-key (asymmetric) or secret-key (symmetric) encryption. The data encryption key (DEK) that provides the basis for the encryption is, itself, encrypted during transmission. The DEK is encrypted using an *interchange key* (IK). DEKs may be generated by the appropriate user agent (UA) or obtained from a key distribution center.

Authentication of sender: by using, e.g., a digital signature

Non-repudiation of message origin: provided public key encryption methods are being used

Content integrity: when sending a message that includes a digital signature and an *MIC (message integrity check)* to help determine whether there has been any tampering

PEM Messages

PEM messages are actually encapsulated in ordinary mail messages. The beginning of the PEM portion is indicated by a specific string. PEM message types are distinguished from each other by values in the message's PEM header. The following three types of messages are defined:

- ENCRYPTED, which means that all four PEM services have been implemented—that is, confidentiality, authentication, data integrity, and (if appropriate) non-repudiation.

- MIC-ONLY, which means that authentication, data integrity, and (if appropriate) non-repudiation are in effect. The message is still encoded in order to protect it from alteration by message transfer agents (MTAs) along the way. The encoding makes the message unreadable by user agents (UAs) that comply with the RFC 822 encoding format but that are not PEM-compliant.

- MIC-CLEAR, which is like MIC-ONLY except that the message is not encoded. Such messages can be read by

UAs that are RFC 822-compliant but not PEM-compliant.

To ensure everything will work, PEM takes the following steps:

- Transforms the data into a version that is so vanilla-flavored it won't crash anyone en route to the destination.

- Takes all necessary steps to get an encryption key (the DEK) for the recipient. The sender must first get a Certificate from a Certification Authority (CA) for each recipient using a public key algorithm for encryption. The sender checks the Certificate to make sure that its validity period has not expired and also to make sure that the Certificate is not on a Certificate Revocation List (CRL), for example, because it has been reported stolen or compromised. The sender also needs to check the authenticity of the CA. With the public key found in the certificate, the sender encrypts the DEK.

- Uses the DEK to encrypt the message.

- Encapsulates the PEM message inside an ordinary mail message. The encrypted material is between lines that read "—BEGIN PRIVACY-ENHANCED MESSAGE—" at the start and "—END PRIVACY-ENHANCED MESSAGE—" at the end. The figure "Encapsulated PEM message" shows this. This encapsulation helps ensure that the encrypted message won't choke any device at an intermediate location. PEM is designed as an end-to-end service.

ENCAPSULATED PEM MESSAGE

RFC 822 Message

RFC 822 Header

To:
From:
Subject:

RFC 822 Body

Blah, Blah, Blah
...
It's supposed to be a secret, but ...

Encapsulated PEM package
-----BEGIN PRIVACY-ENHANCED MESSAGE-----

PEM Header

Proc-type : 4, ENCRYPTED
Content-Domain: RFC822
...
...

PEM message body

... RW5jcnpwdGVkIFRleHRz ...
... Enc ryp ted Te xts ...

-----END PRIVACY-ENHANCED MESSAGE-----

Now remember, PEM's the word...

a b c d e f g h i j k l m n o **P** q r s t u v w x y z

As a well-behaved one, the encapsulation helps keep the encrypted material away from address checkers, such as routers or bridges. Since no intermediate node needs to fiddle with the encrypted portion, PEM can "ensure" content integrity.

For several reasons, PEM has not caught on as quickly as its developers hoped. One of these is the current incompatibility between PEM and MIME (Multipurpose Internet Mail Extensions), which is the other major enhancement of the RFC 822 format.

PRIMARY SOURCES

Various aspects and issues related to PEM are covered in RFCs 1421 through 1424.

COMPARE

PGP (Pretty Good Privacy)

▼
PerfectOffice

PerfectOffice and PerfectOffice Professional are Novell's entries in the integrated office suite for Windows sweepstakes. As such, they compete against SmartSuite from Lotus and against Microsoft Office and Office Professional.

Common Features

The features and tools common to the various applications in PerfectOffice help give the package its integrated feel. Some of the features are shared by all the applications; others are common to only some of them.

DAD (Desktop Application Director): This is the suite's control center, since all the Applications in PerfectOffice can be launched from here. DAD has three customizable toolbars: for PerfectOffice, Control Panel, and Data Sharing. You can add new programs to the DAD bar, and you can also create a DAD bar for each of your program groups.

Common interface: This helps make it easier to work within the different applications. As far as possible, applications use the same interface elements and provide at least the same general layout. The toolbar and other bars also use the same elements wherever possible and use the same icons when appropriate.

Coaches: These are interactive tutorials on specific tasks, resources, or topics. For example, there are WordPerfect coaches to help out with Columns, Graphics, and Footnotes; a Paradox coach provides a quick overview of Paradox. All the applications except Envoy and AppWare support coaches, and all have at least one coach for the application.

Experts: Experts are applets that help you perform an entire task. For example, there is a Create Letter expert in WordPerfect; the Slide Show Expert in Presentation provides help with a central task for this application. WordPerfect and Presentation also work with some special experts—Upgrade Experts— that will take a user through the task of upgrading from an earlier version of the software or from a competitor's product.

QuickTasks: These provide another way to get the program to do your work for you. Any of the 60+ QuickTasks will carry out the task for which it has been defined. You can invoke a QuickTask from within an application or from the PerfectOffice desktop. That is, you don't need to be in any of the applications to invoke a QuickTask. When you invoke one, you'll need to provide some information and answer some questions. The QuickTask will then go off and complete the task—for example, creating a fax, checking mail, scheduling an appointment—on its own. The QuickTask can even start multiple applications while doing its work. So with a few keystrokes and a few items of information, you can Create a Newsletter or a Budget or you can compute a loan amortization. Other predefined QuickTasks include Find File, Create Calendar, Create Agenda, Send File, Finish Document, etc. You can also define your own QuickTasks with the help of a Quick-Task Expert! You can even create two special QuickTasks: "start my day" and "end my day." You could define these to execute your startup and shutdown procedures, for example. These QuickTasks can run any documents, macros, or programs you want, and in whatever order you want.

QuickFiles: This component can be used in place of the Windows File Manager for managing files and directories. With QuickFiles you can launch programs, use QuickFinder to look for files based on word patterns in the name or contents, and create an index of files you need often.

QuickRun and QuickOpen: These utilities keep track of programs and files used recently. When you call these utilities, you'll get a list of the last 10 programs (for QuickRun) or files (for QuickOpen) used. You can launch any of these with a click of the mouse. You must be running DAD to use these utilities.

"How Do I ..." Help: This part of the online help provides information on how to accomplish various tasks. This focus on tasks and how to accomplish them is consistent with the use of Experts and Coaches, and also with the Quick*xxx* (QuickRun, Quick-Open, etc.) series of capabilities built into PerfectOffice.

Drawing Tools: Several of the PerfectOffice applications have their own drawing tools. Of these, the tool included with Presentations has the most features and capabilities. This tool is accessible from any of the other applications in PerfectOffice and from any program that can create OLE objects. You can draw using either vectors or bitmaps.

PerfectOffice Features and Components

Version 3.0 of the PerfectOffice Professional suite includes the following programs:

- QuattroPro 6.0 (spreadsheet)

- WordPerfect 6.1 (word processor)

a b c d e f g h i j k l m n o **p** q r s t u v w x y z

- Envoy 1.0a (document manager)

- Presentations 3.0 (slide show and presentation graphics)

- InfoCentral 1.1 (information manager)

- Paradox 5.0 (database management system)

- AppWare 1.1 (visual application development tools)

The regular version of PerfectOffice has all the applications except Paradox and AppWare.

QuattroPro

QuattroPro 6.0 is the spreadsheet package. In addition to the "standard" number-crunching capabilities for a spreadsheet program—entering, manipulating, and analyzing rows and columns of values—QuattroPro has some features that make it both easier to use and more powerful than your run-of-the-mill spreadsheet program.

QuattroPro includes extensive help about the program, its commands, and objects. The application also includes Coaches and Experts, both of which can provide help accomplishing tasks. Quattro-Pro includes over a dozen preprogrammed QuickTasks as well as predefined *templates* (spreadsheet formats). Users can modify both QuickTasks and templates to suit their needs. In addition, users can edit the properties of QuattroPro objects. Objects include spreadsheet cells or blocks, notebook pages, an entire notebook, or even the entire application. The *ObjectInspector* lets you edit object properties.

WordPerfect

WordPerfect 6.1 is the suite's word processing program. This widely used and well-respected application is powerful, flexible, and comes with resources to make the user's life simpler and more productive. WordPerfect includes a tutorial and an Upgrade Expert to help make it easier to get started.

Once you're working, WordPerfect's QuickCorrect and QuickSelect features make your editing job much easier. With QuickCorrect, you can have the program automatically correct certain kinds of errors—for example, MUltiple Capitals or Capitalizing first letters of each sentence, etc.

QuickSelect makes it easy to mark portions of text—for example, for cutting and pasting. With QuickSelect, you can specify easily whether you want to work with letters, words, sentences, or paragraphs.

Experts such as Make It Fit (for forms) and Table (for document tables), templates such as Calendar, and coaches such as Bookmarks or Endnotes make word processing much easier.

Envoy

Envoy 1.0a is a document manager. This means Envoy can help you view documents, annotate them if you want, and then distribute them on a network. For example, you can create a report or article with WordPerfect and use Envoy to distribute it electronically for comment. Your readers can use Envoy to view the file and to comment on it. Comments can take any of several handy forms: highlighting text, inserting "sticky" notes or bookmarks, using OLE to embed other material, or creating hyperlinks between two sections of the document. After they've gotten their bytes in, your readers can spit the document right back at you—electronically, of course.

Presentations

Presentations 3.0 enables you to create and present slide shows—even interactive ones. You can begin with *masters,* which are pre-designed slides. By beginning with a master, you help ensure that your slides are consistent with respect to backgrounds, colors, and fonts. Individual slides can be created by specifying variations on template slides. Templates for various types of slides—titles, bullet lists, organizational charts, etc.—are available.

Presentations also includes an Expert to help you create the slide show, if you wish. Once you've designed and created the basic slide show, there are various resources and coaches available for editing and revising the slides, and for creating the transitions between slides. You can run your slide show when done, or you can print the slides to a file or printer.

Like WordPerfect, Presentations includes an Upgrade Expert to help you get started with Presentations 3.0 if you've come from an earlier version or if you've defected from a competitor's presentation graphics package. One available QuickTask lets you create a slide show from a WordPerfect outline.

Presentations offers several views on the slides in a collection:

- Slide Editor View, in which slides appear in WYSIWYG (what you see is what you get) format. This is the view for doing detailed editing.

- Slide List View, in which you get a list of all the slides, along with information about each slide. This view provides an administrative perspective, showing the details in verbal form.

- Outline View, in which you see just the text of the presentation in outline form. This view lets you evaluate the clarity and coherence of your ideas and their presentation.

- Slide Sorter View, in which you see thumbnails of each slide. This view is helpful for evaluating the sequence and for possibly rearranging the order of the slides.

Presentations allows you to add speaker notes to a presentation. These elements will not appear on the slides, but you can print out a version for yourself before you begin the show. When you print this, you'll get a small image of the slide with the speaker notes alongside it.

InfoCentral

InfoCentral 1.1 lets you keep track of and make connections between files and even between items within those files. The elements being organized are known as *objects.* An object can be anything that has a name, which leaves it pretty open-ended. Objects can be linked with each other by specifying a connection between them. This connection indicates the relationship between the objects.

Information about objects and connections is stored in an *iBase* (for information base) file. Within InfoCentral, it's easy to see, modify, or delete connections, and it's easy to add, view, edit, or delete objects. InfoCentral's FastFind lets you search for an item of information quickly and easily through a dialog box.

InfoCentral has half a dozen QuickTasks (including Schedule Appointment in InfoCentral and Create an InfoCentral phone list in WordPerfect) and three coaches (for QuickStart, FastFind, and Import) associated with it. This information manager also includes a QuickTour to provide an overview of the application.

Paradox

Paradox 5.0 is a relational database management system (RDBMS). The "database management" part means that Paradox allows you to store, modify, and retrieve information. The "relational database" part says that this information's format and organization will be influenced (or constrained) by a particular model of how information should be organized.

In a relational database, data is organized into tables. Each row is a *record*—for example, a person, company, or book. The database is made up of the information in a collection of such records.

The information consists of values for some or all of the table's columns. Each column is a *field*—for example, last name, company name, or title. It's assumed that the fields are meaningful for the types of records involved. There must also be some field or combination of fields that produces a unique value for every record. This simple or composite field is known as the *key* for the table. The key is used to sort and store the elements of a table.

An RDBMS lets you get information you specify from the database. If information about the same records appears in different tables, Paradox can merge the fields (in pretty much any combination) and provide information about just the fields and records you want. The RDBMS can retrieve the appropriate records and can get the requested fields from whichever table contains them.

To accomplish things in Paradox, you manipulate objects of various sorts. Paradox lets you create and use several types of objects, including:

- Tables, which contain actual data.

- Forms, which you can use to display and enter data.

- Reports, which can display selected data in a specified format.

- Queries, which enable you to retrieve data according to the query. Query by example (QBE) is used in Paradox.

- Scripts, which carry out specified actions under the appropriate conditions. Paradox's ObjectPAL language is used to create script files.

- SQL (Structured Query Language) files, which enable you to write code using SQL.

- Libraries, which serve as repositories for code segments and from which required functions or objects can be borrowed.

- Project Viewer, which provides a more graphical interface for users.

As is true of the other applications, Paradox includes several coaches and experts to help you master important tasks and to get a better overview of the Paradox environment.

AppWare

AppWare 1.1 lets you create programs without programming. By combining and manipulating any of a few dozen objects, and by specifying the behavior of these objects under various conditions, you provide AppWare with enough information to figure out how to generate the code to carry out your instructions.

The objects you're manipulating are actually AppWare Loadable Modules (ALMs)—that is, pre-existing chunks of code. AppWare uses the AppWare Bus (which is included) to connect the modules you've specified and to compile them into an executable program. The AppWare Bus is essentially an engine that manages and coordinates the component ALMs.

The AppWare component in PerfectOffice comes with several ALMs which, together, contain hundreds of objects and functions. Other special-purpose ALMs are also available from third-party sources. The AppWare ALMs can be grouped into the following:

- Essentials, which contains objects and functions related to the Windows environment—for example, objects related to windows, menus, dialog boxes, etc. This ALM collection also contains general programming constructs such as arrays and subroutines.

- Multimedia, which provides objects and functions for handling video and sound.

- Communications, which provides objects and functions for serial connection and communication, file transfers, and terminal emulation.

- Application Linking, which provides the elements required for communications between objects or processes. Support for data exchange methods such as OLE and DDE are included in this group of ALMs.

AppWare also includes ALM Builder resources for creating new ALMs. Once created, you can use these ALMs along with the others. Be sure any sort of program or module is tested thoroughly before you start using it in other work.

Data Exchange

PerfectOffice offers several ways for applications and users to exchange data or other material. For communications between applications, PerfectOffice offers the tried, sometimes trying, and much derided Clipboard. In addition, PerfectOffice supports OLE (Object Linking and Embedding), which provides a much more sophisticated way to link an element into another one. By linking rather than copying, the insert can be updated if the original changes.

For communications between coworkers, PerfectOffice has Envoy, which can be used as an electronic distribution center. Similarly, OBEX (Object Exchange) offers a publish-and-subscribe solution. Users with information to share can publish it; anyone

a b c d e f g h i j k l m n o **p** q r s t u v w x y z

interested can subscribe to the publication. Subscribers are updated whenever there is a new version of the publication.

Performance Management

Performance management is one of five OSI network management domains specified by the ISO and CCITT. This domain is concerned with the following:

- Monitoring the day-to-day network activity

- Gathering and logging data based on this activity, such as utilization, throughput, and delay values

- Storing performance data as historical archives, to serve as a database for planning network optimization and expansion

- Analyzing performance data to identify actual and potential bottlenecks

- Changing configuration settings in order to help optimize network performance

The first two points address the data-collection capabilities expected of a performance-management package. The next two points concern data-analysis capabilities that are used to plan interventions. The last point relates to the control that such a package can exert to change a network's performance. Sophisticated packages can exert control directly; simpler packages require the system administrator to make the actual changes.

Data Gathering

Data is generally gathered by agents, which are associated with particular devices or network segments. These components are designed to monitor their devices and to store or send the observed values to a database from which the network management component can get the information it needs.

Data pertaining to network performance must be gathered over time, and time must be taken into account when examining the information provided. Both the nature and level of network activity change over time, and some data will be tied to specific times. For example, on many networks, the activity level has peaks near the beginning and end of the workday, because those are the times when people log in and out.

Data-Gathering Methods

There are many ways in which data can be gathered, and careful thought must be given to selecting the most appropriate methods for your needs. For example, data collection may use one of the following methods:

- In a *snapshot approach,* values are taken at a single instant in time. This approach is used most commonly when troubleshooting or when gathering "quick and dirty" statistics.

- In a *statistical approach,* the management component looks at network activity at periodic or random intervals. For example, data may be gathered for 30-second periods every five minutes.

- In an *exhaustive approach,* the network's activity is monitored constantly.

For more reliable, long-term performance information, a statistical or exhaustive approach is needed. Exhaustive data gathering produces more reliable data, but requires a larger chunk of the network's bandwidth. With statistical data gathering, more bandwidth is available for transmitting network material but less reliable performance data will be collected.

When you are gathering statistical performance data, it is important to examine assumptions about the data. In particular, many analysis techniques require that sample data points be independent of each other.

Type of Performance Data

The following types of data can be gathered easily and used to help improve network performance:

- Availability, which indicates the amount or proportion of the time that a device or other network object (such as a program or circuit) is available.

- Workload, which can indicate how close to capacity your network is operating. Workload may change quite drastically as a function of time. For example, a network may have a generally low workload, but may reach capacity at certain times of day.

- Response, or responsivity, which provides a measure of how quickly the

network can respond to requests. In general, as workload goes up, responsivity goes down.

- Throughput, which provides a measure of how much information (or, at least, how many bytes) can get across the network. Throughput can be measured in various ways, such as by the number of packets or number of sessions.

- Errors, or failed transmissions, which provide a measure of noise and/or competition on the network. For example, if lots of nodes are clamoring to get transmission rights in an Ethernet network, a significant part of a network's traffic may be error or busy signals. The complement of error measures concerns transmission accuracy; that is, the amount or proportion of time that *no* errors occur in a transmission.

Many performance indicators may be viewed from multiple perspectives and using different measures. Commonly used measures include frequency, relative frequency, duration, or delay. Note that the values on such measures may depend on more than just network activity; for example, the values may also depend on the processing power of the device in question.

For certain types of performance analyses, a management program may actually generate dummy network traffic in order to observe the effects of various levels of network activity on performance indicators.

NETWORK AVERAGE RESPONSE TIMES

For some networks, the average response (how quickly the network responds to requests) may be slow but roughly constant; for other networks, there may be large variations in response time. In extreme cases, users may get dropped from the network if some protocol or device times out because the delay was too long.

Absolute response times depend strongly on the types of devices involved. For example, some types of communications may involve response times of 10 seconds or more—a value that is generally too long for meaningful real-time transactions but that may be perfectly fine for automated activity. Other connections may require response times of less than a second in order to establish or maintain a connection.

Data Presentation

Depending on the management package and its capabilities, performance data may be presented in text or graphics form. Graphics may be histograms or frequency polygons that present the information.

Data may be presented in real-time using either raw or normalized values, or after the fact in either raw or summary form. Various types of data analyses and transformations may also be supported. High-end tools allow a user (who has the appropriate permissions) to query the performance database, usually by using a standardized method such as SQL (Structured Query Language).

Some performance-monitoring packages may present data only if certain threshold values are being approached or exceeded, to warn the system administrator of a potential fault.

Data Analysis

Performance data can be used to fine-tune a network as well as to do troubleshooting. Different types of data analyses may be appropriate, depending on your goal. For example, comparisons over time can provide information that will help you allocate network resources more effectively. In contrast, to find a problem area in a network, you may want to compare performance data from different segments of the network.

Such analyses are not always easy since you will often need to rely on indirect or inferred information. For example, response time bottlenecks may be difficult to measure because there are several places in which bottlenecks might arise.

Performance-Management Package Actions

If a performance indicator approaches or exceeds a threshold value, the performance-management package may take action. This action may be as simple as giving an alarm to call the indicator level to the system administrator's attention. At the other extreme, the management package may change one or more configuration settings. For example, the software may change settings in order to allocate more buffer space or more processing power to the bottleneck point.

In general, interventions and changes in configuration values are more likely to be made through the configuration management component.

BROADER CATEGORY

Network Management

SEE ALSO

Accounting Management; Configuration Management; Fault Management; Security Management

▼
Peripheral

Networks can provide multiple computers with shared access to various peripheral devices, such as modems, faxes, and printers. The table "Common Networking Peripherals" lists the devices commonly connected to networks.

Devices may be attached to the following:

- A file server, which provides access to the peripheral device as a secondary service.

- A workstation used as a special-purpose server specifically to provide access to the peripheral.

COMMON NETWORKING PERIPHERALS	
PERIPHERAL	DESCRIPTION
CD-ROM drive	Provides read-only access to the contents of a huge (660 megabyte) storage area. Such drives are becoming increasingly important as vendors move their software and documentation to compact discs.
Fax machine	Provides fax transmission and reception capabilities for multiple stations. Depending on the particular model, the fax may be able to store faxes, send them to a printer or a print queue (for output as soon as possible), and print them.
Hard disk	Generally internal and controlled by the file server. External hard disks may be attached to supplement storage capacities, particularly if there is no available drive bay in the server. RAID drive systems are a special type of external disk configuration, used to provide fault tolerance and additional data protection. RAID systems may contain up to five hard disks.
Modem	Provides access to telecommunications services by first converting digital signals to acoustic analog form (modulation), then transmitting this information over public or leased telephone lines.
Optical drive	Provides access to WORM (write once, read many) or EO (erasable optical) disks, which store information using light rather than electricity. Such drives may eventually replace tape drives as the backup medium of choice.
Printer	Provides a medium for hard copy output. Print jobs are queued by the print server and are delivered to the printer whenever the printer is ready.
Tape drive	Provides a sequential access medium for storing data that will not need to be retrieved often. Because the tape cartridges can hold considerable storage (over 250 megabytes), such drives are currently the medium of choice for backing up large hard disk systems.

a b c d e f g h i j k l m n o **p** q r s t u v w x y z

- A stand-alone server, such as a printer server or a network modem. These servers are not installed in a computer. Rather, they have their own processor and NIC (network interface card).

- The network, such as a printer with an NIC installed so that the printer can become a network node and can, effectively, be its own server.

For devices in which real-time response is not necessary, user requests for the peripheral device are generally queued up by the server. The requests are then processed as they are encountered in the queue.

Because certain services, such as printing, can demand frequent attention from the CPU (central processing unit), queues may slow down server performance considerably. In such cases, there are advantages to attaching the peripheral to a workstation or to a stand-alone server.

For devices such as tape drives for backups, in which power stability and line quality are essential, the main consideration may be to make sure the device is connected to a machine with a backup power supply or with a line conditioner and surge protector. Another way to ensure that a peripheral is adequately protected against electrical problems is to attach an appropriate protection device (such as a UPS) directly to the peripheral.

WHAT TO LOOK FOR IN A PERIPHERAL

It's important to keep sight of the fact that a peripheral device is being attached to a network, as opposed to being connected to a single-user machine. This fact may influence your product selection.

For example, peripherals that can get overworked (such as printers) will need to be able to handle the workload afforded by the users on a network. Don't try to get away with attaching a printer that's designed to print about 3,000 pages a month to a network with 250 users. If you do, the printer isn't the only thing that's going to be feeling the heat.

Similarly, make sure peripherals on a network have a capacity or speed appropriate for the demands of the network. If you plan to attach a tape backup system to your network, and you hope to do automated backups, then you need to install a system whose tapes can fit the capacity of the hard disks you plan to back up.

Finally, make sure there's no license violation when using devices (such as CD-ROM drives) that may be running products with usage restrictions.

Peripheral Router

A router that serves primarily to connect a network to a larger internetwork. This is in contrast to a central router, which serves as a transfer point for multiple networks.

SEE ALSO
Router

Permanent Virtual Circuit (PVC)

SEE

PVC (Permanent Virtual Circuit)

Permissions

A term used to describe access rights, or privileges, in some networking environments or operating systems. For example, in AppleTalk networks, permissions specify file and folder access rights.

SEE ALSO

Access Rights

Personal Identification Number (PIN)

SEE

PIN (Personal Identification Number)

Personal NetWare

Novell's Personal NetWare is peer-to-peer networking software with added features that make the product easier to manage and more secure than ordinary peer networks. This product is compatible with NetWare versions 2.2 and higher, so that Personal NetWare can be used as a network operating system for its own network.

Personal NetWare, which is included in the Novell DOS 7 package, provides support for the following:

- As many as 50 workstations per server, and up to 50 servers per network, to make 2,500 node networks possible.

- Security measures, such as audit trails and encryption.

- Named pipes as an interprocess communication API (Application Program Interface). This makes it possible to access OS/2 application servers.

- Both the NMS (NetWare Management System) and the SNMP (Simple Network Management Protocol). A Personal NetWare network can be managed either as a stand-alone network or as part of an enterprise network.

- The use of client VLMs (Virtual Loadable Modules) for customizing workstations (that is, clients).

Personal NetWare uses Single Network View, a distributed and replicated database of information about all objects (stations, resources, and so on) on each server. Because there is a single database for the entire network, only a single login to the network is needed. In other peer networks, users usually need to log in to every server they want to use. A single login makes security and access rights easier to check and enforce.

Personal NetWare also has an Auto-Reconnect feature that automatically logs stations back in to a server that went down and has subsequently been put back into service.

Pervasive Computing

Pervasive computing is a central concept in Novell's strategic and product planning. Much of the research and development at Novell is based on the assumption that the future development of computing and networking will be strongly influenced by pervasive computing. In fact, Novell has created a model of pervasive computing.

Most simply, pervasive computing says that eventually computing will be everywhere and that any computer will be able to get in touch with any other computer anytime. A pervasive computing environment provides all users with access to other users or information anytime, and from anywhere. Clearly, pervasive computing must rely on networking—actually, on very large-scale internetworking—to make this access possible.

For this environment, networking must become ubiquitous and as easy to use as the telephone. Network applications can help to provide this ease of use.

For pervasive computing to become a reality, computing and networking technology must be universally reliable. This can be accomplished through the combination of fault-tolerant and self-diagnosing hardware and software.

In Novell's model, a successful pervasive computing environment requires at least the following:

- Network Infrastructure, through which users will get access to services, applications, and communication tools. Programs such as networking operating systems help create and support this infrastructure.

- Network Services, which enable connections and provide information. Such services must be widely distributed, must support multiple platforms, and must be available to both users and programs. Users in this context may be consumers, administrators, or developers.

- Network Access, which enables a computer—at home, at work, or on the road—to make a connection with an access provider. Services provided by or through the access provider will actually enable the user to communicate on the network.

- Network Applications, which must perform their tasks just as they always have, except that these programs may have to perform them on a distributed system. Applications are expected to do their work in a transparent manner so that the user doesn't need to worry about or even know how things are being done.

- Tools and APIs, which enable developers to add to the available tools and resources, and also to change the entire working environment.

- Network Management, which must be able to oversee activities and management on lower levels.

In terms of technology, the change to pervasive computing is evolutionary because people will be able to use what they already have. In terms of the impact it will have on users, the change is revolutionary because it will affect the way people work, play, buy, and sell.

People use operating systems in order to run stand-alone applications. Users can accomplish a great deal without knowing how the operating system works. In the same way, people can use networks to run network-aware programs and do their work without knowing any of the technicalities of networking.

Novell believes computing is moving from a system-centric world to a user-centric one, with applications as the driving force behind the change—just as they have been behind other changes in the past. Applications involving business automation drove technology in the 1960s, business applications were the force in the 1970s, and personal productivity applications boosted changes in the 1980s. Now, in a time of explosive growth in the availability of computing devices, network applications are redefining the way we use computing technology.

▼
Peta

An order of magnitude that corresponds to a quadrillion (10^{15} or 2^{50}).

SEE ALSO
Order of Magnitude

▼
PGP (Pretty Good Privacy)

PGP is an encryption program—and more— developed by Phil Zimmermann. It is easy to use, widely available, and generally free for non-commercial use. There are certain export and usage restrictions, however. PGP can:

- Encrypt files using a private key encryption algorithm (IDEA)

- Send and receive encrypted mail

- Create and verify digital signatures

- Create, manage, certify, and revoke keys

Using PGP

PGP actually uses three keys when doing its work:

- A *public key,* which is associated with a single party (individual or company) but which is publicly known. To be effective for encryption, such a key must be paired with a secret key known only to the owner of the public key. In a public-key encryption strategy, every person who needs to do encryption needs both a public and a secret key.

- A *private key,* which is known only to the key's owner. This key must be kept secret. It is used for decrypting messages from others and also for making digital signatures.

- A *session key,* which is generated at random every time there is a message to encrypt. For reasons of efficiency, PGP actually uses the session key to encrypt the message and then uses the recipient's public key to encrypt the session key. The session key is also secret but is associated with a message rather than with a person.

Ordinarily, when A wants to send an encrypted message to B, A uses B's public key to encrypt it; B uses B's private key to decrypt it. When done in software, this strategy can be quite slow—almost a thousand times slower than a method that uses only a secret key. PGP does things somewhat differently. It uses the recipient's public key only to encrypt a single item—the session key. The rest of the message is encrypted using the secret session key.

Encrypting a Message

During the actual encryption process, PGP does four things:

- Generates a random session key. This is a 128-bit key.

- Uses the International Data Encryption Algorithm (IDEA) and the session key to encrypt the message.

- Uses the RSA encryption algorithm and the recipient's public key to encrypt the session key.

- Bundles the message and the encrypted session key to get the message ready for mailing.

Digital Signatures with PGP

A *digital signature* is a very powerful device for protecting the integrity, and demonstrating the authenticity, of messages. With a digital signature, you can prove that you wrote a message, check whether anyone has changed or tampered with the message, and keep others from signing your name to messages you didn't write.

PGP supports digital signatures, and uses a *message digest function* and your private key to create the signature. The message digest function is a 128-bit value computed from the contents of the message. This same value can be used by the recipient to verify the signature and the integrity of the message.

Key Handling in PGP

PGP asks users to create and enter a *pass phrase* any time they create a public key. Whenever the user wants to use that key, he or she must enter the pass phrase. PGP will use this phrase to decrypt the key from disk. PGP will also require the pass phrase if the user wants to sign a message with a secret key.

Public keys are stored in *key certificates,* with each key getting a separate certificate. A key certificate contains the following kind of information about a key:

- The key itself

- The key's creation date

- User ID(s) for the key's creator

- Possibly a list of digital signatures to vouch for the person

PGP supports *key rings,* which are files containing the public keys of people with whom you might communicate regularly. These files make it easier to keep track of keys. Your private key is *not* kept in the public key files.

Implementations and Distribution

PGP is available for a range of platforms, such as UNIX (various flavors, including Linux and Solaris), Windows, DOS, OS/2, Macintosh, and Amiga.

While the program itself is easy to use, determining what version to use can be quite a chore. This problem is made even more difficult because there are patent, licensing, and even import/export restrictions. Despite this, the program is available from many sites on the Internet. Most of these versions carry licensing restrictions on usage and distribution.

For licensing reasons, version 2.3a was updated and revised. In fact, by the time you're reading this, version 2.3 will be incompatible with any of these later versions. Three variants were spawned:

- PGP 2.4 from ViaCrypt. This is actually a commercial version and has given rise to PGP 2.7.

- PGP 2.6ui and 2.61.ui, which are the "unofficial international" versions. These versions can be used outside of the United States and Canada. Using these versions within those areas might make you guilty of a license violation.

- PGP 2.5, 2.6, 2.6.1, and 2.6.2, which are revised versions created to comply with restrictions.

As of September 1, 1995, version 2.3 files can no longer be read by newer versions of PGP.

PRIMARY SOURCES

PGP documentation and code are available from several locations. A good starting point is http://www.mantis.co.uk/pgp/pgp.html, since this provides home page addresses and other information about getting more material. An excellent source of general information about PGP is Simson Garfinkel's *PGP: Pretty Good Privacy* (O'Reilly and Associates, 1995).

Phase

In periodic signaling, a portion of the entire period, generally used as a reference to offset the start of a signal. The phase is generally expressed in degrees or radians. For example, a 90-degree (or $\pi/2$) phase would be off by one-fourth of the entire period. The *phase angle* represents the phase difference between two signals. For example, two signals with a phase angle of 180 degrees will be complementary.

Phase Jitter

A distortion of a signal's phase caused by random fluctuations in signal frequency. This distortion makes it difficult to synchronize the signal.

Photodetector

In fiber-optic communications, a component that registers incoming light. The quality and sensitivity of such a detector can have a great influence on the transmission properties in a connection.

SEE ALSO

Cable, Fiber-Optic

Photodiode

A component that converts light signals into electrical ones. Photodiodes are used in receivers for fiber-optic communications.

SEE ALSO

Cable, Fiber-Optic

Physical Delivery Access Unit (PDAU)

SEE

PDAU (Physical Delivery Access Unit)

a b c d e f g h i j k l m n o **p** q r s t u v w x y z

Physical Media

In the OSI Reference Model, any physical means for transmitting data. The bottom of the OSI model's physical layer provides an interface to such media. Specifications for the physical media themselves are not part of the OSI model.

Physical Unit (PU)

SEE

PU (Physical Unit)

PIC (Primary Interexchange Carrier)

The IEC (interexchange carrier, or long-distance carrier) that a subscriber uses.

Piggybacking

A transmission method in which acknowledgments for packets received are included in (piggybacked on) an ordinary data packet.

Pin

In some types of cable connectors, a male lead. This lead is generally only one of several (most commonly 9 or 25) that run through a cable.

PIN (Personal Identification Number)

A unique code assigned to an individual for use in transactions on certain types of networks; for example, to do banking transactions through an ATM or to log in to networks that use dynamic passwords.

Ping

In Internet protocol networks, ping is an application used to test whether a remote device is properly connected to a network. Although ping is an acronym (for packet internet groper) that refers to an application, it has achieved word status, and the term is generally used as a verb. For example, "To test whether nodes X and Y can communicate, either X or Y can ping the other."

Ping uses an Echo/Echo Reply exchange, which provides one of the simplest network monitoring schemes. It sends an Echo message using ICMP (Internet Control Message Protocol). If properly connected, the device must respond with an Echo Reply message. The receipt of an Echo Reply indicates a viable connection.

Some versions of ping can also report how long it took to receive the Echo Reply and also the proportion of replies that were lost in transmission. These values can provide information about the traffic and noise levels on the network.

BROADER CATEGORY
Network Management

Pinout

The term pinout refers to the description of the function associated with each pin in a cable. The figure "RS-232C pin assignments" shows the pinout for an RS-232 connection.

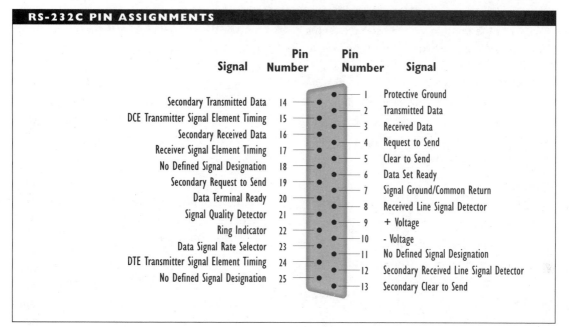

RS-232C PIN ASSIGNMENTS

Signal	Pin Number	Pin Number	Signal
Secondary Transmitted Data	14	1	Protective Ground
DCE Transmitter Signal Element Timing	15	2	Transmitted Data
Secondary Received Data	16	3	Received Data
Receiver Signal Element Timing	17	4	Request to Send
No Defined Signal Designation	18	5	Clear to Send
Secondary Request to Send	19	6	Data Set Ready
Data Terminal Ready	20	7	Signal Ground/Common Return
Signal Quality Detector	21	8	Received Line Signal Detector
Ring Indicator	22	9	+ Voltage
Data Signal Rate Selector	23	10	- Voltage
DTE Transmitter Signal Element Timing	24	11	No Defined Signal Designation
No Defined Signal Designation	25	12	Secondary Received Line Signal Detector
		13	Secondary Clear to Send

Pipe

In many operating environments, a stream that can be shared and, therefore, used to redirect data. For example, output may be redirected from one program through the pipe to become input for another program.

PIR (Protocol-Independent Routing)

Packet routing that is handled independently of the packet format and protocol being used. Such routing provides an alternative to tunneling, in which a packet is wrapped in another format in order to facilitate routing.

PIU (Path Information Unit)

In IBM's SNA network communications, a packet created when the path-control layer adds a transmission header to a basic information unit (BIU) from the transmission-control layer above.

SEE ALSO

SNA (Systems Network Architecture)

Plaintext

Ordinary, unencoded text, which is in contrast to encrypted *ciphertext*.

SEE ALSO

Encryption

PLCP (Physical Layer Convergence Procedure)

In the DQDB network architecture, a function that maps higher-level packets into a uniform format for transmission in a particular configuration. An example of a PLCP is the one for the DS3 services. This line is not a simple extension of the DS1 and DS2 lines below it in the power hierarchy. Instead, the services provide different timing and a different level of tolerance.

SEE ALSO

DQDB (Distributed Queue Dual Bus)

Plenum

An air shaft or duct in a building. This term has given its name to a type of cable—plenum cable—that is run through such a shaft. This cable must meet stringent fire-safety standards, so its jacket is made of material that will not burn easily and will not exude toxic fumes when exposed to heat.

Plesiochronous

In timing synchronization of digital signals, a situation in which corresponding events happen at the same *rate* in two systems (such as a sender and a receiver) but not necessarily at the same time. The clocks on these two systems run at the same speed, but they are not synchronized to the same reference time.

PLS (Physical Layer Signaling)

The topmost component of the physical layer in the OSI and IEEE 802.*x* layer models. This element serves as the interface between the physical layer and the media-access-control (MAC) sublayer above it.

PLS (Primary Link Station)

In environments that use IBM's SDLC (Synchronous Data Link Control) protocol, a primary link station (or just a *primary*) is a node that initiates communications either with another primary or with a secondary link station (SLS).

Plug

A male connector. Specifically, a connector with pins, which plug into the sockets on a female connector (known as a *jack*).

PMD (Physical Media Dependent)

In various networking architectures, most notably FDDI, a physical layer. This layer is responsible for the actual connection between two locations.

PNM (Physical Network Management)

Physical Network Management deals with the maintenance and management of the physical infrastructure of a network. This encompasses the cabling, connectors, power supply, etc. This aspect of network management has received relatively little attention but is becoming more important as computers and networks become integrated with telephones, fax machines, and other devices.

Point-to-Point Connection

In a network, a direct connection between two nodes; that is, a connection without any intervening nodes or switches. In an internetwork, the term refers to a direct connection between two networks.

Polarization

For connectors, the shape or form the connector takes. For example, with unshielded twisted-pair (UTP) wire, the RJ11, RJ45, and MMJ connectors each have a different polarization.

Polling

Polling refers to a process of checking elements, such as computers or queues, in some defined order, to see whether the polled element needs attention (wants to transmit, contains jobs, and so on). In *roll-call polling,* the polling sequence is based on a list of elements available to the controller, or poller. In contrast, in *hub polling,* each element simply polls the next element in the sequence. Polling is used in various computing contexts to control the execution or transmission sequence of the elements involved.

In multitasking operating systems, polling can be used to allocate resources and time to the tasks currently executing. System performance and stability can depend on the way elements are organized. For example, the operating system may maintain a single queue for all the tasks (as in OS/2); or it may use a separate queue for each task (as in Windows NT). In the former case, a task that is hanging or has crashed may affect the performance of other tasks. In the latter case, such tasks will not affect each other's behavior.

In LANs, polling provides a deterministic media-access method in which the server polls each node in succession to determine whether that node wants to access the network. While polling is not very popular for PCs, it is still commonly used in networks that include mainframes and minicomputers.

Being deterministic, such polling is similar to token passing and differs from probabilistic access methods such as CSMA/CD. In a *deterministic* approach, there is a fixed sequence in which tasks are done, which ensures that everyone gets a turn. In a probabilistic approach, the sequence depends on some random or pseudorandom process, so that it is not possible to determine which element will be selected next.

BROADER CATEGORY
Media-Access Method

COMPARE
CSMA/CA; CSMA/CD; Token Passing

POP (Point of Presence)

In telephone communications, the location at which a subscriber's leased or long-distance lines connect to the phone company's lines; that is, the point in a local access transport area (LATA) at which the subscriber's lines connect to an interexchange carrier (IXC). This is usually a central office.

Portable Modem

A compact, external modem that can be transported easily and that can be plugged into the appropriate port on any computer.

Port, Hardware

In general, a hardware port is an access point to a computer, peripheral, network, circuit, switch, or other device. A port provides an electrical and physical interface between a component and the world. There are two fundamental types of ports:

Parallel port: A hardware connection in which there are separate pins defined for all 8 data bits in a character. This means that an entire byte of information can be sent at a time.

Serial port: A hardware connection in which only one pin is available for data transmission in a given direction, so that bits must be transmitted in sequence.

The wiring for a port is almost always associated with a particular physical interface. For example, both Centronics and GPIB ports are associated with interfaces of the same name. There are also numerous standard variants on these port types. For example, RS-232 is a serial port, and SCSI provides a parallel port.

Communication across a port can be established when the appropriate type of device is connected to the port and when there is a compatible device at the other end of the connection.

Port Address or Name

A port address is a bus or memory address associated with a particular hardware port. There will generally be at least enough storage allocated at the port address to handle data being written or read at the port.

A port name can be used instead of an address to refer to a port. The port name is presumably easier to remember than an address. Operating systems sometimes have predefined names associated with certain ports. For example, DOS reserves the names COM1 and LPT1 to refer to the first serial and parallel ports, respectively.

Sharing a Port

A hardware device can be used to allow devices to share a port. Although port-sharing devices make it possible for two or more devices to share a single port, they cannot use the port simultaneously.

SEE ALSO

EPP (Enhanced Parallel Port); SCSI (Small Computer System Interface)

Port, IBM Type 3

An IBM Type 3 port is an enhanced serial port that uses direct memory access (DMA). This port can use an 11.0592 megahertz (MHz) clock, instead of the 1.8432 MHz clock that is used for ordinary serial ports. This gives a maximum serial rate of 691,200 bits per second (bps), although IBM's ports support only up to 345,600 bps.

The enhanced port is backward-compatible with 8250 UART (universal asynchronous receiver/transmitter) data registers but includes additional registers. The port is used in IBM PS/2 models 90 and 95.

Port Selector

The hardware or software that selects a particular port for a communications session. The selection may be made at random or on the basis of a selection criterion.

▼ Port, Software

A memory location that is associated with a hardware port or with a communications channel, and that provides storage for information moving between the memory location and the channel. In connection with the Internet, a port is a value at the transport layer used to distinguish among the multiple applications that may have connections with a single host.

While many port assignments can be arbitrary, certain ports are associated—either by fiat or by convention—with particular applications or services. In fact, the IANA (Internet Assigned Numbers Authority) determines the assignments of port numbers 0 through 1,023. (Until recently, the IANA controlled only numbers between 0 and 255.) For example, the **telnet** remote login service on the Internet is associated with port 23. The table "Selected Port Assignments" shows other preassigned ports in this range. The services and applications listed in the table are each described in their own articles or glosses.

Similarly, previously unassigned port numbers in the range 1,024 through 65,535 can be registered with the IANA by vendors and organizations. For example, port 1,352 is assigned to Lotus Notes.

PRIMARY SOURCES

RFC 1700

SELECTED PORT ASSIGNMENTS	
PORT NUMBER	SERVICE/APPLICATION (DECIMAL)
23	Telnet (remote login service)
80	Gopher (file search service)
88	Kerberos (authentication server)
110	POP3 (Post Office Protocol, version 3)
191	Prospero
194	IRC (Internet Relay Chat)

▼ Port Switching

In a communications session, the process of switching from one port to another, either because the port is malfunctioning or because it is overloaded. Such a switch should be transparent to the parties involved.

▼ POSIX (Portable Operating System Interface)

An IEEE standard that defines the interface between applications and an operating system. Originally developed to provide a common interface for UNIX implementations, POSIX has become more widely adopted, and operating environments ranging from DOS to IBM's MVS (Multiple Virtual Storage) support various parts of the POSIX standard.

a
b
c
d
e
f
g
h
i
j
k
l
m
n
o
p
q
r
s
t
u
v
w
x
y
z

Postamble

In a packet or message, a sequence of bits or fields that follows the actual data, or contents. The postamble, also known as a *trailer,* generally contains a frame check sequence (FCS) or another error-checking field, and may include one or more flags or a predefined bit sequence to indicate the end of a packet. Compare this with the preamble.

Post Office

In a message handling system (MHS), another term for a message store—that is, for an intermediate storage location where messages can be held until they are retrieved by a recipient or sent on their way to a destination.

While storage is the main function of a post office, a useful post office will also be able to keep accounting information about the messages being stored and should even be able to provide summaries of the messages. Users should also be able to selectively retrieve mail from the post office.

On LANs, the post office will generally be accessed using file-sharing or remote-procedure-calling capabilities provided by the (network) operating system. Such methods may be proprietary. In contrast, POP3 (Post Office Protocol, version 3) is used to communicate with a Post Office on the Internet. Similarly, the P7 protocol allows communication with post offices in networks that use the X.400 Message Handling System.

BROADER CATEGORIES
MHS (Message Handling System)

Post, Telephone and Telegraph (PTT)

SEE
PTT (Post, Telephone, and Telegraph)

Power Budget

In a transmission context, the power budget is the difference between the transmitter's power and the receiver's sensitivity. This difference determines the amount of signal loss that can be allowed. The loss restriction, in turn, can determine the maximum distance the signal can travel without cleaning and boosting and may also restrict the number of elements allowed to receive the signal.

For example, if a transmitter can send a 10 decibel (dB) signal and the receiver is capable of detecting a –20 dB signal, the transmission has a power budget of 30 dB.

Power Disturbance

The supply of electrical power can be disrupted by several types of electrical activity. Power disturbances can cause data loss and may also damage equipment. For example, if a hard disk read/write head is close to a surface when a brownout occurs, the head may dip enough to bounce along the surface, possibly damaging the surface and destroying data.

Types of Power Disturbances

Power disturbances can range from a brief surge in power to a total blackout.

Blackout

A blackout is a total loss of electrical power. Blackouts can be caused by lightning, broken power lines, and other natural and man-made disasters.

Brownout

A brownout is a short-term decrease in voltage level. Specifically, a brownout, also known as a *sag*, occurs when the voltage is more than 20 percent below the nominal RMS (root mean square) voltage.

Brownouts can occur when a piece of heavy machinery is turned on and temporarily drains the available power, or when everyone feels the need to run their air conditioners at the same time. According to some sources, brownouts account for almost 90 percent of all power disturbances.

Power companies will sometimes create "rolling brownouts" during peak demand periods. In these planned brownouts, the voltage will be lowered temporarily in different areas for a period of time.

Spike

A spike is a very brief, very large increase in voltage. Specifically, a spike occurs when the voltage is more than twice the nominal peak voltage. Spikes, which are also known as *impulses*, are most often caused by lightning strikes.

Surge

A surge is a short-term increase in voltage. The duration of a surge is longer than for a spike, but the voltage increase is much lower than for a spike. Specifically, a surge occurs if the voltage is more than 10 percent above the nominal RMS voltage for more than $1/120$ second.

Surges are typically caused when the heavy machinery that caused a sag is turned off. Such power disturbances can cause data loss and can impose extra wear and tear on components. Surges account for a small proportion of power disturbances.

Noise

Noise is electrical activity that disrupts or distorts the sine wave pattern on which power is delivered. Noise is typically known as electromagnetic interference (EMI) or radio frequency interference (RFI).

Noise can be caused by any of several factors, including other electrical activity and atmospheric conditions. Noise harms signals and information, not physical components.

Protection against Power Disturbances

There are three general types of protection against power disturbances:

- Isolation, which tries to contain the disturbance before it reaches the protected device. Isolation protects against noise or interference, and also against voltage fluctuations.

- Regulation, which tries to maintain a constant power supply through brownouts, surges, and even blackouts. A UPS (uninterruptible power supply) is arguably the most effective regulation tool.

- Suppression, which tries to guard against unexpected or massive power

a b c d e f g h i j k l m n o **p** q r s t u v w x y z

surges. Surge protectors are the most commonly used suppression tool.

PPP (Point-to-Point Protocol)

In the Internet protocol environment, a protocol for direct communication between two nodes over serial point-to-point links, such as between routers in an internetwork or between a node and a router. PPP is used as a medium-speed access protocol for the Internet. The protocol replaces the older SLIP (Serial Line Internet Protocol).

PRAM (Parameter RAM)

In an AppleTalk network, an area of volatile memory that is used to store important configuration information (such as the node's network address).

Preamble

Material, in a packet or message, that precedes the actual data, or contents. The preamble generally contains various administrative fields, such as fields with source and destination addresses, information about packet type or size, special signals, or bit sequences to indicate the start of a packet.

Premises Distribution System (PDS)

SEE

PDS (Premises Distribution System)

Premises Network

A network confined to a single building, but that covers that building completely.

PRI (Primary Rate Interface)

PRI, also known as primary access interface, is one of two service categories provided for ISDN (Integrated Services Digital Network) networks. The PRI specifies either a 1.536 megabits per second (Mbps) bandwidth in North America and Japan or a 1.984 Mbps bandwidth in Europe.

These bandwidths correspond to T-1 and E-1 lines, respectively. Note that the T-1 and E-1 bandwidths are 1.544 and 2.048 Mbps, respectively. The extra bandwidth covers 8 kilobits per second (kbps) and 64 kbps, respectively, for line-management transmissions.

The PRI bandwidth can be allocated in any of several combinations, depending on whether B or H channels are used. B (bearer) channels are used for data transmissions. H channels are groupings of B and D channels, which are channels used for control and other signaling between sender and receiver.

For T-1 lines, a common split uses 23 B channels and one 64-kbps D channel; for European lines, the corresponding E-1 channel consists of 30 B channels and 1 D channel. These breakdowns are denoted as 23B+D and 30B+D, respectively.

COMPARE

BRI (Basic Rate Interface)

Primary Interexchange Carrier (PIC)

SEE

PIC (Primary Interexchange Carrier)

Primary Link Station (PLS)

SEE

PLS (Primary Link Station)

Print Device

A printer or other output device on a network, and seen as a network object from the perspective of the network. A network print device is configured by loading a printer definition file (*PDF*) into the appropriate print services environment on the network.

Printer, Network

A printer is one of the peripheral devices that can be shared on a network. The printer may be attached to the file server, to a workstation, or to a stand-alone print server device. Or the printer may have a network interface card (NIC) and run its own print server software. This type of printer can connect directly to the network and function as a regular node.

The following features are important for a network printer:

Duty cycle: The workload the printer is able to handle, generally expressed in pages per month (ppm or ppmo). Network printers should have at least 20,000 ppm duty cycles.

Automatic switching: The ability to switch automatically to whatever printing mode or language the current print job requires. For example, one job in a print queue may be in Post-Script and the next may be using Hewlett-Packard's PCL. The printer should be able to handle these jobs without special intervention.

Automatic flushing: The ability to flush any job that contains an error. Without this capability, the printer may hang if it encounters such a job, which will, in turn, stop the printing and cause the print queue to grow.

Paper bins: A network-worthy printer should have a large paper bin—preferably *two* large bins, with the ability to switch automatically when one bin is empty. If the paper bins are too small, someone will need to keep replenishing the supply, or else the print queue will simply keep growing.

Speed: The ability to print quickly enough to keep up with average demand on the network.

BROADER CATEGORY

Peripheral

SEE ALSO

Server

PRINTER ETIQUETTE

A network printer is a shared device. This means that each sharer has a certain responsibility for the care and feeding of the shared device. The rules of etiquette for network printers are to a large extent just common sense and good manners.

- Always restore the printer to its former state after your print job finishes. This includes flushing whatever fonts or macros you download.

- When you pick up your long print job, put into the paper bins one and a half times the paper your job used.

- If your printout is light, indicating that the toner might be nearing the end, inform the system administrator or whoever is responsible for the printer.

Print Queue

On a network, a print queue is a directory that stores print jobs waiting to be printed. The jobs are printed in a first-in-first-out (FIFO) sequence. In Novell's NetWare 4.*x*, the print queue directory is in the QUEUES directory; in earlier versions, the directory is in the SYS:SYSTEM directory.

When a NetWare print queue is created, user ADMIN is assigned as a print queue operator. A print queue operator can change the status of print jobs or delete them from the queue.

Print Spooler

A program or process that can queue print jobs and submit these jobs to the printer when possible. Having a spooler program manage the queue relieves the processor of the task.

Private Automatic Branch Exchange (PABX)

SEE

PABX (Private Automatic Branch Exchange)

Private Branch Exchange (PBX)

SEE

PBX (Private Branch Exchange)

Private Leased Circuit

A leased communication line that provides a permanently available connection between locations.

Privilege Level

In the Intel architecture, any of four rankings (0, 1, 2, or 3) that can be assigned to memory segments to create memory domains. Privilege levels, which are also known as *protection rings,* can be used to keep processes from damaging each other.

Novell's NetWare 4.*x* can use either of two levels: 0 or 3. Novell recommends running the NetWare operating system in level 0 (the OS domain) and running any untested third-party NetWare Loadable Modules (NLMs) in level 3 (the OS_PROTECTED domain) to protect the system. Once an NLM has been proven reliable, it can then be run in the OS domain to improve performance.

PRMD (Private Management Domain)

In the CCITT's X.400 model, a Message Handling System (MHS) or an electronic-mail system operated by a private organization, such as a corporation, a university campus, or a state university system.

SEE ALSO
   X.400

Probe

In an AppleTalk network, a packet sent to the remote end of the network. The probe requests an acknowledgment from the node at the end, which serves to indicate the end of the network and also to acknowledge that the node is functioning.

Process

A program or program portion that is executing on a host computer.

Processing, Centralized

A networking arrangement in which the processing is done by a central server or host node, which also controls the network. This arrangement is suitable for networks in which there is a great disparity in processing power between workstation and server. Mainframe-based networks generally use centralized processing.

Processing, Cooperative

A program-execution technology that allows different tasks in a program to be carried out on different machines. Cooperative processing is important for client/server computing, in which an application front end executes on a client (workstation) and a back end executes on the server.

Processing, Distributed

A networking arrangement in which processing is carried out in multiple and separate locations. Along with the work, control is also decentralized in such a network. There is no central manager, but there may be central monitors or repositories that have information about all relevant network activity.

Profile

In the world of standards and specifications, a profile refers to a subset of a specification or standard. Profiles are created in order to speed product development and implementation. Parts of a specification may be sufficiently stable and practical to warrant implementation—often just for testing. Sometimes, however, profiles are implemented as strategic moves: to establish a presence in an up-and-coming market or to grab a market share as early as possible.

Specifications often have to be implemented in phases for many reasons. A profile implementation can happen, for example, if a technology isn't advanced enough to support a complete specification.

a b c d e f g h i j k l m n o **p** q r s t u v w x y z

Project 21

A project, initiated by the 64-country International Maritime Satellite Organization, for making worldwide mobile communications possible. The project calls for 30 to 40 satellites to blanket the earth. These would make possible point-to-point communications between any two locations on earth. Compare this with the Iridium Project.

Promiscuous Mode

For a network interface card (NIC) driver, an operating mode in which the NIC passes all packets that arrive to higher layers, regardless of whether the packet is addressed to the node. This operating mode makes it possible to pass everything that happens at an NIC on to a network analyzer.

Propagation Delay

The time required for a signal to pass through a component (such as a single device or an entire network) or from one component on a circuit to another. This value is important because the total propagation delay on a network may determine maximum network configurations.

Proprietary Server

A network server that runs a proprietary operating system and that is designed to be used with a particular vendor's hardware and software. Although they were popular as recently as a few years ago, such servers are no longer in vogue. The move is toward generic servers and open systems, which are vendor-independent.

Prospero

On the Internet, a tool for accessing, organizing, and using files that may be located in diverse remote locations. By running a Prospero client on the local machine, a user can get access to Prospero's capabilities. Information about Prospero is available via FTP from prospero.isi.edu.

Protected Mode

The default operating mode for memory allocation and usage for 80286, 80386, and higher processors. In protected mode, multiple processes can execute at the same time. Each process is assigned its own memory area, and no two memory areas overlap, so that programs cannot overwrite each other's work. The 8086 processor operates in *real mode,* which does not afford either multitasking or memory protection.

Protocol

A protocol is a set of predefined rules that govern how two or more processes communicate and interact to exchange data. The processes can be on the same machine or on different machines. For example, a transport-layer program on one machine uses a protocol to talk to the program's counterpart on another machine.

Protocols are generally associated with particular services or tasks, such as data packaging or packet routing. A protocol specifies rules for setting up, carrying out, and terminating a communications connection, and also specifies the format the information packets must have when traveling across this connection.

Some protocols require acknowledgment that an action has been successfully carried out, such as when a packet has been received. Under some circumstances, as in the case of a router going over modem-speed lines, such acknowledgments can slow down a transmission enough to throw off timing requirements for some protocols.

Protocols can be distinguished by several types of properties:

- The *level,* or layer, at which the protocol operates.

- The network architecture for which the protocol is designed. For example, bus-oriented protocols look and behave differently (in their details) than do protocols associated with ring-based networks.

- Whether the protocol is synchronous or asynchronous.

- Whether the protocol is connection-oriented or connectionless.

- Whether the protocol is character- or bit-oriented.

This article discusses these distinctions. Individual protocols and types of protocols are covered in separate entries.

Protocols and Layers

A protocol stack, which consists of the protocols for a particular network architecture, includes protocols at different layers. Details of the protocols reflect the functions and services available at each layer.

Application Layer Protocols

An application layer protocol is any of various protocols that provide services for applications. These protocols are the primary interface between applications and a network. In general, application layer protocols provide some type of access or handling (directory, file, or message) services for a process accessing a network.

The application layer is defined as the topmost in both the seven-layer OSI Reference Model and the five-layer Internet layer model. However, the top Internet layer actually corresponds to the top *three* OSI model layers, so that an Internet-based application layer protocol may have a broader range or a different set of tasks than an OSI application layer protocol.

Examples of application layer protocols include the following:

CMIP and SNMP: OSI and Internet protocols, respectively, for network management and monitoring.

FTAM and FTP: OSI and Internet protocols, respectively, for file transfer and handling. Sun's NFS and AT&T's RFS protocols are comparable.

X.400 and SMTP: OSI and Internet protocols, respectively, for message handling and transfer.

Telnet: Internet protocol for terminal emulation or for providing remote login capabilities.

a b c d e f g h i j k l m n o **p** q r s t u v w x y z

Presentation Layer Protocols

Presentation layer protocols are responsible for providing any conversion, compression, or formatting needed to make data suitable for transmission or use. Practically speaking, the presentation layer and presentation layer protocols rarely appear in pure form. Generally, the presentation layer merges with either the application layer above or the session layer below, or with both.

For example, PostScript may be regarded as a presentation layer protocol—one that provides a format for graphics pages. However, PostScript can also be regarded as an application—a tool for creating page layouts.

Other examples of presentation layer protocols include the following:

- AFP (AppleTalk Filing Protocol), which is the top-level protocol in the AppleTalk protocol suite. As such, AFP also combines application- and presentation-layer services.

- Various TCP/IP protocols, such as FTP (File Transfer Protocol) and SMTP (Simple Mail Transfer Protocol).

Session Layer Protocols

Session layer protocols are responsible for maintaining, synchronizing, and sequencing the dialog in a network connection. As with the presentation layer, session-layer capabilities are often part of other configurations (for example, those that include the presentation layer).

Examples of protocols that provide session-layer services include the following:

- ADSP (AppleTalk Data Stream Protocol), which enables two nodes to establish a reliable connection for data transfer.

- NetBEUI, which is an implementation and extension of NetBIOS. This protocol actually merges into the presentation layer.

- NetBIOS, which actually spans the fifth, sixth, and seventh layers, but which includes capabilities for monitoring sessions to make sure they are running smoothly.

- PAP (Printer Access Protocol), which provides access to a PostScript printer in an AppleTalk network.

Transport Layer Protocols

In the OSI Reference Model, transport layer protocols operate at the fourth, or transport, layer. This layer, or one very similar to it in other models, is important because it sits between the upper layers (which are strongly application-dependent) and the lower ones (which are network-dependent). Depending on whether the packets are being passed down the layers at the sender's end or up the layers at the receiver's end, the transport layer is responsible for ensuring that the packets are sent off or received in the proper sequence and format.

To provide the capabilities required, several classes of transport layer protocols have been defined in the OSI Reference Model.

See the OSI Reference Model article for information about these protocols.

Transport layer protocols include the following:

TCP and UDP: Internet environment and most UNIX-based networks (connection-oriented and connectionless transport services, respectively)

SPX: Novell NetWare environments

PEP: XNS protocol suite from Xerox

VOTS: DEC networks

AEP, ATP, NBP and RTMP: AppleTalk protocol suite

Network Layer Protocols

Network layer protocols are responsible for controlling the flow of data from end to end on the network, from the sender to the receiver. However, these protocols are not guaranteed to deliver the data successfully. To accomplish their tasks, network layer protocols rely on the services of the underlying data-link layer protocols. Network layer protocols can be connection-oriented or connectionless.

Examples of network layer protocols include the following:

CLNP and IP: OSI and Internet protocols, respectively

DDP: AppleTalk protocol

IPX: Novell NetWare protocol

Data-Link Layer Protocols

Data-link layer protocols are any of various protocols that provide network access for users or applications. These protocols are the interface between application programs and a physical network. In general, data-link layer protocols provide the network interface card (NIC) with the bytes to be transmitted onto the network.

Examples of data-link layer protocols include the following:

- Link-access protocols for various network architectures or configurations. For example, ELAP, FLAP, LLAP, and TLAP are the data-link layer protocols in an AppleTalk network. Other commonly used link-access protocols include LAPB and LAPD.

- SDLC from the ISO (and the earlier HDLC, from IBM)

- ARAP, PPP, and SLIP for remote access or for communications over telephone lines

Synchronous versus Asynchronous Protocols

Synchronous protocols rely on timing to identify transmission elements and are most suited for transmissions that occur at a relatively constant rate. Asynchronous protocols, which are more suitable for transmissions that may occur in bursts, rely on special signals (start and stop bits) to mark the individual transmission elements. Both synchronous and asynchronous protocols are data-link layer protocols for transmitting bytes between a DTE (computer) and DCE (modem) or between two computers.

Early synchronous protocols were byte- or character-oriented. For example, the character-oriented Bisync from IBM or the byte-oriented DDCMP from DEC are synchronous protocols. Since timing requires the use of special signals, characters that were used for link control could not be used as data characters. Newer, bit-oriented protocols avoid this problem and are more efficient as a result. Examples of such bit-oriented protocols include SDLC, HDLC, and LAPB.

Most network protocols are asynchronous; most mainframe and terminal-handling protocols are synchronous.

Connectionless versus Connection-Oriented Protocols

Connection-oriented transmissions take place over a single path, so that a destination address is needed only while the path is being determined. After that, the transmission proceeds along the same path.

In connectionless service, data transmissions do not require an established connection between sender and receiver. Instead, packets are sent independently of each other and may take different paths to the destination. Each packet must include the source and destination addresses, however.

Bit-Oriented versus Byte-Oriented Protocols

Character- or byte-oriented protocols use bytes or characters to manage the communications link and for timing. A disadvantage of this method is that the bytes or characters used for the link control cannot be used as ordinary data bytes.

Most early synchronous protocols, such as IBM's Bisync or Digital Equipment Corporation's DDCMP, were byte-oriented.

These have been superseded by more efficient bit-oriented protocols, which can establish timing and manage link controls with individual bits.

Bit-oriented protocols transmit individual bits without regard to their interpretation. Such protocols can establish timing and manage data links using bit signals. Individual bits are used for timing (so that sender and receiver stay in synchrony) and also for link control. Examples of bit-oriented protocols include HDLC, SDLC, and LAPB.

▼ Protocol, AARP (AppleTalk Address Resolution Protocol)

A protocol that maps AppleTalk (network) addresses to Ethernet or Token Ring (physical) addresses. This protocol is based on the widely used ARP protocol that forms part of the TCP/IP protocol suite. It is generally included in the definition for the network's link-access protocol (LAP) rather than functioning as a separate protocol.

▼ Protocol, ADCCP (Advanced Data Communications Control Procedure)

An ANSI-standard (X3.66) communications protocol. ADCCP is bit-oriented, operates at the data-link layer, and is identical to ISO's HDLC (High-level Data Link Control) protocol. Both ADCCP and HDLC are extensions of the older SDLC (Synchronous Data Link Control) developed by IBM in the 1970s.

Protocol, ADSP (AppleTalk Data Stream Protocol)

A session-layer protocol that allows two AppleTalk nodes, usually two Macintoshes, to establish a reliable connection through which data can be transmitted. Once a session is established, the data is transmitted over a single path.

Protocol, AEP (AppleTalk Echo Protocol)

An AppleTalk transport layer protocol used to determine whether two nodes are connected and both available. In general, echo protocols are used to determine whether a particular node is available. They can also be used to get an estimate of the roundtrip time on the network.

Protocol, AFP (AppleTalk Filing Protocol)

An application/presentation layer protocol used between file servers and clients in an AppleShare network and for remote access to an AppleTalk network. AFP is also supported by most non-Macintosh network operating systems. For example, Novell's NetWare for the Macintosh provides AFP support for NetWare file servers.

Protocol, AFS (Andrew File System)

The AFS is a set of file handling protocols that makes it possible to access and use files on a network just as if these files were on your local system. The AFS is generally considered faster and more efficient than the NFS (Network File System), which is currently the most widely used protocol of this sort.

The general consensus is that AFS will eventually replace NFS as the dominant protocol for remote file handling—even though NFS is so strongly entrenched. (The popularity of NFS arises partly because NFS was released at a time when its capabilities were first in demand and partly because NFS supports the TCP/IP protocol suite, which rules on the Internet.)

SEE ALSO

Protocol, NFS (Network File System)

Protocol, ARAP (AppleTalk Remote Access Protocol)

A data-link layer protocol that allows a Macintosh node to access a network from a remote location so that the node can work just as if connected physically to the network.

Protocol, ARP (Address Resolution Protocol)

In the TCP/IP protocol suite, a protocol for mapping between (4-byte) IP addresses and (6-byte) data-link addresses. The IP addresses are network-based; the data-link addresses are hardware-based and are associated with a machine. ARP variants have been developed for a variety of networking environments, including the AppleTalk environment, which supports AARP as the equivalent mapping protocol.

a b c d e f g h i j k l m n o **p** q r s t u v w x y z

▼
Protocol, ASP (AppleTalk Session Protocol)

A session layer protocol in the AppleTalk protocol suite. ASP is used to begin and end a session, send commands from the client to the server, send replies from the latter, and send tickler packets between server and workstation (so that each machine knows that the other is still functioning).

▼
Protocol, ATP (AppleTalk Transaction Protocol)

In Macintosh-based AppleTalk networks, a transport layer protocol that can provide reliable packet transmission. Packets are transported within the framework of a transaction, which is an interaction between a requesting and a responding entity (program or node).

▼
Protocol, AURP (AppleTalk Update Routing Protocol)

In the AppleTalk protocol suite, a routing protocol that uses a link-state algorithm to determine routes through an internetwork. As is characteristic of link-state protocols, AURP reports only changes in the available connections in an internetwork.

▼
Protocol, BGP (Border Gateway Protocol)

In the Internet TCP/IP protocol suite, a protocol for routing packets between networks that use different protocols. This type of protocol is known as an *exterior* gateway protocol (EGP). BGP is an improved version of an older protocol (actually named EGP) and serves as the basis for the ISO's IDRP (Interdomain Routing Protocol).

▼
Protocol, BLAST (Blocked Asynchronous/Synchronous Transmission)

A protocol in which data is transmitted in blocks of a fixed number of bits, rather than as characters or in line-by-line mode. The BLAST protocol is useful in multiplexing situations because it can simplify framing.

▼
Protocol, BOOTP (Bootstrap Protocol)

In the Internet community, a protocol for enabling a diskless workstation to boot and to determine necessary information (such as the node's IP address).

▼
Protocol, BSC (Bisynchronous Communication)

A character-oriented, synchronous protocol for controlling communications at the data-link layer. BSC was developed by IBM in the early 1960s to make communication with its mainframes easier. The BSC protocol supports ASCII and EBCDIC character codes, as well as a special 6-bit transcode (SBT) used only in BSC.

▼
Protocol, CIPX (Compressed IPX)

CIPX is a variant of Novell's IPX (Internet Package Exchange) protocol. CIPX uses a compressed header instead of the 30-octet header characteristic of IPX packets. The compressed header is between one and seven octets if just the IPX header is compressed.

For IPX packets that contain NCP (Network Control Protocol) data, it's possible to compress both the IPX and NCP headers simultaneously. Instead of a 36-octet NCP/IPX header, the CIPX header is between one and eight octets.

Such compression is useful when transmitting over relatively slow WAN (Wide Area Network) lines. The actual compression algorithm to be used must be negotiated between sender and receiver. It's also possible to use header compression in conjunction with a data compression algorithm, which can help further reduce the number of octets that must be transmitted. When both header and data compression are used, the order in which the applications are applied is important. The sender must first use header compression and then data compression; at the receiving end, the algorithms must be applied in reverse order.

PRIMARY SOURCES
RFC 1553

Protocol, Clearinghouse

A presentation-level protocol in the XNS protocol collection from Xerox. Banyan's StreetTalk naming service is a variant of Xerox's Clearinghouse protocol.

Protocol, CLNP (Connectionless Network Protocol)

In the OSI Reference Model, CLNP is the network layer protocol for providing connectionless datagram service. As a provider of connectionless services at the network layer, CLNP is comparable to the IP protocol in the Internet's TCP/IP suite, so it is also known as ISO IP.

Protocol, CLTP (Connectionless Transport Protocol)

In the OSI Reference Model, the transport layer protocol for providing connectionless service. As a provider of connectionless services at the transport layer, CLTP is comparable to the UDP protocol in the Internet's TCP/IP suite.

Protocol, Communication

A communication protocol, or set of guidelines, is used to regulate how two or more endpoints communicate with each other in any legal combination. Communication protocols can be defined at any of several layers in a network layer model. The number and definition of the layers depend on the communications models being used.

In a network, both workstations and servers need to support communication protocols. In most local-area networks (LANs), the server must be able to support protocols at several layers. Some servers support multiple protocol suites so that the server may support more than one communication protocol at each of several layers.

Protocol Converter

A device or a program that translates between two or more protocols, thereby enabling the devices or programs that use the respective protocols to communicate. The term is most commonly applied to devices (such as emulation cards) that provide protocol translations to enable a PC to communicate with a mainframe.

Protocol, CSLIP (Compressed Serial Line Interface Protocol)

CSLIP is a variant of the Serial Line Interface Protocol (SLIP), which is used when transmitting IP (Internet Protocol) packets over serial connections such as phone lines. SLIP and CSLIP are used to encapsulate the IP packets when accessing the Internet over a serial line.

CSLIP uses a compressed packet header and so has less overhead than ordinary SLIP. The compression strategy—known as Van Jacobson compression, after its developer—works by transmitting only differences between successive packets. This makes it possible, in the case of a CSLIP packet, to reduce the header from 24 bytes to 5. While this overhead savings may be only a small percentage of the entire file, it can save a considerable number of bytes when a long document is being transmitted—particularly if the document contains many small packets.

PRIMARY SOURCES

The SLIP protocol is discussed in RFC 1055. Van Jacobson compression is described in RFC 1141.

Protocol, DAP (Directory Access Protocol)

In the CCITT's X.500 Directory Services model, a protocol used for communications between a DUA (directory user agent) and a DSA (directory system agent). These agents represent the user or program and the directory, respectively.

Protocol, Data-Compression

In telecommunications, a data-compression protocol is any of several schemes used to compress data before transmission. These differ from data-compression programs in that the compression at the sending end and the decompression at the receiving end are automatic and completely transparent to the user. In fact, users may not even know the data is being compressed.

Two commonly used compression schemes are the CCITT's V.42bis, which supports transmission rates of up to 38,400 bits per second (bps), and Microcom's MNP 5, which supports rates up to 19,200 bps.

Protocol, DDCMP (Digital Data Communications Messaging Protocol)

A proprietary, byte-oriented protocol used at the data-link layer in DECnet networks. DDCMP can be used for synchronous or asynchronous transmissions.

Protocol, DDP (Datagram Delivery Protocol)

In an internetwork based on Apple's Apple-Talk network software, DDP is a protocol for delivering packets between nodes on different subnetworks. This protocol is responsible for actually getting data from end to end, from the source to the destination.

The packets are actually delivered to sockets, which are addresses associated with particular processes on the node. Thus, a node might receive datagrams intended for different programs. While all delivered to the same machine, the datagrams would go to different processes running on that machine.

Either of two main forms of the DDP packet are used, depending on whether the datagram is being delivered within a network or is going across a router:

- Short DDP is used for datagrams being sent *within* a network.

- Long DDP is used for datagrams traveling *between* networks.

Protocol-Dependent

Describes a process or component that is tied to a particular network layer protocol, such as IP or IPX, and is therefore limited in the types of packets it can process. Simple routers, for example, are protocol-dependent, which means that the router can handle only packets that support a particular protocol. Multiprotocol routers, which can handle any of several protocols, are protocol-independent.

Protocol, DFWMAC (Distributed Foundation Wireless Media Access Control)

A data-link layer protocol for wireless local-area networks, adopted by the IEEE 802.11 committee on wireless networks and designed to provide a common interface between various types of wireless and wired networks.

SEE ALSO
Network, Wireless

Protocol, DHCP (Dynamic Host Configuration Protocol)

On a TCP/IP-based network, DHCP is used to get information about a client host's (i.e., a network node's) configuration from a DHCP server, which is a specially designated network node. This is useful, for example, in situations where clients are assigned IP addresses dynamically, and where these addresses disappear after a session or after the host relinquishes the address.

This is common with Internet Access Providers that assign IP addresses as subscribers connect for a session. The configuration information may not exist until the client requests it. This helps keep down administrative chores.

DHCP is similar—and partially equivalent—to the BOOTP protocol, which is used by diskless hosts to get their predefined address when the host connects to the network. DHCP also has similarities with other configuration transmission or retrieval protocols, including RARP (Reverse Address Resolution Protocol), which is used in diskless workstations from Sun Microsystems. However, DHCP goes beyond both of these protocols in that it can handle more than just fixed addresses.

In addition to being a protocol, DHCP also provides a mechanism for allocating network addresses. In fact, DHCP provides three mechanisms:

- Automatic allocation, in which a permanent IP address is assigned to the host.

a b c d e f g h i j k l m n o **p** q r s t u v w x y z

- Dynamic allocation, in which DHCP assigns a temporary IP address. This mechanism is what distinguishes DHCP from earlier protocols.

- Manual allocation, in which the network administrator assigns the address, and DHCP merely transfers the address.

A client may request a configuration from any available server by broadcasting a DHCPDISCOVER message to accessible servers. After getting any replies (DHCP-OFFER messages), the client selects a server. The selected server's address is included in the DHCPREQUEST message the client sends to all the servers contacted originally. The selected server then begins creating the message with the requested configuration information; the other servers take the Request message as an indication that they have been rejected and that they need not concern themselves with the client any longer.

The modified version of DHCP is being developed for use with the new version of the Internet Protocol (IPv6). The revised DHCP will provide dynamic addressing capabilities for the new 128-bit addressing scheme—just as the current version does for nodes in the 32-bit address space. A separate mechanism—stateless autoconfiguration—will be used to provide predefined addresses, such as those used in local links.

PRIMARY SOURCES

DHCP is discussed in RFCs 1541 (which defines DHCP), 1534, and 1533 (which discuss the relationship between DHCP and BOOTP).

Protocol, Distance-Vector

A distance-vector protocol is any of several routing protocols that use a distance-vector algorithm to determine available connections. With a distance-vector protocol, each router transmits information about the cost of reaching accessible destinations to each of the router's neighbors. Examples of distance-vector protocols include the following:

- RIP (Routing Information Protocol) from the TCP/IP protocol suite, but also used in other suites

- RTMP (Routing Table Maintenance Protocol) from the AppleTalk suite

- IDRP (Interdomain Routing Protocol) from the OSI suite

Distance-vector protocols are in contrast to link-state protocols, which use a different strategy for getting routing information. Distance-vector protocols provide information about the costs of reaching all possible destinations, whereas link-state strategies provide information only about the distances from a router to all its immediate neighbor routers. The distance-vector strategy requires more work when setting up or updating the routing information. In contrast, link-state protocols need to do more work during the actual routing.

BROADER CATEGORY
Protocol, Routing

COMPARE
Protocol, Link-State

Protocol, DLC (Data Link Control)

A protocol used in IBM's SNA architecture to manage the physical connection and to ensure that messages reach their destination.

Protocol, DSP (Directory System Protocol)

In the CCITT X.500 Directory Services model, a protocol used by DSAs (directory system agents) when communicating with each other.

Protocol, ECTP (Ethernet Configuration Test Protocol)

A protocol used to test whether a particular LAN configuration conforms to the requirements for the Blue Book Ethernet (as opposed to the variant defined in IEEE 802.3 documents).

Protocol, EGP (Exterior Gateway Protocol)

In the Internet TCP/IP protocol suite, a class of protocols used for communications between autonomous systems. The two most widely supported EGPs are the exterior gateway protocol (also known as EGP) and the border gateway protocol (BGP). EGP is also a specific exterior gateway protocol (defined in RFC 904), which has since been replaced by the BGP.

Protocol, ELAP (EtherTalk Link Access Protocol)

In the AppleTalk network protocol suite, the data-link layer protocol for EtherTalk

(Apple's implementation of the Ethernet architecture).

Protocol, Error-Correcting

An error-correcting protocol is any of several communications protocols that is capable of both detecting and correcting simple transmission errors. The error detection and correction require the insertion of additional information at predefined points in the transmission. The sender and receiver compute a value using the transmitted data and compare the results.

Commonly used error-correcting protocols include Microcom's MNP 4 and MNP 10, which support rates of up to 9,600 bits per second (bps), and CCITT's v.42, which supports rates of up to 9,600 bps.

Protocol, ES-IS (End System to Intermediate System)

In the OSI network management model, the type of protocol used by a node (an end system) to communicate with a router (an intermediate system).

Protocol, File Transfer

Any of several protocols for transferring files between machines. File transfer is an application-layer service. The file transfer protocol used depends on the type of networks involved. For example, FTAM provides file transfer services for networks that use the OSI Reference Model, and FTP provides these services for TCP/IP protocols.

a
b
c
d
e
f
g
h
i
j
k
l
m
n
o
p
q
r
s
t
u
v
w
x
y
z

Protocol, FLAP (FDDITalk Link Access Protocol)

In the AppleTalk network protocol suite, the data-link layer protocol for FDDITalk (Apple's implementation of the FDDI network architecture).

Protocol, FLIP (Fast Local Internet Protocol)

FLIP is an Internet protocol that was developed as an alternative to TCP and IP for internetworks made up of large-scale distributed systems. FLIP was developed because it offered better security and network management capabilities for distributed systems than did TCP (Transfer Control Protocol) and IP (Internet Protocol).

FLIP was written at the Vrije University in Holland and was originally designed for internetworks using the Amoeba distributed operating system.

Protocol, FTAM (File Transfer, Access, and Management)

In the OSI Reference Model, an application layer protocol and service for remote file access. FTAM enables an application to read, write, or otherwise manage files on a remote machine.

Protocol, FTP (File Transfer Protocol)

In the TCP/IP (or Internet) protocol suite, a file transfer protocol. FTP is an application layer protocol that uses the services of the TCP protocol at the transport layer to move the files. Anonymous FTP is an example of this protocol.

Anonymous FTP is used to download files from public directories. This provides a generic download mechanism. To use anonymous FTP, the user proceeds as follows:

- Run FTP to connect to the host needed.

- Respond with *anonymous* to the request for a user name.

- Respond with the user's electronic-mail (e-mail) address to the password prompt.

As Anonymous, the user will be allowed access to the directory containing the file or files desired. The system will send the requested files to the address specified as the password.

Protocol, HDLC (High-Level Data Link Control)

HDLC is a bit-oriented, data-link layer protocol that has been standardized in several ISO documents (3309, 4335, and 7809) and can support any of the following:

- Half- or full-duplex communications

- Circuit- or packet-switched networks

- Point-to-point or multipoint network topologies

- Transmission over cable or wireless media

HDLC was derived by the ISO from IBM's SDLC protocol in the late 1970s. HDLC uses essentially the same frame structure as SDLC. Also like SDLC, the HDLC protocol is concerned with primary and secondary nodes. A primary, or master, node controls a communication; a secondary node functions in response to a primary's commands. In addition to primaries and secondaries, HDLC supports combined components, which can serve as primary or secondary nodes depending on the situation.

HDLC Transfer Modes

A major difference between HDLC and SDLC is the fact that HDLC can work using any of three different transfer modes and can function at multiple levels. HDLC can work in the following modes:

- NRM (normal response mode), which uses one primary and at least one secondary. Before it can communicate, a secondary must be given permission by the primary. SDLC uses this mode.

- ARM (asynchronous response mode), which uses one primary and at least one secondary. Secondaries do not need permission to communicate with a primary.

- ABM (asynchronous balanced mode), which uses one or more combined nodes. Since each node can be either a primary or a secondary, nodes can communicate without first getting permission. This is the mode that underlies most data-link layer protocols on LANs.

HDLC Operation

A session involving HDLC occurs in three phases:

- One node initiates an interaction by requesting an initialization process, which involves the exchange of packets to establish the type of connection and transfer mode requested.

- The parties exchange information and control packets, known as DPDUs (data-link protocol data units) or frames.

- One node initiates a disconnect operation.

HDLC Frames

A session involves the exchange of three types of frames:

I (**Information**) **frame:** Contains data, generally in the form of packets from higher-level protocols. I frames may also contain error-checking and flow-control information. I frames have both a sending and a receiving sequence number.

S (**Supervisory**) **frame:** Provides a separate way to give commands and exert control in a session.

U (**Unnumbered**) **frame:** Provides additional functions for link control.

The figure "HDLC frame format" shows the format of an HDLC frame.

HDLC FRAME FORMAT

Basic Frame Format

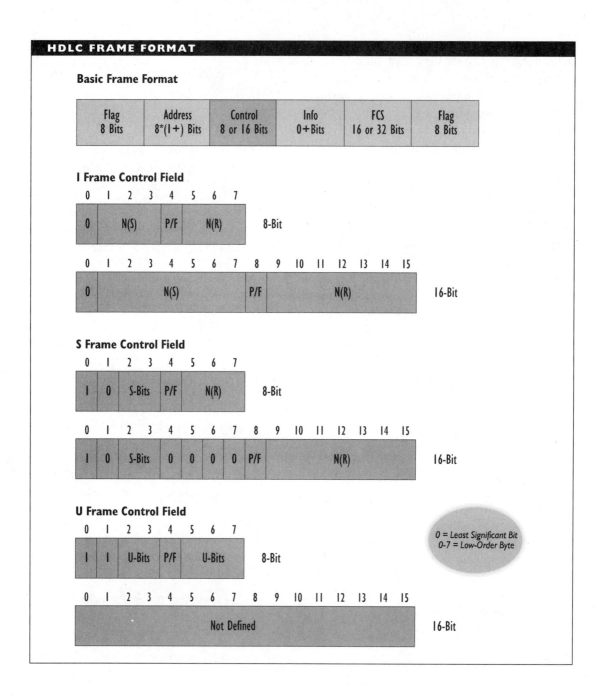

| Flag 8 Bits | Address 8*(1+) Bits | Control 8 or 16 Bits | Info 0+ Bits | FCS 16 or 32 Bits | Flag 8 Bits |

I Frame Control Field

| 0 | 1 | 2 | 3 | 4 | 5 | 6 | 7 |
| 0 | N(S) | | P/F | N(R) | | | | 8-Bit

| 0 | 1 | 2 | 3 | 4 | 5 | 6 | 7 | 8 | 9 | 10 | 11 | 12 | 13 | 14 | 15 |
| 0 | N(S) | | | | | | | P/F | N(R) | | | | | | | 16-Bit

S Frame Control Field

| 0 | 1 | 2 | 3 | 4 | 5 | 6 | 7 |
| 1 | 0 | S-Bits | P/F | N(R) | | | | 8-Bit

| 0 | 1 | 2 | 3 | 4 | 5 | 6 | 7 | 8 | 9 | 10 | 11 | 12 | 13 | 14 | 15 |
| 1 | 0 | S-Bits | 0 | 0 | 0 | 0 | P/F | N(R) | | | | | | | | 16-Bit

U Frame Control Field

| 0 | 1 | 2 | 3 | 4 | 5 | 6 | 7 |
| 1 | 1 | U-Bits | P/F | U-Bits | | | | 8-Bit

0 = Least Significant Bit
0-7 = Low-Order Byte

| 0 | 1 | 2 | 3 | 4 | 5 | 6 | 7 | 8 | 9 | 10 | 11 | 12 | 13 | 14 | 15 |
| Not Defined | | | | | | | | | | | | | | | | 16-Bit

Protocol, HTTP (Hypertext Transfer Protocol)

HTTP is a fast, stateless (amnesiac), and object-oriented protocol used most notably on the World Wide Web (WWW). HTTP is used to allow Web clients and servers to negotiate and interact with each other.

Because it is fast, HTTP is ideal for retrieving and transferring hypermedia materials across distributed systems. Because it is stateless, HTTP does not have any memory of transactions. This is handy for the network traffic patterns found on the WWW—constant connections and disconnections. Because it is object-oriented, it can be used to send generic methods, such as GET and POST, to operate on a variety of data types (HTTP, FTP, gopher, etc.). In fact, new data types can be created and added to HTTP's capabilities.

HTTP Messages

HTTP messages have a Header and possibly a Body. The Header can contain three types of fields:

- General-Header fields, in which the sender can include information such as the date or MIME-version, if applicable.

- Request-Header fields, in which the client can qualify the request. For example, *If-Modified-Since* is a request field that specifies a cutoff date—ignore the request if the object hasn't been modified since the specified date. Note that only clients will include this type of field.

- Entity-Header fields, in which the sender can provide specific information about the object being transferred.

HTTP supports two types of messages: Request (by the client) and Response (by the server). Either of these may be qualified by using the appropriate header fields.

Request Messages

A request message generally takes the form:

```
method object {header
fields} {body}
```

A *method* is a function that can be associated with multiple objects and that may take different forms for some or all of these objects. HTTP request methods include GET, HEAD, and POST.

The object should refer to some type of file or resource. This object is specified by its URI (Universal Resource Identifier). Perhaps the best-known examples of URIs are the URLs (Universal Resource Locators) that represent the addresses of pages on the WWW.

Header fields are optional, as is a message body, but they can't both be left out of a message. GET and HEAD requests don't have bodies because the client doesn't want to send anything other than the request. On the other hand, POST commands *will* generally have a message body, which consists of the material to be posted.

POST is defined in a way that makes it possible to use the same protocol for all the of the following:

- Annotating existing objects

- Posting a message to a mailing list, newsgroup, or bulletin board

- Passing data (from a user-completed form, for example) to a data-processing program

- Adding to a database

Response Messages

In the response message, the server sends back either the requested material or an error message. Actually, the server also sends some type of return code. This will be a three-digit integer beginning with one of the following digits.

1xx (Information): Reserved for future use

2xxx (Success): The action was completed successfully

3xx (Redirection): Further action is needed before the request will be done

4xx (Client error): There may be a possible syntax error in the request or a non-defined request

5xx (Server error): The server was unable to carry out a valid request

HTTP Variants

Because of the unbelievable growth of the WWW, HTTP has been a busy little protocol. With heavy use, various weaknesses and problems with HTTP have appeared. An important shortcoming is HTTP's minimal security features. HTTP can do basic authentication but not encryption. *SHTTP* (Secure HTTP) was developed by EIT to add security features to HTTP. SHTTP supports encryption and security checks.

Another way to improve security when using HTTP is to also use SSL (Secure Socket Layer) from Netscape Communications Corporation. SSL provides security and authentication capabilities by mediating between the TCP/IP transport protocols and service-based protocols (such as HTTP).

PRIMARY SOURCES

Drafts of the HTTP specifications are available through the IETF home page, which is located at http://www.ietf.cnri .reston.va.us/

In particular, documents relating to HTTP and other topics under consideration by the IETF will generally be available from the /ietf-online-proceedings directory of the ftp.ietf.cnri.reston.va.us FTP site.

A PostScript version of an August 1995 draft of the HTTP specifications has the following forbidding title:

```
draft-ietf-http-v10-
spec-02.ps
```

Protocol, ICMP (Internet Control Message Protocol)

In the TCP/IP protocol suite, a protocol used to handle errors at the network layer. ICMP is actually part of the IP, which is the network layer protocol in the TCP/IP suite.

Protocol, IDP (Internet Datagram Packet)

A network-level routing protocol in the XNS protocol suite from Xerox. IDP can be used to route data or packets from any of several transport layer protocols, including RIP (Routing Information Protocol), Echo, PEP (Packet Exchange Protocol), or SPP (Sequenced Packet Protocol). IDP was the basis for the NetWare IPX (Internetwork Packet Exchange) protocol.

Protocol, IDRP (Interdomain Routing Protocol)

An ISO protocol for routing transmissions between different administrative domains. This protocol uses a distance-vector algorithm and is based on the border gateway protocol (BGP), which is used in the TCP/IP suite.

Protocol, IGP (Interior Gateway Protocol)

In the Internet TCP/IP protocol suite, a term for a protocol used by routers *within* an autonomous system to communicate with each other. Within the Internet community, the two most widely supported IGPs are RIP (Routing Information Protocol) and OSPF (Open Shortest Path First). Integrated IS-IS is also an IGP, designed originally for OSI environments.

Protocol, IMAP (Internet Message Access Protocol)

IMAP is a recently introduced protocol for communicating with a post office (temporary e-mail store) in order to store and retrieve e-mail messages in the post office. IMAP runs on top of TCP/IP. It is *not* a protocol for actually sending e-mail.

Introduced in December of 1994, IMAP is actually version 4—that is, it is known as

IMAP4. Previous protocols to accomplish the same tasks had the same acronym but a different expansion: IMAP2 and IMAP3 were known as "Interactive Mail Access Protocols."

PRIMARY SOURCES

IMAP4 is introduced in RFC 1730, and various aspects are discussed in RFCs 1731, 1732, and 1733. IMAP2 and IMAP3 are discussed in RFCs 1176 and 1203, respectively.

Protocol-Independent

Describes a process or device that is not tied to a particular network layer protocol (such as DDP, IP, or IPX). For example, a bridge, which operates at the data-link layer, is protocol-independent. In contrast, older, single-protocol routers are protocol-dependent. This type of router is being replaced by the protocol-independent multi-protocol router.

Protocol, InFlexion

InFlexion is a messaging protocol from Motorola. InFlexion is designed for use in narrowband PCS (Personal Communication Services). The protocol supports transfer rates of up to 112 kbps, and it is two-way. This makes it possible to send messages in both directions in paging networks.

Protocol, Integrated IS-IS

The Integrated IS-IS protocol is used for communications among routers within an autonomous system (AS), or a routing domain. *AS* and *routing domain* are Internet

a b c d e f g h i j k l m n o **p** q r s t u v w x y z

and OSI terms, respectively. An AS consists of a collection of routers that are administered by the same organization and use the same protocol to communicate with each other.

This type of protocol is known as an *interior gateway protocol (IGP)* or an *intradomain routing protocol,* in Internet and OSI terminology, respectively. The Integrated IS-IS protocol can be used in both TCP/IP (Internet) and OSI environments. Another example of an IGP protocol in the TCP/IP suite is the OSPF (Open Shortest Path First) protocol.

▼
Protocol, IP (Internet Protocol)

IP is the widely supported network layer protocol for the Internet. IP is one of the protocols in the TCP/IP protocol suite.

This protocol defines and routes datagrams across the Internet and provides connectionless transport service. The IP protocol uses packet switching and makes a best effort to deliver its packets. The IP protocol uses the services of the data-link layer to accomplish the actual transmission along the path.

IP Packet Header Fields

An IP packet consists of a header and data, known as a *payload.* The payload can be up to 64 kilobytes (KB) and must be at least 512 bytes. The header consists of the following:

Version: The version of IP being used. Version 4 is currently standard. Values of 5 or 6 indicate that special stream protocols are being used.

IHL (Internet header length): The number of 32-bit words used in the header. Padding is used to make sure the header ends on a 32-bit boundary.

ToS (Type of Service): The type of handling and delays that are allowed for the packet. The details of this field are currently in flux.

Total length: The number of bytes in the entire packet, including the header. This value must be between 576 and 65,536, inclusive.

ID: A value created by the sender to identify the packet so its components can be found and reassembled if the packet must be fragmented during its travels. This field is closely tied to the next 2-byte area.

Flags: Three bits that are used to indicate whether the original IP packet has been fragmented and, if so, whether the current packet is the last fragment. The high-order bit is always 0. The middle bit is 0 if the packet may be fragmented and 1 otherwise. The low-order bit is 0 if the packet is the last fragment and 1 otherwise.

Fragment offset: Thirteen bits that specify the location of the fragment in the original packet.

TTL (Time To Live): Originally, this field indicated the number of seconds the packet was allowed to travel in a network before being destroyed. Now it is interpreted as a hop count value and is generally assigned a default value of 32. The contents of this field are decreased at each router to which the packet is passed.

Protocol: This value specifies the higher-level protocol contained in the packet's data field. The table "Assignments for an IP Packet's Protocol Field" lists some of the values that have been assigned to specific protocols or organizations. Note that this list is subject to change. The Internet Assigned Numbers Authority (IANA) is the keeper of the protocol assignments. Official lists are published in the "Assigned Numbers" RFCs. The most recent of these is 1,700. Many of the values not listed are still unassigned.

Checksum: This value is used to make sure the header has not been corrupted or changed during its travels. The value must be updated at each stop-over point because certain fields are changed.

SA (Source Address): The IP address of the sender. This is not the same as an Ethernet or Token Ring address.

DA (Destination Address): The IP address of the destination node.

Options: There may be up to three Option fields. The interpretations for these fields may be defined by the user of the protocol.

Padding: This field is used to make sure the header ends on a 32-bit boundary.

ASSIGNMENTS FOR AN IP PACKET'S PROTOCOL FIELD	
VALUE	PROTOCOL
0	Reserved
1	ICMP Internet Control Message Protocol
2	IGMP (Internet Group Management Protocol)
3	GGP (Gateway-to-Gateway Protocol)
5	ST (Stream Protocol)
6	TCP (Transmission Control Protocol)
8	EGP (Exterior Gateway Protocol)
11	NVP-II (Network Voice Protocol)
17	UDP (User Datagram Protocol)
80	CLNP (ISO Connectionless Protocol)
83	VINES
85	NSFNET-IGP (Internal Gateway Protocol)
88	IGRP (Internet Gateway Routing Protocol)
89	OSPF (Open Shortest Path First)
255	Reserved

Data: This field contains material from a higher-level protocol. The header is shown in the figure "IP datagram header."

IP DATAGRAM HEADER

Version 4 Bits	Header Length 4 Bits	Type of Service 8 Bits	Fragment Length 16 Bits	
Packet ID 16 Bits			Flag 3 Bits	Fragment Offset 13 Bits
TTL (Time to Live) 8 Bits		Protocol ID 8 Bits	Header Checksum 16 Bits	
Source IP Address 32 Bits				
Destination IP Address 32 Bits				
Options 16 Bits			Padding 16 Bits	

PRIMARY SOURCE
RFC 791

BROADER CATEGORIES
TCP/IP Protocol Suite

▼———

Protocol, IPng / IPv6 (Internet Protocol, next generation / version 6)

IPng refers to the proposed successor to IPv4 (Internet Protocol version 4) as the network-layer protocol in the Internet's TCP/IP protocol suite. This is the protocol responsible for routing or delivering packets to their destination.

The phenomenal growth of the Internet has begun to push IP to its limits. Because of this, an IETF (Internet Engineering Task Force) working group was formed to plan the next generation of protocols. In late 1993, an RFC (1550) was released on behalf of this working group. This document asked for white papers from anyone with suggestions for requirements that the new protocol should or must fulfill.

The document also listed 16 issues considered relevant when designing and creating the new protocol. These issues are a combination of technical issues relating to features and (current or imminent) shortcomings in IPv4, policy and administrative issues, and practical issues having to do with implementation and transition. Example issues include:

Scalability: The next version should be able to provide addresses for up to 10^{12} (that's right, a trillion) hosts!

Transition and deployment: The details and considerations of how to switch from one protocol to the next must be planned out.

Mobile hosts: Whether to make it easier for hosts to connect from mobile locations. If so, how to do it?

Robustness and Fault Tolerance: How to ensure that the new version is at least as robust and fault tolerant as the current one.

The solicitation garnered almost 20 RFCs in response—mostly from representatives of different industries or organizations who might be affected by the new protocol. Respondents came from high-tech companies, universities, research centers, consortia, telecommunications and entertainment industries, etc.

Based on this and other feedback, the IETF working group released a draft specification in June of 1995. In this document, the protocol is called IPv6 (IP version 6). This is just a draft and is not yet a standard. In fact, people and groups are still working on alternatives to the IETF specifications, and one of those may actually end up becoming the actual next version of IP.

IPv6 differs from the current version in the following areas:

Addressing capabilities: IPv6 uses 16 octets (128 bits) for addresses (as opposed to 4 octets, or 32 bits, in IPv4). This is more than enough address space for a trillion hosts and is even enough to use different addressing schemes and hierarchies. (To allay any fears of another address shortage

threatening IPv6, note that 128 bits are enough for almost a trillion trillion nonhierarchical addresses for every square meter of surface area on our planet. This ratio drops to about just a few thousand per square meter once bits are allocated for hierarchical groupings—still more than ample room for growth.) IPv6 addresses actually identify interfaces rather than network nodes. A single node can have multiple interfaces, so can be reached through any of multiple addresses. IPv6 also supports a new type of address—an anycast address. Such an address is used when sending a packet to any of a group of interfaces, and it ensures that only one copy of the packet is sent to a node that is associated with multiple addresses on the anycast list.

Address notation: 128 bits provide a lot of possibilities for addresses. IPv6 will, in fact, support several addressing schemes—for back compatibility and to increase the likelihood of a smooth transition to IPv6. The notation for specifying addresses will change, however. IPv6 will use colons (:) instead of periods to separate address elements. Special notation will make it easy to represent addresses that are encapsulated in the longer format—for example, current (32-bit) addresses, which will have many leading zeros when represented as IPv6 addresses.

Header format: The header format has been simplified by dropping some fields or making them optional. This is

a
b
c
d
e
f
g
h
i
j
k
l
m
n
o
p
q
r
s
t
u
v
w
x
y
z

to reduce the overhead from the packet headers.

Header extensions and options: IPv6 provides for several types of optional extension headers, which can provide special instructions for handling a packet. Currently, six extensions are supported: hop-by-hop, routing, fragment, destination options, authentication, and encapsulating security payload. All extensions except hop-by-hop are processed only at the final destination. A hop-by-hop extension is processed at every stop.

Flow labeling capability: IPv6 packets can be labeled as belonging to a particular packet sequence (traffic flow), which may be receiving special processing or which may require a particular type or quality of service.

Authentication and privacy: IPv6 includes extensions that make it possible to provide some security measures with this protocol.

IPv6 Packets

An IPv6 packet consists of header(s) + payload. Between the IP header and the payload, the packet may include up to seven optional headers. (Any of the six extension headers listed earlier—hop-by-hop, routing, etc.—can appear up to one time; the Destination Options header can appear twice.) The presence of such an optional header is indicated by a value in the Next Header field found in the packet (or optional) header. The figure "IPv6 packet" shows the format of such a packet.

The value in the *priority* field specifies what kind of traffic is in the packet. The table "Priority Values" shows the possible types of traffic.

PRIORITY VALUES	
VALUE	**MEANING**
0	uncharacterized traffic
1	filler traffic (e.g., news)
2	unattended data transfer (e.g., e-mail)
3	reserved
4	attended bulk transfer (e.g., FTP, NFS)
5	reserved
6	interactive traffic (e.g., telnet, X)
7	Internet control traffic (e.g., routing protocols, SNMP)

The *flow label* is used to group packets that are to be given the same handling or type of service.

Payload length specifies the number of octets in the the payload portion of the packet. A value of 0 means that the payload is actually being carried as part of a Jumbo payload in the hop-by-hop option. This payload must be larger than 65,535 octets.

The *Next header* field identifies the type of header that follows the IPv6 header. The value will determine whether there are any optional headers before the payload. If this value is zero in the IPv6 header, then the next header is a hop-by-hop header. Otherwise, IPv6 uses the values used in the IPv4 Protocol field. The values associated with

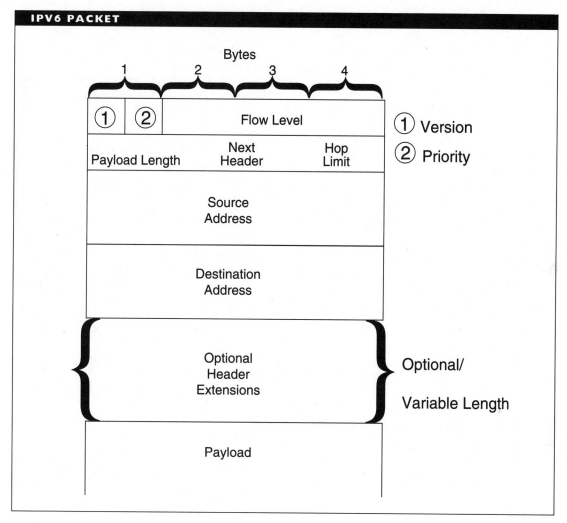

IPV6 PACKET

Bytes

① Version

② Priority

various protocols are listed in the "Assigned Numbers" RFC, the most recent of which is 1,700. (See the table "Assignments for an IP Packet's Protocol Field" in the "Protocol, IP" entry for examples of such values.)

Hop limit is the maximum number of nodes through which the packet can be passed. Each node that passes the packet on will decrement the hop limit value by 1. If this value reaches 0 before the packet reaches its destination, the packet will be discarded. In IPv4, the lifetime of a packet is specified by the TTL (time to live) field. This was originally an actual time limit, but later became a hop count. In IPv6, a packet's lifetime is shortened only by hops between nodes, not by the mere passage of time.

The 128-bit *Source Address* field contains the address of the packet's originator. The details of the addressing scheme to be used with IPv6 are still being worked out.

The 128-bit *Destination Address* field contains the address of the packet's intended recipient. If the packet includes a Routing header, then the destination address may be only an intermediate stop.

The IETF specifications impose constraints and restrictions on the sequence in which certain headers can appear, and make strong recommendations about others. There are also restrictions on the address boundaries for the header fields.

IPv6 is only a draft, and may change— possibly several times—before it is finalized. Nonetheless, it represents a major departure from the current protocol and is designed to enable modification up the line if this seems advisable.

PRIMARY SOURCES

Comments and discussions of IPng can be found in several RFCs, including 1550 (the original solicitation for comments), most of the RFCs in the 1667 through 1688 range, 1705, 1726, and 1753. For IPv6, the IETF drafts can be downloaded through the IETF home page,

http:// www.ietf.cnri. reston.va.us/

or from the /ietf-online-proceedings directory of the ftp.ietf.cnri.reston.va.us FTP site.

▼
Protocol, IPX/SPX (Internetwork Packet Exchange/Sequenced Packet Exchange)

In Novell's NetWare, IPX and SPX are the network protocols responsible for ensuring successful internetwork communications.

IPX

IPX is a network layer protocol, and it is responsible for addressing and routing packets to nodes on other networks. IPX assigns and works with network layer addresses, as opposed to physical layer addresses, which are assigned by the network interface card (NIC) manufacturers. The IPX protocol uses the services of the data-link layer, and it provides services to the SPX (sequenced packet exchange) protocol in the next higher layer.

The IPX protocol is a connectionless protocol. This means that it doesn't need a fixed connection between source and destination. The protocol can send different packets along different routes and doesn't need to worry about the sequencing.

IPX is also a datagram protocol. This means that each packet comes with everything you wanted to know about it. With this information, a higher-level protocol at the receiving end can reassemble the packets in sequence.

IPX Packets

The IPX protocol is based on the IDP (Internet Datagram Packet) protocol from the XNS (Xerox Network System) model. The IPX and IDP packet structures are identical. This structure is shown in the figure "IPX packet structure." Note that the packet has a 30-byte header.

The Length field indicates the total number of bytes in the entire IPX packet. This value must be at least 30 for the header. Note that an IPX packet can be at most 576 bytes if the packet is being routed, which allows for at most 546 bytes of data. The LIP (Large Internet Packet) enhancement

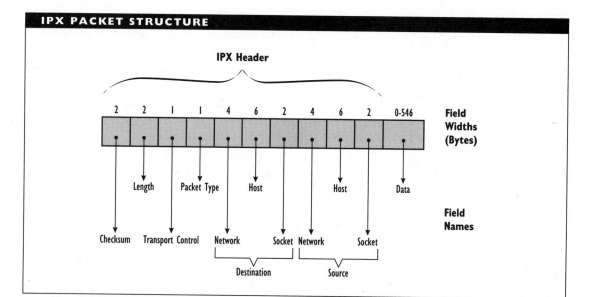

IPX PACKET STRUCTURE

allows larger packet sizes to be transmitted across IPX routers.

The Transport Control field is used to count the number of routers through which the packet passes, known as the *hop count*. The RIP (Routing Information Protocol) is used to monitor this value. If the value reaches 16, the packet is discarded.

The Packet Type field indicates the higher-level protocol to which the packet is being passed. Although 8 bits are allocated for this field, IPX uses just the following values:

- 0 for unknown packet type

- 4 for PEP (Packet Exchange Protocol)

- 5 for SPX (Sequenced Packet Exchange)

- 17 for NCP (NetWare Core Protocol)

The Destination Address field specifies the 4-byte network address of the

destination node. If the sender and destination are on the same network, this value is 0.

The Destination Node field contains the physical address of the destination node. The number of bytes needed for this address depends on the network architecture. For example, Ethernet and Token Ring network nodes use all 6 bytes; ARCnet nodes use only a single byte. For broadcasts, which are packets sent to every node, this field contains only F (hexadecimal) values.

The Destination Socket field contains the address value associated with the higher-layer process. This value is used to specify the location of the interface between the two layers. Values are assigned by Xerox, and vendors can register a value range with Xerox for use in the vendor's products. The following values are of relevance for NetWare networks:

- 1 for RIP (Routing Information Packet)

- 2 for Echo Packet

- 3 for Error Handling

- 451H for NCP File Service Packet

- 452H for SAP (Service Advertising Protocol)

- 453H for Novell RIP, or IPX RIP

- 455H for NetBIOS

- 456H for Diagnostics

The multidigit values, which are in hexadecimal form as indicated by the H, have been assigned for use with NetWare.

The Source Network field contains the network address of the packet's source. If the network is unknown, this value is 0.

The Source Node field contains the physical address of the packet's source. This field is analogous to the Destination Node field, and the same information about physical addresses applies here.

The Source Socket field is analogous to the Destination Socket field in that it contains the address through which the source and destination communicate.

The Data field contains higher-level information being passed up or down in the protocol-layer hierarchy.

SPX

NetWare's transport layer SPX protocol provides a connection-oriented link between nodes. A connection-oriented protocol is one that first establishes a connection between sender and receiver, then transmits the data, and finally breaks the connection. All packets in the transmission are sent in order, and all take the same path. This is in contrast to a connectionless service, in which packets may use different paths.

The SPX protocol ensures that packets arrive at their destination with enough sequence information to reconstruct the message at the receiving end and also to maintain a connection at a specified level of quality. To accomplish this, SPX is responsible for flow control, packet acknowledgment, and similar activities.

An unfortunate disadvantage of a connection-oriented protocol arises when a broadcast packet is to be handled. The protocol must establish a connection with every destination before the packets can be sent. This can be a major undertaking, consuming time and resources.

To avoid such a situation, higher-level NetWare protocols such as NCP (NetWare Core Protocol) can bypass SPX and communicate directly with IPX.

SPX Packets

An SPX packet includes the same header fields as an IPX packet and adds a 12-byte SPX header at the end. These 12 bytes come at the expense of the Data field, so that an SPX packet (without LIP) can contain at most 534 bytes of data. The figure "SPX packet structure" shows the details of the SPX header.

The Connection Control field contains flags to control the flow of data between sender and receiver. Although eight flags are available, only the four high-order bits are defined:

- 10H to mark the last packet in the message

- 20H to signal for attention

- 40H to indicate that an acknowledgment is required

- 80H to identify a system packet

The Datastream Type field indicates whether the packet's Data field contains control information or a packet. If the Data field contains a packet, the Datastream Type will indicate which sort of packet (IPX, IP, and so on).

The Source Connection ID and the Destination Connection ID identify virtual circuits. The source ID is assigned by the sender of the SPX packet. The destination ID is used to demultiplex multiple virtual circuits from a single connection, as for a server.

The Sequence Number is used to number each packet in a message as the packet is sent.

The Acknowledgment Number indicates the sequence number of the packet the receiver expects to receive next. This value implicitly acknowledges any unacknowledged packets with lower sequence numbers. For example, an Acknowledgment Number of 20 indicates that the destination has received and at least implicitly acknowledges 19 packets.

The Allocation Number indicates the number of receive buffers available for a connection. This value is used for end-to-end flow control.

The Data field contains higher-level information being passed up or down in the protocol-layer hierarchy.

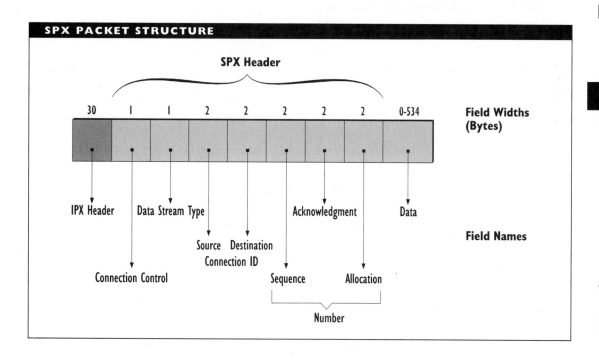

SPX PACKET STRUCTURE

SPX Header

| 30 | 1 | 1 | 2 | 2 | 2 | 2 | 2 | 0-534 | Field Widths (Bytes) |

IPX Header   Data Stream Type   Acknowledgment   Data   Field Names

Connection Control   Source   Destination   Sequence   Allocation
                      Connection ID

Number

Protocol, IS-IS (Intermediate System to Intermediate System)

In the OSI network management model, a routing protocol that routers (intermediate systems) use to communicate with each other. Such a protocol is in contrast to an ES-IS protocol, which is for communication between a node and a router. An IS-IS protocol may be used within an autonomous system (AS) or between ASs. These two cases require IGP and EGP (interior and exterior gateway protocols), respectively.

IS-IS is an example of a link-state protocol. Such protocols can be very efficient because routers exchange routing information only when something has changed. This cuts down on extraneous network traffic.

Protocol, LAPB (Link Access Protocol, Balanced)

A bit-oriented, data-link layer protocol that is used in X.25 connections, such as to connect a terminal or node to a packet-switched network. LAPB is based on the HDLC protocol, and it can support half- or full-duplex communications in a point-to-point link. LAPB supports only the asynchronous balanced mode (ABM) of data transfer.

SEE ALSO
Protocol, HDLC

Protocol, LAPD (Link Access Protocol, D Channel)

A data-link protocol for use on ISDN D channels.

Protocol, LCP (Link Control Protocol)

LCP is one of the three main components of the Point-to-Point Protocol (PPP). PPP is mainly used to provide a way to encapsulate the IP packets while going over serial lines—that is, to get the IP packets over the serial connection and onto the network. LCP is used to set up, handle, and terminate the data link between the two points.

LCP is responsible for tasks such as the following:

- Establishing the link (through an exchange of Configure packets)

- Deciding on the options for encapsulating the (IP) packets

- Dealing with packet size limits or restrictions

- Possibly authenticating the identity of its counterpart (peer) at the other end of the link

- Testing to detect configuration errors such as a link that is looped back

- Testing to make sure the link is operating correctly

- Terminating the link—by exchanging Terminate packets—when finished or when necessary

LCP Packets

LCP uses three kinds of packets: Link Configure, Link Terminate, and Link Maintenance. Each of these comes in variants. For example, the Link Configure packet has four versions: Configure-Request, -Reject, -Ack (acknowledge), and -Nak (negative acknowledge).

- The packet type information is stored in *Code,* the first field of the LCP packet, as shown in the figure "LCP packet." This 8-bit field can take on values that are specified in the most recent "Assigned Numbers" RFC (currently RFC 1700).

- The *Identifier* field is also 8-bit. This value is used when matching requests and replies during an interaction.

- The 16-bit *Length* field indicates the total length of the LCP packet, including the four-octet header.

- The *Data* label for the remainder of the packet serves as a generic term for a variety of contents, depending on the type of LCP packet. Structurally, this field consists of zero or more octets; semantically, the field's interpretation depends on the value of *Code.* Some of the possibilities are discussed below.

For a Configure-Request packet (*Code* = 1), this field consists of zero or more Configuration Options that the LCP wants to negotiate. Each option included has the same (type-length-value, or TLV) format: option type, option length, option details. The table "Configuration Options" lists currently defined options.

CONFIGURATION OPTIONS	
TYPE	OPTION
1	Maximum-receive unit (MRU)
2	Async-Control-Character-Map
3	Protocol
4	Protocol
5	Magic number
6	—Reserved—
7	Protocol field compression
8	Address and control field compression

The format and details of the data field for the options will be determined in part by the option's type.

PRIMARY SOURCES

The LCP is described in RFC 1548. Extensions to the current LCP options are being circulated as RFC 1570.

Protocol, Lightweight

A lightweight protocol is any of a class of protocols designed for use on high-speed internetworks. HSTP (High-Speed Transport Protocol) and XTP (Xpress Transfer Protocol) are examples of lightweight protocols.

Lightweight protocols combine routing and transport services in a more streamlined fashion than do traditional network and transport layer protocols. This makes it possible to transmit more efficiently over high-speed networks, such as ATM or FDDI, and media, such as fiber-optic cable.

Lightweight protocols use various measures and refinements to streamline

LCP PACKET

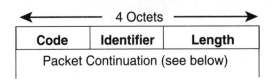

Packet Continuations

Options
Configuration Packet

...

Configuration packets specify one or more options in
this section. Each option has the same format: option
type (1 octet), option length (1 octet), and option data
(variable length).

Data
Terminate Packet

...

Termination packets specify uninterpreted data from the
sender. Length information is provided in the generic part
of the LCP packet header.

Rejected Packet
Code Reject Packet

...

Code-Reject packets include the rejected packet (stripped
of some information).

Rejected Protocol	Rejected Packet
Packet
Reject Packet

...

Protocol-Reject packets also include the rejected packet,
but this is preceded by a 2-octet value indicating the
rejected protocol.

Magic Number
Data

Echo
&
Discard Packets

...

The discard request packet and the Echo packets include a
4-octet magic number, which is used to determine whether
there are any loopbacks in the path. Following this, there may
be zero or more octets of uninterpreted data.

and speed up transmissions, including the following:

- Use of fixed header and trailer sizes. For example, XTP uses identical 40-byte headers and 4-byte trailers for both control and information packets. All the fields in the header are the same size (4 bytes), which also makes packet manipulation easier.

- More efficient use of checksum and error correction. Checksums for XTP are located at the end of the header and at the end of the packet. This makes it possible to compute the checksums while transmitting the packets and to insert the computed value at the appropriate point. In traditional protocols (such as TCP), the packet checksum is in the header, so the packet must be processed twice: first to compute the checksum and then to transmit.

- Error checking is done only at the endpoints, rather than after each transmission, which can save considerable time. Such a cavalier attitude toward error checking is possible because transmission lines are much "cleaner" than they were when the traditional protocols were developed. Also, lightweight protocols make it easy to retransmit only erroneous packets. Traditional protocols demand the retransmission of an erroneous packet and all packets that follow it until the error was detected.

- Use of connection-oriented transmissions to save the overhead of transmitting a destination address with each packet. (A connection-oriented transmission is one in which a path is first established and then used for the duration of the transmission, so that all packets take the same path.)

By using a simple indexing scheme to identify packets for a message, lightweight protocols can use the same path for multiple messages at a time. This approach saves the time required to make routing decisions for each packet and also saves the overhead of address information in each packet and of hop counts (which are used to ensure that a packet is discarded if it does not reach its destination within a predefined number of stops).

Protocol, Link-State

A link-state protocol is any of several routing protocols that use a link-state algorithm to determine available connections. Examples of this type of protocol include the following:

- NLSP (NetWare Link Services Protocol) from Novell's IPX/SPX protocol suite.

- OSPF (Open Shortest Path First) from the TCP/IP suite.

- AURP (AppleTalk Update Routing Protocol) from the AppleTalk suite.

- IS-IS (Intermediate System to Intermediate System) from the OSI suite.

a
b
c
d
e
f
g
h
i
j
k
l
m
n
o
p
q
r
s
t
u
v
w
x
y
z

Link-state protocols are in contrast to distance-vector protocols, which use a different strategy for getting routing information. Distance-vector protocols provide information about the costs of reaching all possible destinations. Link-state approaches provide information only about the distances from a router to all its immediate neighbor routers. The former strategy is more computationally intensive when setting up or updating the routing information; link-state protocols need to do more work during the actual routing.

Link-state protocols send updates only when the network changes, whereas distance-vector protocols send periodic updates. The smaller resulting overhead for link-state protocols makes them better suited for routing over wide-area internetworks. Link-state protocols are also better at dealing with changes to the network.

BROADER CATEGORY
Protocol, Routing

COMPARE
Protocol, Distance-Vector

Protocol, LLAP (LocalTalk Link Access Protocol)

In the AppleTalk network protocol suite, the data-link layer protocol for LocalTalk, Apple's 235 kilobit per second network architecture.

Protocol, LLC (Logical Link Control)

A protocol developed by the IEEE 802.2 committee, which defined the MAC (medium access control) and LLC sublayers of the OSI Reference Model data-link layer. The 802.2 specifications have been replaced by the ISO 8802-2 specifications. An LLC frame is based on the HDLC frame, except that the LLC frame uses different addresses and does not include a CRC field.

Protocol, LMMP (LAN/MAN Management Protocol)

A protocol for network management on local-area networks. LMMP provides the OSI's CMIS/CMIP network management services but implements them directly on the logical-link-control (LLC) sublayer of the data-link layer. LMMP provides application-level services and then bypasses the intervening four layers in order to use the LLC services. This makes it easier to implement LMMP but impossible to use routers. Because of its original name, CMIS/CMIP over LLC, LMMP is also known as CMOL.

Protocol, Low-Level

A protocol below the network layer in the OSI Reference Model. Specifically, a protocol at the physical or data-link layer.

Protocol, LPP (Lightweight Presentation Protocol)

A presentation layer protocol defined for use in the CMOT (CMIP over TCP/IP) network management effort (which was never completed).

Protocol, MLP (Multilink Procedures)

A protocol designed for use with multiple network connections running in parallel. MLP oversees the process of using a point-to-point protocol (such as LAPB or HDLC) in each of the connections. MLP can be used to balance the loads on the connections.

Protocol, Modulation

Modulation protocols are designed for modulating digital signals for transmission over telephone lines. The protocols differ in the rates they support. The following protocols are widely supported:

- Bell 103A and 212A, which support speeds of 300 and 1,200 bits per second (bps), respectively.

- V.21, which supports speeds of 300 bps and which are used by group III fax machines to negotiate.

- V.22 and V.22bis, which support speeds of 600 to 1,200 bps and 2,440 to 4,800 bps, respectively.

- V.32 and V.32bis, which support speeds of 9,600 bps and 7,200 to 14,400 bps, respectively.

- V.FAST, which supports rates between 19,200 and 24,000 bps.

- V.34, which supports rates up to 28,800 bps and even higher with compression.

Protocol, MP (Multilink Point-to-Point Protocol)

MP is a protocol for splitting a signal, sending it along multiple channels, and then reassembling and sequencing it at the common destination for the channels. MP is actually an extension of the Point-to-Point protocol (PPP), and the MP packets are actually handled by PPP as if they belonged to a particular protocol (namely, MP).

MP is a proposed standard from the IETF (Internet Engineering Task Force), and it is generally regarded as more popular than an alternative standard created by BONDING (Bandwidth on Demand Interoperability Group).

PRIMARY SOURCES

RFC 1717

SEE ALSO

Protocol, PPP (Point-to-Point Protocol)

Protocol, NBP (Name Binding Protocol)

An AppleTalk transport layer protocol for mapping logical names to physical addresses.

Protocol, NCP (NetWare Core Protocol)

In Novell's NetWare, NCP is an upper-layer protocol that a NetWare file server uses to deal with workstation requests. NCP actually spans the top three OSI Reference Model layers: application, presentation, and session. The protocol provides capabilities such as the following:

- Creating or breaking a connection for service
- File and directory handling
- Printing
- Security
- Changing drive mappings

When a workstation makes a request that its software will redirect to the server, the workstation software puts the request into the appropriate NCP format and passes the request to the IPX protocol. This protocol passes the packet to the server, which decapsulates (removes the headers and trailers from) the packet, finds the NCP request, and responds to it.

NCP can also be used to communicate directly with the network layer IPX (Internetwork Packet Exchange) protocol under certain conditions. For example, when broadcasting a message (sending the message to all stations on a network), NCP can be used to avoid needing to establish explicit connections with each destination node. The connection-oriented SPX protocol at the transport layer would need to do this, requiring extra time and resources.

BROADER CATEGORY
NetWare

▼
Protocol, NetBEUI (Network Basic Extended User Interface)

A protocol developed originally for use on IBM Token Ring networks. Unlike IBM's original NetBIOS implementation, which used proprietary lower-layer protocols, NetBEUI was designed to communicate with standard (IEEE 802.2 logical-link-control) protocols at the lower layers. NetBEUI protocols are used in Microsoft's LAN Manager and in IBM's LAN Server networks.

▼
Protocol, NetBIOS (Network Basic Input/Output System)

NetBIOS is an interface and an upper-level protocol developed by IBM for use with a proprietary adapter for its PC Network product. NetBIOS provides a standard interface to the lower networking layers. The protocol's functionality actually ranges over the top three layers (session, presentation, and application) in the OSI Reference Model.

Essentially, the protocol provides higher-layer programs with access to the network. The program has been adapted by other network packages (most notably, Microsoft's LAN Manager) and is now widely emulated. Note that not all NetBIOS implementations are equivalent, so you may encounter some incompatibilities.

NetBIOS can also serve as an API (Application Program Interface) for data exchange. As such, it provides programmers with access to resources for establishing a connection between two machines or between two applications on the same machine.

NetBIOS provides four types of services:

- Naming, for creating and checking group and individual names, and for deleting individual names. These names can be either hardware names or symbolic names.

- Datagram support, for connectionless transmissions that make a best effort to deliver packets, but that do not guarantee successful delivery. Packets in this mode are usually no larger than 512 bytes.

- Session support, for transmissions in which a temporary virtual circuit is established for the duration of a session so that delivery of packets can be monitored and verified. In this mode, NetBIOS will guarantee delivery of messages of up to 64 kilobytes.

- General services: for resetting adapter states, canceling application commands when possible, and so on.

SEE ALSO

Protocol, NetBEUI

Protocol, Network Management

A network management protocol is used for monitoring the performance and components of a network. This monitoring is generally performed by special programs, called *agents*. Each agent gathers data about particular functions or components on a single node.

Agent handlers organize, analyze, and filter this information before passing it on to a network manager, which is a special program running (generally) on a dedicated machine.

The following are the two most widely used management protocols:

- SNMP (Simple Network Management Protocol), which was developed for networks that use TCP/IP

- CMIP (Common Management Information Protocol), a protocol from the ISO for use in the OSI Reference Model

Protocol, NFS (Network File System)

NFS is a protocol developed by Sun Microsystems for sharing remote files across UNIX or other networks.

This protocol makes accessing files on remote machines transparent for the user so that the user's ordinary commands will work with these remote files; that is, the user will not even know that the files are anywhere but on the user's local machine.

Similarly, the user's ID will automatically be translated to ensure that it is unique on the network that contains the files. The user's ID must be translated because the user must have access rights to the file. In many cases, files accessible over NFS will have minimal restrictions and will be generally available.

The NFS protocol works at the application level. As such, it is comparable to the FTAM (File Transfer, Access, and Management) protocol in the OSI Reference Model and to AT&T's RFS (Remote File System) protocol in UNIX environments.

To communicate with and give commands on the remote server, NFS relies on remote procedure calls (RPCs). These, in turn, use a generic external data representation (XDR) to move information around. This representation is environment-independent so that files can be passed between operating systems. The information can be translated to the target system's format from the XDR form.

a
b
c
d
e
f
g
h
i
j
k
l
m
n
o
p
q
r
s
t
u
v
w
x
y
z

UDP (User Data Protocol) is most generally used as the actual transport protocol. This protocol is connectionless and unreliable. Packet sequencing and error detection are handled by the NFS protocol.

Because each transaction is considered independent of those that preceded it, NFS is considered a stateless protocol. This is convenient because it makes it unnecessary for sender and receiver to remain synchronized throughout. This, in turn, makes error recovery easier.

NFS also refers to a distributed file system developed by Sun Microsystems for use under its SunOS operating system.

COMPARE
Protocol, FTAM; Protocol, RFS

Protocol, NICE (Network Information and Control Exchange)

A proprietary application layer protocol from Digital Equipment Corporation (DEC). The protocol is used in DECnet networks for testing the network and for getting information about node configurations.

Protocol, NLSP (NetWare Link-State Protocol)

NLSP is a routing protocol in the NetWare IPX/SPX protocol suite. NLSP is an example of a *link-state* protocol, which is particularly well-suited for wide-area routing. This is because link-state protocols broadcast only when something changes, which helps keep network traffic lower. This is in contrast to *distance vector* protocols, which broadcast periodically.

NLSP is designed to replace the less efficient, higher overhead RIP (Routing Information Protocol) and SAP (Services Advertising Protocol). The newer protocol has numerous advantages over RIP and SAP:

Routing: NLSP-based routers know more about the network's layout than RIP-based routers, so that routers can make more intelligent decisions.

Overhead: NLSP has less overhead than RIP or SAP because it broadcasts only when something changes, whereas RIP and SAP broadcast their materials periodically.

Transfer Speed: NLSP supports parallel paths (which makes it possible to split the network load). NLSP also reduces packet sizes by using IPX header compression.

Reliability: Because it supports parallel paths, NLSP can keep network traffic flowing even when a path is down. NLSP checks the integrity of all links regularly.

Network Support: Because it supports up to 127 hops for a packet, NLSP can be used on larger networks than RIP, which supported only up to 15 hops.

Protocol and Media Support: NLSP is back-compatible with RIP and can communicate with RIP-based routers. RIP- and NLSP-based routers can coexist on the same network, although communications must be at a level that the RIP-based router can handle. Similarly, NLSP is also compatible with various network types, including

Ethernet, Token Ring, and point-to-point links.

Protocol, NNTP (Network News Transfer Protocol)

NNTP is the protocol used to distribute news article collections (*newsfeeds*) on the Internet. NNTP is also used to query a news server, which maintains a central database of articles and newsgroups, and to retrieve and post articles to a newsgroup. This database will consist of the Usenet news system and probably some alternative newsgroups that have not found or have not even sought a place in the Usenet newsgroup family.

NNTP uses a reliable data stream (for example, TCP) to distribute and receive articles and also for communications between sender and receiver. NNTP allows interaction between sender and receiver—for example, between two servers with newsfeeds to exchange or between a client host and a news server.

Because of its interactive capabilities, NNTP has advantages over other transfer methods—such as UUCP (UNIX-to-UNIX copy program). For example, if one server has a large newsfeed (newsgroup file collection) to pass to another server, the simplest thing—with UUCP—would be to transfer the entire contents. Because UUCP sends an article regardless of whether the receiving machine already has it, the receiving machine is left to delete any duplicates.

With NNTP, the receiving machine can specify easily which newsgroups and articles it wants—avoiding the unnecessary transmission of what could be dozens of megabytes. This selective capability also comes in handy for clients, who can select just the articles they want to read and skip over anything else.

Although it was proposed almost 10 years ago, NNTP is still just a proposed standard. It is considered an elective protocol, which means that servers need not support it. Nevertheless, it is so widely used on the Internet that, for all practical purposes, it *is* the news transfer protocol.

PRIMARY SOURCES

The original proposal for NNTP is in RFC 977.

Protocol, NSP (Network Services Protocol)

A proprietary transport layer protocol from Digital Equipment Corporation (DEC). NSP is used in DECnet networks.

Protocol, NTP (Network Time Protocol)

NTP is used to synchronize computer clocks on the Internet. This draft standard protocol makes it possible for a server to get the time from a national time source and to distribute the time information to other nodes so that these nodes can adjust their clocks using the primary server as a reference. Hosts can get their time from one of these secondary servers.

NTP is a very complex protocol because it deals with the entire synchronization process—from physical measurement and clocking to dissemination. It also considers algorithms and strategies for improving accuracy—or at least minimizing loss of accuracy—during the multistep process.

a b c d e f g h i j k l m n o **p** q r s t u v w x y z

Depending on the host's location in relation to a time server, NTP is accurate to within 1–50 milliseconds.

Servers can disseminate the time information by unicasts (point-to-point transmissions) or by multicasts (transmission to all parties on a multicast list). The group address and memberships are determined by the Internet Group Management Protocol (IGMP).

PRIMARY SOURCES

NTP version 3 is described in RFC 1305. A simpler, less accurate, variant—SNTP, or simple network time protocol—is proposed in RFC 1769.

Protocol, OSPF (Open Shortest Path First)

In internetworks that use the TCP/IP protocol suite, a routing protocol for passing packets between routers in networks within a given domain. (The *open* in the name is an adjective, not a verb, and is in contrast to *proprietary.*) OSPF is an example of a link-state protocol, in which routers provide updated information only when there is something new to report. OSPF is also an example of an Interior Gateway Protocol (IGP).

Protocol, Packet Burst

In Novell's NetWare, the Packet Burst protocol can be used on top of IPX (Internetwork Exchange Protocol) to send multiple NCP (NetWare Control Protocol) packets. It can send an entire *burst,* without waiting for an acknowledgment after each packet.

Because the protocol monitors the transmission, only lost or erroneous packets need to be retransmitted, not the entire burst. The figure "Communications with and without packet burst" illustrates how Packet Burst works in contrast to other methods. Use of this protocol is sometimes known as operating in *burst mode.*

Protocol, PAP (Printer Access Protocol)

In the AppleTalk protocol suite, the protocol used for communication between nodes (Macintoshes) and printers. PAP is used to set up, maintain, and terminate the connection between node and printer, and also to transfer the data.

Protocol, PEP (Packet Exchange Protocol)

A transport level protocol in the XNS protocol suite from Xerox.

Protocol, PLP (Packet Level Protocol)

A protocol that specifies the details of data transfer between sender and receiver in an X.25 connection. PLP is full duplex and supports error detection and correction, packet sequencing, and transfer-rate adjustment.

Protocol, POP3 (Post Office Protocol, 3)

POP3 is the most recent version of the Post Office Protocol used to provide clients with access to a mail drop (post office) in which messages for the user may be stored.

COMMUNICATIONS WITH AND WITHOUT PACKET BURST

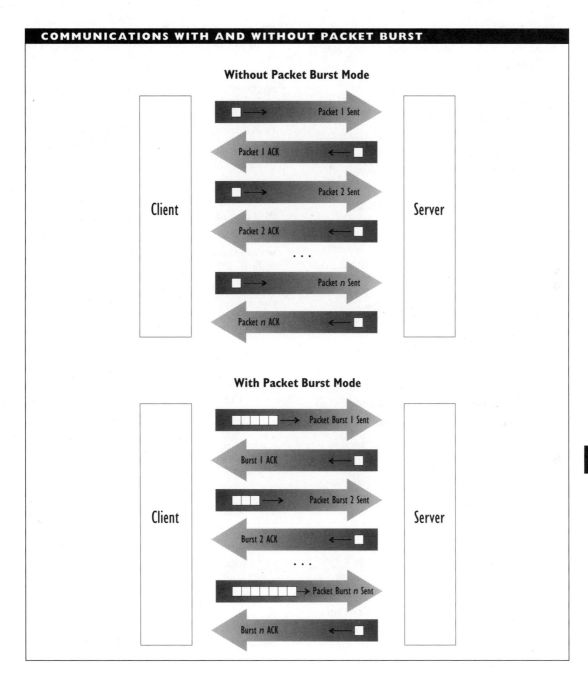

a
b
c
d
e
f
g
h
i
j
k
l
m
n
o
p
q
r
s
t
u
v
w
x
y
z

With POP3, users can retrieve any e-mail messages being held in temporary storage on a POP3 server.

By default, POP3 service is provided on Port 110. POP3 sessions involve the exchange of messages between the client and server. Messages passing between them conform to the message format specified in RFC 822. The session consists of two kinds of messages: commands and responses.

A POP3 session proceeds through several phases:

> **Connection:** The client opens a connection, and the server replies with a positive greeting—for example,

```
S: +OK POP3 server ready
```

> **Authorization:** Once a connection is established, the server requires the client to provide authentication. Two mechanisms are available for doing this. One of these involves encryption and is used when a user doesn't want to be sending passwords.

> **Transaction:** During this phase, the user can check, retrieve, and delete messages. This stage can last for an indefinite period.

> **Update:** When the user gives the QUIT command, the server enters the update stage. All file updates (for example, deletions) requested by the user are actually carried out. Should the connection be lost before the user gives the QUIT command, the server skips the update phase, leaving files as they were before the user began the session.

PRIMARY SOURCES

POP3 is described in RFC 1725.

Protocol, PPP (Point-to-Point Protocol)

PPP is used to transmit TCP/IP packets over telephone lines. The protocol provides a way of encapsulating datagrams so that they can be transmitted over a serial connection. In addition to the encapsulation mechanisms, PPP includes a Link Control Protocol (LCP) component that is used to establish, configure, maintain, and terminate the connection. Finally, PPP includes a collection of Network Control Protocols (NCPs) to deal with the various network layer protocols that might be encountered.

To establish point-to-point communications,

- PPP first uses LCP to establish and test a link, and to agree on a configuration (for example, what packet framing method to use). The LCP may require authentication from its peer at the other end.

- PPP then uses NCP packets to select and configure the network layer protocol(s) being used. Once the protocol information has been established, communications can begin, and PPP can begin transferring packets between the two endpoints.

In a sense, PPP really doesn't do anything but package datagrams and get them from a computer to the other end of a serial connection. Any negotiations or adjustments are made by having PPP send LCP or NCP packets. In its simplest form, the PPP packet consists of a 16-bit *Protocol* field, an *Information* field of variable size, and possibly some padding to round the packet out to an appropriate storage boundary.

The possible values for the *Protocol* field are specified in the most recent "Assigned Numbers" RFC—1700 as of this writing. There are certain restrictions on the values that can be assigned, but in some cases these create groupings that make it easier to categorize the protocol under consideration as being link control, network layer, or network control, for example.

The *Information* field contains the packet being encapsulated. This may be, for example, an IP or an LCP packet. It is assumed that the encapsulated packet will be understood when it is unwrapped at the receiving end.

Note that the Protocol field is the entire PPP header. Since this header doesn't provide any packet length information, the packet needs framing to mark the start and end of the packet. PPP supports standard framing methods such as those provided by HDLC (high-level data link control).

With the growing popularity of the Internet, PPP has become widely used as one of the two main ways for users to get onto the Internet through an Internet Access Provider (IAP). PPP or SLIP (Serial Line Internet Protocol) provides the mechanism for getting packets from the TCP/IP services running on the PC to the IAP and onto the Internet. Of SLIP and PPP, the latter is generally considered the more intelligent and efficient, although objective evidence is hard to come by.

SEE ALSO

IAP (Internet Access Provider); Protocol, SLIP (Serial Line Internet Protocol)

PRIMARY SOURCES

PPP is described in RFC 1661 and in 1570. HDLC framing for PPP is discussed in RFC 1662. Extensions to LCP are discussed in RFC 1570.

Protocol, Proxy

On the World Wide Web (WWW), this protocol is used when a proxy server communicates with information servers through a firewall. A proxy server is one that acts on behalf of another server—for security, efficiency, or other reasons.

For example, if your server is inside a firewall (a protective gateway that filters traffic in order to provide increased security), it won't be able to communicate directly with a Web server in the outside world. Instead, a special server—perhaps part of the gateway itself—will act instead of, or as a proxy for, your server. Your server will pass its request to the proxy. The proxy server will communicate with the Web server, make your requests, and pass the response back to your server—after filtering it, of course.

Protocol, QLLC (Qualified Link Level Control)

A protocol that allows IBM's SNA (Systems Network Architecture) packets to be routed over X.25 links. SNA by itself does not support a network layer protocol and, hence, does not support routing.

a
b
c
d
e
f
g
h
i
j
k
l
m
n
o
p
q
r
s
t
u
v
w
x
y
z

Protocol, RARP (Reverse Address Resolution Protocol)

In the Internet TCP/IP protocol suite, a protocol that maps a hardware address to an Internet address. This protocol is important for diskless workstations, which need to determine their network addresses when the workstations log in to the network.

Protocol, RFS (Remote File System)

AT&T's application layer protocol for handling files on remote machines in a UNIX network. As an application layer protocol, it competes with the FTAM protocol developed for the OSI Reference Model and the NFS protocol developed by Sun Microsystems.

Protocol, RIP (Routing Information Protocol)

A routing protocol in the Novell NetWare protocol suite, RIP is generally known as IPX RIP to distinguish it from the RIP protocol associated with the TCP/IP protocol stack. RIP is a distance-vector protocol, which means it keeps a database of routing information that the protocol broadcasts at intervals. In the same manner, other protocols broadcast theirs, so that each router can update its routing information.

In the Internet TCP/IP protocol suite, RIP is an Interior Gateway Protocol (IGP), which is a protocol used by certain routers to communicate with each other and to determine routes. Like its IPX RIP counterpart, Internet RIP is a distance-vector protocol.

Protocol, Routing

A routing protocol is any of a class of protocols for determining a path between two nodes. The term is generally reserved for internetworking situations in which the two nodes are in different networks, so that routers or bridges are involved.

In an internetwork, the routing elements are known as intermediate systems (IS) and the user stations are known as end systems (ES). ISs use only the three lowest OSI Reference Model layers (physical, data-link, and network); ESs use all seven layers.

Two levels of stations (ES and IS) are sufficient to characterize small internetworks. As the internetwork grows, administration becomes more complex, so additional levels are needed.

For large internetworks, a single organization (corporation, state, or country, for example) may be responsible for multiple routers, or ISs. A group of routers under a common administrator is known as an *autonomous system (AS)* in Internet terminology, or a *routing domain* in the OSI network management model.

The three levels of ES, IS, and AS yield several types of arrangements, each of which may require a different protocol:

- ES-IS communication between workstation and router. This communication generally uses the workstation's native network level protocol, such as IP or IPX.

- IS-IS communication *within* an AS (or routing domain). This communication uses an interior gateway protocol

(IGP). In OSI terminology, this is called an intradomain routing protocol.

- IS-IS communication *between* ASs. This communication uses an exterior gateway protocol (EGP). In OSI terminology, this is an interdomain routing protocol.

The figure "Types of routing arrangements and protocols" shows some of these concepts and how they relate to each other.

Routing protocols may be either static, which means that the route is predetermined and fixed, or dynamic, which means that the route is determined at runtime and may be changed.

Examples of routing protocols include the following:

- BGP (Border Gateway Protocol)
- EGP (Exterior Gateway Protocol)
- Integrated IS-IS (Integrated Intermediate System to Intermediate System)
- OSPF (Open Shortest Path First)
- RIP (Routing Information Protocol)
- RTMP (Routing Table Maintenance Protocol)
- SPF (Shortest Path First)

Protocol, RTMP (Routing Table Maintenance Protocol)

In the AppleTalk protocol suite, a transport layer protocol for tracking and updating the information in the routing table for an internetwork. RTMP is similar to the RIP (Routing Information Protocol) in the TCP/IP

protocol suite and the RIP (Router Information Protocol) used in Novell's NetWare.

Protocol, SDLC (Synchronous Data Link Control)

SDLC is a bit-oriented, data-link layer protocol that can support any of the following:

- Half- or full-duplex communications
- Circuit- or packet-switched networks
- Point-to-point or multipoint network topologies
- Transmission over cable or wireless transmission

SDLC Operation

SDLC was developed in the mid 1970s by IBM for use in IBM's SNA (Systems Network Administration) architecture. Because IBM was interested in facilitating connections between mainframes and terminals, SDLC is more effective for communications between unequal partners, such as a server and a workstation, but not between peers.

These two types of components are known as *primaries* and *secondaries*. Primaries give commands, and secondaries respond. Protocols derived from SDLC also support a third type of component: a combined node can function as either a primary or a secondary, depending on the situation.

Primaries and secondaries can be connected in any of several ways when using SDLC:

- Point-to-point, in which a single primary and a single secondary communicate.

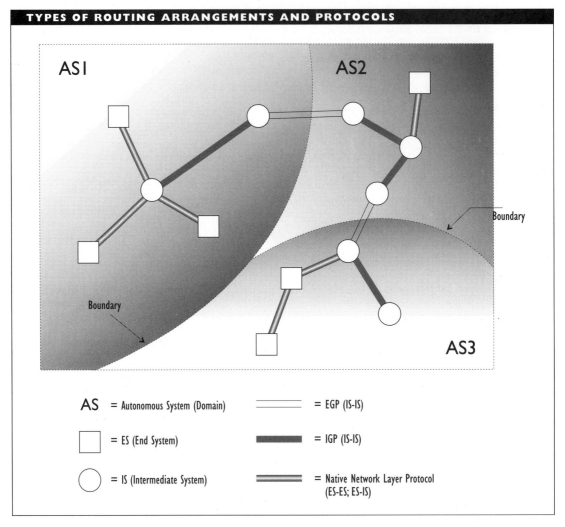

TYPES OF ROUTING ARRANGEMENTS AND PROTOCOLS

AS1

AS2

AS3

Boundary

Boundary

AS = Autonomous System (Domain)

☐ = ES (End System)

◯ = IS (Intermediate System)

= EGP (IS-IS)

= IGP (IS-IS)

= Native Network Layer Protocol (ES-ES; ES-IS)

- Multipoint, in which a single primary communicates with multiple secondaries.

- Loop, in which the primary is one node in a ring of secondaries. Each node is connected to the node immediately in front and in back. Transmissions begin at the primary and are passed from node to node around the loop until the transmission again reaches the primary.

- Hub go-ahead, in which a primary communicates with multiple secondaries using an outbound channel and secondaries communicate with the primary using an inbound channel. The inbound channel may be daisy-chained through each secondary.

An expanded version of SDLC was standardized by ANSI as ADCCP (Advanced Data Communications Control Procedure) and by the ISO as HDLC (High-level Data Link Control).

SDLC Frames

SDLC uses three types of frames: Information, Supervisory, and Unnumbered. Each frame type can occur within the same basic frame structure. The figure "SDLC frame structure" shows these frames.

The frames have the following fields:

Flag: Each SDLC frame begins and ends with an 8-bit flag. These flags always have the same value: 01111110. To ensure that such a bit sequence cannot be encountered anywhere else in an SDLC frame, the sender must insert a 0 after every string of five consecutive 1s. The receiver automatically removes these 0s before passing on the transmitted data. To improve efficiency, the ending flag for one frame can double as the starting flag for the next flag when multiple frames are transmitted in succession.

Address: This 8-bit value contains the address of the secondary that will receive or send the frame. Since all transmissions involve the primary in SDLC, this address is never needed in a frame. SDLC includes provisions for multibyte address fields and also for special addresses to indicate multicasts (in which some secondaries get the frame) or broadcasts (in which all secondaries get the frame).

Control: This 8- or 16-bit field can contain any of three types of values: Information, Supervisory, or Unnumbered. These types are discussed below. Note that *Information* is used as both a frame type and as a field name.

Information: This variable-length field contains the actual data being transmitted. Only certain types of frames have an Information field. Information-type frames include an Information field, as do two types of Unnumbered frames. Supervisory frames do not have Information fields, so they cannot be used for data transmission.

CRC: This 2-byte field contains a cyclical redundancy check (CRC) value based on the Address, Control, and Information fields.

Each of the three frame types includes a poll/find (P/F) bit. This value is set to 1 if the primary wants the secondary to acknowledge receipt of the frame, and 0 otherwise. If the primary sets this bit to 1, the receiver will set the bit to a value that depends on other information in the Control field.

Information-Type Frame

An Information-type frame includes a 3-bit send sequence and a 3-bit receive sequence. (These are 7-bit values when 2 bytes are used for the Control field.) The send sequence represents the number of the next frame the primary will send. The receive sequence represents the number of the next frame the secondary expects to receive.

a
b
c
d
e
f
g
h
i
j
k
l
m
n
o
p
q
r
s
t
u
v
w
x
y
z

SDLC FRAME STRUCTURE

Basic Frame Format

Flag 8 Bits	Address 8*(1+) Bits	Control 8 or 16 Bits	Info 0+ Bits	FCS 16 or 32 Bits	Flag 8 Bits

I Frame Control Field

0 1 2 3 4 5 6 7

0	N(S)	P/F	N(R)	8-Bit

0 1 2 3 4 5 6 7 8 9 10 11 12 13 14 15

0	N(S)	P/F	N(R)	16-Bit

S Frame Control Field

0 1 2 3 4 5 6 7

1	0	S-Bits	P/F	N(R)	8-Bit

0 1 2 3 4 5 6 7 8 9 10 11 12 13 14 15

1	0	S-Bits	0	0	0	0	P/F	N(R)	16-Bit

U Frame Control Field

0 1 2 3 4 5 6 7

1	1	U-Bits	P/F	U-Bits	8-Bit

0 = Least Significant Bit
0-7 = Low-Order Byte

0 1 2 3 4 5 6 7 8 9 10 11 12 13 14 15

1	1	U-Bits	R	U-Bits	P/F	R	16-Bit

In case of error, the secondary stops updating the receive sequence value. The primary can use this value to determine the frame with which to begin retransmitting. Note that the primary must ask for an acknowledgment after every 7 (or 127) frames.

All Information-type frames have a Control field that begins with a 0 bit. Such frames generally have 1 or more bytes in the Information *field*.

Supervisory Frame

A Supervisory frame is used to respond to information frames. The Control field for such frames begins with a bit pattern 10. In addition to the 10 and the P/F bit, the Control field for a Supervisory frame contains a 2-bit function code and a receive sequence value. The function bits specify the purpose of the frame, which can be to indicate any of the following:

- RR (receiver ready), when a secondary is ready to receive a frame.

- RNR (receiver not ready), when a secondary is not ready to receive a frame.

- REJ (reject frame), when an error was detected in a frame.

Supervisory frames do not include an Information field.

Unnumbered Frame

An Unnumbered frame usually serves an administrative purpose, and it is usually sent on its own (rather than as part of a frame sequence). The Control field for such frames begins with an 11-bit pattern. Because Unnumbered frames are not grouped for any reason, there is no need for either send or receive sequence values.

Instead, an Unnumbered frame allocates 5 bits in the Control field to specify a function. The function can specify actions such as initializing or terminating a link, specifying whether the Control field is 1 or 2 bytes, and so on.

Two types of Unnumbered frames can also include an Information field. This field is used to send information relevant to the function being requested.

Protocol, SGMP (Simple Gateway Monitoring Protocol)

In the Internet community, a now obsolete network management protocol. SGMP was a precursor to the SNMP (Simple Network Monitoring Protocol) that has become the most widely used network management protocol for TCP/IP environments.

Protocol, SHTTP (Secure Hypertext Transfer Protocol)

SHTTP is a secure version of the HTTP protocol, which is used to process and transport documents (*Web pages*) on the World Wide Web (WWW). (Web pages are hypertext files and are generally created using the HTML, or hypertext markup language.)

SHTTP provides three major types of security services:

Encryption, which means that the content of messages can be encrypted into what is gibberish for anyone but the person(s) with the mathematical key to decrypt the gibberish back to meaningful text. That is, encryption will ensure that only the person(s) authorized to receive the message—the "key personnel," so to speak—will be able to read it. SHTTP supports any of the popularly used encryption methods, including PEM (Privacy Enhanced Mail) and PGP (Pretty Good Privacy).

Digital Signature, which is one way to prevent message forgery or tampering, and to verify the message source.

Authentication, which provides other mechanisms for testing the integrity of the file (i.e., determining whether anyone has changed it or tampered with it) and verifying that the sender is actually the author.

SHTTP provides end-to-end secure communications, which means it must also be able to ensure the security along the way. SHTTP servers can communicate with both secure and non-secure (i.e., ordinary HTTP) servers. They will not provide secure information to a non-secure server, however.

SHTTP was originally developed at Enterprise Integration Technologies and is currently under consideration by an Internet Engineering Task Force working group. SHTTP represents one strategy for providing security for activity and transactions on the WWW. Another approach currently in use is NetScape's Secure Socket Layer (SSL).

PRIMARY SOURCES

The most current version of the Internet draft documents can be downloaded through the IETF home page,

http://www.ietf.cnri.reston.va.us/

or from the /ietf-online-proceedings directory of the ftp.ietf.cnri.reston.va.us FTP site.

Protocol, SLIP (Serial Line Internet Protocol)

SLIP is a very simple protocol that is used solely for encapsulating and framing IP (Internet Protocol) packets that are being transmitted over serial lines—for example, via modem. Since it is used only in point-to-point connections, SLIP does no packet addressing or error checking.

SLIP is a de facto standard and is used widely by users wishing to connect to the Internet from home through an Internet Access Provider (IAP). Despite its widespread use, SLIP is explicitly not an Internet standard.

A variant protocol—CSLIP, for compressed SLIP—uses a compression scheme (Van Jacobson compression) developed for TCP/IP-based networks. This scheme compresses the packet header from 24 to 5 bytes.

Because it lacks error-correction capabilities and because serial connections can sometimes be quite noisy, SLIP has largely been replaced by the somewhat more capable PPP (Point-to-Point Protocol).

PRIMARY SOURCES

SLIP is discussed in RFC 1055.

Protocol, SMTP (Simple Mail Transfer Protocol)

In the TCP/IP protocol suite, an application layer protocol that provides a simple electronic-mail service. SMTP uses the services of the TCP protocol at the transport layer to send and receive messages.

Protocol, SNAcP (Subnetwork Access Protocol)

In the OSI specifications for the Internal Organization of the Network Layer (IONL), the type of protocol used at the lowest of the three sublayers into which the layer has been subdivided. Such a protocol must provide access to the subnetwork and must be able to transfer data to the subnetwork. The X.25 packet layer protocol is an example of an SNAcP.

Protocol, SNDCP (Subnetwork-Dependent Convergence Protocol)

In the OSI specifications for the Internal Organization of the Network Layer (IONL), the type of protocol used at the middle of the three sublayers into which the layer has been subdivided. Such a protocol must handle any details or problems relating to the subnetwork to which the data is being transferred.

Protocol, SNICP (Subnetwork-Independent Convergence Protocol)

In the OSI specifications for the Internal Organization of the Network Layer (IONL), the type of protocol used at the highest of the three sublayers into which the layer

has been subdivided. Such a protocol must provide the routing and relaying capabilities needed to get data to its destination. The OSI's CLNP (Connectionless-mode Network Protocol) is an example of an SNICP.

Protocol, SNMP (Simple Network Management Protocol)

SNMP is a component of the IP (Internet Protocol) management model. It is the protocol used to represent network management information for transmission. Originally conceived as an interim protocol, to be replaced by the ISO's CMIS/CMIP model, SNMP has proven remarkably durable. In fact, a new and improved version, SNMP version 2, was proposed in 1992.

Two of the authors of SNMPv2, which is just about to be standardized, have asked for an extension from the IETF in order to get a formal evaluation of a stripped-down alternative to SNMPv2.

SNMP Operation

SNMP provides communications at the applications layer in the OSI Reference Model. It was developed for networks that use TCP/IP. This protocol is simple but powerful enough to accomplish its task. SNMP uses a management station and management agents, which communicate with this station. The station is located at the node that is running the network management program.

SNMP agents monitor the desired objects in their environment, package this information in the appropriate manner, and ship it to the management station, either immediately or upon request.

In addition to packets for processing requests and moving packets in and out of a node, the SNMP includes traps. A *trap* is a special packet that is sent from an agent to a station to indicate that something unusual has occurred.

SNMP Community

The SNMP community is the component of the IP network management model that uses management stations and agents. A management agent may be polled by one or more management stations. An SNMP community is a way of grouping selected stations with a particular agent in order to simplify the authentication process the agent must go through when polled. Each community is given a name that is unique for the agent.

The community name is associated with each station included, and it is stored by the agent. All members of an SNMP community share the same authentication code and access rights. They may also share the same SNMP MIB view, which is a selective subset of the information available in the agent's MIB (management information base). Stations in such a community can work only with the attributes included in the MIB view. An MIB view can be created for a single station or for all the stations in an SNMP community.

An agent may have multiple communities, stations may be in more than one community for a single agent, and a station may be part of communities associated with different agents.

By creating and using SNMP communities and MIB views, agents can simplify their work, thereby speeding up network response.

Protocol, SNTP (Simple Network Time Protocol)

SNTP is a variant of the draft standard NTP (Network Time Protocol), which is used to get the correct time from an official source and then disseminate this time information to a subnet of servers. The protocol also enables servers to synchronize their clocks with that of the primary reference server, which gets the time directly from a source.

Whereas NTP is accurate to between 1 and 50 milliseconds at any location on the Internet, SNTP is accurate only to within several hundred milliseconds. SNTP trades off accuracy for simplicity. The authors suggest that SNTP be used only at the outskirts of the Internet—that is, in locations where hosts are unlikely to be providing time information to other hosts. Any host that is disseminating timestamps should use the more accurate NTP.

PRIMARY SOURCES

SNTP is discussed in RFC 1769. The complete NTP is discussed in RFC 1305.

Protocol, SPP (Sequenced Packet Protocol)

A transport level protocol in the XNS protocol suite from Xerox.

Protocol, SSL (Secure Sockets Layer)

SSL is a session level protocol that can be used to encrypt transmissions on the World Wide Web (WWW). SSL and a competing protocol, SHTTP (Secure Hypertext Transfer Protocol), can be used for sensitive transactions or for communications that must be kept secure. SSL provides assurance of privacy by encrypting data; it also provides message and server authentication, and can demand client authentication.

SSL is protocol independent, so it can encapsulate any of the application level protocols—FTP, HTTP, etc.—that might need to use SSL. SSL requires reliable transport, such as that provided by TCP.

SSL was developed at Netscape, and is now under consideration by an IETF (Internet Engineering Task Force).

SSL actually uses two different protocols:

- The SSL Record Protocol, which encapsulates everything that comes through, including SSL Handshake Protocol packets

- The SSL Handshake Protocol, which is used to negotiate and establish security methods and parameters

SSL Record Protocol

The data stream is encapsulated in records, which consist of a header and data. The data may be encrypted or not, and the record may be padded or not.

The data section of an encrypted packet has three parts:

- MAC-DATA, which is a message authentication code that is used to ensure that no one has tampered with the message. This field is 16 bytes when using some of the common authentication algorithms.

- ACTUAL DATA, which is the message that's being sent, and for which all the encryption overhead and work are being carried out.

- PADDING-DATA, which is used to fill out packets—for example, to a boundary value required by the encryption key.

A non-encrypted message contains only the actual data. Both padding and message authentication code are left out.

SSL Handshake Protocol

The SSL handshake protocol is used to set up the security measures that will be used. To do this, the protocol goes through the following phases of negotiation and testing.

- Hello, which is used to determine the capabilities of the parties involved and to select the algorithms that will be used for encryption and authentication.

- Key Exchange, during which the parties exchange material so that both agree on a master key (which will usually be one party's public key).

- Session Key Production, during which the session key or keys are created. These are the keys that will be used to encrypt the current messages. For various reasons, using such a session key to encrypt the message is much faster than using either party's public key. The session key is then encrypted using the master key and included in the message.

- Server Verify, during which the server must prove its authenticity. If the server fails this test, the master key and the session key(s) generated from it are considered untrustworthy, and the session is terminated.

- Client Verify, which is used only if the key exchange algorithm doesn't have such authentication built in. If used, the server requests a certificate from the client.

- Finished, during which the session is terminated.

The most recent complete version of SSL is version 2, but the IETF working group is considering version 3. SSL is not yet a standard, so much of the model is still tentative and is subject to change.

PRIMARY SOURCES

A draft of the most recent version of the specifications is generally available through the Netscape home page:

http://home.netscape.com

Protocol Stack

In networking, a protocol stack is a collection of related protocols used in a particular network. Together, the protocols in a protocol stack cover enough or all of the layers in the communications model being used. Widely used protocol stacks include the following:

- AppleTalk stack, used in Macintosh-based networks

- IPX/SPX stack, used in Novell NetWare networks

- TCP/IP stack, used in UNIX environments, such as the Internet

Protocol stacks are sometimes, loosely, known as a protocol suite. Strictly speaking, however, a protocol stack is a particular implementation of a protocol suite.

Protocol, Stateless

A protocol in which each transaction is independent of its predecessor and its successor so that individual transactions may be repeated without affecting prior or future transactions.

Protocol Suite

In networking, a protocol suite is a collection of related protocols. Together, the protocols in such a suite cover enough or all of the layers in the communications model being used. Widely used protocol suites include the following:

- AppleTalk suite, used in Macintosh-based networks

- IPX suite, used in Novell NetWare networks

- TCP/IP suite, used in UNIX environments, such as the Internet

Protocol, TCP (Transmission Control Protocol)

In the Internet TCP/IP protocol suite, a connection- and stream-oriented transport layer protocol. TCP uses IP (Internet Protocol) at the network layer to deliver packets. TCP's byte stream performs the same kinds of services as Novell's SPX protocol and as the OSI TP4 protocol. In the TCP/IP suite, the UDP (User Datagram Protocol) provides connectionless transport layer service.

Protocol, Telnet

In the TCP/IP protocol suite, an application layer protocol that provides terminal-emulation capabilities. Telnet's services allow users to log in to a remote network from their computer.

Protocol, TFTP (Trivial File Transfer Protocol)

TFTP is a very simple file transfer protocol created for use on the Internet. This protocol is designed for use on top of the connectionless User Datagram Protocol (UDP). TFTP uses a lock-step approach to packet delivery—requiring an acknowledgement for each packet before sending the next one.

TFTP supports just a few types of packets:

- Read Request (RRQ): opcode = 1. Sent when the client wants to download a file.

- Write Request (WRQ): opcode = 2. Sent when the client wants to upload a file or when the packet begins "mail" mode.

- Data (DATA): opcode = 3. Contains up to 512 bytes of actual content. Data fields in data packets are regularly 512 bytes long, but the last packet in a transmission can be shorter.

- Acknowledgement (ACK): opcode = 4. Sent in response to each packet received correctly.

- Error (ERROR): opcode = 5. Sent if something did not work as expected—for example, if a packet was lost or there was an I/O error, etc. Error packets may be sent in reply—instead of an ACK packet—when things do not go as planned.

The only field that all five packet types have in common is their first one: *Opcode*, which is used to identify the type of packet. The figure "TFTP packets" shows that this 16-bit field begins all TFTP packets. Note that only ACK packets are a fixed size.

- *Filename* contains the name of the file to be written or read. This is a string variable in *netascii* format, and is terminated by a zero byte. Netascii is an 8-bit format that is based on a version specified in a USA Standard Code for Information Interchange document, together with modifications based on RFC 764 (Telnet protocol specification).

- *Mode* specifies the data format. This string can be any of three values: "netascii" or "octet" or "mail" in upper, lower, or mixed case. Netascii format uses the 8-bit ascii format mentioned in the previous item; mail is just like netascii except that a username is placed in the *filename* field and each mail transmission begins with a WRQ packet. Octet mode is used to transfer a file using the "native" 8-bit format of the source machine.

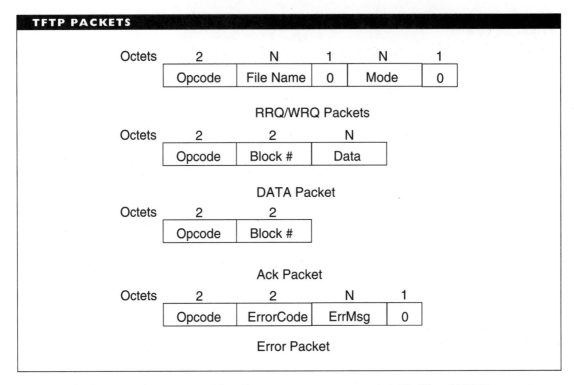

TFTP PACKETS

Octets	2	N	1	N	1
	Opcode	File Name	0	Mode	0

RRQ/WRQ Packets

Octets	2	2	N
	Opcode	Block #	Data

DATA Packet

Octets	2	2
	Opcode	Block #

Ack Packet

Octets	2	2	N	1
	Opcode	ErrorCode	ErrMsg	0

Error Packet

- *Block* # provides a way to identify the successive packets. Block numbers are assigned consecutively, beginning with 1.

- *Data* provides the storage for actual information or content being sent using TFTP. This field can be between 0 and 512 bytes long. Since TFTP uses 512-byte packets, a packet less than 512 bytes is considered the end of the file.

- The 16-bit *ErrorCode* field contains an integer that indicates the type of error. Example error codes include: File not found (1), Disk full or allocation exceeded (3), Illegal TFTP operation (4), and No such user (7).

- *ErrMsg* is a string associated with a particular error code.

TFTP can transfer files, and that's just about it. TFTP really can't do much else—for example, give you a directory listing. The protocol is likely to quit under the slightest of problems. It is, however, very easy to implement, is not resource intensive, and has built-in rate and error control (in the ACK required for each packet).

PRIMARY SOURCES

TFTP is described in RFC 1350.

Protocol, TLAP (TokenTalk Link Access Protocol)

In the AppleTalk protocol suite, the data-link layer protocol for TokenTalk, Apple's implementation of the Token Ring architecture.

Protocol, UDP (User Datagram Protocol)

In the Internet TCP/IP protocol suite, a transport layer protocol. UDP provides connectionless service and it uses IP (Internet Protocol) services at the network layer. As a connectionless protocol, UDP is in contrast to the Internet's TCP (Transport Control Protocol), which provides connection-oriented service. The counterpart to UDP in the OSI protocol collection is TP4 (Transport Protocol Class 4).

Protocol, VOTS (VAX OSI Transport Service)

In the OSI Reference Model, a transport level protocol used on Digital Equipment Corporation (DEC) machines. VOTS can be used in local-area or wide-area networks.

Protocol, VTP (Virtual Terminal Protocol)

In Novell networking environments, VTP is a presentation- and application-layer protocol that provides a model of a general terminal for applications to use.

Protocol, XNS (Xerox Network Services)

XNS is a group of protocols that cover the layers in the OSI Reference Model. The Xerox model uses only five layers, but there is a close relationship between the Xerox and OSI models.

XNS Levels

The XNS levels are as follows:

- Xerox level 0 corresponds to OSI levels 1 and 2 (physical and data-link).

- Xerox level 1 corresponds to OSI level 3 (network).

- Xerox level 2 corresponds to OSI level 4 (transport).

- Xerox level 3 corresponds to OSI levels 5 and 6 (session and presentation).

- Xerox level 4 corresponds to OSI level 7 (application).

XNS Protocols

XNS includes the following protocols, several of which have been adopted or adapted by other network vendors:

- IDP (Internet Datagram Protocol), which serves OSI level 3

- Echo, Error, SPP (Sequenced Packet Protocol), PEP (Packet Exchange Protocol), and RIP (Routing Information Protocol), which serve OSI level 4

a
b
c
d
e
f
g
h
i
j
k
l
m
n
o
p
q
r
s
t
u
v
w
x
y
z

- Courier, which serves OSI level 5
- Clearinghouse, which serves OSI level 6

Protocol, XTP (Xpress Transfer Protocol)

A lightweight protocol developed for use on high-speed networks as a replacement for traditional routing and transport protocols, such as TCP/IP. XTP's packet structure and transmission, error-correction, and control strategies streamline the protocol, saving transmission time and overhead.

SEE ALSO

Protocol, Lightweight

Protocol, ZIP (Zone Information Protocol)

In the AppleTalk protocol suite, a network layer protocol for maintaining a mapping of node names to zones (logical subnetworks). The protocol is used primarily by routers.

Proxy

A proxy, also known as a *proxy agent,* is an element that responds on behalf of another element to a request using a particular protocol. A proxy arrangement is used, for example, when an element does not support a particular protocol and it is not worth the trouble of implementing a protocol stack on that element so that it can support the protocol.

As an example, in the SNMP (Simple Network Management Protocol) component of the IP (Internet Protocol) management model, a management agent can respond on behalf of a network element that does not support SNMP or that is otherwise unable to communicate with the SNMP station. The proxy agent must support SNMP and must also be able to communicate with the represented element.

Proxy ARP

A proxy arrangement in which one device (usually a router) answers address resolution requests on behalf of another device. The proxy agent (the router) is responsible for making sure that packets get to their real destination.

PSN (Packet Switch Node)

In a packet-switching network, a dedicated machine that accepts and routes packets.

PSTN (Public Switched Telephone Network)

A public network that provides circuit switching for users.

PTM (Pulse Time Modulation)

A class of digital modulation methods in which a time-dependent feature of a pulse (for example, width, duration, or position) is varied to encode an analog signal that is being converted to digital form.

PTT (Post, Telephone, and Telegraph)

In most countries, a government agency that provides the named services.

PU (Physical Unit)

In SNA (Systems Network Architecture) networks, a term for a physical device and its resources on a network.

Public-Key Encryption

A data-encryption strategy in which the encryption details depend on two keys: one public and one private. Each person's public key is stored in a key library, from which it will be available to anyone with the appropriate security clearance.

SEE ALSO

Encryption

Pulse

Pulse refers to a brief and rapidly attained variation in the voltage or current level. Pulses are used, for example, to indicate a binary value. A pulse is characterized by the following:

- Amplitude of change.

- Rise and fall times, which represent the amount of time needed to change the level from 10 to 90 percent (rise) of maximum and from 90 percent back down to 10 percent (fall). In an ideal pulse, these values are both zero.

- Duration, or pulse width. The shorter the duration, the faster the transmission speed.

Pulse Carrier

A signal consisting of a series of rapid, constant pulses that is used as the basis for pulse modulation (for example, when converting an analog signal into digital form).

Punch-Down Block

A punch-down block is a device containing metal tabs that puncture the jacket, or casing, on a twisted-pair cable. After puncturing the jacket, these tabs make electrical contact with the wires in the cable. This contact establishes a connection between the block and other blocks or specific devices. The block is connected to other blocks by a cross-connect. By making the appropriate cross-connections, it is possible to link nodes as necessary.

There are punch-down blocks specifically designed for data transmission, as opposed to the telephone company's original 66 punch-down block, which was used for dealing with analog signals. The 66 block is not suitable for use in networks because it is not designed to be disconnected and reconnected over and over (which is likely to happen when configuring a network).

In networking contexts, patch panels are more commonly used as an alternative to punch-down blocks for making cross-connections.

a b c d e f g h i j k l m n o **p** q r s t u v w x y z

PVC (Permanent Virtual Circuit)

In packet-switching networks, a logical path (a virtual circuit) established between two locations. Since the path is fixed, a PVC is the equivalent of a dedicated line, but over a packet-switched network.

SEE ALSO

Virtual Circuit (VC)

PVC (Polyvinylchloride)

A material used in making cable jackets.

QIC (Quarter-Inch Cartridge)

QIC is a set of tape standards defined by the Quarter-Inch Cartridge Drive Standards Organization, a trade association established in 1987.

Two standards are in common use: QIC 40 and QIC 80. Both use the DC-2000 series of minicartridges. QIC 40 writes 10,000 bits per inch on 20 tracks. QIC 80 writes 14,700 bits per inch on 28 tracks. QIC 80 can read QIC 40 tapes, but the reverse is not true. QIC 40 and 80 format tapes are often used to back up small to medium hard-disk systems. Up to about 250 megabytes will fit on a single tape using data compression.

Other higher-density QIC formats allow for higher capacities. QIC 1350 handles up to 1.35 gigabytes (GB) of tape storage, and QIC-2100 is for up to 2.1 GB.

QoS (Quality of Service)

In ATM networks, a set of parameters for describing a transmission. These parameters include values such as allowable delay variation in cell transmission and allowable cell loss (in relation to total cells transmitted). The parameters apply to virtual channel connections (VCC) and virtual path connections (VPC), which specify paths between two entities.

Quad

A cable with four wires, consisting of two twisted pairs, each insulated separately.

Quadbit

A group of 4 bits that are transmitted, processed, or interpreted as a single unit. There are 16 possible quadbit values, as shown in the table "Quadbit Values."

QUADBIT VALUES				
QUADBIT VALUE	BIT 3	BIT 2	BIT 1	BIT 0
0	0	0	0	0
1	0	0	0	1
2	0	0	1	0
3	0	0	1	1
4	0	1	0	0
5	0	1	0	1
6	0	1	1	0
7	0	1	1	1
8	1	0	0	0
9	1	0	0	1
10	1	0	1	0
11	1	0	1	1
12	1	1	0	0
13	1	1	0	1
14	1	1	1	0
15	1	1	1	1

Quantizing

In digital-signal processing, quantizing is the process of converting a PAM (pulse amplitude modulation) signal into PCM (pulse code modulation) form. This converts a signal from a level to a bit sequence.

Quartet Signaling

Quartet signaling is a strategy used in the 100BaseVG Ethernet implementation developed by Hewlett-Packard (HP) and AT&T Microelectronics. The strategy uses four wire pairs simultaneously and relies on the fact that the wire pairs need not be used for sending and receiving at the same time.

The wire availability is guaranteed because demand priority, the media-access method used in 100BaseVG, enables hubs to handle network access for the nodes. Thus, quartet signaling provides four times as many channels as ordinary (10 megabit per second) Ethernet. It also uses a more efficient encoding scheme, 5B/6B encoding, as opposed to the Manchester encoding used by ordinary Ethernet.

The more efficient encoding, together with the four channels and a slightly higher signal frequency, make it possible to increase the bandwidth for an Ethernet network by a factor of 10 (from 10 Mbps to 100 Mbps).

Query Language

In a database management system, a programming language that allows a user to extract and display specific information from the database. For example, SQL is an international database query language that allows the user to create or modify data or the database structure.

SEE ALSO

SQL (Structured Query Language)

Queue

In data handling, a temporary holding structure in which values can be stored until needed. A queue is organized in such a way that the first item added to the queue is also the first item out of the queue. This processing is known as FIFO, for first-in, first-out. Job and print queues are perhaps the best known for those who work with computers.

a b c d e f g h i j k l m n o p q r s t u v w x y z

Radio Frequency Interference (RFI)

SEE

RFI (Radio Frequency Interference)

Radio Paging

A remote signaling method that uses radio waves to contact and activate a paging device, or beeper. This receiver beeps when contacted.

RAID (Redundant Array of Inexpensive Disks)

RAID refers to a system setup that uses multiple drives and writes data across all the disks in a predefined order. Typically, RAID uses four or five drives, but more are not uncommon. The disk array is seen as a single drive by the user. Internally, the multiple drives can be accessed in parallel. RAID is also known as *drive array*.

The rules for reading and writing depend on which of the six RAID levels the system supports. These levels are designated by numerical values from 0 through 5, with each value representing a different way of dealing with the data (not increasing power or speed), as follows:

Level 0: Data striping or disk spanning; block interleaving. In data striping, data is written block by block across each drive, with one block to each drive. An alternative to data striping is disk spanning, in which data blocks are written to the next available disk. If a disk is full or busy, it may be skipped in a particular turn. This RAID level provides no fault tolerance,

since the loss of a hard disk can mean a complete loss of data.

Level 1: Disk mirroring or duplexing. In disk mirroring, a single channel is used to write the same data to two different hard disks. If one drive is damaged, the data is still accessible from the other drive. On the other hand, if the channel fails, both drives are lost. In disk duplexing, data is written to two hard disks using two different channels, which protects the data, unless *both* channels or *both* drives fail.

Level 2: Data striping, bit interleaving. Each bit is written to a different drive, and checksum information is written to special checksum drives. This level is very slow, disk-intensive, and remarkably unreliable (since any of the multiple checksum disks can fail).

Level 3: Data striping, bit interleaving, parity checking. This is the same as level 2, except that a single parity bit is written to a parity drive instead of checksums to checksum drives. It is more reliable than level 2 because there is only one parity drive that can fail.

Level 4: Data striping, block interleaving, parity checking. This is like level 3, except that an entire block (sector) is written to each hard disk each time.

Level 5: Data striping, block interleaving, distributed parity. This is like level 4 except that the parity or checksum information is distributed across the regular disks, rather than being written to special disks. Level 5 allows over-lapping writes, and a disk is accessed only if necessary. This level is faster and also more reliable than the other levels.

In summary, level 0 provides no fault tolerance, since all data is lost if a disk fails. Level 1 provides some fault tolerance if disk duplexing is used. Levels 2 through 5 provide fault tolerance in that a single disk can fail without loss of data. Of these, levels 1 and 5 are most commonly used.

In addition to the cost of the disk drives, a RAID configuration requires a special hard drive controller.

It is arguable whether the amount of increased reliability provided by RAID technology is worth the cost (which is about the same as for an external duplex system). In tests, disk duplexing generally outperformed RAID levels 3 through 5.

COMPARE

SLED (Single Large Expensive Disk)

RAM (Random-Access Memory)

RAM is chip-based working memory, which is the memory used by programs and drivers to execute instructions and to hold data temporarily. RAM chips are distinguished by their access speed, which is on the order of about 70 nanoseconds, and by their capacity, which is currently between 1 and 4 megabytes (MB) per chip set.

Various types of RAM are distinguished in the literature:

- DRAM (dynamic RAM), which must be refreshed periodically in order to

retain its information. Refresh periods are every few milliseconds or so.

- SRAM (static RAM), which retains its contents as long as power is supplied.

- VRAM (video RAM), which is used to provide memory for graphics processing or temporary image storage.

For a discussion of the different classes of RAM (conventional, upper, extended, and expanded), see the Memory article.

RAS (Remote Access Services)

RAS is a Windows NT service that provides limited wide-area networking (WAN) capabilities. For example, RAS allows remote access to a Windows NT network and provides packet-routing capabilities.

Windows NT includes a single-user version of RAS, which allows one user to access the network at a time. Windows NT Advanced Server (NTAS) includes a mutiuser version, which allows up to 64 remote users. The RAS supports various types of WAN connections, including ISDN (Integrated Services Digital Network), modems, and X.25 links.

RAS can route packets using any of several popular protocol stacks, provided these stacks include support for Windows NT NetBIOS.

RBOC (Regional Bell Operating Company)

In telephony, RBOC is a term for any of the seven companies formed as a result of the divestiture of AT&T. The RBOCs are Ameritech, Bell Atlantic, Bell South, NYNEX,

a
b
c
d
e
f
g
h
i
j
k
l
m
n
o
p
q
r
s
t
u
v
w
x
y
z

Pacific Telesis, Southwestern Bell Corporation, and US West.

These RBOCs were created from the 23 BOCs (Bell Operating Companies) that existed before the divestiture. The table "RBOC Information" lists the RBOCs, their domains, and the BOCs from which they were created.

RC5 Encryption Algorithm

RC5 is a secret key encryption algorithm that uses a variable length key and that relies heavily on data-dependent rotations of bit values. The RC5 actually includes separate algorithms for expanding the secret key, doing encryption, and doing decryption.

RC5 can be implemented in many different ways, only some of which are likely to be secure. The algorithm's performance and level of security depend on three parameters:

W: Word size (in bits). This may be 16, 32, or 64.

R: Number of rotation rounds. This may be any whole number between 0 and 255.

B: Number of bytes in the key. This may be any whole number between 0 and 255.

RBOC INFORMATION

RBOC	STATES COVERED	MEMBER BOCs
Ameritech	IL, IN, MI, OH, WI	IL Bell, IN Bell, MI Bell, OH Bell, WI Bell
Bell Atlantic	CT, DE, MD, NJ, PA, WV, VA	Bell of PA, Chesapeake and Potomac of MD, Chesapeake and Potomac of VA, Chesapeake and Potomac of Washington, DC, Chesapeake and Potomac of WV, Diamond State Telephone, NJ Bell
Bell South	AL, FL, GA, KY, LA	South Central Bell
	MS, NC, SC, TN	Southern Bell
NYNEX	MA, ME, NH, NY, RI, VT	New England Telephone, New York Telephone, Southern New England Telephone
Pacific Telesis	CA, NV	NV Bell, Pacific Bell
Southwestern Bell	AR, KS, MO, OK, TX	Southwestern Bell
US West	AZ, CO, ID, MN	Mountain Bell
	MT, NB, NM, ND	Northwestern Bell
	SD, UT, WA, WY	Pacific NW Bell

Different implementations of the algorithm are distinguished by their values on these parameters: RC5-w/r/b. For example, RC5-32/1/1 uses a 32-bit word, but does only one rotation and has only a single byte as the key. This algorithm is *not* secure.

In contrast, RC5-32/16/7 has a 56-bit key and does 16 rotations. These values are comparable to the values for the DES (Data Encryption Standard) algorithm that is currently in use.

Since RC5 is a recently developed algorithm, its behavior for many parameter combinations is still unknown.

BROADER CATEGORIES
Encryption

SEE ALSO
DES (Data Encryption Standard)

RCONSOLE

A Novell NetWare 3.*x* and 4.*x* utility that allows a network supervisor to manage a server from a workstation. The supervisor can give commands and accomplish tasks, just as if the commands were being given directly at the server. In NetWare 4.*x*, RCONSOLE also includes asynchronous capabilities, allowing the supervisor to access the server via modem. In NetWare 3.*x*, the ACONSOLE utility provides asynchronous connections.

RDA (Remote Database Access)

An OSI specification to allow remote access to databases across a network.

Read-after-Write Verification

A Novell NetWare data-verification measure in which the information written to disk is compared with the information in memory. If the two match, the information in memory is released. If they do not match, NetWare's Hot Fix feature assumes the storage location is bad and redirects the information to a safe location in the Hot Fix redirection area.

Read-Only Memory (ROM)

SEE
ROM (Read-Only Memory)

Real Mode

The operating mode for memory allocation and usage for an 8086 processor. This mode can use up to 1 megabyte of memory, and only one process can execute at a time. This is in contrast to the protected mode available in 80286 and later processors. In protected mode, multiple processes can run at the same time, and each process has its own (protected) memory area.

Receive Only (RO)

SEE
RO (Receive Only)

Receiver

One of the three essential components of a communications system. The other two are a transmitter and a communications channel. The receiver's job is to capture or store the transmission, and then convert it to visual or acoustic form.

Reconfiguration Burst

In ARCnet networks, a special bit pattern that is transmitted repeatedly whenever a node wants to force the creation of a new token or when a new node joins a network. Essentially, a reconfiguration burst resets the network.

Rectifier

A device that converts AC (alternating current) into DC (direct current).

Red Book

This term refers to the volumes of telecommunications standards published in 1985 by the CCITT.

Redirection

Redirection is the diversion of data or other signals from a default or intended destination to a new one. In most networking contexts, redirection is transparent to the user. For example, a print request may be redirected from the printer port to a spooler, or a workstation's request for access to a (supposedly) local drive is redirected to the server's disk.

In other contexts, the redirection may be explicit. For example, redirection can be accomplished by using the DOS redirection operators > and >> or the pipe (|) operator.

Redirection Area

In Novell NetWare's Hot Fix feature, an area of the hard disk set aside for storing data that would otherwise be written to bad disk sectors.

Redirector

A redirector is a program that intercepts program or user requests and directs them to the appropriate environment. A networking redirector can direct requests to DOS or to the network interface card (for transmission to the network server).

Similarly, DOS may redirect requests or calls to a network operating system while processing local operating system requests itself. The DOS Requester in Novell NetWare 4.*x* receives redirected commands from DOS and sends them to the network for processing.

SEE ALSO
DOS Requester

Reduced Instruction Set Computing (RISC)

SEE
RISC (Reduced Instruction Set Computing)

Redundancy

A configuration or state with extra components or information. The redundant elements are included to make it possible to compensate for malfunctions or errors. Redundancy may be applied to hardware, software, or information.

Hardware: Duplicate hard disks, servers, or cables are examples of hardware redundancy. Disk mirroring and disk duplexing are two ways to use duplicate hard disks; RAID (redundant array of inexpensive disks) systems provide for up to five hard disks. These types of redundant configurations increase a system's fault tolerance.

Software: The generation of extra copies of critical code segments helps prevent programs from accidentally corrupting the code. For example, copies may be created when the code is needed by different processes.

Information: Redundancy (parity) checks on information being transmitted can detect simple errors. More sophisticated use of information redundancy (such as Hamming coding) can actually correct such transmission errors.

Redwood

Redwood is Banyan's planned networking environment for extended enterprise networks. Based in part on Banyan's existing networking tools (such as StreetTalk and Intelligent Messaging), the Redwood environment will have three major components:

- Click to Information, which provides directory and global naming services. In addition to an enhanced version of StreetTalk, this component will provide X.500 support to facilitate interactions with other networks.

- Business on Mail, which provides database and e-mail services for client/server environments.

- Self-Managing Networks, which relies on Banyan's Distributed Enterprise Management Architecture (or *deMarc*) to provide capabilities for automating some management tasks.

Refractive Index

A measure of the degree to which light will travel at a different speed in a given medium, such as water or a fiber-optic core constructed of a particular type of material. It is also known as *index of refraction*.

Registered Resource

In Novell's NetWare, a resource (such as a disk drive) that can communicate with and provide data for the NetWare Management Agent. When a resource registers, it makes itself, its domain, and its capabilities known to the NetWare Management Agent.

Register Insertion

Register insertion is a media-access method used in some older ring topologies. In register insertion, a node that wants to transmit simply inserts a register (a buffer) into the ring's data stream at an appropriate point in the stream. The inserted register contains the packet to be transmitted (including data, addressing, and error-handling components).

Depending on restrictions, the node may be able to insert its register only during a break in the data stream, or the node may be able to insert its packets before passing a received packet on to the next node. Inserting a register effectively lengthens the logical ring, which means nodes must wait slightly longer for their packets to reach a destination.

The advantage of an insertion strategy is that multiple nodes can be transmitting at the same time. This is in contrast to simple token passing, in which only the node with the token gets access to the network.

The disadvantage of this method is that the ring can become overloaded if many nodes want to transmit at the same time. There is no way to control this, since register insertion does not have any provisions for preventing a node from trying to access the ring.

Register insertion was used in several experimental networks in the 1970s and 1980s, but has been superseded by token passing as the access method of choice for ring networks.

BROADER CATEGORY
Media-Access Method

SEE ALSO
CSMA/CA; CSMA/CD; Polling; Token Passing

Relaying

The process of actually moving data along a path determined by a routing process. The data is relayed between a source and a destination. Relaying is one of the two major functions of the network layer in the OSI Reference Model (another is routing).

Relay Point

In a switching network or system, a point at which packets or messages are switched to other circuits or channels.

Reliable Transfer

In the OSI Reference Model, a transfer mode that guarantees that *either* of the following will happen when a message is transmitted: the message will be transmitted without error, or the sender will be informed if the message could not be transmitted without error.

Reliable Transfer Service Element (RTSE)

SEE
RTSE (Reliable Transfer Service Element)

Remote Access

The ability to access a network or switching system from a long distance, using telephone lines or other channels.

Remote Boot

A process by which a workstation boots using instructions in ROM (read-only memory) and from a server, rather than from a workstation disk. Code for doing this is generally stored in a ROM chip on the workstation.

Remote Computing

Remote computing refers generally to computing done from a distant location. There are two main ways to accomplish this:

Remote node: You dial in through an access server, and become another node on the network. All communications must travel over phone lines between your remote node and the network. This is fine for tasks such as e-mail that don't require large amounts of data to be transferred back and forth. Using a computer as a remote node is also effective when applications are loaded and executed on the remote client. For example, the remote client might have a word processor and other office applications installed. With such a configuration, the work could be done offline, and the remote connection could be used for transferring files. As the remote client, you can connect to anything from a stand-alone PC to a communications server (that is, you can communicate in this way with your computer at home or with the corporate network).

Remote control: You dial from a remote location into your own computer , for example on the network, and you essentially become the keyboard and screen for your computer. The work is done on the host machine (i.e., the one at home); you just see the output. This method is better for working with large databases because the work can

be done on the server, and only the results need to be shipped out to your screen. As the remote client, you control the host's keyboard from the remote site. For example, you would not need an executable version of your word processor to edit a file under this type of connection. Instead, you would use the word processor residing on the host—which can, again, be anything from your stand-alone home PC to a machine on the corporate network.

Remote computing is becoming increasingly popular, but is bringing its own share of logistical problems. For example, a working group—Mobile IP (Internet Protocol)—of the IETF (Internet Engineering Task Force) is trying to determine the best way to allow remote machines to log into the Internet. Among these issues is the question of how to assign Internet addresses.

Remote Connection

A long-distance connection between a workstation and a network; a connection that involves telephone lines and that may require modems. Remote connections often require special timing considerations, because many network transactions must happen within a very limited time period.

Remote Console

A networking utility that enables a network supervisor to manage a server from a workstation or from a remote location using a modem. The supervisor can give commands and accomplish tasks just as if all the commands were being given directly at the server.

SEE ALSO
ACONSOLE; RCONSOLE

Remote Job Entry (RJE)

SEE
RJE (Remote Job Entry)

Remote Network Monitoring (RMON)

SEE
RMON (Remote Network Monitoring)

Remote Operations Service Element (ROSE)

SEE
ROSE (Remote Operations Service Element)

Remote Password Generator (RPG)

SEE
RPG (Remote Password Generator)

Remote Procedure Call (RPC)

SEE
RPC (Remote Procedure Call)

Remote Terminal

A terminal that is located a moderate or great distance from a host or network. A remote terminal is generally connected by telephone lines.

Repeater

A repeater is a hardware device that functions at the physical layer of the OSI Reference Model and that is used to connect two segments of the same network. The figure "Repeaters connect network segments" shows an example of a network with repeaters. This is in contrast to bridges, routers, and gateways, which connect different networks.

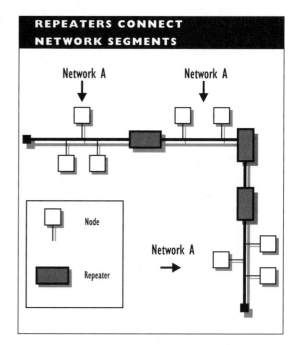

REPEATERS CONNECT NETWORK SEGMENTS

A repeater receives a signal from one segment, cleans and boosts the signal, and then sends it to the other segment. Functionally, a repeater includes both a receiver and a transmitter, with a signal-cleaning component in between. (Compare this to a transceiver, which has the receiver and transmitter as independent components, so that the transceiver can either receive or transmit.)

A repeater may be incorporated into another device, such as a hub or even a node. In that case, the repeater may not be a distinct component, but its function is the same as that of a stand-alone device.

Repeaters can sometimes be used to extend a network beyond the limitations placed on the network's architecture. It is important to note, however, that a repeater can increase segment length only to overcome electrical restrictions; the repeater cannot be used to increase the time limitations inherent in the network's layout. For example, a repeater cannot stretch the network so that a transmission could take more than the allowable slot time to reach all the nodes in an Ethernet network.

Repeaters and Network Architectures

In general, a particular repeater works with only a specific type of network architecture. This has to do with the fact that different architectures use different cabling (for example, coaxial versus twisted-pair) or use cabling with different electrical characteristics (for example, 50-ohm versus 93-ohm resistance).

Note that in an ARCnet network, there is no need for special repeater devices, because active ARCnet hubs serve as repeaters.

Ethernet/802.3

For Ethernet networks, several types of repeaters are used. Repeaters for networks using twisted-pair cabling (10BaseT networks) are generally found in a wiring closet. Repeaters for thick (10Base5) or thin

(10Base2) coaxial cable are likely to be found in the ceiling or wall where the cabling is run. IEEE specifications allow no more than four repeaters in a series between two nodes in an Ethernet network.

A repeater counts as a node on each Ethernet trunk segment it connects. The cable must be terminated independently of the repeater, which does not, in general, serve as a terminator.

In an Ethernet network, repeaters that connect to coaxial cable may be connected to a transceiver. IEEE 802.3 specifications specify that repeaters cannot be connected to transceivers that generate a SQE (signal quality error) test signal. This signal must be absent or disabled on the transceiver.

Multiport repeaters connect several segments. These repeaters generally have an autopartitioning capability, which allows them to disconnect any faulty segments automatically. This effectively quarantines the segment with the faulty node.

Token Ring

For Token Ring architectures, individual nodes serve as repeaters. In addition to "generic" repeaters, *main ring* and *lobe* types of repeaters are distinguished.

Main ring repeaters must be installed in pairs, on the main and the secondary ring, respectively. These repeaters are used when there is more than one MAU (multistation access unit) on the network. Electrical repeaters (such as the IBM 8218 repeater) can extend a ring path by as much as 750 meters (about 2500 feet); fiber-optic repeaters (such as the IBM 8219 and 8220 repeaters) can extend a fiber-optic ring path by as much as 2 kilometers (about 1.25 miles).

a b c d e f g h i j k l m n o p q r s t u v w x y z

A lobe repeater boosts the signal for only a single lobe (a Token Ring node) attached to the MAU. A lobe repeater also extends the distance the lobe can be from the MAU. Each lobe may have its own repeater, although lobe repeaters are not common.

Repeater-Repeater Connections

Repeaters may be connected to other repeaters using IRLs (Inter-repeater links), which are just stretches of cable connecting two repeaters, without any nodes attached. FOIRLs (fiber-optic inter-repeater links) are commonly used to connect network segments on different floors. One reason for this is that fiber-optic cable is impervious to interference from strong electrical or magnetic sources. This is important because cabling between floors is sometimes run through the elevator shaft, and elevator motors can cause considerable interference with electrical signals.

BROADER CATEGORY

Intranetwork Link

COMPARE

Transceiver

Replica

A copy of a partition from the NDS (NetWare Directory Services) for NetWare 4.*x*. Replicas can be distributed across a network to allow faster and easier access to the information in the partition. Having copies of a partition in several locations also provides data protection.

A replica may be read-only or read-write. In the former case, the server can access and use the partition information, but cannot change it in the replica. Such a replica cannot be used to update the partition information. In contrast, the contents of a read-write replica can be changed by the server. Such changes will eventually be incorporated into changes in the partition information.

BROADER CATEGORIES

NDS (NetWare Directory Services); Partition

Repudiation

In network transmissions, denial by a sending node that the message was sent (*origin repudiation*) or by the recipient that the message was received (*destination repudiation*). One security measure that may be used in a network is non-repudiation, which makes it impossible for a sender or receiver to make such denials.

Request For Comments (RFCs)

SEE

RFCs (Request For Comments)

Request/Response Header (RH)

SEE

RH (Request/Response Header)

Request/Response Unit (RU)

SEE

RU (Request/Response Unit)

Request To Send (RTS)

SEE

RTS (Request To Send)

Reservation Protocol

A protocol that allows a node to take exclusive control of a communications channel for a limited period. Such control is needed in certain types of communications, such as communications between a satellite and a receiving station.

Residual Error

In communications, an error that occurs or survives despite the system's error detection and correction mechanisms. For example, a transmission error that does not violate parity might get through if a communication system does not use checksums to test the transmission.

Resistance

In an electrical circuit, the opposition to the flow of electricity.

Resource Fork

The portion of a Macintosh file containing information about the resources (windows, applications, drivers, and so on) used by the file. This information is environment-specific, and is generally meaningless in non-Macintosh implementations (such as DOS).

SEE ALSO
Macintosh

Resources, Network

Resources are the manageable components of a network, including the following:

- Networking hardware, such as servers, workstations, cables, repeaters, hubs, concentrators, and network interface cards (NICs)

- Devices, such as hard disks, printers, modems, and optical drives

- Networking software, such as network operating systems, and networking services (communications, print queues, file services, and so on)

- Auxiliary software, such as drivers, protocols, bridging, routing, and gateway software, monitoring and management software, and applications

- Miscellaneous items, such as processes, security, data structures, users, and volumes

In most network operating systems, resources must be registered in order to be installed or become available through the network. For example, in Novell NetWare environments, a resource such as a gateway package can be registered and installed by loading a NetWare Loadable Module (NLM) containing the gateway's services and functions.

Response Mode

In communications, the mode of the device that receives a call and must respond to it.

COMPARE
Originate Mode

a b c d e f g h i j k l m n o p q **r** s t u v w x y z

Response Time

In networking contexts, response time is the time required for a request at a workstation to reach the server and for the server's response to return to the workstation. Response time is inversely proportional to transmission speed for the network architecture being used.

The minimum return time value is increased by several other factors, including the following:

- Delays introduced by the network interface cards (NICs) in the workstation and the server

- Delays in the server's response (for example, because the CPU is otherwise occupied when the request comes in or as the response is about to go out)

- Delays in accessing the server's hard disk and writing or reading any required data

Restore

To install data and software that has previously been backed up. The restoration process uses the backup media. You will need to restore files if the originals are corrupted. When doing a total restoration, you first need to restore the most recent complete backup, and then restore each of the incremental or differential backups that followed it.

SEE ALSO
Backup

Return Band

In communications using FDM (frequency division multiplexing), a one-directional (simplex) channel over which remote devices respond to a central controller.

Return (Reflection) Loss

In signaling, the amount of a signal that is lost because it is reflected back toward the sender. This value is expressed as a ratio and is measured in decibels (dB).

Return to Zero (RZ)

SEE
RZ (Return to Zero)

Return to Zero Inverted (RZI)

SEE
RZI (Return to Zero Inverted)

RFCs (Request For Comments)

In the Internet community, a series of documents that contain protocol and model descriptions, experimental results, and reviews. All Internet standard protocols are written up as RFCs.

RFI (Radio-Frequency Interference)

Noise in the radio frequency range that interferes with transmissions over copper wire. RFI comes from radio and television transmissions. A stretch of cable (for example, in a network) acts as an antenna for this type of interference.

RH (Request/Response Header)

In SNA (Systems Network Architecture) network communications, a 3-byte element added to a request/response unit (RU) at the transmission control layer to create a basic information unit (BIU).

RI (Ring Indicator)

In the RS-232C specifications, a signal that indicates an incoming call.

RI/RO (Ring In/Ring Out)

In Token Ring multistation access units (MAUs), RI is a port through which another MAU can be connected. The MAU also has a ring out (RO) port through which the MAU can be connected to another MAU. The figure "A small ring network" shows how MAUs can be connected.

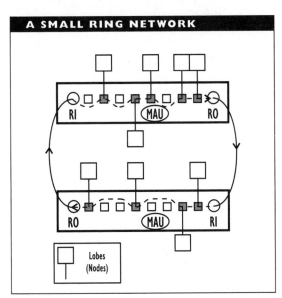

A SMALL RING NETWORK

SEE ALSO
Token Ring

Rights

In networking environments, rights are values, or settings, assigned to an object. These settings determine what the object (such as a user) can do with files, directories, and other resources.

SEE ALSO
Access Rights; NDS (NetWare Directory Services)

Ring

In cabling, one of a twisted-wire pair, with the other wire being known as a tip. A four-pair unshielded twisted-pair cable has four tip/ring pairs. In networking, ring is a logical (and physical) network topology.

SEE ALSO
Topology Ring

Ring In/Ring Out (RI/RO)

SEE
RI /RO (Ring In/ Ring Out)

Ring Indicator (RI)

SEE
RI (Ring Indicator)

RISC (Reduced Instruction Set Computing)

RISC is a computer-design strategy in which the machine logic is based on a small number of simple, general-purpose operations, each of which can be executed very quickly.

The RISC computer architecture was originally limited to high-end workstations, which were expensive but very fast. With technological and other progress, the architecture has become more widely used, and it now can be found even in ordinary computers for personal use. For example, several Macintosh models include a RISC processor.

SEE ALSO

CISC (Complex Instruction Set Computing)

Riser Cable

Cable that runs vertically; for example, between floors in a building. Riser cable often runs through shafts (such as for the elevator). In some cases, such areas can be a source of electrical interference. Consequently, optical fiber (which is impervious to electromagnetic interference) is generally used for riser cable.

Rise Time

The amount of time it takes an electrical signal to go from 10 percent of its level to 90 percent. This value is important, because it helps set an upper limit on the maximum transmission speed that can be supported.

COMPARE

Fall Time

RJE (Remote Job Entry)

RJE is a method in which data and commands are transmitted from a remote location to a centralized (mainframe) host computer that does the processing. Although this method was popular in the mainframe heyday of the 1970s and early 1980s, centralized processing is rapidly being replaced by distributed processing, in which computing power is distributed over a network or internetwork.

RJ-xx

RJ-xx is a modular connection mechanism originally developed by the telephone company. (RJ stands for registered jack.) The connection allows for up to eight wires (used as four pairs). In RJ-xx connections, the jack is the female component and the plug is the male component.

Various RJ configurations are available. These are distinguished by the following:

- Number of wire pairs used (generally two, three, or four)

- Which wire pairs are used (known as the wiring sequence)

- Keying or other modifications to the plug and jack, designed to make correct connections easier and incorrect connections less likely

For example, the telephone company commonly uses two-pair wire in an unkeyed connection. The first wire pair, which uses the two middle positions, carries the voice signal for the primary line.

Strictly speaking, the *RJ* designation applies only to cable that uses a particular wiring scheme (USOC, as described in the Wiring Sequence article). Other wiring sequences have different designations. However, RJ has become a generic designation to describe any type of modular connection.

The following are some commonly used RJ connections:

RJ-11: Four-wire (two-pair) connection. The telephone company version is used for ordinary single-line residential and business telephone lines. The two central wires (green and red) are tip and ring lines, respectively.

RJ-12: Six-wire (three-pair) connection. RJ-11 and RJ-12 connections use the same-sized plug and jack.

RJ-45: Eight-wire (four-pair) connection. The telephone company version is used for connections with multiple lines in the same location. If there is no competition for wires, such a connection can also be used for 10BaseT networks.

An RJ-45 connection uses a larger plug and jack than for RJ-11 or RJ-12. For unkeyed connections, you can connect an RJ-11 or RJ-12 plug to an RJ-45 jack, but you cannot fit an RJ-45 plug into an RJ-11/12 jack.

Although the "user-ends" of RJ-*xx* jacks all look alike, there are two ways of attaching this type of connector to the cable itself. One type of connector has prongs that wrap around the wire when the connector is crimped onto the cable. This type is used with solid, or single-strand, wire. The other type has prongs that pierce the wire when the connector is attached, and it is used for multistrand wire.

RLL (Run-Length Limited)

An encoding scheme for storing data on a disk. RLL uses codes based on the runs of 0 and 1 values, rather than on the individual bit values. This allows data to be stored more efficiently, which increases the effective capacity of the disk. RLL is in contrast to older encoding schemes, such as FM (frequency modulation) and MFM (modified frequency modulation).

rlogin

A remote login service provided as part of the Berkeley UNIX environment. This is an application-layer service, and it is comparable to the Internet's Telnet service.

RMON (Remote Network Monitoring)

RMON is a proposed standard for monitoring and reporting network activity using remote monitors. RMON is designed to supplement the management information obtained and used by the SNMP (Simple Network Management Protocol). In particular, RMON provides functions for getting information about the operation and performance of entire networks or of subnetworks in an internetwork.

Remote monitors are expected to do their work in a way that is minimally disruptive to network activity and that makes minimal demands on the available resources. Much of the information that remote monitors provide is summary information, some of

a b c d e f g h i j k l m n o p q **r** s t u v w x y z

which can be obtained passively (by counting packets, error signals, and so on).

As a supplement to the SNMP management functions and to the data in the MIB-II (management information base, version 2), RMON is included in the global tree under MIB-II. In the notation used to describe elements in the tree, RMON is mib-2 16.

RMON provides MIB elements of its own. The table "Subtrees of the RMON Entry in the Global Tree" lists these MIB elements.

PRIMARY SOURCE
RFC 1271

▼ ─────
RMS (Root Mean Square)

The value of an AC voltage as it is actually measured (for example, by a voltmeter). Empirically, this value is 0.70707... times the peak voltage in the circuit.

▼ ─────
RO (Receive Only)

In communications, a setting to indicate that a device can receive a transmission but cannot transmit it. Printers are probably the most widely used receive-only device.

SUBTREES OF THE RMON ENTRY IN THE GLOBAL TREE	
SUBTREE	**DESCRIPTION**
Statistics	Performance and summary statistics about an entire subnetwork or network, not just a single node.
History	Sample statistics gathered at separate time intervals.
Alarms	Allows the management supervisor to specify when and how alarms are to be used. For example, a monitor may simply gather error information passively, but alert the network manager if the error level reaches a predefined threshold.
Hosts	Statistics about activity between a host and the network or subnetwork.
Host Top N	Summary statistics about the N hosts who are highest in each of several variables.
Traffic Matrix	Provides summary traffic and error information in the form of a matrix, which makes it much easier to find information about particular combinations.
Filters	Used to specify packets or packet types for the monitor to capture. For example, a filter might be specified to look only for packets going to a particular node or host.
Packet Capture	Specifies how the command console can get data from and about network activity.
Events	Contains a list of all the events, or activities, created by the monitor.

Roamer

In telephony, a cellular telephone user who uses services in multiple cells (calling areas). For example, the user and telephone may move between coverage regions. Such roaming behavior can be costly.

ROM (Read-Only Memory)

ROM is chip-based memory whose contents can be executed and read, but cannot be changed. Programs are put into ROM in order to save storage and working memory. Many notebook and special-purpose computers have operating systems and special applications in ROM. Diskless workstations have a ROM chip that enables the workstation to boot from a network server.

The following types of ROM are distinguished in the literature:

- EEPROM (electronically erasable, programmable ROM), which allows old data to be erased simply by writing over it

- EPROM (erasable, programmable ROM), which allows old data to be erased by shining UV (ultraviolet) light on the chip in order to "deprogram" it

- PROM (programmable ROM), which can be programmed once, even by the user, but cannot be changed once programmed

- MROM (mask ROM), which is programmed during the manufacturing process and cannot be modified or reprogrammed

Root Directory

In a hierarchical file system, the highest directory. All other directories are subdirectories of the root.

Root Mean Square (RMS)

SEE

RMS (Root Mean Square)

Root Object

In the NDS global tree, the highest-level object. All country and organization objects are contained in the root object. Granting a user access rights to the root object effectively grants the user rights to the entire Directory tree.

SEE ALSO

NDS (NetWare Directory Services)

ROSE (Remote Operations Service Element)

In the OSI Reference Model, ROSE is a general-purpose ASE (application layer service element) that supports interactive cooperation between two applications. For example, ROSE is used for remote procedure calls or for tasks that require cooperation between a client and a server.

The application requesting the association is known as the *initiator*; that responding to it is the *responder*. The application requesting an operation is known as the *invoker*; that carrying out the operation is the *performer*. An application association provides the context for the cooperation between the two application entities (AEs).

a b c d e f g h i j k l m n o p q **r** s t u v w x y z

When an application association is established, the AEs involved must agree on an operation class and an association class for the interaction. The following five operation classes are defined, based on the type of reply the performer provided and on whether the interaction is synchronous or asynchronous:

- Class 1 (synchronous) reports both success and failure.

- Class 2 (asynchronous) reports both success and failure.

- Class 3 (asynchronous) reports only in case of failure.

- Class 4 (asynchronous) reports only in case of success.

- Class 5 (asynchronous) reports neither success nor failure.

The three association classes are as follows:

Association class 1: Only the initiator can invoke operations.

Association class 2: Only the responder can invoke operations.

Association class 3: Either the initiator or the responder can invoke operations.

The ROSE provides a mechanism for enabling applications to cooperate; however, ROSE does not know how to carry out the actual operations. The details of the operations must be agreed upon by the applications independently of ROSE. Similarly, the processes necessary to carry out the operation must be available once the association is established.

PRIMARY SOURCES
CCITT recommendations X.219 and X.229; ISO document 9072

BROADER CATEGORY
ASE (Application Service Element)

▼ Route Discovery

In network architectures that use source routing, such as Token Ring networks, the process of determining possible routes from a source to a destination node.

▼ Router

The function of a router is to provide a path from a node on one network to a node on another network. The two networks may be separated by several intervening networks and, possibly, by many miles. The figure "Routers connect nodes on different networks" shows an example of networks with routers. The router provides the path by first determining a route and then providing the initial connection for the path.

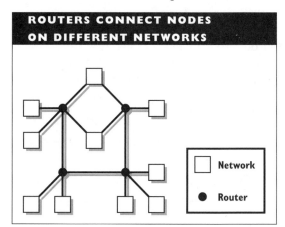

ROUTERS CONNECT NODES ON DIFFERENT NETWORKS

□ Network
● Router

In practice, the routing is provided by a hardware device that operates at the network layer. The router may be internal or a stand-alone unit that has its own power supply. An internal router is implemented on a card that plugs into an expansion slot in a computer. This router uses the computer's power supply (which should be adequate, but is not guaranteed to be so).

The router can find a path for a packet from the router to the packet's destination, and it can forward this packet onto that path. Because it operates at the network layer, a router is dependent on the protocol being used, because this protocol will determine the address format in the packets. Thus, an IP (Internet Protocol) router will not be able to handle packets with addresses in ISO format. A router can work with different data-link layer protocols, but older ones can handle only a single network protocol. Newer, multiprotocol routers can handle several protocols at the same time.

As a result, a router can be used as a packet filter based on network protocols (as well as addresses). Because it is independent of data-link layer protocols, a router can connect networks using different architectures (for example, Ethernet to Token Ring or Ethernet to FDDI).

Router Operation

A router gets a packet from a node or from another router and passes this packet on to a destination specified in an embedded (network layer) packet, which is known as an NPDU (network-layer protocol data unit). To determine the packet's ultimate destination, the router must strip off the data-link frame and determine the destination network address by looking at the NPDU.

The router must then determine the path to this destination, pack the NPDU into a data-link layer packet, and send the packet to the next router or directly to the destination node (if possible and appropriate). This destination is specified in the data-link layer envelope. The envelope may be for a different architecture than the one that sent the packet to the router. In that case, the router must use a data-link layer envelope that differs from the one that delivered the packet.

If the next destination for the packet happens to use a smaller packet size than the router received, the router must break the packet into suitably sized "subpackets" and ship the multiple smaller packets to the next destination. At the receiving end, the smaller packets may need to be reconstituted into the larger packet.

Interpreting Network Addresses

A network address differs from the physical address used by a bridge in that the network address is a logical address that locates a node as part of a (sub)network and also as an individual node within that network.

That network may, in turn, be part of a larger collection of networks. In fact, if the span of the entire conglomeration is large enough, there may be a whole hierarchy of networks, each organized at different levels. For example, the Internet consists of a backbone network whose nodes feed (route to) intermediate-level networks. These may, in turn, feed still more local networks, and so on, down to the destination node.

a
b
c
d
e
f
g
h
i
j
k
l
m
n
o
p
q
r
s
t
u
v
w
x
y
z

A network address may be interpreted as a hierarchical description of a node's location. For example, a node may be the twelfth one in a network on the tenth floor of a building. The building may have 15 floors, each with its own network. The building may be one of 30 in a single city, each with the same network hierarchy. The city's 30-building network may be only one of a dozen cities, each with similar network structures. The entire conglomerate network can be viewed as consisting of 12 city subnetworks, each of which consists of a number of building subnetworks, made up of floor subnetworks, which consist of nodes.

Levels of Routing

Several levels of routers can be defined. For example, a particular city might have building-level routers. Each router knows how to find a path from a node in its building to a node in another building. Basically, the router has the task of getting a packet to the router for the destination building.

When a building-level router receives a packet, the router checks whether it is intended for that building. If so, the router, passes it through to the floor for which the packet is intended. If not, the router determines a path to the destination building. (Note that building-level routers are not concerned with the city portion of an address.)

The conglomerate network might include city-level routers, whose job is to get packets to the destination cities. City-level routers are not concerned with the details of routing a packet to particular buildings in a city.

In this example, level 1 (building-level) routers communicate with other level 1 routers in their own (city) subnetwork. Similarly, level 2 (city-level) routers communicate with each other. In addition, each level 2 router communicates with the level 1 routers in its subnetwork, and each level 1 router communicates with the level 2 router for that city. The figure "Multilevel routers" shows an arrangement with different levels of routers.

Organizing a network universe into levels simplifies the routing task. Routers need to find paths only for the levels they must deal with. The use of levels in this way also increases the number of nodes that can ultimately be part of a conglomerate network. In practice, the levels generally are determined by location (rather than numerical) constraints.

Finding a Path

The router determines how to get to the specified network by communicating with other routers on the network. Because describing a node's location in a very large network can be complicated, locations are generally specified in terms of subnetworks.

Routes are computed using either of two classes of algorithms: distance-vector or link-state.

When using distance-vector algorithms (also known as *Bellman-Ford* or *old ARPAnet routing* algorithms), each router computes the distance between itself and each possible destination. This is accomplished by computing the distance between a router and all its immediate router neighbors, and by taking each neighboring router's computations for the distances between that neighbor and all *its* immediate neighbors. This information must be checked constantly and updated any time there are changes anywhere in the router network. This computational intensity is one drawback of distance-vector algorithms.

MULTILEVEL ROUTERS

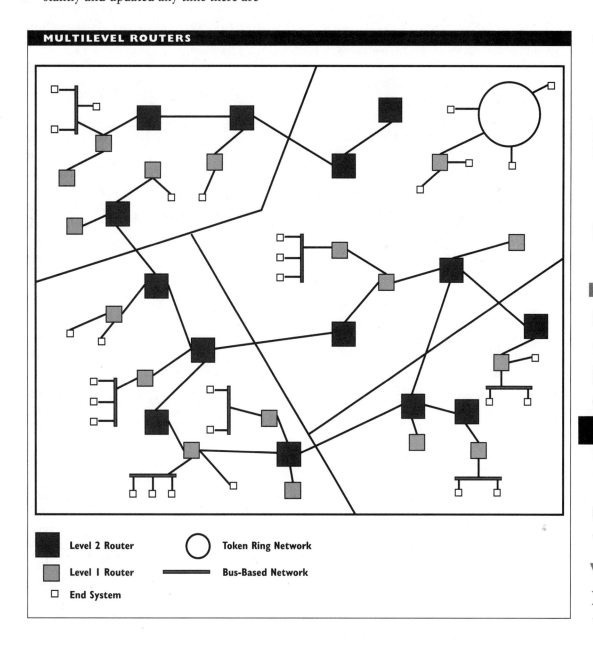

■ Level 2 Router

■ Level 1 Router

□ End System

◯ Token Ring Network

—— Bus-Based Network

a b c d e f g h i j k l m n o p q **r** s t u v w x y z

When using link-state algorithms, each router knows the location of and distance to each of its immediately neighboring routers, and can broadcast this information to all other routers in a link state packet (LSP). Every router transmits its LSP to every other router on the larger network, and each router keeps this information about every other router. If a router updates its LSP, the new version is broadcast and replaces the older versions at each other router.

Selection of an algorithm for a particular application depends on various factors. In general, routing algorithms can be compared in the following terms:

Convergence: How quickly the algorithm yields a route.

Robustness: How drastically the algorithm is affected by incorrect or missing information.

Memory requirements: How much memory will be needed to store all the distance-vector or link-state information.

Load splitting: How easily the algorithm can be extended to include load splitting, in which traffic between the same two routers may be sent across different paths in order to split the traffic more evenly (which can, in turn, increase throughput).

Router Groupings

Several categories of routers are distinguished: single-protocol or multiprotocol, central or peripheral, and local-area network (LAN) or wide-area network (WAN).

Single-Protocol versus Multiprotocol Routers

Because they operate at the network layer, routers are sensitive to the protocol being used. Thus, a router that can handle IP packets cannot handle IPX packets without the addition of special capabilities. Single-protocol routers were the rule for many years.

In the natural course of technological evolution, routers expanded their capabilities with respect to the network level protocols supported. High-end routers can process packets from more than one type of protocol. For example, a router might be able to handle IP, X.25, and IPX protocols. Multiprotocol routers are becoming much more widely used.

The cost of the increased capability is possibly decreased bandwidth in traffic for a particular protocol. That is, if a router needs to process both IP and IPX packets, it will need to split its available time and capacity between the two protocols.

Central Routers versus Peripheral Routers

A router may serve as the transfer point for multiple networks. For example, each network may be connected to a different board in a server or hub. These central routers are at the high end of the price and capability range, and they are usually multiprotocol routers.

In contrast, a peripheral, or branch office, router serves primarily to connect a network to a larger internetwork. These routers are more likely to be at the low end for price and performance. A peripheral router may be limited to a single protocol, particularly if the peripheral router can communicate with a multiprotocol router on the internetwork.

LAN versus WAN Routers

Another common course of technological evolution is to extend the reach of a device over greater distances. In this context, WAN routers, whose job is to find paths over widely distributed networks, are extensions of LAN routers, which connect LANs that are distributed over areas small enough to allow connections without requiring telephone lines. LAN and WAN routers do the same things, but the details of how these tasks are done vary considerably. Most notably, a WAN router needs to support protocols suitable for long-distance access and service (for example, protocols that support X.25). Partly, the development of WAN routers has been waiting for telecommunications lines with a sufficiently large bandwidth to make such routing feasible.

Router Protocols

Like all network components, great and small, routers use protocols to accomplish their work. Router protocols may be concerned with providing a service, greeting neighbors, or routing.

Service protocols provide the packet format used to transmit information across the network layer. IP is the network-layer service for the TCP/IP protocol suite developed for the ARPAnet and still used on the Internet and in many other distributed networks. Other network-layer service protocols include Novell's IPX from the IPX/SPX suite, IDP (Internet Datagram Protocol) from the XNS suite, and the X.25 protocol.

WHAT TO LOOK FOR IN A ROUTER

As with other hardware products, a main source of information about a particular router is the vendor. Useful information about routers includes the following:

- Type of router, such as whether it is a single-protocol or multiprotocol router, a LAN or WAN router, a bridging router (brouter), and so on

- Types of networks connected

- Protocol(s) supported

- Transmission speeds (which may range from 1,200 bits per second to several megabits per second)

- Number of ports

- Interfaces supported (for LANs or WANs)

- Network monitoring and management capabilities

Neighbor-greeting protocols enable nodes and routers to find each other, so that the range of connections can be determined. This information lets nodes know which other nodes and routers are accessible. Neighbor-greeting protocols also provide address-translation capabilities.

ES-IS (End System to Intermediate System) is a neighbor-greeting protocol defined by ISO document 9542. ICMP (Internet Control Message Protocol) and ARP (Address Resolution Protocol) are network-layer routing protocols that also include neighbor-greeting capabilities.

With routing protocols, routers determine paths for packets by communicating with neighboring routers at their level. Routers can request and obtain information about paths from the neighbor to still other routers. IS-IS (Intermediate System to Intermediate System) is a routing protocol specified by the ISO (DP 10589). RIP (Routing Information Protocol) and OPSF (Open Shortest Path First) are routing protocols in the TCP/IP suite.

Common Protocol Areas

As networks grow larger, it becomes increasingly likely that not all parts of the network will use the same protocols. This is particularly true if the network has multiple levels or is spread out, with smaller clusters.

These heterogeneous networks will, however, have areas that use a common protocol. Such areas are known as *routing domains* in OSI terminology, or *autonomous systems* (AS) in TCP/IP specification terminology. See the table "Terminology for Routing Concepts" for a summary of the terms related to routing protocols in the IP and OSI environments.

Intradomain Routing Protocols Protocols for use within a domain are known as *intra*-domain routing protocols. RIP, OSPF, and other widely used protocols operate within a domain. In addition, there are protocols for routing multiple protocols at the same time. Examples are "ships in the night" (SIN) and integrated routing.

Interdomain Routing Protocols A domain may be next to domains that use a different protocol. In this case, it may be necessary to route packets between domains, using inter-domain protocols. The following interd omain routing protocols (IDRPs) serve this purpose.

- EGP (Exterior Gateway Protocol), which is the IP name for a specific protocol that connects different domains. The protocol has flaws, but has been around in the TCP/IP world for a long time.

- BGP (Border Gateway Protocol), which is a revision and improvement of EGP. In addition to being a TCP/IP

TERMINOLOGY FOR ROUTING CONCEPTS		
ISO	**CONCEPT**	**IP**
Intermediate system (IS)	Router	Gateway
End system (ES)	Node	Host
Routing domain	Common protocol area	Autonomous system (AS)
Intradomain routing protocol	Protocol used within a domain	Interior Gateway Protocol (IGP)
Interdomain routing protocol	Protocol used between common protocol areas	Exterior Gateway Protocol (EGP)

protocol, BGP is also the basis for the ISO's IDRP protocol.

- IDRP, which is also the name of a specific interdomain routing protocol. It is based on the BGP protocol.

To do their work, routers can use connectionless or connection-oriented network layer protocols. A connection-oriented protocol first establishes a route and the connection (a virtual circuit, or VC), and then starts transmitting packets along this route. Packets are transmitted in order, and delivery can be guaranteed, since a protocol may require acknowledgment. With connection-oriented protocols, transport-layer services may not be required. The routing algorithm for such protocols is generally proprietary.

The X.25 protocol is a connection-oriented protocol. It specifies the interface between a node (known as a DTE in X.25 terminology) and a router (known as a DCE).

A connectionless protocol, which is also known as a datagram protocol, agrees to make its best effort to transmit a packet to its destination, but does not guarantee to do so. Moreover, packets may get to the same destination by different routes, and they may arrive in a jumbled order. Packets are assembled in the correct order by a transport layer protocol. The routing algorithms for connectionless protocols are generally open (publicly available). IP and CLNP (Connectionless Network Protocol) are two connectionless protocols.

BROADER CATEGORY
Internetwork Link

COMPARE
Bridge; Gateway

SEE ALSO
NetWare Multiprotocol Router; Protocol, Routing

Router, Exterior

In an AppleTalk environment, a router that routes packets to a non-AppleTalk protocol (from which the packets may be transmitted by tunneling). In contrast, an interior router routes packets between AppleTalk networks.

Router, Interior

In an AppleTalk environment, a router that routes packets between AppleTalk networks. In contrast, an exterior router routes packets to a non-AppleTalk protocol.

Routing

Routing is the process of determining an end-to-end path between the sender and the receiver for a packet. This is one of the major functions of the network layer in the OSI Reference Model. (Another function is relaying, which is actually passing packets along the path.)

Types of Routing

The routing task can be performed by the source node (generally an end system) or by the intermediate nodes (generally a router) in the path. These two approaches give rise to two general types of routing: source routing and hop-by-hop routing.

a b c d e f g h i j k l m n o p q **r** s t u v w x y z

Source Routing

In source routing, the source node determines the route and includes it in special fields in the packet being sent. This is also known as *end-to-end routing,* since the entire route to the destination is determined before the packet is sent.

For source routing, the source first needs to determine the route. This is accomplished by sending a discovery, or explorer, packet along each possible path. Once a suitable route has been determined, the intermediate destinations are added to the packet in 2-byte fields. Of these 16 bits, 12 are used to designate the (intermediate) destination network and 4 are used to designate the bridge (that is, the link) to the network. The bridge information is included for two reasons:

- If two networks are linked by more than one bridge, the packet might be sent over all possible links. This would lead to unnecessary network traffic and could eventually lead to network overload as copies of enough packets circulate.

- If a designated link is backed up or moving too slowly, an alternate link to the same destination network can be specified simply by changing the bridge value.

With a source-routing packet, the intermediate routers do not need to do any work. They just need to pass the packet to be specified intermediate routers. However, the success of a source-routing approach depends on the efficiency of the route, and it also requires each intermediate link to be open.

For example, if a link is broken between the time the discovery packet and the actual source-routed packet are sent, the packet will be lost.

Source routing is used in Token Ring networks, and source-routing ability must be built into bridges for such networks, according to the IEEE 802.5 specifications.

Hop-by-Hop Routing

In hop-by-hop routing, the route between source and destination is determined along the way. Each node on the route makes a decision as to where the packet will be sent next. The packet being sent does not contain any special routing information, just the source and destination address. This is also known as *node-to-node routing, border routing,* and sometimes as *intermediate-node routing.* The different names come from different networking environments.

In hop-by-hop routing, each intermediate node needs to know how to reach the next node on a path. The efficiency of the routing depends on the quality of the information available to the intermediate nodes, but this approach is only minimally affected by unforeseen problems such as broken links. Since a router expects to be selecting a route anyway, having a broken link has little effect as long as there are other possible links.

A hop-by-hop approach can also adjust easily to traffic conditions along specific links and can select any available faster link. Internet routing generally uses a hop-by-hop approach.

Computing Routing Information

Two general strategies are available for computing the information used to determine or select routes: distance-vector and link-state.

A distance-vector strategy gets information about the costs of reaching all possible destinations from a router and sends this information to each of the router's neighbors. In contrast, a link-state strategy gets only information about the costs of reaching each of a router's immediate neighbor routers. Commonly used algorithms are available for both of these strategies.

Routing Compared to Other Linkages

Besides routers, bridges and gateways also provide hardware links between networks. Bridges connect similar or identical networks. Gateways connect dissimilar networks.

Bridging functions really just need to know whether the destination is on the local or a remote network. If it is on the local network, the packet is dropped at the bridge; if it is on a different network, the bridge passes the packet over to its other network. The bridging functions do not need to know actual path information.

Gateway functions are more concerned with making sure the packets are in the appropriate formats than with determining the destination. A gateway generally links just a small number of networks or environments. In contrast to packet format, paths are generally simple and fixed, so that routing is not a major issue.

SEE ALSO

Algorithm; Protocol, Distance-Vector; Protocol, Link-State; Protocol, Routing; Router

Routing Buffer

RAM set aside on a Novell NetWare file server for temporarily holding packets until they can be processed by the server or sent onto the network. This is also known as a *communication buffer.*

Routing Domain

In the OSI Reference Model, routing domain is a term for a collection of routers that are part of a larger network but that are under the control of a single organization. The routers *within* a routing domain communicate with each other using a common *intra*domain routing protocol, such as the Integrated IS-IS (Intermediate System to Intermediate System) protocol.

Communication *between* routing domains uses an *inter*domain routing protocol, such as the proposed IDRP (Interdomain Routing Protocol).

In Internet terminology, a routing domain is known as an *autonomous system* (AS). An intradomain routing protocol is known as an *interior gateway protocol* (IGP), and an interdomain routing protocol is known as an *exterior gateway protocol* (EGP).

Routing Table

A table maintained for part of an internetwork. The table contains paths and distances between routers on the internetwork. Distances are generally measured in hops,

a
b
c
d
e
f
g
h
i
j
k
l
m
n
o
p
q
r
s
t
u
v
w
x
y
z

and they may change. As a result, routing tables may be updated frequently.

RPC (Remote Procedure Call)

A mechanism by which a procedure on one computer can be used in a transparent manner by a program running on another machine. This mechanism provides an easy way to implement a client-server relationship. Although the general strategy is similar in different implementations, there are many variants on the RPC model.

RPG (Remote Password Generator)

A device that can be used to generate a unique password every time a user wants to log in to a network. The device uses a special number, which is generated by the network, and the user's personal identification number (PIN) to generate the password.

RSA (Rivesi, Shamir, Adleman) Algorithm

A patented public-key encryption algorithm (named for its inventors). This algorithm could not be cracked for many years, but not for as long as expected. Using the processing capabilities of hundreds of computers and the intelligence of hundreds of colleagues, researchers have determined the keys (prime factors of a very large number) used in this encryption scheme.

SEE ALSO
Encryption

RTS (Request To Send)

A hardware signal sent from a potential transmitter to a destination to indicate that the transmitter wishes to begin a transmission. If the receiver is ready, it sends a clear to send (CTS) signal in return. The RTS/CTS combination is used in the CSMA/CA media-access method used in Apple's Local-Talk network architecture.

RTSE (Reliable Transfer Service Element)

In the OSI Reference Model, an ASE (application layer service element) that helps ensure that PDUs (protocol data units), or packets, are transferred reliably between applications. RTSE services can sometimes survive an equipment failure, because they use transport layer services. In the United States, other sources are usually used instead of RTSE to provide these services.

RU (Request/Response Unit)

In SNA (Systems Network Architecture) network communications, the type of packet exchanged by network addressable units (NAUs), which are network elements with associated ports (or addresses).

Run-Length Limited (RLL)

SEE
RLL (Run-Length Limited)

RZ (Return to Zero)

A signal-encoding method in which the voltage returns to a zero, or neutral, state halfway through each bit interval. This method is self-clocking.

SEE ALSO

Encoding, Signal

RZI (Return to Zero Inverted)

The inverted counterpart of the RZ signal-encoding method. RZI exchanges 1 and 0 in the descriptions. For example, a differential RZI has a signal transition for 0, and no transition for a 1; similarly, a nondifferential RZI uses +5 volts for 0 and −5 volts for 1.

SEE ALSO

Encoding, Signal

a
b
c
d
e
f
g
h
i
j
k
l
m
n
o
p
q
r
s
t
u
v
w
x
y
z

SA (Source Address)

A header field in many types of packets. This value represents the address of the node sending the packet. Depending on the type of address, this field may be 4 or 6 bytes or even longer.

COMPARE

DA (Destination Address)

SAA (Systems Application Architecture)

SAA is an effort on the part of IBM to standardize the conventions, interfaces, and protocols used by applications in all IBM operating environments. The intent was to provide a unified, logical architecture for applications running on machines ranging from a PS/2 up to a System/370.

SAA has four main components:

CUA (Common User Access): This component defines standard interfaces for applications that are window- or character-based. The user will interact with this interface. CUA includes specifications for screen and keyboard layout, and for selection methods using either a keyboard or mouse.

CPI (Common Program Interface): This element defines APIs (Application Program Interfaces) that are consistent across all systems. These are used by developers in their applications. The CPI standards relating to languages and databases follow ANSI specifications.

CCS (Common Communications Support): CCS defines a collection of communications protocols that machines can use to communicate with each other. The most commonly used protocols are LU 6.2 and HLLAPI.

Common Applications: This is concerned with developing common frameworks for the same kinds of applications running in different environments. This component is largely product-oriented, and is more for marketing and appearance than a substantive part of SAA. In fact, some armchair architects do not regard it as part of SAA.

The figure "SAA components" shows how these components fit together with an operating system in a particular environment.

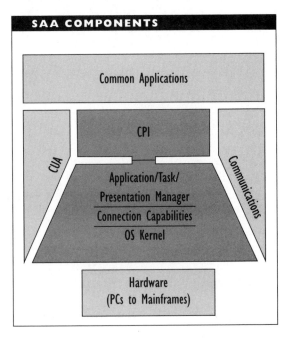

SAA COMPONENTS

Common Applications

CPI

CUA

Communications

Application/Task/
Presentation Manager
Connection Capabilities
OS Kernel

Hardware
(PCs to Mainframes)

SAC (Simplified Access Control)

In the CCITT X.500 Directory Services model, the more restricted of two sets of access control guidelines. The other set is BAC (Basic Access Control).

SEE ALSO

X.500

SAC (Single-Attachment Concentrator)

In FDDI, a concentrator that serves as a termination point for single-attachment stations (SASs) and that attaches to the FDDI ring through a dual-attachment connector (DAC).

SEE ALSO

FDDI (Fiber Distributed Data Interface)

Safety Device

Safety devices are designed to keep a file server or other piece of hardware running smoothly, regardless of power fluctuations or loss. The protection devices buffer, or shield, the hardware from the harsh world of the electrical power line.

Safety devices operate between the power line and the hardware's circuitry. For a network, the biggest natural threat to the hardware comes from the electrical lines. Drastic deviations or fluctuations in the electrical power supply can cause various types of damage, from minimal data loss to fried hardware.

Electrical Threats

As in other areas of life, electrical dangers can come from having too much or too little. Collectively, such disturbances are known as *overvoltages* and *undervoltages*, respectively.

Overvoltages include spikes and surges. Undervoltages include blackouts and brownouts (or sags). According to studies by IBM and by AT&T Bell Labs, undervoltages account for over 90 percent of electrical disturbances, with brownouts accounting for about 87 percent and blackouts for about 5 percent of the total. Overvoltages account for the remaining 8 percent, with spikes accounting for 7 percent and surges for only about 1 percent of all electrical disturbances. See the Power Disturbances article for more information about these types of electrical disturbances.

In most cases, such disturbances occur sporadically. In some areas, voltage variations may be unnervingly frequent. This can be the case if the power supply passes through old lines or if there are malfunctioning components along the line. In some cases, your power company may be able to clean up the power supply.

In addition to these variations in the power supply, several types of noise, or random elements in the power supply, also exist in an electrical system:

- *Common mode noise* is noise arising because of voltage differences between the neutral and ground wires in a system. This type of noise is relatively rare for computer systems, and is almost completely eliminated by noise filters.

a b c d e f g h i j k l m n o p q r **s** t u v w x y z

- *Normal mode noise* is noise arising because of voltage differences between the hot and neutral wires in a system. This type of noise has various sources (other electrical activity on the line, motors being turned on or off, and so on). Some of this noise is handled by noise filters, some is eliminated by various tricks and offsets (such as twisting wire pairs), and some gets through.

- *Intersystem ground noise* is noise that can arise when systems connected to different ground wires communicate. Each ground wire will try to serve as the reference level for both components. This type of noise can be minimized by connecting equipment to a common distribution panel, or frame, because this makes it more likely that the ground values will be the same. In general, noise filters do not help with this kind of noise.

Electrical Safety Devices

Various safety devices have been developed to deal with the most common and the most serious electrical threats:

- Surge protectors, or suppressors, protect a system from excess voltages, such as spikes and surges, and do some noise filtering.

- Line conditioners, or voltage regulators, protect a system from low voltages, such as sags. Some line conditioners also provide surge protection.

- UPS (uninterruptible power supply) devices protect a system when there

is *no* voltage at all—during blackouts. Most UPSs also provide at least some protection against surges, spikes, and sags. During an outage, the connected device runs off the UPS's battery.

- SPS (standby power supply) devices are similar to UPSs, except that the power does not go through the SPS battery during normal operations. When there is a blackout, the SPS will switch to the emergency battery within a few milliseconds.

UPSs and SPSs provide the same protection but use a different method to do so. A UPS delivers power by sending it through a DC battery and then through an inverter to convert back to AC from DC. For a UPS, the *secondary* path is from the power lines to the device being powered, usually after going through a surge suppressor and a noise filter.

An SPS uses the battery and inverter as the secondary path, and the "direct" route from power lines to machine as the primary path. Only if the primary path is blocked does the power come from batteries.

Hybrid devices that combine features of UPS and SPS have been developed.

For more information about a particular safety device, see the separate article about the device.

Testing Safety Devices

Server maintenance should also include regular tests of the UPS or SPS, every six months or so, at the longest. Before starting such a test, you should log everyone off the network, so that no one inadvertently loses any data.

Next, run a batch program that does some busy work but whose actions will not destroy any of your data. For example, you can have your test program read and write a dummy file.

Next, unplug the UPS or SPS from the wall outlet. The network should be running solely on the battery power provided by the UPS or SPS. Depending on the configuration with your UPS, a message may be broadcast informing users that the network will be shut down soon. At the same time, the network software should be writing anything still in its cache, and should be preparing for a system shutdown. The amount of time available before shutdown depends on the network demands and on the performance rating of the UPS.

It is a good idea to drain the battery completely and then recharge it, since such batteries lose their power if they are continually drained a bit, then recharged, drained a bit, recharged, and so on, as happens during everyday functioning in a UPS.

Keep in mind that a UPS' battery lasts only about 5 years. After that time, the battery loses its ability to store charge efficiently.

Be aware that testing a UPS or SPS by disconnecting from the electrical power supply is helpful, but it is not the same as a real

WHAT TO LOOK FOR IN A SAFETY DEVICE

Although safety devices can help with your peace of mind, be aware that no device is completely foolproof. If an electrical disturbance happens once, there is always the chance it will happen again. Just because your surge protector saved you the first time doesn't mean it will save you again.

Surge suppressors, line conditioners, and UPSs vary in the quality of their components. They also vary in the magnitude and number of attacks they can withstand.

You need to have four types of information about a safety device in order to evaluate the device properly and to compare it with similar devices:

- What's the minimum disturbance that will trigger the device?

- What's the maximum disturbance the device can withstand?

- How quickly can the device respond when there is a disturbance?

- How many high-level and low-level disturbances can the device withstand?

For example, some inexpensive surge suppressors are designed to protect your system against a single attack, perhaps two. Such suppressors are intended for use with ordinary appliances (such as toasters), rather than with computer equipment.

When shopping for safety devices, ask for the specifications sheets to find out the magnitude of damage the device can withstand. Make sure any devices you consider are UL-listed.

power disturbance. Studies have shown that the electrical activity when you unplug the UPS or SPS is different from the activity if there is a true power outage.

Determining Power Needs

Rating the power needs for a system is not always an easy task for several reasons. It is sometimes difficult to determine how much power a component draws, and it is easy to forget a component when adding up the power requirements. Also, some devices discuss power in terms of watts (W) and some in terms of volt amps (VA).

The relationship between watts and volt amps is a simple formula. To determine one value from the other, just multiply the starting value by a constant. The problem is that the constant is different for different devices. (For PCs, a volt amp is about 1.5 watts.)

To determine the power requirements for your system, you need to do the following:

- Identify all the components that draw power.

- Determine the power requirements for each component, using the same units when possible, and making any necessary conversions when not.

- Add the values for the individual components.

To be safe, round upwards, so that your estimate will be high, rather than low. The few dollars you save by buying a safety device with less capacity may be lost very quickly if the device is inadequate. Also, you should take expansion into account when computing power requirements.

▼ Sag

A short-term decrease in voltage level. Specifically, a sag occurs when the voltage is more than 20 percent below the nominal RMS voltage, and lasts for a few seconds or longer.

SEE ALSO
Power Disturbance

▼ Salvageable File

In Novell's NetWare, a file deleted but not purged by the user. Salvageable files can be recovered if necessary, because NetWare actually saves the file in a special directory rather than deleting it. In contrast, purged files cannot be recovered.

▼ Sampled Servo (SS)

SEE
SS (Sampled Servo)

▼ SAP (Service Access Point)

In the OSI Reference Model, a SAP is a well-defined location through which an entity at a particular layer can provide services to processes at the layer above.

To indicate the layering, the first letter of the specific layer being discussed is often added before the *SAP*. For example, a transport layer entity provides services to the session layer through a TSAP (or T-SAP). The figure "SAPs and OSI layers" shows how SAPs relate to OSI layers.

SAPS AND OSI LAYERS

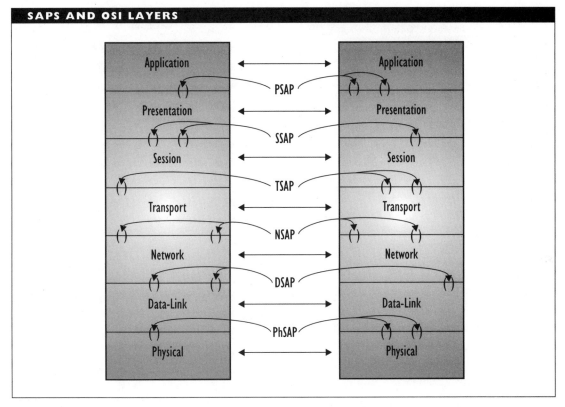

SAP Addresses

Each SAP will have a unique address. This address can also be used as an access point to the service's user, which is the entity at the next higher layer. SAPs are assigned by the IEEE standards office. The table "SAP Addresses for Common Protocols" shows some examples of SAP address values associated with protocols. Addresses are in hexadecimal form.

DSAPs and SSAPs

The IEEE 802.2 specifications refer to SAPs through which network layer processes can request services from the logical-link-control (LLC) sublayer defined by the IEEE. The documents distinguish between source and destination access points. A DSAP (destination service access point) is the address to which the LLC passes information for a network-layer process. An SSAP (source service access point) is the address through which a network-layer process requests LLC services.

The DSAP and SSAP values are included as fields in packets for local-area network (LAN) architectures that conform to IEEE specifications. In practice, these addresses are usually the same, since the process requesting a service is almost always the one that wants the results of that service.

a b c d e f g h i j k l m n o p q r **s** t u v w x y z

SAP ADDRESSES FOR COMMON PROTOCOLS	
PROTOCOL	SAP ADDRESS VALUE (HEXADECIMAL)
IP (ARPAnet)	06
IPX (Novell NetWare)	E0
ISO Network Layer	F5
NetBIOS (IBM)	F0
SNA Group Path Control (IBM)	05
SNA Individual Path Control (IBM)	04
TCP/IP SNAP	AA
XNS (3Com)	80

SEE ALSO
OSI Reference Model

SAP (Service Advertising Protocol)

In Novell's NetWare, a transport layer protocol that servers can use to make their services known on a network. Servers advertise their services using SAP packets. These packets are retrieved and stored by routers. Each router maintains a database of all the servers within "wireshot," and each router broadcasts this information to other routers, typically every 60 seconds or whenever something changes.

Stations that need a service can broadcast SAP request packets. These packets will be answered by the nearest router with information about the requested service.

SAS (Single-Attachment Station)

In FDDI, a station, or node, that lacks the physical ports to attach directly to both the primary and secondary rings. Instead, the SAS attaches to a concentrator (which may be single- or dual-attachment).

SEE ALSO
FDDI (Fiber Distributed Data Interface)

SATAN (Security Analysis Tool for Auditing Networks)

SATAN is a very controversial set of network security tools. It consists of HTML files, shell scripts, and programs written in C, Perl, and Expect. These programs generate additional HTML files that are used to probe networks in order to:

- Determine the network's configuration and weak points
- Probe these weaknesses to determine how vulnerable they make the network
- Generate a report summarizing the network's configuration and weaknesses, and also SATAN's success during its probes

Working with a browser and a World Wide Web (WWW) client, users can have SATAN launch a light, normal, or heavy attack at a target machine or domain. In a light attack, the HTML documents, scripts, and programs are used to report about available host machines and remote procedure call (RPC) services. A normal attack also finds out about the Finger, FTP, Gopher, SMTP, Telnet, and WWW capabilities on the network, since certain features of these services—especially Finger and FTP—make networks particularly vulnerable. A heavy attack will look for other common vulnerabilities, such as trusted hosts or anonymous FTP directories with write permissions.

If vulnerabilities are found, SATAN can make use of expert system tools to investigate further. It can also provide a report of the vulnerabilities. SATAN is extensible, and users can add their own attack or analysis tools.

SATAN's creators—Dan Farmer and Wietse Venema—claim that SATAN finds weaknesses a frighteningly high proportion of the time. Since it was "released" in April 1995, SATAN has apparently been so effective that manufacturers of security products have been known to issue press releases when one of their systems detects or withstands an attack by SATAN.

The release of SATAN has also led to the development of new security products—some of which check for SATAN attacks. In keeping with the terminology, these products have names such as Gabriel.

SATAN on the Loose

SATAN's developers have decided to make the package freely available to anyone interested. Because this includes both sides—security experts and administrators on one side, and crackers on the other—the decision has raised a considerable furor.

SATAN can be a benefit in that it gives system administrators and security specialists a very powerful tool for testing the adequacy of their network security. Once they

find weaknesses, presumably they can fix them. SATAN can be a threat, however, because individuals or organizations trying to gain illegal access to corporate, government, or other sensitive networks get a big helping hand.

A more subtle problem—and possibly more damaging in the long run—is the potential for introducing weaknesses into a network just by using SATAN. The Computer Emergency Response Team (CERT) has issued advisories about SATAN, because certain ways of using the program may lead to security breaches.

It remains to be seen whether SATAN helps improve network security or whether it just makes the network administrator's life more difficult.

PRIMARY SOURCES

The documentation for SATAN is available from the following web site:

ftp://ftp.win.tue.nl/pub/security/
satan_doc.tar.Z

This documentation has several obstacles that "protect" it from readers. First, it is a compressed archive (tar) file. Second, it requires a Web browser (such as Netscape or Mosaic), and version 5 of the Perl language. The documentation actually includes sample data from early trials. (In fact, the documentation consists of the SATAN package with the probing and data retrieval tools removed.) To view the sample data, the developers recommend a fast workstation with 32 MB of memory and at least 64 MB of swap space.

a b c d e f g h i j k l m n o p q r **s** t u v w x y z

▼
Scaling

Expansion of a network by the addition of more nodes. The scalability of a network architecture or operating system should be a major factor in selecting network components.

▼
Scattering

In communications over fiber-optic cable, signal loss that occurs when the light waves in the fiber core strike molecules or slight indentations in the cladding (material surrounding the fiber core).

▼
SCR (Signal-to-Crosstalk Ratio)

In transmissions involving twisted-pair cable, a value that represents the decibel level of a signal in relation to the noise in the cable. Specifically, SCR is calculated as the ratio between the NEXT (near end crosstalk) and the attenuation on a cable. The SCR for an active hub is generally higher than for a passive hub.

▼
SCS (SNA Character String)

In IBM's SNA environment, a printing mode that provides various printing and formatting capabilities.

COMPARE
DSC (Data Stream Compatibility)

SEE ALSO
SNA (Systems Network Architecture)

▼
SCSI (Small Computer System Interface)

SCSI is a high-speed, parallel interface standard that supports hard disks and provides a generic interface for other devices, such as scanners, CD-ROM drives, and other hard disks. SCSI (pronounced "scuzzy") can support drives with very high capacities of more than a gigabyte (GB). A SCSI interface can support up to eight devices in a single expansion slot. Two major versions of the SCSI interface have appeared: SCSI-1 and SCSI-2.

SCSI-1 is the slower, less capable of the pair. This version supports drives of up to 2 GB and transfer rates as high as 5 megabytes per second (MBps). SCSI-2 is faster and supports higher-capacity drives. An ordinary SCSI-2 interface supports transfer rates of up to 10 MBps. A *wide SCSI,* which is a 32-bit interface, can transfer up to 40 MBps. SCSI-2 can support drives with capacities of 3 GB or even more.

SCSI devices can be daisy-chained, so that a single adapter can support a variety of devices. This type of configuration is illustrated in the figure "SCSI chain." In a daisy-chain configuration, it is essential to make sure that every device in the chain has a different address and that the last device in the (electrical) chain is properly terminated.

A SCSI cable may have D-type or Centronics-like connectors at one or both ends. A D-type is a 50-pin connector that looks like the DB-*xx* connectors used for serial ports on PCs, except that the SCSI connector is smaller. Centronics-like connectors are connectors with teeth instead of pins. The table "SCSI Pin Assignments"

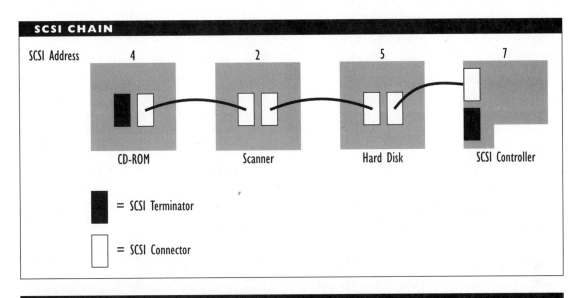

SCSI CHAIN

SCSI Address   4   2   5   7

CD-ROM   Scanner   Hard Disk   SCSI Controller

■ = SCSI Terminator

☐ = SCSI Connector

SCSI PIN ASSIGNMENTS

PIN(S)	DEFINITION
All odd pins except 25	Ground
20, 22, 24, 28, 30, 34	Ground
25	No pin
2, 4, 6, 8, 10, 12, 14, 16	Data lines 0 through 7, respectively
18	Parity line
26	Terminator power
32	Attention
36	Busy
36	Acknowledge
40	Reset
42	Message
44	Select
46	C/D
48	Request
50	I/O

a b c d e f g h i j k l m n o p q r **s** t u v w x y z

shows the pin assignments for a SCSI connection. Pins are numbered from 1 to 50.

SD (Start Delimiter)

A field in a Token Ring data or token packet.

SEE ALSO
Token Ring

SDDI (Shielded Distributed Data Interface)

A networking configuration that implements the FDDI architecture and protocols on shielded twisted-pair (STP) cable. A related implementation is CDDI (copper distributed data interface), which uses unshielded twisted pair (UTP) cable.

SDF (Sub-Distribution Frame)

An intermediate wiring center. For example, an SDF may be used for all the equipment on a particular floor. This type of frame is connected by backbone cable to a main distribution frame (MDF).

SDU (Service Data Unit)

In the OSI Reference Model, a term for a packet that is passed as a service request parameter from one layer to the layer below it. For example, a transport layer process may pass a packet down to the network layer for transmission. The transport layer's packet is an SDU for the network layer.

SEE ALSO
OSI Reference Model

Search Drive

In Novell's NetWare, a drive that is searched if a file is not found in the current directory. A search drive enables a user to work in one directory but access files, such as applications, in other directories, without needing to specify those other directories.

SEE ALSO
Search Mode

Search Engine

A search engine is a program that is designed to traverse some type of search space. In relation to networking, the term is generally applied to a program used to find items—usually documents —on the World Wide Web (WWW).

Web search engines work in a variety of ways. Some use web robots—automated programs—to search through and index the hypertext documents available on the WWW. Others simply gather information from available indexes.

Examples of search engines include WebCrawler, World Wide Web Worm (WWWW), and Lycos.

Search Mode

In Novell's NetWare, search mode is a setting that specifies which search drives should be checked when a program is looking for a data file. The search mode is associated with an executable (.EXE or .COM) file.

NetWare allows the search mode for each file to be set individually. Alternatively, an entry in the NET.CFG file can set the search mode for entire groups of files. The table "NetWare Search Mode Values" shows the modes that are defined.

NETWARE SEARCH MODE VALUES	
MODE	**DESCRIPTION**
0	The program checks NET.CFG for instructions. This is the default value.
1	The program checks the path specified in the file. If none is specified, the program checks the default directory and then all search drives.
2	The program checks the path specified in the file. If none is specified, the program checks only the default directory.
3	The program checks the path specified in the file. If none is specified, the program checks the default directory. If the file open request is read-only, the program also checks the search drives.
4	Reserved for future use.
5	The program searches the specified path and then all search drives. If no path is set, the program searches the default directory and then all search drives.
6	Reserved for future use.
7	The program checks the path specified in the file. If the file open request is read-only, the program checks the search drives. If no path is specified, the program checks the default directory, and then all search drives.

Seat

In computer telephony, a term used to describe an aggregate configuration consisting of a phone line, port, and telephone. As computers and telephones become more integrated, equipment is becoming bundled and priced "per seat" rather than for the individual items.

Secondary Link Station (SLS)

SEE

SLS (Secondary Link Station)

Secret-Key Encryption

A data-encryption strategy that uses a single key, known only to sender and receiver, to encrypt and decrypt transmissions.

SEE ALSO

Encryption

Security

Security is an aspect of network administration concerned with ensuring that the data, circuits, and equipment on a network are used only by authorized users and in authorized ways. More fundamentally, security is concerned with ensuring the following:

Availability: Network components, information, and services are available whenever needed.

Confidentiality: Services and information are available only to those authorized to use them. This availability may differ for different users; that is, certain

a b c d e f g h i j k l m n o p q r **s** t u v w x y z

users may have more privileges and access than others.

Integrity: Components and information are not destroyed, corrupted, or stolen, either through outside intervention or through in-house incompetence.

Threats to Security

The security of a network can be threatened, compromised, or breached with respect to hardware, software, information, and even network operation. In this context, a threat may be defined as a scenario that violates one or more of the security goals. For example, losses of hardware or data are threats to a network's security, as are thefts of passwords or user IDs.

A particular type of threat may or may not be avoidable, and may or may not ever happen. For example, if an unauthorized person has managed to learn a valid user ID and password, the threat is unavoidable, and the network's security is compromised. A compromised network is no longer secure, even though it may not be damaged. If that person uses the stolen information to access the network, the network's security actually will be breached.

To implement effective security measures, it is necessary to determine the possible threats and their consequences, and to develop effective measures against each of these threats.

Threats to network security may be categorized in terms of the network element that is threatened (for example, hardware or software) or in terms of the manner in which the threat affects the network if carried out.

The following are some of the ways threats can be categorized:

- Internal or external. An internal threat derives from hardware or software on the network itself. For example, a malfunctioning or inadequate fan may cause a computer to overheat, damaging its circuits. An external threat derives from a person or from an element outside the network. For example, a disgruntled employee or user with a hammer or a strong magnet could provide a serious external threat.

- Intentional or accidental. An intentional threat has damage to the network as a primary or secondary goal. For example, an industrial or political spy trying to steal or corrupt information represents an intentional threat. In contrast, a power surge or a lightning strike that damages circuitry can be unfortunate, but can hardly be called intentional.

- Active or passive. In an active threat, damage to the network is a main effect. For example, a virus program may format a hard disk on the network, or an industrial spy may delete important network files. In a passive threat, damage to the network is a side effect or an unanticipated result of some other action. For example, the radiation and other signals that emanate from a network during a transmission may be picked up by an unauthorized user and used to obtain information about the network.

Anticipation of all passive threats requires a truly paranoid mind, since some passive threats can be far removed from actual information on the network. For example, a "listener" might be able to draw testable inferences about a network simply by observing transmission traffic patterns on the network.

Threats to Hardware

In this context, hardware refers to a range of objects, including computers, peripherals, cables, telecommunications lines, circuits, and just about any other device or component that someone manages to attach to a network, and through which energy can be sent into the network and information sent from it. Any of these objects may be threatened with destruction, damage, or theft; the object may be rendered temporarily or permanently unusable.

Some of the threats to hardware include the following:

- Theft, as when a computer or another piece of equipment is stolen. In some cases, such as when a hard or floppy disk is stolen, other aspects are also breached.

- Tampering, as when a cable is cut, or jumpers are set to unexpected or incorrect values.

- Destruction, as when a computer's circuitry is fried through an electrical power surge. More subtle forms of destruction can arise through temporary but frequent power decreases or outages or through inadequate ventilation around the computer.

- Damage, as when a cable loses its protection and properties because of humidity and other environmental conditions.

- Unauthorized use, as when someone taps into a cable or a telecommunications line in order to eavesdrop, steal secrets, or send in false information. Similarly, unauthorized access to and use of a node or terminal can also compromise a network.

- Ordinary equipment wear and tear, which is inevitable, but whose progress can be slowed by proper treatment and regular maintenance.

The specific threats to hardware are almost unlimited. Under the proper circumstances, just about anything can pose a threat to a hardware component.

Measures can be taken to avoid (or at least decrease the likelihood of) certain hardware threats. For example, theft or damage by outsiders can be avoided by locking the hardware in a room that is (ideally) inaccessible to all but the system administrator. Similarly, damage through external accidents (such as power disturbances) can be avoided by using surge protectors and other safety devices.

Threats to Software

In this context, software refers to the applications, shells, operating systems, and other programs that execute on and for the network. Data and work files are included in another section, as examples of information.

Threats to software include the following:

- Deletion, as when a program is deliberately or accidentally erased from a hard disk.

- Theft, as when a program is copied by unauthorized users.

- Corruption, as when software is infested by a virus, trojan horse, or worm. Software can also be corrupted in other ways, such as by having a program send a copy of the program's output to an unauthorized file or location.

- Bugs, which may not manifest themselves immediately or which may be very subtle, arising only for certain values or conditions.

Network management programs may be able to watch for efforts to delete or corrupt a program. Management software cannot detect a program bug, but it may be able to recognize the bug's effects.

Threats to Information

In this context, information refers to configurations, files, transmissions, and other data representations. In general, information is used or transformed by the programs discussed as software.

Threats to information include the following:

- Deletion, as when a database is deliberately or inadvertently erased.

- Theft, as when the information in a network transmission is overheard and saved by nodes other than the destination. The information may be intercepted, rather than taken away, so that it is still passed on to its original destination, just as in a normal network transmission. Information theft can also occur as a side effect of hardware theft, such as when a hard disk is stolen.

- Loss, as when data is lost during a network crash, because of a program bug, or because of user error.

- Corruption, as when data is garbled or partially lost. Another form of corruption is data replacement, as when the original data is intercepted and replaced with a modified version.

Some types of information corruption will be detected through cyclic redundancy checks (CRCs) or other error-detection measures. Efforts to delete a data file may be detected by some network management or virus-detection programs. Successful deletions will be detected the next time the file or database is accessed. (Of course, at that point it probably will be too late to do anything about the deletion.)

Threats to Network Operation

Network operation includes both ordinary network activity, such as transmissions, and meta-activity, such as network monitoring and management.

Threats to network operation include the following:

- Interruption, as when a cable connection is broken or a node on certain types of networks goes down.

- Interference, including jamming, as when electrical noise is introduced deliberately or by random external causes.

- Overload, as when network traffic becomes heavy because of too much ordinary activity or because a virus has been introduced and has replicated itself. When the network is overloaded, data packets may be lost or corrupted.

Networks that use optical signaling are much less susceptible to interference and overload.

Causes of Security Threats and Breaches

The following are the main causes of damage to network components or files:

- Unauthorized access to the network, which can result in theft of the hardware, software, or information

- Unauthorized use of network information, as in the case of data interception

- Random events, such as disasters or power anomalies

Random external events generally threaten hardware directly and the contents of the hardware secondarily. Unauthorized access or use generally threatens software and data directly, while threatening hardware mainly as a means to this end (if at all).

Network operation may be disrupted by random external forces (rats, climate, or chemicals destroying a cable section, for example) or by user carelessness or maliciousness.

Security Goals

The most immediate goal of network security efforts is to protect networks from all the types of threats; to make sure that the threatening events do not occur, or at least that they happen as rarely as possible. A second, but equally important goal is to minimize the effects of security breaches once they have occurred.

As stated, a secure network is one that meets these requirements:

- It is always available to authorized users when needed.

- Its contents and resources can be modified only by authorized users.

- Its contents can be read or otherwise displayed only by authorized users.

More specifically, network security measures have the following goals, which together help make for a secure network:

- Prevent malicious damage to network hardware or files; prevent malicious misuse of hardware and software.

- Prevent theft of network components or information.

- Limit accidental damage or destruction of hardware or software, either through user carelessness or environmental events.

- Protect data confidentiality and integrity.

- Prevent unauthorized access to a network and unauthorized use of its resources. This goal includes the more specific one of preventing interception

a
b
c
d
e
f
g
h
i
j
k
l
m
n
o
p
q
r
s
t
u
v
w
x
y
z

or theft of network files or transmissions.

- Provide for recovery from disasters (fire, flood, theft, and so on). There must be provisions for restoring the network data and getting the network back into service.

Security Measures

To accomplish these goals, measures such as the following are taken when implementing and running the network:

- Physically securing hardware from theft, as well as from fire, flood, and other threats.

- Logically securing hardware, such as by using encryption chips on network interface cards. Encryption information must be stored in a separate location, in memory that is not directly accessible to the computer. Hardware security measures are necessary for networks that comply with moderate security levels (such as C2) as specified by the National Security Agency. (These levels are listed later in this article.)

- Use of power-protection devices, such as line conditioners to clean the electrical signals coming into the network components, and uninterruptible or standby power supplies (UPSs or SPSs) to keep the network running long enough to shut down properly in case of a power outage. Depending on the size of the network, only servers and other crucial components (such as hubs or routers) may have UPSs;

"secondary" components may have just line conditioners or surge protectors.

- Use of system fault-tolerant servers, which contain redundant components. If the primary component fails, the secondary one immediately takes over. Networks with the highest degree of system-fault tolerance include auxiliary servers, which can take over if the main server fails.

- Use of redundant cabling, which often complements system fault-tolerant measures, and provides a secondary set of connections for the network. Each node has two network interface cards, with connectors and cables coming off both.

- Doing regular *and frequent* backups onto tape, disk, or optical media. There are numerous backup strategies, ranging from periodic backups of the entire disk contents, incremental or differential backups, and continuous backups. Backup media should *not* be stored at the same location as the original material. Some tape backup systems allow password protection for tapes, so that only authorized persons can restore the backed up material.

- Use of redundant storage, in which multiple copies of information are stored. Again, various strategies are possible, including measures such as disk mirroring, disk duplexing, or the use of RAID (redundant array of inexpensive disks) technology.

- Use of diskless workstations, to prevent users from copying files or logging transmissions to disk.

- Use of callback modems to prevent unauthorized logins from remote locations. This type of modem takes login calls from users, gets the user's access information, then breaks the connection. If the user's login information and telephone number are valid, the modem will call the user back at a predetermined number to allow the user onto the network.

- Writing data to disk only after the targeted disk area is checked. If this area is defective, the material is redirected on the fly to a safe location. To support this feature, an area of the hard disk, usually about 2 percent of the total storage, is set aside.

- Transaction tracking, in which all the materials related to a transaction are kept in memory (or in temporary buffers on disk) and are written only once the transaction is completed. This scheme protects against data loss if the network goes down in the middle of a transaction.

- Use of audit trails, in which all user actions are recorded and stored.

- Controlling access to certain files or directories (for example, the user account and password data).

- Controlling uploading privileges to minimize the likelihood that someone can deliberately or inadvertently load a virus or other damaging program onto the network. Even if such privileges are strictly controlled, virus-detection software should still be used.

- Use of passwords and other user IDs to control access to the network. With dynamic passwords, users get new passwords (generated by a special device) every time they log in to the network.

- Use of host and key authentication in addition to passwords to ensure that all parties involved in a network connection are allowed to be there.

- Allowing users privileges based on the users' status and needs. For example, general users may have access to only files and applications in public directories and perhaps in their own work directories. Similarly, users may be allowed to access the network only at certain times or from certain nodes.

- Encryption of transmissions to prevent (or at least make more difficult) unauthorized theft of information transmitted across the network. Encryption strategies can use public- or secret-key encryption systems. (See the Encryption article for a discussion of the differences among these strategies.) Encryption cannot prevent interception of transmission; it can only make the contents of the transmission more difficult to read.

- Traffic padding, to make the level of network traffic more constant, thus making it more difficult for an eavesdropper to infer network contents.

a
b
c
d
e
f
g
h
i
j
k
l
m
n
o
p
q
r
s
t
u
v
w
x
y
z

- Use of various verification activities, such as message authentication codes (MACs) to determine whether a message has been received as sent. These codes are more sophisticated than ordinary CRCs, because the checksum that is attached is also encrypted. MACs make it much more difficult to intercept and modify a message (including its error-detection fields). Other verification activities include the use of digital signatures, notarization, and origin and destination non-repudiation.

- Recording and reporting efforts to access a network by an unauthorized user (for example, by someone trying to guess a password or trying to log in at an unauthorized time). Such attempts should be reported to the system administrator and the network management facilities, through the use of alarms or other means. (See the Security Management article for more information about security-related alarms.)

- Packet filtering, or transmission of packets only to the destination node. For example, sophisticated hubs and concentrators can determine the destination for a packet, then transmit the packet to that node and transmit gibberish to the other nodes. This makes eavesdropping more difficult, if not impossible.

Most of the preceding security measures can be taken to several levels. Networks that need to conform to government security guidelines must implement particularly stringent and costly security measures. In general, the more security measures and redundancy built into a network, the more expensive the network will be.

Similarly, many of the security measures mentioned may be implemented at any of several functional levels in the OSI Reference Model.

Although the general form of security goals may not change significantly over time, security measures must evolve and change constantly, to keep up with the new methods that are developed to gain unauthorized access to networks and to steal their contents.

Security Levels

Four general security classes are defined in a government publication called the *Trusted Computer System Evaluation Criteria* but more commonly known as the Orange Book. The four classes are, in order of increasing security, as follows:

- Class D (minimal security)
- Class C (discretionary protection)
- Class B (mandatory protection)
- Class A (verified protection)

Class D Security

Class D includes all systems that cannot meet any of the higher security criteria. Systems in this class cannot be considered secure. Examples of class D systems include PC operating systems such as MS DOS or System 7 for the Macintosh.

Class C Security

Class C is divided into C1 and the somewhat more secure C2. Operating systems such as UNIX or network operating systems that provide password protection and access rights might fall into either of these classes (most likely into C1).

C1 security features include the use of passwords or other authentication measures, the ability to restrict access to files and resources, and the ability to prevent accidental destruction of system programs.

In addition to the C1 features, C2 systems include the ability to audit or track all user activity, restrict operations for individual users, and make sure that data left in memory cannot be used by other programs or users.

Class B Security

Class B is divided into three levels. In general, class B systems must be able to provide mathematical documentation of security, actively seek out threats to security, and be able to maintain security even during system failure.

B1 systems must have all the security capabilities of a C2 system and then some. B1 systems must take all available security measures and separate the security-related system components from the ones that are not related to security. B1 documentation must include discussions of the security measures.

B2 systems must have the same as B1, as well as be able to provide a mathematical description of the security system, manage all configuration changes (software updates, and so on) in a secure manner, and check explicitly to make sure new software does not have any backdoors or other ways through which an outsider might try to access the secure system.

B3 systems must have a system administrator in charge of security, and must remain secure even if the system goes down.

Class A Security

A1 systems must be able to verify mathematically that their security system and policy match the security design specifications.

▼
Security Analysis Tool for Auditing Networks (SATAN)

SEE

SATAN (Security Analysis Tool for Auditing Networks)

▼
Security Management

Security management is one of five OSI network management domains specified by the ISO and CCITT. The purpose of security management in the OSI network management model is to provide a secure network as defined in the entry on security and to notify the system administrator of any efforts to compromise or breach this secure network. Very generally, a secure network is one that is always accessible when needed and whose contents can be accessed—read and modified—only by authorized users.

To accomplish these goals, the security management component needs to be able to determine all (actual and potential) access points to the network, and to make sure these points cannot be breached or compromised. If an unauthorized access occurs, the component must be able to provide the system administrator with the information needed to identify and locate the security threat.

Identifying Access Points

The most common access points to a network are the network's nodes, both local and remote. Less obvious access points include cables, air waves, and programs. For example, a potential thief can tap into a transmission line or simply pick a wireless transmission out of the air.

Programs can also be used to get illicit access to a network. For example, a program might be able to log in to network activity in secret or redirect program output to an unauthorized location. Many breaches of large networks (such as the Internet) occur because someone manages to sneak in a program that captures passwords as they move across the network.

In certain network architectures, notably Ethernet and Token Ring networks, all packets pass through every node. In these types of networks, it is easy to steal information from the network just by reading all packets that pass through one's node, regardless of whether the node is the packet's destination. In fact, network monitors operate by simply reading everything that goes by.

Some access points are extremely subtle. These provide information about the network activity through indirect measures, such as analysis of network traffic patterns.

Although these measures may not immediately provide information about the contents of the network traffic, the patterns observed may provide enough of an entry to enable an eavesdropper eventually to decipher the contents.

For example, if a large company regularly sends a long transmission from the payroll computer to a bank the evening before every payday, an industrial spy might reasonably infer that funds are being transferred, and might eventually be able to extract account numbers or other useful information from this transmission, even if the transmission is encrypted.

Securing Access Points

The simplest way to secure an access point is to deny access to unauthorized users or listeners. Depending on the type of access point involved, there are many ways to do this. Some of the most common measures involve an authentication process of the machines, users, message, and/or encryption keys. Other security measures are described in the Security article.

The OSI network management model does not specify how such authentication is to be carried out. As yet, the model does not provide protocols for accomplishing authentication.

Security Alarms

An alarm is a signal used to indicate that something is not functioning as it should. The OSI network management model includes several types of alarms, which are used to indicate fault, performance, and security problems.

Alarms may refer to any of several facets of a network connection, and they should indicate how serious the problem is—that is, they should let the administrator know how quickly something needs to be done about the problem. Five types of security alarms are distinguished, each of which is used for a different network violation:

- Integrity violation, which indicates that network contents or objects have been illegally modified, deleted, or added

- Operational violation, which indicates that a desired object or service could not be used

- Physical violation, which indicates that a physical part of the network (such as a cable) has been damaged or modified without authorization

- Security-mechanism violation, which indicates that the network's security system has been compromised or breached

- Time-domain violation, which indicates that an event has happened outside its allowed or typical time slot

Alarms may be at any of half a dozen severity levels. *Critical* and *major* alarms are given when a condition that affects service has arisen. For a critical alarm, steps must be taken immediately in order to restore the service. For a major alarm, steps must be taken as soon as possible, because the affected service has degraded drastically and is in danger of being lost completely. *Minor* alarms indicate a problem that does not yet affect service, but that may do

so if the problem is not corrected. *Warning* alarms are used to signal a potential problem that may affect service. Depending on the specific case, more diagnostic work may be needed before it makes sense to do something about the potential problem.

Indeterminate alarms are given if it is not possible to determine how serious the problem is. The system administrator will need to make a judgment about the problems that lead to alarms, and may need to decide how to proceed.

A *cleared* alarm is given when a problem has been taken care of. Such an alarm is needed in order to make it possible to automate (much of) the alarm-reporting process.

BROADER CATEGORY
Network Management

SEE ALSO
Accounting Management; Configuration Management; Fault Management; Performance Management

Seed Router

In an AppleTalk internetwork, a router that defines the network number ranges for all other routers in the network. Each AppleTalk internetwork needs at least one seed router.

Seek Time

The amount of time needed to move the read/write heads in a hard disk to a specified sector and track.

COMPARE
Access Time

Segmentation

In networks that conform to the OSI Reference Model, segmentation is the process by which a packet is broken into parts and packed into several packets at a lower layer. Segmentation may be necessary because of packet-size restrictions at certain layers.

When a packet is segmented, the data portion is broken into parts, and each part is combined with the header and with segment sequence information. The packet is passed down to the layer below for further processing (for example, for encapsulation into the lower-layer packets).

The reverse process, removing redundant headers and recombining several segments into the original packet, is known as *reassembly*.

At a larger level, segmentation is also used to describe the situation in which a large local-area network (LAN) is divided into smaller, more manageable ones.

Segmentation is known as *fragmentation* in the Internet community.

Selector

In the OSI Reference Model, a value used at a specific layer to distinguish each of the multiple service access points (SAPs) through which the entity at that level provides services to the layer above it.

Sequenced Packet Protocol (SPP)

SEE

SPP (Sequenced Packet Protocol)

Serial Line Internet Protocol (SLIP)

SEE

Protocol, SLIP (Serial Line Internet Protocol)

Serial Port

A hardware port in which only one pin is available for data transmission in a given direction, so that bits must be transmitted in sequence. The wiring for a port is almost always associated with a particular physical interface (for example, RS-232). A serial port is used most commonly for a modem, printer, or mouse.

Server

Most generally, a server is an entity that provides some type of network service. The server may be hardware, such as a file server in a network, or software, such as network level protocol for a transport level client. The services may be access to files or devices, transport or translation facilities, and so on.

The server provides its service to other machines (workstations) on the network or to other processes. The figure "Context of servers in networks" shows how hardware servers fit into the larger networking scheme.

In a server-based network, the most important hardware server is the *file server*, which controls access to the files and data stored on one or more hard disks. In most cases, local-area networks (LANs) have PC-sized machines as file servers, although minicomputers and mainframes can also be file

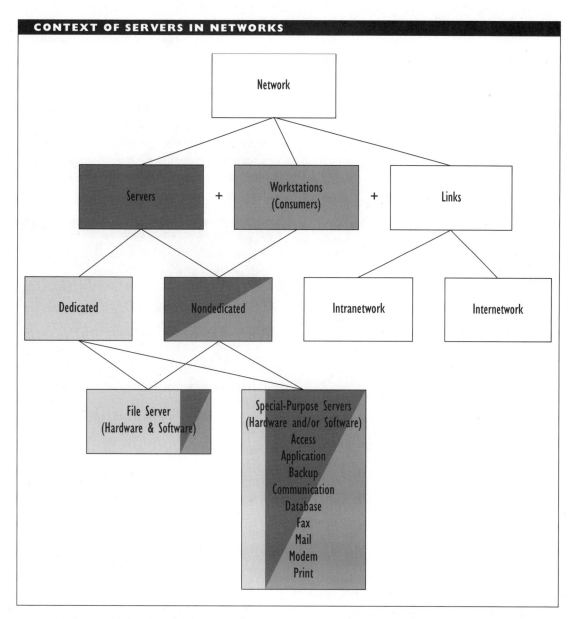

CONTEXT OF SERVERS IN NETWORKS

servers in networks. See the Server, File article for a detailed discussion of file servers.

At the PC level, the architectural choices for workstations and servers include the following:

- Machines using a segmented architecture, based on Intel's $80x86$ chip series. This chip architecture is also used in clone chips from AMD, Cyrix, and other companies, and in the

Pentium, Intel's successor to the $80x86$ family.

- Machines based on Motorola's 68000 family of chips, such as Macintosh or NeXT.

- Machines based on a RISC (reduced instruction set computing) chip set, such as Sun SPARCstations.

Servers do not need to be PCs, although they usually are. Special-purpose servers, such as network modems, can have their own network interface cards (NICs) and can be connected directly to a network. Once connected, the modems can serve as access, or communications, servers.

Dedicated versus Nondedicated Servers

A server may be dedicated or nondedicated. Dedicated servers are used only as a server, not as a workstation. Nondedicated servers are used as both a server and workstation. Networks with a dedicated server are known as *server-based networks;* those with nondedicated servers are known as *peer-to-peer,* or just *peer, networks.*

Dedicated Servers

Dedicated servers cannot be used for ordinary work. In fact, access to the server itself is often limited. In the most security-conscious environments, the server's keyboard is removed, and the server is locked away to prevent any access by unauthorized users.

Most high-end network packages assume a dedicated server. If a network has a dedicated server, this is most likely a file server. In the networking literature, when you see

references to *servers,* without any qualifier, the discussion usually concerns dedicated file servers.

A dedicated file server runs the network operating system (NOS) software, and workstations run smaller programs whose job is to direct user commands to the workstation's operating system or to the server, as appropriate. Both servers and workstations need NICs to function on the network, at least in PC environments.

LOCKING UP THE SERVER

It's not a bad idea to put a dedicated server in a location to which access can be controlled. Removing the keyboard is not an adequate solution if any degree of security is required, since a potential interloper can bring a keyboard.

If the server is locked in a room, make sure the room has adequate ventilation and a clean enough power supply for the hardware. Also be sure to keep a tight rein on the keys to the room.

Nondedicated Servers

A nondedicated server can also be used as a workstation. Using a server as a workstation has several serious disadvantages, however, and is not advised for larger networks.

The following are some of the disadvantages of nondedicated servers compared with dedicated servers:

- Many of the NOSs that allow nondedicated servers run on top of DOS, which makes them extremely slow and clumsy. In contrast, most dedicated servers have software that replaces DOS, at least while the network is up and running. Such systems may also require a separate, non-DOS partition on your hard disk. Since this partition is under the direct control of the NOS (as opposed to being controlled indirectly through DOS), the NOS can arrange and deal with the contents of the partition in a way that optimizes performance.

- Running applications on a DOS machine while it is also supposed to be running a network can lead to a deadly performance degradation.

- Certain tasks will tie up a DOS machine, effectively stopping the network until the task is finished. For some devices that expect responses within a fixed amount of time, such as with modems or fax machines, this can lead to an error or fault condition because of the time-out.

- Adequate security is more difficult to maintain on a nondedicated server.

Generic versus Proprietary Servers

A generic server is one that is designed for use with vendor-independent networking software and hardware components, provided these components conform to industry standards (either official or de facto).

In contrast, a proprietary server runs a proprietary operating system and is designed to be used with a particular vendor's hardware and software. Not too many years ago, several of the major network vendors, such as 3Com, sold proprietary servers. These types of servers are no longer in vogue; the move is toward generic servers. These days,

almost all LANs can be made of generic components.

Server Maintenance

It is important to set up a maintenance schedule for your server and strictly adhere to that schedule. To check the hardware, you should do at least the following things every few weeks (at the very longest interval):

- Clean the server carefully but thoroughly. Cleaning should include removing the dust balls that have accumulated around the fan and inside the machine since the last cleaning.

- Check cabling and connections for tightness and for signs of bending or stress. Do not disconnect connectors unless necessary, since many connectors are rated for a limited number of matings (attachment to another connector).

- If possible, check the cabling with a line analyzer.

- Run thorough diagnostics on the storage medium and on other system components to identify the components that are likely to fail and to deal with these before they actually do fail. Make sure the diagnostic program you plan to use is compatible with the hard disk format and with the networking software you are running.

- Check the quality of your power line by using a line tester. If the line shows lots of surges and/or sags during the testing, you are putting your network (and possibly your net worth) in danger, even if you use line conditioners, surge protectors, or UPSs. These safety devices can protect your system, but not forever. In fact, some surge protectors are designed to withstand only a single large surge.

The tricky part of server maintenance is finding the time to do it, since the network will need to be down, possibly for an extended period. In many cases, server maintenance will need to be done during those early morning hours when other servers all over the country are also being maintained.

Server Backups

Any adequate maintenance work should include regular backups onto tape or perhaps to optical media. Depending on how much work gets done on the network in a day and on how important the work is, backups may need to be done daily or every couple of days. The longer you wait between backups, the more work you can potentially lose.

Superservers

Several manufacturers have developed special-purpose machines that are specifically designed to be file servers. These super-server machines are souped up in one or more ways, including the following:

- Additional RAM, which may be used for whatever purpose the NOS deems most appropriate.

- Multiple processors, which can be used in whatever manner makes the

most sense for the network. Although the current generation of networking software does not take advantage of the processing power, the next generation of NOSs is expected to be able to do so.

- Extra expansion slots, to hold bridges, routers, or NICs.

- Redundant hard drive systems, to speed up disk access and throughput and also for data security.

Special-Purpose Servers

As long as there are developers and users, new services will be provided on networks. As long as services are provided, new types of servers will be specified. The same server machine can perform several of these roles simultaneously. For example, the file server can also serve as a print and fax server. In general, giving the file server double duty is a mixed blessing, and should be given careful consideration before you implement it.

The various special-purpose servers are discussed in separate articles. For example, see the Server, Access article for information about access servers.

BROADER CATEGORY
Hardware

COMPARE
Workstation

SEE ALSO
Server, Access; Server, ACS (Asynchronous Communications Server); Server, Application; Server, ART (Asynchronous Remote Takeover); Server, Backup; Server, Communication; Server, Database;

Server, Fax; Server, File; Server, Modem; Server, Print

Server, Access

An access server is a special type of communications server, designed for handling calls to the network from remote locations. A user dials into the access server, and the user's session appears as if it were running locally. Access servers are generally, but not necessarily, dedicated machines with special hardware for providing access services.

The access server hardware can include multiple cards, housed in a separate box or plugged into a node in the network. Each card has its own processor and may have multiple ports to handle multiple calls simultaneously. When there are multiple cards with CPUs (central processing units), the access server is said to be using a multi-CPU architecture. The processor that provides access to the network is known as the host.

Another way to configure an access server is to use a single card with a multitasking CPU capable of time-sharing. Multiple CPUs cost more but are more reliable, since failure of a single processor will not shut down the access server.

Networked modems have also been used as access servers.

In the mainframe world, an access server, or access hub, provides a way for users at terminals to communicate with a network that has a mainframe or minicomputer as the host machine.

SEE ALSO

Server, Communication

Server, ACS (Asynchronous Communications Server)

An ACS is usually a dedicated PC that provides nodes with access to any of several serial ports or modems. The ports may be connected to mainframes or minicomputers.

When a user on a workstation wants access to a modem or a port, the user simply runs an ordinary communications program in a transparent manner. In order for this to work, one of the following must be the case:

- The communications program must include a redirector (to route the communication process to the appropriate server).

- The workstation must have a special hardware port emulation board installed. In that case, the communications package does not require any special rerouting capabilities (but each workstation does lose an expansion slot).

- You must run a redirection program before starting the communications package. To work with such a software-based redirector, the communications package must be able to use DOS interrupt INT 0x14. Unfortunately, many communications programs bypass this interrupt to access the UART (universal asynchronous receiver/transmitter) directly for faster operation.

SEE ALSO

Server, Communication

a b c d e f g h i j k l m n o p q r **s** t u v w x y z

Server, Application

An application server is generally a dedicated machine that runs applications for workstations. Client-based applications execute on the workstation, and they require any necessary data files to be transferred from the server to the workstation. Using application servers can improve a file server's performance by offloading some of the file server's processing tasks.

Server-based applications run in two chunks: the front end runs on the workstation, and the back end runs on the server. In this way, the workstation can give commands and make requests through the front end, but the actual work and retrieval is done at the back end (on the server). Because of this, only the data processed or returned by the application needs to be sent to the workstation. When working with databases or spreadsheets, this can save considerable time. The tradeoff is that the server is busier because it may have to deal with several application back ends at a time.

Server-based applications are also known as *network-intrinsic,* because they are designed to run in a network environment. In contrast, client-based applications are either *network-aware* or *network-ignorant.* A network-aware application knows that more than one user may be working at the same time and takes any necessary precautions to ensure the users cannot accidentally destroy each other's work by working on the same part of the same file simultaneously.

To avoid problems, do not run network-ignorant applications over a network, because you risk corrupting your files. Also, you may be violating the software license.

Server, Archive

An archive server consists of software to keep track of file usage, to identify files that have not been used in a while (and that are, therefore, candidates for storage on a removable medium). Archiving services are often included with a backup or tape server.

Server, ART (Asynchronous Remote Takeover)

An ART server consists of software to provide a remote caller with access to resources of the local machine or network. The ART server receives input from the remote user and passes it to the local node, as if the input had come from the local keyboard. The server then captures any output at the local node and sends it to the remote location.

The result of all this remote user and server activity is that a keyboard in Kansas, running at an ARTT (Asynchronous Remote Takeover Terminal), can operate a stand-alone or networked computer in Chicago. The ART server will send Chicago's screen output to Kansas for display on the ARTT screen.

Server, Asynchronous Connection Transport

An asynchronous connection transport server consists of software to provide access to resources, such as electronic mail (e-mail) services, over telephone lines. This type of server does not require a dedicated machine.

Server, Backup

A backup server can carry out system shutdowns and backups at regular or specified intervals. The server runs the backup software, which generally can notify all nodes of the impending backup, enable all nodes to end their sessions, and perform the required backup. Software for backups is usually included with the network software. There are also many good backup packages provided by third-party vendors.

Backup servers do not require dedicated machines. Backup services are often provided together with an archive server to keep track of file usage.

Backups may be to disk, tape, or to an optical medium such as WORM (write once, read memory) or EO (erasable optical) disks. In practice, backup to floppy disks is rarely done for networks, because the number of disks and the time required would be prohibitive. Backups to hard disk cartridges are much more common.

In practice, backups must be accompanied by regular and scrupulous disk cleaning and purging. Any files that are no longer used or needed should be removed, to increase the available storage and also decrease the amount of material that must be backed up. (DOS also gets very slow when directories have a large number of files.)

Make sure that the network software you intend to use supports any backup media you intend to use on the network. For example, if you intend to use a WORM drive for backup, make sure the network software's backup utilities support such drives. You

may need special drivers in order to make this support possible.

Server-Based Network

A network in which one or more nodes have special status as dedicated servers. Other nodes (workstations) must go through a server for resources on other machines. This is in contrast to a peer-to-peer network, in which each node may be either server or workstation as the need arises.

SEE ALSO

LAN (Local-Area Network)

Server, Batch-Processing

A batch-processing server consists of software to carry out the tasks specified in batch files. This makes it possible to offload mechanical but time-consuming tasks, such as report generation, to an idle workstation. Batch-processing services are provided by third-party software. A batch-processing server does not require a dedicated machine.

Server, Communication

The term communication server applies to any of several types of servers that provide access to one or more modems and telephone lines. The server also runs the programs needed to establish connections with other machines, prepares files as needed, and sends or receives data. A communication server may be a dedicated machine or it may reside on a workstation.

A communication server may also provide access for remote control programs, which allow users to dial into the network from remote locations. For remote capabilities, special boards are usually required. For heavy remote traffic, you may need to dedicate a machine, known as an *access server,* to this service.

Some communication servers can provide terminal emulation for access to mainframes and minicomputers. Some can also provide connections to remote systems or networks.

Commonly used communication servers include the following:

- Gateways for access to mainframes

- Asynchronous communication servers for access to dial-out modems

- Remote access servers for access *from* remote locations

Communication servers are also known as *dial-in/dial-out* servers.

▼ Server Console

In Novell's NetWare, the console (monitor and keyboard) at which the network supervisor controls and views the activity of the server. From this console, the supervisor can do the following tasks:

- Load and unload NetWare Loadable Modules (NLMs), to change the network's capabilities

- Configure the network

- Send messages

- View network activity

- Shut down the server

When not in use, the server console should always be secured from access. For example, the keyboard and monitor might be locked up in a room.

It is also possible to use a remote keyboard and monitor as a server console. A remote console allows a workstation to serve as the server console at another location.

▼ Server, DAL (Data Access Language)

A DAL server consists of software to provide access to databases using DAL, which is Apple's extension of the SQL (Structured Query Language) database-manipulation language developed originally for use on IBM mainframes.

DAL servers are available for a variety of platforms, ranging from PCs to minicomputers and mainframes. On each platform, the server can provide transparent access to the major database management systems (DBMSs) available on that platform.

A DAL server does not require a dedicated machine.

▼ Server, Database

A database server consists of software to provide access to database records for programs running on other nodes. A database server often runs on the network's file server, but does not require a dedicated machine.

This type of server is useful only if it can do the actual record retrieval and storage on the server, so that it is not necessary to send entire databases between the server and workstation (client). Because of this, database servers are used mainly in client/server local-area networks (LANs), in conjunction with special programs that can run a back-end component to do the work on the server and a front-end interface for a user on the workstation.

An SQL (Structured Query Language) server is a special type of database server designed for use with SQL, which is probably the most commonly used database language.

Server, Directory

Software that provides access to directory information and directory services (DS) for other nodes on the network. A directory server does not require a dedicated machine.

Server, Disk

A disk server consists of a machine and software to control access to one or more hard disks and to any programs and data files stored there. This term has fallen into disuse because of the advent of file servers, which provide disk access as well as other types of services. Disk servers are often, but not necessarily, dedicated machines.

Server, Display

In the X Window graphics environment for UNIX, a display server (also known as an X server) is a hardware-dependent program that runs on the user's machine and that is responsible for controlling the display for whatever work is being done for the user.

A display server is not a server in the same sense as network-related servers are. The terminology for X Window (or X, as it is called) is in contrast to standard networking terminology. In this case, the server is actually the program that is fed data from another process or device, which is usually the role of a client.

In X, the *client* program is actually the one doing whatever task has been requested by the user. The client is a hardware-independent process whose job is to do the requested work and to feed the results to the user's workstation. It is the job of the display server to determine what to do with the results.

The details of the interface for the X window used by the display server are determined by a window manager program. Open Look from Sun Microsystems and Motif from the Open Software Foundation are examples of window managers.

Server, Fax

With a fax server (also known as a *facsimile server*), you can send a fax directly from your workstation, even if the fax machine is attached to a computer in another room or building. A fax server consists of software to provide access to one or more fax machines, and it runs the programs needed to prepare and send a fax or to receive one.

A fax server saves paper, since it is no longer necessary to print a file in order to fax it. The server will take the file, make any required conversions, attach a cover page, queue, and send the fax. A user can accomplish all this without leaving the workstation. Similarly, the fax server will receive faxes, make any required conversions, and store the fax on the file server until the recipient is ready to deal with the fax.

a b c d e f g h i j k l m n o p q r **s** t u v w x y z

Fax servers do not require dedicated machines.

Server, File

A file server exerts considerable control over a network since all transactions go through this component. The figure "File server processing a workstation request" shows one conception of the steps involved when a node (workstation) requests something from a file server.

A file server has one or more network interface cards (NICs), through which it runs the network. Multiple NICs are needed if the server is working with more than one network architecture.

File Server Functions

In addition to controlling access to file and disk resources on a network, a file server is responsible for security and synchronization on the network. Security measures are designed to ensure that only authorized

---

FILE SERVER PROCESSING A WORKSTATION REQUEST

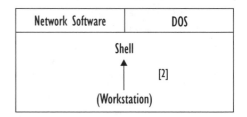

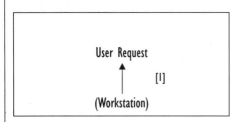

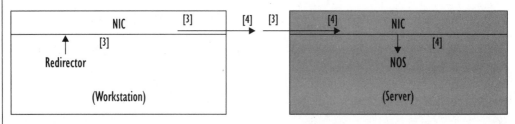

[1] The user at a workstation makes a request, either at the command line or through an application.

[2] This request is intercepted by the network shell running on the workstation to determine whether the request is for DOS or for the network. If it is for DOS, the request is passed on to DOS and the shell's job is finished (for the moment).

[3] Requests passed to the redirector are passed to the NIC, where they are packaged and sent onto the network, using whatever packet format and media-access method are supported by the NIC.

[4] The request is received by an NIC on the server, and it is unpackaged and passed to the network-level protocol being used on the server.

FILE SERVER PROCESSING A WORKSTATION REQUEST (CONTINUED)

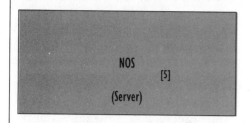

[5] The server processes the request to determine whether the user is allowed to make such a request and, if so, to take whatever steps are necessary to carry it out. This may require sending a response, some data, or even a program to the workstation.

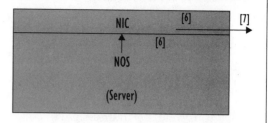

[6] To respond, the server's NOS passes the response to the server's NIC. (The server knows the source of the request and will pass the response to the appropriate NIC in cases where there are multiple NICs in the server.) The NIC packages the response and sends it onto the network.

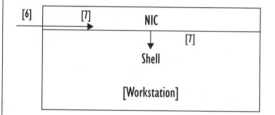

[7] The workstation's NIC catches the response and does whatever unpackaging is necessary to pass the response to the workstation's shell.

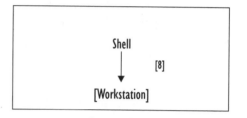

[8] The shell passes the response to the destination application, going through any required protocols or protocol levels to do this.

users can access a particular file. Synchronization measures, such as file or record locking, help ensure that two users cannot do incompatible things to the same file or record simultaneously.

File services are generally implemented in software, and they are a central part of the network operating system (NOS). Depending on the NOS, these services may run on top of the "standard" operating system (for example, DOS, OS/2, or UNIX), rather than being run in a network-based operating system.

File servers for a particular NOS are often named after the NOS. For example, you will see references to an AppleShare or a NetWare server, when the discussion concerns Apple's or Novell's NOSs.

File Server Requirements

An effective file server must be fast, reliable, and provide sufficient storage for all the data and programs users need. The server also needs enough memory to load whatever drivers and other programs are needed to run the network. (Note that other types of servers, such as print or fax servers, may not need heavy-duty hardware.) These needs can be at least partly fulfilled by configuring a file server with the appropriate hardware and software, which are discussed in the following sections.

The system components for the file server should be robust and reliable. The hardware components should be thoroughly tested, and they should have a long mean time before failure (MTBF): several hundred thousands of hours, at least. Some file servers actually have redundant components, so that a backup component can be put into service if the main component fails.

To compensate for all the special requirements for a good file server, you can take a tiny bit of comfort in the fact that you do not need a fancy keyboard or graphics capabilities for your file server. In fact, many file servers have a simple monochrome VGA monitor. If your funds are limited, use the money for RAM (random-access memory) or other server components.

When you are shopping for a file server, it pays to investigate the track record of potential vendors. Also, you should check on the speed and quality of customer support and service. If the server goes down, you will need to get it up and running as quickly as possible.

File Server Processor

A fast 80386 or 80486 processor is essential for a file server. Although some NOSs allow 80286 machines as servers, the greater memory flexibility afforded by the 80386 and 80486 is crucial for bringing the server's performance up to an acceptable level.

Similarly, since the file server will spend a great deal of its time moving data between memory and storage and across the network, you need to make sure the processor can manipulate data in big chunks. For this reason, avoid using the half-width SL processors, which must do their work on "half a bus," as file servers.

Another processor consideration is clock speed, which specifies the number of cycles in a second. Since all actions in ordinary processors take at least a cycle, the shorter this period is, the faster a processor can work.

The original PC had a 4.77 megahertz (MHz) clock speed; high-end machines today have processors with clock speeds of 66 MHz and higher. Again, faster is better only up to a point. Beyond that, other considerations come into play. For example, heat dissipation becomes more difficult, which makes the processor more susceptible to overheating and breakdown.

Also, speeding up the processor does not speed up any other components, so that the processor may need to spend its time waiting. The periods during which the processor waits for other components to catch up are called *wait states*. Each wait state is a cycle on the CPU (central processing unit) clock. In general, a processor with one or more wait states will be slower than a comparable processor without wait states.

File Server Memory

Several megabytes of RAM—4 MB at the very least, preferably 16 MB or more—are also crucial in a file server. Since caching can greatly improve performance, you should use some of the server's memory to create such a cache.

The optimum amount of memory to use for a cache must be determined by empirical means. Larger is better up to a point. When a cache is too small, it will be less likely that the required data is already in the cache area. However, when a cache is too large, the caching software may have too much material to administrate, so that the software spends too much time checking whether something is already in the cache. Different NOSs have different memory requirements.

File Server Storage

A good file server needs at least several hundred megabytes of fast-access hard disk storage. The desirable storage capacity depends on the size of the network. Some experts suggest 50 MB of storage per user as a rough rule of thumb. Smaller allotments are probably fine for most networks, but larger estimates are advisable if future expansion would be a problem. Other considerations regarding hard disks on a file server are discussed later in this article.

Storage becomes even more of an issue with special technologies, such as RAID (redundant array of inexpensive disks), which can provide fault-tolerant storage, at the cost of much greater storage demands.

File Server Power Supply

A properly running server needs a *more than adequate* power supply and a good fan to make sure the working conditions for system components include sufficient power and proper air circulation.

File Server Safety Devices

A UPS (uninterruptible power supply) or SPS (standby power supply), along with surge-suppression and line-conditioning capabilities, are essential for protecting a network from power supply problems. Surge suppression and line conditioning are built into most backup power supplies. See the UPS and SPS articles for a discussion of the criteria and features to consider when selecting and installing these devices.

File Server NICs

Because the file server interacts most heavily with the network, responding to the requests of all the other nodes, it is important to provide this server with the most powerful NIC. Factors that can improve the performance of an NIC include the following:

- Dedicated processor on the NIC, to make the board more capable and more intelligent, thereby enabling the NIC to take over some of the chores that would ordinarily tie up the server's CPU.

- Amount of RAM on the NIC, to serve as a buffer or cache for material moving between the server and the network. The more checking and temporary storage that can be left to the NIC, the less work the server needs to do.

- Size of data bus (8-, 16-, or 32-bit). For the file server, get the widest data bus possible.

- Whether the NIC supports bus mastering, which allows the NIC to seize the system bus when necessary, without bothering the CPU. If so, make sure the bus-mastering schemes used by the computer and the NIC are compatible.

Hard Disks as File Server Components

Since much of a file server's activity involves sending or receiving data files, disk access can easily become a performance bottleneck. Network analyzer and diagnostic programs can provide statistics to help you decide whether the hard disk is being a bottleneck. For example, the statistic for average disk I/O (input/output) operations pending gives a rough idea of how far the hard disk and controller have fallen behind because of demands from the nodes. While there are no hard and fast values, a level of 20 to 25 pending I/O actions is sometimes used as a cut-off point. If there are typically more than this many requests waiting, the hard disk is responsible for at least part of the slow performance.

One way to improve matters is to add a second hard disk controller and associate one or more of the hard drives with this controller. Then the hard disk access can be split over two disks, so that the controllers can work independently of each other.

Once you get a second controller, you can switch from disk mirroring to disk duplexing as a data-protection strategy. The former uses a single controller to write the same data to two different disks; the latter uses separate controllers to do this writing, thereby speeding things up considerably.

With a fast-access hard disk and a suitably sized cache, performance can be improved greatly. A hard disk's speed is reflected in three types of data:

- Access time, which is the average amount of time it takes to move the read/write heads to a specified location and to retrieve the data at that location. The lower the value, the better. Currently, hard disks with average access times of less than 15 milliseconds (msec) are common.

- Seek time, which is the amount of time it takes to move the read heads a track and then to wait until the appropriate sector on the target track is under the read head.

- Transfer rate, which represents the amount of data that can be transferred between the disk and memory in a second. This rate ranges from a few hundred kilobytes per second to 10 megabytes per second for high-end hard disks.

Another hard disk feature that affects server performance is called *sector interleave*. This ratio reflects the ordering of sectors within a track. An interleave of 1:1 indicates that the sectors are arranged consecutively in a track. Other things being equal, this interleave will give the fastest transfer rate. A 2:1 ratio means there is one sector between sectors x and $x+1$; a 3:1 ratio indicates that there are *two* sectors between sectors x and $x+1$, and so on.

For some hard disks it is possible to arrange this ordering—to change the interleave—in order to speed up access to the data in a track. Not all hard disks take kindly to interleave changes. Do not adjust the interleave without making sure your hard disk controller will allow it, and without being fairly sure the new interleave will speed up hard disk performance.

The hard disk controller is another performance factor. The controller mediates between the hard disk and the computer's BIOS and bus. The controller makes the hard disk's read/write heads do what is needed and passes data between the hard disk and BIOS.

Some hard disk controllers have caches of their own to speed up performance; these may or may not conflict with software caches. Even if hardware and software caches do not conflict, adding a software cache may not improve performance significantly. In that case, dropping or decreasing the size of the software cache can free memory that can be put to better use. Determining the optimal cache setup will be an empirical question. Note that 16-bit controllers can transfer twice as much data at a time as 8-bit controllers.

Allocating and Controlling Storage on the File Server

Unfortunately, the storage capacity of a file server is not unlimited. Consequently, you may quickly run into storage problems, in the form of limited available space or extremely large numbers of files.

To avoid storage problems, it is important to estimate storage requirements as accurately as possible when planning the network. As stated, a basic rule of thumb is to allocate about 50 MB of storage per user.

SCSI DRIVES FOR FILE SERVERS

SCSI drives provide the best expansion capability and potential performance for a network file server. You can have up to seven drives on a SCSI host adapter, and the NOS may be able to handle multiple adapters. For example, Novell's Net-Ware allows up to five SCSI host adapters.

The more intelligent SCSI adapters have a connect/disconnect feature that allows the adapter to connect to a drive when that drive needs service, disconnect when done to provide service to another drive, and then reconnect when necessary to the earlier drive. In this way, each drive gets the adapter's attention when the drive needs it, so there is no time lost during waiting.

Once you have your estimate, double it, and use this as a starting point for your storage requirements. If the network is expected to grow, either arrange for the additional storage right away or make sure that the storage capabilities of the server can be expanded.

To keep the file numbers from getting out of hand (and also to limit the amount of storage space being used), you can use the following measures:

- Do not allow users to store games and other "non-network" materials on the server's hard disk. This restriction also helps decrease the likelihood of virus attacks.

- Clean up the directories regularly, removing files that are no longer needed or that have not been used in a long time. The latter files may be allowed to stay unless the storage problems are severe. Before doing file cleaning, warn users so that they can save whichever files they want.

SEE ALSO
Server

Server, Gateway

A gateway server provides a network or an application with access to resources on mainframes or in other remote environments, such as electronic mail (e-mail) services. Gateway servers include software and may also include hardware; and they generally use dedicated machines.

Server, Internet Message

An Internet message server consists of software to provide access to Internet resources over network bridges. This type of server is in contrast to an asynchronous connection transport server, which provides access over telephone lines. This type of server does not require a dedicated machine.

Server, Job

A job server consists of software to manage the tasks queued up in a network or in a special-purpose queue, such as a print or fax queue. Job servers do not require dedicated machines.

Server, LBS (LAN Bridge Server)

In an IBM Token Ring network, a server that consists of software to keep track of and provide access to any bridges connected to the network. An LBS server does not require a dedicated machine.

Server, Mail

A program that manages delivery of mail or other information, upon request. Mail servers are generally implemented at the topmost layer, the applications layer, in the OSI Reference Model. A mail server does not require a dedicated machine.

Server, Modem

A modem server is a type of communication server that provides access to one or more modems. The modem server is a node, which is usually a dedicated machine, on the network. This node has one or more modems attached.

Each other node that wants to use the modem server must have a redirector that can send the communications session and data to the server. Hardware redirectors take up an expansion slot in the workstation, but will work with any communications program. Software redirectors are tied to a specific netware operating system (NOS) and will work only with communications programs that are capable of working with the redirector.

Server, Origin

On the World Wide Web (WWW), an origin server is one on which a particular resource resides or will be created.

Server, Print

A print server provides access to printers and runs the programs needed to create and operate print queues for jobs sent to the printers from the various nodes. Software needed to create a print server is included with the networking software.

Print servers, which may include special hardware, generally support multiple higher-level protocols, and they can usually support multiple printers through serial or parallel connections (or both). For example, the same print server might be able to queue files coming from machines running any of TCP/IP, AppleTalk, or NetWare's IPX/SPX protocols.

In order to use the printer managed by a print server, a workstation must associate an unused port on the workstation with the server's printer, and it must redirect print jobs to this port.

On many networks, file and print services are combined in the same machine, often for simple reasons of economy. There are advantages and disadvantages to this arrangement. The main advantage is that files need not be sent from the file server to the print server machine, and then from there to the printer. The main disadvantage is that even the minimal overhead required to control the print queue and the printing activity will take away CPU (central processing unit) time from other network activity.

Some hardware print servers can also provide terminal services, with the connection to the host through a serial port.

Although it requires frequent CPU access, a print server's effect may not even be noticeable, even if the server is running on the file server.

Print servers sometimes run on dedicated workstations, but this is not allowed under all network operating systems. For example, Novell's NetWare 2.x and 3.x support print

servers on dedicated workstations, but NetWare 4.x does not. Instead, the print server under NetWare 4.x must be run on either the file server or an application server.

PRINT SERVER TIPS

When you're picking a printer to use with a print server, if at all possible, use a fast printer, since there may be several people waiting for their printouts. Keep in mind, however, that your print server must be able to feed the fast printer.

Also, if you have more than a few nodes that might use print services, make sure the printer's duty cycle can handle the load. Don't try to print 30,000 pages a month on a printer with a 3000 copy duty cycle.

On a peer-to-peer network, try to connect the printer to a workstation that is seldom used heavily, because the extra printing work may slow down the workstation's performance.

Server, Proxy

A proxy server is a program that serves as an intermediary between a client and a server. The proxy is a server from the user's point of view, but is a client as far as the target server is concerned.

Proxy servers are used in situations where filtering or shielding is desirable—for example, if a client computer is inside a firewall (protective program) and wants to communicate with a server outside the firewall. In such a situation, the client's request is passed to the proxy server, which communicates with the other side of the firewall. By forcing traffic to go through the proxy server, the firewall software has an easier time filtering.

Once the target server has responded, the proxy server checks the reply and does any required filtering. Then the proxy server passes the reply to the client. As far as the client is concerned, the interaction took place directly between the client and target server.

Server Session Socket (SSS)

SEE

SSS (Server Session Socket)

Server, SQL (Structured Query Language)

An SQL server functions as a database server for systems that use the SQL database manipulation language developed by IBM for use on its mainframes, and then ported to minicomputers and PCs. SQL server software does not require a dedicated machine.

SQL Server is also the name of a relational database management system (RDBMS) developed by Sybase, Inc. This database system is available for several PC and minicomputer platforms, from Sybase as well as from third-party vendors. For example, Microsoft offers SQL Server for OS/2.

Server, Tape

A tape server consists of software to provide capabilities for backing up files to, and restoring them from a tape drive. This type of server may also include archiving capabilities to identify files that have not been used for a specified amount of time and that might therefore be backed up to a removable

medium. A tape server does not require a dedicated machine.

Server, TENNIS (Typical Example of a Needlessly Named Interface Standard)

A component whose job is to prevent services from being captured by the network, thereby leading to a net fault. The TENNIS server monitor keeps track of the number of consecutive net faults. If this number exceeds a predefined limit, the local service is temporarily discontinued, and service access goes to the next component.

Server, Terminal

A terminal server consists of software to provide a transparent connection between a terminal and one or more host computers. At the host end, this connection is through an asynchronous (serial) port. Because the connection is to be transparent, the host needs a separate asynchronous port for each terminal.

To avoid this hardware glut, the host's interface to the terminals may be equipped with a packet assembler/disassembler (PAD). This device provides multiplexing capabilities, so that multiple terminals can be processed through a single input line. Each terminal is associated with a unique virtual circuit (VC), and the PAD uses the VC identity to keep the input from the terminals separate.

A terminal server may provide multiple terminals with access to a host, or it may provide terminals with the ability to switch between sessions on different host machines.

Since each terminal can have settings and features, the PAD must keep a separate configuration file for each VC. The parameter values for terminals used in this way are defined in the CCITT X.3 standard.

Service

A service is a task or operation that is made available through an application or systems program. Operating systems (such as DOS), network operating systems (such as Novell's NetWare), and applications can provide services.

The services that can be provided are limited only by the ability of users and developers to think up new ones. Nevertheless, it is possible to distinguish different classes of service. For example, network services include file services (which control file access and storage), print services, communication services, fax services, archive services, and backup service packages.

A good network operating system (NOS) can provide the entire range of services, either as part of the NOS core or in the form of add-on modules, libraries, or APIs (Application Program Interfaces). The move currently is toward providing highly modular service packages.

According to some analysts, the ultimate outcome will be to make these services independent of particular NOSs, so that developers and possibly even users can create customized service packages.

The concepts of protocol and service are often found together. Specifically, for a given service, there is likely to be a protocol. Standards committees generally create separate specifications for services and protocols.

Service Access Point (SAP)

SEE

SAP (Service Access Point)

Service Advertising Protocol (SAP)

SEE

SAP (Service Advertising Protocol)

Service Data Unit (SDU)

SEE

SDU (Service Data Unit)

Service Point

In IBM's NMA, software through which a non-IBM device or a network can communicate with the NMA network manager. NetView is IBM's NMA management program, and NetView/PC is a service point.

SEE ALSO

NMA (Network Management Architecture)

Service Provider

A service provider, also known as an access provider, is a company or individual that provides telephone access to a network or to another service—for example, to the Internet. For either a flat monthly fee or for an hourly charge, an Internet access provider (an IAP) will provide a telephone number and server through which subscribers can get onto the Internet.

a b c d e f g h i j k l m n o p q r **s** t u v w x y z

Service providers differ in such features as:

- The modem speeds they can handle. Commonly, the issue is whether the provider can handle 28.8 kbps access; higher speeds are possible, as are ISDN connections.

- Whether the access number is a local or 800 number, or whether the access may be a toll call (which would add extra costs).

- The access protocols supported. Some providers let users access the server using ordinary communications software, and then provide network access protocols through the server; other providers support more direct protocols such as SLIP (Serial line Internet Protocol) or PPP (Point-to-Point Protocol).

- The range of Internet usage capabilities supported. At one extreme, providers may support only electronic mail, or e-mail, services. At the other extreme are providers that support any allowable type of access and usage.

- Cost—both startup and monthly costs.

Session

In networking, a logical connection between two nodes, generally a workstation and a server. This connection remains in effect until the task that necessitated the session is completed or some other constraint forces an end to the connection. Depending on the network architectures involved, any of

several session layer protocols may be used to establish, maintain, and break a connection.

Session ID (Session Identifier)

In an AppleTalk network, a unique number associated with each session. The ID is used to identify the session and to distinguish it from other sessions.

SFT (System Fault Tolerance)

Novell's strategy for protecting network data. Novell's NetWare supports three levels of SFT.

Level 1 includes Hot Fix, read-after-write verify, and duplicate directory entry tables (DETs). With the Hot Fix feature, NetWare sets aside a certain amount of the available disk space as a reserved storage area. If a program tries to write data to a bad sector, the Hot Fix feature automatically redirects the output to the special storage area. Hot Fix mode is the default in NetWare. In read-after-write verify, NetWare compares the written material on disk with the material in memory before reusing the memory. The DETs contain information about the server's files and directories, so duplicating them ensures that this important information is available, even if one table becomes corrupted.

Level 2 includes disk mirroring or duplexing. In disk mirroring, data is written to two different hard disks, but over the same channel. Mirroring duplicates data in case one hard disk fails, but does not provide any protection if the hard disk channel fails. Disk duplexing uses two separate channels to write the identical data to two disks. Duplexing thus provides security against either hard disk or disk channel failure.

Level 3 uses duplicate servers, so that all transactions are recorded on both servers. If one server fails, the other will have an identical state, and will, therefore, be able to take over.

Shareable

A shareable file, device, or process is available to multiple users and can be used simultaneously if requested.

Shared Processing

A network configuration in which a single server processes tasks for multiple stations, all of which can communicate with the server. The nodes must share the computing power of the central processor, so the busier the network, the slower tasks will get done.

COMPARE
Distributed Processing

Shell, Network

A general term for networking software that runs on a network workstation and gives the workstation the ability to communicate with the server.

SEE ALSO
DOS Requester; NOS (Network Operating System)

Shield

In coaxial and twisted-pair cabling, a sheath, generally of foil or braided metal, wrapped around a conductor wire and dielectric (insulator). The shield helps to prevent external signals and noise from interfering with the signal being transmitted through the cable.

SEE ALSO
Cable, Coaxial ; Cable, Twisted-Pair

Shielded Distributed Data Interface (SDDI)

SEE
SDDI (Shielded Distributed Data Interface)

Short

In a cable, a condition in which excess current flows between two wires, such as the two wires in a pair, because of an abnormally low resistance between the two wires.

Shortest Path First (SPF)

SEE
SPF (Shortest Path First)

Sideband

A sideband is a frequency band either just above or just below the frequency for the carrier signal used in the modulation process that converts data into analog signals in a modem. The figure "Sidebands lie on either side of a carrier frequency" shows this arrangement.

Since the lower and upper sidebands are symmetrical, one of these is sometimes used either as an additional channel or for diagnostic and management signaling.

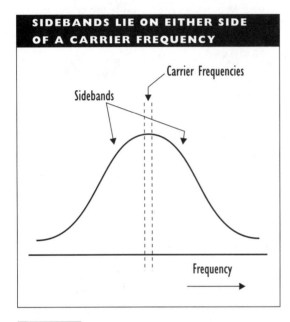

SIDEBANDS LIE ON EITHER SIDE OF A CARRIER FREQUENCY

Signal

An electrical signal takes the form of a change in voltage or current over time. The signal is described by the levels, or amplitudes, that the voltage or current reaches, and by the pattern with which this level changes over time.

The following types of information about amplitudes are distinguished when describing electrical signals:

Peak: The highest level reached by a signal.

Peak-to-peak: The difference between the highest and lowest levels reached by a signal.

Average: A simple arithmetic average of the absolute magnitude of signal levels, without taking positive or negative charge into account.

RMS (root mean square): A weighted measure of amplitude. This is the value actually used when describing a power supply. For example, in the United States, voltage coming out of the wall outlet is about 117 volts RMS, alternating at 60 times a second (at 60 hertz). The peak amplitude for our power supply is actually 165 volts.

Peak values represent single values, whereas average values summarize amplitudes over time.

The signal pattern is described as a waveform that represents level over time. Two types of waveforms are used most commonly in networking contexts:

- **Sine:** The waveform of a "clean" AC signal direct from a reliable power company. Your computer's power supply likes to see such a signal.

- **Square:** The waveform of a "perfectly encoded" digital bit. Such an ideal waveform is produced with instantaneous voltage or current changes. Ideally, your network interface card or a transceiver sends such a signal along the network.

The figure "Common waveforms for electrical signals in networks" illustrates these waveforms.

Different electrical properties are associated with the different waveforms. For example, the average and RMS amplitudes for a square wave are equal to the peak; the average amplitude for a sine wave is less than two-thirds that of the peak (0.637 × peak), and the RMS is 0.707 × peak.

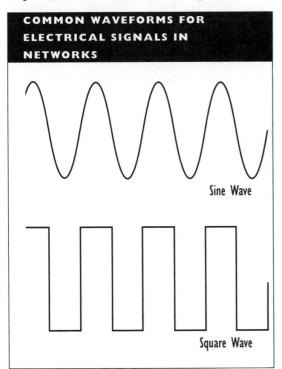

COMMON WAVEFORMS FOR ELECTRICAL SIGNALS IN NETWORKS

Sine Wave

Square Wave

In networking, electrical signals are used in two contexts:

- **Power supply:** The signal that provides electrical power for a network component. Whatever is providing this signal should be providing a sine wave, *not* a square wave.

- **Information transmission:** This is the signal that encodes the data or instructions being transmitted. For digital transmissions, the closer this waveform is to a square wave, the better.

For a digital signal, the rise time (time required for the signal to go from 10 to 90 percent of peak strength) determines the shape of the signal. A square wave has a rise time of 0 seconds; in actual signals, the waveform will be more trapezoidal. (The downside counterpart to rise time is fall time.)

In real-world situations, signals come with noise attached. This noise distorts and weakens the signal, and may result in information loss, transmission errors, and electrical malfunction.

Noise also makes the task of signal amplification, or strengthening, more complicated. You cannot just amplify a weakened signal, because this will amplify the noise as well.

Signal, Analog

An analog signal's values are continuous over time. These values represent a level on some variable, such as voltage or intensity, and they range between a minimum and a maximum value. This is in contrast to a

a
b
c
d
e
f
g
h
i
j
k
l
m
n
o
p
q
r
s
t
u
v
w
x
y
z

digital signal, which takes only a limited number (usually, two) of discrete values.

An analog signal can be periodic or aperiodic. Periodic signals repeat in a regular pattern; aperiodic signals do not. The repetition behavior of a periodic signal is measured in cycles per second, or hertz (Hz).

For example, a 50 Hz signal repeats its pattern 50 times a second. Each repetition is a cycle, and consists of a continuous process in which the signal's value changes continuously from a peak to a trough, and back to the peak. The figure "Features of a periodic signal" illustrates this type of signal.

The amplitude (volume), frequency (pitch), and phase (starting time) for an analog signal can each be varied.

Signal, Digital

A digital signal's possible levels are represented by discrete values within a limited range. These values are created using sequences of 0 and 1 values. The number of possible values that can be represented depends on the number of bits that are allocated to represent a single value. For example, using eight bits, 256 possible values can be represented.

A digital signal must distinguish between two possible values: 0 and 1. At the electrical level, these values are generally represented as different voltage levels. For example, a 1 might be represented by +5 volts and 0 by zero volts; or a 1 might be represented as *either* +5 or −5 volts, with 0 represented as 0 volts. Digital signals are

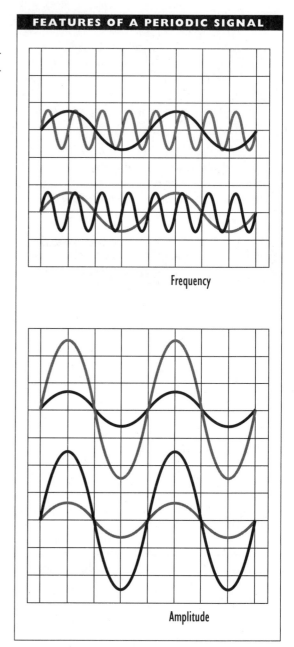

FEATURES OF A PERIODIC SIGNAL

Frequency

Amplitude

FEATURES OF A PERIODIC SIGNAL

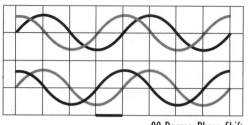

90-Degree Phase Shift

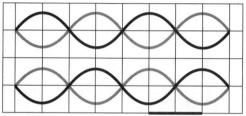

180-Degree Phase Shift

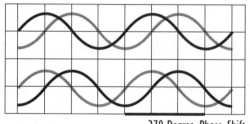

270-Degree Phase Shift

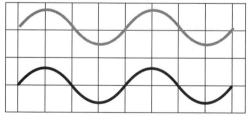

360-Degree Phase Shift (Equivalent to 0-Degree Shift)

sent as square waves, as illustrated in the figure "Square wave patterns representing digital values."

SQUARE WAVE PATTERNS REPRESENTING DIGITAL VALUES

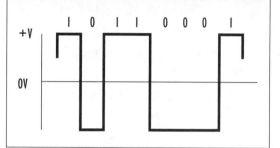

Digital signals are somewhat easier to deal with than analog signals. Because of this, digital circuitry is simpler and cheaper. For various reasons, however, digital circuitry will fail much more abruptly.

SEE ALSO

Encoding, Signal

Signal, Jam

A jam signal is transmitted by an Ethernet node to indicate that there has been a collision on the network. Collisions are usually caused by two nodes trying to send packets at the same time.

The jam signal consists of a 32- or 48-bit transmission whose contents are unspecified except that the contents cannot be identical to the cyclical redundancy check (CRC) value of the partial packet sent prior to the collision.

Each node involved sends a jam signal, and then waits a random amount of time before trying to access the network again.

a b c d e f g h i j k l m n o p q r **s** t u v w x y z

▼ Signal Quality Error (SQE)

SEE

SQE (Signal Quality Error)

▼ Signal-to-Crosstalk Ratio (SCR)

SEE

SCR (Signal-to-Crosstalk Ratio)

▼ Signal-to-Noise Ratio (SNR)

SEE

SNR (Signal-to-Noise Ratio)

▼ Simplified Access Control (SAC)

SEE

SAC (Simplified Access Control)

▼ Simplex

A communications mode in which information can travel in only one direction, as, for example, with a tickertape machine. The receiver may be able to send control and error signals, but no data, to the sender.

COMPARE

Full-Duplex; Half-Duplex

▼ Single-Attachment Concentrator (SAC)

SEE

SAC (Single-Attachment Concentrator)

▼ Single-Attachment Station (SAS)

SEE

SAS (Single-Attachment Station)

▼ Single Large Expensive Disk (SLED)

SEE

SLED (Single Large Expensive Disk)

▼ Single-Mode Fiber

Optical fiber designed to allow just a single path of light through the core. The core for a single-mode fiber is extremely thin—less than 10 microns (millionths of a meter)—which makes the signal extremely clean.

SEE ALSO

Cable, Fiber-Optic

▼ Single Sign On

SEE

SSO (Single Sign On)

▼ Single-Step Multimode Fiber

Optical fiber with a core wide enough to allow multiple light paths (modes) through at a time. Unlike graded-index multimode fiber, single-step fiber has only a single layer of cladding, so that there is an abrupt difference in refractive index between fiber core and cladding.

SEE ALSO

Cable, Fiber-Optic

▼ Skin Effect

When transmitting data at a fast rate over twisted-pair wire, the current tends to flow mostly on the outside surface of the wire. This greatly decreases the cross-section of the wire being used for moving electrons, and thereby *increases* resistance. This, in turn, increases signal attenuation, or loss.

Sky Wave

In radio wave transmissions, a wave that can be transmitted over a great distance before being reflected back to earth. Sky waves, also known as *ionospheric waves,* take advantage of the fact that the ionosphere reflects high-frequency waves in a frequency-dependent manner. The great transmission distances that can be achieved must often use unreliable paths, however.

SLED (Single Large Expensive Disk)

A storage strategy that uses a single, high-capacity disk as the sole storage location. This is the most common strategy, and it is in contrast to the more fault-tolerant RAID (redundant array of inexpensive disks) strategy.

SLIP (Serial Line Internet Protocol)

SEE

Protocol, SLIP (Serial Line Internet Protocol)

Slots

Slots are part of a media-access method used with some older ring topologies. When using this access method, a ring is divided into a number of fixed-size slots, which circulate around the ring. A slot can be empty or in use. This status is determined by the value of a control bit. When an empty slot passes a node in the ring, the node can access the network by setting the slot's control bit and putting a packet (which contains data and addressing and error checking information) into the slot for transmission.

An advantage of slotted rings is that multiple packets can be transmitted at the same time. A disadvantage is the potential for hogging, in which a particular node uses every empty slot that passes by, thereby preventing nodes downstream from gaining access to the network.

Slotted rings have fallen into disuse as token passing and other access methods have become more popular.

BROADER CATEGORY
Media-Access Method

COMPARE
CSMA/CA; CSMA/CD; Demand Priority; Polling; Token Passing

Slotted Ring

A ring topology that uses slots as the media-access method. Slotted Ring networks, such as the Cambridge Ring, were popular in the 1970s, but have largely been replaced by Token Ring networks.

Slot Time

In an Ethernet-based architecture, the maximum time that can elapse between the first and last node's receipt of a packet. To ensure that a node can tell whether the packet it transmitted has collided with another packet, a packet must be longer than the number of bits that can be transmitted in the slot time. For Ethernet networks, this is about half a microsecond, which is long enough to transmit at least 512 bits.

a b c d e f g h i j k l m n o p q r **s** t u v w x y z

SLS (Secondary Link Station)

In environments that use IBM's SDLC (Synchronous Data Link Control) protocol, a secondary link station (or just a *secondary*) is a node that responds to communications initiated by a primary link station (PLS). In SDLC, secondaries cannot initiate communications.

SM (Standby Monitor)

In a Token Ring network, a node that is ready to take over as active monitor (AM)—that is, as the dispenser of the token and de facto network manager—in case the AM fails to do its work in a timely and correct manner. A Token Ring network may have several SMs.

SEE ALSO
Token Ring

SMAE (Systems Management Application Entity)

In the OSI network management model, the component that implements the network management services and activities at the application level in a node.

SEE ALSO
Network Management

Small Computer System Interface (SCSI)

SEE
SCSI (Small Computer System Interface)

SMAP (Systems Management Application Process)

In the OSI network management model, the software that implements the network-management capabilities in a single node, which may be an ordinary station, a router, a bridge, a front-end processor (FEP), or another type of node.

SEE
Network Management

SMASE (Systems Management Application Service Element)

In the OSI network management model, the component that does the work for a systems management application entity (SMAE).

SEE
Network Management

SMDS (Switched Multimegabit Data Service)

SMDS is a connectionless, high-speed, broadband, packet-switched, wide-area network (WAN) service. This service transmits data over public lines at rates between 1.544 and 44.736 megabits per second (mbps), which is much faster than X.25. SMDS can also run over the physical wiring for a metropolitan-area network (MAN). A special version of SMDS—dubbed "skinny SMDS"—has been developed. This variant operates at 56 or 64 kbps.

Access to the network is over DS1 or DS3 lines. The service conforms to IEEE 802.6 standards. Full SMDS services will be made available gradually, over a several-year period.

SMF (Systems Management Function)

In the OSI network management model, any one of a baker's dozen of services available for managing particular network domains.

SEE ALSO
Network Management

SMFA (Systems Management Functional Area)

A term for any one of the five major domains that make up the OSI network management model: accounting management, configuration management, fault management, performance management, and security management.

SEE ALSO
Network Management

SMI (Structure of Management Information)

One of the components in the IP (Internet Protocol) network management model. The SMI specifies how information about managed objects is to be represented. The representation uses a restricted version of the ISO's Abstract Syntax Notation One (ASN.1) system.

SEE ALSO
Network Management

SMS (Storage Management Services)

In Novell's NetWare, SMS is a collection of services for managing data storage and retrieval. These services are provided in a collection of modules and are independent of operating systems and hardware. The following SMS modules are provided:

- SBACKUP, for doing backup and restore operations

- SMDR (Storage Management Data Requester), for passing commands and information between the backup program and TSAs (target service agents)

- Storage device interface, for passing information between SBACKUP and the actual storage devices

- Device drivers, for controlling the actual behavior of the storage or other devices

- Server, database, and workstation TSAs (target service agents) for passing requests, commands, and data between SBACKUP and various other components on the network

- Workstation Manager, for identifying and keeping track of the stations waiting to be backed up

SMS is also an architecture that third-party backup package vendors can use to enable their backup software to work on a NetWare network.

SMT (Station Management)

In the FDDI network architecture, the component concerned with ensuring that various network elements are operating correctly. The three parts to SMT are frame services, connection management, and ring management.

a b c d e f g h i j k l m n o p q r **s** t u v w x y z

SEE ALSO

FDDI (Fiber Distributed Data Interface)

▼

SNA (Systems Network Architecture)

SNA is an all-encompassing architecture designed to enable any IBM machine to communicate with any other. In particular, SNA was developed to enable various machines to communicate with IBM's mainframes. Although SNA was originally introduced in 1974, various capabilities and components have been added over the years.

SNA is both complex and powerful. It can be used to connect machines or networks with very different architectures, provided that both support SNA. It can also be used to pass data between two non-SNA networks.

Various offshoots of SNA (for example, SAA) define standards for application programs, to ensure an interface that can be used within an SNA environment.

SNA was originally released for use in the centralized, master-slave world surrounding IBM mainframes. These machines were used to communicate with terminals (usually dumb terminals), which requested services and resources from the host. All decision making and processing were to be done by the host; all SNA needed to do was enable any type of terminal, controller, printer, or other device to talk to the host. Any interdevice communication would go through the host.

Then came PCs, which are capable of talking to each other directly. In order to enable PCs to communicate with each other without going through the host, IBM added the APPC (Advanced Program-to-Program Communications) capability.

APPC

APPC allows direct communication between certain types of devices (most notably, PCs). To deal with these devices in the SNA hierarchy, a physical unit (type 2.1) and a logical unit (type 6.2) were added. Essentially, a logical unit (LU) is an access point (a logical port) for a device or an application. A physical unit (PU) is a device and software for controlling one or more LUs. PUs and LUs are described in greater detail later in this article.

APPC (or, more precisely, LU 6.2) is a powerful concept because it provides a flexible way to integrate PC networking capabilities with mainframe networking. Allowing direct LU-to-LU connections makes it possible, for example, for two applications *on the same machine* to communicate with each other. This capability also makes it easier to implement client/server computing, in which one part of an application runs on a workstation (the client) and the other part runs on the server.

APPC is actually network-independent, so it can be implemented on non-SNA networks. This independence makes APPC an ideal way to connect dissimilar networks.

SNA as a Layered Architecture

As a layered architecture, SNA divides the world into five main functional layers. It also includes two additional layers as extensions to make comparisons with the OSI Reference Model easier.

The figure "Layers defined for IBM's SNA environment" shows the seven-layer, extended SNA architecture.

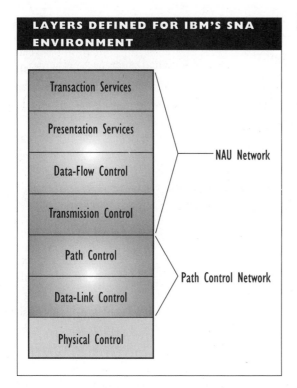

LAYERS DEFINED FOR IBM'S SNA ENVIRONMENT

- Transaction Services
- Presentation Services
- Data-Flow Control — NAU Network
- Transmission Control
- Path Control
- Data-Link Control — Path Control Network
- Physical Control

Physical Control Layer

The physical interface and medium, as well as the electrical properties of the connection, are specified at the lowest layer, physical control, which is *not defined as part of SNA*.

SNA can support both serial and parallel interfaces, and can use coaxial or fiber-optic cable and, in certain places, twisted-pair cable. For example, hosts (mainframes) and front-end processors (FEPs) generally use a parallel interface; terminals or PCs generally use a serial interface. Similarly, the connection between a host and a FEP uses either coaxial or fiber-optic cable, but a PC in a network may be connected to a multistation access unit (MAU) using twisted-pair cable.

Data-Link Control Layer

The lowest layer specified in SNA is the data-link control layer. This layer is responsible for reliable transmission of data across the physical connection. Various protocols are supported at this level, including the following:

- SDLC (Synchronous Data Link Control), arguably the most commonly used protocol for this layer

- X.25, for packet-switched networks and for remote connections

- BSC (Bisynchronous Communications), for older IBM hardware

- LLC (Logical-Link Control) sublayer protocol, defined for token ring and other local-area networks (LANs) in IEEE 802.2

Path Control Layer

Software at the path control layer creates logical connections between the components associated with specific addresses (NAUs, which are described below). This layer consists of three sublayers:

- Transmission group control, which is responsible for identifying and managing all the links between two nodes

- Explicit route control, which performs the actual routing (finds a route between the two nodes in a connection)

- Virtual route control, which manages the logical connection (the virtual route) between connected nodes

a b c d e f g h i j k l m n o p q r **s** t u v w x y z

Each of the links between nodes can be used as a channel for transmission, and all the links between the same two nodes form a transmission group. Transmission groups make it possible to allocate bandwidth (by assigning more channels to the group) and also to balance the transmission load (by allocating transmissions evenly to unused channels in a group).

Transmission Control Layer

The transmission control layer is for managing (establishing, maintaining, and terminating) sessions between nodes. The transmission control layer is responsible for logical routing. (The path control layer is responsible for physical routing.) Among other things, this layer is responsible for making sure that correct transmissions arrive at their destinations and that they do so in the correct order.

The automatic (and user-transparent) encryption and decryption of data is performed at the transmission control layer.

Data-Flow Control

The data-flow control layer defines the general features of the connection (as opposed to the data-link control layer, which defines the specific details of the data transmission). For example, tasks such as the following are handled at this layer:

- A session is defined as half- or full-duplex.

- Mechanisms for enabling recovery from lost or erroneous data are provided.

- Related data is grouped into units.

- Rules for acknowledging packets are specified (such as whether to acknowledge each packet).

- Data transmission may be halted temporarily and then restarted.

Presentation Services Layer

The presentation services layer is responsible for making sure data reaches its destination in an appropriate form. This may require the following:

- Format conversions, such as between ASCII and EBCDIC

- Formatting, such as to display data on a screen

- Data compression and decompression

Transaction Services Layer

The transaction services layer is the layer at which applications communicate with each other, and at which sessions are requested and initiated. Services provided at this layer include the following:

- Distributed data management (DDM), which enables, for example, a node to use a remote database

- Exchange of formatted or unformatted documents using IBM's DCA (Document Content Architecture) and DIA (Document Interchange Architecture)

- Store-and-forward capabilities, for e-mail or other message handling systems, using SNA Distribution Services (SNADS)

Layer Groupings

The middle five layers, which are the main SNA layers, can be grouped into two broad categories, each of which is under the control of a different program:

- Path-control network, which consists of layers 2 and 3 (data-link and path control), and is responsible for moving data through the network. These functions are implemented by the ACF/NCP (Advanced Communications Function/Network Control Program), which generally runs on the SNA network's FEP. By relieving the host of these tasks, the NCP helps improve the network's efficiency.

- NAU network, which provides the functions required to control and manage a network. These functions are implemented by the ACF/VTAM (ACF/Virtual Telecommunications Access Method), which generally runs on the host computer.

SNA Components

SNA has an unusual metaphysics in that some components have both physical and logical status. The objects in an SNA world are nodes, which are distinguished as NAUs.

SNA was created to operate in a hierarchical network, in which the mainframe was at the top of the hierarchy, with terminals at the bottom. Three types of nodes are distinguished in SNA networks:

Host: This is the mainframe running the network (through the ACF/VTAM software). Each host is in charge of a domain, which consists of one or more subareas.

Communications controller: This is an FEP, running the NCP program and the path-control network for the host.

Peripheral: These are the establishment and cluster controllers and the terminals.

An NAU is any entity that can be assigned a network address. Three categories of NAU are distinguished. (Remember, SNA network components may be both hardware and software.)

Physical Units (PUs)

PUs are actual physical devices and also the software that runs these devices. A PU is a node in a network, and also the software that manages the node. As a node, a PU is a connection point to a network, and it can support one or more LUs. The five types of PUs are listed in the table "Physical Unit Types." Interestingly, these are numbered 1, 2.0, 2.1, 4, and 5.

Logical Units (LUs)

LUs are the access points for end-user programs (known as SNA users). SNA users get access to network services through an LU. Essentially, an LU is a logical port, rather than a physical one. An LU is associated with a particular application and, in ordinary usage, is generally equated with this application or with the end-user.

a
b
c
d
e
f
g
h
i
j
k
l
m
n
o
p
q
r
s
t
u
v
w
x
y
z

PHYSICAL UNIT TYPES	
PU TYPE	**DESCRIPTION**
1	A peripheral node. A now obsolete type that represents certain low-end controllers and terminals.
2.0	A peripheral node. An establishment (IBM 3174) or cluster (3274) controller for 3270 terminals. This node can communicate only with a communications controller, or front-end processor, which is a type 4 PU. The node needs the SSCP to establish a session between two LUs.
2.1	A peripheral node. In addition to all the capabilities of a type 2.0 PU, a type 2.1 PU can communicate with another type 2.1 PU and can support one or more type 6.2 LUs. This software can run in any type of computer, including minicomputers or PCs.
4	A subarea node. A communications controller that serves as a front-end processor for a host computer. A type 4 PU can communicate with all other PU types, including other type 4 PUs. Type 4 PUs include IBM 37xx series machines running ACF/NCP.
5	A host processor, usually, a mainframe such as an IBM 370 or 390, running ACF/VTAM as an access method program, and including an SSCP to control the network activity.

In order to make the most effective use of a connection between LUs, several subsystems have been developed, each with its own protocols:

- TSO (time sharing option), which helps make it easier to provide program development services

- CICS (customer information control system), which supports transaction-processing functions

- IMS (information management system), which helps make it easier to access and use databases

- CMS (conversational monitor system), which helps make interactive sessions easier to manage

Often, you will see these subsystems qualified with virtual storage (VS) in their designation, as in *CMS/VS*.

The LU types are listed in the table "Logical Unit Types." Keep in mind that an LU is both the connection and the software controlling the connection; that is, the LU provides the capabilities required to communicate through the specified connection.

The first four LU types (0 through 3) all involve asymmetrical (master-slave) relationships between a program and the device being controlled. Type 4 LUs may be either program-to-program or program-to-device, and they may use either a master/slave or a peer-to-peer relationship. Type 6.x LUs are generally program-to-program and peer-to-peer.

Within SNA, a single PU can support multiple LUs. One consequence of this is that a terminal (or a PC node) may be able to support multiple applications at the same time, simply by having each application associated with a different LU.

LOGICAL UNIT TYPES

LU TYPE	DESCRIPTION
0	User-defined LU. Can be used to support terminals or other devices that are not covered in other types.
1	Printers that support SCS (SNA character string) mode. This is true of just about all printers.
2	Terminals that support the 3270 data stream; for example, IBM models 3278 and 3279.
3	Printers that do not support SCS mode, but that do support data stream compatibility mode (support the 3270 data stream).
4	Peer-to-peer communications using SCS mode; for example, between terminals, or between a terminal and a printer that supports SCS.
6.0	Program-to-program communication between applications (such as database programs) that both use CICS. The applications may be running on the same machine.
6.1	Program-to-program communications between applications running CICS/VS and/or IMS/VS.
6.2	General-purpose program-to-program communication. Uses SNA's general data stream for communications. Such communication does not require a host. LU 6.2 allows communication between two type 2.1 PUs, two type 5 PUs, or between a type 2.1 and a type 5 PU.
7	Communications between a host and a terminal that supports SCS or 5250 data stream.

A session between two NAUs generally involves a primary and a secondary NAU, which have somewhat different functions. Even if the relationship is peer-to-peer, there is a primary and a secondary NAU. In that case, the primary NAU is the one that initiates the communication.

System Service Control Points (SSCPs)

SSCPs provide the services needed to manage an entire network or part of one. An SSCP sits on the host computer along with the VTAM control program, and it controls a domain (a collection of PUs and LUs). The SSCP provides access to services, generally through a PU that is running the NCP. As the control program, the SSCP manages

sessions between LUs as well as managing the PUs.

Component Relationships

The figure "Relationship among SNA components" shows how the various types of SNA components can be related.

All SNA networks require an SSCP. This runs on a type 5 PU, along with the VTAM program. The SSCP on the host machine can load and use an NCP program running on a type 4 PU (an FEP).

The FEP may control other PUs, each of which may control one or more LUs. The LUs communicate with each other through sessions (logical and physical paths), which are set up by the SSCP or possibly by the

a
b
c
d
e
f
g
h
i
j
k
l
m
n
o
p
q
r
s
t
u
v
w
x
y
z

RELATIONSHIP AMONG SNA COMPONENTS

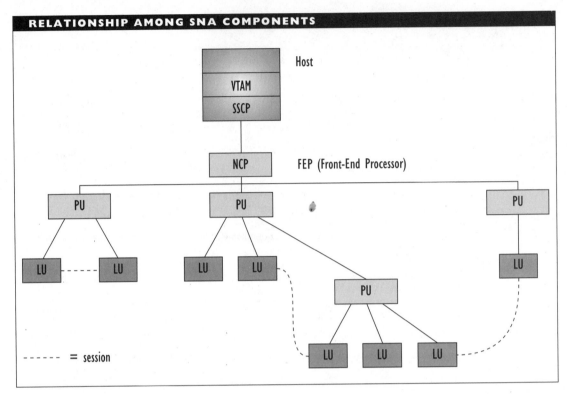

LUs themselves, provided these are type 6.*x* LUs.

Thus, an end-user running a program might attach to an LU at a terminal or through a terminal-emulation program. This LU will be associated with a PU that connects, directly or through intermediate steps, to an FEP and then to the host.

In the case of type 6.*x* LUs—for example, PCs in a Token Ring LAN—the connection need not involve either an FEP or a host.

Links between Devices

SNA supports both local and remote links, depending on how far apart the communicating components are located. Several types of links are commonly used in SNA networks:

Data channels: Very high-speed links (100 megabits per second or so), which are commonly used between a host and a communication controller or between two hosts. The high bandwidth is achieved by using multiple lower-speed data paths in a single channel. Data channels generally use optical fiber.

SDLC (Synchronous Data Link Control): This protocol can be used for communications between a host and nodes or between two nodes over telephone lines. SNA also supports the ISO's HDLC (High-level Data Link Control) protocol, which was adapted from SDLC.

BSC (Binary Synchronous Communications): An obsolescent protocol that is supported because some older IBM hardware uses it.

X.25: This protocol is supported for networks that use packet-switching.

Token Ring: PCs can be connected to a host through a Token Ring network. The network's MAU will be connected to the host (or to an FEP).

One way for a PC to communicate with a mainframe or a minicomputer in SNA is by emulating a particular type of terminal. For example, to communicate with an AS/400 midrange computer, a PC would need to emulate either a 5250 or a 3270 terminal; to communicate with a 3090 mainframe, the PC needs to emulate a 3270 terminal.

SNA Sessions

In SNA, a session is a temporary logical (and physical) link between two NAUs, established for the purpose of communication. The nature of the session and the kinds of information transferred depend on the type of nodes involved. SNA includes sessions for applications and also sessions for network management.

The table "SNA Network Sessions" shows the types of sessions that are allowed in an SNA network. Note that the CP-CP type session is allowed only in networks that use the APPN (Advanced Peer-to-Peer Networking) extension to SNA.

This extension allows PUs or LUs to communicate directly, without needing the help of an SSCP on a host machine. Nodes in an APPN-compatible network each serve as their own control points.

Type 6.2 LU NAUs were introduced with APPN, and these have proven extremely efficient and flexible. Sessions involving type 6.2 LUs are more efficient because they need to transfer less data in a session, and because both the participants in the session can do error recovery.

LU 6.2 sessions are more flexible because even dissimilar systems can communicate. As a result, numerous vendors have added support for LU 6.2 sessions in their products.

Network Management

IBM's most recent and effective network management tool for SNA networks is NetView. This program monitors an SNA network in four areas:

Performance/Accounting: Parameters such as network response times and delays, and resource availability.

Configuration: NetView keeps a record of the physical components on the network and of the logical relationships among these.

Change: NetView can keep track of any type of change to the network, such as the addition or removal of a hardware or a software item.

Problem: NetView detects and deals with any problems that arise on the network. This management task is carried out in five phases: determination,

SNA NETWORK SESSIONS	
SESSION TYPE	**DESCRIPTION**
LU-LU	Communication is between two LUs or between a type 2 LU and a host application. LU-LU sessions are established, maintained, and terminated by the SSCP, unless type 6.*x* LUs are involved.
PU-PU	Communication is between two PUs. A PU-PU session enables one PU to notify another of an event or problem on the network.
SSCP-LU	Communication is between a host (running the SSCP) and a type 2 LU (a terminal). A SSCP-LU session generally precedes or follows the activation of an LU-LU session by the SSCP.
SSCP-PU	Communication is between a host (running the SSCP) and a type 2.0 PU (an establishment controller). A SSCP-PU session generally precedes or follows the establishment of an SSCP-LU session.
SSCP-SSCP	Communication is between two hosts (both running SSCP), and is generally for the purpose of establishing a session across domains, for example, across networks.
CP-CP	Control point to control point communications. Two such sessions are always established at a time: one for transmission in each direction. A CP-CP session requires APPN.

diagnosis, bypass and recovery, resolution, and tracking and control.

Novell's NetWare Management Agent for NetView provides an interface between a NetWare server and NetView. The connection is through a Token Ring network or through NetWare for SAA. With this connection, an administrator can control the NetWare server from a NetView console and execute certain NetView commands on the server. The NetWare server can also send alarms to the NetView host in case of errors. NetWare Management Agent for NetView makes it possible for two different networks to be connected and managed together.

▼
SNA Character String (SCS)

SEE

SCS (SNA Character String)

SNADS (SNA Distribution Services)

SNADS provides store-and-forward file and document-handling capabilities in an IBM SNA (Systems Network Architecture) environment. SNADS uses APPC (Advanced Program-to-Program Communication) protocols to transport data.

SNA Gateway

An SNA gateway is a gateway that enables PCs and other machines on a PC-based network to communicate with IBM mainframes and minicomputers. The gateway provides translation necessary to enable a PC to talk to a host computer as any of the following:

- A 3270 terminal

- A 3287 printer

- An application that can use the LU 6.2 protocol, which is defined to enable programs to communicate

These capabilities require an adapter card. Among other things, this card provides the required emulation capabilities, for the gateway machine and on behalf of any node that can communicate with the gateway.

SNA/SDLC (Systems Network Architecture/Synchronous Data Link Control)

A communications protocol used to transfer data between a host and a controller in an SNA environment.

SNDCP (Subnetwork-Dependent Convergence Protocol)

In the OSI specifications for the Internal Organization of the Network Layer (IONL), the type of protocol used at the middle of the three sublayers into which the layer has been subdivided. A SNDCP protocol must handle any details or problems relating to the subnetwork to which the data is being transferred.

SNICP (Subnetwork-Independent Convergence Protocol)

In the OSI specifications for the Internal Organization of the Network Layer (IONL), the type of protocol used at the highest of the three sublayers into which the layer has been subdivided. A SNICP protocol must provide the routing and relaying capabilities needed to get data to its destination. The OSI's CLNP (Connectionless-mode Network Protocol) is an example of an SNICP.

SNR (Signal-to-Noise Ratio)

In a transmission, SNR is the ratio between the signal and noise levels at a given point, usually at the receiving end of the transmission. The SNR value is generally expressed in decibels (dB).

The SNR can be used to determine how long a cable segment can be before the signal loss is unacceptably high. The SNR also helps determine whether a particular type of cable is appropriate for the intended use.

a b c d e f g h i j k l m n o p q r **s** t u v w x y z

Cable testers, such as those manufactured by MicroTest and by Fluke, can help determine whether a particular type of cable is appropriate in a specific environment.

In general, digital signals have a much higher SNR than analog signals.

Socket

A socket is a general-purpose IPC (interprocess communication) mechanism. It is a logical entity through which a program or process communicates with a network or with another process. Each socket is associated with an address and, usually with some other type of identification.

Sockets were first developed for the UNIX environment, and are part of the BSD UNIX kernel. Sockets are supported, usually in libraries, by other UNIX implementations, for operating systems such as DOS or OS/2, and for network operating systems such as Novell's NetWare and AppleTalk.

Because sockets are generic, different parts of an application can execute on several different machines simultaneously. For example, for a database program, part of the program may run on a file server, which can provide fast access to any of the numerous databases connected to the server. Another part of an application may run on a workstation or on another specialized machine. The program portions communicate with each other using sockets.

Types of socket you may find mentioned in the literature include the following:

- Datagram socket, for sending datagrams (a packet used in connectionless delivery systems that do not guarantee delivery)

- Stream socket, a higher-level mechanism that provides a reliable connection (one that guarantees delivery)

- Raw socket, used for access by low-level protocols, and available only to privileged programs

- DAS (dynamically assigned socket) and SAS (statically assigned socket), used for datagram delivery between nodes in an AppleTalk internetwork

Socket Client

A process or function associated with a socket in a particular network node. The client is said to "own" the socket; that is, it can make use of the socket to request and receive information and network services.

Socket, NetWare

In Novell's NetWare, a socket is part of an IPX internetwork address. A socket is the destination for an IPX packet. Each socket is associated with a unique value. For most sockets, this value is assigned dynamically; however, certain socket values are reserved for Novell's use.

The table "Reserved NetWare Socket Values" shows the reserved socket numbers and their uses. Note that the socket values are expressed in hexadecimal, or base 16, values.

RESERVED NETWARE SOCKET VALUES	
SOCKET VALUE	**RESERVED FOR**
451h	NCP (NetWare Control Protocol)
452h	SAP (Service Advertising Protocol)
453h	RIP (Router Information Protocol)
455h	NetBIOS
456h	Diagnostics
8063h	NVT (Novell Virtual Terminal)
4000-6000h	Temporary sockets

Third-party developers can reserve socket values for use in the developers' products.

Socket Number

In any of various networking environments, such as AppleTalk and Novell's NetWare, a unique value assigned to a socket. The maximum size of such a value depends on the number of bits allocated for the number. For example, AppleTalk socket numbers are 8-bit values. Within this 0–255 range, values between 0 and 127 are reserved by Apple for system devices.

Soft Error

In a Token Ring network, an error that is not considered serious or a threat to the performance or continued operation of the network.

COMPARE
Hard Error

Solaris

Solaris is a UNIX implementation by SunSoft. Solaris is based on SunSoft's own SunOS. SunOS, in turn, is based on UNIX System V Release 4 (SVR4), but adds capabilities such as support for multithreading, symmetric multiprocessing, and real-time processing.

Solaris provides versatile networking support, including support for ONC (Open Network Computing), TCP/IP, NetWare IPX/SPX, and other protocols. Solaris can mount remote file systems automatically when needed, and it includes utilities for configuring network nodes and for installing software across the entire network from a single machine.

Solaris was implemented originally on Sun's SPARC architecture, but has since been ported to the Intel processor family.

SONET (Synchronous Optical Network)

SONET is a high-speed, fiber-optic system, which provides an interface and mechanism for optical transmission of digital information. At the interface, signals are converted from electrical to optical form (and back to electrical form at the destination). It is an ANSI standard. The CCITT counterpart is SDH (Synchronous Digital Hierarchy).

This type of network has the following features:

- Supports transmission rates ranging from 51.84 megabits per second

a b c d e f g h i j k l m n o p q r **s** t u v w x y z

(Mbps) to 2.488 gigabits per second (Gbps). In the digital signal (DS) hierarchy, SONET's basic bandwidth is a DS3 (44.736 Mbps) channel plus overhead. However, SONET also supports the multiplexing of lower-capacity channels, down to the 64 kilobit per second (kbps) DS0 channels.

- Uses an 810-byte (6480-bit) frame as its basic transmission unit, and transmits 80,000 of these per second.

- Uses a four-layer hierarchy to implement and manage the transmission of frames between two endpoints.

- Can adjust timing and framing during operation.

- Supports drop-and-insert capabilities, which make it easier to identify and remove channels going to different destinations. This makes it feasible to multiplex smaller-capacity (as low as 64 kbps) channels into SONET channels.

- Can be used as a carrier service for ATM (Asynchronous Transport Mode) networks.

- Is designed to be usable as a carrier service with up-and-coming communications standards and services, such as broadband ISDN (BISDN).

SONET Network Components

The figure "SONET network components" shows the elements in a SONET network.

The *endpoints* are the source and destination for the DS3 or smaller channels that make up the SONET transmission. A SONET multiplexer combines these various incoming channels into the STM-x channel going out toward the destination.

The paths between the endpoints are constructed of lines, which are, themselves, made from sections. A *section* is a single stretch of fiber-optic cable. The endpoints of a section are transmitters and receivers, which may be in a multiplexer or in a repeater. A repeater simply cleans and strengthens the signal, then sends it on.

A *line* connects two multiplexers. Intermediate multiplexers may be connected to other multiplexers or to endpoints. In either case, these multiplexers may route some of the channels to other networks or to endpoints, or they may add channels from endpoints or other lines. Drop-and-insert actions take place at intermediate multiplexers.

SONET Layers

The SONET standard defines four layers to deal with the tasks involved in getting transmissions from one endpoint to another:

Photonic: Cable, signal, and component specifications are defined at this physical layer. Signals are converted between electrical and optical form.

Section: Frames are created at this layer, and these frames are scrambled, if appropriate. The section layer also monitors the transmission for errors.

Line: This layer is responsible for getting frames from one end of a line to the other. Any timing adjustments, adding, or dropping will be made at this level.

SONET NETWORK COMPONENTS

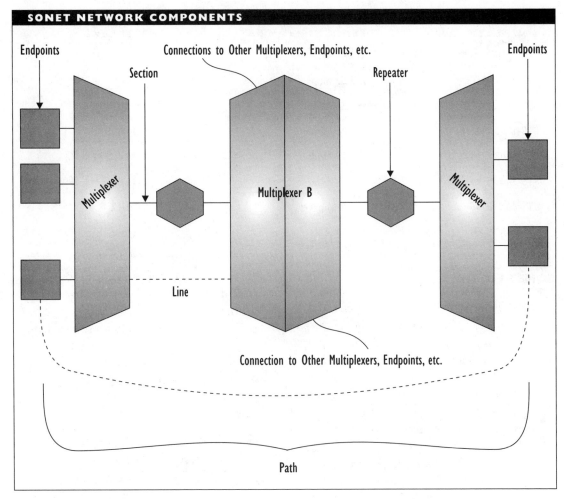

Path: This layer is responsible for getting the transmission from the source to the destination; that is, it is responsible for the overall path.

SONET Transmissions

The table "SONET Channel Capacities" shows the channels defined in the SONET transmission hierarchy. The table also shows the equivalent channels as defined in the CCITT SDH standard, which uses STM (synchronous transfer mode) levels.

At each endpoint, signals must be converted between electrical and optical forms. STS (synchronous transport signal) and OC (optical carrier) are the designations for the electrical and optical channels, respectively. In the SDH hierarchy, the levels are defined as synchronous transport modes.

a b c d e f g h i j k l m n o p q r **s** t u v w x y z

SONET CHANNEL CAPACITIES		
SONET LEVEL	**TRANSMISSION RATE**	**STM LEVEL**
STS-1/OC-1	51.84 Mbps	
STS-3/OC-3	155.52 Mbps	STM-1
STS-9/OC-9	466.56 Mbps	STM-3
STS-12/OC-12	622.08 Mbps	STM-4
STS-18/OC-18	933.12 Mbps	STM-6
STS-24/OC-24	1.244 Gbps	STM-8
STS-36/OC-36	1.866 Gbps	STM-12
STS-48/OC-48	2.488 Gbps	STM-16

SONET Frames

SONET frames have a simple overall structure with complicated details. The figure "A SONET frame" shows the general structure and provides a glimpse into the details.

The 810 bytes in a frame are grouped into nine 90-byte portions, which are transmitted one after the other. In the figure, these are represented as nine rows.

Three bytes in each row are overhead; the remaining 87 bytes are data, or payload. The overhead in three of the rows is allocated for monitoring the section; in the remaining six rows it is for the line.

The remaining bytes contain the payloads for the nine rows. This section of the frame is known as the SPE (synchronous payload environment). One column in the SPE is used for path overhead.

In the figure, enlargements of the overhead sections show the kinds of checking SONET does. Note that both the section and line overhead include channels for communicating. These channels are used to send alarms and other administrative information.

The line overhead includes several bytes for pointers. These are used to allow channels to be dropped or added, and even to allow the SPE to be moved.

A Floating Payload

The fast speeds involved in SONET transmissions mean that precise timing and immediate corrections are crucial. Timing adjustments can be made at the end of a line. Generally, such adjustments are minor, on the order of a byte interval or two.

Such adjustments will wreck the structure of a frame. Fortunately, the SPE can be moved around (relative to the frame boundaries), and can even cross frame boundaries.

The floating payload means that timing adjustments can be made at a very fine level. The drop-and-insert capabilities mean that a frame can be reconstructed at a line endpoint, before being sent down another line.

A SONET FRAME

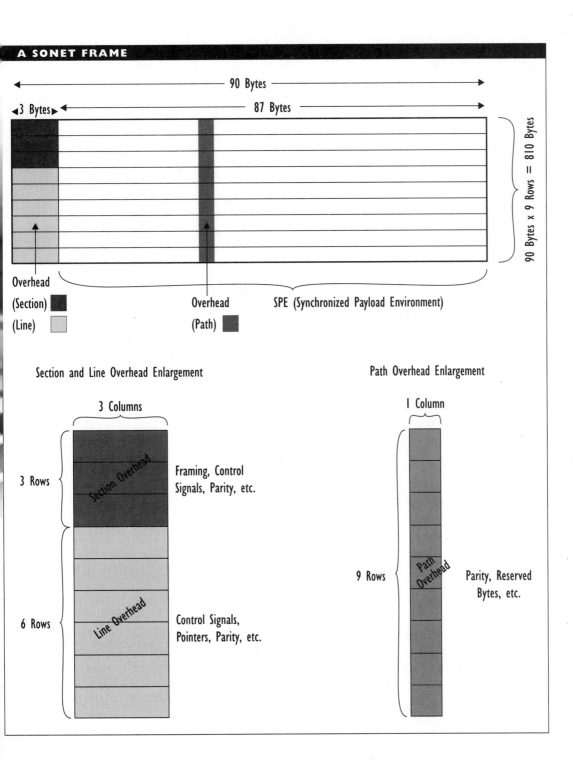

90 Bytes

3 Bytes

87 Bytes

90 Bytes x 9 Rows = 810 Bytes

Overhead

(Section)

(Line)

Overhead

(Path)

SPE (Synchronized Payload Environment)

Section and Line Overhead Enlargement

3 Columns

3 Rows

Section Overhead

Framing, Control
Signals, Parity, etc.

6 Rows

Line Overhead

Control Signals,
Pointers, Parity, etc.

Path Overhead Enlargement

1 Column

9 Rows

Path
Overhead

Parity, Reserved
Bytes, etc.

a b c d e f g h i j k l m n o p q r **s** t u v w x y z

This means, in turn, that the SONET channels can be used efficiently.

Source Address (SA)

SEE

SA (Source Address)

Source Routing

Source routing is a packet-routing strategy used in Token Ring networks. In a source-routing strategy, the route a packet will take between its source and destination is determined in advance by (or for) the source node.

Packet routes are determined by some type of discovery process, in which the node sends a packet onto the network, then waits for the packet's return. By the time it returns to the source node (as the destination), the packet will have picked up travel stickers from each node visited. The sender will be able to determine a path between sender and destination. This routing information is included when a packet is sent around a Token Ring network.

SEE ALSO

Routing

Spanning Tree

In a network, a spanning tree is a path or collection of paths that represent connections between nodes. To be called a spanning tree, the tree must cover every possible path in a network.

A minimal spanning tree is one that covers all possible paths, does so with as few

segments as possible, and makes sure there are no loops (closed paths) in the network.

The IEEE 802.1 recommendations provide an algorithm for finding a spanning tree in any network.

Spectral Width

Spectral width (also known as *laser line width*) is the range of light frequencies (or wavelengths) emitted by a laser. For communications, a narrower width has more desirable properties.

SPF (Shortest Path First)

A routing strategy for passing packets between routers. This strategy is used in Token Ring networks that may include connections to IBM mainframes.

Spike

A very brief, very large increase in voltage. Specifically, a spike occurs when the voltage is more than twice the nominal peak voltage. Spikes (which are also known as *impulses*) are most often caused by lightning strikes.

SEE ALSO

Power Disturbances

Splice

In fiber optics, a permanent connection between two cable segments. The splice can be made by fusing the cores from the two cables together or by attaching the cores to each other by mechanical means. In general, a fusion approach works better than a mechanical one.

Split Cable System

A split cable system is a broadband wiring arrangement in which a single cable's bandwidth is divided between transmission and receiving capabilities. Such a wiring system may be used, for example, in a 10Broad36 broadband Ethernet or a broadband (IEEE 802.4) token bus architecture.

In a split cable system, the cable's frequency spectrum is split with, for example, lower frequencies allocated for incoming transmissions and higher frequencies for outgoing signals. At the head end (the transmission source), a frequency converter translates signals into the appropriate bandwidth, and a bidirectional amplifier passes the frequencies to the appropriate channel (input or output).

The bandwidth in a split cable system need not be distributed equally between the two directions. For example, cable television allocates a much larger part of the bandwidth to outgoing signals, since the subscribers need not communicate with the head end. For local-area networks (LANs), the distribution should be more even. The following splits are commonly used:

Subsplit: Allocates only 25 megahertz (MHz) of bandwidth to transmissions going from node to head end, and over ten times as much bandwidth to output transmissions.

Midsplit: Allocates roughly equal bandwidths to incoming and outgoing transmissions. The split uses bandwidths of over 100 MHz.

Highsplit: Allocates roughly equal bandwidths to incoming and outgoing transmissions. The split uses bandwidths of over 150 MHz for both the incoming and outgoing channels.

COMPARE
Dual Cable System

Split-Horizon Routing

In an AppleTalk Phase 2 network, a strategy for maintaining routing tables. Basically, the strategy involves passing routing table updates only to nodes or routers that can and will actually use the information.

Split Pair

In twisted-pair wiring, split pair refers to sending a signal over wires from two different pairs instead of over wires in the same pair. Since the pairing is what helps cancel the effects of interference, this advantage is lost with split pairs.

SEE ALSO
Wiring Sequence

Splitter

A coupler (an analog device) that breaks a signal into multiple derived signals. An important type of splitter is a wavelength-selective coupler, which splits an incoming signal into outgoing signals based on wavelength.

COMPARE
Combiner

a b c d e f g h i j k l m n o p q r **s** t u v w x y z

Spooler

A spooler is a program that serves as a buffer for material waiting to be processed by a device, such as a printer. The spooler intercepts material being sent (ostensibly) to a particular port, and can store the material until the spooler is ready for the next transmission. The most common type of spooler used is a print spooler.

On a network, the spooler software may run on a workstation or on the print server. For example, in AppleTalk networks, a *background spooler* runs as a background process on the workstation. Such a spooler sends the print jobs to a file.

In contrast, a *spooler/server* runs on the print server and works by serving as the printer for other applications. The spooler then feeds the print jobs to the real printer.

The term spooler comes from spool, which is an acronym for "simultaneous peripheral operation on line."

SPP (Sequenced Packet Protocol)

A transport level protocol in the XNS protocol suite from Xerox.

SPS (Standby Power Supply)

An SPS is an emergency power source that can deliver a limited amount of power to a file server or other device in the event of a blackout (total loss of power).

SPSs are more commonly known as standby UPSs (uninterruptible power supplies). A UPS is a similar, but not identical, device. The main difference is that a UPS always supplies power through a battery, whereas an SPS does so only when there is a power failure.

An SPS includes a battery charger, a battery, and an inverter that can be used to provide the emergency power when necessary. The SPS monitors the power coming in from the power lines. As long as power is coming in, the SPS bypasses the battery component. Instead, the supplied voltage may go through a surge protector and a noise filter before reaching the machine being protected.

Thus, the primary power path in an SPS bypasses the battery, going instead through whatever voltage-cleaning components the SPS has. The secondary path—through a battery charger, a battery, and an inverter—remains idle.

If the SPS detects a blackout, it switches to the battery component. This battery (which must be charged) can provide power for a limited time: anywhere from 5 minutes to over an hour. The amount of time depends on the capacity of the SPS battery and on the power needs of the system being protected. In any case, there should be enough power to enable a file server to shut down the network in an orderly manner.

The switchover from the primary to the secondary (battery/inverter) path takes a few milliseconds (msec), generally fewer than 5 or so. This amount of time is short enough to avoid any data loss, since the computer can run for about 50 msec on power stored in its capacitors. This switching time is also lower than the 8.33 msec "half-cycle" time that represents the interval between pulses of power from the power line. One standard (IEEE 446) for switching times specifies that this period should be no longer than a quarter cycle, which is 4.2 msec. (The cycle time comes from the 60 Hz that is the standard rate at which AC power changes polarity in North American power supplies.)

SPSs are generally less expensive than UPSs, but the money saved may prove to be penny wise and pound foolish. This is because an SPS makes extra demands on the system administrator or whoever is in charge of hardware maintenance.

BROADER CATEGORY

Safety Device

COMPARE

UPS (Uninterruptible Power Supply)

SPS BATTERIES

It is absolutely essential to have a working, fully charged battery available in the event of a power failure. This means the battery must be tested at periodic intervals, and should be fully drained and recharged regularly.

Even if the battery is never used, there will always be some drainage over time. Ironically, drainage increases as the period of non-use does. There's a natural tendency to get complacent the longer one goes without a power outage.

If this leads to looser maintenance, then you could be in for trouble when that blackout finally hits. If the SPS battery hasn't been checked for a long time, the chances become more disconcerting that the battery won't work properly.

Even batteries that are maintained wear out eventually. In general, UPS and SPS batteries should be replaced every 3 to 5 years.

SQE (Signal Quality Error)

In an Ethernet 2.0 or 802.3-based network, a signal sent from the transceiver to the attached machine to indicate that the transceiver's collision-detection circuitry is working. SQE (also known as a *heartbeat*) was introduced to identify nodes incapable of detecting collisions.

SQL (Structured Query Language)

SQL (pronounced either as "sequel" or as individual letters) is a language standardized by the ISO for defining and querying relational databases. SQL is widely used as an interface to databases, and almost all database packages now support SQL. Unfortunately, not all versions of SQL are the same.

User or application requests are handled as *transactions* by SQL. A transaction may involve one or more SQL actions. SQL must be able to complete a transaction completely or not at all. If a transaction cannot be completed, all the actions already performed must be undone. This provides a measure of data protection.

SRAM (Static Random-Access Memory)

A type of chip memory in which information is stored in flip-flop circuits, which retain their value as long as the power is switched on. This is in contrast to DRAM (dynamic RAM), whose contents must be refreshed periodically. SRAM is faster but much more expensive than DRAM, and is used primarily for cache storage, if at all.

a b c d e f g h i j k l m n o p q r **s** t u v w x y z

SS (Sampled Servo)

Sampled servo is a compact disc recording technique in which the contents are stored on a single, spiral track.

COMPARE

CCS (Continuous Composite Servo)

SSO (Single Sign On)

An approach to logins in which a user may need only a single user ID and password in order to access any machine in an enterprise or other network, and even to use any application or service on these machines—provided the user has the appropriate access and usage privileges.

SS7

A standard for out-of-band signaling developed by the CCITT for use in ISDN telephone systems. SS7 (also known as *CCITT 7*) offers fast call setup and sophisticated information and transaction capabilities. For example, SS7 makes call waiting, screening, forwarding, and transfer services available in international networks.

SSCP (System Services Control Point)

A type of node in SNA networks. SSCPs provide the services needed to manage an entire network or part of one.

SEE ALSO

SNA (Systems Network Architecture)

SSS (Server Session Socket)

In an AppleTalk session layer protocol, a field that contains the number of the socket to which the session level packets are to be sent.

Stack Manager

A stack manager is a software process that mediates between a network interface card (NIC) driver and the drivers for higher-level protocols. This type of process is typically loaded in the file server, but may be loaded in a gateway or workstation.

For example, when loaded on a file server, a stack manager could allow the following types of workstations to connect to the server: a DOS workstation running Novell NetWare, a UNIX workstation running TCP/IP, a Macintosh, and an OS/2 workstation running LAN Manager or LAN Server. In this example, the stack manager would need to be able to handle IPX, IP, AppleTalk, and NetBIOS protocols, respectively.

When loaded in a gateway, the stack manager could allow servers from networks running different network operating systems (NOSs) to communicate.

When loaded in a workstation, the stack manager could allow the workstation to access servers running different NOSs. This approach is relatively rare, because the appropriate protocols and shell software must be loaded for each NOS being accessed, in addition to the stack manager.

Stand-Alone Hub

An external hub that requires its own power supply. A stand-alone hub is generally a box with connectors for the nodes that will be attached, and possibly with special connectors for linking to other hubs.

SEE ALSO
Hub

Standby Monitor (SM)

SEE
SM (Standby Monitor)

Standby Power Supply (SPS)

SEE
SPS (Standby Power Supply)

Star Coupler

A coupler that splits a signal into more than two derived signals, as, for example, in a star topology. This is in contrast to a tee coupler, which splits an incoming signal into two outgoing signals.

SEE ALSO
Coupler

StarGroup

StarGroup is a network operating system (NOS) from AT&T. This NOS is adapted from Microsoft's LAN Manager and runs on UNIX systems, although other versions (such as one for the Macintosh) are available. The NOS provides support for the most common protocol families (TCP/IP and ISO), for SNA (Systems Network Architecture) and asynchronous gateways, routers for X.25 networks, and other capabilities.

StarGroup provides extensive network-management capabilities, and it can report management data to AT&T's UNMA (Unified Network Management Architecture) environment or to NetView running in IBM's NMA (Network Management Architecture).

StarKeeper

A network management system from AT&T. StarKeeper provides centralized management of Datakit VCS and ISN (Information Systems Network) switches.

Start Bit

A bit used to establish timing in asynchronous communications. One or more start bits may be appended to the start of every byte. (Start bits are not required for synchronous communications.)

COMPARE
Stop Bit

Start Delimiter (SD)

SEE
SD (Start Delimiter)

STARTUP.NCF

A boot file in a Novell NetWare file server. This file loads the disk driver and name spaces for the server. It can also be used to set other environment variables for the server.

a b c d e f g h i j k l m n o p q r **s** t u v w x y z

Static Random-Access Memory (SRAM)

SEE

SRAM (Static Random-Access Memory)

Station Management (SMT)

SEE

SMT (Station Management)

Statistical Time Division Multiplexing (STDM)

SEE

STDM (Statistical Time Division Multiplexing)

Statistical Multiplexing

A multiplexing strategy in which access is provided only to ports that need or want it. Thus, in any given cycle, one node may have nothing to send, while another node may need to get as much access as possible.

SEE ALSO

Multiplexing

STDA (StreetTalk Directory Assistance)

In StreetTalk, the global network naming system for Banyan's VINES, STDA provides a pop-up window in which a user can see the name of every node or device attached to the network. STDA can also provide addressing facilities for electronic mail and certain types of other information about a particular node or device.

SEE ALSO

StreetTalk

STDM (Statistical Time Division Multiplexing)

A multiplexing technique in which each node is polled and any node with nothing to send is immediately skipped. This helps fill more of the available bandwidth.

SEE ALSO

Multiplexing

STM (Synchronous Transfer Mode)

In broadband ISDN, a transport method that uses time division multiplexing and switching methods to provide each user with up to 50 megabits per second (Mbps) of bandwidth for synchronous transmissions.

STM (Synchronous Transfer Mode)-x

STM-x (where x is the level) is any of several channel capacities defined in the CCITT's SDH (Synchronous Digital Hierarchy), which is the European equivalent of the ANSI SONET (Synchronous Optical Network) standard.

The STM levels represent multiplexed, 44.736 megabits per second (Mbps), DS3 channels + overhead for signaling and framing. For example, the lowest STM capacity, STM-1, has a 155.52 Mbps bandwidth, which multiplexes three 51.84 Mbps channels. The table "STM-x Channel Capacities" shows the rates for the levels in the SDH, as well as the corresponding designations in the SONET hierarchy.

STM-x CHANNEL CAPACITIES

STM LEVEL	TRANSMISSION RATE	SONET LEVEL
	51.84 Mbps	STS-1/OC-1
STM-1	155.52 Mbps	STS-3/OC-3
STM-3	466.56 Mbps	STS-9/OC-9
STM-4	622.08 Mbps	STS-12/OC-12
STM-6	933.12 Mbps	STS-18/OC-18
STM-8	1.244 Gbps	STS-24/OC-24
STM-12	1.866 Gbps	STS-36/OC-36
STM-16	2.488 Gbps	STS-48/OC-48

Stop Bit

A bit used to indicate the end of a character in asynchronous serial communications. One or more stop bits may be appended to the end of every byte. Older devices needed two stop bits to get themselves set again; newer devices require only one. Stop bits are not required for synchronous communications.

COMPARE

Start Bit

Storage Management Services (SMS)

SEE

SMS (Storage Management Services)

Store-and-Forward

A messaging technology in which messages can be held for a time—at the source machine, at an intermediate node, or at the destination machine—and then sent on to their destination.

Store-and-Forward Switch

A switch that first checks a packet's integrity before sending it on to its destination port. The switch gets each packet from the input port, looks up the packet's destination (MAC-level) address, and then sends the packet on. To be useful, such a switch needs enough storage to hold an address table large enough to store every address on the network.

COMPARE

Cut-Through Switching

STREAMS

In Novell's NetWare, STREAMS is a NetWare Loadable Module (NLM) that provides an interface between the NOS (network operating system) and transport layer protocol stacks, such as Novell's own

a b c d e f g h i j k l m n o p q r **s** t u v w x y z

IPX/SPX, the Internet's TCP/IP, IBM's SNA architecture, and networks that conform to the OSI Reference Model.

In addition to the STREAMS NLM, one or more other NLMs are needed to provide STREAMS with access to the other protocol stacks. For example, SPXS.NLM and IPXS.NLM provide access to STREAMS for the transport and network layers, respectively; TCPIP.NLM can mediate between STREAMS and the TCP and UDP protocols.

StreetTalk

StreetTalk is the global naming system for Banyan's VINES network operating system (NOS). StreetTalk includes a database that contains all the necessary information about the network and each node or device on it. The database is updated every 90 seconds by every server on the network.

A StreetTalk name may include three levels of identity: item, group, and organization. Item is the most specific. A node or device may get a name at each of these levels, and these names will be separated by an @. For example, *Hickory@Dickory@Dock* specifies node *Hickory*, which belongs to group *Dickory*, which is part of organization *Dock*.

StreetTalk allows nicknames for nodes and devices.

StreetTalk Directory Assistance (STDA)

SEE

STDA (StreetTalk Directory Assistance)

Structure of Management Information (SMI)

SEE

SMI (Structure of Management Information)

Structured Query Language (SQL)

SEE

SQL (Structured Query Language)

Sub-Distribution Frame (SDF)

SEE

SDF (Sub-Distribution Frame)

Subnet Layers

In the OSI Reference Model, the bottom three layers: physical, data-link, and network. These layers are significant because intermediate systems, which are the devices that relay transmissions between other devices, use only these three layers to pass on transmissions.

SEE ALSO

OSI Reference Model

Subnet Mask

In the IP (Internet Protocol) addressing scheme, a group of selected bits whose values serve to identify a subnetwork. All the members of the subnetwork share the mask value. Once identified using the mask, members of this subnet can be referenced more easily. This is also known as an *address mask*.

Subnetwork

Subnetwork is a term for a network that is part of another network, connected through a gateway, bridge, or router. A subnetwork may include both end systems (nodes) and intermediate systems (routers). The nodes in a subnetwork use a single protocol to communicate with each other. The subnetwork is connected to the larger network through an intermediate system, which may use a routing protocol to communicate with nodes outside the subnetwork.

A local-area network (LAN), or even a group of LANs, connected by bridges or routers, can form a subnetwork. Similarly, a localized X.25 network may be a subnetwork in a larger wide-area network (WAN).

Subnetwork, Level *x*

If an internetwork grows too large, routers may be unable to keep track of all the routing information. This can, under some circumstances, cause errors that are very difficult to fix. To avoid such problems, an oversized internetwork can be divided into areas, each consisting of a number of networks. These areas are called *level 1 subnetworks*, and they are managed by level 1 routers.

To a network elsewhere on the internetwork, all the networks included in a particular level *x* network are treated as part of the same network. For example, a giant reference internetwork might include dozens of networks from a single city, with networks in libraries, schools, research labs,

and so on. For the outside world, all the networks in a city could be grouped into a level 1 subnetwork.

Transmissions to a machine on one of the networks would be sent to a level 1 router for that city. Routers would have the address of that level 1 router, rather than having addresses for each of the networks in the city.

For really large internetworks, several level 1 subnetworks could be grouped into a level 2 subnetwork, handled by level 2 routers.

Arranging a large internetwork hierarchically in this manner makes it possible to build larger internetworks, because routers need to keep track of less information overall. Also, by partitioning level 1 subnetworks, it is possible to isolate any routing or protocol problems that might arise in a subnetwork.

SEE ALSO
Router

Subnetwork-Dependent Convergence Protocol (SNDCP)

SEE
SNDCP (Subnetwork-Dependent Convergence Protocol)

Subnetwork-Independent Convergence Protocol (SNICP)

SEE
SNICP (Subnetwork-Independent Convergence Protocol)

Surface Test

A surface test is a test of a hard disk's surface for bad blocks (areas in which data may become damaged or lost). This type of test can be done as part of the installation process for most network operating systems.

Some hard disk manufacturers perform these tests prior to shipment. If the test identifies bad blocks, these are labeled as bad and the blocks are included in a bad blocks table, so that a program or operating system will not write anything to these regions of the disk.

A surface test may be destructive or nondestructive. In a destructive test, existing data on the disk will be overwritten and lost. In a nondestructive test, data is moved before the section of the disk is tested.

Surge, Electrical

A short-term increase in voltage. The duration of a surge is longer than for a spike, but the voltage increase is much lower than for a spike. Specifically, a surge occurs if the voltage is more than 10 percent above the nominal RMS voltage for more than $1/120$ second.

SEE ALSO
Power Disturbances

Surge, Packet-Switched Network

In packet-switched networks, a surge is a temporary increase in required bandwidth. The increase is measured in relation to a guaranteed bandwidth, known as the *committed information rate* (*CIR*). If you are a subscriber to a packet-switched network, you will be charged for the extra bandwidth.

Surge Suppressor

A surge suppressor is a filter designed to protect computers and other electrical equipment from brief bursts of high voltage, or *surges*. The purpose of a surge suppressor is to deal with the excess voltage and pass on a more normal voltage to the device. Surge suppressors are also known as surge protectors, and less commonly as noise filters.

Surge suppressors differ in the following ways:

- The way in which they deal with the excess voltage

- The speed with which they can deal with the voltage

- The level of voltage they can absorb

- The number of surges they can withstand

- The combinations of power supply wires (hot, neutral, and ground) they protect

Voltage-Diversion Approaches

Less expensive suppressors use a shunt to divert the excess voltage along a separate path. The most popular shunt is a metal-oxide varistor (MOV), and you will see references to "MOV surge suppressors." The shunt approach requires a small amount of time, called the *clamping time,* before the suppressor can go to work.

This grade of surge suppressors is best suited for appliances. Unfortunately, it is also the most widely sold type of surge suppressor. According to some estimates, about 90 percent of surge suppressors are of this type. MOVs have a limited lifetime, and they should be replaced occasionally. How often you will need to replace a MOV depends on the how often it needs to come into service.

A more sophisticated approach uses shunts and noise filtering. This is much more effective (and more expensive) than just a shunt, and it is used in many surge suppressors designed for use with computers.

An isolating design places special components between the power source and the protected device. These devices have particularly high resistance to high voltages, so that the excess signal is effectively blocked by these components. The shunt and noise filtering approach does not require any clamping time or other response delays.

Surge Suppressor Performance

A useful surge suppressor should be fast and effective, reliable and durable.

Underwriters Laboratories has several tests for surge suppressors. The UL 1449 standard sends repeated high-voltage (6000 volts), high-current signals through the surge suppressor, and monitors the voltage that the device lets through.

To be listed, the performance for the first and last tests must be within 10 percent of each other, indicating that the surge protector is durable. Listed devices also get a rating that indicates the voltage that is let through. The best rating is 6000/330 (330 volts are let through with a 6000 volt surge), then 6000/400, 6000/500, and so on.

To be UL-listed, a surge suppressor needs to pass only for the hot-ground wire pair. However, to be really valuable, the suppressor should provide acceptable protection

WHAT TO LOOK FOR IN A SURGE SUPPRESSOR

Consider only UL 1449-listed surge suppressors with 6000/330 (or at worst 6000/400) ratings, especially for use on a network.

Surge suppressors are better than no protection for workstations, but they are not adequate for file servers. A file server should have a UPS (uninterruptible power supply) for protection.

A good indicator of a manufacturer's confidence in its equipment is the warranty offered. Some surge suppressors actually have lifetime warranties. For example, American Power Conversion (APC) will, under certain conditions, provide a $25,000 insurance policy for their surge suppressors and other safety devices.

across *each* pair of lines (hot-ground, hot-neutral, and neutral-ground).

Surge suppressors also do line noise filtering. The UL 1283 standard tests a surge protector's ability to suppress noise at various frequencies. However, a UL 1283 listing is less important than a UL 1449 listing, because the type of noise the UL 1283 tests cover should be filtered out by the shields on your computer anyway, in order to meet FCC (Federal Communication Commission) guidelines for emission levels.

Surge suppressors to which you will attach modems, fax machines, or other devices that will communicate over telephone lines must meet additional standards. These surge protectors should also be UL 497A listed.

BROADER CATEGORY
Safety Device

SVC (Switched Virtual Circuit)

In telecommunications, a circuit, or connection, that is established for a communications session, and that is terminated after the session is over. This is in contrast to a permanent virtual circuit (PVC), which is a connection that is always established.

Switch

A switch is a device that connects material coming in with an appropriate outlet. For example, the input may be packets and the outlet might be an Ethernet bus, as in an Ethernet switch. Or the input might be an electronic mail (e-mail) message in cc:Mail format and the output might be to any of a number of other e-mail formats, as with a mail switch.

A switch needs to have a way of establishing the desired connection, and may also need to translate the input before sending it to an output.

There are two main approaches to the task of matching an input with the desired outlet:

- In a matrix approach, each input channel has a predefined connection with each output channel. To pass something from an input to an output is merely a matter of following the connection.

- In a shared memory approach, the input controller writes the material to a reserved area of memory and the specified output channel reads the material from this memory area.

If the connection requires translation, a switch may translate directly or use an intermediate form. For example, a mail switch may use a common format as the storage format. The specified output channel will translate this "generic" format into the format required for the output channel.

In general, switches are beginning to replace earlier, less flexible internetwork links, such as bridges and gateways. For example, a gateway may be able to connect two different architectures, but a switch may be able to connect several.

Because switches do more work than bridges or gateways, switches need more processing power. Switches may have multiple processors, or they may run on a minicomputer for better performance.

Switch, Data

A location or device in which data can be routed, or switched, to its destination. Data switches are used in switching networks, in which data is grouped and routed on the basis of predetermined criteria.

Switch, Ethernet

An Ethernet switch is a device that can direct network traffic among several Ethernet networks. This type of switch has multiple ports to connect the subnetworks, and it generally has multiple processors to handle the traffic through the switch.

Two types of Ethernet switches are common:

- A store-and-forward switch checks each packet for errors before directing it to the appropriate network. In heavy traffic, this can be time-consuming, and the switch may be overwhelmed; in burst mode, a store-and-forward switch will almost certainly be overwhelmed.

- A cross-point switch directs packets without checking for errors. This type of switch is generally much faster than a store-and-forward switch.

In a sense, an Ethernet switch is just a superbridge for Ethernet networks.

Switched 56

A 56 Kbps, circuit-switched telecommunications service. A switched 56 channel can be leased from long-distance providers, such as AT&T or MCI.

Switched Digital Access

In telecommunications and wide-area networking, a mediated connection to long-distance lines. The local carrier mediates the connection, so that the user is connected directly to the local carrier and from there to the long-distance carrier.

COMPARE
Direct Connect

Switched Multimegabit Data Service (SMDS)

SEE
SMDS (Switched Multimegabit Data Service)

Switched T1

A circuit-switched telecommunications service that provides a 1.544 Mbps bandwidth (that is, a T1 line). Transmissions over this line may go through a multiplexer, or channel bank, where they are broken down and transmitted across slower (for example, 64 Kbps) channels.

COMPARE
Switched 56

Switched Virtual Circuit (SVC)

SEE
SVC (Switched Virtual Circuit)

Switching, Circuit

In circuit switching, a hardware path is set up to establish a connection between two devices. This path stays in effect until the communication is finished, as when one party hangs up the telephone to end a telephone call. Examples of circuit-switching services include the following:

- Switched 56
- Switched T1
- ISDN

COMPARE
Packet Switching

Switching Element

Switching is the process of getting a packet of data into a node and moving this packet along the appropriate path to the packet's

a b c d e f g h i j k l m n o p q r **s** t u v w x y z

destination. More generally, switching is the process of connecting an input to the appropriate output. The goals are to do this as quickly and as inexpensively as possible.

Switching Tasks

Switching involves three tasks:

Mapping: Identifying the desired output channel

Scheduling: Deciding which packet or packets to send in a time slot

Data forwarding: Delivering the packet to the output once it has been scheduled

The switching process is controlled by a switching element, such as the one shown in the figure "A switching element."

Switching Element Components

The switching element has three types of components:

- An input controller (IC) for each input channel, or line. This controller's job is to synchronize each input (which may be a message, packet, or cell, depending on the architecture being used) with the internal clock.

- An output controller (OC) for each output channel. This controller's job is to queue and buffer inputs if there are several being routed to the same output channel.

- An interconnection network, which provides a way of getting from any input channel to any output channel.

The interconnection network can take the form of a matrix with a node for each input-output pair. The interconnection can also be provided by a common memory area to which the input controllers write the input and from which the output controllers read and transmit the input. Bus and ring arrangements may also be used to connect input and output channels.

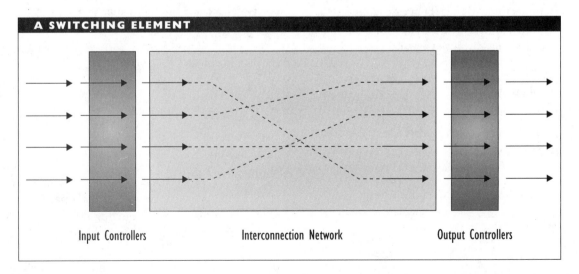

A SWITCHING ELEMENT

Input Controllers   Interconnection Network   Output Controllers

Switching Levels

Switching can take place at any of various levels, and can involve any of the following:

- Hardware circuits, as when making connections for telephone calls

- Messages, such as those in voice and e-mail services, which store a message and forward it to the destination at the appropriate time

- Packets, as in telecommunications services such as X.25 or frame relay

- Cells, as in the ATM network architecture

Cell switching is similar to packet switching, except that it involves fixed-size cells rather than variable-sized packets.

Switching theory, which is concerned with analyzing and optimizing such tasks, is an important and active branch of mathematics, and is likely to grow in prominence as the electronic superhighway is paved.

Switching Hierarchy

In telephony, a hierarchy of switch levels for establishing connections for long-distance calls. Five levels are involved.

SEE ALSO
Exchange

Switching, Message

In message switching, a message makes its way from sender to receiver by being passed through intermediate nodes. Each node will store the entire message and forward it to the next node when the opportunity arises. Under certain types of connections, different parts of the message may take different routes to the destination during transmission.

Synchronization

A timing or version comparison and coordination process. The term is used most commonly to refer to actions by which two or more systems are assigned identical times or by which systems agree on the duration of a bit interval (the time required to send one bit). The term has also come to be used to refer to version comparisons, as when replicas of files or database elements are checked to make sure they contain the same information.

Synchronization Rules

Rules used by file servers to control simultaneous access to a file by multiple stations.

Synchronous

A communications strategy that uses timing to control transmission. A transmission consists of an initial synchronization sequence, followed by a predefined number of bits, each transmitted at a constant rate. Except for the initial synchronization bit, synchronous transmissions do not require any additional bits (as asynchronous methods do). Synchronous transmissions can be fast, but they must be slowed down on noisy lines.

Synchronous Optical Network (SONET)

SEE

SONET (Synchronous Optical Network)

Synchronous Transfer Mode (STM)

SEE

STM (Synchronous Transfer Mode)

Synchronous Transfer Mode (STM)-*x*

SEE

STM (Synchronous Transfer Mode)-*x*

System Attribute

In a file system, such as the one used by DOS, an attribute (or *flag*) that marks a file or directory as usable only by the operating system.

System Connect

The physical connection to a network or a host computer. For example, the system connect in a thin Ethernet network is through a BNC T-connector attached to the network interface card.

System Fault Tolerance (SFT)

SEE

SFT (System Fault Tolerance)

System Services Control Point (SSCP)

SEE

SSCP (System Services Control Point)

System Side

The cabling from the computer or network to the distribution frame.

Systems Application Architecture (SAA)

SEE

SAA (Systems Application Architecture)

Systems Management Application Entity (SMAE)

SEE

SMAE (Systems Management Application Entity)

Systems Management Application Process (SMAP)

SEE

SMAP (Systems Management Application Process)

Systems Management Application Service Element (SMASE)

SEE

SMASE (Systems Management Application Service Element)

Systems Management Function (SMF)

SEE

SMF (Systems Management Function)

Systems Management Functional Area (SMFA)

SEE

SMFA (Systems Management Functional Area)

Systems Network Architecture (SNA)

SEE

SNA (Systems Network Architecture)

Systems Network Architecture/ Synchronous Data Link Control (SNA/SDLC)

SEE

SNA/SDLC (Systems Network Architecture/Synchronous Data Link Control)

SystemView

A comprehensive network management package from IBM. The first parts of SystemView were released in 1990, and components are still being developed. Intended as a replacement for NetView, SystemView is more comprehensive, will support more networking models, and will provide greater flexibility in data presentation than NetView.

a b c d e f g h i j k l m n o p q r **s** t u v w x y z

T

Used as an abbreviation for the prefix *tera*, as in THz (terahertz), TB (terabytes), or Tbps (terabits per second). This order of magnitude corresponds to 2^{40}, which is roughly 10^{12}, or trillions (in the United States counting system).

SEE ALSO

Order of Magnitude

T1 Carrier

In digital communications, T1 is the carrier used in North America, Australia, and Japan. Although originally developed to transmit voice conversations, T1 is also suitable for data and image transmissions, and it is commonly used for such purposes. T1 has a bandwidth of 1.544 megabits per second (Mbps), which comes from two dozen 64 kilobit per second (kbps) channels, together with one 8 kbps framing channel.

The T1 link was developed by AT&T to increase the number of voice calls that could be handled through the existing cables. A T1 carrier can handle 24 conversations simultaneously, using two wire pairs. One pair is used for sending, and the other for receiving, so that a T1 link can operate in full-duplex mode.

The 24 individual channels are each sampled 8,000 times a second, generating an 8 bit value each time. Data from the 24 channels is multiplexed into 192 bit frames, to which a 193rd bit is added for framing purposes. The samples for the 24 channels yield 1.536 Mbps, and 8 kbps is added for framing to make the 1.544 Mbps capacity for a T1 line. (Actually, in the T1 world, the subscriber only gets 56 kbps of every channel; the service provider steals one bit from each value for control purposes.)

The individual 64 kbps channels are known as DS0 (for Digital Signal, level 0) channels. DS0 channels are the building blocks for a T1 carrier and for even higher-speed links. In DS terms, the 24 DS0 channels make up one DS1 channel. The T1 carrier provides the transmission capabilities for the data in the DS1 channel.

T1 lines can be multiplexed into even faster links. The table "The T1 Digital Carrier Hierarchy" shows the T1 hierarchy. The data rates reflect extra channels for framing, control, or signaling.

THE T1 DIGITAL CARRIER HIERARCHY			
SIGNAL LEVEL	CARRIER	#T1 LINKS	DATA RATE
DS1	T1	1	1.544 Mbps
DS1C	T1C	2	3.152 Mbps
DS2	T2	4 (2 × T1C)	6.312 Mbps
DS3	T3	28 (7 × T2)	44.736 Mbps
DS4	T4	168 (6 × T3)	274.176 Mbps

T1 services are still quite expensive. This is partly because they tend to be used for long-distance links and because subscribers must pay a monthly fee based on distance (possibly several dollars per mile). T1 links also have high installation costs.

In Europe, South America, and Mexico, an analogous carrier is defined by the CCITT, designated as E1. This carrier has a bandwidth of 2.048 Mbps.

BROADER CATEGORY

Digital Communications

SEE ALSO

E1 Carrier; Fractional T1

T3 Channel

A communications channel with a bandwidth of 44.736 megabits per second. This channel is the equivalent of 28 T1 channels, or of 672 voice channels, each of 64 kilobits per second. In Europe, this designation has been superseded by the CCITT's DS3 designation.

TA (Terminal Adapter)

A device that mediates between an ISDN (Integrated Services Digital Network) network and devices that are not ISDN-compatible (known as TE2 devices). The TA's output will conform to whichever one of four CCITT standards is appropriate: V.110, V.120, X.30, or X.31.

TAG (Technical Advisory Group)

An IEEE committee whose task is to provide general recommendations and technical guidance for other committees. Perhaps the best known TAGS are the 802.7 and 802.8 committees, which are concerned with issues relating to broadband networks and to the use of fiber-optic cabling in networks, respectively.

Tap

An attachment to a transmission or power line. For example, a tap may be used to add a node to a network. Signals can be received or transmitted through a tap. In a thick Ethernet network, a *vampire tap* is one that actually pierces the cable in order to attach a node to the network.

Tape Drive

A tape drive is a sequential access storage device that is often used for backing up hard disk systems. Because of their large capacity (250 megabyte drives are common) and relatively high speed, tape drives are a popular backup medium for networks.

Most network operating systems include servers for using tape drives as a backup medium, either as part of the basic services or through add-on modules.

Types of Tape Drives

Tape drives come in internal and external forms. Some external drives plug into a parallel port, so they are easier to move from machine to machine to do backups.

Although many tape drive manufacturers have their proprietary compression and storage formats, just about all manufacturers support the QIC-80 format, which has become the standard for tape backup.

a b c d e f g h i j k l m n o p q r s **t** u v w x y z

BUYING TAPES FOR TAPE DRIVES

Fomatting tapes for tape drives is a tedious, time-consuming task. For some types of cartridges, it can take a couple of hours to format, mark, and verify a single tape.

If at all possible, buy preformatted tapes. The price difference is small compared with the time and aggravation saved.

Advantages and Disadvantages of Tape Drives as Backup Media

Tape drives and media are an inexpensive way to back up data. They are also suitable for restoring data when you need to restore an entire tape.

Tape as a storage medium suffers when you want to access specific information on a tape. This is because, unlike hard or floppy disk drives or CD-ROM drives, tape is a sequential-access medium (rather than a random-access medium). This means it can take several minutes to get to the material you want to retrieve from the tape.

BROADER CATEGORY
Peripheral

TAPI (Telephony Applications Program Interface)

TAPI is a set of functions developed by Microsoft for integrating PCs and telephone systems. TAPI supports PBX and Centrex systems, as well as conventional lines. It also supports services such as ISDN or cellular technology. TAPI support is built into Windows 95.

TSAPI, Novell's entry, is a main competitor for TAPI.

BROADER CATEGORY
Computer-Telephony Integration

SEE ALSO
TSAPI (Telephony Services API); Versit

Target

In Novell's NetWare, a server or node that contains data to be backed up or restored. A server or node can be a target only if a Target Service Agent (TSA) is running on the potential target.

SEE ALSO
TSA (Target Service Agent)

Target Coding

In a communications context, the coding (representation) used by the application that receives a transmission. In a network, the receiving application must be running on an end system, which is a node capable of using all seven layers in the OSI Reference Model.

Target Service Agent (TSA)

SEE
TSA (Target Service Agent)

TCNS (Thomas-Conrad Network System)

TCNS is a 100 megabit per second (Mbps) implementation of the ARCnet architecture, developed by Thomas-Conrad. TCNS can use existing ARCnet drivers, but it also includes drivers to make it usable in any of several operating environments, such as Novell's NetWare, Microsoft's LAN Manager, or Banyan's VINES.

TCNS does require special Network Interface Cards (NICs), however. Special NICs are needed because of the higher transmission speed and also because TCNS uses a different encoding scheme than standard ARCnet.

TCNS can use coaxial, Shielded Twisted-Pair (STP), or fiber-optic cable, but it does not support Unshielded Twisted-Pair (UTP). In order to help increase bandwidth, TCNS uses a 4B/5B translation scheme (which converts four signal bits into a five-bit symbol) and then uses a Nonreturn to Zero, Inverted (NRZI) signal-encoding scheme.

BROADER CATEGORY
ARCnet

TCP/IP (Transmission Control Protocol/Internet Protocol) Suite

TCP/IP is a suite of several networking protocols developed for use on the Internet. The suite has proven very popular, and it is also used for most UNIX implementations as well as other platforms. The only real competition for the TCP/IP suite is provided by protocols that have been or are being developed for the emerging OSI Reference Model.

The main protocols in the suite include the following:

- SMTP (Simple Mail Transfer Protocol) provides a simple electronic-mail (e-mail) service. SMTP uses the TCP protocol to send and receive messages.

- FTP (File Transfer Protocol) enables users to transfer files from one machine to another. FTP also uses the services of the TCP protocol at the transport layer to move the files.

- Telnet provides terminal-emulation capabilities and allows users to log in to a remote network from their computers.

- SNMP (Simple Network Management Protocol) is used to control network-management services and to transfer management-related data.

- TCP (Transmission Control Protocol) provides connection- and stream-oriented, transport-layer services. TCP uses the IP to deliver its packets.

- UDP (User Datagram Protocol) provides connectionless transport-layer service. UDP also uses the IP to deliver its packets.

- IP (Internet Protocol) provides routing and connectionless delivery services at the network layer. The IP uses packet switching and makes a best effort to deliver its packets.

TDDI (Twisted-pair Distributed Data Interface)

A network architecture that implements FDDI capabilities and protocols on twisted-pair, copper-based cable.

SEE ALSO
CDDI (Copper-based Distributed Data Interface)

TDM (Time Division Multiplexing)

A transmission scheme in which signals from multiple sources are transmitted "simultaneously" by allocating time slices in sequence to each of the signals. This method is generally used for digital communications.

SEE ALSO
Multiplexing

TDMA (Time Division Multiple Access)

A strategy for making a communications channel available to multiple parties at a time. The strategy allocates each party a time slot, whose duration depends on the number of parties who want to transmit and on the relative importance of the party to whom the time slot is being allocated. Each party's transmissions must be reassembled at the receiving end.

COMPARE
CDMA (Cell Division Multiple Access); FDMA (Frequency Division Multiple Access)

TDR (Time Domain Reflectometry)

A diagnostic method in which a signal of known amplitude and duration is sent along a stretch of cable. Depending on the amount of time the signal takes to return and on the cable's nominal velocity of propagation, a measurement instrument can determine the distance the signal traveled and whether there are any shorts or opens in the cable. A *time domain reflectometer* is a device used to test the integrity of a section of cable before the cable is even unwound.

Tee Coupler

A coupler that splits an incoming signal into two outgoing signals. This is in contrast to a star coupler, which splits the signal into more parts. A tee coupler has three ports. These couplers are used in bus topologies.

SEE ALSO
Coupler

Teleconference

A conference between individuals who are separated by a distance and who are communicating by electronic means. The telecommunications link for a teleconference may be voice only (two-way), one-way video, two-way voice, or two-way video.

Telephony

A term that referred originally to the business of the telephone companies but that has come to refer to the combination and integration of telephone and networking services. For example, providing a link from a network to the telephone lines and using software to interact with the telephone services can be referred to as telephony.

Teleservices

In ISDN (Integrated Services Digital Network), services defined for communications between two endpoints. The following teleservices have been defined:

Telefax: Provides facsimile service compliant with the specifications for Group 4 (digital) faxes. The fax is sent on a B (bearer) channel; control signals are sent over the D (data) channel.

Telephony: Provides speech communication in 3.1 kilohertz (kHz) bandwidths. The conversion is sent over a B channel; control signals are sent over the D channel.

Teletex: Provides text communication capabilities using standardized character sets, formats, and communication protocols. Users can exchange text at 2,400 baud. The user's transmission is over a B channel; control signals are over the D channel. Not to be confused with *teletext*, which is a special type of videotex service.

Telex: Provides interactive text communication capabilities. Telex is older and slower than Teletex.

Videotex: Provides transmission capabilities for both text and graphics. Videotex services are generally one-directional.

Teletext is a one-directional videotex service in which signals are transmitted from a source during certain "quiet" intervals in a television transmission. Originally intended as a service to provide general information (weather, sports updates, and so on), teletext has not yet caught on with the general public. It is, however, popular in business environments.

PRIMARY SOURCE
CCITT Recommendation I.212

▼
Temperature Sensor

A sensor that monitors the temperature inside the computer. If this rises above a predefined level, the sensor automatically turns on or speeds up the computer's fan.

▼
Terminal

A terminal is a device that can be used to communicate with a host computer, such as a mainframe, but that may lack any independent processing capabilities. Several categories of terminals are defined:

Dumb terminal: Lacks any memory or other components needed for doing computations. All processing for the terminal is done by the host or by the host's Front-End Processor (FEP). Dumb terminals have limited flexibility for use because they are not addressable. This means dumb terminals cannot do line sharing and cannot be polled for requests. These restrictions greatly limit the kind of interactions possible with a dumb terminal.

Smart terminal: Has at least limited processing capabilities and can be associated with an address.

Intelligent terminal: Has its own processor, can do its own processing, and can even run programs. PCs often serve as intelligent terminals.

In addition, terminals may be used for synchronous or asynchronous communications. Since the requirements for these two different communications strategies are

a b c d e f g h i j k l m n o p q r s **t** u v w x y z

quite different, synchronous and asynchronous terminals may not be compatible.

If the required type of terminal is not available, it is often possible to provide *terminal emulation* through software, hardware, or both. Through an *emulation*, a PC can be turned into a functionally equivalent replica of the required terminal. In general, asynchronous terminals are easier to emulate than synchronous ones.

Terminal Cluster Controller

A device that connects one or more PCs to a front-end processor for a mainframe computer, most notably in an IBM mainframe network. An alternative uses a gateway to the mainframe.

Terminal Emulation

Terminal emulation is a process by which a computer behaves as if it were a particular model of terminal. For example, terminal emulation may be used in order to enable the PC to communicate with a mainframe machine.

Emulation capabilities can be provided in hardware or software. The use of an emulation adapter card is popular. The speed and performance of these types of boards are sometimes better than for emulation in software, but the price can be prohibitive if many workstations will need to provide access to mainframes.

Terminator

A resistor placed at the end of a segment of cable to prevent signals from being echoed or reflected back toward the incoming signal.

TH (Transmission Header)

In SNA networks, an element added to a basic information unit (BIU) at the path control layer. The BIU, together with the TH, form a path information unit (PIU).

SEE

SNA (Systems Network Architecture)

Three-Way Handshake

A three-way handshake is the process used to synchronize activities when two protocols establish a connection. In a three-way handshake, the following occurs:

- The caller sends a packet requesting a connection. This packet may contain communications parameters that specify the terms under which the caller wants to establish a connection.

- To indicate that it is ready to receive, the called node returns a connect confirmation packet. This packet may contain connection parameters that the called node needs or wants. These parameters may be different from those originally sent by the caller.

- To indicate agreement to the called node's terms, the caller sends an acknowledgment packet. This tells the called node that the terms are acceptable and that the caller is ready to proceed. Under certain conditions, the caller may send an ordinary or a special, expedited data packet instead of the acknowledgment.

Note that *three-way* refers to the number of steps involved rather than to the number of hands. See the Time-Sequence Diagram article for an illustration of the three-way handshake.

Threshold

In network management, an attribute level that is used as a cutoff point between significant or critical and nonsignificant events. For example, an alarm may be given if an error rate goes above a predefined threshold value.

Throughput

A measure of activity or progress in a communications session. The most common measure of throughput is the total number of bits transmitted within a given amount of time, usually a second. This value includes *all* bits transmitted (data, control, and so on), even retransmitted bits. The *effective throughput* is the number of *data* bits transmitted within a given time period.

THT (Token Holding Time)

In FDDI networks, a parameter whose value can be used to adjust access to the network. A high THT value allows a node to keep the token for a long time, which is useful if network activity consists mainly of large file transfers and if rapid access to the network is not critical. In contrast, a small value gives nodes more equal access to the network.

TIA (The Internet Adapter)

The Internet Adapter provides a SLIP (serial line Internet protocol) emulator for UNIX systems. This emulator makes it possible to run Windows browsers, such as Mosaic, from a UNIX shell account. TIA is a shareware program.

TIC (Token Ring Interface Coupler)

A device that enables direct connections from a Token Ring network to various types of mainframe equipment, including front-end processors, AS/400s, and 3174 terminal cluster controllers.

Tight Buffer

In fiber-optic cabling, a layer that is stretched tightly over the cladding to keep the fiber from moving around too much. Tight buffers are commonly used in patch cords and other areas in which the cable is likely to be moved or shaken.

Time-out

As a verb, to time-out means to use too much time to respond in a communication situation, usually resulting in the failure of the task that was being performed. For example, a device, such as a modem or a station on a network, can cause a time-out if it does not acknowledge receipt of a transmission from another device.

Time-outs can be caused by transmission errors, delays due to network traffic, and

a
b
c
d
e
f
g
h
i
j
k
l
m
n
o
p
q
r
s
t
u
v
w
x
y
z

other types of delays. The action taken by the waiting device depends on the configuration. For example, a modem may end the session or retransmit the message.

Time-Sequence Diagram

A time-sequence diagram refers to a technique for graphically representing events over time. In this type of diagram, time is represented on a vertical axis, with the oldest event at the top and the most recent event at the bottom. The information presented horizontally depends on the diagram's content.

The figure "A time-sequence diagram" illustrates an example. The figure shows a three-way handshake in which sender and receiver go through a request and acknowledgment process before the sender begins transmitting data. To make the sequence clear, the events are numbered in the figure.

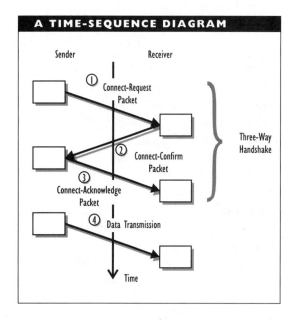

A TIME-SEQUENCE DIAGRAM

Time Synchronization

In Novell's NetWare 4.*x*, time synchronization is a way of ensuring that all servers in a NetWare Directory Services (NDS) Directory are using the same time. Synchronized timing is essential because it provides a way of ordering changes that may have been made to information about objects on the network.

Information about objects changes as a print queue grows or shrinks, a user changes a password, or an application is executed. Since these changes may be recorded in replicas, it is essential to keep track of the timing and sequence of events when updating the Directory.

NetWare 4.*x* uses time synchronization for this purpose. In time synchronization, the NDS marks each event that occurs, along with the exact time of its occurrence, with a unique value, known as a *time stamp*.

To make time stamps useful, the network must ensure that all servers are keeping the same time. To do this, special time servers are designated. These time servers provide the "correct" time to other time servers or to workstations.

NetWare 4.*x* distinguishes three types of time servers that provide time: Single Reference, Reference, and Primary. All other servers that accept time information from these servers are called *secondary* time servers. In any network with more than one time server, the time servers must work together to create a network time. They influence each other until they reach something like an "average" time, and they then deliver this time to all the secondary servers.

Single-Reference Time Server

If one is defined, a Single-Reference time server is the only time server that provides the correct time to all other servers and to workstations. Defining a time server that has such complete authority has two consequences:

- All other servers must be able to contact the Single-Reference time server.

- All other servers on the network must be designated as Secondary time servers, which provide the time information to the workstations.

Single-Reference time servers are generally used for Local-Area Networks (LANs), since it is inconvenient (and expensive) when secondary time servers need to make long-distance calls to find out the time.

Reference Time Server

A Reference time server provides a time for all other Primary servers to work towards as they achieve a network time. A Reference time server may be synchronized with an external time source. It adjusts its internal clock only in relation to such an external source, never to synchronize with other Primary time servers; the Primary servers must adjust to the Reference server.

A network usually has only one Reference time server, and this may or may not be designated as a Single-Reference server. However, if there are two or more Reference servers, each must be synchronized with the same (or with an equivalent) external source. A network probably will not need more than one Reference time server, unless, for example, it has one at each end of a Wide-Area Network (WAN) link.

Reference time servers are used when it is important to have a central time source. A Reference (as opposed to a Single-Reference) time server must have at least one other Primary or Reference time server with which to communicate.

Primary Time Server

A Primary time server synchronizes its clock to a Reference or another Primary time server. Primary time servers participate in a vote, along with Reference and other Primary time servers, to determine the common network time. Once this time is set, Primary time servers adjust their clocks to this time. (Reference time servers do not adjust their clocks, since their time is actually used to determine the network time.)

Primary time servers are useful on large networks, particularly on WANs. By putting a Primary time server in each geographic region, you can minimize the amount of telephone access needed to determine the time. Primary time servers provide the time information to secondary time servers and to workstations. (A Reference server is not necessary, but you must have at least two Primary servers.)

Secondary Time Server

A secondary time server gets time information from a Single Reference, Reference, or Primary time server and provides this information to workstations. Secondary time servers always synchronize their time to that of the time source.

a b c d e f g h i j k l m n o p q r s **t** u v w x y z

Communications among Time Servers

To enable time servers to find each other, the servers can use the SAP (Service Advertising Protocol) to make themselves known. Because of the small amount of extra network traffic generated by SAP packets, this strategy is recommended for small networks and for networks whose configurations are unlikely to change much. The SAP changes dynamically as servers and nodes are added or removed.

An alternative is to configure the network explicitly by specifying the location of all time servers and by specifying which time server each secondary server should contact for information. This strategy is best when the level of SAP traffic begins to impede network performance.

Tip

One of a pair of twisted wires, with the other wire known as the ring. A four-pair unshielded twisted-pair cable has four tip/ring pairs.

Token

In some media-access methods, a special packet that is passed from node to node according to a predefined sequence. The node with the token gets to access the network.

Token Bus

Token Bus is a network architecture defined in the IEEE 802.4 specifications. The Token Bus architecture has never been popular for Local-Area Networks (LANs) of the type found in most offices. It is, however, widely used in manufacturing contexts.

The Token Bus architecture was inspired, in part, by work relating to the automation of manufacturing tasks. This architecture has, in turn, become the basis for the various types of Manufacturing Automation Protocol (MAP) systems that have been developed to help automate operations in industrial contexts.

The 802.4 specifications include physical layer and Media Access Control (MAC) sublayer details for networks that use a bus topology and use token passing as the media-access method. The figure "Context and properties of Token Bus" summarizes this architecture.

The Token Bus architecture supports the following:

- Both carrier band (single-channel) and broadband networks

- Operation over either 75-ohm coaxial cable or fiber-optic cable

- Network speeds of 1, 5, 10, and 20 megabits per second (Mbps), with supported speeds depending on the medium

- Four priority levels for regulating access to the network medium

- Four physical layer medium configurations: two carrier band (full bandwidth), one broadband, and an optical configuration

Physical Media Configurations

According to the 802.4 standard, Token Bus networks can use any of several

a
b
c
d
e
f
g
h
i
j
k
l
m
n
o
p
q
r
s
t
u
v
w
x
y
z

CONTEXT AND PROPERTIES OF TOKEN BUS

Context

Network Architecture
     Ethernet
     ARCnet
     Token Bus ————————————┐
     Token Ring

Token Bus Properties

Defined by IEEE 802.4 specifications

Uses token passing as the media-access method

Uses a physical bus topology, but with nodes connected in a logical ring, based on the token-passing sequence

Supports electrical (coaxial) and fiber-optic cable

Supports carrier band and broadband networks

Supports network speeds of up to 20 Mbps

---

configurations at the physical layer, depending on whether the network uses electrical (75-ohm coaxial) or fiber-optic cable and on whether the network uses the entire bandwidth for a single channel. Selection of a configuration also helps determine the allowable transmission speeds and the topology.

The cable for a Token Bus architecture may support a single channel or multiple channels on the same channel. In carrier band configurations, the entire bandwidth is used for a single modulated transmission; multiplexing is not used to get multiple messages onto the same channel. In contrast, broadband configurations support multiple modulated transmissions on the same cable.

Each of the channels in a broadband configuration will use a different bandwidth for its transmission.

Single-Channel, Phase-Continuous FSK

A single-channel, phase-continuous configuration uses Frequency Shift Keying (FSK) as the modulation technique. In FSK, different frequencies are used to encode different values. The shift from one frequency to another is accomplished by a gradual, continuous change in the frequency (as opposed to an abrupt switch from one frequency to the other).

This method, which is also known as *phase-continuous carrier band,* is the easiest to implement and the least expensive of the four configurations supported for Token Bus architectures. It can be used even with older cable that may already be installed in a building. The disadvantage is that the top speed is only 1 Mbps.

This configuration uses a bus in which all signals are broadcast in all directions. Cable segments are connected using a BNC connector.

Single-Channel, Phase-Coherent FSK

A single-channel, phase-coherent configuration also uses a form of FSK to encode the possible values. In this variant, the frequencies used to encode 1 and 0 values are an integral multiple of the transmission rate. For example, for a 5 Mbps transmission rate, a 1 would be encoded as a 5 MHz frequency and a 0 would be encoded as 10 MHz. For a 10 Mbps network, the frequencies would be 10 and 20 MHz for 1 and 0, respectively.

This method, which is also known as *phase-coherent carrier band,* is more expensive to implement than the phase-continuous carrier band method. It also supports faster networks: either 5 or 10 Mbps. This configuration uses a bus in which all signals are broadcast in all directions. Cable segments are connected using a BNC connector.

Broadband

The primary configuration defined for the Token Bus architecture uses broadband transmissions and a directed bus, or tree, topology. This configuration is based on recommendations from General Motors, whose

work on what has since become the MAP helped inspire the 802.4 standard. The broadband configuration also uses many of the principles and methods associated with cable television transmissions.

In a broadband topology, transmissions are assumed to originate in a special node, known as the *head end.* The signals are sent from the head end to the nodes along the network bus or tree.

The broadband configuration uses a modulation technique that varies both the amplitude and the phase (timing offset) of a signal. The phase variation is actually used to reduce the bandwidth required for the channel, thereby making more channels possible within the total bandwidth. The signal may be scrambled before transmission to avoid loss of synchronization during a long stretch in which a signal does not change.

This configuration can support transmission speeds of 1, 5, or 10 Mbps. Cable segments are connected using an F connector.

Fiber-Optic ASK

Another Token Bus configuration uses optical fiber as the transmission medium. This configuration uses Amplitude Shift Keying (ASK) as the modulation technique. In ASK, values are encoded as changes in the amplitude, or strength, of the carrier signal. In this configuration, the amplitude change is rather severe: a binary 1 is encoded as a pulse of light, and a 0 is no light (a pulse of darkness, so to speak). To avoid the loss of synchronization during a long period of light or darkness, data is first encoded using Manchester encoding to ensure value changes.

This configuration uses a star configuration in which the center of the star may be a node (active star) or a coupler (passive star). In an active star, each node in the star sends its transmissions to the central node, which then broadcasts the transmission to all the other connected nodes. In a passive star, the coupler (signal redirector) at the center is created by fusing the fibers coming from each of the nodes. This fusion creates paths between all nodes so that any transmission from a node will automatically reach all the other nodes.

Fiber-optic configurations are still the most expensive, but they also support the fastest transmission speeds: 5, 10, and 20 Mbps.

Token Bus Operation

Access to the network is determined by the token, a special frame that is passed from node to node in a well-defined sequence. To regulate the sequence in which the token is passed, the nodes involved in the token passing form a logical ring, as shown in the figure "A bus topology with nodes in a logical ring."

Each node passes the token to the node with the next lower ring address. In the figure, the token is passed from node 600 to 400 to 200 to 100. To complete the ring, the node with the lowest address passes to the node with the highest, so that node 100 passes to 600 in the figure. Notice that node 700 is on the bus but it is not part of the ring. Node 700 can receive messages but cannot send any.

Only the node with the token can transmit. When it has the token, a node can send

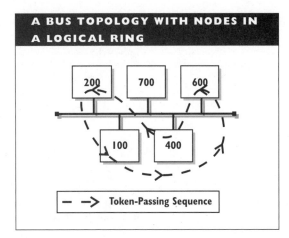

A BUS TOPOLOGY WITH NODES IN A LOGICAL RING

- - -> Token-Passing Sequence

a packet to whatever node it wishes. For example, with the token, node 400 can send a message to node 600. To do so, 400 just needs to broadcast the packet on the bus. Each node on the bus will check the destination address, but only node 600 will bother to read the packet. Node 400 could just as easily have sent a packet to node 700 in this way.

Once node 400 has finished transmitting, it sends the token to node 300. This node can transmit, if it has anything to say.

When token passing is used as a media-access method, networks need considerable monitoring capabilities to keep track of the token. If a token should be lost or corrupted, the network will use mechanisms for forcing an attempt at token recovery and, failing that, for generating a new token to avoid disrupting the network.

To enable nodes to connect to the ring, "sign-up" opportunities are provided at random intervals. Each node will occasionally ask whether any nodes with lower addresses are interested in joining the ring.

Handling Service Priority Levels

The four priority levels for service supported by the Token Bus architecture are named (from highest priority to lowest) 6, 4, 2, and 0.

To ensure that no node hogs the token, restrictions are placed on the amount of time a node may hold a token. This restriction is called the Token Holding Time (THT).

For each priority level, a maximum Token Rotation Time (TRTx) is specified. For example, a value of TRT2 represents how long the token can take to make its way around the ring while still being able to ensure that packets at priority level 2 will be transmitted.

Token Bus Frames

The 802.4 architecture uses a data frame and several types of control frames. The data frame is used for transmitting information from and to higher levels. Control frames help manage, update, and maintain a network. The token is a control frame that plays a central role. The figure "A Token Bus frame" shows the basic structure of a frame and also how the FC field differs for data and control frames.

Control Frames

For control frames, the following fields are used:

Preamble (1+ bytes): Used to synchronize sender and receiver. More bytes are used for faster transmission speeds. For example, 1 byte of synchronization suffices for 1 Mbps networks, but 3 bytes are needed for a 10 Mbps transmission.

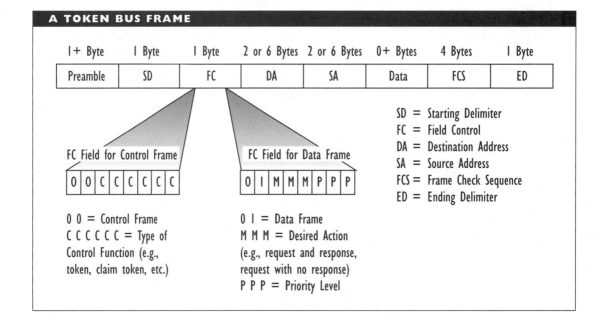

A TOKEN BUS FRAME

1+ Byte	1 Byte	1 Byte	2 or 6 Bytes	2 or 6 Bytes	0+ Bytes	4 Bytes	1 Byte
Preamble	SD	FC	DA	SA	Data	FCS	ED

FC Field for Control Frame

| 0 | 0 | C | C | C | C | C | C |

FC Field for Data Frame

| 0 | 1 | M | M | M | P | P | P |

SD = Starting Delimiter
FC = Field Control
DA = Destination Address
SA = Source Address
FCS = Frame Check Sequence
ED = Ending Delimiter

0 0 = Control Frame
C C C C C C = Type of Control Function (e.g., token, claim token, etc.)

0 1 = Data Frame
M M M = Desired Action (e.g., request and response, request with no response)
P P P = Priority Level

SD (Start Delimiter, 1 byte): Used to indicate the start of a frame. This byte consists of a signal pattern(xx0x x000) that can never occur as data. In this pattern, the x's represent a signal that is not used for data.

FC (Frame Control, 1 byte): Used to specify information about the frame. The first 2 bits indicate whether it is a data (01) or a control (00) frame. In a control frame, the remaining 6 bits specify the command the frame represents. For the token frame, these bits are 001000, from least to most significant bit. In a data frame, the next 3 bits indicate the status of data and transmission and the last 3 bits show the frame's priority level (0, 2, 4, or 6). The status bits represent three possibilities: request with no response expected (the default), request with response expected, or response.

DA (Destination Address): Specifies the node to which the token is being passed. Depending on the type of addresses being used, this field will use either 2 or 6 bytes.

SA (Source Address): Specifies the node passing the token. Depending on the type of addresses being used, this field will use either 2 or 6 bytes.

Data: For control frames, this may contain special settings or commands. For data frames, this contains the material being transmitted between higher layers. Not all types of frames include this field. For example, the token uses 0 bytes for this field.

FCS (Frame Check Sequence, 4 bytes): Used to check whether the frame was received without error.

ED (End Delimiter): Used to indicate the end of the frame. As with the SD field, this will be a unique signal pattern.

Data Frame

A data frame for the Token Bus architecture has the same basic structure as a control frame:

Preamble: Same as for a token frame.

SD (Start Delimiter): Same as for a token frame.

FC (Frame Control): Same as for a token frame, except that this is a data frame.

DA (Destination Address): Same as for token frame.

SA (Source Address): Same as for a token frame.

Data: Contains a Protocol Data Unit (PDU) from a higher layer, generally the Logical-Link Control (LLC) sublayer. This field may be over 8,000 bytes. The restriction is that the FC, DA, SA, Data, and FCS fields together cannot be larger than 8,191 bytes.

FCS (Frame Check Sequence): Same as for a token frame.

ED (End Delimiter): Same as for a token frame.

BROADER CATEGORY

Network Architecture

SEE ALSO

ARCnet; ATM; Ethernet; FDDI; Token Ring

▼
Token Holding Time (THT)

SEE

THT (Token Holding Time)

▼
Token Passing

Token passing is a deterministic media-access method in which a token is passed from node to node, according to a predefined sequence. A *token* is a special packet, or frame. At any given time, the token can be available or in use. When an available token reaches a node that node can access the network. The figure "Summary of the token-passing process" shows this method.

A deterministic access method guarantees that every node will get access to the network within a given length of time, usually on the order of a few hundred microseconds or milliseconds. This is in contrast to a probabilistic access method (such as CSMA/CD), in which nodes check for network activity when they want to access the network, and the first node to claim the idle network gets access to it.

Because each node gets its turn within a fixed period, deterministic access methods are more efficient on networks that have heavy traffic. With such networks, nodes using probabilistic access methods spend much of their time trying to gain access and relatively little time actually transmitting data over the network.

Network architectures that support token passing as an access method include ARCnet, FDDI, and IBM's Token Ring.

Token-Passing Process

To transmit, the node first marks the token as in-use and then transmits a data packet with the token attached. The packet is passed from node to node until the packet reaches its destination. The recipient acknowledges the packet by sending the token back to the sender, who then sets the token to idle and passes it on to the next node in the network.

The next recipient is not necessarily the node that is nearest to the token-passing node. Rather, the next node is determined by some predefined rule. For example, in an ARCnet network, the token is passed from a node to the node with the next higher network address.

Networks that use token passing generally have some provision for setting the priority with which a node gets the token. Higher-level protocols can specify that a message is important and should receive higher priority.

Active and Standby Monitors

A network that uses token passing also requires an active monitor (AM) and one or more Standby Monitors (SMs). The AM keeps track of the token to make sure it has not been corrupted, lost, or sent to a node that has been disconnected from the network. If any of these things happens, the AM generates a new token, and the network is back in business.

The SM makes sure the AM is doing its job and does not break down and get

SUMMARY OF THE TOKEN-PASSING PROCESS

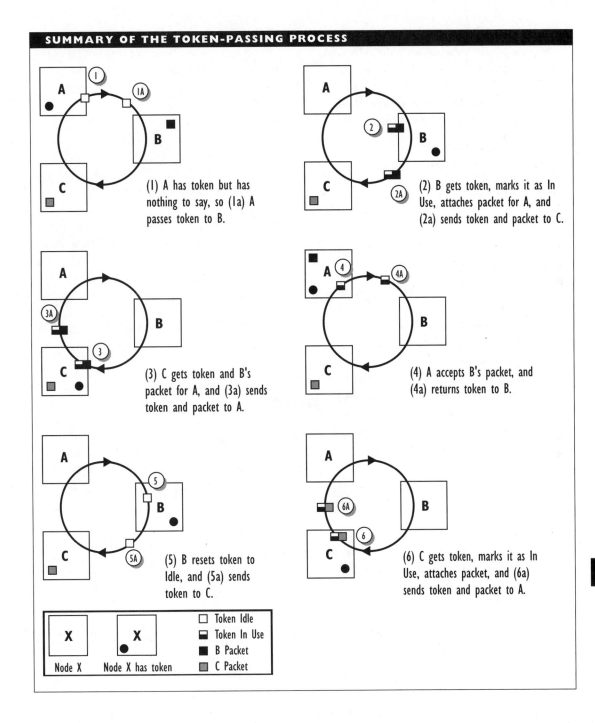

(1) A has token but has nothing to say, so (1a) A passes token to B.

(2) B gets token, marks it as In Use, attaches packet for A, and (2a) sends token and packet to C.

(3) C gets token and B's packet for A, and (3a) sends token and packet to A.

(4) A accepts B's packet, and (4a) returns token to B.

(5) B resets token to Idle, and (5a) sends token to C.

(6) C gets token, marks it as In Use, attaches packet, and (6a) sends token and packet to A.

□	Token Idle
▭	Token In Use
■	B Packet
▩	C Packet

Node X   Node X has token

a b c d e f g h i j k l m n o p q r s **t** u v w x y z

disconnected from the network. If the AM is lost, one of the SMs becomes the new AM, and the network is again in business.

These monitoring capabilities make for complex circuitry on network interface cards that use this media-access method.

BROADER CATEGORY
Media-Access Method

COMPARE
CSMA/CA; CSMA/CD; Demand Priority; Polling

Token Ring

Token Ring is a network architecture that uses a ring network topology and a token-passing strategy to control access to the network. This type of architecture works best with networks that handle heavy data traffic from many users, because of inherent fairness rules in token passing as an access method.

The IEEE 802.5 standard defines the Token Ring architecture and specifies how this architecture operates at the lowest two layers in the OSI Reference Model, which are the physical and data-link layers. All token-ring architectures use the network-access scheme defined by 802.5 and the LLC (Logical-Link Control) sublayer standard defined in an IEEE 802.2 document.

IBM developed its own revised specifications for a token ring architecture. These revisions differ somewhat from the official IEEE 802.5 specifications, but they have become so widely used that discussions of token ring generally mean IBM Token Ring.

IBM is largely responsible for the popularity of the Token Ring architecture because it provides a good way to connect PCs to IBM mainframes. Many of this architecture's more baroque features (such as the frames) are also in the best tradition of the IBM mainframe world.

The figure "Context and properties of Token Ring" summarizes this architecture.

With token passing as the media-access method, the node that has the token gets to access the network, provided the token is available (not being used to transport a packet) when the node receives it. Unlike the CSMA/CD media-access method that Ethernet networks use, token passing is deterministic. This means each node is guaranteed to get a turn sending packets within a pre-defined time or number of cycles.

Token Ring networks have the following features:

- Use a ring as the logical topology, but a star as the physical topology or wiring.

- Operate at either 1 or 4 megabits per second (Mbps), for IEEE 802.5; operate at either 4 or 16 Mbps, for IBM.

- Use baseband signaling, which means that only one signal travels along the line at a time.

- Use the differential Manchester signal-encoding method. Because this method breaks each bit interval into two signals, the clock speed must be twice the transmission speed in order to attain the maximum bandwidth. Thus, a 4 Mbps Token Ring network needs an 8 megahertz (MHz) clock; a 16 Mbps network needs a 32 MHz clock.

CONTEXT AND PROPERTIES OF TOKEN RING

Context

Network Architecture
    Ethernet
    ARCnet
    Token Bus
    Token Ring

Token Ring Properties

Baseband network defined by IEEE 802.5 specifications

Uses token passing as the media-access method

Uses a logical ring topology, arranged in a physical star topology

Node connections reflect the token-passing sequence

Supports electrical (4-wire twisted-pair) and fiber-optic cable

Supports speeds of 1, 4, or 16 Mbps

In the physical topology, lobes are connected to MAUs, which are connected to each other

Requires built-in network-management capabilities to keep track of the token

- Use Shielded Twisted-Pair (STP) or Unshielded Twisted-Pair (UTP) cable or fiber-optic cable, but not coaxial cable. The STP has a 150 ohm resistance, and the UTP has a 100 ohm resistance.

- Use four-wire cable, with two of the wires used for the main ring and two for the secondary ring (which can be used if there is a break in the main ring).

- Have each node (called a *lobe* in IBM terminology) connected to a wiring center, called an MAU (Multistation Access Unit). The wiring inside an MAU creates a ring of the attached nodes.

- Allow MAUs to be connected to each other to create larger rings. Each MAU includes two reserved connectors for making a MAU-MAU connection.

- Allow the use of patch panels, which sit between nodes and MAUs and make it easier to reconfigure the network.

- Require built-in network management facilities because nodes need to be able to determine whether a token has been corrupted, destroyed, or lost.

a
b
c
d
e
f
g
h
i
j
k
l
m
n
o
p
q
r
s
t
u
v
w
x
y
z

- Are controlled by the node that generates the token. This node (which is known as the *active monitor*) is generally the network file server.

Token Ring Components

The components of Token Ring networks include the Network Interface Card (NIC), cable, MAUs, connectors, media filters, and repeaters.

Token Ring NIC

Token Ring NICs are usually designed for 4 Mbps or 16 Mbps operation, or for both. NICs that support both speeds generally require you to select a speed by setting DIP switches or through software.

Because Token Ring networks must do constant network monitoring, NICs for this architecture implement an agent in the chip set. This component communicates with stations in various management roles on the network regarding the node's status and network activity.

Several companies make Token Ring chip sets, and there is some competition to add attractive features to the chip set. This competition also helps drive prices down.

Token Ring Cable

When discussing cabling, the categories defined in the IBM Cable System are generally used. This grouping includes nine types, of which seven are defined. In the literature and in discussions, you will hear references to, for example, Type 1 or Type 3 cable. See the Cable, IBM article for a discussion of this cable system. Note that the IEEE 802.5 specifications do not specify a particular type of cabling.

In a Token Ring network, cable is used for two purposes: for the main ring path (which connects MAUs) and for short runs (lobe to MAU or MAU to patch panel).

STP (IBM Type 1, 2, or possibly 9) cable is generally used for the main ring path. However, the Token Ring specifications also support UTP (for example, Type 3) and fiber-optic (Type 5) cables. For patch or jumper cable, Type 6 cable is commonly used.

MAUs (Multistation Access Units)

MAUs serve as wiring concentrators for several lobes, and they arrange the connections from the lobes into a ring. The IBM 8228 MAU is the "papa" MAU, and most MAUs from other vendors are compatible with this older model. Newer models have more intelligence and monitoring capabilities built into them.

MAUs are simply called *wiring centers* in IEEE 802.5 networks.

Connectors

Token Ring NICs generally have a DB-9 connector for STP cable and may have a modular RJ-45 plug for UTP cable.

MAUs have IBM Data Connectors. This is a special type of connector that self-shorts when disconnected so that the ring inside the MAU is not broken when a lobe is disconnected. Note that a patch cable for an IBM Token Ring network needs a DB-9 or an RJ-*xx* connector at one end and an IBM Data Connector at the other end.

Media Filter and Repeaters

A media filter is needed if you want to connect UTP cable to a DB-9 connector (which is expecting STP cable) on a NIC. This filter removes the high-frequency signals that arise when using UTP and also adjusts the inputs.

Repeaters serve to extend the maximum cable lengths imposed by various power and noise restrictions in a Token Ring network. Different types of repeaters are used for the main ring and for lobes.

Token Ring Layout

Although they use a logical ring structure, Token Ring networks are actually arranged in a star topology with each node connected to a central hub (the MAU), as illustrated in the figure "Token Ring layout."

Depending on where the MAUs are in relation to the nodes, a node may be connected directly to a MAU or to a wallplate. In the latter case, a cable will go from the wall plate to a patch panel and from there to the MAU. Regardless of whether the connection is direct or roundabout, the link to the MAU is through an IBM Data Connector so that the node can be removed from the network without disrupting the ring.

MAUs may be connected to each other using special RI (Ring In) and RO (Ring Out) ports on the MAUs. These connections maintain the ring structure across the MAUs. The RO port from one MAU is connected to the RI port of another. Several MAUs may be linked this way. If there are multiple MAUs, the RO port of the last MAU in the series is connected to the RI port of the first MAU to complete the ring.

Assuming everything is connected correctly, the logical layout of the network should have each node (X) associated directly with exactly two other nodes:

- The node which passes frames and the token to node X in the ring. This node

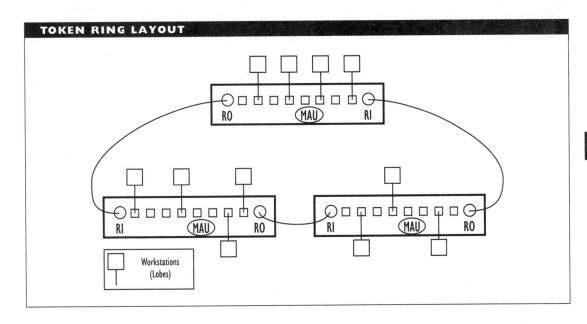

TOKEN RING LAYOUT

is X's Nearest Active Upstream Neighbor (NAUN).

- The node to which X passes frames and the token. This destination neighbor is downstream from X. For symmetry, this node can be called the Nearest Active *Down*stream Neighbor (NADN).

The MAU-MAU connection actually creates a primary, or main, ring and a backup ring. If there is a break in the main ring, it may be possible to bypass the break by going through the backup ring.

Token Ring Restrictions and Limitations

As with other network architectures, there are restrictions on the allowable distances between Token Ring network components and on the number of components allowed on the network.

Token Ring networks have two types of length restrictions: the lobe length and the ring length.

Lobe Length

The lobe length is the distance between a node and a MAU, as follows:

- For Types 1 and 2 cable (both STP), the maximum lobe length is 100 meters (330 feet).

- For types 6 and 9 (also STP), the maximum lobe length is only about 66 meters (220 feet).

- For UTP (such as Type 3 cable), the maximum lobe length is 45 meters (150 feet).

Ring Length

The ring length is the distance between MAUs on the main ring path. Distance calculations and restrictions for this part of a Token Ring network can be complicated. Values depend on the number of repeaters, MAUs, and wiring closets in the network, and these factors are used to compute an Adjusted Ring Length (ARL) for the network.

That caution raised, the following values apply even for simple networks with minimal repeaters, MAUs, and wiring closets:

- For Types 1 and 2 cable, the distance between MAUs can be up to 200 meters (660 feet).

- For Type 3 cable, the distance between MAUs can be up to about 120 meters (400 feet).

- For Type 6 cable, the distance between MAUs can be up to only about 45 meters (140 feet), because this type is intended for use as a patch cable.

- Fiber-optic cable segments can be as long as 1 kilometer (0.6 mile).

There is also a *minimum* distance constraint: lobes must be separated by at least 2.5 meters (8 feet).

Other Token Ring Restrictions

Other restrictions on Token Ring networks include the following:

- At most three cable segments (separated by repeaters) are allowed in a series.

- Each cable segment must be terminated at both ends and grounded at one end.

- In the IEEE 802.5 specifications, a network can have up to 250 lobes.

- In the IBM Token Ring specifications, a network using STP can have up to 260 lobes; one using UTP can have up to 72 lobes.

- At most, 33 MAUs are allowed on the network.

- A network cannot have nodes operating at different speeds. That is, a network may consist of 4 Mbps or 16 Mbps lobes, but not both. You can, however, use a bridge to connect a 4 Mbps to a 16 Mbps Token Ring network.

- To operate a 16 Mbps Token Ring network, you need cable that is rated at least Category 4 in the EIA/TIA-568 classification system.

In many cases, the specific values in the restrictions are imposed because of timing constraints on the network. As such, the quoted values assume a maximal network, so that all signals take the longest possible time to reach their destinations.

In practice, this means that some of the restrictions can be exceeded (but *with caution*), at least slightly, on smaller networks.

Token Ring Operation

In a Token Ring architecture, the token is passed from node to node in a logical ring structure. The token is passed in a fixed direction around the ring. The node with the token is allowed to send a message to another node.

A particular node, usually the network file server, generates the token that starts the network rolling. This node also serves as the Active Monitor (AM) whose job is to keep track of the token and make sure it does not get corrupted or lost. The AM is responsible for several important functions:

- Checking for and detecting lost tokens or frames

- Monitoring frame transmissions

- Purging the ring and creating a new token

- Initiating and monitoring Neighbor Notification (NN)

- Maintaining proper delays in the ring

- Maintaining the master clock

Other nodes serve as Standby Monitors (SMs); their job is to monitor the AM. SMs constantly check for the presence of an AM. If none is detected (or if the AM is not working properly), the SMs go through a token-claiming process to determine a new AM.

Once the ring has been set up, the token-passing process does not require any special intervention from the AM. Each node receives the token from its NAUN and passes it to its NADN.

When a network first starts up, the AM generates a token and initiates a Neighbor Notification (NN) process. This is the process by which each node learns the address

a b c d e f g h i j k l m n o p q r s **t** u v w x y z

of its NAUN and broadcasts its own address to the node's NADN.

Ring nodes can be checked in two different ways for token passing:

- Using *physical ring polling,* each node attached to the network is included, regardless of whether or not that node is currently active (actually logged onto the network).

- Using *active ring polling,* only those nodes that are currently active on the network are included in the token-passing process.

Using the Token

The token is a special type of frame that contains, among other things, a priority value and a monitor setting (which is 0 or 1). A token with a monitor setting of 1 is available for use. Any node with a priority setting greater than or equal to that of the token can grab the token as it goes by on the ring and then transmit a frame.

When a node has grabbed the token and is going to transmit, the node changes the token's monitor setting to 0 (so no other node will try to grab the token). If the active monitor sees a token with a monitor setting of 1 come around, the AM assumes the token is corrupt, destroys it, and creates a new one.

When a node sends a frame onto the network, the frame includes a destination and a source address. The frame is passed from node to node according to the sequence determined by the ring structure. Each node checks to see whether it is the destination for the frame.

If not, the node passes the frame on. If so, the node saves the source address and the data, computes the Cyclic Redundancy Check (CRC) value, changes some bits in the Frame Status field for the data frame, and passes the frame to the node's NADN.

The frame circulates the ring until it returns to the sender, who checks the Frame Status information to make sure the frame was received correctly. If so, the node releases the token and passes it to the NADN.

During the token-passing process, a lobe may claim an available token, let it pass by unclaimed, or request a higher-priority level for the token. A lobe makes this request by setting the reserved priority bits in the token frame to the desired value. When a lobe requests a higher priority, the lobe records the current token priority value in a buffer.

The token continues to circulate with the priority level and the requested priority settings until any of the following happens:

- A lobe with sufficiently high priority grabs the token.

- The unclaimed token reaches the lobe that generated the token.

- A token with a higher priority raises the requested priority level.

In the second case, the starting lobe destroys the token and generates a new one with priority set to the highest requested level. This new token is then sent around the ring, where it can be claimed by the lobe that requested the higher priority.

A lobe may get the token by requesting a higher priority and then claiming the regenerated token. Once the lobe finishes sending its frame and has the token back, that lobe must restore the token's original priority (the token priority setting when the lobe originally requested the higher priority). In short, it is the sender's responsibility to restore a token to the state it had before the sender used it.

Token Ring Activities

Normal repeat mode is the default operation of a lobe in a Token Ring network. When the network is operating normally, each lobe can deal properly with each frame received and can pass the frame on correctly.

In addition to normal repeat mode, several special-purpose activities take place only under certain conditions.

Ring Insertion The five-step ring-insertion process occurs when a lobe wants to join the network. The steps in this process are as follows:

1. Physical connection and lobe media check. The lobe is connected to the network. The connection is checked by having the lobe send a particular type of MAC frame to the MAU and making sure the frame is returned intact.

2. Monitor check. The new lobe checks for the presence of an AM by waiting a specified amount of time to hear one of three types of MAC frames. If the lobe hears one of these frames, it assumes an AM is present and proceeds to the next step. If none of the frames arrives within the specified time, the lobe begins a token-claiming process.

3. Address verification. The lobe checks that its address is unique on the network. This check is also done using a particular type of MAC frame. If successful, the lobe proceeds to the next step; if not, the node disconnects itself from the ring and begins the ring-insertion process again.

4. Neighbor notification. The lobe learns the address of its NAUN and sends its own address to the new lobe's NADN. This process also takes place each time the network is started.

5. Request initialization. The network's Ring Parameter Server (RPS) checks the new lobe's parameters and settings.

NN (Neighbor Notification) The NN process tells each lobe about the upstream neighbor from which the lobe receives frames and the downstream neighbor to which the lobe transmits them. The process uses the Frame Status and Source Address fields in certain types of MAC frames to assign this information to the appropriate lobes.

The NN process is repeated until each lobe has been involved. The AM begins the process by sending the first MAC frame and ends the process by copying the last values from the MAC frame sent by the AM's upstream neighbor.

The AM sends an Active Monitor Present (AMP) MAC frame; the remaining lobes (which are all SMs by default) send Standby Monitor Present (SMP) MAC frames. Each frame is received by one lobe, which becomes the sending lobe's downstream neighbor.

a b c d e f g h i j k l m n o p q r s **t** u v w x y z

Priority Access Each lobe in a Token Ring network has a priority level (0 is lowest, 7 is highest) whose value determines which tokens the lobe can grab. Priority access is the method by which priority values are assigned to the token frame and to a lobe.

A lobe can grab only a token with a priority level less than or equal to the lobe's. Lobes can request priority levels so that they can get the token.

Ring Purge In the ring purge process, the AM dissolves the ring and rebuilds it beginning with the token-claiming process. A ring purge happens under any of the following conditions:

- When the token or a frame is lost or corrupted

- When a particular type of MAC frame is not received within a required amount of time

- When a particular bit in a frame indicates that a lobe has failed to return the token

Token Claiming Through the token-claiming process, an AM is chosen from among the SMs vying for the position. The token-claiming process is initiated under any of the following conditions:

- When the AM does not detect any frames on the ring within a predefined amount of time

- When an SM cannot detect either an AM or a frame within a predefined amount of time

- When a new lobe is added to the ring but that lobe does not detect an AM during the ring insertion process

The process by which a winner emerges from this contest is reminiscent of certain children's games: lobes release and circulate frames using rules based on relative address values, and the first node to get its own frame back three times becomes the AM.

Beaconing Beaconing is a signaling process by which lobes announce the occurrence of hard (serious) errors on the network. A lobe can detect such an error in either itself or in its NAUN.

The Beacon MAC frame sent under these circumstances allows the Ring Error Monitor (REM) to determine the fault domain, which is the logical area in which the error most likely occurred. This area consists of the beaconing lobe, that lobe's NAUN, and the cable between these two lobes.

Further diagnostics rely on monitoring statistics from these and other lobes on the ring.

Network Management

Networks with deterministic media-access methods must be able to make sure the selection mechanism is functioning properly at all times. For Token Ring networks, this means the token must be valid, visible, and circulating.

The mechanism for evaluating the status of the token must also be working correctly. For token ring networks, this means that the AM must be doing its work. If one of the token conditions should be violated and the AM should be unable to detect this, the network could become locked.

To make sure this does not happen, the Token Ring architecture management facilities include some built-in mechanisms: the AM monitors the token, and the other lobes monitor the AM.

Token Ring networks have an extensive set of management capabilities, and each NIC on the network can participate, at least by monitoring network activity. In addition to the AM and SM, Token Ring networks include several other management functions, and the same node may carry out one or more of these functions:

- The CRS (Configuration Report Server) node collects various performance and other numerical information from the nodes and passes this information on to the network manager node.

- The RPS (Ring Parameter Server) node monitors the addresses of all nodes on the ring and of the NAUN for each of these nodes to make sure that all the attachments meet the criteria for a ring. The RPS also sends ring-initialization information to new nodes as they join the ring and sends the information gathered to the network manager.

- The REM (Ring Error Monitor) node gathers reports of any hard or soft errors on the ring and passes this information on to the network manager. (A hard error is serious, and threatens or impairs the network's continued operation; a soft error is considered minor

and no threat to the network's normal operation.) The REM also counts soft error frequency to determine whether they happen often enough to be regarded as potentially serious.

- The LBS (LAN Bridge Server) node monitors the functioning of any bridges on the network and keeps track of the activity across these bridges. The LBS also communicates this data to the network manager.

- The LRM (LAN Reporting Mechanism) node provides the network manager with information about any remote servers on the network.

Note that the REM node is dedicated to its error gathering, and it does not generally function as an ordinary workstation on the network. A protocol analyzer program for Token Ring provides alternatives to or enhancements of the REM's services.

The data collected by each of these management functions is sent to a specially designated node that serves as the network manager. This node's task is to summarize and analyze the collected statistics and to make adjustments in the network's operations as a result of this information. The network manager's capabilities are generally provided as software.

For network management, IBM Token Ring networks use the NMT (Network Management) protocol, which is defined as part of IEEE 802.5. In contrast, FDDI networks, which also use token passing, use SMT (System Management), a somewhat different management protocol.

Token Ring Frames

Token Ring networks send packets, or frames, around the network. There are only four main types of frames in Token Ring networks: Token, LLC, MAC, and Abort Sequence frames. (LLC and MAC frames are both considered data frames.) However, there are 25 types of MAC frames. The figure "Token Ring frame types" shows the frames.

Token Frames

Token frames have three 1-byte fields:

Starting Delimiter: Indicates the start of the frame. It contains a pattern of deliberate signal violations, which are signal patterns that do not occur in normal transmissions, to indicate the start of a frame.

Access Control: Indicates the type of frame, its priority level, and its status. Three bits specify the frame's priority value; 0 is lowest, 7 is highest. A Token bit is set to 0 if the frame is a token and to 1 otherwise. A Monitor bit is set to 1 by the AM, and to 0 whenever a lobe grabs the token. Three bits can be used by a lobe to request a priority level that is required to get access to the network.

Ending Delimiter: Indicates the end of the frame. This field contains a pattern of deliberate signal violations (signal patterns that do not occur in normal transmissions) to indicate the end of a frame.

Abort Sequence Frame

The Abort Sequence frame is used to clear the ring when a faulty frame has been detected. The frame consists of two fields: Starting Delimiter (1 byte) and Ending Delimiter (1 byte). Both of these are the same as in a Token frame.

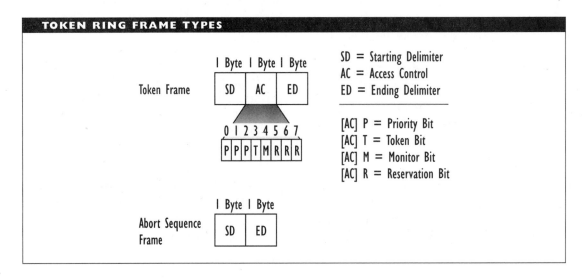

TOKEN RING FRAME TYPES

TOKEN RING FRAME TYPES (CONTINUED)

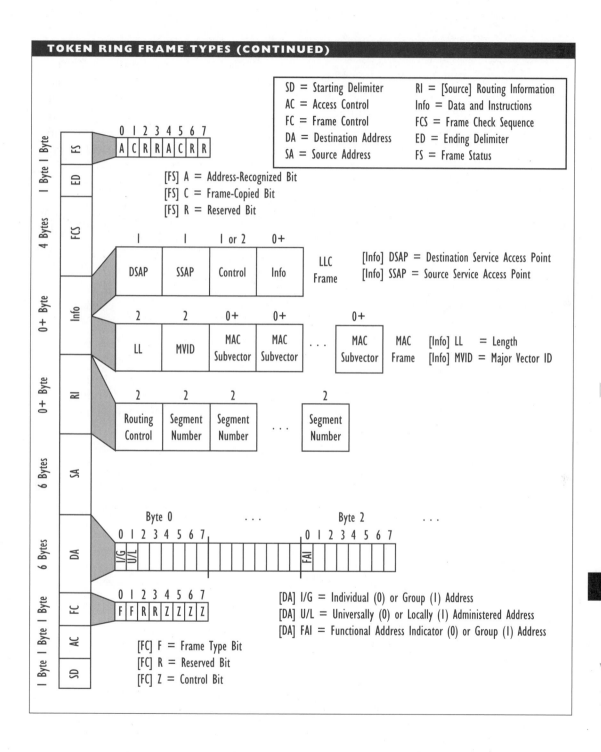

SD = Starting Delimiter   RI = [Source] Routing Information
AC = Access Control   Info = Data and Instructions
FC = Frame Control   FCS = Frame Check Sequence
DA = Destination Address   ED = Ending Delimiter
SA = Source Address   FS = Frame Status

[FS] A = Address-Recognized Bit
[FS] C = Frame-Copied Bit
[FS] R = Reserved Bit

[Info] DSAP = Destination Service Access Point
[Info] SSAP = Source Service Access Point

[Info] LL = Length
[Info] MVID = Major Vector ID

[DA] I/G = Individual (0) or Group (1) Address
[DA] U/L = Universally (0) or Locally (1) Administered Address
[DA] FAI = Functional Address Indicator (0) or Group (1) Address

[FC] F = Frame Type Bit
[FC] R = Reserved Bit
[FC] Z = Control Bit

Data Frames: Common Fields

Both LLC and MAC frames have the same general structure: a header, an optional information field, and a trailer. The header and trailer for LLC and MAC frames differ only in a few bits; the main differences are in the Information field.

Common Header Fields In the header, both types of frames have Starting Delimiter (1 byte) and Access Control (1 byte) fields, which are both the same as for a Token frame (except that the Token bit value is 1 in the Access Control field).

The Frame Control field (1 byte) distinguishes LLC and MAC data frames. The first 2 bits indicate whether the frame is a MAC or LLC frame: 00 is MAC, and 01 is LLC. Values of 10 and 11 are reserved. The next 2 bits are reserved. The last 4 bits are control bits. For LLC frames, these bits are reserved for future use. For MAC frames, the control bits indicate whether the frame should be copied to the lobe's regular input buffer (0000) for normal handling or to an "express" buffer (nonzero value) so that the frame is processed immediately by the MAC sublayer.

The Destination Address field (6 bytes) indicates the address of the lobe to which the frame is being sent. Certain bits in particular bytes have special significance: bit 0 in byte 0 indicates whether the address is an individual (0) or a group (1) address. In group addressing, multiple lobes share the same address for the purpose of communication, so that a frame sent to that location will be received by each lobe that belongs to the group. In individual addressing, each lobe has its own address.

Bit 1 in byte 0 indicates whether the address is administered universally (0) or locally (1). In universal administration, hardware addresses (those assigned to the NIC by the IEEE and the board's manufacturer) are used. In local administration, software or switch-configurable addresses are used.

Bit 0 in byte 2 is special only for locally administered group addresses. This functional address indicator (FAI) bit is 0 if the address is a functional one, and is 1 otherwise. A functional address specifies a lobe with a particular function (Token Ring management or user-defined). The table "Predefined Functional Addresses" indicates predefined addresses for particular lobes.

The Source Address field (6 bytes) indicates the location of the frame's originator. The I/G and U/L bits are also found in the first byte of the Source Address field.

If the frame is addressed to a lobe on another network—a lobe that must be reached using a bridge or a router—the frame will include a Routing Information field. This field will contain information regarding the bridges or routers through which the frame must pass. If this frame is present, the first 2 bytes are routing control, and the remaining bytes are grouped into pairs, each of which identifies a bridge or router.

Common Trailer Fields In the trailer, both LLC and MAC frames have a Frame Check Sequence, an Ending Delimiter field, and a Frame Status field.

The Frame Check Sequence field (4 bytes) contains the results of a 32-bit CRC computation by the sender. This value is used to

PREDEFINED FUNCTIONAL ADDRESSES	
ADDRESS	**SERVER WITH ADDRESS**
C00000000001	Active Monitor (AM)
C00000000002	Ring Parameter Server (RPS)
C00000000008	Ring Error Monitor (REM)
C00000000010	Configuration Report Server (CPS)
C00000000100	Bridge
C00000002000	LAN Manager
C00000800000—C00040000000	User-defined servers

determine whether the frame was received as transmitted. The receiving node also computes a CRC value and compares the computed value with the field's value. If the values match, the frame is assumed to have been received intact.

The Ending Delimiter field (1 byte) is the same as the one used in a Token frame.

The Frame Status field (1 byte) contains information about how the frame fared in its route around the ring. Bits 0 and 4 are Address Recognized bits. These are set to 0 by the sender and are changed to 1 when the destination lobe recognizes the source address. If the frame returns to the sender with these bits still set to 0, the sender assumes the destination node is not on the ring.

Bits 1 and 5 are Copied bits. These are 0 by default but are changed to 1 when the destination lobe copies the frame's contents to its input buffer. If the frame is not received correctly, the destination node sets the Address Recognized bits to 1 but leaves the Copied bits set to 0. The sender will know that the destination is on the ring but that the frame was not received correctly.

The remaining four bits are reserved for future use.

Information Field for LLC Frames An LLC frame is received from the LLC sublayer defined in the IEEE 802.2 standard. This frame contains the packet from the higher-layer protocol, which is being sent as data to another node.

For such a frame, the Information field is known as the PDU (Protocol Data Unit). The PDU is broken down into the DSAP address, SSAP address, and control components.

The DSAP (Destination Service Access Point) address (1 byte) provides information about the process running at the layer that will be receiving the packet. For example, this value is 0xe0 for Novell's NetWare.

The SSAP (Source Service Access Point) address (1 byte) provides information about the process running at the layer that is sending the packet. Again, this value is 0xe0 for Novell's NetWare.

a b c d e f g h i j k l m n o p q r s **t** u v w x y z

The control component's (1 or 2 bytes) value indicates the type of data included in the PDU. This may be ordinary user data, supervisory (command) data, or unnumbered data.

If the data format requires sequence numbering—as when the frame is part of a sequence of frames that, together, constitute a message—2 bytes are used for control information. In that case, the second byte indicates the frame's position in the sequence.

If the first bit in the control component is 0, the PDU contains ordinary information, and the control component uses 2 bytes. Such an I-format PDU is used for connection-oriented communications. In an I-format PDU, the next seven bits represent the frame's location in the transmission sequence. The first bit of the second byte is used by the sender to poll the receiver and by the receiver to respond. The remaining seven bits represent the position in the sequence at which the frame was received.

If the first two bits are 10, the PDU is supervisory, and the control component uses 2 bytes. Such a PDU is used in connection-oriented transmissions (those in which acknowledgments are required). For such an S-format PDU, the next two bits represent any of the following possible values: receive ready (00), reject (01), or receive not ready (10). The next four bits are reserved in this type of PDU. The first bit of the second byte is used for polling and responding (just as for an I-format PDU). The remaining seven bits represent the position in the sequence at which the frame was received.

If the first two bits are 11, the PDU is unnumbered, which may be used for connection-oriented or connectionless services. Such a U-format PDU uses only one byte for the control component. After the 11, such a PDU has two modifier bits (the third and fourth; that is, those in positions 2 and 3), followed by a polling/response bit, followed by three more modifier bits (in positions 5, 6, and 7). The table "Unnnumbered PDU Values" shows the possible modifier values used for connection-oriented or connectionless service. Note that certain values appear twice. The interpretation for the value depends on whether the sender or receiver has set the value.

The remainder of the LLC PDU contains data from a higher-level protocol. The length of this component is limited by time constraints on how long a lobe in the ring may hold on to the token. In practice, the PDU generally has fewer than 4,500 bytes, and may have just a few hundred.

Information Field for MAC Frames MAC frames give commands and provide status information. Of the 25 different MAC frame types defined, 15 can be used by ordinary workstations. The remaining types are used by the AM or by special management servers. The table "Token Ring MAC Frame Types" lists the types defined.

The Information field of a MAC frame has three components:

Length (2 bytes): Specifies the length (in bytes) of the MAC control information provided later in the field.

Major Vector ID (MVID, 2 bytes): Identifies the function of the frame and of the information in the control information component.

UNNUMBERED PDU VALUES		
VALUE (BIT POSITIONS: 23567)	MEANING	COMMUNICATION
00000	UI Command	Connection-oriented
00111	Test Command	Connection-oriented
00111	Test Response	Connection-oriented
11101	XID Command	Connection-oriented
11101	XID Response	Connection-oriented
00010	DISC Command	Connectionless
00110	UA Response	Connectionless
10001	FRMR Response	Connectionless
11000	DM Response	Connectionless
11110	SABME Command	Connectionless

Control Information (0+ bytes): Contains the data and information needed for the frame to do its work.

Extensions and Enhancements

To increase the span of a Token Ring network, you can use repeaters, additional MAUs, and wiring closets. A repeater enables you to run longer stretches of cable by cleaning and boosting the signal at the repeater. These extensions increase the size of the network while increasing the span.

Bridges and Routers

You can also use bridges and routers to increase the reach of a network by providing access to other networks. A bridge can route frames between two Token Ring networks; a router can find an "optimal" path for a frame through any number of networks, some of which may have different architectures.

Although Token Ring and Ethernet bridges perform the same functions, they do so differently. Ethernet bridges are also called learning bridges and transparent bridges because they automatically learn the addresses and network locations of all nodes.

In contrast, Token Ring bridges use source routing. In source routing, the sending lobe first determines the route and then stores this information in the Routing Information field of the frame. The bridge (or router) uses the routing sequence in the field to get the frame to its destination. Because the entire route is stored in the frame, Token Ring bridges can have very high throughput.

Source-routing bridges have a parameter that limits the number of bridges over which a frame can travel. This HCL (Hop Count

a b c d e f g h i j k l m n o p q r s **t** u v w x y z

TOKEN RING MAC FRAME TYPES

MAC FRAMES	DESCRIPTION
Active Monitor Present	The AM generates this frame to initiate the NN process.
Beacon	Any lobe generates this frame when a hard error is detected.
Change Parameters	The CRS generates this to set parameters for a lobe.
Claim Token	Any lobe that wants to participate in the token-claiming process can generate such a frame.
Duplicate Address Test	A new lobe generates this frame to check that the lobe's address will be unique on the ring.
Initialize Ring Station	The RPS generates this in response to the Ring Station Initialization frame generated by a new lobe.
Lobe Test	A new lobe generates this frame to test the connection between the lobe and the MAU.
Remove Ring Station	The CRS generates this to send to a lobe that will be removed from the ring for whatever reason.
Report Active Monitor Error	The AM generates this frame when the AM detects something wrong with itself.
Report NAUN Change	A lobe sends this frame to the CRS when the lobe has been provided with a NAUN address during NN.
Report Neighbor Notification Incomplete	A lobe generates this frame if the lobe does not hear from a NAUN within a predefined amount of time.
Report New Active Monitor	A lobe generates this frame and sends it to the CRS to announce that the lobe is the new AM.
Report Ring Station Address	A lobe sends this frame to the CRS in response to a Request Ring Station Address frame.
Report Ring Station Attachments	A lobe sends this frame to the CRS in response to a Request Ring Station Attachments frame.
Report Ring Station State	A lobe sends this frame to the CRS in response to a Request Ring Station State frame.
Report Soft Error	A lobe generates this frame when the lobe has accumulated more than a predefined number of soft errors, and then sends the frame to the REM.

MAC FRAMES	DESCRIPTION
Report Transmit Forward	A lobe sends this frame to the CRS or to the LAN manager in response to a Transmit Forward frame and to indicate that a path exists from the lobe to the CRS.
Request Ring Station Address	The CRS sends this frame to a lobe when the CRS wants address information from the lobe.
Request Ring Station Attachments	The CRS sends this frame to a lobe to find out what ring functions the lobe can perform.
Request Ring Station State	The CRS sends this frame to a lobe to determine the status of that lobe.
Response	A lobe sends this frame to another lobe to indicate receipt of a frame and to indicate errors in a received frame.
Ring Purge	The AM sends this frame to all lobes to clear the ring and restore Normal Repeat mode.
Ring Station Initialization	A new lobe in the ring generates this frame to announce the lobe's presence and to get any network settings.
Standby Monitor Present	A lobe generates this frame to send to the lobe's NADN as part of the NN process.
Transmit Forward	The CRS or the network manager generates this frame to test the communications path on the network.

Limit) prevents a frame from traveling too long on a network.

Early Token Release

Manufacturers also work to improve network performance by adding features to the NIC chip set or to MAUs. For example, newer Token Ring NICs support ETR (Early Token Release). This is a token-handling variant that makes it possible to have more than one frame traveling around the ring at a time while still using only one token.

Essentially, in ETR, the lobe with the token releases it as soon as the lobe has sent its frame (rather than letting the token circulate with the frame). The frame travels around the ring, with the token's blessing, but without the token. The NADN gets the frame and passes it on, if appropriate. However, this lobe also gets the token, which has been marked as available again.

Because it is available, the lobe can grab the token and send its own frame. The lobe will release the frame to its NADN and will then release the token. This NADN's NADN thus gets the following elements:

- Frame from the original transmitting lobe

- Frame from the original lobe's NADN

- Token

Intelligent MAUs

Manufacturers are making MAUs more intelligent by giving these components more ring monitoring and management capabilities. Some MAUs (such as the LattisNet series from SynOptics) can even manage multiple architectures. Such multiarchitecture MAUs provide routing between the architectures.

Another approach is to make the MAUs more sophisticated at configuring (*and reconfiguring*) themselves, either as lobes are added to the network or on the basis of network activity.

Switched and Dedicated Token Ring

As is the case with other networking architectures, switching technology is becoming increasingly popular. One reason for this is that switches can provide a node with the network's full bandwidth. This helps increase throughput.

Dedicated token ring (DTR) provides a direct connection between a node and the token ring switch so that the node can have the network's full bandwidth.

As another aid to speeding up the architecture, the 802.5 committee defined TXI (Transmit Immediate), to speed up the transmission process.

Full-duplex token ring can provide up to 16 Mbps in each direction.

Token Ring Tools

Hardware tools that can be useful for setting up and maintaining a Token Ring network include crimping and line-testing tools. You can use the crimping tool for crimping wire when making connections.

Use a line-testing tool for testing whether a particular section of cable is working properly. This type of tool comes in all forms and prices. At the low end, for about $25, a simple line monitor will tell you if the line is at least intact. At the very high end ($2,000+), line-testing tools can do very precise measurements using TDR (Time Domain Reflectometry).

In addition to these, a general set of tools (including screwdrivers, chip extractors, and so on) is also essential.

Advantages of Token Ring

Token Ring networks are easy to connect to IBM mainframe-based networks.

Also, even though there is more overhead when using tokens than when using CSMA/CD as an access method, the performance difference is negligible because the bottleneck in a network with heavy traffic is much more likely to be elsewhere. In heavy traffic, nodes on networks using CSMA/CD (for example) will spend a lot of their time resolving collisions, thus adding to the traffic load.

Disadvantages of Token Ring

Components (for example, NICs) tend to be more expensive than for Ethernet or ARCnet architectures.

Also, the Token Ring architecture is not easy to extend to Wide-Area Networks (WANs).

Resources

The specifications for a Token Ring architecture are found in IEEE 802.5 documents. Compared with the documentation generated by the 802.3 and 802.4 committees, these documents are quite sparse and relatively superficial.

The entire 802.5 specifications take fewer than 100 pages; by comparison, it takes 107 pages to cover just the physical medium possibilities in the 802.3 specifications.

ASTRAL (Alliance for Strategic Token Ring Advancement and Leadership) was formed to help develop these new technologies and to help get them accepted as standards. They are another source of information.

BROADER CATEGORY
Network Architecture

COMPARE
ARCnet; ATM; Ethernet; FDDI

TokenTalk

TokenTalk is Apple's implementation of the token ring network architecture for its own AppleTalk environments. TokenTalk has the following features:

- Is defined at the lowest two OSI Reference Model layers: physical and data link

- Uses the TokenTalk Link Access Protocol (TLAP) to get access to the network

- Supports both 4 megabit per second (Mbps) and 16 Mbps networks.

BROADER CATEGORY
AppleTalk; Token Ring

COMPARE
ARCTalk; EtherTalk; LocalTalk

Tool, Network

Tools are devices that make some tasks easier and other tasks possible. Both hardware and software tools are important for creating, running, and maintaining a network.

Several types of hardware tools can be distinguished:

Manufacturing: Tools for creating individual components, such as crimpers and dies for attaching wires to connectors, and tools for splicing, polishing, and attaching optical fiber.

Construction: Tools for assembling or disassembling systems. For example, screwdrivers can be considered construction tools for attaching connectors.

Testing: Tools for testing individual components or for monitoring the performance of a component or system, such as breakout boxes, voltmeters, (milli)ammeters, and line scanners. A versatile piece of equipment, the volt-ohm-milliammeter (VOM) can be used to examine voltage, resistance, and current.

Safety: Tools for making sure components are protected against damage from electrical and other dangers. These types of tools are discussed in the Safety Devices article.

Miscellaneous: Many special-purpose and gerry-rigged tools fit in this category, as do certain "gadgets," or small-scale components that help make things easier. For example, a gadget such as velcro strips can be used to collect and organize cables.

Basic Tool Requirements

The level and range of tools you will need depend on the level of involvement you have with the network. Regardless of the level, a few basic tools will almost certainly make life easier:

- Screwdrivers (flat and Philips head) for opening machines and for attaching connectors

- Pliers for grasping objects and for tightening and loosening nuts

- Chip remover for, ...yes, removing chips from a circuit board

- Tweezers (with long arms) for retrieving screws that fall into the back of the computer as you are removing or attaching the guard on an expansion slot

In addition to these tools, some people might also have use for wire strippers and cutters, and for soldering irons, which may be used to rig up special-purpose circuits or wiring connections.

If you are going to do any troubleshooting at all, you will need a voltmeter or ammeter or both, *with a manual*, to test electrical activity. The manual is essential,

because you will need to look up how to connect the meter. Connecting a meter (or any type of testing device) incorrectly can cause serious damage to sensitive circuitry, both yours and the meter's.

In general, magnets and hammers are not popular around computers, expansion boards, or peripherals. If you must hammer, do it at the keyboard.

Tools for Installing and Attaching Cable

If you will be involved with installing the cable, as well as hooking up the computers, you may need other, more specialized tools as well.

For example, it is rarely feasible, and even more rarely advisable, to get all your cable pre-cut and pre-attached (to the connectors). You may need to make your own cable, or rather, cable ends. To do this, you need to attach the cable to the connector, make sure the cable and connector fit snugly, and then test the cable.

To attach connectors to cable, you need the following tools:

- A crimping tool, or crimper, for pressing the cable and connector together

- A die for the specified cable/connection pair, to make sure cable and connector fit properly

You can buy preconfigured installation tool kits from vendors such as Jensen Tools or Black Box. These kits can range in price from one or two hundred to several thousand dollars.

If you are actually going to be installing the cable—hanging it in the ceiling or running it through a plenum in a wall or under the floor—you will need industrial-strength tools, since some of the parts you will install may need to support dozens of pounds of cable.

Tools for Testing Cables

Voltmeters and ammeters provide readings (of voltage and current, or amperage, respectively) by tapping into the circuit and recording electrical activity as it occurs. The recorded values may or may not provide details about what is happening along the lines or on the network.

Scanners are much more sophisticated testing tools. Some of the capabilities of top-of-the-line scanners include the following:

- Check for faults (shorts or opens) in a cable.

- Test a cable's compliance with any of several network architectures, such as Ethernet, Token Ring, ARCnet, and electronics standards, such as UL (Underwriters Laboratories).

- Monitor performance and electrical activity, given the type of cable and architecture involved.

- Test the cable's wiring sequence.

- Generate and print a summary of the information obtained.

A powerful scanner can test for wire quality (for example, to find the best pair of wires in a cable for a connection), for the quality of the connections between cable segments or between cable and device.

At the lower end, scanners will at least be able to test for noise, crosstalk (in particular, Near End Crosstalk, or NEXT), signal attenuation, resistance, cable length, and so on.

Tools for Installing and Attaching Fiber-Optic Cable

Working with optical fiber creates special requirements not found when dealing with electrical cable. These special requirements, in turn, create a need for special tools.

The procedure for connecting or splicing two sections of fiber is somewhat different than for copper wire.

For connectors, the fiber must be glued into a ferrule (a tube used for guiding the fiber and for keeping it from moving), then the ends must be cut and polished in an appropriate manner. Polishing machines are used to make the fiber ends smooth, and special microscopes can be used to check the polishing job. Even for "high-tech" fiber-optic connections, something as lowly as epoxy is needed to attach the fiber core to the side of a ferrule.

In addition, the same kinds of tools as for copper wire may be needed: cable strippers and pliers for taking the outer sheaths off the cable, crimping tools, and so on. Most fiber-optic installation kits also include a duster (to make sure the pieces of fiber are clean before being joined). Special fluid may also be used to adjust the reflectivity of the fiber or cladding.

For splicing, the fibers are joined directly and permanently. One way of doing this to fuse the two pieces of fiber together by applying heat to melt the fibers slightly and then joining them before the fibers cool. Special machines, called fusion splicers, are used to do this.

a b c d e f g h i j k l m n o p q r s **t** u v w x y z

Tools for Testing Fiber-Optic Cable

Equipment for testing the integrity of fiber-optic cable and the quality of the signal must gather optical (rather than electrical) data. Consequently, special equipment is needed. Ironically, this equipment gets its information from electrical signals. These signals are created by converting the optical signal to electrical form.

An optical power meter is the analog to the VOM mentioned earlier. This device can determine the power of a signal in decibels (dB) or in decibels referenced to a milliwatt (dBm). The latter provides a standardized way of specifying signal strength.

An Optical Time-Domain Reflectometer (OTDR) serves as the foundation for higher-end cable testers. The optical time domain reflectome*try* that underlies this device uses the light scattered back from a signal (or light bounced back for a test signal) and allows sophisticated measurements on the light.

These devices cost several thousand dollars but can provide valuable information, such as signal loss per unit distance and signal loss at splices or over connectors.

TOP (Technical Office Protocol)

TOP is an architecture that provides standards for the representation and exchange of messages, documents, and other files in office settings. TOP provides APIs (Application Program Interfaces) for a variety of file types, including electronic mail (e-mail), office documents, and graphics files. These APIs are built upon the seven-layer OSI Reference Model.

THE "CARDWARE" TOOL

A useful type of tool might be called "cardware" by analogy with hardware and software. One of the most effective tools for accomplishing anything is an ability to get the resources or information needed for a particular task.

Forms, checklists, or question collections can be invaluable for getting information. Committing items or questions to paper makes it easier to examine the entire collection to determine whether it gets all the necessary information or points.

By doing this in advance—preferably testing, evaluating, and revising it as necessary—you can provide a reference against which to compare competing options or products.

Such forms and questionnaires are found in magazines, technical and marketing brochures, and even advertisements. You can sometimes put together a useful checklist of desirable features by collecting comparisons from the manufacturers of each of the products.

Like the closely related MAP (Manufacturing Automation Protocol), TOP is an effort to provide standardized protocols and services for use in real-world contexts that involve the reliable and efficient exchange of formatted data or access to such data from remote locations.

TOP APIs

The figure "TOP APIs, OSI layers, and protocols" shows the APIs defined for TOP and also shows how these relate to the OSI Reference Model layers and to various protocols.

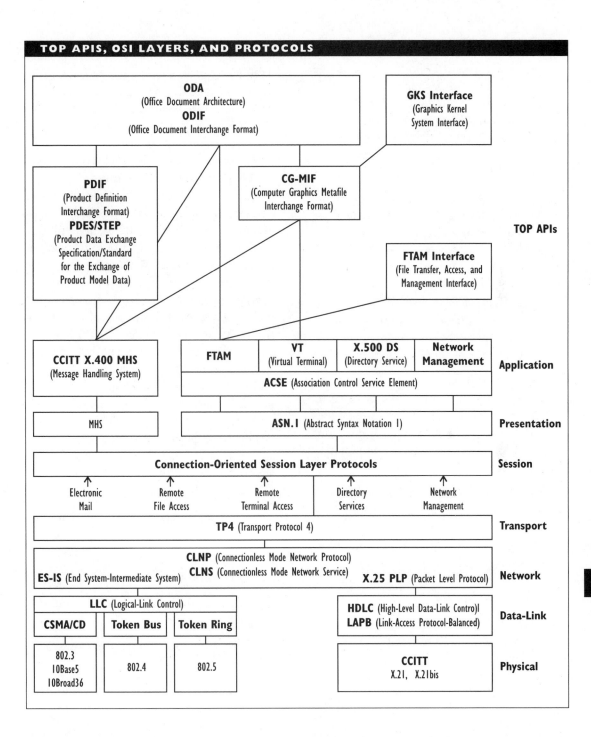

TOP APIS, OSI LAYERS, AND PROTOCOLS

ODA (Office Document Architecture)
ODIF (Office Document Interchange Format)

GKS Interface (Graphics Kernel System Interface)

PDIF (Product Definition Interchange Format)
PDES/STEP (Product Data Exchange Specification/Standard for the Exchange of Product Model Data)

CG-MIF (Computer Graphics Metafile Interchange Format)

FTAM Interface (File Transfer, Access, and Management Interface)

TOP APIs

CCITT X.400 MHS (Message Handling System)

FTAM | **VT** (Virtual Terminal) | **X.500 DS** (Directory Service) | **Network Management**

ACSE (Association Control Service Element)

Application

MHS | **ASN.1** (Abstract Syntax Notation 1)

Presentation

Connection-Oriented Session Layer Protocols

Session

Electronic Mail | Remote File Access | Remote Terminal Access | Directory Services | Network Management

TP4 (Transport Protocol 4)

Transport

CLNP (Connectionless Mode Network Protocol)
CLNS (Connectionless Mode Network Service)
ES-IS (End System-Intermediate System)
X.25 PLP (Packet Level Protocol)

Network

LLC (Logical-Link Control)
CSMA/CD | **Token Bus** | **Token Ring**

HDLC (High-Level Data-Link Control)
LAPB (Link-Access Protocol-Balanced)

Data-Link

802.3 10Base5 10Broad36 | 802.4 | 802.5

CCITT X.21, X.21bis

Physical

a b c d e f g h i j k l m n o p q r s **t** u v w x y z

TOP provides APIs for the following:

- PDIF (Product Definition Interchange Format) provides support for the description standards IGES (Initial Graphics Exchange Standard) and PDES/STEP (Product Description Exchange Standard/Standard for the Exchange of Product Model Data).

- ODA/ODIF (Office Document Architecture/Office Document Interchange Format) provides support for the creation and exchange of formatted and compound documents. (*Compound* documents contain multiple types of content, such as character and vector or raster graphics.) Certain of these formats can be used to create documents for the PDIF APIs.

- CGMIF (Computer Graphics Metafile Interchange Format) provides a vector-based representation for graphics files. This format can be used for describing graphics elements in compound documents.

- GKS (Graphics Kernel System) Interface provides a collection of primitive objects and functions for creating two- and three-dimensional graphics objects. In the TOP architecture, GKS objects are also represented in the CGMIF.

- FTAM (File Transfer, Access, and Management) Interface provides an interface for an FTAM application, which can be used to initiate and carry out the actual file transfer.

OSI Layers in the TOP Architecture

TOP APIs are designed to use protocols and services that conform to existing standards. To help provide flexibility in this use, the bottom four and the top three layers are each treated as a group.

The communications-based layers—from the physical layer to the transport layer—support one Wide-Area Network (WAN) and three Local-Area Network (LAN) architectures: Ethernet (802.3), Token Bus (802.4), and Token Ring (802.5) LAN architectures and the X.25 WAN interface.

TOP supports the data-link layer protocols appropriate to the various architectures, including support for the Logical-Link Control (LLC) sublayer specified by IEEE 802.2 for the LAN architectures. The TOP architecture supports connectionless protocols and services at the network and transport layers, but also supports the connection-oriented X.25 Packet Level Protocol.

For the application-oriented layers (session, presentation, and application), TOP supports several types of applications:

- Electronic Mail using the CCITT X.400 Message Handling System (MHS)

- Remote File Access using the OSI FTAM protocol

- Remote Terminal Access using the OSI's VT (Virtual Terminal) protocol

- Network directory services using OSI protocols

- Network management services using OSI protocols

Both TOP and MAP are currently undergoing scheduled revisions after a 6-year evaluation period for versions 3.0 of both TOP and MAP.

Topology, Backbone Bridge

A backbone topology provides a method for using bridges among multiple networks. A backbone topology connects each pair of networks directly using a bridge.

For example, in a three network (A, B, and C) setup, three bridges would be used: to connect A and B, A and C, and B and C. The figure "A backbone bridge topology" illustrates this example.

This connection topology is in contrast to a cascaded bridge topology, in which two bridges are used (A to B and B to C) so that network A needs to go through network B to communicate with network C. A backbone bridge topology saves work for each

network; a cascaded bridge topology saves on equipment.

COMPARE
Topology, Cascaded Bridge

Topology, Bus

Bus refers to a physical and a logical topology. As a logical topology, a bus is distinguished by the fact that packets are broadcast so that every node gets the message at the same time. Ethernet networks are the best examples of a logical bus topology.

As a physical topology, a bus describes a network in which each node is connected to a common line: the backbone, or trunk. A bus usually has the file server at one end, with the main trunk line extending from this point. (Although the metaphor of a backbone is useful, it should not be taken literally; just as in the real world, not all

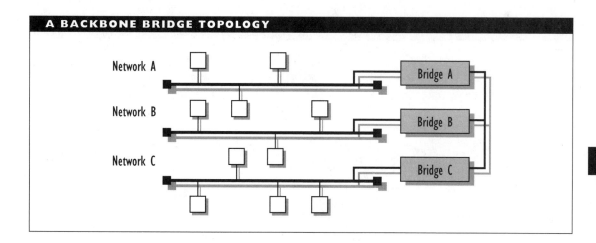

A BACKBONE BRIDGE TOPOLOGY

Network A

Network B

Network C

Bridge A

Bridge B

Bridge C

network backbones are straight.) The figure "A bus topology" illustrates this layout.

Nodes are attached to this trunk line, and every node can hear each packet as it goes past. Packets travel in both directions along the backbone and need not go through the individual nodes. Rather, each node checks the packet's destination address to determine whether the packet is intended for the node.

When the signal reaches the end of the trunk line, a terminator absorbs the packet to keep it from traveling back again along the bus line, possibly interfering with other messages already on the line. Each end of a trunk line must be terminated so that signals are removed from the bus when they reach the end.

Thin and thick Ethernet are the best examples of a physical bus topology. Twisted-pair Ethernet (10Base-T Ethernet)

uses a logical bus topology, but a star for its physical topology.

In a bus topology, nodes should be far enough apart that they do not interfere with each other. If the backbone cable is long, it may be necessary to boost the signal strength. The maximum length of the backbone is limited by the size of the time interval that constitutes "simultaneous" packet reception.

Bus Topology Advantages

Bus topologies offer the following advantages:

- A bus uses relatively little cable compared to other topologies and arguably has the simplest wiring arrangement.

- Since nodes just attach to the main line, it's easy to add or remove nodes

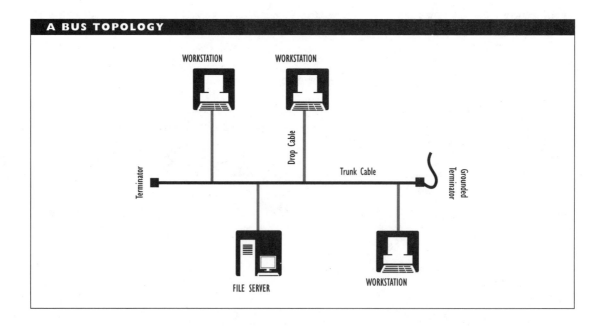

A BUS TOPOLOGY

WORKSTATION WORKSTATION

Drop Cable

Terminator

Trunk Cable

Grounded Terminator

FILE SERVER WORKSTATION

from a bus. This makes it easy to extend a bus topology.

- Architectures based on this topology are simple and flexible.

Bus Topology Disadvantages

Bus topology disadvantages include the following:

- Diagnosis/troubleshooting (fault-isolation) can be difficult.

- The bus trunk can be a bottleneck when network traffic gets heavy. This is because nodes can spend much of their time trying to access the network.

Topology, Cascaded Bridge

A cascaded bridge topology is a method for providing bridges among multiple networks. A cascaded topology uses one network (B) as an access point to another network (C) from a third network (A). Thus, instead of providing a direct bridge between A and C, a cascaded bridge topology saves a bridge by making network A go through B to communicate with C. The figure "A cascaded bridge topology" illustrates this layout.

A cascaded topology saves on equipment but adds to work. This approach is in contrast to a backbone bridge topology, in which there are direct bridges between each pair of networks. In the example, A would be connected directly to B and directly to C with separate bridges, and B would be connected to C with yet another bridge.

COMPARE
Topology, Backbone Bridge

Topology, Distributed Star

A distributed star topology is a physical topology that consists of two or more hubs, each of which is the center of a star arrangement. The figure "A distributed star topology" illustrates this layout.

This type of topology is common, and it is generally known simply as a *star topology*. A good example of such a topology is an

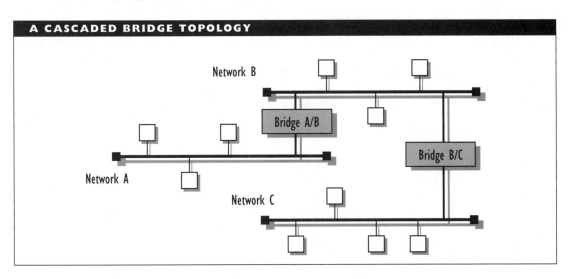

A CASCADED BRIDGE TOPOLOGY

Network B

Bridge A/B

Bridge B/C

Network A

Network C

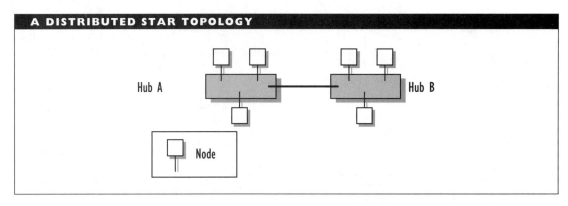

A DISTRIBUTED STAR TOPOLOGY

Hub A

Hub B

Node

ARCnet network with at least one active hub and one or more active or passive hubs.

Topology, Hybrid

A physical topology that is actually a combination of two or more different physical topologies. The best known example is the star-wired ring topology that is used to implement IBM Token Ring networks.

SEE ALSO

Topology, Star-Wired Ring

Topology, Logical

A logical topology defines the logical layout of a network. This specifies how the elements in the network communicate with each other and how information is transmitted, or the path information takes through a network.

The two main logical topologies are bus and ring. These are each associated with different types of media-access methods, which determine how a node gets to transmit information along the network.

In a bus topology, information is broadcast, and every node gets the information at the same time. "Same time" for a bus topology is defined as the amount of time it actually takes a signal to cover the entire length of cable. This time interval limits the maximum speed and size for the network. Supposedly, nodes read only messages intended for them. To broadcast, a node needs to wait until the network is temporarily idle. Ethernet networks are the best examples of a logical bus topology.

In a ring topology, each node hears from exactly one node and talks to exactly one other node. Information is passed sequentially from node to node. In a ring topology, information is passed sequentially in an order determined by a predefined process. A polling or token mechanism is used to determine who has transmission rights, and a node can transmit only when it has this right. A Token Ring network is the best example of a logical ring topology.

Topology, Mesh

A mesh topology is a physical topology in which there are at least two paths to and from every node. The figure "A mesh topology" illustrates this layout.

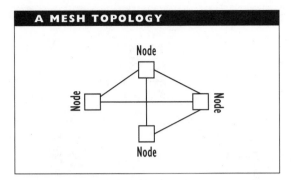

A MESH TOPOLOGY

This type of topology is advantageous in hostile environments in which connections are easily broken. If a connection is broken in this layout, at least one substitute path is always available.

A more restrictive definition requires each node to be connected directly to every other node. Because of the severe connection requirements, such restrictive mesh topologies are feasible only for small networks.

Topology, Physical

A physical topology defines the wiring layout for a network. This specifies how the elements in the network are connected to each other *electrically*. This arrangement will determine what happens if a node on the network fails.

Categories of Physical Topologies

There are numerous physical topologies because hybrid topologies are possible. These are created from two or more different physical topologies. Physical topologies fall into three main categories:

- Those which implement a logical bus topology. These include bus, star, and tree topologies. In a star topology,

multiple nodes are connected to a central hub. This hub may be connected to another hub or to the network's file server. In a tree topology, two or more buses may be daisy-chained (strung together) or a bus may be split into two or more buses at a hub.

- Those which implement a logical ring topology. Logical ring topologies are implemented by physical rings, which are actually rare in pure form. This is because a physical ring is extremely susceptible to failures. When a node in a physical ring goes down, the entire network goes down. For this reason, logical rings are generally implemented by a hybrid star-wired ring topology.

- Hybrids, which implement a combination of physical topologies. The best known of these is a star-wired ring, which is used for IBM Token Ring networks. The FDDI architecture also allows a variety of hybrid topologies, such as a dual ring of trees. Hybrid topologies are used to overcome weaknesses or restrictions in one or the other component topology.

The various physical topologies are described in separate articles.

Multipoint versus Point-to-Point Connections

Physical topologies can also be categorized by the manner in which nodes are connected to each other. In particular, they can be categorized by how workstations are connected to a server on the network.

In a point-to-point connection, two nodes are linked directly. A mesh topology is a specific type of point-to-point connection in which there are at least two direct paths to every node. (A more restrictive definition of a mesh topology requires that every node be connected directly to every other node.)

In a multipoint connection (also called a *multidrop connection*), multiple nodes are connected to a single node (for example, to a hub or gateway), which is, in turn, connected to another (for example, to a server or host).

Topology, Ring

A ring topology is a logical and a physical topology. As a logical topology, a ring is distinguished by the fact that packets are transmitted sequentially from node to node, in a predefined order. Nodes are arranged in a closed loop so that the initiating node is the last one to receive a packet. Token Ring networks are the most widely used example of a logical ring topology.

As a physical topology, a ring describes a network in which each node is connected to two other nodes. Information traverses a one-way path so that a node receives packets from exactly one node and transmits them to exactly one other node. A packet travels around the ring until it returns to the node that originally sent the packet. In a ring topology, each node can act as a repeater, boosting the signal before sending it on. The figure "A ring topology" illustrates this layout.

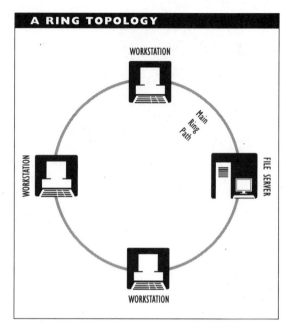

A RING TOPOLOGY

WORKSTATION

Main Ring Path

WORKSTATION

FILE SERVER

WORKSTATION

Each node checks whether the packet's destination node matches the node's address. When the packet reaches its destination, the node accepts the message, then sends it back to the sender to acknowledge receipt.

Since ring topologies use token passing to control access to the network, the token is returned to sender with the acknowledgment. The sender then releases the token to the next node on the network. If this node has nothing to say, the node passes the token on to the next node, and so on. When the token reaches a node with a packet to send, that node sends its packet.

Physical ring networks are rare because this topology has considerable disadvantages compared to a more practical star-wired ring hybrid, which is described in a separate article.

The advantages of a ring topology are that the cable requirements are fairly minimal and no wiring center or closet is needed.

The disadvantages of this topology include the following:

- If any node goes down, the entire ring goes down.

- Diagnosis/troubleshooting (fault isolation) is difficult because communication is only one-way.

- Adding or removing nodes disrupts the network.

▼
Topology, Star

A star topology is a physical topology in which multiple nodes are connected to a central component, generally known as a hub. The figure "A star topology" illustrates this layout. Despite appearances, such a wiring scheme actually implements a logical bus topology.

The hub of a star generally is just a wiring center; that is, a common termination point for the nodes, with a single connection continuing from the hub. In rare cases, the hub may actually be a file server, with all its nodes attached directly to the server.

As a wiring center, a hub may, in turn, be connected to a file server, a wall plate, or to another hub. All signals, instructions, and data going to and from each node must pass through the hub to which the node is connected.

The telephone company wiring system is the best known example of a star topology, with lines to individual subscribers (such as yourself or your employer) coming from a central location. In the LAN world, low impedance ARCnet networks are probably the best example of a star topology.

One advantage of a star topology is that troubleshooting and fault isolation are easy.

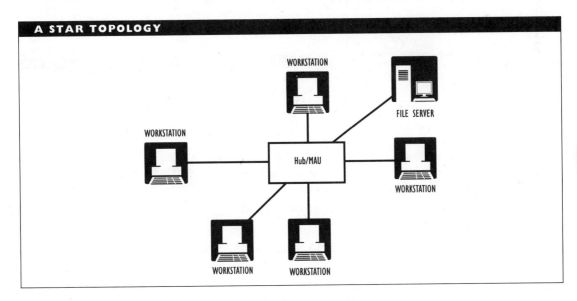

A STAR TOPOLOGY

WORKSTATION

FILE SERVER

WORKSTATION

Hub/MAU

WORKSTATION

WORKSTATION

WORKSTATION

a b c d e f g h i j k l m n o p q r s **t** u v w x y z

Also, it is easy to add or remove nodes and to modify the cable layout.

A disadvantage of this topology is that if the hub fails, the entire network fails. Sometimes a backup central machine is included to make it possible to deal with such a failure. Also, a star topology requires a lot of cable.

Topology, Star-Wired Ring

A star-wired ring topology, also known as a *hub topology,* is a hybrid physical topology that combines features of the star and ring topologies. Individual nodes are connected to a central hub, as in a star network. Within the hub, however, the connections are arranged into an internal ring. Thus, the hub constitutes the ring, which must remain intact for the network to function. The figure "A star-wired ring topology" illustrates this layout.

The hubs, known as *Multistation Access Units (MAUs)* in Token Ring network terminology, may be connected to other hubs. In this arrangement, each internal ring is opened and connected to the attached hubs to create a larger, multi-hub ring.

The advantage of using star wiring instead of simple ring wiring is that it is easy to disconnect a faulty node from the internal ring. The IBM Data Connector is specially designed to close a circuit if an attached node is disconnected physically or electrically. By closing the circuit, the ring remains intact, but with one less node.

IBM Token Ring networks are the best-known example of a star-wired ring topology at work. In Token Ring networks, a secondary ring path can be established and used if part of the primary path goes down.

The advantages of a star-wired ring topology include the following:

- Troubleshooting, or fault isolation, is relatively easy.

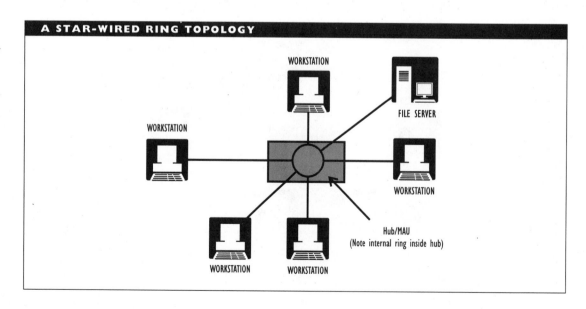

A STAR-WIRED RING TOPOLOGY

WORKSTATION

FILE SERVER

WORKSTATION

WORKSTATION

WORKSTATION

WORKSTATION

Hub/MAU
(Note internal ring inside hub)

- The modular design makes it easy to expand the network and makes layouts extremely flexible.

- Individual hubs can be connected to form larger rings.

- Wiring to the hub is flexible.

The disadvantages are that, because of the extreme flexibility for the arrangement, configuration and cabling may be complicated.

Topology, Tree

A tree topology, also known as a distributed bus or a branching tree topology, is a hybrid physical topology that combines features of star and bus topologies. Several buses may be daisy-chained together, and there may be branching at the connections (which will be hubs). The starting end of the tree is known as the *root* or *head* end. The figure "A tree topology" illustrates this layout.

This type of topology is used in delivering cable television services.

The advantages of a tree topology are that the network is easy to extend by just adding another branch and that fault isolation is relatively easy.

The disadvantages are as follows:

- If the root goes down, the entire network goes down.

- If any hub goes down, all branches off of that hub go down.

- Access becomes a problem if the entire conglomerate becomes too big.

ToS (Type of Service)

A field in an IP (Internet Protocol) packet, or datagram, header. The contents of this byte specify the kind of transmission desired, with respect to delay, throughput, and reliability. Part of this byte specifies a priority for the datagram's handling. The details of this field are being reconsidered by the Internet Engineering Task Force (IETF).

A TREE TOPOLOGY

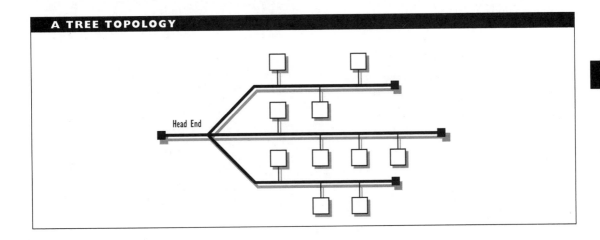

Head End

TPDDI (Twisted-Pair Distributed Data Interface)

A network architecture, also known as CDDI, that implements the FDDI specifications on electrical (rather than optical) twisted-pair cable. This FDDI variant is being considered by the ANSI FDDI committee (X3T9.5).

TP-PMD (Twisted-Pair, Physical Media Dependent)

The 100 megabit per second, FDDI standard as implemented on unshielded twisted-pair (UTP) cable.

Traceroute

A program that can create a map of the path taken by a packet as it goes from source to destination. Traceroute is used as a tool when troubleshooting a network.

SEE ALSO

RFC 1470 ("FYI on a Network Management Tool Catalog, Tools for Monitoring and Debugging TCP/IP Internets and Interconnected Devices")

Traffic

In networking, the level of network activity. For example, one measure of traffic is the number of messages sent over the network at a given time or within a given interval.

Traffic Descriptor

In the ATM architecture, an element that specifies parameters for a Virtual Channel or Path Connection (VCC or VPC). These parameter values can be negotiated by the entities involved in the connection. A traffic descriptor is also known as a *user-network contract*.

Trailer

In packets transmitted on a network, a packet portion that follows the data contained in the packet. Trailer portions generally include error-detection fields (for example, FCS or CRC). Most administrative and control information relevant to the packet is in the packet's *header*, which *precedes* the data portion.

Transaction

A transaction is an interaction between a client and a server. For example, a transaction may be a request, the transfer of data, or the termination of a connection. An ATM (Automated Teller Machine) session is an example of a transaction.

The transaction is the smallest complete action when using SQL (Structured Query Language) to search or modify a database. In SQL, if any step in the transaction cannot be carried out, the entire transaction fails, and all the intermediate steps in the transaction are undone.

Transceiver

A transceiver, from *trans*mitter/*receiver*, is a device that can both receive and transmit a signal. On a network, most computers are connected to the network using a transceiver.

The transceiver may be on a Network Interface Card (NIC), or it may be an external component. For example, the transceiver for a thin Ethernet network is on the NIC. A transceiver for thick Ethernet is external, and it attaches to a drop cable (which goes to the node) and to the network cable.

In fiber-optics, a transceiver is similar to a repeater in that both consist of a transmitter and a receiver. The difference is that these components are in parallel for a transceiver and in series for a repeater (with the receiver first, then the signal-cleaning component, then the transmitter).

In the IEEE specifications, a transceiver is known as a Medium Attachment Unit (MAU), not to be confused with a Multistation Access Unit, which is the MAU in a Token Ring network.

BROADER CATEGORY
Intranetwork link

SEE ALSO
Repeater

Transfer Mode

In telecommunications, the manner in which data is transmitted and/or switched in a network. For example, ATM (Asynchronous Transfer Mode) transmits asynchronously, and uses both circuit- and packet-switching techniques to route data.

Transfer Time

In connection with an SPS, the amount of time required to switch to the SPS' auxiliary power in case of a power outage to a network node. Look for times less than 5 milliseconds or so.

SEE ALSO
UPS (Uninterruptible Power Supply); SPS (Standby Power Supply)

Transmission Code

A set of rules for representing data, usually characters. Commonly used transmission codes include EBCDIC (an 8-bit code used on all IBM mainframes) and ASCII (a 7-bit code commonly used on PCs).

Transmission Header (TH)

SEE
TH (Transmission Header)

Transmission Medium

The physical medium through which a data, voice, or another type of transmission moves to reach its destination. Common transmission media include conductive (usually, copper) wire, optical fiber, and air.

Transmission Mode

A transmission mode describes the manner in which a communication between a sender and a receiver can take place. The following modes are defined:

Simplex: Communication goes in one direction only, and the sender can use the entire communication channel. A ticker-tape machine is an example.

Half-duplex: Communication can go in both directions, but in only one

a b c d e f g h i j k l m n o p q r s **t** u v w x y z

direction at a time. The sender can use the entire channel. In order to change direction, a special signal must be given and acknowledged. The time required to turn over control to the other side is called the line turnaround (or just turnaround) time. Turnaround time can become significant in certain transmissions. A CB connection is an example.

Full-duplex: Communication can go in both directions simultaneously, but each part gets to use only half the channel. Modem connections are an example.

Echo-plex: An error-checking mode in which characters typed for transmission are sent back to the screen from the receiver to permit direct comparison with what was typed.

Transmission, Parallel

Parallel is a transmission mode in which the bits that make up a byte are all transmitted at the same time; each bit is transmitted on a different wire. The figure "Parallel transmission" shows this method. This is in contrast to serial transmission, in which bits are transmitted one at a time, in sequence.

Parallel transmissions are commonly used for communicating with printers and external LAN adapters, and for internal communications on the computer's bus.

COMPARE

Transmission, Serial

PARALLEL TRANSMISSION

Bit		DB-25 Pin
0	1	2
1	1	3
2	0	4
3	0	5
4	1	6
5	1	7
6	0	8
7	0	9

Transmission, Serial

Serial is a digital transmission mode in which bytes are broken down into individual bits. These bits are then transmitted one after the other in a predefined sequence (least to most significant bits or vice versa). The bits are reassembled into a byte at the receiving end. The figure "Serial transmission, with both least and most significant bits first" shows this method. Serial transmissions are in contrast to parallel transmissions, in which multiple bits are transmitted at the same time, each on different wires.

Serial transmissions are used for communicating with modems (for telecommunications), some printers, and some mouse devices.

SERIAL TRANSMISSION, WITH BOTH LEAST AND MOST SIGNIFICANT BITS FIRST

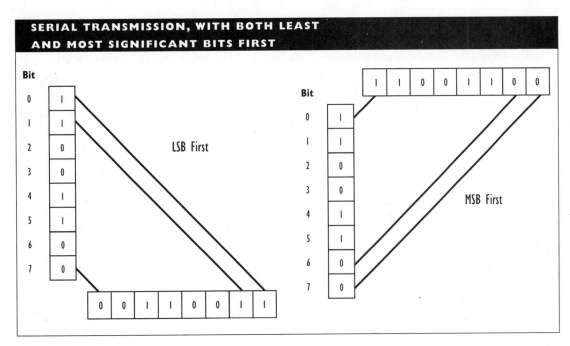

COMPARE
Transmission, Parallel

Transmission, Single-Frequency

Single-frequency is a transmission method using radio waves. In single-frequency transmissions, the signal is encoded within a narrow frequency range. With such a signal, all the energy is concentrated at a particular frequency range.

A single-frequency signal is susceptible to jamming and eavesdropping. Depending on the frequency range being used, you may need a license to operate a single-frequency network.

Motorola's Altair system is an example of a single-frequency network. These types of radio wave networks operate within a frequency range that requires licensing, but the vendor takes care of that. For the Altair system, Motorola must also assign a frequency within which to operate, to ensure that the network does not interfere with another single-frequency network in the area. The Altair network operates as an Ethernet network.

BROADER CATEGORIES
Network, Wireless; Radio Wave Transmission

COMPARE
Transmission, Spread-Spectrum

Transmission, Spread-Spectrum

Spread-spectrum is a form of radio transmission in which the signal is distributed over a broad frequency range, or spectrum. The distribution pattern is based on either frequency hopping or on direct sequence coding.

With frequency hopping, a transmitter will send at a particular frequency for a few milliseconds, then switch to another frequency for a few milliseconds, and so on. The frequency sequence is selected at random. The receiver must know the random number sequence and must be able to adjust and fine-tune just as rapidly and accurately as the transmitter. This type of signal is impossible to jam or eavesdrop unless the frequency hopping sequence is known.

With direct-sequence coding, the information to be transmitted is modified by a multibit binary chipping code. The chipping code spreads the signal out over a broader frequency range, with more chips (bits) in the code corresponding to a broader range. As with frequency hopping, this type of transmission is impossible to jam or overhear unless the chipping code is known.

Spread-spectrum signals are extremely unlikely to interfere with other transmissions, since the other transmission would need to be using the same spreading algorithm. Spread-spectrum networks do not require licensing, at least not within the frequency range covered by such products. WaveLAN from NCR, RangeLAN from Proxim, and Netwave from Xircom are examples of networks that use spread-spectrum technology.

BROADER CATEGORY

Network, Wireless; Radio Wave Transmission

COMPARE

Transmission, Single-Frequency

Transparent

Used as an adjective in connection with computer use, something that is taken care of without requiring any instructions or attention from the user. For example, the media-access process in a network transmission is transparent to the user.

Transparent Mode

A terminal-display mode in which control characters are displayed literally, rather than being interpreted as commands. For example, in transparent mode, a beep character (Ctrl+G, or ASCII 7) sent to the terminal (or to a PC emulating a terminal) would be displayed as a Ctrl+G character; there would be no beep.

Tree Structure

A tree is a flexible data structure that can be used to represent information that is hierarchically organized, such as a corporate structure or an elimination tournament schedule.

As a data structure, a tree consists of a topmost element called the *root* and one or more elements that are defined directly below this root.

The root may represent the topmost element in the content area being represented (for example, a corporate head). The root is often left as an abstract entity, which means that it is an element that serves a purpose but that has no particular content associated with it.

The elements below the root are known as *children* of the root. A child element may, itself, be a tree, and the child can have child trees of its own. Or the child element may be an end element, known as a *leaf*. A leaf element has no children.

Directories of various types are often represented using a tree structure. For example, directories for hierarchical file systems, such as the one used by DOS, and for naming services, such as the NetWare Directory Services (NDS) used in NetWare 4.*x,* are represented using trees.

The NDS contains information about all objects (users, devices, queues, and so on) on the network. This information is stored in the Directory tree, or just Directory (with an uppercase *D*). In the Directory, the topmost element is the root object. Below this are one or more children, known as containers. See the NDS article for more information about the Directory tree.

Trojan Horse

A program that looks harmless but that contains hidden instructions to destroy files, programs, or File Allocation Tables (FATs). The instructions may be "time bombs," which are triggered by certain dates, times, or user commands.

SEE ALSO
Virus; Worm

Trouble Ticket

In network fault management, a trouble ticket is an error log. Trouble tickets are a useful logging method for distributed systems.

When a fault arises somewhere on a distributed network, a nearby administrator may take responsibility for dealing with it. This administrator can fill out a trouble ticket to indicate that the fault has been detected and is being worked on. When the fault has been resolved, the administrator can add the date of the resolution to the trouble ticket.

Trouble tickets can be stored in a problem library, and they can serve as both reference information and performance data.

BROADER CATEGORY
Network Management

TSA (Target Service Agent)

A TSA is a Novell NetWare program that helps move data between a host and a target server. A *host* is any server with storage and a storage controller. A *target* is a server with data to be backed up or restored.

Specifically, a TSA runs on a target and communicates with the SBACKUP utility on the host, as follows:

1. SBACKUP on the host sends a request to the TSA on the target. The TSA translates the request into a form the target's Operating System (OS) will be able to handle.

2. In the second step, the TSA actually passes the request on to the target OS. The target OS performs the appropriate action on the data.

3. The target OS returns any output or results to the TSA, which now converts them into a form suitable for the host. In fact, NetWare uses the SMS (Storage

Management Services) to create hardware and operating system-independent representations.

4. The TSA passes the results and data to SBACKUP for the host.

The figure "A TSA at work" shows the elements of a session with SBACKUP and a TSA.

TSAPI (Telephony Services API)

A collection of functions for communicating with telephones, PBXs, and other telecommunications devices and for enabling networks to make use of these devices. The TSAPI was developed by AT&T and Novell to help bring about true Computer-Telephony Integration (CTI).

BROADER CATEGORY

CTI (Computer-Telephony Integration)

SEE ALSO

TAPI (Telephony API); Versit

TSR (Terminate-and-Stay-Resident) Program

A program that is loaded into memory and stays there, usually dormant, until activated by a condition or a key sequence.

TTL (Transistor-Transistor Logic)

A very fast (versions operating at over 100 megahertz are available) but relatively power-hungry logic family for digital circuitry. Compare TTL with ECL, which is used for very high-speed applications, and CMOS, which is used for applications in which low-power consumption is needed.

TTRT (Target Token Rotation Time)

In FDDI networks, a parameter whose value specifies how long it will take before every node on a network gets access to the token.

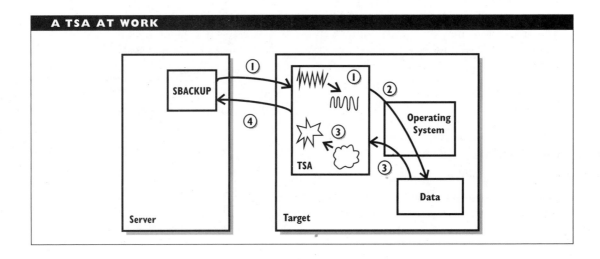

A TSA AT WORK

TTS (Transaction Tracking System)

TTS is a Novell NetWare software safety mechanism used to protect file integrity in database applications. In TTS, database transactions are carried out completely or not at all.

TTS works using *automatic rollback* to accomplish its tasks. Automatic rollback restores the starting state if a transaction fails before completion. Backing out of a transaction enables the user or application to completely abandon an uncompleted transaction in a database so that no changes are made to the database. Automatic roll-back helps ensure that a record is never changed partially in a transaction.

TTS can help prevent errors under conditions such as the following:

- Loss of power to either the server or the workstation during a transaction

- Other hardware failure in either server or workstation during a transaction

- Hardware failure to a non-node component, such as a cable, hub, or repeater

- Software failure, such as a hung system

TTS works only with files in which information is stored in records and in which record locking can be used. This applies to database files and to some electronic-mail (e-mail) and workgroup schedule files. TTS will not work with ordinary text files such as those created with a word processor.

BROADER CATEGORY
NetWare

Tunneling

Tunneling is a method for avoiding protocol restrictions by wrapping packets from one protocol in a packet for another and then transmitting this wrapped, or encapsulated, packet over a network that supports the wrapper protocol.

For example, an SDLC (Synchronized Data Link Control) packet from an SNA (Systems Network Architecture) network expects to be transmitted in a connection-oriented manner (over a predefined path). In contrast, on some Local-Area Networks (LANs), packets are transmitted in a connectionless manner (by whatever path is most expedient). To move SDLC packets over LANs, these packets may be wrapped in a TCP/IP protocol.

Similarly, the Apple Internet Router (AIR) can wrap an AppleTalk packet inside X.25 or TCP/IP packets.

Tunneling is also known as *protocol encapsulation* and *synchronous pass-through*.

Turbo FAT Index Table

In the DOS file system as used by NetWare, a turbo FAT (File Allocation Table) index table is created when a file gets too large for an ordinary FAT. The turbo FAT index that Novell's NetWare creates for such a file will speed up access to the file.

TUXEDO

Novell's TUXEDO software provides a high-level interface for client-server and transaction-management services, such as Online Transaction Processing (OLTP). TUXEDO provides a functional layer between applications and database management systems or othertransaction-based systems.

The additional layer supplies a common interface that developers can use, and it also provides a buffer between applications and services. This buffer makes it easier to redirect or otherwise filter transmissions, thereby making it easy to protect data. For example, TUXEDO uses the layer to redirect a client's request to an appropriate server, which will handle the transaction. Instead of transmitting data across the network, TUXEDO transmits requests and functions.

Applications communicate using a data-presentation service known as *typed buffers*. Typed buffers provide an intermediate representation for data, which can be translated from and to any format supported by TUXEDO. By separating the applications from the internal representations, TUXEDO helps make network and remote access easier for applications.

Other TUXEDO features and capabilities include the following:

- Use of a naming service so that clients can refer to services by name instead of needing to specify the service's location

- Support for DOS, Microsoft Windows 3.1, OS/2, and Macintosh workstations

- The ability to transfer data among platforms that differ in the way they represent data (for example, DOS, UNIX, and mainframe environments)

- Support for message queuing by applications

- Use of an authentication system to verify a user's identity

- Transaction monitoring and management

- Replication of servers and services across multiple nodes to help ensure that the requested services will always be available

- Support for load balancing and for automatic recovery and server restarts after a fault

- Support for service migration, by which a service is moved from one server to another when error or load conditions dictate

UA (User Agent)

In the CCITT X.400 Message Handling System (MHS), the UA is an application process that provides access for a human user to a Message Transfer System (MTS).

SEE ALSO

X.400

UAL (User Access Line)

In an X.25 network, the UAL is the line that provides a connection between a DTE (computer) and a network, with the user's DCE (digital service unit, modem, or multiplexer) serving as the interface to the network.

UAL (User Agent Layer)

In the 1984 version of the X.400 Message Handling System (MHS) recommendations, the UAL is the upper sublayer of the OSI application layer. Users interact with the UAL, and the UAL, in turn, communicates with the MTL (message transfer layer) below it.

SEE ALSO

X.400

UAM (User Authentication Method)

In an AppleTalk network, the UAM identifies users for a file server before giving the users access to services. Depending on the authentication method being used, this can be done on the basis of either an unencrypted password sent over the network or a random number from which the user's password can be derived by decrypting at the server's end.

UART (Universal Asynchronous Receiver/Transmitter)

The UART is the chip that does the nitty-gritty work for serial communications. The UART is located on either the motherboard or on a serial interface card.

UART Functions

The UART performs the following tasks:

- Converts parallel input from a program to serial form for transmission

- Adds any required start, stop, and parity bits to the byte

- Monitors the serial port's status by reading the appropriate control pins

- Controls the timing for the transmission

- Maintains and administrates a buffer to speed up processing

- At the receiving end, strips framing bits from the transmitted character

- At the receiving end, converts serial input to parallel form, before passing the character on to a program

Because of all the tasks a UART needs to do, this component can easily become a bottleneck in a communication. If the data is being transmitted too quickly from the program, the UART may be overrun, so that bits (and even bytes) are lost. To help protect against such loss, UARTs have buffers that can be used to store bits while the UART is tending to other tasks.

UART Versions

The early PCs used the 8-bit 8250 UART, which had 1-byte buffers for receiving and transmitting. Beginning about 1985, when AT clones became available, the 8250 was replaced by the faster, more powerful, 16-bit 16450 UART.

The 16-bit version is capable of transmissions up to 115,200 bits per second (bps). Although this is faster than the best throughput of ordinary modems, the UART must have complete control of the computer's resources to achieve this speed.

To deal with the greater demands imposed on the processor by programs and to make the UART effective even in multi-user and multitasking environments, a new version of the UART was introduced: the 16550A. Even though this chip represents a major deviation from earlier models, the difference is only internal. In fact, the 16550A plugs into a socket designed for the 16450. (Not all UARTs are in sockets; some are part of the board itself.)

A major difference between the 16450 and 16550 UARTs is the 16-byte buffers (for receiving and transmitting) on a 16550. These buffers are not used until activated by software that can make use of the 16550's features. Until that happens, the 16550 behaves just like a 16450.

The buffers save considerable time because the UART needs to stop transmission much less often. This means the UART must compete less with other devices for the central processing unit's (CPU's) attention. In systems running a multitasking

environment or those with high-speed microprocessors (such as the 80486), the faster UART may be the only way to get high-speed communications to work properly.

The 16550 has more intelligent circuitry for checking when it needs to do work and when it needs to signal other devices. In addition, the 16550 can run about 20 percent faster than the 16450. These enhancements give the 16550 UART a 256 kilobit per second (Kbps) throughput under optimal conditions.

UMB (Upper Memory Block)

In the DOS environment, the UMB refers to part or all of the memory in the area between 640 kilobytes and 1 megabyte. With the help of memory managers, UMBs are allocated for storing drivers, video or other buffers, and other items, which frees conventional memory and gives programs more room in which to execute.

SEE ALSO

Memory

UNA (Upstream Neighbor's Address)

In a Token Ring network, the address of the node from which a given node receives frames. Because of the ring structure, this address is unique at any given time in the network's operation.

SEE ALSO

Token Ring

a
b
c
d
e
f
g
h
i
j
k
l
m
n
o
p
q
r
s
t
u
v
w
x
y
z

▼
Undervoltage

As in other areas of life, electrical dangers can come from having too much or too little. Collectively, such disturbances are known as overvoltages and undervoltages, respectively. An undervoltage is a condition in which the voltage supply is below its nominal level.

SEE ALSO
Power Disturbance

▼
UNI (User-to-Network Interface)

In ATM networks, one of three levels of interface. The other two are network-to-network (NNI) and user-to-user (UUI).

▼
Unicode

Unicode is a 16-bit character code, which supports up to 64,000 different characters. A 16-bit representation is particularly useful for languages with large alphabets or other basic units (for example, Asian languages). The Unicode specifications were developed by the Unicode Consortium. Most of the commonly used character codes (such as ASCII or EBCDIC) are encoded somewhere in Unicode's data-banks and can, therefore, be used.

Character representation using Unicode is in contrast to the code-page strategy currently used in most DOS and Microsoft Windows environments. Each code page is 8 bits and has room for just 256 characters.

The NetWare Directory database in Novell's NetWare 4.x uses Unicode format to store information about objects and their attributes.

▼
Unified Messaging

Unified messaging, also known as *integrated messaging,* is a local-area network (LAN) based telephony service in which various kinds of messages or information can be accessed in a transparent manner. The types of information that can be handled include electronic mail (e-mail), fax, image, video, and voice transmissions.

With unified messaging, the telephony services can find and display the messages regardless of the format. This search-and-display process, known as a *launch,* may require certain applications. For example, the process may need an application that can display a particular type of message. Any required applications will be started up automatically.

▼
Unified Network Management Architecture (UNMA)

SEE
UNMA (Unified Network Management Architecture)

▼
Uniform Service Ordering Code (USOC)

SEE
USOC (Uniform Service Ordering Code)

▼
Uninterruptible Power Supply (UPS)

SEE
UPS (Uninterruptible Power Supply)

Universal Asynchronous Receiver/Transmitter (UART)

SEE

UART (Universal Asynchronous Receiver/Transmitter)

Universal In-Box

A single location that can be used as a delivery point for all forms of electronic communications for a user, including e-mail, faxes, and other types of messages. A universal in-box makes computer-telephony integration easier to use and more appealing to ordinary users.

Universal Resource Locator (URL)

SEE

URL (Universal Resource Locator)

UNIX

UNIX is a 32-bit, multiuser, multitasking operating system. It was originally developed at AT&T's Bell Labs in 1969 to implement a space invaders game on some unused hardware. The operating system has since been implemented on hardware ranging from PCs to Crays; it has acquired hundreds of commands, tools, and utilities over the years.

UNIX development has proceeded along two major strains: the AT&T System releases (with the most recent major release being System V) and the UC Berkeley System Distribution (BSD) releases (with the most recent major release being 4). The various UNIX strains and variants were combined at

the UNIX Software Operation (now UNIX Systems Group, a division of Novell). In recognition of the two UNIX strains, the most recent combined version is System V Release 4.2, known as SVR4.2.

The UNIX environment provides several types of networking resources, including the uucp (UNIX-to-UNIX copy) program and the TCP/IP protocol suite. UNIX also makes distributed computing easier, and it forms a major part of the Internet software infrastructure. The X Window System developed at MIT provides the basis of a graphical interface for UNIX.

UNIX variants, work-alikes, and extensions abound. The following is a partial list:

- A/UX (Macintosh)
- AIX (IBM)
- Coherent (Intel)
- LINUX (Intel)
- MACH (various)
- MINIX (various)
- NeXTSTEP (NeXT and Intel)
- Solaris (RISC and Intel)
- ULTRIX (DEC)
- UnixWare (Intel)
- Xenix (Intel)
- Yggdrasil (Intel)

UnixWare

UnixWare is Novell's implementation of the 32-bit multiuser, multitasking, and multithreading UNIX operating system.

a b c d e f g h i j k l m n o p q r s t **u** v w x y z

UnixWare is based on UNIX System V Release 4.2 MP (SVR4.2 MP). In addition to providing a full UNIX implementation, UnixWare includes extensions that enable easy integration with NetWare networks.

Two versions of UnixWare are marketed: UnixWare Personal Edition and UnixWare Application Server. The former is intended for use on workstations or stand-alone machines; the latter can be used to run programs that might otherwise be executed on a mainframe.

UnixWare Application Server

UnixWare Application Server offers the following features:

- Uses the X Window graphics environment (version X11 R5) to provide a graphical user interface (GUI). Unix-Ware also supports other APIs (Application Program Interfaces) for running X Window applications.

- Offers binary and/or source compatibility with several popular UNIX implementations, including SCO UNIX and XENIX (binary), Solaris, and Berkeley UNIX (source).

- Supports multiple file systems, including several UNIX file systems and the widely supported NFS (Network File System). UnixWare Application Server also supports the CDFS (Compact Disc File System).

- Runs DOS applications and real mode Microsoft Windows applications.

- Supports UNIX networking protocols: TCP/IP and NFS (FTP, SMTP, SNMP, Telnet, PPP, SLIP, and NIS).

- Supports the protocols of a NetWare client, including IPX/SPX, NCP, RIP, SAP, ODI, MHS, and Packet Burst.

- Meets the criteria for a C2 security classification and has many of the features required for the more stringent B2 security level. An auditing package called UnixWare C2 Auditing is available as an optional add-on.

- Supports fault-tolerance and data-protection measures, including support for RAID (redundant array of inexpensive disks), disk mirroring, and disk striping. The Veritas Advanced File System supports on-line administration (backups, volume mounting and unmounting, defragmentation, and so on), which also adds to the fault-tolerant capabilities.

- Supports Novell Virtual Terminal (NVT) to provide access to UNIX applications for various types of clients (DOS, OS/2, Microsoft Windows, Macintosh, and UNIX).

- Provides direct access to NetWare services for applications. This is accomplished through the NWCalls API.

- Supports open systems and industry standards, including IEEE POSIX 1003.1, *X/Open Portability Guide* (XPG3 and XPG4), Intel Application Binary Interface (iABI), and the System V Interface Definition, issue 3 (SVID3).

- Supports add-on services that can provide capabilities such as remote login, access to server-based applications, and network management.

Because it supports preemptive multitasking, UnixWare is suited for use as a server for mission-critical applications, such as on-line transaction processing (OLTP). A UnixWare machine can function as an application server while a NetWare machine functions as the file server. In such a configuration, UnixWare runs as an NCP client on the NetWare network.

Because of its ability to work smoothly with a NetWare network and its utility as an application server, Novell is positioning UnixWare as an important component as enterprise computing environments move from reliance on mainframes to greater reliance on PC-based computing power.

UnixWare Personal Edition

The Personal Edition version of UnixWare will run on stand-alone machines or workstations. This version lacks some of the more advanced features, such as built-in NFS support and support for CD-ROM drives. In many cases, the features are available as optional add-ons.

UnixWare Personal Edition supports various automatic processes, including automatic mounting of file systems and automatic authentication to the file server. The Personal Edition includes the DOS Requester and gets access to NetWare utilities through this Requester.

Unloading

The process of removing the contents (usually a program, module, or other file) from an allocated area of memory. For example, a program is unloaded from working memory when execution finishes. In Novell's NetWare versions 3.*x* and 4.*x*, unloading refers to the unlinking of a NetWare Loadable Module (NLM) from the NetWare operating system.

UNMA (Unified Network Management Architecture)

UNMA is an architecture developed by AT&T to provide a unified framework for AT&T's conception of network management tasks. The UNMA is medium- and vendor-independent, and relies on distributed (rather than centralized, or mainframe-based) processing.

The architecture is based on OSI protocols, serves as an operating environment for AT&T's Accumaster Integrator network management package, and provides a framework for dealing with the nine major management functions in AT&T's model:

- Accounting management

- Configuration management

- Fault management

- Performance management

- Security management

- Integrated control

- Operations support

- Planning capability

a b c d e f g h i j k l m n o p q r s t **u** v w x y z

- Programmability

The first five of these function areas are identical to those specified in the OSI network management model.

UNMA Components

UNMA consists of five main components:

- A unified user interface, which provides a graphics-based summary of the network's operation. This is the level with which the user interacts directly.

- An integrated network management system, which actually does the network management. In the UNMA, this role is filled by Accumaster Integrator, as described in the next section.

- Element management systems (EMSs), which serve essentially as local network managers. They are managers for a part of the entire network, such as for a local-area network (LAN), a mainframe, or a telecommunications link. The integrated management system supervises EMS operation and communicates with these components using the network management protocol.

- A network management protocol (NMP), which is based on OSI protocols and designed to enable the management package to perform all the tasks included in AT&T's definition of network management.

- Network elements, which are the components operating at the user level. In UNMA, a network element can be anything from a node to a LAN, from a modem to a PBX (private branch exchange), an IXC (interexchange carrier), or an entire PTT (Post, Telephone, and Telegraph).

These elements are shown in the figure "Structure of AT&T's UNMA."

Accumaster Integrator

Accumaster Integrator is the actual network management package within UNMA. The package is a "supermanager" in that it can monitor both hardware and logical network activity. Given AT&T's leading role in telecommunications, it should not be surprising that Accumaster Integrator can manage various types of telecommunications setups, including PBXs, X.25 network connections, Dataphone systems, and IXCs, in addition to the usual network elements (nodes, LANs, and so on).

Accumaster Integrator has powerful graphics-based reporting and display capabilities, and it can distinguish between important and noncritical alarms on the network.

Although Accumaster Integrator is based on the OSI network management model, it offers support for other models. In particular, support is available through third-party products for IBM's SNA (Systems Network Architecture) and for the NMA (Network Management Architecture) based on this model. Other products provide support for the SNMP (Simple Network Management

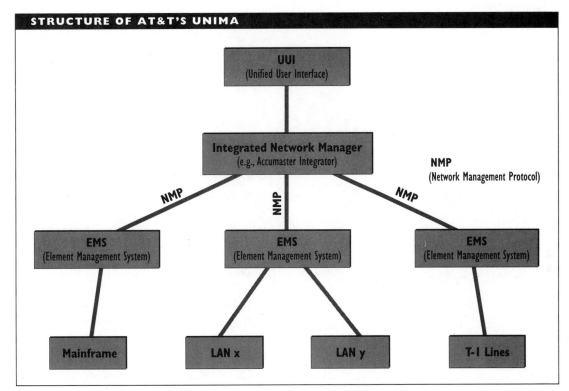

STRUCTURE OF AT&T'S UNIMA

UUI
(Unified User Interface)

Integrated Network Manager
(e.g., Accumaster Integrator)

NMP
(Network Management Protocol)

NMP

NMP

NMP

EMS
(Element Management System)

EMS
(Element Management System)

EMS
(Element Management System)

Mainframe

LAN x

LAN y

T-1 Lines

Protocol) supported in TCP/IP-based network management.

SEE ALSO

EMA (Enterprise Management Architecture); Network Management; NMA (Network Management Architecture)

Upgrade

An upgrade provides a mechanism for converting from one version of a program or package to another, more recent one. For example, Novell supports the following types of upgrades to NetWare 4.*x*:

- Migration, in which servers are converted from NetWare 2.*x* or 3.*x* to NetWare 4.*x* or another netware operating system

- In-place upgrade, which uses SERVER.EXE to upgrade from NetWare 2.*x* to NetWare 3.*x* and then uses the 4.*x* upgrade programs to continue the upgrade process

As a verb, upgrade refers to the process of performing the installation of a newer software version or of a more powerful hardware component.

Uplink

In telecommunications, a communications link between one or more earth stations and a satellite; also, the process of transmitting from an earth station to the satellite.

COMPARE
Downlink

Upload

To transfer data (such as a file) from a PC or other machine to a host machine. For example, the target machine may be a mainframe or a bulletin board system (BBS) computer. In general, an upload transfers from a remote machine to a central one. This process requires a communications protocol that both host and recipient can understand and use.

Upper Memory Block (UMB)

SEE
UMB (Upper Memory Block)

UPS (Uninterruptible Power Supply)

A UPS is an emergency power source that can deliver a limited amount of power to a file server or other device in the event of a blackout (total loss of power).

UPSs are sometimes known as online UPSs to distinguish them from SPSs (standby power supplies), which are also known as *offline UPSs*. An SPS is similar, but not identical, to a UPS. The main difference is that a UPS always supplies power through a battery, whereas an SPS does so only when there is a power failure.

UPS Operation

A UPS provides power to a file server through its battery and an inverter (which converts the battery's direct current to alternating current). That is, a UPS takes power from the lines and uses it to charge a battery.

CONSEQUENCES OF ONLINE POWER

An online power supply has several consequences:

- Since a server will get more than just emergency power from the UPS, the UPS must be able to provide power that is at least as clean as the power company's. In practice, this means the UPS must be able to produce a true sine wave pattern, rather than providing just a square wave as a rough approximation. Ask potential vendors to send you typical wave patterns produced by their devices or check on these for yourself. To do that properly, you'll need an oscilloscope.

- There is a 25 to 30 percent loss of power as it goes through the battery and the inverter. Thus, the UPS must work harder than the power company to supply the file server (or whatever) with its power. (A standby power supply, in contrast, loses only about 2 percent of the power.)

- A busy UPS generates a considerable amount of heat as it loses the power. This heat causes wear and tear on the UPS components, including the battery. This wear shortens the effective lifetime of the components. Some manufacturers house the battery in a separate box to protect it from the heat, and thereby extend the battery's life.

The UPS then feeds the server by sending power from the battery through an inverter to create the alternating current the computer's power supply expects. The UPS's battery is kept full by a battery charger that is also part of the UPS.

A UPS with a bad battery can actually suck power from the lines as it tries to charge the battery. This can cause voltage sags in other devices. Similarly, a UPS operating in an environment with a low voltage supply will not be able to charge the battery, which may also get drained to provide extra power.

UPSs typically work as battery chargers during normal operation. If there is something wrong with the battery, the UPS may draw more than its share of power, to the detriment of other equipment on the same line.

In a UPS, the primary power path is through the battery. Should the battery stop working, a standard online UPS has a secondary path: the one the power company supplies. In other words, the secondary path is the path that would exist if there were no UPS attached.

UPS Special Features

A UPS should have an inverter shutdown capability so that the battery will not continue to be drained. After the UPS has shut down the machine, the battery should also be shut down.

UPSs can be monitored and put to work if necessary. Monitoring capabilities are included in most network operating systems, but they can generally be added if not provided. UPS monitors can record values for various indicators of power requirements and supply. See the UPS Monitoring article for more information.

Some UPSs can perform automatic network shutdowns in case of a blackout. This is a great help because it enables networks to be shut down properly even if no one is around during a power outage. Shutdown capability is often provided in an optional board that is plugged into the server (or whatever machine is being protected).

Variant Power Supplies

The (online) UPS and the SPS represent two "pure" ends of a spectrum that includes various hybrids and special variants. These hybrids each have their own distinctive features, advantages, and disadvantages:

- An *online without bypass* variant operates like a regular UPS, except that the entire system goes down if the UPS breaks down, because there is no secondary path. This means that the power supply is through the UPS or nothing. Such a device is cheaper to make but riskier to use.

- A *standby online* hybrid always has the inverter online but puts the battery into action only when necessary. This has the instantaneous switchover of an online UPS and the small power requirements of an SPS. This variant has no secondary path.

- A *line interactive* variant has the inverter and battery always online, but the battery is used only when needed. During normal operation, the inverter charges the battery and feeds the file server. In a blackout, the inverter draws power from the battery to feed the server.

a b c d e f g h i j k l m n o p q r s t u v w x y z

- A *standby ferro* is a standby power supply with a special transformer that protects against noise and overvoltages. This variant has the same power loss and heat generation as an online power supply.

UPS Maintenance

A UPS battery is working all the time, which is going to take its toll. To ensure that the battery is working properly, it is a good idea to test it every few months. It is also important periodically to discharge the battery completely and then charge it again. Testing and discharging can both be done at the same time.

When you are testing the battery, back up the network before you begin the test. Then follow the recommendations of the UPS manufacturer regarding testing. In most cases, the recommendation will be to pull the plug on the UPS. The effects of just pulling the plug are not exactly the same as in the case of a real power outage, because along with the UPS, other equipment or machinery connected to the lines will be drawing the last remaining power. This is a more severe trial than simply pulling the plug. Nevertheless, such a test is better than none.

Even with regular maintenance, UPS batteries need to be replaced every few years.

Centralized versus Distributed UPSs

The device or devices protected by a UPS depend on where the UPS is connected. A centralized UPS is intended to provide power protection for an entire network with a single power supply. This type of UPS is rare, because its power requirements are enormous. Such a UPS must be able to provide more than the total power consumed by the components during normal operation. This is because each node can draw more than 20 times its average power requirements at startup. The UPS battery would be quickly drained each morning as the stations logged in one by one.

The more common solution is to use distributed UPSs, which means a separate UPS for every device that needs special protection. This gets expensive, cluttered, and hot (especially if all the machines are in the same room).

Mainly because of the expense, many locations protect only file servers and possibly certain other key components, such as routers, hubs, or hard disk subsystems.

BROADER CATEGORY
Safety Device

COMPARE
SPS (Standby Power Supply)

UPS Monitoring

UPS monitoring is a network operating system (NOS) service that enables the NOS to keep track of an attached UPS to determine when backup power is being provided. The server can shut down the network before the backup power supply is exhausted.

For ISA (Industry Standard Architecture) and EISA (Extended Industry Standard Architecture) architectures, the UPS monitoring software needs an interface board to do the actual monitoring; with MicroChannel Architecture (formerly MCA) machines, the UPS can be monitored through the mouse port.

Various UPS vendors offer more sophisticated monitoring than the services provided by the NOS. These products may also provide automatic battery tests and power supply diagnostics.

Upstream Neighbor's Address (UNA)

SEE
UNA (Upstream Neighbor's Address)

Up Time

The time during which a machine or other device is functioning. Even when functioning, a machine is not necessarily available for use, however. This may happen, for example, when the demand for a device makes it impossible to accommodate all the requests. A device that is unavailable because of heavy activity level is still said to be "up."

COMPARE
Down Time

URL (Universal Resource Locator)

A URL provides a means of identifying a document on the Internet. The following is an example of a URL:

http://cuiwww.unige.ch/meta-index.html

This URL has three main parts:

- Information about the document type and about the protocol used to transport it. On the World Wide Web (WWW) the most common value is

http, as in the example. This indicates that the Hypertext Transfer Protocol (HTTP) is being used—probably to transport a hypertext document written using HTML (Hypertext Markup Language). Other possible values include FTP, Gopher, and file. The protocol information is almost always followed by a colon and two forward slashes (://).

- The next element is the domain name of the machine on which the document is found. In the example, this is cuiwww.unige.ch, which is a web server at the university of Geneva (unige) in Switzerland (ch).

- The final element is the document's name. This name must be represented as an absolute path to the file. In the example, the document is named meta-index.html and is found in the root directory of the machine.

URLs are an example of the more general Universal Resource Identifiers (URI), which also encompass Universal Resource Names (URNs).

PRIMARY SOURCES
URLs are discussed in RFC 1738.

US Classification Levels

The US Classification levels provide a set of classification categories specified by the United States government and used in datagrams transmitted across the Internet. A datagram's classification level is specified in an 8-bit value. The levels are shown in the table "US Classification Levels."

a b c d e f g h i j k l m n o p q r s t **u** v w x y z

US CLASSIFICATION LEVELS	
BIT SEQUENCE	**LEVEL**
0000 0001	Reserved
0011 1101	Top secret
0101 1010	Secret
1001 0110	Confidential
0110 0110	Reserved
1100 1100	Reserved
1010 1011	Unclassified
1111 0001	Reserved

Note that 8 bits have been allocated to represent just eight possible classifications (only four of which are currently used). With 8 bits, it is possible to make the values different enough that a receiver could identify a value even if multiple bits in the sequence were incorrect. (In terms of error-correction strategies, the selected bit sequences differ from every other selected sequence in at least four positions.)

Usenet

Usenet is a global news distribution service that relies on the Internet for much of its news traffic. Usenet works by using news servers that agree to share and distribute *newsfeeds* (grouped collections of news articles).

Usenet sites mirror (maintain copies of) or distribute articles from newsgroups, which are named article collections in seven top-level categories and in thousands of subcategories:

- *comp* deals with computer science and related topics.

- *news* contains announcements and information about Usenet and news-related software.

- *rec* contains newsgroups for hobbies, arts, crafts, music, and other recreational activities.

- *sci* contains newsgroups concerned with scientific research, advances, and applications for scientific fields other than computer science.

- *soc* deals with topics of social relevance—with "social" defined just about any way you want it to be.

- *talk* contains debate and heated—or long-winded—discussion about controversial topics.

- *misc* contains categories that don't fit into any of the others in the list.

There are thousands of newsgroups that don't fall into any of the Usenet categories. these are grouped under *alt* and several dozen other headings.

User Access Line (UAL)

SEE
UAL (User Access Line)

User Agent (UA)

SEE
UA (User Agent)

User Agent Layer (UAL)

SEE

UAL (User Agent Layer)

User Authentication Method (UAM)

SEE

UAM (User Authentication Method)

User-Network Contract

In the ATM architecture, a user-network contract (also known as a *traffic descriptor*) is an element that specifies parameters for a virtual channel or path connection (VCC or VPC). These parameter values can be negotiated by the entities involved in the connection.

User Object

In the NetWare Directory Services (NDS) for NetWare 4.*x*, a user object is a leaf object that represents a specific user. The following properties are associated with a user object, and these properties will have specific values for the user:

- User's login name

- User's group membership (if any)

- Home directories, which serve as personal workspaces for the user

- Trustee rights, which control access to directories and files

- Security equivalences, which give a user the same rights as another user has or had

- Print job configurations

- Account management

- User login scripts

- User account restrictions

SEE ALSO

NDS (NetWare Directory Services)

User Profile

A record specifying a user's access and usage rights on a server.

User-to-Network Interface (UNI)

SEE

UNI (User-to-Network Interface)

USOC (Uniform Service Ordering Code)

A commonly used sequence for wire pairs.

SEE ALSO

Wiring Sequence

uucp

An application layer protocol for transferring files between UNIX systems. The uucp (for UNIX-to-UNIX copy program) protocol is dial-up and store-and-forward, so that its services are limited. uucp is available for just about every operating environment. It is commonly used as a low-end access protocol for the Internet.

a b c d e f g h i j k l m n o p q r s t **u** v w x y z

Value-Added Network (VAN)

SEE

VAN (Value-Added Network)

Value-Added Process (VAP)

SEE

VAP (Value-Added Process)

VAN (Value-Added Network)

A commercial network that includes services or features added to existing networks. Users can buy access to these VANs.

VAP (Value-Added Process)

In Novell's NetWare 2.*x*, a process that runs on top of the network operating system to provide additional services without interfering with normal network operations. A VAP can run only on a network server or on a router.

COMPARE

NLM (NetWare Loadable Module)

Variable Bit Rate (VBR)

SEE

VBR (Variable Bit Rate)

VBI (Vertical Blank Interval)

A nonvisible component of the signal sent to televisions, the VBI is currently used only for closed captioning. But the VBI can also be used for signaling other purposes. A new product—Malachi, from En Technology—will use the VBI for downloading software to users.

VBR (Variable Bit Rate)

In ATM networks, a VBR connection transmits at varying rates, such as in bursts. VBR connections use class B, C, or D services and are used for data (as opposed to voice) transmissions, whose contents are not constrained by timing restrictions.

SEE ALSO

ATM (Asynchronous Transfer Mode)

VC (Virtual Circuit)

In long-distance communications, a virtual circuit is a temporary connection between two points. This type of circuit will appear as a dedicated line to the user, but will actually be using packet switching to accomplish transmissions. The virtual circuit is maintained as long as the connection exists. A different virtual circuit may be established each time a call is made.

Virtual circuits are used in contrast to leased lines, in which a dedicated connection between two particular points is always available. X.25 and frame relay both use virtual circuits.

In the X.25 environment, a virtual circuit is a logical connection between a DTE (computer) and a DCE (digital service unit, modem, or multiplexer). This type of connection can be a switched virtual circuit (SVC) or a permanent virtual circuit (PVC). The SVC can connect to a different DTE at the other end each time. The PVC always connects to the same DTE at the other end.

VCC (Virtual Channel Connection)

In ATM, a VCC is a logical connection between two entities (which may be users or networks). This is the basic switching level for ATM and is analogous to a virtual circuit (VC) in an X.25 network.

VCCs have the following features:

- May be switched (established as needed) or dedicated (semipermanent)

- Preserve the order in which cells are transmitted; that is, if cells A, B, and C are transmitted in that sequence, they are received in the same order at the other end

- Provide a quality of service (QoS) that is specified by parameters concerning such features as variations in cell delays and cell losses (in relation to total cells transmitted)

- Have performance parameters that can be negotiated by the entities involved in a connection

The parameters that apply for a VCC are specified in a *traffic descriptor,* also called a *user-network contract.* Although the details have not yet been standardized, a user-network contract is expected to specify values such as peak transmission rate and maximum burst length.

A group of VCCs can be allocated for the same connection, to provide the desired bandwidth for the connection. This type of VCC cluster is known as a *virtual path connection* (*VPC*). All channels in a given VPC are routed together, which helps reduce management overhead. Certain VCCs in a VPC may be reserved for network use.

VCI (Virtual Channel Identifier)

In an ATM network, a value associated with a single virtual channel connection (VCC) for a particular user. The VCI is used to route a cell to and from the user. A given VCC may have different VCIs at the sending and receiving ends. In a sense, this value represents a service access point (SAP).

COMPARE
VPI (Virtual Path Identifier)

VCPI (Virtual Control Program Interface)

An interface developed by Quarterdeck Systems, Phar Lap Software, and other vendors. VCPI provides specifications to enable DOS programs to run in protected mode on 80386 and higher machines and to execute cooperatively with other operating environments (most notably, DESQview). As the first *DOS extender,* VCPI became a *de facto* standard. VCPI is incompatible with DPMI (DOS Protected Mode Interface), an alternative DOS extender standard developed by Microsoft.

Velocity of Propagation (VOP)

SEE
VOP (Velocity of Propagation)

Vendor Independent Messaging (VIM)

SEE

VIM (Vendor Independent Messaging)

Veronica (Very Easy Rodent-Oriented Netwide Index to Computerized Archives)

An Internet service for gopher environments. Veronica searches all gopher servers for any menus that contain items that match specified search criteria. The string specifying the search criteria can include substrings and also Boolean operators (AND, NOT, OR).

SEE ALSO

Gopher

Versit

A consortium formed by Apple, AT&T, IBM, and Siemens Rolm Communications to create a specification for CTI (Computer-Telephony Integration). This would enable computers, networks, and PDAs (Personal Digital Assistants) to communicate with telephones, PBXs, and other devices. To help bring this about, the Versit participants are developing specifications for an application program interface (API) for telephony. This is a set of functions that make possible communications between computers and telephony devices.

SEE ALSO

TAPI (Telephony API); TSAPI (Telephony Services API)

Vertical Blank Interval (VBI)

SEE

VBI (Vertical Blank Interval)

Very Small Aperture Terminal (VSAT)

SEE

VSAT (Very Small Aperture Terminal)

VESA (Video Electronics Standards Association)

An association of video adapter and display manufacturers, which has developed standards for display formats (such as the Super VGA graphics standard) and also for a system bus, called the VL, or VESA local, bus. Like its main competitor, the PCI bus, the VL bus standard is capable of 64-bit operation and can also support much faster clock speeds than earlier bus designs.

Videoconferencing

Videoconferencing refers to multiparty communications involving both video and audio. Videoconferencing may use special-purpose hardware, ordinary telephone services, or computer-based hardware and software. Until recently, acceptable quality video and sound required huge (for the period) bandwidths. This situation has improved as image and voice compression methods have become more efficient.

A video codec (coder/decoder) is needed for translating between the video images and their digital representation. Standards and specifications for videoconferencing and also for codecs and the information they must process are formulated in the CCITT H.200 and H.300 series of documents.

Video Electronics Standards Association (VESA)

SEE

VESA (Video Electronics Standards Association)

VIM (Vendor Independent Messaging)

VIM is an API (Application Program Interface) for use between application programs and the various types of messaging-related services available. Applications include programs such as electronic mail (e-mail), scheduling, and workflow. Services include message store-and-forward and directory services.

Details of the API depend on the service being provided. For example, when used for directory or messaging services, VIM allows use of multiple databases (known as *address books*) and either direct or indirect addressing when specifying a message recipient.

The VIM API was developed by a consortium of vendors, including Apple, Borland, Lotus, and Novell. VIM is comparable in function to Microsoft's MAPI (Messaging API) and also to the XDS (X.500 Directory Services) API from X/Open and the X.400 API Association.

VINES (Virtual Networking System)

VINES is a distributed network operating system (NOS) from Banyan Systems. It is built on a UNIX operating environment and shares many of that operating system's features, including its distributed nature and its extensibility. However, VINES is flexible and can deal with most of the popular operating and networking environments. Moreover, the UNIX system is covered by VINES and is unavailable, so that any networking or system services must be provided by VINES.

VINES can support up to four network interface cards (NICs) per server. If the cards support different topologies, VINES can automatically perform any necessary protocol binding or translation when moving packets between the LANs supported by different cards. Protocol binding is accomplished using Microsoft's NDIS (Network Driver Interface Specification). This provides a standard interface for NIC, or adapter, drivers, so that multiple adapters can be connected, each with access to the available protocol stacks.

VINES provides access to files and directories across the network. The VINES file system (VFS) can support views compatible with any of several popular file systems, including those for DOS, OS/2, and Macintosh environments. This means that workstations running these environments can keep their files in native format. VINES also provides locking and synchronization capabilities to ensure that multiple users do not try to access the same material at the same time.

a b c d e f g h i j k l m n o p q r s t u **v** w x y z

Other VINES features and services include the following:

- Support for multiple servers and enterprise networks.

- Backup and archiving capabilities, including support for various types of backup media.

- Support for named pipes, sockets, and NetBIOS emulation to provide connectivity in a range of environments.

- Drivers for, and shared access to, various physical devices (hard disks and other storage media, printers, communications equipment, and so on).

- Network-wide security services that provide user authentication services and that use access rights lists associated with files and resources to determine who is allowed to use which resources. A VINES administrator can also specify when and how each user may use a file or resource.

- Both local and network-wide management and monitoring capabilities, including the optional ability to monitor (in real time) the network from the server console or from any network PC. Basic or optional management components can provide statistics about both local-area network (LAN) and wide-area network (WAN) interfaces.

- Server-to-server connections for LANs or WANs. WAN connections can be over X.25, ISDN, T1, SNA, dial-up, or leased lines.

- Support for the VINES protocol stack and optional support for other popular protocol stacks, including OSI, TCP/IP, and AppleTalk stacks. In addition, VINES offers NetBIOS emulation, which provides generic support for other layered networking environments.

- Intelligent messaging (IM), which provides a generalized information transfer capability that encompasses electronic mail and message handling, bulletin board systems, calendar, scheduling, and reporting activity, fax services, and workflow automation. The IM service supports a proprietary Banyan Mail Service (BMS) as well as many popular third-party mail packages for DOS, Macintosh, Microsoft Windows, and other environments.

- Symmetric multiprocessing capabilities, which support multiple processors working independently of each other but all communicating with the NOS. This allows the NOS to allocate different tasks to different processors.

- Asynchronous communication capabilities for remote networking and optional gateway services for communicating with SNA and other networking environments. The ICA (intelligent communications adapter) provides serial connections from a VINES server to other environments, including mainframe hosts, public or private data networks, or other VINES servers. The VINES ATE (asynchronous terminal emulation) services allow workstations to connect to mainframe hosts.

The figure "VINES architecture" shows the main protocols supported in the VINES architecture.

Much of the flexibility and power of VINES can be attributed to the fact that VINES services are all coordinated with the StreetTalk Directory service. StreetTalk is a distributed and replicated global directory service that provides users with transparent access to resources anywhere on the network, regardless of the server providing the resource. The NetWare Directory Services (NDS) in Novell's NetWare 4.*x* provide comparable network services. These global directory services are in contrast to server-based naming services, such as the NetWare bindery, which is used in NetWare versions 3.*x* and earlier.

VINES ARCHITECTURE

Layer 7: Application Layer	VINES File Service	VINES Applications Services
Layer 6: Presentation Layer	VINES Remote Procedure Calls (RPCs)	Server Message Block (SMB)
Layer 5: Session Layer	Socket Interface	

Layer 4: Transport Layer	VINES Interprocess Communications (VIPC)	VINES Sequenced Packet Protocol (VSPP)	Transmission Control Protocol (TCP)	User Datagram Protocol (UDP)
Layer 3: Network Layer	VINES Internet Protocol (VIP)	VINES Internet Control Protocol (VICP)	Internet Protocol (IP)	X.25
Layer 2: Data-Link Layer	Network Driver Interface Specification (NDIS)	X.25 HDLC		
Layer 1: Physical Layer	Network Interface Card and Cabling			

a b c d e f g h i j k l m n o p q r s t u **v** w x y z

VINES comes in several versions, ranging from a five-user version to one that will handle an unlimited number of nodes. In addition, a symmetric multiprocessing version is available for use on servers with multiple central processing units (CPUs).

Virtual

Ad hoc, as in a virtual circuit, which is created as needed, or in virtual memory, which can be taken from an available buffer for temporary use when needed.

Virtual Channel Connection (VCC)

SEE

VCC (Virtual Channel Connection)

Virtual Channel Identifier (VCI)

SEE

VCI (Virtual Channel Identifier)

Virtual Circuit (VC)

SEE

VC (Virtual Circuit)

Virtual Control Program Interface (VCPI)

SEE

VCPI (Virtual Control Program Interface)

Virtual Loadable Module (VLM)

SEE

VLM (Virtual Loadable Module)

Virtual Networking System (VINES)

SEE

VINES (Virtual Networking System)

Virtual Path Connection (VPC)

SEE

VPC (Virtual Path Connection)

Virtual Path Identifier (VPI)

SEE

VPI (Virtual Path Identifier)

Virtual Telecommunications Access Method (VTAM)

SEE

VTAM (Virtual Telecommunications Access Method)

Virtual Terminal (VT)

SEE

VT (Virtual Terminal)

Virus

A virus is a small bit of computer code that is self-replicating and that is designed to hide inside other programs. The virus travels with these programs, and it is invoked whenever the program is invoked. Because the virus is self-replicating, it will make a copy of itself whenever the program is invoked, and it can then infest other programs or files.

In addition to self-replication, the virus may also include instructions to cause unexpected effects or damage to a computer or its files. There are thousands of different viruses loose, and new ones appear almost daily. Virus scanning and destruction programs must be updated periodically to handle new viruses as they appear.

Viruses can be categorized by where they reside and by how they work. Viruses generally infect either or both of two locations:

- File viruses infect files—generally executable ones. When these files are executed or opened, the virus begins to spread.

- Boot sector viruses infect the disk's boot sector. This means that they will replicate every time the machine boots.

- Multipartite viruses infect both locations.

A few of the strategies used by viruses include:

- Stealth viruses, which modify system functions or seize interrupts in order to help hide themselves. Whenever a program, such as a virus scanning program, requests the co-opted function, the virus intercepts the call and handles the response.

- Polymorphic viruses, which change themselves whenever they replicate to confound anti-virus programs that look for distinctive signatures (bit patterns) of known viruses. Encrypted

viruses may be considered a special case of polymorphic virus: everything in the virus is encrypted except for the code needed to decrypt the virus prior to activating it. This decryption code may be altered each time.

- Armored viruses, which try to take defensive measures when a program tries to disassemble or otherwise analyze the virus.

SEE ALSO

Trojan Horse; Worm

VLM (Virtual Loadable Module)

In Novell NetWare environments, a VLM is a module that runs on a DOS workstation and that enables the workstation to communicate with the server. Two classes of VLMs are defined: a *child VLM* handles a group of functions for a particular implementation, and a multiplexer VLM finds the appropriate child VLM for a given task.

The VLMs listed in the table "NetWare 4.*x* VLMs" are used in the NetWare 4.*x* DOS Requester. These VLMs are loaded and managed by a DOS Requester module named VLM.EXE.

Since VLM.EXE is just a TSR (terminate-and-stay-resident) program manager, any TSR program written to conform to the VLM specifications can be treated as a module, which means that the VLM capabilities can be extended.

SEE ALSO

DOS Requester

NETWARE 4.X VLMS	
VLM	**FUNCTION**
AUTO.VLM	Used to reconnect automatically to the server if a connection has been lost. AUTO.VLM rebuilds the connection and its configuration information when the malfunctioning device is back on line. Currently, AUTO.VLM works only with NetWare 4.x Directory Services, but will eventually support Bindery Services (for earlier NetWare versions).
BIND.VLM	Used for Bindery Services from NetWare 3.x and earlier. Either NDS.VLM or BIND.VLM or both will be loaded, depending on the kinds of NetWare servers on the network.
CONN.VLM (Connection Table Manager)	Maintains the connections and connection information for the DOS Requester and allocates these connections. Anywhere between 2 and 50 connections can be supported, and the number can be set during configuration. The default is 8, because this is the maximum number of connections supported by the network shell program used with NetWare 3.x. CONN makes the table information available to other modules and can also provide statistics for network management.
FIO.VLM (File Input/Output)	Used for accessing files on the network. FIO.VLM provides file cache capabilities for more efficient access, Large Internet Packets (LIP) for more flexible packaging of transmissions, and Packet Burst mode for more efficient transmission.
GENERAL.VLM	Contains various functions used in other modules. Functions are available to provide server, queue, and connection information, to handle search drive mappings, and to deal with machine names.
IPXNCP.VLM	Builds the appropriate packets and passes these packets to the IPX protocol for transmission over the network. IPXNCP.VLM is a child process that is managed by TRAN.VLM.
NDS.VLM	Used for NetWare 4.x Directory Services. Either NDS.VLM or BIND.VLM or both will be loaded, depending on the kinds of NetWare servers on the network.
NETX.VLM	Used to provide compatibility with utilities from pre-4.x NetWare versions. This module need not be loaded if the network involves only NetWare 4.x servers or if only applications (but no NetWare utilities) from earlier versions are called.

VLM	FUNCTION
NMR.VLM (NetWare Management Responder)	Uses VLM.EXE's memory management capabilities to load and provide diagnostic capabilities for management software. NMR can gather information about the workstation configuration and also about the ODI services.
NWP.VLM (NetWare Protocol)	Uses child modules to connect to available services and to handle logins and logouts.
PNW.VLM	Used with Personal NetWare servers.
PRINT.VLM	Provides printer redirection for both Bindery and NetWare Directory Services.
REDIR.VLM	Serves as the DOS Redirector for the VLM architecture.
RSA.VLM	Provides packet encryption capabilities based on the RSA algorithm.
SECURITY.VLM	Used to provide security features. This module provides a message digest algorithm to help provide protection at the transport layer.
TRAN.VLM	Provides the ability to handle different transport layer protocols. By default, TRAN has only the IPXNCP.VLM module to manage, but others can be added by third parties. TRAN is a multiplexer VLM.

Voice Mail

Voice mail provides a system for recording, storing, retrieving, and delivering electronic voice messages.

Volume

In networking, a volume refers to the highest level in a file server's directory and file structure. For example, a large hard disk can be divided into several volumes during installation of the network operating system. Conversely, a volume may be distributed over multiple disks.

In Novell's NetWare, a volume is a fixed amount of physical hard disk space. The SYS volume is created automatically during NetWare installation. Other NetWare volumes can be created using INSTALL.

A NetWare volume can be divided logically into directories, and physically into volume segments. Volume segments can be on different hard disks, and each volume can have up to 32 volume segments. A hard disk can have at most eight volume segments. In NetWare versions 3.x and later, it is possible to add segments to a volume provided that there is sufficient storage and there are not too many entries to add.

When the NetWare server boots, each available volume is mounted. *Mounting* makes the volume visible to the operating system and also loads certain information for the subsequent use of the volume.

a
b
c
d
e
f
g
h
i
j
k
l
m
n
o
p
q
r
s
t
u
v
w
x
y
z

▼
VOP (Velocity of Propagation)

In a network, a value that indicates the signal speed as a proportion of the maximum speed theoretically possible. This value varies with cable and with architecture. Values for electrically based local-area networks range from about 60 to 85 percent of maximum.

SEE ALSO

NVP (Nominal Velocity of Propagation)

▼
VPC (Virtual Path Connection)

In ATM, a VPC provides a cluster of logical connections between two entities (users or networks). Each individual connection is known as a VCC, and all the channels in a particular VPC connect the same two entities. These VCCs are also routed together.

SEE ALSO

VCC (Virtual Channel Connection)

▼
VPI (Virtual Path Identifier)

In an ATM network, a VPI is a value associated with a particular virtual path connection (VPC).

COMPARE

VCI (Virtual Channel Identifier)

▼
VSAT (Very Small Aperture Terminal)

A relatively small (up to about 2 meters) satellite dish, used for digital communications.

▼
VT (Virtual Terminal)

In the OSI Reference Model, virtual terminal is an application layer service that makes it possible to emulate the behavior of a particular terminal. This type of emulation enables an application to communicate with a remote system, such as a mainframe or minicomputer host, without needing to worry about the type of hardware sending or receiving the communications. The virtual terminal provides an intermediate base with which both the host and the PC can communicate.

The host will use the host's native language to communicate with the PC through the virtual terminal. The virtual terminal will convert any communications from the host into an intermediate form and then into a form compatible with the protocols the PC is using.

OSI Classes of Service for Virtual Terminals

The OSI virtual terminal services specify what properties and capabilities a virtual terminal should have. The OSI specifies three classes of virtual terminal service:

Basic: A text-oriented service that provides basic capabilities such as line editing, scrolling, and so on. Basic mode can also handle certain block- or page-oriented commands.

Forms: A text-oriented service with access to certain predefined form templates and with the ability to communicate with forms-based terminals (such as the IBM 3270 terminals).

Graphics: A service that provides graphics capabilities and that can handle image-oriented terminals.

Other Virtual Terminal Choices

In addition to these classes of service, virtual terminal also offers choices for the following:

Modes of operation: Half-duplex or full-duplex. In half-duplex, transmissions go in only one direction at a time, so that only one party can send at a time. In full-duplex, both sides can be talking simultaneously.

Delivery control method: None, simple, or quarantine. In simple delivery control, the user can request delivery of any undelivered packets. In quarantine delivery control, the data is held until explicitly released.

Echo control: Remote or local.

PRIMARY SOURCES
ISO documents 9040 and 9041

BROADER CATEGORY
ASE (Application Service Element)

▼ VTAM (Virtual Telecommunications Access Method)

In IBM's SNA (Systems Network Architecture) environment, software that controls the communications services. VTAM runs on a mainframe under IBM's MVS or VM operating systems and supports several popular communications protocols, including Token Ring and SDLC (Synchronous Data Link Control).

a
b
c
d
e
f
g
h
i
j
k
l
m
n
o
p
q
r
s
t
u
v
w
x
y
z

WAIS (Wide Area Information Service)

On the Internet, a service that can search specified locations (*sources*) for files that contain specified terms (*keywords*). WAIS (pronounced "weighs") returns a list of files that satisfy the search criteria. WAIS allows the use of one or more keywords, which can be combined using simple relationships (AND, OR, or NOT).

WAN (Wide-Area Network)

A WAN is a network whose elements may be separated by distances great enough to require telephone communications. The WAN supports communications between such elements. For most WANs, the long-distance bandwidth is relatively slow: on the order of kilobits per second (kbps) as opposed to megabits per second (Mbps) for local-area networks (LANs). For example, an Ethernet LAN has a 10 Mbps bandwidth; a WAN using part or all of a T1 carrier has a bandwidth determined by the number of 64 kbps channels the WAN is using—up to 24 such channels for a maximum T1 bandwidth of 1.544 Mbps (including control bits).

There is no specified upper limit to the radius of a WAN, but in practice, machines distributed over areas larger than a state almost certainly belong to different networks that are connected to each other. Such a setup is known as an *internetwork*. Thus, although they are simply called WANs, these are more accurately wide-area *inter*networks (WAIs). One of the oldest, best-known, and most widely used examples of a WAI is the Department of Defense's ARPAnet, from which we have inherited many of the important concepts and protocols used in networking.

Centralized versus Distributed WANs

WANs can be centralized or distributed. A centralized WAN generally consists of a mainframe (or minicomputer) host connected over telephone or dedicated lines to terminals at remote sites. The terminals are usually dumb. Centralized WANs generally use polling to control access to the network.

A distributed WAN may include intelligent nodes, which are nodes that have processing capabilities independent of their connection to a host mainframe. The ARPAnet was one of the first distributed WANs.

WANs do not always involve mainframes. In fact, WANs consisting solely of PC-based networks (such as Novell NetWare LANs) are fairly common.

WAN Connection Approaches

Three types of approaches are used to connect WANs:

- Circuit switching, which provides a fixed connection (at least for the duration of a call or session), so that each packet takes the same path. Examples of this approach include ISDN, Switched 56, and Switched T1.

- Packet switching, which establishes connections during the transmission process so that different packets from the same transmission may take different routes and may arrive out of sequence at the destination. Examples of this approach are X.25, frame relay, and ATM.

- Leased lines, which can provide a dedicated connection for private use.

Watchdog

In Novell's NetWare, a special packet used to make sure a workstation is still connected to the NetWare server. A watch-dog packet is sent if the server has not heard from a node in a predefined amount of time. If the workstation does not respond to any of the repeated requests within a preset amount of time, the server assumes the workstation is no longer connected and clears the entry for the station in the network configuration file.

WATS (Wide-Area Telecommunication Service)

A long-distance service that provides discounted rates. WATS lines may be inbound, outbound, or both. Inbound and outbound services require separate subscriptions, but may share the same line. The 1-800 service is the best-known example of WATS service.

Wavelength

The distance an electrical or light signal travels in a single cycle. Specific wavelengths or wavelength ranges may be used to encode particular transmissions. For light signals, there is an inverse relationship between wavelength and frequency: the greater the wavelength, the smaller the frequency, and vice versa.

Wavelength Division Multiplexing (WDM)

SEE

WDM (Wavelength Division Multiplexing)

Wavelength-Selective Coupler

A splitter coupler breaks a light signal into multiple derived signals. An important type of splitter is a wavelength-selective coupler, which splits an incoming signal into outgoing signals based on wavelength.

SEE ALSO

Coupler

WBC (Wideband Channel)

In an FDDI network, a WBC is a channel with a bandwidth of 6.144 megabits per second (Mbps). The FDDI bandwidth can support 16 WBCs. In FDDI-II, a WBC can be allocated either for packet- or circuit-switched service.

If it is used for packet-switched service, the channel is merged with the other WBCs allocated this way. This aggregate is known as the *packet data channel*. This is the channel that transmits data in an FDDI network. The channel has a minimum bandwidth of 768 kilobits per second (kbps) and a maximum of about 99 Mbps.

If a WBC is used for circuit-switched service, it may be allocated entirely to a single connection, or the WBC may be broken into slower channels, each of which can then be used to connect a different pair of nodes.

a b c d e f g h i j k l m n o p q r s t u v **w** x y z

WDM (Wavelength Division Multiplexing)

A multiplexing method in which different signals are transmitted at different wavelengths along the same wire or fiber.

SEE ALSO

Multiplexing

WebCrawler

WebCrawler is a search engine for the World Wide Web (WWW). A search engine is a program that can search an index to find pages that contain the strings or expressions specified by the user.

WebCrawler was developed by Brian Pinkerton at the University of Washington and uses *web robots,* which are somewhat intelligent programs designed to retrieve information from the Web. (Web robots are examples of *knowbots,* which are information retrieval programs.)

When building an index of Web pages, WebCrawler uses several knowbots at a time. Each knowbot begins with one or more documents and determines all the links from those documents. The knowbot's goal is to identify and index all the links in the original documents, then all the links in the documents to which the original documents connect, and so on. The information retrieved by the knowbots is indexed, and this is the database WebCrawler searches when a user accesses it with a query.

The WebCrawler home page contains an interesting example of netiquette (considerate behavior on the Internet). When searching through Web pages, the knowbots can use either of two strategies: depth first or breadth first. The first way involves searching down and following links to their conclusion. In practice, this means that the knowbot will be retrieving lots of pages from the same site—effectively hogging the site and perhaps preventing other Web searchers from accessing the pages at that location.

In contrast, the breadth first strategy used by Pinkerton's knowbots means that they move from site to site. This is not a big deal on the Internet—that is, it doesn't necessarily make the search process any slower. It does, however, avoid tying up what may be a popular resource.

The home page for WebCrawler is: http://www.biotech.washington.edu/WebCrawler/WebQuery.html

Web Home Page

A Web home page is the starting point for a hypertext document accessible through the World Wide Web (WWW). Home pages may belong to individuals, corporations, or other organizations. They can be used to:

- Provide access to information about a concept or product.

- Provide information about a company and its products.

- Provide information about an individual.

- Provide quick access to pages that are of interest to the page's owner.

- Provide ways to enter and request information.

Web Robot

A Web robot is an electronic assistant pro-grammed to retrieve information on the World Wide Web (WWW). Web robots are examples of *knowbots* (from knowledge robot), which are intelligent retrieval programs.

Several search engines on the Web use Web robots—for example, Oliver McBryan's Word Wide Web Worm (WWWW) and Brian Pinkerton's WebCrawler. Such pro-grams use Web robots to index documents specified on a list. The robot then follows up all links in these documents, all links in the follow-up documents, and so forth.

Web robots are also known as *Web crawlers* and *digital agents*.

Whiteboard

A term used to describe products that use only software to provide conferencing capa-bilities that enable conference members to work cooperatively on a document.

White Pages Directory

On the Internet, a database containing name and address information for users on a server or network. White pages directories may be found through the Gopher and the Whois servers. The user-based white pages are in contrast to the service-oriented yellow pages.

WIN (Wireless In-Building Network)

A wireless network that is confined to a single building.

Window

In the context of optical communications, a wavelength region that has a relatively high transmittance (transmission capability) and that is surrounded by regions with low transmittancy. Such window regions are used for transmissions.

Windows for Workgroups

Microsoft's Windows for Workgroups is an extension of Microsoft Windows 3.1 that provides peer-to-peer networking capabili-ties. These capabilities make it easier to share files, directories, and resources among multiple machines.

Windows for Workgroups differs from traditional peer-to-peer networking pack-ages (such as LANtastic or NetWare Lite) in that a Windows for Workgroups machine can be either a server or a workstation, depending on the context. In fact, a com-puter can be a server for one machine and a workstation when dealing with a different machine. This is similar to newer peer-based networking software (such as Novell's Per-sonal NetWare and Hayes Microcomputer's LANstep). Windows for Workgroups also has more sophisticated security capabilities.

Windows for Workgroups requires a net-work interface card (NIC), or a network adapter for each node, and the appropriate cabling. These components are needed to create the physical network over which the software will work. Windows for Work-groups supports Ethernet (thick, thin, and twisted-pair versions) and Token Ring net-work adapters.

a b c d e f g h i j k l m n o p q r s t u v **w** x y z

In addition to enhancements on many of the features provided by Windows 3.1, Windows for Workgroups provides the following features:

- File, directory, application, and printer sharing. Shared directories are marked with a special icon in the File Manager. The owner of a file or directory can see who is using the file at a given time.

- Support for passwords and other access restrictions to directories. Only shared directories are visible to network components. The owner of a directory can set the following access restrictions on the directory: no access allowed, read access only, password required for access, or full access.

- Connectivity with servers for Novell NetWare and for Microsoft LAN Manager.

- Toolbars to simplify commands.

The Windows for Workgroups package also includes the following programs:

- Microsoft Mail, a program that provides electronic mail (e-mail) services. In addition to being able to send and receive mail, users can do file transfer by attaching files to messages.

- Schedule+, a program that serves both as a personal calendar and notebook, and also as a group scheduling tool. Schedule+ uses Microsoft Mail for deliveries and also relies on certain Mail files for address and membership information.

- Chat, an accessory for communicating in real time with another user. Unlike Mail, which provides a store-and-forward capability, Chat sessions are live. They take place on a split screen in which one window is for the user's writing, and the other is for receiving information.

- Net Watcher, an accessory to determine how local network resources are being used by other members of a workgroup.

- WinMeter, an accessory to report on central processing unit (CPU) usage. WinMeter reports the proportion of processing that is network-based.

Windows 95

Windows 95 is the long awaited successor to the DOS and Windows 3.1 environments. Unlike Windows 3.1, which is just a graphical user interface that runs on top of DOS, Windows 95 is an operating system that runs with a special version of DOS. Specifically, Windows 95 is a 32-bit operating system with a graphical interface, built-in network support (including support for the most popular protocol stacks), and a flat memory space.

Windows 95 supports preemptive multitasking and multithreading. Multitasking refers to the ability to work on more than one task almost simultaneously; preemptive indicates that the multitasking is under the operating system's control. That is, Windows 95 decides when to switch processor time to a new task. This is in contrast to *cooperative multitasking,* in which applications are responsible for handing off task control properly to the next allocation. (Windows 3.1 uses cooperative multitasking.) Multithreading means that Windows can be running multiple parts of a program, provided the program is written properly.

Windows 95 is back-compatible with its 16-bit predecessors, DOS and Windows 3.*x*. This means it can run properly behaved (and even some badly behaved) DOS and Windows programs. In fact, Windows 95 offers several ways to run DOS programs, with different degrees of DOS autonomy (see below).

The Windows 95 Environment

Like Windows 3.1, Windows 95 has a graphical interface. Beyond that, the two don't have much in common. For example, the Program Manager from Windows 3.1 has been replaced by a Desktop metaphor and a Start button. Applications or folders—formerly directories—on the Desktop are accessible by clicking on the corresponding icons. Programs and files are also accessible through the Start button, which is found in the corner of the Windows screen.

Various interface niceties and additions make it easier to move around and accomplish things. For example, *shortcuts* are simple ways to start a task. Another component—Explorer—provides all the capabilities of File Manager and then some. Explorer provides easy access to the contents of all the devices accessible from your computer.

My Computer provides easy access to various details and levels of your computer. Most of the resources and information are accessible by other means. The true benefit of My Computer is gathering everything in one location.

In a networking context, My Briefcase enables you to make sure that you always have the most current versions of files on the computer you're using. This makes it easier to move from machine to machine without having to worry about version control all the time.

Windows 95 supports installable file systems and long file names. Installable file systems means that the operating system can, or will be able to, understand and use different types of file organizations. Currently, Windows 95 supports only the DOS FAT system and VFAT, which is the Windows 95 extension of FAT. It is likely that drivers will soon be available for the NTFS used by Windows NT and the HPFS used by OS/2.

Long file name support means that Windows 95 names are not limited to the 8.3 (name.extension) format used by DOS and Windows 3.*x* files. Be aware, however, that files with long names may not be accessible to DOS programs and may, in fact, be destroyed, corrupted, or lost by certain kinds of DOS programs.

Windows 95 contains new utilities, including:

- CD Player, which lets you play audio CDs on your computer's CD-ROM drive. With CD Player you can control track sequence, speed, etc.

- Fax, which lets you send and receive faxes.

a b c d e f g h i j k l m n o p q r s t u v **w** x y z

- HyperTerminal, which is a full-featured communications package that replaces Terminal from earlier Windows versions.

- Phone Dialer, which lets you dial a number using your modem and then speak to the party on a regular telephone. With Phone Dialer you can log calls automatically.

- Sound Recorder, which lets you record through a microphone connected to the PC.

- WordPad, which is a word processor for editing unformatted files (.INF, .INI, or .TXT, for example), and also Word for Windows files. WordPad replaces Write.

Other Windows 95 Components

Windows 95 includes two major components, one of which has created considerable controversy. These components are Microsoft Exchange and the controversial Microsoft Network (MSN).

Microsoft Exchange

Microsoft Exchange provides a central location for handling all messaging functions—electronic mail, Internet or information service traffic, faxes, etc. Microsoft Exchange can serve both as a repository and as a launch center for messages. That is, Exchange can store messages in an Inbox until the user is ready to deal with them; it can also send outgoing messages using whatever services the user specifies. Exchange can even forward messages between message functions. For example, you can send an e-mail message or a downloaded file as a fax.

In order to use Microsoft Exchange, however, it must first be configured and connected. For example, your computer should be connected to a network and you must be registered with the mail and fax services on the network. If you use online services, you must also enter information about these. E-mail addresses and other access information should be entered in the Exchange address book which, incidentally, can serve as a common address book for all your messaging activities.

Microsoft Network

Microsoft's online service package is included with Windows 95, and this has led to loud protests from other developers and vendors. These groups claim that Microsoft is getting an undue advantage by being able to include MSN with the operating system and making it easy for users to register with the service.

MSN provides the usual gamut of services currently expected of online service providers:

- Electronic mail

- Chat forums for online conversations and bulletin boards for message exchanges

- Access to the Internet, and even to CompuServe

- Libraries of articles, programs, graphics, and other types of files

- Information services about various topics, including news, finances, and weather

- Information about new Microsoft products

Accessing MSN

As with any other service provider, you must open an account before you can use MSN. This is done in a one-time registration process. After logging on to MSN, you can access the various services and offerings through MSN Central, which serves as a starting point. MSN Central provides access through the following choices:

- MSN Today, which lists current events and topics.

- E-Mail, which loads Microsoft Exchange and your Inbox.

- Favorite Places, which provides quick access to the services and forums you visit most frequently. You can add new items to the folder that contains this list.

- Member Assistance, which provides access to various kinds of help—for new and veteran members.

- Categories, which provides access to folders about various topics.

Running Windows 95

When you start up Windows 95, you can control the environment to which you'll boot:

- Pressing F4 during the boot process will load the operating system you

used prior to installing Windows 95, provided you left the system on your computer. For example, if this was DOS, you can run Windows 3.1 on top of it.

- Pressing F5 will boot a *fail-safe* version of Windows 95. This is a version with a minimal system and with only essential drivers. Use this boot when you're having configuration difficulties.

- Pressing F8 will get you a menu from which you can select how you want to boot.

Once you're in Windows 95, you can still run DOS programs. There are three ways to do this:

- From an MS-DOS prompt, which runs your program in a Windows 95 DOS window. In this mode Windows 95 plays DOS.

- In MS-DOS Mode, which shuts down Windows 95 but runs the version of DOS that works with Windows 95.

- From earlier versions of DOS, provided these are still installed on your system.

Windows 95 also provides another nice feature: Remote Access Service (RAS). This allows you to call into a network or a stand-alone machine (that also supports RAS) from a remote location. The machine from which you logged in can then operate as a network client just as if it were onsite, except that transmissions will be considerably slower. A machine using the RAS functions as a remote node communicating with

a
b
c
d
e
f
g
h
i
j
k
l
m
n
o
p
q
r
s
t
u
v
w
x
y
z

a network. Such connections generally involve a modem, which can be a bottleneck because of the relatively low-transmission speeds. Given this, the quality of a RAS connection will depend on the nature of the connection. If the remote machine is just giving instructions so that most of the work is being done at the remote location, then the slow modem connection will play a minor role. On the other hand, if the session involves transferring large files, then the modem can be a painful bottleneck.

Windows 95 and Networking

Windows 95 provides other networking capabilities in addition to MSN. It provides built-in support for peer-to-peer networking and also supports several of the most common protocol stacks: TCP/IP, IPX/SPX, NetBEUI, and both NDIS and ODI driver interfaces (for network adapter cards).

In supporting the Internet Protocol Stack (TCP/IP), Windows 95 also supports several of the Internet services, including FTP (File Transfer Protocol), Telnet (a remote terminal emulation protocol), SLIP and PPP (serial access protocols).

In short, Windows 95 makes your computer ready for work on just about any kind of network.

Windows NT

Microsoft's Windows NT is a 32-bit, preemptive, multitasking operating system with built-in networking capabilities and security services. Windows NT is designed to be portable, and runs on CISC (complex instruction set computing), RISC (reduced instruction set computing), and symmetric multiprocessor computer architectures. Windows NT's modular design makes it easier to extend by adding new modules and also easier to port to other machines by isolating hardware-dependent elements in separate modules.

The Windows NT architecture consists of the following components:

- The Hardware Abstraction Layer (HAL) is software that serves as the interface to particular hardware at one end but provides a hardware-independent interface to other Windows NT components. The HAL is generally provided by the hardware manufacturer.

- The kernel manages the most fundamental tasks: thread dispatching, hardware-exception handling, and processor synchronization. The kernel also implements low-level, hardware-dependent functions. Processes running in the kernel cannot be preempted.

- The Windows NT Executive provides an interface between the environment subsystems in the outside world (of users and other machines) and the kernel. The Executive provides several types of services, as shown in the figure "Windows NT Architecture."

- Environment subsystems, which represent environments that might want to run on top of Windows NT. Supported subsystems include those for OS/2, POSIX, and Win32 (which is the Windows NT subsystem).

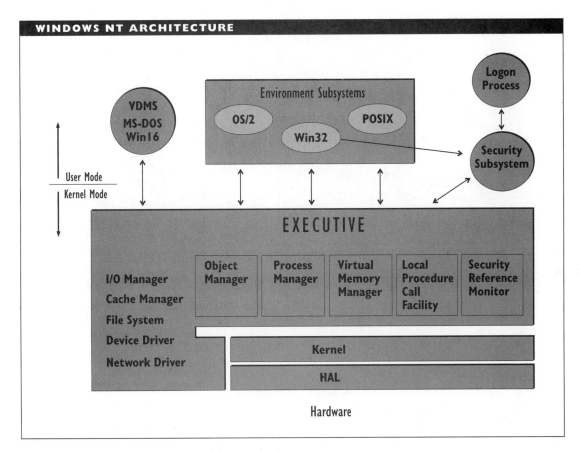

WINDOWS NT ARCHITECTURE

- VDMs (Virtual DOS Machines), which provide support for DOS or for 16-bit Windows applications by creating virtual machines and then implementing the desired environment within such a machine.

I/O Manager is first among equals in the Executive component breakdown. This element provides a cache manager, file system support, and a common interface for device and higher-level network drivers.

Windows NT Networking

The Windows NT networking architecture has a layered design that makes it easier to provide support for multiple networking environments. Through use of generic interfaces, Windows NT also provides support for environment combinations across the layers. The figure "Windows NT and OSI Layers" shows how Windows NT's networking components relate to the layers in the OSI Reference Model.

The device drivers at the bottom of the architecture provide the interface to particular hardware. These drivers can work with

WINDOWS NT AND OSI LAYERS

OSI Layer	Windows NT Component
Application	Environment Subsystems
Presentation	Providers
	Executive Services
Session	Redirector / Server
Transport	TDI
Network	Transport Protocols: NBF (NetBEUI), TCP/IP, DLC, NWLink (IPX/SPX)
Data-Link	NDIS
	NIC Drivers
Physical	

multiple transport layer protocols because of the NDIS (Network Device Interface Specification) interface. NDIS enables any of the protocol stacks supported to communicate with any NDIS-conformant network interface card (NIC) and allows any NIC to communicate with supported protocol stacks.

Windows NT supports several transport layer protocol stacks:

- NBF (NetBEUI Format), which is used in OS/2-based network operating systems (such as LAN Manager and LAN Server).

- TCP/IP (Transport Control Protocol/Internet Protocol), which is used in UNIX and other environments. Support for TCP/IP enables a Windows NT computer to function as a TCP/IP client.

- NWLink, which is a version of Novell's IPX/SPX protocols. With NWLink, a Windows NT machine can function as a NetWare client.

- DLC (Data Link Control), which provides access to mainframe environments.

The Transport Driver Interface (TDI) provides the second boundary at which it is possible to mix and match networking environments. The protocol stacks below this interface can be used in sessions with any valid server or redirector.

At the session layer, the Windows NT redirector and server components provide the functionality for the workstation and server, respectively. These components are implemented as file system drivers. Redirectors for both NT and other networking environments can be loaded simultaneously so that a Windows NT machine can be connected to other networks. For example, redirectors for Novell's NetWare and Banyan's VINES are available.

A provider is also needed for each network supported through a redirector. The provider operates at the session and application layers, in contrast to the redirector, which operates at the session layer.

Windows NT includes support for distributed applications, such as mail, scheduling, and database services. Applications can use NetBIOS, Windows Sockets, named pipes, mail slots, and remote procedure calls (RPCs) to provide or communicate with distributed applications.

Servers and Advanced Servers

Depending on the size and purpose of a Windows NT network, it may consist of workgroups or of domains. A *workgroup* is a group of users who share information and resources. A workgroup network consists of a server and several workstations.

A *domain* consists of several servers with a common security policy and a shared user database. The server in charge of such a network is known as a *domain controller*. A domain controller must run the Windows NT Advanced Server software.

Windows NT Advanced Servers provide support for additional client types. In particular, Windows NT Advanced Servers support Macintosh and RAS (Remote Access Service) clients. The latter makes it possible for remote PCs to get full access to the Windows NT network. The RAS capabilities include security, with authentication of all remote access clients.

Windows NT computers can be NetWare clients, and Windows NT Advanced Servers can function as application servers for the NetWare network. Because of its support for TCP/IP and for distributed computing, a Windows NT network can work with UNIX systems. Similarly, support for the DLC (Data Link Control) protocol makes it possible to connect Windows NT networks and IBM mainframes.

Windows NT Security

Security and authentication checks are made during the login process (which uses a secure communications channel) and also during network operations (for example, when a user or process needs to access a service).

In addition to the security process during login, Windows NT includes a local security subsystem and a Security Reference Monitor. The monitor is part of the Windows NT Executive, and it is responsible for making

a
b
c
d
e
f
g
h
i
j
k
l
m
n
o
p
q
r
s
t
u
v
w
x
y
z

sure the local security subsystem's requirements are enforced.

Winsock

Winsock (for Windows sockets) is the name given to an API (Application Program Interface) that implements the TCP/IP protocol stack in a Windows environment. Windows programs—for example, the Chameleon Sampler or commercial programs from Net-Manage and other companies—that provide access to the Internet must all have access to a TCP/IP stack. Most of these programs use some version of Winsock.

Wireless Components

Wireless networks use the same functional components as networks that use a physical medium. Specifically, wireless nodes need transmitters and receivers, just like wired nodes.

However, wireless components may take somewhat different forms and may turn up in unusual locations in wireless networks. For example, a network may use antennas located at strategic points to broadcast and capture signals across the network. In wireless communications, each node may have its own antenna, or a single antenna may serve a limited area. Antennas will generally be placed in open, unobstructed areas in order to avoid objects that can block incoming or outgoing signals.

BROADER CATEGORY
Hardware

SEE ALSO
Network, Wireless

Wireless Modem

A modem that transmits over a wireless network rather than over telephone lines.

SEE ALSO
Modem

Wire, Solid

Solid wire is electrical wire whose central, conducting element is a single strand of (usually) copper or some other conductive material. This is in contrast to stranded wire, whose conductor wire consists of dozens, perhaps hundreds, of thin copper strands wrapped tightly around each other.

Wire, Stranded

Electrical wire whose central, conducting element consists of many thin strands of (usually) copper or some other conductive material. These strands are rolled tightly around each other. This is in contrast to solid wire, whose conductor wire consists of a single, (relatively) large diameter copper (or other conductive) wire.

Wiring Center

Wiring center is a general term for any of several components that serve as common termination points for one or more nodes and/or other wiring centers. The wiring center will connect to a higher-level wiring collector, to either an intermediate distribution frame (IDF) or a main distribution frame (MDF).

Functions of Wiring Centers

The main functions of a wiring center are electrical. The wiring center collects lines in a common location in order to continue the connection more easily from there. Any network-specific features or benefits (such as signal routing flexibility) are likely to be the result of special intelligence or capabilities built into the wiring center.

Collecting multiple cables at a common location makes the following tasks easier:

- Installing cabling

- Tracking down faults

- Cleaning and boosting signals (if appropriate)

- Controlling (limiting) the transmission of packets and the dissemination of information

- Dealing with any necessary electrical conversions involving particular nodes

Over time, various capabilities and services have migrated from the server to wiring centers. This helps decrease the server's workload. It also makes certain security measures easier to implement. For example, an intelligent hub can send a packet to its destination and can broadcast a nonsense packet to nondestination nodes. In networks such as Ethernet and ARCnet, all packets are broadcast to all nodes. Nodes are supposed to ignore packets not intended for the nodes, but there is no way to prevent an eavesdropping node from reading everything that comes through.

Types of Wiring Centers

Hubs, concentrators, and MAUs (multistation access units) have all been referred to as wiring centers. In part, terminology is tied to network architecture.

MAU is the term for a common termination point in a Token Ring network. Individual nodes (or lobes, in Token Ring terminology) can connect to the MAU in whatever sequence is most convenient. Internally, the MAU orders the connected lobes to produce a ring structure, as required by the network architecture.

MAUs have two additional ports, called RI (ring in) and RO (ring out), through which they can be connected to other MAUs. These ports make it possible to maintain the ring structure over the larger, multi-MAU network.

Hub is the term for a component that serves as a termination point for multiple nodes that all use the same network architecture (for example, Ethernet or ARCnet). Hubs differ in the amount of intelligence they have and in whether they can boost a signal.

A *concentrator* is a "superhub," which can connect lines from different architectures and with different cabling. For example, a concentrator may be used as the termination point for the nodes on multiple networks, and these networks may use different architectures.

The boundaries between the two are fuzzy, but the main differences between hubs and concentrators are in the number of nodes the component can handle, the number of network architectures it can handle, and the component's price.

a b c d e f g h i j k l m n o p q r s t u v **w** x y z

Hubs, concentrators, and MAUs represent the basic wiring centers. There are all sorts of exotic variants of these types, with specialized capabilities and properties added by vendors.

BROADER CATEGORIES

Hardware; Intranetwork Link

SEE ALSO

Concentrator; Hub

Wiring Closet

In a premises wiring layout, a wiring closet is one in which cables are gathered, usually in one or more punch-down blocks or in a distribution frame. These cables connect the various areas in an office or building to the central wiring and from there to the telephone or power company wiring.

Wiring, Legacy

Wiring that is already installed in a business or residence. This wiring may or may not be suitable for networking purposes.

Wiring, Premises

A wiring system that provides the "behind the scenes" wiring for an entire house or office building. This wiring generally runs between outlets and any wiring centers or distribution frames. Users connecting devices to the outlets need to provide the cables to do so.

Wiring Sequence

In twisted-pair cabling, the wiring sequence is the order in which the wire pairs are attached to pins in the connector. (In a pair of wires, one wire is known as the *tip* and the other as the *ring*.)

Several standard wiring sequences exist, as shown in the figure "Commonly used wiring sequences."

Each of the standard schemes was developed by a different organization or standards committee, and each is intended for different purposes:

- USOC (Uniform Service Ordering Code) is a sequence originally developed by the telephone company. The tip/ring pairs are nested, with tip 1 and ring 1 (denoted as T1 and R1, respectively) occupying the middle two connections. In an 8-wire (4-pair) arrangement, these correspond to wires 4 and 5. This pair is nested inside T2 and R2, which is nested inside T3 and R3, and so on. The advantage of such nesting is that a 6-wire plug (such as an RJ-12) can be plugged into an 8-wire jack (such as an RJ-45).

- The 10BaseT sequence is used in Ethernet networks running over unshielded twisted-pair (UTP) cable. Note that, by design, the middle pair (wires 4 and 5) is not used because voice connections are generally made in this tip/ring pair in telephone cable. By not using these wires, the 10BaseT sequence is compatible with 3- or 4-pair telephone cable (at least with respect to wiring).

COMMONLY USED WIRING SEQUENCES

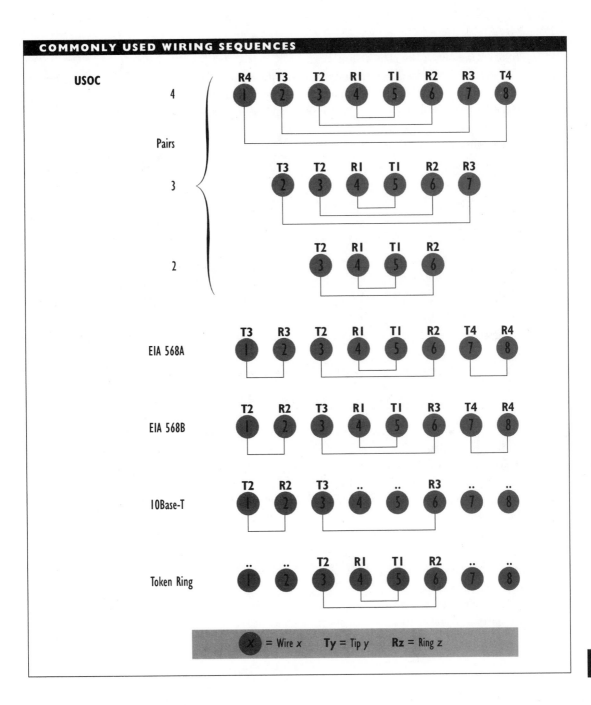

USOC

4

Pairs

3

2

EIA 568A

EIA 568B

10Base-T

Token Ring

X = Wire x   **Ty** = Tip y   **Rz** = Ring z

- The Token Ring sequence is used in Token Ring networks. The sequence uses pairs 1 and 2 in the four center locations. Note that this wiring scheme makes it impossible to use telephone cable for both voice and a Token Ring network at the same time.

- The EIA-568A sequence was developed as part of the EIA/TIA-568 specifications for UTP. This particular variant was designed to be backward-compatible with the USOC sequence, at least for 4-wire cable (T1/R1 and T2/R2). The remaining two pairs are grouped at opposite sides of the cable.

- The EIA-568B sequence is also used as the sequence for AT&T's Premises Distribution System (PDS). This is a widely used configuration, in part because it is compatible with the wiring sequence specified for 10BaseT network cabling.

The interference-protection properties of twisted-pair cable come from *pairing* the wires. The advantages of pairing are lost if a signal is carried over wires from two different pairs. This is known as the *split-pair* problem and can happen if one wiring sequence (such as USOC) is used in a situation that calls for a different sequence (such as Ethernet). For example, the T2 and R2 pair for 10BaseT Ethernet would be split over two pairs in a USOC wiring sequence.

CABLE QUALITY

It is important to find out which wiring scheme is being used in any cable you plan to use or buy, and to make sure all the cable uses the same scheme.

Try to make sure the connector and wire types have been matched correctly. A "piercing" connector may not penetrate the solid wire, which means the attachment is more likely to become loose and flaky with time, particularly if the wire is frequently bent or subjected to other stresses near the connector end.

The chances of connector and cable being mismatched are greater with cheaper cable. *Let the buyer beware.*

Workflow Software

Software for describing or managing the steps needed to complete a transaction or other type of task. Examples of workflow software include flowcharting and other "electronic pencil" programs, CASE (computer-assisted software engineering) or CAM (computer-assisted manufacturing) software, and programs based on an underlying model of management or process, such as software for automating the steps in a manufacturing or an assembly context.

Workgroup

A workgroup is a group of individuals who share files, data, and possibly applications. Workgroups are generally defined around an office, a project, or a group of tasks. The individuals who make up a workgroup may change as a project (for example) progresses or as tasks change.

Workgroup members can use local-area networks (LANs), electronic mail (e-mail), or other message-handling services to share information. Some applications (such as database, spreadsheet, and word processing programs) come in special workgroup versions that are specifically designed to allow such collaborative interactions. In other cases, an ordinary application may use an engine program that provides workgroup capabilities for the application.

In addition to allowing users to share information, many workgroup programs can also exchange information easily with other applications. Workgroup programs are often combined into suites that encompass a range of computing tasks. (Note that the different applications in such a suite may be associated with different members of a workgroup if the workgroup is formed by task.)

The Borland Office for Windows package is an example of a suite of workgroup programs. The package includes workgroup versions of Paradox for Windows, Quattro Pro, and WordPerfect in a single environment. (The latter two products are now owned by Novell.) Borland Office programs use an Object Exchange (OBEX) engine to drive the Workgroup Desktop. Users and applications can exchange information by going through the Workgroup Desktop.

Workstation

In a PC network, a workstation is a client machine. In general, a workstation is a consumer of network services, although it is not uncommon for a workstation to serve as a special-purpose server, such as a server for a printer or backup tape drive.

In general, workstations can be viewed as interchangeable units, which need not be particularly powerful unless they are being used for a resource-intensive purpose. In contrast, a file server should be a high-speed, powerful machine that can deal with dozens of requests at once.

Each workstation needs a network interface card (NIC) that is compatible with the workstation's hardware and with the NIC used by the network's server. External and PCMCIA NICs are available so that even a machine with minimal capabilities (such as a palmtop) can be used as a workstation. Laptops have some important advantages as workstations—most notably, portability—and are becoming more common in networks.

Unlike a server (which runs a network operating system, or NOS), a workstation runs a special type of program that coordinates operations with the workstation's native operating system. The details of this program's operation depend on the type of workstation software involved. For example, a network shell program performs the following tasks:

- Intercepts all user and application commands

- Determines whether the command is for the local operating system (such as DOS, OS/2, or UNIX) or for the network

- Routes the command to the local operating system or to the NIC for processing and transmission onto the network

- Passes transmissions from the network (via the NIC) to the application running on the workstation

LAPTOPS AS WORKSTATIONS

Laptops can serve as workstations on a LAN, but special adapters or measures are usually necessary. There are several ways to connect a laptop to a LAN: through a docking station, external LAN adapter, or a PCMCIA card.

A docking station is essentially an expansion box that turns a laptop into a desktop. You can also use a docking station to connect a laptop to a larger display or to a better keyboard. The docking station has expansion slots, into which you can put whatever types of cards you want. To use the attached laptop on a LAN, you need to plug a NIC into one of the expansion slots. Docking stations are hardware-dependent, and they generally work with only a single model laptop from a single manufacturer.

An external LAN adapter (NIC) attaches to the laptop's parallel port. This can be pocket size (portable) or desk size. The desk size version may support multiple types of cable in the same unit; the pocket size adapter will have room for only a single type of connector.

External NICs generally include a pass-through parallel port, which provides an additional parallel port to replace the one bound to the external adapter. (Note, however, that this additional port will be accessible only if it can be assigned a valid and accessible address.) The pocket size adapter does not include a parallel port; the adapter can be used with a parallel port multiplexer, however. Because they communicate through the parallel port, external adapters don't need an address and IRQ line, which make setup much easier. External adapters use the IEEE addressing algorithm (just like other types of NICs), so they get node addresses just like any other machine.

Unlike a docking station, external NICs are hardware-independent (as is the case for ordinary NICs). This makes it possible to use such adapters with just about any laptop.

External adapters are slower because the parallel port is slower. Fortunately, these adapters won't slow down other network activity, because such tasks as token passing are handled right onboard (without going to the port).

Prices for an external NIC depend on the protocol being supported. ARCnet is cheapest; Token Ring is most expensive.

PCMCIA cards make it possible to link a smaller computer (such as a notebook) to a network.

Newer laptops have the EPP (enhanced parallel port), which supports burst speeds of up to 16 Mbps. Support for this port is built into Intel's 386.25 SL chip set, which is currently popular for laptops.

In contrast, a program such as the Net-Ware DOS Requester used in NetWare 4.*x* functions much differently. The DOS Requester consists of about a dozen Virtual Loadable Modules (VLMs), each of which is responsible for certain tasks related to networking and also to the coordination of operations between the operating system and the Requester. For example, the DOS Requester includes VLMs for handling network security, file access, protocol management, redirecting tasks based on communications with the operating system, and so on. See the VLM article for a summary of the individual modules.

The better communication between DOS and a Requester (as opposed to a shell) means less redundancy in functions, which saves memory and also helps improve performance.

For the most part, workstation programs communicate at the network layer of the OSI Reference Model, and they use protocols such as Novell's IPX or the Internet's IP to communicate with the driver for the NIC. Certain Requester modules operate at the transport layer.

In general, a workstation does not need to know much about the resources on a network, other than that they are available. This information is available from the server, which will generally mediate between the workstation and a particular resource.

BROADER CATEGORY

Computer

COMPARE

Server

▼
Workstation, Diskless

A diskless workstation is designed specifically for use on networks. It has no disk drive (either floppy or hard), but it does have a keyboard, screen, some memory, booting instructions in ROM, and a network interface card (NIC).

The workstation software needed to connect to the network must be loaded somehow, either from ROM (read-only memory) or from the server. In the latter case, the software is loaded through the NIC. Most NICs have a socket into which a bootable ROM chip can be inserted to enable the diskless workstation to boot without help from the server.

A diskless workstation is closed, which means there is no way to upload anything from the workstation or download anything to it. A diskless workstation cannot pass a virus onto the network, nor can a user bootleg software off the network. Because of this, diskless workstations afford greater security than ordinary workstations. For this reason, such workstations are popular in networks where security is a problem or where it is crucial.

Beyond increased security, diskless workstations have little to offer. They are not significantly cheaper than ordinary PCs but have much more limited utility. Because the instructions in ROM are generally tied to a particular release of the networking software, the ROM chip must be upgraded every time there is a change in software versions. At $50 or more dollars per node, such an upkeep cost is considerable. However, they may provide greater reliability of the

a b c d e f g h i j k l m n o p q r s t u v **w** x y z

nodes because there are no drives to get dirty or break down.

Worm

A program that is designed to infiltrate an operating system and to keep replicating itself. Eventually, there are so many copies of the worm floating around that the computer cannot do any work, and a system crash results.

SEE ALSO

Trojan Horse; Virus

WOS (Workstation Operating System)

The native operating system on a workstation in a network. Whereas the file server will run a network operating system, workstations can generally continue to run their usual operating systems. The networking software can run as terminate-and-stay resident (TSR) programs or as applications on top of the WOS.

WOSA (Windows Open Services Architecture)

A system-level interface for connecting applications to services (regardless of whether these services are provided on a network).

WWW (World Wide Web)

The World Wide Web has grown from a distributed document lending service for a group of high energy physicists to the world's largest library—at least in geographical extent. WWW—known simply as the Web—is the name for a network of links to hypertext documents. Documents are known as *Web pages,* and the starting point in a document or for a corporation is known as the *home page.*

Information about the documents and access to them are controlled and provided by Web servers. At the user's end, a Web client takes the user's requests and passes them on to the server. Such a client is generally a *browser* program—that is, a hypertext reader program. Browsers and server communicate using a transfer protocol—generally HTTP (Hypertext Transfer Protocol). Netscape Navigator, various flavors of Mosaic, and Cello are all examples of Web browsers.

Web pages are identified by their URLs (Uniform Resource Locators), which are a form of Web address and document description. For example, the following is the URL for the Sybex home page:

http://www.sybex.com

This URL has two components. The first part (*http*) indicates the protocol being used for the documents to be retrieved. In this case, the *http* refers to the hypertext transfer protocol, which is used to transport hypertext files across the Internet. Other protocols that are generally handled by browsers include FTP and Gopher.

The second part specifies the domain name for the machine on which the home page is found. In this case it's a machine named *sybex.com,* which is accessed through a Web server (*www*).

Searching and Accessing the Web

There are currently over seven million documents on the Web, and about two dozen publishers are competing with each other to sell products that make it easy for users with Internet accounts to add to this by setting up their own Web pages.

There are various online resources for searching the Web. Some are organized by content, and others use search engines to carry out open-ended queries.

Search Engine Index

Undoubtedly one of the most useful Web tools available is a document containing links to search engines on the WWW. If you're just getting started, or if you've forgotten what's available, then this is the Web page you should visit first:

http://cuiwww.unige.ch/meta-index.html

Yahoo

Yahoo is one of the first information sources for the Web and is still one of the most popular. It is organized by topics but also allows users to search by keywords. By having you narrow down your search to a content area, Yahoo can speed up its work. Yahoo's home page is

http://www.yahoo.com

WWWW

The World Wide Web Worm, or the Worm, is one of the most popular Web search engines. It works by sending out a *Web robot* to search through Web pages. The robot searches and indexes all documents on its list, all documents to which there are links from the original documents, all links from the links, etc.

It is located at:

http://www.cs.colorado.edu/home/mcbryan/WWWW.html

NIKOS

NIKOS (New Internet KnOwledge System) is a text-based search engine developed by California Polytechnic Institute and Rockwell Network Systems. When it returns its results, NIKOS orders them on the basis of how relevant they are likely to be.

The NIKOS home page is:

http://www.rns.com/cgi-bin/nikos

Harvest

Harvest is an example of what may be the next generation of Web searchers: a program that indexes Web page content as well as titles, authors, and key words. It is billed as an information discovery and access system, and is an experiment in finding and delivering complex information efficiently.

Harvest uses a two-level search process to make things more efficient. At the information end, *gatherers* have relatively specific search tasks based on user queries. The gatherers return their results to *brokers*, who organize and package the information for the consumers, or users.

Brokers are monitored, and if a broker gives out the same information frequently, that information is copied to a cache by a special server program known as a *replicator*. By caching the information, Harvest uses fewer resources the next time someone wants that information.

The Harvest home page is:

http://rd.cs.colorado.edu/harvest/

The Growth of the Web

The WWW is growing at an astounding pace. From a few thousand Web pages in 1989, the Web has grown to over seven million (and counting). Averaged, this amounts to about 3,000 documents per day over the entire period. In fact, the Web is growing at a considerably faster pace now. For example, it is rumored that during one period the database in the NIKOS Web search engine grew at the rate of five entries per *minute*—about 7,000 per day.

This growth is likely to continue for a while, especially as new users master their Web Publishing kits and load their own Web pages.

SEE ALSO

Browsers; HTML (Hypertext Markup Language)

PRIMARY SOURCES

One useful place to start finding out about WWW is with the FAQ (Frequently Asked Questions) file. This is available from:

http://sunsite.unc.edu/boutell/faq/www_faq.html

Any of the Web Kits described in Appendix B also provide helpful information about the WWW and about interesting pages.

WWWW (World Wide Web Worm)

A search program for the World Wide Web (WWW). WWWW was developed by Oliver McBryan at the University of Colorado, and it works by sending out a Web robot to search documents. The robot begins by searching documents on a list, then searching all documents accessible through the original documents, etc.

WWWW is one of the most popular search engines, and was chosen the Best Navigational Tool at the Best of the Web '94 contest. The home page for WWWW is:

http://www.cs.colorado.edu/home/mcbryan/WWWW.html

Other search engine products include Lycos, NIKOS, WebCrawler, and Yahoo.

X.25

X.25 is a set of recommendations defined by the CCITT for transmitting data over a packet-switched network. It provides a CCITT-standard *interface* to packet-switched networks and has become the most widely used interface for wide-area networks (WANs).

This interface encompasses the three lower layers in the OSI Reference Model. At the physical layer, the X.25 standard assumes an X.21 interface, but can also support V.35 and the EIA RS232-D interfaces. At the data-link layer, X.25 assumes LAPB (Link Access Protocol, Balanced) is being used but also supports other protocols, such as the older LAP and IBM's Bisync (BSC) protocol. At the network layer, X.25 uses PLP (Packet-Level Protocol).

X.25 is suitable for data (but not voice) transmissions. It defines procedures for exchanging data between a DTE (such as a computer) and the network. The connection to this network is represented by a DTE, which may be a modem, multiplexer, or PAD (packet assembler/disassembler). Asynchronous devices (such as a PC) can be connected to the X.25 network through the use of a PAD.

X.25 uses LCNs (logical channel numbers) to distinguish the connections between DTEs at either end of a communication. These LCNs make it possible to send a packet into a packet-switched network at one end (with no control over the packet's journey) and then to pick the packet out at the receiving end.

The interface supports transmission speeds of up to 64 kilobits per second

(kbps). The 1992 revision of the X.25 recommendations has increased the throughput to 2 megabits per second (Mbps), but this faster X.25 is not yet widely used. X.25 also has a relatively high overhead for error checking and packet sequencing.

X.25 does *not* specify how a packet should be shipped across the network. In fact, X.25 has nothing at all to say about the details of the network transmissions. The WAN itself is represented as a network "cloud" (an assumed connection). X.25 is responsible for getting packets into that cloud at one end and for retrieving them at the other end.

X.400

X.400 is a message handling standard defined by the CCITT. X.400 has been through two major versions and a revision:

- The original 1984 draft, referred to as X.400/84, provides the basic definitions and model. This version has been implemented for years. Unfortunately, the model has major shortcomings.

- A 1988 version, referred to as X.400/88, addresses most of the major flaws in the 1984 draft, but is not yet widely implemented.

A round of revisions in 1992 addressed additional flaws and ambiguities, and also defined two new types of message contents: EDI (Electronic Data Interchange) messages for use in business transactions and record keeping, and voice messages.

The notion of a Message Handling System (MHS) figures prominently in both versions, but the details of an MHS are somewhat different. Similarly, both versions include a Message Transfer Service (MTS) as an MHS component, but the contents of this MTS differ.

The X.400/84 version dealt only with MHS interfaces for end users. In X.400/88, an MHS is an object that has interfaces for communicating with end users, with other CCITT and special services, and possibly with other networks.

The X.400 recommendations series addresses the contents and workings of the MHS and the manner in which the MHS communicates with outside entities. The documents say nothing about how to implement these recommendations.

The MHS contains several other objects as components, including the MTS. The figure "1984/1988-version composite of the structure of an MHS" shows the structure of an MHS. Shaded portions are included only in X.400/88; the remaining elements are included in both versions.

X.400 Components

The MHS consists of the following elements:

UA (User Agent): An application process (AP) that provides an end-user with access to the MTS. UAs are used in both versions.

AU (Access Unit): A process that provides a gateway between the MTS and other

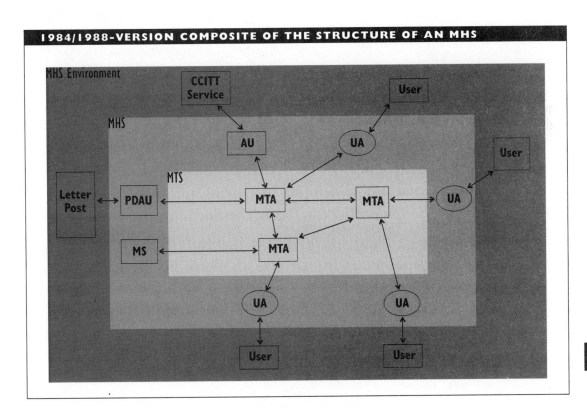

1984/1988-VERSION COMPOSITE OF THE STRUCTURE OF AN MHS

CCITT services. AUs are used in only the 88 version.

PDAU (Physical Delivery Access Unit): A type of AU that provides a gateway between the MTS and services that involve physical delivery. PDAUs are used in only the 88 version.

MS (Message Store): An archive used as temporary storage for messages until they can be forwarded to their destination. The Message Store Access Protocol (MSAP) is used to communicate with this store. MSs are used in only the 88 version.

MTS (Message Transfer System): A process that transfers messages between users. The MTS relies on its own components (MTAs) to accomplish this transfer. MTSs are used in both versions.

MTA (Message Transfer Agent): A component of the MTS, the MTA forwards messages to another MTA or the destination entity (which may be a UA, MS, AU, or PDAU). MTAs are used in both versions, but the details differ.

MHS Element Distribution

The MHS elements can be distributed in several ways. These variants differ in the location of MTAs and of the elements that provide interfaces for the MHS (for example, UAs and AUs). The 1984 version provides only UAs for such interfaces.

The elements can be distributed as follows:

- Only interfaces on the machine, as when workstations access the MHS through a server. In this case, the server has the MTA, and the workstations need to run only user agents.

- Only MTA on the machine, such as on the server that is providing MHS access to the workstations described in the previous item.

- MTA and interfaces on the same machine, as when the access is through a terminal.

Management Domains

To make electronic mail (e-mail) truly useful, it must be global, which means the MHS must be able to span the entire world. In order to deal with a worldwide MHS, X.400 defines management domains (MDs).

A management domain is a limited—but not necessarily contiguous—area whose message handling capabilities operate under the control of a management authority. Two types of management domains are defined:

ADMD (Administration Management Domain): A network area operated by the CCITT. For example, an ADMD may be a national Post, Telegraph, and Telephone (PTT) service.

PRMD (Private Management Domain): A network area operated by a private organization, such as a university campus or a state university system.

ADMDs can connect PRMDs, but a PRMD cannot connect two ADMDs.

X.400 and the OSI Reference Model

The relationship between X.400 and the OSI Reference Model depends on the X.400 version. The 1984 version covered the presentation and application layers. In addition, X.400/84 subdivided the application layer into an upper user agent layer (UAL) and a lower message transfer layer (MTL). Users interact with the UAL, and the UAL in turn communicates with the MTL below it. User agent entities (UAEs) carry out the layer-related functions at the UAL. The 1984 version defines the interpersonal messaging protocol (known as P2) for communications between UAEs.

The 1988 version discards the sublayers and confines the definition of the model to the application layer. This makes it much easier to implement the 1988 version.

X.400 and Electronic Commerce

One of the major accomplishments of the 1988–1992 sessions was the creation of the X.435 standard. This document defines a messaging system for electronic data interchange (EDI), which is a standard that businesses have adopted for their use. X.435 specifies EDI services, as well as defining EDI messages, agents, and message stores.

It is expected that more and more businesses will begin using EDI for their business transactions and internal record keeping. If that happens, business will move to EDI at an even faster rate because companies get the most benefits from EDI when their clients also use it.

PRIMARY SOURCES

The ITU X.400 series of documents define the MHS. For example, X.400 provides an overview of MHS; X.402 describes the architecture; X.411 and X.413 describe the abstract services; and X.419 describes the protocols. Several of the F.400 documents are also relevant.

X.500

The CCITT X.500 Directory Services specifications provide standards and guidelines for representing, accessing, and using information stored in a Directory. In this context, a Directory contains information about objects. These objects may be files (as in a file system directory listing), network entities (as in a network naming service such as Banyan's StreetTalk or Novell's NetWare Directory Services), or other types of entities. To distinguish an X.500 Directory from the more commonly encountered file system directory in Novell's literature, the X.500 variant is written with an uppercase *D*.

Functions of a Directory Service

X.500 Directory Services are application-layer processes. Directory services can be used for various tasks, including the following:

- Providing a global, unified naming service for all elements in a network.

- Translating between network names and addresses.

- Providing descriptions of objects in a directory. The descriptions are listings of attributes and values associated with the objects.

- Providing unique names for all objects in the Directory. All aliases for an object evaluate to the object's unique name.

Depending on the context in which the Directory service is being used, the information may be organized as a name space or as an address book. The latter format is used in electronic mail (e-mail) or messaging services and is more likely to be tied to a particular product.

Directory Information Bases (DIBs)

The information for a Directory service is stored in a Directory Information Base (DIB). This information is organized in terms of entries and attributes. The entries correspond to the objects in a network; the attributes correspond to properties associated with the objects. The information is represented using ASN.1 (Abstract Syntax Notation 1).

Information in the DIB is organized in a tree structure, known as the Directory Information Tree (DIT). The DIT represents the logical organization of the Directory's contents. Each node in the tree represents an object type. Intermediate nodes (elements with subtrees derived from them) generally serve an organizational function. The subtrees of such an intermediate node represent objects derived from the node's object type. Leaf nodes, which are elements with no subtrees, correspond to specific objects. The figure "An example of a DIT" shows a tree.

The Relative Distinguished Name (RDN) is among the attributes associated with each object in a directory. The RDN specifies an object's local name, which may or may not

be unique. In the example in the figure, C=US is an RDN, as are OU=UCSC and CN=B Slug. Because there are restrictions on the ways objects in a directory can be related to each other, the labels associated with each object provide information about the object's relative location in the DIT:

- C, which represents Country, and is the highest (most general) grouping field in the DIT. Such a field can be located only directly below the root.

- O, which represents Organization, and is the next most general grouping field (after Country). If present, an O field must be located either directly below the root or directly below a Country node.

- OU, which represents Organizational Unit, and is an intermediate-level grouping field. An OU field can appear only below an O field.

- CN, which represents Common Name, and is the bottom-level field. A CN field can be used only with a leaf node.

The rules specifying allowable locations for different fields are part of the schema for a directory. A schema represents the rules that define the types of relationships allowed between objects in the Directory. Although they are mentioned in the 1988 version, only the 1992 X.500 includes formal elaboration of the schema rules.

Each object has a unique location in the DIT. To identify an object uniquely, you just need to specify all the names on the path to the object. To do this, list every RDN on the path from the root to the object. This chain

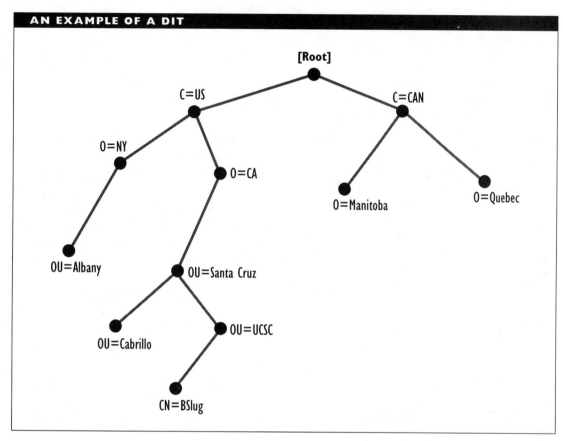

AN EXAMPLE OF A DIT

of RDNs is the object's unique Distinguished Name, or DN. In the figure, C=US, O=CA, OU=Santa Cruz, OU=UCSC, CN=B Slug is the DN for the leaf element named CN=B Slug.

A DIB may be distributed across a network or an internetwork. To simplify access and use, parts or all of a Directory may be replicated at multiple locations in a network or internetwork. When replicas exist, decisions need to be made about how to handle updates. Three possibilities exist for making changes to the Directory:

- No changes are allowed to either the original or any replicas.

- Changes must be made in the original, which must then periodically inform all replicas of the update. This is known as a master/shadow arrangement because shadow is a term for a replica. This concept was introduced in the 1992 X.500 specifications.

- Changes may be made in either the original or in a replica. Other locations will be updated on whatever schedule is in effect. For some networks, updates must be immediate; for others, updates are made at periodic intervals. This is known as a peer-to-peer update mechanism. Despite the same name, such a mechanism is not necessarily related to a peer-to-peer network.

A DIB may be modified or updated frequently. If replicas are also being modified, then synchronization of the changes is essential. Synchronization ensures that all versions of the Directory information are up to date and that everyone is using the same version. The actual updating depends on the availability of a common time frame as a reference. The reference time need not be correct; it just has to be shared by the DIB and all replicas. See the Time Synchronization article for an example of the use of reference times.

Using DIBs

To access the information in a DIB, X.500 provides Directory User and Directory System Agents (DUAs and DSAs, respectively). An end user can get information from a Directory service by working through a DUA. The DUA communicates with a DSA, whose task is to access and deal with the actual DIB. The DUA communicates with a DSA using a DAP (Directory Access Protocol).

Communication between DUA and DSA uses any of three ports that are defined in X.500: Read, Search, or Modify. (A *port* is an access to a service from the perspective of the user of a protocol.) Each of these ports can handle a limited number and range of actions:

- The Read port can handle Read, Compare, and Abandon.

- The Search port can handle List and Search.

- The Modify port can handle Add Entry, Remove Entry, Modify Entry, and Modify RDN.

In some cases, particularly with a distributed Directory, DSAs may use each other for help. Such interactions use the DSP (Directory System Protocol). The figure "Accessing a DIB" shows these elements. In addition to the two protocols shown in the figure, the 1992 X.500 specifications introduce two new protocols, both of which are used for interactions between DSAs: DISP (Directory Information Shadowing Protocol) and DOP (Directory Operational Binding Management Protocol).

The 1988 version of the X.500 recommendations relied on the authentication services to prevent unauthorized access to Directory information or elements. The 1992 revision adds access controls as a mechanism. With this, a Directory can have access control lists associated with it. These lists determine who is allowed access to Directory elements and also the kinds of access that will be allowed.

X.500 Security Measures

To help ensure that unauthorized users do not get access to the DIB, steps are taken to authenticate each user. The X.500 authentication framework specifies two levels of authentication:

- Simple authentication, which requires just a valid password from the user

ACCESSING A DIB

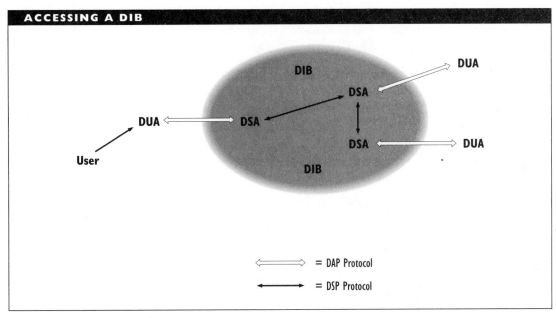

- Strong authentication, which uses encryption to help safeguard information

In addition, the authentication framework supports the use of digital signatures to help prevent message or information forgery, and the use of certificates (public keys with enciphered information) to ensure that the encryption keys are unique and known only to authorized parties.

The State of X.500

Directories of the sort defined in X.500 have been around a long time. For example, the Domain Naming Service in the Internet community and Novell's NetWare Directory Services (NDS) in version 4.x of NetWare provide such services.

Such Directory or naming services generally adopt the X.500 architecture (entries and attributes organized in a tree structure)

and some amount of the X.500 functionality. The ASN.1 notation is less likely to be adapted in such implementations.

Implementation of X.500 specifications has been slow partly because developers were waiting for the 1992 revisions for both X.500 and for the X.400 Message Handling Services (MHS), which rely heavily on X.500 services. Now that updates to both the MHS and the Directory Services standards have appeared, the expectation is that such services will be implemented more rapidly.

SEE ALSO

NDS (NetWare Directory Services); StreetTalk; X.400

xB/tB Encoding

xB/tB encoding is a general label for any of several data-translation schemes that can serve as a preliminary to signal encoding in telecommunications or networking contexts.

In xB/tB, every group of x bits is represented as a y-bit symbol. This symbol is associated with a bit pattern that is then encoded using a standard signal encoding method (usually NRZI).

The following are commonly used translation schemes of this sort:

- 4B/5B, used in FDDI networks

- 5B/6B, used in the 100BaseVG fast Ethernet standard proposed by Hewlett-Packard

- 8B/10B, used in SNA (Systems Network Administration) networks

XDR (External Data Representation)

An abstract (machine-independent) syntax for describing data structures. XDR was developed by Sun Microsystems as part of their Network File System (NFS), and it is comparable in function to the Abstract Syntax Notation One (ASN.1) used in the OSI Reference Model.

Xmodem

Xmodem is a popular file transfer protocol available in many off-the-shelf and shareware communications packages, as well as on many bulletin board systems (BBSs).

Xmodem divides the data for the transmission into blocks. Each block consists of the start-of-header character, a block number, 128 bytes of data, and a checksum.

An extension to Xmodem, called *Xmodem-CRC,* adds a more stringent

error-checking method by using a cyclical redundancy check (CRC) to detect transmission errors.

SEE ALSO
Kermit; Ymodem; Zmodem

XMS (Extended Memory Specification)

Microsoft's specifications for extended memory. In order to access extended memory, programs should use an XMS driver (for example, HIMEM.SYS).

SEE ALSO
Memory

XON/XOFF

In asynchronous communications, characters used to control the flow of data. The XOFF (ASCII 19, or Ctrl-S) tells the sender to stop transmitting until further notice; the XON (ASCII 17, or Ctrl-Q) tells the sender to resume transmission after an XOFF.

Ymodem

Ymodem is a popular file transfer protocol available in many off-the-shelf and shareware communications packages, as well as on many bulletin board systems (BBSs). Ymodem is a variation of the Xmodem protocol.

This protocol divides the data to be transmitted into blocks. Each block consists of the start-of-header character, a block number, 1 kilobyte of data, and a checksum. Ymodem also incorporates the capabilities to send multiple files in the same session and to abort file transfer during the transmission.

Ymodem's larger data block results in less overhead for error control than required by Xmodem; however, if the block must be retransmitted because the protocol detects an error, there is more data to resend.

SEE ALSO

Kermit; Xmodem; Zmodem

▼
Zero-Slot LAN

A zero-slot LAN is a local-area network (LAN) that uses one of the existing serial or parallel ports on the computer rather than a special network interface card (NIC) plugged into the computer's expansion bus.

Because zero-slot LANs can transmit only as fast as the computer's output port, they are considerably slower than networks that use network-specific hardware and software. The maximum length of each cable segment is also severely limited, so zero-slot LANs can connect only two or three computers.

The advantage of a zero-slot LAN is its low cost compared with dedicated network systems; however, the prices of newer peer-to-peer networks are beginning to negate this advantage.

▼
ZIS (Zone Information Socket)

In an AppleTalk network, a socket (access point) associated with the zone information protocol (ZIP) services.

▼
ZIT (Zone Information Table)

In an AppleTalk network, a ZIT maps the zone name(s) associated with each subnetwork in a network or internetwork.

▼
Zmodem

A popular file transfer protocol available in many off-the-shelf and shareware communications packages, as well as on many bulletin board systems. Zmodem is similar to Xmodem and Ymodem but is designed to handle larger data transfers with fewer errors. Zmodem also includes a feature called checkpoint restart, which allows an interrupted transmission to resume at the point of interruption rather than starting again at the beginning of the transmission.

SEE ALSO
Kermit; Xmodem; Ymodem

▼
Zone

In an AppleTalk network or internetwork, a logical subset of nodes which, together, form a subdivision. A zone can have a name associated with it, and a node can be part of one or more zones. The zone name is used to simplify routing and service advertising. A zone can encompass multiple networks and can cross network boundaries (that is, apply to parts of several networks).

APPENDICES

Acronyms and Abbreviations

It has been said that with only a thousand different words you can express any idea in English. If this is true, then the following acronym list has enough entries to make several languages. Acronyms have become a language of their own, and they are bandied about and used just like ordinary words. Because they have become such an integral part of any discussion related to computer topics, and particularly to networking, we have tried to provide a list that is as comprehensive as possible. The list has grown by about 1,900 entries since the first edition, and the acronym/abbreviation population grows daily. If you can't find an acronym here, try finding it at the following location on the Internet:

http://www.ucc.ie/info/net/acronyms/acro.html

Be aware that some acronyms are from other languages. The expansions for these may look odd because they are translations.

32BFA	32-bit File Access
4GL	Fourth Generation Language
A	Ampere
A/D	Analog/Digital
AA	Application Association
AA	Auto Answer
AAA	Autonomous Administrative Area
AAI	Administration Authority Identifier
AAL	ATM Adaptation Layer
AALM	ATM Adaptation Layer Management
AAL-PCI	ATM Adaptation Layer Protocol Control Information
AAL-SDU	ATM Adaptation Layer Service Data Unit
AALx	AAL Protocol x (x=1, 2, 3, 4, or 5)
AAP	Alternate Access Providers
AAP	Association of American Publishers
AAR	Automatic Alternate Routing
AARNet	Australian Academic Research Network
AARP	AppleTalk Address Resolution Protocol
AAU	Audio Access Unit
AAUI	Apple Attachment Unit Interface
AB	Abort Session
ABATS	Automatic Bit Access Test System
ABI	Application Binary Interface
ABM	Asynchronous Balanced Mode
ABME	Asynchronous Balanced Mode Extended
ABP	Alternate Bipolar
ABR	Answer Bid Ratio
ABR	Available Bit Rate
ABS	Abort Session
ABS	Average Busy Season
ABT	Abort Timer

ABT	Answer Back Tone	ACEF	Access Control Enforcement Function
AC	Accept Session	ACET	Advisory Committee on Electronics and Telecommunications
AC	Access Control		
AC	Acoustic Coupler		
AC	Alternating Current	ACF	Access Control Field
AC	Application Context	ACF	Advanced Communications Function
AC	Association Control		
ACA	Automatic Circuit Assurance	ACF/NCP	Advanced Communications Function/Network Control Program
ACB	Access Control Block		
ACB	Adapter Control Block	ACF/TCAM	Advanced Communications Function/Telecommunications Access Method
ACB	Application Control Block		
ACBH	Average Consistent Busy Hour		
ACC	Automatic Callback Calling	ACF/VTAM	Advanced Communications Function/Virtual Telecommunications Access Method
ACCS	Automated Calling-Card Service		
ACD	Adaptive Call Distributor	ACF/VTAME	Advanced Communications Function/Virtual Telecommunications Access Method Entry
ACD	Automatic Call Distributor (or Distribution)		
		ACH	Automated Clearing House
ACDF	Access Control Decision Function	ACH CCD	Automated Clearing House Cash Concentration or Disbursement
ACDI	Asynchronous Communication Device Interface		
		ACI	Access Control Information
ACE	Access Connection Element	ACIA	Access Control Inner Areas
ACE	Access Control Entry	ACIA	Asynchronous Communication Interface Adapter
ACE	Advanced Computing Environment		
		ACID	Atomicity, Consistency, Isolation, and Durability
ACE	Adverse Channel Enhancement		
		ACK	Acknowledgment
ACE	Asynchronous Communication Element	ACK0	Positive Acknowledgment

ACK1	Positive Acknowledgment	ACTLU	Activate Logical Unit
ACL	Access Control List	ACTPU	Activate Physical Unit
ACM	Address Complete Message	ACTS	Automated Computer Time Service
ACM	Association for Computing Machinery	ACTS	Automatic Coin Telephone System
ACP	Access Control Points	ACU	Autocall Unit
ACP	Allied Communications Publication	AD	Activity Discard
ACP	Ancillary Control Process	AD	Addendum
ACPM	Association Control Protocol Machine	AD	Administrative Domain
ACR	Abandon Call and Retry	ADA	Activity Discard Acknowledgment
ACR	Attenuation to Crosstalk Ratio	ADAPSO	Association of Data Processing Service Organizations
ACS	Access Control Store		
ACS	Asynchronous Communications Server	ADB	Apple Desktop Bus
		ADC	Analog-to-Digital Converter
ACSA	Access Control Specific Area	ADC	Analysis Data Concentrator
ACSE	Application Control Service Element	ADCCP	Advanced Data Communications Control Procedures
ACSE	Association Control Service Element	ADCU	Association of Data Communications Users
ACSNET	Australian Computer Science Network	ADDMD	Administrative Directory Management Domain
ACSP	Access Control Specific Point	ADF	Access Control Decision Function
ACT	Activity (bit)		
ACTAS	Alliance of Computer-Based Telephony Application Suppliers	ADI	Access Control Decision Information
		ADI	Application Directory
ACTGA	Attendant Control of Trunk Group Access	ADM	Adaptive Delta Modulation

ADMD	Administration Management Domain
ADN	Advanced Digital Network
ADP	Automatic Data Processing
ADPCM	Adaptive Differential Pulse Code Modulation
ADSI	Analog Display Services Interface
ADSL	Asymmetrical Digital Subscriber Line
ADSP	AppleTalk Data Stream Protocol
ADT	Abstract Data Type
AE	Activity End
AE	Application Entity
AEA	Activity End Acknowledgment
AEB	Analog Expansion Bus
AEC	Adaptive Echo Cancellation
AEF	Access Control Enforcement Function
AEF	Address Extension Facility
AEIMP	Apple Event Interprocess Messaging Protocol
AEP	AppleTalk Echo Protocol
AEP	Application Environment Profile
AET	Application Entity Title
AF	Address Field
AF	Audio Frequency

AF	Auxiliary Facility
AFC	Automatic Frequency Control
AFI	AppleTalk Filing Interface
AFI	Authority and Format Identifier
AFII	Association for Font Information Interchange
AFIPS	American Federation of Information Processing Societies
AFNOR	Association Francaise de Normalisation
AFP	Advanced Function Printing
AFP	AppleTalk Filing Protocol
AFRP	ARCNET Fragmentation Protocol
AFS	Andrew File System
AFSK	Audio Frequency Shift Keying
AFT	Application File Transfer
AGBH	Average Group Busy Hour
AGC	Automatic Gain Control
AGS	Asynchronous Gateway Server
AHT	Average Holding Times
AI	Artificial Intelligence
AI	Authentication Information
AIA	Aerospace Industries Association
AIAG	Automotive Industry Action Group
AID	Attention Identifier

AIFF	Advanced Integrated File Format	ALAP	ARCTalk Link Access Protocol
AIFF	Amiga Image File Format	ALI	Automatic Location Information
AIFF	Audio Interchange File Format	ALM	AppWare Loadable Module
AIFF	Audio Interface File Format	ALO	At Least Once
AIIM	Association for Information and Image Management	ALP	Abstract Local Primitive
AIM	Analog Intensity Modulation	ALS	Application Layer Structure
AIM	Apple, IBM, Motorola (Alliance)	ALT	Automatic Link Transfer
AIM	Asynchronous Interface Module	ALU	Application Layer User
AIM	ATM Inverse Multiplexer	ALU	Arithmetic Logical Unit
AIN	Advanced Intelligent Network	AM	Accounting Management
AIO	Asynchronous Input/Output	AM	Active Monitor
AIOD	Automatic Identification of Outward Dialing	AM	Amplitude Modulation
AIR	Adaptive Increase Rate	AM/PSK	Amplitude Modulation with Phase Shift Keying
AIR	Apple Internet Router	AMA	Automatic Message Accounting
AIS	Advanced Integrated Synthesis	AMD	Advanced Micro Devices
AIS	Alarm Indication Signal	AME	Asynchronous Modem Eliminator
AIS	Automatic Intercept System	AMF	Account Metering Function
AIS-E	Alarm Indication Signal, External	AM-FDM	Amplitude Modulated-Frequency Division Multiplexed
AIX	Advanced Interactive Executive	AMH	Application Message Handling
AK	Acknowledge	AMI	Alternate Mark Inversion
AKA	Also Known As	AMII	Agile Manufacturing Information Infrastructure
AL	Access Link		
AL	Application Layer		

AMIS	Audio Messaging Interchange Standard	ANSI	American National Standards Institute
AMM	Agent Management Module	ANTC	Advanced Networking Test Center
AMP	Active Monitor Present	AOCE	Apple Open Collaborative Environment
AMPS	Advanced Mobile Phone Service	AOL	America Online
AMS	Audiovisual Multimedia Service	AOM	Application OSI Management
AMT	Address Mapping Table	AOS	Alternate Operator Service
AMVFT	Amplitude Modulated Voice Frequency Telegraph	AOS	Alternate Option Selection
AM-VSB	Amplitude Modulation Vestigial Sideband	AOS	Automated Office Systems
		AOSIP	Airline Open Systems Interconnection Profile
ANBH	Average Network Busy Hour	AOW	Asia and Oceania Workshop
AND	Automatic Network Dialing	AP	Administrative Point
ANDOS	All-or-Nothing Disclosure of Secrets	AP	Application Process
ANF	AppleTalk Networking Forum	AP	Application Profile
ANI	Automatic Number Identification	APAR	Authorized Program Analysis Report
ANM	Advanced Network Management	APB	Alpha Primary Bootstrap
ANM	Answer Message	APC	Adaptive Predictive Coding
ANN	Auditing Network Needs	APC	Asynchronous Procedure Call
ANS	American National Standard	APCC	American Public Communications Council
ANSA	Advanced Network Systems Architecture	APCI	Application-layer Protocol Control Information
ANSC	American National Standards Committee	APD	Avalanche Photodiode
		APDU	Application Protocol Data Unit
		API	Application Program Interface

APIA	Application Program Interface Association	AR	Activity Resume
APL	A Programming Language	ARA	Attribute Registration Authority
APLI	ACSE Presentation Library Interface	ARAP	AppleTalk Remote Access Protocol
APLT	Advanced Private Line Termination	ARD	Application Remote Database
APM	Advanced Power Management	ARDIS	Advanced National Radio Data Service
APP	Application	ARE	All Routes Explorer
APP	Application Portability Profile	ARF	Alarm Reporting Function
APPC	Advanced Program-to-Program Communications	ARF	Automatic Reconfiguration Facility
APPC/PC	Advanced Program-to-Program Communications/Personal Computers	ARGO	A Really Good Open System Interconnection
APPI	Advanced Program-to-Program Internetworking	ARI	Address Recognized Indicator Bit
APPL	Application Program	ARL	Access Rights List
APPN	Advanced Peer-to-Peer Networking	ARL	Adjusted Ring Length
		ARL	Attendant Release Loop
APS	Application Processing Services	ARM	Asynchronous Response Mode
APS	Asynchronous Protocol Specification (Alliance)	ARO	After Receipt of Order
		ARP	Address Resolution Protocol
APS	Automatic Protection Switching	ARPA	Advanced Research Projects Agency
APT	Application Process Title	ARPANET	Advanced Research Projects Agency Network
APT	Application Programmer's Toolkit	ARQ	Automatic Repeat Request
APTS	Advanced Public Transportation Service	ARR	Attributes for Representing Relationships
APU	Audio Presentation Unit	ARR	Automatic Repeat Request

ARS	Alternate (also Automatic) Route Selection	ASK	Amplitude Shift Keying
ART	Asynchronous Remote Takeover	ASM	Address Space Manager
		ASN	Abstract Syntax Notation
ART	Automatic Revision Tracking	ASN	Advance Ship Notice
ARTT	Asynchronous Remote Takeover Terminal	ASN.1	Abstract Syntax Notation One
		ASO	Application Service Object
ARU	Audio Response Unit	ASP	Abstract Service Primitive
AS	Activity Start	ASP	AppleTalk Session Protocol
AS	Application System	ASP	Association of Shareware Publishers
AS/400	Application System/400		
ASAI	Adjunct Switch Application Interface	ASPI	Advanced SCSI Programming Interface
		ASR	Answer Seizure Ratio
ASB	Asynchronous Balanced Mode	ASR	Automatic Send/Receive
ASC	Accredited Standards Committee	ASR	Automatic Speech Recognition
ASCII	American Standard Code for Information Interchange	AST	Asynchronous System Trap
		ASTLVL	Asynchronous System Trap Level
ASDC	Abstract Service Definition Convention	ASTM	American Society for Testing Materials
ASDU	Application-layer Service Data Unit	ASTRAL	Alliance for Strategic Token Ring Advancement and Leadership
ASE	Application Service Element		
ASI	Adapter Support Interface	ASVD	Analog Simultaneous Voice/ Data
ASI	Alternate Space Inversion		
ASI	Application Software Interface	ASYNC	Asynchronous Transmission
ASIC	Application-Specific Integrated Circuit	AT	Advanced Technology
		AT&T	American Telephone and Telegraph
ASIS	American Society for Industrial Security		

ATA	ARCnet Trade Association	ATM-SDU	Asynchronous Transfer Mode Service Data Unit
ATA	AT Attachment	ATP	Advanced Technology Program
ATAPI	AT Attachment Packet Interface	ATP	AppleTalk Transaction Protocol
ATAS	Analog Test Access System	ATP	Application Transaction Processing
ATASPI	AT Attachment Software Programming Interface	ATPS	AppleTalk Print Services
ATB	All Trunks Busy	ATQ	AppleTalk Transition Queue
ATC	Authorized Training Center	ATS	Abstract Test Suite
ATD	Association of Telecommunications Dealers	ATT	Applied Transmission Technologies
ATD	Asynchronous Time Division	ATTIS	AT&T Information Systems
ATDM	Asynchronous Time Division Multiplexing	ATU-C	ADSL-3 Terminal Unit at CO
ATDP	Attention Dial Pulse	ATU-R	ADSL-3 Terminal Unit at Remote Site
ATDT	Attention Dial Tone	AU	Access Unit
ATE	Asynchronous Terminal Emulation	AU	Adaptive Unit
ATIS	Advanced Traveler Information Systems	AU	Administrative Unit
ATIS	Alliance for Telecommunications Industry Solutions	AUC	Authentication Center
		AUC	Authentication Certificate
ATM	Abstract Test Method	AUG	Administrative Unit Group
ATM	Asynchronous Transfer Mode	AU-i	Administrative Unit-i
ATM	Automatic Teller Machine	AUI	Attachment (also Auxiliary) Unit Interface
ATMARP	ATM Address Resolution Protocol	AUP	Acceptable Use Policy
ATME	Automatic Transmission Measuring Equipment	AURP	AppleTalk Update Routing Protocol
		AUTODIN	Automatic Digital Network

AUU	ATM User-to-User (Flag)		BBC	Broadband Bearer Capability
AV	Audio-Visual		BBH	Bouncing Busy Hour
AVA	Attribute Value Assertion		BBS	Bulletin Board System
AVCS	Advanced Vehicle Control Systems		BC	Begin Chain
			BC	Blind Copy
AVD	Alternative Voice/Data		BC	Block Check
AVI	Audio Visual Interleaved		Bcc	Blind Courtesy (also Carbon) Copy
AVN	Automated Voice Network			
AVS	Advanced Vector Synthesis		BCC	Block Check Character
AVS	APPC/VM VTAM Support		BCD	Binary Coded Decimal
AVT	Application Virtual Terminal		BCD	Blocked Calls Delayed
AWC	Association for Women in Computing		BCDBS	Broadband Connectionless Data Bearer Service
AWG	American Wire Gauge		BCH	Blocked Calls Held
AWT	Abstract Window Toolkit		BCN	Backward Congestion Notification
B8ZS	Bipolar with 8 Zero Substitution		BCN	Beacon
BAC	Basic Access Control		BCNU	Be Seeing You
BACM	Basic Access Control Model		BCOB	Broadband Class of Bearer
BAPI	Bridge Application Program Interface		BCP	Business Communications Project
BAS	Basic Activity Subset		BCP	Byte-Control Protocols
BAS	Bit-rate Allocation Signal		BCR	Blocked Calls Released
BASIC	Beginners All-Purpose Symbolic Instruction Code		BCS	Basic Combined Subset
			BCS	Business Communications Systems
BAUD	Bits At Unit Density			
BB	Begin Bracket		BCVT	Basic Class Virtual Terminal
BB&N	Bolt, Beranek & Newman		BCW	Burst Code-Word

BDE	Borland Database Engine
BDLC	Burroughs Data Link Control
BDN	Bell Data Network
BDR	Backup Designated Router
BDS	Building Distribution System
BDT	Bureau of Telecommunications Development
BEC	Backward Error Correction
BECN	Backward Explicit Congestion Notification
BEITA	Business Equipment and Information Technology Association
Bellcore	Bell Communications Research
BEM	Bug-eyed Monster
BER	Basic Encoding Rules
BER	Bit Error Rate (or Ratio)
BER	Box Event Records
BERT	Bit Error Rate Tester
BF	Boundary Function
BF	Bridge Function
BF	Framing Bit
BFT	Binary File Transfer
BFt	Terminal Framing Bit
BGP	Border Gateway Protocol
BGT	Broadcast and Group Translators
BHCA	Busy Hour Call Attempts
BIA	Burned-In Address

BIAS	Burroughs Integrated Adaptive System
BIB	Bus Interface Board
BICI SAAL	Broadband Inter-Carrier Interface Signaling ATM Adaptation Layer
B-ICI	Broadband Inter-Carrier Interface
BICMOS	Bipolar Complementary Metal-Oxide Semiconductor
BICSI	Building Industry Construction Standards Institute
BIH	Bureau International de L'Heure (International Time Bureau)
BIM	Business and Information Modeling (Task Group)
BIMOS	Bipolar Metal-Oxide Semiconductor
BIND	Berkeley Internet Name Domain
BIOS	Basic Input/Output System
BIP	Bit Interleave Parity
BIPS	Billion Instructions Per Second
BIP-x	Bit Interleaved Parity-x
BIS	Bracket Initiation Stopped
BIS	Business Intelligence Systems
B-ISDN	Broadband Integrated Services Digital Network
BISDN	Broadband Integrated Services Digital Network

B-ISDN PRM	B-ISDN Protocol Reference Model	BMP	Bitmap
B-ISPBX	B-ISDN Private Branch Exchange	BMS	Banyan Mail Services
		BMS	Basic Mapping Support
BISSI	Broadband Inter-switching System Interface	BMU	Basic Measurement Unit
		BN	Backward Notification
B-ISUP	Broadband ISDN User's Part	BN	Boundary Node
BISYNC	Bisynchronous (or Binary Synchronous) Communications	BN	Bridge Number
		BNA	Burroughs Network Architecture
BIT	Basic Interconnection Test	BNC	Bayonet Nut (also Navy) Connector
BIT	Binary Digit		
BITNET	Because It's Time Network	BNC	Bayonet-Neill-Concelnan
BIU	Basic Information Unit	BNF	Backus-Naur Form
BIU	Bus Interface Unit	BNN	Boundary Network Node
BKERT	Block Error Rate Tester	BNT	Broadband Network Termination
BLAST	Blocked Asynchronous/ Synchronous Transmission	B-NT1	B-ISDN Network Termination 1
BLER	Block Error Rate (or Ratio)	B-NT2	B-ISDN Network Termination 2
BLERT	Block Error Rate Tester		
BLF	Busy Lamp Field	BOA	Basic Object Adapter
B-LLI	Broadband Lower Layer Information	BOC	Bell Operating Company
		BOF	Birds of a Feather
BLNT	Broadband Local Network Technology	BOI	Basic Operators Interface
		BOM	Beginning of Message
BLOB	Binary Large Object	BOM	Bill of Materials
BLU	Basic Link Unit	BONDING	Bandwidth on Demand Interoperability Group
BMA	Broadcast Multiple Access		
BMOS	Bytex Matrix Operating System		

BONT	Broadband Optical Network Termination		BSC	Binary Synchronous Communication
BOOTP	Bootstrap Protocol		BSC	Binary Synchronous Control
BOP	Bit-Oriented Protocol		BSC	Binary Synchronous, or Bisync, Communication
BOPS	Billion Operations Per Second			
BPDU	Bridge Protocol Data Unit		BSD	Berkeley Software Distribution
BPF	Band-pass Filter		BSE	Basic Service Element
BPL	Break Point Location		BSI	British Standards Institute
BPNRZ	Bipolar Non-Return-to-Zero		BSMTP	Batch Simple Message Transfer Protocol
BPP	Bridge Port Pair		BSN	Broadband Service Node
BPR	Business Process Reengineering		BSR	Board of Standards Review
BPRZ	Bipolar Return-to-Zero		BSRF	Basic System Reference Frequency
bps	Bits Per Second			
Bps	Bytes Per Second		BSS	Basic Synchronized Subset
BPSK	Binary Phase Shift Keying		BSS	Broadband Switching System
BPSS	Bell Packet Switching System		BSVC	Broadcast Switched Virtual Connection
BPV	Bipolar Violation			
BRA	Basic Rate Access		BT	British Telecom
BRB	Be Right Back		BT	Bulk Transfer (Service Class)
BRI	Basic Rate Interface		BT	Burst Tolerance
BRP	Business Recovery Plan		B-TA	B-ISDN Terminal Adapter
BRS	Big Red Switch		BTA	Business Technology Association
BS	Back Space			
BS	Base Station		BTAG	Begin Tag
BSA	Basic Service Arrangement		BTAM	Basic Telecommunications Access Method
BSC	Base Station Controller		BTE	Broadband Terminal Equipment

B-TE1	B-ISDN Terminal Equipment 1
B-TE2	B-ISDN Terminal Equipment 2
BTM	Bulk Transfer and Manipulation (Service Class)
BTR	Bit Transfer Rate
BTS	Base Transceiver Station
BTU	Basic Transmission Unit
BTV	Business Television
BTW	By The Way
BUAF	Big Ugly ASCII Font
BUAG	Big Ugly ASCII Graphic
BUS	Broadcast and Unknown Server
BW	Bandwidth
C/SCC	Computer/Standards Coordinating Committee (IEEE Computer Society)
CA	Cell Arrival
CA	Cellular Automata
CA	Certificate (or Certification) Authority
CA	Channel Adapters (or Attachment)
CAC	Canadian Advisory Committee
CAC	Carrier Access Code
CAC	Connection Admission Control
CACS	Customer Administration Communication System
CAD	Computer-Aided Design

CAD/CAM	Computer-Aided Design/Computer-Aided Manufacturing
CAE	Common Application Environment
CAE	Computer-Aided Engineering
CAF	Channel Auxiliary Facility
CAFM	Computer-Aided Facility Management
CAI	Common Air Interface
CAI	Computer-Aided Instruction
CALC	Customer Access Line Charge
CalREN	California Research and Education Network
CALS	Computer-Aided Acquisition and Logistic Support
CAM	Channel Access Method
CAM	Computer Association of Manufacturers
CAM	Computer-Aided Manufacturing
CAMA	Centralized Automatic Message Accounting
CAMC	Customer Access Maintenance Center
CAMP	Corporate Association for Microcomputer Professionals
CAN	Campus-Area Network
CAN	Central Administration and Naming
CAP	Carrierless Amplitude/Phase

CAP	Competitive Access Provider
CAP	Computer-Aided Publishing
CAP	Customer Administration Panel
CARL	Colorado Alliance of Research Libraries
CARO	Computer Antivirus Research Organization
CAS	Centralized Attendant System (or Service)
CAS	Communicating Application Specification
CASE	Common Application Service Element
CASE	Computer-Assisted Software Engineering
CAT	Common Authentication Technology
CATV	Cable Television
CATV	Community Antenna Television
CAU	Controlled Access Unit
CAU/LAM	Controlled Access Unit/Lobe Attachment Module
CAV	Constant Angular Velocity
CB	Citizens Band
CBC	Certified Business Credential
CBC	Cipher Block Chaining
CBCPD	Cipher Block Chaining of Plaintext Difference
CBDS	Connectionless Broadband Data Service
CBE	Certified Banyan Engineer
CBEMA	Computer and Business Equipment Manufacturers' Association
CBF	Computer-Based Fax
CBI	Certified Banyan Instructor
CBMS	Computer-Based Messaging System
CBO	Continuous Bitstream-Oriented
CBQ	Class-based Queuing
CBR	Constant Bit Rate
CBS	Certified Banyan Specialist
CBT	Computer-Based Training
CBW	Crypt Breaker's Workbench
CBX	Computerized Branch Exchange
CC	Carbon Copy
CC	Chain Command
CC	Clearing Center
CC	Cluster Controller
CC	Connection Confirm
CC	Continuity Cell
CC	Country Code
CC	Courtesy Copy
CCA	Conceptual (or Common) Communication Area

CCAF	Call Control Access (or Agent) Function	CCITT	Consultative Committee for International Telegraphy and Telephony
CCB	Channel Control Block	CCL	Connection Control Language
CCB	Connection Control Block	CCO	Context Control Object
CCC	Clear Channel Capability	CCPS	Consultative Council for Postal Studies
CCD	Cash Concentration and Disbursement	CCR	Commitment, Concurrency, and Recovery
CCDN	Corporate Consolidated Data Network	CCR	Current Cell Rate
CCE	Collaborative Computing Environment	CCR	Customer Controlled Reconfiguration
CCEP	Commercial COMSEC Endorsement Program	CCRSE	Commitment, Concurrency, and Recovery Service Element
CCF	Connection (or Call) Control Function	CCS	Centum (Hundreds) Call Seconds
CCH	Control Channel	CCS	Common Channel Signal (or Signaling)
CCH	Harmonization Coordination Committee	CCS	Common Communications Support
CCH/SP	CCH Permanent Secretariat	CCS	Console Communication Service
CCI	Client Communication Interface	CCS	Continuous Composite Servo
CCIA	Computer and Communication Industry Association	CCS7	Common Channel Signaling 7
CCIR	Comité Consultatif Internationale de Radiocommunications (International Consultative Committee for Radio Communications)	CCSA	Common Control Switching Arrangement
		CCSS7	Common Channel Signaling System 7
CCIRN	Coordinating Council on International Research Networks	CCT	CNMA Conformance Testing
CCIS	Common Channel Interoffice Signaling	CCTA	Central Computer and Telecommunications Agency

CCTV	Closed-Circuit TV	CDI	Custom Device Interface
CCU	Central Control Unit	CDM	Custom Device Module
CCU	Communications Control Unit	CDMA	Code Division Multiple Access
CCW	Channel Command Word	CDO	Community Dial Office
CD	Capability Data	CDPD	Cellular Digital Packet Data
CD	Carrier Detect	CDR	Call Detail Recording
CD	Chain Data	CD-R	Compact Disc Recordable
CD	Change Directory	CDRH	Center for Devices and Radiological Health
CD	Collision Detection		
CD	Committee Draft	CDRM	Cross-Domain Resource Manager
CD	Compact Disc		
CD	Current Data	CD-ROM	Compact Disk-Read Only Memory
CD+G	Compact Disc Plus Graphics	CD-ROM XA	Compact Disc Read-Only Memory Extended Architecture
CDA	Capability Data Acknowledgment		
CDCCP	Control Data Communications Control Procedure	CDRSC	Cross-Domain Resource
		CD-RTOS	Compact Disc Real-Time Operating System
CDCS	Cambridge Distributed Computing System		
		CDS	Central Directory Server
CD-DA	Compact Disc, Digital Audio	CDS	Conceptual Data Store
CDDI	Copper Distributed Data Interface	CDS	Current Directory Structure
		CDT	Cell Delay Tolerance
CDE	Common Desktop Environment	CDV	Cell Delay Variation
CDF	Configuration Data Flow	CDVT	Cell Delay Variation Tolerance
CDFS	CD-ROM File System	CD-WO	Compact Disc, Write Once
CDI	Change Direction Indicator	CE	Communications Entity
CD-I	Compact Disc Interactive	CE	Connection Element

CEBI	Conditional End Bracket Indicator	CF	Control Function
		CF	Conversion Facility
CEC	Commission of European Communities	CFAC	Call Forwarding All Calls
		CFB	Cipher Feedback
CEI	Comparably Efficient Interconnection	CFG	Configuration
CEI	Connection Endpoint Identifier	CFGR	Configuration
CELP	Code Excited Linear Predictive Coding	CFV	Call for Votes
		CGA	Color Graphics Adapter
CEN	Comité Européen de Normalisation (European Committee for Standardization)	CGI	Common Gateway Interface
		CGI	Computer Graphics Interface
CENELEC	Comité Européen de Normalisation Électrique (European Committee for Electrical Standardization)	CGM	Computer Graphics Metafile
		CGMIF	Computer Graphics Metafile Interchange Format
CENTREX	Central Exchange	CGPM	Conference Générale des Poids et Mesures (General Conference on Weights and Measures)
CEP	Connection Endpoint		
CEPI	Connection Endpoint Identifier	CGSA	Cellular Geographic Serving Area
CEPT	Comité Européen des Administrations des Postes et des Télécommunications (European Committee for the Administration of Post and Telecommunications)	CH	Correspondent Host
		CHILL	CCITT High-Level Language
		CHPID	Channel Path Identifier
		CHRP	Common Hardware Reference Platform
CEQ	Customer Equipment	CHT	Call Holding Time
CER	Cell Error Ratio	CI	Certified Instructor
CERT	Computer Emergency Response Team	CI	Component Integration
		CI	Computer Interconnect
CES	Circuit Emulation Service	CI	Congestion Indicator
CET	Computer-Enhanced Telephony		

CI	Connect Indication
C-i	Container-i
CI	Copy Inhibit
CIAC	Computer Incident Advisory Capability
CICS	Customer Information Control System (also Communication Subsystem)
CICSPARS	CICS Performance Analysis Reporting System
CID	Command (or Connection) Identifier
CIDR	Classless Interdomain Routing
CIE	Commercial Internet Exchange
CIE	Commission Internationale de l'Eclairage
CIE	Customer-Initiated Entry
CIGOS	Canadian Interest Group on Open Systems
CIJE	Current Index to Journals in Education
CIM	CompuServe Information Manager
CIM	Computer-Integrated Manufacturing
CIMAP	Circuit Installation Maintenance Access Package
CIME	Customer Installation Maintenance Entities

CIMITI	Center for Information Management and Information Technology Innovation
CIO	Chief Information Officer
CIP	Carrier Identification Parameter
CIPX	Compressed IPX (Protocol)
CIR	Committed Information Rate
CIRC	Cross-Interleaved Reed-Solomon Code
CIS	CompuServe Information Services
CISC	Complex Instruction Set Computer
CITEC	Center for Information Technology & Communications
CIU	Communications Interface Unit
CIUG	California ISDN Users' Group
CIX	Commercial Internet Exchange
CL	Connectionless
CLA	Central Legitimization Agency
CLASS	Cooperative Library Agency for Systems and Services
CLASS	Custom Local-Area Signaling Services
CLAW	Common Link Access to Workstation
CLB	Common Logic Board
CLI	Command Line Interface

CLI	Connectionless Internetworking		CLU	Control Logical Unit
CLIB	C Library		CLV	Constant Linear Velocity
CLID	Calling Line Identification		Cm	Centimeter
CLIP	Calling Line Identification Presentation		CM	Configuration Management
			CM/2	Communications Manager for OS/2
CLIR	Calling Line Identification Restriction		CMA	Communication Managers Association
CLIST	Command List		CMC	Common Mail Calls
CLLM	Consolidated Link-Layer Management		CMC	Common Messaging Calls
CLNAP	Connectionless Network Access Protocol		CMC	Communication Management Cupcake
CLNP	Connectionless Network Protocol		CMC	Computer-Mediated Communication
CLNS	Connectionless-Mode Network Service		CMC	Connection Management Computer
CLP	Cell Loss Priority		CME	Circuit Multiplication Equipment
CLR	Cell Loss Ratio		CME	Component Management Entity
CLS	Clear Screen		CMI	Coded Mark Inversion
CLS	Connectionless Service		CMIP	Common Management Information (also Interface) Protocol
CLSDST	Close Destination			
CLSF	Connectionless Service Functions		CMIPDU	Common Management Information Protocol Data Unit
CL-TK	Claim Token		CMIPM	Common Management Information Protocol Machine
CLTP	Connectionless Transport Protocol			
CLTS	Connectionless Transport Service		CMIS	Common Management Information (also Interface) Service
CLU	Command Line Utility			

CMISE	Common Management Information Service Element	CNI	Certified NetWare Instructor
CML	Current-Mode Logic	CNI	Coalition for Networked Information
CMOL	CMIP Over Logical Link Control	CNIDR	Clearinghouse for Networked Information Discovery and Retrieval
CMOS	Complementary Metal-Oxide Semiconductor	CNM	Communication Network Management
CMOT	Common Management Information Services and Protocol Over TCP/IP	CNM	Customer Network Management
CMR	Cell Misinsertion Rate	CNMA	Communications Network for Manufacturing Applications
CMS	Conversational Monitor System	CNMI	Communication Network Management Interface
CMT	Connection Management	CNN	Composite Network Node
CN	Common Name	CNOS	Computer Network Operating System
CN	Common Node		
CN	Connect	CNRI	Corporation for National Research Initiatives
CN	Copy Network		
CN	Country Name	CNRS	Centre Nationale de Récherche Scientifique (National Center for Scientific Research)
CN	Customer Network		
CNA	Certified NetWare Administrator	CNS	Complementary Network Services
CNC	Concentrator		
CNCP	Canadian National Canadian Pacific	CNT	Communications Name Table
		CO	Central Office
CNE	Certified NetWare Engineer	CO	Connection Oriented
CNEPA	CNE Professional Association	CO	Customer Owned
CNET	Centre National d'Études des Telecommunications (National Center for the Study of Telecommunications)	CoA	(RARE) Council of Administration
		COA	Care-of-Agent

COAX	Coaxial Cable	COM	Continuation of Message
COBOL	Common Business-Oriented Language	COMBS	Customer-Oriented Message Buffer System
COC	Central Office Connections	COMPU-SEC	Computer Security
COCF	Connection-Oriented Convergence Function	COMSEC	Communications Security
		COMSPEC	Command Specifier
COCOM	Coordinating Committee for Multilateral Export Control	CON	Concentrator
COCOT	Customer-Owned Coin-Operated Telephone	CONCERT	Communications for North Carolina Education, Research, and Technology
COD	Connection-Oriented Data	CONF	Confirm
CODASYL	Computer Data Systems Language	CONS	Connection-Oriented Network Service
CODASYL-DBTG	Computer Data Systems Language Data Base Task Group	COPP	Connection-Oriented Presentation Protocol
CODEC	Coder/Decoder	COPS	Computer Oracle and Password System
CODLS	Connection-Mode Data Link Service	COPS	Connection-Oriented Presentation Service
COH	Connection Overhead	COR	Confirmation of Receipt
COI	Connection-Oriented Internetworking	CORA	Canadian OSI Registration Authority
COIN	Columbia Online Information Network	CORBA	Common Object Request Broker Architecture
COLP	Connected Line Identification Presentation	COS	Call Originate Status
COLR	Connected Line Identification Restriction	COS	Class of Service
		COS	Corporation for Open Systems
COM	Common (also Component) Object Model	COSAC	Canadian Open Systems Applications Criteria
COM	Computer Output Microfilm		

COSE	Common Open Software Environment
COSE	Common Operating System Environment
COSINE	Cooperation for Open Systems Interconnection Networking-Europe
COSM	Class of Service Manager
COSMOS	Computer System for Mainframe Operations
COSN	Consortium for School Networking
COSS	Connection-Oriented Session Service
COSSS	Committee on Open Systems Support Services
COT	Central Office Trunks
COTF	Classroom of the Future
COTP	Connection-Oriented Transport Protocol
COTS	Commercial Off-the-Shelf (Software)
COTS	Connection-Oriented Transport Service
COW	Character-Oriented Windows
CP	Circularly Polarized
CP	Connect Presentation
CP	Connection Processor
CP	Control Point
CP	Control Program

CP	Customer Premises
CPA	Connect Presentation Accept
CPAAL5	Common Part of ATM Adaptation Layer-5
CPC	Certified Professional Credential
CPCB	Control Program (or Point) Control Block
CPCS	Common Part Convergence Sublayer
CPD	Computer Privacy Digest
CPE	Convergence Protocol Entity
CPE	Customer Premises Equipment
CPF	Control Program Facility
CPFM	Continuous Phase Frequency Modulation
CPH	Characters Per Hour
CPI	Common Part Indicator
CPI	Common Programming Interface
CPI	Computer to PABX (Private Automatic Branch Exchange) Interface
CPI	Computer-to-PBX (Private Branch Exchange) Interface
CPIC	Common Programming Interface for Communications
CPI-C	Common Programming Interface with C Language
CPIW	Customer-Provided Inside Wiring

CPM	Cost Per Minute
CPMS	Control Point Management Services
CPMU	COSINE Project Management Unit
CPN	Calling Party Number
CPN	Customer Premises Network
CPODA	Contention Priority-Oriented Demand Assignment
CPP	Certified Perfect Partners
CPR	Connect Presentation Reject
CPS	Characters Per Second
CPS	Cycles Per Second
CPSR	Computer Professionals for Social Responsibility
CPU	Central Processing Unit
CPUC	California Public Utilities Commission
CR	Carriage Return
CR	Command Response
CR	Connect Request
CRC	Cyclic Redundancy Check
CRCG	Common Routing Connection Group
CREN	Corporation for Research and Educational Networking
CRF	Cable Retransmission Facility
CRF	Communication-Related (also Connection-Related) Function

CRF(VC)	Virtual Channel Connection-Related Function
CRF(VP)	Virtual Path Connection-Related Function
CRL	Certificate Revocation List
CRLF	Carriage Return, Line Feed
CRQ	Call Request
CRS	Cell Relay Service
CRS	Configuration Report Server
CRSO	Cellular Radio Switching Office
CRT	Cathode Ray Tube
CRV	Call Reference Value
CS	Carrier Selection
CS	Check Sequence
CS	Circuit Switching
CS	Configuration Services
CS	Console
CS	Convergence Sublayer
CS	Coordinated Single-Layer
CS1	Capability Set 1
CS2	Capability Set 2
CSA	Canadian Standards Association
CSA	Carrier (also Common) Service Area
CSA	Common Storage Area
CSCW	Computer-Supported Cooperative Work

CSDC	Circuit-Switched Digital Capability
CSDN	Circuit-Switched Data Network
CSE	(Wordperfect) Certified System Engineer
CSE	Coordinated Single-Layer Embedded
CSELT	Centro Studi E Laborateri Tele-communicazioni (Telecommunications Study Center and Laboratory)
CSFS	Cable Signal Fault Signature
CSI	Convergence Sublayer Indication
CSL	Call Support Layer
CSL	Computer Systems Laboratory
CSLIP	Compressed Serial Line Interface Protocol
CSMA	Carrier Sense Multiple Access
CSMA/CA	Carrier Sense Multiple Access/ Collision Avoidance
CSMA/CD	Carrier Sense Multiple Access/ Collision Detection
CSMA/CP	Carrier Sense Multiple Access/ Collision Prevention
CSMC	Communications Services Management Council
CS-MUX	Carrier-Switched Multiplexer
CS-MUX	Circuit-Switching Multiplexer
CSN	Carrier Service Node
CSN	Colorado Supernet
CSNET	Computer Science Network
CSO	Central Services Organization
CSO	Central Switching Office
CSO	Composite Second Order
CSO	Computing Services Office
CSP	Communications Scanner Processor
CSPDN	Circuit-Switched Public Data Network
CS-PDU	Convergence Sublayer Protocol Data Unit
CSPP	Computer Systems Policy Project
CSPRSG	Cryptographically Secure Pseudo-random Sequence Generator
CSPS	Constrained System Parameter Stream
CSR	Centrex Station Rearrangement
CSR	Customer Service Record
CSRSS	Client Server Runtime Subsystem
CSS	Conceptual Signaling and Status
CSS	Control Signaling and Status (Store)
CSS	Controlled Slip Second
CSSFE	Controlled Slip Second, Far End

CSTA	Computer-Supported Telephony (also Telecommunications) Application	CTIP	Commission on Computing, Telecommunications, and Information Policies
CSTC	Computer Security Technology Center	CTL	Control
CSTO	Computer Systems Technology Office	CTNE	Compañia Telefónica Nacional de España (National Telephone Company of Spain)
CSU	Central Switching Unit	CTRG	Collaboration Technology Research Group
CSU	Channel Service Unit		
CSU/DSU	Channel Service Unit/Data Service Unit	CTS	Clear to Send
		CTS	Common Transport Semantics
CSV	Comma-Separated Variable	CTS	Communications Technology Satellite
CT	Collection Time		
CTAK	Cipher Text Auto Key	CTS	Conformance Testing Service
CTB	Communications Toolbox	CTS-LAN	Conformance Testing Service Local-Area Network
CTB	Composite Triple Beat		
CTC	Channel-to-Channel	CTSM	Conformance Test System Manual
CTCA	Channel-to-Channel Adapter	CTS-WAN	Conformance Testing System for Wide-Area Networks
CTCP	Communication and Transport Control Program		
		CTTC	Coax to the Curb
CTD	Cell Transfer Delay	CTTH	Coax to the Home
CTD	Cumulative Transit Delay	CTV	Cell Tolerance Variation
CTERM	Command Terminal Protocol	CTX	Corporate Trade Exchange
CTERM	Communications Terminal (Protocol)	CU	See You
		CUA	Channel Unit Address
CTF	Central Tabulating Facility	CUA	Common User Access
CTI	Computer-Telephone Integration	CUG	Cluster (also Closed) User Group
		CUI	Common User Interface

CUL	See You Later	DACD	Directory Access Control Domain
CUT	Control Unit Terminal	DACS	Digital Access and Cross-Connect System
CV	Code Violation		
CVCP	Code Violation, CP-Bit Parity	DACTPU	Deactivate Physical Unit
CVCRC	Code Violation, Cyclical Redundancy Check	DAD	Desktop Application Director
CVFE	Code Violation, Far End	DAD	Draft Addendum
CVO	Commercial Vehicle Operation	DAF	Destination Address Field
CVP	Code Violation, "P" Bit	DAF	Directory Authentication Framework
CVSD	Continuous Variable Slope Delta Modulation	DAF	Distributed Application Framework
CVT	Communications Vector Table	DAK	Data Acknowledge
CVTC	Conversational Voice Technologies Corporation	DAL	Data Access Language
		DAL	Data Access Line
CW	Call Waiting	DAM	Data Access Manager
CWARC	Canadian Workplace Automation Research Center	DAM	Draft Amendment
CWI	Centrum Voor Wiskunde En Informatica (Center for Mathematics and Informatics)	DAMA	Demand (or Data) Assigned Multiple Access
		DAN	Departmental Area Network
CWIS	Campus-Wide Information System	DAP	Data Access Protocol
DA	Data Available	DAP	Directory Access Protocol
DA	Desk Accessory	DAP	Document Application Profile
DA	Destination Address	DARPA	Defense Advanced Research Projects Agency
DAA	Data Access Arrangement	DARTnet	Defense Advanced Research Testbed Network
DAC	Data Authentication Code		
DAC	Digital-to-Analog Converter	DAS	Disk Array Subsystem
DAC	Dual Attachment Concentrator	DAS	Dual Address Space

DAS	Dual-Attachment Station	DCA	Defense Communications Agency
DAS	Dynamically Assigned Sockets	DCA	Digital Communication Associates
DASD	Direct Access Storage Device (Hard Disk in IBMese)	DCA	Document Content Architecture
DASS	Design Automation Standards Subcommittee	DCA	Dynamic Channel Assignment
DASS	Distributed Authentication Security Service	DCAA	Dual Call Auto Answer
DAT	Digital Audio Tape	DCB	Data Control Block
DAT	Duplicate Address Test	DCB	Directory Cache Buffer
DAT	Dynamic Address Translation	DCB	Disk Coprocessor Board
DATC	Drake Authorized Training Centers	DCC	Data Communications Channel
dB	Decibel	DCC	Data Country Code
DB2/2	Data Base 2 for OS/2	DCC	Digital Compact Cassette
DBA	Database Administrator	DCC	Distributed Computing and Communications
DBCS	Double-Byte Character Set	DCD	Data Carrier Detect
DBK	Definition Block	DCE	Data Circuit-Terminating Equipment
DBMS	Database Management System		
DBS	Data Base Service	DCE	Data Communications Equipment
DBS	Direct Broadcast Satellite		
DBTG	Data Base Task Group	DCE	Distributed Computing Environment
DBX	Digital Branch Exchange		
DC	Data Chaining	DCEC	Defense Communications Engineering Center
DC	Direct Current	DCE-RPC	Distributed Computing Environment Remote Procedure Call
DC	Disconnect Confirm		
DC	Distribution Center		
		DCF	Data Communications Function

DCF	Distributive Computing Facility	DDCMP	Digital Data Communications Messaging Protocol
DCIU	Data Communications Interface Unit	DDD	Direct Distance Dialing
DCL	Digital Command Language	DDDB	Distributed Directory Database
DCME	Digital Circuit Multiplication Equipment	DDE	Dynamic Data Exchange
DCMS	Digital Circuit Multiplication System	DDF	Data Description File
		DDFII	Data Description File for Information Interchange
DCN	Data Communication Network	DDGL	Device-Dependent Graphics Layer
DCO	Digitally Controlled Oscillator	DDI	Direct Dialing in
DCP	Digital Communications Protocol	DDK	Device Development Kit
DCPSK	Differentially Coherent Phase Shift Keying	DDL	Data Definition (or Description) Language
DCR	Direct Current Resistance	DDL	Data Direct Link
DCS	Data Circuit Switches	DDM	Direction Division Multiplexing
DCS	Defined Context Set	DDM	Distributed Data Management
DCS	Digital Cellular System	DDN	Defense Data (or Department) Network
DCS	Digital Cross-Connect System		
DCS	Distributed Computing System	DDName	Data Definition Name
DCSS	Discontinuous Shared Segment	DDN-NIC	Defense Data Network Network Information Center
DCT	Discrete Cosine Transform		
DD	Depacketization Delay	DDP	Datagram Delivery Protocol
DDA	Domain Defined Attribute	DDP	Distributed Data Processing
DDB	Directory (also Distributed) Database	DDR	Data Descriptive Record
		DDS	Dataphone Digital Service
DDBMS	Distributed Database Management System	DDS	Digital Data Service
		DDS	Digital Directory System

DDS	Direct Digital Service	DESIRE	Directory of European Information Security Standard Requirements
DDS	Document Distribution Services		
DE	Directory Entry	DET	Directory Entry Table
DE	Discard Eligibility	DEUNA	Digital Ethernet Unibus Network Adapter
DEA	Data Encryption Algorithm	DF	Don't Fragment
DEA	Directory Entry Attribute	DFB	Distributed Feedback (Laser)
DEB	Directory Entry Block	DFC	Data Flow Control
DEC	Digital Equipment Corporation	DFD	Data Flow Diagram
DECdns	DEC Distributed Name Service	DFEP	Diagnostic Front End Processor
DECdts	Digital Equipment Corporation Distributed Time Service	DFI	Digital Signal Processing Format Identifier
DECmcc	DEC Management Control Center	DFL	Distributed Feedback Laser
DECnet	Digital Equipment Corporation Network Architecture	DFN	Deutsches Forschungsnetz
DEF	Direct Equipment Failure	DFR	Document Filing and Retrieval
DEK	Data Encryption (also Exchange) Key	DFS	Distributed File System
		DFSK	Differential Frequency Shift Keying
DELNI	Digital Equipment Corporation Local Network Interconnect	DFSM	Dispersion Flattened Signal Mode
DELTA	Distributed Electronic Telecommunications Archive	DFT	Distributed Function Terminal
DEMPR	DEC Multiport Repeater	DFWMAC	Distributed Foundation Wireless Medium Access Control
DEMUX	Demultiplexer		
DER	Distinguished Encoding Rules	DGSE	Direction Générale de la Securité
DES	Data Encryption Standard	DH	DMPDU Header
DES	Destination End System	DHA	Destination Hardware Address
DES	Distributed End System		

DHCP	Dynamic Host Configuration Protocol		DISA	Data Interchange Standards Association
DI	Delete Inhibit		DISA	Defense Information Systems Agency
DI	Document Imaging			
DIA	Document Interchange Architecture		DISA	Direct Inward Switch Access
			DISC	Disconnect
DIB	Device-Independent Bitmap		DISERF	Data Interchange Standards Education and Research Foundation
DIB	Directory Information Base			
DIBI	Device Independent Backup Interface		DISN	Defense Information Systems Network
DIC	Data Integrity Check		DISOSS	Distributed Office Supported System
DID	Destination ID			
DID	Direct Inward Dialing		DISP	Directory Information Shadow Protocol
DIF	Data (or Documentation) Interchange Format		DISP	Draft International Standardized Profile
DIG	Domain Information Groper			
DIGI	Deutsche Interessengemeinschaft Internet (German Special Interest Group for Internet)		DIT	Directory Information Tree
			DIU	Distribution Interchange Unit
			DIVE	Direct Interface Video Extension
DIGL	Device-Independent Graphics Layer			
			DIVE API	Direct Interface Video Extension API
DIGS	Device-Independent Graphics Services			
			DIW	D-Inside Wire
DIN	Deutsches Institut Fur Normung (German Institute for Standardization)		DIX	Digital Intel Xerox
			DL	Data Link
DIP	Dual In-Line Package		DL	Distribution List
DIPE	Distributed Interactive Processing Environment		DLA	Defense Logistic Agency
			DLC	Data Link Control
DIS	Draft International Standard		DLC	Digital Loop Carrier

DLC	Dynamic Load Control	DM	Document Manipulation (Service Class)
DLCEP	Data Link Connection Endpoint	DMA	Direct Memory Access
DLCF	Data Link Control Field	DMA	Document Management Alliance
DLCI	Data Link Connection Identifier	DMAC	Direct Memory Access Controller
DLE	Data Link Escape	DMD	Directory Management Domain
DLL	Data Link Layer		
DLL	Dynamic Link Library	DMDD	Distributed Multiplexing Distributed Demultiplexing
DLM	Data Line Monitor		
DLO	Data Line Occupied	DME	Distributed Management Environment
DLPDU	Data Link Protocol Data Unit	DMI	Definition of Management Information
DLPI	Data Link Provider Interface		
DLS	Data Link Services	DMI	Desktop Management Interface
DLS	Document Library Services	DMI	Digital Multiplexed Interface
DLSAP	Data Link Layer Service Access Point	DML	Data Manipulation Language
DLSDU	Data Link Layer Service Data Unit	DMO	Domain Management Organization
DLSw	Data Link Switching	DMPDU	Derived Medium Access Control Protocol Data Unit
DLT	Digital Linear Tape	DMS	Defense Messaging System
DLTG	Delegate Liaison Task Group	DMS	Document Management Service
DLU	Dependent (or Destination) Logical Unit		
DLUR	Dependent Logical Unit Requestor	DMSP	Distributed Mail System Protocol
		DMT	Discrete Multitone
DLUS	Dependent Logical Unit Server	DMTF	Desktop Management Task Force
DM	Delta Modulation		
DM	Disconnected Mode	DMUX	Double Multiplexer

DN	Distinguished Name	DOMS	Distributed Object Management System
DN	Distribution Network	DOMSAT	Domestic Satellite Service
DNA	Digital (also Distributed) Network Architecture	DONACS	Department of the Navy Automation and Communication System
DNC	Digital Node Controller		
DNC	Dynamic Network Controller	DOP	Directory Operational Protocol
DNDS	Distributed Network Design System	DOS	Disk Operating System
DNHR	Dynamic Nonhierarchical Routing	DOV	Data Over Voice
		DP	Data Processing
DNIC	Data Network Identification Code	DP	Demarcation Point
DNIS	Dialed Number Identification Service	DP	Draft Proposal
		DP	Dual Processor
DNP	Distributed Network Processing	DPA	Demand Protocol Architecture
DNR	Data Network Routing	DPA	Document Printing Application
DNS	Domain Name System	dpANS	Draft Proposed American National Standard
DOAM	Distributed Office Applications Model	DPC	Data Processing Center
DOAPI	DOS Open API	DPC	Deferred Procedure Call
DOC	Dynamic Overload Control	DPCM	Differential Pulse Code Modulation
DOD	Department of Defense	DPG	Dedicated Packet Group
DOD	Direct Outward Dialing	DPI	Dots Per Inch
DOE	Department of Energy	DPL	Dedicated Private Line
DOIT	Disabilities, Opportunities, Internetworking, Technology	DPL	Distribution Services Primary Link
DOMF	Distributed Object Management Facility	DPLL	Digital Phase-Locked Loop
		DPMI	DOS Protected Mode Interface

DPMS	Display Power Management Signaling	DS	Directory (also Digital) Service
DPMS	DOS Protected Mode Services	DS	Distributed Single-layer
DPO	Dial Pulse Originating	DS	Document Storage
DPSK	Differential Phase Shift Keying	DS	Draft Standard
DPT	Dial Pulse Terminating	DS0	Digital Signal, Level 0
DQDB	Distributed Queue Dual Bus	DS1	Digital Signal, Level 1
DR	Definite Response	DS1C	Digital Signal, Level 1C
DR	Delivery Report	DS2	Digital Signal, Level 2
DR	Disconnect Request	DS3 PLCP	Digital Signal, Level 3 Physical Layer Convergence Protocol
DR	Dynamic Reconfiguration	DS3	Digital Signal, Level 3
DRAM	Dynamic Random-Access Memory	DS4	Digital Signal, Level 4
DRDA	Distributed Relational Data Architecture	DSA	Dedicated Switched Access
		DSA	Destination Software Address
DRDS	Dynamic Reconfiguration Data Set	DSA	Digital (Equipment Corporation) Storage Architecture
DRN	Data Routing Network	DSA	Digital Signature Algorithm
DRP	DECnet Routing Protocol	DSA	Directory Service (or System) Agent (or Area)
DRP	Directory Replication Protocol	DSA	Directory System Alert
DRPF	Decimal Reference Publication Format	DSA	Distributed Systems Architecture
DRS	Data Rate Selector	DSAP	Data Link Service Access Point
DRSLST	Directed Search List	DSAP	Destination Service Access Point
DS	Dansk Standardiseringsrad (Danish Board for Standardization)	DSB	Double Sideband
DS	Desired State	DSBFC	Double Sideband Full Carrier
DS	Digital Section	DSBSC	Double Sideband Suppressed Carrier

DSC	Data Stream Compatibility	DSP	Defense Standardized Profit
DSC	Direct Satellite Communications	DSP	Digital Signal Processor
DSC	Document Structure Conventions	DSP	Directory System Protocol
		DSP	Domain Specific Part
DSD	Data Structure Definition	DSPU	Downstream Physical Unit
DSD	Direct Store Delivery	DSR	Data Set Ready
DSDS	Dataphone Switched Digital Service	DSS	Decision Support Systems
		DSS	Digital Signal Standard
DSE	Data Switching Equipment	DSS	Digital Signature Standard
DSE	Data-Specific Entry	DSS	Digital Subscriber Service
DSE	Data-Switching Exchange	DSS	Direct Station Selection
DSE	Distributed Single-layer Embedded	DSS	Domain SAP Service
DSE	Distributed System Environment	DSS/BLF	Direct Station Selection/Busy Lamp Field
DSE	DSA Specific Entry	DSSI	Digital (DEC) Small Systems Interconnect
DSI	Digital Speech Interpolation	DSSSL	Document Style, Semantics, and Specification Language
DSID	Destination Signaling Identifier		
DSL	Digital Subscriber Line	DSTINIT	Data Services Task Initialization
DSLO	Distributed System License Option	DSTU	Draft Standard for Trial Use
DSM	Dedicated Server Module	DSU	Data Service Unit
DSM	Digital Storage Media	DSU	Digital Services Unit
DSM	Distributed Switching Matrix	DSU/CSU	Data Service Unit/Channel Service Unit
DSMA	Digital Sense Multiple Access		
DSN	Delivery Status Notification	DSUN	Distribution Services Unit Name
DSOM	Distributed System Object Model	DSX	Digital Signal Cross-Connect

DSx	Digital Signal, Level x (x = 0, 1, 1C, 2, 3, or 4)	DTS	Decoding Time Stamp
		DTS	Digital Termination Service
DSX1/3	Digital Signal Cross-Connect Between Levels 1 and 3	DTS	Digital Transmission System
DT	Data	DTSS	Digital Time Synchronization Service
DT	Data Transfer		
DT	Detection Threshold	DTSX	Data Transport Station for X.25
DT	DMPDU Trailer	DU	Data Unit
DTAM	Document Transfer and Manipulation	DUA	Directory User Agent
DTAM-PM	Document Transfer and Manipulation Protocol Machine	DUV	Data Under Voice
		DVE	Digital Video Effect
		DVI	Digital Video Interactive
DTAMSE	Document Transfer and Manipulation Service Element	DVMRP	Distance Vector Multicast Routing Protocol
DTAS	Digital Test Access System	DVT	Destination Vector Table
DTD	Document Type Definition	DWO	Digital Waveform Oscillator
DTE	Data Terminal Equipment	DX	Directory Exchange
DTI	Department of Trade and Industry (UK)	DXC	Digital Cross-Connect
		DXI	Data Exchange Interface
DTMF	Desktop Management Task Force	E/O	Electro-optical
		EA	Expedited Acknowledgment
DTMF	Dual Tone Multifrequency	EA	Extended Attribute
DTP	Desktop Publishing	EA	External Access (equipment)
DTP	Distributed Transaction Processing	EAB	Extended Addressing Bit
DTR	Data Terminal Ready	EAN	Electronic Article Number
DTR	Dedicated Token Ring	EAN	European Academic Network
DTR	Draft Technical Report	EAOG	European ADMD Operators Group
DTS	Data Transfer System		

EARN	European Academic and Research Network
EAROM	Electrically Alterable Read-Only Memory
EAS	Extended Area Service
EASINet	European Academic Supercomputer Initiative Network
EAX	Electronic Automatic Exchange
EB	End Bracket
EB	Erlang B
EBCDIC	Extended Binary Coded Decimal Interchange Code
EBIOS	Extended BIOS
EBONE	European Backbone
EC	Electronic Commerce
EC	European Community (or Commission)
ECAT	Electronic Commerce Action Team
ECB	Electronic Cookbook
ECC	Enhanced Error Checking and Correction
ECC	Error-Correcting Code
ECE	Economic Commission for Europe
ECF	Enhanced Connectivity Facilities
ECH	Echo Canceller with Hybrid
ECITC	European Committee for Information-Technology Testing and Certification
ECL	Emitter-Coupled Logic
ECL	End Communication Layer
ECM	Error-Correcting Mode
ECMA	European Computer Manufacturers Association
ECN	Explicit Congestion Notification
ECNE	Enterprise Certified NetWare Engineer
ECO	Echo-Controlled Object
ECOS	Extended Communications Operating System
ECP	Extended Capabilities Port
ECPA	Electronic Communications Privacy Act
ECR	Efficient Consumer Response
ECSA	Exchange Carriers Standards Association
ECTEI	European Conference of Telecommunications and Electronics Industries
ECTF	Enterprise Computer Technology Forum
ECTP	Ethernet Configuration Test Protocol
ECU	European Currency Unit
ED	End Delimiter
ED	EWOS Document

ED	Exception Data
ED	Expedited Data
EDA	Electronic Document Authorization
EDA	Embedded Document Architecture
EDAC	Error Detection and Correction
E-DDP	Extended Datagram Delivery Protocol
EDE	Encrypt-Decrypt-Encrypt
EDF	Execution Diagnostic Facility
EDFA	Erbium-Doped Fiber Amplifiers
EDGAR	Electronic Data Gathering, Archiving, and Retrieval
EDI	Electronic Data Interchange
EDIA	Electronic Data Interchange Association
EDICUSA	Electronic Data Interchange Council of the United States
EDIF	Electronic Data Interchange Format
EDIFACT	Electronic Data Interchange for Finance, Administration, Commerce and Transport
EDIM	Electronic Data Interchange User Agent Message
EDIME	Electronic Data Interchange Messaging Environment
EDIMG	Electronic Data Interchange Messaging

EDI-MS	Electronic Data Interchange Message Store
EDIMS	Electronic Data Interchange Messaging System
EDIN	Electronic Data Interchange Notification
EDIUA	Electronic Data Interchange User Agent
EDL	Edit Decision List
EDLIS	Exchange of Dylan Lyrics Internet Service
EDM	Electronic Document Management
EDMD	Electronic Document Message Directory
EDN	Expedited Data Negotiation
EDO	Extended Data Out
EDP	Electronic Data Processing
EDSD	Electronic Document Segment Directory
EEB	Extended Erlang B
EEC	European Economic Community (or Commission)
EEI	External Environment Interface
EEMA	Electrical and Electronic Manufacturing Association
EEMA	European Electronic Mail Association
EEMAC	Electrical and Electronic Manufacturing Association of Canada

EEPG	European Engineering Planning Group
EEPROM	Electrically Erasable Programmable Read Only Memory
EER	Enhanced E-R (Data Model)
EETDN	End-to-End Transit Delay Negotiation
EETLA	Extraordinarily Extended Three Letter Acronym
EFCI	Explicit Forward Congestion Indicator
EFD	Event Forwarding Discriminator
EFF	Electronic Frontier Foundation
EFLA	Extended Four-letter Acronym
EFM	Eight-to-fourteen Modulation
EFS	End Frame Sequence
EFS	Error Free Second
EFS	Extended Facility Set
EFS	External File System
EFT	Electronic Funds Transfer
EFTA	European Free Trade Association
EG	Envelope Generator
EG	Experts Group
EGA	Enhanced Graphics Adapter
EG-CAE	Experts Group for Command Application Environment
EG-CT	Experts Group for Conformance Testing

EG-DIR	Experts Group on Directory
EG-FT	Experts Group on File Transfer
EG-LIB	Experts Group for Library
EG-LL	Experts Group Lower Layers
EG-MHS	Experts Group for MHS
EG-MMS	Experts Group Manufacturing Message Specification
EG-NM	Experts Group for Network Management
EG-ODA	Experts Group for Office Document Architecture
EGP	Exterior Gateway Protocol
EG-TP	Experts Group on Transaction Processing
EG-VT	Experts Group on Virtual Terminal
EHA	European Harmonization Activity
EHF	Extremely High Frequency
EHLLAPI	Extended High-Level Language Applications Program Interface
EIA	Electronic Industries Association
EIB	Enterprise Information Base
EIES	Electronic Information Exchange System
EIGRP	Enhanced IGRP
EINET	Enterprise Integration Network
EINOS	Enhanced Interactive Network Optimization System

EIRP	Effective Isotropic Radiated Power	EMP	Electromagnetic Pulse
EIS	Electronic Information Security	EMPC	Electromagnetic Pulse Cannon
EIS	Executive Information Systems	EMPM	Electronic Manuscript Preparation and Markup
EISA	Extended Industry Standard Architecture	EMPT	Electromagnetic Pulse Transformer
EIT	Encoded Information Type	EMS	Expanded Memory Specification
EIUF	European ISDN Users' Forum	EMUG	European MAP/TOP Users' Group
EKE	Encrypted Key Exchange		
EKTS	Electronic Key Telephone System	EMWAC	European Microsoft Windows NT Academic Center
ELAN	Emulated (also ESPRIT) Local-Area Network	EMX	Enterprise Mail Exchange
ELAP	EtherTalk Link Access Protocol	EN	End Node
ELEPL	Equal Level Echo Path Loss	EN	European Norm
ELS	Entry Level System	ENA	Extended Network Addressing
EMA	Electronic Mail Association	ENDIF	Enterprise Network-Data Interconnectivity Family (Working Group)
EMA	Electronic Messaging Association		
EMA	Enterprise Management Architecture	ENE	Enterprise Networking Event
		ENQ	Inquiry
EMB	Embedded Memory Block	ENS	Enterprise Naming (also Network) Service
EMC	Electromagnetic Capacity		
EMC	Electronic Medical Claims	ENS	European Nervous System
EMF	Electromotive Force	ENSDU	Expedited Network Service Data Unit
EMI	Electromagnetic Interference		
EMM	Expanded Memory Manager	ENTELEC	Energy Telecommunications and Electrical Association
EMOS1	East Mediterranean Optical System 1	EO	End Office
		EO	Erasable Optic

EOA	End of Address		EPROM	Erasable Programmable Read Only Memory
EOB	End of Burst		EPS	Encapsulated PostScript
EOC	Embedded Operations Channel		EPSCS	Enhanced-Private Switched Communications Service
EOC	End of Content			
EOF	Extremely Old Fart		EPSF	Encapsulated PostScript Format
EOI	End of Interrupts			
EOM	End of Message		EQEEB	Equivalent Queue Extended Erlang B
EON	End of Number			
EOS	Element of Service		E-R	Entity-relationship (Data Model)
EOS	Enterprise Object Software		ER	Error
EOT	End of Text (or Transmission)		ER	Exception Response
EOTC	European Organization for Testing and Certification		ER	Explicit Route
EP	Echo Protocol		ERA	Entity-Relationship-Attribute
EP	Emulation Program		ERD	Event Report Discriminator
EP	Extended Play		ERE	Echo Return Loss
EPA	Environmental Protection Agency		EREP	Environmental Recording, Editing, and Printing
EPABX	Electronic Private Automatic Branch Exchange		ERF	Event Report Function
EPHOS	European Procurement Handbook for Open Systems		ERIC	Educational Resources Information Service
EPIC	Electronic Privacy Information Center		ERL	Echo Return Loss
EPOS	Electronic Point of Sale		ERMF	Event Report Management Function
EPP	Enhanced Parallel Port		ERP	Error-Recovery Procedure
EPRI	Electrical Power Research Institute		ERS	Evaluated Receipt Settlement
			ERT	Equivalent Random Theory
			ES	End System

ES	Errored Second
ESA	Enhanced Subarea Addressing
ESA	Enterprise System Architecture
ESA	Errored Second, Type A
ESA	European Space Agency
ESAFE	Errored Second, Type A, Far End
ESB	Errored Second, Type B
ESBFE	Errored Second, Type B, Far End
ESCON	Enterprise System Connection Architecture
ESCP	Errored Second, CP-bit Parity
ESCR	Elementary Stream Clock Reference
ESCRC	Errored Second, Cyclic Redundancy Check
ESD	Electronic Software Distribution
ESD	Electrostatic Discharge
ESDI	Enhanced Small Device Interface
ES-ES	End System to End System
ESF	Extended Superframe Format
ESFE	Errored Second, Far End
ESH	End-System Hello
ES-IS	End System to Intermediate System
ESL	Electronic Software Licensing
ESL	Enhanced Signaling Link
ESMR	Enhanced Specialized Mobile Radio
ESMTP	Extended Simple Mail Transfer Protocol
ESN	Electronic Serial Number
ESN	Electronic Switched Network
ESnet	Energy Sciences Network
ESP	Enhanced Service Provider
ESP	Errored Second, P-bit
ESPRIT	European Strategic Project for Research on Information Technology
ESS	Electronic Switching System
ESTELLE	Extended State Transition Language
ET	Exchange Termination
ETAG	End Tag
ETB	End of Text (or Transmission) Block
ETCO	European Telecommunications Consultancy Organization
ETCOM	European Testing for Certification of Office and Manufacturing Equipment
ETE	End-to-End
ETG	EWOS Technical Guide
ETIS	Electronic Telephone Inquiry System
ETL	Electronic Testing Laboratory

ETLA	Extended Three Letter Acronym
ETN	Electronic Tandem Network
ETR	Early Token Release
ETRI-PEC	Electronics and Telecommunications Research Institute-Protocol Engineering Center
ETS	European Telecommunications Standards
ETS	Executable Test Suite
ETSDU	Expedited Transport Service Data Unit
ETSI	European Telecommunications Standards Institute
ETTM	Electronic Toll and Traffic Management
ETX	End of Text
EUNET	European UNIX Network
EUROSINET	European Open System Interconnect Network
EUTELSAT	European Telecommunications Satellite
EUUG	European UNIX Users Group
EV	Extreme Value
EVE	European Videoconferencing Equipment
EVE	Extensible VAX Editor
EVE	Extreme Value Engineering
EVS	European Videoconferencing Service

EWICS	European Workshop on Industrial Computer Systems
EWOS	European Workshop for Open Systems
EX	Expedited
EXLIST	Exit List
EXM	Exit Message
EXOS	Extension Outside
EXT	External Trace
f2f	Face to Face
FACT	Federation of Automated Coding Technologies
FAD	Frame Assembler/Disassembler
FADU	File Access Data Unit
FAIS	Factory Automation Interconnection System
FAL	File Access Listener
FAN	Facility Area Network
FAPL	Format and Protocols Language
FAQ	Frequently Asked Questions
FAQL	Frequently Asked Question List
FARNET	Federation of American Research Networks
FAS	Frame Alignment Sequence
FAT	File Allocation (also Access) Table
FAX	Facsimile

FBE	Free Buffer Enquiry		FDL	Facility Data Link
FC	Feedback Control		FDL	File Definition Language
FC	Frame Check (or Control)		FDM	Frequency Division Multiplexing
FCA	Fiber Channel Association		FDMA	Frequency Division Multiple Access
FCB	File Cache Buffer			
FCC	Federal Communications Commission		FDR	Field Definition Record
FCCSET	Federal Coordinating Council on Science, Engineering, and Technology		FDT	Formal Description Technique
			FDX	Full Duplex
			FE	Function Element
FCG	Format Computer Graphics		FEBE	Far End Block Error
FCI	Frame Copied Indicator Bit		FEC	Field Entry Condition
FCS	Fast Circuit Switching		FEC	Forward Error Correction
FCS	Fiber Channel Standard		FECN	Forward Explicit Congestion Notification
FCS	Frame Check Sequence			
FCSI	Fiber Channel Systems Initiative		FED-STD	Federal Standard
			FEE	Fast Elliptic Encryption
FC-x	Fiber Channel, Level x (x = 0, 1, 2, 3, or 4)		FEE	Field Entry Event
			FEI	Field Entry Instruction
FDCO	Field Definition Control Object		FEICO	Field Entry Instruction Control Object
FDD	Frequency Division Duplex			
FDDI	Fiber Distributed Data Interface		FEIR	Field Entry Instruction Record
			FEP	Front End Processor
FDDI-FO	Fiber Distributed Data Interface Follow-On		FEPCO	Field Entry Pilot Control Object
FDFA	Federal Department of Foreign Affairs		FEPG	Federal Engineering Planning Group
FDHM	Full Duration Half Maximum		FEPR	Field Entry Pilot Record
FDI	Format Directory		FER	Field Entry Reaction

FERF	Far End Receive Failure	FITL	Fiber in the Loop
FERPM	FTAM Error Recovery Protocol Machine	FIX	Federal Information (also Internet) Exchange
FEXT	Far End Crosstalk	FL	First Level
FF	Form Feed	FLAP	FDDITalk Link Access Protocol
FFOL	FDDI Follow-On LAN	FLIH	First-Level Interrupt Handler
FFT	Fast Fourier Transform	FLIP	Fast Local Internet Protocol
FFT	Final Form Text	FLP	FastLink Pulse
FG	Frame Ground	FM	Fault Management
FG	Functional Group	FM	Frequency Modulation
FGND	Frame Ground	FM	Function Management
FH	Frame Handler	FMBS	Frame-Mode Bearer Service
FHD	Fixed-Head Disk	FMD	Function Management Data
FI	File Interchange	FM-FDM	Frequency Modulated-Frequency Division Multiplexed
FID	Format Identifier		
FIFO	First In, First Out		
FIGS	Figures Shift	FMH	Function Management Header
FIM	Fiber Interface Module	FMS	File Management System
FIN	Finish Flag	FMV	Full Motion Video
FIPS	Federal Information Processing Standard	FMVFT	Frequency Modulation Voice Frequency Telegraph
FIR	Fast Infrared	FN	Finish
FIR	Finite Impulse Response	FN	Forward Notification
FIRL	Fiber-Optic Inter-Repeater Link	FNC	Federal Networking Council
		FNOI	Further Notice of Inquiry
FIRST	Forum on Incident Response and Security Teams	FNP	Front-End Network Processor
FISUS	Fill in Signal Units	FNPRM	Further Notice of Proposed Rule Making

FO	Fiber Optics
FOAF	Friend of a Friend
FOC	Fiber Optic Communications
FOCS	Foundations of Computer Science
FOD	Format Office Document
FOIRL	Fiber Optic Inter-Repeater Link
FOOBAR	FTP Operation Over Big Address Records
FOPG	Federal Networking Council Open Systems Interconnection Planning Group
FOT	Frequency of Optimum Traffic
FOTS	Fiber Optic Transmission System
FOX	Field Operational X.500
FP	Functional Profile
FPASD	Facsimile Packet Assembler/ Disassembler
FPF	Facility Parameter Field
FPLMTS	Future Public Land Mobile Telecommunication System
FPODA	Fixed Priority-Oriented Demand Assignment
FPS	Fast Packet Switching
FPS	Frames Per Second
FPSNW	File and Print Service for NetWare
FPU	Floating Point Unit

FQA	Frequently Questioned Acronym
FQDN	Fully Qualified Domain Name
FQPCID	Fully Qualified Procedure Correlation Identifier
FR	Frame Relay
FR&O	First Report and Order
FRAD	Frame Relay Access Device
FREDMAIL	Free Educational Electronic Mail
FRF	Frame Relay Forum
FRFH	Frame Relay Frame Handler
FRICC	Federal Research Internet Coordination Committee
FRMR	Frame Reject
FRS	Flexible Route Selection
FRS	Frame Relay Service
FRSE	Frame Relay Switching Equipment
FR-SSCS	Frame Relaying Service-specific Convergence Sublayer
FRTE	Frame Relay Terminal Equipment
FS	File Server
FS	Frame Status
FS	Functional Standard
FSF	Free Software Foundation
FSGML	Format Standard Generalized Markup Language

FSIOP	File Server I/O Processor
FSK	Frequency Shift Keying
FSL	Free Space Loss
FSM	Finite State Machine
FSN	Full Service Network
FSP	File Service Process
FSS	Fully Separated Subsidiary
FSTG	Functional Standardization Taxonomy Group
FSU	File Support Utility
FT	Fault Tolerant
Ft	Foot
FT1	Fractional T1
FTAM	File Transfer, Access, and Management
FTF	Face to Face
FTP	File Transfer Protocol
FTS	Federal Telecommunications System
FTS	File Transfer Service
FTSC	Federal Telecommunications Standards Committee
FTTC	Fiber to the Curb
FTTH	Fiber to the Home
FTTN	Fiber to the Node
FU	Functional Unit
FUBAR	Fouled Up Beyond All Recognition

FUNI	Frame User Network Interface
FWHM	Full Width at Half Maximum
FWIW	For What It's Worth
FX	Foreign Exchange
FYI	For Your Information
G	Giga-
GA	Go Ahead
GAN	Global-Area Network
GAO	Government Accounting Office
GAP	Gateway Access Protocol
GAP	Generic Address Parameter
GATED	GATE Daemon
Gb	Gigabit
GB	Gigabyte
Gbps	Gigabits Per Second
GBps	Gigabytes Per Second
GCID	Global Call Identifier
GCID-IE	Global Call Identifier—Information Element
GCM	Generalized Control Model
GCRA	Generic Cell Rate Algorithm
GCS	Group Control System
gd&r	Grinning, Ducking, and Running
GDAP	Government Document Application Profile
GDDM	Graphical Data Display Manager

GDES	Generalized Data Encryption Standard	GN	Given Name
GDMI	Generic Definition of Management Information	GNM	Generic Network Model
		GNMP	Government Network-Management Profile
GDMO	Guidelines for the Definition of Managed Objects	GNU	GNU's Not UNIX
GDS	Generalized Data Stream	GO	Geometrical Optics
GDS	Graphics Data Syntax	GOES	Geostationary Orbit Environment Satellite
GE	Group of Experts	GoS	Grade of Service
GEMDES	Government Electronic Messaging and Document Exchange Service	GOSIP	Government Open Systems Interconnection Profile
GEN	Generation	GPD	General Purpose Discipline
GFC	Generic Flow Control	GPIB	General Purpose Interface Bus
GFI	General Format Identifier	GPL	General Public License
GFID	General Format Identifier	GPN	Government Packet Network
GGP	Gateway-to-Gateway Protocol	GPS	Global Positioning Satellite (or Service)
GHz	Gigahertz	GPV	General Public Virus
GID	Group ID	GQ	Generation Qualifier
GIF	Graphic Interchange Format	GR/PS	Graphical Representation/ Phrase Representation
GIGO	Garbage In, Garbage Out		
GKS	Graphical Kernel System	GRC	Generic Reference Configuration
GL	Generation Language (e.g., 4GL)	GRD	GOSIP Register Database
GMHS	Global Message Handling Service	GRIN	Graded Indices
		GSA	General Services Administration
GMSC	Gateway Mobile Services Switching Center	GSM	Groupe Spécial Mobile
GMT	Greenwich Mean Time	GSN	Government Satellite Network

GSS/RSS	Generation Support Statement/Reception Support Statement	HAND	Have A Nice Day
GSTN	General Switch Telephone Network	HASP	Houston Automatic Spooling Priority
GT	Give Token	HBA	Host Bus Adapter
GTA	Give Token Acknowledgment	HC	Hyperchannel
GTA	Government Telecommunications Agency	HCD	Hardware Configuration Definition
GTC	Give Token Confirm	HCFA	Health Care Finance Administration
GTE	General Telephone and Electronics	HCL	Hop Count Limit
GTF	Generalized Trace Facility	HCS	Hard Clad Silica
GTIS	Government Telecommunications and Informatics Services	HCS	Header Check Sequence
		HCSS	High-Capacity Storage System
GTN	Government Telecommunications Network	HD	Hard Disk
GUI	Graphical User Interface	HDB3	High-Density Bipolar—Three Zeros
GUS	Guide to the Use of Standards	HDCD	High Density Compact Disc
GWNCP	Gateway Network Control Program	HDLC	High-Level Data Link Control
GWSSCP	Gateway System Services Control Point	HDSL	High-bit-rate Digital Subscriber Line
		HDT	Host Digital Terminal
H	Hexadecimal	HDTV	High Definition Television
HAA	Home Address Agent	HD-WDM	Wave Division Multiplexing
HAI	Host Adapter Interface	HDX	Half Duplex
HAL	Hardware Abstraction Layer	HE	Head End
HAM	Host Adapter Module	HEC	Header Error Control (or Correction or Check)
HAM	Hybrid Access Method		
HAN	House Area Network	HEL	Header Extension Length

HEMP	High-altitude Electromagnetic Pulse
HEMS	High-Level Entity Monitoring System
HERF	High Energy Radio Frequency
Hex	Hexadecimal
HF	High Frequency
HFC	Hybrid Fiber-optic Coaxial (Networks)
HFO	High-Frequency Oscillator
HFS	Hierarchical File System
HICOM	High Technology Communication
HID/LOD	High-Density/ Low-Density Tariff
HILI	Higher-Level Interface
HIPPI	High-Performance Parallel Interface
HI-SAP	Hybrid Isochronous-MAC Service Access Point
HLC	Higher-Layer Compatibility
HLF	Higher-Layer Function
HLLAPI	High-Level Language Application Program Interface
HLPI	Higher-Level Protocol Identifier
HLR	Home Location Register
HMA	High Memory Area
HMI	Hub Management Interface
HMI	Human-Machine Interface
HML	Human-Machine Language
HMP	Host Monitoring Protocol
HMUX	Hybrid Multiplexer
HN	Host to Network
HNDS	Hybrid Network Design System
HOB	Hierarchical Operational Binding
HOL	Head of Line
HP	Hewlett-Packard
HPAD	Host Packet Assembler/ Disassembler
HPCA	High-Performance Computing Act
HPCC	High-Performance Computing and Communications
HPF	High-Pass Filter
HPFS	High-Performance File System
HPIB	Hewlett-Packard Interface Bus
HPM	High-Power Microwave
HPN	High-Performance Network
HPPI	High-Performance Parallel Interface
HPR	High-Performance Routing
HPSS	High-Performance Switching System
Hr	Hour
HRC	Hybrid Ring Control

HRPF	Hexadecimal Reference Publication Format	iABI	Intel Application Binary Interface
HRX	Hypothetical Reference Connection	IAC	Inter-Application Communication
HS	Half Session	IAC	International Advisory Committee
HSC	Hierarchical Storage Controller	IAC	Interpret As Command
HSDC	High-Speed Data Card	IADCS	Interactivity Defined Context Set
HSDN	High-Speed Data Network		
HSLAN	High-Speed Local-Area Network	IAM	Initial Address Message
HSM	Hardware-Specific Module	IAN	Integrated Analog Network
HSM	Hierarchical Storage Management (or Manager)	IANA	Internet Assigned Numbers Authority
HSSI	High-Speed Serial Interface	IANAL	I Am Not A Lawyer
HSV	Hue/Saturation/Value	IAOG	International ADMD Operators Group
HT	Horizontal Tab		
HTML	Hypertext Mark-up Language	IAP	Inner Administrative Point
HTTP	Hypertext Transfer Protocol	IAP	Internet Access Provider
HVAC	Heating, Ventilation and Air Conditioning	IAPP	Industrial Automation Planning Panel
Hz	Hertz	IAR	Initial Address Reject
I/G	Individual/Group	IAS	Interactive Application System
I/O	Input/Output	IAU	International Astronomical Union
IA	Implementation Agreement		
IA	International Alphabet	IBCN	Integrated Broadband Communication Network
IA5	International Alphabet 5	IBM	International Business Machines
IAA	Initial Address Acknowledgement		
IAB	Internet Activities Board	IBMNM	IBM Network Management
		IC	Input Controller

IC	Integrated Circuit		ICN	International Cooperating Network
IC	Interexchange Carrier		ICOS	International Club for Open Systems
ICA	Intelligent (also Integrated) Communications Adapter		ICOT	ISDN Conformance Testing
ICA	International Communications Association		ICP	Initial Connection Protocol
ICAC	Industrial Commercial Advisory Council		ICP	Interconnect Control Program
ICADD	International Committee for Acceptable Document Designs		ICP	Internet Control Protocol
ICC	International Chamber of Commerce		ICP	Interprocess Communications Protocol
ICC	International Communication Conference		ICPT	Intercept Tone
ICC	International Control Center		ICST	Institute for Computer Science and Technology
ICCA	Independent Computer Consultants Association		ICSU	Internal Channel Service Unit
ICCB	Internet Configuration Control Board		ICSW	ISDN CPE and Software Workgroup
ICCF	Interactive Computing and Control Facility		ICTYBT-IWHTKY	I Could Tell You but Then I Would Have to Kill You
ICD	International Code Designator		ICV	Integrity Check Value
ICF	Isochronous Convergence Function		ICW	Interrupt Continuous Wave
ICI	Incoming Call Identification		ID	Identifier
ICI	Interexchange Carrier Interface		ID	Internet Draft
ICI	Interface Control Information		IDA	Indirect Data Addressing
ICLID	Incoming Called Identification		IDA	Integrated Digital Access
ICMP	Internet Control Message Protocol		IDAPI	Integrated Database Application Programming Interface
			IDC	Insulation Displacement Contact

IDC	International Data Corporation	IDSA	Interactive Digital Software Association
IDCMA	Independent Data Communication Manufacturers' Association	IDT	Interrupt Descriptor (also Dispatch) Table
IDCT	Inverse Discrete Cosine Transform	IDU	Interface Data Unit
IDD	International Direct Dialing	IE	Information Element
IDE	Integrated (or Intelligent) Drive Electronics	IEC	Interexchange Carrier
		IEC	International Electrotechnical Commission
IDF	Intermediate Distribution Frame	IEE	Institute of Electrical Engineers
IDG	Inter-Dialog Gap	IEEE	Institute of Electrical and Electronics Engineers
IDI	Initial Domain Identifier	IEEE-USA/CCIP	IEEE Committee on Communications and Information Policy
IDL	Interface Definition Language		
IDM	Integrated Diagnostic Modem	IEICE	Institute of Electronics, Information, and Communication Engineers
IDMS	Image and Document Management Services		
IDN	Integrated Digital Network	IEN	Internet Engineering (also Experiment) Note
IDN	Interface Definition Notation		
IDP	Initial Domain Part	IEPG	Intercontinental Engineering Planning Group
IDP	Integrated Detector Pre-amplifier	IES	Information Exchange System
IDP	Internet Datagram Protocol	IESG	Internet Engineering Steering Group
IDP	Internetwork Datagram Packet (or Protocol)		
IDPR	Interdomain Policy Routing	IETF	Internet Engineering Task Force
IDRA	International Digital Radio Association	IEV	International Electrotechnical Vocabulary
		IF	Intermediate Frequency
IDRP	Inter-Domain Routing Protocol	IFG	Interframe Gap

IFIP	International Federation for Information Processing	IK	Interchange Key
		IKE	IBM Kiosk for Education
IFOBS	International Forum on Open Bibliographic Systems	ILAC	International Laboratory Accreditation Conference
IFRB	International Frequency Registration Board	ILD	Injection Laser Diode
IFS	Installable File System	ILMI	Interim Link Management Interface
IFS	Internal File System	ILU	Independent Logical Unit
IFU	Interworking Functional Unit	IM	Intelligent Messaging
IGC	Institute for Global Communications	IM	Intensity Modulation
IGES	Initial Graphics Exchange Specification	IMAC	Isochronous Media Access Control
IGMP	Internet Group Management Protocol	IMAP	Internet Message Access Protocol
IGOSS	Industry and Government Open Systems Specification	IMCO	In My Considered Opinion
		IMHO	In My Humble Opinion
IGP	Interior Gateway Protocol	IMIL	International Management Information Library
IGRP	Internet Gateway Routing Protocol	IML	Initial Microcode Load
IHL	Internet Header Length	IMNSHO	In My Not So Humble Opinion
I-H-U	I Heard You	IMO	In My Opinion
IIA	Information Interchange Architecture	IMP	Information Management Plan
		IMP	Interface Message Processor
IIM	Inventory Information Management	IMPACT	Information Market Policy Actions
IINREN	Interagency Interim National Research and Education Network	IMPATT	Impact Avalanche and Transit Time
IIW	ISDN Implementors' Workshop	IMPDU	Initial MAC Protocol Data Unit

IMPS	Interface Message Processors	INTAP	Interoperability Technology Association for Information Processing
IMR	Intensive Mode Recording		
IMR	Internet Monthly Report	INTELSAT	International Telecommunications Satellite Organization
IMS	Image Management Service		
IMS	Information Management Systems	INTUG	International Telecommunications Users' Group
IMS/VS	Information Management System/Virtual Storage	INWATS	Inward Wide-Area Telephone Service
IMSI	International Mobile Subscriber Identity	IO	Input/Output
		IOC	Input/Output Control
IMSP	Independent Manufacturer Support Program	IOC	Interoffice Channel
IMTS	Improved Mobile Telephone Service	IOCDS	Input/Output Configuration Data Set
IM-UAPDU	Interpersonal Messaging User Agent Protocol Data Unit	IOCP	Input/Output Control (or Configuration) Program
IMVOD	Impulse VOD	IOD	Identified Outward Dialing
In	Inch	IOM	Input/Output Module
IN	Intelligent Network	IONL	Internal Organization of the Network Layer
InARP	Inverse Address-Resolution Protocol	IOP	Input/Output Processor
INCA	Integrated Network Communication Architecture	IOP	Interoperability
		IOPD	Input/Output Problem Determination
IND	Indication		
INFOSEC	Information Systems Security	IOS	Intermediate Open System
INIT	Initials	IP	Internet Protocol
INMARSAT	International Maritime Satellite Service	IPAE	Internet Protocol Address Encapsulation
INN	Intermediate Network Node	IPC	Interprocess Communication
INT	Interrupt		

IPCP	Internet Protocol Control Protocol	IPS	Image Processing Server
		IPS	Information Processing System
IPCS	Interactive Problem Control System	IPSIT	International Public Sector Information Technology
IPD	Internet Protocol Datagram	IPSJ	Information Processing Society of Japan
IPDS	Intelligent Printer Data Stream		
IPDU	Internetwork Protocol Data Unit	IPX	Internetwork Packet Exchange
		IPX/SPX	Internetwork Packet Exchange/ Sequenced Packet Exchange
IPE	In-band Parameter Exchange		
IPI	Initial Protocol Identifier	IR	Infrared
IPI	Intelligent Peripheral Interface	IR	Internet Registry
IPICS	ISP Implementation Conformance System	IR	Internet (or Internetwork) Router
IPL	Initial Program Load	IRC	International Record Carrier
IPL	Interactive Services Primary Layer	IRC	Internet Relay Chat
		IRD	Information Resource Dictionary
IPM	Impulses Per Minute		
IPM	Interpersonal Messaging	IrDA	Infrared Data Association
IPMS	Interpersonal Messaging Service (or System)	IRDS	Information Resource Dictionary System
IPM-UA	Interpersonal Messaging User Agent	IRF	Intermediate Routing Function
		IRL	Inter-Repeater Link
IPN	Integrated Packet Network	IRM	Inherited Rights Mask
IPN	Interpersonal Notification	IRN	Intermediate Routing Node
IPng	Internet Protocol, Next Generation	IRP	Internal Reference Point
		IRQ	Interrupt Request Line
IPR	Isolated Pacing Response	IRQL	Interrupt Request Level
IPRA	Internet Policy Registration Authority	IRSG	Internet Research Steering Group
IPRL	ISPICS Requirements List		

IRTF	Internet Research Task Force	ISM	Industrial, Scientific, and Medical
IRV	International Reference Version	ISN	Information Systems Network
IS	Information Systems	ISN	Initial Sequence Number
IS	Intermediate System	ISN	Internet Society News
IS	International (also Internet) Standard	ISO	International Standardization Organization
ISA	Industry Standard Architecture	ISO/CS	International Standardization Organization Central Secretariat
ISACA	Information Systems Audit and Control Association		
ISAM	Indexed Sequential Access Method	ISOC	Internet Society
ISC	International Switching Center	ISODE	International Standardization Organization Development Environment
ISC	Intersystem Communications in CICS		
ISCA	Intelligent Synchronous Communications Adapter	ISORM	International Standardization Organization Reference Model
		ISP	Information Service Provider
ISCC	Intelligent System Control Console	ISP	International Standard (or Standardized) Profile
ISCF	Inter-System Control Facility	ISP	Internet Service Provider
ISD	International Subscriber Dialing	ISPATS	International Standardized Profile Abstract Test Suite
ISDN	Integrated Services Digital Network	ISPBX	Integrated Service Private Branch Exchange
ISE	Integrated Storage Element	ISPC	International Sound-program Center
ISH	Intermediate System Hello		
ISI	Information Sciences Institute	ISPETS	International Standardized Profile Executable Test Suite
ISI	Inter-Symbol Interference	ISPF	Interactive System Productivity Facility
IS-IS	Intermediate System to Intermediate System		

ISPICS	International Standardized Profile Implementation-Conformance Statement
ISPIXIT	ISP Protocol Implementation Extra Information for Testing
ISPSN	Initial Synchronization Point Serial Number
ISPT	Instituto Superiore Poste E Telecommunicazioni (Superior Institute for Post and Telecommunications)
ISPX	ISDN Private Branch Exchange
ISR	Intermediate Session Routing
ISR	Interrupt Service Routine
ISRC	International Standard Recording Code
ISS	Internet Security Scanner
ISSB	Information Systems Standards Board
ISSI	Interswitching System Interface
ISSO	Information Systems Security Organization
ISTE	International Society for Technology in Education
ISU	Integrated Service Unit
ISUP	ISDN User Part
ISV	Independent Software Vendor
IT	Information Technology
IT	Information Type
IT	Intelligent Terminal

ITA	International Telegraph Alphabet
ITAA	Information Technology Association of America
ITAEGC	Information Technology Advisory Experts' Group on Certification
ITAEGS	Information Technology Advisory Experts' Group on Standardization
ITAEGT	Information Technology Advisory Experts' Group on Telecommunications
ITB	Intermediate Text Block
ITC	Independent Telephone Company
ITCA	International Teleconferencing Association
ITCC	Information Technology Consultative Committee
ITDM	Intelligent Time-Division Multiplexer
ITE	Information Technology Equipment
ITFS	Instructional Television Fixed Service
ITI	Industrial Technology Institute
ITI	Interactive Terminal Interface
ITIMS	In-Service Transmission Impairment Measurement Set
ITR	Internet Talk Radio

ITRC	Information Technology Requirements Council
ITS	Institute for Telecommunication Sciences
ITS	Invitation to Send
ITSB	Image Technology Standards Board
ITSC	Inter-regional Telecommunications Standards Conference
ITSEC	Information Technology Security Evaluation Criteria
ITSP	Information Technology and System Planning
ITSTC	Information Technology Steering Committee
ITT	Invitation to Transmit
ITU	International Telecommunications Union
ITUA	Independent T1 Users' Association
ITU-T	International Telecommunications Union, Telecommunications Sector
ITV	Interactive TV
IUCV	Interuser Communication Vehicle
IUMA	Internet Underground Music Archive
IUPAC	International Union of Pure and Applied Chemistry
IUT	Implementation Under Test

IUW	ISDN User's Workshop
IVD	Integrated Voice and Data
IVDMS	Integrated Voice and Data Multiplexers
IVDT	Integrated Voice/Data Terminal
IVDTE	Integrated Voice/Data Terminal Equipment
IVHS	Intelligent Vehicle Highway Systems
IVMO	Initial Value Managed Object
IVOD	Interactive Voice on Demand
IVR	Interactive Voice Response
IVS	Interactive Video Service
IVSN	Interactive Video Services Network
IVT	Interrupt Vector Table
IW	Information Warehouse
IWBNI	It Would Be Nice If
IWF	Interworking Function
IWU	Intermediate Working Unit
IWU	Internetworking Unit
IXC	Interexchange Carrier or Channel
IXI	International X.25 Interconnect
IYFEG	Insert Your Favorite Ethnic Group
JAM	Just A Minute
JANET	Joint Academic Network

JBIG	Joint Bi-level Imaging Group	JTC	Joint Technical Committee
JCG	Joint Coordination Group	JTC1	Joint Technical Committee 1
JCL	Job Control Language	JTM	Job Transfer and Manipulation
JDA	Joint Development Agreement	Jughead	Jonzy's Universal Gopher Hierarchy Excavation and Display
JEDI	Joint Electronic Data Interchange	JUNET	Japanese UNIX Network
JEDI	Joint Environment for Digital Imaging	JVTOS	Joint Viewing and Tele-Operation Service
JEMA	Japanese Electric Machinery Association	k	Kilo-
		KAK	Key-Auto-Key
JES	Job Entry Subsystem	KAU	Key Station Adapter Unit
JES 2	Job Entry Subsystem 2	Kb	Kilobit
JES 3	Job Entry Subsystem 3	KB	Kilobyte
JIPS	JANET Internet Protocol Service	Kbps	Kilobits Per Second
JISC	Japanese Industrial Standards Committee	KBps	Kilobytes Per Second
		KDC	Key Distribution Center
JIT	Just in Time	KDD	Kokusai Denshin Denwa
JITC	Joint Interoperability Test Center	KDS	Keyboard Display Station
		KHz	Kilohertz
JITEC	Joint Information Technology Experts Committee	KIBO	Knowledge In, Bullshit Out
		KIS	Knowbot Information Service
JMUG	Japanese MAP/TOP User Group	KISS	Keep It Safely Secure
JNT	Joint Network Team	KISS	Keep It Simple, Stupid
JPEG	Joint Photographic Experts Group	km	Kilometer
		KMP	Key Management Protocol
JRAG	Joint Registration Advisory Group	KSO	Keyboard Send Only
JSA	Japan Standards Association	KSR	Keyboard Send and Receive

KSU	Key Service Unit		LAPS	LAN Adapter and Protocol Support
KTS	Key Telephone System		LAPX	Link Access Procedure, Half Duplex
KTU	Key Telephone Unit			
LAA	Locally-Administered Address		LASER	Light Amplification by Stimulated Emission of Radiation
LAB	Latency Adjustment Buffer			
LAB	Line Attachment Base		LAT	Local-Area Transport
LAD	Local-Area Disk		LATA	Local Access and Transport Area
LAL	Leased Access Line			
LAM	Lobe Attachment Module		LAVC	Local-Area VAX Cluster
LAMA	Local Automatic Message Accounting		LAWN	Local-Area Wireless Network
			LB	Leaky Bucket
LAN	Local-Area Network		LBRV	Low Bit Rate Voice
LAN/RM	Local-Area Networks Reference Model		LBS	LAN Bridge Server
			LBT	Listen Before Talk
LANAO	LAN Automation Option		LC	Link Control
LANDA	Local-Area Network Dealer Association		LC	Local Channel
			LCC	Lost Calls Cleared
LANE	Local-Area Network Emulation		LCD	Line Current Disconnect
			LCD	Liquid Crystal Display
LANRES	Local-Area Network Resource Extension Services		LCD	Lost Calls Delayed
LANSUP	LAN Adapter NDIS Support		LCF	Log Control Function
LAP	Link Access Procedure (or Protocol)		LCGN	Logical Channel Group Number
LAPB	Link Access Procedure, Balanced		LCI	Logical Channel Identifier (or Identification)
LAPD	Link Access Procedure, D Channel		LCM	Line Concentrating Module
			LCM	Logical Control Module
LAPM	Link Access Procedure, Modem		LCN	Logical Channel Number

LCP	Link Control Protocol		LEN	Low-Entry Networking
LCR	Least Cost Routing		LEOS	Low Earth Orbit Satellite
LCR	Line Control Register		LES	LAN Emulation Server
LD	LAN Destination		LF	Largest Frame
LD	Laser Diode		LF	Line Feed
LDAP	Lightweight Directory Access Protocol		LF	Low Frequency
			LFC	Local Function Capabilities
LDDB	Local Directory Database		LFM	Link Framing Module
LDDI	Local Distributed Data Interface		LFN	Long Fat Network
			LFO	Low-Frequency Oscillator
LDDS	Limited Distance Data Service		LFSID	Local Form Session Identifier
LDM	Limited Distance Modem		LGC	Line Group Controller
LDN	Listed Directory Number		LGN	Logical Group Number
LE	LAN Emulation		LH	Link Header
LE	Local Exchange		LHT	Long Holding Time
LEA	Light Extender Amplifier		LI	Length Indicator
LEAF	Law-Enforcement Access Field		LIB	Line Interface Base
LEARP	LAN Emulation Address Resolution Protocol		LIC	Line Interface Coupler
			LID	Local Injection/Detection
LEC	LAN Emulation Client		LIDB	Line Information Database
LEC	Local Exchange Carrier		LIFO	Last In, First Out
LECC	Layered Error-Correction Code		LIJP	Leaf-initiated Join Parameter
LECID	LAN Emulation Client Identifier		LIM	Line Interface Module
			LIM	Lotus, Intel, Microsoft
LECS	LAN Emulation Configuration Server		LIMS	Lotus, Intel, Microsoft Specifications
LED	Light-Emitting Diode			
LEN	Large Extension Node		LIP	Large Internet Packet

LIPX	Large Internetwork Packet Exchange	LMMP	LAN/MAN Management Protocol
LIT	Line Insulation Test	LMMS	LAN/MAN Management Service
LIU	Line Interface Unit		
LIV	Link Integrity Violation	LMU	LAN Manager for UNIX
LIVT	Link Integrity Verification Test	LMX	L Multiplex
LIW	Long Instruction Word	LNA	Low Noise Amplifier
LL2	Link Level 2	LND	Local Number Dialing
LLAP	LocalTalk Link Access Protocol	LNM	LAN Network Manager
LLATMI	Lower Layer Asynchronous Transfer Mode Interface	LO	Line Occupancy
		LOB	Line of Business
LLC	Logical Link Control	LOC	Loss of Cell Delineation
LLC	Lower Layer Compatibility	LOCIS	Library of Congress Information Service
LLC/SNAP	Logical Link Control, Subnetwork Access Protocol		
LLC1	Logical Link Control Type 1	LOCKD	LOCK Daemon
LLC2	Logical Link Control Type 2	LOF	Loss of Frame
LLCS	Logical Link Control Security	LOL	Laughing Out Loud
LLP	Lower Layer Protocol	LOS	Line of Sight
		LOSS	Loss of Signal
LLPDU	Logical Link Protocol Data Unit	LOTOS	Language for Temporal Ordering Specification
LLS	LAN-Like Switching	LP	Linearly Polarized
LLSIG	Lower Layer Special Interest Group	LPAR	Logical Partition
		LPC	Linear Predictive Coding
LLWANP	LAN-to-LAN Wide Area Network Program	lpd	Line Printer Daemon
LM	Layer Management	LPDA	Link Problem Determination Application
LME	Layer Management Entity	LPF	Low-Pass Filter
LMI	Local Management Interface		

LPN	Local Packet Network	LSL	Link Support Layer
LPP	Lightweight Presentation Protocol	LSN	Logical Session Number
		LSP	Link State Packet
LPR	Line Printer	LSR	Leaf Setup Request
LPVS	Link Packetized Voice Server	LSRR	Loose Source and Record Route
LQA	Line Quality Analysis		
LRC	Longitudinal Redundancy Check	LSS	Low-Speed Scanner
		LSSU	Link Status Signal Unit
LRM	LAN Reporting Mechanism	LT	Line (or Local or Loop) Termination
LRU	Least Recently Used		
LS	Licensing Service	LT	Lower Tester
LS	Link Station	LTA	Line Turnaround
LS	Local Single-layer	LTB	Last Trunk Busy
LS/LC	Line Stabilizer/Line Conditioner	LTD	Local Test Desk
		LTE	Line Terminating Entity
LSA	Limited Space-charge Accumulation	LTE	Line Terminating Equipment
		LTE	Local Telephone Exchange
LSAP	Link Service Access Point	LTH	Length Field
LS-API	Licensing Server Application Program Interface	LTM	LAN Traffic Monitor
		LTRS	Letter Shift
LSB	Least Significant Bit (or Byte)	LU	Logical Unit
LSB	Lower Sideband	LUA	Logical Unit Application
LSD	Line Sharing Device	LUT	Look-Up Table
LSDU	Link Service Data Unit	LUW	Logical Units of Work
LSE	Local Single-layer Embedded	LWG	LAN WorkGroup
LSE	Local System Environment	LWS	Linear Whitespace
LSEL	Link Selector	LWSP	Logical White Space
LSI	Large Scale Integration		

LWT	Listen While Talk
M	Mandatory
M	Mega-
m	Meter
MA	Maintenance and Adaptation
MA	Medium Adaptor
MAA	Major Acknowledgment
MAAP	Management and Administration Panels
MAC	Medium Access Control
MAC	Message Authentication Code
MAC	Multiplexed Analog Components
MACE	Macintosh Audio Compression and Expansion
MACF	Multiple Association Control Function
MACSTAR	Multiple Access Customer Station Rearrangement
MACU	Multidrop Auto Call Unit
MADE	Manufacturing Automation and Design Engineering
MAN	Metropolitan-Area Network
MAP	Major Point
MAP	Manufacturing Automation Protocol
MAP/TOP	Manufacturing Automation Protocol/Technical and Office Protocol

MAPDU	Management Application Protocol Data Unit
MAPI	Mail (also Messaging) Application Program Interface
MARC	Machine-Readable Cataloging
MASC	Mobitex Asynchronous Communications (Protocol)
MASE	Message Administration Service Element
MATD	Maximum Acceptable Transit Delay
MATR	Minimum Average Time Requirement
MAU	Medium Attachment Unit
MAU	Multistation Access Unit
MAW	Microsoft At Work
Mb	Megabit
MB	Megabyte
MB	Memoryless Behavior
mb/s	Megabits Per Second
MBA	MASSBUS Adapter
MBA	Master of Business Administration
Mbps	Megabits Per Second
MBps	Megabytes Per Second
MBS	Maximum Burst Size
MBZ	Must Be Zero
MBZS	Maximum Bandwidth Zero Suppression

MCA	MicroChannel Architecture	MD	Mini-Disc
MCC	Microelectronics and Computer Technology Corporation	MD	Multiple Dissemination
		MD5	Message Digest 5
MCC	Mission Control Center	MDBS	Mobile Database System
MCD	Maintenance Cell Description	MDC	Manipulation Detecting Code
MCF	Medium Access Control (MAC) Convergence Function	MDD	Multidimensional Database
		MDF	Main Distribution Frame
MCI	Media Control Interface	MDI	Multiple Document Interface
MCI	Microwave Communications Inc.	MDIS	Mobile Data Intermediate System
MCI	Multimedia Command Interface	MDN	Mobile Data Network
MCO	Multiplexer Control Option	MDR	Message Detail Recording
MCP	MAC Convergence Protocol	MDS	Mail Delivery System
MCP	Microsoft Certified Professional	MDS	Multiple Dataset System
		MDS	Multipoint Distribution Service
MCPS	Microsoft Certified Product Specialist	MDSE	Message Delivery Service Element
MCR	Minimum Cell Rate	MDTS	Modem Diagnostic and Test System
MCR	Monitor Console Routine		
MCS	Maintenance Control Subsystem	ME	Mapping Entity
		ME	Mobile Equipment
MCTD	Mean Cell Transfer Delay	MEA	Mail-Enabled Application
MCU	Mobile Control Unit	MED	Maximum Excess Delay
MCVD	Modified Chemical Vapor Deposit	MEGO	My Eyes Glaze Over
MD	Make Directory	MERS	Most Economic Route Selection
MD	Management Domain	MES	Manufacturing Execution System
MD	Mediation Device		

M-ES	Mobile End System	Mi	Mile
MESA	Manufacturing Execution System Association	MIA	Minor Acknowledgment
MF	Mediation Function	MIB	Management (also Message) Information Base
MF	Medium Frequency	MIC	Medium Interface Cable (also Connector)
MF	More Fragments		
MF	Multiple Frequency	MIC	Message Identification Code
MFA	Management Functional Areas	MIC	Message Integrity Check
MFD	Master File Directory	MICR	Magnetic Ink Character Recognition
MFJ	Modified Final Judgment		
MFM	Modified Frequency Modulation	MICS	Management Information Conformance Statement
MFOTS	Military Fiber-Optic Transmission System	MID	Message ID
		MID	Multiplexing Identifier
MFS	Macintosh File System	MIDA	Message Interchange for Distributed Application
MFS	Message Formatting Service	MIDI	Musical Instrument Digital Interface
MFT	Mixed Form Text		
MG	Motor Generators	MIF	Management Information File (or Form)
MH	Message Handling		
MH	Mobile Host	MIFF	Management Information Format File
MHD	Moving Head Disk		
MHP	Message Handling Protocol	MIL	Management Information Library
MHS	Message Handling System (or Service)	MILNET	Military Network
		MIL-STD	Military Standard
MHS-SE	Message Handling System Service Element	MIM	Management Information Model
MHTS	Message Handling Test System	MIME	Multipurpose Internet Mail Extension
MHz	Megahertz		

Min	Minute
MIN	Multipath Interconnection Network
MIN	Multiple Interaction Negotiation
MIN	Multistage Interconnection Networks
MIND	Modular Interactive Network Designer
MIO	Multiple Port Information Outlet
MIP	Minor Point
MIPS	Millions of Instructions Per Second
MIR	Maximum Information Rate
MIS	Management Information Systems
MIT	Management Information Tree
MIT	Massachusetts Institute of Technology
MITI	Ministry of International Trade and Industry
MLA	Master License Agreement
MLFA	Machine-learned Fragment Analysis
MLI	Multiple Link Interface
MLID	Multiple Link Interface Driver
MLN	Main Listed Number
MLP	Multilink Procedures

MLPP	Multilevel Precedence and Preemption
MLS	Multilevel Security
MLS	Multiple Listing Service
MLT	Multiple Logical Terminals
Mm	Millimeter
MMAC	Multimedia Access Center
MMC	Multimedia Marketing Council
MMD	Multimedia Document
MMDF	Multichannel Memorandum Distribution Facility
MMDS	Multichannel Multipoint Distribution Service
MMF	Multimode Fiber
MMFS	Manufacturing Message Format Standard
MMHS	Military Message Handling System
MMI	Man-Machine Interface
MMJ	Modified Modular Jack
MML	Man-Machine Language
MMPM/2	Multimedia Presentation Manager/2
MMS	Manufacturing Message Service
MMS	Manufacturing Message Specification (or Standard)
MMT	Multimedia Multiparty Teleconferencing
MMU	Memory Management Unit

MNCS	Multipoint Network Control System	MOSS	Maintenance and Operator Subsystem
MNDS	Multinetwork Design System	MOT	Managed Object to Test
MNP	Microcom Networking Protocol	MOT	Means of Testing
MO	Magneto-Optical	MOTAS	Member of the Appropriate Sex
MO	Managed Object	motd	Message of the Day
MOAC	Message Origin Authentication Check	MOTIS	Message-Oriented Text Interchange System
MOC	Manufacturing Outreach Center	MOTOS	Member of the Opposite Sex
MOC	Mission Operations Computer	MOTSS	Member of the Same Sex
MOCS	Managed-Object Conformance Statement	MOV	Metal Oxide Varistor
		MP	Machine Processable
MODEM	Modulator Demodulator	MP	Managing Process
MOLIS	Minority Online Information Service	MP	Mobile Professional
		MP	Modem Port
MOO	Multiuser Simulated Environment, Object-Oriented	MPAF	Midpage Allocation Field
		MPC	Multipath Channel
MOOSE	Multiuser Object-Oriented Shared Environment	MPCC	Multiprotocol Communications Controller
MOP	Maintenance (also Management) Operations Protocol	MPDT	Multipeer Data Transmission
MorF	Male or Female	MPDU	Message Protocol Data Unit
MOS	Mean Opinion Score	MPEG	Moving Pictures Experts Group
MOS	Metal Oxide Semiconductor	MPG	Multiplayer Game
MOSFET	Metal Oxide Semiconductor Field Effect Transistor	MPG	Multiple Preferred Guests
MOSPF	Multicast Open Shortest Path First Protocol	MPI	Multiple Protocol Interface
		MPL	Multi-Schedule Private Line

MPP	Massively Parallel Processing	MRPII	Manufacturing Resource Planning
MPP	Multiple-Protocol Package	MRSE	Message Retrieval Service Element
MPR	Multiport Repeater	MS	Management Services
MPR	Multiprotocol Router	MS	Message Store
MPSA	Multiprocessor Server Architecture	MS	Meta-Signaling
MPST	Memory Process Scheduling Table	Ms	Millisecond
MPT	Ministry of Posts and Telecommunications	MS	Mobile Station
		MS	More Segments
MPT	Multiport Transceiver	MSA	Metropolitan Service Area
MPTM	Multiparty Test Method	MS-AIS	Multiplex Section Alarm Indication Signal
MPTN	Multiprotocol Transport Network	MSAP	MAC Service Access Point
MPU	Multiprocessor Unix	MSAP	Management Service Access Point
MPW	Macintosh Programmer's Workbench	MSAP	Message Store Access Protocol
MPX	Multiplexer	MSAT	Mobile Satellite
MQ	Message Queue	MSAU	Multistation Access Unit
MQE	Managed Query Environment	MSB	Most Significant Bit (or Byte)
MQI	Message Queuing Interface	MSC	Mobile (Services) Switching Center
MR	Magnetoresistive		
MR	Message Retrieval	MSCP	Mass Storage Control Protocol
MRCI	Microsoft Real-time Compression Interface	MSD	Microwave Semiconductor Device
MRCS	Multirate Circuit Switching	MSDOS	Microsoft Disk Operating System
MRI	Magnetic Resonance Imaging		
MRM	Maximum Rights Mask	MSF	Measurement Summarization Function
MRO	Multiregion Operation		

MS-FERF	Multiplex Section Far End Receive Failure	MST	Multiplex Slotted and Token Ring
MSG	Message	MSU	Management Service Unit
MSHP	Maintain System History Program	MSU	Message Signal Unit
MSI	Medium Scale Integration	MSU	Microsoft University
MSL	Mirrored-Server Link	MSU	Modem-Sharing Unit
MSM	Matrix Switch Module	MSVC	Meta-Signaling Virtual Channel
MSN	Microsoft Network	MT	Measured Time
MSN	Monitoring (Cell) Sequence Number	MT	Message Transfer
MSN	Multiple Systems Networking	MT	Message Type
MSNF	Multiple Systems Networking Facility	MTA	Message Transfer Agent
MSOH	Multiplex Section Overhead	MTACP	Magnetic Tape Ancillary Control Process
MSP	Maintenance Service Provider	MTAE	Message Transfer Agent Entity
MSP	Message Security Protocol	MTAU	Metallic Test Access Unit
MSP	Mid-level Service Provider	MTBF	Mean Time Between Failures
MSS	Maritime Satellite Service	MTC	Man Tended Capability
MSS	Mass Storage Service	MTC	Manufacturing Technology Center
MSS	Metropolitan Switching System	MTCN	Minimum Throughput Class Negotiation
MSS	Mobile Satellite Service	MTL	Message Transfer Layer
MSS	Modem Substitution Switch	MTP	Message Transfer Part (also Protocol)
MSSE	Message Submission Service Element	MTR	Minimum Time Requirement
MSSSE	Message Submission and Storage Service Element	MTS	Message Telecommunications Service
MST	Minimum Spanning Tree	MTS	Message Transfer Service

MTS	Mobile Telephone Service	MVL	Major Vector Length
MTSE	Message Transfer Service Element	MVS	Multiple Virtual Storage
		MVS/TSO	Multiple Virtual Storage/Time Sharing Option
MTSL	Message Transfer Sublayer		
MTSO	Mobile Telephone Switching Office	MVS/XA	Multiple Virtual Storage/ Extended Architecture
MTTA	Multi-Tenant Telecommunications Association	MVT	Multiprogramming with Variable Number of Tasks
MTTR	Mean Time to Repair	MX	Mail Exchanger
MTU	Maximum Transmission Unit	N	Normal
MTU	Message Transfer Unit	NA	Numerical Aperture
MTX	Mobile Telephone Exchange	NAC	Network Access Controller
MUD	Multiuser Dimension (or Dungeon)	NAC	Network Applications Consortium
MUF	Maximum Usable Frequency	NACHA	National Automated Clearinghouse Association
MULTICS	Multiplexed Information and Computing Service	NACS	NetWare Asynchronous Communications Server
MUP	Multiple Uniform Naming Convention Provider	NADF	North American Directory Forum
MUS	Multiuser System		
MUSE	Multiuser Simulated Environment	NAEB	North American EDIFACT Board
MUSH	Multiuser Simulated Hallucination	NAEC	Novell Authorized Education Center
MUX	Multiplexer	NAK	Negative Acknowledgment
MVC	Multicast Virtual Circuit	NAM	Network Access Method
MVI	Major Vector Identifier	NAM	Numerical Assignment Modules
MVID	Major Vector ID		
MVIP	Multivendor Integration Protocol	NAMAS	National Measurement Accreditation Services

NAMS	Network Analysis and Management System
NAMTUG	North American MAP/TOP Users' Group
NAN	Neighborhood (also National) Area Network
NANP	North American Numbering Plan
NAPLPS	North American Presentation Level Protocol Syntax
NARM	National Association of Recording Merchandisers
NARUC	National Association of Regulatory Utilities Commission
NAS	Network Access Signaling
NAS	Network Application Support
NASA	National Aeronautics and Space Administration
NASC	Novell Authorized Service Center
NASI	NetWare Asynchronous Services Interface
NASTD	National Association of State Telecommunications Directors
NATA	National Association of Testing Authorities
NATA	North American Telecommunications Association
NATD	National Association of Telecommunication Dealers
NAU	Network Access Unit
NAU	Network Addressable Unit
NAUN	Nearest Active (or Addressable) Upstream Neighbor
NBEC	Non-Bell Exchange Carrier
NBMA	Non-Broadcast Multiple Access
NBP	Name Binding Protocol
NBS	National Bureau of Standards
NC	Network Connection
NC	Numerical Controller
NCB	Network (also Node) Control Block
NCC	National Computing Center
NCC	Network Control Center
NCCF	Network Communications Control Facility
NCEP	Network Connection Endpoint
NCF	NetWare Command File
NCIC	Network Control Interface Channel
NCL	Network Control Language
NCM	Network Connection Management
NCMS	Network Control and Management System
NCO	National Coordination Office
NCO/HPCC	National Coordination Office High Performance Computing and Communications
NCP	NetWare Core Protocol

NCP	Network Control Program (also Point)	NDM	Network Database Management
NCR	National Cash Register	NDMS	NetWare Distributed Management Services
NCR-DNA	NCR (Corp.) Distributed Network Architecture	NDN	Non-Delivery Notification
NCS	National Communications Systems	NDPS	NetWare Distributed Print Services
NCS	NetWare Connect Services	NDS	NetWare Directory Services
NCS	Network Computing (also Control) System	NDT	Net Data Throughput
NCSA	National Center for Supercomputing Applications	NDTS	Network Diagnostic and Test System
NCSA	National Computer Security Association	NE	Network Element
NCSC	National Computer Security Center	NEAP	Novell Education Academic Partner
NCSI	Network Communications Services Interface	NEBS	Network Equipment Building System
NCSL	National Computer Systems Laboratory	NEC	National Electric Code
NCT	Network Control Terminal	NEF	Network Element Function
NCTE	Network Channel Termination Equipment	NEMA	National Electrical Manufacturers Association
NCUG	National Centrex Users' Group	NEP	Noise-Equivalent Power
ND	Network Digit	NEST	Novell Embedded Systems Technology
NDD	NetWare Directory Database	NET	Network-Entity Title
NDF	NCP/EP Definition Facility	NET	Norme Européenne de Télécommunications (European Standard for Telecommunications)
NDIS	Network Driver Interface Specification		
NDL	Network Database Language	NetBEUI	NetBIOS Extended User Interface

NetBIOS	Network Basic Input/Output System	NIIT	National Information Infrastructure Testbed
NetDDE	Network Dynamic Data Exchange	NIM	Network Interface Module
		NiMH	Nickel Metal Hydride
NETID	Network ID	NIOD	Network Inward/Outward Dialing
NETUCON	NetWare Users' Conference		
NEWS	Network Error Warning System	NIS	Names Information Socket
		NIS	Network Information Services
NEXT	Near End Crosstalk or Near End Differential Crosstalk	N-ISDN	Narrowband ISDN
		NISO	National Information Standards Association
NF	Not Finished		
NFF	No Form Feed	NIST	National Institute of Standards and Technology
NFS	Network File System		
NH	Non-busy Hour	NIST-APP	National Institute of Standards and Technology-Application Portability Profile
NHOB	Non-specific Hierarchical Operational Binding		
NHRP	Next Hop Resolution Protocol	NIU	Network Interface Unit
NI	Network Interface	NIUF	National ISDN Users' Forum
NIB	Node Identification (or Initialization) Block	NIUF	North American ISDN Users' Forum
NIC	Network Information Center	NJE	Network Job Entry
NIC	Network Interface Card	NL	Network Layer
NICE	Network Information and Control Exchange	NLDM	Network Logical Data Manager
NID	Network Interface Device	NLM	NetWare Loadable Module
NID	Next ID	NLP	NetWare Lite Protocol
NIF	Network Information File	NLS	National Language Support
NII	National Information Infrastructure	NLSP	NetWare Link Service Protocol
		Nm	Nanometer

NM	Network Management
NMA	NetWare Management Agent (also Architecture)
NMC	Network Management Center
NMCC	Network Management Control Center
NME	Network Management Entity
NMF	Network Management Forum
NMI	Non-Maskable Interrupt
NMP	Network Management Protocol
NMR	NetWare Management Responder
NMS	Network Management System (or Station)
NMSIG	Network Management Special Interest Group
NMSL/C	NetWare Management Server Link/Cable Option
NMSL/F	NetWare Management Server Link/Fiber Option
NMT	Nordic Mobile Telephone
NMTS	National Message Transfer System
NMVT	Network Management Vector Transport
NN	Negative Notification
NN	Network Node
nn	No News
NND	National Number Dialing

NNI	Netherlands Normatization Institute
NNI	Network-Node Interface
NNI	Network-to-Network Interface
NNS	NetWare Name Service
NNT	NetView-NetView Task
NNTP	Network News Transfer Protocol
NNTPD	Network News Transfer Protocol Daemon
NOC	Network Operations Center
NOF	Node Operator Facility
NOI	Notice of Inquiry
NOOP	Network OSI Operations
NOS	Network Operating System
Np	Neper
NP	Network Provider (also Performance)
NP	New Project
NPA	NetWare Peripheral Architecture
NPA	Network Professional Association
NPA	Numbering Plan Area
NPAI	Network Protocol Address Information
NPAP	Network Printing Alliance Protocol
NPC	Network Parameter Control

NPC	North Pacific Cable		NS	Network Service
NPCI	Network Protocol Control Information		NS	Network Signaling
			NS	Number of Sends
NPDA	Network Problem Determination Application		NSA	National Security Agency
NPDU	Network Protocol Data Unit		NSA	Next Station Addressing
NPF	Network Partitioning Facility		NSAI	National Standards Authority of Ireland
NPL	National Physical Laboratory		NSAP	Network Service Access Point
NPM	NetView Performance Monitor		NSDU	Network Layer Service Data Unit
NPRM	Notice of Proposed Rule Making		NSE	Network Support Encyclopedia
NPSI	Network Packet Switch Interface		NSEL	Network Selector
NPTN	National Public Telecommunications (or Telecomputing) Network		NSEP	National Security and Emergency Preparedness
			NSF	National Science Foundation
NR	Negative Response		NSF	Network Search Function
NR	Number of Receives		NSFnet	National Science Foundation Network
NREN	National Research and Education Network		NSI	NASA Science Internet
NRL	Naval Research Laboratory		NSM	NetWare Services Manager
NRM	Network Resource Management		NSP	NATO Standardized Profile
NRM	Normal Response Mode		NSP	NetWare Lite Sideband Protocol
NRS	Name Registration Scheme		NSP	Network Service Part (SS7)
NRZ	Non-Return to Zero		NSP	Network Service Provider
NRZI	Non-Return to Zero, Inverted		NSP	Network Services Protocol
NRZ-L	Non-Return to Zero-Level		NSPC	National Sound Program Center
Ns	Nanosecond		NSR	Non-Source Routed

NSS	Nodal Switching System	NTS	NetWare Technical Support
NSSA	Not So Stubby Area	NTS	Network Tracking System
NSSDU	Normal Session Service Data Unit	NTSA	Networking Technical Support Alliance
NSSII	Network Supervisory System I	NTSC	National Television Systems Committee
NSSR	Non-Specific Subordinate Reference	NTT	Nippon Telegraph and Telephone
NT	Network Termination	NTU	Network Terminating Unit
NT	New Technology	NUA	Network Users' Association
NT1	Network Termination 1	NUC	NetWare Unix Client
NT12	Network Termination 1+2	NUCFS	NetWare UNIX Client File System
NT2	Network Termination 2		
NTD	Network Tools for Design	NUI	NetWare Users International
NTFS	New Technology (NT) File System	NUI	Network User Identification
		NVE	Network-Visible Entity
NTI	Novell Technology Institute	NVLAP	National Voluntary Laboratory Accreditation Program
NTIA	National Telecommunication and Information Administration	NVOD	Near Realtime Voice on Demand
NTIA/USA	National Telecommunication and Information Administration/USA	NVP	Network Voice Protocol
		NVP	Nominal Velocity of Propagation
NTIS	National Technical Information Service	NVRAM	Non-Volatile Random Access Memory
NTM	Network Traffic Management	NVT	Novell (also Network) Virtual Terminal
NTN	Network Terminal Number		
NTO	Network Terminal Option	NVTS	Network Virtual Terminal Service
NTP	Network Time Protocol		
NTPF	Number of Terminals Per Failure	NWI	New Work Item

NWS	National Weather Service	OC1	Optical Carrier, Level 1
NYSERNet	New York State Education and Research Network	OCA	Open Communication Architecture
O	Optional	OCB	Out-going Calls Barred
O	Organization	OCC	Other Charges or Credits
O&M	Operation and Maintenance	OCC	Other Common Carriers
O/R	Originator/Recipient	OCE	Open Collaborative Environment
OA	Office Automation		
OA	Operator Assistance	OC-i	Optical Carrier, Level i
OAAC	Objects and Attributes for Access Control	OCLC	Online Computer Learning (also Library) Center
OAC	Operational Amplifier Characteristics	OCR	Optical Character Recognition
		OCS	Operator Console Services
OAI	Open Application Interface	OCX	OLE Custom Control
OAM	Operation and Maintenance	ODA	Open (also Office) Document Architecture
OAM	Operations, Administration, and Maintenance (Functions)		
		ODBC	Open Database Connectivity
OAM&P	Operations, Administration, Maintenance, and Provisioning	ODBMS	Object DBMS
		ODD	Operator Distance Dialing
OAMC	Operation and Maintenance Center	ODETTE	Organization for Data Exchange by Teletransmission in Europe
OAMC	Operation, Administration, and Maintenance Center		
		ODI	Open Data-link Interface
OASIS	Online Access to the Standards Information Service	ODIF	Office Document Interchange Format
OBEX	Object Exchange	ODINSUP	Open Data-link Interface/ Network Driver Interface Specification Support
OBI	Online Book Initiative		
OC	Optical Carrier		
OC	Output Controller	ODK	Office Developers Kit
		ODL	Object Definition Language

ODMA	Open Document Management API	OLAP	Online Analytical Processing
ODN	Optical Distribution Network	OLE	Object Linking and Embedding
ODP	Open Distributed Processing	OLI	Originating Line Information
ODS	Open Data Services	OLRT	Online Real Time
OECD	Organization for Economic Cooperation and Development	OLT	Optical Line Termination
		OLTP	Online Transaction Processing
OEDIPE	OSI EDI for Energy Providers	OLU	Originating Logical Unit
OEM	Original Equipment Manufacturer	OM	Object Management
		OM	Optical Modulator
OFB	Output Feedback	OMA	Object Management Architecture
OFBNLF	Output Feedback with a Nonlinear Function	OMAP	Operations, Management, and Administration Part (SS7)
OFNP	Optical Fiber, Non-conductive Plenum	OMC	Operations and Maintenance Center
OFNR	Optical Fiber, Non-conductive Riser	OMF	Object Management Function
OFTEL	Office of Telecommunications	OMG	Object Management Group
OFTP	ODETTE File Transfer Protocol	OMI	Open Messaging Interface
		ONA	Open Network Architecture
OGT	Outgoing Trunk	ONC	Open Network Computing
OH	Off Hook	ONI	Operator Number Identification
OHQ	Off-Hook Queue		
Oic	Oh, I See	ONITA	Of No Interest to Anybody
OID	Object Identifier	ONMS	Open Network Management System
OIM	Optical Index Modulation		
OIM	OSI Internet Management	ONN	Open Network Node
OIT	Object Identifier Tree	ONP	Open Network Provision
OIW	OSI Implementers Workshop	ONU	Optical Network Unit

OO	Over and Out	OS/2	Operating System/2
OOBE	Out-of-Box Experience	OS/400	Operating System/400 (for AS/400)
OOD	Object-Oriented Design		
OODB	Object-Oriented Database	OSA	Open Scripting Architecture
OOF	Out of Frame	OSAK	OSI Application Kernel
OOK	On-Off Keying	OSC	Operating System Control
OOP	Object-Oriented Programming	OSE	Open Systems Environment
OOS	Out of Service	OSF	Open Software Foundation
OOUI	Object-Oriented User Interface	OSF	Operations Systems Function
OPCR	Original Program Clock Reference	OSI	Open Systems Interconnection
		OSI/CS	OSI Communications Subsystem
OPDU	Operation Protocol Data Unit	OSID	Origination Signaling Identifier
OPEN	Open Protocol Enhanced Network	OSIE	OSI Environment
OPM	Organization and Procedures Manual	OSILL	Open System Interconnection, Lower Layers
OPNDST	Open Destination	OSINet	OSI Network
OPS	Off Premises Station	OSIRM	Open Systems Interconnection Reference Model
OPX	Off Premises Extension		
OQL	Object Query Language	OSIUL	Open System Interconnection, Upper Layers
O-QPSK	Offset Quadrature Phase Shift Keying	OSME	Open Systems Message Exchange
ORAP	O/R Address Prefix	OSNS	Open Systems Network Services
ORB	Object Request Broker		
O-ROM	Optical Read-Only Memory	OSPF	Open Shortest Path First
ORT	Overload Recovery Time	OSS	Operational Support System
ORWG	Open Routing Working Group	OSSWG	Office System Standards Work Group
OS	Operating System		

OSTC	Open Systems Testing Consortium	P3	Protocol 3 (Submission and Delivery Protocol in X.400)
OSTP	Office of Science and Technology Policy	P5	Protocol 5 (Teletext Access Protocol in X.400)
OSWS	Operating System Workstation	P7	Protocol 7 (Message Store Access Protocol in X.400)
OTA	Office of Technology Assessment	PA	Prearbitrated
OTDR	Optical Time Domain Reflectometer	PA	Public Address
		PAA	Peer Access Approval
OTL	OSI Testing Liaison	PABX	Private Automatic Branch Exchange
Otoh	On the Other Hand		
OTQ	Out-going Trunk Queuing	PAC	Privilege Attribute Certificate
Otth	On the Third Hand	PACCEPT	Presentation Accept
OU	Organizational Unit	PACS	Picture Archiving and Communication System
OUI	Organizational Unit Identifier		
OURS	Open User Recommended Solution	PAD	Packet Assembler/ Disassembler
		PAE	Peer Access Enforcement
OVD	Optical Video Disk	PAEB	Pan American EDIFACT Board
OW/AF	Object Windows for AppWare Foundation	PAF	Prearbitrated Function
OWF	One-Way Function	PAGODA	Profile Alignment Group for Office Document Architecture
OWF	Optimum Working Frequency		
OWRTS	Open-Wire Radio Transmission System	PAI	Protocol Address Information
		PAL	Phase Alternate Line
OWTL	Open-Wire Transmission Line	PAM	Pulse Amplitude Modulation
P/F	Poll/Final Bit	PAN	Peripheral Area Network
P1	Protocol 1 (Message Transfer Function in X.400)	PANS	Pretty Amazing New Stuff
		PAP	Printer Access Protocol
P2	Protocol 2 (Interpersonal Messaging in X.400)	PAR	Peak-to-Average Ratio

PAR	Positive Acknowledgment with Retransmission	PCI	Peripheral Component Interface
PARADISE	Piloting a Researcher's Directory Service in Europe	PCI	Presentation Context Identifier
PARC	Palo Alto Research Center	PCI	Program (or Protocol) Control Information
PATG	Procedures and Awareness Task Group	PCI	Program-Controlled Interruption
PATS	Parameterized Abstract Test Suite	PCI	Programmable Communication Interface
PAX	Private Automatic Exchange	PCM	Pulse Code Modulation
PBX	Private Branch Exchange	PCMCIA	Personal Computer Memory Card International Association
PC	Path Control	PCN	Personal Communications Network
PC	Personal Computer		
PC	Priority Control	PCO	Point of Control and Observation
PC	Protocol Count		
PCA	Policy Certification Authority	PCONNECT	Presentation Connect
PCA	Program Calibration Area	PCPM	Programmable Call Progress Monitoring
PCAMI	Personal Computing Asset Management Institute		
		PCR	Peak Cell Rate
PCB	Printed Circuit Board	PCR	Program Clock Reference
PCCU	Physical Communications Control Unit	PCS	Personal Communications Services
PCE	Presentation Connection Endpoint	PCS	Plastic Clad Silica
		PCSA	Personal Computer System Architecture
PCEI	Presentation Connection Endpoint Identifier		
PCEO	Personal Computer Enhancement Operation	PCSN	Private Circuit-Switching Network
PCEP	Presentation Connection Endpoint	PCTE	Portable Common Tools Environment

PCTR	Protocol Conformance Test Report		PDM	Pulse Duration Modulation
PCU	Packet Control Unit		PDN	Packet (also Public) Data Network
PCVS	Point-to-Point Switched Virtual Connection		PDN	Passive Distribution Network
PD	Packetization Delay		PDP	Parallel Data Processor
PD	Physical Delivery		PDP	Professional Developer's Program
PD	Public Domain		PDP	Programmable Data Processor
PDA	Personal Digital (also Data) Assistant		PDS	Parallel Data Structure
			PDS	Phase Distortion Synthesis
PDAD	Proposed Draft Addendum		PDS	Physical Delivery Service
PDAM	Proposed Draft Amendment		PDS	Premises Distribution System
PDAU	Physical Delivery Access Unit		PDS	Processor Direct Slot
PDB	Process Data Block		PDTR	Proposed Draft Technical Report
PDC	Packet Data Channel			
PDD	Physical Device Driver		PDU	Packet (or Payload or Protocol) Data Unit
PDES	Product Data Exchange Standard		PDV	Presentation Data Value
PDF	Package (also Printer) Definition File		PEB	PCM Expansion Bus
			PEDI	Protocol for Electronic Data Interchange
PDF	Portable Document Format			
PDF	Program Development Facility		PELS	Picture Elements
PDH	Plesiochronous Digital Hierarchy		PEM	Privacy Enhanced Mail
			PEP	Packet Exchange Protocol
PDIAL	Public Dial-up Internet Access List		PEP	Platform Environment Profile
			PEPY	Presentation Element Parser, YACC
PDIF	Product Definition Interchange Format			
			PER	Packed Encoding Rules
PDISP	Proposed Draft International Standardized Profile		PER	Program Event Recording

PERL	Practical Extraction and Report Language	PI	Peripherals Interface
PES	Packetized Elementary Stream	PI	Protocol Identification
PES	Proposed Encryption Standard	PIA	Peripheral Interface Adapter
PETS	Parameterized Executable Test Suite	PIC	Personal Identification Code
PFD	Privacy Forum Digest	PIC	Personal Intelligent Communicators
PFEP	Programmable Front-End Processor	PIC	Primary Interexchange Carrier
PFM	Pulse Frequency Modulation	PIC	Programmable Interrupt Controller
PGF	Presentation Graphics Feature	PICS	Protocol Implementation Conformance Statement
PGI	Parameter Group Identifier	PICT	Picture
PGP	Pretty Good Privacy	PID	Packet (also Protocol) Identifier
PH	Packet Handler (or Handling)	PID	Personal ID
PH	Packet Header	PIDX	Petroleum Industry Data Exchange
PhC	Physical-layer Connection	PIF	Phase Interface Fading
PhCEP	Physical Connection Endpoint	PIF	Program Information File
PHIGS	Programmer Hierarchical Interactive Graphics System	PIFT	Protocol Interbank File Transfer
PhL	Physical Layer	PIM	Personal Information Manager
PhPDU	Physical-layer Protocol Data Unit	PIM	Port Interface Module
PhS	Physical-layer Service	PIM	Protocol-Independent Multicast
Ph-SAP	Physical-layer Service Access Point	PIN	Personal Identification Number
PhSDU	Physical-layer Protocol Data Unit	PIN	Positive Intrinsic Negative Photodiode
PHY	Physical Layer	PIN	Procedure Interrupt Negative
PI	Parameter Identifier		

Pine	Pine Is Not Elm	PLMN	Public Land Mobile Network
Ping	Packet Internet Groper	PL-OAM	Physical Layer Operation and Maintenance (Cell)
PIP	P Internet Protocol		
PIP	Program Initialization Parameters	plotka	Press Lots of Keys to Abort
		PLP	Packet-Layer Protocol (or Procedure)
PIR	Protocol Independent Routing		
PIT	Programmable Interrupt Timer	PLS	Physical Layer Signaling
pita	Pain in the Arse	PLS	Primary Link Station
PITR	Product Inter-operation Test Report	PLSAP	Physical Layer Service Access Point
PIU	Path Information Unit	PLU	Primary Logical Unit
PIXEL	Picture Element	PLV	Production Level Video
PIXIT	Protocol Implementation Extra Information for Testing	PM	Performance Management
		PM	Phase Modulation
PKCS	Public Key Cryptography System (or Standard)	PM	Physical Medium
		PM	Protocol Machine
PKE	Public Key Encryption	PMA	Performance Measurement Analysis
PKP	Public Key Partners		
PL	Physical Layer	PMA	Physical Medium Attachment
PL	Presentation Layer	PMA	Program Memory Area
PL	Private Line	PMAC	Packet Media Access Controller
PLC	Programmable Logic Controller	PMBX	Private Manual Branch Exchange
PLCP	Physical Layer Convergence Procedure (or Protocol)		
		PMD	Physical Media Dependent
PLD	Phase Lock Demodulator	PML	Permitted Maximum Level
PLIP	Parallel Line Internet Protocol	PMMU	Paged Memory Management Unit
PLK	Primary Link		
PLL	Phase-Locked Loop	PMN	Performance Monitoring

PMS	Public Message Service	POS	Passive Optical Splitter
PMSP	Preliminary Message Security Protocol	POS	Point of Sale
		POSI	Promoting OSI
PMT	Packet-Mode Terminal	POSIX	Portable Operating System Interface Extension
PMT	Photo Multiplier Tube		
PMTU	Path Maximum Transmission Unit	POT	Point of Termination
		POTS	Plain Old Telephone Service
PMX	Packet Multiplexer	POWER	Performance Optimization with Enhanced RISC
PMX	Private Message Exchange		
PN	Personal Name	PPC	Program-to-Program Communication
PN	Positive Notification		
PNA	Private Network Adapter	PPCI	Presentation Protocol Control Information
PNC	Personal Number Calling		
PND	Present Next Digit	PPDU	Presentation Protocol Data Unit
PNIC	Private Network Identification Code		
		PPL	Plain Position Indicator
PNM	Physical Network Management	PPM	Pages Per Minute (or Month)
P-NNI	Private Network-to-Network Interface	PPM	Presentation Protocol Machine
		PPM	Principal Period Maintenance
POAC	Probe Origin Authentication Check	PPM	Pulse Position Modulation
		PPN	Private Packet Network
POH	Path Overhead	PPO	Primary Program Operator
POI	Path Overhead Indicator	PPP	Point to Point Protocol
POI	Program Operator Interface	PPPI	Production Planning Process Industries
PON	Passive Optical Network		
POP	Point of Presence	PPS	Packets (or Pulses) Per Second
POP	Post Office Protocol	PPSDN	Public Packet-Switched Data Network
POP3	Post Office Protocol, Version 3		

PPSN	Public Packet Switched Network	PS	PostScript
		PS	Presentation Service
PPTM	Protocol Profile Testing Methodology	PS	Print Server
		PS	Proposed Standard
PR	Prepare	PS/2	Personal System 2
PR/SM	Processor Resource/Systems Manager	PS/VP	Personal System/Value Point
PRA	Parabolic Reflector Antenna	PSAP	Presentation Service Access Point
PRA	Primary Rate Access		
PRAM	Parameter RAM	PSAP	Public Safety (or Service) Answering Point
PRB	Packet Receive Buffer	PSC	Print Server Control
PRB	Procedures Review Board	PSC	Protection Switching Circuit
PRDMD	Private Directory-Management Domain	PSC	Public Service Commission
PREFUSE	Presentation Refuse	PSD	Power Spectral Density
PRG	Purge	PSD	Protection Switching Duration
PRI	Primary Rate Interface	PSDN	Packet-Switched Data Network
PRID	Protocol Identifier	PSDN	Public Switched Data Network
PRM	Protocol Reference Model	PSDU	Presentation Service Data Unit
PRMD	Private Mail Domain	PSE	Packet Switching Exchange
PRMD	Private Management Domain	PSE	Power Series Expansion
PRML	Partial-Response Maximum-Likelihood (Technology)	PSEL	Presentation Selector
		PSH	Push (Flag)
PROFS	Professional Office System	PSI	Packet Switching Interface
P-ROM	Partial Read-Only Memory	PSI	Performance Summary Interval
PROM	Programmable Read-Only Memory	PSI	Process to Support Interoperability
PRTM	Printing Response Time Monitor	PSI	Program-Specific Information
		PSID	Product-Set Identification

PSK	Phase Shift Keying	PTNX	Private Telecommunications Network Exchange
PSM	Phase Shift Modulation	PTP	Point-To-Point
PSN	Packet Switched Network (or Node)	PTR	Pointer
PSN	Packet Switching Node	PTS	Presentation Time Stamp
PSN	Private Switching Network	PTS	Profile Test Specification
PSP	Presentation Services Process	PTT	Post, Telephone, and Telegraph
PSPDN	Packet Switched Public Data Network	PTTXAU	Public Teletex Access Unit
PSRG	Privacy and Security Research Group	PTXAU	Public Telex Access Unit
		PU	Physical Unit
PSTN	Public Switched Telephone Network	PU	Presentation Unit
		PUC	Public Utility Commission
PSW	Program Status Word	PUCP	Physical Unit Control Point
PT	Pass Through	PUMS	Physical Unit Management Service
PT	Payload Type		
PT	Please Token	PUT	Program Update Tape
PTAN	Performance Testing Alliance for Networks	PV	Parameter Value
		PVC	Polyvinyl Chloride
PTC	Public Telephone Companies	PVC	Private (or Permanent) Virtual Circuit
PTE	Path Terminating Entity		
PTF	Program Temporary Fix	PVCC	Permanent Virtual Channel Connection
PTI	Payload Type Identifier		
PTLXAU	Public Telex Access Unit	PVD	Point of Video Delivery
PTM	Packet Transfer Mode	PVN	Private Virtual Network
PTM	Pulse Time Modulation	PVPC	Permanent Virtual Path Connection
PTN	Personal Telecommunications Number		
		PVT	Permanent Virtual Terminal
PTN	Public Telephone Network	PWGSC	Public Works and Government Services Canada

PWL	Power Indicator
PWM	Pulse Width Modulation
PWS	Programmable Workstation
Q	Queue
QA	Queue Arbitrated
QAF	Queued Arbitrated Function
QAM	Quadrature Amplitude Modulation
QBE	Query by Example
QC	Quiesce Complete
QD	Queuing Delay
qdu	Quantization Distortion Unit
QEC	Quiesce at End of Chain
QFA	Quick File Access
QIC	Quarter-Inch Cartridge
QLLC	Qualified Link Level Control
QLLC	Qualified Logical Link Control
QMF	Query Management Facility
QoS	Quality of Service
qotd	Quote of the Day
QPSK	Quadrature Phase Shift Keying
QPSX	Queued Packet and Synchronous Circuit Exchange
QPW	Quattro Pro for Windows
QR	Quick Response
QTAM	Queued Telecommunications Access Method

QWEST	Quantum-Well Envelope State Transition
QWL	Quantum-Well Laser
R	Reminder
RA	Rate Adapter
RA	Read Audit
RA	Recognition Arrangement
RA	Registration Authority
RA0	Rate Adapter 0
RA1	Rate Adapter 1
RA2	Rate Adapter 2
RAB	Record Access Block
RACE	Research and Development of Advanced Communication in Europe
RACF	Resource Access Control Facility
RAD	Rapid Application Development
RADAR	Radio Detection and Ranging
RAG	Registration and Advisory Group
RAI	Remote Alarm Indicator
RAID	Redundant Array of Inexpensive Disks
RAM	Random-Access Memory
RARC	Regional Administrative Conference

RARE	Réseaux Associes Pour la Récherche Européenne (Associated Network for European Research)	RDF	Rate Decrease Factor
		RDI	Remote Defect Identification (or Indication)
RARP	Reverse Address Resolution Protocol	RDI	Restricted Digital Information
RAS	Remote Access Services	RDL-SQL	Relational Database Language-Structured Query Language
RBHC	Regional Bell Holding Company	RDM	Remote Document Management
RBOC	Regional Bell Operating Company	RDN	Relative Distinguished Name
		RDP	Reliable Data Protocol
RBS	Robbed Bit Signaling	RDS	Remote Data Scope
RC	Routing Control	RDT	Recall Dial Tone
RCAC	Remote Computer Access Communications Service	RDT	Referenced Data Transfer
		RDT	Resource Definition Table
RCD	Receiver-Carrier Detector	RE	Reference Equivalent
RCF	Remote Call Forwarding	RE	Routing Element
RCS	Resource Constructor Set	REC	RARE Executive Committee
RCV	Receiver	RECFMS	Record Formatted Maintenance Statistics
RD	Receive Data		
RD	Remove Directory	REJ	Reject
RD	Request a Disconnect	REL	Release Message
RD	Route Descriptor	REM	Ring Error Monitor
RD	Routing Domain	REMF	Reverse Electromagnetic Force
RDA	Remote Database (also Document) Access	REN	Ringer Equivalence Number
		REQ	Request
RDAU	Remote Data Access Unit	RES	Reserved
RDBMS	Relational (also Remote) Database Management System	RESP	Response
RDC	Remote Data Concentrator	RESYNC	Resynchronization

RET	Resolution Enhancement Technology		RI	Ring Indication
RETLA	Really Extended Three Letter Acronym		RI	Routing Indicator (or Information)
REXX	Restructured Extended Executor		RIB	Routing Information Base
RF	Radio Frequency		RIF	Routing Information Field
RFC	Radio Frequency Choke		RII	Route Information Indicator
RFC	Request for Comments		RIM	Request Initialization Mode
RFD	Regional Frequency Divider		RIP	Router (or Routing) Information Protocol
RFD	Request for Discussion		RIPE	Réseaux IP Européene
RFI	Radio Frequency Interference		RIPEM	Riordan's Privacy Enhanced Mail
RFI	Request for Information		RISC	Reduced Instruction Set Computing
RFP	Request for Proposal		RISE	Retrieval and Interchange of Standards in Europe
RFQ	Request for Quotation		RJ	Registered Jack
RFS	Remote File Server (or System)		RJ	Reject
RFT	Revisable Format Text		RJE	Remote Job Entry
RG	Radio Government		RL	Real Life
RG	Rapporteur Group		RLC	Release Complete
RG	Regenerator		RLCM	Remote Line Concentrating Module
RGB	Red Green Blue		RLIN	Research Libraries Information Network
RGO	Royal Greenwich Observatory			
RH	Request (or Response) Header		RLL	Run-Length Limited
RHOB	Relevant Hierarchical Operational Binding		RLM	Remote Line Module
RI	Reference Implementation		RLSD	Received Line Signal Detector
RI	Rename Inhibit		RM	Reference Model
RI	Ring In			

RM	Resource Manager (or Management)	ROAC	Report Origin Authentication Check
RMATS	Remote Maintenance and Testing System	ROAD	Routing and Addressing (Group)
RMDM	Reference Model of Data Management	RODM	Resource Object Data Manager
RMF	Remote Management Facility	ROER	Remote Operations Error
RMHS	Remote Message Handling Service	rofl	Rolling on the Floor, Laughing
		ROH	Receiver Off-Hook
RM-ODP	Reference Model for Open Distributed Processing	ROI	Return on Investment
RMON	Remote Network Monitoring	ROIV	Remote Operations Invoke
RMON-MIB	Remote Network Monitoring Management Information Base	ROLC	Routing Over Large Clouds
		ROM	Read-Only Memory
RMS	Record Management Services	ROPM	Remote Operations Protocol Machine
RMS	Repetitive Motion Syndrome		
RMS	Root Mean Square	RORE	Remote Operations Return Error
RMT	Ring Management	RORJ	Remote Operations Reject
rn	Read News	RORS	Remote Operations Response
RN	Receipt Notification	ROS	Read-Only Store
RN	Reference Noise	ROS	Remote Operations Service
RNAS	Request Network Address Segment	ROSE	Remote Operations Service Element
RNE	Réseau National d'Essai (National Network for Testing)	ROTFL	Rolling on the Floor Laughing
RNR	Receiver Not Ready	ROTL	Remote Office Test Line
RO	Receive Only	RPC	Registered Protective Circuitry
RO	Remote Operations	RPC	Remote Procedure Call
RO	Ring Out	RPE	Remote Peripheral Equipment
		RPG	Remote Password Generator

RPG	Report Program Generator	RSCS	Remote Spooling and Control Subsystem
RPL	Remote Procedure (or Program) Load	RSCV	Route Selection Control Vector
RPL	Request Parameter List	RSE	Remote Single-layer Embedded
RPM	Revolutions Per Minute	RSF	Remote Support Facility
RPOA	Recognized Private (or Public) Operating Agency	RSI	Repetitive Stress Injury
		RSL	Received Signal Level
RPQ	Request for Price Quotation	RSN	Real Soon Now
RPS	Ring Parameter Service	RSO	Regional Standards Organization
RR	Receive Ready		
RRIP	Rock Ridge Interchange Protocol (Specifications)	RSOH	Regenerator Section Overhead
		RSP	Response
RRISI	Realtors Regional Information System Inc.	RS-PCM	Resynthesized Pulse Code Modulation
RRQ	Read Request	RS-PPDU	Resynchronize Presentation Protocol Data Unit
RRT	Reverse Recovery Time		
RS	Recommended Standard	RSPX	Remote Sequenced Packet Exchange
RS	Relay System		
RS	Remote Single-layer	RSS	Route Selection Services
RS	Resume Session	RST	Reset Flag
RS	Ring Station	RSU	Remote Switching Unit
RS-#	Recommended Standard #	RSVP	(Resource) Reservation Protocol
RSA	Resume Acknowledgment		
RSA	Rivest, Shamir, Adleman	RSX	Real-time Resource Sharing Executive
RSA-PPDU	Resynchronize Acknowledge Presentation Protocol Data Unit	RT	Reliable Transfer
		RT	Report
RSC	Remote Switching Center	RT	Routing Table
		RT	Routing Type

RTAB	Reliable Transfer Abort
RTBM	Read the Bloody Manual
RTC	RARE Technical Committee
RTDS	Real Time Data System
RTEL	Reverse Telnet
RTF	Rich Text Format
RTFAQ	Read the Frequently Asked Questions
RTFM	Read the FLWO (Four-Letter Word Omitted) Manual
RTM	Read the Manual
RTM	Read the Monitor
RTMP	Routing Table Maintenance Protocol
RTNR	Ringing Tone No Reply
RTOAC	Reliable Transfer Open Accept
RTORJ	Reliable Transfer Open Reject
RTORQ	Reliable Transfer Open Request
RTPM	Reliable Transfer Protocol Machine
RTR	Ready to Receive
RTS	Reliable Transfer Service
RTS	Request to Send
RTS	Residual Time Stamp
RTSE	Reliable Transfer Service Element
RTT	Round-Trip Time

RTTP	Reliable Transfer Token Response
RU	Remote Unit
RU	Request (or Response) Unit
RUA	Remote User Agent
RUP	Routing Update Protocol
RUIP	Remote User Information Program
RVI	Reverse Interrupt
RW	Read-Write
RWCC	Regional Workshop Coordinating Committee
RZ	Return to Zero
RZI	Return to Zero, Inverted
S	Second
S	Shareable
SA	Sequenced Application
SA	Source Address
SA	Study Administration
SA	Subarea
SAA	Specific Administrative Area
SAA	Standards Association of Australia
SAA	Systems Application Architecture
SAAL	Signaling ATM Adaptation Layer
SAB	Subnetwork-Access Boundary

SABM	Set Asynchronous Balanced Mode
SABME	Set Asynchronous Balanced Mode Extended
SABRE	Semi-Automatic Business Research Environment
SAC	Simplified Access Control
SAC	Single-Attachment Concentrator
SACF	Single Association Control Function
SACK	Selective Acknowledgment
SAF	Single Association Control Function (SACF) Auxiliary Facility
SAF	Subnetwork Access Facility
SAFENET	Survivable Adaptable Fiber-optic Embedded Network
SAG	SQL (Structured Query Language) Access Group
SAGE	Semi-Automatic Ground Environment
SAK	Selective Acknowledgment
SALI	Source Address Length Indicator
SALMON	SNA Application Monitor
SAMBE	Set Asynchronous Mode Balanced Extended
SAMMS	Standard Automated Material Management System
SAO	Single Association Object

SAP	Service Access Point
SAP	Service Advertising Protocol
SAPI	Service Access Point Identifier
SAR	Segmentation and Reassembly
SARF	Security Alarm Reporting Function
SARM	Set Asynchronous Response Mode
SAS	Single-Attachment Station
SAS	Statistically Assigned Sockets
SAS	SWITCH Access System
SASE	Special Application Service Element
SASFE	SEF/AIS Alarm Signal, Far End
SASO	Saudi Arabian Standards Organization
SATAN	Security Analysis Tool for Auditing Networks
SATF	Security Audit Trail Function
SATF	Shared-Access Transfer Facility
SATS	Selected Abstract Test Suite
SAW	Surface Acoustic Wave
SBA	Set Buffer Address
SBC	System Broadcast Channel
SBCS	Single-Byte Character Set
SBI	Stop Bracket Initiation
SBK	System Builder's Kit
SBS	Satellite Business Systems

SBT	System Backup Tape Drive	SCM	Session Control (or Connection) Manager
SC	Session Connection (or Control)	SCO	Santa Cruz Operation
SC	Subcommittee	SCP	Service (or System) Control Point
SC	Subscriber Connector		
SCA	Short Code Address	SCPC	Single Channel Per Channel
SCA	Subsidiary Communication Authorization	SCR	Secure Conversion
		SCR	Silicon Control Rectifiers
SCA	Systems Communication Architecture	SCR	Sustainable Cell Rate
SCADA	Supervisory Control and Data Acquisition	SCS	Satellite Communications Systems
SCAI	Switch to Computer Application Interface	SCS	Silicon Controlled Switches
		SCS	SNA Character String
SCB	Session Control Block	SCS	SWITCH Central System
SCC	Satellite Communications Control	SCS	System Communication Services
SCC	Specialized Common Carrier	SCS	System Conformance Statement
SCC	Standards Council of Canada	SCSA	Signal Computing System Architecture
SCCP	Signaling Connection Control Part	SCSI	Small Computer System Interface
SCE	System Control Element		
SCEF	Service Creation Environment Function	SCTO	Soft Carrier Turn-Off
		SCTR	System Conformance Test Report
SCEP	Session Connection Endpoint		
SCF	Service Control Function	SCUSA	Standards Council of the USA
SCFM	Sub-Carrier Frequency Modulation	SD	Start Delimiter
		SDA	Security Domain Authority
SCIF	Single-Console Image Facility	SDA	Swappable Data Area
SCL	Switch to Computer Link		

SDAP	Standard Document Application Profile	SDN	Software Defined Network
SDD	Software Description Database	SDNS	Secure Data Network System
SDDI	Shielded Data Distributed Interface	SDO	Standards Development Organization
S-DDP	Short Datagram Delivery Protocol	SDRP	Source Demand Routing Protocol
SDE	Submission and Delivery Entity	SDSAF	Switched Digital Services Applications Forum
SDF	Screen Definition Facility	SDSE	Shadowed Directory Service Area (DSA) Specific Entry
SDF	Service Data Function	SDT	Start Data Traffic
SDG	Software Development Group	SDT	Structured Data Transfer
SDH	Synchronous Digital Hierarchy	SDU	Service Data Unit
SDI	Supplier Declaration of Inter-operation	SE	Session Entity
SDIF	SGML Document Interchange Format	SE	Sweden
		SE	Switching Element
SDIF	Standard Document Interchange Format	SEA	SoftSolutions Enterprise Administrator
SDK	Software Developer's Kit	SEAL	Simple and Efficient Adaptation Layer
SDL	Specification and Description Language	Sec	Second
SDL	System Description Language	SECAM	Systeme En Couleur Avec Memoire
SDL/GR	Specification and Description Language/Graphical Representation	SEF	Source Explicit Forwarding
		SEF	Standard Exchange Format
SDL/PR	Specification and Description Language/Phrase Representation	SEF/AIS	Severely Errored Framing/ Alarm Indication Signal
SDLC	Synchronous Data Link Control	SEK	Swedish Electrical Commission
		SEN	Software Engineering Notes
SDM	Space-Division Multiplexing		

SES	Severely Errored Second	SGM	Segmentation Message
SESFE	Severely Errored Second, Far End	SGML	Standard Generalized Markup Language
SESP	Severely Errored Second, Path	SGML-B	Standard Generalized Markup Language-Binary
SET	Shock, Excited-Tones	SGMP	Simple Gateway Management (or Monitoring) Protocol
SETS	Selected Executable Test Suite		
SF	Single Frequency	SGND	Signal Ground
SF	Summarization Function	SH	Shared
SF	Switching Fabric	SH	Switch Hook
SFD	Simple Formattable Document	SHA	Secure Hash Algorithm
SFD	Start of Frame Delimiter	SHF	Super-High Frequency
SFET	Synchronous Frequency Encoding Technique	SHT	Short Holding Time
		SHTTP	Secure Hypertext Transport Protocol
SFI	Single Frequency Interface		
SFNOI	Second Further Notice of Inquiry	SI	SPDU Identifier
		SI	Step Index
SFQL	Structured Full-text Query Language	SIA	Stable Implementation Agreements
SFS	Shared File System		
SFS	Suomen Standardisoimisliitto (Standards Association of Finland)	SIC	Standard Industrial Codes
		SICS	Service Implementation Conformance Statement
SFT	System Fault Tolerance	SID	Signaling Identifier
SFU	Store and Forward Unit	SID	Source Identifier
SG	Study Group	SID	Sudden Ionospheric Disturbance
SGFS	Special Group on Functional Standardization		
		SID	Switch Interface Device
SGISP	Special Group on International Standardized Profiles	SIDF	Standard Interface Data Format

SIDF	System Independent Data Format	SIS	Structured Information Store
SIF	Source Input Format	SITA	Society for International Telecommunications for Aeronautics
SIG	Special Interest Group		
SIGCOMM	Special Interest Group on Data Communications	SIVR	Speaker-Independent Voice Recognition
SIL	Semiconductor Injection Laser	SKID	Secret Key Identification
SILS	Standard for Interoperable LAN Security	SL	Session Layer
		SL	Sink Loss
SIM	Set Initialization Mode	SLC	Semiconductor Laser Configurations
SIM	Society for Information Management	SLED	Single Large Expensive Disk
SIMM	Single In-line Memory Module	SLI	Suppress Length Indication
SIMP	Satellite Information Message Protocol	SLIC	Standard Language for Implementation Conventions
SINA	Static Integrated Network Access	SLIP	Serial Line Internet Protocol
		SLR	Service Level Reporter
SIO	Security Information Object	SLS	Sequential Logic Systems
SIO	Start Input/Output	SLU	Secondary Logical Unit
SIP	SMDS Interface Protocol	SM	Session Manager
SIPP	Simple Internet Protocol Plus	SM	Standby Monitor
SIR	Signal (to Co-Channel) Interference Ratio	SM	Synchronous Multiplexer
SIR	Speaker-Independent Recognition	SMA	Sub-Miniature Assembly
		SMAE	Systems Management Application Entity
SIR	Sustained Information Rate	SMAF	Service Management Access (or Agent) Function
SIS	Standardiserings-kommissionen in Sverige (Swedish Standards Committee)	SMAP	Systems Management Application Process

SMAS	Switched Maintenance Access System	SMFA	Systems Management Functional Area
SMASE	Systems Management Application Service Element	SMI	Structure of Management Information
SMATV	Satellite Master Antenna Television	SMI	System Management Interrupt
SMB	Server Message Block	SMIB	Stored Message Information Base
SMC	Secretariat Management Committee	SMIB	System Management Information Base
SMC	Sleep Mode Connection	SMIS	Specific Management Information Service
SMC	Standard Microsystems Corporation	SMISE	Specific Management Information Service Element
SMD	Storage Module Device	SMK	Shared Management Knowledge
SMDL	Standard Music Description Language	SMO	System Management Overview
SMDR	Station Message Detail Recording	SMP	Session Management Protocol
SMDR	Storage Management Data Requester	SMP	Standby Monitor Present
SMDS	Switched Multimegabit Data Service	SMP	Symmetric Multiprocessing
SME	Society of Manufacturing Engineers	SMP	System Modification Program
SME	Storage Management Engine	SMPDU	Service Message Protocol Data Unit
SMF	Service (also Systems) Management Function	SMPDU	System Management Protocol Data Unit
SMF	Simple Message Format	SMPTE	Society of Motion Picture and Television Engineers
SMF	Single-Mode Fiber	SMR	Specialized Mobile Radio
SMF	Standard Message (or Messaging) Format	SMRT	Signal Message Rate Timing
SMF	Standard MIDI File	SMS	Service-Management System
		SMS	Short Message Services

SMS	Storage Management Services (also Subsystem)	SNI	SNA Network Interconnection (or Interface)
SMS	Systems Management Server	SNI	Subscriber Network Interface
SMSA	Standard Metropolitan Statistical Area	SNICF	Subnetwork-Independent Convergence Facility
SMSDI	Storage Management Services Device Interface	SNICP	Subnetwork-Independent Convergence Protocol
SMSP	Storage Management Services Protocol	SNMP	Simple Network Management Protocol
SMT	Station Management	SNMPv2	Simple Network Management Protocol Version 2
SMTP	Simple Mail Transfer Protocol		
SN	Sequence Number	SNP	Sequence Number Protection
SN	Subarea Node	SNPA	Subnetwork Point of Attachment
SN	Subnetwork	SNR	Signal-to-Noise Ratio
SNA	Systems Network Architecture	SNRM	Set Normal Response Mode
SNA/SDLC	Systems Network Architecture/ Synchronous Data Link Control	SNS	Satellite Navigation System
		SNS	Secondary Network Server
SNAcF	Subnetwork Access Function	SO	Significant Other
SNAcP	Subnetwork Access Protocol	SOA	Safe Operating Area
SNADS	Systems Network Architecture Distribution Services	SOA	Semiconductor Optical Amplifier
SNAP	Subnetwork Access Protocol	SOGITS	Senior Officials' Group for Information Technology Standardization
SNARE	Subnetwork Address-Resolution Entity		
SNCP	Single Node Control Point	SOGT	Senior Officials' Group for Telecommunications
SNDCF	Subnetwork-Dependent Convergence Facility	SOH	Section Overhead
		SOH	Start of Header
SNDCP	Subnetwork-Dependent Convergence Protocol	SOHO	Small Office/Home Office

SOM	Start of Message
SOM	System Object Model
SOMA	Semantic Object Modeling Approach
SON	Sent (or Send) Outside the Node
SONET	Synchronous Optical Network
SOP	Standard Operating Procedure
SP	Security Protocol
SP	Service Provider
SP	Signaling Point
SP	Space Character
SP	System Performance
SPA	Software Publishers Association
SPAG	Standards Promotion and Application Group
SPAN	System Performance Analysis
SPARC	Scalable Performance Architecture
SPARC	Standards Planning and Review Committee
SPC	Signaling Point Code
SPC	Stored Program Control
SPCS	Service Point Command Service
SPDL	Standard Page Description Language
SPDU	Session Protocol Data Unit

SPE	Synchronous Payload Envelope
SPEDE	SAMMS Procurement by Electronic Data Exchange
SPF	Shortest Path First
SPI	Security Profile Inspector
SPI	Subsequent Protocol Identifier
SPID	Service Protocol Identifier
SPIRIT	Service Provider Integrated Requirements for Information Technology
SPL	Service Provider Link
SPM	Session Protocol Machine
SPMF	Servo Play-Mode Function
SPN	Signal Processor Network
SPN	Subscriber Premises Network
SPOOL	Simultaneous Peripheral Operation On-Line
SPP	Sequenced Packet Protocol
SPS	Stand-by Power Supply
SPSN	Synchronization-Point Serial Number
SPTS	Single Program Transport Stream
SPTV	Still Picture Television
SPX	Sequenced Packet Exchange
SQD	Signal Quality Detector
SQE	Signal Quality Error
SQL	Structured Query Language

SQUID	Super-conducting Quantum Interference Device	SSA	Subschema Specific Area
SR	Source Routing	SSAP	Session (also Source) Service Access Point
SRAM	Static Random-Access Memory	SSB	Single Sideband
SRB	Source Route Bridging	SSBSC	Single Sideband Suppressed Carrier
SREJ	Selective Reject		
SRES	Signed Response	SSCF	Service Specific Coordination Function
SRF	Specialized Resource Function	SSCOP	Service Specific Connection Oriented Protocol
SRF	Specifically Routed Frame		
SRH	SNARE Request Hello	SSCP	System Services Control Point
SRI	Stanford Research Institute	SSCS	Service Specific Convergence Sublayer
SRL	Signal Return Loss		
SRM	Self-Routing Module	SSDU	Session Service Data Unit
SRM	System Resource Manager	SSEL	Session Selector
SRT	Source Routing Transparent	SSF	Service Switching Function
SRTS	Synchronous Residual Time Stamp	SSI	Small-Scale Integration
		SSI	Subsystem Support Interface
SR-UAPDU	Status Report-User Agent Protocol Data Unit	SSL	Secure Socket Layer
		SSM	Single-Segment Message
SS	Sampled Servo	SSN	Switched Service Network
SS	Server-to-Server	SSO	Single Sign on
SS	Session Service	SSO	Structure, Sequence, and Organization (of a Program)
SS	Signaling System		
SS	Start/Stop	SSP	Service Switching Point
SS	Switching System	SSP	System Support Program
SS6	Signaling System 6	SSS	Server Session Socket
SS7	Signaling System 7	SST	Single Sideband Transmitter
SSA	Serial Storage Architecture		

SSTDMA	Spacecraft Switched Time Division Multiple Access	STMF	State Management Function
ST	Segment Type	STM-i	Synchronous Transport Module i
ST	Sequence Terminal	STO	Security Through Obscurity
ST	Straight Tip	STP	Service Transaction Program
STA	Spanning Tree Algorithm	STP	Shielded Twisted Pair
STACK	Start Acknowledgement	STP	Signal Transfer Point
STANAG	Standard Agreement	STR	Synchronous Transmit Receive
STB	Start of Text Block	STS	Shared Tenant Service
STC	Switching and Testing Center	STS	Synchronous Time Stamp
STC	System Time Clock	STS	Synchronous Transport Signal
STD	Standard	STS-3c	Synchronous Transport System, with Level 3 Concatenated
STD	Subscriber Trunk Dialing		
STD	Synchronous Time Division	STS-i	Synchronous Transport Signal, Level i
STD	System Time Decoder		
STDA	StreetTalk Directory Assistance	STT	Set-Top Terminal
STDM	Statistical Time Division Multiplexing	STV	Subscription Television
		STX	Start of Text
STE	Signal Terminal Equipment	SU	Service User
STE	Spanning Tree Explorer	SU	Signaling Unit
STEP	Software Test and Evaluation Panel	SUA	Stored Upstream Address
STEP	Standard for the Exchange of Product Model Data	SUABORT	Session User Abort
		SUDS	Software Updates Distribution Service
STF	Standard Transaction Format		
STI	Single Tuned Interstage	SUSP	System Use Sharing Protocol
STM	Station Management	SUT	System Under Test
STM	Synchronous Transfer Mode	SVA	Shared Virtual Area

SVC	Signaling Virtual Channel	SYNC	Synchronization
SVC	Switched Virtual Circuit	SYSCON	System Configuration
SVC	Switched Voice Circuit	T	Tera-
SVCI	Switched Virtual Circuit Identifier	TA	Terminal Adapter
		TA	Transferred Account
SVD	Simultaneous Voice/Data	TAAS	Trunk Answer From Any Station
SVGA	Super VGA		
SVI	Subvector Identifier	TAC	Technical Assistance Center
SVID	System V Interface Definition	TAC	Terminal Access Controller
SVL	Subvector Length	TACIT	Transition and Coexistence Including Testing (Working Group)
SVP	Subvector Parameter		
SVP	Switched Virtual Path	TACS	Total Access Communication System
SVR	(UNIX) System V Release		
SVS	Switched Virtual Circuit	TADP	Tests and Analyses of Data Protocols
SVVS	System V Verification Suite		
SWAIS	Simple Wide-Area Information Server	TAF	Terminal Access Facility
		TAG	Technical Advisory Group
SWAN	Satellite Wide-Area Network	TAG	Technical Assessment (Task) Group
SWC	Serving Wire Center		
SWG	Special Working Group	TANSTAAFL	There Ain't No Such Thing as a Free Lunch
SWIFT	Society for Worldwide International Financial Telecommunications		
		TAP	Trace Analysis Program
		TAPI	Telephony Application Program Interface
SWO	Standards Writing Organization		
		TARR	Test Action Request Receiver
SWRL	Southwest Regional Labs	TAS	Telephone Access Server
SXS	Step-by-Step Switch	TAS	Telephone Answering Service
SYN	Synchronize Flag	TASI	Time Assignment Speech Interpolation

TAT	Theoretical Arrival Time	TCB	Task Control Block
TAT	Trans-Atlantic Telecom	TCB	Transmission Control Block
TAU	Telematic Access Unit	TCC	Transmission Control Code
Tb	Terabit	TCCC	Technical Committee for Computer Communications
TB	Terabyte		
TB	Transparent Bridging	TCE	Transit Connection Element
TB	Treasury Board	TCEP	Transport Connection Endpoint
TBA	Trunk Bridger Amplifier		
TBC	Time-Base Corrector	TCH	Traffic Channel
TBC	Token Bus Controller	TCI	Test Cell Input
TBITS	Treasury Board Information Technology Standard	Tcl	Tool Command Language (pronounced "tickle")
Tbps	Terabits Per Second	TCM	Time Compression Multiplexing
TBps	Terabytes Per Second	TCM	Trellis Coded Modulation
TBS	Treasury Board Secretariat	TCN	Telecommunications Networks
TC	Technical Committee	TCN	Throughput Class Negotiation
TC	Terminal Controller	TCNS	Thomas-Conrad Network System
TC	Test Conductor		
TC	Transaction Capabilities	TCO	Test Cell Output
TC	Transmission Convergence Sublayer	TCP	Test Coordination Procedure
		TCP	Transmission Control Protocol
TC	Transport Connection	TCP/IP	Transmission Control Protocol/ Internet Protocol
TCA	Telecommunications Association		
		TCRF	Transit Connection-Related Function
TCAM	Telecommunications Access Method		
		TCS	Transmission Convergence Sublayer
TCAP	Transaction Capability Application Part		
		TCS-1	Trans-Caribbean System-1

TCSEC	Trusted Computer System Evaluation Criteria
TCT	Terminal Control Table (in CICS)
TCU	Transmission Control Unit
TCU	Trunk Coupling Unit
TD	Transmit Data
TD	Typed Data
TDB	Task Database
TDCC	Transportation Data Coordinating Committee
TDD	Time Division Duplex
TDDI	Twisted-pair Distributed Data Interface
TDED	Trade Data Elements Directory
TDF	Trunk Distribution Frame
TDI	Transit Delay Indication
TDI	Transport Device (or Driver) Interface
TDID	Trade Data Interchange Directory
TDJ	Transfer Delay Jitter
TDM	Time Division Multiplexing
TDM	Topology Database Manager
TDMA	Time Division Multiple Access
TDR	Time Domain Reflectometer
TDS	Transit Delay Selection
TDSAI	Transit Delay Selection and Indication

TE	Terminal Equipment
TE1	Terminal Equipment Type 1
TE2	Terminal Equipment Type 2
TEDIS	Trade Electronic Data Interchange System
TEHO	Tail End Hop Off
TEI	Terminal End-point Identifier
TELCO	Telephone Company
TELNET	Telecommunications Network
TELSET	Telephone Set
TEM	Transverse Electromagnetic
TEMPEST	Transient Electromagnetic Pulse Emanation Standardizing
TEN	Telephone Equipment Network
TEP	Transport Endpoint
TERC	Technology Education Research Center
TERC	Telecommunications Equipment Re-marketing Council
TFA	Transparent File Access
TFP	TOPS Filing Protocol
TFTP	Trivial File Transfer Protocol
TG	Task Group
TG	Transmission Group
TGB	Trunk Group Busy
TGS	Ticket-Granting Server (or Service)
TGT	Ticket-granting Ticket

TGW	Trunk Group Warning	TIRPC	Transport Independent Remote Procedure Call
TH	Transmission Header	TIU	Telematic Internetworking Unit
THD	Ten High Day	TIU	Trusted Interface Unit
THD	Total Harmonic Distortion	Tk	Toolkit
THEnet	Texas Higher Education Network	TL	Transport Layer
THT	Token Holding Time	TLA	Three Letter Acronym
THz	Terahertz	TLAP	TokenTalk Link Access Protocol
TI	Time in	TLF	Trunk Line Frame
TIA	Telecommunications Industry Association	TLFF	Technical Level Feeders Forum
TIA	Telematic Internetworking Application	TLI	Transport Layer (or Library) Interface
TIA	the Internet Adapter	TLMA	Telematic Agent
TIAS	Telematic Internetworking Abstract Service	TLMAU	Telematic Access Unit
TIB	Task Information Base	TLP	Transmission Level Point
TIC	Token-ring Interface Coupler	TLSPP	Transport Layer Sequenced Packet Protocol
TID	Transaction ID	TLV	Type-Length-Value
TID	Traveling Ionospheric Disturbance	TLX	Telex
TIE	Translated Image Environment	TLXAU	Telex Access Unit
TIFF	Tagged Image File Format	TM	Terminal Management
TIMS	Transmission Impairment Measuring Sets	TM	Traffic Management
TIP	Terminal Interface Package (also Processor)	TMF	Test Management Function
		TMN	Telecommunications Management Network
TIRIS	Texas Instruments Registration and Information System	TMP	Test-Management Protocol
		TMPDU	Test-Management Protocol Data Unit

TMS	Telecommunications Message Switcher	TP	Transaction Processing
TMS	Telephone Management System	TP	Transport Protocol
TMS	Time-Multiplexed Switching	TP	Twisted Pair
TMSCP	Tape Mass Storage Control Program	TP0	Transport Protocol Class 0
TMSI	Temporary Mobile Subscriber Identity	TP1	Transport Protocol Class 1
		TP2	Transport Protocol Class 2
TM-SWG	Traffic Management (Sub-Working Group)	TP3	Transport Protocol Class 3
		TP4	Transport Protocol Class 4
TMU	Transmission Message Unit	TPA	Telematic Protocol Architecture
TN	Transport Network	TPA	Trading Partner Agreement
TNC	Terminal Node Connector (also Controller)	TPAD	Terminal Packet Assembler/ Disassembler
TNC	The Networking Center	TPC	Trans-Pacific Cable
TNC	Threaded Navy (also Nut) Connector	TPCC	Third-Party Call Control
TNC	Threaded Neill-Concelnan Connector	TPDDI	Twisted Pair Distributed Data Interface
		TPDU	Transport Protocol Data Unit
TNIC	Transit Network Identification Code	TPE	Transmission Path Endpoint
TNS	Transaction Network Service	TPE	Twisted Pair Ethernet
TNS	Transit Network Selection	TPF	Transaction Processing Facility
TO	Test Object	TPI	Transport Protocol Interface
TO	Time Out	TPPMD	Twisted Pair, Physical Media Dependent
TOP	Technical and Office Protocol	TPS	Transactions Per Second
TOS	Technical and Office Systems	TPS	Two-Processor Switch
ToS	Type of Service	TPSP	Transaction Processing Service Provider
TP	Terminal Portability		

TPSU	Transaction Processing Service User	TS	Time Stamp
TPSUI	Transaction Processing Service User Invocation	TS	Traffic Shaping
		TS	Transaction Services
TPT	Third-Party Transfer	TS	Transport Service (also Stream)
TPTAE	Third-Party Transfer Application Entity	TS	Transport Stream
TPx	Transport Protocol, Class x (x=0, 1, 2, 3, or 4)	TSA	Target Service Agent
		TSA	Technical Support Alliance
TQM	Total Quality Management	TSAF	Transport Services Access Facility
TR	Technical Report	TSAP	Transport Service Access Point
TR	Test Responder	TSAPI	Telephony Services Application Program Interface
TR	Token Ring		
TR	Tributaries	TSC	Transmission Subsystem Controller
TRA	Token-Ring Adapter	TSCF	Target System Control Facility
TRAC	Technical Recommendation Application Committee	TSDS	Transaction Set Development System
TRADA-COMS	Trading Data Communications Standards	TSDU	Transport-layer Service Data Unit
TRIB	Transmission Rate in Bits	TSE	Terminal Switching Exchange
TRIL	Token Ring Interoperability Lab	TSEL	Transport Selector
TRIP	Transcontinental ISDN Project	TSI	Time-Slot Interchange
TROPIC	Token Ring Protocol Interface Controller	TSO	Terminating Service Office
		TSO	Time-Sharing Option
TRS	Topology and Routing Services	TSO/E	Time-Sharing Option/Extension
TRSS	Token Ring Subsystem		
TRT	Token Rotation Timer	TSPS	Traffic Service Position System
TS	Time Slot	TSR	Telemarketing Service Representative

TSR	Terminate and Stay Resident	TTX	Teletex
TSS	Time-Sharing System	TTXAU	Teletex Access Unit
TSS	Transmission Subsystem	TTY	Teletypewriter
TSS&TP	Test Suite Structure and Test Purposes	TUBA	TCP and UDP Over Bigger Addresses
TSSDU	Typed Data Session Service Data Unit	TUCC	Triangle University Computing Center
TTA	Telecommunication Technology Association	TUG	TeX User's Group
		TUG-i	Tributary Unit Group-i
TTC	Telecommunications Technical Committee	TU-i	Tributary Unit-i
		TUP	Telephone User Part
TTC	Telecommunications Technology Council	TUR	Traffic Usage Recorder
TTCN	Tree and Tabular Combined Notation	TV	Television
		TVA	Time Variant Amplifier
TTCN.GR	Tree and Tabular Combined Notation, Graphical Representation	TVC	Trunk Verification by Customer
		TVF	Time Variant Filter
TTCN.MP	Tree and Tabular Combined Notation, Machine Processable	TVRO	Television Receive Only
TTD	Target Transit Delay	TVS	Trunk Verification by Station
TTD	Temporary Text Delay	TWA	Two-Way Alternate
TTL	Time to Live	TWAIN	Toolkit Without An Important Name
TTL	Transistor-Transistor Logic		
TTN	Tandem Tie-line Network	TWIG	Technical Wizard Interest Group
TTP	Timed-Token Protocol		
TTP	Transport Test Platform	TWS	Two-Way Simultaneous
TTRT	Target Token Rotation Time	TWX	Teletypewriter Exchange
TTS	Transaction Tracking System	TXI	Transmit Immediate
TTTN	Tandem Tie-Trunk Network	TXK	Telephone Exchange Crossbar

TXS	Telephone Exchange Strowger	UCC	Uniform Commercial Code
TYMNET	Timeshare Inc. Network	UCD	Uniform Call Distribution
TZD	Time Zone Difference	UCL	University College, London
U/L	Universal/Local	UCS	Uniform Communications Standard (also System)
UA	Universal Access		
UA	Unnumbered Acknowledgment	UCS	Universal Component System
UA	Unsequenced Application	UCS/WINS	Uniform Communication System/Warehouse Information Network Standard
UA	User Account		
UA	User Agent	UCW	Ubit Control Word
UAE	User Agent Entity	UD	Unit Data
UAL	User Agent Layer	UDI	Unrestricted Digital Information
UAM	User Authentication Method		
UAOS	User Alliance for Open Systems	UDLC	Universal Data Link Control
UAPDU	User Agent Protocol Data Unit	UDP	User Datagram Protocol
UART	Universal Asynchronous Receiver Transmitter	UDT	Unstructured Data Transfer
		UE	User Element
UAS	Unavailable Second	UFS	UNIX File System
UASFE	Unavailable Second, Far End	UHF	Ultra-High Frequency
UASL	User Agent Sublayer	UI	Unit Interval
UBCIM	Universal Bibliographic Control/International MARC	UI	UNIX International
		UI	Unnumbered Information
UBR	Unspecified Bit Rate	UI	Unnumbered Interrupt
UCA	Utilities Communication Architecture	UI	User Interface
UCB	Unit Control Block	UID	User ID
UCB	University of California, Berkeley	UIS	Universal Information Services
		UKRA	United Kingdom Registration Authority
UCC	Uniform Code Council		

UL	Underwriters' Laboratories		UNTDI	United Nations Trade Data Interchange
UL	Urban Legend		UoD	Universe of Discourse
UL	User Location		UoW	Unit of Work
ULA	Upper-Layer Architecture		UP	Unnumbered Poll
ULCC	University of London Computing Centre		UPC	Uniform (also Universal) Product Code
ULCT	Upper-Layer Conformance Testing		UPC	Usage Parameter Control
ULP	Upper-Layer Protocol (or Process)		UPS	Uninterruptible Power Supply
			UPT	Universal Personal Telecommunications
UMB	Upper Memory Block		UPTN	Universal Personal Telecommunication Number
UME	UNI Management Entity			
UMPDU	User Message Protocol Data Unit		UPU	Universal Postal Union
UMTS	Universal Mobile Telephone Service		URG	Urgent Flag
			URI	Uniform Resource Identifier
UN	United Nations		URL	Uniform Resource Locators
UN/ECE	United Nations Economic Commission for Europe		URN	Uniform Resource Name
			URSI	Union Radio-Scientifique Internationale (International Union of Radio Sciences)
UNA	Upstream Neighbors Address			
UNC	Uniform Naming Convention		USA	Undedicated Switch Access
UNI	User-Network Interface		USART	Universal Synchronous/Asynchronous Receiver/Transmitter
UNISON-1	Unidirectional Synchronous Optical Network 1			
UNJEDI	United Nations Joint EDI		USB	Upper Sideband
UNMA	Unified Network Management Architecture		USE	UnixWare Support Encyclopedia
UNO	Universal Network Object		USITA	United States Independent Telephone Association
UNSM	UN/EDIFACT Standard Message		USL	UNIX System Laboratories

USNC	United States National Committee	VAD	Value-Added Distributor
USO	UNIX Software Operation	VADS	Value-Added Data Services
USOC	Uniform Service Order Code	VAMPIRE	Voice-Actuated Medical Practice Image Recorder
USP	United States Pharmacopia	VAN	Value-Added Network
USRA	Universities Space Research Association	VAP	Value-Added Process
USRT	Universal Synchronous Receiver Transmitter	VAR	Value-Added Reseller
		VARP	VINES Address Resolution Protocol
USS	Unformatted System Services	VAS	Value-Added Service
USV	User Services	VAS	Video Application Signaling
UT	Universal Time	VAST	Variable Architecture Synthesis Technology
UT	Unsequenced Terminal		
UT	Upper Tester	VAU	Video Access Unit
UTAM	Unlicensed Transition and Management	VAX	Virtual Address Extension
		VAXBI	VAX Bus Interface
UTC	Universal Coordinated Time	VBA	Visual Basic for Applications
UTOPIA	Universal Test and Operations PHY Interface for ATM	VBR	Variable Bit Rate
UTP	Unshielded Twisted Pair	VBX	Visual Basic (Custom) Control
UTTP	Unshielded Telephone Twisted Pair	VBX	Visual Basic Extension
		VC	Virtual Call
UUCP	UNIX to UNIX Copy Program	VC	Virtual Channel
UUS	User-to-User Signaling	VCC	Virtual Channel Connection
V	Volt	VCCE	Virtual Channel Connection Endpoint
V+TU	Voice Plus Teleprinter Unit		
VAB	Visual Application Builder	VCI	Virtual Channel Identifier
VAC	Value-Added Carrier	VCI	Virtual Circuit Identifier
VAC	Voltage AC	VCI	Virtual Connection Identifier

VC-i	Virtual Container i		VF	Voice Frequency
VCL	Virtual Channel Link		VFRP	VINES Fragmentation Protocol
VCNS	VTAM Common Network Services		VFS	VINES File System
			VFS	Virtual File Store (or System)
VCPI	Virtual Control Program Interface		VFT	Voice Frequency Telegraph
			VfW	Video for Windows
VCS	Virtual Circuit Switch		VG	Voice Grade
VDA	Variable Digital Amplifier		VGA	Video Graphics Array
VDC	Voltage DC		VHF	Very High Frequency
VDD	Virtual Device Driver		VICP	VINES Internet Control Protocol
VDD	Virtual Display Device			
VDF	Variable Digital Filter		VIM	Vendor Independent Messaging
VDI	Virtual Device Interface		VINES	Virtual Networking System
VDM	Virtual DOS Machine		VIP	Video Information Provider
VDMAD	Virtual Direct Memory Access Device		VIP	VINES Internet Protocol
			VIP	Visual Information Processing
VDMM	Virtual DOS Machine Manager		VIPC	VINES Interprocess Communications
VDT	Video Dialtone			
VDT	Video Display Terminal		VIP-NI	Video Information Provider Network Interface
VDU	Video Display Unit			
Veronica	Very Easy Rodent-Oriented Net-wide Index to Computer-ized Archives		VIT	VTAM Internal Trace
			VITAL	Virtually Integrated Technical Architecture Lifecycle
VESA	Video Equipment Standards Association		VIU	Video Information User
VEST	VAX Environment Software Translator		VIU-NI	Video Information User Network Interface
VEX	Video Extensions for X-Windows		VIW	VIP-video Information Warehouse
			VKD	Virtual Keyboard Device

VL	VESA Local	VMT	Virtual Memory Table
VL	Virtual Link	VMTP	VDT Message Transfer Part
VLAN	Virtual Local-Area Network	VMTP	Versatile Message Transaction Protocol
VLF	Virtual Look Aside Facility		
VLM	Virtual Loadable Module	VMTP-T	VDT Message Transfer Part Translator
VLR	Visitor Location Register		
VLSI	Very Large-Scale Integration	VNA	Virtual Network Architecture
VM	Virtual Machine (also Memory)	VNET	Virtual Network
		VNL	Via Net Loss
VM	Voice Messaging	VNLF	Via Net Loss Factor
VM/CMS	Virtual Machine/Conversation Monitor System	VOD	Video on Demand
		VOM	Volt-Ohm-Meter
VM/ESA	Virtual Machine/Enterprise Systems Technology	VOP	Velocity of Propagation
		VOTS	VAX OSI Transport Service
VM/SP	Virtual Machine/System Product	VP	Virtual Path
		VPC	Virtual Path Connection
VM/SP HPO	Virtual Machine/System Product, High-Performance Option	VPCE	Virtual Path Connection Endpoint
VM/XA	Virtual Machine/Extended Architecture	VPCI/VCI	Virtual Path Connection Identifier/Virtual Channel Identifier
VMBP	Virtual Machine Break Point	VPI	Virtual Path Identifier
VMD	Virtual Manufacturing Device	VPICD	Virtual Programmable Interrupt Control Device
VMD	Virtual Mouse Device		
VMDBK	Virtual Machine Definition Block	VPL	Virtual Path Link
		VPN	Virtual Private Network
VMI	Vendor-managed Inventory	VPU	Video Presentation Unit
VMM	Virtual Machine Manager	VR	Virtual Router
VMS	Virtual Memory System	VRAM	Video Random-Access Memory
VMS	Voice Message System		

VRC	Vertical Redundancy Check	VTAM	Virtual Telecommunication Access Method
VRPWS	Virtual Router Pacing Window Size	VTC	Virus Test Center
VRTP	VINES Routing Transport Protocol	VTD	Virtual Timer Device
		VTE	Virtual Terminal Environment
VRU	Voice Response Unit	VTP	Virtual Terminal Protocol
VRUP	VINES Routing Update Protocol	VTPM	Virtual Terminal Protocol Machine
VS	Virtual Storage (also Scheduling)	VTPP	Variable Team Pricing Plan
		VTS	Virtual Terminal Service
VSAM	Virtual Index Sequential Access Method	VTSE	Virtual Terminal Service Element
VSAM	Virtual Storage Access Method	VU	Volume Unit
VSAT	Very Small Aperture Terminal	VVIEF	VAX Vector Instruction Emulation Facility
VSB	Vestigial Sideband		
VSCCP	VDT Signaling Connection Control Part	VxD	Virtual Device Driver
		VxFS	Veritas File System
VSCP	VDT Session Control Part	W3C	World Wide Web Consortium
VSCS	VM/SNA Console Support	WA	Write Audit
VSE	Virtual Storage Extended	WACA	Write Access Connection Acceptor
VSE/ESA	Virtual Storage Extended/ Enterprise System Architecture	WACIA	Write Access Connection Initiator
VSF	Voice Store-and-Forward		
VSPC	Visual Storage Personal Computing	WACK	Wait for Acknowledgment
		WAIS	Wide-Area Information Service
VSPP	VINES Sequenced Packet Protocol	WAITS	Wide-Area Information Transfer System
VSWR	Voltage Standing Wave Radio	WAIUG	Washington-Area ISDN Users' Group
VT	Vertical Tab		
VT	Virtual Terminal		

WAN	Wide-Area Network	WINS	Warehouse Information Network Standard
WANDD	Wide-Area Network Device Driver	WINS	Windows Naming Service
WARC	World Administrative Radio Conference	WKSH	Windowing Korn Shell
WATS	Wide-Area Telephone Service	WMF	Workload Monitoring Function
WAVAR	Write Access Variable	WMRM	Write Many, Read Many
WBC	Wideband Channel	WNIM	Wide-Area Network Interface Module
WCC	World Congress on Computing		
WD	Working Document (or Draft)	WOAPI	Windows Open Application Program Interface
WDM	Wavelength Division Multiplexing	WORM	Write Once, Read Many
WELAC	Western Europe Laboratory Accreditation Cooperation	WOS	Workstation Operation System
		WOSA	Windows Open System Architecture
WELL	Whole Earth 'Lectronic Link		
WEP	Well-known Entry Point	WP	White Pages
WFMTUG	World Federation of MAP/TOP Users' Group	WP	Working Party
		WPG	WordPerfect Graphics
WfW	Windows for Workgroups	WPM	Words Per Minute
WG	Working Group	WPS	Workplace Shell
WIBNI	Wouldn't It Be Nice If	WP/WC	We Play, We Chat
WIMP	Windows Icons, Mice (or Menu), and Pointers	WRQ	Write Request
		WRT	With Respect To
WIN	Wissenschaftsnetz (Science Network)	WRU	Who Are You
WINCS	WWMCCS Intercomputer Network Communication Subsystem	WSF	Workstation Function
		WTAPI	Writing Tools Application Program Interface
WINDO	Wide Information Network for Data Online	WTDM	Wavelength Time Division Multiplexing

WTSC	World Telecommunication Standardization Conference
WUI	Western Union International
WWMCCS	Worldwide Military Command and Control System
WWW	World Wide Web
WWWW	World Wide Web Worm
WYSIAYG	What You See Is All You Get (pronounced "whizzy-egg")
WYSIWYG	What You See Is What You Get (pronounced "whizzy-wig")
X	The X Window System
XA	Extended Architecture
XALS	Extended Application-Layer Structure
XAPIA	X.400 API Association
XCF	Cross-system Coupling Facility
XDF	Extended Distance Facility
Xdm	X Display Manager
XDR	External Data Representation
Xds	X Display Server
XDS	X/Open Directory Services API
XFCN	External Function
XID	Exchange ID
XIP	Execute in Place
XIWT	Cross-Industry Working Team
XMH	X Mail Handler
XMIT	Transmit

XMS	Extended Memory Specification
XNA	Xerox Network Architecture
XNS	Xerox Network Services
XO	Exactly Once
XOFF	Transmitter Off
XON	Transmitter on
XPD	Cross Polarization Discrimination
XPG	X.400 Promotion Group
XPG	X/Open Portability Guide
XPSDU	Expedited Presentation Service Data Unit
XQL	Xtructured Query Language
XRF	Extended Recovery Facility
XSSDU	Expedited Session Service Data Unit
XT	Extended Technology
XTC	External Transmit Clock
XTI	X/Open Transport-layer Interface
XTP	Express Transfer Protocol
YAA	Yet Another Acronym
YABA	Yet Another Bloody Acronym
YAFIYGI	You Asked for It, You Got It
YAHOO	Yet Another Hierarchically Officious Oracle
YAUN	Yet Another UNIX Nerd
YHBT	You Have Been Trolled

YHBT. - YHL. HAND.	You Have Been Trolled. You Have Lost. Have A Nice Day.
YHL	You Have Lost
YMMV	Your Mileage May Vary
YMU	Y-Net Management Unit
YP	Yellow Pages
YR	Yeah, Right
ZIF	Zero Insertion Force
ZIP	Zone Information Protocol
ZIS	Zone Information Socket
ZIT	Zone Information Table
ZMA	Zone Multicast Access

Bibliography and
Other Resources

APPENDIX

B

There are thousands of books about networking, telecommunications, and related topics. The standards organizations alone have produced hundreds of documents. In addition, there are many other types of information sources. These sources include consultants, periodicals, technical reports and newsletters, training centers, and films.

Primary Sources

Three classes of primary sources can be helpful to network developers, administrators, and users:

- Documents and recommendations from standards committees

- Internal manufacturers' documentation about architectures and about software or hardware products

- Manufacturers' and vendors' technical reports and research papers about products, protocols, and standards

Standards Documentation

Copies of standards documents are available either from the committees or organizations themselves or from their distributors. The following list provides information on how to contact such sources. We have tried to make certain the information in the list is correct and up-to-date, but things change. So don't be surprised if you try to contact one of these sources and find that the phone number, or even the address, has changed.

ANSI (American National Standards Institute)
11 West 42nd Street, 13th Floor
New York, NY 10036
(212) 642-4900;
(202) 639-4090 (Washington DC Office)

CSA (Canadian Standards Association)
178 Rexdale Boulevard
Rexdale, Ontario M9W 1R3
Canada
(416) 747-4000

ECMA (European Computer Manufacturers Association)
114 Rue de Rhone
CH-1204 Geneva
Switzerland

EIA (Electrical Industries Association)
2001 Eye Street, NW
Washington, DC 20006
(202) 457-4966

FIPS (Federal Information Processing Standard)
U.S. Department of Commerce
National Technical Information Service
5285 Port Royal Road
Springfield, VA 22161

IEEE (Institute of Electrical and Electronics Engineers)
345 East 47th Street
New York, NY 10017
(212) 705-7900

ISO (International Standardization
Organization)
Central Secretariat
1, Rue de Varembe
CH-1204 Geneva
Switzerland

ISO (U.S. Office)
c/o ANSI (American National Standards
Institute)
11 West 42nd Street, 13th Floor
New York, NY 10036
(212) 642-4900;
(202) 639-4090 (Washington, DC Office)

ITU (International Telecommunications
Union)
General Secretariat
Place des Nations
CH-1211 Geneva 20
Switzerland

ITU (U.S. Office)
c/o U.S. Department of Commerce
National Technical Information Service
5285 Port Royal Road
Springfield, VA 22161
(703) 487-4650

Other Sources for Standards and Recommendations

The following resellers and distributors also
provide documentation from standards
committees:

Global Engineering Documents
1990 M Street NW, Suite 400
Washington, DC 20036
(800) 854-7179

Information Handling Services
P.O. Box 1154
15 Inverness Way East
Englewood, CO 80150
(800) 525-7052; (303) 790-0600

Phillips Business Information
1201 Seven Locks Road, Suite 300
Potomac, MD 20854
(800) 777-5006

United Nations Bookshop
General Assembly Building
Room GA 32B
New York, NY 10017
(800) 553-3210; (212) 963-7680

ITU (U.S. Office)
c/o U.S. Department of Commerce
National Technical Information Service
5285 Port Royal Road
Springfield, VA 22161
(703) 487-4650

InfoMagic, Inc.
11950 N. Highway 89
Flagstaff, AZ 86004
(800) 800-6613; (520) 526-9565
Fax: (520) 526-9573
E-Mail: info@infomagic.com
Web: http://www.infomagic.com

InfoMagic sells CDs containing various
documentation, including the RFCs that
serve as standards in the Internet community
and much of the ITU (formerly, the CCITT)
documentation. While there are gaps in
the standards, the 2-CD collection is well
organized and indispensable if you need to
consult any of the included documents

often or if you'll need any number of the documents.

They also have discs containing various Internet tools, and *World Wide Catalog,* an interesting disc about the World Wide Web that can be used even if you don't have an Internet account.

The discs, which are updated every six months or so, cost about $30–$40. While you can get the materials yourself, it would take you weeks to do so.

▼
Secondary Sources

The following books are informative secondary sources about topics related, broadly or narrowly, to networking or to the Internet. These are by no means the only good sources for such information, but they do provide a start for readers who want to go beyond this book. The references range from introductory to advanced treatments.

Apple Computer. *Inside Macintosh: Networking* (1994, Addison-Wesley).

Apple Computer. *Technical Introduction to the Macintosh Family,* 2nd ed. (1992, Addison-Wesley).

Aronson, Larry. *HTML Manual of Style* (1994, Ziff-Davis Press).

Bach, Maurice J. *The Design of the UNIX Operating System* (1986, Prentice-Hall).

Black, Uyless. *OSI: A Model for Computer Communications* (1991, Prentice-Hall).

Black, Uyless. *The V Series Recommendations* (1991, McGraw-Hill).

Black, Uyless. *The X Series Recommendations* (1991, McGraw-Hill).

Blum, Daniel J. & Litwack, David M. *The E-Mail Frontier* (1995, Addison-Wesley).

Branwyn, Gareth et al. *Internet Roadside Attractions* (1995, Ventana Press).

Brown, Kevin, Brown, Kenyon & Brown, Kyle. *Mastering Lotus Notes* (1995, Sybex).

Brown, Wendy E. & Simpson, Colin MacLeod (eds.). *The OSI Dictionary of Acronyms and Related Abbreviations* (1993, McGraw-Hill).

Cady, Glee Harrah & McGregor, Pat. *Mastering the Internet* (1995, Sybex).

Cedeno, Nancy. *The Internet Tool Kit* (1995, Sybex).

Chappell, Laura. *Novell's Guide to NetWare LAN Analysis* (1993, Novell Press).

Chappell, Laura A. & Spicer, Roger L. *Novell's Guide to Multiprotocol Networking* (1994, Novell Press).

Cheswick, William R. & Bellovin, Steven M. *Firewalls and Internet Security* (1994, Addison-Wesley).

Chellis, James. *The CNA Study Guide for Netware 4* (1996, Network Press).

Clarke, David James IV. *The CNA Study Guide* (1995, Network Press).

Colonna-Romano, John & Srite, Patricia. *The Middleware Source Book* (1995, Digital Press).

Comer, Douglas E. *Internetworking with TCP/IP,* Volume 1, 2nd ed. (1991, Prentice-Hall).

Coulouris, George, Dollimore, Jean & Kindberg, Tim. *Distributed Systems: Concepts and Design,* 2nd ed. (1994, Addison-Wesley).

Cowart, Robert. *Mastering Windows 95* (1995, Sybex).

Crumlish, Christian. *A Guided Tour of the Internet* (1995, Sybex).

Crumlish, Christian. *The Internet Dictionary* (1995, Sybex).

Currid, Cheryl C. & Saxon, Stephen. *Novell's Guide to NetWare 4.0 Networks* (1993, Novell Press).

Day, Michael. *Downsizing to NetWare* (1992, New Riders Publishing).

Day, Michael & Neff, Ken. *Troubleshooting NetWare for the 386* (1991, M&T Books).

Derfler, Frank Jr. *PC Magazine Guide to Connectivity,* 2nd ed. (1992, Ziff-Davis Press).

Dienes, Sheila S. *Microsoft Office Professional, Instant Reference* (1995, Sybex).

Duntemann, Jeff, Pronk, Ron & Vincent, Patrick. *Web Explorer Pocket Companion* (1995, Coriolis Group).

Dyson, Peter. *Mastering OS/2 Warp* (1995, Sybex).

Dyson, Peter. *The Network Press Dictionary of Networking* (1995, Network Press).

Eager, Bill. *Using the World Wide Web* (1994, Que).

Eddy, Sandra E. *The Compact Guide to Lotus SmartSuite* (1995, Sybex).

Fahey, Tom. *net.speak, the internet dictionary* (1994, Hayden Books).

Falk, Bennett. *The Internet Roadmap,* 2nd ed. (1995, Sybex).

Feldman, Len. *Windows NT: The Next Generation* (1993, Sams).

Flanagan, William A. *The Guide to T-1 Networking,* 4th ed. (1990, Telecom Library).

Fraase, Michael & James, Phil. *The Windows Internet Tour Guide* (1995, Ventana Press).

Freedman, Alan. *The Computer Glossary,* 6th ed. (1993, Amacom).

Garfinkel, Simson. *PGP: Pretty Good Privacy* (1995, O'Reilly & Associates).

Gaskin, James E. *The Complete Guide to NetWare 4* (1995, Network Press).

Gilster, Paul. *The Internet Navigator* (1993, John Wiley & Sons).

Graham, Ian. *HTML Sourcebook* (1995, Wiley).

Green, James Harry. *The Business One Irwin Handbook of Telecommunications,* 2nd ed. (1992, Irwin).

Hahn, Harley & Stout, Rick. *The Internet Complete Reference* (1994, Osborne McGraw-Hill).

Halsall, Fred. *Data Communications, Computer Networks, and OSI,* 3rd ed. (1994, Addison-Wesley).

Handel, Rainer & Huber, Manfred N. *Integrated Broadband Networks* (1991, Addison-Wesley).

Harbaugh, Logan G. *Novell's Problem-Solving Guide for NetWare Systems* (1993, Novell Press).

Harris, Stuart & Kidder, Gayle. *Netscape Quick Tour* (1995, Ventana Press).

Hebrawi, Baha. *OSI Upper Layer Standards and Practice* (1993, McGraw-Hill).

Hecht, Jeff. *Understanding Fiber Optics* (1987, Sams).

Herbon, Gamal B. *Designing NetWare Directory Services* (1994, M&T Books).

Howe, Denis. *Free On-Line Dictionary of Computing* (1993, Denis Howe). Available on the Internet by FTP or Gopher from wombat.doc.ic.ac.uk (146.169.22.42).

Heslop, Brent & Budnick, Larry. *HTML Publishing on the Internet, for Windows* (1995, Ventana Press).

Hoffman, Paul E. *The Internet Instant Reference,* 2nd ed. (1995, Sybex).

Hopkins, Gerald L. *The ISDN Literacy Book* (1995, Addison-Wesley).

Hughes, Jeffrey F. & Thomas, Blair W. *Novell's QuickPath to NetWare 4.1 Networks* (1995, Novell Press).

Huitema, Christian. *Routing in the Internet* (1995, Prentice-Hall).

Jordan, Larry & Churchill, Bruce. *Communications and Networking for the IBM PC and Compatibles,* 4th ed. (1992, Brady).

Khan, Ahmed S. *The Telecommunications Fact Book and Illustrated Dictionary* (1992, Delmar Publishers).

Kosiur, Dave & Jones, Nancy E. H. *Macworld Networking Handbook* (1992, IDG Books).

Krol, Ed. *The Whole Internet User's Guide & Catalog* (1994, O'Reilly & Associates).

LeJeune, Urban A. *Netscape & HTML Explorer* (1995, Coriolis Group).

Leinwand, Allan & Fang, Karen. *Network Management, a Practical Perspective* (1993, Addison-Wesley).

Liebing, Edward. *NetWare User's Guide* (1993, M&T Books).

Lindberg, Kelley J. P. *Novell's Guide to Managing Small NetWare Networks* (1993, Novell Press).

Linnell, Dennis. *The SAA Handbook* (1990, Addison-Wesley).

Lynch, Daniel C. & Rose, Marshall T. *Internet System Handbook* (1993, Addison-Wesley).

Mansfield, Ron. *The Compact Guide to Microsoft Office Professional* (1995, Sybex).

Margulies, Edwin. *Client Server Computer Telephony* (1994, Flatiron Publishing).

Matthews, Carole Boggs & Matthews, Martin. *Windows 95 Instant Reference* (1995, Sybex).

Merrin, Robin. *The Mosaic Roadmap* (1995, Sybex).

Microsoft Press. *Windows NT Resource Guide* (1993, Microsoft Press).

Microsoft Press. *Computer Dictionary* (1991, Microsoft Press).

Miller, Mark A. *Internetworking* (1991, M&T Books).

Miller, Mark A. *LAN Protocol Handbook* (1992, M&T Books).

Miller, Mark A. *Troubleshooting Internetworks* (1991, M&T Books).

Miller, Mark A. *Troubleshooting TCP/IP* (1992, M&T Books).

Minasi, Mark, Anderson, Christa, & Creegan, Elizabeth. *Mastering Windows NT Server 3.51* (1996, Sybex).

Motorola. *The Basics Book of Frame Relay* (1993, Addison-Wesley).

Motorola. *The Basics Book of Information Networking* (1992, Addison-Wesley).

Motorola. *The Basics Book of ISDN,* 2nd ed. (1992, Addison-Wesley).

Motorola. *The Basics Book of OSI and Network Management* (1993, Addison-Wesley).

Motorola. *The Basics Book of X.25 Packet Switching,* 2nd ed. (1992, Addison-Wesley).

Nassar, Dan. *Token Ring Troubleshooting* (1992, NRP).

Negus, Chris & Schumer, Larry. *Novell's Guide to UnixWare 2,* 2nd ed. (1994, Sybex).

Netrix. *The Buyer's Guide to Frame Relay Networking,* 3rd ed. (1992, Netrix Corporation).

Newton, Harry. *Newton's Telecom Dictionary,* 7th ed. (1994, Flatiron Publishing).

NeXT Computer, Inc. *NeXTSTEP Network and System Administration* (1992, Addison-Wesley).

Novell Systems Research Department. *Novell's Application Notes for NetWare 4.01* (1993, Novell Press).

Ousterhout, John K. *Tcl and the Tk Toolkit* (1994, Addison-Wesley).

Partridge, Greg. *Gigabit Networking* (1994, Addison-Wesley).

Pecar, Joseph A., O'Connor, Roger J. & Garbin, David A. *The McGraw-Hill Telecommunications Factbook* (1993, McGraw-Hill).

Perlman, Radia. *Interconnections: Bridges and Routers* (1992, Addison-Wesley).

Piscitello, David M. & Chapin, A. Lyman. *Open Systems Networking: TCP/IP and OSI* (1993, Addison-Wesley).

Plattner, B. et al. *X400 Message Handling* (1991, Addison-Wesley).

Potts, William F. *McGraw-Hill Data Communications Dictionary* (1993, McGraw-Hill).

Radicati, Sara. *X.500 Directory Services* (1994, Van Nostrand Reinhold).

Ruley, John D. *Networking Windows NT* (1994, John Wiley & Sons).

Russell, Deborah & Gangemi, G. T. Sr. *Computer Security Basics* (1991, O'Reilly & Associates).

Sasser, Susan, Ralston, Mary & McLaughlin, Robert. *Troubleshooting Your LAN* (1992, MIS Press).

Schank, Jeffrey D. *Novell's Guide to Client-Server Applications and Architecture* (1995, Sybex).

Schatt, Sam. *Understanding Local Area Networks,* 3rd ed. (1993, Sams).

Schatt, Stan. *Understanding Network Management* (1993, Windcrest).

Schneier, Bruce. *Applied Cryptography* (1994, Wiley).

Schulman, Andrew. *Unauthorized Windows 95, Developer's Resource Kit* (1994, IDG).

Sidhu, Gursharan S., Andrews, Richard F. & Oppenheimer, Alan B. *Inside AppleTalk,* 2nd ed. (1990, Addison-Wesley).

Simpson, Alan, Olson, Elizabeth & Weisskopf, Gene. *The Compact Guide to PerfectOffice* (1995, Sybex).

Sochats, Ken & Williams, Jim. *The Networking and Communications Desk Reference* (1992, Sams).

Stallings, William. *Handbook of Computer-Communications Standards* (1987, Macmillan).

Stallings, William. *Local and Metropolitan Area Networks,* 4th ed. (1993, Macmillan).

Stallings, William. *Networking Standards: A Guide to OSI, ISDN, LAN, and MAN Standards* (1993, Addison-Wesley).

Stallings, William. *SNMP, SNMPv2, and CMIP* (1993, Addison-Wesley).

Sterling, Donald J. Jr. *Technician's Guide to Fiber Optics,* 2nd ed. (1993, Delmar).

Stevens, W. Richard. *TCP/IP Illustrated, Volume 1: The Protocols* (1994, Addison-Wesley).

Strayer, W. Timothy, Dempsey, Bert J. & Weaver, Alfred C. *XTP: The Xpress Transfer* (1992, Addison-Wesley).

Tanenbaum, Andrew S. *Computer Networks* (1988, Prentice-Hall).

Tauber, Daniel A. & Kienan, Brenda. *Surfing the Internet with Netscape* 2nd ed. (1996, Sybex).

Taylor, D. Edgar. *The McGraw-Hill Internetworking Handbook* (1995, McGraw-Hill).

Turlington, Shannon R. *Waking the World Wide Web* (1995, Ventana Press).

Vincent, Patrick. *Free Stuff from the World Wide Web* (1995, Coriolis Group).

Wright, Gary R. & Stevens, W. Richard. *TCP/IP Illustrated, Volume 2: The Implementation* (1995, Addison-Wesley).

Yggdrasil Computing. *The Linux Bible: The GNU Testament,* 3rd ed. (1995, Yggdrasil).

Internet Resources

The Internet, the world's largest network, grows at a faster pace than its local counterparts. Given its popularity, it's not surprising that new products and resources are appearing daily.

Whenever products flood the market, there's a huge variation in quality. In this section, I've tried to list some of the basic Internet products that seemed better than most. These are not necessarily the only good products on the market. Rather, they're products with which I'm familiar or which have been recommended by persons whose judgment I trust.

The selection of products is not exhaustive. That would be an impossible presentation because Internet products may be appearing at an even faster rate than acronyms. Rather, the selection is designed to give some idea of the kinds of products that are out there.

The Internet as Its Own Resource

Probably the best place to learn about the Internet is on the Internet. There are thousands of documents, programs, and other resources accessible through the World Wide Web or by other means. Of course, there's a catch-22: to explore the Internet to learn how to use it, you first have to know how to use it so you can explore it.

That's where products such as those in the following sections come in: They can introduce you to the Internet and get you started. The Internet or Web Surfer kits provide both software and suggestions for things to do on the Internet. The videos and tutorials can help make the Internet a more familiar place and can help you develop a sense for how to do things.

Videos and Tutorials

Several videos are available, some with interactive disks or CDs. The videos can provide exposure to the Internet through example sessions. This can help make the Internet a bit more familiar without having to commit to finding an access provider and getting an account.

A very well done series of CDs from MindQ provides introductions to the Internet through interactive tutorials and access to the Internet. Depending on whether you have an Internet Access Provider, the "direct" access will be to the real Internet or to a simulated one. The disc, *Internet: A Knowledge Odyssey,* comes in three versions:

- Basic, which provides tutorials, glossaries, access to a database of over 2,000 Web sites, and tools for accessing the Internet.

- Business, which is professionally oriented with information about businesses and business activities on the Internet. It also includes tools for creating Web pages and for building your own Web site.

- Home, which emphasizes more of the playful resources available on the Internet.

Internet Packages

Since everyone wants to get onto the Internet, publishers and software vendors are rushing to provide customers with products to help. They've been coming out with software and book packages for at least four types of users:

- Beginners, who are just trying to get started and who know little about the Internet. In many cases, the main attraction for such users is likely to be the World Wide Web because it is the flashiest of the Internet resources and is, in many ways, the easiest to use.

- Intermediate users, who are experienced at using computers and possibly even familiar with networks, but who haven't had a chance to explore the Internet.

- Advanced users, who know what they want and just need to find the right tools.

- Small businesses and entrepreneurs, who would like to get onto the Internet to explore or exploit its potential. These users want to see how the Internet can help them in their business. With respect to Internet familiarity, members of this group could fall into any of the other groups.

Judging by the pace at which products come out, publishers consider this a very lucrative market. What makes this even more interesting is the fact that you can get a perfectly fine set of tools for using the Internet just by downloading them from the Internet itself. In fact, some of the same companies that are selling Internet software are also giving versions of it away.

One reason they can get away with this is that there's often enough value-added material in the commercial versions to make the investment—between $40 and $150 or so—worthwhile. For example, the commercial products often include one or more books about the Internet or the World Wide Web. Note that the software components in some of the commercial products sometimes include the same software you could download from the Internet—it's just packaged nicely and perhaps has additional printed documentation. For example, many of the packages include NetManage's Chameleon Sampler for the Internet utilities (FTP, Telnet, Mail). Also, these packages generally include coupons and other offers to provide additional values for some users.

Introductory and Intermediate-Level Products

At the lower end, several publishers have offerings that deserve serious consideration. These introductory packages take three general forms:

- Internet kits or Internets-in-a-box, which generally provide everything you need to get started on the Internet, including the software you need to communicate with the Internet. In addition to the SLIP or PPP software, the packages will include some type of TCP/IP protocol suite—generally as a Winsock (Windows socket) API. Also, the package will contain a browser (hypertext reader) and some subset of popular Internet tools—usually at least FTP, Telnet, and Gopher clients. The access software makes it easy for you to sign on with an Internet Access Provider (IAP)—particularly with the provider that will be the default unless you specify otherwise. In some cases, the provider will be the publisher itself, so that opening an Internet account with them will, in fact, provide them with additional income from you. In other cases, it will be a provider with dial-up lines throughout the country or with toll-free lines available. (Note that subscribers may need to pay some type of fee or surcharge for using the 800 line, so be wary and always ask about charges, even if it's an 800 number.) Internet kits generally cost from $60 to $150, with most toward the lower end.

- Web Explorer kits generally include less material than Internet kits. They include a browser and perhaps some software for creating or editing HTML (Hypertext Markup Language) files. (HTML is used to create hypertext documents.) One variant of this type of product that is becoming popular is a browser with HTML editing abilities bundled in.

- Web Authoring kits, which include an HTML editor—often some variant of HoTMetaL, which is one of the most widely-used HTML editors. At the low end, these products are generally limited in power and ease of use. But, for someone just getting started with the Internet, the Web, or HTML, these products are probably just right.

In general, the books included in the introductory packages are catalogs or travelogues of neat places to visit on the Internet and cool things to do there. The packages may also include a more technical book showing how to do certain things on the Internet. For example, the packages that provide tools for writing Web pages must also discuss HTML.

The following Internet kit-type products all have merits and deserve a look:

- *Internet Membership Kit* v2.0 from Ventana Media comes with two books, a disk, a CD, and a good selection of software, including Ventana's own version of Mosaic.

- *All in One Web Surfer Kit* from the Coriolis Group includes three handy books and a short manual, together with a CD containing Internet access and browser software, as well as HTML editing tools.

- *Internet Suite* from Quarterdeck is a new arrival on the scene. Internet Suite comes with Quarterdeck Mosaic, which is a completely rewritten version of the publicly available Mosaic browser, and also includes Quarterdeck's versions of FTP, Telnet, Mail, and News programs.

- *Internet in a Box* from CompuServe's Spry/Internet division is arguably the grand-daddy of these packages, but it is still going strong. This product includes safe shopping capabilities. A related product, *Internet in a Box for Kids,* includes filtering software to prevent kids from accessing areas of the Internet that would be inappropriate for them.

- NetManage—who gives away Chameleon Sampler free of charge—also makes a commercial product: *Internet Chameleon,* which is a more powerful relative of the Sampler. Whereas the Sampler has half a dozen or more utilities, *Internet Chameleon* has almost 20.

- *Cyberjack* from Delrina is another new product. For Windows 95, it takes advantage of the new operating system to offer multitasking and multi-threading. Delrina includes IRC (chat) software, and has a Guidebook component that provides visual icons to identify and provide instant access to

over a hundred of the "coolest" Web sites.

- *Emissary* from The Wollongong Group is another newcomer. It also provides the usual Internet programs, but in a well-integrated environment.

Many book publishers have Web Explorer products. In many cases, you can choose between a package with Netscape's Navigator or a version with the Mosaic browser. The following are among the better examples of such products:

- *Mosaic and Web Explorer* and *Netscape and HTML Explorer* from the Coriolis Group.

- *World Wide Web Kit* in Mosaic or Netscape versions from Ventana Media.

- *Mosaic in a Box* from CompuServe's Spry/Internet division. This product also comes in a version for Windows 95.

- *Quarterdeck Mosaic* from Quarterdeck Systems. This component is included in the *Internet Suite.*

Similarly, Web Authoring kits are becoming increasingly popular as people find out how inexpensive it can be to have a Web home page and also how easy it can be to create Web pages with the right tools. There's quite a range in the power of such authoring kits, with high-end products commanding prices that are several times the price of the low-end ones. The following packages all have something to offer:

- *Internet Publishing Kit* from Ventana Media includes versions of several popular HTML editors, as well as HTML assistants (for word processing packages) and conversion tools. Note that, in some cases, the software versions are also available free on the Internet—but only if you hunt them down and clean them up. One of the two CDs includes electronic versions of two of the books included in the package.

- *All-in-one Web Surfing Kit* from the Coriolis Group. This kit was mentioned in an earlier context but fits just as well here.

- *Spider* from Incontext Systems includes an HTML editor with a Web browser. This editor is generally considered very powerful but easy to use. The company's *Incontext* product is an SGML editor.

- *Web Author* from Quarterdeck Systems is an add-on module for Word for Windows 6.0. With this component you can create HTML files in Word.

- *Panorama Pro* from SoftQuad actually supports SGML (Standardized General Markup Language), the more powerful language on which HTML is based.

Many of these publishers will also be happy to rent you space for your newly authored Web page. Most access providers also have provisions for such space rental.

Advanced Products

At the advanced and more specialized end you'll find more powerful (and usually more expensive) programs. These programs can help make publishing on the Web easier as well as enable you to create more complex or entertaining Web pages.

For example, in the Web publishing area, *WebAnchor* from Iconovex can read through HTML files, analyze the content, present several types of summaries, and then add anchors to the HTML files to make the various locations more easily accessible. The indexes created make it easier for users to find exactly the information they want, thereby saving search time and frustration.

In the Internet access area, you can find more advanced products such as:

- NetManage's *Chameleon 4.5* and *Chameleon* integrated with *Ecco Pro* Personal Information Management software.

- *SuperHighway Access for Windows* from Frontier Technologies Corporation, which offers more powerful features in several of the programs included in the package. For example, *SuperHighway* supports the MIME extensions to allow handling of multimedia in electronic mail. It also includes such auxiliary programs as Archie, Jughead, and Veronica, which make Gopher searches more efficient.

Web Server programs are also more advanced products, which are likely to be of interest to would-be Internet entrepreneurs. With these products, you can turn your computer into an accessible Web server, assuming you can arrange the logistics with your access provider. Once you've created your Web pages, you can keep them on your own machine and still let users access them.

Web Server from Quarterdeck and *Serving the Web* from Coriolis Group are two relatively inexpensive Web Server packages.

Internet Products Vendor List

The following vendor list covers just the vendors discussed here. Be aware that numbers, addresses, and even companies can change:

CompuServe Spry/Internet
(800) 777-9638
http://www.spry.com

The Coriolis Group
(800) 410-0192; (602) 483-0192
http://www.coriolis.com

Delrina
(800) 813-8161
http://www.delrina.com

Frontier Technologies Corp.
(800) 929-3054
http://www.frontiertech.com

InContext Corp.
(800) 263-0127
http://www.incontext.ca

Iconovex Corporation
(800) 943-0292
http://www.iconovex.com

MindQ
(800) 646-3008

NetManage
(408) 973-7171
http://www.netmanage.com

Quarterdeck Corporation
(800) 354-3222
http://www.qdeck.com

SoftQuad Inc.
Ventana Media
(800) 743-5369; (919) 942-0220
http://www.vmedia.com

The Wollongong Group
(800) 872-8649
http://www.twg.com

Miscellaneous Sources

Other sources of information are available to meet several needs:

- Getting basic background and general information, either about an area or a specific product

- Getting more advanced information and training

- Staying up-to-date on what is going on in an area or with a product

Background Information

For general background information or a basic introduction, and for relatively stable information, the most useful resources are books, films, online tutorials, and introductory workshops or seminars. Introductory courses are often available through local user groups, universities, and schools.

Advanced Training

Courses or workshops at conferences or through professional training centers are excellent resources for more advanced or specialized training. Vendors may either provide such training through their own divisions or may certify third-party trainers.

For example, Novell authorizes training centers to give courses leading to recognition as a Certified NetWare Engineer or Administrator or as an Enterprise Certified NetWare Engineer. Once certified, such individuals can provide consulting and other services to end users and other customers.

In some regions, advanced training may also be available through local user groups or local universities. This is more likely in areas with large user groups (such as Boston or New York) or where many people are employed in the computer industry.

Staying Up-to-Date

The world of networking changes daily, so staying current is a major challenge. (The same is true of the computing industry in general, which changes just as quickly as, or perhaps even more quickly than, the networking industry.)

Most networking vendors have BBSs (bulletin board systems) or a forum on at least one of the online services (such as CompuServe, America Online, or BIX). Vendor BBSs are generally free (except for the telephone charges), but forums available

through computer services generally include an online charge as well. To get information about such online resources, call the vendor.

Novell's NetWire, accessible through CompuServe, is one of the most comprehensive collections of online resources. *Using NetWire* by Laura Chappell and Brent Larson (1992, Know, Inc., P.O. Box 50507, Provo, UT 84605-0507) tells how to access NetWire through CompuServe.

Membership in professional associations or user groups can also provide an information channel. The CNEPA (Certified NetWare Engineer Professional Association) and NUI (NetWare Users International) are two examples of such groups.

For those with smaller budgets or a more casual interest, the various networking and computer magazines can help keep you up-to-date on developments.

Index

Note to the Reader: **Boldface** numbers indicate pages where you will find the principal discussion of a topic or the definition of a term. *Italic* page numbers indicate pages where topics are illustrated in figures.

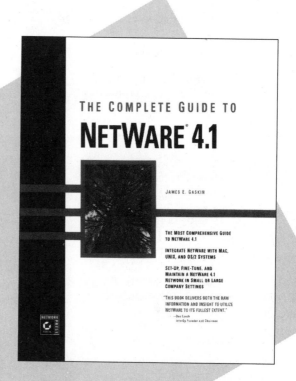